CIVIL AIRCRAFT
MARKINGS 2012

REVISED 63rd EDITION

Allan S. Wright

MIDLAND

An imprint of
Ian Allan Publishing

www.ianallanpublishing.co.uk

Contents

This 62nd edition first published 2012

ISBN 978 1 85780 357 0

Published by Midland Publishing

an imprint of Ian Allan Publishing Ltd, Hersham, Surrey KT12 4RG.
Printed in England by Ian Allan Printing Ltd, Hersham, Surrey KT12 4RG.

Visit the Ian Allan Publishing website at
www.ianallanpublishing.com

Distributed in the United States of America and Canada by BookMasters Distribution Services

Cover: Rossiya Antonov An-148-100B airliner RA-61703 on final-approach to Gatwick, UK at 12.35 on 25th November 2011 on the daily Rossiya flight-number SDM297 from St Petersburg, Russia. ©*Aviation-images.com*

Advertising: Dave Smith, Tel/Fax 01775 767184
6 Sunningdale Avenue, Spalding, Lincs, PE9 2PP, UK.

Introduction

The familiar 'G' prefixed four-letter registration system was adopted in 1919 after a short-lived spell with serial numbers commencing at K-100. Until July 1928 the UK allocations were issued in the G-Exxx range but, as a result of further international agreements, this series ended at G-EBZZ, the replacement being G-Axxx. From this point registrations were issued in a reasonably orderly manner through to G-AZZZ, the position reached in July 1972. There were, however, two exceptions. In order to prevent possible confusion with signal codes, the G-AQxx sequence was omitted, while G-AUxx was reserved for Australian use originally. In recent years however, individual requests for a mark in the latter range have been granted by the Authorities.

Although the next logical sequence was started at G-Bxxx, it was not long before the strictly applied rules relating to aircraft registration began to be relaxed. Permission was readily given for personalised marks to be issued, incorporating virtually any four-letter combination, while re-registration also became a common feature – a practice almost unheard of in the past. In this book, where this has taken place at some time, all previous UK identities carried appear in parenthesis after the operator's/owner's name. For example, during its career Twin Squirrel G-LNTY has also carried the identities G-ECOS, G-DORL and G-BPVB.

Some aircraft have also been allowed to wear military markings without displaying their civil identity. In this case the serial number actually carried is shown in parenthesis after the type's name. For example Auster 6A G-ARRX flies in military colours as VF512, its genuine previous identity. As an aid to the identification of such machines, a conversion list is provided.

Other factors caused a sudden acceleration in the number of registrations allocated by the Civil Aviation Authority in the early 1980s. The first surge followed the discovery that it was possible to register plastic bags, and other items even less likely to fly, on payment of the standard fee. This erosion of the main register was checked in early 1982 by the issue of a special sequence for such devices commencing with G-FYAA. Powered hang-gliders provided the second glut of allocations as a result of the decision that these types should be officially registered. Although a few of the early examples penetrated the current in-sequence register, in due course all new applicants were given marks in special ranges, this time G-MBxx, G-MGxx, G-MJxx, G-MMxx, G-MNxx, G-MTxx, G-MVxx, G-MWxx, G-MYxx and G-MZxx. It took some time before all microlights displayed an official mark but gradually the registration was carried, the size and position depending on the dimensions of the component to which it was applied.

There was news of a further change in mid-1998 when the CAA announced that with immediate effect microlights would be issued with registrations in the normal sequence alongside aircraft in other classes. In addition, it meant that owners could also apply for a personalised identity upon payment of the then current fee of £170 from April 1999, a low price for those wishing to display their status symbol. These various changes played their part in exhausting the current G-Bxxx range after some 26 years, with G-BZxx coming into use before the end of 1999. As this batch approached completion the next series to be used began at G-CBxx instead of the anticipated G-CAxx. The reason for this step was to avoid the re-use of marks issued in Canada during the 1920s, although a few have appeared more recently as personalised UK registrations.

Another large increase in the number of aircraft registered has resulted from the EU-inspired changes in glider registration. After many years of self-regulation by the British Gliding Association, new gliders must now comply with EASA regulations and hence receive registrations in the main G-Cxxx sequence. The phasing-in of EASA registration for the existing glider fleet has been a fairly lengthy process but has now come to an end and as at the beginning of 2012 there were over 2,250 examples on the Register.

September 2007 saw the issue of the 50,000th UK aircraft registration with G-MITC being allocated to a Robinson R44 Raven. The total number of aircraft on the Register has risen over the past 25 years from just under 10,000 at the beginning of 1985 to in excess of 21,300 by January 2009. Numbers have fallen back slightly since that time with the figure as at 1st January 2012 standing at 20,040.

Non-airworthy and preserved aircraft are shown with a star (★) after the type.

The three-letter codes used by airlines to prefix flight numbers are included for those carriers most likely to appear in or over the UK. Radio frequencies for the larger airfields/airports are also listed.

ASW

ACKNOWLEDGEMENTS: Once again thanks are extended to the Registration Department of the Civil Aviation Authority for its assistance and allowing access to its files and thanks are also given to all those who have contributed items for possible use in this edition.

Classic Aircraft

Best in classic aviation

With a superb new look, 12 exciting issues a year and the work of the best writers and photographers in the business, *Classic Aircraft* is the magazine for the true aviation aficionado. Continuing the rich history of *Aircraft Illustrated*, established over 40 years ago, *Classic Aircraft* offers a contemporary take on the greatest years of aviation, the glory days of charismatic aircraft. From the most famous historic airliners to the most exciting military jets of all time, our coverage is second to none.

Classic Aircraft places an unrivalled focus on the classic aircraft of the post-war years, covering the developments in military aviation and fascinating operations during the Cold War period, and the huge changes that swept through the airline world as mass air travel became a reality. But there's much more to the history in *Classic Aircraft* than that. We cover World War Two, the inter-war period, World War One and the pioneer aviators; we also look at modern-day aviation happenings with a unique historical slant. Whatever the subject, stunning archive imagery accompanies informed, in-depth articles from leading authors and revealing 'from the cockpit' stories. Aviation writing gets no better.

International Civil Aircraft Markings

A2-	Botswana	OB-	Peru
A3-	Tonga	OD-	Lebanon
A4O-	Oman	OE-	Austria
A5-	Bhutan	OH-	Finland
A6-	United Arab Emirates	OK-	Czech Republic
A7-	Qatar	OM-	Slovakia
A8-	Liberia	OO-	Belgium
A9C-	Bahrain	OY-	Denmark
AP-	Pakistan	P-	North Korea
B-	China/Taiwan/Hong Kong/Macao	P2-	Papua New Guinea
C-	Canada	P4-	Aruba
C2-	Nauru	PH-	Netherlands
C3-	Andorra	PJ-	Netherlands Antilles
C5-	Gambia	PK-	Indonesia
C6-	Bahamas	PP-	Brazil
C9-	Mozambique	PR-	Brazil
CC-	Chile	PT-	Brazil
CN-	Morocco	PU-	Brazil
CP-	Bolivia	PZ-	Surinam
CS-	Portugal	RA-	Russia
CU-	Cuba	RDPL-	Laos
CX-	Uruguay	RP-	Philippines
D-	Germany	S2-	Bangladesh
D2-	Angola	S5-	Slovenia
D4-	Cape Verde Islands	S7-	Seychelles
D6-	Comores Islands	S9-	São Tomé
DQ-	Fiji	SE-	Sweden
E3-	Eritrea	SP-	Poland
E5-	Cook Islands	ST-	Sudan
EC-	Spain	SU-	Egypt
EI-	Republic of Ireland	SX-	Greece
EK-	Armenia	T2-	Tuvalu
EP-	Iran	T3-	Kiribati
ER-	Moldova	T7-	San Marino
ES-	Estonia	T8A-	Palau
ET-	Ethiopia	T9-	Bosnia and Herzegovina
EW-	Belarus	TC-	Turkey
EX-	Kyrgyzstan	TF-	Iceland
EY-	Tajikistan	TG-	Guatemala
EZ-	Turkmenistan	TI-	Costa Rica
F-	France, inc Colonies and Protectorates	TJ-	Cameroon
G-	United Kingdom	TL-	Central African Republic
H4-	Solomon Islands	TN-	Republic of Congo
HA-	Hungary	TR-	Gabon
HB-	Switzerland and Liechtenstein	TS-	Tunisia
HC-	Ecuador	TT-	Tchad
HH-	Haiti	TU-	Ivory Coast
HI-	Dominican Republic	TY-	Benin
HK-	Colombia	TZ-	Mali
HL-	South Korea	UK-	Uzbekistan
HP-	Panama	UN-	Kazakhstan
HR-	Honduras	UR-	Ukraine
HS-	Thailand	V2-	Antigua
HZ-	Saudi Arabia	V3-	Belize
I-	Italy	V4	St. Kitts & Nevis
J2-	Djibouti	V5-	Namibia
J3-	Grenada	V6-	Micronesia
J5-	Guinea Bissau	V7-	Marshall Islands
J6-	St. Lucia	V8-	Brunei
J7-	Dominica	VH-	Australia
J8-	St. Vincent	VN-	Vietnam
JA-	Japan	VP-A	Anguilla
JU-	Mongolia	VP-B	Bermuda
JY-	Jordan	VP-C	Cayman Islands
LN-	Norway	VP-F	Falkland Islands
LV-	Argentina	VP-G	Gibraltar
LX-	Luxembourg	VP-L	British Virgin Islands
LY-	Lithuania	VP-M	Montserrat
LZ-	Bulgaria	VQ-B	Bermuda
M-	Isle of Man	VQ-H	Saint Helena/Ascension
N-	United States of America	VQ-T	Turks & Caicos Islands

VT-	India	5A-	Libya
XA-	Mexico	5B-	Cyprus
XB-	Mexico	5H-	Tanzania
XC-	Mexico	5N-	Nigeria
XT-	Burkina Faso	5R-	Malagasy Republic (Madagascar)
XU-	Cambodia	5T-	Mauritania
XW-	Laos	5U-	Niger
XY-	Myanmar	5V-	Togo
YA-	Afghanistan	5W-	Western Samoa (Polynesia)
YI-	Iraq	5X-	Uganda
YJ-	Vanuatu	5Y-	Kenya
YK-	Syria	6O-	Somalia
YL-	Latvia	6V-	Senegal
YN-	Nicaragua	6Y-	Jamaica
YR-	Romania	7O-	Yemen
YS-	El Salvador	7P-	Lesotho
YU-	Serbia	7Q-	Malawi
YV-	Venezuela	7T-	Algeria
Z-	Zimbabwe	8P-	Barbados
Z3-	Macedonia	8Q-	Maldives
ZA-	Albania	8R-	Guyana
ZK-	New Zealand	9A-	Croatia
ZP-	Paraguay	9G-	Ghana
ZS-	South Africa	9H-	Malta
3A-	Monaco	9J-	Zambia
3B-	Mauritius	9K-	Kuwait
3C-	Equatorial Guinea	9L-	Sierra Leone
3D-	Swaziland	9M-	Malaysia
3X-	Guinea	9N-	Nepal
4K-	Azerbaijan	9Q-	Congo Kinshasa
4L-	Georgia	9U-	Burundi
4O-	Montenegro	9V-	Singapore
4R-	Sri Lanka	9XR-	Rwanda
4X-	Israel	9Y-	Trinidad and Tobago

Aircraft Type Designations & Abbreviations

(for example PA-28 Piper Type 28)

A.	Beagle, Auster, Airbus
AAC	Army Air Corps
AA-	American Aviation, Grumman American
AB	Agusta-Bell
AESL	Aero Engine Services Ltd
AG	American General
An	Antonov
ANEC	Air Navigation & Engineering Co
ANG	Air National Guard
AS	Aérospatiale
A.S.	Airspeed
A.W.	Armstrong Whitworth
B.	Blackburn, Bristol, Boeing, Beagle
BA	British Airways
BAC	British Aircraft Company
BAC	British Aircraft Corporation
BAe	British Aerospace
BAPC	British Aviation Preservation Council
BAT	British Aerial Transport
B.K.	British Klemm
BN	Britten-Norman
Bo	Bolkow
Bü	Bücker
CAARP	Co-operatives des Ateliers Aéronautiques de la Région Parisienne
CAC	Commonwealth Aircraft Corporation
CAF	Canadian Air Force
CASA	Construcciones Aeronautics SA
CCF	Canadian Car & Foundry Co
CEA	Centre-Est Aviation
CH.	Chrislea
CHABA	Cambridge Hot-Air Ballooning Association
CLA.	Comper
CP.	Piel
CUAS	Cambridge University Air Squadron
Cycl	Cyclone
D.	Druine
DC-	Douglas Commercial
DH.	de Havilland
DHA.	de Havilland Australia
DHC.	de Havilland Canada
DR.	Jodel (Robin-built)
EE	English Electric
EAA	Experimental Aircraft Association
EMB	Embraer Empresa Brasileira de Aeronautica SA
EoN	Elliotts of Newbury
EP	Edgar Percival
ETPS	Empire Test Pilots School
F.	Fairchild, Fokker
F.A.A.	Fleet Air Arm
FFA	Flug und Fahrzeugwerke AG
FH	Fairchild-Hiller
FrAF	French Air Force
FRED	Flying Runabout Experimental Design
Fw	Focke-Wulf
G.	Grumman
GA	Gulfstream American
GAL.	General Aircraft
GC	Globe Aircraft
GECAS	General Electric Capital Aviation Services
GY	Gardan
H	Helio
HM.	Henri Mignet
HP.	Handley Page
HPR.	Handley Page Reading
HR.	Robin
HS.	Hawker Siddeley

ICA	Intreprinderea de Constructii Aeronau
IHM	International Helicopter Museum
I.I.I.	Iniziative Industriali Italiane
IL	Ilyushin
ILFC	International Lease Finance Corporation
IMCO	Intermountain Manufacturing Co
IWM	Imperial War Museum
KR	Rand-Robinson
L.	Lockheed
L.A.	Luton, Lake
LET	Letecky Narodny Podnik
LLP	Limited Liability Partnership
L.V.G.	Luft-Verkehrs Gesellschaft
M.	Miles, Mooney
MBA	Micro Biplane Aviation
MBB	Messerschmitt-Bölkow-Blohm
McD	McDonnell
MDH	McDonnell Douglas Helicopters
MH.	Max Holste
MHCA	Manhole Cover
MJ	Jurca
MS.	Morane-Saulnier
NA	North American
NC	Nord
NE	North East
P.	Hunting (formerly Percival), Piaggio
PA-	Piper
PC.	Pilatus
PZL	Panstwowe Zaklady Lotnicze
QAC	Quickie Aircraft Co
R.	Rockwell
RAF	Rotary Air Force
RAAF	Royal Australian Air Force
RAFGSA	Royal Air Force Gliding & Soaring Association
RCAF	Royal Canadian Air Force
RF	Fournier
R.N.	Royal Navy
S.	Short, Sikorsky
SA,SE,SO	Sud-Aviation, Aérospatiale, Scottish Aviation
SAAB	Svenska Aeroplan Aktieboleg
SC	Short
SCD	Side Cargo Door
SNCAN	Société Nationale de Constructions Aéronautiques du Nord
SOCATA	Société de Construction d'Avions de Tourisme et d'Affaires
SpA	Societa per Azioni
SPP	Strojirny Prvni Petiletky
S.R.	Saunders-Roe, Stinson
SS	Special Shape
ST	SOCATA
SW	Solar Wings
T.	Tipsy
TB	SOCATA
Tu	Tupolev
UH.	United Helicopters (Hiller)
UK	United Kingdom
USAF	United States Air Force
USAAC	United States Army Air Corps
USN	United States Navy
V.	Vickers-Armstrongs
VLM	Vlaamse Luchttransportmaatschappij
VS.	Vickers-Supermarine
WA	Wassmer
WAR	War Aircraft Replicas
WHE	W.H.Ekin
WS	Westland
Z.	Zlin

British Civil Aircraft Registrations

Reg.	Type (†False registration)	Owner or Operator	Notes
G-AAAH†	DH.60G Moth (replica) (BAPC 168) ★	Yorkshire Air Museum/Elvington	
G-AAAH	DH.60G Moth ★	Science Museum *Jason*/South Kensington	
G-AACA†	Avro 504K (BAPC 177) ★	Brooklands Museum of Aviation/Weybridge	
G-AACN	HP.39 Gugnunc ★	Science Museum/Wroughton	
G-AADR	DH.60GM Moth	E. V. Moffatt	
G-AAEG	DH.60G Gipsy Moth	I. B. Grace	
G-AAHI	DH.60G Moth	Nigel John Western Reid Discretionary Settlement 2008	
G-AAHY	DH.60M Moth	D. J. Elliott	
G-AAIN	Parnall Elf II	The Shuttleworth Collection/Old Warden	
G-AAJT	DH.60G Moth	M. R. Paul	
G-AALY	DH.60G Moth	K. M. Fresson	
G-AAMX	DH.60GM Moth ★	RAF Museum/Hendon	
G-AAMY	DH.60GMW Moth	Totalsure Ltd	
G-AANG	Blériot XI	The Shuttleworth Collection/Old Warden	
G-AANH	Deperdussin Monoplane	The Shuttleworth Collection/Old Warden	
G-AANI	Blackburn Monoplane	The Shuttleworth Collection/Old Warden	
G-AANJ	L.V.G. C VI (7198/18)	Aerospace Museum/Cosford	
G-AANL	DH.60M Moth	R. A. Palmer	
G-AANO	DH.60GMW Moth	A. W. & M. E. Jenkins	
G-AANV	DH.60G Moth	R. A. Seeley	
G-AAOK	Curtiss Wright Travel Air 12Q	Shipping & Airlines Ltd	
G-AAOR	DH.60G Moth	B. R. Cox	
G-AAPZ	Desoutter I (mod.)	The Shuttleworth Collection	
G-AATC	DH.80A Puss Moth	R. A. Palmer	
G-AAUP	Klemm L.25-1A	J. I. Cooper	
G-AAWO	DH.60G Moth	I. C. Reid	
G-AAXG	DH 60M Moth	S. H. Kidston	
G-AAXK	Klemm L.25-1A ★	C. C. Russell-Vick (stored)	
G-AAYT	DH.60G Moth	P. Groves	
G-AAYX	Southern Martlet	The Shuttleworth Collection	
G-AAZG	DH.60G Moth	C. C. & J. M. Lovell	
G-AAZP	DH.80A Puss Moth	R. P. Williams	
G-ABAA	Avro 504K ★	Manchester Museum of Science & Industry	
G-ABAG	DH.60G Moth	A. & P. A. Wood	
G-ABBB	B.105A Bulldog IIA (K2227) ★	RAF Museum/Hendon	
G-ABDA	DH.60G Moth	R. A. Palmer	
G-ABDW	DH.80A Puss Moth (VH-UQB) ★	Museum of Flight/East Fortune	
G-ABDX	DH.60G Moth	M. D. Souch	
G-ABEV	DH.60G Moth	S. L. G. Darch	
G-ABHE	Aeronca C.2	N. S. Chittenden	
G-ABLM	Cierva C.24 ★	De Havilland Heritage Museum/London Colney	
G-ABLS	DH.80A Puss Moth	R. A. Seeley	
G-ABMR	Hart 2 (J9941) ★	RAF Museum/Hendon	
G-ABNT	Civilian C.A.C.1 Coupe	Shipping & Airlines Ltd	
G-ABNX	Redwing 2	Redwing Syndicate	
G-ABOI	Wheeler Slymph ★	Midland Air Museum/Coventry	
G-ABOX	Sopwith Pup (N5195)	C. M. D. & A. P. St. Cyrien	
G-ABSD	DHA.60G Moth	M. E. Vaisey	
G-ABUL†	DH.82A Tiger Moth ★	F.A.A. Museum/Yeovilton (G-AOXG)	
G-ABUS	Comper CLA.7 Swift	R. C. F. Bailey	
G-ABVE	Arrow Active 2	Real Aircraft Co	
G-ABWD	DH.83 Fox Moth	R. I. Souch	
G-ABWP	Spartan Arrow	R. T. Blain	
G-ABXL	Granger Archaeopteryx ★	J. R. Granger	
G-ABYA	DH.60G Gipsy Moth	M. J. Saggers	
G-ABZB	DH.60G-III Moth Major	G. M. Turner & N. Child	
G-ACBH	Blackburn B.2 ★	–/Redhill	
G-ACCB	DH.83 Fox Moth	E. A. Gautrey	
G-ACDA	DH.82A Tiger Moth	B. D. Hughes	
G-ACDC	DH.82A Tiger Moth	Tiger Club Ltd	
G-ACDI	DH.82A Tiger Moth	Doublecube Aviation LLP	
G-ACEJ	DH.83 Fox Moth	I. G. Barnett & G. R. Williams	
G-ACET	DH.84 Dragon	G. Cormack	
G-ACGT	Avro 594 Avian IIIA ★	Yorkshire Light Aircraft Ltd/Leeds	
G-ACGZ	DH.60G-III Moth Major	N. H. Lemon	

Notes	Reg.	Type	Owner or Operator
	G-ACIT	DH.84 Dragon ★	Science Museum/Wroughton
	G-ACLL	DH.85 Leopard Moth	V. M & D. C. M. Stiles
	G-ACMA	DH.85 Leopard Moth	P. A. Vacher
	G-ACMD	DH.82A Tiger Moth	M. J. Bonnick
	G-ACMN	DH.85 Leopard Moth	M. R. & K. E. Slack
	G-ACNS	DH.60G-III Moth Major	C. T. Parry
	G-ACOJ	DH.85 Leopard Moth	Norman Aeroplane Trust
	G-ACSP	DH.88 Comet ★	T. M., M. L., D. A. & P. M. Jones
	G-ACSS	DH.88 Comet ★	The Shuttleworth Collection Grosvenor House/ Old Warden
	G-ACSS†	DH.88 Comet (replica) ★	G. Gayward (BAPC216)
	G-ACSS†	DH.88 Comet (replica) ★	The Galleria Hatfield (BAPC257)
	G-ACTF	Comper CLA.7 Swift ★	The Shuttleworth Collection/Old Warden
	G-ACUS	DH.85 Leopard Moth	R. A. & V. A. Gammons
	G-ACUU	Cierva C.30A (HM580) ★	G. S. Baker/Duxford
	G-ACUX	S.16 Scion (VH-UUP) ★	Ulster Folk & Transport Museum
	G-ACVA	Kay Gyroplane ★	Museum of Flight/East Fortune
	G-ACWM	Cierva C.30A (AP506) ★	IHM/Weston-super-Mare
	G-ACWP	Cierva C.30A (AP507) ★	Science Museum/South Kensington
	G-ACXB	DH.60G-III Moth Major	D. F. Hodgkinson
	G-ACXE	B.K. L-25C Swallow	J. G. Wakeford
	G-ACYK	Spartan Cruiser III ★	Museum of Flight (front fuselage)/East Fortune
	G-ACZE	DH.89A Dragon Rapide	Chewton Glen Aviation Ltd (G-AJGS)
	G-ADAH	DH.89A Dragon Rapide ★	Manchester Museum of Science & Industry Pioneer
	G-ADEV	Avro 504K (H5199)	The Shuttleworth Collection/Old Warden (G-ACNB)
	G-ADGP	M.2L Hawk Speed Six	R. A. Mills
	G-ADGT	DH.82A Tiger Moth (BB697)	The Tiger Club 1990 Ltd
	G-ADGV	DH.82A Tiger Moth	M. van Dijk & M. R. Van der Straaten (G-BACW)
	G-ADHD	DH.60G-III Moth Major	M. E. Vaisey
	G-ADIA	DH.82A Tiger Moth	S. J. Beaty
	G-ADJJ	DH.82A Tiger Moth	J. M. Preston
	G-ADKC	DH.87B Hornet Moth	A. J. Davy
	G-ADKK	DH.87B Hornet Moth	R. M. Lee
	G-ADKL	DH.87B Hornet Moth	P. R. & M. J. F. Gould
	G-ADKM	DH.87B Hornet Moth	S. G. Collyer
	G-ADLY	DH.87B Hornet Moth	Totalsure Ltd
	G-ADMT	DH.87B Hornet Moth	D. C. Reid
	G-ADMW	M.2H Hawk Major (DG590) ★	RAF Museum Storage & Restoration Centre/ RAF Stafford
	G-ADND	DH.87B Hornet Moth (W9385)	D. M. & S. M. Weston
	G-ADNE	DH.87B Hornet Moth	G-ADNE Group
	G-ADNL	M.5 Sparrowhawk ★	A. P. Pearson
	G-ADNZ	DH.82A Tiger Moth (DE673)	D. C. Wall
	G-ADOT	DH.87B Hornet Moth ★	De Havilland Heritage Museum/London Colney
	G-ADPC	DH.82A Tiger Moth	D. J. Marshall
	G-ADPJ	B.A.C. Drone ★	M. J. Aubrey
	G-ADPS	B.A. Swallow 2	J. F. Hopkins
	G-ADRA	Pietenpol Air Camper	A. J. Mason
	G-ADRG†	Mignet HM.14 (replica) ★	Lower Stondon Transport Museum (BAPC77)
	G-ADRR	Aeronca C.3	S. J. Rudkin
	G-ADRX†	Mignet HM.14 (replica) ★	S. Copeland Aviation Group (BAPC231)
	G-ADRY†	Mignet HM.14 (replica) (BAPC29)★	Brooklands Museum of Aviation/Weybridge
	G-ADVU†	Mignet HM.14 (replica) ★	North East Aircraft Museum/Usworth (BAPC211)
	G-ADWJ	DH.82A Tiger Moth	K. F. Crumplin
	G-ADWO	DH.82A Tiger Moth (BB807) ★	Solent Sky, Southampton
	G-ADWT	M.2W Hawk Trainer	R. Earl & B. Morris
	G-ADXS	Mignet HM.14 ★	Thameside Aviation Museum/Shoreham
	G-ADXT	DH.82A Tiger Moth	Conciair Ltd
	G-ADYS	Aeronca C.3	E. P. & P. A. Gliddon
	G-ADYV†	Mignet HM.14 (replica) ★	P. Ward (BAPC243)
	G-ADZW†	Mignet HM.14 (replica) ★	Solent Sky/Southampton (BAPC253)
	G-AEBB	Mignet HM.14 ★	The Shuttleworth Collection/Old Warden
	G-AEBJ	Blackburn B-2	BAe Systems (Operations) Ltd
	G-AEDB	B.A.C. Drone 2	R. E. Nerou & P. L. Kirk
	G-AEDU	DH.90 Dragonfly	Norman Aeroplane Trust
	G-AEEG	M.3A Falcon Skysport	P. R. Holloway
	G-AEEH	Mignet HM.14 ★	Aerospace Museum/Cosford
	G-AEFG	Mignet HM.14 (BAPC75) ★	N. H. Ponsford/Breighton
	G-AEFT	Aeronca C.3	N. S. Chittenden

Reg.	Type	Owner or Operator	Notes
G-AEGV	Mignet HM.14 ★	Midland Air Museum/Coventry	
G-AEHM	Mignet HM.14 ★	Science Museum/Wroughton	
G-AEJZ	Mignet HM.14 (BAPC120) ★	Aero Venture	
G-AEKR	Mignet HM.14 (BAPC121) ★	Doncaster Museum & Art Gallery	
G-AEKV	Kronfeld Drone ★	Brooklands Museum of Aviation/Weybridge	
G-AEKW	M.12 Mohawk ★	RAF Museum	
G-AELO	DH.87B Hornet Moth	M. J. Miller	
G-AEML	DH.89 Dragon Rapide	Fundacion Infante de Oreans/Spain	
G-AENP	Hawker Hind (K5414) (BAPC78)	The Shuttleworth Collection	
G-AEOA	DH.80A Puss Moth	P. & A. Wood/Old Warden	
G-AEOF†	Mignet HM.14 (BAPC22) ★	Aviodrome/Lelystad, Netherlands	
G-AEOF	Rearwin 8500	Shipping & Airlines Ltd	
G-AEPH	Bristol F.2B (D8096)	The Shuttleworth Collection	
G-AERV	M.11A Whitney Straight	R. A. Seeley	
G-AESB	Aeronca C.3	R. J. M. Turnbull	
G-AESE	DH.87B Hornet Moth	B. R. Cox	
G-AESZ	Chilton D.W.1	R. E. Nerou	
G-AETA	Caudron G.3 (3066) ★	RAF Museum/Hendon	
G-AETG	Aeronca 100	J. Teagle and Partners	
G-AEUJ	M.11A Whitney Straight	R. E. Mitchell	
G-AEVS	Aeronca 100	R. A. Fleming	
G-AEXD	Aeronca 100	M. A. & N. Mills	
G-AEXF	P.6 Mew Gull	Real Aircraft Co	
G-AEXT	Dart Kitten II	K. G. G. Howe	
G-AEXZ	Piper J-2 Cub	M. & J. R. Dowson	
G-AEZF	S.16 Scion 2 ★	Acebell Aviation/Redhill	
G-AEZJ	P.10 Vega Gull	D. P. H. Hulme	
G-AFAP†	CASA C.352L ★	Aerospace Museum/Cosford	
G-AFBS	M.14A Hawk Trainer 3 ★	G. D. Durbridge-Freeman/Duxford (G-AKKU)	
G-AFCL	B. A. Swallow 2	C. P. Bloxham	
G-AFDO	Piper J-3F-60 Cub	R. Wald	
G-AFDX	Hanriot HD.1 (HD-75) ★	RAF Museum/Hendon	
G-AFEL	Monocoupe 90A	M. Rieser	
G-AFFD	Percival Q-6 ★	B. D. Greenwood	
G-AFFH	Piper J-2 Cub	M. J. Honeychurch	
G-AFFI†	Mignet HM.14 (replica) (BAPC76) ★	Yorkshire Air Museum/Elvington	
G-AFGD	B. A. Swallow 2	A. T. Williams & ptnrs	
G-AFGE	B. A. Swallow 2	A. A. M. & C. W. N. Huke	
G-AFGH	Chilton D.W.1.	M. L. & G. L. Joseph	
G-AFGI	Chilton D.W.1.	K. A. A. McDonald	
G-AFGM	Piper J-4A Cub Coupé	P. H. Wilkinson	
G-AFGZ	DH.82A Tiger Moth	M. R. Paul (G-AMHI)	
G-AFHA	Mosscraft MA.1. ★	C. V. Butler	
G-AFIN	Chrislea LC.1 Airguard (BAPC203) ★	T. W. J. Carnall	
G-AFIR	Luton LA-4 Minor	J. Cresswell	
G-AFIU	Parker CA-4 Parasol ★	The Aeroplane Collection/Hooton Park	
G-AFJA	Watkinson Dingbat ★	A. T. Christian	
G-AFJB	Foster-Wikner G.M.1. Wicko	J. Dible	
G-AFJR	Tipsy Trainer 1	M. E. Vaisey (stored)	
G-AFJU	M.17 Monarch	Museum of Flight/East Fortune	
G-AFJV	Mosscraft MA.2 ★	C. V. Butler	
G-AFNI	DH.94 Moth Minor	J. Jennings	
G-AFOB	DH.94 Moth Minor	K. Cantwell	
G-AFOJ	DH.94 Moth Minor	H. Long	
G-AFPN	DH.94 Moth Minor	A. A. A. Maitland & R. S. Jones	
G-AFRZ	M.17 Monarch	R. E. Mitchell/Sleap (G-AIDE)	
G-AFSC	Tipsy Trainer 1	D. M. Forshaw	
G-AFSV	Chilton D.W.1A	R. E. Nerou	
G-AFTA	Hawker Tomtit (K1786)	The Shuttleworth Collection	
G-AFTN	Taylorcraft Plus C2 ★	Leicestershire County Council Museums/Snibston	
G-AFUP	Luscombe 8A Silvaire	R. Dispain	
G-AFVE	DH.82A Tiger Moth (T7230)	J. Mainka	
G-AFWH	Piper J-4A Cub Coupé	C. W. Stearn & R. D. W. Norton	
G-AFWI	DH.82A Tiger Moth	P. R. Harvey	
G-AFWT	Tipsy Trainer 1	N. Parkhouse	
G-AFYD	Luscombe 8F Silvaire	J. D. Iliffe	
G-AFYO	Stinson H.W.75	M. Lodge	
G-AFZA	Piper J-4A Cub Coupe	R. A. Benson	
G-AFZK	Luscombe 8A Silvaire	M. G. Byrnes	
G-AFZL	Porterfield CP.50	P. G. Lucas & S. H. Sharpe	
G-AFZN	Luscombe 8A Silvaire	M. Payne	
G-AGAT	Piper J-3F-50 Cub	A. S. Bathgate	

Notes	Reg.	Type	Owner or Operator
	G-AGBN	GAL.42 Cygnet 2 ★	Museum of Flight/East Fortune
	G-AGEG	DH.82A Tiger Moth	Norman Aeroplane Trust
	G-AGHY	DH.82A Tiger Moth	P. Groves
	G-AGIV	Piper J-3C-65 Cub	J-3 Cub Group
	G-AGJG	DH.89A Dragon Rapide	M. J. & D. J. T. Miller
	G-AGLK	Auster 5D	C. R. Harris
	G-AGMI	Luscombe 8A Silvaire	Oscar Flying Group
	G-AGNJ	DH.82A Tiger Moth	B. P. Borsberry & ptnrs
	G-AGNV	Avro 685 York 1 (TS798) ★	Aerospace Museum/Cosford
	G-AGOS	R.S.4 Desford Trainer (VZ728) ★	Leicestershire County Council Museums
	G-AGPG	Avro 19 Srs 2 ★	The Aeroplane Collection/Hooton Park
	G-AGPK	DH.82A Tiger Moth	T. K. Butcher
	G-AGRU	V.498 Viking 1A ★	Brooklands Museum of Aviation/Weybridge
	G-AGSH	DH.89A Dragon Rapide 6	Bournemouth Aviation Museum
	G-AGTM	DH.89A Dragon Rapide 6	Air Atlantique Ltd
	G-AGTO	Auster 5 J/1 Autocrat	M. J. Barnett & D. J. T. Miller
	G-AGTT	Auster J/1 Autocrat	C. Norfolk
	G-AGVG	Auster 5 J/1 Autocrat (modified)	P. J. & S. J. Benest
	G-AGXN	Auster J/1N Alpha	Gentleman's Aerial Touring Carriage Group
	G-AGXU	Auster J/1N Alpha	L. J. Kingscott
	G-AGXV	Auster J/1 Autocrat	B. S. Dowsett & I. M. Oliver
	G-AGYD	Auster J/1N Alpha	P. D. Hodson
	G-AGYH	Auster J/1N Alpha	I. M. Staves
	G-AGYK	Auster J/1 Autocrat	Autocrat Syndicate
	G-AGYT	Auster J/1N Alpha	P. J. Barrett
	G-AGYU	DH.82A Tiger Moth (DE208)	S. A. Firth
	G-AGYY	Ryan ST3KR (27)	H. de Vries/Holland
	G-AGZZ	DH.82A Tiger Moth	M. C. Jordan
	G-AHAG	DH.89A Rapide	D. E. Findon
	G-AHAL	Auster J/1N Alpha	Wickenby Aviation
	G-AHAM	Auster J/1 Autocrat	C. P. L. Jenkin
	G-AHAN	DH.82A Tiger Moth	Tiger Associates Ltd
	G-AHAP	Auster J/1 Autocrat	W. D. Hill
	G-AHAT	Auster J/1N Alpha ★	Dumfries & Galloway Aviation Museum
	G-AHAU	Auster 5 J/1 Autocrat	Andreas Auster Group
	G-AHBL	DH.87B Hornet Moth	Shipping and Airlines Ltd
	G-AHBM	DH.87B Hornet Moth	P. A. & E. P. Gliddon
	G-AHCL	Auster J/1N Alpha (modified)	N. Musgrave
	G-AHCN	Auster J/1N Alpha	C. L. Towell & A. G. Boon
	G-AHCR	Gould-Taylorcraft Plus D Special	D. E. H. Balmford & D. R. Shepherd
	G-AHEC	Luscombe 8A Silvaire	C. G. Dodds
	G-AHED	DH.89A Dragon Rapide (RL962) ★	RAF Museum Storage & Restoration Centre/RAF Stafford
	G-AHGD	DH.89A Dragon Rapide (Z7288)	S. G. Jones
	G-AHGW	Taylorcraft Plus D (LB375)	C. V. Butler
	G-AHGZ	Taylorcraft Plus D (LB367)	M. Pocock
	G-AHHH	Auster J/1 Autocrat	H. A. Jones
	G-AHHT	Auster J/1N Alpha	A. C. Barber & N. J. Hudson
	G-AHIP	Piper J-3C-65 Cub	A. D. Pearce
	G-AHIZ	DH.82A Tiger Moth	C.F.G. Flying Ltd
	G-AHKX	Avro 19 Srs 2	The Shuttleworth Collection
	G-AHKY	Miles M.18 Series 2 ★	Museum of Flight/East Fortune
	G-AHLK	Auster 3 (NJ889)	J. H. Powell-Tuck
	G-AHLT	DH.82A Tiger Moth	M. P. Waring
	G-AHNR	Taylorcraft BC-12D	Bumble Bee Group
	G-AHOO	DH.82A Tiger Moth	J. T. & A. D. Milsom
	G-AHPZ	DH.82A Tiger Moth	N. J. Wareing
	G-AHRI	DH.104 Dove 1 ★	Newark Air Museum
	G-AHSA	Avro 621 Tutor (K3241)	The Shuttleworth Collection
	G-AHSD	Taylorcraft Plus D (LB323)	A. L. Hall-Carpenter
	G-AHSP	Auster J/1 Autocrat	R. M. Weeks
	G-AHSS	Auster J/1N Alpha	A. M. Roche
	G-AHST	Auster J/1N Alpha	A. C. Frost
	G-AHTE	P.44 Proctor V	D. K. Tregilgas
	G-AHTW	A.S.40 Oxford (V3388) ★	Skyfame Collection/Duxford
	G-AHUF	DH.Tiger Moth	Dream Ventures Ltd
	G-AHUG	Taylorcraft Plus D	D. Nieman
	G-AHUI	M.38 Messenger 2A ★	The Aeroplane Collection/Hooton Park
	G-AHUJ	M.14A Hawk Trainer 3 (R1914) ★	Strathallan Aircraft Collection
	G-AHUN	Globe GC-1B Swift	R. J. Hamlett
	G-AHUV	DH.82A Tiger Moth	A. D. Gordon
	G-AHVU	DH.82A Tiger Moth	J. B. Steel

Reg.	Type	Owner or Operator	Notes
G-AHVV	DH.82A Tiger Moth	M. Arter	
G-AHXE	Taylorcraft Plus D (LB312)	J. M. C. Pothecary	
G-AIBE	Fulmar II (N1854) ★	F.A.A. Museum/Yeovilton	
G-AIBH	Auster J/1N Alpha	M. J. Bonnick	
G-AIBM	Auster J/1 Autocrat	R. Greatrex	
G-AIBR	Auster J/1 Autocrat	P. R. Hodson	
G-AIBW	Auster J/1N Alpha	C. R. Sunter	
G-AIBX	Auster J/1 Autocrat	Wasp Flying Group	
G-AIBY	Auster J/1 Autocrat	D. Morris	
G-AICX	Luscombe 8A Silvaire	The 2177 Flying Group	
G-AIDL	DH.89A Dragon Rapide 6 (TX310)	Air Atlantique Ltd	
G-AIDN	VS.502 Spitfire Tr.VII (MT818)	P. M. Andrews	
G-AIDS	DH.82A Tiger Moth	K. D. Pogmore & T. Dann	
G-AIEK	M.38 Messenger 2A (RG333)	G. B. E. Pearce	
G-AIFZ	Auster J/1N Alpha	M. D. Ansley	
G-AIGD	Auster V J/1 Autocrat	R. B. Webber	
G-AIGF	Auster J/1N Alpha	A. R. C. Mathie	
G-AIGT	Auster J/1N Alpha	R. R. Harris	
G-AIIH	Piper J-3C-65 Cub	The G-AIIH Group	
G-AIJI	Auster J/1N Alpha ★	C. J. Baker	
G-AIJM	Auster J/4	N. Huxtable	
G-AIJT	Auster J/4 Srs 100	Aberdeen Auster Flying Group	
G-AIKE	Auster 5	R. H. Cooper & T. K. Rumble	
G-AIPR	Auster J/4	M. A. & N. Mills	
G-AIPV	Auster J/1 Autocrat	W. P. Miller	
G-AIRC	Auster J/1 Autocrat	Z. J. Rockey	
G-AIRK	DH.82A Tiger Moth	J. S. & P. R. Johnson	
G-AISA	Tipsy B Srs 1	S. Slater	
G-AISC	Tipsy B Srs 1	Wagtail Flying Group	
G-AISS	Piper J-3C-65 Cub	K. W. Wood & F. Watson	
G-AIST	VS.300 Spitfire 1A (AR213/PR-D)	Spitfire The One Ltd	
G-AISX	Piper J-3C-65 Cub	Cubfly	
G-AITB	A.S.10 Oxford (MP425) ★	RAF Museum/Hendon	
G-AIUA	M.14A Hawk Trainer 3 (T9768) ★	D. S. Hunt	
G-AIUL	DH.89A Dragon Rapide 6	I. Jones	
G-AIXA	Taylorcraft Plus D (LB264)★	RAF Museum/Hendon	
G-AIXJ	DH.82A Tiger Moth	D. Green	
G-AIXN	Benes-Mraz M.1C Sokol	A. J. Wood	
G-AIYG	SNCAN Stampe SV.4B	J. E. Henny/Belgium	
G-AIYR	DH.89A Dragon Rapide (HG691)	Spectrum Leisure Ltd	
G-AIYS	DH.85 Leopard Moth	R. A. & V. A. Gammons	
G-AIZE	Fairchild F.24W Argus 2 (FS628) ★	Aerospace Museum/Cosford	
G-AIZG	VS.236 Walrus 1 (L2301) ★	F.A.A. Museum/Yeovilton	
G-AIZU	Auster J/1 Autocrat★	C. J. & J. G. B. Morley	
G-AJAD	Piper J-3C-65 Cub	C. R. Shipley	
G-AJAE	Auster J/1N Alpha	J. & B. F. Wolfe	
G-AJAJ	Auster J/1N Alpha	G-AJAJ Group	
G-AJAM	Auster J/2 Arrow	D. A. Porter	
G-AJAP	Luscombe 8A Silvaire	M. Flint	
G-AJAS	Auster J/1N Alpha	P. Ferguson & L. & R. Ferguson-Dalling	
G-AJCP	D.31 Turbulent	B. R. Pearson	
G-AJDW	Auster J/1 Autocrat	D. R. Hunt	
G-AJEB	Auster J/1N Alpha ★	The Aeroplane Collection/Hooton Park	
G-AJEE	Auster J/1 Autocrat	A. C. Whitehead	
G-AJEH	Auster J/1N Alpha	J. T. Powell-Tuck	
G-AJEI	Auster J/1N Alpha	J. Siddall	
G-AJEM	Auster J/1 Autocrat	A. L. Aish	
G-AJES	Piper J-3C-65 Cub (330485:C-44)	D. E. Jarvis	
G-AJGJ	Auster 5 (RT486)	British Classic Aircraft Restoration Flying Group	
G-AJHS	DH.82A Tiger Moth	Vliegend Museum/Netherlands	
G-AJIH	Auster J/1 Autocrat	A. J. Collins	
G-AJIS	Auster J/1N Alpha	Husthwaite Auster Group	
G-AJIT	Auster J/1 Kingsland Autocrat	G-AJIT Group	
G-AJIU	Auster J/1 Autocrat	M. D. Greenhalgh	
G-AJIW	Auster J/1N Alpha	W. C. Walters	
G-AJJP	Fairey Jet Gyrodyne (XJ389) ★	Museum of Berkshire Aviation/Woodley	
G-AJJS	Cessna 120	Juliet Sierra Group	
G-AJJT	Cessna 120	Juliet Tango Group	
G-AJJU	Luscombe 8E Silvaire	Enstone Luscombe Group	
G-AJKB	Luscombe 8E Silvaire	T. Carter	
G-AJOC	M.38 Messenger 2A ★	Ulster Folk & Transport Museum	

Notes	Reg.	Type	Owner or Operator
	G-AJOE	M.38 Messenger 2A	P. W. Bishop
	G-AJON	Aeronca 7AC Champion	J. M. Gale
	G-AJOV†	Westland WS-51 Dragonfly ★	Aerospace Museum/Cosford
	G-AJOZ	Fairchild F.24W Argus 2 ★	Yorkshire Air Museum/Elvington
	G-AJPI	Fairchild F.24R-41a Argus 3 (314887)	R. Sijben/Netherlands
	G-AJRB	Auster J/1 Autocrat	R. W. Vince
	G-AJRE	Auster J/1 Autocrat (Lycoming)	Air Tech Spares
	G-AJRH	Auster J/1N Alpha ★	Charnwood Museum/Loughborough
	G-AJRS	M.14A Hawk Trainer 3 (P6382:C)	The Shuttleworth Collection
	G-AJTW	DH.82A Tiger Moth (N6965:FL-J)	J. A. Barker
	G-AJUE	Auster J/1 Autocrat	P. H. B. Cole
	G-AJUL	Auster J/1N Alpha	M. J. Crees
	G-AJVE	DH.82A Tiger Moth	R. A. Gammons
	G-AJWB	M.38 Messenger 2A	P. W. Bishop
	G-AJXC	Auster 5	R. D. Helliar-Symonds, K. A. & S. E. W. Williams
	G-AJXV	Auster 4 (NJ695)	B. A. Farries
	G-AJXY	Auster 4	X-Ray Yankee Group
	G-AJYB	Auster J/1N Alpha	P. J. Shotbolt
	G-AKAT	M.14A Hawk Trainer 3 (T9738)	R. A. Fleming
	G-AKAZ	Piper J-3C-65 Cub (57-G)	Frazerblades Ltd
	G-AKBO	M.38 Messenger 2A	D. O. Blackburn & P. A. Fenton
	G-AKDF	M.38 Messenger 2A	C. W. P. Turner
	G-AKDK	M.65 Gemlni 1A	C. W. P. Turner
	G-AKDN	DHC.1A-1 Chipmunk	P. S. Derry/Canada
	G-AKDW	DH.89A Dragon Rapide ★	De Havilland Heritage Museum/London Colney
	G-AKEL	M.65 Gemini 1A ★	Ulster Folk & Transport Museum
	G-AKEN	M.65 Gemlni 1A	C. W. P. Turner
	G-AKEX	Percival Proctor III	M. Biddulph (G-AKIU)
	G-AKGE	M.65 Gemini 3C ★	Ulster Folk & Transport Museum
	G-AKHP	M.65 Gemini 1A	M. Hales
	G-AKHU	M.65 Gemini 1A	C. W. P. Turner
	G-AKHZ	M.65 Gemini 7 ★	The Aeroplane Collection/Hooton Park
	G-AKIB	Piper J-3C-90 Cub (480015:M-44)	M. C. Bennett
	G-AKIF	DH.89A Dragon Rapide	Airborne Taxi Services Ltd
	G-AKIN	M.38 Messenger 2A	Sywell Messenger Group
	G-AKIU	P.44 Proctor V	Air Atlantique Ltd
	G-AKKB	M.65 Gemini 1A	D. R. Gray
	G-AKKH	M.65 Gemini 1A	J. S. Allison
	G-AKKR	M.14A Magister (T9707) ★	Museum of Army Flying/Middle Wallop
	G-AKKY	M.14A Hawk Trainer 3 (L6906)★ (BAPC44)	Museum of Berkshire Aviation/Woodley
	G-AKLW	Short SA.6 Sealand 1 ★	Ulster Folk & Transport Museum
	G-AKOW	Auster 5 (TJ569) ★	Museum of Army Flying/Middle Wallop
	G-AKPF	M.14A Hawk Trainer 3 (N3788)	P. R. Holloway
	G-AKRA	Piper J-3C-65 Cub	W. R. Savin
	G-AKRP	DH.89A Dragon Rapide 4	Eaglescott Dominie Group
	G-AKSY	Auster 5 (TJ534)	A. Brier
	G-AKSZ	Auster 5C	P. W. Yates & R. G. Darbyshire
	G-AKTH	Piper J-3C-65 Cub	A. G. A. Obertelli & G. W. S. Turner
	G-AKTI	Luscombe 8A Silvaire	C. Chambers
	G-AKTO	Aeronca 7BCM Champion	R. M. Davies
	G-AKTP	PA-17 Vagabond	Golf Tango Papa Group
	G-AKTR	Aeronca 7AC Champion	M. J. Whitwell
	G-AKTS	Cessna 120	M. Isterling
	G-AKTT	Luscombe 8A Silvaire	S. J. Charters
	G-AKUE	DH.82A Tiger Moth	D. F. Hodgkinson
	G-AKUF	Luscombe 8E Silvaire	M. O. Loxton
	G-AKUJ	Luscombe 8E Silvaire	P. R. Bentley
	G-AKUK	Luscombe 8A Silvaire	O. R. Watts
	G-AKUL	Luscombe 8A Silvaire	E. A. Taylor
	G-AKUM	Luscombe 8F Silvaire	D. A. Young
	G-AKUN	Piper J-3F-65 Cub	W. R. Savin
	G-AKUO	Aeronca 11AC Chief	L. W. Richardson
	G-AKUP	Luscombe 8E Silvaire	D. A. Young
	G-AKUR	Cessna 140	J. Greenaway & C. A. Davies
	G-AKUW	Chrislea CH.3 Super Ace 2	J. & S. Rickett
	G-AKVF	Chrislea CH.3 Super Ace 2	Aviation Heritage Ltd
	G-AKVM	Cessna 120	N. Wise & S. Walker
	G-AKVN	Aeronca 11AC Chief	P. A. Jackson
	G-AKVO	Taylorcraft BC-12D	A. Weir
	G-AKVP	Luscombe 8A Silvaire	J. M. Edis
	G-AKVR	Chrislea CH.3 Skyjeep 4	R. B. Webber

Reg.	Type	Owner or Operator	Notes
G-AKVZ	M.38 Messenger 4B	Shipping & Airlines Ltd	
G-AKWS	Auster 5A-160 (RT610)	M. C. Hayes	
G-AKWT	Auster 5 ★	C. Baker	
G-AKXP	Auster 5 (NJ633)	M. J. Nicholson	
G-AKXS	DH.82A Tiger Moth	J. & G. J. Eagles	
G-AKZN	P.34A Proctor 3 (Z7197) ★	RAF Museum/Hendon	
G-ALAR	Miles M.38 Messenger 4A	C. W. P. Turner	
G-ALAX	DH.89A Dragon Rapide ★	Durney Aeronautical Collection/Andover	
G-ALBJ	Auster 5	B. M. Vigor	
G-ALBK	Auster 5	K. Wheatcroft	
G-ALBN	Bristol 173 (XF785) ★	RAF Museum Storage & Restoration Centre/Cardington	
G-ALCK	P.34A Proctor 3 (LZ766) ★	Skyfame Collection/Duxford	
G-ALCU	DH.104 Dove 2 ★	Midland Air Museum/Coventry	
G-ALDG	HP.81 Hermes 4 ★	Duxford Aviation Society (fuselage only)	
G-ALEH	PA-17 Vagabond	A. D. Pearce	
G-ALFA	Auster 5	A. E. Jones	
G-ALFU	DH.104 Dove 6 ★	Duxford Aviation Society	
G-ALGA	PA-15 Vagabond	S. T. Gilbert	
G-ALGT	VS.379 Spitfire F.XIVH (RM689)	Rolls-Royce PLC	
G-ALIJ	PA-17 Vagabond	G-ALIJ Flying Group	
G-ALIW	DH.82A Tiger Moth	F. R. Curry	
G-ALJF	P.34A Proctor 3	J. F. Moore	
G-ALJL	DH.82A Tiger Moth	R. I. & D. Souch	
G-ALJR	Abbott-Baynes Scud III	L. P. Woodage	
G-ALLF	Slingsby T.30A Prefect (ARK)	J. F. Hopkins & K. M. Fresson	
G-ALMA	Piper J3C-65 Cub	M. J. Butler (G-BBXS)	
G-ALNA	DH.82A Tiger Moth	R. J. Doughton	
G-ALND	DH.82A Tiger Moth (N9191)	J. T. Powell-Tuck	
G-ALOD	Cessna 140	H. Merkado	
G-ALSP	Bristol 171 Sycamore (WV783) ★	RAF Museum/Hendon	
G-ALSS	Bristol 171 Sycamore (WA576) ★	Dumfries & Galloway Aviation Museum	
G-ALST	Bristol 171 Sycamore (WA577) ★	North East Aircraft Museum/Usworth	
G-ALSW	Bristol 171 Sycamore (WT933) ★	Newark Air Museum	
G-ALSX	Bristol 171 Sycamore (G-48-1) ★	IHM/Weston-super-Mare	
G-ALTO	Cessna 140	T. M. Jones & ptnrs	
G-ALUC	DH.82A Tiger Moth	D. R. & M. Wood	
G-ALWB	DHC.1 Chipmunk 22A	D. M. Neville	
G-ALWF	V.701 Viscount ★	Duxford Aviation Society *RMA Sir John Franklin*	
G-ALWS	DH.82A Tiger Moth	A. P. Benyon	
G-ALWW	DH.82A Tiger Moth	D. E. Findon	
G-ALXT	DH.89A Dragon Rapide ★	Science Museum/Wroughton	
G-ALXZ	Auster 5-150	G-ALXZ Syndicate	
G-ALYB	Auster 5 (RT520) ★	South Yorkshire Aviation Museum/Doncaster	
G-ALYG	Auster 5D	A. L. Young	
G-ALYW	DH.106 Comet 1 ★	RAF Exhibition Flight (fuselage converted to 'Nimrod')	
G-ALZE	BN-1F ★	M. R. Short/Solent Sky, Southampton	
G-ALZO	A.S.57 Ambassador ★	Duxford Aviation Society	
G-AMAW	Luton LA-4 Minor	The Real Aeroplane Co.Ltd	
G-AMBB	DH.82A Tiger Moth	J. Eagles	
G-AMCK	DH.82A Tiger Moth	Liverpool Flying School Ltd	
G-AMCM	DH.82A Tiger Moth	A. K. & J. I. Cooper	
G-AMDA	Avro 652A Anson 1 (N4877:MK-V) ★	Skyfame Collection/Duxford	
G-AMEN	PA-18 Super Cub 95	The G-AMEN Flying Group	
G-AMHF	DH.82A Tiger Moth	A. J. West	
G-AMHJ	Douglas C-47A Dakota 6 (KG651) ★	Assault Glider Association/Shawbury	
G-AMIV	DH.82A Tiger Moth	Air Fighter Academy GmbH	
G-AMKU	Auster J/1B Aiglet	P. G. Lipman	
G-AMLZ	P.50 Prince 6E ★	The Jetstream Club	
G-AMMS	Auster J/5K Aiglet Trainer	R. B. Webber	
G-AMNN	DH.82A Tiger Moth	I. J. Perry	
G-AMOG	V.701 Viscount ★	Museum of Flight/East Fortune	
G-AMPG	PA-12 Super Cruiser	A. G. & S. M. Measey	
G-AMPI	SNCAN Stampe SV.4C	T. W. Harris	
G-AMPO	Douglas C-47B (FZ626/YS-DH) ★	(gate guardian)/RAF Lyneham	
G-AMPY	Douglas C-47B (KK116)	Air Atlantique Ltd/Coventry	
G-AMPZ	Douglas C-47B ★	Air Service Berlin GmbH/Tempelhof	
G-AMRA	Douglas C-47B	Air Atlantique Ltd	
G-AMRF	Auster J/5F Aiglet Trainer	D. A. Hill	
G-AMRK	G.37 Gladiator I (K7985)	The Shuttleworth Collection	

Notes	Reg.	Type	Owner or Operator
	G-AMSG	SIPA 903	S. W. Markham
	G-AMSN	Douglas C-47B ★	Aceball Aviation/Redhill
	G-AMTA	Auster J/5F Aiglet Trainer	J. D. Manson
	G-AMTF	DH.82A Tiger Moth (T7842)	H. A. D. Monro
	G-AMTK	DH.82A Tiger Moth	S. W. McKay & M. E. Vaisey
	G-AMTM	Auster J/1 Autocrat	R. J. Stobo (G-AJUJ)
	G-AMTV	DH.82A Tiger Moth	G-AMTV Flying Group
	G-AMUF	DHC.1 Chipmunk 21	Redhill Tailwheel Flying Club Ltd
	G-AMUI	Auster J/5F Aiglet Trainer	R. B. Webber
	G-AMVD	Auster 5 (TJ652)	M.Hammond
	G-AMVP	Tipsy Junior	A. R. Wershat
	G-AMVS	DH.82A Tiger Moth	J. T. Powell-Tuck
	G-AMXA	DH.106 Comet 2 (nose only) ★	(stored)
	G-AMYD	Auster J/5L Aiglet Trainer	R. D. Thomasson
	G-AMYJ	Douglas C-47B (KN353) ★	Yorkshire Air Museum/Elvington
	G-AMZI	Auster J/5F Aiglet Trainer	J. F. Moore
	G-AMZT	Auster J/5F Aiglet Trainer	D. Hyde, J. W. Saull & J. C. Hutchinson
	G-ANAF	Douglas C-47B	Air Atlantique Ltd
	G-ANAP	DH.104 Dove 6 ★	Brunel Technical College/Lulsgate
	G-ANCF	B.175 Britannia 308 ★	Bristol Aero Collection (stored)/Kemble
	G-ANCS	DH.82A Tiger Moth	C. E. Edwards & E. A. Higgins
	G-ANCX	DH.82A Tiger Moth	E. N. K. Lison
	G-ANDE	DH.82A Tiger Moth	D. A. Nisbet
	G-ANDM	DH.82A Tiger Moth	N. J. Stagg
	G-ANEH	DH.82A Tiger Moth (N6797)	G. J. Wells
	G-ANEL	DH.82A Tiger Moth	Totalsure Ltd
	G-ANEM	DH.82A Tiger Moth	P. J. Benest
	G-ANEN	DH.82A Tiger Moth	G-ANEN Group
	G-ANEW	DH.82A Tiger Moth	K. F. Crumplin
	G-ANEZ	DH.82A Tiger Moth	C. D. J. Bland
	G-ANFH	Westland WS-55 Whirlwind ★	IHM/Weston-super-Mare
	G-ANFI	DH.82A Tiger Moth (DE623)	G. P. Graham
	G-ANFL	DH.82A Tiger Moth	Felthorpe Tiger Group Ltd
	G-ANFM	DH.82A Tiger Moth	Reading Flying Group
	G-ANFP	DH.82A Tiger Moth	G. D. Horn
	G-ANFU	Auster 5 (NJ719) ★	North East Aircraft Museum/Usworth
	G-ANFV	DH.82A Tiger Moth (DF155)	R. A. L. Falconer
	G-ANGK	Cessna 140A	M. J. Whiteman-Haywood
	G-ANHK	DH.82A Tiger Moth	J. D. Iliffe
	G-ANHR	Auster 5	H. L. Swallow
	G-ANHS	Auster 4 (MT197)	Mike Tango Group
	G-ANHU	Auster 4	J. Mainka
	G-ANHX	Auster 5D	D. J. Baker
	G-ANIE	Auster 5 (TW467)	R. T. Ingram
	G-ANIJ	Auster 5D (TJ672)	G. M. Rundle
	G-ANIS	Auster 5	J. Clarke-Cockburn
	G-ANJA	DH.82A Tiger Moth	A. D. Hodgkinson
	G-ANJD	DH.82A Tiger Moth	D. O. Lewis
	G-ANKK	DH.82A Tiger Moth (T5854)	Halfpenny Green Tiger Group
	G-ANKT	DH.82A Tiger Moth (K2585)	The Shuttleworth Collection
	G-ANKV	DH.82A Tiger Moth (T7793) ★	Westmead Business Group/Croydon Airport
	G-ANKZ	DH.82A Tiger Moth (N6466)	T. D. Le Mesurier
	G-ANLD	DH.82A Tiger Moth	K. Peters
	G-ANLS	DH.82A Tiger Moth	P. A. Gliddon
	G-ANLW	Westland WS-51/2 Widgeon ★	Norfolk & Suffolk Museum/Flixton
	G-ANMO	DH.82A Tiger Moth (K4259:71)	R. J. Moore & B. S. Floodgate
	G-ANMY	DH.82A Tiger Moth (DE470)	Dog Easy Ltd
	G-ANNB	DH.82A Tiger Moth	J. P. Brown
	G-ANNE	DH.82A Tiger Moth	C. R. Hardiman
	G-ANNG	DH.82A Tiger Moth	P. F. Walter
	G-ANNI	DH.82A Tiger Moth (T6953)	C. E. Ponsford & ptnrs
	G-ANNK	DH.82A Tiger Moth	D. R. Wilcox
	G-ANOA	Hiller UH-12A ★	Redhill Technical College
	G-ANOD	DH.82A Tiger Moth	P. G. Watson
	G-ANOH	DH.82A Tiger Moth	N. Parkhouse
	G-ANOK	SAAB S.91C Safir ★	A. F. Galt & Co (stored)
	G-ANOM	DH.82A Tiger Moth	T. G. I. Dark
	G-ANON	DH.82A Tiger Moth (T7909)	M. Kelly
	G-ANOO	DH.82A Tiger Moth	R. K. Packman
	G-ANOV	DH.104 Dove 6 ★	Museum of Flight/East Fortune
	G-ANPE	DH.82A Tiger Moth	I. E. S. Huddleston/Clacton (G-IESH)
	G-ANPK	DH.82A Tiger Moth	A. D. Hodgkinson

Reg.	Type	Owner or Operator	Notes
G-ANPP	P.34A Proctor 3	C. P. A. & J. Jeffrey	
G-ANRF	DH.82A Tiger Moth	C. D. Cyster	
G-ANRM	DH.82A Tiger Moth (DF112)	Spectrum Leisure Ltd	
G-ANRN	DH.82A Tiger Moth	J. J. V. Elwes	
G-ANRP	Auster 5 (TW439)	S. D. & S. P. Allen	
G-ANRX	DH.82A Tiger Moth ★	De Havilland Heritage Museum/London Colney	
G-ANSM	DH.82A Tiger Moth	Douglas Aviation	
G-ANTE	DH.82A Tiger Moth (T6562)	G-ANTE Flyers Ltd	
G-ANTK	Avro 685 York ★	Duxford Aviation Society	
G-ANUO	DH.114 Heron 2D (G-AOXL) ★	Westmead Business Group/Croydon Airport	
G-ANUW	DH.104 Dove 6 ★	Jet Aviation Preservation Group	
G-ANVY	P.31 Proctor 4	J. W. Tregilgas	
G-ANWB	DHC.1 Chipmunk 21	G. Briggs	
G-ANXB	DH.114 Heron 1B ★	Newark Air Museum	
G-ANXC	Auster J/5R Alpine	Alpine Group	
G-ANXR	P.31C Proctor 4 (RM221)	N. H. T. Cottrell	
G-ANZT	Thruxton Jackaroo (T7798)	D. J. Neville & P. A. Dear	
G-ANZU	DH.82A Tiger Moth	M. I. Lodge	
G-ANZZ	DH.82A Tiger Moth	T. K. Butcher	
G-AOAA	DH.82A Tiger Moth	R. C. P. Brookhouse	
G-AOBG	Somers-Kendall SK.1	P. W. Bishop	
G-AOBH	DH.82A Tiger Moth (NL750)	P. Nutley	
G-AOBJ	DH.82A Tiger Moth	A. D. Hodgkinson	
G-AOBU	P.84 Jet Provost T.1 (XD693)	T. J. Manna	
G-AOBX	DH.82A Tiger Moth	David Ross Flying Group	
G-AOCP	Auster 5 ★	C. J. Baker (stored)	
G-AOCR	Auster 5D (NJ673)	T. Taylor	
G-AOCU	Auster 5	S. J. Ball	
G-AODA	Westland S-55 Srs 3 ★	IHM/Weston-super-Mare	
G-AODR	DH.82A Tiger Moth	G-AODR Group (G-ISIS)	
G-AODT	DH.82A Tiger Moth (R5250)	R. A. Harrowven	
G-AOEH	Aeronca 7AC Champion	A. Gregori	
G-AOEI	DH.82A Tiger Moth	C.F.G. Flying Ltd	
G-AOEL	DH.82A Tiger Moth ★	Museum of Flight/East Fortune	
G-AOES	DH.82A Tiger Moth	K. A. & A. J. Broomfield	
G-AOET	DH.82A Tiger Moth	Venom Jet Promotions Ltd	
G-AOEX	Thruxton Jackaroo	A. T. Christian	
G-AOFE	DHC.1 Chipmunk 22A (WB702)	W. J. Quinn	
G-AOFJ	Auster J/1N Alpha	L. J. Kingscott	
G-AOFS	Auster J/5L Aiglet Trainer	P. N. A. Whitehead	
G-AOGA	M.75 Aries ★	Irish Aviation Museum (stored)	
G-AOGI	DH.82A Tiger Moth	W. J. Taylor	
G-AOGR	DH.82A Tiger Moth (XL714)	R. J. S. G. Clark	
G-AOGV	Auster J/5R Alpine	R. E. Heading	
G-AOHY	DH.82A Tiger Moth (N6537)	S. W. Turley	
G-AOHZ	Auster J/5P Autocar	A. D. Hodgkinson	
G-AOIM	DH.82A Tiger Moth	C. R. Hardiman	
G-AOIR	Thruxton Jackaroo	K. A. & A. J. Broomfield	
G-AOIS	DH.82A Tiger Moth (R5172)	J. K. Ellwood	
G-AOJH	DH.83C Fox Moth	Connect Properties Ltd	
G-AOJJ	DH.82A Tiger Moth (DF128)	E. & K. M. Lay	
G-AOJK	DH.82A Tiger Moth	R. J. Willies	
G-AOJR	DHC.1 Chipmunk 22	G. J-H. Caubergs & N. Marien/Belgium	
G-AOJT	DH.106 Comet 1 (F-BGNX) ★	De Havilland Heritage Museum (fuselage only)	
G-AOKH	P.40 Prentice 1	J. F. Moore	
G-AOKL	P.40 Prentice 1 (VS610)	The Shuttleworth Collection	
G-AOKO	P.40 Prentice 1 ★	Aero Venture	
G-AOKZ	P.40 Prentice 1 (VS623) ★	Midland Air Museum/Coventry	
G-AOLK	P.40 Prentice 1 ★	RAF Museum	
G-AOLU	P.40 Prentice 1 (VS356)	N. J. Butler	
G-AORB	Cessna 170B	Cranetec Engineering North Ltd	
G-AORG	DH.114 Heron 2	Duchess of Brittany (Jersey) Ltd	
G-AORW	DHC.1 Chipmunk 22A	Skylark Aviation Ltd	
G-AOSF	DHC.1 Chipmunk 22 (WB571:34)	D. A. W. Sensmeier/Germany	
G-AOSK	DHC.1 Chipmunk 22 (WB726)	L. J. Irvine	
G-AOSY	DHC.1 Chipmunk 22 (WB585:M)	Chippy Sierra Yankee Group	
G-AOTD	DHC.1 Chipmunk 22 (WB588)	S. Piech	
G-AOTF	DHC.1 Chipmunk 23 (Lycoming)	The Royal Air Force Gliding and Soaring Association	
G-AOTI	DH.114 Heron 2D ★	De Havilland Heritage Museum/London Colney	
G-AOTK	D.53 Turbi	TK Flying Group	
G-AOTR	DHC.1 Chipmunk 22	Ace Leasing Ltd	

Notes	Reg.	Type	Owner or Operator
	G-AOTY	DHC.1 Chipmunk 22A (WG472)	A. A. Hodgson
	G-AOUJ	Fairey Ultra-Light ★	IHM/Weston-super-Mare
	G-AOUO	DHC.1 Chipmunk 22 (Lycoming)	The Royal Air Force Gliding and Soaring Association
	G-AOUP	DHC.1 Chipmunk 22	A. R. Harding
	G-AOUR	DH.82A Tiger Moth ★	Ulster Folk & Transport Museum
	G-AOVF	B.175 Britannia 312F ★	Aerospace Museum/Cosford
	G-AOVS	B.175 Britannia 312F ★	Airport Fire Section/Luton
	G-AOVT	B.175 Britannia 312F ★	Duxford Aviation Society
	G-AOVW	Auster 5	B. Marriott
	G-AOXN	DH.82A Tiger Moth	S. L. G. Darch
	G-AOZH	DH.82A Tiger Moth (K2572)	M. H. Blois-Brooke
	G-AOZL	Auster J/5Q Alpine	R. M. Weeks
	G-AOZP	DHC.1 Chipmunk 22	S. J. Davies
	G-APAF	Auster 5 (TW511)	J. J. J. Mostyn (G-CMAL)
	G-APAH	Auster 5	T. J. Goodwin
	G-APAJ	Thruxton Jackaroo	J. T. H. Page
	G-APAL	DH.82A Tiger Moth (N6847)	P. J. Shotbolt
	G-APAM	DH.82A Tiger Moth	R. P. Williams
	G-APAO	DH.82A Tiger Moth (R4922)	H. J. Maguire
	G-APAP	DH.82A Tiger Moth (R5136)	Blue Eye Aviation Ltd
	G-APAS	DH.106 Comet 1XB ★	Aerospace Museum/Cosford
	G-APBE	Auster 5	R. B. Woods
	G-APBI	DH.82A Tiger Moth	C. J. Zeal
	G-APBO	D.53 Turbi	R. C. Hibberd
	G-APBW	Auster 5	C. R. W. Brown/France
	G-APCB	Auster J/5Q Alpine	A. A. Beswick
	G-APCC	DH.82A Tiger Moth	L. J. Rice/Henstridge
	G-APDB	DH.106 Comet 4 ★	Duxford Aviation Society
	G-APEP	V.953C Merchantman ★	Brooklands Museum of Aviation/Weybridge
	G-APFA	D.54 Turbi	F. J. Keitch
	G-APFJ	Boeing 707-436 ★	Museum of Flight/East Fortune
	G-APFU	DH.82A Tiger Moth	Leisure Assets Ltd
	G-APFV	PA-23-160 Apache	J. L. Thorogood (G-MOLY)
	G-APHV	Avro 19 Srs 2 (VM360) ★	Museum of Flight/East Fortune
	G-APIE	Tipsy Belfair B	D. Beale
	G-APIH	DH.82A Tiger Moth	K. Stewering
	G-APIK	Auster J/1N Alpha	J. H. Powell-Tuck
	G-APIM	V.806 Viscount ★	Brooklands Museum of Aviation/Weybridge
	G-APIT	P.40 Prentice 1 (VR192) ★	WWII Aircraft Preservation Society/Lasham
	G-APIY	P.40 Prentice 1 (VR249) ★	Newark Air Museum
	G-APIZ	D.31 Turbulent	R. G. Meredith
	G-APJB	P.40 Prentice 1 (VR259)	Air Atlantique Ltd
	G-APJJ	Fairey Ultra-light ★	Midland Aircraft Preservation Society
	G-APJZ	Auster J/1N Alpha	P. G. Lipman
	G-APKM	Auster J/1N Alpha	C. M. Tyers
	G-APLG	Auster J/5L Aiglet Trainer ★	Solway Aviation Society
	G-APLO	DHC.1 Chipmunk 22A (WD379)	Lindholme Aircraft Ltd
	G-APLU	DH.82A Tiger Moth	M. E. Vaisey
	G-APMB	DH.106 Comet 4B ★	Gatwick Handling Ltd (ground trainer)
	G-APMH	Auster J/1U Workmaster	M. R. P. Thorogood
	G-APMX	DH.82A Tiger Moth	Foley Farm Flying Group
	G-APMY	PA-23 Apache 160 ★	Aero Venture
	G-APNJ	Cessna 310 ★	Chelsea College/Shoreham
	G-APNT	Currie Wot	B. J. Dunford
	G-APNZ	D.31 Turbulent	J. Knight
	G-APPA	DHC.1 Chipmunk 22	D. M. Squires
	G-APPL	P.40 Prentice 1	S. J. Saggers
	G-APPM	DHC.1 Chipmunk 22 (WB711)	S. D. Wilch
	G-APRL	AW.650 Argosy 101 ★	Midland Air Museum/Coventry
	G-APRO	Auster 6A	A. F. & H. Wankowski
	G-APRR	Super Aero 45	M. J. O'Donnell
	G-APRS	SA Twin Pioneer Srs 3	Aviation Heritage Ltd (G-BCWF)
	G-APRT	Taylor JT.1 Monoplane	R. A. Keech
	G-APSA	Douglas DC-6A	Air Atlantique Ltd
	G-APSR	Auster J/1U Workmaster	D. & K. Aero Services Ltd
	G-APTR	Auster J/1N Alpha	C. R. Shipley
	G-APTU	Auster 5	G-APTU Flying Group
	G-APTW	Westland WS-51/2 Widgeon ★	North East Aircraft Museum/Usworth
	G-APTY	Beech G.35 Bonanza	G. E. Brennand
	G-APTZ	D.31 Turbulent	The Tiger Club (1990) Ltd
	G-APUD	Bensen B.7M (modified) ★	Manchester Museum of Science & Industry

Reg.	Type	Owner or Operator	Notes
G-APUE	L.40 Meta Sokol	S. E. & M. J. Aherne	
G-APUP	Sopwith Pup (replica) (N5182) ★	RAF Museum/Hendon	
G-APUR	PA-22 Tri-Pacer 160	S. T. A. Hutchinson	
G-APUW	Auster J/5V-160 Autocar	E. A. J. Hibbard	
G-APUY	D.31 Turbulent	C. Jones	
G-APVF	Putzer Elster B (97+04)	A. Wiseman	
G-APVG	Auster J/5L Aiglet Trainer	R. E. Tyers	
G-APVN	D.31 Turbulent	R. Sherwin	
G-APVS	Cessna 170B	N. Simpson Stormin' Norman	
G-APVU	L.40 Meta Sokol	S. E. & M. J. Aherne	
G-APVZ	D.31 Turbulent	The Tiger Club (1990) Ltd	
G-APWA	HPR.7 Herald 101 ★	Museum of Berkshire Aviation/Woodley	
G-APWJ	HPR.7 Herald 201 ★	Duxford Aviation Society	
G-APWN	Westland WS-55 Whirlwind 3 ★	Midland Air Museum/Coventry	
G-APWY	Piaggio P.166 ★	Science Museum/Wroughton	
G-APXJ	PA-24 Comanche 250	T. Wildsmith	
G-APXR	PA-22 Tri-Pacer 160	A. Troughton	
G-APXT	PA-22 Tri-Pacer 150 (modified)	A. E. Cuttler	
G-APXU	PA-22 Tri-Pacer 125 (modified)	G-APXU Syndicate	
G-APXW	EP.9 Prospector (XM819) ★	Museum of Army Flying/Middle Wallop	
G-APXX	DHA.3 Drover 2 (VH-FDT) ★	WWII Aircraft Preservation Society/Lasham	
G-APYB	Tipsy T.66 Nipper 3	B. O. Smith	
G-APYD	DH.106 Comet 4B ★	Science Museum/Wroughton	
G-APYG	DHC.1 Chipmunk 22	P. A. & J. M. Doyle	
G-APYI	PA-22 Tri-Pacer 135	D. R. Gibby	
G-APYT	Champion 7FC Tri-Traveller	B. J. Anning	
G-APZJ	PA-18 Super Cub 150	S. G. Jones	
G-APZL	PA-22 Tri-Pacer 160	B. Robins	
G-APZX	PA-22 Tri-Pacer 150	V. A. Holliday	
G-ARAD	Luton LA-5 Major ★	North East Aircraft Museum	
G-ARAM	PA-18 Super Cub 150	Skymax (Aviation) Ltd	
G-ARAN	PA-18 Super Cub 150	Cubs Flight Group	
G-ARAS	Champion 7FC Tri-Traveller	Alpha Sierra Flying Group	
G-ARAT	Cessna 180C	S. D. Pryke & J. Graham	
G-ARAW	Cessna 182C Skylane	Ximango UK	
G-ARAX	PA-22 Tri-Pacer 150	J. W. Iliffe	
G-ARAZ	DH.82A Tiger Moth (R4959:59)	D. A. Porter	
G-ARBE	DH.104 Dove 8	M. Whale & M. W. A. Lunn	
G-ARBG	Tipsy T.66 Nipper 2	D. Shrimpton	
G-ARBM	Auster V J1B Aiglet	A. D. Hodgkinson	
G-ARBO	PA-24 Comanche 250	Tatenhill Aviation Ltd	
G-ARBS	PA-22 Tri-Pacer 160 (tailwheel)	S. D. Rowell	
G-ARBV	PA-22 Tri-Pacer 160	L. M. Williams	
G-ARBZ	D.31 Turbulent	G. Richards	
G-ARCF	PA-22 Tri-Pacer 150	M. J. Speakman	
G-ARCS	Auster D6/180	R. J. Fray	
G-ARCT	PA-18 Super Cub 95	A. H. Diver	
G-ARCV	Cessna 175A	R. Francis & C. Campbell	
G-ARCW	PA-23 Apache 160	F. W. Ellis	
G-ARCX	A.W. Meteor 14 ★	Museum of Flight/East Fortune	
G-ARDB	PA-24 Comanche 250	P. Crook	
G-ARDD	CP.301C1 Emeraude	K. N. P. Higgs	
G-ARDE	DH.104 Dove 6 ★	T. E. Evans	
G-ARDJ	Auster D.6/180	P. N. A. Whitehead	
G-ARDO	Jodel D.112	W. R. Prescott	
G-ARDS	PA-22 Caribbean 150	N. P. McGowan & C. A. Donaldson	
G-ARDV	PA-22 Tri-Pacer 160	M. D. N. Fisher	
G-ARDY	Tipsy T.66 Nipper 2	J. K. Davies	
G-ARDZ	Jodel D.140A	M. J. Wright	
G-AREA	DH.104 Dove 8 ★	De Havilland Heritage Museum/London Colney	
G-AREH	DH.82A Tiger Moth	C. D. Cyster & A. J. Hastings	
G-AREI	Auster 3 (MT438)	R. B. Webber	
G-AREL	PA-22 Caribbean 150	The Caribbean Flying Club	
G-AREO	PA-18 Super Cub 150	E. P. Parkin	
G-ARET	PA-22 Tri-Pacer 160	L. A. Runnalls	
G-AREV	PA-22 Tri-Pacer 160	D. J. Ash	
G-AREX	Aeronca 15AC Sedan	R. J. M. Turnbull	
G-ARFB	PA-22 Caribbean 150	The Tri Pacer Group	
G-ARFD	PA-22 Tri-Pacer 160	J. R. Dunnett	
G-ARFG	Cessna 175°	G. C. Rogers	
G-ARFI	Cessna 150A	J. D. Woodward	
G-ARFO	Cessna 150A	A. P. Amor	

Notes	Reg.	Type	Owner or Operator
	G-ARFT	Jodel DR.1050	R. Shaw
	G-ARFV	Tipsy T.66 Nipper 2	J. J. Austin
	G-ARGG	DHC.1 Chipmunk 22 (WD305)	D. Curtis
	G-ARGO	PA-22 Colt 108	D. R. Smith
	G-ARGV	PA-18 Super Cub 180	Wolds Gliding Club Ltd
	G-ARGY	PA-22 Tri-Pacer 160	A. & I. Bazin (G-JEST)
	G-ARGZ	D.31 Turbulent	The Tiger Club (1990) Ltd
	G-ARHB	Forney F-1A Aircoupe	K. J. Peacock & S. F. Turner
	G-ARHC	Forney F-1A Aircoupe	D. J. Hewitt
	G-ARHL	PA-23 Aztec 250	C. J. Freeman
	G-ARHM	Auster 6A	R. C. P. Brookhouse
	G-ARHN	PA-22 Caribbean 150	Popham Flying Group
	G-ARHR	PA-22 Caribbean 150	A. R. Wyatt
	G-ARHW	DH.104 Dove 8	Aviation Heritage Ltd
	G-ARHX	DH.104 Dove 8 ★	North East Aircraft Museum
	G-ARHZ	D.62 Condor	E. Shouler
	G-ARID	Cessna 172B	L. M. Edwards
	G-ARIF	Ord-Hume O-H.7 Minor Coupé ★	M. J. Aubrey
	G-ARIH	Auster 6A (TW591)	M. C. Jordan
	G-ARIK	PA-22 Caribbean 150	A. Taylor
	G-ARIL	PA-22 Caribbean 150	S. Eustathiou
	G-ARJB	DH.104 Dove 8	M. Whale & M. W. A. Lunn
	G-ARJE	PA-22 Colt 108	C. I. Fray
	G-ARJF	PA-22 Colt 108	M. J. Avery
	G-ARJH	PA-22 Colt 108	F. Vogels/France
	G-ARJR	PA-23 Apache 160G ★	Instructional airframe/Kidlington
	G-ARJS	PA-23 Apache 160G	Bencray Ltd/Blackpool
	G-ARJT	PA-23 Apache 160G	J. H. Ashcroft
	G-ARJU	PA-23 Apache 160G	Man Air Ltd
	G-ARKG	Auster J/5G Autocar	A. G. Boon & C. L. Towell
	G-ARKJ	Beech N35 Bonanza	G. D. E. Macdonald
	G-ARKK	PA-22 Colt 108	R. D. Welfare
	G-ARKM	PA-22 Colt 108	G. Cannon
	G-ARKN	PA-22 Colt 108	R. Redfern & M. Barker
	G-ARKP	PA-22 Colt 108	J. P. A. Freeman
	G-ARKS	PA-22 Colt 108	R. A. Nesbitt-Dufort
	G-ARLB	PA-24 Comanche 250	D. Heater (G-BUTL)
	G-ARLG	Auster D.4/108	Auster D4 Group
	G-ARLK	PA-24 Comanche 250	R. P. Jackson
	G-ARLP	Beagle A.61 Terrier 1	Gemini Flying Group
	G-ARLR	Beagle A.61 Terrier 2	M. Palfreman
	G-ARLU	Cessna 172B Skyhawk ★	Instructional airframe/Irish Air Corps
	G-ARLZ	D.31A Turbulent	A. D. Wilson
	G-ARMC	DHC.1 Chipmunk 22A (WB703)	John Henderson Children's Trust
	G-ARMF	DHC.1 Chipmunk 22A (WZ868:H)	D. M. Squires
	G-ARMG	DHC.1 Chipmunk 22A	M. F. Cuming
	G-ARML	Cessna 175B Skylark	D. Stephens
	G-ARMN	Cessna 175B Skylark	G-ARMN Group
	G-ARMO	Cessna 172B Skyhawk	A. J. Tobias
	G-ARMR	Cessna 172B Skyhawk	Sunsaver Ltd/Barton
	G-ARMZ	D.31 Turbulent	The Tiger Club (1990) Ltd
	G-ARNB	Auster J/5G Autocar	R. F. Tolhurst
	G-ARND	PA-22 Colt 108	J. L. & J. E. D. Rogerson
	G-ARNE	PA-22 Colt 108	The Shiny Colt Group
	G-ARNG	PA-22 Colt 108	F. B. Rothera
	G-ARNJ	PA-22 Colt 108	R. A. Keech
	G-ARNK	PA-22 Colt 108 (tailwheel)	S. J. Smith
	G-ARNL	PA-22 Colt 108	J. A. Dodsworth
	G-ARNO	Beagle A.61 Terrier 1 ★ (VX113)	–/Sywell
	G-ARNP	Beagle A.109 Airedale	S. W. & M. Isbister
	G-ARNY	Jodel D.117	G-ARNY Flying Group
	G-ARNZ	D.31 Turbulent	The Tiger Club (1990) Ltd
	G-AROA	Cessna 172B Skyhawk	D. E. Partridge
	G-AROC	Cessna 175B	A. J. Symes (G-OTOW)
	G-AROJ	Beagle A.109 Airedale ★	D. J. Shaw (stored)
	G-ARON	PA-22 Colt 108	M. Hayter
	G-AROO	Forney F-1A Aircoupe	W. J. McMeekan
	G-AROW	Jodel D.140B	A. R. Crome
	G-AROY	Boeing Stearman A75N.1	I. T. Whitaker-Bethel & J. Mann
	G-ARPH	HS.121 Trident 1C ★	Museum of Flight/East Fortune
	G-ARPK	HS.121 Trident 1C ★	Manchester Airport Authority
	G-ARPO	HS.121 Trident 1C ★	CAA Fire School/Teesside
	G-ARRD	Jodel DR.1050	P. R. Watkins

Reg.	Type	Owner or Operator	Notes
G-ARRE	Jodel DR.1050	West of Leicester Flyers	
G-ARRI	Cessna 175B	G-ARRI Partnership	
G-ARRL	Auster J/1N Alpha	A. C. Ladd	
G-ARRM	Beagle B.206-X ★	Bristol Aero Collection (stored)	
G-ARRO	Beagle A.109 Airedale	M. & S. W. Isbister	
G-ARRS	CP.301A Emeraude	J. F. Sully	
G-ARRT	Wallis WA-116-1	K. H. Wallis	
G-ARRU	D.31 Turbulent	D. G. Huck	
G-ARRX	Auster 6A (VF512)	J. E. D. Mackie	
G-ARRY	Jodel D.140B	C. Thomas	
G-ARRZ	D.31 Turbulent	T. A. Stambach	
G-ARSG	Roe Triplane Type IV (replica)	The Shuttleworth Collection/Old Warden	
G-ARSL	Beagle A.61 Terrier 1 (VF581)	D. J. Colclough	
G-ARSU	PA-22 Colt 108	Sierra Uniform Flying Group	
G-ARTH	PA-12 Super Cruiser	R. I. Souch	
G-ARTJ	Bensen B.8M ★	Museum of Flight/East Fortune	
G-ARTL	DH.82A Tiger Moth (T7281)	F. G. Clacherty	
G-ARTT	MS.880B Rallye Club	R. N. Scott	
G-ARTZ	McCandless M.4 gyroplane	W. R. Partridge	
G-ARUG	Auster J/5G Autocar	D. P. H. Hulme	
G-ARUH	Jodel DR.1050	A. F. Vizoso	
G-ARUI	Beagle A.61 Terrier	T. W. J. Dann	
G-ARUL	LeVier Cosmic Wind	P. G. Kynsey	
G-ARUV	CP.301A Emeraude	S. D. Glover	
G-ARUY	Auster J/1N Alpha	D. Burnham	
G-ARUZ	Cessna 175C	Cardiff Skylark Group	
G-ARVM	V.1101 VC10 ★	Brooklands Museum of Aviation/Weybridge	
G-ARVO	PA-18 Super Cub 95	M. Ali	
G-ARVT	PA-28 Cherokee 160	Red Rose Aviation Ltd	
G-ARVU	PA-28 Cherokee 160	Barton Mudwing Ltd	
G-ARVV	PA-28 Cherokee 160	G. E. Hopkins	
G-ARVZ	D.62B Condor	A. A. M. Huke	
G-ARWB	DHC.1 Chipmunk 22 (WK611)	Thruxton Chipmunk Flying Club	
G-ARWR	Cessna 172C	Devanha Flying Group	
G-ARWS	Cessna 175C	M. D. Fage	
G-ARXB	Beagle A.109 Airedale	S. W. & M. Isbister	
G-ARXD	Beagle A.109 Airedale	D. Howden	
G-ARXG	PA-24 Comanche 250	R. F. Corstin	
G-ARXH	Bell 47G	A. B. Searle	
G-ARXP	Luton LA-4 Minor	R. M. Weeks	
G-ARXT	Jodel DR.1050	CJM Flying Group	
G-ARXU	Auster 6A (VF526)	A. B. Taylor-Roberts and E. M. Le Gresley	
G-ARXW	MS.885 Super Rallye	M. J. Kirk	
G-ARYB	HS.125 Srs 1 ★	Midland Air Museum/Coventry	
G-ARYC	HS.125 Srs 1 ★	De Havilland Heritage Museum/London Colney	
G-ARYD	Auster AOP.6 (WJ358) ★	Museum of Army Flying/Middle Wallop	
G-ARYH	PA-22 Tri-Pacer 160	C. Watt	
G-ARYK	Cessna 172C	A. Winnicott	
G-ARYR	PA-28 Cherokee 180	G-ARYR Flying Group	
G-ARYS	Cessna 172C	M. S. Johnston	
G-ARYV	PA-24 Comanche 250	D. C. Hanss	
G-ARYZ	Beagle A.109 Airedale	C. W. Tomkins	
G-ARZB	Wallis WA-116 Srs 1	K. H. Wallis	
G-ARZS	Beagle A.109 Airedale	M. & S. W. Isbister	
G-ARZW	Currie Wot	B. R. Pearson	
G-ASAA	Luton LA-4 Minor	M. J. Aubrey (stored)	
G-ASAI	Beagle A.109 Airedale	K. R. Howden	
G-ASAJ	Beagle A.61 Terrier 2 (WE569)	T. Bailey	
G-ASAL	SA Bulldog Srs 120/124	Pioneer Flying Co Ltd	
G-ASAU	MS.880B Rallye Club	M. S. Lonsdale	
G-ASAX	Beagle A.61 Terrier 2	A. D. Hodgkinson	
G-ASAZ	Hiller UH-12E4 (XS165)	Hields Aviation/Sherburn	
G-ASBA	Phoenix Currie Wot	J. C. Lister	
G-ASBH	Beagle A.109 Airedale	D. T. Smollett	
G-ASCC	Beagle E3 Mk 11 (XP254)	R. Warner	
G-ASCD	Beagle A.61 Terrier 2 (TJ704) ★	Yorkshire Air Museum/Elvington	
G-ASCH	Beagle A.61 Terrier 2	G-ASCH Group	
G-ASCM	Isaacs Fury II (K2050)	R. F. Redknap	
G-ASCZ	CP.301A Emeraude	I. Denham-Brown	
G-ASDF	Edwards Gyrocopter ★	B. King	
G-ASDK	Beagle A.61 Terrier 2	J. Swallow (G-ARLM)	
G-ASDY	Wallis WA-116/F	K. H. Wallis	
G-ASEA	Luton LA-4A Minor	D. Underwood	

G-ASEB – G-ASSV

Notes	Reg.	Type	Owner or Operator
	G-ASEB	Luton LA-4A Minor	S. R. P. Harper
	G-ASEO	PA-24 Comanche 250	Oxbridge Investments Ltd
	G-ASEP	PA-23 Apache 235	Arrowstate Ltd
	G-ASEU	D.62A Condor	W. M. Grant
	G-ASFA	Cessna 172D	Fly BPL.com
	G-ASFD	L-200A Morava	M. Emery
	G-ASFK	Auster J/5G Autocar	B. C. C. Harrison
	G-ASFL	PA-28 Cherokee 180	G-ASFL Group
	G-ASFR	Bölkow Bö.208A1 Junior	S. T. Dauncey
	G-ASFX	D.31 Turbulent	E. F. Clapham & W. B. S. Dobie
	G-ASGC	V.1151 Super VC10 ★	Duxford Aviation Society
	G-ASHD	Brantly B.2A ★	IHM/Weston-super-Mare
	G-ASHS	SNCAN Stampe SV.4C	J. W. Beaty
	G-ASHT	D.31 Turbulent	C. W. N. Huke
	G-ASHU	PA-15 Vagabond (modified)	The Calybe Flying Group
	G-ASHX	PA-28 Cherokee 180	Powertheme Ltd
	G-ASIB	Cessna F.172D	S. J. Ducker
	G-ASII	PA-28 Cherokee 180	T. N. & T. R. Hart & R. W. S. Matthews
	G-ASIJ	PA-28 Cherokee 180	MK Aero Support Ltd
	G-ASIL	PA-28 Cherokee 180	R. Plant & J. Wesson
	G-ASIS	Jodel D.112	W. R. Prescott
	G-ASIT	Cessna 180	R. A. Seeley
	G-ASIY	PA-25 Pawnee 235	The Royal Air Force Gliding and Soaring Association
	G-ASJL	Beech H.35 Bonanza	R. L. Dargue
	G-ASJV	VS.361 Spitfire IX (MH434/PK-K)	Merlin Aviation Ltd
	G-ASJZ	Jodel D.117A	M. A. Watts
	G-ASKC	DH.98 Mosquito 35 (TA719) ★	Skyfame Collection/Duxford
	G-ASKK	HPR.7 Herald 211 ★	Norwich Aviation Museum
	G-ASKL	Jodel D.150	J. M. Graty
	G-ASKP	DH.82A Tiger Moth	Tiger Club (1990) Ltd
	G-ASKT	PA-28 Cherokee 180	T. J. Herbert
	G-ASLH	Cessna 182F	A. L. Brown & A. L. Butcher
	G-ASLV	PA-28 Cherokee 235	Aces High Ltd
	G-ASLX	CP.301A Emeraude	J. J. Reilly
	G-ASMA	PA-30 Twin Comanche 160 C/R	K. Cooper
	G-ASME	Bensen B.8M	R. M. Harris
	G-ASMF	Beech D.95A Travel Air	M. J. A. Hornblower
	G-ASMJ	Cessna F.172E	Aeroscene Ltd
	G-ASML	Luton LA-4A Minor	R. W. Vince
	G-ASMM	D.31 Tubulent	W. J. Browning
	G-ASMS	Cessna 150A	M. & W. Long
	G-ASMT	Fairtravel Linnet 2	P. Harrison
	G-ASMV	CP.1310-C3 Super Emeraude	P. F. D. Waltham
	G-ASMW	Cessna 150D	Dukeries Aviation
	G-ASMY	PA-23 Apache 160 ★	R. D. Forster
	G-ASMZ	Beagle A.61 Terrier 2 (VF516)	B. Andrews
	G-ASNC	Beagle D.5/180 Husky	Peterborough & Spalding Gliding Club Ltd
	G-ASNI	CP.1310-C3 Super Emeraude	D. Chapman
	G-ASNK	Cessna 205	Justgold Ltd
	G-ASNW	Cessna F.172E	G-ASNW Group
	G-ASNY	Campbell-Bensen B.8M gyroplane ★	R. Light & T. Smith
	G-ASOH	Beech 95-B55A Baron	G. Davis & C. Middlemiss
	G-ASOI	Beagle A.61 Terrier 2	G.D.B. Delmege
	G-ASOK	Cessna F.172E	D. W. Disney
	G-ASOL	Bell 47D ★	North East Aircraft Museum
	G-ASOM	Beagle A.61 Terrier 2	GASOM.org (G-JETS)
	G-ASOX	Cessna 205A	S. M. C. Harvey
	G-ASPF	Jodel D.120	G. W. Street
	G-ASPP	Bristol Boxkite (replica)	The Shuttleworth Collection/Old Warden
	G-ASPS	Piper J-3C-90 Cub	A. J. Chalkley/Blackbushe
	G-ASPV	DH.82A Tiger Moth (T7794)	P. Zanardo
	G-ASRB	D.62B Condor	B. J. Douglas/Ireland
	G-ASRC	D.62C Condor	C. R. Isbell
	G-ASRK	Beagle A.109 Airedale	Bio Pathica Ltd/Lydd
	G-ASRO	PA-30 Twin Comanche 160	D. W. Blake
	G-ASRT	Jodel 150	P. Turton
	G-ASRW	PA-28 Cherokee 180	G. N. Smith
	G-ASSM	HS.125 Srs 1/522 ★	Science Museum/South Kensington
	G-ASSP	PA-30 Twin Comanche 160	P. H. Tavener
	G-ASSS	Cessna 172E	P. R. March & P. Turner/Filton
	G-ASST	Cessna 150D	F. R. H. Parker
	G-ASSV	Kensinger KF	C. I. Jefferson

Reg.	Type	Owner or Operator	Notes
G-ASSW	PA-28 Cherokee 140	E. R. Curry	
G-ASSY	D.31 Turbulent	R. C. Bailey	
G-ASTG	Nord 1002 Pingouin II	R. J. Fray	
G-ASTI	Auster 6A	S. J. Partridge	
G-ASTL	Fairey Firefly I (Z2033) ★	F.A. A. Museum/Yeovilton	
G-ASTP	Hiller UH-12C ★	IHM/Weston-super-Mare	
G-ASUB	Mooney M.20E Super 21	S. C. Coulbeck	
G-ASUD	PA-28 Cherokee 180	G-ASUD Group	
G-ASUE	Cessna 150D	D. Huckle	
G-ASUG	Beech E18S ★	Museum of Flight/East Fortune	
G-ASUI	Beagle A.61 Terrier 2	A. L. Aish	
G-ASUP	Cessna F.172E	GASUP Air	
G-ASUR	Dornier Do 28A-1	N. J. Taafe	
G-ASUS	Jurca MJ.2B Tempete	R. Targonski	
G-ASVG	CP.301B Emeraude	K. R. H. Wingate	
G-ASVM	Cessna F.172E	R. H. Bennett	
G-ASVO	HPR.7 Herald 214 ★	Archive Visitor Centre/Shoreham (cockpit section)	
G-ASVP	PA-25 Pawnee 235	Banbury Gliding Club Ltd	
G-ASVZ	PA-28 Cherokee 140	T. D. Jackman	
G-ASWJ	Beagle 206 Srs 1 (8449M) ★	Brunel Technical College/Bristol	
G-ASWN	Bensen B.8M	D. R. Shepherd	
G-ASWX	PA-28 Cherokee 180	Gasworks Flying Group Ltd	
G-ASXC	SIPA 903	B. L. Procter (G-DWEL)	
G-ASXD	Brantly B.2B	Lousada PLC	
G-ASXI	Tipsy T.66 Nipper 3	P. G. Blenkinsopp	
G-ASXJ	Luton LA-4A Minor	C. R. Greenaway	
G-ASXS	Jodel DR.1050	R. A. Hunter	
G-ASXU	Jodel D.120A	G-ASXU Group	
G-ASXX	Avro 683 Lancaster 7 (NX611) ★	Panton Family Trust/East Kirkby	
G-ASXZ	Cessna 182G Skylane	Last Refuge Ltd	
G-ASYD	BAC One-Eleven 475 ★	Brooklands Museum of Aviation/Weybridge	
G-ASYG	Beagle A.61 Terrier 2 (VX927)	Terrane Auster Group	
G-ASYJ	Beech D.95A Travel Air	Crosby Aviation (Jersey) Ltd	
G-ASYP	Cessna 150E	Henlow Flying Group	
G-ASZB	Cessna 150E	R. J. Scott	
G-ASZD	Bölkow Bö.208A2 Junior	M. J. Ayers	
G-ASZE	Beagle A.61 Terrier 2	D. R. Ockleton	
G-ASZR	Fairtravel Linnet 2	R. Hodgson	
G-ASZS	Gardan GY-80 Horizon 160	ZS Group	
G-ASZU	Cessna 150E	L. J. Baker, R. Hall & C. Davies	
G-ASZV	Tipsy T.66 Nipper 2	D. H. Greenwood	
G-ASZX	Beagle A.61 Terrier 1 (WJ368)	R. B. Webber	
G-ATAF	Cessna F.172F	Summit Media Ltd	
G-ATAG	Jodel DR.1050	T. M. Dawes-Gamble	
G-ATAS	PA-28 Cherokee 180	ATAS Group	
G-ATAU	D.62B Condor	M. C. Burlock	
G-ATAV	D.62C Condor	V. A. Holliday	
G-ATBG	Nord 1002 (NJ+C11)	Ardmore Aviation Service	
G-ATBH	Aero 145	P. D. Aberbach	
G-ATBI	Beech A.23 Musketeer	Three Musketeers Flying Group	
G-ATBJ	Sikorsky S-61N	British International	
G-ATBL	DH.60G Moth	The R. W. Beaty (Farms) Ltd Unapproved Pension Scheme for Mr. S. J. Beaty	
G-ATBP	Fournier RF-3	D. McNicholl	
G-ATBS	D.31 Turbulent	J. A. Lear	
G-ATBU	Beagle A.61 Terrier 2	T. Jarvis	
G-ATBW	Tipsy T.66 Nipper 2	Stapleford Nipper Group	
G-ATBX	PA-20 Pacer 135	G. D. & P. M. Thomson	
G-ATBZ	Westland WS-58 Wessex 60 ★	IHM/Weston-super-Mare	
G-ATCC	Beagle A.109 Airedale	J. R. Bowden	
G-ATCD	Beagle D.5/180 Husky	T. C. O'Gorman	
G-ATCE	Cessna U.206	A. J. Hickling	
G-ATCJ	Luton LA-4A Minor	T. D. Boyle	
G-ATCL	Victa Airtourer 100	A. D. Goodall	
G-ATCN	Luton LA-4A Minor	The Real Aeroplane Co.Ltd	
G-ATCX	Cessna 182 ★	Softnotes Ltd	
G-ATDA	PA-28 Cherokee 160	Portway Aviation Ltd/Shobdon	
G-ATDN	Beagle A.61 Terrier 2 (TW641)	S. J. SaggersBiggin Hill	
G-ATDO	Bölkow Bö.208C1 Junior	P. Thompson	
G-ATEF	Cessna 150E	Swans Aviation	
G-ATEM	PA-28 Cherokee 180	G. D. Wyles	
G-ATEP	EAA Biplane ★	E. L. Martin (red)/Guernsey	

Notes	Reg.	Type	Owner or Operator
	G-ATEV	Jodel DR.1050	J. C. Carter & J. L. Altrip
	G-ATEW	PA-30 Twin Comanche 160	Air Northumbria (Woolsington) Ltd
	G-ATEZ	PA-28 Cherokee 140	EFI Aviation Ltd
	G-ATFD	Jodel DR.1050	G-ATFD Group
	G-ATFF	PA-23 Aztec 250C	T. J. Wassell
	G-ATFG	Brantly B.2B ★	Museum of Flight/East Fortune
	G-ATFM	Sikorsky S-61N	British International
	G-ATFR	PA-25 Pawnee 150	Borders (Milfield) Gliding Club Ltd
	G-ATFV	Agusta-Bell 47J-2A ★	Caernarfon Air World
	G-ATFY	Cessna F.172G	J. M. Vinall
	G-ATGN	Thorn Coal Gas Balloon	British Balloon Museum/Newbury
	G-ATGP	Jodel DR.1050	Madley Flying Group
	G-ATGY	Gardan GY-80 Horizon	D. H. Mackay
	G-ATHA	PA-23 Apache 235 ★	Brunel Technical College/Bristol
	G-ATHD	DHC.1 Chipmunk 22 (WP971)	Spartan Flying Group Ltd
	G-ATHK	Aeronca 7AC Champion	The Chase Flying Group
	G-ATHM	Wallis WA-116 Srs 1	Wallis Autogyros Ltd
	G-ATHN	Nord 1101 Noralpha ★	E. L. Martin (stored)/Guernsey
	G-ATHR	PA-28 Cherokee 180	Azure Flying Club Ltd
	G-ATHT	Victa Airtourer 115	Cotswold Flying Group
	G-ATHU	Beagle A.61 Terrier 1	J. A. L. Irwin
	G-ATHV	Cessna 150F	Cessna Hotel Victor Group
	G-ATHZ	Cessna 150F	R. D. Forster
	G-ATIC	Jodel DR.1050	T. A. Major
	G-ATIG	HPR.7 Herald 214 ★	Norwich Airport towing trainer
	G-ATIN	Jodel D.117	A. Ayre
	G-ATIR	AIA Stampe SV.4C	A. Trueman
	G-ATIS	PA-28 Cherokee 160	D. E. Skertchly
	G-ATIZ	Jodel D.117	R. A. Smith
	G-ATJA	Jodel DR.1050	Bicester Flying Group
	G-ATJC	Victa Airtourer 100 (modfied)	Aviation West Ltd
	G-ATJG	PA-28 Cherokee 140	C. A. McGee
	G-ATJL	PA-24 Comanche 260	S. J. Ollier
	G-ATJN	Jodel D.119	J. Upex
	G-ATJV	PA-32 Cherokee Six 260	Wingglider Ltd
	G-ATKH	Luton LA-4A Minor	H. E. Jenner
	G-ATKI	Piper J-3C-65 Cub	B. Ryan
	G-ATKT	Cessna F.172G	R. J. D. Blois
	G-ATKX	Jodel D.140C	Kilo Xray Syndicate
	G-ATLA	Cessna 182J Skylane	J. W. & J. T. Whicher
	G-ATLB	Jodel DR.1050/M1	Le Syndicate du Petit Oiseau
	G-ATLM	Cessna F.172G	Air Fotos Aviation Ltd
	G-ATLP	Bensen B.8M	R. F. G. Moyle
	G-ATLT	Cessna U.206A	Skydive UK Ltd
	G-ATLV	Jodel D.120	G. Constantine & A. Y. Leung
	G-ATMC	Cessna F.150F	G. H. Farrah & D. Cunnane
	G-ATMH	Beagle D.5/180 Husky	Dorset Gliding Club Ltd
	G-ATMM	Cessna F.150F	Cranfield Aviation Training School Ltd
	G-ATMT	PA-30 Twin Comanche 160	Montagu-Smith & Co Ltd
	G-ATNB	PA-28 Cherokee 180	Ken Macdonald and Co
	G-ATNE	Cessna F.150F	T. P. Hancock
	G-ATNL	Cessna F.150F	PVI Power Services Ltd
	G-ATNV	PA-24 Comanche 260	K. Powell
	G-ATOH	D.62B Condor	Three Spires Flying Group
	G-ATOI	PA-28 Cherokee 140	R. Ronaldson
	G-ATOJ	PA-28 Cherokee 140	A Flight Aviation Ltd
	G-ATOK	PA-28 Cherokee 140	ILC Flying Group
	G-ATOM	PA-28 Cherokee 140	A. Flight Aviation Ltd
	G-ATON	PA-28 Cherokee 140	Stirling Flying Syndicate
	G-ATOO	PA-28 Cherokee 140	Caralair Aviation
	G-ATOP	PA-28 Cherokee 140	P. R. Coombs
	G-ATOR	PA-28 Cherokee 140	Aligator Group
	G-ATOT	PA-28 Cherokee 180	P. A. Layzell
	G-ATOU	Mooney M.20E Super 21	DbProf Doo
	G-ATOY	PA-24 Comanche 260 ★	Museum of Flight/East Fortune
	G-ATOZ	Bensen B.8M	C. R. Gordon
	G-ATPN	PA-28 Cherokee 140	M. F. Hatt & ptnrs
	G-ATPT	Cessna 182J Skylane	C. Beer t/a Papa Tango Group
	G-ATPV	JB.01 Minicab	M. J. Cook
	G-ATRG	PA-18 Super Cub 150	Lasham Gliding Society Ltd
	G-ATRK	Cessna F.150F	Falcon Aviation Ltd
	G-ATRL	Cessna F.150F	A. A. W. Stevens
	G-ATRM	Cessna F.150F	J. Redfearn

Reg.	Type	Owner or Operator	Notes
G-ATRR	PA-28 Cherokee 140	Blue Sky Investments Ltd	
G-ATRW	PA-32 Cherokee Six 260	Pringle Brandon Architects	
G-ATRX	PA-32 Cherokee Six 260	F. Chakroun	
G-ATSI	Bölkow Bö.208C1 Junior	GATSI Bolkow Ltd	
G-ATSL	Cessna F.172G	C. S. & C. S. Soojeri	
G-ATSR	Beech M.35 Bonanza	C. B. Linton	
G-ATSX	Bölkow Bö.208C1 Junior	Little Bear Ltd	
G-ATSY	Wassmer Wa.41 Super Baladou IV	McLean Aviation	
G-ATSZ	PA-30 Twin Comanche 160B	Sierra Zulu Aviation Ltd	
G-ATTB	Wallis WA-116-1 (XR944)	D. A. Wallis	
G-ATTD	Cessna 182J	M. F. C. Perez	
G-ATTI	PA-28 Cherokee 140	G-ATTI Flying Group	
G-ATTK	PA-28 Cherokee 140	G-ATTK Flying Group/Southend	
G-ATTM	Jodel DR.250-160	C. P. Tomkinson	
G-ATTN	Piccard HA Balloon ★	Science Museum/South Kensington	
G-ATTR	Bölkow Bö.208C1 Junior	S. Luck	
G-ATTV	PA-28 Cherokee 140	D. B. & M. E. Meeks	
G-ATTX	PA-28 Cherokee 180	IPAC Aviation Ltd	
G-ATUB	PA-28 Cherokee 140	G-ATUB Group	
G-ATUF	Cessna F.150F	D. P. Williams	
G-ATUG	D.62B Condor	C. Gill	
G-ATUH	Tipsy T.66 Nipper 1	M. D. Barnard & C. Voelger	
G-ATUI	Bölkow Bö.208C1 Junior	M. J. Grundy	
G-ATUL	PA-28 Cherokee 160	Barry Fielding Aviation Ltd	
G-ATVF	DHC.1 Chipmunk 22 (WD327)	The Royal Air Force Gliding and Soaring Association	
G-ATVK	PA-28 Cherokee 140	R. F. Cresswell	
G-ATVO	PA-28 Cherokee 140	G. R. Bright	
G-ATVP	Vickers FB.5 Gunbus replica (2345) ★	RAF Museum/Hendon	
G-ATVS	PA-28 Cherokee 180	D. S. Olson	
G-ATVW	D.62B Condor	G. G. Roberts	
G-ATVX	Bölkow Bö.208C1 Junior	A. M. Witt	
G-ATWA	Jodel DR.1050	One Twenty Group	
G-ATWB	Jodel D.117	Andrewsfield Whisky Bravo Group	
G-ATWJ	Cessna F.172F	J. P. A. Freeman/Headcorn	
G-ATXA	PA-22 Tri-Pacer 150	S. Hildrop	
G-ATXD	PA-30 Twin Comanche 160B	C. A. Denovan	
G-ATXJ	HP.137 Jetstream 300 ★	Fire Service training airframe/Cardiff	
G-ATXN	Mitchell-Proctor Kittiwake 1	R. G. Day/Biggin Hill	
G-ATXO	SIPA 903	C. H. Morris	
G-ATXX	McCandless M.4 gyroplane ★	Ulster Folk & Transport Museum	
G-ATXZ	Bölkow Bö.208C1 Junior	G-ATXZ Group	
G-ATYM	Cessna F.150G	B. G. De Wert	
G-ATYN	Cessna F.150G	J. S. Grant	
G-ATYS	PA-28 Cherokee 180	D. G. Baverstock	
G-ATZM	Piper J-3C-90 Cub	N. D. Marshall	
G-ATZS	Wassmer Wa.41 Super Baladou IV	G-ATZS Flying Group	
G-ATZY	Cessna F.150G	Aircraft Engineers Ltd	
G-AVAR	Cessna F.150G	J. A. Rees	
G-AVAW	D.62B Condor	Condor Aircraft Group	
G-AVAX	PA-28 Cherokee 180	A. F. Prosser	
G-AVBG	PA-28 Cherokee 180	M. C. Plomer-Roberts	
G-AVBH	PA-28 Cherokee 180	T. R. Smith (Agricultural Machinery) Ltd	
G-AVBS	PA-28 Cherokee 180	Bravo Sierra Flying Group	
G-AVBT	PA-28 Cherokee 180	J. F. Mitchell	
G-AVCM	PA-24 Comanche 260	R. F. Smith/Stapleford	
G-AVCN	BN-26A-8 Islander	Britten-Norman Aircraft Preservation Society	
G-AVCV	Cessna 182J Skylane	University of Manchester, School of Earth, Atmospheric and Environmental Sciences	
G-AVDA	Cessna 182K Skylane	F. W. Ellis	
G-AVDG	Wallis WA-116 Srs 1	K. H. Wallis	
G-AVDS	Beech 65-B80 Queen Air ★	Airport Fire Service/Filton	
G-AVDT	Aeronca 7AC Champion	D. & N. Cheney	
G-AVDV	PA-22-150 Tri-Pacer	P. Bower	
G-AVDY	Luton LA-4A Minor	J. Goodband	
G-AVEC	Cessna F.172 ★	S. M. Furner	
G-AVEF	Jodel 150	Heavy Install Ltd	
G-AVEH	SIAI-Marchetti S.205	EH Aviation	
G-AVEM	Cessna F.150G	M. A. Watts	
G-AVEN	Cessna F.150G	J. M. Hough	
G-AVEO	Cessna F.150G	Execflyer (G-DENA)	
G-AVER	Cessna F.150G	LAC Flying School	
G-AVEU	Wassmer Wa.41 Baladou IV	The Baladou Flying Group	

Notes	Reg.	Type	Owner or Operator
	G-AVEX	D.62B Condor	C. A. Macleod
	G-AVEY	Currie Super Wot	C. K. Farley
	G-AVEZ	HPR.7 Herald 210 ★	Rescue trainer/Norwich
	G-AVFB	HS.121 Trident 2E ★	Duxford Aviation Society
	G-AVFE	HS.121 Trident 2E ★	Belfast Airport Authority
	G-AVFH	HS.121 Trident 2E ★	De Havilland Heritage Museum (fuselage only)/ London Colney
	G-AVFM	HS.121 Trident 2E ★	Brunel Technical College/Bristol
	G-AVFR	PA-28 Cherokee 140	R. R. Orr
	G-AVFU	PA-32 Cherokee Six 300	Trixstar Farms Ltd
	G-AVFX	PA-28 Cherokee 140	A. E. Fielding
	G-AVFZ	PA-28 Cherokee 140	G-AVFZ Flying Group
	G-AVGA	PA-24 Comanche 260	G. McD. Moir
	G-AVGC	PA-28 Cherokee 140	D. Matthews
	G-AVGE	PA-28 Cherokee 140	J. D. C. Lea
	G-AVGI	PA-28 Cherokee 140	Merseyflight Air Training School
	G-AVGU	Cessna F.150G	R. D. Luper
	G-AVGY	Cessna 182K Skylane	G. Appelback
	G-AVGZ	Jodel DR.1050	A. F. & S. Williams
	G-AVHH	Cessna F.172	Bristol & Wessex Helicopters Ltd
	G-AVHL	Jodel DR.105A	Seething Jodel Group
	G-AVHM	Cessna F.150G	D. A. & W. D. Hill
	G-AVHT	Auster AOP.9 (WZ711)	C. W. Romkins LtdSeething Jodel Group
	G-AVHY	Fournier RF.4D	I. G. K. Mitchell
	G-AVIA	Cessna F.150G	American Airplane Breakers
	G-AVIB	Cessna F.150G	Far North Aviation
	G-AVIC	Cessna F.172 ★	Leeside Flying Ltd
	G-AVIL	Alon A.2 Aircoupe (VX147)	G. D. J. Wilson
	G-AVIN	MS.880B Rallye Club	D. G. Palmer
	G-AVIP	Brantly B.2B	Eaglescott Brantly Group
	G-AVIS	Cessna F.172 ★	J. P. A. Freeman
	G-AVIT	Cessna F.150G	P. Cottrell
	G-AVIZ	Scheibe SF.25A Motorfalke	Spilsby Gliding Trust
	G-AVJF	Cessna F.172H	J. A. & D. T. A. Rees
	G-AVJJ	PA-30 Twin Comanche 160B	A. H. Manser
	G-AVJK	Jodel DR.1050/M1	Juliet Kilo Syndicate
	G-AVJO	Fokker E.III (replica) (422/15)	Flying Aces Movie Aircraft Collection
	G-AVJV	Wallis WA-117 Srs 1	K. H. Wallis (G-ATCV)
	G-AVJW	Wallis WA-118 Srs 2	K. H. Wallis (G-ATPW)
	G-AVKD	Fournier RF-4D	Lasham RF4 Group
	G-AVKE	Gadfly HDW.1 ★	IHM/Weston-super-Mare
	G-AVKG	Cessna F.172H	P. R. Brown-John
	G-AVKI	Slingsby T.66 Nipper 3	Team Nipper
	G-AVKK	Slingsby T.66 Nipper 3	C. Watson
	G-AVKP	Beagle A.109 Airedale	D. R. Williams
	G-AVKR	Bölkow Bö.208C1 Junior	L. Hawkins
	G-AVLB	PA-28 Cherokee 140	M. Wilson
	G-AVLC	PA-28 Cherokee 140	D. P. McCullagh
	G-AVLE	PA-28 Cherokee 140	G. E. Wright
	G-AVLF	PA-28 Cherokee 140	Woodbine Group
	G-AVLG	PA-28 Cherokee 140	R. J. Everett
	G-AVLI	PA-28 Cherokee 140	Lima India Aviation Group
	G-AVLJ	PA-28 Cherokee 140	Cherokee Aviation Holdings Jersey Ltd
	G-AVLM	Beagle B.121 Pup 3	T. M. & D. A. Jones
	G-AVLN	Beagle B.121 Pup 2	Dogs Flying Group
	G-AVLO	Bölkow Bö.208C1 Junior	G. D. Price & P. R. Teager
	G-AVLT	PA-28-140 Cherokee	Transcourt Ltd and Turweston Flying School Ltd (G-KELC)
	G-AVLW	Fournier RF-4D	J. C. A. C. da Silva
	G-AVLY	Jodel D.120A	M. E. Wills & N. V. de Candole
	G-AVMA	Gardan GY-80 Horizon 180	Z. R. Hildick
	G-AVMB	D.62B Condor	L. J. Dray
	G-AVMD	Cessna 150G	Bagby Aviation Flying Group
	G-AVMF	Cessna F. 150G	J. F. Marsh
	G-AVMJ	BAC One-Eleven 510ED ★	European Aviation Ltd (cabin trainer)
	G-AVMK	BAC One-Eleven 510ED ★	Gravesend College (fuselage only)
	G-AVMO	BAC One-Eleven 510ED ★	Museum of Flight/East Fortune
	G-AVMU	BAC One-Eleven 510ED ★	Duxford Aviation Society
	G-AVNC	Cessna F.150G	J. Turner
	G-AVNE	Westland WS-58 Wessex Mk 60 Srs 1 ★	IHM/Weston-super-Mare
	G-AVNN	PA-28 Cherokee 180	G-AVNN Flying Group
	G-AVNO	PA-28 Cherokee 180	November Oscar Flying Group

Reg.	Type	Owner or Operator	Notes
G-AVNS	PA-28 Cherokee 180	P. T. Osborne	
G-AVNU	PA-28 Cherokee 180	D. Durrant	
G-AVNW	PA-28 Cherokee 180	Len Smith's (Aviation) Ltd	
G-AVNY	Fournier RF-4D	J. B. Giddins (G-IVEL)	
G-AVNZ	Fournier RF-4D	C. D. Pidler	
G-AVOA	Jodel DR.1050	D. A. Willies/Cranwell	
G-AVOH	D.62B Condor	Condor Group	
G-AVOM	CEA Jodel DR.221	Avon Flying Group	
G-AVOO	PA-18 Super Cub 150	Dublin Gliding Club Ltd	
G-AVOZ	PA-28 Cherokee 180	Oscar Zulu Flying Group	
G-AVPD	Jodel D.9 Bébé ★	S. W. McKay (stored)	
G-AVPI	Cessna F.172H	Air-Tech	
G-AVPJ	DH.82A Tiger Moth	C. C. Silk	
G-AVPM	Jodel D.117	L. B. Clark & J. C. Haynes	
G-AVPN	HPR.7 Herald 213 ★	Yorkshire Air Museum/Elvington	
G-AVPO	Hindustan HAL-26 Pushpak	B. Johns	
G-AVPV	PA-18 Cherokee 180	K. A. Passmore	
G-AVPY	PA-25 Pawnee 235C	Southdown Gliding Club Ltd	
G-AVRK	PA-28 Cherokee 180	Just Plane Trading Ltd	
G-AVRS	Gardan GY-80 Horizon 180	N. M. Robbins	
G-AVRU	PA-28-Cherokee 180	Lanpro	
G-AVRW	Gardan GY-20 Minicab	Kestrel Flying Group	
G-AVRZ	PA-28 Cherokee 180	Mantavia Group Ltd	
G-AVSA	PA-28 Cherokee 180	P. A. Wells	
G-AVSB	PA-28 Cherokee 180	D. L. Macdonald	
G-AVSC	PA-28 Cherokee 180	G-AVSC Syndicate	
G-AVSD	PA-28 Cherokee 180	C. B. D. Owen	
G-AVSE	PA-28 Cherokee 180	F. Glendon/Ireland	
G-AVSF	PA-28 Cherokee 180	Monday Club	
G-AVSI	PA-28 Cherokee 140	G-AVSI Flying Group	
G-AVSP	PA-28 Cherokee 180	C. J. d'Oyly	
G-AVSR	Beagle D.5/180 Husky	G. R. Greenfield & S. D. J. Holwill	
G-AVTC	Slingsby Nipper T.66 RA.45 Srs 3	J. Crawford	
G-AVTP	Cessna F.172H	Tango Papa Group	
G-AVTT	Ercoupe 415D	Wright's Farm Eggs Ltd	
G-AVUG	Cessna F.150H	Skyways Flying Group	
G-AVUH	Cessna F.150H	A. G. McLaren	
G-AVUO	Luton LA4 Minor	M. E. Vaisey	
G-AVUS	PA-28 Cherokee 140	AVUS Group	
G-AVUT	PA-28 Cherokee 140	Bencray Ltd	
G-AVUU	PA-28 Cherokee 140	A. Jahanfar & ptnrs	
G-AVUZ	PA-32 Cherokee Six 300	Ceesix Ltd	
G-AVVC	Cessna F.172H	Babs Flying Group	
G-AVVJ	MS.893A Rallye Commodore	M. Powell	
G-AVVO	Avro 652A Anson 19 (VL348)★	Newark Air Museum	
G-AVWA	PA-28 Cherokee 140	SFG Ltd	
G-AVWD	PA-28 Cherokee 140	M. Howells	
G-AVWI	PA-28 Cherokee 140	L. M. Veitch	
G-AVWJ	PA-28 Cherokee 140	M. R. Booker	
G-AVWL	PA-28 Cherokee 140	G-AVWL Group	
G-AVWM	PA-28 Cherokee 140	P. E. Preston & Partners	
G-AVWO	PA-28R Cherokee Arrow 180	Whiskey Oscar Group	
G-AVWR	PA-28R Cherokee Arrow 180	G-AVWR Flying Group	
G-AVWT	PA-28R Cherokee Arrow 180	O. D. Mihalop	
G-AVWU	PA-28R Cherokee Arrow 180	M. Ali & S. Din	
G-AVWV	PA-28R Cherokee Arrow 180	Strathtay Flying Group	
G-AVWY	Fournier RF-4D	J. P. Marriott	
G-AVXA	PA-25 Pawnee 235	S. Wales Gliding Club Ltd	
G-AVXD	Slingsby T.66 Nipper 3	J. A. Brompton	
G-AVXF	PA-28R Cherokee Arrow 180	G-AVXF Group	
G-AVXW	D.62B Condor	C. Willmott	
G-AVXY	Auster AOP.9	G. J. Siddall	
G-AVXZ	PA-28 Cherokee 140 ★	ATC Hayle (instructional airframe)	
G-AVYB	HS.121 Trident 1E-140 ★	SAS training airframe/Hereford	
G-AVYK	Beagle A.61 Terrier 3	R. Burgun	
G-AVYL	PA-28 Cherokee 180	G-AVYL Flying Group	
G-AVYM	PA-28 Cherokee 180	N. B. Le-Grys	
G-AVYR	PA-28 Cherokee 140	R. M Weeks	
G-AVYS	PA-28R Cherokee Arrow 180	R. J. Schreiber	
G-AVYT	PA-28R Cherokee Arrow 180	G. N. Smith	
G-AVYV	Jodel D.120	L. S. Johnson	
G-AVZB	Aero Z-37 Cmelak ★	Science Museum/Wroughton	
G-AVZI	Bölkow Bö.208C1 Junior	C. F. Rogers	

Notes	Reg.	Type	Owner or Operator
	G-AVZP	Beagle B.121 Pup 1	T. A. White/Bagby
	G-AVZR	PA-28 Cherokee 180	Lincoln Aero Club Ltd
	G-AVZU	Cessna F.150H	R. D. Forster
	G-AVZV	Cessna F.172H	E. L. King. & D. S. Lightbown
	G-AVZW	EAA Biplane Model P	C. Edmondson
	G-AWAC	Gardan GY-80 Horizon 180	P. B. Hodgson
	G-AWAJ	Beech 95-D55 Baron	B. F. Whitworth
	G-AWAT	D.62B Condor	R. E. Matthews
	G-AWAU	Vickers FB.27A Vimy (replica) (F8614) ★	RAF Museum/Hendon
	G-AWAW	Cessna F.150F ★	Science Museum/South Kensington
	G-AWAX	Cessna 150D	G-AWAX Group
	G-AWAZ	PA-28R Cherokee Arrow 180	G-AWAZ Flying Group
	G-AWBA	PA-28R Cherokee Arrow 180	March Flying Group
	G-AWBB	PA-28R Cherokee Arrow 180	P. J. Young
	G-AWBC	PA-28R Cherokee Arrow 180	Anglo Aviation (UK) Ltd
	G-AWBE	PA-28 Cherokee 140	B. E. Boyle
	G-AWBG	PA-28 Cherokee 140	G-AWBG Group
	G-AWBJ	Fournier RF-4D	J. B. Giddins & D. M. Hook
	G-AWBM	D.31 Turbulent	D. E. Wood
	G-AWBN	PA-30 Twin Comanche 160B	Stourfield Investments Ltd
	G-AWBS	PA-28 Cherokee 140	R. A. Ballard
	G-AWBT	PA-30 Twin Comanche 160B ★	Instructional airframe/Cranfield
	G-AWBU	Morane-Saulnier N (replica) (MS824)	Flying Aces Movie Aircraft Collection
	G-AWBX	Cessna F.150H	F. B. & J. W. Wolfe
	G-AWCM	Cessna F.150H	R. Garbett
	G-AWCN	Cessna FR.172E	B. & C. Stobart-Hook
	G-AWCP	Cessna F.150H (tailwheel)	C. E. Mason
	G-AWDA	Slingsby T.66 Nipper 3	J. A. Cheesebrough
	G-AWDO	D.31 Turbulent	R. N. Crosland
	G-AWDP	PA-28 Cherokee 180	B. H. & P. M. Illston
	G-AWDR	Cessna FR.172E	B. A. Wallace
	G-AWDU	Brantly B.2B	N. J. M. Freeman
	G-WEA	Beagle B.121 Pup Srs.1	G. V. Crowe
	G-AWEF	SNCAN Stampe SV.4B	RAF Buchanan
	G-AWEI	D.62B Condor	P. A. Gange
	G-AWEK	Fournier RF-4D	M. P. J. Hill
	G-AWEL	Fournier RF-4D	A. B. Clymo
	G-AWEM	Fournier RF-4D	B. J. Griffin
	G-AWEP	Barritault JB-01 Minicab	R. K. Thomas
	G-AWES	Cessna 150H	D. W. Vincent
	G-AWEV	PA-28 Cherokee 140	Norflight Ltd
	G-AWEX	PA-28 Cherokee 140	Reconnaisance Ventures Ltd
	G-AWEZ	PA-28R Cherokee Arrow 180	R. G. E. Simpson
	G-AWFB	PA-28R Cherokee Arrow 180	J. C. Luke
	G-AWFC	PA-28R Cherokee Arrow 180	A. Simpson
	G-AWFD	PA-28R Cherokee Arrow 180	D. J. Hill
	G-AWFF	Cessna F.150H	R. A. Marven
	G-AWFJ	PA-28R Cherokee Arrow 180	Parplon Ltd
	G-AWFN	D.62B Condor	J. James
	G-AWFO	D.62B Condor	T. A. & R. E. Major
	G-AWFP	D.62B Condor	Blackbushe Flying Club
	G-AWFT	Jodel D.9 Bébé	W. H. Cole
	G-AWFW	Jodel D.117	C. J. Rodwell
	G-AWFZ	Beech A23 Musketeer	Bob Crowe Aircraft Sales Ltd
	G-AWGA	Beagle A.109 Airedale ★	(stored)
	G-AWGD	Cessna F.172H	Rutland Flying School
	G-AWGK	Cessna F.150H	G. E. Allen
	G-AWGN	Fournier RF-4D	R. J. Grimstead
	G-AWGZ	Taylor JT.1 Monoplane	R. L. Sambell
	G-AWHB	CASA 2-111D (6J+PR) ★	Aces High Ltd/North Weald
	G-AWHE	Hispano HA.1112 M1L	Spitfire Ltd
	G-AWHX	Rollason Beta B.2	S. G. Jones
	G-AWHY	Falconar F.11-3	Why Fly Group (G-BDPB)
	G-AWIF	Brookland Mosquito 2	C. A. Reeves
	G-AWII	VS.349 Spitfire VC (AR501)	The Shuttleworth Collection
	G-AWIR	Midget Mustang	E. C. Murgatroyd
	G-AWIT	PA-28 Cherokee 180	G-AWIT Ltd
	G-AWIV	Airmark TSR.3	P. K. Jenkins
	G-AWIW	SNCAN Stampe SV.4B	R. E. Mitchell
	G-AWJE	Slingsby T.66 Nipper 3	K G. G. Howe
	G-AWJV	DH.98 Mosquito TT Mk 35 (TA634) ★	De Havilland Heritage Museum/London Colney
	G-AWJX	Zlin Z.526 Trener Master	P. A. Colman

Reg.	Type	Owner or Operator	Notes
G-AWKD	PA-17 Vagabond	C. C. & J. M. Lovell	
G-AWKO	Beagle B.121 Pup 1	J. Martin	
G-AWKP	Jodel DR.253	G-AWKP Group	
G-AWKX	Beech A65 Queen Air ★	(Instructional airframe)/Shoreham	
G-AWLF	Cessna F.172H	Gannet Aviation	
G-AWLG	SIPA 903	S. W. Markham	
G-AWLI	PA-22 Tri-Pacer 150	A. P. S. Maynard & S. Myla	
G-AWLO	Boeing Stearman E75	N. D. Pickard	
G-AWLP	Mooney M.20F	I. C. Lomax	
G-AWLR	Slingsby T.66 Nipper 3	T. D. Reid	
G-AWLS	Slingsby T.66 Nipper 3	G. A. Dunster & B. Gallagher	
G-AWLX	Auster 5 J/2 Arrow	W. J. Taylor	
G-AWLZ	Fournier RF-4D	Nympsfield RF-4 Group	
G-AWMD	Jodel D.11	J. R. Cooper	
G-AWMF	PA-18 Super Cub 150 (modified)	Booker Gliding Club Ltd	
G-AWMN	Luton LA-4A Minor	S. Penfold	
G-AWMR	D.31 Turbulent	J. R. D. Bygraves	
G-AWMT	Cessna F.150H	Strategic Synergies Ltd	
G-AWNT	BN-2A Islander	Precision Terrain Surveys Ltd	
G-AWOE	Aero Commander 680E	J. M. Houlder	
G-AWOF	PA-15 Vagabond	C. M. Hicks	
G-AWOH	PA-17 Vagabond	A. Lovejoy & K. Downes	
G-AWOT	Cessna F.150H	D. I. Flory	
G-AWOU	Cessna 170B	S. Billington	
G-AWOX	Westland WS-58 Wessex 60 (150225) ★	Paintball Adventure West/Bristol	
G-AWPH	P.56 Provost T.1	J. A. D. Bradshaw	
G-AWPJ	Cessna F.150H	W. J. Greenfield	
G-AWPN	Shield Xyla	J. P. Gilbert	
G-AWPU	Cessna F.150J	LAC Flying School	
G-AWPW	PA-12 Super Cruiser	AK Leasing (Jersey) Ltd	
G-AWPZ	Andreasson BA-4B	J. M. Vening	
G-AWRP	Cierva Rotorcraft ★	IHM/Weston-super-Mare	
G-AWRS	Avro 19 Srs. 2 (TX213) ★	North East Aircraft Museum/Usworth	
G-AWRY	P.56 Provost T.1 (XF836)	A. J. House	
G-AWSA	Avro 652A Anson 19 (VL349) ★	Norfolk & Suffolk Aviation Museum/Flixton	
G-AWSH	Zlin Z.526 Trener Master	P. A. Colman	
G-AWSL	PA-28 Cherokee 180D	A. H. & A. H. Brown	
G-AWSM	PA-28 Cherokee 235	Aviation Projects Ltd	
G-AWSN	D.62B Condor	M. K. A. Blyth	
G-AWSP	D.62B Condor	R. Q. & A. S. Bond	
G-AWSS	D.62A Condor	N. J. & D. Butler	
G-AWST	D.62B Condor	J. R. Bell	
G-AWSV	Skeeter 12 (XM553)	Maj. M. Somerton-Rayner	
G-AWSW	Beagle D.5/180 Husky (XW635)	Windmill Aviation	
G-AWTL	PA-28 Cherokee 180D	G. Lloyd & M. Day	
G-AWTP	Schleicher Ka 6E	Papa Victor Syndicate	
G-AWTS	Beech A.23 Musketeer	J. G. Edwards & K. D. Maal	
G-AWTV	Beech 19A Musketeer Sport	J. Whittaker	
G-AWTX	Cessna F.150J	R. D. Forster	
G-AWUB	Gardan GY-201 Minicab	R. A. Hand	
G-AWUE	Jodel DR.1050	K. W. Wood & F. M. Watson	
G-AWUJ	Cessna F.150H	I. M. Ashpole & N. Sutton	
G-AWUL	Cessna F.150H	A. J. Baron	
G-AWUN	Cessna F.150H	G-AWUN Group	
G-AWUO	Cessna F.150H	K. A. O'Neill	
G-AWUT	Cessna F.150J	Aerospace Resources Ltd	
G-AWUU	Cessna F.150J	C. D. London	
G-AWUX	Cessna F.172H	G-AWUX Group	
G-AWUZ	Cessna F.172H	Five Percent Flying Group	
G-AWVA	Cessna F.172H	Barton Air Ltd	
G-AWVC	Beagle B.121 Pup 1	J. J. West	
G-AWVE	Jodel DR.1050/M1	E. A. Taylor	
G-AWVG	AESL Airtourer T.2	C. J. Schofield	
G-AWVN	Aeronca 7AC Champion	Champ Flying Group	
G-AWVZ	Jodel D.112	D. C. Stokes	
G-AWWE	Beagle B.121 Pup 2	Pup Flyers	
G-AWWM	Gardan GY-201 Minicab	P. J. Brayshaw	
G-AWWN	Jodel DR.1050	The G-AWWN Group	
G-AWWP	Aerosport Woody Pusher III	M. S. Bird & R. D. Bird	
G-AWWU	Cessna FR.172F	Westward Airways (Lands End) Ltd	
G-AWXR	PA-28 Cherokee 180D	Aero Clube da Costa Verde/Portugal	
G-AWXS	PA-28 Cherokee 180D	C. R. & S. A. Hardiman	
G-AWXX	Westland Wessex 60 Srs 1	D. Brem-Wilson	

Notes	Reg.	Type	Owner or Operator
	G-AWXY	MS.885 Super Rallye	K. Henderson/Hibaldstow
	G-AWXZ	SNCAN Stampe SV.4C	Bianchi Aviation Film Services Ltd
	G-AWYB	Cessna FR.172F	M.P. & S. T. Barnard & M. S. Macdonald
	G-AWYJ	Beagle B.121 Pup 2	H. C. Taylor
	G-AWYL	Jodel DR.253B	T. C. Van Lonkhuyzen
	G-AWYO	Beagle B.121 Pup 1	B. R. C. Wild
	G-AWYY	Slingsby T.57 Camel replica (B6401) ★	F.A.A. Museum/Yeovilton
	G-AWZI	HS.121 Trident 3B ★	A. Lee/FAST Museum (nose only)/Farnborough
	G-AWZJ	HS.121 Trident 3B ★	Dumfries & Galloway Museum
	G-AWZK	HS.121 Trident 3B ★	Trident Preservation Society/Manchester
	G-AWZM	HS.121 Trident 3B ★	Science Museum/Wroughton
	G-AWZP	HS.121 Trident 3B ★	Manchester Museum of Science & Industry (nose only)
	G-AWZX	HS.121 Trident 3B ★	BAA Airport Fire Services/Gatwick
	G-AXAB	PA-28 Cherokee 140	Bencray Ltd
	G-AXAN	DH.82A Tiger Moth (EM720)	D. & S. A. Firth
	G-AXAS	Wallis WA-116T	K. H. Wallis (G-AVDH)
	G-AXAT	Jodel D.117A	P. S. Wilkinson
	G-AXBF	Beagle D.5/180 Husky	M. C. R. Wills
	G-AXBJ	Cessna F.172H	Atlantic Bridge Aviation Ltd
	G-AXBW	DH.82A Tiger Moth (T5879:RUC-W)	G-AXBW Ltd
	G-AXBZ	DH.82A Tiger Moth	W. J. de Jong Cleyndert
	G-AXCA	PA-28R Cherokee Arrow 200	W. H. Nelson
	G-AXCG	Jodel D.117	D. J. Millin
	G-AXCM	MS.880B Rallye Club	D. C. Manifold
	G-AXCX	Beagle B.121 Pup 2	L. A. Pink
	G-AXCY	Jodel D.117A	R. S. Marom
	G-AXDI	Cessna F.172H	M. F. & J. R. Leusby
	G-AXDK	Jodel DR.315	R. D. Bennett
	G-AXDN	BAC-Sud Concorde 01 ★	Duxford Aviation Society
	G-AXDV	Beagle B.121 Pup 1	T. A. White
	G-AXDZ	Cassutt Racer IIIM	A. Chadwick
	G-AXED	PA-25 Pawnee 235	Wolds Gliding Club Ltd
	G-AXEH	B.125 Bulldog 1 ★	Museum of Flight/East Fortune
	G-AXEI	Ward Gnome ★	Real Aeroplane Club/Breighton
	G-AXEO	Scheibe SF.25B Falke	P. F. Moffatt
	G-AXEV	Beagle B.121 Pup 2	D. S. Russell & D. G. Benson
	G-AXFG	Cessna 337D	County Garage (Cheltenham) Ltd
	G-AXFN	Jodel D.119	T. A. Appleby
	G-AXGE	MS.880B Rallye Club	R. P. Loxton
	G-AXGG	Cessna F.150J	A. J. Simpson
	G-AXGP	Piper J-3C-90 Cub	A. P. Acres
	G-AXGR	Luton LA-4A Minor	B. A. Schlussler
	G-AXGS	D.62B Condor	SAS Flying Group
	G-AXGV	D.62B Condor	Hawkaero Flying Group
	G-AXGZ	D.62B Condor	R. M. Schweitzer
	G-AXHA	Cessna 337A	I. M. Latiff
	G-AXHC	SNCAN Stampe SV.4C	D. L. Webley
	G-AXHO	Beagle B.121 Pup 2	L. W. Grundy
	G-AXHP	Piper J-3C-65 Cub (480636:A-58)	Witham (Specialist) Vehicles Ltd
	G-AXHR	Piper J-3C-65 Cub (329601:D-44)	D. J. Dash
	G-AXHS	MS.880B Rallye Club	B. & A. Swales
	G-AXHT	MS.880B Rallye Club	P. M. Murray
	G-AXHV	Jodel D.117A	Derwent Flying Group
	G-AXIA	Beagle B.121 Pup 1	C. K. Parsons
	G-AXIE	Beagle B.121 Pup 2	J. P. Thomas
	G-AXIO	PA-28 Cherokee 140B	G. W. Mountford
	G-AXIR	PA-28 Cherokee 140B	R. W. Howard
	G-AXIW	Scheibe SF.25B Falke	M. Pedley
	G-AXIX	Glos-Airtourer 150	S. Alexander
	G-AXJB	Omega 84 balloon	Southern Balloon Group
	G-AXJH	Beagle B.121 Pup 2	The Henry Flying Group
	G-AXJI	Beagle B.121 Pup 2	J. J. Sanders & J. A. Walley
	G-AXJJ	Beagle B.121 Pup 2	M. L. Jones & ptnrs
	G-AXJO	Beagle B.121 Pup 2	J. A. D. Bradshaw
	G-AXJR	Scheibe SF.25B Falke	Falke Syndicate
	G-AXJV	PA-28 Cherokee 140B	Seahawk Flying Group
	G-AXJX	PA-28 Cherokee 140B	K. Wilson
	G-AXKH	Luton LA-4A Minor	M. E. Vaisey
	G-AXKJ	Jodel D.9	The Hinton D9 Group
	G-AXKO	Westland-Bell 47G-4A	M. Gallagher
	G-AXKS	Westland Bell 47G-4A ★	Museum of Army Flying/Middle Wallop

Reg.	Type	Owner or Operator	Notes
G-AXKX	Westland Bell 47G-4A	R. A. Dale	
G-AXLI	Slingsby T.66 Nipper 3	D. & M. Shrimpton	
G-AXLS	Jodel DR.105A	Axle Flying Club	
G-AXLZ	PA-18 Super Cub 95	R. J. Quantrell	
G-AXMA	PA-24 Comanche 180	B. C. Faulkner	
G-AXMD	Omega O-56 balloon ★	British Balloon Museum/Newbury	
G-AXMT	Bücker Bü 133 Jungmeister	R. A. Fleming/Breighton	
G-AXMW	Beagle B.121 Pup 1	DJP Engineering (Knebworth) Ltd	
G-AXMX	Beagle B.121 Pup 2	Bob The Beagle Group	
G-AXNJ	Wassmer Jodel D.120	Clive Flying Group	
G-AXNN	Beagle B.121 Pup 2	Gabrielle Aviation Ltd	
G-AXNP	Beagle B.121 Pup 2	J. W. Ellis & R. J. Hemmings	
G-AXNR	Beagle B.121 Pup 2	AXNR Group	
G-AXNS	Beagle B.121 Pup 2	Derwent Aero Group	
G-AXNW	SNCAN Stampe SV.4C	C. S. Grace	
G-AXNX	Cessna 182M	T. Latky & C.Csilla	
G-AXNZ	Pitts S.1C Special	November Zulu Group	
G-AXOG	PA-E23 Aztec 250D	G. H. Nolan	
G-AXOH	MS.894 Rallye Minerva	T. A. D. Crook	
G-AXOJ	Beagle B.121 Pup 2	Pup Flying Group	
G-AXOR	PA-28 Cherokee 180D	Oscar Romeo Aviation Ltd	
G-AXOS	MS.894A Rallye Minerva	R. S. M. Fendt	
G-AXOT	MS.893 Rallye Commodore 180	P. Evans	
G-AXOZ	Beagle B.121 Pup 1	R. J. Ogborn	
G-AXPA	Beagle B.121 Pup 1	Papa-Alpha Group	
G-AXPC	Beagle B.121 Pup 2	T. A. White	
G-AXPF	Cessna F.150K	D. R. Marks	
G-AXPG	Mignet HM.293	W. H. Cole (stored)	
G-AXPZ	Campbell Cricket	W. R. Partridge	
G-AXRC	Campbell Cricket	L. R. Morris	
G-AXRP	SNCAN Stampe SV-4C	C. C. Manning (G-BLOL)	
G-AXRR	Auster AOP.9 (XR241)	R. B. Webber	
G-AXRT	Cessna FA.150K (tailwheel)	C. C. Walley	
G-AXSF	Nash Petrel	Nash Aircraft Ltd	
G-AXSG	PA-28 Cherokee 180	The Tago Island Co Ltd	
G-AXSI	Cessna F.172H	Eastcoast Farm Equipment (G-SNIP)	
G-AXSM	Jodel DR.1051	T. R. G. & M. S. Barnby	
G-AXSW	Cessna FA.150K	R. J. Whyham	
G-AXSZ	PA-28 Cherokee 140B	White Wings Flying Group	
G-AXTA	PA-28 Cherokee 140B	G-AXTA Aircraft Group	
G-AXTC	PA-28 Cherokee 140B	G-AXTC Group	
G-AXTJ	PA-28 Cherokee 140B	K. Patel	
G-AXTL	PA-28 Cherokee 140B	Bristol and West Aeroplane Club Ltd	
G-AXTO	PA-24 Comanche 260	J. L. Wright	
G-AXTX	Jodel D.112	C. Sawford	
G-AXUA	Beagle B.121 Pup 1	P. Wood	
G-AXUB	BN-2A Islander	Headcorn Parachute Club Ltd	
G-AXUC	PA-12 Super Cruiser	J. J. Bunton	
G-AXUF	Cessna FA.150K	B. T. Walsh	
G-AXUJ	Auster J/1 Autocrat	P. Gill (G-OSTA)	
G-AXUK	Jodel DR.1050	Downland Flying Group	
G-AXUM	HP.137 Jetstream 1 ★	Sodeteg Formation/France	
G-AXVB	Cessna F.172H	R. & J. Turner	
G-AXVK	Campbell Cricket	B. Jones	
G-AXVM	Campbell Cricket	D. M. Organ	
G-AXVN	McCandless M.4	W. R. Partridge	
G-AXWA	Auster AOP.9 (XN437)	C. M. Edwards	
G-AXWT	Jodel D.11	C. S. Jackson	
G-AXWV	Jodel DR.253	R. Friedlander & D. C. Ray	
G-AXWZ	PA-28R Cherokee Arrow 200	Whisky Zulu Group	
G-AXXC	CP.301B Emeraude	J. C. & R. D. P. Cadle	
G-AXXV	DH.82A Tiger Moth (DE992)	C. N. Wookey	
G-AXXW	Jodel D.117	M. Breen & D. Carr	
G-AXYK	Taylor JT.1 Monoplane	O. C. Pope	
G-AXYU	Jodel D.9 Bébé	P. Turton	
G-AXZD	PA-28 Cherokee 180E	G. M. Whitmore	
G-AXZF	PA-28 Cherokee 180E	M. Arthur	
G-AXZH	Glasflugel H201B Standard Libelle	M. C. Gregorie	
G-AXZM	Slingsby T.66 Nipper 3	G. R. Harlow	
G-AXZO	Cessna 180	The Cessna 180 Group	
G-AXZP	PA-E23 Aztec 250D	D. M. Harbottle	
G-AXZT	Jodel D.117	P. Guest	
G-AXZU	Cessna 182N	W. Gollan	

Notes	Reg.	Type	Owner or Operator
	G-AYAB	PA-28 Cherokee 180E	J. R. Green
	G-AYAC	PA-28R Cherokee Arrow 200	Fersfield Flying Group
	G-AYAJ	Cameron O-84 balloon	E. T. Hall
	G-AYAL	Omega 56 balloon ★	British Balloon Museum/Newbury
	G-AYAN	Slingsby Motor Cadet III	G. Hill & R. Moyse
	G-AYAR	PA-28 Cherokee 180E	A. Jahanfar/Southend
	G-AYAT	PA-28 Cherokee 180E	G-AYAT Flying Group
	G-AYAW	PA-28 Cherokee 180E	D. G., P. G. & R. J. Taylor
	G-AYBD	Cessna F.150K	Apollo Aviation Advisory Ltd
	G-AYBG	Scheibe SF.25B Falke	Anglia Sailplanes
	G-AYBO	PA-23 Aztec 250D	A. G. Gutknecht/Austria
	G-AYBP	Jodel D.112	G. J. Langston
	G-AYBR	Jodel D.112	I. S. Parker
	G-AYCC	Campbell Cricket	D. J. M. Charity
	G-AYCF	Cessna FA.150K	E. J. Atkins
	G-AYCG	SNCAN Stampe SV.4C	N. Bignall
	G-AYCJ	Cessna TP.206D	White Knuckle Airways Ltd
	G-AYCK	AIA Stampe SV.4C	The Real Flying Co Ltd (G-BUNT)
	G-AYCN	Piper J-3C-65 Cub	W. R. & B. M. Young
	G-AYCO	CEA DR.360	Charlie Oscar Club
	G-AYCP	Jodel D.112	J. A. Carey
	G-AYCT	Cessna F.172H	J. R. Benson
	G-AYDI	DH.82A Tiger Moth	Delta India Group
	G-AYDR	SNCAN Stampe SV.4C	D. J. Ashley
	G-AYDV	Coates Swalesong SA11	The Real Aeroplane Co.Ltd
	G-AYDW	Beagle A.61 Terrier 2	A. S. Topen
	G-AYDX	Beagle A.61 Terrier 2	T. S. Lee
	G-AYDY	Luton LA-4A Minor	J. Dible/Ireland
	G-AYDZ	Jodel DR.200	Zero One Group
	G-AYEB	Jodel D.112	J. Evans
	G-AYEC	CP.301A Emeraude	Redwing Flying Group
	G-AYEE	PA-28 Cherokee 180E	Demero Ltd & Transcourt Ltd
	G-AYEF	PA-28 Cherokee 180E	Pegasus Flying Group
	G-AYEG	Falconar F-9	A. L. Smith
	G-AYEH	Jodel DR.1050	H. L. M. Williams
	G-AYEJ	Jodel DR.1050	J. M. Newbold
	G-AYEN	Piper J-3C-65 Cub	P. Warde & C. F. Morris
	G-AYET	MS.892A Rallye Commodore 150	A. T. R. Bingley
	G-AYEW	Jodel DR.1051	J. R. Hope
	G-AYFC	D.62B Condor	A. R. Chadwick
	G-AYFD	D.62B Condor	B. G. Manning
	G-AYFE	D.62C Condor	M. Soulsby
	G-AYFF	D.62B Condor	H. Stuart
	G-AYFJ	MS.880B Rallye Club	Rallye FJ Group
	G-AYFV	Crosby BA-4B	A. R. C. Mathie
	G-AYGA	Jodel D.117	J. W. Bowes
	G-AYGB	Cessna 310Q ★	Instructional airframe/Perth
	G-AYGC	Cessna F.150K	Alpha Aviation Group
	G-AYGD	Jodel DR.1051	J. F. M. Barlett & J. P. Liber
	G-AYGE	SNCAN Stampe SV.4C	L. J. Proudfoot & ptnrs
	G-AYGG	Jodel D.120	J. M. Dean
	G-AYGX	Cessna FR.172G	Reims Rocket Group
	G-AYHA	AA-1 Yankee	S. J. Carr
	G-AYHX	Jodel D.117A	A. P. Chapman & L. E. Cowling
	G-AYIA	Hughes 369HS ★	G. D. E. Bilton/Sywell
	G-AYIG	PA-28 Cherokee 140C	G. K. Clarkson
	G-AYII	PA-28R Cherokee Arrow 200	Double India Group
	G-AYIJ	SNCAN Stampe SV.4B	D. Savage
	G-AYJA	Jodel DR.1050	G. Connell
	G-AYJB	SNCAN Stampe SV.4C	F. J. M. & J. P. Esson
	G-AYJD	Alpavia-Fournier RF-3	Juliet Delta Group
	G-AYJP	PA-28 Cherokee 140C	Transcourt Ltd and Demero Ltd
	G-AYJR	PA-28 Cherokee 140C	Transcourt Ltd and Turweston Flying School
	G-AYJY	Isaacs Fury II	T. E. W. Terrell
	G-AYKD	Jodel DR.1050	G. Wright
	G-AYKJ	Jodel D.117A	R. J. Hughes
	G-AYKK	Jodel D.117	J. M. Whitham
	G-AYKS	Leopoldoff L.7 Colibri	W. B. Cooper
	G-AYKT	Jodel D.117	D. I. Walker
	G-AYKW	PA-28 Cherokee 140C	P. W. Carlton
	G-AYKZ	SAI KZ-8	R. E. Mitchell
	G-AYLA	Glos-Airtourer 115	D. S. P. Disney

Reg.	Type	Owner or Operator	Notes
G-AYLC	Jodel DR.1051	E. W. B. Trollope	
G-AYLF	Jodel DR.1051 (modified)	R. Twigg	
G-AYLL	Jodel DR.1050	C. Joly	
G-AYLP	AA-1 Yankee	D. Nairn	
G-AYLV	Jodel D.120	M. R. Henham	
G-AYME	Fournier RF-5	R. D. Goodger	
G-AYMK	PA-28 Cherokee 140C	W. E. Mould	
G-AYMO	PA-23 Aztec 250C	J. A. D. Richardson	
G-AYMP	Currie Wot	R. C. Hibberd	
G-AYMR	Lederlin 380L	P. J. Brayshaw	
G-AYMU	Jodel D.112	M. R. Baker	
G-AYMV	Western 20 balloon	R. G. Turnbull	
G-AYNA	Phoenix Currie Wot	D. R. Partridge	
G-AYND	Cessna 310Q	Source Group Ltd	
G-AYNF	PA-28 Cherokee 140C	BW Aviation Ltd	
G-AYNJ	PA-28 Cherokee 140C	M. Corbett	
G-AYNN	Cessna 185B	Bencray Ltd	
G-AYNP	Westland WS-55 Whirlwind Srs 3 ★	IHM/Weston-super-Mare	
G-AYOW	Cessna 182N Skylane	I. F. Ellis, L. M. Hall & C. J. R. Vernon	
G-AYOZ	Cessna FA.150L	P. D. Stell	
G-AYPE	MBB Bö.209 Monsun	Papa Echo Ltd	
G-AYPG	Cessna F.177RG	D. P. McDermott	
G-AYPH	Cessna F.177RG	M. L. & T. M. Jones	
G-AYPJ	PA-28 Cherokee 180	R. B. Petrie	
G-AYPM	PA-18 Super Cub 95 (115373)	R. Horner	
G-AYPO	PA-18 Super Cub 95	A. W. Knowles	
G-AYPS	PA-18 Super Cub 95	D. Racionzer	
G-AYPU	PA-28R Cherokee Arrow 200	Monalto Investments Ltd	
G-AYPV	PA-28 Cherokee 140D	Ashley Gardner Flying Club Ltd	
G-AYPZ	Campbell Cricket	A. Melody	
G-AYRG	Cessna F.172K	I. G. Harrison	
G-AYRH	MS.892A Rallye Commodore 150	S. O'Ceallaigh & J. Barry	
G-AYRI	PA-28R Cherokee Arrow 200	J. C. Houdret	
G-AYRM	PA-28 Cherokee 140D	M. J. Saggers	
G-AYRO	Cessna FA.150L Aerobat	Fat Boys Flying Club	
G-AYRS	Jodel D.120A	L. R. H. D'Eath	
G-AYRT	Cessna F.172K	P. E. Crees	
G-AYRU	BN-2A-6 Islander	Hebridean Air Services Ltd	
G-AYSB	PA-30 Twin Comanche 160C	M. J. Abbott	
G-AYSH	Taylor JT.1 Monoplane	C. J. Lodge	
G-AYSK	Luton LA-4A Minor	B. A. Schlussler & S. J. Rudkin	
G-AYSX	Cessna F.177RG	A. P. R. Dean	
G-AYSY	Cessna F.177RG	S. A. Tuer	
G-AYTA	SOCATA MS.880B Rallye Club ★	Manchester Museum of Science & Industry	
G-AYTR	CP.301A Emeraude	I. D. Worthington	
G-AYTT	Phoenix PM-3 Duet	R. B. Webber & J. K. Houlgrave	
G-AYTV	Jurca Tempete	C. W. Kirk	
G-AYUB	CEA DR.253B	Rothwell Group	
G-AYUH	PA-28 Cherokee 180F	Broadland Flying Group Ltd	
G-AYUJ	Evans VP-1	T. N. Howard	
G-AYUM	Slingsby T.61A Falke	M. H. Simms	
G-AYUN	Slingsby T.61A Falke	G-AYUN Group	
G-AYUP	Slingsby T.61A Falke	P. R. Williams	
G-AYUR	Slingsby T.61A Falke	R. Hanningan & R. Lingard	
G-AYUS	Taylor JT.1 Monoplane	S. P. Collins	
G-AYUT	Jodel DR.1050	G. Bell	
G-AYUV	Cessna F.172H	Justgold Ltd	
G-AYVO	Wallis WA-120 Srs 1	K. H. Wallis	
G-AYVP	Woody Pusher	J. R. Wraight	
G-AYWA	Avro 19 Srs 2 ★	N. K. Geddes	
G-AYWD	Cessna 182N	Wild Dreams Group	
G-AYWH	Jodel D.117A	D. Kynaston	
G-AYWM	Glos-Airtourer Super 150	Star Flying Group	
G-AYWT	AIA Stampe SV.4C	R. A. Palmer	
G-AYXP	Jodel D.117A	G. N. Davies	
G-AYXS	SIAI-Marchetti S205-18R	P. J. Bloore & J. M. Biles	
G-AYXT	WS-55 Whirlwind Srs 2 (XK940:911) ★	IHM/Weston-super-Mare	
G-AYXU	Champion 7KCAB Citabria	E. V. Moffatt & J. S. Peplow	
G-AYYL	Slingsby T.61A Falke	Brightman Industries Ltd	
G-AYYO	Jodel DR.1050/M1	Bustard Flying Club Ltd	
G-AYYT	Jodel DR.1050/M1	R. Johnston	
G-AYYU	Beech C23 Musketeer	G-AYYU Group	

G-AYZH – G-AZKE

BRITISH CIVIL REGISTRATIONS

Notes	Reg.	Type	Owner or Operator
	G-AYZH	Taylor JT.2 Titch	T. D. Gardner
	G-AYZI	SNCAN Stampe SV.4C	D. M. & P. A. Fenton
	G-AYZJ	Westland WS-55 Whirlwind HAS.7 ★	Newark Air Museum (XM685)
	G-AYZK	Jodel DR.1050/M1	D. G. Hesketh
	G-AYZS	D.62B Condor	M. N. Thrush
	G-AYZU	Slingsby T.61A Falke	A. J. Harpley
	G-AYZW	Slingsby T.61A Falke	Y-ZW Group
	G-AZAB	PA-30 Twin Comanche 160B	Bickertons Aerodromes Ltd
	G-AZAJ	PA-28R Cherokee Arrow 200B	P. Woulfe
	G-AZAW	Gardan GY-80 Horizon 160	J. W. Foley
	G-AZAZ	Bensen B.8M ★	F.A.A. Museum/Yeovilton
	G-AZBB	MBB Bö.209 Monsun 160FV	J. A. Webb
	G-AZBE	Glos-Airtourer Super 150	R. G. Vincent
	G-AZBI	Jodel 150	R. J. Wald
	G-AZBL	Jodel D.9 Bébé	J. Hill
	G-AZBN	Noorduyn AT-16 Harvard IIB (FT391)	Swaygate Ltd
	G-AZBU	Auster AOP.9 (XR246)	Auster Nine Group
	G-AZCB	SNCAN Stampe SV.4C	M. Coward
	G-AZCK	Beagle B.121 Pup 2	P. Crone
	G-AZCL	Beagle B.121 Pup 2	Flew LLP & J. M. Henry
	G-AZCN	Beagle B.121 Pup 2	E. J. Spencer, D. M. Callagham & G. Wildgoose
	G-AZCP	Beagle B.121 Pup 1	M. R. Badmington
	G-AZCT	Beagle B.121 Pup 1	J. Coleman
	G-AZCU	Beagle B.121 Pup 1	A. A. Harris
	G-AZCV	Beagle B.121 Pup 2	N. R. W. Long
	G-AZCZ	Beagle B.121 Pup 2	L. & J. M. Northover
	G-AZDD	MBB Bö.209 Monsun 150FF	Double Delta Flying Group
	G-AZDE	PA-28R Cherokee Arrow 200B	Metair Ltd
	G-AZDG	Beagle B.121 Pup 2	D. J. Sage & J. R. Heaps
	G-AZDJ	PA-32 Cherokee Six 300	K. J. Mansbridge & D. C. Gibbs
	G-AZDX	PA-28 Cherokee 180F	M. Cowan
	G-AZDY	DH.82A Tiger Moth	J. B. Mills
	G-AZEE	MS.880B Rallye Club	J. Shelton
	G-AZEF	Jodel D.120	P. R. Sears
	G-AZEG	PA-28 Cherokee 140D	Ashley Gardner Flying Club Ltd
	G-AZEU	Beagle B.121 Pup 2	G. M. Moir
	G-AZEV	Beagle B.121 Pup 2	G. H. Matthews
	G-AZEW	Beagle B.121 Pup 2	D. Ridley
	G-AZEY	Beagle B.121 Pup 2	M. E. Reynolds
	G-AZFA	Beagle B.121 Pup 2	J. Smith
	G-AZFC	PA-28 Cherokee 140D	WLS Flying Group
	G-AZFF	Jodel D.112	J. Bolger/Ireland
	G-AZFI	PA-28R Cherokee Arrow 200B	G-AZFI Ltd
	G-AZFM	PA-28R Cherokee Arrow 200B	P. J. Jenness
	G-AZFR	Cessna 401B	R. E. Wragg
	G-AZGA	Jodel D.120	A. P. Hatton
	G-AZGC	SNCAN Stampe SV.4C	D. J. Ashley
	G-AZGE	SNCAN Stampe SV.4C	Tiger Airways
	G-AZGF	Beagle B.121 Pup 2	K. Singh
	G-AZGL	MS.894A Rallye Minerva	The Cambridge Aero Club Ltd
	G-AZGY	CP.301B Emeraude	R. H. Braithwaite
	G-AZGZ	DH.82A Tiger Moth (NM181)	R. J. King
	G-AZHB	Robin HR.100/200B	J. F. Gould
	G-AZHC	Jodel D.112	Aerodel Flying Group
	G-AZHD	Slingsby T.61A Falke	R. J. Shallcrass
	G-AZHH	SA 102.5 Cavalier	D. W. Buckle
	G-AZHI	Glos-Airtourer Super 150	Flying Grasshoppers Ltd
	G-AZHK	Robin HR.100/200B	G. I. Applin (G-ILEG)
	G-AZHR	Piccard Ax6 balloon	C. Fisher
	G-AZHT	AESL Airtourer (modified)	Aviation West Ltd
	G-AZHU	Luton LA-4A Minor	W. Cawrey
	G-AZIB	ST-10 Diplomate	W. B. Bateson
	G-AZII	Jodel D.117A	J. S. Brayshaw
	G-AZIJ	Jodel DR.360	F. M. Carter
	G-AZIL	Slingsby T.61A Falke	D. W. Savage
	G-AZIP	Cameron O-65 balloon	Dante Balloon Group
	G-AZJC	Fournier RF-5	Seighford RF5 Group
	G-AZJE	Ord-Hume JB-01 Minicab	Kayee Flyers
	G-AZJV	Cessna F.172L	G-AZJV Flying Group
	G-AZJY	Cessna FRA.150L	J. S. Davis
	G-AZKC	MS.880B Rallye Club	L. J. Martin
	G-AZKE	MS.880B Rallye Club	D. A. Thompson & J. D. Headlam/Germany

34

Reg.	Type	Owner or Operator	Notes
G-AZKO	Cessna F.337F	G. James	
G-AZKP	Jodel D.117	Moray Flying Group	
G-AZKS	AA-1A Trainer	I. R. Matterface	
G-AZKW	Cessna F.172L	D. Stewart	
G-AZKZ	Cessna F.172L	R. D. & E. Forster	
G-AZLE	Boeing N2S-5 Kaydet (1102:102)	A. E. Paulson	
G-AZLF	Jodel D.120	M. S. C. Ball	
G-AZLH	Cessna F.150L	W. Ali	
G-AZLN	PA-28 Cherokee 180F	Enstone Sales & Services Ltd and J. Logan	
G-AZLV	Cessna 172K	G-AZLV Flying Group	
G-AZLY	Cessna F.150L	R. B. McLain	
G-AZMC	Slingsby T.61A Falke	P. J. R. White	
G-AZMD	Slingsby T.61C Falke	Tandem Gliding Syndicate	
G-AZMJ	AA-5 Traveler	W. R. Partridge	
G-AZMX	PA-28 Cherokee 140 ★	NE Wales Institute of Higher Education (Instructional airframe)/Flintshire	
G-AZMZ	MS.893A Rallye Commodore 150	J. Palethorpe	
G-AZNK	SNCAN Stampe SV.4A	November Kilo Group	
G-AZNL	PA-28R Cherokee Arrow 200D	B. P. Liversidge	
G-AZNO	Cessna 182P	M. S. Williams	
G-AZNT	Cameron O-84 balloon	P. Glydon	
G-AZOA	MBB Bö.209 Monsun 150FF	M. W. Hurst	
G-AZOB	MBB Bö.209 Monsun 150FF	J. A. Webb	
G-AZOE	Glos-Airtourer 115	G-AZOE 607 Group	
G-AZOF	Glos-Airtourer Super 150	R. C. Thursby & C. Goldsmith	
G-AZOG	PA-28R Cherokee Arrow 200D	Southend Flying Club	
G-AZOL	PA-34-200 Seneca II	Stapleford Flying Club Ltd	
G-AZOS	Jurca MJ.5-H1 Sirocco	P. J. Tanulak	
G-AZOU	Jodel DR.1050	Horsham Flying Group	
G-AZOZ	Cessna FRA.150L	J. E. Jones	
G-AZPA	PA-25 Pawnee 235	Black Mountains Gliding Club Ltd	
G-AZPC	Slingsby T.61C Falke	D. Heslop & J. R. Kimberley	
G-AZPF	Fournier RF-5	R. Pye	
G-AZPH	Craft-Pitts S-1S Special ★	Science Museum/South Kensington	
G-AZPX	Western O-31 balloon	Zebedee Balloon Service Ltd	
G-AZRA	MBB Bö.209 Monsun 150FF	Alpha Flying Ltd	
G-AZRH	PA-28 Cherokee 140D	Trust Flying Group	
G-AZRI	Payne Free Balloon	C. A. Butter & J. J. T. Cooke	
G-AZRK	Fournier RF-5	A. B. Clymo & J. F. Rogers	
G-AZRL	PA-18 Super Cub 95	J. S. & P. R. Johnson	
G-AZRM	Fournier RF-5	Romeo Mike Group	
G-AZRN	Cameron O-84 balloon	C. J. Desmet/Belgium	
G-AZRP	Glos-Airtourer 115	B. F. Strawford	
G-AZRS	PA-22 Tri-Pacer 150	R. H. Hulls	
G-AZRZ	Cessna U.206F	Cornish Parachute Club Ltd	
G-AZSA	Stampe et Renard SV.4B	M. R. Dolman	
G-AZSC	Noorduyn AT-16 Harvard IIB (43:SC)	Goodwood Road Racing Co Ltd	
G-AZSF	PA-28R Cherokee Arrow 200D	Smart People Don't Buy Ltd	
G-AZTA	MBB Bö.209 Monsun 150FF	A. J. Court	
G-AZTF	Cessna F.177RG	R. Burgun	
G-AZTM	AESL Airtourer T2	Victa Restoration Group	
G-AZTS	Cessna F.172L	R. Murray & A. Bagley-Murray	
G-AZTV	Stolp SA.500 Starlet	G. R. Rowland	
G-AZTW	Cessna F.177RG	I. M. Richmond & G. R. Waller	
G-AZUM	Cessna F.172L	Fowlmere Flyers	
G-AZUT	MS.893A Rallye Commodore 180	J. Palethorpe	
G-AZUY	Cessna E.310L	W. B. Bateson	
G-AZUZ	Cessna FRA.150L	D. J. Parker	
G-AZVA	MBB Bö.209 Monsun 150FF	M. P. Brinkmann	
G-AZVB	MBB Bö.209 Monsun 150FF	E. & P. M. L. Cliffe	
G-AZVF	MS.894A Rallye Minerva	Minerva Flying Group	
G-AZVG	AA-5 Traveler	G-AZVG Group	
G-AZVH	MS.894A Rallye Minerva	P. L. Jubb	
G-AZVI	MS.892A Rallye Commodore	G. C. Jarvis	
G-AZVL	Jodel D.119	A. K. & K. B. Raven	
G-AZVP	Cessna F.177RG	C. R. Brown	
G-AZWB	PA-28 Cherokee 140	G-AZWB Flying Group	
G-AZWD	PA-28 Cherokee 140	BJ Services (Midlands) Ltd	
G-AZWF	SAN Jodel DR.1050	Cawdor Flying Group	
G-AZWS	PA-28R Cherokee Arrow 180	K. M. Turner	
G-AZWT	Westland Lysander IIIA (V9367)	The Shuttleworth Collection	
G-AZWY	PA-24 Comanche 260	Keymer Son & Co Ltd	
G-AZXB	Cameron O-65 balloon	R. J. Mitchener & P. F. Smart	

Notes	Reg.	Type	Owner or Operator
	G-AZXD	Cessna F.172L	R. J. R. Williams & D. Palmer
	G-AZXG	PA-23 Aztec 250D ★	Instructional airframe/Cranfield
	G-AZYA	Gardan GY-80 Horizon 160	R. G. Whyte
	G-AZYB	Bell 47H-1 ★	IHM/Weston-super-Mare
	G-AZYD	MS.893A Rallye Commodore	Staffordshire Gliding Club Ltd
	G-AZYF	PA-28-180 Cherokee D	AZYF Group
	G-AZYS	CP.301C-1 Emeraude	C. G. Ferguson & D. Drew
	G-AZYU	PA-23 Aztec 250E	L. J. Martin
	G-AZYY	Slingsby T.61A Falke	J. A. Towers
	G-AZYZ	Wassmer Wa.51A Pacific	C. R. Buxton/France
	G-AZZO	PA-28-140 Cherokee	R. J. Hind
	G-AZZR	Cessna F.150L	N. J. Wakeling
	G-AZZV	Cessna F.172L	Zentelligence Ltd
	G-AZZZ	DH.82A Tiger Moth	S. W. McKay
	G-BAAD	Evans Super VP-1	Breighton VP-1 Group
	G-BAAF	Manning-Flanders MF1 (replica)	Aviation Film Services Ltd
	G-BAAI	MS.893A Rallye Commodore	R. D. Taylor
	G-BAAT	Cessna 182P	T. E. Earl
	G-BAAW	Jodel D.119	Alpha Whiskey Flying Group
	G-BABC	Cessna F.150L	B. B. Singh
	G-BABD	Cessna FRA.150L (modified)	Anglia Flight
	G-BABE	Taylor JT.2 Titch	M. Bonsall
	G-BABG	PA-28 Cherokee 180	Mendip Flying Group
	G-BABK	PA-34-200 Seneca II	D. F. J. Flashman
	G-BACB	PA-34-200 Seneca II	Milbrooke Motors
	G-BACE	Fournier RF-5	G-BACE Fournier Group
	G-BACJ	Jodel D.120	Wearside Flying Association
	G-BACL	Jodel 150	G-BACL Flying Group
	G-BACN	Cessna FRA.150L	F. Bundy
	G-BACO	Cessna FRA.150L	T. E. C. Cushing
	G-BADC	Rollason Beta B.2A	A. P. Grimley
	G-BADH	Slingsby T.61A Falke	I. F. Wells
	G-BADJ	PA-E23 Aztec 250E	C. Papadakis
	G-BADM	D.62B Condor	Delta Mike Condor Group
	G-BADV	Brochet MB50	W. B. Cooper
	G-BADW	Pitts S-2A Special	R. E. Mitchell
	G-BADZ	Aerotek Pitts S-2A Special	R. F. Warner
	G-BAEB	Robin DR.400/160	G. D. Jones
	G-BAEE	Jodel DR.1050/M1	R. Little
	G-BAEM	Robin DR.400/125	M. A. Webb
	G-BAEN	Robin DR.400/180	R. H. & C. R. Partington
	G-BAEO	Cessna F.172M	L. W. Scattergood
	G-BAEP	Cessna FRA.150L (modified)	A. M. Lynn
	G-BAER	Cosmic Wind	A. G. Truman
	G-BAET	Piper J-3C-65 Cub	C. J. Rees
	G-BAEU	Cessna F.150L	L. W. Scattergood
	G-BAEV	Cessna FRA.L150L	B. Doyle
	G-BAEW	Cessna F.172M ★	Westley Aircraft
	G-BAEY	Cessna F.172M	Skytrax Aviation Ltd
	G-BAEZ	Cessna FRA.150L	Donair Flying Club Ltd
	G-BAFA	AA-5 Traveler	C. F. Mackley
	G-BAFG	DH.82A Tiger Moth	Akerios International Business Co.Ltd
	G-BAFL	Cessna 182P	R. B. Hopkinson & A. S. Pike
	G-BAFP	Robin DR.400/160	J. C. Bacon
	G-BAFT	PA-18 Super Cub 150	C. A. M. Neidt
	G-BAFU	PA-28 Cherokee 140	C. F. Dukes & W. T. Johnson
	G-BAFV	PA-18 Super Cub 95	T. F. & S. J. Thorpe
	G-BAFW	PA-28 Cherokee 140	A. J. Peters
	G-BAFX	Robin DR.400/140	R. Foster
	G-BAGB	SIAI Marchetti SF.260	V. Balzer
	G-BAGC	Robin DR.400/140	O. C. Baars
	G-BAGF	Jodel D.92 Bébé	E. Evans
	G-BAGG	PA-32 Cherokee Six 300E	A. D. Hoy
	G-BAGN	Cessna F.177RG	R. W. J. Andrews
	G-BAGR	Robin DR.400/140	J. D. Last
	G-BAGS	Robin DR.400/180 2+2	M. Whale & M. W. A. Lunn
	G-BAGT	Helio H.295 Courier	D. C. Hanss
	G-BAGX	PA-28 Cherokee 140	I. Lwanga
	G-BAGY	Cameron O-84 balloon	P. G. Dunnington
	G-BAHD	Cessna 182P Skyline	Lambley Flying Group
	G-BAHF	PA-28 Cherokee 140	Warwickshire Aviation Ltd
	G-BAHH	Wallis WA-121	K. H. Wallis

Reg.	Type	Owner or Operator	Notes
G-BAHI	Cessna F.150H	MJP Aviation & Sales	
G-BAHJ	PA-24 Comanche 250	K. Cooper	
G-BAHL	Robin DR.400/160	J. B. McVeighty	
G-BAHP	Volmer VJ.22 Sportsman	Seaplane Group	
G-BAHS	PA-28R Cherokee Arrow 200-II	A. R. N. Morris	
G-BAHX	Cessna 182P	M. D. J. Moore	
G-BAIG	PA-34-200-2 Seneca	Mid-Anglia School of Flying	
G-BAIH	PA-28R Cherokee Arrow 200-II	M. G. West	
G-BAIK	Cessna F.150L	M. Sollitt	
G-BAIS	Cessna F.177RG	Cardinal Syndicate	
G-BAIW	Cessna F.172M	W. J. Greenfield	
G-BAIZ	Slingsby T.61A Falke	Falke Syndicate	
G-BAJA	Cessna F.177RG	D. W. Ward	
G-BAJB	Cessna F.177RG	J. D. Loveridge	
G-BAJC	Evans VP-1	S. J. Greer	
G-BAJE	Cessna 177	Dynamic Aviation BV	
G-BAJN	AA-5 Traveler	P. J. Stead	
G-BAJO	AA-5 Traveler	Montgomery Aviation Ltd	
G-BAJR	PA-28 Cherokee 180	Spectrum Bravo Flying Group	
G-BAJZ	Robin DR.400/125	Rochester Aviation Ltd	
G-BAKH	PA-28 Cherokee 140	Blue Sky Investments Ltd	
G-BAKJ	PA-30 Twin Comanche 160B	G. D. Colover	
G-BAKM	Robin DR.400/140	D. V. Pieri	
G-BAKN	SNCAN Stampe SV.4C	M. Holloway	
G-BAKR	Jodel D.117	R. W. Brown	
G-BAKV	PA-18 Super Cub 150	W. J. Murray	
G-BAKW	Beagle B.121 Pup 2	Cunning Stunts Flying Group	
G-BALD	Cameron O-84 balloon	C. A. Gould	
G-BALF	Robin DR.400/140	G. & D. A. Wasey	
G-BALG	Robin DR.400/180	S. G. Jones	
G-BALH	Robin DR.400/140B	G-BALH Flying Group	
G-BALJ	Robin DR.400/180	D. A. Batt & D. de Lacey-Rowe	
G-BALN	Cessna T.310Q	O'Brien Properties Ltd	
G-BAMB	Slingsby T.61C Falke	H. J. Bradley	
G-BAMC	Cessna F.150L	K. Evans	
G-BAML	Bell 206B Jet Ranger II ★	Aero Venture	
G-BAMR	PA-16 Clipper	G-BAMR Flying Group	
G-BAMS	Robin DR.400/160	G-BAMS Ltd	
G-BAMT	CEA DR400/160	S. G. Jones	
G-BAMU	Robin DR.400/160	The Alternative Flying Group	
G-BAMV	Robin DR.400/180	K. Jones & E. A. Anderson	
G-BAMY	PA-28R Cherokee Arrow 200-II	C. B. Clark	
G-BANA	Robin DR.221	G. T. Pryor	
G-BANB	Robin DR.400/180	M. Ingvardsen	
G-BANC	Gardan GY-201 Minicab	C. R. Shipley	
G-BANU	Wassmer Jodel D.120	C. H. Kilner	
G-BANV	Phoenix Currie Wot	K. Knight	
G-BANW	CP.1330 Super Emeraude	P. S. Milner	
G-BANX	Cessna F.172M	Oakfleet 2000 Ltd	
G-BAOJ	MS.880B Rallye Club	R. E. Jones	
G-BAOM	MS.880B Rallye Club	P. J. D. Feehan	
G-BAOP	Cessna FRA.150L	R. D. Forster	
G-BAOU	AA-5 Traveler	R. C. Mark	
G-BAPB	DHC.1 Chipmunk 22	G. V. Bunyan	
G-BAPI	Cessna FRA.150L	Marketing Management Services International Ltd	
G-BAPJ	Cessna FRA.150L	M. D. Page	
G-BAPL	PA-23 Turbo Aztec 250E	Donington Aviation Ltd	
G-BAPP	Evans VP-1 Series 2	D. H. G. Cotter	
G-BAPR	Jodel D.11	J. F. M. Bartlett	
G-BAPS	Campbell Cougar ★	IHM/Weston-super-Mare	
G-BAPV	Robin DR.400/160	J. D. & M. Millne	
G-BAPW	PA-28R Cherokee Arrow 180	A.G. Bourne & M. W. Freeman	
G-BAPX	Robin DR.400/160	G-BAPX Group	
G-BAPY	Robin HR.100/210	G-BAPY Group	
G-BARC	Cessna FR.172J	Severn Valley Aviation Group	
G-BARF	Jodel D.112 Club	V. Hughes	
G-BARH	Beech C.23 Sundowner	G. Moorby & J. Hinchcliffe	
G-BARN	Taylor JT.2 Titch	R. G. W. Newton	
G-BARP	Bell 206B JetRanger 2	Western Power Distribution (South West) PLC	
G-BARS	DHC.1 Chipmunk 22 (1377)	J. Beattie & R. M. Scarre	
G-BARZ	Scheibe SF.28A Tandem Falke	K. Kiely	
G-BASH	AA-5 Traveler	BASH Flying Group	
G-BASJ	PA-28-180 Cherokee	Bristol Aero Club	

Notes	Reg.	Type	Owner or Operator
	G-BASL	PA-28-140 Cherokee	P. N. Clynes
	G-BASM	PA-34-200 Seneca II	M. Gipps
	G-BASN	Beech C.23 Sundowner	S. R. Ford
	G-BASO	Lake LA-4 Amphibian	Uulster Seaplane Association Ltd
	G-BASP	Beagle B.121 Pup 1	B. J. Coutts
	G-BATC	MBB Bö.105D	South Georgia Heritage Trust
	G-BATJ	Jodel D.119	Clipgate TJ Group
	G-BATN	PA-23 Aztec 250E	Marshall of Cambridge Ltd
	G-BATV	PA-28 Cherokee 180D	J. N. Rudsdale
	G-BATW	PA-28 Cherokee 140	C. D. Sainsbury
	G-BAUC	PA-25 Pawnee 235	Southdown Gliding Club Ltd
	G-BAUH	Jodel D.112	G. A. & D. Shepherd
	G-BAVB	Cessna F.172M	T. S. Sheridan-McGinnitty
	G-BAVH	DHC.1 Chipmunk 22	Portsmouth Naval Gliding Club
	G-BAVL	PA-23 Aztec 250E	S. P. & A. V. Chillott
	G-BAVO	Boeing Stearman N2S (26)	R. C. McCarthy
	G-BAVR	AA-5 Traveler	G. E. Murray
	G-BAWG	PA-28R Cherokee Arrow 200-II	Solent Air Ltd
	G-BAWK	PA-28 Cherokee 140	J. Stanley
	G-BAXE	Hughes 269A	Reethorpe Engineering Ltd
	G-BAXK	Thunder Ax7-77 balloon ★	A. R. Snook
	G-BAXS	Bell 47G-5	C. R. Johnson
	G-BAXU	Cessna F.150L	M. W. Sheppardson
	G-BAXV	Cessna F.150L	CBM Associates Consulting Ltd
	G-BAXY	Cessna F.172M	Eaglesoar Ltd
	G-BAXZ	PA-28 Cherokee 140	G-BAXZ (87) Syndicate
	G-BAYL	SNCAN Nord 1101 Norecrin ★	(stored)/Chirk
	G-BAYO	Cessna 150L	J. A. & D. T. A. Rees
	G-BAYP	Cessna 150L	Yankee Papa Flying Group
	G-BAYR	Robin HR.100/210	P. D. Harries
	G-BAZC	Robin DR.400/160	S. G. Jones
	G-BAZM	Jodel D.11	A. F. Simpson
	G-BAZS	Cessna F.150L	L. W. Scattergood
	G-BAZT	Cessna F.172M	Aviation South West Ltd
	G-BBAW	Robin HR.100/210	F. A. Purvis
	G-BBAX	Robin DR.400/140	G. J. Bissex & P. H. Garbutt
	G-BBAY	Robin DR.400/140	J. C. Stubbs
	G-BBBB	Taylor JT.1 Monoplane	M. C. Arnold
	G-BBBC	Cessna F.150L	W. J. Greenfield
	G-BBBI	AA-5 Traveler	Go Baby Aviation Group
	G-BBBN	PA-28 Cherokee 180	Estuary Aviation Ltd
	G-BBBW	FRED Srs 2	M. Palfreman
	G-BBBY	PA-28 Cherokee 140	W. R. & R. Davies
	G-BBCH	Robin DR.400/2+2	The Cotswold Aero Club Ltd
	G-BBCI	Cessna 150H	A. M. & F. Alam
	G-BBCN	Robin HR.100/210	J. C. King
	G-BBCS	Robin DR.400/140	B. N. Stevens
	G-BBCY	Luton LA-4A Minor	A. W. McBlain
	G-BBCZ	AA-5 Traveler	Mercantile Developments Ltd
	G-BBDC	PA-28-140 Cherokee	G-BBDC Group
	G-BBDE	PA-28R Cherokee Arrow 200-II	R. L. Coleman, P. Knott & Istec Services Ltd
	G-BBDG	BAC-Aérospatiale Concorde 100 ★	Brooklands Museum
	G-BBDH	Cessna F.172M	J. D. Woodward
	G-BBDL	AA-5 Traveler	Delta Lima Flying Group
	G-BBDM	AA-5 Traveler	Jackeroo Aviation Group
	G-BBDO	PA-23 Turbo Aztec 250E	J. W. Anstee
	G-BBDP	Robin DR.400/160	Robin Lance Aviation Associates Ltd
	G-BBDS	PA-31 Turbo Navajo	Jota Aircraft Leasing Ltd (G-SKKB)
	G-BBDT	Cessna 150H	J. G. N. Wilson
	G-BBDV	SIPA S.903	Eatonair Group
	G-BBEA	Luton LA-4 Minor	D. S. Evans
	G-BBEB	PA-28R Cherokee Arrow 200-II	F. J. Stimpson & M. J. Potter
	G-BBEC	PA-28 Cherokee 180	P. & M. Corrigan
	G-BBEN	Bellanca 7GCBC Citabria	C. A. G. Schofield
	G-BBFD	PA-28R Cherokee Arrow 200-II	C. H. Rose & M. J. Green
	G-BBFL	Gardan GY-201 Minicab	R. Smith
	G-BBFV	PA-32 Cherokee Six 260	G-BBFV Syndicate
	G-BBGC	MS.893E Rallye 180GT	P. M. Nolan
	G-BBGI	Fuji FA.200-160	A and P West
	G-BBHF	PA-23 Aztec 250E	G. J. Williams
	G-BBHI	Cessna 177RG	T. G. W. Bunce
	G-BBHJ	Piper J-3C-65 Cub	Wellcross Flying Group

Reg.	Type	Owner or Operator	Notes
G-BBHK	Noorduyn AT-16 Harvard IIB (FH153)	M. Kubrak	
G-BBHY	PA-28 Cherokee 180	Air Operations Ltd	
G-BBIF	PA-23 Aztec 250E	Marshall of Cambridge Aerospace Ltd	
G-BBIH	Enstrom F-28A-UK	Friebe France Aeronautique SARL	
G-BBII	Fiat G-46-3B (4-97/MM52801)	G-BBII Ltd	
G-BBIL	PA-28 Cherokee 140	Saxondale Group	
G-BBIO	Robin HR.100/210	R. P. Caley	
G-BBIX	PA-28 Cherokee 140	Sterling Aviation Ltd	
G-BBJI	Isaacs Spitfire (RN218)	S. Vince	
G-BBJU	Robin DR.400/140	J. C. Lister	
G-BBJV	Cessna F.177RG	P. R. Powell	
G-BBJX	Cessna F.150L	L. W. Scattergood	
G-BBJY	Cessna F.172M	D. G. Wright	
G-BBJZ	Cessna F.172M	L. P. Burrow	
G-BBKA	Cessna F.150L	W. M. Wilson	
G-BBKB	Cessna F.150L	Justgold Ltd	
G-BBKE	Cessna F.150L	G. J. Smith	
G-BBKG	Cessna FR.172J	R. Wright	
G-BBKI	Cessna F.172M	C. W. & S. A. Burman	
G-BBKL	CP.301A Emeraude	Piel G-BBKL	
G-BBKX	PA-28 Cherokee 180	DRA Flying Club Ltd	
G-BBKY	Cessna F.150L	F. W. Astbury	
G-BBKZ	Cessna 172M	KZ Flying Group	
G-BBLH	Piper J-3C-65 Cub (31145:G-26)	Shipping & Airlines Ltd	
G-BBLS	AA-5 Traveler	A. Grant	
G-BBLU	PA-34-200 Seneca II	R. H. R. Rue	
G-BBMB	Robin DR.400/180	Regent Flying Group	
G-BBMH	EAA. Sports Biplane Model P.1	G-BBMH Flying Group	
G-BBMJ	PA-23 Aztec 250E	Nationwide Caravan Rental Services Ltd	
G-BBMN	DHC.1 Chipmunk 22	R. Steiner	
G-BBMO	DHC.1 Chipmunk 22 (WK514)	Mike Oscar Group	
G-BBMR	DHC.1 Chipmunk 22 (WB763:14)	P. J. Wood	
G-BBMT	DHC.1 Chipmunk 22	MT Group	
G-BBMV	DHC.1 Chipmunk 22 (WG348)	S. P. Tilling	
G-BBMW	DHC.1 Chipmunk 22 (WK628)	G. Fielder & A. Wilson	
G-BBMZ	DHC.1 Chipmunk 22	G-BBMZ Chipmunk Syndicate	
G-BBNA	DHC.1 Chipmunk 22 (Lycoming)	Coventry Gliding Club Ltd	
G-BBNC	DHC.1 Chipmunk T.10 (WP790) ★	De Havilland Heritage Museum/London Colney	
G-BBND	DHC.1 Chipmunk 22 (WD286)	Bernoulli Syndicate	
G-BBNH	PA-34-200 Seneca II	M. G. D. Baverstock & ptnrs	
G-BBNI	PA-34-200 Seneca II	M. P. Grimshaw	
G-BBNJ	Cessna F.150L	M. C. Bellamy	
G-BBNT	PA-31-350 Navajo Chieftain	Atlantic Bridge Aviation Ltd	
G-BBNZ	Cessna F.172M	J. H. Sandham Aviation	
G-BBOA	Cessna F.172M	J. D & A. M. Black	
G-BBOH	Pitts S-1S Special	Venom Jet Promotions Ltd	
G-BBOL	PA-18 Super Cub 150	N. Artt	
G-BBOO	Thunder Ax6-56 balloon	K. Meehan Tigerjack	
G-BBOR	Bell 206B JetRanger 2	M. J. Easey	
G-BBPP	PA-28 Cherokee 180	Big Red Kite Ltd (G-WACP)	
G-BBPS	Jodel D.117	A. Appleby	
G-BBPX	PA-34-200 Seneca II	The G-BBPX Flying Group	
G-BBPY	PA-28 Cherokee 180	Sunsaver Ltd	
G-BBRA	PA-23 Aztec 250D	P. A. R. Marin	
G-BBRB	DH.82A Tiger Moth (DF198)	R. Barham	
G-BBRC	Fuji FA.200-180	BBRC Ltd	
G-BBRI	Bell 47G-5A	Alan Mann Aviation Group Ltd	
G-BBRN	Procter Kittiwake 1 (XW784/VL)	H. M. Price	
G-BBRZ	AA-5 Traveler	B. McIntyre	
G-BBSA	AA-5 Traveler	Usworth 84 Flying Associates Ltd	
G-BBSS	DHC.1A Chipmunk 22	Coventry Gliding Club Ltd	
G-BBSW	Pietenpol Air Camper	J. K. S. Wills	
G-BBTB	Cessna FRA.150L	Solent School of Flying	
G-BBTG	Cessna F.172M	Triple X Flying Group	
G-BBTH	Cessna F.172M	Tayside Aviation Ltd	
G-BBTJ	PA-23 Aztec 250E	J. A. & R. H. Cooper	
G-BBTK	Cessna FRA.150L	Cleveland Flying School Ltd	
G-BBTY	Beech C23 Sundowner	G-BBTY Group	
G-BBUE	AA-5 Traveler	Tatenhill Aviation Ltd	
G-BBUJ	Cessna 421B	Aero VIP Companhia de Transportes & Servicios Aereos SA/Portugal	
G-BBUT	Western O-65 balloon	R. G. Turnbull	
G-BBUU	Piper J-3C-65 Cub	C. Stokes	

Notes	Reg.	Type	Owner or Operator
	G-BBVF	SA Twin Pioneer Srs 3 ★	Museum of Flight/East Fortune
	G-BBVO	Isaacs Fury II (S1579)	C. E. Brookes
	G-BBXB	Cessna FRA.150L	D. C. & M. Laycock
	G-BBXW	PA-28-151 Cherokee Warrior	Bristol Aero Club
	G-BBXY	Bellanca 7GCBC Citabria	R. R. L. Windus
	G-BBXZ	Evans VP-1	R. W. Burrows
	G-BBYB	PA-18 Super Cub 95	A. L. Walker
	G-BBYH	Cessna 182P	Ramco (UK) Ltd
	G-BBYM	HP.137 Jetstream 200 ★	Aerospace Museum/Cosford (G-AYWR)
	G-BBYP	PA-28 Cherokee 140	E. Williams
	G-BBYS	Cessna 182P	G-BBYS Group
	G-BBYU	Cameron O-56 balloon	British Balloon Museum
	G-BBZF	PA-28-140 Cherokee	D. Franzan
	G-BBZH	PA-28R Cherokee Arrow 200-II	G. Higgins, C. Harte and I. O'Brien
	G-BBZN	Fuji FA.200-180	D. Kynaston & ptnrs
	G-BBZV	PA-28R Cherokee Arrow 200-II	P. B. Mellor
	G-BCAH	DHC.1 Chipmunk 22 (WG316)	Century Aviation Ltd
	G-BCAP	Cameron O-56 balloon ★	Balloon Preservation Group/Lancing
	G-BCAR	Thunder Ax7-77 balloon ★	British Balloon Museum/Newbury
	G-BCAZ	PA-12 Super Cruiser	A. D. Williams
	G-BCBG	PA-23 Aztec 250E	M. J. L. Batt
	G-BCBH	Fairchild 24R-46A Argus III	Dreamticket Promotions Ltd
	G-BCBJ	PA-25 Pawnee 235	Deeside Gliding Club (Aberdeenshire) Ltd
	G-BCBL	Fairchild 24R-46A Argus III (HB751)	F. J. Cox
	G-BCBR	AJEP/Wittman W.8 Tailwind	D. P. Jones
	G-BCBX	Cessna F.150L	P. Lodge & J. G. McVey
	G-BCBZ	Cessna 337C	J. Haden
	G-BCCC	Cessna F.150L	D. J. Parkinson
	G-BCCE	PA-23 Aztec 250E	Golf Charlie Echo Ltd
	G-BCCF	PA-28 Cherokee 180	Charlie Foxtrot Aviation
	G-BCCK	AA-5 Traveler	Prospect Air Ltd
	G-BCCR	CP.301A Emeraude (modified)	D. C. Stokes
	G-BCCX	DHC.1 Chipmunk 22 (Lycoming)	The Royal Air Force Gliding and Soaring Association
	G-BCCY	Robin HR.200/100	M. E. Hicks
	G-BCDK	Partenavia P.68B	Mach 014 SAS Di Albertario Michele and Co/Italy
	G-BCDL	Cameron O-42 balloon	D. P. & Mrs B. O. Turner Chums
	G-BCDN	F.27 Friendship Mk 200 ★	Instructional airframe/Norwich
	G-BCDY	Cessna FRA.150L	R. L. Nunn & T. R. Edwards
	G-BCEB	Sikorsky S-61N Mk II	Veritair Ltd
	G-BCEE	AA-5 Traveler	P. J. Marchant
	G-BCEF	AA-5 Traveler	G-BCEF Group
	G-BCEN	BN-2A-26 Islander	Reconnaissance Ventures Ltd
	G-BCEP	AA-5 Traveler	A. A. Kind & P. Ragan
	G-BCER	Gardan GY-201 Minicab	D. Beaumont
	G-BCEU	Cameron O-42 balloon	P. Glydon
	G-BCEY	DHC.1 Chipmunk 22 (WG465)	Gopher Flying Group
	G-BCFF	Fuji FA-200-160	S. A. Cole
	G-BCFR	Cessna FRA.150L	Foxtrot Romeo Group
	G-BCFW	SAAB 91D Safir	D. R. Williams
	G-BCFY	Luton LA-4A Minor	M. P. Wiseman
	G-BCGB	Bensen B.8	A. Melody
	G-BCGC	DHC.1 Chipmunk 22 (WP903)	Henlow Chipmunk Group
	G-BCGH	SNCAN NC.854S	Nord Flying Group
	G-BCGI	PA-28 Cherokee 140	John West Consulting Ltd
	G-BCGJ	PA-28 Cherokee 140	Demero Ltd & Transcourt Ltd
	G-BCGM	Jodel D.120	S. M. Kenyon-Roberts
	G-BCGN	PA-28 Cherokee 140	C. F. Hessey
	G-BCGS	PA-28R Cherokee Arrow 200	Arrow Aviation Group
	G-BCGW	Jodel D.11	G. H. Chittenden
	G-BCHL	DHC.1 Chipmunk 22A (WP788)	Shropshire Soaring Ltd
	G-BCHP	CP.1310-C3 Super Emeraude	G. Hughes & A. G. Just (G-JOSI)
	G-BCHT	Schleicher ASK.16	Dunstable K16 Group
	G-BCID	PA-34-200 Seneca II	Shenley Farms (Aviation) Ltd
	G-BCIH	DHC.1 Chipmunk 22 (WD363)	P. J. Richie
	G-BCIJ	AA-5 Traveler	Arrow Association
	G-BCIR	PA-28-151 Warrior	R. W. Harris
	G-BCJM	PA-28 Cherokee 140	APB Leasing Ltd
	G-BCJN	PA-28 Cherokee 140	Bristol and Wessex Aeroplane Club Ltd
	G-BCJO	PA-28R Cherokee Arrow 200	R. Ross
	G-BCJP	PA-28 Cherokee 140	J. Wilson

Reg.	Type	Owner or Operator	Notes
G-BCKN	DHC.1A Chipmunk 22 (Lycoming)	The Royal Air Force Gliding and Soaring Association	
G-BCKS	Fuji FA.200-180AO	G. J. Ward	
G-BCKT	Fuji FA.200-180	A. G. Dobson	
G-BCKU	Cessna FRA.150L	Mid America (UK) Ltd	
G-BCKV	Cessna FRA.150L	M. Bonsall	
G-BCLI	AA-5 Traveler	BCLI Group	
G-BCLL	PA-28 Cherokee 180	S. C. Hardman	
G-BCLS	Cessna 170B	N. Simpson	
G-BCLT	MS.894A Rallye Minerva 220	K. M. Bowen	
G-BCLU	Jodel D.117	G-BCLU Group	
G-BCLW	AA-1B Trainer	C. R. White	
G-BCMD	PA-18 Super Cub 95	P. Stephenson	
G-BCMJ	Squarecraft Cavalier SA.102-5	N. F. Andrews	
G-BCMT	Isaacs Fury II	R.W. Burrows	
G-BCNC	Gardan GY-201 Minicab	J. R. Wraight	
G-BCNP	Cameron O-77 balloon	P. Spellward	
G-BCNX	Piper J-3C-65 Cub (540)	K. J. Lord	
G-BCNZ	Fuji FA.200-160	W. Dougan	
G-BCOB	Piper J-3C-65 Cub (329405:A-23)	C. Marklew-Brown	
G-BCOI	DHC.1 Chipmunk 22 (WP970:12)	M. J. Diggins	
G-BCOL	Cessna F.172M	November Charlie Flying Group	
G-BCOM	Piper J-3C-65 Cub	Dougal Flying Group	
G-BCOO	DHC.1 Chipmunk 22	T. G. Fielding & M. S. Morton	
G-BCOR	SOCATA Rallye 100ST	T. J. Horsley	
G-BCOU	DHC.1 Chipmunk 22 (WK522)	P. J. Loweth	
G-BCOY	DHC.1 Chipmunk 22	Coventry Gliding Club Ltd	
G-BCPD	Gardan GY-201 Minicab	P. R. Cozens	
G-BCPG	PA-28R Cherokee Arrow 200-II	Roses Flying Group	
G-BCPH	Piper J-3C-65 Cub (329934:B-72)	G. Earl	
G-BCPJ	Piper J-3C-65 Cub	J. W. Widdows	
G-BCPK	Cessna F.172M	D. C. C. Handley	
G-BCPN	AA-5 Traveler	G-BCPN Group	
G-BCPU	DHC.1 Chipmunk 22	P. Waller	
G-BCRB	Cessna F.172M	Wingstask 1995Ltd	
G-BCRE	Cameron O-77 balloon ★	Balloon Preservation Group/Lancing	
G-BCRL	PA-28-151 Warrior	BCRL Ltd	
G-BCRR	AA-5B Tiger	S. Waite	
G-BCRX	DHC.1 Chipmunk 22 (WD292)	P. J. Tuplin & M. I. Robinson	
G-BCSA	DHC.1 Chipmunk 22 (Lycoming)	The Royal Air Force Gliding and Soaring Association	
G-BCSL	DHC.1 Chipmunk 22	Chipmunk Flyers Ltd	
G-BCSX	Thunder Ax7-77 balloon	C. Wolstenholm	
G-BCTF	PA-28-151 Warrior	The St. George Flight Training Ltd	
G-BCTI	Schleicher ASK 16	Tango India Syndicate	
G-BCTK	Cessna FR.172J	M. G. E. Morton	
G-BCTT	Evans VP-1	E. R. G. Ludlow	
G-BCUB	Piper J-3C-65 Cub	A. L. Brown	
G-BCUF	Cessna F.172M	Howell Plant Hire & Construction	
G-BCUH	Cessna F.150M	M. G. Montgomerie	
G-BCUJ	Cessna F.150M	J. T. Mountain	
G-BCUL	SOCATA Rallye 100ST	C. A. Ussher & Fountain Estates Ltd	
G-BCUO	SA Bulldog Srs 120/122	Cranfield University	
G-BCUS	SA Bulldog Srs 120/122	Falcon Group	
G-BCUV	SA Bulldog Srs 120/122 (XX704)	Flew LLP	
G-BCUW	Cessna F.177RG	S. J. Westley	
G-BCUY	Cessna FRA.150M	J. C. Carpenter	
G-BCVB	PA-17 Vagabond	A. T. Nowak	
G-BCVC	SOCATA Rallye 100ST	W. Haddow	
G-BCVE	Evans VP-2	D. Masterson & D. B. Winstanley	
G-BCVF	Practavia Pilot Sprite	D. G. Hammersley	
G-BCVG	Cessna FRA.150L	G-BCVG Flying Group	
G-BCVH	Cessna FRA.150L	M. A. James	
G-BCVJ	Cessna F.172M	Rothland Ltd	
G-BCVY	PA-34-200T Seneca II	Oxford Aviation Academy (Oxford) Ltd	
G-BCWB	Cessna 182P	M. F. Oliver & A. J. Mew	
G-BCWH	Practavia Pilot Sprite	R. Tasker	
G-BCWK	Alpavia Fournier RF-3	T. J. Hartwell	
G-BCXB	SOCATA Rallye 100ST	The Rallye Group	
G-BCXE	Robin DR.400/2+2	Weald Air Services Ltd	
G-BCXJ	Piper L-4J Cub (480752:E-39)	W. Readman	
G-BCXN	DHC.1 Chipmunk 22 (WP800)	G. M. Turner	
G-BCYH	DAW Privateer Mk. 3	G-BCYH Group	

Notes	Reg.	Type	Owner or Operator
	G-BCYK	Avro CF.100 Mk 4 Canuck (18393) ★	Imperial War Museum/Duxford
	G-BCYM	DHC.1 Chipmunk 22 (WK577)	G-BCYM Group
	G-BCYR	Cessna F.172M	P. Barton, R. Ryan & P. Wayman
	G-BCZM	Cessna F.172M	Cornwall Flying Club Ltd
	G-BCZO	Cameron O-77 balloon	W. O. T. Holmes
	G-BDAD	Taylor JT.1 Monoplane	C. S. Whitwell
	G-BDAG	Taylor JT.1 Monoplane	N. R. Osborne
	G-BDAH	Evans VP-1	G. H. J. Geurts
	G-BDAI	Cessna FRA.150M	B. K. & W. G. Ranger
	G-BDAK	Rockwell Commander 112	M. C. Wilson
	G-BDAO	SIPA S.91	S. B. Churchill
	G-BDAP	AJEP Tailwind	J. Whiting
	G-BDAR	Evans VP-1	R. F. Powell
	G-BDAY	Thunder Ax5-42S1 balloon	T. M. Donnelly Meconium
	G-BDBF	FRED Srs 2	G. E. & R. E. Collins
	G-BDBH	Bellanca 7GCBC Citabria	C. J. Gray
	G-BDBI	Cameron O-77 balloon	C. Jones
	G-BDBS	Short SD3-30 ★	Ulster Aviation Society
	G-BDBU	Cessna F.150M	S. Collins
	G-BDBV	Jodel D.11A	Seething Jodel Group
	G-BDBZ	Westland WS-55 Whirlwind (XJ398) ★	Aeroventure/Doncaster
	G-BDCD	Piper J-3C-85 Cub (480133:B-44)	Cubby Cub Group
	G-BDCI	CP.301A Emeraude	D. L. Sentance
	G-BDDD	DHC.1 Chipmunk 22	DRA Aero Club Ltd
	G-BDDF	Jodel D.120	J. V. Thompson
	G-BDDG	Jodel D.112	J. Pool & D. G. Palmer
	G-BDDS	PA-25 Pawnee 235	Vale of Neath Gliding Club
	G-BDDX	Whittaker MW2B Excalibur ★	Cornwall Aero Park/Helston
	G-BDDZ	CP.301A Emeraude	E. C. Mort
	G-BDEC	SOCATA Rallye 100ST	J. Fingleton
	G-BDEH	Jodel D.120A	EH Group
	G-BDEI	Jodel D.9 Bébé	The Noddy Group
	G-BDEU	DHC.1 Chipmunk 22 (WP808)	Skylark Aviation Ltd
	G-BDEX	Cessna FRA.150M	A. P. F. Tucker
	G-BDEY	Piper J-3C-65 Cub	Ducksworth Flying Club
	G-BDEZ	Piper J-3C-65 Cub	M. Housley
	G-BDFB	Currie Wot	J. Jennings
	G-BDFH	Auster AOP.9 (XR240)	R. B. Webber
	G-BDFR	Fuji FA.200-160	M. S. Bird
	G-BDFU	Dragonfly MPA Mk 1 ★	Museum of Flight/East Fortune
	G-BDFY	AA-5 Traveler	Grumman Group
	G-BDGB	Gardan GY-20 Minicab	S. Burchfield
	G-BDGH	Thunder Ax7-77 balloon	R. J. Mitchener & P. F. Smart
	G-BDGM	PA-28-151 Cherokee Warrior	J. Tonge
	G-BDHK	Piper J-3C-65 Cub (329417)	Knight Flying Group
	G-BDIE	Rockwell Commander 112	J. McAleer & R. J. Adams
	G-BDIG	Cessna 182P	A. J. Macdonald
	G-BDIH	Jodel D.117	N. D. H. Stokes
	G-BDIX	DH.106 Comet 4C ★	Museum of Flight/East Fortune
	G-BDJD	Jodel D.112	J. E. Preston
	G-BDJG	Luton LA-4A Minor	Very Slow Flying Club
	G-BDJP	Piper J-3C-90 Cub	S. T. Gilbert
	G-BDJR	SNCAN Nord NC.858	R. F. M. Marson
	G-BDKC	Cessna A185F	Bridge of Tilt Co Ltd
	G-BDKD	Enstrom F-28A	P. J. Price
	G-BDKH	CP.301A Emeraude	T. A. S. Rayner
	G-BDKJ	K & S SA.102.5 Cavalier	D. A. Garner
	G-BDKM	SIPA 903	S. W. Markham
	G-BDKW	Rockwell Commander 112A	J. T. Klaschka
	G-BDLO	AA-5A Cheetah	S. & J. Dolan
	G-BDLT	Rockwell Commander 112	D. L. Churchward
	G-BDLY	K & S SA.102.5 Cavalier	P. R. Stevens
	G-BDMS	Piper J-3C-65 Cub (FR886)	A. T. H. Martin
	G-BDMW	Jodel DR.100A	Mike Whisky Group
	G-BDNC	Taylor JT.1 Monoplane	D. W. Mathie
	G-BDNG	Taylor JT.1 Monoplane	R. B. McComish
	G-BDNT	Jodel D.92 Bébé	R. J. Stobo
	G-BDNU	Cessna F.172M	J. & K. G. McVicar
	G-BDNW	AA-1B Trainer	N. A. Baxter
	G-BDNX	AA-1B Trainer	M. Clark & M. W. Olliver
	G-BDOD	Cessna F.150M	OD Group
	G-BDOE	Cessna FR.172J	A. W. Todd

Reg.	Type	Owner or Operator	Notes
G-BDOG	SA Bulldog Srs 200	D. C. Bonsall	
G-BDOL	Piper J-3C-65 Cub	L. R. Balthazor	
G-BDOW	Cessna FRA.150	Joystick Aviation Ltd	
G-BDPA	PA-28-151 Warrior	Aircraft Engineers Ltd	
G-BDPJ	PA-25 Pawnee 235B	Swift Aerobatic Display Team	
G-BDRD	Cessna FRA.150M	Aircraft Engineers Ltd	
G-BDRF	Taylor JT.1 Monoplane	D. J. Couzens	
G-BDRG	Taylor JT.2 Titch	D. R. Gray	
G-BDRJ	DHC.1 Chipmunk 22 (WP857)	WP857 Trust	
G-BDRK	Cameron O-65 balloon	R. J. Mitchener & P. F. Smart	
G-BDSB	PA-28-181 Archer II	Testair Ltd	
G-BDSF	Cameron O-56 balloon	J. H. Greensides	
G-BDSH	PA-28 Cherokee 140 (modified)	The Wright Brothers Flying Group	
G-BDSK	Cameron O-65 balloon	Southern Balloon Group Carousel II	
G-BDSM	Slingsby T.31B Cadet III	F. C. J. Wevers/Netherlands	
G-BDTB	Evans VP-1	P. W. Boyes	
G-BDTL	Evans VP-1	T. W. Carnall	
G-BDTO	BN-2A Mk III-2 Trislander	Aurigny Air Services Ltd (G-RBSI/G-OTSB)	
G-BDTU	Omega III gas balloon	R. G. Turnbull	
G-BDTV	Mooney M.20F	S. Redfearn	
G-BDTX	Cessna F.150M	F. W. Ellis	
G-BDUI	Cameron V-56 balloon	D. C. Johnson	
G-BDUL	Evans VP-1 Srs.2	J. C. Lindsay	
G-BDUM	Cessna F.150M	P. B. Millington	
G-BDUN	PA-34-200T Seneca II	R. Paris	
G-BDUO	Cessna F.150M	D. W. Locke	
G-BDUY	Robin DR.400/140B	J. G. Anderson	
G-BDUZ	Cameron V-56 balloon	Zebedee Balloon Service	
G-BDVA	PA-17 Vagabond	I. M. Callier	
G-BDVB	PA-15 (PA-17) Vagabond	B. P. Gardner	
G-BDVC	PA-17 Vagabond	A. R. Caveen	
G-BDWE	Flaglor Scooter	P. King	
G-BDWH	SOCATA Rallye 150ST	M. A. Jones	
G-BDWJ	SE-5A (replica) (F8010:Z)	D. W. Linney	
G-BDWM	Mustang scale replica (FB226)	D. C. Bonsall	
G-BDWO	Howes Ax6 balloon	R. B. & C. Howes	
G-BDWP	PA-32R-300 Cherokee Lance	A. Belcastro & I. Bardelli/Italy	
G-BDWX	Jodel D.120A	R. P. Rochester	
G-BDWY	PA-28-140 Cherokee E	N. Grantham	
G-BDWZ	Slingsby T-59J Kestrel	T. J. Wilkinson	
G-BDXX	SNCAN NC.858S	K. M. Davis	
G-BDYG	P.56 Provost T.1 (WV493) ★	Museum of Flight/East Fortune	
G-BDZA	Scheibe SF.25E Super Falke	Hereward Flying Group	
G-BDZC	Cessna F.150M	A. M. Lynn	
G-BDZD	Cessna F.172M	R. J. A. Durie	
G-BDZG	Slingsby T.59H Kestrel	R. E. Gretton	
G-BEAB	Jodel DR.1051	R. C. Hibberd	
G-BEAC	PA-28 Cherokee 140	R. Murray & A. Bagley-Murray	
G-BEAD	WG.13 Lynx ★	Instructional airframe/Middle Wallop	
G-BEAG	PA-34-200T Seneca II	Oxford Aviation Academy (Oxford) Ltd	
G-BEAH	Auster J/2 Arrow	Bedwell Hey Flying Group	
G-BEBC	Westland WS-55 Whirlwind 3 (XP355) ★	Norwich Aviation Museum	
G-BEBG	WSK-PZL SDZ-45A Ogar	The Ogar Syndicate	
G-BEBN	Cessna 177B	P. M. A. Croton	
G-BEBR	GY-201 Minicab	A. R. Hawes	
G-BEBS	Andreasson BA-4B	N. J. W. Reid	
G-BEBU	Rockwell Commander 112A	I. Hunt	
G-BEBZ	PA-28-151 Warrior	Airways Flight Training (Exeter) Ltd	
G-BECA	SOCATA Rallye 100ST	N. G. Ogborne	
G-BECB	SOCATA Rallye 100ST	D. H. Tonkin	
G-BECK	Cameron V-56 balloon	N. H. & A. M. Ponsford	
G-BECN	Piper J-3C-65 Cub (480480:E-44)	G. Denney	
G-BECT	CASA 1.131E Jungmann 2000 (A-57)	Alpha 57 Group	
G-BECW	CASA 1.131E Jungmann 2000 (A-10)	C. M. Rampton	
G-BECZ	CAARP CAP-10B	C. M. Thompson	
G-BEDA	CASA 1.131E Jungmann 2000	L. Atkin & M. G. Kates	
G-BEDB	Nord 1203 Norecrin ★	B. F. G. Lister (stored)/Chirk	
G-BEDD	Jodel D.117A	Dubious Group	
G-BEDF	Boeing B-17G-105-VE (124485:DF-A)	B-17 Preservation Ltd	
G-BEDG	Rockwell Commander 112	G-BEDG Group	
G-BEDJ	Piper J-3C-65 Cub (44-80594)	R. Earl	
G-BEDP	BN-2A Mk.III-2 Trislander	Blue Island Air	

Notes	Reg.	Type	Owner or Operator
	G-BEDV	V.668 Varsity T.1 (WJ945) ★	Duxford Aviation Society
	G-BEEE	Thunder Ax6-56A balloon ★	British Balloon Museum/Newbury
	G-BEEH	Cameron V-56 balloon	Sade Balloons Ltd
	G-BEEI	Cameron N-77 balloon	A. P. Griffiths
	G-BEER	Isaacs Fury II (K2075)	R. S. C. Andrews
	G-BEEU	PA-28 Cherokee 140F	E. Merkado
	G-BEFA	PA-28-151 Warrior	Verran Freight
	G-BEFF	PA-28 Cherokee 140F	E. Merkado
	G-BEGG	Scheibe SF.25E Super Falke	G-BEGG Motorfalke
	G-BEHH	PA-32R Cherokee Lance 300	K. Swallow
	G-BEHU	PA-34-200T Seneca II	Pirin Aeronautical Ltd
	G-BEHV	Cessna F.172N	Edinburgh Air Centre Ltd
	G-BEIF	Cameron O-65 balloon	C. Vening
	G-BEIG	Cessna F.150M	R. D. Forster & M. S. B. Thorp
	G-BEII	PA-25 Pawnee 235D	Burn Gliding Club Ltd
	G-BEIL	SOCATA Rallye 150T	The Rallye Flying Group
	G-BEIP	PA-28-181 Archer II	S. Pope
	G-BEIS	Evans VP-1	P. J. Hunt
	G-BEJK	Cameron S-31 balloon	Rango Balloon and Kite Company
	G-BEJV	PA-34-200T Seneca II	Oxford Aviation Academy (Oxford) Ltd
	G-BEKL	Bede BD-4E-150	F. E.Tofield
	G-BEKM	Evans VP-1	G. J. McDill
	G-BEKN	Cessna FRA.150M	T. J. Lynn
	G-BEKO	Cessna F.182Q	G. J. & F. J. Leese
	G-BELT	Cessna F.150J	A. Kumar (G-AWUV)
	G-BEMB	Cessna F.172M	Stocklaunch Ltd
	G-BEMM	Slingsby T.31B Motor Cadet III	E. and P. McEvoy
	G-BEMW	PA-28-181 Archer II	Touch & Go Ltd
	G-BEMY	Cessna FRA.150M	J. R. Power
	G-BEND	Cameron V-56 balloon	Dante Balloon Group
	G-BENJ	Rockwell Commander 112B	BENJ Flying Group
	G-BENK	Cessna F.172M	Bulldog Aviation Ltd
	G-BEOD	Cessna 180H	I. Addy
	G-BEOE	Cessna FRA.150M	W. J. Henderson
	G-BEOH	PA-28R-201T Turbo Arrow III	Gloucestershire Flying Club
	G-BEOI	PA-18 Super Cub 150	Southdown Gliding Club Ltd
	G-BEOK	Cessna F.150M	KPOW Ltd
	G-BEOL	Short SC.7 Skyvan 3 variant 100	Invicta Aviation Ltd
	G-BEOX	Lockheed 414 Hudson IV (A16-199) ★	RAF Museum/Hendon
	G-BEOY	Cessna FRA.150L	J. N. Ponsford
	G-BEOZ	A.W.650 Argosy 101 ★	Aeropark/East Midlands
	G-BEPF	SNCAN Stampe SV.4A	C. C. Rollings & F. J. Hodson
	G-BEPV	Fokker S.11-1 Instructor (174)	S. W. & M. Isbister & C. Tyers
	G-BEPY	Rockwell Commander 112B	T. L. Rippon
	G-BERA	SOCATA Rallye 150ST	A. C. Stamp
	G-BERC	SOCATA Rallye 150ST	Severn Valley Aero Group
	G-BERI	Rockwell Commander 114	K. B. Harper
	G-BERN	Saffrey S-330 balloon	B. Martin
	G-BERT	Cameron V-56 balloon	Southern Balloon Group Bert
	G-BERY	AA-1B Trainer	R. H. J. Levi
	G-BETD	Robin HR.200/100	C. L. Wilsher
	G-BETE	Rollason B.2A Beta	T. M. Jones
	G-BETF	Cameron 'Champion' SS balloon ★	British Balloon Museum/Newbury
	G-BETL	PA-25 Pawnee 235D	Cambridge University Gliding Trust Ltd
	G-BETM	PA-25 Pawnee 235D	Yorkshire Gliding Club (Pty) Ltd
	G-BEUA	PA-18 Super Cub 150	London Gliding Club (Pty) Ltd
	G-BEUD	Robin HR.100/285R	E. A. & L. M. C. Payton
	G-BEUI	Piper J-3C-65 Cub	M. C. Jordan
	G-BEUP	Robin DR.400/180	Samuels LLP
	G-BEUU	PA-18 Super Cub 95	F. Sharples
	G-BEUX	Cessna F.172N	Multiflight Ltd
	G-BEUY	Cameron N-31 balloon	J. J. Daly
	G-BEVB	SOCATA Rallye 150ST	M. Smullen
	G-BEVC	SOCATA Rallye 150ST	Wolds Flyers Syndicate
	G-BEVG	PA-34-200T-2 Seneca	Direct Aviation Management Ltd
	G-BEVO	Sportavia-Pützer RF-5	M. Hill
	G-BEVP	Evans VP-2	G. Moscrop & R. C. Crowley
	G-BEVS	Taylor JT.1 Monoplane	D. Hunter
	G-BEVT	BN-2A Mk III-2 Trislander	Aurigny Air Services Ltd
	G-BEVW	SOCATA Rallye 150ST	S. W. Brown
	G-BEWN	DH.82A Tiger Moth	H. D. Labouchere
	G-BEWO	Zlin Z.326 Trener Master	P. A. Colman
	G-BEWR	Cessna F.172N	P. Lodge & J. G. McVey

Reg.	Type	Owner or Operator	Notes
G-BEWX	PA-28R-201 Arrow III	Three Greens Arrow Group	
G-BEWY	Bell 206B JetRanger 3	Polo Aviation Ltd (G-CULL)	
G-BEXN	AA-1C Lynx	I. H. Seach-Allen	
G-BEXW	PA-28-181 Cherokee	J. O'Keeffe	
G-BEYA	Enstrom 280C	P. George	
G-BEYB	Fairey Flycatcher (replica) (S1287) ★	F.A.A. Museum/Yeovilton	
G-BEYF	HPR.7 Herald 401 ★	Jet Heritage Museum/Bournemouth	
G-BEYL	PA-28 Cherokee 180	Yankee Lima Group	
G-BEYT	PA-28 Cherokee 140	J. N. Plange	
G-BEYV	Cessna T.210M	P. Mason & R. Turnell	
G-BEYW	Taylor JT.1 Monoplane	R. A. Abrahams	
G-BEYZ	Jodel DR.1051/M1	M. L. Balding	
G-BEZC	AA-5 Traveler	C. M. O'Connell	
G-BEZE	Rutan Vari-Eze	S. K. Cockburn	
G-BEZF	AA-5 Traveler	The G-BEZF Flying Group	
G-BEZG	AA-5 Traveler	M. D. R. Harling	
G-BEZH	AA-5 Traveler	Zulu Hotel Group	
G-BEZI	AA-5 Traveler	C. J. & L. Campbell	
G-BEZK	Cessna F.172H	S. Jones	
G-BEZL	PA-31-310 Turbo Navajo C	2 Excel Aviation Ltd	
G-BEZO	Cessna F.172M	Staverton Flying School @ Skypark Ltd	
G-BEZP	PA-32 Cherokee Six 300D	T. P. McCormack & J. K. Zealley	
G-BEZR	Cessna F.172M	J. P. Birnie	
G-BEZV	Cessna F.172M	Insch Flying Group	
G-BEZY	Rutan Vari-Eze	I. J. Pountney	
G-BEZZ	Jodel D.112	G-BEZZ Jodel Group	
G-BFAF	Aeronca 7BCM (7797)	D. C. W. Harper	
G-BFAH	Phoenix Currie Wot	R. W. Clarke	
G-BFAI	Rockwell Commander 114	P. Ellingford & K. Eves	
G-BFAK	GEMS MS.892A Rallye Commodore 150	J. M. Hedges	
G-BFAP	SIAI-Marchetti S.205-20R	A. O. Broin	
G-BFAS	Evans VP-1	A. I. Sutherland	
G-BFAW	DHC.1 Chipmunk 22	M. L. J. Goff	
G-BFAX	DHC.1 Chipmunk 22 (WG422)	M. F. Humphries	
G-BFBA	Jodel DR.100A	A. F. Vizoso	
G-BFBB	PA-23 Aztec 250E	D. Byrne	
G-BFBE	Robin HR.200/100	A. C. Pearson	
G-BFBM	Saffery S.330 balloon	B. Martin	
G-BFBR	PA-28-161 Warrior II	Phoenix Aviation	
G-BFBU	Partenavia P.68B	Reconnaissance Ventures Ltd	
G-BFBY	Piper J-3C-65 Cub	M. Shaw	
G-BFCT	Cessna Tu.206F	D. I. Schellingerhout	
G-BFDC	DHC.1 Chipmunk 22 (WG475)	N. F. O'Neill	
G-BFDE	Sopwith Tabloid (replica) (168) ★	RAF Museum/Hendon	
G-BFDF	SOCATA Rallye 235E	M. A. Wratten	
G-BFDI	PA-28-181 Archer II	Truman Aviation Ltd	
G-BFDK	PA-28-161 Warrior II	S. T. Gilbert	
G-BFDL	Piper J-3C-65 Cub (454537:J-04)	T. Holtbrook & B. A. Nicholson	
G-BFDO	PA-28R-201T Turbo Arrow III	J. Blackburn & J. Driver	
G-BFEB	Jodel 150	Jodel EB Group	
G-BFEF	Agusta-Bell 47G-3B1	I. F. Vaughan	
G-BFEH	Jodel D.117A	J. A. Crabb	
G-BFEK	Cessna F.152	Staverton Flying School @ Skypark Ltd	
G-BFEV	PA-25 Pawnee 235	Trent Valley Aerotowing Club Ltd	
G-BFFE	Cessna F.152-II	A. J. Hastings	
G-BFFJ	Sikorsky S-61N Mk II	Veritair Ltd *Tresco*	
G-BFFP	PA-18 Super Cub 150 (modified)	East Sussex Gliding Club Ltd	
G-BFFT	Cameron V-56 balloon	R. I. M. Kerr & D. C. Boxall	
G-BFFW	Cessna F.152	Aircraft Engineers Ltd	
G-BFGD	Cessna F.172N-II	Wannabe Flyers	
G-BFGG	Cessna FRA.150M	J. M. Machin	
G-BFGH	Cessna F.337G	T. Perkins	
G-BFGK	Jodel D.117	B. F. J. Hope	
G-BFGL	Cessna FA.152	E-Pane Ltd	
G-BFGS	MS.893E Rallye 180GT	Chiltern Flyers Ltd	
G-BFGX	Cessna FRA.150M	Aircraft Engineers Ltd	
G-BFGZ	Cessna FRA.150M	C. M. Barnes	
G-BFHH	DH.82A Tiger Moth	P. Harrison & M. J. Gambrell	
G-BFHI	Piper J-3C-65 Cub	N. Glass & A. J. Richardson	
G-BFHP	Champion 7GCAA Citabria	Citabriation Group	
G-BFHR	Jodel DR.220/2+2	J. E. Sweetman	
G-BFHU	Cessna F.152-II	D. J. Cooke & Co Ltd	
G-BFHV	Cessna F.152-II	Falcon Flying Services	

Notes	Reg.	Type	Owner or Operator
	G-BFIB	PA-31 Turbo Navajo	Richard Hannon Ltd
	G-BFID	Taylor JT.2 Titch Mk III	N. Jamieson
	G-BFIE	Cessna FRA.150M	J. P. A. Freeman
	G-BFIG	Cessna FR.172K XPII	Tenair Ltd
	G-BFIJ	AA-5A Cheetah	T. H. & M. G. Weetman
	G-BFIN	AA-5A Cheetah	Aircraft Engineers Ltd
	G-BFIP	Wallbro Monoplane 1909 (replica) ★	Norfolk & Suffolk Aviation Museum/Flixton
	G-BFIT	Thunder Ax6-56Z balloon	J. A. G. Tyson
	G-BFIU	Cessna FR.172K XP	The G-BFIU Flying Group
	G-BFIV	Cessna F.177RG	C. Fisher
	G-BFIX	Thunder Ax7-77A balloon	R. Owen
	G-BFIY	Cessna F.150M	R. J. Scott
	G-BFJR	Cessna F.337G	Teal Aviation
	G-BFJZ	Robin DR.400/140B	Weald Air Services Ltd
	G-BFKB	Cessna F.172N	Shropshire Flying Group
	G-BFKF	Cessna FA.152	Aerolease Ltd
	G-BFKL	Cameron N-56 balloon	Merrythought Toys Ltd Merrythought
	G-BFLU	Cessna F.152	Swiftair Maintenance Ltd
	G-BFLX	AA-5A Cheetah	A. M. Verdon
	G-BFLZ	Beech 95-A55 Baron	R. Tang
	G-BFMG	PA-28-161 Warrior II	J. G. Fricker & N. T. Oakman
	G-BFMH	Cessna 177B	Aerofoil Aviation Ltd
	G-BFMK	Cessna FA.152	The Leicestershire Aero Club Ltd
	G-BFMR	PA-20 Pacer 125	J. Knight
	G-BFMX	Cessna F.172N	A2Z Wholesale Fashion Jewellery Ltd
	G-BFNG	Jodel D.112	NG Group
	G-BFNI	PA-28-161 Warrior II	Lion Services
	G-BFNK	PA-28-161 Warrior II	White Waltham Airfield Ltd
	G-BFNM	Globe GC-1B Swift	M. J. Butler
	G-BFOE	Cessna F.152	Redhill Air Services Ltd
	G-BFOF	Cessna F.152	ACS Engineering Ltd
	G-BFOG	Cessna 150M	B. F. Spafford
	G-BFOJ	AA-1 Yankee	N. W. Thomas
	G-BFOP	Jodel D.120	R. J. Wesley & G. D. Western
	G-BFOU	Taylor JT.1 Monoplane	G. Bee
	G-BFOV	Cessna F.172N	D. J. Walker
	G-BFPA	Scheibe SF.25B Falke	Tay Forth Falke Syndicate
	G-BFPH	Cessna F.172K	Linc-Air Flying Group
	G-BFPO	Rockwell Commander 112B	Doerr International Ltd
	G-BFPR	PA-25 Pawnee 235D	The Windrushers Gliding Club Ltd
	G-BFPS	PA-25 Pawnee 235D	Kent Gliding Club Ltd
	G-BFPZ	Cessna F.177RG Cardinal	O. C. Baars
	G-BFRD	Bowers Fly-Baby 1A	R. A. Phillips
	G-BFRI	Sikorsky S-61N	British International
	G-BFRR	Cessna FRA.150M	Romeo Romeo Flying Group
	G-BFRS	Cessna F.172N	Aerocomm Ltd
	G-BFRV	Cessna FA.152	Cristal Air Ltd
	G-BFRY	PA-25 Pawnee 260	Yorkshire Gliding Club (Pty) Ltd
	G-BFSA	Cessna F.182Q	Ensiform Aviation Ltd
	G-BFSC	PA-25 Pawnee 235D	Essex Gliding Club Ltd
	G-BFSD	PA-25 Pawnee 235D	Deeside Gliding Club (Aberdeenshire) Ltd
	G-BFSR	Cessna F.150J	W. Ali
	G-BFSS	Cessna FR.172G	Albedale Farms Ltd
	G-BFSY	PA-28-181 Archer II	Downland Aviation
	G-BFSZ	PA-28-161 Warrior II	R. J. Whyham (G-KBPI)
	G-BFTA	PA-28-161 Warrior II	D. A. G. Roseblade
	G-BFTC	PA-28R-201T Turbo Arrow III	Top Cat Flying Group
	G-BFTF	AA-5B Tiger	F. C. Burrow Ltd
	G-BFTG	AA-5B Tiger	D. Hepburn & G. R. Montgomery
	G-BFTH	Cessna F.172N	T. W. Oakley
	G-BFTX	Cessna F.172N	Tri Society
	G-BFUB	PA-32RT-300 Lance II	Jolida Holdings Ltd
	G-BFUD	Scheibe SF.25E Super Falke	SF25E Syndicate
	G-BFUZ	Cameron V-77 balloon	Servowarm Balloon Syndicate
	G-BFVG	PA-28-181 Archer II	H. A. Schlosser
	G-BFVH	DH.2 (replica) (5964)	S. W. Turley
	G-BFVS	AA-5B Tiger	G-BFVS Flying Group
	G-BFVU	Cessna 150L	Aviation South West Ltd
	G-BFWB	PA-28-161 Warrior II	Mid-Anglia School of Flying
	G-BFWD	Currie Wot (C3009)	D. Silsbury & B. Proctor
	G-BFXF	Andreasson BA.4B	P. N. Birch
	G-BFXG	D.31 Turbulent	E. J. I. Musty & M. J. Whatley
	G-BFXK	PA-28 Cherokee 140	The G-BFXK Owners Group

Reg.	Type	Owner or Operator	Notes
G-BFXL	Albatros D.5a replica (D5397/17) ★	F.A.A. Museum/Yeovilton	
G-BFXR	Jodel D.112	R. G. Marshall	
G-BFXS	Rockwell Commander 114	Romeo Whiskey Ltd	
G-BFXW	AA-5B Tiger	Campsol Ltd	
G-BFXX	AA-5B Tiger	W. R. Gibson	
G-BFYA	MBB Bö.105DB	Alan Mann Aviation Group Ltd	
G-BFYC	PA-32RT-300 Lance II	A. A. Barnes	
G-BFYI	Westland-Bell 47G-3B1	K. P. Mayes	
G-BFYK	Cameron V-77 balloon	L. E. Jones	
G-BFYL	Evans VP-2	W. C. Brown	
G-BFYM	PA-28-161 Warrior II	E. T. Hawkins	
G-BFYO	SPAD XIII (replica) (4513:1) ★	American Air Museum/Duxford	
G-BFYW	Slingsby T.65A Vega	S. A. Whitaker	
G-BFZB	Piper J-3C-85 Cub (480723:E5-J)	M. S. Pettit	
G-BFZD	Cessna FR.182RG	R. B. Lewis & Co	
G-BFZH	PA-28R Cherokee Arrow 200	C. S. & C. S. Soojeri	
G-BFZM	Rockwell Commander 112TC	J. A. Hart & R. J. Lamplough	
G-BFZO	AA-5A Cheetah	J. W. Cross	
G-BFZU	Cessna FA.152	BJ Aviation Ltd	
G-BFZV	Cessna F.172M	The Army Flying Association	
G-BGAA	Cessna 152 II	PJC Leasing Ltd	
G-BGAB	Cessna F.152 II	TG Aviation Ltd	
G-BGAE	Cessna F.152 II	Aerolease Ltd	
G-BGAF	Cessna FA.152	G-BGAF Group	
G-BGAG	Cessna F.172N	R. Clarke	
G-BGAJ	Cessna F.182Q II	B. Blumberg	
G-BGAX	PA-28 Cherokee 140	G-BGAX Group	
G-BGAZ	Cameron V-77 balloon	C. J. Madigan & D. H. McGibbon	
G-BGBA	Robin R.2100A	Cotswold Aviation Services Ltd	
G-BGBE	Jodel DR.1050	J. A. & B. Mawby	
G-BGBF	Druine D.31 Turbulent	T. A. Stambach	
G-BGBG	PA-28-181 Archer II	Harlow Printing Ltd	
G-BGBI	Cessna F.150L	T. J. Gilpin & P. M. Cobban	
G-BGBK	PA-38-112 Tomahawk	Truman Aviation Ltd	
G-BGBN	PA-38-112 Tomahawk	Bonus Aviation Ltd	
G-BGBR	Cessna F.172N	Willowair Flying Club	
G-BGBV	Slingsby T65A Vega	Vega Syndicate BGA2800	
G-BGBW	PA-38-112 Tomahawk	Truman Aviation Ltd	
G-BGBZ	Rockwell Commander 114	G. W. Dimmer	
G-BGCB	Slingsby T.65A Vega	P. W. Williams	
G-BGCM	AA-5A Cheetah	G. & S. A. Jones	
G-BGCO	PA-44-180 Seminole	BAE Systems (Operations) Ltd	
G-BGCU	Slingsby T.65A Vega	K. Challinor	
G-BGCY	Taylor JT.1 Monoplane	A. T. Lane	
G-BGEH	Monnett Sonerai II	D. & V. T. Hubbard	
G-BGEI	Baby Great Lakes	M. T. Taylor	
G-BGFC	Evans VP-2	S. W. C. Hollins	
G-BGFF	FRED Srs 2	I Pearson & P. C. Appleton	
G-BGFI	AA-5A Cheetah	D. Chowanietz & A. Necker	
G-BGFJ	Jodel D.9 Bébé	O. G. Jones	
G-BGFT	PA-34-200T Seneca II	Oxford Aviation Academy (Oxford) Ltd	
G-BGFX	Cessna F.152	Redhill Air Services Ltd	
G-BGGA	Bellanca 7GCBC Citabria	L. A. King	
G-BGGB	Bellanca 7GCBC Citabria	Citabria Syndicate	
G-BGGC	Bellanca 7GCBC Citabria	G-BGGC RPA Memorial Group	
G-BGGD	Bellanca 8GCBC Scout	B. Walker & Co (Dursley) Ltd	
G-BGGE	PA-38-112 Tomahawk	Truman Aviation Ltd	
G-BGGI	PA-38-112 Tomahawk	Truman Aviation Ltd	
G-BGGL	PA-38-112 Tomahawk	Bonus Aircraft Ltd	
G-BGGM	PA-38-112 Tomahawk	Bonus Aircraft Ltd	
G-BGGO	Cessna F.152	East Midlands Flying School Ltd	
G-BGGP	Cessna F.152	East Midlands Flying School Ltd	
G-BGGU	Wallis WA-116/RR	K. H. Wallis	
G-BGGW	Wallis WA-112	K. H. Wallis	
G-BGHF	Westland WG.30 ★	IHM/Weston-super-Mare	
G-BGHI	Cessna F.152	V. R. McCready	
G-BGHJ	Cessna F.172N	Air Plane Ltd	
G-BGHM	Robin R.1180T	P. Price	
G-BGHP	Beech 76 Duchess	Magneta Ltd	
G-BGHS	Cameron N-31 balloon	G. Gray	
G-BGHT	Falconar F-12	C. R. Coates	
G-BGHU	NA T-6G Texan (115042:TA-042)	C. E. Bellhouse	

Notes	Reg.	Type	Owner or Operator
	G-BGHY	Taylor JT.1 Monoplane	G. W. Hancox
	G-BGHZ	FRED Srs 2	A. J. Perry
	G-BGIB	Cessna 152 II	Redhill Air Services Ltd
	G-BGIG	PA-38-112 Tomahawk	Air Claire Ltd
	G-BGIU	Cessna F.172H	A. G. Arthur
	G-BGIY	Cessna F.172N	Air Claire Ltd
	G-BGJU	Cameron V-65 Balloon	J. A. Folkes
	G-BGKC	SOCATA Rallye 110ST	J. H. Cranmer
	G-BGKO	Gardan GY-20 Minicab	K. D. PEARCE
	G-BGKS	PA-28-161 Warrior II	Curtis Moore Aviation Ltd
	G-BGKT	Auster AOP.9 (XN441)	Kilo Tango Group
	G-BGKU	PA-28R-201 Arrow III	Aerolease Ltd
	G-BGKV	PA-28R-201 Arrow III	R. Haverson & A. K. Lake
	G-BGKY	PA-38-112 Tomahawk	APB Leasing Ltd
	G-BGKZ	Auster J/5F Aiglet Trainer	R. B. Webber
	G-BGLA	PA-38-112 Tomahawk	Norwich School of Flying
	G-BGLB	Bede BD-5B ★	Science Museum/Wroughton
	G-BGLF	Evans VP-1 Srs 2	B. A. Schlussler
	G-BGLG	Cessna 152	L. W. Scattergood
	G-BGLK	Monnett Sonerai 2L	J. Bradley
	G-BGLO	Cessna F.172N	J. R. Isabel
	G-BGLZ	Stits SA-3A Playboy	A. J. Collins
	G-BGME	SIPA 903	M. Emery (G-BCML)
	G-BGMJ	Gardan GY-201 Minicab	G-BGMJ Group
	G-BGMP	Cessna F.172G	B. M. O'Brien
	G-BGMR	Gardan GY-20 Minicab	P. A. Hall
	G-BGMS	Taylor JT.2 Titch	M. A. J. Spice
	G-BGMT	SOCATA Rallye 235E	C. G. Wheeler
	G-BGMV	Scheibe SF.25B Falke	I. P. Manley
	G-BGND	Cessna F.172N	A. J. M. Freeman
	G-BGNT	Cessna F.152	Aerolease Ltd
	G-BGNV	GA-7 Cougar	G. J. Bissex & D. D. Saint
	G-BGOD	Colt 77A balloon	C. Allen & M. D. Steuer
	G-BGOG	PA-28-161 Warrior II	W. D. Moore & F. J. Morris
	G-BGOL	PA-28R-201T Turbo Arrow III	R. G. Jackson
	G-BGON	GA-7 Cougar	Plane Talking Ltd
	G-BGOR	AT-6D Harvard III (14863)	P. Meyrick
	G-BGPB	CCF T-6J Texan (1747)	1959 Ltd
	G-BGPD	Piper J-3C-65 Cub (479744:M-49)	P. R. Whiteman
	G-BGPH	AA-5B Tiger	Shipping & Airlines Ltd
	G-BGPI	Plumb BGP-1	B. G. Plumb
	G-BGPJ	PA-28-161 Warrior II	W. Lancs Warrior Co Ltd
	G-BGPL	PA-28-161 Warrior II	Demero Ltd & Transcourt Ltd
	G-BGPM	Evans VP-2	The Old Fokkers Flying Group
	G-BGPN	PA-18 Super Cub 150	A. R. Darke
	G-BGRE	Beech A200 Super King Air	Martin-Baker (Engineering) Ltd
	G-BGRI	Jodel DR.1051	R. G. Hallam
	G-BGRM	PA-38-112 Tomahawk	C. R. Salway
	G-BGRO	Cessna F.172M	Cammo Aviation
	G-BGRR	PA-38-112 Tomahawk	P. J. Montgomery
	G-BGRT	Steen Skybolt	O. Meier
	G-BGRX	PA-38-112 Tomahawk	Bonus Aviation Ltd
	G-BGSA	Morane MS.892E-150	D. C. Tonkin
	G-BGSH	PA-38-112 Tomahawk	Hatfield Ltd
	G-BGSJ	Piper J-3C-65 Cub	A. J. Higgins
	G-BGSV	Cessna F.172N	Southwell Air Services Ltd
	G-BGSW	Beech F33 Debonair	C. Wood
	G-BGSY	GA-7 Cougar	N. D. Anderson
	G-BGTC	Auster AOP.9 (XP282)	Terranne Auster Group
	G-BGTI	Piper J-3C-65 Cub	A. P. Broad
	G-BGUB	PA-32 Cherokee Six 300E	D. P. & E. A. Morris
	G-BGVB	Robin DR.315	P. J. Leggo
	G-BGVE	CP.1310-C3 Super Emeraude	R. Whitwell
	G-BGVH	Beech 76 Duchess	Velco Marketing
	G-BGVK	PA-28-161 Warrior II	Aviation South West Ltd
	G-BGVN	PA-28RT-201 Arrow IV	John Wailing Ltd
	G-BGVS	Cessna F.172M	Orkney Flying Club
	G-BGVV	AA-5A Cheetah	W. A. Davidson
	G-BGVY	AA-5B Tiger	R. J. C. Neal-Smith
	G-BGVZ	PA-28-181 Archer II	M. & W. Walsh
	G-BGWC	Robin DR.400/180	M. A. Newman
	G-BGWM	PA-28-181 Archer II	Thames Valley Flying Club Ltd
	G-BGWN	PA-38-112 Tomahawk	J. R. Davison

Reg.	Type	Owner or Operator	Notes
G-BGWO	Jodel D.112	G. R. Pybus	
G-BGWR	Cessna U.206A	Parachuting Aircraft Ltd (G-DISC)	
G-BGWV	Aeronca 7AC Champion	RFC Flying Group	
G-BGWZ	Eclipse Super Eagle ★	F.A.A. Museum/Yeovilton	
G-BGXA	Piper J-3C-65 Cub (329471:F-44)	P. King	
G-BGXC	SOCATA TB10 Tobago	M. H. & S. H. Cundey	
G-BGXD	SOCATA TB10 Tobago	D. F. P. Finan	
G-BGXO	PA-38-112 Tomahawk	Goodwood Terrena Ltd	
G-BGXR	Robin HR.200/100	J. R. Cross	
G-BGXS	PA-28-236 Dakota	G-BGXS Group	
G-BGXT	SOCATA TB10 Tobago	J. L. Alexander	
G-BGYH	PA-28-161 Warrior II	Paper Space Ltd	
G-BGYN	PA-18 Super Cub 150	B. J. Dunford	
G-BGZF	PA-38-112 Tomahawk	APB Leasing Ltd	
G-BHAA	Cessna 152 II	Herefordshire Aero Club Ltd	
G-BHAD	Cessna A.152	T. W. Gilbert	
G-BHAI	Cessna F.152	Scottish Aircraft Sales	
G-BHAJ	Robin DR.400/160	Rowantask Ltd	
G-BHAR	Westland-Bell 47G-3B1	T. J. Wright	
G-BHAV	Cessna F.152	T. M. & M. L. Jones	
G-BHAW	Cessna F.172N	J. Smith	
G-BHAX	Enstrom F-28C-UK-2	PVS (Barnsley) Ltd	
G-BHAY	PA-28RT-201 Arrow IV	Alpha Yankee Ltd	
G-BHBA	Campbell Cricket	S. N. McGovern	
G-BHBE	Westland-Bell 47G-3B1 (Soloy)	T. R. Smith (Agricultural Machinery) Ltd	
G-BHBG	PA-32R Cherokee Lance 300	E. Schiewe	
G-BHBT	Marquart MA.5 Charger	Bravo Tango Group	
G-BHBZ	Partenavia P.68B	Reconnaissance Ventures	
G-BHCC	Cessna 172M	D. Wood-Jenkins	
G-BHCE	Jodel D.112	C. E. & M. G. Cookson	
G-BHCM	Cessna F.172H	J. Dominic	
G-BHCP	Cessna F.152	Eastern Air Executive Ltd	
G-BHCZ	PA-38-112 Tomahawk	J. E. Abbott	
G-BHDD	V.668 Varsity T.1 (WL626:P) ★	Aeropark/East Midlands	
G-BHDE	SOCATA TB10 Tobago	Alpha-Alpha Ltd	
G-BHDK	Boeing B-29A-BN (461748:Y) ★	Imperial War Museum/Duxford	
G-BHDM	Cessna F.152 II	Big Red Kite Ltd	
G-BHDP	Cessna F.182Q II	Zone Travel Ltd	
G-BHDS	Cessna F.152 II	Tayside Aviation Ltd	
G-BHDV	Cameron V-77 balloon	P. Glydon	
G-BHDW	Cessna F.152 II	Aircraft Engineers Ltd	
G-BHDX	Cessna F.172N	GDX Ltd	
G-BHDZ	Cessna F.172N	Abbey Security Services Ltd	
G-BHEC	Cessna F.152 II	Stapleford Flying Club Ltd	
G-BHED	Cessna FA.152	TG Aviation Ltd	
G-BHEG	Jodel 150	D. M. Griffiths	
G-BHEK	CP.1315-C3 Super Emeraude	D. B. Winstanley	
G-BHEL	Jodel D.117	M. A. Child	
G-BHEM	Bensen B.8M	G. C. Kerr	
G-BHEN	Cessna FA.152	Leicestershire Aero Club Ltd	
G-BHEU	Thunder Ax7-65 balloon	J. A. W. Dyer	
G-BHEV	PA-28R Cherokee Arrow 200	7-Up Group	
G-BHEX	Colt 56A balloon	A. S. Dear & ptnrs	
G-BHFC	Cessna F.152	JH Sandham Aviation	
G-BHFE	PA-44-180 Seminole	Bonus Aviation Ltd	
G-BHFG	SNCAN Stampe SV.4C	A. D. R. Northeast & S. A. Cook	
G-BHFH	PA-34-200T Seneca II	Oxford Aviation Academy (Oxford) Ltd	
G-BHFI	Cessna F.152	BAe (Warton) Flying Club	
G-BHFJ	PA-28RT-201T Turbo Arrow IV	S. A. Cook & D. R. Northeast	
G-BHFK	PA-28-151 Warrior	Ilkeston Car Sales Ltd	
G-BHGC	PA-18 Super Cub 150	Vectis Gliding Club Ltd	
G-BHGF	Cameron V-56 balloon	P. Smallward	
G-BHGJ	Jodel D.120	Q. M. B. Oswell	
G-BHGO	PA-32 Cherokee Six 260	L. C. Myall	
G-BHGY	PA-28R Cherokee Arrow 200	Truman Aviation Ltd	
G-BHHB	Cameron V-77 balloon	R. Powell	
G-BHHE	Jodel DR.1051/M1	P. Bridges & P. C. Matthews	
G-BHHG	Cessna F.152 II	TG Aviation Ltd	
G-BHHH	Thunder Ax7-65 balloon	J. M. J. Roberts	
G-BHHK	Cameron N-77 balloon ★	British Balloon Museum	
G-BHHN	Cameron V-77 balloon	Itchen Valley Balloon Group	
G-BHHX	Jodel D.112	J. Anderson & R. Broad	
G-BHIB	Cessna F.182Q	The G-BHIB Flying Group	

Notes	Reg.	Type	Owner or Operator
	G-BHII	Cameron V-77 balloon	R. V. Brown
	G-BHIJ	Eiri PIK-20E-1 (898)	P. M. Yeoman
	G-BHIN	Cessna F.152	Target Aviation Ltd
	G-BHIR	PA-28R Cherokee Arrow 200	Factorcore Ltd
	G-BHIS	Thunder Ax7-65 balloon	Hedgehoppers Balloon Group
	G-BHIY	Cessna F.150K	G. J. Ball
	G-BHJF	SOCATA TB10 Tobago	Tyas Aviation Ltd
	G-BHJI	Mooney M.20J	Otomed APS/Denmark
	G-BHJK	Maule M5-235C Lunar Rocket	M. K. H. Bell
	G-BHJN	Fournier RF-4D	RF-4 Group
	G-BHJO	PA-28-161 Warrior II	Brackla Flying Group
	G-BHJS	Partenavia P.68B	Flew LLP
	G-BHJU	Robin DR.400/2+2	Ageless Aeronautics
	G-BHKR	Colt 12A balloon ★	British Balloon Museum/Newbury
	G-BHKT	Jodel D.112	G. Dawes
	G-BHLE	Robin DR.400/180	A. V. Harmer
	G-BHLH	Robin DR.400/180	G-BHLH Group
	G-BHLJ	Saffery-Rigg S.200 balloon	I. A. Rigg
	G-BHLT	DH.82A Tiger Moth	Skymax (Aviation) Ltd
	G-BHLU	Fournier RF-3	G. Sabatino
	G-BHLW	Cessna 120	L. W. Scattergood
	G-BHLX	AA-5B Tiger	M. D. McPherson
	G-BHMA	SIPA 903	H. J. Taggart
	G-BHMG	Cessna FA.152	R. J. Williamson
	G-BHMJ	Avenger T.200-2112 balloon	R. Light *Lord Anthony 1*
	G-BHMK	Avenger T.200-2112 balloon	P. Kinder *Lord Anthony 2*
	G-BHMT	Evans VP-1	R. T. Callow
	G-BHMY	F.27 Friendship Mk.200 ★	Norwich Aviation Museum
	G-BHNA	Cessna F.152 II	Eastern Air Executive Ltd
	G-BHNC	Cameron O-65 balloon	D. & C. Bareford
	G-BHNK	Jodel D.120A	K. R. Daly
	G-BHNL	Jodel D.112	M. D. Mold
	G-BHNO	PA-28-181 Archer II	B. J. Richardson
	G-BHNP	Eiri PIK-20E-1	D. A. Sutton
	G-BHNV	Westlan-Bell 47G-3B1	S. W. Hutchinson
	G-BHNX	Jodel D.117	M. J. A. Trudgill
	G-BHOA	Robin DR.400/160	T. L. Trott
	G-BHOJ	Colt 12A balloon	J. A. Folkes
	G-BHOL	Jodel DR.1050	S. J. Pearson
	G-BHOM	PA-18 Super Cub 95	Oscar Mike Flying Group
	G-BHOR	PA-28-161 Warrior II	Oscar Romeo Flying Group
	G-BHOT	Cameron V-65 balloon	Dante Balloon Group
	G-BHOZ	SOCATA TB9 Tampico	G-BHOZ Flying Group
	G-BHPK	Piper J-3C-65 Cub (238410:A-44)	L-4 Group
	G-BHPL	CASA 1.131E Jungmann 1000 (E3B-350:05-97) ★	A. Burroughes
	G-BHPS	Jodel D.120A	T. J. Price
	G-BHPZ	Cessna 172N	O'Brien Properties Ltd
	G-BHRC	PA-28-161 Warrior II	Sherwood Flying Club Ltd
	G-BHRH	Cessna FA.150K	Merlin Flying Club Ltd
	G-BHRO	Rockwell Commander 112	R. A. Blackwell
	G-BHRR	CP.301A Emeraude	T. W. Offen
	G-BHRW	Jodel DR.221	Dauphin Flying Club
	G-BHSB	Cessna 172N	J. W. Cope & M. P. Wimsey
	G-BHSD	Scheibe SF.25E Super Falke	Upwood Motorglider Group
	G-BHSE	Rockwell Commander 114	604 Sqdn Flying Group Ltd
	G-BHSN	Cameron N-56 balloon	I. Bentley
	G-BHSS	Pitts S-1S Special	N. Leis
	G-BHSY	Jodel DR.1050	T. R. Allebone
	G-BHTA	PA-28-236 Dakota	Dakota Ltd
	G-BHTC	Jodel DR.1050/M1	G. Clark
	G-BHUB	Douglas C-47A (315509:W7-S) ★	Imperial War Museum/Duxford
	G-BHUE	Jodel DR.1050	M. J. Harris
	G-BHUG	Cessna 172N	G-BHUG Group
	G-BHUI	Cessna 152	South Warwickshire School of Flying Ltd
	G-BHUJ	Cessna 172N	Uniform Juliet Group
	G-BHUM	DH.82A Tiger Moth	S. G. Towers
	G-BHUU	PA-25 Pawnee 235	Booker Gliding Club Ltd
	G-BHVF	Jodel 150A	Groupe Ariel
	G-BHVP	Cessna 182Q	G. S. Chapman
	G-BHVR	Cessna 172N	Victor Romeo Group
	G-BHVV	Piper J-3C-65 Cub	C. A. Ward
	G-BHWA	Cessna F.152	Lincoln Enterprises Ltd

Reg.	Type	Owner or Operator	Notes
G-BHWB	Cessna F.152	Lincoln Enterprises Ltd	
G-BHWH	Weedhopper JC-24A	G. A. Clephane	
G-BHWK	MS.880B Rallye Club	P. Sharpe	
G-BHWY	PA-28R Cherokee Arrow 200-II	Kilo Foxtrot Flying Group	
G-BHWZ	PA-28-181 Archer II	M. A. Abbott	
G-BHXA	SA Bulldog Srs 120/1210	Air Plan Flight Equipment Ltd	
G-BHXD	Jodel D.120	D. A. Garner	
G-BHXK	PA-28 Cherokee 140	S. A. Finlay	
G-BHXS	Jodel D.120	Plymouth Jodel Group	
G-BHXY	Piper J-3C-65 Cub (44-79609:44-S)	F. W. Rogers	
G-BHYA	Cessna R.182RG II	J-P. Jarier	
G-BHYC	Cessna 172RG II	IB Aeroplanes Ltd	
G-BHYD	Cessna R.172K XP II	Sylmar Aviation Services Ltd	
G-BHYG	PA-34-200T Seneca II	Oxford Aviation Academy (Oxford) Ltd	
G-BHYI	SNCAN Stampe SV.4A	D. Hicklin	
G-BHYP	Cessna F.172M	Avior Ltd	
G-BHYR	Cessna F.172M	G-BHYR Group	
G-BHYV	Evans VP-1	I. P. Manley	
G-BHYX	Cessna 152 II	Stapleford Flying Club Ltd	
G-BHZE	PA-28-181 Archer II	Zegruppe Ltd	
G-BHZH	Cessna F.152	Plymouth Flying School Ltd	
G-BHZK	AA-5B Tiger	ZK Group	
G-BHZO	AA-5A Cheetah	PG Air	
G-BHZR	SA Bulldog Srs 120/1210	White Knuckle Air Ltd	
G-BHZS	SA Bulldog Srs 120/1210	Air Plan Flight Equipment Ltd	
G-BHZT	SA Bulldog Srs 120/1210	D. M. Curties	
G-BHZU	Piper J-3C-65 Cub	J. K. Tomkinson	
G-BHZV	Jodel D.120A	G-BHZV Group	
G-BIAC	SOCATA Rallye 235E	G-BIAC Flying Group	
G-BIAH	Jodel D.112	P. A. Gange	
G-BIAI	WMB.2 Windtracker balloon	I. Chadwick	
G-BIAP	PA-16 Clipper	G-BIAP Flying Group	
G-BIAR	Rigg Skyliner II balloon	I. A. Rigg	
G-BIAU	Sopwith Pup (replica) (N6452) ★	F.A.A. Museum/Yeovilton	
G-BIAX	Taylor JT.2 Titch	D. M. Bland	
G-BIAY	AA-5 Traveler	P. Moderate	
G-BIBA	SOCATA TB9 Tampico	TB Aviation Ltd	
G-BIBN	Cessna FA.150K	B. V. Mayo	
G-BIBO	Cameron V-65 balloon	D. M. Hoddinott	
G-BIBS	Cameron P-20 balloon	Cameron Balloons Ltd	
G-BIBT	AA-5B Tiger	Horizon Aviation Ltd	
G-BIBW	Cessna F.172N	Shields Estates Ltd	
G-BIBX	WMB.2 Windtracker balloon	I. A. Rigg	
G-BICD	Auster 5	T. R. Parsons	
G-BICE	NA AT-6C Harvard IIA (41-33275:CE)	C. M. L. Edwards	
G-BICG	Cessna F.152 II	Falcon Flying Services	
G-BICM	Colt 56A balloon	Avon Advertiser Balloon Club	
G-BICP	Robin DR.360	B. McVeighty	
G-BICR	Jodel D.120A	Beehive Flying Group	
G-BICS	Robin R.2100A	I. Young	
G-BICU	Cameron V-56 balloon	Black Pearl Balloons	
G-BICW	PA-28-161 Warrior II	Charlie Whisky Flying Group	
G-BICX	Maule M5-235C Lunar Rocket	I. S. McLeod & J. L. Yourell	
G-BIDD	Evans VP-1	J. Hodgkinson	
G-BIDF	Cessna F.172P	C. J. Chaplin & N. J. C. Howard	
G-BIDG	Jodel 150A	D. R. Gray	
G-BIDH	Cessna 152 II	Hull Aero Club Ltd (G-DONA)	
G-BIDI	PA-28R-201 Arrow III	T. A. N. Brierley & A. Lidster	
G-BIDJ	PA-18A Super Cub 150	Flight Solutions Ltd	
G-BIDK	PA-18 Super Cub 150	Mapesbury Capital Partners Ltd	
G-BIDO	CP.301A Emeraude	A. R. Plumb	
G-BIDV	Colt 14A balloon ★	British Balloon Museum/Newbury	
G-BIDW	Sopwith 1½ Strutter (replica) (A8226) ★	RAF Museum/Hendon	
G-BIDX	Jodel D.112	P. Turton	
G-BIEJ	Sikorsky S-76A	Bristow Helicopters Ltd	
G-BIEN	Jodel D.120A	H. J. Morton/France	
G-BIEO	Jodel D.112	Clipgate Flyers	
G-BIES	Maule M5-235C Lunar Rocket	William Proctor Farms	
G-BIET	Cameron O-77 balloon	G. M. Westley	
G-BIEY	PA-28-151 Warrior	M. J. Isaac	
G-BIFA	Cessna 310R II	J. S. Lee	
G-BIFB	PA-28 Cherokee 150C	P. Coombs	

Notes	Reg.	Type	Owner or Operator
	G-BIFO	Evans VP-1	D. C. Unwin
	G-BIFP	Colt 56A balloon	J. W. Adkins
	G-BIFY	Cessna F.150L	Bonus Aviation Ltd
	G-BIGJ	Cessna F.172M	Cirrus Aviation Ltd
	G-BIGK	Taylorcraft BC-12D	N. P. St. J. Ramsay
	G-BIGL	Cameron O-65 balloon	P. L. Mossman
	G-BIGR	Avenger T.200-2112 balloon	R. Light
	G-BIGX	Bensen B.8M	W. C. Turner
	G-BIHD	Robin DR.400/160	G. I. J. Thomson & R. A. Hawkins
	G-BIHF	SE-5A (replica) (F943)	C. J. Zeal
	G-BIHI	Cessna 172M	E-Plane Ltd
	G-BIHO	DHC.6 Twin Otter 310	Isles of Scilly Skybus Ltd
	G-BIHT	PA-17 Vagabond	B. Carter
	G-BIHU	Saffrey S.200 balloon	B. L. King
	G-BIHX	Bensen B.8M	P. P. Willmott
	G-BIIA	Fournier RF-3	C. J. Riley
	G-BIIB	Cessna F.172M	Civil Service Flying Club (Biggin Hill) Ltd
	G-BIID	PA-18 Super Cub 95	D. A. Lacey
	G-BIIE	Cessna F.172P	Alan Mann Aviation Group Ltd
	G-BIIK	MS.883 Rallye 115	N. J. Garbett
	G-BIIT	PA-28-161 Warrior II	Tayside Aviation Ltd
	G-BIIV	PA-28-181 Archer II	J. Thuret/France
	G-BIIZ	Great Lakes 2T-1A Sport Trainer	Circa 42 Ltd
	G-BIJB	PA-18 Super Cub 150	James Aero Ltd
	G-BIJD	Bölkow Bö.208C Junior	Sikh Sydicate
	G-BIJE	Piper J-3C-65 Cub	R. L. Hayward & A. G. Scott
	G-BIJS	Luton LA-4A Minor	I. J. Smith
	G-BIJU	CP-301A Emeraude	Eastern Taildraggers Flying Group (G-BHTX)
	G-BIJV	Cessna F.152 II	Falcon Flying Services
	G-BIJW	Cessna F.152 II	Falcon Flying Services
	G-BIJX	Cessna F.152 II	Falcon Flying Services
	G-BIKC	Boeng 757-236F	DHL Air Ltd
	G-BIKE	PA-28R Cherokee Arrow 200	R. Taylor
	G-BIKF	Boeing 757-236F	DHL Air Ltd
	G-BIKG	Boeing 757-236F	DHL Air Ltd
	G-BIKI	Boeing 757-236F	DHL Air Ltd
	G-BIKJ	Boeing 757-236F	DHL Air Ltd
	G-BIKK	Boeing 757-236F	DHL Air Ltd
	G-BIKM	Boeing 757-236F	DHL Air Ltd
	G-BIKN	Boeing 757-236F	DHL Air Ltd
	G-BIKO	Boeing 757-236F	DHL Air Ltd
	G-BIKP	Boeing 757-236F	DHL Air Ltd
	G-BIKS	Boeing 757-236F	DHL Air Ltd
	G-BIKU	Boeing 757-236F	DHL Air Ltd
	G-BIKV	Boeing 757-236F	DHL Air Ltd
	G-BIKZ	Boeing 757-236F	DHL Air Ltd
	G-BILB	WMB.2 Windtracker balloon	B. L. King
	G-BILE	Scruggs BL.2B balloon	P. D. Ridout
	G-BILG	Scruggs BL.2B balloon	P. D. Ridout
	G-BILH	Slingsby T.65C Vega	R. F. Barber
	G-BILI	Piper J-3C-65 Cub (454467:J-44)	G-BILI Flying Group
	G-BILL	PA-25 Pawnee 235	Pawnee Aviation
	G-BILR	Cessna 152 II	APB Leasing Ltd
	G-BILS	Cessna 152 II	Mona Flying Club
	G-BILU	Cessna 172RG	Full Sutton Flying Centre Ltd
	G-BILZ	Taylor JT.1 Monoplane	A. Petherbridge
	G-BIMK	Tiger T.200 Srs 1 balloon	M. K. Baron
	G-BIMM	PA-18 Super Cub 150	Spectrum Leisure Ltd
	G-BIMN	Steen Skybolt	R. J. Thomas
	G-BIMT	Cessna FA.152	Staverton Flying School @ Skypark Ltd
	G-BIMU	Sikorsky S-61N	Bristow Helicopters Ltd
	G-BIMX	Rutan Vari-Eze	D. G. Crow
	G-BIMZ	Beech 76 Duchess	R. P. Smith
	G-BINL	Scruggs BL.2B balloon	P. D. Ridout
	G-BINM	Scruggs BL.2B balloon	P. D. Ridout
	G-BINR	Unicorn UE.1A balloon	Unicorn Group
	G-BINS	Unicorn UE.2A balloon	Unicorn Group
	G-BINT	Unicorn UE.1A balloon	D. E. Bint
	G-BINX	Scruggs BL.2B balloon	P. D. Ridout
	G-BINY	Oriental balloon	J. L. Morton
	G-BIOA	Hughes 369D	AH Helicopter Services Ltd
	G-BIOB	Cessna F.172P	Network Mapping UK Ltd
	G-BIOC	Cessna F.150L	W. H. Milner

Reg.	Type	Owner or Operator	Notes
G-BIOI	Jodel DR.1051/M	A. A. Alderdice	
G-BIOJ	Rockwell Commander 112TCA	A. T. Dalby	
G-BIOK	Cessna F.152	A. D. H. Macdonald	
G-BIOM	Cessna F.152	J. B. P. E. Fernandes	
G-BIOU	Jodel D.117A	M. R. Routh	
G-BIOW	Slingsby T.67A	A. B. Slinger	
G-BIPA	AA-5B Tiger	Tri-Star Developments Ltd	
G-BIPH	Scruggs BL.2B balloon	C. M. Dewsnap	
G-BIPI	Everett gyroplane	C. A. Reeves	
G-BIPN	Fournier RF-3	G-BIPN Group	
G-BIPT	Jodel D.112	C. R. Davies	
G-BIPV	AA-5B Tiger	Echo Echo Ltd	
G-BIPW	Avenger T.200-2112 balloon	B. L. King	
G-BIRD	Pitts S-1D Special	N. E. Smith	
G-BIRE	Colt 56 Bottle SS balloon	D. J. Stagg	
G-BIRH	PA-18 Super Cub 135 (R-163)	Banbury Gliding Club Ltd	
G-BIRI	CASA 1.131E Jungmann 1000	D. Watt	
G-BIRL	Avenger T.200-2112 balloon	R. Light	
G-BIRP	Arena Mk 17 Skyship balloon	A. S. Viel	
G-BIRT	Robin R.1180TD	W. D'A. Hall	
G-BIRW	MS.505 Criquet (F+IS) ★	Museum of Flight/East Fortune	
G-BISG	FRED Srs 3	T. Littlefair	
G-BISH	Cameron V-65 balloon	P. J. Bish	
G-BISL	Scruggs BL.2B balloon	P. D. Ridout	
G-BISM	Scruggs BL.2B balloon	P. D. Ridout	
G-BISS	Scruggs BL.2C balloon	P. D. Ridout	
G-BIST	Scruggs BL.2C balloon	P. D. Ridout	
G-BISX	Colt 56A balloon	C. D. Steel	
G-BISZ	Sikorsky S-76A	Bristow Helicopters Ltd	
G-BITA	PA-18 Super Cub 150	Intrepid Aviation Co	
G-BITE	SOCATA TB10 Tobago	M. A. Smith	
G-BITF	Cessna F.152 II	G-BITF Owners Group	
G-BITH	Cessna F.152 II	J. R. Hyde (G-TFSA)	
G-BITK	FRED Srs 2	D. J. Wood	
G-BITM	Cessna F.172P	Dreamtrade Ltd	
G-BITO	Jodel D.112D	A. Dunbar	
G-BITY	FD.31T balloon	A. J. Bell	
G-BIUM	Cessna F.152	Eastern Air Executive Ltd	
G-BIUP	SNCAN NC.854S	J. Greenaway & T. D. Cooper	
G-BIUY	PA-28-181 Archer II	J. S. Devlin & Z. Islam	
G-BIVA	Robin R.2112	D. M. Croucher	
G-BIVB	Jodel D.112	N. M. Harwood	
G-BIVC	Jodel D.112	M. J. Barmby	
G-BIVF	CP.301C-3 Emeraude	T. C. Darters	
G-BIVK	Bensen B.8M	M. J. Atyeo	
G-BIWB	Scruggs RS.5000 balloon	P. D. Ridout	
G-BIWC	Scruggs RS.5000 balloon	P. D. Ridout	
G-BIWF	Warren balloon	P. D. Ridout	
G-BIWG	Zelenski Mk 2 balloon	P. D. Ridout	
G-BIWJ	Unicorn UE.1A balloon	B. L. King	
G-BIWK	Cameron V-65 balloon	I. R. Williams & R. G. Bickerdike	
G-BIWN	Jodel D.112	C. R. Coates & P. K. Morley	
G-BIWR	Mooney M.20F	M. Broady	
G-BIWU	Cameron V-65 balloon	W. Rousell & J. Tyrrell	
G-BIWW	AA-5 Traveler	Dix-Sept Aviation Ltd	
G-BIWY	Westland WG.30 ★	Instructional airframe/Yeovil	
G-BIXA	SOCATA TB9 Tampico	W. Maxwell	
G-BIXB	SOCATA TB9 Tampico	B. G. Adams	
G-BIXH	Cessna F.152	Northumbria Flying School Ltd	
G-BIXL	P-51D Mustang (472216:HO-M)	R. Lamplough	
G-BIXN	Boeing Stearman A75N1 (FJ777)	V. S. E. Norman	
G-BIXW	Colt 56B balloon	N. A. P. Bates	
G-BIXX	Pearson Srs 2 balloon	D. Pearson	
G-BIXZ	Grob G-109	Hinton Pilot Flight Training Ltd	
G-BIYI	Cameron V-65 balloon	Sarnia Balloon Group	
G-BIYJ	PA-18 Super Cub 95	S. Russell	
G-BIYK	Isaacs Fury II	S. M. Roberts	
G-BIYP	PA-20 Pacer 125	A. W. Hoy & S. W. M. Johnson	
G-BIYR	PA-18 Super Cub 150 (R-151)	Delta Foxtrot Flying Group	
G-BIYU	Fokker S.11.1 Instructor (E-15)	Fokker Syndicate	
G-BIYW	Jodel D.112	A. Appleby	
G-BIYX	PA-28 Cherokee 140	W. B. Bateson	
G-BIYY	PA-18 Super Cub 95	A. E. & W. J. Taylor	

Notes	Reg.	Type	Owner or Operator
	G-BIZE	SOCATA TB9 Tampico	B. Higgins
	G-BIZF	Cessna F.172P	R. S. Bentley
	G-BIZG	Cessna F.152	M. A. Judge
	G-BIZI	Robin DR.400/120	Headcorn Flying School Ltd
	G-BIZK	Nord 3202 (78)	A. I. Milne
	G-BIZM	Nord 3202	Global Aviation Ltd
	G-BIZO	PA-28R Cherokee Arrow 200	Lemas Air
	G-BIZR	SOCATA TB9 Tampico	Fenland Flying Group (G-BSEC)
	G-BIZV	PA-18 Super Cub 95 (18-2001)	J. P. Nugent
	G-BIZW	Champion 7GCBC Citabria	G. Read & Sons
	G-BIZY	Jodel D.112	Wayland Tunley & Associates
	G-BJAD	FRED Srs 2 ★	Newark (Nottinghamshire & Lincolnshire) Air Museum
	G-BJAE	Lavadoux Starck AS.80 ★	D. J. & S. A. E. Phillips/Coventry
	G-BJAF	Piper J-3C-65 Cub	P. J. Cottle
	G-BJAG	PA-28-181 Archer II	C. R. Chubb
	G-BJAJ	AA-5B Tiger	Draycott Tiger Club
	G-BJAL	CASA 1.131E Jungmann 1000	G-BJAL Group
	G-BJAO	Bensen B.8M	A. P. Lay
	G-BJAP	DH.82A Tiger Moth (K2587)	K. Knight
	G-BJAS	Rango NA.9 balloon	A. Lindsay
	G-BJAV	Gardan GY-80 Horizon 160	W. R.Maloney
	G-BJAY	Piper J-3C-65 Cub	D. W. Finlay
	G-BJBK	PA-18 Super Cub 95	M. S. Bird
	G-BJBM	Monnett Sonerai I	I. Pearson
	G-BJBO	Jodel DR.250/160	Wiltshire Flying Group
	G-BJBW	PA-28-161 Warrior II	152 Group
	G-BJCA	PA-28-161 Warrior II	U. Kleinheyer
	G-BJCF	CP.1310-C3 Super Emeraude	K. M. Hodson & C. G. H. Gurney
	G-BJCI	PA-18 Super Cub 150 (modified)	The Borders (Milfield) Gliding Club Ltd
	G-BJCW	PA-32R-301 Saratoga SP	Golf Charlie Whisky Ltd
	G-BJDE	Cessna F.172M	J. K. P. Amor
	G-BJDF	MS.880B Rallye 100T	P. W. Johnson
	G-BJDJ	HS.125 Srs 700B	TAG Farnborough Engineering Ltd (G-RCDI)
	G-BJDK	European E.14 balloon	Aeroprint Tours
	G-BJDW	Cessna F.172M	J. Rae
	G-BJEE	BN-2T Turbine Islander	Cormack (Aircraft Services) Ltd
	G-BJEF	BN-2B-26 Islander	Cormack (Aircraft Services) Ltd
	G-BJEI	PA-18 Super Cub 95	H. J. Cox
	G-BJEJ	BN-2T Turbine Islander	Islander Aircraft Ltd
	G-BJEL	SNCAN NC.854	C. A. James
	G-BJEV	Aeronca 11AC Chief (897)	R. F. Willcox
	G-BJEX	Bölkow Bö.208C Junior	G. D. H. Crawford
	G-BJFC	European E.8 balloon	P. D. Ridout
	G-BJFE	PA-18 Super Cub 95	P. H. Wilmot-Allistone
	G-BJFM	Jodel D.120	J. V. George
	G-BJGM	Unicorn UE.1A balloon	D. Eaves & P. D. Ridout
	G-BJGX	Sikorsky S-76A	Bristow Helicopters Ltd
	G-BJGY	Cessna F.172P	K. & S. Martin
	G-BJHB	Mooney M.20J	Zitair Flying Club Ltd
	G-BJHK	EAA Acro Sport	M. R. Holden
	G-BJHV	Voisin Replica ★	Brooklands Museum of Aviation/Weybridge
	G-BJIA	Allport balloon	D. J. Allport
	G-BJIC	Dodo 1A balloon	P. D. Ridout
	G-BJID	Osprey 1B balloon	P. D. Ridout
	G-BJIG	Slingsby T.67A	A. D. Hodgkinson
	G-BJIV	PA-18 Super Cub 180	Yorkshire Gliding Club (Pty) Ltd
	G-BJKF	SOCATA TB9 Tampico	G-BJKF Group
	G-BJKW	Wills Aera II	J. K. S. Wills
	G-BJLC	Monnett Sonerai IIL	P. O. Yeo
	G-BJLX	Cremer balloon	P. W. May
	G-BJLY	Cremer balloon	P. Cannon
	G-BJML	Cessna 120	R. A. Smith
	G-BJMR	Cessna 310R	J. H. Sandham Aviation
	G-BJMW	Thunder Ax8-105 balloon	G. M. Westley
	G-BJMX	Jarre JR.3 balloon	P. D. Ridout
	G-BJMZ	European EA.8A balloon	P. D. Ridout
	G-BJNA	Arena Mk 117P balloon	P. D. Ridout
	G-BJND	Osprey Mk 1E balloon	A. Billington & D. Whitmore
	G-BJNG	Slingsby T.67AM	D. F. Hodgkinson
	G-BJNN	PA-38-112 Tomahawk	Carlisle Flight Training Ltd
	G-BJNY	Aeronca 11CC Super Chief	P. I. & D. M. Morgans

Reg.	Type	Owner or Operator	Notes
G-BJNZ	PA-23 Aztec 250F	Bonus Aviation Ltd (G-FANZ)	
G-BJOB	Jodel D.140C	T. W. M. Beck & M. J. Smith	
G-BJOE	Jodel D.120A	H. Davies	
G-BJOT	Jodel D.117	R. A. Kilbride	
G-BJOV	Cessna F.150K	G-BJOV Flying Group	
G-BJPI	Bede BD-5G	M. D. McQueen	
G-BJRA	Osprey Mk 4B balloon	E. Osborn	
G-BJRG	Osprey Mk 4B balloon	A. E. de Gruchy	
G-BJRH	Rango NA.36 balloon	N. H. Ponsford	
G-BJRP	Cremer balloon	M. D. Williams	
G-BJRR	Cremer balloon	M. D. Williams	
G-BJRV	Cremer balloon	M. D. Williams	
G-BJSS	Allport balloon	D. J. Allport	
G-BJST	CCF T-6J Harvard IV (KF729)	M. F. Cuming, J. G. Fricker & N. T. Oakman	
G-BJSV	PA-28-161 Warrior II	Airways Flight Training (Exeter) Ltd	
G-BJSW	Thunder Ax7-65 balloon	J. Edwards	
G-BJSZ	Piper J-3C-65 Cub	K. Gilbert	
G-BJTB	Cessna A.150M	Cirrus Aviation Ltd	
G-BJTP	PA-18 Super Cub 95 (115302:TP)	J. T. Parkins	
G-BJTY	Osprey Mk 4B balloon	A. E. de Gruchy	
G-BJUB	BVS Special 01 balloon	P. G. Wild	
G-BJUD	Robin DR.400/180R	Lasham Gliding Society Ltd	
G-BJUR	PA-38-112 Tomahawk	Truman Aviation Ltd	
G-BJUS	PA-38-112 Tomahawk	J. D. Williams	
G-BJUV	Cameron V-20 balloon	P. Spellward	
G-BJVC	Evans VP-2	S. J. Greer & S. E. Clarke	
G-BJVH	Cessna F.182Q	R. J. de Courcy Cuming	
G-BJVJ	Cessna F.152	Henlow Flying Club	
G-BJVK	Grob G-109	B. Kimberley	
G-BJVM	Cessna 172N	R. D. & M. S. B. Forster	
G-BJVS	CP.1310-C3 Super Emeraude	N. F. Harris	
G-BJVT	Cessna F.152	Northumbria Flying School Ltd	
G-BJVV	Robin R.1180	J. Owens	
G-BJWH	Cessna F.152 II	J. D. Baines	
G-BJWI	Cessna F.172P	Flew LLP	
G-BJWO	BN-2A-26 Islander	Metachem Diagnostics Ltd (G-BAXC)	
G-BJWT	Wittman W.10 Tailwind	Tailwind Group	
G-BJWV	Colt 17A balloon	D. T. Meyes	
G-BJWW	Cessna F.172N	Air Charter & Travel Ltd	
G-BJWX	PA-18 Super Cub 95	R. A. G. Lucas	
G-BJWY	S-55 Whirlwind HAR.21(WV198) ★	Solway Aviation Museum/Carlisle	
G-BJWZ	PA-18 Super Cub 95	G-BJWZ Syndicate	
G-BJXB	Slingsby T.67A	X-Ray Bravo Ltd	
G-BJXK	Fournier RF-5	RF5 Syndicate	
G-BJXP	Colt 56B balloon	H. J. Anderson	
G-BJXR	Auster AOP.9	I. Churm & J. Hanson	
G-BJXX	PA-23 Aztec 250E	V. Bojovic	
G-BJXZ	Cessna 172N	T. M. Jones	
G-BJYD	Cessna F.152 II	N. J. James	
G-BJYF	Colt 56A balloon	A. J. Moore	
G-BJYK	Jodel D.120A	M. R. Baker	
G-BJZB	Evans VP-2	R. B. McComish	
G-BJZF	DH.82A Tiger Moth	M. I. Lodge	
G-BJZN	Slingsby T.67A	ZN Group	
G-BJZR	Colt 42A balloon	Selfish Balloon Group	
G-BKAE	Jodel D.120	C. Long	
G-BKAF	FRED Srs 2	N. Glass	
G-BKAM	Slingsby T.67M Firefly160	R. C. B. Brookhouse	
G-BKAO	Jodel D.112	H. Haigh	
G-BKAS	PA-38-112 Tomahawk	Hinton Pilot Flight Training Ltd	
G-BKAY	Rockwell Commander 114	D. L. Bunning	
G-BKAZ	Cessna 152	L. W. Scattergood	
G-BKBD	Thunder Ax3 balloon	P. Donkin	
G-BKBF	MS.894A Rallye Minerva 220	K. A. Hale, L. C. Clark & P. Mickleborough	
G-BKBN	SOCATA TB10 Tobago	P. M. Clayton & D. Turner	
G-BKBP	Bellanca 7GCBC Scout	M. G. & J. R. Jefferies	
G-BKBS	Bensen B8MV	L. Harrison	
G-BKBV	SOCATA TB10 Tobago	T. C. H. Wright	
G-BKBW	SOCATA TB10 Tobago	Merlin Aviation	
G-BKCC	PA-28 Cherokee 180	DR Flying Club Ltd	
G-BKCE	Cessna F.172P II	The Leicestershire Aero Club Ltd	
G-BKCI	Brügger MB.2 Colibri	M. R. Walters	

Notes	Reg.	Type	Owner or Operator
	G-BKCN	Currie Wot	N. A. A. Podmore
	G-BKCV	EAA Acro Sport II	R. J. Bower
	G-BKCW	Jodel D.120	Dundee Flying Group (G-BMYF)
	G-BKCX	Mudry/CAARP CAP-10B	G. P. Gorvett
	G-BKCZ	Jodel D.120A	I. K. Ratcliffe
	G-BKDC	Monnett Sonerai II	K. J. Towell
	G-BKDH	Robin DR.400/120	Marine & Aviation Ltd
	G-BKDJ	Robin DR.400/120	S. Pritchard & I. C. Colwell
	G-BKDK	Thunder Ax7-77Z balloon	A. J. Byrne
	G-BKDP	FRED Srs 3	M. Whittaker
	G-BKDR	Pitts S-1S Special	J. H. Milne & T. H. Bishop
	G-BKDT	SE-5A (replica) (F943) ★	Yorkshire Air Museum/Elvington
	G-BKDX	Jodel DR.1050	H. D. Colliver
	G-BKEP	Cessna F.172M	R. M. Dalley
	G-BKER	SE-5A (replica) (F5447:N)	N. K. Geddes
	G-BKET	PA-18 Super Cub 95	H. M. MacKenzie
	G-BKEV	Cessna F.172M	Derby Arrows
	G-BKEW	Bell 206B JetRanger 3	N. R. Foster
	G-BKEY	FRED Srs 3	G. S. Taylor
	G-BKFC	Cessna F.152 II	C. Walton Ltd
	G-BKFG	Thunder Ax3 Maxi Sky Chariot balloon	Cameron Balloons Ltd
	G-BKFI	Evans VP-1	P. L. Naylor
	G-BKFL	Aerosport Scamp	J. Sherwood
	G-BKFM	QAC Quickie 1	G. E. Meakin
	G-BKFR	CP.301C Emeraude	Devonshire Flying Group
	G-BKFW	P.56 Provost T.1 (XF597)	Sylmar Aviation & Services Ltd
	G-BKGA	MS.892E Rallye 150GT	C. J. Spradbery
	G-BKGB	Jodel D.120	B. A. Ridgway
	G-BKGC	Maule M.6-235	The Vale of the White Horse Gliding Centre Ltd
	G-BKGD	Westland WG.30 Srs.100 ★	IHM/Weston-super-Mare
	G-BKGL	Beech D.18S (1164:64)	A. T. J. Darrah
	G-BKGM	Beech D.18S (HB275)	L. S. Williams
	G-BKGR	Cameron O-65 balloon	K. Kidner & L. E. More
	G-BKGW	Cessna F.152-II	Leicestershire Aero Club Ltd
	G-BKHG	Piper J-3C-65 Cub (479766:D-63)	H. C. Cox
	G-BKHW	Stoddard-Hamilton Glasair IIRG	P. J. Mansfield
	G-BKHY	Taylor JT.1 Monoplane	B. C. J. O'Neill
	G-BKHZ	Cessna F.172P	L. R. Leader
	G-BKIB	SOCATA TB9 Tampico	G. A. Vickers
	G-BKIC	Cameron V-77 balloon	C. A. Butler
	G-BKIF	Fournier RF-6B	Tiger Airways
	G-BKII	Cessna F.172M	Sealand Aerial Photography Ltd
	G-BKIJ	Cessna F.172M	Cirrus Aviation Ltd
	G-BKIK	Cameron DG-19 airship ★	Balloon Preservation Group/Lancing
	G-BKIR	Jodel D.117	R. Shaw & D. M. Hardaker
	G-BKIS	SOCATA TB10 Tobago	Wessex Flyers
	G-BKIT	SOCATA TB9 Tampico	Cavendish Aviation UK Ltd
	G-BKIU	Colt 17A Cloudhopper balloon	S. R. J. Pooley
	G-BKIY	Thunder Ax3 balloon ★	Balloon Preservation Group/Lancing
	G-BKIZ	Cameron V-31 balloon	A. P. S. Cox
	G-BKJB	PA-18 Super Cub 135	W. S. Stanley
	G-BKJF	MS.880B Rallye 100T	R. Neeson
	G-BKJS	Jodel D.120A	B. F. Baldock & T. J. Nicholson
	G-BKJW	PA-23 Aztec 250E	Alan Williams Entertainments Ltd
	G-BKKN	Cessna 182R	R A. Marven
	G-BKKO	Cessna 182R	E. L. King & D. S. Lightbown
	G-BKKZ	Pitts S-1D Special	P. G. Gabriele
	G-BKLO	Cessna F.172M	Stapleford Flying Club Ltd
	G-BKMA	Mooney M.20J Srs 201	Foxtrot Whisky Aviation
	G-BKMB	Mooney M.20J Srs 201	G-BKMB Flying Group
	G-BKMG	Handley Page O/400 (replica)	The Paralyser Group
	G-BKMT	PA-32R-301 Saratoga SP	P. Ashworth
	G-BKNO	Monnett Sonerai IIL	S. Hardy
	G-BKNP	Cameron V-77 balloon	P. Lesser/Sweden
	G-BKNZ	CP.301A Emeraude	J. A. Thomas
	G-BKOA	SOCATA MS.893E Rallye 180GT	M. Jarrett
	G-BKOB	Z.326 Trener Master	A. L. Rae
	G-BKOK	BN-2B-26 Islander	Cormack (Aircraft Services) Ltd
	G-BKOT	Wassmer Wa.81 Piranha	B. N. Rolfe
	G-BKOU	P.84 Jet Provost T.3 (XN637)	G-BKOU/2 Ltd
	G-BKPA	Hoffmann H-36 Dimona	J. D. Hanton & R. Matthews
	G-BKPB	Aerosport Scamp	B. R. Thompson
	G-BKPC	Cessna A.185F	Black Knights Parachute Centre

Reg.	Type	Owner or Operator	Notes
G-BKPD	Viking Dragonfly	E. P. Browne & G. J. Sargent	
G-BKPE	Jodel DR.250/160	M. Hales	
G-BKPS	AA-5B Tiger	A. E. T. Clarke	
G-BKPX	Jodel D.120A	D. M. Garrett & C. A. Jones	
G-BKPY	SAAB 91B/2 Safir (56321:U-AB) ★	Newark Air Museum	
G-BKPZ	Pitts S-1T Special	D. A. Slater	
G-BKRA	NA T-6G Texan (51-15227)	First Air Ltd	
G-BKRF	PA-18 Super Cub 95	K. M. Bishop	
G-BKRH	Brügger MB.2 Colibri	M. R. Benwell	
G-BKRK	SNCAN Stampe SV.4C	Strathgadie Stampe Group	
G-BKRL	Chichester-Miles Leopard ★	Bournemouth Aviation Museum	
G-BKRN	Beechcraft D.18S (43-35943)	A. A. Marshall & P. L. Turland	
G-BKRZ	Dragon G-77 balloon	J. R. Barber	
G-BKSC	Saro Skeeter AOP.12 (XN351) ★	R. A. L. Falconer	
G-BKSD	Colt 56A balloon	R. L. Wright	
G-BKSE	QAC Quickie Q.1	M. D. Burns	
G-BKST	Rutan Vari-Eze	R. Towle	
G-BKSX	SNCAN Stampe SV.4C	C. A. Bailey & J. A. Carr	
G-BKTA	PA-18 Super Cub 95	M. J. Dyson	
G-BKTH	CCF Hawker Sea Hurricane IB (Z7015)	The Shuttleworth Collection	
G-BKTM	PZL SZD-45A Ogar	Hinton Ogar Group	
G-BKTV	Cessna F.152	ACS Aviation Ltd	
G-BKTZ	Slingsby T.67M Firefly	P. R. Elvidge (G-SFTV)	
G-BKUE	SOCATA TB9 Tampico	Fife TB9ers	
G-BKUI	D.31 Turbulent	E. Shouler	
G-BKUR	CP.301A Emeraude	T. Harvey	
G-BKVA	SOCATA Rallye 180T	Norfolk Gliding Club Ltd	
G-BKVC	SOCATA TB9 Tampico	J. P. Gough	
G-BKVF	FRED Srs 3	G. E. & R. E. Collins	
G-BKVG	Scheibe SF.25E Super Falke	G-BKVG Ltd	
G-BKVK	Auster AOP.9 (WZ662)	J. K. Houlgrave	
G-BKVL	Robin DR.400/160	Tatenhill Aviation Ltd	
G-BKVM	PA-18 Super Cub 150 (115684)	D. G. Caffrey	
G-BKVO	Pietenpol Air Camper	M. C. Hayes	
G-BKVP	Pitts S-1D Special	S. A. Smith	
G-BKVT	PA-23 Aztec 250E	BKS Surveys Ltd (G-HARV)	
G-BKVW	Airtour 56 balloon	L. D. & H. Vaughan	
G-BKWD	Taylor JT.2 Titch	J. F. Sully	
G-BKWR	Cameron V-65 balloon	Window on the World Ltd	
G-BKWY	Cessna F.152	Northumbria Flying School Ltd	
G-BKXA	Robin R.2100	M. Wilson	
G-BKXD	SA.365N Dauphin 2	CHC Scotia Ltd	
G-BKXF	PA-28R Cherokee Arrow 200	P. L. Brunton	
G-BKXM	Colt 17A balloon	R. G. Turnbull	
G-BKXN	ICA-Brasov IS-28M2/80HP	R. J. S. Charnley	
G-BKXO	Rutan LongEz	M. G. Parsons	
G-BKXP	Auster AOP.6	B. J. Ellis	
G-BKXR	D.31A Turbulent	G. C. Bridges	
G-BKZE	AS.332L Super Puma	CHC Scotia Ltd	
G-BKZF	Cameron V-56 balloon	C. F. Sanger-Davies	
G-BKZG	AS.332L Super Puma	CHC Scotia Ltd	
G-BKZI	Bell 206B JetRanger 2	Bucklefields Business Devlopments Ltd	
G-BKZT	FRED Srs 2	U. Chakravorty	
G-BKZV	Bede BD-4A	T. S. Smith	
G-BLAC	Cessna FA.152	W. Ali	
G-BLAF	Stolp SA.900 V-Star	P. K. Dale	
G-BLAH	Thunder Ax7-77-1 balloon	T. M. Donnelly	
G-BLAI	Monnett Sonerai 2L	T. Simpon	
G-BLAM	Jodel DR.360	D. J. Durell	
G-BLAT	Jodel 150	G-BLAT Flying Group	
G-BLCC	Thunder Ax7-77Z balloon	W. J. Treacy & P. Murphy/Ireland	
G-BLCG	SOCATA TB10 Tobago	Contrarios Services Ltd (G-BHES)	
G-BLCH	Colt 65D balloon	S. Charlish	
G-BLCI	EAA Acro Sport	M. R. Holden	
G-BLCM	SOCATA TB9 Tampico	K. J. Steele & D. J. Hewitt	
G-BLCT	Jodel DR.220 2+2	F. N. P. Maurin	
G-BLCU	Scheibe SF.25B Falke	Charlie Uniform Syndicate	
G-BLCV	Hoffmann H-36 Dimona	R. & M. Weaver	
G-BLCW	Evans VP-1	K. Lewis	
G-BLDB	Taylor JT.1 Monoplane	J. P. J. Hefford	
G-BLDD	WAG-Aero CUBy AcroTrainer	M. P. Wiseman	
G-BLDG	PA-25 Pawnee 260C	Ouse Gliding Club Ltd	

Notes	Reg.	Type	Owner or Operator
	G-BLDK	Robinson R22	Flight Academy (Gyrocopters) Ltd
	G-BLDN	Rand-Robinson KR-2	P. R. Diffey
	G-BLDV	BN-2B-26 Islander	Loganair Ltd
	G-BLES	Stolp SA.750 Acroduster Too	C. J. Kingswood
	G-BLFI	PA-28-181 Archer II	Bonus Aviation Ltd
	G-BLFZ	PA-31-310 Turbo Navajo C	London Executive Aviation Ltd
	G-BLGH	Robin DR.300/180R	Booker Gliding Club Ltd
	G-BLGS	SOCATA Rallye 180T	A. Waters
	G-BLGV	Bell 206B JetRanger 3	Heliflight (UK) Ltd
	G-BLHH	Jodel DR.315	S. J. Luck
	G-BLHI	Colt 17A balloon	J. A. Folkes
	G-BLHJ	Cessna F.172P	J. H. Sandham Aviation
	G-BLHM	PA-18 Super Cub 95	A. G. Edwards
	G-BLHN	Robin HR.100/285	K. A. & L. M. C. Payton
	G-BLHR	GA-7 Cougar	W. B. Orde-Powlett
	G-BLHS	Bellanca 7ECA Citabria	A. J. Wilkins
	G-BLHW	Varga 2150A Kachina	Wilburton Flying Group
	G-BLID	DH.112 Venom FB.50 (J-1605) ★	P. G. Vallance Ltd
	G-BLIK	Wallis WA-116/F/S	K. H. Wallis
	G-BLIT	Thorp T-18 CW	A. P. Tyrwhitt-Drake
	G-BLIW	P.56 Provost T.51 (177)	A. D. M. & K. B. Edie
	G-BLIX	Saro Skeeter Mk 12 (XL809)	K. M. Scholes
	G-BLIY	MS.892A Rallye Commodore	A. J. Brasher
	G-BLJM	Beech 95-B55 Baron	A. Nitsche/Germany
	G-BLJO	Cessna F.152	J. S. Develin & Z. Islam
	G-BLKA	DH.112 Venom FB.54 (WR410:N) ★	De Havilland Heritage Museum/London Colney
	G-BLKM	Jodel DR.1051	Kilo Mike Group
	G-BLKY	Beech 95-58 Baron	R. A. Perrot
	G-BLLA	Bensen B.8M	K. T. Donaghey
	G-BLLB	Bensen B.8M	D. H. Moss
	G-BLLD	Cameron O-77 balloon	G. Birchall
	G-BLLH	Jodel DR.220A 2+2	M. D. Hughes
	G-BLLN	PA-18 Super Cub 95	N. M. Zullo
	G-BLLO	PA-18 Super Cub 95	D. G. Margetts
	G-BLLP	Slingsby T.67B	Air Navigation and Trading Co Ltd
	G-BLLR	Slingsby T.67B	R. L. Brinklow
	G-BLLS	Slingsby T.67B	K. Davis
	G-BLLW	Colt 56B balloon	G. Fordyce & ptnrs
	G-BLLZ	Rutan LongEz	R. S. Stoddart-Stones
	G-BLMA	Zlin 326 Trener Master	G. P. Northcott
	G-BLMC	Avro 698 Vulcan B.2A ★	Aeropark/East Midlands
	G-BLME	Robinson R22HP	Heli Air Ltd
	G-BLMG	Grob G.109B	Mike Golf Syndicate
	G-BLMI	PA-18-95 Super Cub	M. R. Masters
	G-BLMN	Rutan LongEz	J. Laszlo
	G-BLMP	PA-17 Vagabond	D. & M. Shrimpton.
	G-BLMR	PA-18 Super Cub 150	M. Vickers
	G-BLMT	PA-18 Super Cub 135	I. S. Runnalls
	G-BLMW	T.66 Nipper 3	S. L. Millar
	G-BLMZ	Colt 105A balloon	M. D. Dickinson
	G-BLNO	FRED Srs 3	L. W. Smith
	G-BLOR	PA-30 Twin Comanche 160	R. L. C. Appleton
	G-BLOS	Cessna 185A (also flown with floats)	D. C. Minshaw
	G-BLOT	Colt Ax6-56B balloon	H. J. Anderson
	G-BLOV	Thunder Ax5-42 Srs 1 balloon	A. G. R. Calder
	G-BLPA	Piper J-3C-65 Cub	A. C. Frost
	G-BLPB	Turner TSW Hot Two Wot	Papa Bravo Group
	G-BLPE	PA-18 Super Cub 95	A. A. Haig-Thomas
	G-BLPF	Cessna FR.172G	S. Culpin
	G-BLPG	Auster J/1N Alpha (16693:693)	Annic Marketing (G-AZIH)
	G-BLPH	Cessna FRA.150L	J. D. Baines
	G-BLPI	Slingsby T.67B	RAF Wyton Flying Group Ltd
	G-BLPP	Cameron V-77 balloon	R. J. Gooch
	G-BLRA	BAe 146-100	BAE Systems (Corporate Air Teavel) Ltd
	G-BLRC	PA-18 Super Cub 135	Supercub Group
	G-BLRF	Slingsby T.67C	R. C. Nicholls
	G-BLRL	CP.301C-1 Emeraude	A. M. Smith
	G-BLRM	Glaser-Dirks DG.400	J. A. & W. S. Y. Stephen
	G-BLSD	DH.112 Venom FB.54 (J-1758) ★	R. Lamplough/North Weald
	G-BLSX	Cameron O-105 balloon	B. J. Petteford
	G-BLTA	Thunder Ax7-77A	K. A. Schlussler
	G-BLTC	D.31A Turbulent	S. J. Butler
	G-BLTK	Rockwell Commander 112TC	Commander TC Group

Reg.	Type	Owner or Operator	Notes
G-BLTM	Robin HR.200/100	Barton Robin Group	
G-BLTN	Thunder Ax7-65 balloon	A. H. Symonds	
G-BLTR	Scheibe SF.25B Falke	V. Mallon/Germany	
G-BLTS	Rutan LongEz	R. W. Cutler	
G-BLTV	Slingsby T.67B	R. L. Brinklow	
G-BLTW	Slingsby T.67B	Cheshire Air Training Services Ltd	
G-BLTY	Westland WG.30 Srs 160	D. Brem-Wilson	
G-BLUI	Thunder Ax7-65 balloon	S. Johnson	
G-BLUV	Grob G.109B	109 Flying Group	
G-BLUX	Slingsby T.67M Firefly 200	R. L. Brinklow	
G-BLUZ	DH.82B Queen Bee (LF858)	The Bee Keepers Group	
G-BLVB	Airtour AH-56 balloon	J. J. Daly	
G-BLVI	Slingsby T.67M Firefly Mk II	Brooke Park Ltd	
G-BLVK	CAARP CAP-10B	E. K. Coventry	
G-BLVL	PA-28-161 Warrior II	TG Aviation Ltd	
G-BLVS	Cessna 150M	D. H. G. Penney	
G-BLVW	Cessna F.172H	R. Holloway	
G-BLWD	PA-34-200T Seneca 2	Bencray Ltd	
G-BLWF	Robin HR.100/210	M. D. Parker	
G-BLWH	Fournier RF-6B-100	F. J. Hodson & C. C. Rollings	
G-BLWM	Bristol M.1C (replica) (C4994) ★	RAF Museum/Hendon	
G-BLWP	PA-38-112 Tomahawk	APB Leasing Ltd	
G-BLWT	Evans VP-1	N. Clark	
G-BLWY	Robin R.2160D	Charlie Yankee Ltd	
G-BLXA	SOCATA TB20 Trinidad	Trinidad Flyers Ltd	
G-BLXG	Colt 21A balloon	A. Walker	
G-BLXH	Fournier RF-3	J. E. Dallison	
G-BLXI	CP.1310-C3 Super Emeraude	R. Howard	
G-BLXO	Jodel 150	P. R. Powell	
G-BLXR	AS.332L Super Puma	Bristow Helicopters Ltd	
G-BLYD	SOCATA TB20 Trinidad	Yankee Delta Corporation Ltd	
G-BLYP	Robin 3000/120	Weald Air Services	
G-BLYT	Airtour AH-77 balloon	I. J. Taylor & R. C. Kincaid	
G-BLZA	Scheibe SF.25B Falke	Zulu Alpha Syndicate	
G-BLZH	Cessna F.152 II	P. D'Costa	
G-BLZP	Cessna F.152	East Midlands Flying School Ltd	
G-BMAD	Cameron V-77 balloon	M. A. Stelling	
G-BMAO	Taylor JT.1 Monoplane	S. J. Alston	
G-BMAX	FRED Srs 2	D. A. Arkley	
G-BMAY	PA-18 Super Cub 135	R. W. Davies	
G-BMBB	Cessna F.150L	E. T. Hawkins	
G-BMBJ	Schempp-Hirth Janus CM	BJ Flying Group	
G-BMBW	Bensen B.8MR	M. E. Vahdat	
G-BMBZ	Scheibe SF.25E Super Falke	K. E. Ballington	
G-BMCC	Thunder Ax7-77 balloon	A. K. & C. M. Russell	
G-BMCD	Cameron V-65 balloon	R. Lillyman	
G-BMCG	Grob G.109B	D. K. R. Draper	
G-BMCI	Cessna F.172H	A. B. Davis	
G-BMCN	Cessna F.152	Cristal Air Ltd	
G-BMCS	PA-22 Tri-Pacer 135	T. A. Hodges	
G-BMCV	Cessna F.152	Leicestershire Aero Club Ltd	
G-BMCW	AS.332L Super Puma	Bristow Helicopters Ltd	
G-BMCX	AS.332L Super Puma	Bristow Southeast Asia Ltd	
G-BMDB	SE-5A (replica) (F235:B)	D. Biggs	
G-BMDE	Pietenpol AirCamper	P. B. Childs	
G-BMDJ	Price Ax7-77S balloon	R. A. Benham	
G-BMDK	PA-34-220T Seneca III	Air Medical Fleet Ltd	
G-BMDP	Partenavia P.64B Oscar 200	S. T. G. Lloyd	
G-BMDS	Jodel D.120	N. Lynch	
G-BMEA	PA-18 Super Cub 95	M. J. Butler	
G-BMEH	Jodel 150 Special Super Mascaret	R. J. & C. J. Lewis	
G-BMET	Taylor JT.1 Monoplane	M. K. A. Blyth	
G-BMEU	Isaacs Fury II	I. G. Harrison	
G-BMEX	Cessna A.150K	R. J. Grantham & D. Boatswain	
G-BMFD	PA-23 Aztec 250F	Giles Aviation Ltd (G-BGYY)	
G-BMFG	Dornier Do.27A-4	Dornier 27 Group	
G-BMFI	PZL SZD-45A Ogar	S. L. Morrey	
G-BMFP	PA-28-161 Warrior II	Bravo-Mike-Fox-Papa Group	
G-BMFU	Cameron N-90 balloon	J. J. Rudoni	
G-BMFY	Grob G.109B	P. J. Shearer	
G-BMGB	PA-28R Cherokee Arrow 200	Malmesbury Specialist Cars	
G-BMGC	Fairey Swordfish Mk II (W5856)	F.A.A. Museum/Yeovilton	

Notes	Reg.	Type	Owner or Operator
	G-BMGG	Cessna 152 II	Falcon Flying Services
	G-BMGR	Grob G.109B	G-BMGR Group
	G-BMHA	Rutan LongEz	S. F. Elvins
	G-BMHC	Cessna U.206F	H. and R. Morley
	G-BMHL	Wittman W.8 Tailwind	H. J. Bennet
	G-BMHS	Cessna F.172M	Tango X-Ray Flying Group
	G-BMHT	PA-28RT-201T Turbo Arrow	G-BMHT Flying Group
	G-BMID	Jodel D.120	G-BMID Flying Group
	G-BMIG	Cessna 172N	BMIG Group
	G-BMIM	Rutan LongEz	R. M. Smith
	G-BMIO	Stoddard-Hamilton Glasair RG	P. Bint & L. McMahon
	G-BMIP	Jodel D.112	F. J. E. Brownsill
	G-BMIR	Westland Wasp HAS.1 (XT788) ★	Park Aviation Supply/Charlwood
	G-BMIS	Monnett Sonerai II	S. R. Edwards
	G-BMIV	PA-28R-201T Turbo Arrow III	Firmbeam Ltd
	G-BMIW	PA-28-181 Archer II	Oldbus Ltd
	G-BMIX	SOCATA TB20 Trinidad	Aviation Surrey Ltd
	G-BMIY	Oldfield Baby Great Lakes	J. B. Scott (G-NOME)
	G-BMIZ	Robinson R22 Beta	Castlehill Aviation Ltd
	G-BMJA	PA-32R-301 Saratoga SP	H. Merkado
	G-BMJB	Cessna 152	Endrick Aviation LLP
	G-BMJC	Cessna 152 II	T. Brogden
	G-BMJD	Cessna 152 II	Donair Flying Club Ltd
	G-BMJL	Rockwell Commander 114	D. J. & S. M. Hawkins
	G-BMJN	Cameron O-65 balloon	P. M. Traviss
	G-BMJO	PA-34-220T Seneca III	Fastnet Jet Alliance Ltd
	G-BMJR	Cessna T.337H	John Roberts Services Ltd (G-NOVA)
	G-BMJX	Wallis WA-116X	K. H. Wallis
	G-BMJY	Yakovlev C18M (07)	W. A. E. Moore
	G-BMKB	PA-18 Super Cub 135	Cubair Flight Training Ltd
	G-BMKC	Piper J-3C-65 Cub (329854:R-44)	P. R. Monk
	G-BMKD	Beech C90A King Air	ATC (Lasham) Ltd
	G-BMKF	Jodel DR.221	S. T. & L. A. Gilbert
	G-BMKG	PA-38-112 Tomahawk II	APB Leasing Ltd
	G-BMKI	Colt 21A balloon	A. C. Booth
	G-BMKJ	Cameron V-77 balloon	R. C. Thursby
	G-BMKK	PA-28R-200 Cherokee Arrow II	P. M. Murray
	G-BMKP	Cameron V-77 balloon	R. Bayly
	G-BMKR	PA-28-161 Warrior II	Field Flying Group (G-BGKR)
	G-BMKY	Cameron O-65 balloon	A. R. Rich
	G-BMLJ	Cameron N-77 balloon	C. J. Dunkley
	G-BMLK	Grob G.109B	Brams Syndicate
	G-BMLL	Grob G.109B	G-BMLL Flying Group
	G-BMLM	Beech 95-58 Baron	Atlantic Bridge Aviation Ltd
	G-BMLS	PA-28R-201 Arrow III	R. M. Shorter
	G-BMLT	Pietenpol Air Camper	W. E. R. Jenkins
	G-BMLW	Cameron O-77 balloon	M. L. & L. P. Willoughby
	G-BMLX	Cessna F.150L	J. P. A. Freeman
	G-BMMF	FRED Srs 2	R. C. Thomas
	G-BMMI	Pazmany PL.4A	P. I. Morgans
	G-BMMK	Cessna 182P	G. G. Weston
	G-BMMM	Cessna 152 II	Falcon Flying Services Ltd
	G-BMMP	Grob G.109B	G-BMMP Syndicate
	G-BMMV	ICA-Brasov IS-28M2A	C. D. King
	G-BMMW	Thunder Ax7-77 balloon	P. A. George
	G-BMNL	PA-28R Cherokee Arrow 200	Mid America (UK) Ltd
	G-BMNV	SNCAN Stampe SV.4D	Wessex Aviation & Transport Ltd
	G-BMOE	PA-28R Cherokee Arrow 200	Piper Leasing Ltd
	G-BMOF	Cessna U206G	Wild Geese Skydiving Centre
	G-BMOG	Thunder Ax7-77 balloon	R. M. Boswell
	G-BMOH	Cameron N-77 balloon	P. J. Marshall & M. A. Clarke
	G-BMOI	Partenavia P.68B	Ravenair Aircraft Ltd
	G-BMAD	ARV Super 2	R. E. Griffiths
	G-BMOL	PA-23 Aztec 250D	LDL Enterprises (G-BBSR)
	G-BMOT	Bensen B.8M	M. Fontolan
	G-BMPC	PA-28-181 Archer II	C. J. & R. J. Barnes
	G-BMPD	Cameron V-65 balloon	R. P. E. Phillips
	G-BMPL	Optica Industries OA.7 Optica	J. K. Edgley
	G-BMPP	Cameron N-77 balloon	The Sarnia Balloon Group
	G-BMPR	PA-28R-201 Arrow III	T. J. Brammer & D. T. Colley
	G-BMPS	Strojnik S-2A	G. J. Green
	G-BMPY	DH.82A Tiger Moth	N. M. Eisenstein
	G-BMRA	Boeing 757-236F	DHL Air Ltd

Reg.	Type	Owner or Operator	Notes
G-BMRB	Boeing 757-236F	DHL Air Ltd	
G-BMRC	Boeing 757-236F	DHL Air Ltd	
G-BMRD	Boeing 757-236F	DHL Air Ltd	
G-BMRE	Boeing 757-236F	DHL Air Ltd	
G-BMRF	Boeing 757-236F	DHL Air Ltd	
G-BMRH	Boeing 757-236F	DHL Air Ltd	
G-BMRJ	Boeing 757-236F	DHL Air Ltd	
G-BMSB	VS.509 Spitfire IX (MJ627:9G-P)	M. S. Bayliss (G-ASOZ)	
G-BMSC	Evans VP-2	R. S. Acreman	
G-BMSD	PA-28-181 Archer II	H. Merkado	
G-BMSE	Valentin Taifun 17E	D. O'Donnell	
G-BMSF	PA-38-112 Tomahawk	B. Catlow	
G-BMSG	SAAB 32A Lansen ★	J. E. Wilkie/Cranfield	
G-BMSL	FRED Srs 3	T. C. Darters	
G-BMTA	Cessna 152 II	ACS Aviation Ltd	
G-BMTB	Cessna 152 II	Sky Leisure Aviation (Charters) Ltd	
G-BMTC	AS.355F1 Twin Squirrel	Cambridge & Essex Air Support Unit (G-SASU/G-BSSM/G-BKUK/G-EPOL)	
G-BMTJ	Cessna 152 II	The Pilot Centre Ltd	
G-BMTO	PA-38-112 Tomahawk	A. Sanja	
G-BMTU	Pitts S-1E Special	N. A. A. Pogmore	
G-BMTX	Cameron V-77 balloon	J. A. Langley	
G-BMUD	Cessna 182P	M. E. Taylor	
G-BMUG	Rutan LongEz	A. G. Sayers	
G-BMUJ	Colt Drachenfisch balloon	Virgin Airship & Balloon Co Ltd	
G-BMUO	Cessna A.152	Sky Leisure Aviation (Charters) Ltd	
G-BMUT	PA-34-200T Seneca II	G-DAD Air Ltd	
G-BMUU	Thunder Ax7-77 balloon	A. R. Hill	
G-BMUZ	PA-28-161 Warrior II	Northumbria Flying School Ltd	
G-BMVA	Scheibe SF.25B Falke	Kent Gliding Club Ltd	
G-BMVB	Cessna F.152	M. P. Barnard	
G-BMVG	QAC Quickie Q.1	N. Ciattoni	
G-BMVL	PA-38-112 Tomahawk	G. W. Mountford	
G-BMVM	PA-38-112 Tomahawk	Brimpton Flying Group	
G-BMVT	Thunder Ax7-77A balloon	M. L. & L. P. Willoughby	
G-BMVU	Monnett Moni	Stacey Aviation Ltd	
G-BMWF	ARV Super 2	G. E. Collard	
G-BMWR	Rockwell Commander 112	M. & J. Edwards	
G-BMWU	Cameron N-42 balloon ★	I. Chadwick	
G-BMWV	Putzer Elster B	Magpie Group	
G-BMXA	Cessna 152 II	ACS Aviation Ltd	
G-BMXB	Cessna 152 II	C. I. J. Young	
G-BMXC	Cessna 152 II	MK Aero Support Ltd	
G-BMYC	SOCATA TB10 Tobago	J. C. Woolard	
G-BMYD	Beech A36 Bonanza	Rocel BV	
G-BMYG	Cessna FA.152	Greer Aviation Ltd	
G-BMYI	AA-5 Traveler	W. C. & S. C. Westran	
G-BMYU	Jodel D.120	A. J. L. Gordon	
G-BMZF	WSK-Mielec LiM-2 (MiG-15bis) (01420) ★	F.A.A. Museum/Yeovilton	
G-BMZN	Everett gyroplane	T. A. Holmes	
G-BMZS	Everett gyroplane	L. W. Cload	
G-BMZW	Bensen B.8MR	P. D. Widdicombe	
G-BNAI	Wolf W-II Boredom Fighter (146-11083)	C. M. Bunn	
G-BNAJ	Cessna 152 II	Galair Ltd	
G-BNAN	Cameron V-65 balloon	Rango Balloon and Kite Company	
G-BNAW	Cameron V-65 balloon	A. Walker	
G-BNBW	Thunder Ax7-77 balloon	I. S. & S. W. Watthews	
G-BNBY	Beech 95-B55A Baron	J. Butler/France (G-AXXR)	
G-BNCB	Cameron V-77 balloon	C. W. Brown	
G-BNCM	Cameron N-77 balloon	C. A. Stone	
G-BNCO	PA-38-112 Tomahawk	D. K. Walker	
G-BNCR	PA-28-161 Warrior II	Airways Aero Associations Ltd	
G-BNCS	Cessna 180	C. Elwell Transport Ltd	
G-BNCX	Hawker Hunter T.7 (XL621) ★	Brooklands Museum of Aviation/Weybridge	
G-BNCZ	Rutan LongEz	D. G. Foreman	
G-BNDE	PA-38-112 Tomahawk	B. R. Nurthen	
G-BNDG	Wallis WA-201/R Srs1	K. H. Wallis	
G-BNDN	Cameron V-77 balloon	A. Hornshaw	
G-BNDP	Brügger MB.2 Colibri	A. C. Barber	
G-BNDR	SOCATA TB10 Tobago	Monavion.fr	
G-BNDT	Brügger MB.2 Colibri	D. W. Rees	

Notes	Reg.	Type	Owner or Operator
	G-BNDV	Cameron N-77 balloon	R. E. Jones
	G-BNDW	DH.82A Tiger Moth	C. R. Hardiman
	G-BNEE	PA-28R-201 Arrow III	Britannic Management Aviation
	G-BNEL	PA-28-161 Warrior II	S. C. Westran
	G-BNEN	PA-34-200T Seneca II	CE Ventures Ltd
	G-BNEO	Cameron V-77 balloon	J. G. O'Connell
	G-BNEV	Viking Dragonfly	N. W. Eyre
	G-BNFG	Cameron O-77 balloon	Capital Balloon Club Ltd
	G-BNFI	Cessna 150J	A. Waters
	G-BNFN	Cameron N-105 balloon	P. Glydon
	G-BNFO	Cameron V-77 balloon	M. B. Young
	G-BNFP	Cameron O-84 balloon	M. Clarke
	G-BNFR	Cessna 152 II	A. Jahanfar
	G-BNFV	Robin DR.400/120	J. P. A. Freeman
	G-BNGE	Auster AOP.6 (TW536)	N. D. Sharpe
	G-BNGJ	Cameron N-77 balloon	S. W. K. Smeeton
	G-BNGN	Cameron N-77 balloon	N. Dykes
	G-BNGO	Thunder Ax7-77 balloon	J. S. Finlan
	G-BNGT	PA-28-181 Archer II	Edinburgh Flying Club Ltd
	G-BNGV	ARV Super 2	N. A. Onions & L. J. Russell
	G-BNGW	ARV Super 2	Southern Gas Turbines Ltd
	G-BNGY	ARV Super 2	S. C. Smith (G-BMWL)
	G-BNHB	ARV Super 2	C. J. Challener
	G-BNHG	PA-38-112 Tomahawk II	Highland Aviation Training Ltd
	G-BNHJ	Cessna 152 II	The Pilot Centre Ltd
	G-BNHK	Cessna 152 II	Wayfarers Flying Group
	G-BNHL	Colt beer glass SS balloon	J. A. Viner
	G-BNHN	Colt Ariel Bottle SS balloon ★	British Balloon Museum
	G-BNHT	Fournier RF-3	G-BNHT Group
	G-BNID	Cessna 152 II	MK Aero Support Ltd
	G-BNII	Cameron N-90 balloon	Topless Balloon Group
	G-BNIK	Robin HR.200/120	G-BNIK Group
	G-BNIM	PA-38-112 Tomahawk	Air Claire Ltd
	G-BNIN	Cameron V-77 balloon	Cloud Nine Balloon Group
	G-BNIO	Luscombe 8A Silvaire	India Oscar Group
	G-BNIP	Luscombe 8A Silvaire	M. J. Diggins
	G-BNIU	Cameron O-77 balloon	Terre d'Envoi Blois Montgolfiere/France
	G-BNIV	Cessna 152 II	Cristal Air Ltd
	G-BNIW	Boeing Stearman PT-17	R. C. Goold
	G-BNJB	Cessna 152 II	Aerolease Ltd
	G-BNJC	Cessna 152 II	Stapleford Flying Club Ltd
	G-BNJH	Cessna 152 II	ACS Aviation Ltd
	G-BNJL	Bensen B.8MR	S. Ram
	G-BNJT	PA-28-161 Warrior II	Hawarden Flying Group
	G-BNJX	Cameron N-90 balloon	Mars UK Ltd
	G-BNJZ	Cassutt Racer IIIM	J. Stringer
	G-BNKC	Cessna 152 II	Herefordshire Aero Club Ltd
	G-BNKD	Cessna 172N	P. J. Craig & A. D. Evans
	G-BNKE	Cessna 172N	Kilo Echo Flying Group
	G-BNKH	PA-38-112 Tomahawk	S. J. Miles
	G-BNKI	Cessna 152 II	RAF Halton Aeroplane Club Ltd
	G-BNKP	Cessna 152 II	Spectrum Leisure Ltd
	G-BNKR	Cessna 152 II	Blue Sky Investments Ltd
	G-BNKS	Cessna 152 II	APB Leasing Ltd
	G-BNKT	Cameron O-77 balloon	A. A. Brown
	G-BNKV	Cessna 152 II	Cristal Air Ltd
	G-BNLA	Boeing 747-436	British Airways
	G-BNLD	Boeing 747-436	British Airways
	G-BNLE	Boeing 747-436	British Airways
	G-BNLF	Boeing 747-436	British Airways
	G-BNLG	Boeing 747-436	British Airways
	G-BNLH	Boeing 747-436	British Airways
	G-BNLI	Boeing 747-436	British Airways
	G-BNLJ	Boeing 747-436	British Airways
	G-BNLK	Boeing 747-436	British Airways
	G-BNLL	Boeing 747-436	British Airways
	G-BNLM	Boeing 747-436	British Airways
	G-BNLN	Boeing 747-436	British Airways
	G-BNLO	Boeing 747-436	British Airways
	G-BNLP	Boeing 747-436	British Airways
	G-BNLR	Boeing 747-436	British Airways
	G-BNLS	Boeing 747-436	British Airways
	G-BNLT	Boeing 747-436	British Airways

Reg.	Type	Owner or Operator	Notes
G-BNLU	Boeing 747-436	British Airways	
G-BNLV	Boeing 747-436	British Airways	
G-BNLW	Boeing 747-436	British Airways	
G-BNLX	Boeing 747-436	British Airways	
G-BNLY	Boeing 747-436	British Airways	
G-BNLZ	Boeing 747-436	British Airways	
G-BNMB	PA-28-151 Warrior	Azure Flying Club Ltd	
G-BNMD	Cessna 152 II	T. M. Jones	
G-BNME	Cessna 152 II	M. Bonsall	
G-BNMF	Cessna 152 II	Redhill Air Services Ltd	
G-BNMG	Cameron O-77 balloon	J. H. Turner	
G-BNMH	Pietenpol Air Camper	N. M. Hitchman	
G-BNMI	Colt Flying Fantasy SS balloon	Air 2 Air Ltd	
G-BNML	Rand-Robinson KR-2	P. J. Brookman	
G-BNMO	Cessna TR.182RG	R. Taggart	
G-BNMX	Thunder Ax7-77 balloon	S. A. D. Beard	
G-BNNA	Stolp SA.300 Starduster Too	Banana Group	
G-BNNE	Cameron N-77 balloon	R. D. Allen, L. P. Hooper & M. J. Streat	
G-BNNO	PA-28-161 Warrior II	I. A. Anderson	
G-BNNT	PA-28-151 Warrior	S. T. Gilbert & D. J. Kirkwood	
G-BNNU	PA-38-112 Tomahawk	Percival Aircraft Company (Bournemouth) Ltd	
G-BNNX	PA-28R-201T Turbo Arrow III	Bristol Flying Centre Ltd	
G-BNNY	PA-28-161 Warrior II	Falcon Flying Services	
G-BNNZ	PA-28-161 Warrior II	R. West	
G-BNOB	Wittman W.8 Tailwind	D. G. Hammersley	
G-BNOF	PA-28-161 Warrior II	Tayside Aviation Ltd	
G-BNOH	PA-28-161 Warrior II	Sherburn Aero Club Ltd	
G-BNOJ	PA-28-161 Warrior II	BAE Systems (Warton) Flying Club Ltd	
G-BNOM	PA-28-161 Warrior II	J. H. Sandham Aviation	
G-BNON	PA-28-161 Warrior II	Tayside Aviation Ltd	
G-BNOP	PA-28-161 Warrior II	BAE Systems (Warton) Flying Club Ltd	
G-BNPE	Cameron N-77 balloon	R. N. Simpkins	
G-BNPF	Slingsby T.31M	S. Luck & ptnrs	
G-BNPH	P.66 Pembroke C.1 (WV740)	A. G. & G. A. G. Dixon	
G-BNPM	PA-38-112 Tomahawk	Papa Mike Aviation	
G-BNPO	PA-28-181 Archer II	Bonus Aviation Ltd	
G-BNPV	Bowers Fly-Baby 1B	J. G. Day	
G-BNPY	Cessna 152 II	G. Tennant	
G-BNRA	SOCATA TB10 Tobago	Double D Airgroup	
G-BNRG	PA-28-161 Warrior II	Glenn Aviation Ltd	
G-BNRL	Cessna 152 II	Bulldog Aviation Ltd	
G-BNRP	PA-28-181 Archer II	Bonua Aviation Ltd	
G-BNRR	Cessna 172P	Wentworth Productions	
G-BNRX	PA-34-200T Seneca II	Truman Aviation Ltd	
G-BNRY	Cessna 182Q	K. F. & S. J. Farey	
G-BNSG	PA-28R-201 Arrow III	The Leicestershire Aero Club Ltd	
G-BNSI	Cessna 152 II	Sky Leisure Aviation (Charters) Ltd	
G-BNSL	PA-38-112 Tomahawk II	Lomac Aviators Ltd	
G-BNSM	Cessna 152 II	Cornwall Flying Club Ltd	
G-BNSN	Cessna 152 II	The Pilot Centre Ltd	
G-BNSO	Slingsby T.67M Firefly Mk II	R. M. Rennoldson	
G-BNSP	Slingsby T.67M Firefly Mk II	N. J. Heard	
G-BNSR	Slingsby T.67M Firefly Mk II	Slingsby SR Group	
G-BNST	Cessna 172N	CSG Bodyshop	
G-BNSU	Cessna 152 II	Channel Aviation Ltd	
G-BNSV	Cessna 152 II	Channel Aviation Ltd	
G-BNSY	PA-28-161 Warrior II	R. A. Brown	
G-BNSZ	PA-28-161 Warrior II	S. Magrabi	
G-BNTC	PA-28RT-201T Turbo Arrow IV	Redhill Air Services Ltd	
G-BNTD	PA-28-161 Warrior II	S. Tew	
G-BNTP	Cessna 172N	Westnet Ltd	
G-BNTZ	Cameron N-77 balloon	Balloon Team	
G-BNUL	Cessna 152 II	Big Red Kite Ltd	
G-BNUN	Beech 95-58PA Baron	SMB Aviation Ltd	
G-BNUO	Beech 76 Duchess	Pace Projects Ltd and Professional Flight Simulation Ltd	
G-BNUT	Cessna 152 Turbo	Stapleford Flying Club Ltd	
G-BNUX	Hoffmann H-36 Dimona	Buckminster Dimona Syndicate	
G-BNUY	PA-38-112 Tomahawk II	D. C. Storey	
G-BNVB	AA-5A Cheetah	Pelican Project Management Ltd	
G-BNVE	PA-28-181 Archer II	Solent Flight Ltd	
G-BNVT	PA-28R-201T Turbo Arrow III	Victor Tango Group	
G-BNWA	Boeing 767-336ER	British Airways	

Notes	Reg.	Type	Owner or Operator
	G-BNWB	Boeing 767-336ER	British Airways
	G-BNWC	Boeing 767-336ER	British Airways
	G-BNWD	Boeing 767-336ER	British Airways
	G-BNWH	Boeing 767-336ER	British Airways
	G-BNWI	Boeing 767-336ER	British Airways
	G-BNWM	Boeing 767-336ER	British Airways
	G-BNWN	Boeing 767-336ER	British Airways
	G-BNWO	Boeing 767-336ER	British Airways
	G-BNWR	Boeing 767-336ER	British Airways
	G-BNWS	Boeing 767-336ER	British Airways
	G-BNWT	Boeing 767-336ER	British Airways
	G-BNWU	Boeing 767-336ER	British Airways
	G-BNWV	Boeing 767-336ER	British Airways
	G-BNWW	Boeing 767-336ER	British Airways
	G-BNWX	Boeing 767-336ER	British Airways
	G-BNWY	Boeing 767-336ER	British Airways
	G-BNWZ	Boeing 767-336ER	British Airways
	G-BNXE	PA-28-161 Warrior II	M. S. Brown
	G-BNXK	Nott-Cameron ULD-3 balloon	J. R. P. Nott (G-BLJN)
	G-BNXL	Glaser-Dirks DG.400	M. Lee
	G-BNXM	PA-18 Super Cub 95	C. J. Gowthorpe
	G-BNXT	PA-28-161 Warrior II	Falcon Flying Services
	G-BNXU	PA-28-161 Warrior II	Friendly Warrior Group
	G-BNXV	PA-38-112 Tomahawk	W. B. Bateson
	G-BNXX	SOCATA TB20 Trinidad	J. C. Taylor
	G-BNXZ	Thunder Ax7-77 balloon	Hale Hot Air Balloon Group
	G-BNYD	Bell 206B JetRanger 3	Toby Blackwell Ltd
	G-BNYK	PA-38-112 Tomahawk	Lomac Aviators Ltd
	G-BNYL	Cessna 152 II	V. J. Freeman
	G-BNYM	Cessna 172N	Kestrel Syndicate
	G-BNYO	Beech 76 Duchess	Multiflight Ltd
	G-BNYP	PA-28-181 Archer II	R. D. Cooper
	G-BNYZ	SNCAN Stampe SV.4E	Bianchi Film Aviation Services Ltd
	G-BNZB	PA-28-161 Warrior II	Falcon Flying Services Ltd
	G-BNZC	DHC.1 Chipmunk 22 (18671:671)	The Shuttleworth Collection
	G-BNZK	Thunder Ax7-77 balloon	T. D. Marsden
	G-BNZL	Rotorway Scorpion 133	J. R. Wraight
	G-BNZM	Cessna T.210N	A. J. M. Freeman
	G-BNZN	Cameron N-56 balloon	H. B. Pilo/Sweden
	G-BNZO	Rotorway Executive	J. S. David
	G-BNZV	PA-25 Pawnee 235	Aeroklub Alpski Letalski Center Lesce/Slovenia
	G-BNZZ	PA-28-161 Warrior II	Providence Aviation Ltd
	G-BOAA	BAC-Aérospatiale Concorde 102 ★	Museum Of Flight East Fortune (G-N94AA)
	G-BOAB	BAC-Aérospatiale Concorde 102 ★	Preserved at Heathrow (G-N94AB)
	G-BOAC	BAC-Aérospatiale Concorde 102 ★	Displayed in viewing area Manchester International (G-N94AC)
	G-BOAF	BAC-Aérospatiale Concorde 102 ★	Bristol Aero Collection/Filton (G-N94AF)
	G-BOAH	PA-28-161 Warrior II	Aircraft Engineers Ltd
	G-BOAI	Cessna 152 II	Aviation Spirit Ltd
	G-BOAL	Cameron V-65 balloon	N. H. & A. M. Ponsford
	G-BOAU	Cameron V-77 balloon	G. T. Barstow
	G-BOBA	PA-28R-201 Arrow III	Bravo Aviation Ltd
	G-BOBR	Cameron N-77 balloon	Trigger Concepts Ltd
	G-BOBT	Stolp SA.300 Starduster Too	G-BOBT Group
	G-BOBV	Cessna F.150M	S. Adlington & D. Harris
	G-BOBY	Monnett Sonerai II	R. G. Hallam
	G-BOCG	PA-34-200T Seneca II	Oxford Aviation Academy (Oxford) Ltd
	G-BOCI	Cessna 140A	Charlie India Aviators
	G-BOCK	Sopwith Triplane (replica) (N6290)	The Shuttleworth Collection
	G-BOCL	Slingsby T.67C	Richard Brinklow Aviation Ltd
	G-BOCM	Slingsby T.67C	Richard Brinklow Aviation Ltd
	G-BOCN	Robinson R22 Beta	Northmore Aviation Ltd
	G-BODB	PA-28-161 Warrior II	Sherburn Aero Club Ltd
	G-BODC	PA-28-161 Warrior II	Sherburn Aero Club Ltd
	G-BODD	PA-28-161 Warrior II	L. W. Scattergood
	G-BODE	PA-28-161 Warrior II	Sherburn Aero Club Ltd
	G-BODI	Glasair III Model SH-3R	A. P. Durston
	G-BODO	Cessna 152	Enstone Sales and Services Ltd
	G-BODP	PA-38-112 Tomahawk	B. Petrie
	G-BODR	PA-28-161 Warrior II	Airways Aero Associations Ltd
	G-BODS	PA-38-112 Tomahawk	Coulson Flying Services Ltd
	G-BODT	Jodel D.18	L. D. McPhillips

Reg.	Type	Owner or Operator	Notes
G-BODU	Scheibe SF.25C Falke	Hertfordshire County Scout Council	
G-BODY	Cessna 310R	Reconnaissance Ventures Ltd	
G-BODZ	Robinson R22 Beta	Langley Aviation Ltd	
G-BOEE	PA-28-181 Archer II	J. C. & G. M. Brinkley	
G-BOEH	Jodel DR.340	Piper Flyers Group	
G-BOEK	Cameron V-77 balloon	R. I. M. Kerr & ptnrs	
G-BOEM	Pitts S-2A	M. Murphy	
G-BOEN	Cessna 172M	R. Chynoransky & M. Novansky	
G-BOER	PA-28-161 Warrior II	B. Boult	
G-BOET	PA-28RT-201 Arrow IV	B. C. Chambers (G-IBEC)	
G-BOFC	Beech 76 Duchess	Magenta Ltd	
G-BOFF	Cameron N-77 balloon	R. S. McKibbin	
G-BOFL	Cessna 152 II	GEM Integrated Solutions Ltd	
G-BOFM	Cessna 152 II	GEM Integrated Solutions Ltd	
G-BOFW	Cessna A.150M	D. F. Donovan	
G-BOFY	PA-28 Cherokee 140	R. A. Brown	
G-BOFZ	PA-28-161 Warrior II	Northumbria Flying School Ltd	
G-BOGI	Robin DR.400/180	A. L. M. Shepherd	
G-BOGK	ARV Super 2	M. K. Field	
G-BOGM	PA-28RT-201T Turbo Arrow IV	RJP Aviation	
G-BOGO	PA-32R-301T Saratoga SP	Diff Air KFT	
G-BOGY	Cameron V-77 balloon	A. Reimann & P. Spellward	
G-BOHA	PA-28-161 Warrior II	Phoenix Aviation	
G-BOHD	Colt 77A balloon	D. B. Court	
G-BOHF	Thunder Ax8-84 balloon	J. A. Harris	
G-BOHH	Cessna 172N	ASL Aviation	
G-BOHI	Cessna 152 II	Cirrus Aviation Ltd	
G-BOHJ	Cessna 152 II	Airlaunch	
G-BOHM	PA-28 Cherokee 180	B. F. Keogh & R. A. Scott	
G-BOHO	PA-28-161 Warrior II	Egressus Flying Group	
G-BOHR	PA-28-151 Warrior	R. M. E. Garforth	
G-BOHT	PA-38-112 Tomahawk	St. George Flight Training Ltd	
G-BOHU	PA-38-112 Tomahawk	D. A. Whitmore	
G-BOHV	Wittman W.8 Tailwind	D. H. Greenwood	
G-BOHW	Van's RV-4	A. Mercy	
G-BOIB	Wittman W.10 Tailwind	C. R. Nash	
G-BOIC	PA-28R-201T Turbo Arrow III	M. J. Pearson	
G-BOID	Bellanca 7ECA Citabria	D. Mallinson	
G-BOIG	PA-28-161 Warrior II	D. Vallence-Pell	
G-BOIK	Air Command 503 Commander	F. G. Shepherd	
G-BOIL	Cessna 172N	Upperstack Ltd	
G-BOIO	Cessna 152	Sandham Aviation	
G-BOIR	Cessna 152	Shropshire Aero Club Ltd	
G-BOIT	SOCATA TB10 Tobago	G-BOIT Flying Group	
G-BOIV	Cessna 150M	India Victor Group	
G-BOIX	Cessna 172N	JR Flying Ltd	
G-BOIY	Cessna 172N	L. W. Scattergood	
G-BOIZ	PA-34-200T Seneca II	S. F. Tebby & Son	
G-BOJB	Cameron V-77 balloon	I. M. & S. D. Warner	
G-BOJI	PA-28RT-201 Arrow IV	Arrow Two Group	
G-BOJK	PA-34-220T Seneca III	Redhill Flying Club (G-BRUF)	
G-BOJM	PA-28-181 Archer II	R. P. Emms	
G-BOJS	Cessna 172P	Paul's Planes Ltd	
G-BOJU	Cameron N-77 balloon	M. A. Scholes	
G-BOJW	PA-28-161 Warrior II	J. R. Pearce	
G-BOJZ	PA-28-161 Warrior II	Falcon Flying Services	
G-BOKA	PA-28-201T Turbo Dakota	CBG Aviation Ltd	
G-BOKB	PA-28-161 Warrior II	Apollo Aviation Advisory Ltd	
G-BOKH	Whittaker MW7	I. Pearson	
G-BOKW	Bolkow Bo.208C Junior	L. S. Johnson	
G-BOKX	PA-28-161 Warrior II	Shenley Farms (Aviation) Ltd	
G-BOKY	Cessna 152 II	D. F. F. & J. E. Poore	
G-BOLB	Taylorcraft BC-12-65	C. E. Tudor	
G-BOLC	Fournier RF-6B-100	J. D. Cohen	
G-BOLD	PA-38-112 Tomahawk	G-BOLD Group	
G-BOLE	PA-38-112 Tomahawk	Double S Group	
G-BOLG	Bellanca 7KCAB Citabria	B. R. Pearson	
G-BOLI	Cessna 172P	Boli Flying Club	
G-BOLL	Lake LA-4 Skimmer	M. C. Holmes	
G-BOLN	Colt 21A balloon	G. Everett	
G-BOLO	Bell 206B JetRanger	Hargreaves Leasing Ltd	
G-BOLP	Colt 21A balloon	Spirit Balloons Ltd	
G-BOLR	Colt 21A balloon	C. J. Sanger-Davies	

Notes	Reg.	Type	Owner or Operator
	G-BOLS	FRED Srs 2	I. F. Vaughan
	G-BOLT	Rockwell Commander 114	I. R. Harnett
	G-BOLU	Robin R.3000/120	Mistral Aviation Ltd
	G-BOLV	Cessna 152 II	Synergy Aircraft Leasing Ltd
	G-BOLW	Cessna 152 II	G-BOLW Flying Group
	G-BOLY	Cessna 172N	Simair Ltd
	G-BOMB	Cassutt Racer IIIM	D. Hart
	G-BOMN	Cessna 150F	P. A. Chamberlaine
	G-BOMO	PA-38-112 Tomahawk II	APB Leasing Ltd
	G-BOMP	PA-28-181 Archer II	H. Merkado
	G-BOMS	Cessna 172N	Penchant Ltd
	G-BOMU	PA-28-181 Archer II	J. Sawyer
	G-BOMY	PA-28-161 Warrior II	BOMY Group
	G-BOMZ	PA-38-112 Tomahawk	G-BOMZ Aviation
	G-BONC	PA-28RT-201 Arrow IV	G-BONC Flying Group
	G-BONG	Enstrom F-28A-UK	Chobham Helicopters Ltd
	G-BONP	CFM Streak Shadow	G. J. Chater
	G-BONR	Cessna 172N	D. I. Craikl
	G-BONS	Cessna 172N	BONS Group
	G-BONT	Slingsby T.67M Mk II	Etico
	G-BONU	Slingsby T.67B	R. L. Brinklow
	G-BONW	Cessna 152 II	Lincoln Aero Club Ltd
	G-BONY	Denney Kitfox Model 1	R. Dunn & P. F. Hill
	G-BONZ	Beech V35B Bonanza	P. M. Coulten
	G-BOOB	Cameron N-65 balloon	P. J. Hooper
	G-BOOC	PA-18 Super Cub 150	S. A. C. Whitcombe
	G-BOOD	Slingsby T.31M Motor Tutor	R. G. Webster
	G-BOOE	GA-7 Cougar	R. J. Moller
	G-BOOF	PA-28-181 Archer II	H. Merkado
	G-BOOG	PA-28RT-201T Turbo Arrow IV	Simair Ltd
	G-BOOH	Jodel D.112	J. G. Bright
	G-BOOI	Cessna 152	Stapleford Flying Club Ltd
	G-BOOL	Cessna 172N	Just Plane Trading Ltd
	G-BOOW	Aerosport Scamp	D. A. Weldon/Ireland
	G-BOOX	Rutan LongEz	I. R. Wilde
	G-BOOZ	Cameron N-77 balloon	J. E. F. Kettlety
	G-BOPA	PA-28-181 Archer II	Flyco Ltd
	G-BOPC	PA-28-161 Warrior II	Aeros Ltd
	G-BOPD	Bede BD-4	S. T. Dauncey
	G-BOPH	Cessna TR.182RG	J. M. Mitchell
	G-BOPO	Brooklands OA.7 Optica	J. K. Edgley
	G-BOPR	Brooklands OA.7 Optica	Aeroelvira Ltd
	G-BOPT	Grob G.115	LAC Flying School
	G-BOPU	Grob G.115	LAC Flying School
	G-BORB	Cameron V-77 balloon	M. H. Wolff
	G-BORD	Thunder Ax7-77 balloon	D. D. Owen
	G-BORE	Colt 77A balloon	J. D. & C. J. Medcalf
	G-BORG	Campbell Cricket	R. L. Gilmore
	G-BORK	PA-28-161 Warrior II	The Warrior Group (G-IIIC)
	G-BORL	PA-28-161 Warrior II	Westair Flying School Ltd
	G-BORM	HS.748 Srs 2B ★	Airport Fire Service/Exeter
	G-BORN	Cameron N-77 balloon	I. Chadwick
	G-BORS	PA-28-181 Archer II	Aircraft Grouping Ltd
	G-BORW	Cessna 172P	Briter Aviation Ltd
	G-BORY	Cessna 150L	D. H. G. Penney
	G-BOSB	Thunder Ax7-77 balloon	A. M. Holly
	G-BOSD	PA-34-200T Seneca II	Bristol Flying Centre Ltd
	G-BOSE	PA-28-181 Archer II	G-BOSE Group
	G-BOSJ	Nord 3400 (124)	A. I. Milne
	G-BOSM	Jodel DR.253B	A. G. Stevens
	G-BOSN	AS.355F1 Twin Squirrel	Helicopter Services
	G-BOSO	Cessna A.152	J. S. Develin & Z. Islam
	G-BOTD	Cameron O-105 balloon	P. J. Beglan/France
	G-BOTF	PA-28-151 Warrior	G-BOTF Group
	G-BOTG	Cessna 152 II	Donington Aviation Ltd
	G-BOTH	Cessna 182Q	P. E. Gethin
	G-BOTI	PA-28-151 Warrior	Falcon Flying Services
	G-BOTK	Cameron O-105 balloon	N. Woodham
	G-BOTN	PA-28-161 Warrior II	Apollo Aviation Advisory
	G-BOTO	Bellanca 7ECA Citabria	G-BOTO Group
	G-BOTP	Cessna 150J	R. F. Finnis & C. P. Williams
	G-BOTU	Piper J-3C-65 Cub	T. L. Giles
	G-BOTV	PA-32RT-300 Lance II	Robin Lance Aviation Association Ltd

Reg.	Type	Owner or Operator	Notes
G-BOTW	Cameron V-77 balloon	M. R. Jeynes	
G-BOUE	Cessna 172N	P. Gray & G. N. R. Bradley	
G-BOUF	Cessna 172N	B. P. & M. I. Sneap	
G-BOUJ	Cessna 150M	UJ Flying Group	
G-BOUK	PA-34-200T Seneca II	C. J. & R. J. Barnes	
G-BOUL	PA-34-200T Seneca II	Oxford Aviation Academy (Oxford) Ltd	
G-BOUM	PA-34-200T Seneca II	Oxford Aviation Academy (Oxford) Ltd	
G-BOUN	Rand-Robinson KR-2	P. J. Brookman	
G-BOUT	Colomban MC.12 Cri-Cri	C. K. Farley	
G-BOUV	Bensen B.8MR	L. R. Phillips	
G-BOUZ	Cessna 150G	Atlantic Bridge Aviation Ltd	
G-BOVB	PA-15 Vagabond	J. R. Kimberley	
G-BOVK	PA-28-161 Warrior II	Multiflight Ltd	
G-BOVU	Stoddard-Hamilton Glasair III	B. R. Chaplin	
G-BOVX	Hughes 269C	Arrow Aviation Services Ltd	
G-BOWB	Cameron V-77 balloon	R. A. Benham	
G-BOWE	PA-34-200T Seneca II	Oxford Aviation Academy (Oxford) Ltd	
G-BOWM	Cameron V-56 balloon	R. S. Breakwell	
G-BOWN	PA-12 Super Cruiser	T. L. Giles	
G-BOWO	Cessna R.182	D. A. H. Morris (G-BOTR)	
G-BOWP	Jodel D.120A	J. M. Pearson	
G-BOWV	Cameron V-65 balloon	R. A. Harris	
G-BOWY	PA-28RT-201T Turbo Arrow IV	J. S. Develin & Z. Islam	
G-BOWZ	Bensen B.80V	W. W. Heslop	
G-BOXA	PA-28-161 Warrior II	Channel Islands Aero Club (Jersey) Ltd	
G-BOXC	PA-28-161 Warrior II	Bravo Aviation Ltd	
G-BOXG	Cameron O-77 balloon	R. A. Wicks	
G-BOXH	Pitts S-1S Special	G. R. Cotterell	
G-BOXJ	Piper J-3C-65 Cub	A. Bendkowski	
G-BOXR	GA-7 Cougar	Plane Talking Ltd	
G-BOXT	Hughes 269C	Goldenfly Ltd	
G-BOXU	AA-5B Tiger	Marcher Aviation	
G-BOXV	Pitts S-1S Special	C. Waddington	
G-BOXW	Cassutt Racer Srs IIIM	D. I. Johnson	
G-BOYB	Cessna A.152	Modi Aviation Ltd	
G-BOYC	Robinson R22 Beta	Yorkshire Helicopters	
G-BOYF	Sikorsky S-76B	Darley Stud Management Co Ltd	
G-BOYH	PA-28-151 Warrior	R. Nightingale	
G-BOYI	PA-28-161 Warrior II	G-BOYI Group	
G-BOYL	Cessna 152 II	Redhill Air Services Ltd	
G-BOYM	Cameron O-84 balloon	M. P. Ryan	
G-BOYO	Cameron V-20 balloon	J. L. Hilditch & T. Ward	
G-BOYP	Cessna 172N	I. D. & D. Brierley	
G-BOYV	PA-28RT-201T Turbo Arrow III	N. Halsall	
G-BOYX	Robinson R22 Beta	R. Towle	
G-BOZI	PA-28-161 Warrior II	Aerolease Ltd	
G-BOZN	Cameron N-77 balloon	Calarel Developments Ltd	
G-BOZO	AA-5B Tiger	J. Willis	
G-BOZR	Cessna 152 II	GEM Integrated Solutions Ltd	
G-BOZS	Pitts S-1C Special	S. D. Blakey	
G-BOZV	CEA DR.340 Major	C. J. Turner & S. D. Kent	
G-BOZW	Bensen B.8M	M. E. Wills	
G-BOZY	Cameron RTW-120 balloon	Magical Adventures Ltd	
G-BOZZ	AA-5B Tiger	Dolphin Property (Management) Ltd	
G-BPAA	Acro Advanced	B. O. & F. A. Smith	
G-BPAB	Cessna 150M	M. T. Farmer	
G-BPAF	PA-28-161 Warrior II	S. T. & T. W. Gilbert	
G-BPAJ	DH.82A Tiger Moth	P. A. Jackson (G-AOIX)	
G-BPAL	DHC.1 Chipmunk 22 (WG350)	K. F. & P. Tomsett (G-BCYE)	
G-BPAW	Cessna 150M	G-BPAW Group	
G-BPAY	PA-28-181 Archer II	D. A. C. Smith	
G-BPBJ	Cessna 152 II	W. Shaw & P. G. Haines	
G-BPBK	Cessna 152 II	Swiftair Maintenance Ltd	
G-BPBM	PA-28-161 Warrior II	Redhill Air Services Ltd	
G-BPBO	PA-28RT-201T Turbo Arrow IV	S. R. Eagle	
G-BPBP	Brügger MB.2 Colibri	D. A. Preston	
G-BPBW	Cameron O-105 balloon	A. Waters	
G-BPCA	BN-2B-26 Islander	Loganair Ltd (G-BLNX)	
G-BPCF	Piper J-3C-65 Cub	B. M. O'Brien	
G-BPCI	Cessna R.172K	N. A. Bairstol	
G-BPCK	PA-28-161 Warrior II	Compton Abbas Airfield Ltd	
G-BPCL	SA Bulldog Srs 120/128 (HKG-6)	Isohigh Ltd	

Notes	Reg.	Type	Owner or Operator
	G-BPCR	Mooney M.20K	T. & R. Harris
	G-BPCX	PA-28-236 Dakota	Blue Yonder Aviation Ltd
	G-BPDE	Colt 56A balloon	J. E. Weidema/Netherlands
	G-BPDG	Cameron V-77 balloon	H. Crawley
	G-BPDJ	Chris Tena Mini Coupe	J. J. Morrissey
	G-BPDM	CASA 1.131E Jungmann 2000(781-32)	J. D. Haslam
	G-BPDT	PA-28-161 Warrior II	Channel Islands Aero Club (Jersey) Ltd
	G-BPDV	Pitts S-1S Special	G-BPDV Syndicate
	G-BPEM	Cessna 150K	D. Wright
	G-BPEO	Cessna 152 II	Global Skies Ltd
	G-BPES	PA-38-112 Tomahawk II	Sherwood Flying Club Ltd
	G-BPEZ	Colt 77A balloon	J. W. Adkins
	G-BPFB	Colt 77A balloon	C. J. Freeman
	G-BPFC	Mooney M.20C	It's Plane Crazy Ltd
	G-BPFD	Jodel D.112	M. & S. Mills
	G-BPFH	PA-28-161 Warrior II	M. H. Kleiser
	G-BPFI	PA-28-181 Archer II	F. Teagle
	G-BPFL	Davis DA-2	P. E. Barker
	G-BPFM	Aeronca 7AC Champion	D. Boyce
	G-BPFZ	Cessna 152 II	Devon and Somerset Flight Training Ltd
	G-BPGC	Air Command 532 Elite	A. G. W. Davis
	G-BPGD	Cameron V-65 balloon	Gone With The Wind Ltd
	G-BPGE	Cessna U.206C	Scottish Parachute Club
	G-BPGF	Thunder Ax7-77 balloon	M. Schiavo
	G-BPGH	EAA Acro Sport II	M. F. Humphries
	G-BPGK	Aeronca 7AC Champion	D. A. Crompton & G. C. Holmes
	G-BPGT	Colt AS-80 Mk II airship	P. Porati/Italy
	G-BPGU	PA-28-181 Archer II	G. Underwood
	G-BPGZ	Cessna 150G	J. B. Scott
	G-BPHG	Robin DR.400/180	P. A. Giblett & B. Brenton
	G-BPHH	Cameron V-77 balloon	C. D. Aindow
	G-BPHI	PA-38-112 Tomahawk	J. S. Devlin & Z. Islam
	G-BPHJ	Cameron V-77 balloon	C. W. Brown
	G-BPHK	Whittaker MW7	J. S. Shufflebottom
	G-BPHL	PA-28-161 Warrior II	J. D. Swales
	G-BPHO	Taylorcraft BC-12	B. J. Swanton
	G-BPHP	Taylorcraft BC-12-65	Bluebird Group
	G-BPHR	DH.82A Tiger Moth (A17-48)	N. Parry
	G-BPHU	Thunder Ax7-77 balloon	R. P. Waite
	G-BPHX	Cessna 140	M. J. Medland
	G-BPHZ	MS.505 Criquet (DM+BK)	Aero Vintage Ltd
	G-BPIF	Bensen-Parsons 2-place gyroplane	B. J. L. P. & W. J. A. L. de Saar
	G-BPII	Denney Kitfox	T. P. Lowe
	G-BPIK	PA-38-112 Tomahawk	Carlisle Flight Training Ltd
	G-BPIP	Slingsby T.31 Motor Cadet III	V. K. Meers
	G-BPIR	Scheibe SF.25E Super Falke	A. P. Askwith
	G-BPIT	Robinson R22 Beta	NA Air Ltd
	G-BPIU	PA-28-161 Warrior II	Golf India Uniform Group
	G-BPIV	B.149 Bolingbroke Mk IVT (R3821)	Blenheim (Duxford) Ltd
	G-BPIZ	AA-5B Tiger	D. A. Horsley
	G-BPJB	Schweizer 269C	Escola de Aviacao Aerocondor SA
	G-BPJG	PA-18 Super Cub 150	M. W. Stein
	G-BPJK	Colt 77A balloon	P. Lavelle
	G-BPJP	PA-28-161 Cadet	Aviation Rentals
	G-BPJS	PA-28-161 Cadet	Plane Talking Ltd
	G-BPJU	PA-28-161 Cadet	Aviation Rentals
	G-BPJW	Cessna A.150K	G. Duck
	G-BPJZ	Cameron O-160 balloon	M. L. Gabb
	G-BPKF	Grob G.115	Swiftair Maintenance Ltd
	G-BPKK	Denney Kitfox Mk 1	C. P. Moss
	G-BPKM	PA-28-161 Warrior II	R. Cass
	G-BPKR	PA-28-151 Warrior	Redhill Air Services Ltd
	G-BPKT	Piper J.5A Cub Cruiser	A. J. Greenslade
	G-BPLH	Jodel DR.1051	C. K. Farley
	G-BPLM	AIA Stampe SV.4C	C. J. Jessonl
	G-BPLR	BN-2B-20 Islander	Hebridean Air Services Ltd
	G-BPLV	Cameron V-77 balloon	V. Grenier/France
	G-BPLZ	Hughes 369HS	M. A. & R. J. Fawcett
	G-BPMB	Maule M5-235C Lunar Rocket	Maule Flying group
	G-BPME	Cessna 152 II	Hinde Holdings Ltd
	G-BPMF	PA-28-151 Warrior	Mike Foxtrot Group
	G-BPML	Cessna 172M	N. A. Bilton
	G-BPMM	Champion 7ECA Citabria	H. J. Taggart

Reg.	Type	Owner or Operator	Notes
G-BPMU	Nord 3202B	E. C. Murgatroyd (G-BIZJ)	
G-BPMW	QAC Quickie Q.2	P. M. Wright (G-OICI/G-OGKN)	
G-BPMX	ARV Super 2	R. A. Collins	
G-BPNI	Robinson R22 Beta	Heliflight (UK) Ltd	
G-BPNO	Zlin Z.326 Trener Master	J. A. S. Bailey & S. T. Logan	
G-BPOA	Gloster Meteor T.7 (WF877) ★	39 Restoration Group	
G-BPOB	Sopwith Camel F.1 (replica) (B2458:R)	Flying Aces Movie Aircraft Collection	
G-BPOM	PA-28-161 Warrior II	POM Flying Group	
G-BPOS	Cessna 150M	S. G. Lewis	
G-BPOT	PA-28-181 Archer II	P. S. Simpson	
G-BPOU	Luscombe 8A Silvaire	J. L. Grayer	
G-BPPA	Cameron O-65 balloon	Rix Petroleum Ltd	
G-BPPE	PA-38-112 Tomahawk	First Air Ltd	
G-BPPF	PA-38-112 Tomahawk	Bristol Strut Flying Group	
G-BPPJ	Cameron A-180 balloon	D. J. Farrar	
G-BPPK	PA-28-151 Warrior	Jazzlink Ltd	
G-BPPO	Luscombe 8A Silvaire	P. Dyer	
G-BPPP	Cameron V-77 balloon	Sarnia Balloon Group	
G-BPPY	Hughes 269B	M. D. Leeney	
G-BPPZ	Taylorcraft BC-12D	G. C. Smith	
G-BPRA	Aeronca 11AC Chief	C. S. Tolchard	
G-BPRC	Cameron 77 Elephant SS balloon	A. Schneider/Germany	
G-BPRD	Pitts S-1C Special	Parrot Aerobatic Group	
G-BPRI	AS.355F1 Twin Squirrel	MW Helicopters Ltd (G-TVPA)	
G-BPRJ	AS.355F1 Twin Squirrel	PLM Dollar Group Ltd	
G-BPRL	AS.355F1 Twin Squirrel	MW Helicopters Ltd	
G-BPRM	Cessna F.172L	BJ Aviation Ltd (G-AZKG)	
G-BPRN	PA-28-161 Warrior II	Air Navigation & Trading Co Ltd	
G-BPRX	Aeronca 11AC Chief	J. E. S. Turner	
G-BPRY	PA-28-161 Warrior II	White Wings Aviation Ltd	
G-BPSH	Cameron V-77 balloon	P. G. Hossack	
G-BPSJ	Thunder Ax6-56 balloon	V. Hyland	
G-BPSL	Cessna 177	K. S. Herbert	
G-BPSO	Cameron N-90 balloon	J. Oberprieler/Germany	
G-BPSR	Cameron V-77 balloon	K. J. A. Maxwell	
G-BPSS	Cameron A-120 balloon	Anglian Countryside Balloons Ltd	
G-BPTA	Stinson 108-2	M. L. Ryan	
G-BPTD	Cameron V-77 balloon	J. Lippett	
G-BPTE	PA-28-181 Archer II	J. S. Develin & Z. Islam	
G-BPTG	Rockwell Commander 112TC	B. Ogunyemi	
G-BPTI	SOCATA TB20 Trinidad	N. Davis	
G-BPTL	Cessna 172N	D. A. Gathercole	
G-BPTS	CASA 1.131E Jungmann 1000 (E3B-153:781-75)	E. P. Parkin	
G-BPTU	Cessna 152	A. M. Alam	
G-BPTV	Bensen B.8	C. Munro	
G-BPTZ	Robinson R22 Beta	Kuki Helicopter Sales Ltd and S. J. Nicholls	
G-BPUA	EAA Sport Biplane	E. J. & M. P. Hill	
G-BPUB	Cameron V-31 balloon	M. T. Evans	
G-BPUF	Thunder Ax6-56Z balloon	R. C. & M. A. Trimble (G-BHRL)	
G-BPUL	PA-18 Super Cub 150	C. D. Duthy-James	
G-BPUM	Cessna R.182RG	R. C. Chapman	
G-BPUP	Whittaker MW7	J. H. Beard	
G-BPUR	Piper J-3L-65 Cub ★	Hawker Restorations Ltd	
G-BPUU	Cessna 140	D. R. Speight	
G-BPUW	Colt 90A balloon	S. Sonnenberg/Germany	
G-BPVA	Cessna 172F	S. Lancashire Flyers Group	
G-BPVE	Bleriot IX (replica) (1) ★	Bianchi Aviation Film Services Ltd/Booker	
G-BPVH	Cub Aircraft J-3C-65 Prospector	D. E. Cooper-Maguire	
G-BPVI	PA-32R-301 Saratoga SP	M. T. Coppen	
G-BPVK	Varga 2150A Kachina	D. W. Parfrey	
G-BPVM	Cameron V-77 balloon	J. Dyer	
G-BPVN	PA-32R-301T Turbo Saratoga SP	R. Weston	
G-BPVO	Cassutt Racer IIIM	K. P. Rusling	
G-BPVW	CASA 1.131E Jungmann 2000	C. & J-W. Labeij/Netherlands	
G-BPVZ	Luscombe 8E Silvaire	J. W. Macdonald, S. M. Thomas & A. P. Wilkie	
G-BPWB	Sikorsky S-61N	Bristow Helicopters Ltd/HM Coastguard	
G-BPWC	Cameron V-77 balloon	R. F. Davey	
G-BPWE	PA-28-161 Warrior II	RPR Associates Ltd	
G-BPWG	Cessna 150M	GB Pilots Wilsford Group	
G-BPWI	Bell 206B JetRanger 3	Warren Aviation	
G-BPWK	Sportavia Fournier RF-5B	G-BPWK Flying Group	
G-BPWL	PA-25 Pawnee 235	M. H. Sims	

Notes	Reg.	Type	Owner or Operator
	G-BPWM	Cessna 150L	P. D. Button
	G-BPWN	Cessna 150L	A. J. & N. J. Bissex
	G-BPWP	Rutan LongEz (modified)	D. A. Field
	G-BPWR	Cessna R.172K	J. A. & D. T. A. Rees
	G-BPWS	Cessna 172P	Chartstone Ltd
	G-BPXA	PA-28-181 Archer II	Cherokee Flying Group
	G-BPXE	Enstrom 280C Shark	A. Healy
	G-BPXG	Colt 45A balloon	Zebedee Balloon Service Ltd
	G-BPXJ	PA-28RT-201T Turbo Arrow IV	J. & M. Holubecki-France
	G-BPXX	PA-34-200T Seneca II	Yorkshire Aviation Ltd
	G-BPXY	Aeronca 11AC Chief	P. L. Turner
	G-BPYJ	Wittman W.8 Tailwind	J. P. & Y. Mills
	G-BPYL	Hughes 369D	Morcorp (BVI) Ltd
	G-BPYN	Piper J-3C-65 Cub	The Aquila Group
	G-BPYR	PA-31-310 Turbo Navajo	Excel Aviation Ltd
	G-BPYS	Cameron O-77 balloon	D. J. Goldsmith
	G-BPYT	Cameron V-77 balloon	M. H. Redman
	G-BPYV	Cameron V-77 balloon	R. J. Shortall
	G-BPYY	Cameron A-180 balloon	G. D. Fitzpatrick
	G-BPYZ	Thunder Ax7-77 balloon	J. E. Astall
	G-BPZA	Luscombe 8A Silvaire	M. J. Wright
	G-BPZB	Cessna 120	Cessna 120 Group
	G-BPZC	Luscombe 8A Silvaire	C. C. & J. M. Lovell
	G-BPZD	SNCAN NC.858S	Zula Delta Syndicate
	G-BPZE	Luscombe 8E Silvaire	M. A. Watts
	G-BPZM	PA-28RT-201 Arrow IV	Airways Flight Training (Exeter) Ltd (G-ROYW/G-CRTI)
	G-BPZP	Robin DR.400/180R	S. G. Jones
	G-BPZS	Colt 105A balloon	L. E. Giles
	G-BPZU	Scheibe SF.25C Falke	Southdown Gliding Club Ltd
	G-BPZY	Pitts S-1C Special	J. S. Mitchell
	G-BPZZ	Thunder Ax8-105 balloon	Capricorn Balloons Ltd
	G-BRAA	Pitts S-1C Special	R. J. Hodder
	G-BRAK	Cessna 172N	Falcon Flying Services Ltd
	G-BRAM	Mikoyan MiG-21PF (503) ★	FAST Museum/Farnborough
	G-BRAR	Aeronca 7AC Champion	R. B. Armitage
	G-BRBA	PA-28-161 Warrior II	B. Willis
	G-BRBB	PA-28-161 Warrior II	M. A. & A. J. Bell
	G-BRBC	NA T-6G Texan	A. P. Murphy
	G-BRBD	PA-28-151 Warrior	Compton Abbas Airfield Ltd
	G-BRBE	PA-28-161 Warrior II	KN Singles and Twins Aviation
	G-BRBG	PA-28 Cherokee 180	P. M. Carter
	G-BRBH	Cessna 150H	J. Maffia & H. Merkado
	G-BRBI	Cessna 172N	Skyhawk Flying Group
	G-BRBJ	Cessna 172M	N. Foster
	G-BRBK	Robin DR.400/180	R. Kemp
	G-BRBL	Robin DR.400/180	Upavon Chipmunk Group
	G-BRBM	Robin DR.400/180	R. W. Davies
	G-BRBN	Pitts S-1S Special	G-BRBN Flying Group
	G-BRBO	Cameron V-77 balloon	M. B. Murby
	G-BRBP	Cessna 152	Just Plane Trading Ltd
	G-BRBV	Piper J-4A Cub Coupe	P. Clarke
	G-BRBW	PA-28 Cherokee 140	Air Navigation and Trading Co Ltd
	G-BRBX	PA-28-181 Archer II	Trent 199 Flying Group
	G-BRCA	Jodel D.112	R. C. Jordan
	G-BRCE	Pitts S-1C Special	M. P. & S. T. Barnard
	G-BRCF	Montgomerie-Bensen B.8MR	J. S. Walton
	G-BRCJ	Cameron H-20 balloon	P. A. Sweatman
	G-BRCM	Cessna 172L	S. G. E. Plessis & D. C. C. Handley
	G-BRCO	Cameron H-20 balloon	P. Lawman
	G-BRCT	Denney Kitfox Mk 2	M. L. Roberts
	G-BRCV	Aeronca 7AC Champion	P. I. and D. M. Morgans
	G-BRCW	Aeronca 11AC Chief	R. B. Griffin
	G-BRDD	Avions Mudry CAP-10B	T. A. Smith
	G-BRDF	PA-28-161 Warrior II	White Waltham Airfield Ltd
	G-BRDG	PA-28-161 Warrior II	Falcon Flying Services
	G-BRDJ	Luscombe 8A Silvaire	P. G. Stewart
	G-BRDM	PA-28-161 Warrior II	White Waltham Airfield Ltd
	G-BRDO	Cessna 177B	Cardinal Aviation
	G-BRDT	Cameron DP-70 airship	Balloon Promotion SAS
	G-BRDV	Viking Wood Products Spitfire Prototype replica (K5054) ★	Solent Sky, Southampton

Reg.	Type	Owner or Operator	Notes
G-BRDW	PA-24 Comanche 180	I. P. Gibson	
G-BREA	Bensen B.8MR	D. J. Martin	
G-BREB	Piper J-3C-65 Cub	J. R. Wraight	
G-BREH	Cameron V-65 balloon	S. E. & V. D. Hurst	
G-BREL	Cameron O-77 balloon	R. A. Patey	
G-BREP	PA-28RT-201 Arrow IV	Jetstream Executive Travel Ltd	
G-BREU	Montgomerie-Bensen B.8MR	J. S. Firth	
G-BREX	Cameron O-84 balloon	P. Hegarty	
G-BREY	Taylorcraft BC-12D	BREY Group	
G-BREZ	Cessna 172M	L. A. Mills	
G-BRFB	Rutan LongEz	A. R. Oliver	
G-BRFC	Percival P.57 Sea Prince T.Mk.1 (WP321)	A. & G. A. Gainsford-Dixon	
G-BRFF	Colt 90A balloon	Amber Valley Aviation	
G-BRFI	Aeronca 7DC Champion	A. C. Lines	
G-BRFJ	Aeronca 11AC Chief	J. M. Mooney	
G-BRFL	PA-38-112 Tomahawk	A. D. Pocock	
G-BRFM	PA-28-161 Warrior II	British Disabled Flying Association	
G-BRFO	Cameron V-77 balloon	Hedge Hoppers Balloon Group	
G-BRFW	Montgomerie-Bensen B.8 2-seat	A. J. Barker	
G-BRFX	Pazmany PL.4A	D. E. Hills	
G-BRGD	Cameron O-84 balloon	R. G. Russell	
G-BRGE	Cameron N-90 balloon	Oakfield Farm Products Ltd	
G-BRGF	Luscombe 8E Silvaire	Luscombe Flying Group	
G-BRGI	PA-28 Cherokee 180	R. A. Buckfield	
G-BRGT	PA-32 Cherokee Six 260	D. A. Hitchcock	
G-BRGW	Gardan GY-201 Minicab	R. G. White	
G-BRHA	PA-32RT-300 Lance II	Lance G-BRHA Group	
G-BRHG	Colt 90A balloon	R. D. Allen	
G-BRHO	PA-34-200 Seneca	Andrews Professional Colour Laboratories Ltd	
G-BRHP	Aeronca O-58B Grasshopper (31923)	C. J. Willis/Italy	
G-BRHR	PA-38-112 Tomahawk	D. C. Hanss	
G-BRHX	Luscombe 8E Silvaire	J. Lakin	
G-BRHY	Luscombe 8E Silvaire	A. R. W. Taylor	
G-BRIE	Cameron N-77 balloon	S. F. Redman	
G-BRIH	Taylorcraft BC-12D	IH Flying Group	
G-BRIJ	Taylorcraft F-19	M. W, Olliver	
G-BRIK	T.66 Nipper 3	P. R. Bentley	
G-BRIL	Piper J-5A Cub Cruiser	D. J. Bone	
G-BRIO	Turner Super T-40A	S. Bidwell	
G-BRIR	Cameron V-56 balloon	H. G. Davies & C. Dowd	
G-BRIV	SOCATA TB9 Tampico Club	S. J. Taft	
G-BRIY	Taylorcraft DF-65 (42-58678:IY)	S. R. Potts	
G-BRJA	Luscombe 8A Silvaire	A. D. Keen	
G-BRJC	Cessna 120	M. J. Medland	
G-BRJK	Luscombe 8A Silvaire	C. J. L. Peat & M. Richardson	
G-BRJL	PA-15 Vagabond	A. R. Williams	
G-BRJN	Pitts S-1C Special	W. Chapel	
G-BRJT	Cessna 150H	Juliet Tango Group	
G-BRJV	PA-28-161 Cadet	Northumbria Flying School Ltd	
G-BRJX	Rand-Robinson KR-2	J. R. Bell	
G-BRJY	Rand-Robinson KR-2	R. E. Taylor	
G-BRKC	Auster J/1 Autocrat	J. W. Conlon	
G-BRKH	PA-28-236 Dakota	T. A. White	
G-BRKR	Cessna 182R	A. R. D. Brooker	
G-BRKW	Cameron V-77 balloon	T. J. Parker	
G-BRKY	Viking Dragonfly Mk II	G. D. Price	
G-BRLB	Air Command 532 Elite	F. G. Shepherd	
G-BRLF	Campbell Cricket (replica)	J. L. G. McLane	
G-BRLG	PA-28RT-201T Turbo Arrow IV	P. Lodge & J. G. McVey	
G-BRLI	Piper J-5A Cub Cruiser	Little Bear Ltd	
G-BRLL	Cameron A-105 balloon	P. A. Sweatman	
G-BRLO	PA-38-112 Tomahawk	St. George Flight Training Ltd	
G-BRLP	PA-38-112 Tomahawk	Highland Aviation Training Ltd	
G-BRLR	Cessna 150G	Blue Skys Aviation (NE) Ltd	
G-BRLS	Thunder Ax7-77 balloon	E. C. Meek	
G-BRMA	WS-51 Dragonfly HR.5 (WG719) ★	IHM/Weston-super-Mare	
G-BRMB	B.192 Belvedere HC.1	IHM/Weston-super-Mare	
G-BRME	PA-28-181 Archer II	Blue Sky Investments Ltd	
G-BRML	PA-38-112 Tomahawk	J. S. Willcocks	
G-BRMT	Cameron V-31 balloon	B. Reed	
G-BRMU	Cameron V-77 balloon	K. J. & G. R. Ibbotson	
G-BRMV	Cameron O-77 balloon	P. D. Griffiths	

Notes	Reg.	Type	Owner or Operator
	G-BRNC	Cessna 150M	Penny Hydraulics Ltd
	G-BRND	Cessna 152 II	T. M. & M. L. Jones
	G-BRNE	Cessna 152 II	Redhill Air Services Ltd
	G-BRNK	Cessna 152 II	D. C. & M. Bonsall
	G-BRNN	Cessna 152 II	Eastern Air Executive Ltd
	G-BRNT	Robin DR.400/180	C. E. Ponsford & ptnrs
	G-BRNU	Robin DR.400/180	November Uniform Travel Syndicate Ltd
	G-BRNV	PA-28-181 Archer II	N. S. Lyndhurst
	G-BRNW	Cameron V-77 balloon	N. Robertson & G. Smith
	G-BRNX	PA-22 Tri-Pacer 150	S. N. Askey
	G-BROE	Cameron N-65 balloon	A. I. Attwood
	G-BROG	Cameron V-65 balloon	R. Kunert
	G-BROI	CFM Streak Shadow Srs SA	R. C. Ford
	G-BROJ	Colt 31A balloon	N. J. Langley
	G-BROO	Luscombe 8E Silvaire	P. R. Bush
	G-BROR	Piper J-3C-65 Cub	White Hart Flying Group
	G-BROX	Robinson R22 Beta	J. G. Burgess
	G-BROY	Cameron V-77 balloon	C. B. McDougall
	G-BROZ	PA-18 Super Cub 150	P. G. Kynsey
	G-BRPE	Cessna 120	W. B. Bateson
	G-BRPF	Cessna 120	G. A. Robson
	G-BRPG	Cessna 120	I. C. Lomax
	G-BRPH	Cessna 120	J. A. Cook
	G-BRPK	PA-28 Cherokee 140	G-BRPK Group
	G-BRPL	PA-28-140 Cherokee	Aircraft Grouping Ltd
	G-BRPM	T.66 Nipper 3	J. H. H. Turner
	G-BRPP	Brookland Hornet (modified)	B. J. L. P. & W. J. A. L. de Saar
	G-BRPR	Aeronca O-58B Grasshopper (31952)	A. F. Kutz
	G-BRPS	Cessna 177B	E. Janssen & A. Lietaert
	G-BRPT	Rans S.10 Sakota	M. D. Moaby
	G-BRPU	Beech 76 Duchess	Plane Talking Ltd
	G-BRPV	Cessna 152	Eastern Air Executive Ltd
	G-BRPX	Taylorcraft BC-12D	G-BRPX Group
	G-BRPY	PA-15 Vagabond	J. & V. Hobday
	G-BRPZ	Luscombe 8A Silvaire	C. A. Flint
	G-BRRA	VS.361 Spitfire LF.IX	P. M. Andrews
	G-BRRB	Luscombe 8E Silvaire	J. Nicholls
	G-BRRF	Cameron O-77 balloon	K. P. & G. J. Storey
	G-BRRK	Cessna 182Q	Werewolf Aviation Ltd
	G-BRRR	Cameron V-77 balloon	K. P. & G. J. Storey
	G-BRRU	Colt 90A balloon	Reach For The Sky Ltd
	G-BRRY	Robinson R22 Beta	Alan Mann Aviation Group Ltd
	G-BRSA	Cameron N-56 balloon	J. F. Till
	G-BRSD	Cameron V-77 balloon	M. E. Granger
	G-BRSE	PA-28-161 Warrior II	Falcon Flying Services Ltd
	G-BRSF	VS.361 Spitfire HF.9c (RR232)	M. B. Phillips
	G-BRSJ	PA-38-112 Tomahawk II	APB Leasing Ltd
	G-BRSL	Cameron N-56 balloon	S. Budd
	G-BRSP	Air Command 532 Elite	G. M. Hobman
	G-BRSW	Luscombe 8A Silvaire	Bloody Mary Aviation
	G-BRSX	PA-15 Vagabond	M. R. Holden
	G-BRSY	Hatz CB-1	Eaglescott Hatz Biplane Group
	G-BRTD	Cessna 152 II	152 Group
	G-BRTJ	Cessna 150F	A. G. Arthur
	G-BRTL	Hughes 369E	Road Tech Computer Systems Ltd
	G-BRTP	Cessna 152 II	R. Lee
	G-BRTT	Schweizer 269C	Fairthorpe Ltd
	G-BRTV	Cameron O-77 balloon	S. D. Wrighton
	G-BRTW	Glaser-Dirks DG.400	I. J. Carruthers
	G-BRTX	PA-28-151 Warrior	Spectrum Flying Group
	G-BRUB	PA-28-161 Warrior II	Flytrek Ltd
	G-BRUD	PA-28-181 Archer II	FlyBPL.com
	G-BRUG	Luscombe 8E Silvaire	N. W. Barratt
	G-BRUH	Colt 105A balloon	D. C. Chipping/Portugal
	G-BRUJ	Boeing Stearman A.75N1 (6136:205)	R. M. Hughes
	G-BRUM	Cessna A.152	A. J. Gomes
	G-BRUN	Cessna 120	A. R. M. Eagle, J. A. Longworth & J. Peake (G-BRDH)
	G-BRUO	Taylor JT.1 Monoplane	S. T. S. Bygrave
	G-BRUV	Cameron V-77 balloon	T. W. & R. F. Benbrook
	G-BRUX	PA-44-180 Seminole	M. Ali
	G-BRVB	Stolp SA.300 Starduster Too	G-VB Group
	G-BRVE	Beech D.17S	Patina Ltd

Reg.	Type	Owner or Operator	Notes
G-BRVF	Colt 77A balloon	J. Adkins	
G-BRVG	NA SNJ-7 Texan (27)	D. Gilmour/Intrepid Aviation Co	
G-BRVH	Smyth Model S Sidewinder	B. D. Deleporte	
G-BRVI	Robinson R22 Beta	York Helicopters	
G-BRVJ	Slingsby T.31 Motor Cadet III	B. Outhwaite	
G-BRVL	Pitts S-1C Special	M. F. Pocock	
G-BRVN	Thunder Ax7-77 balloon	D. L. Beckwith	
G-BRVO	AS.350B Ecureuil	Rotorhire LLP	
G-BRVY	Thunder Ax8-90 balloon	G. E. Morris	
G-BRVZ	Jodel D.117	L. Holland	
G-BRWA	Aeronca 7AC Champion	J. R. Edwards	
G-BRWB	NA T-6G Texan (526)	R. Clifford	
G-BRWD	Robinson R22 Beta	Hughes Plant Ltd	
G-BRWP	CFM Streak Shadow	R. Biffin	
G-BRWR	Aeronca 11AC Chief	A. W. Crutcher	
G-BRWT	Scheibe SF.25C Falke	Booker Gliding Club Ltd	
G-BRWU	Luton LA-4A Minor	R. B. Webber	
G-BRWV	Brügger MB.2 Colibri	M. P. Wakem	
G-BRWX	Cessna 172P	R. A. Brown & A. C. Dove	
G-BRWZ	Cameron 90 Macaw SS balloon	Forbes Global Inc	
G-BRXA	Cameron O-120 balloon	R. J. Mansfield	
G-BRXD	PA-28-181 Archer II	D. D. Stone	
G-BRXE	Taylorcraft BC-12D	B. T. Morgan & W. J. Durrad	
G-BRXF	Aeronca 11AC Chief	Aeronca Flying Group	
G-BRXG	Aeronca 7AC Champion	X-Ray Golf Flying Group	
G-BRXH	Cessna 120	BRXH Group	
G-BRXL	Aeronca 11AC Chief (42-78044)	P. L. Green	
G-BRXN	Montgomerie-Bensen B.8MR	C. M. Frerk	
G-BRXP	SNCAN Stampe SV.4C (modified)	T. Brown	
G-BRXS	Howard Special T Minus	F. A. Bakir	
G-BRXV	Robinson R22 Beta	Heliflight (UK) Ltd	
G-BRXW	PA-24 Comanche 260	Oak Group	
G-BRXY	Pietenpol Air Camper	P. S. Ganczakowski	
G-BRZA	Cameron O-77 balloon	S. Nother	
G-BRZB	Cameron A-105 balloon	Headland Services Ltd	
G-BRZD	Hapi Cygnet SF-2A	C. I. Coghill	
G-BRZG	Enstrom F-28A	Duxburys Ltd	
G-BRZI	Cameron N-180 balloon	Eastern Balloon Rides	
G-BRZK	Stinson 108-2	Voyager G-BRZK Syndicate	
G-BRZL	Pitts S-1D Special	T. R. G. Barnby	
G-BRZS	Cessna 172P	YP Flying Group	
G-BRZW	Rans S.10 Sakota	D. L. Davies	
G-BRZX	Pitts S-1S Special	Zulu Xray Group	
G-BRZZ	CFM Streak Shadow	J. A. Weston	
G-BSAI	Stoddard-Hamilton Glasair III	K. J. & P. J. Whitehead	
G-BSAJ	CASA 1.131E Jungmann 2000	P. G. Kynsey	
G-BSAK	Colt 21A balloon	M. D. Mitchell	
G-BSAS	Cameron V-65 balloon	P. Donkin	
G-BSAV	Thunder Ax7-77 balloon	I. G. & C. A. Lloyd	
G-BSAW	PA-28-161 Warrior II	Haimoss Ltd	
G-BSAZ	Denney Kitfox Mk 2	A. J. Lloyd & ptnrs	
G-BSBA	PA-28-161 Warrior II	Falcon Flying Services Ltd	
G-BSBG	CCF Harvard IV (20310:310)	A. P. St. John	
G-BSBI	Cameron O-77 balloon	D. M. Billing	
G-BSBR	Cameron V-77 balloon	R. P. Wade	
G-BSBT	Piper J-3C-65 Cub	A. R. Elliott	
G-BSBV	Rans S.10 Sakota	S. Bain	
G-BSBW	Bell 206B JetRanger 3	Castle Air Ltd	
G-BSBZ	Cessna 150M	P. J. Gallagher & P. Gallogly	
G-BSCC	Colt 105A balloon	A. F. Selby	
G-BSCE	Robinson R22 Beta	Carpets Direct (GB) Ltd	
G-BSCG	Denney Kitfox Mk 2	A. Levitt	
G-BSCH	Denney Kitfox Mk 2	G. R. Moore	
G-BSCI	Colt 77A balloon	J. L. & S. Wrigglesworth	
G-BSCK	Cameron H-24 balloon	J. D. Shapland	
G-BSCM	Denney Kitfox Mk 2	H. D. Colliver (G-MSCM)	
G-BSCN	SOCATA TB20 Trinidad	B. W. Dye	
G-BSCO	Thunder Ax7-77 balloon	F. J. Whalley	
G-BSCP	Cessna 152 II	Moray Flying Club (1990) Ltd	
G-BSCS	PA-28-181 Archer II	Wingtask 1995 Ltd	
G-BSCV	PA-28-161 Warrior II	Southwood Flying Group	
G-BSCW	Taylorcraft BC-65	G. Johnson	

Notes	Reg.	Type	Owner or Operator
	G-BSCX	Thunder Ax8-105 balloon	S. Charlish
	G-BSCY	PA-28-151 Warrior	Take Flight Aviation Ltd
	G-BSCZ	Cessna 152 II	The RAF Halton Aeroplane Club Ltd
	G-BSDA	Taylorcraft BC-12D	D. G. Edwards
	G-BSDD	Denney Kitfox Mk 2	D. C. Crawley
	G-BSDH	Robin DR.400/180	R. L. Brucciani
	G-BSDI	Corben Junior Ace Model E	G. N. Holland
	G-BSDJ	Piper J-4E Cub Coupe	D. M. Hook
	G-BSDK	Piper J-5A Cub Cruiser	J. E. Mead
	G-BSDL	SOCATA TB10 Tobago	Delta Lima Group
	G-BSDN	PA-34-200T Seneca II	Jetstream Executive Travel Ltd
	G-BSDO	Cessna 152 II	J. Vickers
	G-BSDP	Cessna 152 II	Paul's Planes Ltd
	G-BSDS	Boeing Stearman E75 (118)	L. W. Scattergood
	G-BSDW	Cessna 182P	Parker Diving Ltd
	G-BSDZ	Enstrom 280FX	Rotormotive Ltd
	G-BSED	PA-22 Tri-Pacer 160 (modified)	M. D. N. Fisher
	G-BSEE	Rans S.9	R. P. Hothersall
	G-BSEF	PA-28 Cherokee 180	I. D. Wakeling
	G-BSEG	Ken Brock KB-2 gyroplane	S. J. M. Ledingham
	G-BSEJ	Cessna 150M	C. L. Day
	G-BSEK	Robinson R22	S. J. Strange
	G-BSEL	Slingsby T.61G Super Falke	D. G. Holley
	G-BSEP	Cessna 172	EPAviation
	G-BSER	PA-28 Cherokee 160	Yorkair Ltd
	G-BSEU	PA-28-181 Archer II	K. R. Taylor
	G-BSEV	Cameron O-77 balloon	P. B. Kenington
	G-BSEX	Cameron A-180 balloon	Heart of England Balloons
	G-BSEY	Beech A36 Bonanza	P. Malam-Wilson
	G-BSFA	Aero Designs Pulsar	P. F. Lorriman
	G-BSFD	Piper J-3C-65 Cub	P. E. S. Latham
	G-BSFE	PA-38-112 Tomahawk II	ACS Aviation Ltd
	G-BSFF	Robin DR.400/180R	Lasham Gliding Society Ltd
	G-BSFP	Cessna 152T	The Pilot Centre Ltd
	G-BSFR	Cessna 152 II	Galair Ltd
	G-BSFV	Woods Woody Pusher	M. G. Parsons
	G-BSFW	PA-15 Vagabond	J. R. Kimberley
	G-BSFX	Denney Kitfox Mk 2	F. Colman
	G-BSGB	Gaertner Ax4 Skyranger balloon	B. Gaertner
	G-BSGD	PA-28 Cherokee 180	R. J. Cleverley
	G-BSGF	Robinson R22 Beta	L. B. Clark
	G-BSGG	Denney Kitfox Mk 2	C. G. Richardson
	G-BSGH	Airtour AH-56B balloon	A. R. Hardwick
	G-BSGJ	Monnett Sonerai II	J. L. Loweth
	G-BSGK	PA-34-200T Seneca II	Aeros Holdings Ltd
	G-BSGL	PA-28-161 Warrior II	Keywest Air Charter Ltd
	G-BSGP	Cameron N-65 balloon	R. Leslie
	G-BSGS	Rans S.10 Sakota	M. R. Parr
	G-BSGT	Cessna T.210N	E. A. T. Brenninkmeyer
	G-BSHA	PA-34-200T Seneca II	Justgold Ltd
	G-BSHC	Colt 69A balloon	Magical Adventures Ltd
	G-BSHD	Colt 69A balloon	F. W. Ewer
	G-BSHH	Luscombe 8E Silvaire	S. L. Lewis
	G-BSHI	Luscombe 8F Silvaire	D. Kelly
	G-BSHK	Denney Kitfox Mk 2	D. Doyle & C. Aherne
	G-BSHO	Cameron V-77 balloon	D. J. Duckworth & J. C. Stewart
	G-BSHP	PA-28-161 Warrior II	Aviation Rentals
	G-BSHR	Cessna F.172N	Deep Cleavage Ltd (G-BFGE)
	G-BSHY	EAA Acro Sport I	R. J. Hodder
	G-BSIC	Cameron V-77 balloon	T. R. Tillson
	G-BSIF	Denney Kitfox Mk 2	R. J. Humphries
	G-BSIG	Colt 21A Cloudhopper balloon	C. J. Dunkley
	G-BSIH	Rutan LongEz	W. S. Allen
	G-BSII	PA-34-200T Seneca II	R. L. Burt
	G-BSIJ	Cameron V-77 balloon	G. B. Davies
	G-BSIM	PA-28-181 Archer II	Falcon Flying Services Ltd
	G-BSIO	Cameron 80 Shed SS balloon	R. E. Jones
	G-BSIU	Colt 90A balloon	S. Travaglia/Italy
	G-BSIY	Schleicher ASK.14	P. W. Andrews
	G-BSIZ	PA-28-181 Archer II	P. J. Gerrard & M. J. Cunliffe
	G-BSJU	Cessna 150M	A. C. Williamson
	G-BSJX	PA-28-161 Warrior II	MK Aero Support Ltd
	G-BSJZ	Cessna 150J	M. H. Campbell

Reg.	Type	Owner or Operator	Notes
G-BSKA	Cessna 150M	R. J. Cushing	
G-BSKG	Maule MX-7-180	A. J. Lewis	
G-BSKW	PA-28-181 Archer II	R. J. Whyham	
G-BSLA	Robin DR.400/180	A. B. McCoig	
G-BSLH	CASA 1.131E Jungmann 2000	M. A. Warden	
G-BSLI	Cameron V-77 balloon	R. S. McKibbin	
G-BSLK	PA-28-161 Warrior II	R. A. Rose	
G-BSLM	PA-28 Cherokee 160	R. Fulton	
G-BSLT	PA-28-161 Warrior II	L. W. Scattergood	
G-BSLU	PA-28 Cherokee 140	W. E. Lewis	
G-BSLV	Enstrom 280FX	B. M. B Roumier	
G-BSLW	Bellanca 7ECA Citabria	J. S. Flavell	
G-BSLX	WAR Focke-Wulf Fw 190 (replica) (4+)	Fw 190 Gruppe	
G-BSMD	Nord 1101 Noralpha (+14)	J. W. Hardie	
G-BSME	Bölkow Bö.208C1 Junior	D. J. Hampson	
G-BSMG	Montgomerie-Bensen B.8M	A. C. Timperley	
G-BSMK	Cameron O-84 balloon	G-BSMK Shareholders	
G-BSMM	Colt 31A balloon	D. V. Fowler	
G-BSMN	CFM Streak Shadow	P. J. Porter	
G-BSMT	Rans S-10 Sakota	T. D. Wood	
G-BSMU	Rans S.6 Coyote II	A. Wright (G-MWJE)	
G-BSMV	PA-17 Vagabond (modified)	A. Cheriton	
G-BSNE	Luscombe 8E Silvaire	C. B. Buscombe, R. Goldsworthy & G. Vitta	
G-BSNF	Piper J-3C-65 Cub	D. A. Hammant	
G-BSNG	Cessna 172N	A. J. & P. C. MacDonald	
G-BSNJ	Cameron N-90 balloon	D. P. H. Smith/France	
G-BSNT	Luscombe 8A Silvaire	Luscombe Quartet	
G-BSNU	Colt 105A balloon	Gone Ballooning	
G-BSNX	PA-28-181 Archer II	Redhill Air Services Ltd	
G-BSNZ	Cameron O-105 balloon	J. Francis	
G-BSOF	Colt 25A balloon	J. M. Bailey	
G-BSOG	Cessna 172M	P. J. Meakin	
G-BSOJ	Thunder Ax7-77 balloon	R. J. S. Jones	
G-BSOK	PA-28-161 Warrior II	A. Oxenham	
G-BSOM	Glaser-Dirks DG.400	G-BSOM Group	
G-BSON	Green S.25 balloon	J. J. Green	
G-BSOO	Cessna 172F	The Oscar Oscar Group	
G-BSOR	CFM Streak Shadow Srs SA	A. Parr	
G-BSOT	PA-38-112 Tomahawk II	APB Leasing Ltd	
G-BSOU	PA-38-112 Tomahawk II	D. J. Campbell	
G-BSOX	Luscombe 8AE Silvaire	P. S Lanary	
G-BSOZ	PA-28-161 Warrior II	S. P. Donoghue & R. F. W. Holder	
G-BSPA	QAC Quickie Q.2	G. V. McKirdy & B. K. Glover	
G-BSPE	Cessna F.172P	T. W. Williamson	
G-BSPG	PA-34-200T Seneca II	Andrews Professional Colour Laboratories Ltd	
G-BSPK	Cessna 195A	A. G. & D. L. Bompas	
G-BSPL	CFM Streak Shadow Srs SA	G. L. Turner	
G-BSPN	PA-28R-201T Turbo Arrow III	Wendex Vehicle Rental Ltd	
G-BSRD	Cameron N-105 balloon	A. Ockelmann	
G-BSRH	Pitts S-1C Special	C. D. Swift	
G-BSRI	Lancair 235	G. Lewis	
G-BSRK	ARV Super 2	D. M. Blair	
G-BSRL	Campbell Cricket Mk.4 gyroplane	M. Brudnicki	
G-BSRP	Rotorway Executive	R. J. Baker	
G-BSRR	Cessna 182Q	C. M. Moore	
G-BSRT	Denney Kitfox Mk 2	M. J. Freeman	
G-BSRX	CFM Streak Shadow	C. M. Webb	
G-BSSA	Luscombe 8E Silvaire	Luscombe Flying Group	
G-BSSB	Cessna 150L	D. T. A. Rees	
G-BSSC	PA-28-161 Warrior II	Sky Blue Flight Training	
G-BSSF	Denney Kitfox Mk 2	S. R. Eskins	
G-BSSI	Rans S.6 Coyote II	J. Currell (G-MWJA)	
G-BSSK	QAC Quickie Q.2	R. Greatrex	
G-BSSP	Robin DR.400/180R	Soaring (Oxford) Ltd	
G-BSST	BAC-Sud Concorde 002 ★	F.A.A. Museum/Yeovilton	
G-BSSV	CFM Streak Shadow	R. W. Payne	
G-BSSW	PA-28-161 Warrior II	D. J. Skidmore & E. F. Rowland	
G-BSSY	Polikarpov Po-2	Richard Shuttleworth Trustees	
G-BSTC	Aeronca 11AC Chief	J. Armstrong & D. Lamb	
G-BSTE	AS.355F2 Twin Squirrel	Oscar Mayer Ltd	
G-BSTH	PA-25 Pawnee 235	Scottish Gliding Union Ltd	
G-BSTI	Piper J-3C-65 Cub	J. A. Scott	
G-BSTK	Thunder Ax8-90 balloon	M. Williams	

Notes	Reg.	Type	Owner or Operator
	G-BSTL	Rand-Robinson KR-2	C. S. Hales & N. Brauns
	G-BSTM	Cessna 172L	G-BSTM Group
	G-BSTO	Cessna 152 II	Plymouth Flying School Ltd
	G-BSTP	Cessna 152 II	FR Aviation Ltd
	G-BSTR	AA-5 Traveler	B. D. Jones
	G-BSTT	Rans S.6 Coyote II	D. G. Palmer
	G-BSTX	Luscombe 8A Silvaire	C. Chambers
	G-BSTY	Thunder Ax8-90 balloon	R. O. Leslie
	G-BSTZ	PA-28 Cherokee 140	Air Navigation & Trading Co Ltd
	G-BSUA	Rans S.6 Coyote II	A. J. Todd
	G-BSUB	Colt 77A balloon	F. W. Ewer
	G-BSUD	Luscombe 8A Silvaire	I. G. Harrison
	G-BSUF	PA-32RT-300 Lance II	S. A. Fell & J. Gibbs
	G-BSUK	Colt 77A balloon	A. J. Moore
	G-BSUO	Scheibe SF.25C Falke	Portmoak Falke Syndicate
	G-BSUU	Colt 180A balloon	British School of Ballooning
	G-BSUV	Cameron O-77 balloon	J. F. Trehern
	G-BSUW	PA-34-200T Seneca II	NPD Direct Ltd
	G-BSUX	Carlson Sparrow II	D. Harker
	G-BSUZ	Denney Kitfox Mk 3	C. E. Ponsford
	G-BSVB	PA-28-181 Archer II	K. A. Boost
	G-BSVE	Binder CP.301S Smaragd	Smaragd Flying Group
	G-BSVF	PA-28-161 Warrior II	Airways Aero Associations Ltd
	G-BSVG	PA-28-161 Warrior II	Airways Aero Associations Ltd
	G-BSVH	Piper J-3C-65 Cub	C. R. & K. A. Maher
	G-BSVI	PA-16 Clipper	Clipper Aviation
	G-BSVK	Denney Kitfox Mk 2	C. Cox
	G-BSVM	PA-28-161 Warrior II	EFG Flying Services
	G-BSVN	Thorp T-18	D. Prentice
	G-BSVP	PA-23-250 Aztec F	S. G. Spier
	G-BSVR	Schweizer 269C	M. K. E. Askham
	G-BSVS	Robin DR.400/100	D. McK. Chalmers
	G-BSWB	Rans S.10 Sakota	F. A. Hewitt
	G-BSWC	Boeing Stearman E75 (112)	Richard Thwaites Aviation Ltd
	G-BSWF	PA-16 Clipper	Durham Clipper Group
	G-BSWG	PA-17 Vagabond	P. E. J. Sturgeon
	G-BSWH	Cessna 152 II	Airspeed Aviation Ltd
	G-BSWI	Rans S.10 Sakota	J. M. Mooney
	G-BSWL	Slingsby T.61F Venture T.2	Bidford Gliding Ltd
	G-BSWM	Slingsby T.61F Venture T.2	Venture Gliding Group
	G-BSWR	BN-2T-26 Turbine Islander	Police Service of Northern Ireland
	G-BSWV	Cameron N-77 balloon	S. Charlish
	G-BSWX	Cameron V-90 balloon	B. J. Burrows
	G-BSWY	Cameron N-77 balloon	Nottingham Hot Air Balloon Club
	G-BSXA	PA-28-161 Warrior II	Falcon Flying Services
	G-BSXB	PA-28-161 Warrior II	S. R. Mendes
	G-BSXC	PA-28-161 Warrior II	N. Ibrahim
	G-BSXD	Soko P-2 Kraguj (30146)	S. M. Johnston
	G-BSXI	Mooney M.20E	D. H. G. Penney
	G-BSXM	Cameron V-77 balloon	C. A. Oxby
	G-BSXS	PA-28-181 Archer II	de Banke Aviation LLP
	G-BSXT	Piper J-5A Cub Cruiser	R. G. Trute
	G-BSYA	Jodel D.18	K. Wright
	G-BSYF	Luscombe 8A Silvaire	Atlantic Aviation
	G-BSYG	PA-12 Super Cruiser	Fat Cub Group
	G-BSYH	Luscombe 8A Silvaire	N. R. Osborne
	G-BSYI	AS.355F1 Twin Squirrel	Layang Layang Aerospace Sdn Bhd
	G-BSYJ	Cameron N-77 balloon	Chubb Fire Ltd
	G-BSYO	Piper J-3C-90 Cub	C. R. Reynolds & J. D. Fuller (G-BSMJ/G-BRHE)
	G-BSYU	Robin DR.400/180	P. D. Smoothy
	G-BSYV	Cessna 150M	E-Plane Ltd
	G-BSYW	Cessna 150M	Cada Vliegtuilgen BV/Netherlands
	G-BSYY	PA-28-161 Warrior II	British Disabled Flying Association
	G-BSYZ	PA-28-161 Warrior II	Yankee Zulu Group
	G-BSZB	Stolp SA.300 Starduster Too	D. T. Gethin
	G-BSZC	Beech C-45H (51-11701A:AF258)	Weston Ltd
	G-BSZD	Robin DR.400/180	Alfa Flight
	G-BSZF	Jodel DR.250/160	J. B. Randle
	G-BSZG	Stolp SA.100 Starduster	D. F. Chapman
	G-BSZH	Thunder Ax7-77 balloon	T. J. Wilkinson
	G-BSZI	Cessna 152 II	Eglinton Flying Club Ltd
	G-BSZJ	PA-28-181 Archer II	M. L. A. Pudney & R. D. Fuller
	G-BSZM	Montgomerie-Bensen B.8MR	A. McCredie

Reg.	Type	Owner or Operator	Notes
G-BSZO	Cessna 152	Flight Center Ltd	
G-BSZT	PA-28-161 Warrior II	Golf Charlie Echo Ltd	
G-BSZV	Cessna 150F	C. A. Davis	
G-BSZW	Cessna 152	S. T. & T. W. Gilbert	
G-BTAG	Cameron O-77 balloon	R. A. Shapland	
G-BTAK	EAA Acrosport II	S. E. Ford	
G-BTAL	Cessna F.152 II	Hertfordshire Aero Club Ltd	
G-BTAM	PA-28-181 Archer II	Tri-Star Farms Ltd	
G-BTAT	Denney Kitfox Mk 2	M. Lawton	
G-BTAW	PA-28-161 Warrior II	Piper Flying Group	
G-BTAZ	Evans VP-2 ★	Norwich Aviation Museum	
G-BTBA	Robinson R22 Beta	Heliflight (UK) Ltd	
G-BTBB	Thunder Ax8-105 S2 balloon	G. J. Boulden	
G-BTBC	PA-28-161 Warrior II	Synergy Aircraft Leasing Ltd	
G-BTBG	Denney Kitfox Mk 2	G. N. Lawder	
G-BTBH	Ryan ST3KR (854)	R. C. Piper	
G-BTBJ	Cessna 190	R. H. Reeves	
G-BTBL	Montgomerie-Bensen B.8MR	AES Radionic Surveillance Systems	
G-BTBP	Cameron N-90 balloon	M. Catalani/Italy	
G-BTBU	PA-18 Super Cub 150	Betty Bu Syndicate	
G-BTBW	Cessna 120	M. J. Willies	
G-BTBY	PA-17 Vagabond	F. M. Ward	
G-BTCB	Air Command 582 Sport	G. Scurrah	
G-BTCC	Grumman F6F-3 Hellcat (40467:19)	Patina Ltd	
G-BTCD	P-51D-25-NA Mustang (413704:87-H)	Pelham Ltd	
G-BTCE	Cessna 152	S. T. Gilbert	
G-BTCH	Luscombe 8E Silvaire	G-BTCH Flying Group	
G-BTCI	PA-17 Vagabond	T. R. Whittome	
G-BTCJ	Luscombe 8AE Silvaire	R. Bentley	
G-BTCM	Cameron N-90 balloon	G. Everett (G-BMPW)	
G-BTCS	Colt 90A balloon	Branded Sky Ltd	
G-BTCZ	Cameron Chateau 84 balloon	Balleroy Developpement SAS	
G-BTDA	Slingsby T.61G Falke	G-BTDA Group	
G-BTDC	Denney Kitfox Mk 2	K. R. H. Wingate	
G-BTDD	CFM Streak Shadow	S. H. Merrony	
G-BTDE	Cessna C-165 Airmaster	R. H. Screen	
G-BTDI	Robinson R22	S. Klinge	
G-BTDN	Denney Kitfox Mk 2	M. G. Rummey	
G-BTDR	Aero Designs Pulsar	R. A. Blackwell	
G-BTDS	Colt 77A balloon	C. P. Witter Ltd	
G-BTDT	CASA 1.131E Jungmann 2000	T. A. Reed	
G-BTDV	PA-28-161 Warrior II	Falcon Flying Services Ltd	
G-BTDW	Cessna 152 II	J. H. Sandham Aviation	
G-BTDZ	CASA 1.131E Jungmann 2000	R. J. & M. Pickin	
G-BTEA	Cameron N-105 balloon	M. W. A. Shemilt	
G-BTEE	Cameron O-120 balloon	D. L. Smith	
G-BTEL	CFM Streak Shadow	J. E. Eatwell	
G-BTES	Cessna 150H	C. Burt-Brown & G. G. Saint	
G-BTET	Piper J-3C-65 Cub	City of Oxford Flying Group	
G-BTEU	SA.365N-2 Dauphin	CHC Scotia Ltd	
G-BTEW	Cessna 120	J. H. Milne & T. H. Bishop	
G-BTFA	Denney Kitfox Mk 2	K. R. Peek	
G-BTFC	Cessna F.152 II	Aircraft Engineers Ltd	
G-BTFE	Bensen-Parsons 2-seat gyroplane	D. C. Ellis	
G-BTFG	Boeing Stearman A75N1 (441)	TG Aviation Ltd	
G-BTFJ	PA-15 Vagabond	B. McCready	
G-BTFK	Taylorcraft BC-12D	A. O'Rourke	
G-BTFL	Aeronca 11AC Chief	BTFL Group	
G-BTFM	Cameron O-105 balloon	Edinburgh University Hot Air Balloon Club	
G-BTFO	PA-28-161 Warrior II	Flyfar Ltd	
G-BTFP	PA-38-112 Tomahawk	St.George Flight Training Ltd	
G-BTFT	Beech 58 Baron	Fastwing Air Charter Ltd	
G-BTFU	Cameron N-90 balloon	J. J. Rudoni & A. C. K. Rawson	
G-BTFV	Whittaker MW7	S. J. Luck	
G-BTFX	Bell 206B JetRanger 2	Amcay Ltd	
G-BTGD	Rand-Robinson KR-2 (modified)	B M. Neary	
G-BTGI	Rearwin 175 Skyranger	J. M. Fforde	
G-BTGJ	Smith DSA-1 Miniplane	G. J. Knowles	
G-BTGL	Light Aero Avid Flyer	M. G. Dovey	
G-BTGM	Aeronca 7AC Champion	A. J. McLuskie	
G-BTGO	PA-28 Cherokee 140	Demero Ltd & Transcourt Ltd	
G-BTGR	Cessna 152 II	A. J. Gomes	

Notes	Reg.	Type	Owner or Operator
	G-BTGS	Stolp SA.300 Starduster Too	G. N. Elliott & ptnrs (G-AYMA)
	G-BTGT	CFM Streak Shadow	I. Heunis (G-MWPY)
	G-BTGW	Cessna 152 II	Stapleford Flying Club Ltd
	G-BTGX	Cessna 152 II	Stapleford Flying Club Ltd
	G-BTGY	PA-28-161 Warrior II	Stapleford Flying Club Ltd
	G-BTGZ	PA-28-181 Archer II	Nick Deyong Ltd
	G-BTHE	Cessna 150L	J. E. Preston
	G-BTHF	Cameron V-90 balloon	N. J. & S. J. Langley
	G-BTHI	Robinson R22 Beta	Summerline Aviation Ltd
	G-BTHK	Thunder Ax7-77 balloon	M. S.Trend
	G-BTHM	Thunder Ax8-105 balloon	Montgolfieres Club de L'Orme/France
	G-BTHP	Thorp T.211	M. Gardner
	G-BTHX	Colt 105A balloon	PSH Skypower Ltd
	G-BTHY	Bell 206B JetRanger 3	Suffolk Helicopters Ltd
	G-BTID	PA-28-161 Warrior II	Aviation South West Ltd
	G-BTIE	SOCATA TB10 Tobago	Aviation Spirit Ltd
	G-BTIF	Denney Kitfox Mk 3	D. S. Lally
	G-BTIG	Montgomerie-Bensen B.8MR	G. H. Leeming
	G-BTII	AA-5B Tiger	Red Row Investments Ltd
	G-BTIJ	Luscombe 8E Silvaire	S. J. Hornsby
	G-BTIL	PA-38-112 Tomahawk	B. J. Pearson
	G-BTIM	PA-28-161 Cadet	Plane Talking Ltd
	G-BTIO	SNCAN Stampe SV.4C	M. D. & C. F. Garratt
	G-BTIR	Denney Kitfox Mk 2	R. B. Wilson
	G-BTIV	PA-28-161 Warrior II	Warrior Group/Eaglescott
	G-BTJA	Luscombe 8E Silvaire	M. W. Rudkin
	G-BTJB	Luscombe 8E Silvaire	M. Loxton
	G-BTJC	Luscombe 8F Silvaire	M. Colson
	G-BTJD	Thunder Ax8-90 S2 balloon	P. Richardson
	G-BTJF	Thunder Ax10-180 balloon	Airborne Adventures Ltd
	G-BTJH	Cameron O-77 balloon	M. Saveri
	G-BTJL	PA-38-112 Tomahawk	J. S. Devlin & Z. Islam
	G-BTJO	Thunder Ax9-140 balloon	G. P. Lane
	G-BTJS	Montgomerie-Bensen B.8MR	T. A. Holmes
	G-BTJU	Cameron V-90 balloon	Flambe Balloons Ltd
	G-BTJX	Rans S.10 Sakota	P. C. Avery
	G-BTKA	Piper J-5A Cub Cruiser	M. J. Walker
	G-BTKB	Renegade Spirit 912	P. J. Calvert
	G-BTKD	Denney Kitfox Mk 4	R. A. Hills
	G-BTKG	Light Aero Avid Flyer	T. Wade/Ireland
	G-BTKL	MBB Bö.105DB-4	Gryphon Aviation Ltd
	G-BTKP	CFM Streak Shadow	C. A. Sargent & C. D. Creasey
	G-BTKT	PA-28-161 Warrior II	Biggin Hill Flying Club Ltd
	G-BTKV	PA-22 Tri-Pacer 160	R. A. Moore
	G-BTKX	PA-28-181 Archer II	D. J. Perkins
	G-BTLB	Wassmer Wa.52 Europa	The G-BTLB Group
	G-BTLG	PA-28R Cherokee Arrow 200	P. J. Moore
	G-BTLL	Pilatus P.3-03	R. E. Dagless
	G-BTLM	PA-22 Tri-Pacer 160	F & H (Aircraft)
	G-BTLP	AA-1C Lynx	Partlease Ltd
	G-BTMA	Cessna 172N	East of England Flying Group Ltd
	G-BTMK	Cessna R.172K XPII	K. E. Halford
	G-BTMO	Colt 69A balloon	Thunder & Colt
	G-BTMP	Campbell Cricket	P. W. McLaughlin
	G-BTMR	Cessna 172M	Linley Aviation Ltd
	G-BTMT	Denney Kitfox Mk 1	L. G. Horne
	G-BTMV	Everett Srs 2 gyroplane	L. Armes
	G-BTMW	Zenair CH.701 STOL	L. Lewis
	G-BTNA	Robinson R22 Beta	Attitude Aerobatics Ltd
	G-BTNC	AS.365N-2 Dauphin 2	CHC Scotia Ltd
	G-BTNE	PA-28-161 Warrior II	Fly Welle Ltd
	G-BTNH	PA-28-161 Warrior II	Falcon Flying Services Ltd (G-DENH)
	G-BTNO	Aeronca 7AC Champion	B. J. & B. G. Robe
	G-BTNR	Denney Kitfox Mk 3	High Notions Flying Group
	G-BTNT	PA-28-151 Warrior	Azure Flying Club Ltd
	G-BTNV	PA-28-161 Warrior II	G. M. Bauer & A. W. Davies
	G-BTNW	Rans S.6-ESA Coyote II	R. C. Holmes
	G-BTOC	Robinson R22 Beta	Swift Helicopter Services Ltd
	G-BTOG	DH.82A Tiger Moth	TOG Group
	G-BTOL	Denney Kitfox Mk 3	P. J. Gibbs
	G-BTON	PA-28 Cherokee 140	Group G-BTON
	G-BTOO	Pitts S-1C Special	T. L. Davis
	G-BTOP	Cameron V-77 balloon	J. J. Winter

Reg.	Type	Owner or Operator	Notes
G-BTOT	PA-15 Vagabond	J. E. D. Rogerson	
G-BTOU	Cameron O-120 balloon	J. J. Daly	
G-BTOW	SOCATA Rallye 180GT	M. Jarrett	
G-BTOZ	Thunder Ax9-120 S2 balloon	H. G. Davies	
G-BTPA	BAe ATP	Atlantic Airlines Ltd	
G-BTPC	BAe ATP	Atlantic Airlines Ltd	
G-BTPE	BAe ATP	Atlantic Airlines Ltd	
G-BTPF	BAe ATP	Atlantic Airlines Ltd	
G-BTPG	BAe ATP	Atlantic Airlines Ltd	
G-BTPH	BAe ATP	Atlantic Airlines Ltd	
G-BTPJ	BAe ATP	Deutsche Leasing Sverige AB	
G-BTPL	BAe ATP	European Turboprop Management AB	
G-BTPT	Cameron N-77 balloon	H. J. Andrews	
G-BTPV	Colt 90A balloon	Balloon Preservation Group	
G-BTPX	Thunder Ax8-90 BALLOON	B. J. Ross	
G-BTRC	Light Aero Avid Speedwing	Grangecote Ltd	
G-BTRF	Aero Designs Pulsar	P. F. Crosby & C. Smith	
G-BTRG	Aeronca 65C Super Chief	A. Welburn	
G-BTRI	Aeronca 11CC Super Chief	P. A. Wensak	
G-BTRK	PA-28-161 Warrior II	Stapleford Flying Club Ltd	
G-BTRL	Cameron N-105 balloon	J. Lippett	
G-BTRO	Thunder Ax8-90 balloon	Capital Balloon Club Ltd	
G-BTRR	Thunder Ax7-77 balloon	P. J. Wentworth	
G-BTRS	PA-28-161 Warrior II	Airwise Flying Group	
G-BTRT	PA-28R Cherokee Arrow 200-II	Romeo Tango Group	
G-BTRU	Robin DR.400/180	R. H. Mackay	
G-BTRW	Slingsby T.61F Venture T.2	RW Group	
G-BTRY	PA-28-161 Warrior II	Oxford Aviation Academy (Oxford) Ltd	
G-BTRZ	Jodel D.18	A. P. Aspinall	
G-BTSB	Corben Baby Ace D	M. R Overall	
G-BTSJ	PA-28-161 Warrior II	Plymouth Flying School Ltd	
G-BTSN	Cessna 150G	M. L. F. Langrick	
G-BTSP	Piper J-3C-65 Cub	A. Corcoran	
G-BTSR	Aeronca 11AC Chief	J. M. Miller	
G-BTSV	Denney Kitfox Mk 3	R. J. Folwell	
G-BTSW	Colt AS-80 Mk II airship	Gefa-Flug GmbH/Germany	
G-BTSX	Thunder Ax7-77 balloon	C. Moris-Gallimore/Portugal	
G-BTSY	EE Lightning F.6 (XR724) ★	Lightning Association	
G-BTSZ	Cessna 177A	Henlow Aviation Ltd	
G-BTTD	Montgomerie-Bensen B.8MR	A. J. P Herculson	
G-BTTE	Cessna 150L	C. Wilson & W. B. Murray	
G-BTTL	Cameron V-90 balloon	A. J. Baird	
G-BTTO	BAe ATP	Atlantic Airlines Ltd (G-OEDE)	
G-BTTR	Aerotek Pitts S-2A Special	Yellowbird Adventures Ltd	
G-BTTW	Thunder Ax7-77 balloon	J. Kenny	
G-BTTY	Denney Kitfox Mk 2	C. J. Haste	
G-BTTZ	Slingsby T.61F Venture T.2	G-BTTZ Group	
G-BTUA	Slingsby T.61F Venture T.2	Shenington Gliding Club	
G-BTUB	Yakovlev C.11	G. G. L. James	
G-BTUC	EMB-312 Tucano ★	Ulster Aviation Heritage	
G-BTUG	SOCATA Rallye 180T	Herefordshire Gliding Club Ltd	
G-BTUH	Cameron N-65 balloon	J. S. Russon	
G-BTUK	Aerotek Pitts S-2A Special	S. H. Elkington	
G-BTUL	Aerotek Pitts S-2A Special	J. M. Adams	
G-BTUM	Piper J-3C-65 Cub	G-BTUM Syndicate	
G-BTUR	PA-18 Super Cub 95 (modified)	N. T. Oakman	
G-BTUS	Whittaker MW7	C. T. Bailey	
G-BTUV	Aeronca A65TAC Defender	S. Hudson, P. McLoughlin & F. McMorrow	
G-BTUW	PA-28-151 Warrior	T. S. Kemp	
G-BTUZ	American General AG-5B Tiger	R. V. Grocott	
G-BTVA	Thunder Ax7-77 balloon	C. M. Waters	
G-BTVC	Denney Kitfox Mk 2	M. J. Downes	
G-BTVE	Hawker Demon I (K8203)	Demon Displays Ltd	
G-BTVV	Cessna FA.337G	C. Keane	
G-BTVW	Cessna 152 II	TGD Leasing Ltd	
G-BTVX	Cessna 152 II	The Flight Centre 2010 Ltd	
G-BTWB	Denney Kitfox Mk 3	J. & O. Houlihan (G-BTTM)	
G-BTWC	Slingsby T.61F Venture T.2	The Royal Air Force Gliding and Soaring Association	
G-BTWD	Slingsby T.61F Venture T.2	York Gliding Centre	
G-BTWE	Slingsby T.61F Venture T.2	Aston Down G-BTWE Syndicate	
G-BTWF	DHC.1 Chipmunk 22 (WK549)	J. A. Simms	
G-BTWI	EAA Acro Sport I	J. O'Connell	

Notes	Reg.	Type	Owner or Operator
	G-BTWJ	Cameron V-77 balloon	C. Gingell & M. Holden-Wadsworth
	G-BTWL	WAG-Aero Acro Sport Trainer	F. Horan
	G-BTWV	Cameron O-90 balloon	The Cybele Flying Group
	G-BTWX	SOCATA TB9 Tampico	T. I. Murtough
	G-BTWY	Aero Designs Pulsar	R. Bishop
	G-BTWZ	Rans S.10 Sakota	J. T. Phipps
	G-BTXD	Rans S.6-ESA Coyote II	A. I. Sutherland
	G-BTXF	Cameron V-90 balloon	G. Thompson
	G-BTXI	Noorduyn AT-16 Harvard IIB (FE695)	Patina Ltd
	G-BTXK	Thunder Ax7-65 balloon	A. F. Selby
	G-BTXM	Colt 21A Cloudhopper balloon	H. J. Andrews
	G-BTXS	Cameron O-120 balloon	Southern Balloon Group
	G-BTXT	Maule MXT-7-180 Star Rocket	G-BTXT Group
	G-BTXX	Bellanca 8KCAB Decathlon	Tatenhill Aviation Ltd
	G-BTXZ	Zenair CH.250	G-BTXZ Group
	G-BTYC	Cessna 150L	Polestar Aviation Ltd
	G-BTYH	Pottier P.80S	R. G. Marshall
	G-BTYI	PA-28-181 Archer II	Godiva Imaging Ltd
	G-BTYT	Cessna 152 II	Cristal Air Ltd
	G-BTYX	Cessna 140	R. F. Richards
	G-BTYY	Curtiss Robin C-2	R. R. L. Windus
	G-BTZA	Beech F33A Bonanza	G-BTZA Group
	G-BTZB	Yakovlev Yak-50 (10 yellow)	D. H. Boardman
	G-BTZD	Yakovlev Yak-1 (1342)	Historic Aircraft Collection Ltd
	G-BTZE	LET Yakovlev C.11	M. V. Rijkse
	G-BTZO	SOCATA TB20 Trinidad	A. P. Howells
	G-BTZP	SOCATA TB9 Tampico	M. W. Orr
	G-BTZS	Colt 77A balloon	P. T. R. Ollivere
	G-BTZV	Cameron V-77 balloon	D. J. & H. M. Brown
	G-BTZX	Piper J-3C-65 Cub	ZX Cub Group
	G-BTZY	Colt 56A balloon	S. J. Wardle
	G-BTZZ	CFM Streak Shadow	D. R. Stennett
	G-BUAA	Corben Baby Ace D	C. E. Brookes
	G-BUAB	Aeronca 11AC Chief	J. Reed
	G-BUAC	Slingsby T.31 Motor Cadet III	D. A. Wilson & C. R. Partington
	G-BUAF	Cameron N-77 balloon	Zebedee Balloon Service Ltd
	G-BUAG	Jodel D.18	A. L. Silcox
	G-BUAI	Everett Srs 3 gyroplane	D. Stevenson
	G-BUAJ	Cameron N-90 balloon	High Road Balloons
	G-BUAM	Cameron V-77 balloon	N. Florence
	G-BUAT	Thunder Ax9-120 balloon	J. Fenton
	G-BUAV	Cameron O-105 balloon	D. & T. Dorrell
	G-BUAX	Rans S.10 Sakota	P. D. J. Brown
	G-BUBL	Thunder Ax8-105 balloon ★	British Balloon Museum/Newbury
	G-BUBN	BN-2B-26 Islander	Isles of Scilly Skybus Ltd
	G-BUBS	Lindstrand LBL-77B balloon	B. J. Bower
	G-BUBT	Stoddard Hamilton Glasair IIS RG	D. Bonucchi
	G-BUBU	PA-34-220T Seneca III	Brinor (Holdings) Ltd
	G-BUBW	Robinson R22 Beta	Plane Talking Ltd
	G-BUBY	Thunder Ax8-105 S2 balloon	T. M. Donnelly
	G-BUCA	Cessna A.150K	BUCA Group
	G-BUCC	CASA 1.131E Jungmann 2000 (BU+CC)	P. L. Gaze (G-BUEM)
	G-BUCG	Schleicher ASW.20L (modified)	W. B. Andrews
	G-BUCH	Stinson V-77 Reliant	Gullwing Trading Ltd
	G-BUCI	Auster AOP.9 (XP242)	Historic Aircraft Flight Reserve Collectio
	G-BUCK	CASA 1.131E Jungmann 1000 (BU+CK)	Jungmann Flying Group
	G-BUCM	Hawker Sea Fury FB.11	Patina Ltd
	G-BUCO	Pietenpol Air Camper	A. James
	G-BUCT	Cessna 150L	North East Flight Training Ltd
	G-BUDA	Slingsby T.61F Venture T.2	The Royal Air Force Gliding and Soaring Association
	G-BUDC	Slingsby T.61F Venture T.2 (ZA652)	T.61 Group
	G-BUDE	PA-22 Tri-Pacer 135 (tailwheel)	P. Robinson
	G-BUDF	Rand-Robinson KR-2	M. Stott
	G-BUDI	Aero Designs Pulsar	R. W. L. Oliver
	G-BUDK	Thunder Ax7-77 balloon	W. Evans
	G-BUDL	Auster 3 (NX534)	K. B. Owen
	G-BUDN	Cameron 90 Shoe SS balloon	Magical Adventures Ltd
	G-BUDO	PZL-110 Koliber 150	A. S. Vine
	G-BUDR	Denney Kitfox Mk 3	N. J. P. Mayled

Reg.	Type	Owner or Operator	Notes
G-BUDS	Rand-Robinson KR-2	D. W. Munday	
G-BUDT	Slingsby T.61F Venture T.2	G-BUDT Group	
G-BUDU	Cameron V-77 balloon	T. M. G. Amery	
G-BUDW	Brügger MB.2 Colibri	S. P. Barrett (G-GODS)	
G-BUEC	Van's RV-6	A. H. Harper	
G-BUED	Slingsby T.61F Venture T.2	617 VGS Group	
G-BUEF	Cessna 152 II	Channel Aviation	
G-BUEG	Cessna 152 II	Aviation South West Ltd	
G-BUEI	Thunder Ax8-105 balloon	K. P. Barnes	
G-BUEK	Slingsby T.61F Venture T.2	G-BUEK Group	
G-BUEN	VPM M-14 Scout	J. L. G. McLane	
G-BUEP	Maule MX-7-180	N. J. B. Bennett	
G-BUEW	Rans S-6 Coyote II	C. Cheeseman (G-MWYE)	
G-BUFG	Slingsby T.61F Venture T.2	Hinton Pilot Flight Training Ltd	
G-BUFH	PA-28-161 Warrior II	Solent School of Flying	
G-BUFR	Slingsby T.61F Venture T.2	East Sussex Gliding Club Ltd	
G-BUFV	Light Aero Avid Speedwing Mk.4	M. & B. Gribbin	
G-BUFY	PA-28-161 Warrior II	Bickertons Aerodromes Ltd	
G-BUGE	Bellanca 7GCAA Cltabria	V. Vaughan & N. O'Brien	
G-BUGG	Cessna 150F	C. P. J. Taylor & D. M. Forshaw	
G-BUGI	Evans VP-2	D. P. Busby & A. Temple	
G-BUGJ	Robin DR.400/180	W. E. R. Jenkins	
G-BUGL	Slingsby T.61F Venture T.2	VMG Group	
G-BUGP	Cameron V-77 balloon	R. Churcher	
G-BUGS	Cameron V-77 balloon	S. J. Dymond	
G-BUGT	Slingsby T.61F Venture T.2	Bambi Aircraft Group	
G-BUGV	Slingsby T.61F Venture T.2	Oxfordshire Sportflying Ltd	
G-BUGW	Slingsby T.61F Venture T.2	Hinton Pilot Flight Training Ltd	
G-BUGY	Cameron V-90 balloon	Dante Balloon Group	
G-BUGZ	Slingsby T.61F Venture T.2	Dishforth Flying Group	
G-BUHA	Slingsby T.61F Venture T.2 (ZA634:C)	Saltby Flying Group	
G-BUHB	BAe.146-300	Trident Aviation Leasing Services Jersey) Ltd	
G-BUHM	Cameron V-77 balloon	L. A. Watts	
G-BUHO	Cessna 140	W. B. Bateson	
G-BUHR	Slingsby T.61F Venture T.2	Connel Motor Glider Group	
G-BUHS	Stoddard-Hamilton Glasair SH TD-1	T. F. Horrocks	
G-BUHU	Cameron N-105 balloon	Unipart Balloon Club	
G-BUHZ	Cessna 120	The Cessna 120 Group	
G-BUIF	PA-28-161 Warrior II	Northumbria Flying School Ltd	
G-BUIG	Campbell Cricket (replica)	J. A. English	
G-BUIH	Slingsby T.61F Venture T.2	Falcon Gliding Group	
G-BUIJ	PA-28-161 Warrior II	OPS Aero Support Services	
G-BUIK	PA-28-161 Warrior II	Falcon Flying Services	
G-BUIL	CFM Streak Shadow	A. A. Castleton	
G-BUIN	Thunder Ax7-77 balloon	P. C. Johnson	
G-BUIP	Denney Kitfox Mk 2	Avcomm Developments Ltd	
G-BUIR	Light Aero Avid Speedwing Mk 4	S. J. Handley	
G-BUIU	Cameron V-90 balloon	H. Micketeit/Germany	
G-BUIZ	Cameron N-90 balloon	Balloon Preservation Flying Group	
G-BUJA	Slingsby T.61F Venture T.2	The Royal Air Force Gliding and Soaring Association	
G-BUJB	Slingsby T.61F Venture T.2	Falke Syndicate	
G-BUJE	Cessna 177B	FG93 Group	
G-BUJH	Colt 77B balloon	R. P. Cross & R. Stanley	
G-BUJI	Slingsby T.61F Venture T.2	Solent Venture Syndicate Ltd	
G-BUJJ	Avid Speedwing	S. Hazelden	
G-BUJK	Montgomerie-Bensen B.8MR	P. C. W. Raine	
G-BUJM	Cessna 120	Cessna 120 Flying Group	
G-BUJN	Cessna 172N	Warwickshire Aviation Ltd	
G-BUJO	PA-28-161 Warrior II	Falcon Flying Services	
G-BUJP	PA-28-161 Warrior II	Phoenix Aviation	
G-BUJV	Light Aero Avid Speedwing Mk 4	C. Thomas	
G-BUJW	Thunder Ax8-90 S2 balloon	G. J. Grimes	
G-BUJX	Slingsby T.61F Venture T.2	The Burn Gliding Club Ltd	
G-BUJZ	Rotorway Executive 90 (modified)	M. P. Swoboda	
G-BUKB	Rans S.10 Sakota	M. K. Blatch	
G-BUKF	Denney Kitfox Mk 4	Kilo Foxtrot Group	
G-BUKH	D.31 Turbulent	J. G. Wilkins	
G-BUKI	Thunder Ax7-77 balloon	Virgin Balloon Flights	
G-BUKK	Bücker Bü 133C Jungmeister (U-80)	E. J. F. McEntee	
G-BUKO	Cessna 120	K. Handley	
G-BUKP	Denney Kitfox Mk 2	RNAV Europe Ltd	
G-BUKR	MS.880B Rallye Club 100T	G-BUKR Flying Group	

Notes	Reg.	Type	Owner or Operator
	G-BUKU	Luscombe 8E Silvaire	Silvaire Flying Group
	G-BUKY	CCF Harvard IVM (52-8543)	R. A. Fleming
	G-BUKZ	Evans VP-2	P. R. Farnell
	G-BULB	Thunder Ax7-77 balloon	G. B. Davies
	G-BULC	Light Aero Avid Flyer Mk 4	C. Nice
	G-BULF	Colt 77A balloon	P. Goss & T. C. Davies
	G-BULG	Van's RV-4	V. D. Long
	G-BULH	Cessna 172N Skyhawk II	FlyBPL.com
	G-BULJ	CFM Streak Shadow	C. C. Brown
	G-BULL	SA Bulldog Srs 120/128 (HKG-5)	N. V. Sills
	G-BULN	Colt 210A balloon	H. G. Davies
	G-BULO	Luscombe 8A Silvaire	B. W. Foulds
	G-BULT	Campbell Cricket	A. T. Pocklington
	G-BULY	Light Aero Avid Flyer	J. G. Stewart
	G-BULZ	Denney Kitfox Mk 2	T. G. F. Trenchard
	G-BUMP	PA-28-181 Archer II	A. J. Keen
	G-BUNB	Slingsby T.61F Venture T.2	The Royal Air Force Gliding and Soaring Association
	G-BUNC	PZL-104 Wilga 35	R. F. Goodman
	G-BUND	PA-28RT-201T Turbo Arrow IV	E. Culot
	G-BUNG	Cameron N-77 balloon	A. Kaye
	G-BUNO	Lancair 320	J. Softley
	G-BUNV	Thunder Ax7-77 balloon	R. M. Garnett & R. Stone
	G-BUOA	Whittaker MW6-S Fatboy Flyer	H. N. Graham
	G-BUOB	CFM Streak Shadow	J. M. Hunter
	G-BUOD	SE-5A (replica) (B595:W)	M. D. Waldron/Belgium
	G-BUOE	Cameron V-90 balloon	A. Derbyshire
	G-BUOF	D.62B Condor	R. P. Loxton
	G-BUOI	PA-20-135 Pacer	Foley Farm Flying Group
	G-BUOK	Rans S.6-ESA Coyote II	M. Morris
	G-BUOL	Denney Kitfox Mk 3	D. C. & M. Brooks
	G-BUON	Light Aero Avid Aerobat	I. A. J. Lappin
	G-BUOR	CASA 1.131E Jungmann 2000	M. I. M. S. Voest/Netherlands
	G-BUOW	Aero Designs Pulsar XP	T. J. Hartwell
	G-BUPA	Rutan LongEz	N. G. Henry
	G-BUPB	Stolp SA.300 Starduster Too	J. R. Edwards & J. W. Widdows
	G-BUPC	Rollason Beta B.2	C. A. Rolph
	G-BUPF	Bensen B.8R	P. W. Hewitt-Dean
	G-BUPI	Cameron V-77 balloon	S. M. Sherwin (G-BOUC)
	G-BUPM	VPM M-16 Tandem Trainer	A. Kitson
	G-BUPP	Cameron V-42 balloon	L. J. Schoeman
	G-BUPR	Jodel D.18	R. W. Burrows
	G-BUPU	Thunder Ax7-77 balloon	R. C. Barkworth & D. G. Maguire/USA
	G-BUPV	Great Lakes 2T-1A	R. J. Fray
	G-BUPW	Denney Kitfox Mk 3	S. G. Metcalfe
	G-BURD	Cessna F.172N	Tayside Aviation Ltd
	G-BURE	Jodel D.9	N. P. St.J. Ramsay
	G-BURG	Colt 77A balloon	P. A. & M. Still
	G-BURH	Cessna 150E	C. A. Davis
	G-BURI	Enstrom F-28C	D. W. C. Holmes
	G-BURJ	HS.748 Srs.2A	Clewer Aviation Ltd
	G-BURL	Colt 105A balloon	J. E. Rose
	G-BURN	Cameron O-120 balloon	G. Gray
	G-BURP	Rotorway Executive 90	N. K. Newman
	G-BURR	Auster AOP.9	Annic Aviation
	G-BURS	Sikorsky S-76A	Premiair Aviation Services Ltd (G-OHTL)
	G-BURT	PA-28-161 Warrior II	Paul's Planes Ltd
	G-BURZ	Hawker Nimrod II (K3661:362)	Historic Aircraft Collection Ltd
	G-BUSG	Airbus A.320-211	GA Telesis Ireland Ltd
	G-BUSH	Airbus A.320-211	SASOF TR-44 Aviation Ireland Ltd
	G-BUSI	Airbus A.320-211	SASOF TR-44 Aviation Ireland Ltd
	G-BUSJ	Airbus A.320-211	British Airways
	G-BUSK	Airbus A.320-211	SASOF TR-44 Aviation Ireland Ltd
	G-BUSN	Rotorway Executive 90	J. A. McGinley
	G-BUSR	Aero Designs Pulsar	S. S. Bateman & R. A. Watts
	G-BUSS	Cameron 90 Bus SS balloon	Magical Adventures Ltd
	G-BUSV	Colt 105A balloon	M. N. J. Kirby
	G-BUSW	Rockwell Commander 114	J. Vicoll
	G-BUTB	CFM Streak Shadow	H. O. Maclean & S. MacKechnie
	G-BUTD	Van's RV-6	N. W. Beadle
	G-BUTE	Anderson EA-1 Kingfisher	T. Crawford (G-BRCK)
	G-BUTF	Aeronca 11AC Chief	Fox Flying Group
	G-BUTG	Zenair CH.601HD	A. J. Thomas

Reg.	Type	Owner or Operator	Notes
G-BUTH	CEA DR.220 2+2	Phoenix Flying Group	
G-BUTJ	Cameron O-77 balloon	D. Hoddinott	
G-BUTK	Murphy Rebel	A. J. Gibson	
G-BUTM	Rans S.6-116 Coyote II	J. D. Sinclair-Day	
G-BUTT	Cessna FA150K	Ag-Raum GmbH/Germany (G-AXSJ)	
G-BUTX	CASA 1.133C Jungmeister (ES.1-4)	Bucker Flying Group	
G-BUTY	Brügger MB.2 Colibri	R. M. Lawday	
G-BUTZ	PA-28 Cherokee 180C	M. H. Canning (G-DARL)	
G-BUUA	Slingsby T.67M Firefly Mk II	M. Geroschus	
G-BUUB	Slingsby T.67M Firefly Mk II	The Leicestershire Aero Club Ltd	
G-BUUC	Slingsby T.67M Firefly Mk II	Swiftair Maintenance Ltd	
G-BUUE	Slingsby T.67M Firefly Mk II	J. R. Bratty	
G-BUUF	Slingsby T.67M Firefly Mk II	Tiger Airways	
G-BUUI	Slingsby T.67M Firefly Mk II	Bustard Flying Club Ltd	
G-BUUJ	Slingsby T.67M Firefly Mk II	Durham Tees Flight Training Ltd	
G-BUUK	Slingsby T.67M Firefly Mk II	Avalanche Aviation Ltd	
G-BUUM	PA-28RT-201 Arrow IV	CCHM Aviation Ltd	
G-BUUP	BAe ATP	Atlantic Airlines Ltd	
G-BUUR	BAe ATP	Atlantic Airlines Ltd	
G-BUUU	Cameron Bottle SS balloon ★	British Balloon Museum/Newbury	
G-BUUX	PA-28 Cherokee 180D	Aero Group 78	
G-BUVA	PA-22-135 Tri-Pacer	Oaksey VA Group	
G-BUVE	Colt 77B balloon	G. D. Philpot	
G-BUVL	Fisher Super Koala	A. D. Malcolm	
G-BUVM	CEA DR.250/160	G-BUVM Group	
G-BUVN	CASA 1.131E Jungmann 2000(BI-005)	W. Van Egmond/Netherlands	
G-BUVO	Cessna F.182P	Romeo Mike Flying Group (G-WTFA)	
G-BUVR	Christen A.1 Husky	A. E. Poulson	
G-BUVT	Colt 77A balloon	N. A. Carr	
G-BUVW	Cameron N-90 balloon	P. Spellward	
G-BUVX	CFM Streak Shadow	T. J. Shaw	
G-BUWE	SE-5A (replica) (C9533:M)	Airpark Flight Centre Ltd	
G-BUWF	Cameron N-105 balloon	R. E. Jones	
G-BUWH	Parsons 2-seat gyroplane	R. V. Brunskill	
G-BUWI	Lindstrand LBL-77A balloon	Capital Balloon Club Ltd	
G-BUWJ	Pitts S-1C Special	M. A. Sims	
G-BUWK	Rans S.6-116 Coyote II	R. Warriner	
G-BUWL	Piper J-4A	M. L. Ryan	
G-BUWR	CFM Streak Shadow	T. Harvey	
G-BUWS	Denney Kitfox Mk 2	J. E. Brewis	
G-BUWT	Rand-Robinson KR-2	G. Bailey-Woods	
G-BUWU	Cameron V-77 balloon	T. R. Dews	
G-BUXA	Colt 210A balloon	Balloon School International Ltd	
G-BUXC	CFM Streak Shadow	N. R. Beale	
G-BUXD	Maule MXT-7-160	I. D. McClelland	
G-BUXI	Steen Skybolt	BUXI Group	
G-BUXK	Pietenpol Air Camper	B. M. D. Nelson	
G-BUXL	Taylor JT.1 Monoplane	P. J. Hebdon	
G-BUXN	Beech C23 Sundowner	Private Pilots Syndicate	
G-BUXS	MBB Bö.105DBS/4	Bond Air Services (G-PASA/G-BGWP)	
G-BUXW	Thunder Ax8-90 S2 balloon	Nottingham Hot Air Balloon Club	
G-BUXX	PA-17 Vagabond	R. H. Hunt	
G-BUXY	PA-25 Pawnee 235	Bath, Wilts & North Dorset Gliding Club Ltd	
G-BUYB	Aero Designs Pulsar	A. P. Fenn	
G-BUYC	Cameron 80 Concept balloon	R. P. Cross	
G-BUYD	Thunder Ax8-90 balloon	S. & P. McGuigan	
G-BUYF	Falcon XP	M. J. Hadland	
G-BUYK	Denney Kitfox Mk 4	M. S. Shelton	
G-BUYL	RAF 2000GT gyroplane	M. H. J. Goldring	
G-BUYO	Colt 77A balloon	S. F. Burden/Netherlands	
G-BUYS	Robin DR.400/180	G-BUYS Flying Group	
G-BUYU	Bowers Fly-Baby 1A	R. Metcalfe	
G-BUYY	PA-28 Cherokee 180	G-BUYY Group	
G-BUZA	Denney Kitfox Mk 3	A. O'Brien/Ireland	
G-BUZB	Aero Designs Pulsar XP	S. M. Lancashire	
G-BUZC	Everett Srs 3A gyroplane	M. P. L'Hermette	
G-BUZG	Zenair CH.601HD	R. M. Ballard	
G-BUZH	Aero Designs Star-Lite SL-1	C. A. McDowall	
G-BUZK	Cameron V-77 balloon	Zebedee Balloon Service Ltd	
G-BUZM	Light Aero Avid Flyer Mk 3	R. McLuckie & O. G. Jones	
G-BUZO	Pietenpol Air Camper	D. A. Jones	
G-BUZR	Lindstrand LBL-77A balloon	Lindstrand Technologies Ltd	
G-BUZT	Kolb Twinstar Mk 3	J. A. G. Robb	

Notes	Reg.	Type	Owner or Operator
	G-BUZV	Ken Brock KB-2 gyroplane	K. Hughes
	G-BUZZ	Agusta-Bell 206B JetRanger 2	Rivermead Aviation Ltd
	G-BVAB	Zenair CH.601HDS	B. N. Rides
	G-BVAC	Zenair CH.601HD	J. A. Tyndall & S. Wisedale
	G-BVAF	Piper J-3C-65 Cub	N. M. Hitchman
	G-BVAH	Denney Kitfox Mk.3	S. Allinson
	G-BVAI	PZL-110 Koliber 150	B. G. Ell
	G-BVAM	Evans VP-1	Breighton VP-1 Group
	G-BVAO	Colt 25A balloon	M. E. Dworski
	G-BVAW	Staaken Z-1 Flitzer (D-692)	L. R. Williams
	G-BVAY	Rutan Vari-Eze	D. A. Young
	G-BVAZ	Montgomerie-Bensen B.8MR	N. Steele
	G-BVBF	PA-28-151 Warrior	R. K. Spence
	G-BVBK	Colt Flying Coffe Jar SS balloon	M. E. White
	G-BVBR	Light Aero Avid Speedwing	J. M. Baldwin & O. Kotova
	G-BVBS	Cameron N-77 balloon	Heart of England Balloons
	G-BVCA	Cameron N-105 balloon	Kent Ballooning
	G-BVCG	Van's RV-6	A. W. Shellis & I. C. Smit
	G-BVCL	Rans S.6-116 Coyote II	R. L. N. Lucey
	G-BVCN	Colt 56A balloon	J. A. W. Dyer
	G-BVCO	FRED Srs 2	I. W. Bremner
	G-BVCP	Piper CP.1 Metisse	B. M. Diggins
	G-BVCS	Aeronca 7BCM Champion	A. C. Lines
	G-BVCT	Denney Kitfox Mk 4	A. F. Reid
	G-BVCY	Cameron H-24 balloon	A. C. K. Rawson & J. J. Rudoni
	G-BVDB	Thunder Ax7-77 balloon	S. J. Hollingsworth & M. K. Bellamy (G-ORDY)
	G-BVDC	Van's RV-3	B. S. Carpenter
	G-BVDH	PA-28RT-201 Arrow IV	J. Germanos
	G-BVDI	Van's RV-4	J. Glen-Davis Gorman
	G-BVDJ	Campbell Cricket (replica)	S. Jennings
	G-BVDM	Cameron 60 Concept balloon	M. P. Young
	G-BVDO	Lindstrand LBL-105A balloon	K. Graham
	G-BVDP	Sequoia F.8L Falco	N. M. Turner
	G-BVDR	Cameron O-77 balloon	N. J. Logue
	G-BVDS	Lindstrand LBL-69A balloon	Lindstrand Hot-Air Balloons Ltd
	G-BVDT	CFM Streak Shadow	L. P. Harper
	G-BVDW	Thunder Ax8-90 balloon	S. C. Vora
	G-BVDX	Cameron V-90 balloon	R. K. Scott
	G-BVDY	Cameron 60 Concept balloon	P. Baker/Ireland
	G-BVDZ	Taylorcraft BC-12D	N. Rushen
	G-BVEA	Mosler Motors N.3 Pup	G-BVEA Group (G-MWEA)
	G-BVEH	Jodel D.112	M. L. Copland
	G-BVEL	Evans VP-1 Srs.2	M. J. & S. J. Quinn
	G-BVEN	Cameron 80 Concept balloon	R. M. Powell
	G-BVEP	Luscombe 8A Master	B. H. Austen
	G-BVER	DHC.2 Beaver 1 (XV268)	Seaflite Ltd (G-BTDM)
	G-BVEV	PA-34-200 Seneca	G-BVEV Flying Group
	G-BVEW	Lindstrand LBL-150A balloon	S. J. Colin
	G-BVEY	Denney Kitfox Mk 4-1200	J. H. H. Turner
	G-BVEZ	P.84 Jet Provost T.3A (XM479)	Newcastle Jet Provost Co Ltd
	G-BVFA	Rans S.10 Sakota	D. S. Wilkinson
	G-BVFB	Cameron N-31 balloon	P. Lawman
	G-BVFF	Cameron V-77 balloon	R. J. Kerr & G. P. Allen
	G-BVFM	Rans S.6-116 Coyote II	F. B. C. de Beer
	G-BVFO	Light Aero Avid Speedwing	T. G. Solomon
	G-BVFR	CFM Streak Shadow	M. A. Kelly
	G-BVFS	Slingsby T.31M	S. R. Williams
	G-BVFU	Cameron 105 Sphere SS balloon	Stichting Phoenix/Netherlands
	G-BVFZ	Maule M5-180C Lunar Rocket	R. C. Robinson
	G-BVGA	Bell 206B JetRanger3	Findon Air Services
	G-BVGB	Thunder Ax8-105 S2 balloon	E. K. Read
	G-BVGE	WS-55 Whirlwind HAR.10 (XJ729)	J. F. Kelly/Ireland
	G-BVGF	Shaw Europa	A. Graham & G. G. Beal
	G-BVGH	Hawker Hunter T.7 (XL573)	M. Stott
	G-BVGI	Pereira Osprey II	D. Westoby
	G-BVGJ	Cameron C-80 balloon	J. M. J. & V. F. Roberts
	G-BVGK	Lindstrand LBL Newspaper SS balloon	H. Holmqvist
	G-BVGO	Denney Kitfox Mk 4-1200	P. Madden
	G-BVGP	Bücker Bü 133 Jungmeister (U-95)	M. V. Rijkse
	G-BVGT	Auster J/1 (modified)	K. D. & C. S. Rhodes
	G-BVGW	Luscombe 8A Silvaire	J. Smith
	G-BVGX	Thunder Ax8-90 S2 balloon	G-BVGX Group/New Zealand

Reg.	Type	Owner or Operator	Notes
G-BVGY	Luscombe 8E Silvaire	A. G. Carrick	
G-BVGZ	Fokker Dr.1 (replica) (450/17) ★	R. A. Fleming	
G-BVHC	Grob G.115D-2 Heron	Tayside Aviation Ltd	
G-BVHD	Grob G.115D-2 Heron	Tayside Aviation Ltd	
G-BVHE	Grob G.115D-2 Heron	Tayside Aviation Ltd	
G-BVHF	Grob G.115D-2 Heron	Tayside Aviation Ltd	
G-BVHG	Grob G.115D-2 Heron	Tayside Aviation Ltd	
G-BVHI	Rans S.10 Sakota	J. D. Amos	
G-BVHJ	Cameron A-180 balloon	S. J. Boxall	
G-BVHK	Cameron V-77 balloon	A. R. Rich	
G-BVHL	Nicollier HN.700 Menestrel II	W. Dobinson & D. Hawkins	
G-BVHM	PA-38-112 Tomahawk	Hinton Pilot Flight Training Ltd (G-DCAN)	
G-BVHO	Cameron V-90 balloon	N. W. B. Bews	
G-BVHR	Cameron V-90 balloon	G. P. Walton	
G-BVHS	Murphy Rebel	S. T. Raby	
G-BVHV	Cameron N-105 balloon	Kent Ballooning	
G-BVIA	Rand-Robinson KR-2	K. Atkinson	
G-BVIE	PA-18 Super Cub 95 (modified)	J. C. Best (G-CLIK/G-BLMB)	
G-BVIF	Montgomerie-Bensen B.8MR	R. M. & D. Mann	
G-BVIK	Maule MXT-7-180 Star Rocket	Graveley Flying Group	
G-BVIL	Maule MXT-7-180 Star Rocket	K. & S. C. Knight	
G-BVIS	Brügger MB.2 Colibri	B. H. Shaw	
G-BVIV	Light Aero Avid Speedwing	S. Styles	
G-BVIW	PA-18-Super Cub 150	I. H. Logan	
G-BVIZ	Shaw Europa	The Europa Group	
G-BVJF	Montgomerie-Bensen B.8MR	D. M. F. Harvey	
G-BVJG	Cyclone AX3/K	J. Gilroy (G-MYOP)	
G-BVJK	Glaser-Dirks DG.800A	J. S. Forster	
G-BVJN	Shaw Europa	JN Europa Group	
G-BVJT	Cessna F.406	Nor Leasing	
G-BVJU	Evans VP-1	BVJU Flying Club & Associates	
G-BVJX	Marquart MA.5 Charger	A. E. Cox	
G-BVKB	Boeing 737-59D	bmi Baby	
G-BVKF	Shaw Europa	T. R. Sinclair	
G-BVKG	Colt Flying Hot Dog SS balloon	Longbreak Ltd/USA	
G-BVKK	Slingsby T.61F Venture T.2	Buckminster Gliding Club Ltd	
G-BVKL	Cameron A-180 balloon	Dragon Balloon Co Ltd	
G-BVKM	Rutan Vari-Eze	J. P. G. Lindquist/Switzerland	
G-BVKU	Slingsby T.61F Venture T.2	G-BVKU Syndicate	
G-BVLA	Lancair 320	Eaglescott Lancair Group	
G-BVLD	Campbell Cricket (replica)	C. Berry	
G-BVLF	CFM Starstreak Shadow SS-D	J. C. Pratelli	
G-BVLG	AS.355F1 Twin Squirrel	PLM Dollar Group PLC	
G-BVLH	Shaw Europa	D. Barraclough	
G-BVLL	Lindstrand LBL-210A balloon	Airborne Balloon Flights Ltd	
G-BVLN	Aero Designs Pulsar XP	D. A. Campbell	
G-BVLP	PA-38-112 Tomahawk	J. Hornby	
G-BVLR	Van's RV-4	RV4 Group	
G-BVLT	Bellanca 7GCBC Citabria	Slade Associates	
G-BVLU	D.31 Turbulent	C. D. Bancroft	
G-BVLV	Shaw Europa	Euro 39 Group	
G-BVLX	Slingsby T.61F Venture T.2	The Royal Air Force Gliding and Soaring Association	
G-BVMA	Beech 200 Super King Air	Dragonfly Aviation Services LLP (G-VPLC)	
G-BVME	AS.365N2 Dauphin 2	CHC Scotia Ltd	
G-BVMH	WAG-Aero Sport Trainer (39624:D-39)	J. Mathews	
G-BVMJ	Cameron 95 Eagle SS balloon	R. D. Sargeant	
G-BVMM	Robin HR.200/100	Gloster Aero Group	
G-BVMN	Ken Brock KB-2 gyroplane	G-BVMN Group	
G-BVMR	Cameron V-90 balloon	I. R. Comley	
G-BVMU	Yakovlev Yak-52 (09 yellow)	Ascendances SPRL/Belgium	
G-BVNG	DH.60G-III Moth Major	P. & G. Groves	
G-BVNI	Taylor JT-2 Titch	G. de Halle	
G-BVNS	PA-28-181 Archer II	Scottish Airways Flyers (Prestwick) Ltd	
G-BVNU	FLS Aerospace Sprint Club	M. D. R. Elmes	
G-BVNY	Rans S.7 Courier	D. M. Byers-Jones	
G-BVOC	Cameron V-90 balloon	H. W. R. Stewart	
G-BVOH	Campbell Cricket (replica)	A. Kitson	
G-BVOI	Rans S.6-116 Coyote II	M. J. Whiteman-Haywood	
G-BVOK	Yakovlev Yak-52 (55 grey)	Trans Holdings Ltd	
G-BVOP	Cameron N-90 balloon	October Gold Ballooning Ltd	
G-BVOR	CFM Streak Shadow	J. M. Chandler	
G-BVOS	Shaw Europa	Durham Europa Group	

Notes	Reg.	Type	Owner or Operator
	G-BVOW	Shaw Europa	H. P. Brooks
	G-BVOY	Rotorway Executive 90	C. H. Drake
	G-BVOZ	Colt 56A balloon	British School of Ballooning
	G-BVPA	Thunder Ax8-105 S2 balloon	Firefly Balloon Promotions
	G-BVPD	CASA 1.131E Jungmann 2000	D. Bruton
	G-BVPM	Evans VP-2 Coupé	P. Marigold
	G-BVPN	Piper J-3C-65 Cub	C. Sarcelet (G-TAFY)
	G-BVPS	Jodel D.112	P. J. Swain
	G-BVPV	Lindstrand LBL-77B balloon	P. G. Hill
	G-BVPW	Rans S.6-116 Coyote II	T. B. Woolley
	G-BVPX	Bensen B.8 (modified) Tyro Gyro	A. W. Harvey
	G-BVPY	CFM Streak Shadow	R. J. Mitchell
	G-BVRA	Shaw Europa	N. E. Stokes
	G-BVRH	Taylorcraft BL.65	M. J. Kirk
	G-BVRL	Lindstrand LBL-21A balloon	M. E. & T. J. Orchard
	G-BVRU	Lindstrand LBL-105A balloon	C & R Jemmett
	G-BVRV	Van's RV-4	A. Troughton
	G-BVRZ	PA-18 Super Cub 95	R. W. Davison
	G-BVSB	TEAM mini-MAX	D. G. Palmer
	G-BVSD	SE.3130 Alouette II (V-54)	M. J. Cuttell
	G-BVSF	Aero Designs Pulsar	R. J. & J. A. Freestone
	G-BVSN	Light Aero Avid Speedwing	R. C. Bowley
	G-BVSP	P.84 Jet Provost T.3A (XM370)	H. G. Hodges & Son Ltd
	G-BVSS	Jodel D.150	A. P. Burns
	G-BVST	Jodel D.150	A. Shipp/Breighton
	G-BVSX	TEAM mini-MAX 91	J. A. Clark
	G-BVSZ	Pitts S-1E (S) Special	H. J. Morton
	G-BVTA	Tri-R Kis	A. F. Prosser
	G-BVTC	P.84 Jet Provost T.5A (XW333)	Global Aviation Ltd
	G-BVTD	CFM Streak Shadow	M. Walton
	G-BVTL	Colt 31A balloon	A. Lindsay
	G-BVTM	Cessna F.152 II	RAF Halton Aeroplane Club (G-WACS)
	G-BVTN	Cameron N-90 balloon	P. Zulehner/Austria
	G-BVTV	Rotorway Executive 90	D. W. J. Lee
	G-BVTW	Aero Designs Pulsar	R. J. Panther
	G-BVTX	DHC.1 Chipmunk 22A (WP809)	TX Flying Group
	G-BVUA	Cameron O-105 balloon	Wickers World Ltd
	G-BVUC	Colt 56A balloon	J. F. Till
	G-BVUG	Betts TB.1 (Stampe SV.4C)	H. F. Fekete (G-BEUS)
	G-BVUH	Thunder Ax6-65B balloon	K. B. Chapple
	G-BVUI	Lindstrand LBL-25A balloon	J. W. Hole
	G-BVUK	Cameron V-77 balloon	H. G. Griffiths & W. A. Steel
	G-BVUM	Rans S.6-116 Coyote II	M. Á. Abbott
	G-BVUN	Van's RV-4	D. J. Harvey
	G-BVUT	Evans VP-1 Srs. 2	M. J. Barnett
	G-BVUU	Cameron C-80 balloon	T. M. C. McCoy
	G-BVUV	Shaw Europa	R. J. Mills
	G-BVUZ	Cessna 120	T. K. Duffy
	G-BVVA	Yakovlev Yak-52	S. T. G. Lloyd
	G-BVVB	Carlson Sparrow II	L. M. McCullen
	G-BVVE	Jodel D.112	M. Balls
	G-BVVG	Nanchang CJ-6A (68)	Nanchang CJ6A Group
	G-BVVH	Shaw Europa	T. G. Hoult
	G-BVVI	Hawker Audax I (K5600)	Aero Vintage Ltd
	G-BVVK	DHC.6 Twin Otter 310	Loganair Ltd/British Airways
	G-BVVL	EAA Acro Sport II	G-BVVL Syndicate
	G-BVVM	Zenair CH.601HD	D. Macdonald
	G-BVVN	Brügger MB.2 Colibri	N. F. Andrews
	G-BVVP	Shaw Europa	I. Mansfield
	G-BVVR	Stits SA-3A Playboy	R. B. Armitage
	G-BVVS	Van's RV-4	E. G. & N. S. C. English
	G-BVVU	Lindstrand LBL Four SS balloon	Magical Adventures Ltd/USA
	G-BVVW	Yakovlev Yak-52	M. Blackman
	G-BVVZ	Corby CJ-1 Starlet	P. V. Flack
	G-BVWB	Thunder Ax8-90 S2 balloon	M. A. Stelling & K. C. Tanner
	G-BVWC	EE Canberra B.6 (WK163)	Classic Aviation Projects Ltd
	G-BVWI	Cameron light bulb SS balloon	Mobberley Balloon Collection
	G-BVWM	Shaw Europa	Europa Syndicate
	G-BVWW	Lindstrand LBL-90A balloon	J. D. A. Shields
	G-BVWY	Porterfield CP.65	R. L. Earl & B. Morris
	G-BVWZ	PA-32-301 Saratoga	The Saratoga (WZ) Group
	G-BVXA	Cameron N-105 balloon	R. E. Jones
	G-BVXC	EE Canberra B.6 (WT333) ★	Classic Aviation Projects Ltd/Bruntingthorpe

Reg.	Type	Owner or Operator	Notes
G-BVXD	Cameron O-84 balloon	Hedge Hoppers Balloon Group	
G-BVXE	Steen Skybolt	J. Buglass (G-LISA)	
G-BVXJ	CASA 1.133 Jungmeister	A. C. Mercer	
G-BVXK	Yakovlev Yak-52 (26 grey)	E. Gavazzi	
G-BVXM	AS.350B Ecureuil	The Berkeley Leisure Group Ltd	
G-BVXR	DH.104 Devon C.2 (XA880)	M. Whale & M. W. A. Lunn	
G-BVXS	Taylorcraft BC-12D	XRay Sierra Group	
G-BVYF	PA-31-350 Navajo Chieftain	J. A. Rees & D. T. Rees (G-SAVE)	
G-BVYG	CEA DR.300/180	Ulster Gliding Club Ltd	
G-BVYK	TEAM mini-MAX	A. G. Ward	
G-BVYM	CEA DR.300/180	London Gliding Club (Pty) Ltd	
G-BVYO	Robin R.2160	D. J. S. McClean	
G-BVYP	PA-25 Pawnee 235B	Bidford Airfield Ltd	
G-BVYU	Cameron A-140 balloon	S. Charlish	
G-BVYX	Light Aero Avid Speedwing Mk 4	J. E. Lipman	
G-BVYY	Pietenpol Air Camper	Pietenpol G-BVYY Group	
G-BVYZ	Stemme S.10V	L. Gubbay	
G-BVZD	Tri-R Kis Cruiser	J. M. Angiolini & G. Melling	
G-BVZE	Boeing 737-59D	bmi Baby	
G-BVZJ	Rand-Robinson KR-2	G. M. Rundle	
G-BVZN	Cameron C-80 balloon	S. J. Clarke	
G-BVZO	Rans S.6-116 Coyote II	P. J. Brion	
G-BVZR	Zenair CH.601HD	R. A. Perkins	
G-BVZT	Lindstrand LBL-90A balloon	J. Edwards	
G-BVZV	Rans S.6-116 Coyote II	A. H. & F. A. Macaskill	
G-BVZX	Cameron H-34 balloon	R. H. Etherington	
G-BVZZ	DHC.1 Chipmunk 22 (WP795)	Portsmouth Naval Gliding Club	
G-BWAC	Waco YKS-7	D. N. Peters	
G-BWAD	RAF 2000GT gyroplane	A. Melody	
G-BWAF	Hawker Hunter F.6A (XG160:U) ★	Bournemouth Aviation Museum/Bournemouth	
G-BWAG	Cameron O-120 balloon	P. M. Skinner	
G-BWAH	Montgomerie-Bensen B.8MR	J. B. Allan	
G-BWAI	CFM Streak Shadow	C. M. James	
G-BWAJ	Cameron V-77 balloon	T. J. Wilkinson	
G-BWAN	Cameron N-77 balloon	I. Chadwick	
G-BWAO	Cameron C-80 balloon	M. D. Freeston & S. Mitchell	
G-BWAP	FRED Srs 3	G. A. Shepherd	
G-BWAR	Denney Kitfox Mk 3	I. Wightman	
G-BWAT	Pietenpol Air Camper	P. W. Aitchison	
G-BWAU	Cameron V-90 balloon	K. M. & A. M. F. Hall	
G-BWAV	Schweizer 269C	Helihire	
G-BWAW	Lindstrand LBL-77A balloon	D. Bareford	
G-BWBI	Taylorcraft F-22A	R. T. G. Preston	
G-BWBT	Lindstrand LBL-90A balloon	British Telecommunications PLC	
G-BWBZ	ARV-1 Super 2	M. P. Holdstock	
G-BWCA	CFM Streak Shadow	I. C. Pearson	
G-BWCK	Everett Srs 2 gyroplane	B. F. Pearson	
G-BWCS	P.84 Jet Provost T.5 (XW293:Z)	J. H. Ashcroft	
G-BWCT	Tipsy T.66 Nipper 1	J. S. Hemmings & C. R. Steer	
G-BWCV	Shaw Europa	G. C. McKirdy	
G-BWCY	Murphy Rebel	S. Burrow	
G-BWDB	ATR-72-202	Aurigny Air Services Ltd	
G-BWDH	Cameron N-105 balloon	M. A. Scholes	
G-BWDM	Lindstrand LBL-120A balloon	A. N. F. Pertwee	
G-BWDP	Shaw Europa	S. Attubato	
G-BWDS	P.84 Jet Provost T.3A (XM424)	Aviation Heritage Ltd	
G-BWDT	PA-34-220T Seneca III	H. R. Chambers (G-BKHS)	
G-BWDX	Shaw Europa	J. Robson	
G-BWDZ	Sky 105-24 balloon	Blue Sky Syndicate	
G-BWEA	Lindstrand LBL-120A balloon	S. R. Seager	
G-BWEB	P.84 Jet Provost T.5A (XW422:3)	XW422 Group	
G-BWEE	Cameron V-42 balloon	A. J. Davey/Germany	
G-BWEF	SNCAN Stampe SV.4C	Acebell G-BWEF Syndicate (G-BOVL)	
G-BWEG	Shaw Europa	R. J. Marsh	
G-BWEM	VS.358 Seafire L.IIIC (RX168)	Mark One Partners LLC	
G-BWEN	Macair Merlin GT	D. A. Hill	
G-BWEU	Cessna F.152 II	Affair Aircraft Leasing LLP	
G-BWEW	Cameron N-105 balloon	Unipart Balloon Club	
G-BWEY	Bensen B.8	F. G. Shepherd	
G-BWEZ	Piper J-3C-65 Cub (436021)	J. G. McTaggart	
G-BWFG	Robin HR.200/120B	Air Atlantique Ltd	
G-BWFH	Shaw Europa	G. C. Grant	

|

Notes	Reg.	Type	Owner or Operator
	G-BWFJ	Evans VP-1	J. M. Vinall
	G-BWFK	Lindstrand LBL-77A balloon	Balloon Preservation Flying Group
	G-BWFM	Yakovlev Yak-50	Fox Mike Group
	G-BWFN	Hapi Cygnet SF-2A	G-BWFN Group
	G-BWFO	Colomban MC.15 Cri-Cri	K. D. & C. S. Rhodes
	G-BWFT	Hawker Hunter T.8M (XL602)	Global Aviation Services Ltd
	G-BWFX	Shaw Europa	A. D. Stewart
	G-BWFZ	Murphy Rebel	D. K. Shead (G-SAVS)
	G-BWGA	Lindstrand LBL-105A balloon	R. Thompson
	G-BWGF	P.84 Jet Provost T.5A (XW325)	Viper Jet Provost Group Ltd
	G-BWGJ	Chilton DW.1A	T. J. Harrison
	G-BWGL	Hawker Hunter T.8C (XJ615)	Stichting Hawker Hunter Foundation/Netherlands
	G-BWGO	Slingsby T.67M Firefly 200	R. Gray
	G-BWGS	BAC.145 Jet Provost T.5A (XW310)	M. P. Grimshaw
	G-BWGU	Cessna 150F	Goodair Leasing Ltd
	G-BWGY	HOAC Katana DV.20	JL Flying Ltd
	G-BWHA	Hawker Hurricane IIB (Z5252)	Historic Flying Ltd
	G-BWHD	Lindstrand LBL-31A balloon	M. R. Noyce & R. P. E. Phillips
	G-BWHF	PA-31-325 Navajo	Awyr Cymru Cyf
	G-BWHI	DHC.1 Chipmunk 22A (WK624)	N. E. M. Clare
	G-BWHK	Rans S.6-116 Coyote II	S. J. Wakeling
	G-BWHM	Sky 140-24 balloon	C. J. S. Limon
	G-BWHP	CASA 1.131E Jungmann (S4+A07)	J. F. Hopkins
	G-BWHR	Tipsy Nipper T.66 Srs 1	L. R. Marnef
	G-BWHS	RAF 2000 gyroplane	B. J. Payne
	G-BWHU	Westland Scout AH.1 (XR595)	N. J. F. Boston
	G-BWIA	Rans S.10 Sakota	I. D. Worthington
	G-BWIB	SA Bulldog Srs 120/122 (XX514)	B. I. Robertson/USA
	G-BWID	D.31 Turbulent	N. Huxtable
	G-BWII	Cessna 150G	J. D. G. Hicks (G-BSKB)
	G-BWIJ	Shaw Europa	R. Lloyd
	G-BWIK	DH.82A Tiger Moth (NL985)	P. J. Lawton
	G-BWIL	Rans S-10	S. H. Leahy
	G-BWIP	Cameron N-90 balloon	K. C. Tanner
	G-BWIR	Dornier 328-100	Suckling Airways (Cambridge) Ltd
	G-BWIV	Shaw Europa	T. G. Ledbury
	G-BWIW	Sky 180-24 balloon	T. M. Donnelly
	G-BWIX	Sky 120-24 balloon	J. M. Percival
	G-BWIZ	QAC Quickie Tri-Q 200	M. C. Davies
	G-BWJB	Thunder Ax8-105 balloon	Justerini & Brooks Ltd
	G-BWJG	Mooney M.20J	S. Nahum
	G-BWJH	Shaw Europa	I. R. Willis
	G-BWJM	Bristol M.1C (replica) (C4918)	The Shuttleworth Collection
	G-BWJW	Westland Scout AH.Mk.1 (XV130)	S. Dadak & G. Sobell
	G-BWJY	DHC.1 Chipmunk 22 (WG469)	K. J. Thompson
	G-BWKE	Cameron AS-105GD airship	W. Arnold/Germany
	G-BWKF	Cameron N-105 balloon	M. Buono/Italy
	G-BWKK	Auster A.O.P.9 (XP279)	C. A. Davis & D. R. White
	G-BWKT	Stephens Akro Laser	P. D. Begley
	G-BWKU	Cameron A-250 balloon	British School of Ballooning
	G-BWKV	Cameron V-77 balloon	C. A. Bryant
	G-BWKW	Thunder Ax8-90 balloon	Gone With The Wind Ltd
	G-BWKZ	Lindstrand LBL-77A balloon	J. H. Dobson
	G-BWLD	Cameron O-120 balloon	D. Pedri & ptnrs/Italy
	G-BWLF	Cessna 404	Reconnaisance Ventures Ltd (G-BNXS)
	G-BWLJ	Taylorcraft DCO-65 (42-35870/129)	B. J. Robe
	G-BWLL	Murphy Rebel	F. W. Parker
	G-BWLM	Sky 65-24 balloon	W. J. Brogan
	G-BWLY	Rotorway Executive 90	P. W. & I. P. Bewley
	G-BWMB	Jodel D.119	C. Hughes
	G-BWMC	Cessna 182P	Iscavia Ltd
	G-BWMF	Gloster Meteor T.7 (WA591)	Aviation Heritage Ltd
	G-BWMH	Lindstrand LBL-77B balloon	M. Gallagher
	G-BWMI	PA-28RT-201T Turbo Arrow IV	O. Cowley
	G-BWMJ	Nieuport 17/2B (replica) (N1977:8)	R. Gauld-Galliers & M. R. Lancombe
	G-BWMK	DH.82A Tiger Moth (T8191)	APB Leasing Ltd
	G-BWMN	Rans S.7 Courier	P. I. Lewis
	G-BWMO	Oldfield Baby Lakes	D. Maddocks (G-CIII)
	G-BWMS	DH.82A Tiger Moth	Foundation Early Birds/Netherlands
	G-BWMU	Cameron 105 Monster Truck SS balloon	Magical Adventures Ltd/Canada
	G-BWMV	Colt AS-105 Mk II airship	D. Stuber/Germany
	G-BWMX	DHC.1 Chipmunk 22 (WG407:67)	407th Flying Group
	G-BWMY	Cameron Bradford & Bingley SS balloon	Magical Adventures Ltd/USA

Reg.	Type	Owner or Operator	Notes
G-BWNB	Cessna 152 II	South Warwickshire School of Flying	
G-BWNC	Cessna 152 II	South Warwickshire School of Flying	
G-BWND	Cessna 152 II	South Warwickshire School of Flying Ltd & G. Davies	
G-BWNI	PA-24 Comanche 180	W. A. Stewart	
G-BWNJ	Hughes 269C	L. R. Fenwick	
G-BWNK	D,H,C,1 Chipmunk 22 (WD390)	WD390 Group	
G-BWNM	PA-28R Cherokee Arrow 180	M. & R. C. Ramnial	
G-BWNO	Cameron O-90 balloon	T. Knight	
G-BWNP	Cameron 90 Club SS balloon	L. P. Hooper & A. R. Hardwick	
G-BWNS	Cameron O-90 balloon	I. C. Steward	
G-BWNT	DHC.1 Chipmunk 22 (WP901)	P. G. D. Bell & A. Stafford	
G-BWNU	PA-38-112 Tomahawk	Kemble Aero Club Ltd	
G-BWNY	Aeromot AMT-200 Super Ximango	Powell-Brett Associates Ltd	
G-BWNZ	Agusta A109C	Anglo Beef Processors Ltd	
G-BWOB	Luscombe 8F Silvaire	P. R. Bush	
G-BWOF	P.84 Jet Provost T.5	Techair London Ltd	
G-BWOH	PA-28-161 Cadet	Plane Talking Ltd	
G-BWOI	PA-28-161 Cadet	Aviation Rentals	
G-BWOJ	PA-28-161 Cadet	Aviation Rentals	
G-BWOK	Lindstrand LBL-105G balloon	Lindstrand Hot Air Balloons Ltd	
G-BWOR	PA-18 Super Cub 135	C. D. Baird	
G-BWOT	P.84 Jet Provost T.3A (XN459)	M. Soor	
G-BWOV	Enstrom F-28A	P. A. Goss	
G-BWOW	Cameron N-105 balloon	Skybus Ballooning	
G-BWOY	Sky 31-24 balloon	C. Wolstenholme	
G-BWOZ	CFM Streak Shadow SA	J. A. Lord	
G-BWPC	Cameron V-77 balloon	H. Vaughan	
G-BWPE	Murphy Renegade Spirit UK	J. Hatswell/France	
G-BWPF	Sky 120-24 balloon	J. Francis	
G-BWPH	PA-28-181 Archer II	H. Merkado	
G-BWPJ	Steen Skybolt	D. Houghton	
G-BWPP	Sky 105-24 balloon	The Sarnia Balloon Group	
G-BWPS	CFM Streak Shadow SA	P. J. Mogg	
G-BWPT	Cameron N-90 balloon	G.Everett	
G-BWPZ	Cameron N-105 balloon	D. M. Moffat	
G-BWRA	Sopwith LC-1T Triplane (replica) (N500)	J. G. Brander (G-PENY)	
G-BWRC	Light Aero Avid Speedwing	C. G. Thompson	
G-BWRO	Shaw Europa	G-BWRO Group	
G-BWRR	Cessna 182Q	A. & R. Reid	
G-BWRS	SNCAN Stampe SV.4C	G. P. J. M. Valvekens/Belgium	
G-BWRT	Cameron 60 Concept balloon	Zebedee Balloon Service Ltd	
G-BWRZ	Lindstrand LBL-105A balloon	N. Dykes	
G-BWSB	Lindstrand LBL-105A balloon	R. Calvert-Fisher	
G-BWSC	PA-38-112 Tomahawk II	The Hawstead Flying Group	
G-BWSD	Campbell Cricket	R. F. G. Moyle	
G-BWSG	P.84 Jet Provost T.5 (XW324/K)	J. Bell	
G-BWSH	P.84 Jet Provost T.3A (XN498)	Global Aviation Ltd	
G-BWSI	K & S SA.102.5 Cavalier	B. W. Shaw	
G-BWSJ	Denney Kitfox Mk 3	J. M. Miller	
G-BWSL	Sky 77-24 balloon	D. Baggley	
G-BWSN	Denney Kitfox Mk 3	M. J. Laundy	
G-BWSU	Cameron N-105 balloon	A. M. Marten	
G-BWSV	Yakovlev Yak-52	M. W. Fitch	
G-BWTB	Lindstrand LBL-105A balloon	Servatruc Ltd	
G-BWTC	Zlin Z.242L	S. W. Turley	
G-BWTD	Zlin Z.242L	Oxford Aviation Academy (Oxford) Ltd	
G-BWTE	Cameron O-140 balloon	Cameron Flights Southern Ltd	
G-BWTG	DHC.1 Chipmunk 22 (WB671:910)	R. G. T. de Man/Netherlands	
G-BWTH	Robinson R22 Beta	Helicopter Services	
G-BWTJ	Cameron V-77 balloon	A. J. Montgomery	
G-BWTK	RAF 2000 GTX-SE gyroplane	M. Love	
G-BWTN	Lindstrand LBL-90A balloon	J. A. Lomas	
G-BWTO	DHC.1 Chipmunk 22 (WP984)	Skycraft Services Ltd	
G-BWTW	Mooney M.20C	T. J. Berry	
G-BWUA	Campbell Cricket	N. J. Orchard	
G-BWUB	PA-18S Super Cub 135	Caledonian Seaplanes Ltd	
G-BWUE	Hispano HA.1112M1L	Historic Flying Ltd (G-AWHK)	
G-BWUH	PA-28-181 Archer III	A. Davis	
G-BWUJ	Rotorway Executive 162F	Southern Helicopters Ltd	
G-BWUK	Sky 160-24 balloon	Cameron Flights Southern Ltd	
G-BWUL	Noorduyn AT-16 Harvard IIB	G-BWUL Flying Group	
G-BWUN	DHC.1 Chipmunk 22 (WD310)	T. Henderson	

Notes	Reg.	Type	Owner or Operator
	G-BWUP	Shaw Europa	V. Goddard
	G-BWUS	Sky 65-24 balloon	N. A. P. Bates
	G-BWUT	DHC.1 Chipmunk 22 (WZ879)	Herbert Aviation Ltd
	G-BWUU	Cameron N-90 balloon	Bailey Balloons Ltd
	G-BWUV	DHC.1 Chipmunk 22A (WK640)	A. C. Darby
	G-BWUZ	Campbell Cricket (replica)	K. A. Touhey
	G-BWVB	Pietenpol Air Camper	E. B. Toulson
	G-BWVC	Jodel D.18	R. W. J. Cripps
	G-BWVF	Pietenpol Air Camper	N. Clark
	G-BWVI	Stern ST.80	I. Pearson
	G-BWVM	Colt AA-1050 balloon	B. B. Baxter Ltd
	G-BWVN	Whittaker MW7	E. Stinton
	G-BWVR	Yakovlev Yak-52 (52 yellow)	I. Parkinson
	G-BWVS	Shaw Europa	D. R. Bishop
	G-BWVT	DHA.82A Tiger Moth	R. Jewitt
	G-BWVU	Cameron O-90 balloon	J. Atkinson
	G-BWVV	Jodel D.18	J. C. Field
	G-BWVY	DHC.1 Chipmunk 22 (WP896)	N. Gardner
	G-BWVZ	DHC.1 Chipmunk 22A (WK590)	D. Campion/Belgium
	G-BWWA	Ultravia Pelican Club GS	J. S. Aplin
	G-BWWB	Shaw Europa	P. Levi
	G-BWWC	DH.104 Dove 7 (XM223)	Air Atlantique Ltd
	G-BWWE	Lindstrand LBL-90A balloon	B. J. Newman
	G-BWWF	Cessna 185A	T. N. Bartlett & S. M. C. Harvey
	G-BWWG	SOCATA Rallye 235E	J. J. Frew
	G-BWWI	AS.332L Super Puma	Bristow Helicopters Ltd
	G-BWWJ	Hughes 269C	R. J. Scott (G-BMYZ)
	G-BWWK	Hawker Nimrod I (S1581)	Patina Ltd
	G-BWWL	Colt Flying Egg SS balloon	Magical Adventures Ltd/USA
	G-BWWN	Isaacs Fury II (K8303:D)	J. S. Marten-Hale
	G-BWWP	Rans S.6-116 Coyote II	H. R. Carey
	G-BWWT	Dornier 328-100	Suckling Airways (Cambridge) Ltd
	G-BWWU	PA-22 Tri-Pacer 150	K. M. Bowen
	G-BWWW	BAe Jetstream 3102	British Aerospace PLC
	G-BWWX	Yakovlev Yak-50	D. P. McCoy/Ireland
	G-BWWY	Lindstrand LBL-105A balloon	M. J. Smith
	G-BWXA	Slingsby T.67M Firefly 260	Swift Aircraft Ltd
	G-BWXB	Slingsby T.67M Firefly 260	Swift Aircraft Ltd
	G-BWXC	Slingsby T.67M Firefly 260	Swift Aircraft Ltd
	G-BWXD	Slingsby T.67M Firefly 260	Swift Aircraft Ltd
	G-BWXE	Slingsby T.67M Firefly 260	Swift Aircraft Ltd
	G-BWXF	Slingsby T.67M Firefly 260	Swift Aircraft Ltd
	G-BWXG	Slingsby T.67M Firefly 260	Swift Aircraft Ltd
	G-BWXH	Slingsby T.67M Firefly 260	Swift Aircraft Ltd
	G-BWXI	Slingsby T.67M Firefly 260	Swift Aircraft Ltd
	G-BWXJ	Slingsby T.67M Firefly 260	Swift Aircraft Ltd
	G-BWXK	Slingsby T.67M Firefly 260	Swift Aircraft Ltd
	G-BWXL	Slingsby T.67M Firefly 260	Swift Aircraft Ltd
	G-BWXM	Slingsby T.67M Firefly 260	Swift Aircraft Ltd
	G-BWXN	Slingsby T.67M Firefly 260	Swift Aircraft Ltd
	G-BWXP	Slingsby T.67M Firefly 260	D. S. McGregor
	G-BWXR	Slingsby T.67M Firefly 260	Swift Aircraft Ltd
	G-BWXS	Slingsby T.67M Firefly 260	Swift Aircraft Ltd
	G-BWXT	Slingsby T.67M Firefly 260	Swift Aircraft Ltd
	G-BWXU	Slingsby T.67M Firefly 260	Swift Aircraft Ltd
	G-BWXV	Slingsby T.67M Firefly 260	A. D. Hoy
	G-BWXX	Slingsby T.67M Firefly 260	Swift Aircraft Ltd
	G-BWXY	Slingsby T.67M Firefly 260	Swift Aircraft Ltd
	G-BWXZ	Slingsby T.67M Firefly 260	Swift Aircraft Ltd
	G-BWYB	PA-28 Cherokee 160	I. M. Latiff
	G-BWYD	Shaw Europa	F. H. Mycroft
	G-BWYI	Denney Kitfox Mk3	D. R. Piercy
	G-BWYK	Yakovlev Yak-50	Foley Farm Flying Group
	G-BWYN	Cameron O-77 balloon	W. H. Morgan (G-ODER)
	G-BWYO	Sequoia F.8L Falco	M. C. R. Sims
	G-BWYR	Rans S.6-116 Coyote II	K. W. Scrivens
	G-BWYU	Sky 120-24 balloon	Aerosauras Balloons Ltd
	G-BWZA	Shaw Europa	T. G. Cowlishaw
	G-BWZG	Robin R.2160	Sherburn Aero Club Ltd
	G-BWZJ	Cameron A-250 balloon	Balloon Club of Great Britain
	G-BWZU	Lindstrand LBL-90B balloon	K. D. Pierce
	G-BWZX	AS.332L Super Puma	Bristow Helicopters Ltd
	G-BWZY	Hughes 269A	Reeve Newfields Ltd (G-FSDT)

Reg.	Type	Owner or Operator	Notes
G-BXAB	PA-28-161 Warrior II	TG Aviation Ltd (G-BTGK)	
G-BXAC	RAF 2000 GTX-SE gyroplane	J. A. Robinson	
G-BXAF	Pitts S-1D Special	N. J. Watson	
G-BXAH	CP.301A Emeraude	A. P. Goodwin	
G-BXAJ	Lindstrand LBL-14A balloon	Oscair Project AB/Sweden	
G-BXAK	Yakovlev Yak-52 (44 black)	J. Calverley	
G-BXAN	Scheibe SF-25C Falke	C. Falke Syndicate	
G-BXAO	Avtech Jabiru SK	P. J. Thompson	
G-BXAS	Avro RJ100	Trident Jet (Jersey) Ltd	
G-BXAU	Pitts S-1 Special	L. Westnage	
G-BXAV	Yakovlev Yak-52	N. J. Stillwell	
G-BXAX	Cameron N-77 balloon ★	Balloon Preservation Group	
G-BXAY	Bell 206B JetRanger 3	Viewdart Ltd	
G-BXBA	Cameron A-210 balloon	Reach For The Sky Ltd	
G-BXBB	PA-20 Pacer 150	M. E. R. Coghlan	
G-BXBK	Avions Mudry CAP-10B	S. Skipworth	
G-BXBL	Lindstrand LBL-240A balloon	Firefly Balloon Promotions	
G-BXBM	Cameron O-105 balloon	Bristol University Hot Air Ballooning Society	
G-BXBU	Avions Mudry CAP-10B	J. F. Cosgrave & H. R. Pearson	
G-BXBZ	PZL-104 Wilga 80	J. H. Sandham Aviation	
G-BXCA	Hapi Cygnet SF-2A	J. D. C. Henslow	
G-BXCC	PA-28-201T Turbo Dakota	Greer Aviation Ltd	
G-BXCD	TEAM mini-MAX 91A	A. Maltby	
G-BXCG	Jodel DR.250/160	CG Group	
G-BXCJ	Campbell Cricket (replica)	A. G. Peel	
G-BXCN	Sky 105-24 balloon	Nottingham Hot-Air Balloon Club	
G-BXCO	Colt 120A balloon	J. R. Lawson	
G-BXCP	DHC.1 Chipmunk 22 (WP859)	M. P. O'Connor	
G-BXCT	DHC.1 Chipmunk 22 (WB697)	Wickenby Aviation	
G-BXCU	Rans S.6-116 Coyote II	S. C. Ord	
G-BXCV	DHC.1 Chipmunk 22 (WP929)	Ardmore Aviation Services Ltd/Hong Kong	
G-BXCW	Denney Kitfox Mk 3	M. J. Blanchard	
G-BXDA	DHC.1 Chipmunk 22 (WP860)	D. C. Mowat	
G-BXDB	Cessna U.206F	D. A. Howard (G-BMNZ)	
G-BXDD	RAF 2000GTX-SE gyroplane	R. Harris	
G-BXDE	RAF 2000GTX-SE gyroplane	B. Jones	
G-BXDF	Beech 95-B55 Baron	Chesh-Air Ltd	
G-BXDG	DHC.1 Chipmunk 22 (WK630)	Felthorpe Flying Group	
G-BXDH	DHC.1 Chipmunk 22 (WD331)	B. K. & W. G. Ranger	
G-BXDI	DHC.1 Chipmunk 22 (WD373)	Sunrise Global Aviation Ltd	
G-BXDM	DHC.1 Chipmunk 22 (WP840)	G. Hubsch	
G-BXDN	DHC.1 Chipmunk 22 (WK609)	W. D. Lowe, G. James & L. A. Edwards	
G-BXDO	Rutan Cozy	J. Foreman	
G-BXDP	DHC.1 Chupmunk 22 (WK642)	Gipsy Captains	
G-BXDR	Lindstrand LBL-77A balloon	British Telecommunications PLC	
G-BXDS	Bell 206B JetRanger III	Toby Blackwell Ltd (G-TAMF/G-OVBJ)	
G-BXDT	Robin HR.200/120B	Multiflight Ltd	
G-BXDU	Aero Designs Pulsar	M. P. Board	
G-BXDV	Sky 105-24 balloon	N. A. Carr	
G-BXDY	Shaw Europa	D. G. & S. Watts	
G-BXDZ	Lindstrand LBL-105A balloon	D. J. & A. D. Sutcliffe	
G-BXEC	DHC.1 Chipmunk 22 (WK633)	D. S. Hunt	
G-BXEJ	VPM M-16 Tandem Trainer	AES Radionic Surveillance Systems	
G-BXEN	Cameron N-105 balloon	E. Ghio/Italy	
G-BXES	P.66 Pembroke C.1 (XL954)	Air Atlantique Ltd	
G-BXEX	PA-28-181 Archer II	R. Mayle	
G-BXEZ	Cessna 182P	Forhawk Ltd	
G-BXFB	Pitts S-1 Special	J. F. Dowe	
G-BXFC	Jodel D.18	B. S. Godbold	
G-BXFE	Avions Mudry CAP-10B	Avion Aerobatic Ltd	
G-BXFG	Shaw Europa	A. Rawicz-Szczerbo	
G-BXFI	Hawker Hunter T.7 (WV372)	Hunter Flying Ltd	
G-BXFK	CFM Streak Shadow	A. G. Sindrey	
G-BXFN	Colt 77A balloon	Charter Ballooning Ltd	
G-BXGA	AS.350B2 Ecureuil	PLM Dollar Group Ltd	
G-BXGD	Sky 90-24 balloon	Servo & Electronic Sales Ltd	
G-BXGG	Shaw Europa	D. J. Joyce	
G-BXGH	Diamond Katana DA20-A1	M. Dorrian	
G-BXGL	DHC.1 Chipmunk 22	Airways Aero Associations Ltd	
G-BXGM	DHC.1 Chipmunk 22 (WP928:D)	Chipmunk G-BXGM Group	
G-BXGO	DHC.1 Chipmunk 22 (WB654:U)	Trees Group	
G-BXGP	DHC.1 Chipmunk 22 (WZ882)	Eaglescott Chipmunk Group	
G-BXGS	RAF 2000 gyroplane	C. R. Gordon	

Notes	Reg.	Type	Owner or Operator
	G-BXGT	I.I.I. Sky Arrow 650T	J. S. C. Goodale
	G-BXGV	Cessna 172R	Skyhawk Group
	G-BXGX	DHC.1 Chipmunk 22 (WK586:V)	I. J. Flitcroft
	G-BXGY	Cameron V-65 balloon	Dante Balloon Group
	G-BXGZ	Stemme S.10V	D. Tucker & K. Lloyd
	G-BXHA	DHC.1 Chipmunk 22 (WP925)	H. M. & S. Roberts
	G-BXHE	Lindstrand LBL-105A balloon	L. H. Ellis
	G-BXHF	DHC.1 Chipmunk 22 (WP930:J)	Hotel Fox Syndicate
	G-BXHH	AA-5A Cheetah	A. W. Daffin
	G-BXHJ	Hapi Cygnet SF-2A	I. J. Smith
	G-BXHL	Sky 77-24 balloon	R. K. Gyselynck
	G-BXHO	Lindstrand Telewest Sphere SS balloon	Magical Adventures Ltd
	G-BXHR	Stemme S.10V	J. H. Rutherford
	G-BXHT	Bushby-Long Midget Mustang	K. Manley
	G-BXHU	Campbell Cricket Mk 6	P. J. Began
	G-BXHY	Shaw Europa	Jupiter Flying Group
	G-BXIA	DHC.1 Chipmunk 22 (WB615)	Dales Aviation
	G-BXIC	Cameron A-275 balloon	Aerosaurus Balloons LLP
	G-BXIE	Colt 77B balloon	L. C. Sanders
	G-BXIF	PA-28-161 Warrior II	Piper Flight Ltd
	G-BXIG	Zenair CH.701 STOL	A. J. Perry
	G-BXIH	Sky 200-24 balloon	Kent Ballooning
	G-BXII	Shaw Europa	D. A. McFadyean
	G-BXIJ	Shaw Europa	R. James
	G-BXIM	DHC.1 Chipmunk 22 (WK512)	A. B. Ashcroft & P. R. Joshua
	G-BXIO	Jodel DR.1050M	R. S. Palmer
	G-BXIT	Zebedee V-31 balloon	Zebedee Balloon Service Ltd
	G-BXIX	VPM M-16 Tandem Trainer	P. P. Willmott
	G-BXIY	Blake Bluetit (BAPC37)	M. J. Aubrey
	G-BXIZ	Lindstrand LBL-31A balloon	J. S. Russon
	G-BXJB	Yakovlev Yak-52	Yak Display Group
	G-BXJC	Cameron A-210 balloon	British School of Ballooning
	G-BXJD	PA-28 Cherokee 180C	M. G. A. Hussein
	G-BXJG	Lindstrand LBL-105B balloon	C. E. Wood
	G-BXJH	Cameron N-42 balloon	D. M. Hoddinott
	G-BXJJ	PA-28-161 Cadet	Plane Talking Ltd
	G-BXJM	Cessna 152	ACS Aviation Ltd
	G-BXJO	Cameron O-90 balloon	Dragon Balloon Co Ltd
	G-BXJP	Cameron C-80 balloon	A. Sarrasin
	G-BXJS	Schempp-Hirth Janus CM	Janus Syndicate
	G-BXJT	Sky 90-24 balloon	J. G. O'Connell
	G-BXJV	Diamond Katana DA20-A1	Enniskillen Flying School Ltd
	G-BXJW	Diamond Katana DA20-A1	Enniskillen Flying School Ltd
	G-BXJY	Van's RV-6	D. J. Sharland
	G-BXJZ	Cameron C-60 balloon	J. M. Stables
	G-BXKF	Hawker Hunter T.7(XL577/V)	R. F. Harvey
	G-BXKL	Bell 206B JetRanger 3	Swattons Aviation Ltd
	G-BXKM	RAF 2000 GTX-SE gyroplane	A. H. Goddard
	G-BXKO	Sky 65-24 balloon	Ecole de Pilotage Franche-Comte Montgolfieres/France
	G-BXKU	Colt AS-120 Mk II airship	D. C. Chipping/Portugal
	G-BXKW	Slingsby T.67M Firefly 200	J-F Jansen & A. Huygens
	G-BXKX	Auster V	J. A. Clark
	G-BXLF	Lindstrand LBL-90A balloon	W. Rousell & J. Tyrrell
	G-BXLG	Cameron C-80 balloon	S. M. Anthony
	G-BXLK	Shaw Europa	R. G. Fairall
	G-BXLN	Fournier RF-4D	P. W. Cooper
	G-BXLO	P.84 Jet Provost T.4 (XR673/L)	Century Aviation Ltd
	G-BXLP	Sky 90-24 balloon	A. P. Jay & R. S. McKibbin
	G-BXLS	PZL-110 Koliber 160A	D. C. Bayes
	G-BXLT	SOCATA TB200 Tobago XL	C., G. & J. Fisher & D. Fitton
	G-BXLW	Enstrom F.28F	Rhobur Ltd
	G-BXLY	PA-28-151 Warrior	Multiflight Ltd (G-WATZ)
	G-BXMF	Cassutt Racer IIIM	P. R. Fabish
	G-BXMG	RAF 2000 GTX gyroplane	J. S. Wright
	G-BXMM	Cameron A-180 balloon	High Road Balloons
	G-BXMV	Scheibe SF.25C Falke 1700	K. E. Ballington
	G-BXMX	Currie Wot	M. R. Coreth
	G-BXMY	Hughes 269C	R. J. Scott
	G-BXNA	Light Aero Avid Flyer	A. P. Daines
	G-BXNC	Shaw Europa	J. K. Cantwell
	G-BXNN	DHC.1 Chipmunk 22 (WP983:B)	E. N. Skinner
	G-BXNS	Bell 206B JetRanger 3	Sterling Helicopters Ltd

Reg.	Type	Owner or Operator	Notes
G-BXNT	Bell 206B JetRanger 3	Sterling Helicopters Ltd	
G-BXOA	Robinson R22 Beta	MG Group Ltd	
G-BXOC	Evans VP-2	H. J. & E. M. Cox	
G-BXOF	Diamond Katana DA20-A1	M. Dorrian	
G-BXOI	Cessna 172R	E. J. Watts	
G-BXOJ	PA-28-161 Warrior III	Craigard Property Trading Ltd	
G-BXOM	Isaacs Spitfire	S. Vince	
G-BXON	Auster AOP.9	C. J. & D. J. Baker	
G-BXOT	Cameron C-70 balloon	Dante Balloon Group	
G-BXOU	CEA DR.360	J. A. Lofthouse	
G-BXOW	Colt 105A balloon	F. M. H. Audenaert	
G-BXOX	AA-5A Cheetah	R. L. Carter & P. J. Large	
G-BXOY	QAC Quickie Q.235	C. C. Clapham	
G-BXOZ	PA-28-181 Archer II	Spritetone Ltd	
G-BXPC	Diamond Katana DA20-A1	Cubair Flight Training Ltd	
G-BXPD	Diamond Katana DA20-A1	Cubair Flight Training Ltd	
G-BXPI	Van's RV-4	S. T. G. Lloyd	
G-BXPK	Cameron A-250 balloon	Alba Ballooning Ltd	
G-BXPL	PA-28 Cherokee 140	Take Flight Aviation Ltd	
G-BXPM	Beech 58 Baron	Foyle Flyers Ltd	
G-BXPP	Sky 90-24 balloon	S. J. Farrant	
G-BXPR	Colt 110 Can SS balloon	P. O. Wagner/Germany	
G-BXPT	Ultramagic H-77 balloon	G. D. O. Bartram/Andorra	
G-BXRA	Avions Mudry CAP-10B	J. W. Scott	
G-BXRB	Avions Mudry CAP-10B	T. T. Duhig	
G-BXRC	Avions Mudry CAP-10B	Group Alpha	
G-BXRD	Enstrom 280FX	K. Payne & M. A. Stephenson	
G-BXRF	CP.1310-C3 Super Emeraude	D. T. Gethin	
G-BXRM	Cameron A-210 balloon	Dragon Balloon Co Ltd	
G-BXRO	Cessna U.206G	M. Penny	
G-BXRP	Schweizer 269C	AH Helicopter Services Ltd	
G-BXRR	Westland Scout AH.1	M. Soor	
G-BXRS	Westland Scout AH.1 (XW613)	B-N Group Ltd	
G-BXRT	Robin DR.400-180	T. P. Usborne	
G-BXRV	Van's RV-4	Cleeve Flying Grouip	
G-BXRY	Bell 206B JetRanger	Corbett Holdings Ltd	
G-BXRZ	Rans S.6-116 Coyote II	M. P. Hallam	
G-BXSC	Cameron C-80 balloon	N. A. Apsey	
G-BXSD	Cessna 172R	R. Paston	
G-BXSE	Cessna 172R	MK Aero Support Ltd	
G-BXSG	Robinson R22 Beta II	Rivermead Aviation Ltd	
G-BXSH	Glaser-Dirks DG.800B	R. O'Conor	
G-BXSI	Avtech Jabiru SK	P. F. Gandy	
G-BXSP	Grob G.109B	Deeside Grob Group	
G-BXSR	Cessna F172N	N. C. K. G. Copeman	
G-BXST	PA-25 Pawnee 235C	The Northumbria Gliding Club Ltd	
G-BXSU	TEAM mini-MAX 91A	I. A. Coates (G-MYGL)	
G-BXSV	SNCAN Stampe SV.4C	B. A. Bower	
G-BXSX	Cameron V-77 balloon	D. R. Medcalf	
G-BXSY	Robinson R22 Beta II	N. M. G. Pearson	
G-BXTB	Cessna 152	Durham Tees Flight Training Ltd	
G-BXTD	Shaw Europa	P. R. Anderson	
G-BXTF	Cameron N-105 balloon	Flying Pictures Ltd	
G-BXTG	Cameron N-42 balloon	P. M. Watkins & S. M. M. Carden	
G-BXTH	Westland Gazelle HT.1 (XW866)	Armstrong Aviation Ltd	
G-BXTI	Pitts S-1S Special	Fly Hire Ltd	
G-BXTJ	Cameron N-77 balloon	Chubb Fire Ltd Chubb	
G-BXTO	Hindustan HAL-6 Pushpak	P. Q. Benn	
G-BXTS	Diamond Katana DA20-A1	I. M. Armitage & D. J. Short	
G-BXTT	AA-5B Tiger	M. N. Stevens	
G-BXTV	Bug Mk.4 helicopter	B. R. Cope	
G-BXTW	PA-28-181 Archer III	Davison Plant Hire	
G-BXTY	PA-28-161 Cadet	Flew LLP	
G-BXTZ	PA-28-161 Cadet	Flew LLP	
G-BXUA	Campbell Cricket Mk.5	A. W. Harvey	
G-BXUC	Robinson R22 Beta	Rivermead Aviation Ltd/Switzerland	
G-BXUF	Agusta-Bell 206B JetRanger 3	SJ Contracting Services Ltd	
G-BXUG	Lindstrand Baby Bel SS balloon	K-H. Gruenauer/Germany	
G-BXUH	Lindstrand LBL-31A balloon	Balloon Preservation Flying Groupt	
G-BXUI	Glaser-Dirks DG.800B	J. Le Coyte	
G-BXUM	Shaw Europa	D. Bosomworth	
G-BXUO	Lindstrand LBL-105A balloon	Lindstrand Technologies Ltd	
G-BXUS	Sky 65-24 balloon	PSH Skypower Ltd	

Notes	Reg.	Type	Owner or Operator
	G-BXUU	Cameron V-65 balloon	M. D. Freeston & S. Mitchell
	G-BXUW	Cameron Colt 90A balloon	Zycomm Electronics Ltd
	G-BXUX	Brandli Cherry BX-2	M. F. Fountain
	G-BXUY	Cessna 310Q	G. A. Vickers
	G-BXVA	SOCATA TB200 Tobago XL	Archer Two Ltd
	G-BXVB	Cessna 152 II	PJC (Leasing) Ltd
	G-BXVD	CFM Streak Shadow SA	I. J. C. Burman
	G-BXVG	Sky 77-24 balloon	M. Wolf
	G-BXVK	Robin HR.200/120B	Modi Aviation Ltd
	G-BXVM	Van's RV-6A	J. C. Lomax
	G-BXVO	Van's RV-6A	P. J. Hynes & M. E. Holden
	G-BXVP	Sky 31-24 balloon	T. Dudman
	G-BXVR	Sky 90-24 balloon	P. Hegarty
	G-BXVS	Brügger MB.2 Colibri	G. T. Snoddon
	G-BXVT	Cameron O-77 balloon	R. P. Wade
	G-BXVU	PA-28-161 Warrior II	Jet Connections Ltd
	G-BXVV	Cameron V-90 balloon	Floating Sensations Ltd
	G-BXVX	Rutan Cozy	G. E. Murray
	G-BXVY	Cessna 152	Stapleford Flying Club Ltd
	G-BXWA	Beech 76 Duchess	Aviation South West Ltd
	G-BXWB	Robin HR.100/200B	W. A. Brunwin
	G-BXWG	Sky 120-24 balloon	M. E. White
	G-BXWH	Denney Kitfox Mk.4-1200	M. G. Porter
	G-BXWK	Rans S.6-ESA Coyote II	P. B. Davey
	G-BXWL	Sky 90-24 balloon	D. J. Baggley
	G-BXWO	PA-28-181 Archer II	J. S. Develin & Z. Islam
	G-BXWP	PA-32 Cherokee Six 300	R. J. Sharpe
	G-BXWR	CFM Streak Shadow	M. A. Hayward (G-MZMI)
	G-BXWT	Van's RV-6	R. C. Owen
	G-BXWU	FLS Aerospace Sprint 160	Aeroelvia Ltd
	G-BXWV	FLS Aerospace Sprint 160	Aeroelvia Ltd
	G-BXWX	Sky 25-16 balloon	C. O'Neill & G. Davis
	G-BXXG	Cameron N-105 balloon	R. N. Simpkins
	G-BXXH	Hatz CB-1	R. D. Shingler
	G-BXXI	Grob G.109B	M. N. Martin
	G-BXXJ	Colt Flying Yacht SS balloon	Magical Adventures Ltd/USA
	G-BXXK	Cessna FR.172N	J. A. Havers and R. A. Blackwell
	G-BXXL	Cameron N-105 balloon	Flying Pictures Ltd
	G-BXXN	Robinson R22 Beta	Helicopter Services
	G-BXXO	Lindstrand LBL-90B balloon	G. P. Walton
	G-BXXP	Sky 77-24 balloon	T. R. Wood
	G-BXXS	Sky 105-24 balloon	Flying Pictures Ltd
	G-BXXT	Beech 76 Duchess	Pridenote Ltd
	G-BXXU	Colt 31A balloon	Sade Balloons Ltd
	G-BXXW	Enstrom F-28F	D. A. Marks (G-SCOX)
	G-BXYE	CP.301-C1 Emeraude	D. T. Gethin
	G-BXYF	Colt AS-105 GD airship	LN Flying Ltd
	G-BXYI	Cameron H-34 balloon	S. P. Harrowing
	G-BXYJ	Jodel DR.1050	G-BXYJ Group
	G-BXYM	PA-28 Cherokee 235	Redfly Aviation Ltd
	G-BXYO	PA-28RT-201 Arrow IV	W. R. Tupling-Prest
	G-BXYP	PA-28RT-201 Arrow IV	G. I. Cooper
	G-BXYT	PA-28RT-201 Arrow IV	Falcon Flying Services Ltd
	G-BXYX	Van's RV-6A	A. G. Palmer
	G-BXZA	PA-38-112 Tomahawk	Aviatlantic
	G-BXZB	Nanchang CJ-6A (2632019)	Wingglider Ltd
	G-BXZF	Lindstrand LBL-90A balloon	B. T. Harris
	G-BXZI	Lindstrand LBL-90A balloon	J. A. Viner
	G-BXZK	MDH MD-900 Explorer	Dorset Police Air Support Unit
	G-BXZO	Pietenpol Air Camper	P. J. Cooke
	G-BXZU	Micro Aviation Bantam B.22-S	M. E. Whapham & R. W. Hollamby
	G-BXZV	CFM Streak Shadow	M. D. O'Brien
	G-BXZY	CFM Streak Shadow Srs DD	Cloudbase Aviation Services Ltd
	G-BYAL	Boeing 757-28AER	Thomson Airways Ltd
	G-BYAO	Boeing 757-204ER	Thomson Airways Ltd
	G-BYAP	Boeing 757-204ER	Thomson Airways Ltd
	G-BYAT	Boeing 757-204ER	Thomson Airways Ltd
	G-BYAU	Boeing 757-204ER	Thomson Airways Ltd
	G-BYAV	Taylor JT.1 Monoplane	D. M. Lockley
	G-BYAW	Boeing 757-204ER	Thomson Airways Ltd
	G-BYAX	Boeing 757-204ER	Thomson Airways Ltd
	G-BYAY	Boeing 757-204ER	Thomson Airways Ltd

Reg.	Type	Owner or Operator	Notes
G-BYAZ	CFM Streak Shadow	A. G. Wright	
G-BYBC	Agusta-Bell 206B JetRanger 2	Sky Charter UK Ltd (G-BTWW)	
G-BYBD	Cessna F.172H	D. G. Bell & J. Cartmell (G-OBHX/G-AWMU)	
G-BYBE	Jodel D.120A	J. M. Alexander	
G-BYBF	Robin R.2160i	D. J. R. Lloyd-Evans	
G-BYBH	PA-34-200T Seneca II	Goldspear (UK) Ltd	
G-BYBI	Bell 206B JetRanger 3	Castle Air Ltd	
G-BYBJ	Medway Hybred 44XLR	M. Gardner	
G-BYBK	Murphy Rebel	J. R. Howard	
G-BYBL	Gardan GY-80 Horizon 160D	M. J. Sutton	
G-BYBM	Avtech Jabiru SK	P. J. Hatton	
G-BYBN	Cameron N-77 balloon	M. G. Howard	
G-BYBO	Medway Hybred 44XLR Eclipser	C. Hershaw	
G-BYBP	Cessna A.185F	G. M. S. Scott	
G-BYBR	Rans S.6-116 Coyote II	S. & A. F. Williams	
G-BYBS	Sky 80-16 balloon	B. K. Rippon	
G-BYBU	Renegade Spirit UK	R. L. Williams	
G-BYBV	Mainair Rapier	M. W. Robson	
G-BYBX	Slingsby T.67M Firefly 260	Slingsby Advanced Composites Ltd	
G-BYBY	Thorp T.18C Tiger	P. G. Mair	
G-BYBZ	Jabiru SK	D. Licheri	
G-BYCA	PA-28 Cherokee 140D	R. Steptoe	
G-BYCD	Cessna 140 (modified)	G. P. James	
G-BYCF	Robinson R22 Beta II	Aero Maintenance Ltd	
G-BYCJ	CFM Shadow Srs DD	P. I. Hodgson	
G-BYCM	Rans S.6-ES Coyote II	E. W. McMullan	
G-BYCN	Rans S.6-ES Coyote II	T. J. Croskery	
G-BYCP	Beech B200 Super King Air	London Executive Aviation Ltd	
G-BYCS	Jodel DR.1051	CS Group	
G-BYCV	Meridian Maverick 430	I. J. H. Morgan	
G-BYCW	Mainair Blade 912	P. C. Watson	
G-BYCX	Westland Wasp HAS.1	BN Helicopters Ltd	
G-BYCY	I.I.I. Sky Arrow 650T	K. A. Daniels	
G-BYCZ	Avtech Jabiru SK	SK Group	
G-BYDB	Grob G.115B	J. B. Baker	
G-BYDE	VS.361 Spitfire LF. IX (PT879)	P. A. Teichman	
G-BYDF	Sikorsky S-76A	Brecqhou Development Ltd	
G-BYDG	Beech C24R Sierra	Professional Flight Simulation Ltd	
G-BYDJ	Colt 120A balloon	D. K. Hempleman-Adams	
G-BYDK	SNCAN Stampe SV.4C	Bianchi Aviation Film Services Ltd	
G-BYDL	Hawker Hurricane IIB (Z5207)	P. J. Lawton	
G-BYDT	Cameron N-90 balloon	R. M. Stanley	
G-BYDV	Van's RV-6	B. F. Hill	
G-BYDY	Beech 58 Baron	Pilot Services Flying Group Ltd	
G-BYDZ	Pegasus Quantum 15-912	A. Mundy	
G-BYEA	Cessna 172P	M. Gates	
G-BYEC	Glaser-Dirks DG.800B	The 23 Syndicate	
G-BYEE	Mooney M.20K	Double Echo Flying Group	
G-BYEH	CEA Jodel DR.250	S. T. Scully	
G-BYEJ	Scheibe SF-28A Tandem Falke	D. Shrimpton	
G-BYEK	Stoddard Hamilton Glastar	M. W. Meynell	
G-BYEL	Van's RV-6	D. Millar	
G-BYEM	Cessna R.182 RG	Bickertons Aerodromes Ltd	
G-BYEO	Zenair CH.601HDS	J. R. Clarke	
G-BYER	Cameron C-80 balloon	J. M. Langley	
G-BYES	Cessna 172P	Redhill Air Services Ltd	
G-BYEW	Pegasus Quantum 15-912	D. Martin	
G-BYEY	Lindstrand LBL-21 Silver Dream balloon	Oscair Project Ltd/Sweden	
G-BYFA	Cessna F.152 II	Redhill Air Services Ltd (G-WACA)	
G-BYFC	Avtech Jabiru SK	M. Flint	
G-BYFF	Pegasus Quantum 15-912	Kemble Flying Club	
G-BYFI	CFM Starstreak Shadow SA	J. A. Cook	
G-BYFJ	Cameron N-105 balloon	R. J. Mercer	
G-BYFK	Cameron Printer 105 SS balloon	Mobberley Balloon Collection	
G-BYFL	Diamond HK.36 TTS	Seahawk Gliding Club	
G-BYFM	Jodel DR.1050M-1 (replica)	A. J. Roxburgh	
G-BYFR	PA-32R-301 Saratoga II HP	Buckleton Ltd	
G-BYFT	Pietenpol Air Camper	G. Everett	
G-BYFU	Lindstrand LBL-105B balloon	ULM Decouverte/France	
G-BYFV	TEAM mini-MAX 91	W. E. Gillham	
G-BYFX	Colt 77A balloon	Wye Valley Aviation Ltd	
G-BYFY	Avions Mudry CAP-10B	R. N. Crosland	
G-BYGA	Boeing 747-436	British Airways	

Notes	Reg.	Type	Owner or Operator
	G-BYGB	Boeing 747-436	British Airways
	G-BYGC	Boeing 747-436	British Airways
	G-BYGD	Boeing 747-436	British Airways
	G-BYGE	Boeing 747-436	British Airways
	G-BYGF	Boeing 747-436	British Airways
	G-BYGG	Boeing 747-436	British Airways
	G-BYHC	Cameron Z-90 balloon	S. M. Sherwin
	G-BYHE	Robinson R22 Beta	Helicopter Services Ltd
	G-BYHG	Dornier 328-100	Suckling Airways (Cambridge) Ltd
	G-BYHH	PA-28-161 Warrior III	Stapleford Flying Club Ltd
	G-BYHI	PA-28-161 Warrior II	T. W. & W. S. Gilbert
	G-BYHJ	PA-28R-201 Arrow	Flew LLP
	G-BYHK	PA-28-181 Archer III	T-Air Services
	G-BYHL	DHC.1 Chipmunk 22 (WG308)	M. R. & I. D. Higgins
	G-BYHO	Mainair Blade 912	T. Porter & D. Whiteley
	G-BYHP	CEA DR.253B	HP Flying Group
	G-BYHR	Pegasus Quantum 15-912	I. D. Chantler
	G-BYHS	Mainair Blade 912	T. J. Grange, R. Beard & K. Meechan
	G-BYHT	Robin DR.400/180R	Deeside Robin Group
	G-BYHU	Cameron N-105 balloon	ABC Flights Ltd
	G-BYHV	Raj Hamsa X'Air 582	M. G. Adams
	G-BYHY	Cameron V-77 balloon	P. Spellward
	G-BYIA	Avtech Jabiru SK	M. D. Doyle
	G-BYIB	Rans S.6-ES Coyote II	W. Anderson
	G-BYID	Rans S.6-ES Coyote II	R. M. Watson
	G-BYIE	Robinson R22 Beta II	Heli Air Ltd
	G-BYII	TEAM mini-MAX	G. Wilkinson
	G-BYIJ	CASA 1.131E Jungmann 2000	R. N. Crosland
	G-BYIK	Shaw Europa	P. M. Davis
	G-BYIL	Cameron N-105 balloon	Oakfield Farm Products Ltd
	G-BYIM	Avtech Jabiru UL	A. & J. McVey
	G-BYIN	RAF 2000 gyroplane	J. R. Legge
	G-BYIO	Colt 105A balloon	N. Charbonnier/Italy
	G-BYIP	Aerotek Pitts S-2A Special	D. P. Heather-Hayes
	G-BYIR	Aerotek Pitts S-1S Special	S. Kramer
	G-BYIS	Pegasus Quantum 15-912	D. J. Ramsden
	G-BYIU	Cameron V-90 balloon	H. Micketeit/Germany
	G-BYIV	Cameron PM-80 balloon	A. Schneider/Germany
	G-BYIW	Cameron PM-80 balloon	Team Ballooning/Germany
	G-BYIX	Cameron PM-80 balloon	A. Schneider/Germany
	G-BYIY	Lindstrand LBL-105B balloon	J. H. Dobson
	G-BYIZ	Pegasus Quantum 15-912	J. D. Gray
	G-BYJA	RAF 2000 GTX-SE	C. R. W. Lyne
	G-BYJB	Mainair Blade 912	D. C. Haslam
	G-BYJC	Cameron N-90 balloon	A. G. Merry
	G-BYJD	Avtech Jabiru UL	M. W. Knights
	G-BYJE	TEAM Mini-MAX 91	T. A. Willcox
	G-BYJF	Thorpe T.211	AD Aviation Ltd
	G-BYJG	Lindstrand LBL-77A balloon	Lindstrand Hot-Air Balloons Ltd
	G-BYJH	Grob G.109B	A. J. Buchanan
	G-BYJI	Shaw Europa	M. Gibson (G-ODTI)
	G-BYJK	Pegasus Quantum 15-912	K. D. Smith
	G-BYJL	Aero Designs Pulsar	F. A. H. Ashmead
	G-BYJM	Cyclone AX2000	R. W. Kraike
	G-BYJN	Lindstrand LBL-105A balloon	B. Meeson
	G-BYJO	Rans S.6-ES Coyote II	K. N. Cobb
	G-BYJP	Aerotek Pitts S-1S Special	Eaglescott Pitts Group
	G-BYJR	Lindstrand LBL-77B balloon	B. M. Reed
	G-BYJS	SOCATA TB20 Trinidad	A. P. Bedford
	G-BYJT	Zenair CH.601HD	J. D. T. Tannock
	G-BYJW	Cameron Sphere 105 balloon	Balleroy Developpement SAS
	G-BYJX	Cameron C-70 balloon	B. Perona
	G-BYKA	Lindstrand LBL-69A balloon	B. Meeson
	G-BYKB	Rockwell Commander 114	A. Walton
	G-BYKC	Mainair Blade 912	G. W. Cameron & C. S. Harrison
	G-BYKD	Mainair Blade 912	D. C. Boyle
	G-BYKF	Enstrom F-28F	S. C. Severeyns & G. T. Williams
	G-BYKG	Pietenpol Air Camper	K. B. Hodge
	G-BYKI	Cameron N-105 balloon	J. A. Leahy/Ireland
	G-BYKJ	Westland Scout AH.1	Austen Associates
	G-BYKK	Robinson R44	Dragonfly Aviation
	G-BYKL	PA-28-181 Archer II	Transport Command Ltd
	G-BYKP	PA-28R-201T Turbo Arrow IV	D. W. Knox & D. L. Grimes

Reg.	Type	Owner or Operator	Notes
G-BYKS	Leopoldoff L-6 Colibri	I. M. Callier	
G-BYKT	Pegasus Quantum 15-912	N. J. Howarth	
G-BYKU	BFC Challenger II	K. W. Seedhouse	
G-BYKW	Lindstrand LBL-77B balloon	K. Allemand/France	
G-BYKX	Cameron N-90 balloon	G. Davis	
G-BYLB	D. H. 82A Tiger Moth	P. A. Layzell	
G-BYLC	Pegasus Quantum 15-912	A. Cordes	
G-BYLD	Pietenpol Air Camper	S. Bryan	
G-BYLI	Nova Vertex 22 hang glider	M. Hay	
G-BYLJ	Letov LK-2M Sluka	W. J. McCarroll	
G-BYLL	Sequoia F.8L Falco	N. J. Langrick	
G-BYLO	T.66 Nipper Srs 1	M. J. A. Trudgill	
G-BYLP	Rand-Robinson KR-2	C. S. Hales	
G-BYLS	Bede BD-4	G. H. Bayliss	
G-BYLT	Raj Hamsa X'Air 582	T. W. Phipps	
G-BYLV	Thunder Ax8-105 S2 balloon	kb Voli Di Chiozzi Bartolomeo EC SAS/Italy	
G-BYLW	Lindstrand LBL-77A balloon	Associazione Gran Premio Italiano	
G-BYLX	Lindstrand LBL-105A balloon	Italiana Aeronavi/Italy	
G-BYLY	Cameron V-77 balloon (1)	R. Bayly/Italy (G-ULIA)	
G-BYLZ	Rutan Cozy	W. S. Allen	
G-BYMB	Diamond Katana DA20-C1	S. Staniulis & A. Zakaras	
G-BYMD	PA-38-112 Tomahawk II	M. A. Petrie	
G-BYMF	Pegasus Quantum 15-912	G. R. Stockdale	
G-BYMG	Cameron A-210 balloon	Cloud Nine Balloon Co	
G-BYMH	Cessna 152	PJC (Leasing) Ltd	
G-BYMI	Pegasus Quantum 15	N. C. Grayson	
G-BYMJ	Cessna 152	PJC (Leasing) Ltd	
G-BYMK	Dornier 328-100	Suckling Airways (Cambridge) Ltd	
G-BYMN	Rans S.6-ESA Coyote II	R. Fitzpatrick	
G-BYMO	Campbell Cricket	P. G. Rawson	
G-BYMP	Campbell Cricket Mk 1	J. J. Fitzgerald	
G-BYMR	Raj Hamsa X'Air R100(3)	W. Drury	
G-BYMU	Rans S.6-ES Coyote II	I. R. Russell & S. Palmer	
G-BYMV	Rans S.6-ES Coyote II	T. P. R. Wright	
G-BYMW	Boland 52-12 balloon	C. Jones	
G-BYMX	Cameron A-105 balloon	H. Reis/Germany	
G-BYMY	Cameron N-90 balloon	A. Cakss	
G-BYNA	Cessna F.172H	D. M. White (G-AWTH)	
G-BYND	Pegasus Quantum 15	W. J. Upton	
G-BYNE	Pilatus PC-6/B2-H4 Turbo Porter	D. M. Penny	
G-BYNF	NA-64 Yale I (3349)	R. S. Van Dijk	
G-BYNI	Rotorway Exec 90	M. Bunn	
G-BYNK	Robin HR.200/160	Penguin Flight Group	
G-BYNM	Mainair Blade 912	J. P. Hanlon & A. C. McAllister	
G-BYNN	Cameron V-90 balloon	Cloud Nine Balloon Group	
G-BYNP	Rans S.6-ES Coyote II	R. J. Lines	
G-BYNS	Avtech Jabiru SK	D. K. Lawry	
G-BYNU	Cameron Thunder Ax7-77 balloon	J. A. W. Dyer	
G-BYNW	Cameron H-34 balloon	I. M. Ashpole	
G-BYNX	Cameron RX-105 balloon	Cameron Balloons Ltd	
G-BYNY	Beech 76 Duchess	Magenta Ltd	
G-BYOB	Slingsby T.67M Firefly 260	Stapleford Flying Club Ltd	
G-BYOD	Slingsby T.67C	D. I. Stanbridge	
G-BYOG	Pegasus Quantum 15-912	M. D. Hinge	
G-BYOH	Raj Hamsa X'Air 582 (1)	J. Owen	
G-BYOI	Sky 80-16 balloon	I. S. & S. W. Watthews	
G-BYOJ	Raj Hamsa X'Air 582 (1)	S. E. J. M. McDonald	
G-BYOK	Cameron V-90 balloon	D. S. Wilson	
G-BYOM	Sikorsky S-76C (modified)	Starspeed Ltd (G-IJCB)	
G-BYON	Mainair Blade	R. Campbell-Moore	
G-BYOO	CFM Streak Shadow	G. R. Eastwood	
G-BYOR	Raj Hamsa X'Air 582(7)	R. Dilkes	
G-BYOT	Rans S.6-ES Coyote II	G. Shaw	
G-BYOU	Rans S.6-ES Coyote II	P. G. Bright & P. L. Parker	
G-BYOV	Pegasus Quantum 15-912	M. Howland	
G-BYOW	Mainair Blade	M. Taylor & T. Smith	
G-BYOX	Cameron Z-90 balloon	D. R. Rawlings	
G-BYOZ	Mainair Rapier	A. G. Lomas	
G-BYPB	Pegasus Quantum 15-912	Cleaprop Microlight School Ltd	
G-BYPD	Cameron A-105 balloon	Headland Hotel Ltd	
G-BYPE	Gardan GY-80 Horizon 160D	P. B. Hodgson	
G-BYPF	Thruster T.600N	M. A. Beadman	
G-BYPG	Thruster T.600N	M. A. Roxburgh	

Notes	Reg.	Type	Owner or Operator
	G-BYPH	Thruster T.600N	D. M. Canham
	G-BYPJ	Pegasus Quantum 15-912	M. Watson
	G-BYPL	Pegasus Quantum 15-912	IP. Lister
	G-BYPM	Shaw Europa XS	G. F. Stratton
	G-BYPN	MS.880B Rallye Club	R. Edwards and D. & S. A. Bell
	G-BYPO	Raj Hamsa X'Air 582 (1)	D. W. Willis
	G-BYPR	Zenair CH.601HD Zodiac	R. Line
	G-BYPT	Rans S.6-ES Coyote II	G. P. & P. T. Willcox
	G-BYPU	PA-32R-301 Saratoga SP	AM Blatch Electrical Contractors Ltd
	G-BYPW	Raj Hamsa X'Air 583 (3)	K. J. Kimpton
	G-BYPY	Ryan ST3KR (001)	T. Curtis-Taylor
	G-BYPZ	Rans S.6-116 Super 6	R. A. Blackbourne
	G-BYRC	Westland WS-58 Wessex HC.2 (XT671)	D. Brem-Wilson
	G-BYRG	Rans S.6-ES Coyote II	S. J. Macmillan
	G-BYRJ	Pegasus Quantum 15-912	C. W. Docksey
	G-BYRK	Cameron V-42 balloon	R. Kunert
	G-BYRO	Mainair Blade	P. W. F. Coleman
	G-BYRR	Mainair Blade 912	G. R. Sharples
	G-BYRU	Pegasus Quantum 15-912	L. M. Westwood
	G-BYRV	Raj Hamsa X'Air 582 (1)	A. D. Russell
	G-BYRX	Westland Scout AH.1 (XT634)	Edwalton Aviation Ltd
	G-BYRY	Slingsby T.67M Firefly 200	PI Air Services SPRL/Belgium
	G-BYRZ	Lindstrand LBL-77M balloon	Challenge Transatlantique/France
	G-BYSA	Shaw Europa XS	R. L. Hitchcock
	G-BYSE	Agusta-Bell 206B JetRanger 2	C. I. Motors Ltd (G-BFND)
	G-BYSF	Avtech Jabiru UL	P. F. Morgan
	G-BYSG	Robin HR.200/120B	Modi Aviation Ltd
	G-BYSI	WSK-PZL Koliber 160A	J. & D. F. Evans
	G-BYSJ	DHC.1 Chipmunk 22 (WB569:R)	C. H. Green
	G-BYSK	Cameron A-275 balloon	Balloon School (International) Ltd
	G-BYSM	Cameron A-210 balloon	Balloon School (International) Ltd
	G-BYSN	Rans S.6-ES Coyote II	S. J. Smith
	G-BYSP	PA-28-181 Archer II	Take Flight Aviation Ltd
	G-BYSS	Medway Rebel SS	K. A. Sutton
	G-BYSV	Cameron N-120 balloon	S. Simmington
	G-BYSX	Pegasus Quantum 15-912	D. W. Ormond
	G-BYSY	Raj Hamsa X'Air 582 (1)	J. M. Davidson
	G-BYTB	SOCATA TB20 Trinidad	Watchman Aircraft Ltd
	G-BYTC	Pegasus Quantum 15-912	R. J. Marriott
	G-BYTI	PA-24 Comanche 250	M. Carruthers & G. Auchterlonie
	G-BYTJ	Cameron C-80 balloon	A. J. Gregory
	G-BYTK	Avtech Jabiru UL	G. R. Phillips
	G-BYTL	Mainair Blade 912	P. B. Spencer & J. T. Burrow
	G-BYTM	Dyn' Aero MCR-01	I. Lang & E. J. Clarke
	G-BYTN	DH.82A Tiger Moth (N6720:VX)	R. Merewood & J. W. Freckington
	G-BYTR	Raj Hamsa X'Air 582 (1)	B. Wyatt
	G-BYTS	Montgomerie-Bensen B.8MR gyroplane	C. Seaman
	G-BYTU	Mainair Blade 912	J. E. Morgan
	G-BYTV	Avtech Jabiru UK	M. G. Speers
	G-BYTW	Cameron O-90 balloon	Sade Balloons Ltd
	G-BYTZ	Raj Hamsa X'Air 582 (1)	R. Armstrong
	G-BYUA	Grob G.115E Tutor	Babcock Aerospace Ltd
	G-BYUB	Grob G.115E Tutor	Babcock Aerospace Ltd
	G-BYUC	Grob G.115E Tutor	Babcock Aerospace Ltd
	G-BYUD	Grob G.115E Tutor	Babcock Aerospace Ltd
	G-BYUE	Grob G.115E Tutor	Babcock Aerospace Ltd
	G-BYUF	Grob G.115E Tutor	Babcock Aerospace Ltd
	G-BYUG	Grob G.115E Tutor	Babcock Aerospace Ltd
	G-BYUH	Grob G.115E Tutor	Babcock Aerospace Ltd
	G-BYUI	Grob G.115E Tutor	Babcock Aerospace Ltd
	G-BYUJ	Grob G.115E Tutor	Babcock Aerospace Ltd
	G-BYUK	Grob G.115E Tutor	Babcock Aerospace Ltd
	G-BYUL	Grob G.115E Tutor	Babcock Aerospace Ltd
	G-BYUM	Grob G.115E Tutor	Babcock Aerospace Ltd
	G-BYUN	Grob G.115E Tutor	Babcock Aerospace Ltd
	G-BYUO	Grob G.115E Tutor	Babcock Aerospace Ltd
	G-BYUP	Grob G.115E Tutor	Babcock Aerospace Ltd
	G-BYUR	Grob G.115E Tutor	Babcock Aerospace Ltd
	G-BYUS	Grob G.115E Tutor	Babcock Aerospace Ltd
	G-BYUU	Grob G.115E Tutor	Babcock Aerospace Ltd
	G-BYUV	Grob G.115E Tutor	Babcock Aerospace Ltd
	G-BYUW	Grob G.115E Tutor	Babcock Aerospace Ltd
	G-BYUX	Grob G.115E Tutor	Babcock Aerospace Ltd

Reg.	Type	Owner or Operator	Notes
G-BYUY	Grob.G.115E Tutor	Babcock Aerospace Ltd	
G-BYUZ	Grob G.115E Tutor	Babcock Aerospace Ltd	
G-BYVA	Grob G.115E Tutor	Babcock Aerospace Ltd	
G-BYVB	Grob G.115E Tutor	Babcock Aerospace Ltd	
G-BYVC	Grob G.115E Tutor	Babcock Aerospace Ltd	
G-BYVD	Grob G.115E Tutor	Babcock Aerospace Ltd	
G-BYVE	Grob G.115E Tutor	Babcock Aerospace Ltd	
G-BYVF	Grob G.115E Tutor	Babcock Aerospace Ltd	
G-BYVG	Grob G.115E Tutor	Babcock Aerospace Ltd	
G-BYVH	Grob G.115E Tutor	Babcock Aerospace Ltd	
G-BYVI	Grob G.115E Tutor	Babcock Aerospace Ltd	
G-BYVJ	Grob G.115E Tutor	Babcock Aerospace Ltd	
G-BYVK	Grob G.115E Tutor	Babcock Aerospace Ltd	
G-BYVL	Grob G.115E Tutor	Babcock Aerospace Ltd	
G-BYVM	Grob G.115E Tutor	Babcock Aerospace Ltd	
G-BYVO	Grob G.115E Tutor	Babcock Aerospace Ltd	
G-BYVP	Grob G.115E Tutor	Babcock Aerospace Ltd	
G-BYVR	Grob G.115E Tutor	Babcock Aerospace Ltd	
G-BYVS	Grob G.115E Tutor	Babcock Aerospace Ltd	
G-BYVT	Grob G.115E Tutor	Babcock Aerospace Ltd	
G-BYVU	Grob G.115E Tutor	Babcock Aerospace Ltd	
G-BYVV	Grob G.115E Tutor	Babcock Aerospace Ltd	
G-BYVW	Grob G.115E Tutor	Babcock Aerospace Ltd	
G-BYVX	Grob G.115E Tutor	Babcock Aerospace Ltd	
G-BYVY	Grob G.115E Tutor	Babcock Aerospace Ltd	
G-BYVZ	Grob G.115E Tutor	Babcock Aerospace Ltd	
G-BYWA	Grob G.115E Tutor	Babcock Aerospace Ltd	
G-BYWB	Grob G.115E Tutor	Babcock Aerospace Ltd	
G-BYWC	Grob G.115E Tutor	Babcock Aerospace Ltd	
G-BYWD	Grob G.115E Tutor	Babcock Aerospace Ltd	
G-BYWE	Grob G.115E Tutor	Babcock Aerospace Ltd	
G-BYWF	Grob G.115E Tutor	Babcock Aerospace Ltd	
G-BYWG	Grob G.115E Tutor	Babcock Aerospace Ltd	
G-BYWH	Grob G.115E Tutor	Babcock Aerospace Ltd	
G-BYWI	Grob G.115E Tutor	Babcock Aerospace Ltd	
G-BYWJ	Grob G.115E Tutor	Babcock Aerospace Ltd	
G-BYWK	Grob G.115E Tutor	Babcock Aerospace Ltd	
G-BYWL	Grob G.115E Tutor	Babcock Aerospace Ltd	
G-BYWM	Grob G.115E Tutor	Babcock Aerospace Ltd	
G-BYWN	Grob G.115E Tutor	Babcock Aerospace Ltd	
G-BYWO	Grob G.115E Tutor	Babcock Aerospace Ltd	
G-BYWP	Grob G.115E Tutor	Babcock Aerospace Ltd	
G-BYWR	Grob G.115E Tutor	Babcock Aerospace Ltd	
G-BYWS	Grob G.115E Tutor	Babcock Aerospace Ltd	
G-BYWT	Grob G.115E Tutor	Babcock Aerospace Ltd	
G-BYWU	Grob G.115E Tutor	Babcock Aerospace Ltd	
G-BYWV	Grob G.115E Tutor	Babcock Aerospace Ltd	
G-BYWW	Grob G.115E Tutor	Babcock Aerospace Ltd	
G-BYWX	Grob G.115E Tutor	Babcock Aerospace Ltd	
G-BYWY	Grob G.115E Tutor	Babcock Aerospace Ltd	
G-BYWZ	Grob G.115E Tutor	Babcock Aerospace Ltd	
G-BYXA	Grob G.115E Tutor	Babcock Aerospace Ltd	
G-BYXB	Grob G.115E Tutor	Babcock Aerospace Ltd	
G-BYXC	Grob G.115E Tutor	Babcock Aerospace Ltd	
G-BYXD	Grob G.115E Tutor	Babcock Aerospace Ltd	
G-BYXE	Grob G.115E Tutor	Babcock Aerospace Ltd	
G-BYXF	Grob G.115E Tutor	Babcock Aerospace Ltd	
G-BYXG	Grob G.115E Tutor	Babcock Aerospace Ltd	
G-BYXH	Grob G.115E Tutor	Babcock Aerospace Ltd	
G-BYXI	Grob G.115E Tutor	Babcock Aerospace Ltd	
G-BYXJ	Grob G.115E Tutor	Babcock Aerospace Ltd	
G-BYXK	Grob G.115E Tutor	Babcock Aerospace Ltd	
G-BYXL	Grob G.115E Tutor	Babcock Aerospace Ltd	
G-BYXM	Grob G.115E Tutor	Babcock Aerospace Ltd	
G-BYXN	Grob G.115E Tutor	Babcock Aerospace Ltd	
G-BYXO	Grob G.115E Tutor	Babcock Aerospace Ltd	
G-BYXP	Grob G.115E Tutor	Babcock Aerospace Ltd	
G-BYXS	Grob G.115E Tutor	Babcock Aerospace Ltd	
G-BYXT	Grob G.115E Tutor	Babcock Aerospace Ltd	
G-BYXW	Medway Eclipser	G. A. Hazell	
G-BYXX	Grob G.115E Tutor	Babcock Aerospace Ltd	
G-BYXY	Grob G.115E Tutor	Babcock Aerospace Ltd	
G-BYXZ	Grob G.115E Tutor	Babcock Aerospace Ltd	

Notes	Reg.	Type	Owner or Operator
	G-BYYA	Grob G.115E Tutor	Babcock Aerospace Ltd
	G-BYYB	Grob G.115E Tutor	Babcock Aerospace Ltd
	G-BYYC	Hapi Cygnet SF-2A	G. H. Smith
	G-BYYE	Lindstrand LBL-77A balloon	C. Wilkinson
	G-BYYG	Slingsby T.67C	The Pathfinder Flying Club Ltd
	G-BYYL	Avtech Jabiru UL 450	M. J. Hillier & W. J. Lee
	G-BYYM	Raj Hamsa X'Air 582 (1)	S. M. S. Smith
	G-BYYN	Pegasus Quantum 15-912	V. Gledhill
	G-BYYO	PA-28R -201 Arrow III	Stapleford Flying Club Ltd
	G-BYYP	Pegasus Quantum 15	D. A. Linsey-Bloom
	G-BYYR	Raj Hamsa X'Air 582 (4)	T. D. Bawden
	G-BYYT	Avtech Jabiru UL 450	A. C. Cale and A. J. Young.
	G-BYYX	TEAM mini-MAX 91	P. S. Lewinton
	G-BYYY	Pegasus Quantum 15-912	Clearprop Microlight School Ltd
	G-BYYZ	Staaken Z-21A Flitzer	T. White
	G-BYZA	AS.355F2 Twin Squirrel	MMAir Ltd
	G-BYZB	Mainair Blade	A. M. Thornley
	G-BYZF	Raj Hamsa X'Air 582 (1)	R. P. Davies
	G-BYZG	Cameron A-275 balloon	Cameron Flights Southern Ltd
	G-BYZL	Cameron GP-65 balloon	P. Thibo
	G-BYZO	Rans S.6-ES Coyote II	Golf Zulu Oscar Group
	G-BYZP	Robinson R22 Beta	T. I. McGlone
	G-BYZR	I.I.I. Sky Arrow 650TC	G-BYZR Flying Group
	G-BYZS	Avtech Jabiru UL-450	N. Fielding
	G-BYZT	Nova Vertex 26	M. Hay
	G-BYZU	Pegasus Quantum 15	N. I. Clifton
	G-BYZV	Sky 90-24 balloon	P. Farmer
	G-BYZW	Raj Hamsa X'Air 582 (2)	J. Magill
	G-BYZX	Cameron R-90 balloon	D. K. Hempleman-Adams
	G-BYZY	Pietenpol Aircamper	D. M. Hanchett
	G-BYZZ	Robinson R22 Beta II	Mid-Atlantic Helicopters Ltd
	G-BZAB	Mainair Rapier	B. Myers
	G-BZAE	Cessna 152	APB Leasing Ltd
	G-BZAG	Lindstrand LBL-105A balloon	A. M. Figiel
	G-BZAI	Pegasus Quantum 15	S. I. Close
	G-BZAK	Raj Hamsa X'Air 582 (1)	G. L. Daniels
	G-BZAL	Mainair Blade 912	J. Potts
	G-BZAM	Europa	D. U. Corbett
	G-BZAP	Avtech Jabiru UL-450	I. J. Grindley & D. R. Griffiths
	G-BZAR	Denney Kitfox 4-1200 Speedster	N. J. France (G-LEZJ)
	G-BZAS	Isaacs Fury II (K5673)	N. C. Stone
	G-BZAT	Avro RJ100	Trident Jet (Jersey) Ltd
	G-BZAX	Avro RJ100	Triangle Regional Aircraft Leasing Ltd
	G-BZAY	Avro RJ100	Triangle Regional Aircraft Leasing Ltd
	G-BZAZ	Avro RJ100	Triangle Regional Aircraft Leasing Ltd
	G-BZBC	Rans S.6-ES Coyote II	A. J. Baldwin
	G-BZBE	Cameron A-210 balloon	Dragon Balloon Co Ltd
	G-BZBF	Cessna 172M	L. W. Scattergood
	G-BZBH	Thunder Ax6-65 balloon	P. J. Hebdon & A. C. Fraser
	G-BZBI	Cameron V-77 balloon	C. & A. I. Gibson
	G-BZBJ	Lindstrand LBL-77A balloon	P. T. R. Ollivere
	G-BZBL	Lindstrand LBL-120A balloon	East Coast Balloons Ltd
	G-BZBO	Stoddard-Hamilton Glasair III	M. B. Hamlett/France
	G-BZBP	Raj Hamsa X'Air 582 (1)	J. L. B. Roy
	G-BZBR	Pegasus Quantum 15-912	P. D. Neilson
	G-BZBS	PA-28-161 Warrior III	Aviation Rentals
	G-BZBT	Cameron H-34 Hopper balloon	D. G. Such
	G-BZBU	Robinson R22	I. C. Macdonald
	G-BZBW	Rotorway Executive 162F	Southern Helicopters Ltd
	G-BZBX	Rans S.6-ES Coyote II	P. J. Taylor
	G-BZBZ	Jodel D.9	P. A. Gasson
	G-BZDA	PA-28-161 Warrior III	Aviation Rentals
	G-BZDC	Mainair Blade	E. J. Wells & P. J. Smith
	G-BZDD	Mainair Blade 912	G. Devlin
	G-BZDE	Lindstrand LBL-210A balloon	Toucan Travel Ltd
	G-BZDF	CFM Streak Shadow SA	W. M. Moylan
	G-BZDH	PA-28R Cherokee Arrow 200-II	G-BZDH Ltd
	G-BZDJ	Cameron Z-105 balloon	BWS Security Systems Ltd
	G-BZDK	X'Air 582(2)	B. Park
	G-BZDM	Stoddard-Hamilton Glastar	F. G. Miskelly
	G-BZDN	Cameron N-105 balloon	I. R. Warrington & P. A. Foot
	G-BZDP	SA Bulldog Srs 120/121 (XX551:E)	R. M. Raikes

Reg.	Type	Owner or Operator	Notes
G-BZDR	Tri-R Kis	J. M. & J. A. Jackson	
G-BZDS	Pegasus Quantum 15-912	K. C. Yeates	
G-BZDT	Maule MXT-7-180	Strongcrew Ltd	
G-BZDV	Westland Gazelle HT.2	D. A. Gregory	
G-BZEA	Cessna A.152	Sky Leisure Aviation (Charters) Ltd	
G-BZEB	Cessna 152	Sky Leisure Aviation (Charters) Ltd	
G-BZEC	Cessna 152	Sky Leisure Aviation (Charters) Ltd	
G-BZED	Pegasus Quantum 15-912	D. Crozier	
G-BZEE	Agusta-Bell 206B JetRanger 2	Rocket Aviation Ltd	
G-BZEG	Mainair Blade	R. P. Cookson	
G-BZEJ	Raj Hamsa X'Air 582 (7)	H-Flight X'Air Flying Group	
G-BZEL	Mainair Blade 912	T. McCormack	
G-BZEN	Avtech Jabiru UL-450	N. W. Cawley	
G-BZEP	SA Bulldog Srs 120/121 (XX561:7)	A. J. Amato	
G-BZER	Raj Hamsa X'Air R100 (1)	N. P. Lloyd & H. Lloyd-Jones	
G-BZES	Rotorway Executive 90	Southern Helicopters Ltd (G-LUFF)	
G-BZET	Robin HR.200/120B	Bulldog Aviation Ltd	
G-BZEU	Raj Hamsa X'Air 582 (2)	D. E. Foster	
G-BZEW	Rans S.6-ES Coyote II	M. J. Wooldridge	
G-BZEY	Cameron N-90 balloon	Northants Auto Parts and Service Ltd	
G-BZEZ	CFM Streak Shadow	G. J. Pearce	
G-BZFA	Avro 146 RJ70	Trident Turboprop (Dublin) Ltd	
G-BZFB	Robin R.2112A	T. F. Wells	
G-BZFC	Pegasus Quantum 15-912	G. Addison	
G-BZFD	Cameron N-90 balloon	David Hataway Holdings Ltd	
G-BZFG	Sky 105 balloon	Virgin Airship & Balloon Co Ltd	
G-BZFH	Pegasus Quantum 15-912	D. W. Adams	
G-BZFI	Avtech Jabiru UL	Group Family	
G-BZFN	SA Bulldog Srs 120/121 (XX667:16)	Risk Logical Ltd	
G-BZFP	DHC.6 Twin Otter 310	Loganair Ltd/Flybe.com	
G-BZFR	Extra EA.300/L	T. C. Beadle	
G-BZFS	Mainair Blade 912	D. F. Clorley	
G-BZFT	Murphy Rebel	N. A. Evans	
G-BZFU	Lindstrand LBL HS-110 HA Airship	Lindstrand Hot Air Balloons Ltd	
G-BZFV	Zenair CH.601UL	M. E. Caton	
G-BZGA	DHC.1 Chipmunk 22 (WK585)	The Real Flying Co Ltd	
G-BZGB	DHC.1 Chipmunk 22 (WZ872:E)	Silverstar Aviation Ltd	
G-BZGF	Rans S.6-ES Coyote II	C. A. Purvis & D. F. Castle	
G-BZGH	Cessna F.172N	Golf Hotel Group	
G-BZGJ	Thunder Ax10-180 S2 balloon	Merlin Balloons	
G-BZGK	NA OV-10B Bronco (99+32)	Aircraft Restoration Co Ltd	
G-BZGL	NA OV-10B Bronco (99+26)	Aircraft Restoration Co Ltd	
G-BZGM	Mainair Blade 912	D. Avery	
G-BZGO	Robinson R44	Flight Academy (Gyrocopters) Ltd	
G-BZGR	Rans S.6-ES Coyote II	J. M. Benton	
G-BZGS	Mainair Blade 912	M. J. Holmes	
G-BZGT	Avtech Jabiru UL-450	J. White	
G-BZGV	Lindstrand LBL-77A balloon	J. H. Dryden	
G-BZGW	Mainair Blade	M. Liptrot	
G-BZGX	Raj Hamsa X'Air 582 (6)	P. J. Gleeson	
G-BZGY	Dyn'Aéro CR.100	B. Appleby	
G-BZGZ	Pegasus Quantum 15-912	D. W. Beech	
G-BZHA	Boeing 767-336ER	British Airways	
G-BZHB	Boeing 767-336ER	British Airways	
G-BZHC	Boeing 767-336ER	British Airways	
G-BZHE	Cessna 152	International Artists Sports Management Ltd	
G-BZHF	Cessna 152	Modi Aviation Ltd	
G-BZHG	Tecnam P92 Echo	R. W. F. Boarder	
G-BZHJ	Raj Hamsa X'Air 582 (7)	S. Hardy	
G-BZHL	Noorduyn AT-16 Harvard IIB	R. H. Cooper & S. Swallow	
G-BZHN	Pegasus Quantum 15-912	A. M. Sirant	
G-BZHO	Pegasus Quantum 15	T. H. Beales	
G-BZHR	Avtech Jabiru UL-450	G. W. Rowbotham & W. Turner	
G-BZHT	PA-18A Super Cub 150	Lakes Gliding Club	
G-BZHU	Wag-Aero Sport Trainer	Teddy Boys Flying Group	
G-BZHV	PA-28-181 Archer III	R. M. & T. A. Limb	
G-BZHX	Thunder Ax11-250 S2 balloon	Wizard Balloons Ltd	
G-BZHY	Mainair Blade 912	M. Morris	
G-BZIA	Raj Hamsa X'Air 700 (1)	J. L. Pritchett	
G-BZIC	Lindstrand LBL Sun SS balloon	Ballongaventyr 1 Sakne AB/Sweden	
G-BZID	Montgomerie-Bensen B.8MR	A. Gault	
G-BZIG	Thruster T.600N	Ultra Air Ltd	
G-BZIH	Lindstrand LBL-31A balloon	Skyart Balloons	

Notes	Reg.	Type	Owner or Operator
	G-BZII	Extra EA.300/1	P. F. Brice
	G-BZIJ	Robin DR.400/500	Rob Airways Ltd
	G-BZIK	Cameron A-250 balloon	Breckland Balloons Ltd
	G-BZIL	Colt 120A balloon	Champagne Flights
	G-BZIM	Pegasus Quantum 15-912	S. Jelley
	G-BZIO	PA-28-161 Warrior III	Aviation Rentals
	G-BZIP	Montgomerie-Bensen B.8MR	C. D. Prebble
	G-BZIS	Raj Hamsa X'Air 582 (2)	T. Welch
	G-BZIT	Beech 95-B55 Baron	Propellorhead Aviation Ltd
	G-BZIV	Avtech Jabiru UL	V. R. Leggott
	G-BZIW	Pegasus Quantum 15-912	J. M. Hodgson
	G-BZIX	Cameron N-90 balloon	M. Stefanini & P. Marmugi/Italy
	G-BZIY	Raj Hamsa X'Air 582 (2)	A. L. A. Gill
	G-BZIZ	Ultramagic H-31 balloon	G. D. O. Bartram
	G-BZJA	Cameron 90 Fire SS balloon	Chubb Fire Ltd
	G-BZJC	Thruster T.600N	M. H. Moulai
	G-BZJD	Thruster T.600T	The Valentine Syndicate
	G-BZJG	Cameron A-400 balloon	Cameron Balloons Ltd
	G-BZJH	Cameron Z-90 balloon	Balloon SpA
	G-BZJI	Nova X-Large 37 paraplane	M. Hay
	G-BZJJ	Robinson R22 Beta	E. Sorvillo/Italy
	G-BZJM	VPM M-16 Tandem Trainer	D. Wood
	G-BZJN	Mainair Blade 912	L. Campbell & M. A. Haughey
	G-BZJO	Pegasus Quantum 15	W. C. Bryan
	G-BZJP	Zenair CH.701UL	B. J. Fallows
	G-BZJV	CASA 1-131E Jungmann 1000	R. A. Cumming
	G-BZJW	Cessna 150F	P. Ligertwood
	G-BZJZ	Pegasus Quantum 15	S. Baker
	G-BZKC	Raj Hamsa X'Air 582 (11)	J. E. Evans
	G-BZKD	Stolp Starduster Too	P. & C. Edmunds
	G-BZKE	Lindstrand LBL-77B balloon	H. Cresswell
	G-BZKF	Rans S.6-ES Coyote II	A. W. Lowrie
	G-BZKL	PA-28R-201 Arrow III	M. A. & M. H. Cromati
	G-BZKO	Rans S-6-ES Coyote II	G. Millar
	G-BZKU	Cameron Z-105 balloon	N. A. Fishlock
	G-BZKV	Cameron Sky 90-24 balloon	Omega Selction Services Ltd
	G-BZKW	Ultramagic M-27 balloon	T. G. Church
	G-BZLC	WSK-PZL Koliber 160A	G. F. Smith
	G-BZLE	Rans S.6-ES Coyote II	B. M. Davis
	G-BZLF	CFM Shadow Srs CD	D. W. Stacey
	G-BZLG	Robin HR.200/120B	Flew LLP
	G-BZLH	PA-28-161 Warrior II	Aviation Rentals
	G-BZLK	Slingsby T.31M Motor Tutor	G. Smith
	G-BZLL	Pegasus Quantum 15-912	A. J. Thomson
	G-BZLP	Robinson R44	T. A. Wells
	G-BZLS	Cameron Sky 77-24 balloon	D. W. Young
	G-BZLU	Lindstrand LBL-90A balloon	A. E. Lusty
	G-BZLV	Avtech Jabiru UL-450	G. Dalton
	G-BZLX	Pegasus Quantum 15-912	D. McCabe & M. Harris
	G-BZLY	Grob G.109B	R. W. Hegmann
	G-BZLZ	Pegasus Quantum 15-912	A. S. Martin
	G-BZMB	PA-28R-201 Arrow III	Thurrock Arrow Group
	G-BZMC	Avtech Jabiru UL	D. Maddison
	G-BZMD	SA Bulldog Srs 120/121 (XX554)	Mad Dog Flying Group
	G-BZME	SA Bulldog Srs 120/121 (XX698:9)	S. J. Whitworth
	G-BZMF	Rutan LongEz	Go-Ez Group
	G-BZMG	Robinson R44	Audisio Automobili Cuneo SRL
	G-BZMH	SA Bulldog Srs 120/121 (XX692:A)	M. E. J. Hingley
	G-BZMJ	Rans S-6-ES Coyote II	R. J. G. Clark
	G-BZML	SA Bulldog Srs 120/121 (XX693:07)	I. D. Anderson
	G-BZMM	Robin DR.400/180R	N. A. C. Norman
	G-BZMO	Robinson R22 Beta	Time Select Ltd
	G-BZMR	Raj Hamsa X'Air 582 (2)	M. Grime
	G-BZMS	Mainair Blade	T. R. Villa
	G-BZMT	PA-28-161 Warrior III	Aviation Rentals
	G-BZMW	Pegasus Quantum 15-912	A. W. Micklem
	G-BZMY	SPP Yakovlev Yak C-11	Classic Displays Ltd
	G-BZMZ	CFM Streak Shadow	J. F. F. Fouche
	G-BZNB	Pegasus Quantum 15	M. P. & R. A. Wells
	G-BZNC	Pegasus Quantum 15-912	D. E. Wall
	G-BZND	Sopwith Pup (replica) (N5199)	M. A. Goddard
	G-BZNE	Beech B300 Super King Air	Skyhopper LLP
	G-BZNF	Colt 120A balloon	N. Charbonnier/Italy

Reg.	Type	Owner or Operator	Notes
G-BZNH	Rans S.6-ES Coyote II	S. R. A. Brierley	
G-BZNJ	Rans S.6-ES Coyote II	R. A. McKee	
G-BZNK	Morane Saulnier MS.315-D2	R. H. Cooper & S. Swallow	
G-BZNM	Pegasus Quantum 15	J. T. Davies	
G-BZNN	Beech 76 Duchess	Flew LLP	
G-BZNP	Thruster T.600N	J. D. Gibbons	
G-BZNS	Mainair Blade	A. G. Laycock	
G-BZNU	Cameron A-300 balloon	Balloon School (International) Ltd	
G-BZNV	Lindstrand LBL-31A balloon	G. R. Down	
G-BZNW	Isaacs Fury II (K2048)	S. M. Johnston	
G-BZNX	SOCATA MS.880B Rallye Club	Air & Ground Aviation Ltd	
G-BZNY	Shaw Europa XS	W. J. Harrison	
G-BZOB	Slepcev Storch (6G-ED)	B. J. Chester-Master	
G-BZOD	Pegasus Quantum 15-912	V. J. Vaughan	
G-BZOE	Pegasus Quantum 15	J. Needham	
G-BZOF	Montgomerie-Bensen B.8MR gyroplane	S. J. M. Ledingham	
G-BZOG	Dornier 328-100	Suckling Airways (Cambridge) Ltd	
G-BZOI	Nicollier HN.700 Menestrel II	S. J. McCollum	
G-BZOL	Robin R.3000/140	S. D. Baker	
G-BZON	SA Bulldog Srs 120/121 (XX528:D)	D. J. Critchley	
G-BZOO	Pegasus Quantum 15-912	A. J. Maxfield	
G-BZOP	Robinson R44	CN Joinery and Building Services Ltd	
G-BZOR	TEAM mini-MAX 91	T. P. V. Sheppard	
G-BZOU	Pegasus Quantum 15-912	D. T. Moeller	
G-BZOV	Pegasus Quantum 15-912	D. Turner	
G-BZOW	Whittaker MW7	G. W. Peacock	
G-BZOX	Cameron Colt 90B balloon	D. J. Head	
G-BZOY	Beech 76 Duchess	Aviation Rentals	
G-BZOZ	Van's RV-6	M. & S. Sheppard	
G-BZPA	Mainair Blade 912S	J. McGoldrick	
G-BZPD	Cameron V-65 balloon	P. Spellward	
G-BZPG	Beech C24R Sierra 200	Wycombe Air Centre Ltd	
G-BZPH	Van's RV-4	G-BZPH RV-4 Group	
G-BZPI	SOCATA TB20 Trinidad	K. M. Brennan	
G-BZPJ	Beech 76 Duchess	K. O'Connor	
G-BZPK	Cameron C-80 balloon	D. L. Homer	
G-BZPN	Mainair Blade 912S	G. R. Barker	
G-BZPP	Westland Wasp HAS.1 (XT793:456)	C. J. Marsden	
G-BZPR	Ultramagic N-210 balloon	Cameron Flights Southern Ltd	
G-BZPS	SA Bulldog Srs 120/121 (XX658:07)	A. J. Robinson & M. J. Miller	
G-BZPT	Ultramagic N-210 balloon	South Downs Ballooning Ltd	
G-BZPV	Lindstrand LBL-90B balloon	D. P. Hopkins	
G-BZPW	Cameron V-77 balloon	J. Vonka	
G-BZPX	Ultramagic S-105 balloon	Scotair Balloons	
G-BZPY	Ultramagic H-31 balloon	Scotair Balloons	
G-BZPZ	Mainair Blade	D. & M. Bailey	
G-BZRA	Rans S.6-ES Coyote II	M. Allen	
G-BZRB	Mainair Blade	K. J. Barnard	
G-BZRJ	Pegasus Quantum 15-912	G-BZRJ Group	
G-BZRO	PA-30 Twin Comanche C	Gloucester Comanche Group	
G-BZRP	Pegasus Quantum 15-912	T. P. Williams	
G-BZRR	Pegasus Quantum 15-912	R. Carlin	
G-BZRS	Eurocopter EC 135T2	Bond Air Services Ltd	
G-BZRT	Beech 76 Duchess	Aviation Rentals	
G-BZRV	Van's RV-6	N. M. Hitchman	
G-BZRW	Mainair Blade 912S	G. J. E. Alcorn	
G-BZRY	Rans S.6-ES Coyote II	A. G. Smith	
G-BZRZ	Thunder Ax11-250 S2 balloon	A. C. K. Rawson & J. J. Rudoni	
G-BZSB	Pitts S-1S Special	A. D. Ingold	
G-BZSC	Sopwith Camel F.1 (replica)	The Shuttleworth Collection	
G-BZSE	Hawker Hunter T.8B (WV322:Y)	Towerdrive 2000 Ltd	
G-BZSG	Pegasus Quantum 15-912	S. Andrews	
G-BZSH	Ultramagic H-77 balloon	P. M. G. Vale	
G-BZSI	Pegasus Quantum 15	D. G. Cull	
G-BZSM	Pegasus Quantum 15	C. A. Brock	
G-BZSO	Ultramagic M-77C balloon	C. C. Duppa-Miller	
G-BZSP	Stemme S.10	A. Flewelling & L. Bleaken	
G-BZSS	Pegasus Quantum 15-912	T. R. Marsh	
G-BZST	Jabiru SPL-450	D. J and L. Rhys	
G-BZSX	Pegasus Quantum 15-912	G. L. Hall	
G-BZSY	SNCAN Stampe SV.4A	G. J. N. Valvekens/Belgium	
G-BZSZ	Avtech Jabiru UL-450	M. P. Gurr & D. R. Burridge	
G-BZTA	Robinson R44	Jarretts Motors Ltd	

Notes	Reg.	Type	Owner or Operator
	G-BZTC	TEAM mini-MAX 91	G. G. Clayton
	G-BZTD	Thruster T.600T 450 JAB	B. O. McCartan
	G-BZTF	Yakovlev Yak-52	KY Flying Group
	G-BZTH	Shaw Europa	T. J. Houlihan
	G-BZTJ	CASA Bü 133C Jungmeister	R. A. Seeley
	G-BZTK	Cameron V-90 balloon	E. Appollodorus
	G-BZTM	Mainair Blade	P. A. Houston
	G-BZTN	Europa XS	R. S. Gent
	G-BZTR	Mainair Blade	D. J. Porter
	G-BZTS	Cameron 90 Bertie Bassett SS balloon	Trebor Bassett Ltd
	G-BZTT	Cameron A-275 balloon	Cameron Flights Southern Ltd
	G-BZTU	Mainair Blade 912	C. T. Halliday
	G-BZTV	Mainair Blade 912S	R. D. McManus
	G-BZTW	Hunt Wing Avon 582 (1)	T. S. Walker
	G-BZTX	Mainair Blade 912	K. A. Ingham
	G-BZTY	Avtech Jabiru UL	R. P. Lewis
	G-BZUB	Mainair Blade	J. Campbell
	G-BZUC	Pegasus Quantum 15-912	G. Breen/Portugal
	G-BZUD	Lindstrand LBL-105A balloon	A. Nimmo
	G-BZUE	Pagasus Quantum 15-912	P. O'Rourke
	G-BZUF	Mainair Rapier	B. Craig
	G-BZUG	RL.7A XP Sherwood Ranger	J. G. Boxall
	G-BZUH	Rans S.6-ES Coyote II	C. Parkinson
	G-BZUI	Pegasus Quantum 15-912	A. P. Slade
	G-BZUK	Lindstrand LBL-31A balloon	G. R. J. Luckett/USA
	G-BZUL	Avtech Jabiru UL	J. G. Campbell
	G-BZUO	Cameron A-340HL balloon	Anglian Countryside Balloons Ltd
	G-BZUP	Raj Hamsa X'Air Jabiru(3)	P. O'Hagan
	G-BZUU	Cameron C-90 balloon	D. C. Ball
	G-BZUV	Cameron H-24 balloon	J. N. Race
	G-BZUX	Pegasus Quantum 15	C. Gorvett
	G-BZUY	Van's RV-6	Uniform Yankee Group
	G-BZUZ	Hunt Avon-Blade R.100 (1)	C. F. Janes
	G-BZVA	Zenair CH.701UL	M. W. Taylor
	G-BZVB	Cessna FR.172H	Victor Bravo Group (G-BLMX)
	G-BZVE	Cameron N-133 balloon	A. Bellini
	G-BZVI	Nova Vertex 24 hang glider	M. Hay
	G-BZVJ	Pegasus Quantum 15	R. Blackhall
	G-BZVK	Raj Hamsa X'Air 582 (2)	M. Donnelly
	G-BZVM	Rans S.6-ES Coyote II	D. P. Sudworth
	G-BZVN	Van's RV-6	Syndicate RV6 G-BZVN
	G-BZVR	Raj Hamsa X'Air 582 (4)	R. F. E. Berry
	G-BZVT	I.I.I. Sky Arrow 650T	D. J. Goldsmith
	G-BZVU	Cameron Z-105 balloon	The Mall Balloon Team Ltd
	G-BZVV	Pegasus Quantum 15-912	S. Runcie
	G-BZVW	Ilyushin IL-2 Stormovik	S. Swallow & R. H. Cooper
	G-BZVX	Ilyushin IL-2 Stormovik	S. Swallow & R. H. Cooper
	G-BZWB	Mainair Blade 912	L. Parker
	G-BZWC	Raj Hamsa X'Air Falcon 912 (1)	T. A. Dobbins
	G-BZWG	PA-28 Cherokee 140	H. Merkado
	G-BZWH	Cessna 152	H. Merkado
	G-BZWJ	CFM Streak Shadow	T. A. Morgan
	G-BZWK	Avtech Jabiru SK	G. M. Bolger
	G-BZWM	Pegasus XL-Q	D. T. Evans
	G-BZWN	Van's RV-8	A. J. Symms & R. D. Harper
	G-BZWR	Mainair Rapier	M. A. Steele
	G-BZWS	Pegasus Quantum 15-912	G-BZWS Syndicate
	G-BZWT	Technam P.92-EM Echo	R. F. Cooper
	G-BZWU	Pegasus Quantum 15-912	C. A. Reynolds
	G-BZWV	Steen Skybolt	D. E. Blaxland
	G-BZWX	Whittaker MW5D Sorcerer	J. Bate
	G-BZWZ	Van's RV-6	A. P. Mardlin
	G-BZXA	Raj Hamsa X'Air V2 (1)	J. Bulpin
	G-BZXB	Van's RV-6	B. J. King-Smith & D. J. Akerman
	G-BZXC	SA Bulldog Srs 120/121 (XX612:A, 03)★	Carnegie College
	G-BZXI	Nova Philou 26 hang glider	M. Hay
	G-BZXK	Robin HR.200/120B	Flew LLP
	G-BZXM	Mainair Blade 912	A. D. Taylor
	G-BZXN	Avtech Jabiru UL-450	D. A. Hall
	G-BZXO	Cameron Z-105 balloon	D. K. Jones & K. D. Thomas
	G-BZXP	Kiss 400-582 (1)	A. Fairbrother
	G-BZXR	Cameron N-90 balloon	F. R. Battersby
	G-BZXS	SA Bulldog Srs 120/121 (XX631:W)	K. J. Thompson

Reg.	Type	Owner or Operator	Notes
G-BZXT	Mainair Blade 912	Barton 912 Flyers	
G-BZXV	Pegasus Quantum 15-912	P. I. Oliver	
G-BZXW	VPM M-16 Tandem Trainer	P. J. Troy-Davies (G-NANA)	
G-BZXX	Pegasus Quantum 15-912	D. J. Johnston & D. Ostle	
G-BZXY	Robinson R44	Helicopter Services Ltd	
G-BZXZ	SA Bulldog Srs 120/121 (XX629:V)	D. Haworth	
G-BZYA	Rans S.6-ES Coyote II	M. R. Osbourn	
G-BZYD	Westland Gazelle AH.1 (XZ239)	Aerocars Ltd	
G-BZYG	Glaser-Dirks DG.500MB	R. C. Bromwich	
G-BZYI	Nova Phocus 123 hang glider	M. Hay	
G-BZYK	Avtech Jabiru UL	Cloudbase Aviation G-BZYK	
G-BZYM	Raj Hamsa X'Air 700 (1A)	R. R. Celentano	
G-BZYN	Pegasus Quantum 15-912	J. Cannon	
G-BZYR	Cameron N-31 balloon	C. J. Sanger-Davies	
G-BZYS	Micro Aviation Bantam B.22-S	D. L. Howell	
G-BZYT	Interavia 80TA	J. King	
G-BZYU	Whittaker MW6 Merlin	K. J. Cole	
G-BZYV	Snowbird Mk.V 582 (1)	M. A. Oakley	
G-BZYW	Cameron N-90 balloon	M. Catalani	
G-BZYX	Raj Hamsa X'Air 700 (1A)	A. M. Sutton	
G-BZYY	Cameron N-90 balloon	M. E. Mason	
G-BZZD	Cessna F.172M	R. H. M. Richardson-Bunbury (G-BDPF)	
G-CAHA	PA-34-200T Seneca II	TGD Leasing Ltd	
G-CALL	PA-23 Aztec 250F	J. D. Moon	
G-CAMM	Hawker Cygnet (replica)	Richard Shuttleworth Trustees	
G-CAMP	Cameron N-105 balloon	Hong Kong Balloon & Airship Club	
G-CAMR	BFC Challenger II	P. R. A. Walker	
G-CAPI	Mudry/CAARP CAP-10B	PI Group (G-BEXR)	
G-CAPX	Avions Mudry CAP-10B	H. J. Pessall	
G-CARS†	Pitts S-2A Special (replica)★	Toyota Ltd	
G-CBAB	SA Bulldog Srs 120/121 (XX543:F)	J. N. R. Davidson, L. C. T. George & P. J. R. Hill	
G-CBAD	Mainair Blade 912	J. Stocking	
G-CBAF	Lancair 320	L. H. & M. van Cleeff	
G-CBAK	Robinson R44	CEL Electrical Logistics Ltd	
G-CBAL	PA-28-161 Warrior II	Azure Flying Club Ltd	
G-CBAN	SA Bulldog Srs 120/121 (XX668:1)	C. Hilliker	
G-CBAP	Zenair CH.601UL	A. G. Marsh	
G-CBAR	Stoddard-Hamilton Glastar	C. M. Barnes	
G-CBAS	Rans S.6-ES Coyote II	S. Stockill	
G-CBAT	Cameron Z-90 balloon	British Telecommunications PLC	
G-CBAU	Rand-Robinson KR-2	C. B. Copsey	
G-CBAV	Raj Hamsa X'Air V.2 (1)	D. W. Stamp & G. J. Lampitt	
G-CBAW	Cameron A-300 balloon	D. K. Hempleman-Adams	
G-CBAX	Tecnam P92-EA Echo	L. Collier	
G-CBAZ	Rans S.6-ES Coyote II	E. S. Wills	
G-CBBB	Pegasus Quantum 15-912	F. A. Dimmock	
G-CBBC	SA Bulldog Srs 120/121 (XX515:4)	Bulldog Support Ltd	
G-CBBF	Beech 76 Duchess	Flew LLP	
G-CBBG	Mainair Blade	G-CBBG Flying Group	
G-CBBH	Raj Hamsa X'Air 582 (11)	S. P. Macdonald	
G-CBBK	Robinson R22	R. J. Everett	
G-CBBL	SA Bulldog Srs 120/121 (XX550:Z)	A. Cunningham	
G-CBBM	Savannah VG Jabiru (1)	C. E. Passmore	
G-CBBN	Pegasus Quantum 15-912	G-CBBN Flying Group	
G-CBBO	Whittaker MW5D Sorcerer	P. J. Gripton	
G-CBBP	Pegasus Quantum 15-912	C. E. Thompson	
G-CBBS	SA Bulldog Srs 120/121 (XX694:E)	Newcastle Aerobatic Academy Ltd	
G-CBBT	SA Bulldog Srs 120/121 (XX695:3)	Newcastle Bulldog Group Ltd	
G-CBBW	SA Bulldog Srs 120/121 (XX619:T)	S. E. Robottom-Scott	
G-CBCB	SA Bulldog Srs 120/121 (XX537:C)	M. W. Minary The General Aviation Trading Co Ltd	
G-CBCD	Pegasus Quantum 15	I. A. Lumley	
G-CBCF	Pegasus Quantum 15-912	P. A. Bromley	
G-CBCH	Zenair CH.701UL	L. G. Millen	
G-CBCI	Raj Hamsa X'Air 582 (2)	C. P. Lincoln	
G-CBCK	Tipsy T.66 Nipper Srs 3	N. M. Bloom (G-TEDZ)	
G-CBCL	Stoddard-Hamilton Glastar	M. I. Weaver	
G-CBCM	Raj Hamsa X'Air 700 (1A)	M. Ellis	
G-CBCP	Van's RV-6A	G-CBCP Group	
G-CBCR	SA Bulldog Srs 120/121 (XX702:P)	D. Wells	
G-CBCV	SA Bulldog Srs 120/121 (XX699:F)	C. A. Patter	

Notes	Reg.	Type	Owner or Operator
	G-CBCX	Pegasus Quantum 15	D. W. Allen
	G-CBCY	Beech C24R Sierra Super	Wycombe Air Centre Ltd
	G-CBCZ	CFM Streak Shadow SLA	J. O'Malley-Kane
	G-CBDC	Thruster T.600N 450-JAB	P. M. Yeoman
	G-CBDD	Mainair Blade	G. Hird
	G-CBDG	Zenair CH.601HD	R. E. Lasnier
	G-CBDH	Flight Design CT2K	K. Tuck
	G-CBDI	Denney Kitfox Mk.2	J. G. D. Barbour
	G-CBDJ	Flight Design CT2K	P. J. Walker
	G-CBDK	SA Bulldog Srs 120/121 (XX611:7)	J. N. Randle
	G-CBDL	Mainair Blade	M. D. Howe
	G-CBDM	Tecnam P92-EM Echo	J. J. Cozens
	G-CBDN	Mainair Blade	T. Peckham
	G-CBDP	Mainair Blade 912	D. S. Parker
	G-CBDS	SA Bulldog Srs 120/121 (XX707:4)	J. R. Parry
	G-CBDU	Quad City Challenger II	E. J. Brooks
	G-CBDV	Raj Hamsa X'Air 582	M. R. Cumpston
	G-CBDX	Pegasus Quantum 15	P. Sinkler
	G-CBDZ	Pegasus Quantum 15-912	J. J. Brutnell
	G-CBEB	Kiss 400-582 (1)	M. Harris
	G-CBEC	Cameron Z-105 balloon	A. L. Ballarino/Italy
	G-CBED	Cameron Z-90 balloon	John Aimo Balloons SAS/Italy
	G-CBEE	PA-28R Cherokee Arrow 200	IHC Ltd
	G-CBEF	SA Bulldog Srs 120/121 (XX621:H)	A. M. Farmer & J. A. Ingram
	G-CBEH	SA Bulldog Srs 120/121 (XX521:H)	J. E. Lewis
	G-CBEI	PA-22 Colt 108	D. Sharp
	G-CBEJ	Colt 120A balloon	The Cotswold Balloon Co. Ltd
	G-CBEK	SA Bulldog Srs 120/121 (XX700:17)	B. P. Robinson
	G-CBEM	Mainair Blade	K. W. Bodley
	G-CBEN	Pegasus Quantum 15-912	S. Clarke
	G-CBES	Shaw Europa XS	M. R. Hexley
	G-CBEU	Pegasus Quantum 15-912	S. D. Cox
	G-CBEV	Pegasus Quantum 15-912	A. S. R. Czajka
	G-CBEW	Flight Design CT2K	Shy Talk Group
	G-CBEX	Flight Design CT2K	A. G. Quinn
	G-CBEY	Cameron C-80 balloon	D. V. Fowler
	G-CBEZ	Robin DR.400/180	K. V. Field
	G-CBFA	Diamond DA40 Star	Lyrastar Ltd
	G-CBFE	Raj Hamsa X'Air V.2 (1)	T. D. Wolstenholme
	G-CBFF	Cameron O-120 balloon	T. M. C. McCoy
	G-CBFH	Thunder Ax8-105 S2 balloon	D. V. Fowler & A. N. F. Pertwee
	G-CBFJ	Robinson R44	HJS Helicopters Ltd
	G-CBFK	Murphy Rebel	P. J. Gibbs
	G-CBFM	SOCATA TB21 Trinidad	Exec Flight Ltd
	G-CBFN	Robin DR.100/200B	Foxtrot November Group
	G-CBFO	Cessna 172S	P. Gray
	G-CBFP	SA Bulldog Srs 120/121 (XX636:Y)	R. Nisbet & A. R. Dix
	G-CBFU	SA Bulldog Srs 120/121 (XX628:9)	J. R. & S. J. Huggins
	G-CBFW	Bensen B.8	A. J. Thomas
	G-CBFX	Rans S.6-ES Coyote II	A. E. Ciantar
	G-CBFY	Cameron Z-250 balloon	M. L. Gabb
	G-CBGB	Zenair CH.601UL	J. F. Woodham
	G-CBGC	SOCATA TB10 Tobago	Tobago Aviation Ltd
	G-CBGD	Zenair CH.701UL	I. S. Walsh
	G-CBGE	Tecnam P92-EM Echo	J. P. Spiteri
	G-CBGG	Pegasus Quantum 15	T. E. Davies
	G-CBGH	Teverson Bisport	M. J. Larroucau
	G-CBGJ	Aeroprakt A.22 Foxbat	M. McCall
	G-CBGL	MH.1521M Broussard	MAXB Group
	G-CBGO	Murphy Maverick 430	C. R. Ellis & E. A. Wrathall
	G-CBGP	Ikarus C.42 FB UK	C. F. Welby
	G-CBGR	Avtech Jabiru UL-450	R. G. Kirkland
	G-CBGS	Cyclone AX2000	JAT Group
	G-CBGU	Thruster T.600N 450-JAB	B. R. Cardosi
	G-CBGV	Thruster T.600N 450	Freshwater Microlights
	G-CBGW	Thruster T.600N 450-JAB	A. R. Pluck
	G-CBGX	SA Bulldog Srs 120/121 (XX622:B)	Henfield Lodge Ltd
	G-CBGZ	Westland Gazelle HT.2 (ZB646:59/CU)	D. Weatherhead Ltd
	G-CBHA	SOCATA TB10 Tobago	Oscar Romeo Aviation Ltd
	G-CBHB	Raj Hamsa X'Air 582 (5)	F. G. Shepherd
	G-CBHC	RAF 2000 GTX-SE gyroplane	A. J. Thomas
	G-CBHD	Cameron Z-160 balloon	Ballooning 50 Degrees Nord/Luxembourg
	G-CBHG	Mainair Blade 912S	B. S. Hope

Reg.	Type	Owner or Operator	Notes
G-CBHI	Shaw Europa XS	Active Aviation Ltd	
G-CBHJ	Mainair Blade 912	B. C. Jones	
G-CBHK	Pegasus Quantum 15 (HKS)	B. Dossett	
G-CBHM	Mainair Blade 912	F. J. Thorne	
G-CBHN	Pegasus Quantum 15-912	G. G. Cook	
G-CBHO	Gloster Gladiator II (N5719)	Retro Track & Air (UK) Ltd	
G-CBHP	Corby CJ-1 Starlet	D. H. Barker	
G-CBHR	Lazer Z200	The Space Creative Partnership Ltd	
G-CBHT	Dassault Falcon 900EX	TAG Aviation (UK) Ltd (G-GPWH)	
G-CBHU	RL.5A Sherwood Ranger	G-CBHU Group	
G-CBHW	Cameron Z-105 balloon	Bristol Chamber of Commerce, Industry & Shipping	
G-CBHX	Cameron V-77 balloon	N. A. Apsey	
G-CBHY	Pegasus Quantum 15-912	A. Hope	
G-CBHZ	RAF 2000 GTX-SE gyroplane	M. P. Donnelly	
G-CBIB	Flight Design CT2K	T. R. Villa	
G-CBIC	Raj Hamsa X'Air V2 (2)	J. T. Blackburn & D. R. Sutton	
G-CBID	SA Bulldog Srs 120/121(XX549:6)	Red Dog Group/Bulldog Group	
G-CBIE	Flight Design CT2K	B. M. Jones & S. R. McKiernan	
G-CBIF	Avtech Jabiru SPL-450	S. N. J. Huxtable	
G-CBIH	Cameron Z-31 balloon	Gone With The Wind Ltd	
G-CBIJ	Ikarus C.42 FB UK Cyclone	J. A. Smith	
G-CBIL	Cessna 182K	E. Bannister (G-BFZZ)	
G-CBIM	Lindstrand LBL-90A balloon	R. K. Parsons	
G-CBIN	TEAM mini-MAX 91	A. R. Mikolaczyk	
G-CBIO	Thruster T.600N 450-JAB	Sandown Microlights	
G-CBIP	Thruster T.600N 450-JAB	D. R. Seabrook	
G-CBIR	Thruster T.600N 450-JAB	E. G. White	
G-CBIS	Raj Hamsa X'Air 582 (2)	P. T. W. T. Derges	
G-CBIT	RAF 2000 GTX-SE gyroplane	Terrafirma Services Ltd	
G-CBIU	Cameron 95 Flame SS balloon	PSH Skypower Ltd	
G-CBIV	Skyranger 912 (1)	R. K. W. Moss	
G-CBIW	Lindstrand LBL-310A balloon	C. E. Wood	
G-CBIX	Zenair CH.601UL	R. A. & B. M. Roberts	
G-CBIY	Aerotechnik EV-97 Eurostar	R. Soltysik	
G-CBIZ	Pegasus Quantum 15-912	B. Cook	
G-CBJD	Stoddard-Hamilton Glastar	K. F. Farey	
G-CBJE	RAF 2000 GTX-SE gyroplane	V. G. Freke	
G-CBJG	DHC.1 Chipmunk 20 (1373)	C. J. Rees	
G-CBJH	Aeroprakt A.22 Foxbat	H. Smith	
G-CBJJ	SA Bulldog Srs 120/121 (XX525)	G. V. Crowe, T. Marnix & H. V. Snick	
G-CBJL	Kiss 400-582 (1)	R. E. Morris	
G-CBJM	Avtech Jabiru SP-470	G. R. T. Elliott	
G-CBJN	RAF 2000 GTX-SE gyroplane	R. Hall	
G-CBJO	Pegasus Quantum 15-912	M. Johnson	
G-CBJP	Zenair CH.601UL	R. E. Peirse	
G-CBJR	Aerotechnik EV-97A Eurostar	Madley Flying Group	
G-CBJS	Cameron C-60 balloon	N. Ivison	
G-CBJT	Mainair Blade	C. Roadnight	
G-CBJV	Rotorway Executive 162F	R. J. Green	
G-CBJW	Ikarus C.42 Cyclone FB UK	G. D. Jones	
G-CBJX	Raj Hamsa X'Air Falcon J22	N. & E. Hart	
G-CBJZ	Westland Gazelle HT.3	K. G. Theurer/Germany	
G-CBKA	Westland Gazelle HT.3 (XZ937:Y)	J. Windmill	
G-CBKB	Bücker Bü 181C Bestmann	W. R. & G. D. Snadden	
G-CBKD	Westland Gazelle HT.2	Flying Scout Ltd	
G-CBKE	Kiss 400-582 (1)	T. H. Parr	
G-CBKF	Easy Raider J2.2 (1)	R. R. Armstrong	
G-CBKG	Thruster T.600N 450 JAB	Silver Shadow Group	
G-CBKI	Cameron Z-90 balloon	Wheatfields Park Ltd	
G-CBKJ	Cameron Z-90 balloon	Invista (UK) Holdings Ltd	
G-CBKK	Ultramagic S-130 balloon	Hayrick Ltd	
G-CBKL	Raj Hamsa X'Air 582 (1)	Caithness X-Air Group	
G-CBKM	Mainair Blade 912	N. Purdy	
G-CBKN	Mainair Blade 912	D. S. Clews	
G-CBKO	Mainair Blade 912S	S. J. Taft	
G-CBKR	PA-28-161 Warrior III	Yeovil Auto Tuning	
G-CBKS	Kiss 400-582 (1)	S. Kilpin	
G-CBKU	Ikarus C.42 Cyclone FB UK	C. Blackburn	
G-CBKW	Pegasus Quantum 15-912	W. G. Coulter	
G-CBKY	Avtech Jabiru SP-470	P. R. Sistern	
G-CBLA	Aero Designs Pulsar XP	J. P. Kynaston	
G-CBLB	Technam P.92-EM Echo	R. Lewis-Evans	

Notes	Reg.	Type	Owner or Operator
	G-CBLD	Mainair Blade 912S	N. E. King
	G-CBLE	Robin R.2120U	Flew LLP
	G-CBLF	Raj Hamsa X'Air 582 (11)	B. J. Harper & P. J. Soukup
	G-CBLK	Hawker Hind	Aero Vintage Ltd
	G-CBLL	Pegasus Quantum 15-912	G. J. McNally
	G-CBLM	Mainair Blade 912	A. S. Saunders
	G-CBLN	Cameron Z-31 balloon	P. M. Oggioni
	G-CBLO	Lindstrand LBL-42A balloon	R. J. Clements
	G-CBLP	Raj Hamsa X'Air Falcon	A. C. Parsons
	G-CBLS	Fiat CR.42	Fighter Collection Ltd
	G-CBLT	Mainair Blade 912	B. J. Bader
	G-CBLU	Cameron C-90 balloon	A. G. Martin
	G-CBLW	Raj Hamsa X'Air Falcon 582(3)	R. G. Halliwell
	G-CBLX	Kiss 400-582 (1)	I. G. Parker
	G-CBLY	Grob G.109B	G-CBLY Syndicate
	G-CBLZ	Rutan LongEz	S. K. Cockburn
	G-CBMA	Raj Hamsa X'Air 582 (10)	K. G. Winter
	G-CBMB	Cyclone Ax2000	T. H. Chadwick
	G-CBMC	Cameron Z-105 balloon	B. R. Whatley
	G-CBMD	IDA Bacau Yakovlev Yak-52 (10 yellow)	R. J. Hunter
	G-CBME	Cessna F.172M	Skytrax Aviation Ltd
	G-CBMI	Yakovlev Yak-52	I. A. Harding
	G-CBMK	Cameron Z-120 balloon	G. Davies
	G-CBML	DHC.6 Twin Otter 310	Isles of Scilly Skybus Ltd
	G-CBMM	Mainair Blade 912	W. L. Millar
	G-CBMO	PA-28 Cherokee 180	C. Woodliffe
	G-CBMP	Cessna R.182	Orman (Carrolls Farm) Ltd
	G-CBMR	Medway Eclipser	D. S. Blofeld
	G-CBMT	Robin DR.400/180	A. C. Williamson
	G-CBMU	Whittaker MW6-S Fat Boy Flyer	F. J. Brown
	G-CBMV	Pegasus Quantum 15	G. Poulett
	G-CBMW	Zenair CH.701 UL	I. Park
	G-CBMX	Kiss 400-582 (1)	C. D. Gates
	G-CBMZ	Aerotechnik EV-97 Eurostar	J. C. O'Donnell
	G-CBNA	Flight Design CT2K	J. R. Fyfe
	G-CBNB	Eurocopter EC 120B	Arenberg Consultadoria E Servicos LDA/Madeira
	G-CBNC	Mainair Blade 912	A. C. Rowlands
	G-CBNF	Rans S.7 Courier	M. Henderson
	G-CBNG	Robin R.2112	R. K. Galbally & E. W. Russell
	G-CBNI	Lindstrand LBL-180A balloon	Cancer Research UK
	G-CBNJ	Raj Hamsa X'Air 912 (1)	P. S. Chapman
	G-CBNL	Dyn'Aéro MCR-01 Club	D. H. Wilson
	G-CBNO	CFM Streak Shadow	D. J. Goldsmith
	G-CBNT	Pegasus Quantum 15-912	B. H. Goldsmith
	G-CBNV	Rans S.6-ES Coyote II	J. D. Henderson
	G-CBNW	Cameron N-105 balloon	Bailey Balloons
	G-CBNX	Mongomerie-Bensen B.8MR	A. C. S. M. Hart
	G-CBNZ	TEAM hi-MAX 1700R	A. P. S. John
	G-CBOA	Auster B.8 Agricola Srs 1	C. J. Baker
	G-CBOC	Raj Hamsa X'Air 582 (5)	A. J. McAleer
	G-CBOE	Hawker Hurricane IIB	P. J. Tuplin & P. W. Portelli
	G-CBOF	Shaw Europa XS	I. W. Ligertwood
	G-CBOG	Mainair Blade 912S	OG Group
	G-CBOK	Rans S.6-ES Coyote II	I. Johnson
	G-CBOM	Mainair Blade 912	G. Suckling
	G-CBOO	Mainair Blade 912S	Oscar Oscar Group
	G-CBOP	Avtech Jabiru UL-450	D. W. Batchelor
	G-CBOR	Cessna F.172N	Vetsonic LLP
	G-CBOS	Rans S.6-ES Coyote II	J. T. Athulathmudali
	G-CBOW	Cameron Z-120 balloon	Turner Balloons Ltd
	G-CBOY	Pegasus Quantum 15-912	Charlie Boy Syndicate
	G-CBOZ	IDA Bacau Yakovlev Yak-52	T. M. Boxall
	G-CBPC	Sportavia-Putzer RF-5B Sperber	Lee RF-5B Group
	G-CBPD	Ikarus C.42 Cyclone FB UK	Waxwing Group
	G-CBPE	SOCATA TB10 Tobago	A. F. Welch
	G-CBPI	PA-28R-201 Arrow III	M. J. Richardson
	G-CBPL	TEAM mini-MAX 93	P. R. G. Morley
	G-CBPM	Yakovlev Yak-50 (50 black)	P. W. Ansell
	G-CBPP	Avtech Jabiru UL-450	D. G. Bennett
	G-CBPR	Avtech Jabiru UL-450	F. B. Hall
	G-CBPU	Raj Hamsa X'Air R100(3)	O. Sanda
	G-CBPV	Zenair CH.601UL	R. D. Barnard
	G-CBPW	Lindstrand LBL-105A balloon	A. C. Elson

Reg.	Type	Owner or Operator	Notes
G-CBRB	Ultramagic S-105 balloon	I. S. Bridge	
G-CBRC	Jodel D.18	B. W. Shaw	
G-CBRD	Jodel D.18	J. D. Haslam	
G-CBRE	Mainair Blade 912	J. Jones	
G-CBRF	Ikarus C.42 FB100 VLA	T. W. Gale	
G-CBRG	Cessna 560XL Citation Excel	Queensway Aviation Ltd	
G-CBRJ	Mainair Blade 912S	R. W. Janion	
G-CBRK	Ultramagic M-77 balloon	R. T. Revel	
G-CBRM	Mainair Blade	M. H. Levy	
G-CBRO	Robinson R44	R. D. Jordan	
G-CBRR	Aerotechnik EV-97A Eurostar	T. O. Powley	
G-CBRT	Murphy Elite	T. W. Baylie	
G-CBRV	Cameron C-90 balloon	C. J. Teall	
G-CBRW	Aerostar Yakovlev Yak-52 (50 grey)	Max-Alpha Aviation GmbH/Germany	
G-CBRX	Zenair CH.601UL Zodiac	C. J. Meadows	
G-CBRZ	Kiss 400-582(1)	J. J. Ryan/Ireland	
G-CBSF	Westland Gazelle HT.2	Falcon Aviation Ltd	
G-CBSH	Westland Gazelle HT.3 (XX406:P)	Alltask Ltd	
G-CBSI	Westland Gazelle HT.3 (XZ934:U)	P. S. Unwin	
G-CBSK	Westland Gazelle HT.3 (ZB627:A)	Falcon Flying Group	
G-CBSL	IDA Bacau Yakovlev Yak-52 (67 red)	N. & A. D. Barton	
G-CBSO	PA-28-181 Archer II	Archer One Ltd	
G-CBSP	Pegasus Quantum 15-912	K. D. MacCuish	
G-CBSR	Yakovlev Yak-52	Grovinvest Srl	
G-CBSS	IDA Bacau Yakovlev Yak-52	E. J. F. Verhellen/Belgium	
G-CBSU	Avtech Jabiru UL	K. R. Crawley	
G-CBSV	Montgomerie-Bensen B.8MR	J. A. McGill	
G-CBSZ	Mainair Blade 912S	W. Gray	
G-CBTB	I.I.I. Sky Arrow 650TS	J. S. Hudson	
G-CBTD	Pegasus Quantum 15-912	D. Baillie	
G-CBTE	Mainair Blade 912|S	K. J. Miles	
G-CBTG	Ikarus C42 FB UK Cyclone	G-CBTG Flying Group	
G-CBTK	Raj Hamsa X'Air 582 (5)	A. P. Lambert	
G-CBTL	Monnett Moni	G. Dawes	
G-CBTM	Mainair Blade	D. A. A. Hewitt	
G-CBTN	PA-31 Navajo C	Durban Aviation Services Ltd	
G-CBTO	Rans S.6-ES Coyote II	C. G. Deeley	
G-CBTR	Lindstrand LBL-120A balloon	R. H. Etherington	
G-CBTS	Gloster Gamecock (replica)	Retro Track & Air (UK) Ltd	
G-CBTT	PA-28-181 Archer II	Citicourt Aviation Ltd (G-BFMM)	
G-CBTW	Mainair Blade 912	K. J. Austwick	
G-CBTX	Denney Kitfox Mk.2	G. I. Doake	
G-CBUA	Extra EA.230	S. Pedersen	
G-CBUC	Raj Hamsa X'Air 582 (5)	M. N. Watson	
G-CBUD	Pegasus Quantum 15-912	G. N. S. Farrant	
G-CBUE	Ultramagic N-250 balloon	Elinore French Ltd	
G-CBUF	Flight Design CT2K	N. A. Thomas	
G-CBUG	Technam P.92-EM Echo	J. J. Bodnarec	
G-CBUI	Westland Wasp HAS.1 (XT420:606)	The Helicopter Squadron Ltd	
G-CBUJ	Raj Hamsa X'Air 582 (10)	M. A. Curtis	
G-CBUK	Van's RV-6A	P. G. Greenslade	
G-CBUN	Barker Charade	D. R. Wilkinson & T. Coldwell	
G-CBUO	Cameron O-90 balloon	W. J. Treacy & P. M. Smith	
G-CBUP	VPM M-16 Tandem Trainer	J. S. Firth	
G-CBUR	Zenair CH.601UL	R. Simpson	
G-CBUS	Pegasus Quantum 15	J. Liddiard	
G-CBUU	Pegasus Quantum 15-912	D. & P. Allman	
G-CBUW	Cameron Z-133 balloon	Balloon School (International) Ltd	
G-CBUX	Cyclone AX2000	I. D. Worthington	
G-CBUY	Rans S.6-ES Coyote II	I. L. Johnson	
G-CBUZ	Pegasus Quantum 15	D. G. Seymour	
G-CBVA	Thruster T.600N 450	D. J. Clingan	
G-CBVB	Robin R.2120U	Flew LLP	
G-CBVC	Raj Hamsa X'Air 582 (5)	D. J. Rooney	
G-CBVD	Cameron C-60 balloon	Phoenix Balloons Ltd	
G-CBVF	Murphy Maverick	H. A. Leek	
G-CBVG	Mainair Blade 912S	A. M. Buchanan	
G-CBVH	Lindstrand LBL-120A balloon	Line Packaging & Display Ltd	
G-CBVK	Schroeder Fire Balloons G balloon	S. Travaglia	
G-CBVM	Aerotechnik EV-97 Eurostar	M. Sharpe	
G-CBVN	Pegasus Quik	C. Kearney	
G-CBVR	Skyranger 912 (2)	S. H. Lunney	
G-CBVS	Skyranger 912 (2)	S. C. Cornock	

Notes	Reg.	Type	Owner or Operator
	G-CBVT	Yakovlev Yak-52	M. A. G. Lopez
	G-CBVU	PA-28R Cherokee Arrow 200-II	S. Crowley
	G-CBVU	Cameron N-120 balloon	John Aimo Balloons SAS/Italy
	G-CBVX	Cessna 182P	P. & A. de Weerdt
	G-CBVY	Ikarus C.42 Cyclone FB UK	M. J. Hendra & Gossage
	G-CBVZ	Flight Design CT2K	A. N. D. Arthur
	G-CBWA	Flight Design CT2K	G-CBWA Group
	G-CBWB	PA-34-200T Seneca II	Fairoaks Airport Ltd
	G-CBWD	PA-28-161 Warrior III	J. Wright
	G-CBWE	Aerotechnik EV-97 Eurostar	J. & C. W. Hood
	G-CBWG	Aerotechnik EV-97 Eurostar	K. Dickson
	G-CBWI	Thruster T. 600N 450	P. L. Jarvis
	G-CBWJ	Thruster T. 600N 450	Voliamo Group
	G-CBWK	Ultramagic H-77 balloon	H. C. Peel
	G-CBWN	Campbell Cricket Mk.6	P. G. Rawson
	G-CBWO	Rotorway Executive 162F	Handyvalue Ltd
	G-CBWP	Shaw Europa	T. W. Greaves
	G-CBWS	Whittaker MW6 Merlin	D. W. McCormack
	G-CBWU	Rotorway Executive 162F	F. A. Cavaciuti
	G-CBWV	Falconar F-12A Cruiser	A. Ackland
	G-CBWW	Skyranger 912 (2)	N. S. Wellsl
	G-CBWY	Raj Hamsa X'Air 582 (6)	J. C. Rose
	G-CBWZ	Robinson R22 Beta	Plane Talking Ltd
	G-CBXA	Raj Hamsa X'Air 582 (5)	K. & K. P. Kormi
	G-CBXB	Lindstrand LBL-150A balloon	M. A. Webb
	G-CBXC	Ikarus C.42 Cyclone FB UK	J. A. Robinson
	G-CBXE	Easy Raider J2.2 (3)	D. A. Lord
	G-CBXF	Easy Raider J2.2 (2)	M. R. Grunwell
	G-CBXG	Thruster T.600N 450	Newtownards Microlight Group
	G-CBXJ	Cessna 172S	Steptoe and Sons Properties Ltd
	G-CBXK	Robinson R22 Mariner	Tiger Helicopters Ltd
	G-CBXM	Mainair Blade	B. A. Coombe
	G-CBXN	Robinson R22 Beta II	N. M. G. Pearson
	G-CBXR	Raj Hamsa X-Air Falcon 582 (1)	A. R. Rhodes
	G-CBXS	Skyranger J2.2 (1)	C. J. Erith
	G-CBXU	TEAM mini-MAX 91A	C. D. Hatcher
	G-CBXV	Mainair Blade	D. C. Peto
	G-CBXW	Shaw Europa XS	R. G. Fairall
	G-CBXZ	Rans S.6-ES Coyote II	D. Tole
	G-CBYB	Rotorway Executive 162F	Clark Contracting
	G-CBYC	Cameron Z-275 balloon	P. Baker
	G-CBYD	Rans S.6-ES Coyote II	R. Burland
	G-CBYE	Pegasus Quik	C. E. Morris
	G-CBYF	Mainair Blade	J. Ayre
	G-CBYH	Aeroprakt A.22 Foxbat	G. C. Moore
	G-CBYI	Pegasus Quantum 15-503	The G-BCYI Group
	G-CBYJ	Steen Skybolt	The Skybolt Group
	G-CBYM	Mainair Blade	S. Webb
	G-CBYN	Shaw Europa XS	G. M. Tagg
	G-CBYO	Pegasus Quik	C. J. Roper & P. F. Mayo
	G-CBYP	Whittaker MW6-S Fat Boy Flyer	R. J. Grainger
	G-CBYS	Lindstrand LBL-21 balloon France	B. M. Reed/France
	G-CBYT	Thruster T.600N 450	P. Bartle & J. Paterson
	G-CBYU	PA-28-161 Warrior II	Stapleford Flying Club Ltd
	G-CBYV	Pegasus Quantum 15-912	G-CBYV Syndicate
	G-CBYW	Hatz CB-1	T. A. Hinton
	G-CBYY	Robinson R44	AMS Aviation Ltd
	G-CBYZ	Tecnam P92-EM Echo-Super	B. Weaver
	G-CBZA	Mainair Blade	M. Lowe
	G-CBZB	Mainair Blade	A. Bennion
	G-CBZD	Mainair Blade	G. F. Jones
	G-CBZE	Robinson R44	Alps (Scotland) Ltd
	G-CBZF	Robinson R22 Beta	Fly Executive Ltd
	G-CBZG	Rans S.6-ES Coyote II	W. Chang
	G-CBZH	Pegasus Quik	B. D. Searle
	G-CBZI	Rotorway Executive 162F	T. D. Stock
	G-CBZJ	Lindstrand LBL-25A balloon	Pegasus Ballooning
	G-CBZK	Robin DR.400/180	R. A. Fleming
	G-CBZL	Westland Gazelle HT.3	Armstrong Aviation Ltd
	G-CBZM	Avtech Jabiru SPL-450	M. E. Ledward
	G-CBZN	Rans S.6-ES Coyote II	R. G. Morris
	G-CBZP	Hawker Fury 1 (K5674)	Historic Aircraft Collection
	G-CBZR	PA-28R-201 Arrow III	Plane Talking Ltd/Elstree

Reg.	Type	Owner or Operator	Notes
G-CBZS	Aurora	J. Lynden	
G-CBZT	Pegasus Quik	A. P. Portsmouth	
G-CBZU	Lindstrand LBL-180A balloon	European Balloon Co.Ltd	
G-CBZW	Zenair CH.701UL	T. M. Siles	
G-CBZX	Dyn' Aero MCR-01 ULC	A. C. N. Freeman & M. P. Wilson	
G-CBZZ	Cameron Z-275 balloon	A. C. K. Rawson & J. J. Rudoni	
G-CCAB	Mainair Blade	A. J. Morris	
G-CCAC	Aerotech EV-97 Eurostar	D. C. Lugg	
G-CCAD	Mainair Pegasus Quik	L. A. Hosegood & M. J. Mawle	
G-CCAE	Avtech Jabiru UL-450	D. Logan	
G-CCAF	Skyranger 912 (1)	D. W. & M. L. Squire	
G-CCAG	Mainair Blade 912	W. Cope	
G-CCAK	Zenair CN.601HD	A. Kimmond	
G-CCAL	Technam P.92-EA Echo	M. Rudd	
G-CCAM	Mainair Blade	M. Richardson	
G-CCAP	Robinson R22 Beta II	Development Charter Ltd	
G-CCAR	Cameron N-77 balloon	D. P. Turner	
G-CCAS	Pegasus Quik	Caunton Alpha Syndicate	
G-CCAT	AA-55A Cheetah	A. Ohringer (G-OAJH/G-KILT/G-BJFA)	
G-CCAU	Eurocopter EC 135T1	Eurocopter UK Ltd	
G-CCAV	PA-28-181 Archer II	Archer II Ltd	
G-CCAW	Mainair Blade 912	A. D. Carr	
G-CCAY	Cameron Z-42 balloon	P. Stern	
G-CCAZ	Mainair Pegasus Quik	J. P. Floyd	
G-CCBA	Skyranger R.100	Fourstrokes Group	
G-CCBB	Cameron N-90 balloon	S. C. A. & L. D. Craze	
G-CCBC	Thruster T.600N 450	E. J. Girling & J. A. E. Bowen	
G-CCBF	Maule M.5-235C	C. G. Sims (G-NHVH)	
G-CCBG	Skyranger V.2 + (1)	P. R. Mailer & F. Stannard	
G-CCBH	PA-28 Cherokee 236	J. R. Hunt, M. Kenny & S. M. Packer	
G-CCBI	X'Air R100 (2)	O. Sanda	
G-CCBJ	Skyranger 912 (2)	C. S. Robinson	
G-CCBK	Aerotechnik EV-97 Eurostar	B. S. Waycott	
G-CCBL	Agusta-Bell 206B JetRanger 3	Formula Karting Ltd	
G-CCBM	Aerotechnik EV-97 Eurostar	W. Graves	
G-CCBN	Scale Replica SE-5a (80105/19)	V. C. Lockwood	
G-CCBR	Jodel D.120	A. Dunne & M. Munnelly	
G-CCBT	Cameron Z-90 balloon	I. J. Sharpe	
G-CCBV	Cameron Z-225 balloon	New Spirit Baloons ASBL, Luxembourg	
G-CCBW	Sherwood Ranger	A. L. Virgoe	
G-CCBX	Raj Hamsa X'Air 133 (2)	R. G. Cheshire	
G-CCBY	Avtech Jabiru UL-450	D. M. Goodman	
G-CCBZ	Aero Designs Pulsar	J. M. Keane	
G-CCCA	VS.509 Spitfire Tr.IX	Historic Flying Ltd (G-BHRH/G-TRIX)	
G-CCCB	Thruster T.600N 450	G-CCCB Flying Group	
G-CCCD	Mainair Pegasus Quantum 15	R. N. Gamble	
G-CCCE	Aeroprakt A.22 Foxbat	P. Sykes	
G-CCCF	Thruster T.600N 450	G. A. Fowler	
G-CCCG	Mainair Pegasus Quik	D. Seiler	
G-CCCH	Thruster T600N 450	P. J. Scullion	
G-CCCI	Medway Eclipse R	C. Dunford	
G-CCCJ	Nicollier HN.700 Menestrel II	G. A. Rodmell	
G-CCCK	Skyranger 912 (2)	P. L. Braniff	
G-CCCM	Skyranger 912 (2)	I. A Forrest & C. K. Richardson	
G-CCCN	Robin R.3000/160	DR Flyers 2	
G-CCCO	Aerotechnik EV-97A Eurostar	D. R. G. Whitelaw	
G-CCCP	IDA Yakovlev Yak-52	A. Heidtmann	
G-CCCR	Best Off Sky Ranger 912(2)	E. Foster & J. H. Peet	
G-CCCU	Thruster T.600N 450	A. F. Cashin	
G-CCCV	Raj Hamsa X'Air Falcon 133 (1)	G. J. Boyer	
G-CCCW	Pereira Osprey 2	D. J. Southward	
G-CCCY	Skyranger 912 (2)	A. Watson	
G-CCDB	Mainair Pegasus Quik	A. Pritchard	
G-CCDD	Mainair Pegasus Quik	M. P. Hadden & M. H. Rollins	
G-CCDF	Mainair Pegasus Quik	R. P. McGann	
G-CCDG	Skyranger 912 (1)	Freebird Group	
G-CCDH	Skyranger 912 (2)	M. L. Willmington	
G-CCDJ	Raj Hamsa X'Air Falcon 582 (2)	P. White	
G-CCDK	Pegasus Quantum 15-912	S. Brock	
G-CCDL	Raj Hamsa X'Air Falcon 582 (2)	G. M. Brown	
G-CCDM	Mainair Blade	P. R. G. Morley	
G-CCDO	Mainair Pegasus Quik	S. T. Welsh	

BRITISH CIVIL REGISTRATIONS

Notes	Reg.	Type	Owner or Operator
	G-CCDP	Raj Hamsa X'Air R.100 (3)	F. J. McGuigan
	G-CCDR	Raj Hamsa X'Air Falcon Jabiru	P. D. Sibbons
	G-CCDS	Nicollier HN.700 Menestrel II	B. W. Gowland
	G-CCDU	Tecnam P92-EM Echo	B. N. Thresher
	G-CCDV	Thruster T.600N 450	G. C. Hobson
	G-CCDW	Skyranger 582 (1)	Debts R Us Family Group
	G-CCDX	Aerotechnik EV-97 Eurostar	J. M. Swash
	G-CCDY	Skyranger 912 (2)	N. H. Copperthwaite
	G-CCDZ	Pegasus Quantum 15-912	K. D. Baldwin
	G-CCEA	Mainair Pegasus Quik	G. D. Ritchie
	G-CCEB	Thruster T.600N 450	Thruster Air Services Ltd
	G-CCED	Zenair CH.601UL	R. P. Reynolds
	G-CCEE	PA-15 Vagabond	I. M. Callier (G-VAGA)
	G-CCEF	Shaw Europa	C. P. Garner
	G-CCEH	Skyranger 912 (2)	ZC Owners
	G-CCEJ	Aerotechnik EV-97 Eurostar	N. A. Quintin
	G-CCEK	Kiss 400-582 (1)	R. C. Hinkins & M. Thurlbourn
	G-CCEL	Avtech Jabiru UL	S. K. Armstrong
	G-CCEM	Aerotechnik EV-97 Eurostar	Oxenhope Flying Group
	G-CCEN	Cameron Z-120 balloon	R. Hunt
	G-CCEO	Thunder Ax10-180 S2 balloon	P. Heitzeneder/Austria
	G-CCEP	Raj Hamsa X'Air Falcon Jabiru	F. J. Csuka
	G-CCES	Raj Hamsa X'Air 3203(1)	G. V. McCloskey
	G-CCET	Nova Vertex 28 hang glider	M. Hay
	G-CCEU	RAF 2000 GTX-SE gyroplane	N. G. Dovaston
	G-CCEW	Mainair Pegasus Quik	N. F. Mackenzie
	G-CCEY	Raj Hamsa X'582 (11)	P. F. F. Spedding
	G-CCEZ	Easy Raider J2.2	P. J Clegg
	G-CCFA	Kiss 400-582 (1)	A. E. Barron
	G-CCFB	Mainair Pegasus Quik	P. Bailey
	G-CCFC	Robinson R44 II	H. J. Walters
	G-CCFD	BFC Challenger II	W. Oswald
	G-CCFE	Tipsy Nipper T.66 Srs 2	R. A. Weller
	G-CCFG	Dyn'Aéro MCR-01 Club	P. H. Milward
	G-CCFI	PA-32 Cherokee Six 260	McManus Truck & Trailer Spares Ltd
	G-CCFJ	Kolb Twinstar Mk.3	D. Travers
	G-CCFK	Shaw Europa	C. R. Knapton
	G-CCFL	Mainair Pegasus Quik	P. G. Mallon
	G-CCFO	Pitts S-1S Special	R. J. Anderson
	G-CCFS	Diamond DA40D Star	R. H. Butterfield
	G-CCFT	Mainair Pegasus Quantum 15-912	D. A. Bannister
	G-CCFU	Diamond DA40D Star	Jetstream Aviation Academy/Greece
	G-CCFV	Lindstrand LBL-77A balloon	Alton Aviation Ltd
	G-CCFW	WAR Focke-Wulf Fw.190	D. B. Conway
	G-CCFX	EAA Acrosport 2	C. D. Ward
	G-CCFY	Rotorway Executive 162F	Southern Helicopters Ltd
	G-CCFZ	Ikarus C.42 FB UK	B. W. Drake
	G-CCGB	TEAM mini-MAX	A. D, Pentland
	G-CCGC	Mainair Pegasus Quik	R. W. Street
	G-CCGE	Robinson R22 Beta	Patriot Aviation Ltd
	G-CCGF	Robinson R22 Beta	Multiflight Ltd
	G-CCGG	Jabiru Aircraft Jabiru J400	S. C. E Twiss
	G-CCGH	Supermarine Aircraft Spitfire Mk.26 (AB196)	Cokebusters Ltd
	G-CCGK	Mainair Blade	C. M. Babiy & M. Hurn
	G-CCGM	Kiss 450-582 (1)	A. I. Lea
	G-CCGO	Medway AV8R	G. Cousins
	G-CCGP	Bristol Type 200	R. L. Holman
	G-CCGR	Raj Hamsa X'Air 133 (1)	A. Greenwell
	G-CCGS	Dornier 328-100	Suckling Airways (Cambridge) Ltd
	G-CCGT	Cameron Z-425 balloon	A. A. Brown
	G-CCGU	Van's RV-9A	B. J. Main & ptnrs
	G-CCGW	Shaw Europa	D. Buckley
	G-CCGY	Cameron Z-105 balloon	Cameron Balloons Ltd
	G-CCGZ	Cameron Z-250 balloon	Cameron Flights Southern Ltd
	G-CCHA	Diamond DA40D Star	Diamond Hire UK Ltd
	G-CCHD	Diamond DA40D Star	Flying Time Ltd
	G-CCHH	Pegasus Quik	C. A. Green
	G-CCHI	Mainair Pegasus Quik	M. R. Starling
	G-CCHJ	Kiss 400-582 (1)	H. C. Jones
	G-CCHL	PA-28-181 Archer iii	Archer Three Ltd
	G-CCHM	Kiss 450	M. J. Jessup
	G-CCHN	Corby CJ.1 Starlet	N. S. Dell

Reg.	Type	Owner or Operator	Notes
G-CCHO	Mainair Pegasus Quik	M. Allan	
G-CCHP	Cameron Z-31 balloon	M. H. Redman	
G-CCHR	Easy Raider 583 (1)	M. P. Wiseman	
G-CCHS	Raj Hamsa X'Air 582	N. H. Gokul	
G-CCHT	Cessna 152	J. S. Devlin & Z. Islam	
G-CCHV	Mainair Rapier	K. L. Smith	
G-CCHW	Cameron Z-77 balloon	A. Murphy	
G-CCHX	Scheibe SF.25C Falke	Lasham Gliding Society Ltd	
G-CCHY	Bücker Bü 131 Jungmann (A+12)	M. V. Rijkse	
G-CCID	Jabiru Aircraft Jabiru J400	G-CCID Syndicate	
G-CCIF	Mainair Blade	S. P. Moores	
G-CCIG	Aero Designs Pulsar	P. Maguire	
G-CCIH	Mainair Pegasus Quantum 15	T. Smith	
G-CCII	ICP Savannah Jabiru (3)	D. Chaloner	
G-CCIJ	PA-28R Cherokee Arrow 180	S. A. Hughes	
G-CCIK	Skyranger 912 (2)	M. D. Kirby	
G-CCIO	Skyranger 912 (2)	B. Berry	
G-CCIR	Van's RV-8	N. W. Charles	
G-CCIS	Scheibe SF.28A Tandem Falke	The Tandem-Falke Syndicate	
G-CCIT	Zenair CH.701UL	J. A. R. Hughes	
G-CCIU	Cameron N-105 balloon	W. W. Leitlein	
G-CCIV	Mainair Pegasus Quik	G. H. Ousby	
G-CCIW	Raj Hamsa X'Air 582 (2)	N. Watts	
G-CCIY	Skyranger 912 (2)	L. F. Tanner	
G-CCIZ	PZL-110 Koliber 160A	J. P. Nugent	
G-CCJA	Skyranger 912 (2)	C. Day	
G-CCJB	Zenair CH.701 STOL	E. G. Brown	
G-CCJD	Mainair Pegasus Quantum 15	P. Clark	
G-CCJF	Cameron C-90 balloon	Balloon School International Ltd	
G-CCJH	Lindstrand LBL-90A balloon	J. R. Hoare	
G-CCJI	Van's RV-6	A. Jenkins	
G-CCJJ	Medway Pirana	P. K. Bennett	
G-CCJK	Aerostar Yakovlev Yak-52	G-CCJK Group	
G-CCJL	Super Marine Aircraft Spitfire XXVI	M. W. Hanley & P. M. Whitaker	
G-CCJM	Mainair Pegasus Quik	P. Crosby	
G-CCJN	Rans S.6ES Coyote II	D. L. Frankland, J. M. Kirtley & T. W. Stewart	
G-CCJO	ICP-740 Savannah Jabiru 4	R. & I. Fletcher	
G-CCJT	Skyranger 912 (2)	Juliet Tango Group	
G-CCJU	ICP MXP-740 Savannah Jabiru (4)	A. R. & M. A. Baxter	
G-CCJV	Aeroprakt A.22 Foxbat	Foxbat UK015 Syndicate	
G-CCJW	Skyranger 912 (2)	J. R. Walter	
G-CCJX	Shaw Europa XS	J. S. Baranski	
G-CCJY	Cameron Z-42 balloon	D. J. Griffin	
G-CCKF	Skyranger 912 (2)	D. McCabe & M. Harris	
G-CCKG	Skyranger 912 (2)	J. Young	
G-CCKH	Diamond DA40D Star	Flying Time Ltd	
G-CCKI	Diamond DA40D Star	S. C. Horwood	
G-CCKJ	Raj Hamsa X'Air 133 (3)	G. A. Davidson	
G-CCKL	Aerotechnik EV-97A Eurostar	G-CCKL Group	
G-CCKM	Mainair Pegasus Quik	W. T. Milburn & P. A. Kershaw	
G-CCKN	Nicollier HN.700 Menestrel II	C. R. Partington	
G-CCKP	Robin DR.400/120	Duxford Flying Group	
G-CCKR	Pietenpol Air Camper	C. R. Thompson	
G-CCKT	Hapi Cygnet SF-2	P. W. Abraham	
G-CCKV	Isaacs Fury II	S. T. G. Ingram	
G-CCKW	PA-18 Super Cub 135	P. A. Layzell (G-GDAM)	
G-CCKX	Lindstrand LBL-210A balloon	Alba Ballooning Ltd	
G-CCKY	Lindstrand LBL-240A balloon	Cameron Flights Southern Ltd	
G-CCKZ	Customcraft A-25 balloon	M. J. Axtell	
G-CCLF	Best Off Skyranger 912 (2)	J. Bannister & N. J. Sutherland	
G-CCLG	Lindstrand LBL-105A balloon	M. A. Derbyshire	
G-CCLH	Rans S.6-ES Coyote II	K. R. Browne	
G-CCLM	Mainair Pegasus Quik	D. J. Shippen & C. C. Colclough	
G-CCLO	Ultramagic H-77 balloon-	J. P. Moore	
G-CCLP	ICP MXP-740 Savannah	C. J. Powell & A. H. Watkins	
G-CCLR	Schleicher Ash 26E	M. T. Burton & A. Darby	
G-CCLS	Comco Ikarus C.42 FB UK	B. D. Wykes	
G-CCLU	Best Off Skyranger 912	C. M. Babiy	
G-CCLV	Diamond DA40D Star	N. Harrison	
G-CCLW	Diamond DA40D Star	Shacklewell Diamond Group	
G-CCLX	Mainair Pegasus Quik	J. W. Edwards	
G-CCMC	Jabiru Aircraft Jabiru UL 450	J. Horan	
G-CCMD	Mainair Pegasus Quik	J. T. McCormack	

Notes	Reg.	Type	Owner or Operator
	G-CCME	Mainair Pegasus Quik	Caunton Graphites Syndicate
	G-CCMH	M.2H Hawk Major	J. A. Pothecary
	G-CCMI	SA Bulldog Srs 120/121 (XX513:10)	H. R. M. Tyrrell (G-KKKK)
	G-CCMJ	Easy Raider J2.2 (1)	G. F. Clews
	G-CCMK	Raj Hamsa X'Air Falcon	G. J. Digby
	G-CCML	Mainair Pegasus Quik	D. Renton
	G-CCMM	Dyn'Aéro MCR-01 ULC Banbi	J. D. Harris
	G-CCMN	Cameron C-90 balloon	A.E. Austin
	G-CCMO	Aerotechnik EV-97A Eurostar	T. Booth
	G-CCMP	Aerotechnik EV-97A Eurostar	E. K. McAlinden
	G-CCMR	Robinson R22 Beta	G. F. Smith
	G-CCMS	Mainair Pegasus Quik	Barton Charlie Charlie Group
	G-CCMT	Thruster T.600N 450	S. P. McCaffrey
	G-CCMU	Rotorway Executive 162F	D. J. Fravigar & J. Smith
	G-CCMW	CFM Shadow Srs.DD	M. Wilkinson
	G-CCMX	Skyranger 912 (2)	K. J. Cole
	G-CCMZ	Best Off Skyranger 912 (2)	D. D. Appleford
	G-CCNA	Jodel DR.100A (Replica)	R. Everitt
	G-CCNB	Rans S.6ES Coyote II	M. S. Lawrence
	G-CCNC	Cameron Z-275 balloon	J. D. & K. Griffiths
	G-CCND	Van's RV-9A	K. S. Woodard
	G-CCNE	Mainair Pegasus Quantum 15	G. D. Barker
	G-CCNF	Raj Hamsa X'Air 582 Falcon 133	R. E. Williams
	G-CCNG	Flight Design CT2K	A. Cheshire
	G-CCNH	Rans S.6ES Coyote II	J. E. Howard
	G-CCNJ	Skyranger 912 (2)	J. D. Buchanan
	G-CCNL	Raj Hamsa X'Air Falcon 133(1)	S. E. Vallance
	G-CCNM	Mainair Pegasus Quik	J. G. McMinn
	G-CCNN	Cameron Z-90 balloon	J. H. Turner
	G-CCNP	Flight Design CT2K	M. J. Hawkins
	G-CCNR	Skyranger 912 (2)	K. Washbourne
	G-CCNS	Skyranger 912 (2)	G. G. Rowley
	G-CCNT	Ikarus C.42 FB80	November Tango Group
	G-CCNU	Skyranger J2.2 (2)	P. D. Priestley
	G-CCNV	Cameron Z-210 balloon	J. A. Cooper
	G-CCNW	Mainair Pegasus Quantum Lite	J. Childs
	G-CCNX	CAB CAP-10B	Arc Input Ltd
	G-CCNY	Robinson R44	J. & S. J. Strange
	G-CCNZ	Raj Hamsa X'Air 133 (1)	A. Tucker
	G-CCOB	Aero C.104 Jungmann	C. W. Tomkins
	G-CCOC	Mainair Pegasus Quantum 15	S. I. P. Hardman
	G-CCOF	Rans S.6-ESA Coyote II	A. J. Wright & M. Govan
	G-CCOG	Mainair Pegasus Quik	A. O. Sutherland
	G-CCOK	Mainair Pegasus Quik	A. R. Walker
	G-CCOM	Westland Lysander IIIA (V9312)	Propshop Ltd
	G-CCOP	Ultramagic M-105 balloon	M. E. J. Whitewood
	G-CCOR	Sequoia F.8L Falco	D. J. Thoma
	G-CCOS	Cameron Z-350 balloon	Wickers World Ltd
	G-CCOT	Cameron Z-105 balloon	Airborne Adventures Ltd
	G-CCOU	Mainair Pegasus Quik	D. E. J. McVicker
	G-CCOV	Shaw Europa XS	B. C. Barton
	G-CCOW	Mainair Pegasus Quik	R. F. Dye & G. S. B. Airth
	G-CCOY	NA AT-6D Harvard II	Classic Flying Machine Collection Ltd
	G-CCOZ	Monnett Sonerai II	W. H. Cole
	G-CCPA	Kiss 400-582(1)	C.P. Astridge
	G-CCPC	Mainair Pegasus Quik	P. M. Coppola
	G-CCPD	Campbell Cricket Mk.4	T. H. Geake
	G-CCPE	Steen Skybolt	C. Moore
	G-CCPF	Skyranger 912 (2)	A. R. Tomlinson
	G-CCPG	Mainair Pegasus Quik	A.W. Lowrie
	G-CCPH	EV-97 TeamEurostar UK	A. H. Woolley
	G-CCPJ	EV-97 TeamEurostar UK	J. S. Webb
	G-CCPK	Murphy Rebel	B. A. W. Bridgewater
	G-CCPL	Skyranger 912 (2)	G-CCPL Group
	G-CCPM	Mainair Blade 912	P. S. Davies
	G-CCPN	Dyn'Aéro MCR-01 Club	M. Sibson
	G-CCPO	Cameron N-77 balloon	A. M. Daniels (G-MITS)
	G-CCPP	Cameron 70 Concept balloon	Sarnia Balloon Group
	G-CCPS	Ikarus C.42 FB100 VLA	H. Cullens
	G-CCPT	Cameron Z-90 balloon	Charter Ballooning Ltd
	G-CCPV	Jabiru J400	J. R. Lawrence & M. J. Worrall
	G-CCPW	BAe Jetstream 3102	Linksair Ltd
	G-CCPX	Diamond DA400 Star	R. T. Dickinson

Reg.	Type	Owner or Operator	Notes
G-CCPY	Hughes 369D	Alpha Properties (London) Ltd	
G-CCPZ	Cameron Z-225 balloon	Cameron Flights Southern Ltd	
G-CCRA	Glaser-Dirks DG-800B	R. Fischer	
G-CCRB	Kolb Twinstar Mk.3 (modified)	M. Daly	
G-CCRC	Cessna Tu.206G	D. M. Penny	
G-CCRF	Mainair Pegasus Quantum 15	N. F. Taylor	
G-CCRG	Ultramagic M-77 balloon	Wickers World Ltd	
G-CCRH	Cameron Z-315 balloon	B. J. Palfreyman	
G-CCRI	Raj Hamsa X'Air 582 (5)	B. M. Tibenham	
G-CCRJ	Shaw Europa	J. F. Cliff	
G-CCRK	Luscombe 8A Silvaire	J. R. Kimberley	
G-CCRN	Thruster T.600N 450	R. A. Wright	
G-CCRP	Thruster T.600N 450	M. M. Lane (G-ULLY)	
G-CCRR	Skyranger 912 (1)	M. Cheetham	
G-CCRS	Lindstrand LBL-210A balloon	Aerosaurus Ballooning Ltd	
G-CCRT	Mainair Pegasus Quantum 15	N. Mitchell	
G-CCRV	Skyranger 912 (2)	A. C. Thomson	
G-CCRW	Mainair Pegasus Quik	S. O. Hutchinson	
G-CCRX	Jabiru UL-450	M. Everest	
G-CCSA	Cameron Z-350 balloon	Ballooning Network Ltd	
G-CCSD	Mainair Pegasus Quik	S. J. M. Morling	
G-CCSF	Mainair Pegasus Quik	D. G. Barnes & A. Sorah	
G-CCSG	Cameron Z-275 balloon	Wickers World Ltd	
G-CCSH	Mainair Pegasus Quik	N. C. Milnes	
G-CCSI	Cameron Z-42 balloon	IKEA Ltd	
G-CCSJ	Cameron A-275 balloon	Dragon Balloon Co Ltd	
G-CCSL	Mainair Pegasus Quik	A. J. Harper	
G-CCSN	Cessna U.206G	K. Brady	
G-CCSO	Raj Hamsa X'Air Falcon	D. G. McHugh	
G-CCSP	Cameron N-77 balloon	Ballongforeningen Oscair I Goteberg/Sweden	
G-CCSR	Aerotechnik EV-97A Eurostar	Sierra Romeo Flying Group	
G-CCSS	Lindstrand LBL-90A balloon	British Telecom	
G-CCST	PA-32R-301 Saratoga	G. R. Balls	
G-CCSU	IDA Bacau Yakovlev Yak-52	S. Ullrich/Germany	
G-CCSV	ICP MXP-740 Savannah Jabiru (1)	R. D. Wood	
G-CCSW	Nott PA balloon	J. R. P.Nott	
G-CCSX	Skyranger 912	T. Jackson	
G-CCSY	Mainair Pegasus Quik	I. K. Macleod	
G-CCTA	Zenair CH.601UL Zodiac	G. E. Reynolds	
G-CCTB	BAe. RJ100	Trident Jet Leasing (Ireland) Ltd	
G-CCTC	Mainair Pegasus Quik	D. R. Purslow	
G-CCTD	Mainair Pegasus Quik	R. N. S. Taylor	
G-CCTE	Dyn'Aéro MCR-01 Banbi	B. J. Mills & N. J. Milnes	
G-CCTF	Aerotek Pitts S-2A Special	Stampe and Pitts Flying Group	
G-CCTG	Van's RV-3B	A. Donald	
G-CCTH	Aerotechnik EV-97 TeamEurostar UK	M. W. Fitch	
G-CCTI	Aerotechnik EV-97 Teameurostar	Flylight Airsports Ltd	
G-CCTL	Robinson R44 II	B. Daly	
G-CCTM	Mainair Blade	J. N. Hanso	
G-CCTN	Ultramagic T-180 balloon	A. Derbyshire	
G-CCTO	Aerotechnik EV-97 Eurostar	A. J. Bolton	
G-CCTP	Aerotechnik EV-97 Eurostar	P. E. Rose	
G-CCTR	Skyranger 912	G. Lampit & D. W. Stamp	
G-CCTS	Cameron Z-120 balloon	F. R. Hart	
G-CCTT	Cessna 172S	ACS Engineering Ltd	
G-CCTU	Mainair Pegasus Quik	J. J. C. Parrish & I. D. Smart	
G-CCTV	Rans S.6ESA Coyote II	G. & S. Simons	
G-CCTW	Cessna 152	R. J. Dempsey	
G-CCTX	Rans S.8ES Coyote II	T. Osbourne	
G-CCTZ	Mainair Pegasus Quik 912S	S. Baker	
G-CCUA	Mainair Pegasus Quik	C. Gane	
G-CCUB	Piper J-3C-65 Cub	G. Cormack	
G-CCUE	Ultramagic T-180 balloon	Cameron Flights Southern Ltd	
G-CCUF	Skyranger 912(2)	R. E. Parker	
G-CCUH	RAF 2000 GTX-SE gyroplane	J. H. Haverhals	
G-CCUI	Dyn'Aéro MCR-01 Banbi	J. T. Morgan	
G-CCUK	Agusta A109-II	Eastern Atlantic Helicopters Ltd	
G-CCUL	Shaw Europa XS	Europa 6	
G-CCUO	Hughes 369D	Claremont Air Services	
G-CCUP	Wessex 60 Mk.2 (XR502:Z)	D. Brem-Wilson & J. Buswell	
G-CCUR	Mainair Pegasus Quantum 15-912	D. W. Power & D. James	
G-CCUT	Aerotechnik EV-97 Eurostar	Doctor and the Medics	
G-CCUY	Shaw Europa	N. Evans	

Notes	Reg.	Type	Owner or Operator
	G-CCUZ	Thruster T.600N 450	Fly 365 Ltd
	G-CCVA	Aerotechnik EV-97 Eurostar	K. J. Scott
	G-CCVF	Lindstrand LBL-105 balloon	Alan Patterson Design
	G-CCVH	Curtiss H-75A-1 (82:8)	The Fighter Collection
	G-CCVI	Zenair CH.701 SP	The 701 Group
	G-CCVJ	Raj Hamsa X'Air Falcon 133	I. S. Doig
	G-CCVK	Aerotechnik EV-97 TeamEurostar UK	J. Holditch
	G-CCVL	Zenair CH.601XL Zodiac	A. Y-T. Leungr & G. Constantine
	G-CCVM	Van's RV-7A	J. G. Small
	G-CCVN	Jabiru SP-470	Teesside Aviators Group
	G-CCVP	Beech 58	Richard Nash Cars Ltd
	G-CCVR	Skyranger 912(2)	M. J. Batchelor
	G-CCVS	Van's RV-6A	J. Edgeworth (G-CCVC)
	G-CCVT	Zenair CH.601UL Zodiac	P. Millar
	G-CCVU	Robinson R22 Beta II	Fly Excecutive Ltd
	G-CCVW	Nicollier HN.700 Menestrel II	B. F. Enock
	G-CCVX	Mainair Tri Flyer 330	J. A. Shufflebotham
	G-CCVZ	Cameron O-120 balloon	T. M. C. McCoy
	G-CCWC	Skyranger 912	W. Goldsmith
	G-CCWE	Lindstrand LBL-330A balloon	Adventure Balloons Ltd
	G-CCWF	Raj Hamsa X'Air 133	F. Loughran
	G-CCWH	Dyn'Aéro MCR-01 Bambi	B. J. Mills & N. J. Mines
	G-CCWJ	Robinson R44 II	Saxon Logistics Ltd
	G-CCWL	Mainair Blade	M. E. Rushworth
	G-CCWM	Robin DR.400/180	M. R. Clark
	G-CCWO	Mainair Pegasus Quantum 15-912	R. Fitzgerald
	G-CCWP	Aerotechnik EV-97 TeamEurostar UK	Sky Blue Flight Training
	G-CCWR	Mainair Pegasus Quik	A. Harding
	G-CCWU	Skyranger 912	W. J. Byrd
	G-CCWV	Mainair Pegasus Quik	W. J. Dawson
	G-CCWW	Mainair Pegasus Quantum 15-912	I. W. Barlow
	G-CCWZ	Raj Hamsa X'Air Falcon 133	M. A. Evans
	G-CCXA	Boeing Stearman A75N-1 Kaydet (669)	Skymax (Aviation) Ltd
	G-CCXB	Boeing Stearman B75N1	C. D. Walker
	G-CCXC	Avion Mudry CAP-10B	Skymax (Aviation) Ltd
	G-CCXD	Lindstrand LBL-105B balloon	Silver Ghost Balloon Club
	G-CCXE	Cameron Z-120 balloon	M. R. Andreas
	G-CCXF	Cameron Z-90 balloon	R. G. March & T. J. Maycock
	G-CCXG	SE-5A (replica) (C5430)	C. Morris
	G-CCXH	Skyranger J2.2	M. J. O'Connor
	G-CCXK	Pitts S-1S Special	P. G. Bond
	G-CCXM	Skyranger 912(1)	C. J. Finnigan
	G-CCXN	Skyranger 912(1)	S. E. Garner & G. P. Martin
	G-CCXO	Corgy CJ-1 Starlet	S. C. Ord
	G-CCXP	ICP Savannah Jabiru	B. J. Harper
	G-CCXR	Mainair Pegasus Blade	J. McErlain
	G-CCXS	Montgomerie-Bensen B.8MR	A. Morgan
	G-CCXT	Mainair Pegasus Quik	C. Turner
	G-CCXU	Diamond DA40D Star	R. J. & L. Hole
	G-CCXV	Thruster T.600N 450	Caunton Thruster Group
	G-CCXW	Thruster T.600N 450	G-CCXW Syndicate
	G-CCXX	AG-5B Tiger	P. D. Lock
	G-CCXZ	Mainair Pegasus Quik	K. J. Sene
	G-CCYB	Escapade 912(1)	B. E. & S. M. Renehan
	G-CCYC	Robinson R44 II	Derg Developments Ltd/Ireland
	G-CCYE	Mainair Pegasus Quik	J. Lane
	G-CCYG	Robinson R44	Moorland Windows
	G-CCYI	Cameron O-105 balloon	Media Balloons Ltd
	G-CCYJ	Mainair Pegasus Quik	YJ Syndicate
	G-CCYL	MainairPegasus Quantum 15	A. M. Goulden
	G-CCYM	Skyranger 912	I. Pilton
	G-CCYO	Christen Eagle II	P. C. Woolley
	G-CCYP	Colt 56A balloon	Magical Adventures Ltd
	G-CCYR	Ikarus C.42 FB80	Airbourne Aviation Ltd
	G-CCYS	Cessna F.182Q	S. Dyson
	G-CCYU	Ultramagic S-90 balloon	A. R. Craze
	G-CCYX	Bell 412	RCR Aviation Ltd
	G-CCYY	PA-28-161 Warrior II	Flightcontrol Ltd
	G-CCYZ	Dornier EKW C3605	CW Tomkins Ltd
	G-CCZA	SOCATA MS.894A Rallye Minerva 220	R. N. Aylett
	G-CCZB	Mainair Pegasus Quantum 15	A. Johnson
	G-CCZD	Van's RV-7	D. Powell
	G-CCZI	Cameron A-275 balloon	Balloon School (International) Ltd

Reg.	Type	Owner or Operator	Notes
G-CCZJ	Raj Hamsa X' Air Falcon 582	P. A. Lindford	
G-CCZK	Zenair CH.601 UL Zodiac	R. J. Hopkins	
G-CCZL	Ikarus C-42 FB80	Shadow Aviation Ltd	
G-CCZM	Skyranger 912S	D. Woodward	
G-CCZN	Rans S.6-ES Coyote II	R. D. Proctor	
G-CCZO	Mainair Pegasus Quik	P. G. Penhaligan	
G-CCZP	Super Marine Aircraft Spitfire 26 (JF343:JW-P)	J. W. E. Pearson	
G-CCZR	Medway Raven Eclipse R	K. A. Sutton	
G-CCZS	Raj Hamsa X'Air Falcon 582	A. T. Kilpatrick	
G-CCZT	Van's RV-9A	Zulu Tango Flying Group	
G-CCZU	Diamond DA40D Star	Diamond Aircraft UK Ltd	
G-CCZV	PA-28-151 Warrior	P. D. P. Deal	
G-CCZW	Mainair Pegasus Blade	P. J. Webster	
G-CCZX	Robin DR.400/180	M. Conrad	
G-CCZY	Van's RV-9A	Mona RV-9 Group	
G-CCZZ	Aerotechnik EV-97 Eurostar	B. M Starck & J. P. Aitken	
G-CDAA	Mainair Pegasus Quantum 15-912	I. A. Macadam	
G-CDAB	Glasair Super IISRG	W. L. Hitchins	
G-GDAC	Aerotechnik EV-97 TeamEurostar	Nene Valley Microlights Ltd	
G-CDAD	Lindstrand LBL-25A balloon	G. J. Madelin	
G-CDAE	Van's RV-6A	K. J. Fleming	
G-CDAG	Mainair Blade	K. I. Making	
G-CDAI	Robin DR.400/140B	D. Hardy & J. Sambrook	
G-CDAK	Zenair CH.601 UK Zodiac	W. K. Evans	
G-CDAL	Zenair CH.601UL Zodiac	R. J. Howell	
G-CDAO	Mainair Pegasus Quantum 15 -912	J. C. Duncan	
G-CDAP	Aerotechnik EV-97 TeamEurostar UK	Mainair Microlight School Ltd	
G-CDAR	Mainair Pegasus Quik	A. R. Pitcher	
G-CDAT	ICP MXP-740 Savannah Jabiru	G. M. Railson	
G-CDAW	Robinson R22 Beta	Airtask Group PLC	
G-CDAX	Mainair Pegasus Quik	L. Hurman	
G-CDAY	Skyranger 912	G-CDAY Group	
G-CDAZ	Aerotechnik EV-97 Eurostar	M. C. J. Ludlow	
G-CDBA	Skyranger 912(S)	P. J. Brennan	
G-CDBB	Mainair Pegasus Quik	G. Hall	
G-CDBC	Aviation Enterprises Magnum	Aviation Enterprises Ltd	
G-CDBD	Jabiru J400	I. D. Rutherford	
G-CDBE	Montgomerie-Bensen B.8M	P. Harwood	
G-CDBG	Robinson R22 Beta	Jepar Rotorcraft	
G-CDBJ	Yakovlev Yak-3	C. E. Bellhouse	
G-CDBK	Rotorway Executive 162F	Car Builder Solutions Ltd	
G-CDBM	Robin DR.400/180	C. M. Simmonds	
G-CDBO	Skyranger 912	G-CDBO Flying Group	
G-CDBR	Stolp SA.300 Starduster Too	R. J. Warren	
G-CDBS	MBB Bö.105DBS-4	Bond Air Services Ltd	
G-CDBU	Ikarus C.42 FB100	S. E. Meehan	
G-CDBV	Skyranger 912S	K. Hall	
G-CDBX	Shaw Europa XS	R. Marston	
G-CDBY	Dyn'Aero MCR-01 ULC	A. Thornton	
G-CDBZ	Thruster T.600N 450	J. A. Lynch	
G-CDCB	Robinson R44 II	Microwave Sales and Services Ltd	
G-CDCC	Aerotechnik EV-97A Eurostar	R. E. & & N. G. Nicholson	
G-CDCD	Van's RVF-9A	RV9ers	
G-CDCE	Avions Mudry CAP-10B	The Tiger Club (1990) Ltd	
G-CDCF	Mainair Pegasus Quik	T. J. Gayton-Polley	
G-CDCG	Ikarus C.42 FB UK	N. E. Ashton & R. H. J. Jenkins	
G-CDCH	Skyranger 912(2)	G. C. Long	
G-CDCI	Pegasus Quik	S. G. Murray	
G-CDCK	Mainair Pegasus Quik	R. Solomons	
G-CDCM	Ikarus C.42 FB UK	S. T. Allen	
G-CDCO	Ikarus C.42 FB UK	G. S. Gee-Carter & K. A. O'Neill	
G-CDCP	Avtech Jabiru J400	M. W. T. Wilson	
G-CDCR	Savannah Jabiru(1)	T. Davidson	
G-CDCS	PA-12 Super Cruiser	D. Todorovic	
G-CDCT	Aerotechnik EV-97 TeamEurostar UK	G. R. Nicholson	
G-CDCU	Mainair Pegasus Blade	W. S. Clare	
G-CDCV	Robinson R44 II	Heli Air Ltd	
G-CDCW	Escapade 912 (1)	P. Nicholls	
G-CDCX	Citation 750	Pendley Aviation LLP	
G-CDDA	SOCATA TB20 Trinidad	Oxford Aviation Academy (Oxford) Ltd	
G-CDDB	Grob/Schemmp-Hirth CS-11	K. D. Barber/France	
G-CDDF	Mainair Pegasus Quantum 15-912	B. C. Blackburn & J. L. Dalgetty	

Notes	Reg.	Type	Owner or Operator
	G-CDDG	PA-26-161 Warrior II	Smart People Don't Buy Ltd
	G-CDDH	Raj Hamsa X'Air Falcon	G. Loosley
	G-CDDI	Thruster T.600N 450	R. Nayak
	G-CDDK	Cessna 172M	M. H. & P. R. Kavern
	G-CDDL	Cameron Z-350 balloon	Balloon School (International) Ltd
	G-CDDM	Lindstrand LBL 90A balloon	A. M. Holly
	G-CDDN	Lindstrand LBL 90A balloon	Flying Enterprises
	G-CDDO	Raj Hamsa X'Air 133(2)	S. Bain
	G-CDDP	Lazer Z.230	A. Smith
	G-CDDR	Skyranger 582(1)	M. Jones
	G-CDDS	Zenair CH.601HD	S. Foreman
	G-CDDT	SOCATA TB20 Trinidad	Oxford Aviation Academy (Oxford) Ltd
	G-CDDU	Skyranger 912(2)	J. S. G. Down & R. Newton
	G-CDDV	Cameron Z-250 balloon	Alba Ballooning Ltd
	G-CDDW	Aeroprakt A.22 Foxbat	M. Raflewski
	G-CDDX	Thruster T.600N 450	P. A. G. Harper
	G-CDDY	Van's RV-8	The AV8ors
	G-CDEA	SAAB 2000	Air Kilroe Ltd
	G-CDEB	SAAB 2000	Eastern Airways
	G-CDED	Robinson R22 Beta	Flight Solutions Ltd
	G-CDEF	PA-28-161 Cadet	Western Air (Thruxton) Ltd
	G-CDEH	ICP MXP-740 Savannah	P. E. Terrell
	G-CDEM	Raj Hamsa X' Air 133	R. J. Froud
	G-CDEN	Mainair Pegasus Quantum 15 912	J. D. J. Spragg
	G-CDEO	PA-28 Cherokee 180	VVB Engineering Services Ltd
	G-CDEP	Aerotechnik EV-97 TeamEurostar	Echo Papa Group
	G-CDER	PA-28-161 Warrior II	Archer Five Ltd
	G-CDET	Culver LCA Cadet	J. Gregson
	G-CDEV	Escapade 912 (1)	M. B. Devenport
	G-CDEW	Pegasus Quik	K. M. Sullivan
	G-CDEX	Shaw Europa	K. Martindale
	G-CDEZ	Robinson R44 II	Heli Air Ltd
	G-CDFA	Kolb Twinstar Mk3 Extra	S. Soar & W. A. Douthwaite
	G-CDFC	Ultramagic S-160 balloon	S. E. Hurst
	G-CDFD	Scheibe SF.25C Falke	The Royal Air Force Gliding and Soaring Association
	G-CDFG	Mainair Pegasus Quik	D. Gabbott
	G-CDFI	Colt 31A balloon	A. M. Holly
	G-CDFJ	Skyranger 912	L. A. Hosegood
	G-CDFK	Jabiru UL-450	J. A. Ellis
	G-CDFL	Zenair CH.601UL	Caunton Zodiac Group
	G-CDFM	Raj Hamsa X'Air 582 (5)	W. A. Keel-Stocker
	G-CDFN	Thunder Ax7-77 balloon	E. Rullo/Italy
	G-CDFO	Pegasus Quik	The Foxtrot Oscars
	G-CDFP	Skyranger 912 (2)	J. M. Gammidge
	G-CDFR	Mainair Pegasus Quantum 15	A. Jopp
	G-CDFU	Rans S.6-ES	P. W. Taylor
	G-CDFY	Beech B.200 Super King Air	BAE Systems Marine Ltd
	G-CDGA	Taylor JT.1 Monoplane	R. M. Larimore
	G-CDGB	Rans S.6-116 Coyote	S. Penoyre
	G-CDGC	Pegasus Quik	A. T. K. Crozier
	G-CDGD	Pegasus Quik	I. D. & V. A. Milne
	G-CDGE	Edge XT912-IIIB	M. R. Leyshon
	G-CDGF	Ultramagic S-105 balloon	D. & K. Bareford
	G-CDGG	Dyn'Aéro MCR-01 Club	N. Rollins
	G-CDGH	Rans S.6-ES Coyote	G-CDGH Group
	G-CDGI	Thruster T600N 450	R. North
	G-CDGN	Cameron C-90 balloon	M. C. Gibbons
	G-CDGO	Pegasus Quik	J. C. Townsend
	G-CDGP	Zenair CH 601XL	T. J. Bax
	G-CDGR	Zenair CH 701UL	I. A. R. Sim
	G-CDGS	AG-5B Tiger	M. R. O'B. Thompson
	G-CDGT	Montgomerie-Parsons Two Place g/p	J. B. Allan
	G-CDGU	VS.300 Spitfire I (X4276)	Peter Monk Ltd
	G-CDGW	PA-28-181 Archer III	Rutland Flying Group
	G-CDGX	Pegasus Quantum 15-912	S. R. Green
	G-CDGY	VS.349 Spitfire Mk VC	Aero Vintage Ltd
	G-CDHA	Skyranger 912S(1)	A. T. Cameron
	G-CDHC	Slingsby T67C	N. J. Morgan
	G-CDHE	Skyranger 912(2)	Barton Syndicate
	G-CDHF	PA-30 Twin Comanche B	Reid International (Guernsey) Ltd
	G-CDHG	Mainair Pegasus Quik	T. W. Pelan
	G-CDHH	Robinson R44 II	Abwood Homes/Ireland

Reg.	Type	Owner or Operator	Notes
G-CDHJ	Lindstrand LBL-90B balloon	Lindstrand Hot Air Balloons Ltd	
G-CDHM	Pegasus Quantum 15	S. T. Hayes	
G-CDHN	Lindstrand LBL-317A balloon	Aerosaurus Balloons Ltd	
G-CDHO	Raj Hamsa X'Air 133 (1)	G. P. Masters	
G-CDHP	Lindstrand LBL-150A balloon	Floating Sensations Ltd (G-OHRH)	
G-CDHR	Ikarus C.42 FB80	Airbourne Aviation Ltd	
G-CDHU	Skyranger 912 (2)	G-CDHU Group	
G-CDHX	Aeroprakt A.22 Foxbat	N. E. Stokes	
G-CDHY	Cameron Z-90 balloon	D. M. Roberts	
G-CDHZ	Nicollier HN.700 Menestrel II	G. E. Whittaker	
G-CDIA	Thruster T.600N 450	T. Davidson	
G-CDIB	Cameron Z-350Z balloon	Ballooning Network Ltd	
G-CDIF	Mudry CAP-10B	J. D. Gordon	
G-CDIG	Aerotechnik EV-97 Eurostar	M. Sanders	
G-CDIH	Cameron Z-275 balloon	Bailey Balloons Ltd	
G-CDIJ	Skyranger 912 (2)	India Juliet Flying Group	
G-CDIL	Pegasus Quantum 15-912	G. J. Prisk	
G-CDIO	Cameron Z-90 balloon	Slowfly Montgolfiere SNC/Italy	
G-CDIP	Skyranger 912S(1)	J. Parke	
G-CDIR	Mainair Pegasus Quantum 15-912	W. Traynor-Keen	
G-CDIS	Cessna 150F	S. P. Fox	
G-CDIT	Cameron Z-105 balloon	Bailey Balloons Ltd	
G-CDIU	Skyranger 912S(1)	C. P. Dawes & J. English	
G-CDIV	Lindstrand LBL-90A balloon	The Packhouse Ltd	
G-CDIX	Ikarus C.42 FB.100	T. G. Greenhill & J. G. Spinks	
G-CDIY	Aerotechnik EV-97A Eurostar	R. E. Woolsey	
G-CDIZ	Escapade 912(1)	E. G. Bishop & E. N. Dunn	
G-CDJB	Van's RV-4	W. D. Garlick & R. J. Napp	
G-CDJC	Skyranger 912 (2)	J. L. A. Campell	
G-CDJD	ICP MXP-740 Savannah Jabiru (4)	D. W. Mullin	
G-CDJE	Thruster T.600N 450	C. H. Ford	
G-CDJF	Flight Design CT2K	P. A. James	
G-CDJG	Zenair 601UL Zodiac	D. Garcia	
G-CDJI	Ultramagic M-120 balloon	The Ballooning Business Ltd	
G-CDJJ	IAV Yakovlev Yak-52	J. J. Miles	
G-CDJK	Ikarus C.42 FB 80	Cornish Aviation Ltd	
G-CDJL	Avtech Jabiru J400	J. Gardiner	
G-CDJM	Zenair CH.601XL	S. A. Rennison	
G-CDJN	RAF 2000 GTX-SE gyroplane	D. J. North	
G-CDJO	DH.82A Tiger Moth	D. Dal Bon	
G-CDJP	Skyranger 912(2)	I. A. Cunningham	
G-CDJR	Aerotechnik EV-97 TeamEurostar	K. C. Lye & M. D. White	
G-CDJU	CASA 1.131E Jungmann Srs.1000	P. Gaskell	
G-CDJV	Beech A.36 Bonanza	Atlantic Bridge Aviation Ltd/Lydd	
G-CDJW	Van's RV-7	J. B. Shaw	
G-CDJX	Cameron N-56 balloon	Cameron Balloons Ltd	
G-CDJY	Cameron C-80 balloon	British Airways PLC	
G-CDKA	SAAB 2000	Eastern Airways	
G-CDKB	SAAB 2000	Eastern Airways	
G-CDKE	Rans S6-ES Coyote II	J. E. Holloway	
G-CDKF	Escapade 912 (1)	Kilo Fox Flying Group	
G-CDKH	Skyranger 912S (1)	C. Lenaghan	
G-CDKI	Skyranger 912S (1)	J. M. Hucker	
G-CDKJ	Silence Twister	A. H. R. Stansfield	
G-CDKK	Mainair Pegasus Quik	P. M. Knight	
G-CDKL	Escapade 912 (2)	M. A. Hodgson & D. Maidment	
G-CDKM	Pegasus Quik	P. Lister	
G-CDKN	ICP MXP-740 Savannah Jabiru (4)	J. Bate	
G-CDKO	ICP MXP-740 Savannah Jabiru (4)	C. Jones & B. Hunter	
G-CDKP	Avtech Jabiru UL-D Calypso	Rochester Microlights Ltd	
G-CDKX	Skyranger J.2 .2 (1)	E. Lewis	
G-CDKY	Robinson R44	Highland Charter Company	
G-CDKZ	Thunder Ax10-160 S2 balloon	Cameron Flights Southern Ltd	
G-CDLA	Mainair Pegasus Quik	C. R. Stevens	
G-CDLB	Cameron Z-120 balloon	J. A. Hibberd and Tchemma Products	
G-CDLC	CASA 1.131E Jungmann 2000	R. D. Loder	
G-CDLD	Mainair Pegasus Quik 912S	W. Williams	
G-CDLG	Skyranger 912 (2)	D. J. Saunders	
G-CDLI	Airco DH.9 (E8894)	Aero Vintage Ltd	
G-CDLJ	Mainair Pegasus Quik	J. S. James & R. S. Keyser	
G-CDLK	Skyranger 912S	L. E. Cowling	
G-CDLL	Dyn'Aéro MCR-01 ULC	D. Cassidy	
G-CDLR	ICP MXP / 740 Savannah Jabiru (4)	A. J. Burton & P. Read	

BRITISH CIVIL REGISTRATIONS

Notes	Reg.	Type	Owner or Operator
	G-CDLS	Jabiru Aircrraft Jabiru J400	Kestrel Group
	G-CDLT	Raytheon Hawker 800XP	Gama Aviation Ltd
	G-CDLW	Zenair ZH.601UL Zodiac	W. A. Stphen
	G-CDLY	Cirrus SR20	Partside Aviation Ltd
	G-CDLZ	Mainair Pegasus Quantum 15-912	C. M. Jeffrey & J. L. Dalgetty
	G-CDMA	PA-28-151 Warrior	A. Cabre
	G-CDMC	Cameron Z-105 balloon	First Flight
	G-CDMD	Robin DR.400/500	P. R. Liddle
	G-CDME	Van's RV-7	M. W. Elliott
	G-CDMF	Van's RV-9A	J. R. Bowden
	G-CDMG	Robinson R22 Beta	Heli Aitch Be Ltd
	G-CDMH	Cessna P.210N	J. G. Hinley
	G-CDMJ	Mainair Pegasus Quik	M. J. R. Dean
	G-CDMK	Montgomerie-Bensen B8MR	P. Rentell
	G-CDML	Mainair Pegasus Quik	Ducky Group
	G-CDMM	Cessna 172P Skyhawk	Cristal Air Ltd
	G-CDMN	Van's RV-9	G. J. Smith
	G-CDMO	Cameron S Can-100 balloon	A. Schneider/Germany
	G-CDMP	Best Off Skyranger(1)	J. A. Charlton
	G-CDMS	Ikarus C,42 FB 80	Airbourne Aviation Ltd
	G-CDMT	Zenair CH.601XL Zodiac	B. A. Ritchie
	G-CDMU	Mainair Pegasus Quik	T. M. Bolton & S. D. Jones
	G-CDMV	Best Off Skyranger 912S(1)	D. O'Keeffe & K. E. Rutter
	G-CDMX	PA-28-161 Warrior II	S. Collins
	G-CDMY	PA-28-161 Warrior II	J. S. Develin & Z. Islam
	G-CDMZ	Mainair Pegasus Quik	R. Solomons
	G-CDNA	Grob G.109A	Army Gliding Association
	G-CDND	GA-7 Cougar	C. J. Chaplin
	G-CDNE	Best Off Skyranger 912S(1)	G-CDNE Syndicate
	G-CDNF	Aero Design Pulsar 3	D. Ringer
	G-CDNG	Aerotechnik EV-97 TeamEurostar UK	H. Wilson
	G-CDNH	Mainair Pegasus Quik	C. D. Andrews
	G-CDNI	Aerotechnik EV-97 TeamEurostar UK	G-CDNI Group
	G-CDNJ	Colomban MC-15 Cri Cri	Cri Cri Group
	G-CDNM	Aerotechnik EV-97 TeamEurostar UK	H. C. Lowther
	G-CDNO	Westland Gazelle AH.1 (XX432)	Falcon Aviation Ltd
	G-CDNP	Aerotechnik EV-97 TeamEurostar UK	Eaglescott Eurostar Group
	G-CDNR	Ikarus C.42 FB1000	M. T. Sheelan
	G-CDNS	Westland Gazelle AH.1 (XZ321)	Falcon Aviation Ltd
	G-CDNT	Zenair CH.601XL Zodiac	W. McCormack
	G-CDNW	Ikarus C.42 FB UK	W. Gabbott
	G-CDNY	Jabiru SP-470	G. Lucey
	G-CDNZ	Ultramagic M-120 balloon	R. H. Etherington/Italy
	G-CDOA	EV-97 TeamEurostar UK	A. Costello & J. Cunliffe
	G-CDOB	Cameron C-90 balloon	G. D. & S. M. Philpot
	G-CDOC	Mainair Quik GT450	D. M. Broom
	G-CDOE	Avro 146 RJ70	Trident Turboprop (Dublin) Ltd
	G-CDOF	Avro 146 RJ70	Trident Turboprop (Dublin) Ltd
	G-CDOG	Lindstrand LBL-Dog SS balloon	ABC Flights Ltd
	G-CDOJ	Schweizer 269C-1	Alan Mann Aviation Group Ltd
	G-CDOK	Ikarus C.42 FB 100	M Aviation Ltd
	G-CDOM	Mainair Pegasus Quik	G-CDOM Flying Group
	G-CDON	PA-28-161 Warrior II	G-CDON Group
	G-CDOO	Mainair Pegasus Quantum 15-912	O. C. Harding
	G-CDOP	Mainair Pegasus Quik	H. A. Duthie & R. C. Tadman
	G-CDOR	Mainair Blade	J. D. Otter
	G-CDOT	Ikarus C.42 FB 100	A. C. Anderson
	G-CDOV	Skyranger 912(2)	B. Richardson
	G-CDOY	Robin DR.400/180R	Lasham Gliding Society Ltd
	G-CDOZ	EV-97 TeamEurostar UK	J. P. McCall
	G-CDPA	Alpi Pioneer 300	N. D. White
	G-CDPB	Skyranger 982(1)	N. S. Bishop
	G-CDPD	Mainair Pegasus Quik	M. D. Vearncombe
	G-CDPE	Skyranger 912(2)	D. Workman
	G-CDPG	Crofton Auster J1-A	P. & T. Groves
	G-CDPH	Tiger Cub RL5A LW Sherwood Ranger ST	K. F. Crumplin
	G-CDPI	Zenair CH.601UL Zodiac	W. W. Burgess
	G-CDPJ	Van's RV-8	P. Johnson
	G-CDPL	EV-97 TeamEurostar UK	C. I. D. H Garrison
	G-CDPN	Ultramagic S-105	D. J. MacInnes
	G-CDPP	Ikarus C42 FB UK	H. M. Owen
	G-CDPR	PA-18 Super Cub 95	F. Lamouroux

Reg.	Type	Owner or Operator	Notes
G-CDPS	Raj Hamsa X'Air 133	N. Brown	
G-CDPV	PA-34-200T Seneca II	Globebrow Ltd	
G-CDPW	Mainair Pegasus Quantum 15-912	T. P. R. Wright	
G-CDPY	Shaw Europa	A. Burrill	
G-CDPZ	Flight Design CT2K	M. E. Henwick	
G-CDRC	Cessna 182Q Skylane	R. S. Hill and Sons	
G-CDRD	AirBorne XT912-B Edge/Streak III-B	Fly NI Ltd	
G-CDRF	Cameron Z-90 balloon	Chalmers Ballong Corps	
G-CDRG	Mainair Pegasus Quik	R. J. Gabriel	
G-CDRH	Thruster T.600N	Carlisle Thruster Group	
G-CDRI	Cameron O-105 balloon	Snapdragon Balloon Group	
G-CDRJ	Tanarg/Ixess 15 912S(1)	M. Delves-Yates	
G-CDRN	Cameron Z-225 balloon	Balloon School (International) Ltd	
G-CDRO	Ikarus C42 F880	Airbourne Aviation Ltd	
G-CDRP	Ikarus C42 FB80	D. S. Parker	
G-CDRR	Mainair Pegasus Quantum 15-912	G. J. Crago	
G-CDRS	Rotorway Executive 162F	R. C. Swann	
G-CDRT	Mainair Pegasus Quik	R. Tetlow	
G-CDRU	CASA 1.131E Jungmann 2000	P. Cunniff	
G-CDRV	Van's RV-9A	R. J. Woodford	
G-CDRW	Mainair Pegasus Quik	G. L. Fearon	
G-CDRX	Cameron Z-225 balloon	Balloon School (International) Ltd	
G-CDRY	Ikarus C42 FB100 VLA	R. J. Mitchell	
G-CDRZ	Balóny Kubíček BB22 balloon	Club Amatori Del Volo In Montgolfiera	
G-CDSA	Mainair Pegasus Quik	G-CDSA Group	
G-CDSB	Alpi Pioneer 200	T. A. & P. M. Pugh	
G-CDSC	Scheibe SF.25C Rotax-Falke	Devon & Somerset Motorglider Group	
G-CDSD	Alpi Pioneer 300	J. A. Ball	
G-CDSF	Diamond DA40D Star	Flying Time Ltd	
G-CDSH	ICP MXP-740 Savannah Jabiru(5)	J. P. Bell & T. N. Huggins-Haig	
G-CDSK	Reality Escapade Jabiru(3)	R. H. Sear	
G-CDSM	P & M Aviation Quik GT450	S. L. Cogger	
G-CDSN	Raj Hamsa X'Air Jabiru(3)	S. P. Heard	
G-CDSO	Thruster T.600N	The Red Barons	
G-CDSS	Mainair Pegasus Quik	P. A. Bass	
G-CDST	Ultramagic N-250 balloon	Cameron Flights Southern Ltd	
G-CDSU	Robinson R22	Sloane Helicopters Ltd	
G-CDSW	Ikarus C.42 FB UK	R. W. Skelton & J. Toner	
G-CDSX	EE Canberra T.Mk.4 (VN799)	Aviation Heritage Ltd	
G-CDSY	Robinson R44	D. Romagnoli	
G-CDTA	EV-97 TeamEurostar UK	R. D. Stein	
G-CDTB	Mainair Pegasus Quantum 15-912	D. W. Corbett	
G-CDTD	Eurocopter AS350B2 Ecureuil	TEC Aircraft Leasing GmbH & Co KG	
G-CDTG	Diamond DA42 Twin Star	Aviation Rentals	
G-CDTH	Schempp-Hirth Nimbus 4DM	M. A. V. Gatehouse	
G-CDTI	Messerschmitt Bf.109E (4034)	Rare Aero Ltd	
G-CDTJ	Escapade Jabiru(1)	R. N. R. Bellamy	
G-CDTL	Avtech Jabiru J-400	M. I. Sistern	
G-CDTO	P & M Quik GT450	J. R. Houston	
G-CDTP	Skyranger 912S (1)	P. M. Whitaker	
G-CDTR	P & M Quik GT450	M. G. Freeman	
G-CDTT	Savannah Jabiru(4)	M. J. Day	
G-CDTU	EV-97 TeamEurostar UK	G-CDTU Group	
G-CDTV	Tecnam P2002 EA Sierra	S. A. Noble	
G-CDTX	Cessna F.152	J. S. Develin & Z. Islam	
G-CDTY	Savannah Jabiru (5)	H. Cooke & B. Robertson	
G-CDTZ	Aeroprakt A.22 Foxbat	P. C. Piggott & M. E. Hughes	
G-CDUE	Robinson R44	Scotia Helicopters Ltd	
G-CDUH	P & M Quik GT450	A. P. & P. R. Santus	
G-CDUJ	Lindstrand LBL 31A balloon	J. M. Frazer	
G-CDUK	Ikarus C.42 FB UK	D. M. Lane	
G-CDUL	Skyranger 912S (2)	T. W. Thiele & C. D. Hogbourne	
G-CDUS	Skyranger 912S (1)	G. Devlin & J. Northage	
G-CDUT	Jabiru J400	T. W. & A. Pullin.	
G-CDUU	P & M Quik GT450	Caunton Charlie Delta Group	
G-CDUV	Savannah Jabiru(5)	D. M. Blackman	
G-CDUW	Aeronca C3	N. K. Geddes	
G-CDUX	PA-32 Cherokee Six 300	D. J. Mason	
G-CDUY	Thunder & Colt 77A balloon	G. Birchall	
G-CDVA	Skyranger 912 (2)	S. J. Dovey	
G-CDVB	Agusta A.109E Power	Agusta Westland Ltd	
G-CDVD	Aerotechnik EV-97A Eurostar	P. Ritchie	
G-CDVF	Rans S.6-ES Coyote II	S. G. Beeson	

Notes	Reg.	Type	Owner or Operator
	G-CDVG	Pegasus Quik	C. M. Lewis
	G-CDVH	Pegasus Quantum 15	M. J. Hyde
	G-CDVI	Ikarus C42 FB80	Airbourne Aviation Ltd
	G-CDVJ	Montgomerie-Bensen B8MR	D. J. Martin
	G-CDVK	Savannah Jabiru (5)	M. Peters
	G-CDVL	Alpi Pioneer 300	J. D. Clabon
	G-CDVN	P & M Quik GT450	P. Warrener
	G-CDVO	P & M Quik	D. Sykes
	G-CDVR	P & M Quik GT450	N. H. McCorquodale
	G-CDVS	Europa XS	J. F. Lawn
	G-CDVT	Van's RV-6	P. J. Wood
	G-CDVU	Aerotechnik EV-97 TeamEurostar	W. D. Kyle & T. J. Dowling
	G-CDVV	SA Bulldog Srs. 120/121 (XX626:02, W)	W. H. M. Mott
	G-CDVX	TP-47G-10-GU Thunderbolt (42-25068)	Patina Ltd
	G-CDVZ	P & M Quik GT450	S. M. Green & M. D. Peacock
	G-CDWB	Skyranger 912(2)	V. J. Morris
	G-CDWD	Cameron Z-105 balloon	Bristol University Ballooning Society
	G-CDWE	Nord NC.856 Norvigie	R. H. & J. A. Cooper
	G-CDWG	Dyn'Aéro MCR-01 Club	S. E. Gribble
	G-CDWH	Curtiss P-40B	The Fighter Collection
	G-CDWI	Ikarus C42 FB80	The Scottish Flying Club
	G-CDWJ	Flight Design CTSW	B. W. T. Rood
	G-CDWK	Robinson R44	B. Morgan
	G-CDWL	Raj Hamsa X'Air 582 (5)	The CDWL Flying Group
	G-CDWM	Skyranger 912S (1)	R. W. Marshall
	G-CDWN	Ultramagic N-210 balloon	S. R. Seager
	G-CDWO	P & M Quik GT450	G. W. Carwardine
	G-CDWP	P & M Quik GT450	J. R. North
	G-CDWR	P & M Quik GT450	G-CDWR Group
	G-CDWS	P & M Quik GT450	H. N. Barrott
	G-CDWT	Flight Design CTSW	R. Scammell
	G-CDWU	Zenair CH.601UL Zodiac	A. D. Worrall
	G-CDWW	P & M Quik GT450	J. H. Bradbury
	G-CDWX	Lindstrand LBL 77A balloon	LSB Public Relations Ltd
	G-CDWY	Agusta A109S Grand	Sportsdirect.com Retail Ltd
	G-CDWZ	P & M Quik GT450	B. J. Holloway
	G-CDXA	Robinson R44 Raven	Northumbria Helicopters Ltd
	G-CDXD	Medway SLA100 Executive	A. J. Baker
	G-CDXF	Lindstrand LBL 31A balloon	R. S. Mohr
	G-CDXG	P & M Pegasus Quantum 15-912	A. P. Hutchinson
	G-CDXH	Avro RJ100	Trident Jet Leasing (Ireland) Ltd
	G-CDXI	Cessna 182P	B. G. McBeath
	G-CDXJ	Jabiru J400	J. C. Collingwood
	G-CDXK	Diamond DA42 Twin Star	A. M. Healy
	G-CDXL	Flight Design CTSW	A. K. Paterson
	G-CDXN	P & M Quik GT450	Microflight Aviation Ltd
	G-CDXO	Zenair CH.601UL Zodiac	T. W. Lorimer
	G-CDXP	Aerotechnik EV-97 Eurostar	R. J. Crockett
	G-CDXR	Replica Fokker DR.1	J. G. Day
	G-CDXS	Aerotechnik EV-97 Eurostar	J. C. Rose
	G-CDXT	Van's RV-9	T. M. Storey
	G-CDXU	Chilton DW.1A	M. Gibbs
	G-CDXV	Campbell Cricket Mk.6A	W. G. Spencer
	G-CDXW	Cameron Orange 120 SS balloon	You've Been Tangooed
	G-CDXX	Robinson R44 Raven II	Emsway Developments Ltd
	G-CDXY	Skystar Kitfox Mk.7	D. E. Steade
	G-CDYB	Rans S.6-ES Coyote II	D. E. Rubery
	G-CDYD	Ikarus C42 FB80	C42 Group
	G-CDYI	BAe Jetstream 4100	Eastern Airways
	G-CDYL	Lindstrand LBL-77A balloon	J. H. Dobson
	G-CDYM	Murphy Maverick 430	M. R. Cann
	G-CDYO	Ikarus C42 FB80	B. Goodridge
	G-CDYP	Aerotechnik EV-97 TeamEurostar UK	R. V. Buxton & R. Cranborne
	G-CDYR	Bell 206L-3 LongRanger III	Yorkshire Helicopters
	G-CDYT	Ikarus C42 FB80	J. W. D. Blythe
	G-CDYU	Zenair CH.701UL	A. Gannon
	G-CDYX	Lindstrand LBL-77B balloon	H. M. Savage
	G-CDYY	Alpi Pioneer 300	B. Williams
	G-CDYZ	Van's RV-7	Holden Group Ltd
	G-CDZA	Alpi Pioneer 300	J. F. Dowe
	G-CDZB	Zenair CH.601UL Zodiac	L. J. Dutch
	G-CDZD	Van's RV-9A	D. King
	G-CDZG	Ikarus C42-FB80	Mainair Microlight School Ltd

Reg.	Type	Owner or Operator	Notes
G-CDZH	Boeing 737-804	Thomsonfly	
G-CDZI	Boeing 737-804	Thomsonfly	
G-CDZL	Boeing 737-804	Thomsonfly (G-BYNC)	
G-CDZM	Boeing 737-804	Thomsonfly (G-BYNB)	
G-CDZO	Lindstrand LBL-60X balloon	R. D. Parry	
G-CDZR	Nicollier HN.700 Menestrel II	G-CDZR Flying Group	
G-CDZS	Kolb Twinstar Mk.3 Extra	P. W. Heywood	
G-CDZT	Beech B200 Super King Air	BAE Systems Ltd	
G-CDZU	ICP MXP-740 Savannah Jabiru (5)	P. J. Cheney	
G-CDZW	Cameron N-105 balloon	Backetorp Byggconsult AB	
G-CDZY	Medway SLA 80 Executive	Medway Microlights	
G-CDZZ	Rotorsport UK MT-03	S. J. Boxall	
G-CEAE	Boeing 737-229	European Skybus Ltd	
G-CEAH	Boeing 737-229	European Aviation Ltd	
G-CEAK	Ikarus C42 FB80	Barton Heritage Flying Group	
G-CEAM	Aerotechnik EV-97 TeamEurostar UK	Flylight Airsports Ltd	
G-CEAN	Ikarus C42 FB80	C. P. Roche	
G-CEAO	Jurca MJ.5 Sirocco	P. S. Watts	
G-CEAR	Alpi Pioneer 300	A. Parker	
G-CEAT	Zenair CH.601HDS Zodiac	T. B. Smith	
G-CEAU	Robinson R44	Mullahead Property Co Ltd	
G-CEAV	Ultramagic M-105 balloon	G. Everett	
G-CEAX	Ultramagic S-130 balloon	Anglian Countryside Balloons Ltd	
G-CEAY	Ultramagic H-42 balloon	J. D. A. Shields	
G-CEBA	Zenair CH.601XL Zodiac	P. G. Morris	
G-CEBC	ICP MXP-740 Savannah Jabiru (5)	E. W. Chapman	
G-CEBE	Schweizer 269C-1	Millburn World Travel Services Ltd	
G-CEBF	Aerotechnik EV-97A Eurostar	M. Lang	
G-CEBG	Balóny Kubíček BB26 balloon	P. M. Smith	
G-CEBH	Tanarg/Ixess 15 912S (1)	D. A. Chamberlain	
G-CEBI	Kolb Twinstar Mk.3	R. W. Livingstone	
G-CEBK	PA-31-350 Navajo Chieftain	De Jong Management BV	
G-CEBL	Balóny Kubíček BB20GP balloon	Associazione Sportiva Aerostatica Lombada/Italy	
G-CEBM	P & M Quik GT450	G. Oliver	
G-CEBN	Avro RJ100	Trident Jet Leasing (Ireland) Ltd	
G-CEBO	Ultramagic M-65C balloon	M. J. Woodcock	
G-CEBP	EV-97 TeamEurostar UK	T. R. Southall	
G-CEBT	P & M Quik GT450	A. J. Riddell	
G-CEBW	P-51D Mustang	Dental Insurance Solutions Ltd	
G-CEBZ	Zenair CH.601UL Zodiac	I. M. Ross & A Watt	
G-CECA	P & M Quik GT450	A. Weatherall	
G-CECC	Ikarus C42 FB80	G-CECC Group	
G-CECD	Cameron C-90 balloon	S. P. Harrowing	
G-CECE	Jabiru UL-D	ST Aviation Ltd	
G-CECF	Just/Reality Escapade Jabiru (3)	M. M. Hamer	
G-CECG	Jabiru UL-D	R. K. Watson	
G-CECH	Jodel D.150	W. R. Prescott	
G-CECI	Pilatus PC-6/B2-H4 Turbo Porter	D. M. Penny	
G-CECJ	Aeromot AMT-200S Super Ximango	C. J. & S. C. Partridge	
G-CECK	ICP MXP-740 Savannah Jabiru (5)	K. W. Eskins	
G-CECL	Ikarus C42 FB80	C. Lee	
G-CECO	Hughes 269C	H. Larcombe	
G-CECP	Best Off Skyranger 912(2)	A. Asslanian	
G-CECS	Lindstrand LBL-105A balloon	R. P. Ashford	
G-CECU	Boeing 767-222	UK International Airlines Ltd	
G-CECV	Van's RV-7	D. M. Stevens	
G-CECX	Robinson R44	Dolphin Property (Management) Ltd	
G-CECY	EV-97 Eurostar	M. R. M. Welch	
G-CECZ	Zenair CH.601XL Zodiac	J. A. Kentzer	
G-CEDB	Just/Reality Escapade Jabiru (4)	P. Travis	
G-CEDC	Ikarus C42 FB100	P. D. Ashley	
G-CEDE	Flight Design CTSW	F. Williams & J. A. R. Hartley	
G-CEDF	Cameron N-105 balloon	Bailey Balloons Ltd	
G-CEDG	Robinson R44	P. J. Barnes	
G-CEDI	Best Off Skyranger 912(2)	L. Call & G. Finney	
G-CEDJ	Aero Designs Pulsar XP	P. F. Lorriman	
G-CEDK	Cessna 750 Citation X	The Duke of Westminster	
G-CEDL	TEAM Minimax 91	A. J. Weir	
G-CEDN	Pegasus Quik	R. G. Beecham	
G-CEDO	Raj Hamsa X'Air Falcon 133(2)	R. J. Thomas	
G-CEDR	Ikarus C42 FB80	Newtownards Microlight Group	
G-CEDT	Tanarg/Ixess 15 912S(1)	N. S. Brayn	

BRITISH CIVIL REGISTRATIONS

Notes	Reg.	Type	Owner or Operator
	G-CEDV	Evektor EV-97 TeamEurostar UK	Airborne Aviation Ltd
	G-CEDW	TEAM Minimax 91	J. K. Buckingham
	G-CEDX	Evektor EV-97 TeamEurostar UK	C. P. Davis
	G-CEDZ	Best Off Skyranger 912(2)	J. E. Walendowski & I. Bell
	G-CEEB	Cameron C-80 balloon	Cameron Balloons Ltd
	G-CEEC	Raj Hamsa X'Air Hawk	B. G. King
	G-CEED	ICP MXP-740 Savannah Jabiru(5)	A. C. Thompson
	G-CEEE	Robinson R44	C. R. Caswell
	G-CEEG	Alpi Pioneer 300	D. McCormack
	G-CEEI	P & M Quik GT450	R. A. Hill
	G-CEEJ	Rans S-7S Courier	J. M. Lister
	G-CEEK	Cameron Z-105 balloon	PSH Skypower Ltd
	G-CEEL	Ultramagic S-90 balloon	San Paolo Company SRL
	G-CEEM	P & M Quik GT450	D. P. Sayer
	G-CEEN	PA-28-161 Cadet	Plane Talking Ltd
	G-CEEO	Flight Design CTSW	E. McCallum
	G-CEEP	Van's RV-9A	M. P. Comley, N. Horseman & K. Rose
	G-CEER	ELA 07R	F. G. Shepherd
	G-CEES	Cameron C-90 balloon	P. C. May
	G-CEEU	PA-28-161 Cadet	Plane Talking Ltd
	G-CEEV	PA-28-161 Warrior III	Plane Talking Ltd
	G-CEEW	Ikarus C42 FB100	D. McCartan
	G-CEEX	ICP MXP-740 Savannah Jabiru(5)	G. M. Teasdale
	G-CEEY	PA-28-161 Warrior III	Plane Talking Ltd
	G-CEEZ	PA-28-161 Warrior III	Plane Talking Ltd
	G-CEFA	Ikarus C42 FB100 VLA	J. Morrisroe
	G-CEFB	Ultramagic H-31 balloon	P. Dickinson
	G-CEFC	Super Marine Spitfire 26	D. R. Bishop
	G-CEFJ	Sonex	R. W. Chatterton
	G-CEFK	Evektor EV-97 TeamEurostar UK	P. Morgan
	G-CEFM	Cessna 152	Cristal Air Ltd
	G-CEFP	Jabiru J430	G. Hammond
	G-CEFS	Cameron C-100 balloon	Gone With The Wind Ltd
	G-CEFT	Whittaker MW5-D Sorcerer	W. Bruce
	G-CEFV	Cessna 182T Skylane	G. H. Smith and Son
	G-CEFY	ICP MXP-740 Savannah Jabiru(4)	B. Hartley
	G-CEFZ	Evektor EV-97 TeamEurostar UK	Robo Flying Group
	G-CEGE	Fairchild SA.226TC Metro II	BCA Charters Ltd
	G-CEGG	Lindstrand LBL-25A Cloudhopper balloon	C. G. Dobson
	G-CEGH	Van's RV-9A	M. E. Creasey
	G-CEGI	Van's RV-8	C. W. N. & A. A. M. Huke
	G-CEGJ	P & M Quik GT450	Flylight Airsports Ltd
	G-CEGK	ICP MXP-740 Savannah VG Jabiru(1)	S. Woolmington
	G-CEGL	Ikarus C42 FB100	FES Autogas Ltd
	G-CEGO	Evektor EV-97A Eurostar	N. J. Keeling, R. F. McLachlan & J. A. Charlton
	G-CEGP	Beech 200 Super King Air	Cega Air Ambulance UK Ltd (G-BXMA)
	G-CEGR	Beech 200 Super King Air	Henfield Lodge Ltd
	G-CEGS	PA-28-161 Warrior II	White Waltham Airfield Ltd
	G-CEGT	P & M Quik GT450	J. Plenderleith
	G-CEGU	PA-28-151 Warrior	Aviation Rentals
	G-CEGV	P & M Quik GT450	Flexwing Ruffians Group
	G-CEGW	P & M Quik GT450	P. Barrow
	G-CEGY	ELA 07R	A. Buchanan
	G-CEGZ	Ikarus C42 FB80	A. D. Tomlins
	G-CEHC	P & M Quik GT450	G. H. Sharwood-Smith
	G-CEHD	Best Off Skyranger 912(2)	A. A. Howland & J. V. Clew
	G-CEHE	Medway SLA 100 Executive	R. P. Stoner
	G-CEHG	Ikarus C42 FB100	C. J. Hayward & C. Walters
	G-CEHI	P & M Quik GT450	A. Costello
	G-CEHL	EV-97 TeamEurostar UK	Poet Pilot (UK) Ltd
	G-CEHM	Rotorsport UK MT-03	R. C. Slight
	G-CEHN	Rotorsport UK MT-03	P. A. Harwood
	G-CEHR	Auster AOP.9	J. Cooke & R. B. Webber
	G-CEHS	CAP.10B	G. Hutchinson
	G-CEHT	Rand KR-2	P. P. Geoghegan
	G-CEHV	Ikarus C42 FB80	Mainair Microlight School Ltd
	G-CEHW	P & M Quik GT450	G-CEHW Group
	G-CEHX	Lindstrand LBL-9A balloon	P. Baker
	G-CEHZ	Edge XT912-B/Streak III-B	J. Horan
	G-CEIA	Rotorsport UK MT-03	M. P Chetwynd-Talbot
	G-CEIB	Yakovlev Yak-18A	R. A. Fleming
	G-CEID	Van's RV-7	A. Moyce
	G-CEIE	Flight Design CTSW	D. K. Ross

Reg.	Type	Owner or Operator	Notes
G-CEIG	Van's RV-7	W. K. Wilkie	
G-CEIH	Avro RJ100	Trident Jet Leasing (Ireland) Ltd	
G-CEII	Medway SLA80 Executive	F. J. Clarehugh	
G-CEIK	Ultramagic M-90 balloon	M. R. W. Steyaert	
G-CEIL	Bassett Escapade 912(2)	D. E. Bassett	
G-CEIS	Jodel DR.1050	G. R. Richardson	
G-CEIT	Van's RV-7	S. S. Gould	
G-CEIV	Tanarg/Ixess 15 912S(2)	W. R. Cross	
G-CEIW	Europa	R. Scanlan	
G-CEIX	Alpi Pioneer 300	R. F. Bond	
G-CEIY	Ultramagic M-120 balloon	Societa Cooperativa Sociale Il Paraticchio/Italy	
G-CEIZ	PA-28-161 Warrior II	India Zulu Flying Group	
G-CEJA	Cameron V-77 balloon	G. Gray (G-BTOF)	
G-CEJC	Cameron N-77 balloon	D. J. Stagg	
G-CEJD	PA-28-161 Warrior III	Western Air (Thruxton) Ltd	
G-CEJE	Wittman W.10 Tailwind	R. A. Povall	
G-CEJF	PA-28-161 Cadet	Aviation Rentals	
G-CEJG	Ultramagic M-56 balloon	Dragon Balloon Co.Ltd	
G-CEJI	Lindstrand LBL-105A balloon	Richard Nash Cars Ltd	
G-CEJJ	P & M Quik GT450	Juliet Juliet Group	
G-CEJK	Lindstrand LBL-260A balloon	Cameron Flights Southen Ltd	
G-CEJL	Ultramagic H-31 balloon	Robert Wiseman Dairies PLC	
G-CEJN	Mooney M.20F	G. R. Wakeley	
G-CEJR	Cameron Z-90 balloon	KB Voli Di Chiozzi Bartolomeo EC SAS/Italy	
G-CEJT	Cameron Z-31 balloon	Atlantic Ballooning BVBA/Belgium	
G-CEJV	PA-28-161 Cadet	Aviation Rentals	
G-CEJW	Ikarus C42 FB80	M. I. Deeley	
G-CEJX	P & M Quik GT450	P. Stewart & A. J. Huntly	
G-CEJY	Aerospool Dynamic WT9 UK	R. G. Bennett	
G-CEJZ	Cameron C-90 balloon	M. J. Woodcock	
G-CEKA	Robinson R-44 II	P. L. Lunnon	
G-CEKB	Taylor JT.1 Monoplane	C. J. Bush	
G-CEKC	Medway SLA100 Executive	B. W. Webb	
G-CEKD	Flight Design CTSW	M. K. Arora	
G-CEKE	Robin DR400/180	M. F. Cuming	
G-CEKG	P & M Quik GT450	G-CEKG Flying Group	
G-CEKI	Cessna 172P	N. Houghton	
G-CEKJ	Evektor EV-97A Eurostar	C. W. J. Vershoyle-Greene	
G-CEKK	Best Off Sky Ranger Swift 912S(1)	M. S. Schofield & B. W. G. Stanbridge	
G-CEKO	Robin DR400/100	R. J. Hopkins	
G-CEKS	Cameron Z-105 balloon	Phoenix Balloons Ltd	
G-CEKT	Flight Design CTSW	Charlie Tango Group	
G-CEKV	Europa	K. Atkinson	
G-CEKW	Jabiru J430	J430 Syndicate	
G-CELA	Boeing 737-377	Jet 2	
G-CELB	Boeing 737-377	Jet 2	
G-CELC	Boeing 737-377	Jet 2 (G-OBMA)	
G-CELD	Boeing 737-377	Jet 2 (G-OBMB)	
G-CELE	Boeing 737-377	Jet 2 (G-MONN)	
G-CELF	Boeing 737-377	Jet 2	
G-CELG	Boeing 737-377	Jet 2	
G-CELH	Boeing 737-330	Jet 2	
G-CELI	Boeing 737-330	Jet 2	
G-CELJ	Boeing 737-330	Jet 2	
G-CELK	Boeing 737-330	Jet 2	
G-CELM	Cameron C-80 balloon	L. Greaves	
G-CELO	Boeing 737-33AQC	Jet 2	
G-CELP	Boeing 737-330QC	Jet 2	
G-CELR	Boeing 737-330QC	Jet 2	
G-CELS	Boeing 737-377	Jet 2	
G-CELU	Boeing 737-377	Jet 2	
G-CELV	Boeing 737-377	Jet 2	
G-CELW	Boeing 737-377	Jet 2	
G-CELX	Boeing 737-377	Jet 2	
G-CELY	Boeing 737-377	Jet 2	
G-CELZ	Boeing 737-377	Jet 2	
G-CEMA	Alpi Pioneer 200	D. M. Bracken	
G-CEMB	P & M Quik GT450	D. W. Logue	
G-CEMC	Robinson R44 Raven II	Helicentre Holdings Ltd	
G-CEMD	PA-28-161 Warrior II	Steptoe and Son Properties Ltd	
G-CEME	Evektor EV-97 Eurostar	F. W. McCann	
G-CEMF	Cameron C-80 balloon	Linear Communications Consultants Ltd	
G-CEMG	Ultramagic M-105 balloon	Comunicazione In Volo SRL/Italy	

Notes	Reg.	Type	Owner or Operator
	G-CEMI	Europa XS	B. D. A. Morris
	G-CEMK	Boeing 767-222	UK International Airlines Ltd
	G-CEML	P & M Pegasus Quik	C. J. Kew
	G-CEMM	P & M Quik GT450	M. A. Rhodes
	G-CEMO	P & M Quik GT450	L. E. Craig
	G-CEMR	Mainair Blade 912	A. D. Cameron
	G-CEMS	MDH MD900 Explorer	Yorkshire Air Ambulance Ltd.
	G-CEMT	P & M Quik GT450	W. Barden & S. E. Robinson
	G-CEMU	Cameron C-80 balloon	J. G. O'Connell
	G-CEMV	Lindstrand LBL-105A balloon	R. G. Turnbull
	G-CEMW	Lindstrand LBL Bananas balloon	Top Banana Balloon Team (G-OCAW)
	G-CEMX	P & M Pegasus Quik	S. J. Meehan
	G-CEMY	Alpi Pioneer 300	J. C. A. Garland & P. F. Salter
	G-CEMZ	Pegasus Quik	D. Jessop
	G-CENA	Dyn'Aero MCR-01 ULC Banbi	I. N. Drury & D. Goodman
	G-CENB	Evektor EV-97 TeamEurostar UK	K. J. Gay
	G-CENC	Christen Eagle II	Tefo Teknik AB/Sweden
	G-CEND	Evektor EV-97 TeamEurostar UK	Flylight Airsports Ltd
	G-CENE	Flight Design CTSW	The CT Flying Group
	G-CENG	SkyRanger 912(2)	R. A. Knight
	G-CENH	Tecnam P2002-EA Sierra	M. W. Taylor
	G-CENI	Supermarine Spitfire Mk.26	D. B. Smith
	G-CENJ	Medway SLA 951	M. Ingleton
	G-CENK	Schempp-Hirth Nimbus 4DT	R. A. Christie
	G-CENL	P & M Quik GT450	P. Von Sydow & S. Baker
	G-CENM	Evektor EV-97 Eurostar	N. D. Meer
	G-CENO	Aerospool Dynamic WT9 UK	R. O. Lewthwaite
	G-CENP	Ace Magic Laser	A. G. Curtis
	G-CENR	ELA 07S	M. S. Gough
	G-CENS	SkyRanger Swift 912S(1)	M. & N. D. Stannard
	G-CENV	P & M Quik GT450	RAF Microlight Flying Association
	G-CENW	Evektor EV-97A Eurostar	Southside Flyers
	G-CENX	Lindstrand LBL-360A	Wickers World Ltd
	G-CENZ	Aeros Discus/Alize	J. D. Buchanan
	G-CEOB	Pitts S-1 Special	I. Gallagher & P. A. Moslin
	G-CEOC	Tecnam P2002-EA Sierra	M. A. Lomas
	G-CEOF	PA-28R-201 Arrow	J. H. Sandham Aviation
	G-CEOG	PA-28R-201 Arrow	A. J. Gardiner
	G-CEOH	Raj Hamsa X'Air Falcon ULP(1)	Miles Blackburn Ltd
	G-CEOI	Cameron C-60 balloon	M. E. White
	G-CEOJ	Eurocopter EC 155B	Starspeed Ltd
	G-CEOL	Flylight Lightfly-Discus	A. Bill
	G-CEOM	Jabiru UL-450	J. R. Caylow
	G-CEON	Raj Hamsa X'Air Hawk	K. S. Campbell
	G-CEOO	P & M Quik GT450	S. Moran
	G-CEOP	Aeroprakt A22-L Foxbat	J. G. Miller
	G-CEOS	Cameron C-90 balloon	British School of Ballooning
	G-CEOT	Dudek ReAction Sport/Bailey Quattro 175	J. Kelly
	G-CEOU	Lindstrand LBL-31A balloon	Lindstrand Hot Air Balloons Ltd
	G-CEOV	Lindstrand LBL-120A balloon	Lindstrand Hot Air Balloons Ltd
	G-CEOW	Europa XS	R. W. Wood
	G-CEOX	Rotorsport UK MT-03	A. J. Saunders
	G-CEOY	Schweizer 269C-1	CSL Industrial Ltd
	G-CEOZ	Paramania Action GT26/PAP Chariot Z	A. M. Shepherd
	G-CEPL	Super Marine Spitfire Mk.26	S. R. Marsh
	G-CEPM	Jabiru J430	T. R. Sinclair
	G-CEPN	Kolb Firefly	I. Brewster
	G-CEPP	P & M Quik GT450	W. M. Studley
	G-CEPR	Cameron Z-90 balloon	Sport Promotion SRL/Italy
	G-CEPS	TL2000UK Sting Carbon	C. E. & R. P. Reeves
	G-CEPU	Cameron Z-77 balloon	Liquigas SPA
	G-CEPV	Cameron Z-77 balloon	Liquigas SPA
	G-CEPW	Alpi Pioneer 300	N. K. Spedding
	G-CEPX	Cessna 152	Cristal Air Ltd
	G-CEPY	Ikarus C42 FB80	L. Lay
	G-CEPZ	DR.107 One Design	CEPZ Flying Group
	G-CERB	SkyRanger Swift 912S(1)	J. J. Littler
	G-CERC	Cameron Z-350 balloon	Ballooning Network Ltd
	G-CERD	D.H.C.1 Chipmunk 22	A. C. Darby
	G-CERE	Evektor EV-97 TeamEurostar UK	Airbourne Aviation Ltd
	G-CERF	Rotorsport UK MT-03	P. J. Robinson
	G-CERH	Cameron C-90 balloon	A. Walker
	G-CERI	Shaw Europa XS	S. J. M. Shepherd

Reg.	Type	Owner or Operator	Notes
G-CERK	Van's RV-9A	P. E. Brown	
G-CERL	Ultramagic M-77 balloon	A. M. Holly	
G-CERN	P & M Quik GT450	P. M. Jackson	
G-CERO	Agusta A109C	Castle Air Ltd (G-OBEK/G-CDDJ)	
G-CERP	P & M Quik GT450	G. R. Cassie, A. J. L. Coulson, D. A. Howe & S. O. Kennedy	
G-CERT	Mooney M.20K	J. A. Nisbet	
G-CERV	P & M Quik GT450	East Fortune Flyers	
G-CERW	P & M Pegasus Quik	D. J. Cornelius	
G-CERX	Hawker 850XP	Hangar 8 Management Ltd	
G-CERY	SAAB 2000	Eastern Airways	
G-CERZ	SAAB 2000	Eastern Airways	
G-CESA	Replica Jodel DR.1050	T. J. Bates	
G-CESD	SkyRanger Swift 912S(1)	S. E. Dancaster	
G-CESF	EV-97 TeamEurostar UK	W. F. Whitfield	
G-CESG	P & M Quik GT450	L. Greco	
G-CESH	Cameron Z-90 balloon	M. Rowlands	
G-CESI	Aeroprakt A22-L Foxbat	D. J. Ashley	
G-CESJ	Raj Hamsa X'Air Hawk	J. Bolton & R. Shewan	
G-CESM	TL2000UK Sting Carbon	E. Stephenson	
G-CESR	P & M Quik GT450	G. Kerr	
G-CESS	Cessna F.172G	V. Bojovic (G-ATGO)	
G-CEST	Robinson R44	Scotia Helicopters Ltd	
G-CESU	Robinson R22 Beta	M. Boni	
G-CESV	EV-97 TeamEurostar UK	N. Jones	
G-CESW	Flight Design CTSW	J. Whiting	
G-CESX	Cameron Z-31 balloon	I. M. Ashpole	
G-CESY	Cameron Z-31 balloon	I. M. Ashpole	
G-CESZ	CZAW Sportcruiser	S. Eccles	
G-CETB	Robin DR.400/180	QR Flying Club	
G-CETD	PA-28-161 Warrior III	Plane Talking Ltd	
G-CETE	PA-28-161 Warrior III	Plane Talking Ltd	
G-CETF	Flight Design CTSW	P and M Aviation Ltd	
G-CETK	Cameron Z-145 balloon	R. H. Etherington	
G-CETL	P & M Quik GT450	J. I. Greenshields	
G-CETM	P & M Quik GT450	I. Burnside	
G-CETN	Hummel Bird	A. A. Haseldine	
G-CETO	Best Off Sky Ranger Swift 912S(1)	J. & B. Hudson	
G-CETP	Van's RV-9A	D. Boxall & S. Hill	
G-CETR	Ikarus C42 FB100	A. E. Lacy-Hulbert	
G-CETS	Van's RV-7	TS Group	
G-CETT	Evektor EV-97 TeamEurostar UK	Tango Tango Group	
G-CETU	Best Off Sky Ranger Swift 912S(1)	A. Raithby & N. McCusker	
G-CETV	Best Off Sky Ranger Swift 912S(1)	C. J. Johnson	
G-CETX	Alpi Pioneer 300	J. M. P. Ree	
G-CETY	Rans S-6-ES Coyote II	J. North	
G-CETZ	Ikarus C42 FB100	Airways Airsports Ltd	
G-CEUE	BN-2B-20 Islander	Britten-Norman Aircraft Ltd	
G-CEUF	P & M Quik GT450	G. T. Snoddon	
G-CEUH	P & M Quik GT450	North West Turf Ltd	
G-CEUJ	SkyRanger Swift 912S(1)	J. P. Batty & J. R. C. Brightman	
G-CEUL	Ultramagic M-105 balloon	R. A. Vale	
G-CEUM	Ultramagic M-120 balloon	Bridges Van Hire Ltd	
G-CEUN	Orlican Discus CS	The Royal Air Force Gliding and Soaring Association	
G-CEUR	Schempp-Hirth Ventus 2cT	G. Coppin	
G-CEUT	Hoffman H-36 Dimona II	M. Tolson	
G-CEUU	Robinson R44 II	A. Stafford-Jones	
G-CEUV	Cameron C-90 balloon	A. M. Holly	
G-CEUW	Zenair CH.601XL Zodiac	J. S. Griffiths	
G-CEUZ	P & M Quik GT450	B. S. Smy	
G-CEVA	Ikarus C42 FB80	The Scottish Flying Group	
G-CEVB	P & M Quik GT450	N. Hartley & J. L. Guy.	
G-CEVC	Van's RV-4	P. A. Brook	
G-CEVD	Rolladen-Schneider LS3	Victor Delta Syndicate	
G-CEVE	Centrair 101A	T. P. Newham	
G-CEVG	P & M Pegasus Quik	Bartn Quik Group	
G-CEVH	Cameron V-65 balloon	J. A. Atkinson	
G-CEVJ	Alpi Pioneer 200	B. W. Bartlett	
G-CEVK	Schleicher Ka 6CR	K6 Syndicate	
G-CEVL	Fairchild M-62A-4 Cornell	UK Cornell Group	
G-CEVM	Tecnam P2002-EA Sierra	R. C. Mincik	
G-CEVN	Rolladen-Schneider LS7	N. Gaunt & B. C. Toon	

Notes	Reg.	Type	Owner or Operator
	G-CEVO	Grob G.109B	T.J. Wilkinson
	G-CEVP	P & M Quik GT450	L. Wenham
	G-CEVS	EV-97 TeamEurostar UK	Hotel Victor Flying Group
	G-CEVT	Dudek Reaction 27/Bailey Quattro 175	J. Kelly
	G-CEVU	Savannah VG Jabiru(4)	B. L. Cook
	G-CEVV	Rolladen-Schneider LS3	LS3 307 Syndicate
	G-CEVW	P & M Quik GT450	R. W. Sutherland
	G-CEVX	Aeriane Swift Light PAS	J. S. Firth
	G-CEVY	Rotorsport UK MT-03	P. Robinson
	G-CEVZ	Centrair ASW-20FL	B. Watkins
	G-CEWC	Schleicher ASK-21	London Gliding Club Proprietary Ltd
	G-CEWD	P & M Quik GT450	J. Murphy
	G-CEWE	Schempp-Hirth Nimbus 2	T. Clark
	G-CEWF	Jacobs V35 Airchair balloon	D. J. Farrar
	G-CEWG	Aerola Alatus-M	Flylight Airsports Ltd
	G-CEWH	P & M Quik GT450	B. W. Hunter
	G-CEWI	Schleicher ASW-19B	S. R. Edwards
	G-CEWK	Cessna 172S	Skytrek Aviation Services
	G-CEWL	Alpi Pioneer 200	G-CEWL Ltd
	G-CEWM	DHC.6 Twin Otter 300	Isles of Scilly Skybus Ltd
	G-CEWN	Diamond DA-42 Twin Star	Airedale Mechanical and Electrical Ltd
	G-CEWO	Schleicher Ka 6CR	DQS Group
	G-CEWP	Grob G.102 Astir CS	R. D. Slater
	G-CEWR	Aeroprakt A22-L Foxbat	C. S. Bourne & G. P. Wiley
	G-CEWS	Zenair CH.701SP	G. E. MacCuish
	G-CEWT	Flight Design CTSW	A and R. W. Osborne
	G-CEWU	Ultramagic H-77 balloon	P. C. Waterhouse
	G-CEWW	Grob G.102 Astir CS	M. R. Woodiwiss
	G-CEWX	Cameron Z-350 balloon	Original Bristol FM Ltd
	G-CEWY	Quicksilver GT500	R. J. Scott
	G-CEWZ	Schempp-Hirth Discus bT	J. F. Goudie
	G-CEXL	Ikarus C42 FB80	Syndicate C42-1
	G-CEXM	Best Off Sky Ranger Swift 912S(1)	A. F. Batchelor
	G-CEXN	Cameron A-120 balloon	Dragon Balloon Company Ltd
	G-CEXO	PA-28-161 Warrior III	Durham Tees Flight Training Ltd
	G-CEXP	HPR.7 Herald 209 ★	Towing and rescue trainer/Gatwick
	G-CEXX	Rotorsport UK MT-03	D. B. Roberts
	G-CEYC	DG Flugzeugbau DG-505 Elan Orion	Scottish Gliding Union Ltd
	G-CEYD	Cameron N-31 balloon	Black Pearl Balloons (G-LLYD)
	G-CEYE	PA-32R-300 Cherokee Lance	G. R. & S. W. Case
	G-CEYF	Eurocopter EC135 T1	Starspeed Ltd (G-HARP)
	G-CEYG	Cessna 152	S. J. & T. Powell and A. H. Haynes
	G-CEYH	Cessna 152	Cornwall Flying Club Ltd
	G-CEYK	Europa XS	A. B. Milne
	G-CEYL	Bombardier BD-700-1A10 Global Express	Aravco Ltd
	G-CEYM	Van's RV-6	R. B. Skinner
	G-CEYN	Grob G.109B	G-CEYN Flying Group
	G-CEYO	Aerospatiale AS.350B2 Ecureuil	FBS Ltd
	G-CEYP	North Wing Design Stratus/ATF	J. S. James
	G-CEYR	Rotorsport UK MT-03	N. Wright
	G-CEYU	SA.365N1 Dauphin 2	Multiflight Ltd
	G-CEYX	Rotorsport UK MT-03	N. Creveul
	G-CEYY	EV-97 TeamEurostar UK	N. J. James
	G-CEYZ	Sikorsky S-76C	Bristow Helicoipters Ltd
	G-CEZA	Ikarus C42 FB80	P. Harper & P. J. Morton
	G-CEZB	Savannah VG Jabiru(1)	D. D. J. Rossdale
	G-CEZD	EV-97 TeamEurostar	G. P. Jones
	G-CEZE	Best Off Sky Ranger Swift 912S	G-CEZE Group
	G-CEZF	EV-97 TeamEurostar UK	D. J. Dick
	G-CEZG	Diamond DA.42 Twin Star	Diamond Aircraft UK Ltd
	G-CEZH	Aerochute Dual	G. Stokes
	G-CEZI	PA-28-161 Cadet	Chalrey Ltd
	G-CEZK	Stolp S.750 Acroduster Too	R. I. M. Hague
	G-CEZL	PA-28-161 Cadet	Chalrey Ltd
	G-CEZM	Cessna 152	Cristal Air Ltd
	G-CEZN	Pacific Airwave Pulse 2/Skycycle	G. W. Cameron
	G-CEZO	PA-28-161 Cadet	Chalrey Ltd
	G-CEZR	Diamond DA.40D Star	Flying Time Ltd
	G-CEZS	Zenair CH.601HDS Zodiac	R. Wyness
	G-CEZT	P & M Aviation Quik GT450	B. C. Blackburn
	G-CEZU	CFM Streak Shadow SA	M. R. Foreman
	G-CEZV	Zenair CH.601HDS Zodiac	G. Waters
	G-CEZW	Jodel D.150 Mascaret	N. J. Kilford

Reg.	Type	Owner or Operator	Notes
G-CEZX	P & M Aviation Quik GT450	N. J. Braund	
G-CEZZ	Flight Design CTSW	S. Emery	
G-CFAG	Rotorsport UK MT-03	M. D. Cole	
G-CFAJ	DG-300 Elan	S. Marriott	
G-CFAK	Rotorsport UK MT-03	R. M. Savage	
G-CFAM	Schempp-Hirth Nimbus 3/24.5	Nimbus III Syndicate J15	
G-CFAO	Rolladen-Schneider LS4	V. R. Roberts	
G-CFAP	Interplane ZJ-Viera	Flylight Airsports Ltd	
G-CFAR	Rotorsport UK MT-03	P. M. Twose	
G-CFAS	Escapade Jabiru(3)	C. G. N. Boyd	
G-CFAT	P & M Aviation Quik GT450	T. G. Jackson	
G-CFAU	Cameron Z-105 balloon	High On Adventure Balloons Ltd	
G-CFAV	Ikarus C42 FB80	P. E. Scopes	
G-CFAW	Lindstrand LBL-35A Cloudhopper balloon	A. Walker	
G-CFAX	Ikarus C42 FB80	R. E. Parker & B. Cook	
G-CFAY	Sky 120-24 balloon	G. B. Lescott	
G-CFBA	Schleicher ASW-20BL	C. R. Little	
G-CFBB	Schempp-Hirth Standard Cirrus	L. Dale	
G-CFBC	Schleicher ASW-15B	CFBC Group	
G-CFBE	Ikarus C42 FB80	C. A. Hasell	
G-CFBF	Lindstrand LBL 203T gas balloon	S and D Leisure (Europe) Ltd	
G-CFBH	Glaser-Dirks DG-100G Elan	IBM Gliding Club	
G-CFBJ	Rotorsport UK MT-03	C-More Flying Ltd	
G-CFBK	BAC 167 Strikemaster Mk.80A (1125)	Trans Holdings Ltd	
G-CFBL	Best Off Sky Ranger Swift 912S(1)	D. Hemmings	
G-CFBM	P & M Quantum 15-912	F. W. & N. A. Milne	
G-CFBN	Glasflugel Mosquito B	S. R. & J. Nash	
G-CFBO	Reality Escapade Jabiru(3)	J. F. Thornton	
G-CFBP	BAe 125 Srs.700A	Hawker 700 Ltd	
G-CFBS	Best Off Sky Ranger Swift 912S(1)	A. J. Tyler	
G-CFBT	Schempp-Hirth Ventus bT	488 (Gransden) Group	
G-CFBV	Schleicher ASK-21	London Gliding Club Proprietary Ltd	
G-CFBW	DG-100G Elan	G-CFBW Syndicate	
G-CFBX	Beech C90GTI King Air	J. M. Lynch	
G-CFBY	Best Off Sky Ranger Swift 912S(1)	J. A. Armin	
G-CFBZ	Schleicher Ka 6CR	R. H. W. Martyn	
G-CFCA	Schempp-Hirth Discus b	M. R. Hayden	
G-CFCB	Centrair 101	T. J. Berriman	
G-CFCC	Cameron Z-275 balloon	Ballooning Network Ltd	
G-CFCD	SkyRanger Swift 912S(1)	D. & L. Payn	
G-CFCE	Raj Hamsa X'Air Hawk	B. M. Tibenham	
G-CFCF	Aerochute Dual	C. J. Kendal & S. G. Smith	
G-CFCH	Campbell Cricket Mk.4	E. J. Barton	
G-CFCI	Cessna F.172N	J. Blacklock	
G-CFCJ	Grob G.102 Astir CS	A. J. C. Beaumont & P. Hardwick	
G-CFCK	Best Off Sky Ranger 912S(1)	C. M. Sperring	
G-CFCL	Rotorsport UK MT-03	M. D. Reece	
G-CFCM	Robinson R44	A. J. Brough	
G-CFCN	Schempp-Hirth Standard Cirrus	P. C. Bunniss	
G-CFCP	Rolladen-Schneider LS6-a	R. E. Robertson	
G-CFCR	Schleicher Ka-6E	R. F. Whittaker	
G-CFCS	Schempp-Hirth Nimbus 2C	J. Luck & P. Dolling	
G-CFCT	EV-97 TeamEurostar UK	Sutton Eurostar Group	
G-CFCU	Lindstrand LBL-203T gas balloon	Lindstrand Aeroplatforms Ltd	
G-CFCV	Schleicher ASW-20	M. J. Davis	
G-CFCW	Rotorsport UK MT-03	C. M. Jones	
G-CFCX	Rans S-6-ES Coyote II	D. & S. Morrison	
G-CFCY	Best Off Sky Ranger Swift 912S(1)	M. E. & T. E. Simpson	
G-CFCZ	P & M Quik GT450	P. K. Dale	
G-CFDA	Schleicher ASW-15	7 Delta Group	
G-CFDC	P & M Aviation Quik GT450	P. R. Davies	
G-CFDE	Schempp-Hirth Ventus bT	P. Clay	
G-CFDF	Ultramagic S-90 balloon	Edinburgh University Hot Air Balloon Club	
G-CFDG	Schleicher Ka 6CR	Delta-Golf Group	
G-CFDI	Van's RV-6	M. D. Challoner	
G-CFDJ	EV-97 TeamEurostar UK	J. D. J. Spragg & M. Jones	
G-CFDK	Rans S-6-ES Coyote II	Conair Sports Ltd	
G-CFDL	P & M QuikR	P and M Aviation Ltd	
G-CFDM	Schempp-Hirth Discus b	J. L. & T. G. M. Whiting	
G-CFDN	Best Off Sky Ranger Swift 912S(1)	D. A. Perkins	
G-CFDO	Flight Design CTSW	D. I. Waller	
G-CFDP	Flight Design CTSW	N. Fielding	

Notes	Reg.	Type	Owner or Operator
	G-CFDS	TL2000UK Sting Carbon	TL Sting G-CFDS Group
	G-CFDT	Aerola Alatus-M	B. T. Green
	G-CFDU	BB03 Trya/BB103	J. M. Macleod
	G-CFDV	Sikorsky S-76C	Bristow Helicopters Ltd
	G-CFDX	PZL-Bielsko SZD-48-1 Jantar Standard 2	The Jantar Syndicate
	G-CFDY	P &M Quik GT450	C. N. Thornton
	G-CFDZ	Flight Design Exxtacy/Alize	N. C. O. Watney
	G-CFEA	Cameron C-90 balloon	A. M. Holly
	G-CFEB	Cameron C-80 balloon	A. M. Holly
	G-CFED	Van's RV-9	E. Taylor & P. Robinson
	G-CFEE	Evektor EV-97 Eurostar	G.CFEE Flying Group
	G-CFEF	Grob G.102 Astir CS	Oxford University Gliding Club
	G-CFEG	Schempp-Hirth Ventus b/16.6	P. Ottomaniello
	G-CFEH	Centrair 101 Pegase	Booker Gliding Club Ltd
	G-CFEJ	Schempp-Hirth Discus b	Lima Charlie Syndicate
	G-CFEK	Cameron Z-105 balloon	R. M. Penny (Plant Hire and Demolition) Ltd
	G-CFEL	EV-97 Eurostar	S. R. Green
	G-CFEI	RAF 2000 GTX-SE	A. M. Wells
	G-CFEM	P & M Aviation Quik GT450	A. M. King
	G-CFEN	PZL-Bielsko SZD-50-3 Puchacz	The Northumbria Gliding Club Ltd
	G-CFEO	EV-97 Eurostar	J. B. Binks
	G-CFER	Schempp-Hirth Discus b	S. R. Westlake
	G-CFES	Schempp-Hirth Discus b	P. W. Berridge
	G-CFET	Van's RV-7	J. Astor
	G-CFEV	P & M Pegasus Quik	W. T. Davis
	G-CFEX	P & M Quik GT450	H. Wilson
	G-CFEY	Aerola Alatus-M	M. S. Hayman
	G-CFEZ	CZAW Sportcruiser	J. F. Barber & J. R. Large
	G-CFFA	Ultramagic M-90 balloon	Proxim SPA/Italy
	G-CFFB	Grob G.102 Astir CS	M. H. Simms
	G-CFFC	Centrair 101A	B. Douglas
	G-CFFE	EV-97 TeamEurostar UK	M. Lawton
	G-CFFF	Pitts S-1S Special	P. J. Roy
	G-CFFG	Aerochute Dual	R. J. Watkin
	G-CFFH	Aeros Discus 15T Dragonfly	D. Wilson
	G-CFFJ	Flight Design CTSW	R. Germany
	G-CFFL	Lindstrand LBL-317A balloon	Aerosarus Balloons Ltd
	G-CFFN	P & M Quik GT450	Kent County Scout Council
	G-CFFO	P & M Quik GT450	D. E. McGauley
	G-CFFS	Centrair 101A	W. Murray
	G-CFFT	Schempp-Hirth Discus b	R. Maskell
	G-CFFU	Glaser-Dirks DG-101G Elan	FFU Group
	G-CFFV	PZL-Bielsko SZD-51-1 Junior	Herefordshire Gliding Club Ltd
	G-CFFX	Schempp-Hirth Discus b	P. J. Richards
	G-CFFY	PZL-Bielsko SZD-51-1 Junior	Scottish Gliding Union Ltd
	G-CFGA	VS Spitfire VIII	The Pembrokeshire Spitfire Aeroplane Company Ltd
	G-CFGB	Cessna 680 Citation Sovereign	Keepflying LLP
	G-CFGC	Demoiselle	R. B. Hewing
	G-CFGD	P & M Quik GT450	D. J. Revell
	G-CFGE	Stinson 108-1 Voyager	M. J. Medland
	G-CFGF	Schempp-Hirth Nimbus 3T	R. E. Cross
	G-CFGG	Rotorsport UK MT-03	C. M. Jones
	G-CFGH	Jabiru J160	D. F. Sargant & D. J. Royce
	G-CFGI	VS.358 Seafire Mk.II (MB293)	Mark One Partners LLC
	G-CFGJ	VS.300 Spitfire I (N3200)	Mark One Partners LLC
	G-CFGK	Grob G.102 Astir CS	P. Allingham
	G-CFGM	Ikarus C42	R. S. O'Carroll
	G-CFGN	VS.300 Spitfire IA	Mark One Partners LLC
	G-CFGO	Best Off Sky Ranger Swift 912S	C. Lamb
	G-CFGP	Schleicher ASW-19	A. E. Prime
	G-CFGR	Schleicher ASK-13	Portsmouth Naval Gliding Centre
	G-CFGT	P & M Aviation Quik GT450	G. I. Taylor
	G-CFGU	Schempp-Hirth Standard Cirrus	D. Higginbottom
	G-CFGV	P & M Quik GT450	R. Bennett
	G-CFGX	EV-97 TeamEurostar UK	Golf XRay Group
	G-CFGY	Rotorsport UK MT-03	G. J. Slater & N. D. Leak
	G-CFGW	Centrair 101A	L. P. Smith
	G-CFGZ	Flight Design CTSW	B. Gorvett
	G-CFHB	Micro Aviation B.22J Bantam	P. Rayson
	G-CFHC	Micro Aviation B.22J Bantam	B. J. Syson
	G-CFHD	Schleicher ASW-20 BL	O. Boskano
	G-CFHF	PZL-Bielsko SZD-51-1	Black Mountains Gliding Club

Reg.	Type	Owner or Operator	Notes
G-CFHG	Schempp-Hirth Mini Nimbus C	R. W. & M. P. Weaver	
G-CFHI	Van's RV-9	J. R. Dawe	
G-CFHJ	Centrair 101A Pegase	Booker Gliding Club Ltd	
G-CFHK	Aeroprakt A22-L Foxbat	R. Bellew	
G-CFHL	Rolladen-Schneider LS4	I. P. Hicks	
G-CFHM	Schleicher ASK-13	Lasham Gliding Society Ltd	
G-CFHN	Schleicher K 8B	The Nene Valley Gliding Club Ltd	
G-CFHO	Grob G.103 Twin Astir II	The Surrey Hills Gliding Club Ltd	
G-CFHP	Ikarus C42 FB80	Airbourne Aviation Ltd	
G-CFHR	Schempp-Hirth Discus b	M. Fursedon, J. Jervis & T. Turner	
G-CFHS	Tchemma T01/77 balloon	D. J. Farrar	
G-CFHU	Robinson R22 Beta	Cameron and Brown Partnership	
G-CFHW	Grob G.102 Astir CS	P. Haliday	
G-CFHX	Schroeder Fire Balloons G22/24 balloon	T. J. Ellenrieder	
G-CFHY	Fokker Dr.1 Triplane replica	P. G. Bond	
G-CFHZ	Schleicher Ka 6CR	G. D. Leatherland	
G-CFIA	Best Off Sky Ranger Swift 912S(1)	D. I. Hall	
G-CFIC	Jodel DR.1050/M1	J. H. & P. I. Kempton	
G-CFID	Tanarg/Ixess 15 912S	D. Smith	
G-CFIE	Rotorsport UK MT-03	A. McCredie	
G-CFIF	Christen Eagle II	CFG Flying Group	
G-CFIG	P & M Aviation Quik GT450	J. Whitfield	
G-CFIH	Piel CP.1320	I. W. L. Aikman	
G-CFII	DH.82A Tiger Moth	Motair LLP	
G-CFIJ	Christen Eagle II	U. Wendt	
G-CFIK	Lindstrand LBL-60X balloon	A. M. Holly	
G-CFIL	P & M Aviation Quik GT450	S. N. Catchpole	
G-CFIM	P & M Aviation Quik GT450	A. Szczepanek	
G-CFIO	Cessna 172S	Skytrek Air Services	
G-CFIP	Raj Hamsa X'Air Falcon 700(1)	E. Maguire	
G-CFIS	Jabiru UL-D	O. Matthews	
G-CFIT	Ikarus C42 FB100	N. Hammerton	
G-CFIU	CZAW Sportcruiser	G. Everett & D. Smith	
G-CFIW	Balony Kubicek BB20XR balloon	H. C. J. Williams	
G-CFIY	Ikarus C42 FB100	D. M. Robbins	
G-CFIZ	Best Off Sky Ranger 912(2)	J. A. Hartshorne	
G-CFJA	Embraer EMB-135BJ Legacy	TAG Aviation (UK) Ltd	
G-CFJB	Rotorsport UK MT-03	N. J. Hargreaves	
G-CFJC	Sikorsky S-76C	Bristow Helicopters Ltd	
G-CFJF	Schempp-Hirth SHK-1	J. F. Mills	
G-CFJG	Best Off Sky Ranger Swift 912S(1)	C. M. Gray	
G-CFJH	Grob G.102 Astir CS77	P. Hardman	
G-CFJI	Ultramagic M-105 balloon	Comunicazione In Volo Srl/Italy	
G-CFJJ	Best Off Sky Ranger Swift 912S(1)	J. J. Ewing	
G-CFJK	Centrair 101A	D. Lewis	
G-CFJL	Raj Hamsa X'Air Hawk	G. L. Craig	
G-CFJM	Rolladen-Schneider LS4-a	K. Woods & S. Hill	
G-CFJN	Diamond DA.40D Star	Atlantic Flight Training Ltd	
G-CFJO	Diamond DA.40D Star	Atlantic Flight Training Ltd	
G-CFJP	Cameron N-56 balloon	V. J. M. L de Gail	
G-CFJR	Glaser-Dirks DG-300 Club Elan	W. Palmer & H. Smith	
G-CFJS	Glaser-Dirks DG-300 Club Elan	K. L. Goldsmith	
G-CFJU	Raj Hamsa X'Air Hawk	R. J. Minns & H. M. Wooldridge	
G-CFJV	Schleicher ASW-15	R. Abercrombie	
G-CFJW	Schleicher K7	K7 Group	
G-CFJX	DG-300 Elan	Crown Service Gliding Club	
G-CFJZ	Schempp-Hirth SHK-1	B. C. Irwin & R. H. Hanna	
G-CFKA	Rotorsport UK MT-03	Yorkshire Gyro Syndicate	
G-CFKB	CZAW Sportcruiser	B. S. Williams	
G-CFKD	Raj Hamsa X'Air Falcon Jabiru(2)	A. M. Fawthrop	
G-CFKE	Raj Hamsa X'Air Hawk	S. Rance	
G-CFKF	Cameron Z-210 balloon	First Flight	
G-CFKG	Rolladen-Schneider LS4-a	FKG Group	
G-CFKH	Zenair CH.601XL Zodiac	M. A. Baker	
G-CFKI	Cameron Z-120 balloon	KB Voli Di Chiozzi Bartolomeo EC SAS/Italy	
G-CFKJ	P & M Aviation Quik GT450	B. Geary	
G-CFKK	Flylight Dragonfly	C. G. Langham	
G-CFKL	Schleicher ASW-20 BL	J. Ley	
G-CFKM	Schempp-Hirth Discus b	Lasham Gliding Society Ltd	
G-CFKN	Lindstrand GA22 Mk.II airship	Lindstrand Technologies Ltd	
G-CFKO	P & M Aviation Quik GT450	D. W. C. Beer	
G-CFKP	Performance Designs Barnstormer/ Voyager	M. R. M. Harrall	

Notes	Reg.	Type	Owner or Operator
	G-CFKR	P & M Aviation Pegasus Quik	R. D. Ballard
	G-CFKS	Flight Design CTSW	D. J. M. Williams
	G-CFKT	Schleicher K 8B	FKT Group
	G-CFKU	P & M Aviation Quik GT450	C. A. Hasell
	G-CFKV	Savannah VG Jabiru(1)	D. Thorpe & K. N. Rigley
	G-CFKW	Alpi Pioneer 200	P. Rayson
	G-CFKX	Cameron Z-160 balloon	Virgin Balloon Flights
	G-CFKY	Schleicher Ka 6CR	J. A. Timmis
	G-CFKZ	Europa XS	N. P. Davis
	G-CFLA	P & M Aviation Quik GT450	D. Blake
	G-CFLB	Paratoys 28/Lowboy 313	P. R. Nation
	G-CFLC	Glaser-Dirks DG-300 Club Elan	J. L.Hey
	G-CFLD	Ikarus C42 FB80	L. McWilliams
	G-CFLE	Schempp-Hirth Discus b	D. A. Humphreys & S. J. A. McCracken
	G-CFLF	Rolladen-Schneider LS4-a	D. Lamb
	G-CFLG	CZAW Sportcruiser	D. A. Buttress
	G-CFLH	Schleicher K8B	The South Wales Gliding Club Ltd
	G-CFLI	Europa Aviation Europa	A. & E. Bennett
	G-CFLK	Cameron C-90 balloon	J. R. Rivers-Scott
	G-CFLL	EV-97 Eurostar	D. R. Lewis
	G-CFLM	P & M Pegasus Quik	JAG Flyers
	G-CFLN	Best Off Sky Ranger Swift 912S(1)	D. Bletcher
	G-CFLO	Rotorsport UK MT-03	R. G. Mulford
	G-CFLP	D.31 Turbulent	Eaglescott Turbulent Group
	G-CFLR	P & M Aviation Quik GT450	N. J. Lister
	G-CFLS	Schleicher Ka 6CR	University College London Union
	G-CFLU	SAAB 2000	Eastern Airways
	G-CFLV	SAAB 2000	Eastern Airways
	G-CFLW	Schempp-Hirth Standard Cirrus 75	J. Pack
	G-CFLX	DG-300 Club Elan	R. Emms
	G-CFLZ	Scheibe SF-27A Zugvogel V	SF Group
	G-CFMA	BB03 Trya/BB103	D. Sykes
	G-CFMB	P & M Aviation Quik GT450	Countermine PLC
	G-CFMC	Van's RV-9A	G-CFMC Flying Group
	G-CFMD	P & M Aviation Quik GT450	Wilson G. Jamieson Ltd
	G-CFME	SOCATA TB10 Tobago	Charles Funke Associates Ltd
	G-CFMH	Schleicher ASK-13	Lasham Gliding Society Ltd
	G-CFMI	Best Off Sky Ranger 912(1)	P. Shelton
	G-CFMM	Cessna 172S	Cristal Air Ltd
	G-CFMN	Schempp-Hirth Ventus cT	FMN Glider Syndicate
	G-CFMO	Schempp-Hirth Discus b	P. D. Bagnall
	G-CFMP	Europa XS	M. P. Gamble
	G-CFMR	Ultramagic V-14 balloon	M. W. A. Shemilt
	G-CFMS	Schleicher ASW-15	Loughborough Students Union Gliding Club
	G-CFMT	Schempp-Hirth Standard Cirrus	J. M. Brooke
	G-CFMU	Schempp-Hirth Standard Cirrus	A. Harrison & J. Gammage
	G-CFMV	Aerola Alatus-M	M. Housley
	G-CFMW	Scheibe SF-25C	The Windrushers Gliding Club Ltd
	G-CFMX	PA-28-161 Warrior II	Stapleford Flying Club Ltd
	G-CFMY	Rolladen-Schneider LS7	G-CFMY Group
	G-CFNB	Cameron TR-70 balloon	Balslooning Team BVBA/Belgium
	G-CFNC	Flylight Dragonfly	W. G. Minns
	G-CFND	Schleicher Ka 6E	C. Scutt & P. Bryant
	G-CFNE	PZL-Bielsko SZD-38A Jantar 1	T. Robson, J. Murray & I. Gordon
	G-CFNF	Robinson R44 II	S. G. Dykes
	G-CFNG	Schleicher ASW-24	P. H. Pickett
	G-CFNH	Schleicher ASW-19	S. N. & P. E. S. Longland
	G-CFNI	Airborne Edge XT912-B/Streak III-B	Fly NI Ltd
	G-CFNK	Slingsby T.65A Vega	I. P. Goldstraw & V. Luscombe-Mahoney
	G-CFNL	Schempp-Hirth Discus b	A. S. Ramsay & P. P. Musto
	G-CFNM	Centrair 101B Pegase	D. T. Hartley
	G-CFNO	Best Off Sky Ranger Swift 912S(1)	J. W. Taylor
	G-CFNP	Schleicher Ka 6CR	P. Pollard-Wilkins
	G-CFNR	Schempp-Hirth Discus b	J. I. H. Mitcheson
	G-CFNS	Glaser-Dirks DG-300 Club Elan	P. E. Williams, K. F. Byrne & J. M. Price
	G-CFNT	Glaser-Dirks DG-600	G-CFNT Group
	G-CFNU	Rolladen Schneider LS4-a	R. J. Simpson
	G-CFNV	CZAW Sportcruiser	N. D. McAllister & M. Owen
	G-CFNW	EV-97 TeamEurostar UK	The Scottish Aero Club Ltd
	G-CFNX	Tanarg/Ixess 13 912S(1)	Flylight Airsports Ltd
	G-CFNY	Flylight Dragonfly	M. J. Jessop
	G-CFNZ	Airborne Edge XT912-B/Streak III-B	P. Walton
	G-CFOB	Schleicher ASW-15B	A. W. Marr

Reg.	Type	Owner or Operator	Notes
G-CFOC	Glaser-Dirks DG200/17	R. & C. Nunn	
G-CFOF	Scheibe SF-27A Zugvogel V	S. Maddex	
G-CFOG	Ikarus C42 FB UK	P. D. Coppin	
G-CFOH	GA Gulfstream IV	Gama Aviation Ltd	
G-CFOI	Cessna 172N	P. Fearon	
G-CFOJ	Eurocopter EC.155 B1	Starspeed Ltd	
G-CFOK	Grob G.103C Twin III Acro	York Gliding Centre Ltd	
G-CFOL	Ultramagic M-90 balloon	M. G. Howard	
G-CFOM	Scheibe SF27A	K. A. Ford & R. D. Noon	
G-CFON	Wittman W8 Tailwind	C. F. O'Neill	
G-CFOO	P & M Aviation Quik R	Microavionics	
G-CFOP	Cameron Hopping Bag 120 SS balloon	J. Ravibalan	
G-CFOR	Schleicher K 8B	Dorset Gliding Club Ltd	
G-CFOS	Flylight Dragonfly	P. S. Bendall	
G-CFOT	PZL-Bielsko SZD-48-3 Jantar Standard 3	T. Greenwood	
G-CFOU	Schleicher K7	Vectis Gliding Club Ltd	
G-CFOV	CZAW Sportcruiser	J. G. Murphy	
G-CFOW	Best Off Sky Ranger Swift 912S(1)	A. Chappell	
G-CFOX	Marganski MDM-1	Fox Syndicate	
G-CFOY	Schempp-Hirth Discus b	B. W. Mills, J. W. Slater & R. F. Dowty	
G-CFOZ	Rolladen-Schneider LS1-f	L51 Group	
G-CFPA	CZAW Sportcruiser	T. W. Lorimer	
G-CFPB	Schleicher ASW-15B	G-CFPB Syndicate	
G-CFPD	Rolladen-Schneider LS7	LS7 Group	
G-CFPE	Schempp-Hirth Ventus cT	R. Palmer	
G-CFPF	Scheibe L-Spatz 55	N. C. Stone	
G-CFPG	AMS-Flight Carat A	A. Collinson	
G-CFPH	Centrair ASW-20F	GB2 Syndicate	
G-CFPI	P & M Aviation Quik GT450	G-CFPI Group	
G-CFPJ	CZAW Sportcruiser	S. R. Winter	
G-CFPL	Schempp-Hirth Ventus c	R. V. Barrett	
G-CFPM	PZL-Bielsko SZD-51-1 Junior	Kent Gliding Club Ltd	
G-CFPN	Schleicher ASW-20	M. Rayner	
G-CFPP	Schempp-Hirth Nimbus 2B	R. Jones & R. Murfitt	
G-CFPR	P & M Aviation Quik R	A. G. N. Coulon	
G-CFPS	Sky 25-16 balloon	G. B. Lescott	
G-CFPT	Schleicher ASW-20	L. Hornsey and L. Weeks Syndicate	
G-CFPW	Glaser-Dirks DG-600	P. B. Gray	
G-CFPZ	Sikorsky S-76C	Bristow Helicopters (International) Ltd	
G-CFRC	Schempp-Hirth Nimbus 2B	Tim and Martin Nimbus 2B Group	
G-CFRE	Schleicher Ka 6E	K6-FRE Syndicate	
G-CFRF	Lindstrand LBL-31A	RAF Halton Hot Air Balloon Club	
G-CFRH	Schleicher ASW-20CL	J. N. Wilton	
G-CFRI	Ultramagic N-355 balloon	Kent Ballooning	
G-CFRJ	Schempp-Hirth Standard Cirrus	J. Francis & P. Gould	
G-CFRK	Schleicher ASW-15B	ASW 15B Syndicate	
G-CFRL	Grob G.102 Astir CS	The South Wales Gliding Club Ltd	
G-CFRM	SkyRanger Swift 912S(1)	R. K. & T. A. Willcox	
G-CFRN	Rotorsport UK MTO Sport	P. E. Scopes	
G-CFRP	Centrair 101A Pegase	C. Bessent	
G-CFRR	Centrair 101A	G-CFRR Syndicate	
G-CFRS	Scheibe Zugvogel IIIB	G-CFRS Flying Group	
G-CFRT	EV-97 TeamEurostar UK	G. J. Slater & N. D. Leak	
G-CFRV	Centrair 101A	P. J. Britten	
G-CFRW	Schleicher ASW-20L	R. M. Green	
G-CFRX	Centrair 101A	S. Woolrich	
G-CFRY	Zenair CH 601UL	C. K. Fry	
G-CFRZ	Schempp-Hirth Standard Cirrus	S. G. Lapworth & N. E. Smith	
G-CFSB	Tecnam P2002-RG Sierra	W. J. Gale and Son	
G-CFSD	Schleicher ASK-13	Portsmouth Naval Gliding Centre	
G-CFSE	Cameron H-340HL balloon	Balloon School (International) Ltd	
G-CFSF	P & M Aviation QuikR	C. J. Gordon	
G-CFSG	Van's RV-9	R. A. L. Hubbard	
G-CFSH	Grob G.102 Astir CS Jeans	Buckminster Gliding Club Ltd	
G-CFSI	Aerola Alatus-M	T. J. Birkbeck	
G-CFSJ	Jabiru J160	D. P. Bird	
G-CFSK	Dyn'Aero MCR-01 VLA Sportster	S. Collins	
G-CFSL	Kubicek BB-26Z balloon	M. R. Jeynes	
G-CFSM	Cessna 172Q	Zentelligence Ltd	
G-CFSN	Aerola Alatus-M	B. K. Harrison	
G-CFSR	DG-300 Elan	A. P. Montague	
G-CFSS	Schleicher Ka 6E	FSS Syndicate	
G-CFST	Schleicher ASH-25E	D. Tucker & K. H. Lloyd	

Notes	Reg.	Type	Owner or Operator
	G-CFSW	Skyranger Swift 912S(1)	S. B. & L. S. Williams
	G-CFSX	Savannah VG Jabiru(1)	J. P. Swadling
	G-CFTA	Ace Magic Laser	P and M Aviation Ltd
	G-CFTB	Schleicher Ka 6CR	D. J. Baldwin
	G-CFTC	PZL-Bielsko SZD-51-1 Junior	Seahawk Gliding Club
	G-CFTD	Schleicher ASW-15B	G-CFTD Flying Group
	G-CFTE	P & M Aviation Quik R	M. E. Fowler
	G-CFTF	Roe 1 Triplane Replica	E. A. Verdon-Roe
	G-CFTG	P & M Aviation Quik R	A. V. Cosser
	G-CFTH	PZL-Bielsko SZD-50-3 Puchacz	Buckminster Gliding Club Ltd
	G-CFTI	Evektor EV-97A Eurostar	R. J. Dance
	G-CFTJ	Aerotechnik EV-97A Eurostar	C. B. Flood
	G-CFTK	Grob G.102 Astir CS Jeans	Ulster Gliding Club Ltd
	G-CFTL	Schleicher ASW-20CL	J. S. & S. V. Shaw
	G-CFTM	Cameron C-80 balloon	P. A. Meecham
	G-CFTN	Schleicher K 8B	Mendip Gliding Club Ltd
	G-CFTO	Ikarus C42 FB80	Fly Hire Ltd
	G-CFTP	Schleicher ASW-20CL	D. J. Pengilley & M. S. Hawkins
	G-CFTR	Grob G.102 Astir CS77	The University of Nottingham Students Union
	G-CFTS	Glaser-Dirks DG-300 Club Elan	FTS Syndicate
	G-CFTT	Van's RV-7	R. I. & D. J. Blain
	C-CFTU	Flylight Dragonfly	R. J. Cook
	G-CFTV	Rolladen-Schneider LS7-WL	D. Hilton
	G-CFTW	Schempp-Hirth Discus b	230 Syndicate
	G-CFTX	Jabiru J160	R. K. Creasey
	G-CFTY	Rolladen-Schneider LS7-WL	J. A. Thomson & A. Burgess
	G-CFTZ	Evektor EV-97 Eurostar	G. G. Bevis
	G-CFUA	Van's RV-9A	I. M. Macleod
	G-CFUB	Schleicher Ka 6CR	C. Boyd
	G-CFUD	Skyranger Swift 912S(1)	G-CFUD Group
	G-CFUE	Alpi Pioneer 300 Hawk	A. Dayani
	G-CFUF	Ultramagic N-300 balloon	Merlin Balloons
	G-CFUG	Grob G.109B	Portsmouth Naval Gliding Centre
	G-CFUH	Schempp-Hirth Ventus c	C. G. T. Huck
	G-CFUI	Hunt Wing/Avon 503(4)	R. F. G. Moyle
	G-CFUJ	Glaser-Dirks DG-300 Elan	Foxtrot Uniform Juliet Group
	G-CFUL	Schempp-Hirth Discus b	Discus 803 Syndicate
	G-CFUN	Schleicher ASW-20CL	D. C. W. Sanders
	G-CFUP	Schempp-Hirth Discus b	Lasham Gliding Society Ltd
	G-CFUR	Schempp-Hirth Ventus cT	A. P. Carpenter
	G-CFUS	PZL-Bielsko SZD-51-1 Junior	Scottish Gliding Union Ltd
	G-CFUT	Glaser-Dirks DG-300 Club Elan	M. J. Barnett
	G-CFUU	DG-300 Club Elan	S. K. Ruffell
	G-CFUV	Rolladen-Schneider LS7-WL	E. Alston
	G-CFUW	Rotorsport UK MTO Sport	D. A. Robertson
	G-CFUX	Cameron C-80 balloon	A. M. Holly
	G-CFUY	PZL-Bielsko SZD-50-3 Puchacz	The Bath, Wilts and North Dorset Gliding Club
	G-CFUZ	CZAW Sportcruiser	M. W. Bush
	G-CFVA	P & M Quik GT450	Countermine PLC
	G-CFVC	Schleicher ASK-13	Mendip Gliding Club Ltd
	G-CFVE	Schempp-Hirth Nimbus 2	L. Mitchell
	G-CFVF	Kiss 400-582(1)	J. D. Pinkney
	G-CFVG	Rotorsport UK MTO Sport	K. J. Whitehead
	G-CFVH	Rolladen-Schneider LS7	C. C. & J. C. Marshall
	G-CFVI	Evektor EV-97 TeamEurostar	Nene Valley Microlights Ltd
	G-CFVJ	Cvjetkovic CA-65 Skyfly	D. Hunter
	G-CFVK	Skyranger HKS(1)	B. Barrass
	G-CFVL	Scheibe Zugvogel IIIB	The G-CFVL Flying Group
	G-CFVM	Centrair 101A Pegase	S. H. North
	G-CFVN	Centrair 101A Pegase	G-CFVN Group
	G-CFVO	Beech B.200 Super King Air	Unity Aviation Ltd
	G-CFVP	Centrair 101A Pegase	Foxtrot Victor Papa Group
	G-CFVR	Europa XS	K. A. O'Neill
	G-CFVT	Schempp-Hirth Nimbus 2	I. Dunkley
	G-CFVU	Schleicher ASK-13	The Vale of the White Horse Gliding Centre Ltd
	G-CFVV	Centrair 101A Pegase	Cambridge Gliding Club Ltd
	G-CFVW	Schempp-Hirth Ventus bT	A. D. Johnson
	G-CFVX	Cameron C-80 balloon	A. M. Holly
	G-CFVY	Cameron A-120 balloon	Rocket M edia (UK) Ltd
	G-CFVZ	Schleicher Ka 6E	N. R. Bowers & R. C. Fisher
	G-CFWA	Schleicher Ka 6CR	C. C. Walley
	G-CFWB	Schleicher ASK-13	Cotswold Gliding Club
	G-CFWC	Grob G.103C Twin III Acro	The South Wales Gliding Club Ltd

Reg.	Type	Owner or Operator	Notes
G-CFWD	Rotorsport UK MTO Sport	Gower Gyronautics	
G-CFWE	PZL-Bielsko SZD-50-3 Puchacz	Deeside Gliding Club (Aberdeenshire) Ltd	
G-CFWF	Rolladen-Schneider LS7	G. B. Hibberd	
G-CFWH	Scheibe SF27A	A. S. Carter	
G-CFWI	Kubicek BB-22Z balloon	V. Gounon	
G-CFWJ	P & M Quik GT450	D. Little	
G-CFWK	Schempp-Hirth Nimbus-3DT	29 Syndicate	
G-CFWL	Schleicher K8B	A. S. Burton	
G-CFWM	Glaser-Dirks DG-300 Club Elan	FWM Group	
G-CFWN	P & M Quik GT450	G-CFWN Group	
G-CFWO	Murphy Maverick 430	S. P. Rice	
G-CFWP	Schleicher ASW-19B	980 Syndicate	
G-CFWS	Schleicher ASW-20C	662 Syndicate	
G-CFWT	PZL-Bielsko SZD-50-3 Puchacz	Coventry Gliding Club Ltd	
G-CFWU	Rolladen-Schneider LS7-WL	Whiskey Uniform Group	
G-CFWV	Van's RV-7	S. J. Carr & D. K. Sington	
G-CFWW	Schleicher ASH-25E	G-CFWW Syndicate	
G-CFWY	Centrair 101A Pegase	S. Foster	
G-CFWZ	Schleicher ASW-19B	G-CFWZ Flying Group	
G-CFXA	Grob G.104 Speed Astir IIB	A. V. Jupp & D. C. White	
G-CFXB	Schleicher K 8B	R. Sansom	
G-CFXC	Schleicher Ka 6E	A. K. Bailey & G. Pook	
G-CFXD	Centrair 101A Pegase	D. G. England & R. Banks	
G-CFXF	Magni M-16C Tandem Trainer	M. W. King	
G-CFXG	Flylight Dragonfly	N. L. Stammers	
G-CFXH	Schleicher K 7	Vale of Neath Gliding Club	
G-CFXI	Lindstrand LBL Box balloon	A. M. Holly	
G-CFXJ	Schleicher ASW-24	G. S. J. Bambrook & A. Purcell	
G-CFXK	Flylight Dragonfly	P. J. Clegg	
G-CFXL	Lindstrand LBL-90A balloon	A. M. Holly	
G-CFXM	Schempp-Hirth Discus bT	G. R. E. Bottomley	
G-CFXN	CZAW Sportcruiser	R. Underwood & J. D. Boyce	
G-CFXO	PZL-Bielsko SZD-50-3 Puchacz	Coventry Gliding Club Ltd	
G-CFXP	Lindstrand LBL-105A balloon	Shaun Bradley Project Services Ltd	
G-CFXR	Lindstrand LBL-105A balloon	Lindstrand Hot Air Balloons Ltd	
G-CFXS	Schleicher Ka 6E	B. C. F. Wade & R. B. Woodhouse	
G-CFXT	Naval Aircraft Factory N3N-3	R. H. & J. A. Cooper	
G-CFXU	Schleicher Ka-6E	FXU Syndicate	
G-CFXW	Schleicher K8B	The South Wales Gliding Club Ltd	
G-CFXX	P & M Quik R	M. C. Shortman	
G-CFXY	Schleicher ASW-15B	E. L. Armstrong	
G-CFXZ	P & M Quik R	I. Jones	
G-CFYA	PZL-Bielsko SZD-50-3 Puchacz	Cairngorm Gliding Club	
G-CFYB	Rolladen-Schneider LS7	A. T. Macdonald & V. P. Haley	
G-CFYC	Schempp-Hirth Ventus b	G. Smith	
G-CFYD	Aeroprakt A22-L Foxbat	A. P. Fenn	
G-CFYE	Scheibe Zugvogel IIIB	R. Staines	
G-CFYF	Schleicher ASK-21	London Gliding Club Proprietary Ltd	
G-CFYG	Glasflugel Club Libelle 205	FYG Syndicate	
G-CFYH	Rolladen-Schneider LS4-a	G. W. & C. A. Craig	
G-CFYI	Grob G.102 Astir CS	A. C. Arthurs & P. T. Raisbeck	
G-CFYJ	Schempp-Hirth Standard Cirrus	FYJ Syndicate	
G-CFYK	Rolladen-Schneider LS7-WL	R. R. Ward	
G-CFYL	PZL-Bielsko SZD-50-3 Puchacz	Deesside Gliding Club (Aberdeenshire) Ltd	
G-CFYM	Schempp-Hirth Discus bT	B. F. Laverick-Smith	
G-CFYN	Schempp-Hirth Discus b	N. White & P. R. Foulger	
G-CFYO	P & M Quik R	M. H. Bond	
G-CFYP	FBM & W Silex M/Flyke/Monster	A. J. R. Carver	
G-CFYR	LET L-23 Super Blanik	G-CFYR Group	
G-CFYS	Dynamic WT9 UK	E. M. Middleton	
G-CFYT	Beech 58 Baron	Conciair Ltd	
G-CFYU	Glaser-Dirks DG-100 Elan	I. M. & C. Shepherd	
G-CFYV	Schleicher ASK-21	The Bristol Gliding Club Proprietary Ltd	
G-CFYW	Rolladen-Schneider LS7	C. Bessant	
G-CFYX	Schempp-Hirth Discus b	Discus FYX Group	
G-CFYY	Schleicher ASK-13	Lasham Gliding Society Ltd	
G-CFYZ	Schleicher ASH-25	A. J. Nurse	
G-CFZA	PZL-Bielsko SZD-51-1	Booker Gliding Club Ltd	
G-CFZB	Glasflugel H201B Standard Libelle	J. C. Meyer	
G-CFZD	Jabiru J430	C. J. Judd & A. Macknish	
G-CFZF	PZL-Bielsko SZD-51-1 Junior	Devon and Somerset Gliding Club Ltd	
G-CFZG	Colt 77A balloon	K. A. O'Kines	
G-CFZH	Schempp-Hirth Ventus c	FZH Group	

Notes	Reg.	Type	Owner or Operator
	G-CFZI	Savannah Jabiru (5)	J. T., A. L. & O. D. Lewis
	G-CFZJ	VS.388 Seafire F.46	C. T. Charleston
	G-CFZK	Schempp-Hirth Standard Cirrus	S. Lucas & R. Burgoyne
	G-CFZL	Schleicher ASW-20 CL	A. L. & R. M. Housden
	G-CFZM	Avro RJ85	Triangle Regional Aircraft Leasing Ltd
	G-CFZO	Schempp-Hirth Nimbus 3	954 Syndicate
	G-CFZP	PZL-Bielsko SZD-51-1 Junior	Portsmouth Naval Gliding Centre
	G-CFZR	Schleicher Ka 6CR	I. McHardy
	G-CFZS	Cameron A-140 balloon	Eastern Safaris Europe Ltd
	G-CFZT	Ace Magic Laser	P and M Aviation Ltd
	G-CFZV	Rolladen-Schneider LS7	W. M. Davies
	G-CFZW	Glaser-Dirks DG-300 Club Elan	D. O'Flanagan, G. Rogers & G. Stilgoe
	G-CFZX	Rotorsport UK MTO Sport	Gyro-I Ltd
	G-CFZZ	LET L-33 Solo	The Andreas L33 Group
	G-CGAA	Flylight Dragonfly	G. Adkins
	G-CGAB	AB Sportine LAK-12 Lietuva	W. T. Emery
	G-CGAC	P & M Quik GT450	A. Gillett
	G-CGAD	Rolladen-Schneider LS3	P. B. Turner
	G-CGAF	Schleicher ASK-21	Lasham Gliding Society Ltd
	G-CGAG	Scleicher ASK-21	Stratford on Avon Gliding Club Ltd
	G-CGAH	Schempp-Hirth Standard Cirrus	J. W. Williams
	G-CGAI	Raj Hamsa X'Air Hawk	P. J. Kilshaw
	G-CGAJ	Alpi Pioneer 400	C. Rusalen
	G-CGAK	Acrosport II	P. D. Sibbons
	G-CGAL	P & M Quik R	R. A. Keene
	G-CGAM	Schleicher ASK-21	Oxford University Gliding Club
	G-CGAN	Glasflugel H301 Libelle	S. & C. A. Noujaim
	G-CGAO	DHC.1 Chipmunk 22	P. Jeffery
	G-CGAP	Schempp-Hirth Ventus bT	J. R. Greenwell
	G-CGAR	Rolladen-Schneider LS6-c	A. Warbrick
	G-CGAS	Schempp-Hirth Ventus cT	G. M. J. Monaghan
	G-CGAT	Grob G.102 Astir CS	N. J. Hooper
	G-CGAU	Glasflugel H201B Standard Libelle	G-CGAU Group
	G-CGAV	Scheibe SF-27A Zugvogel V	GAV Syndicate
	G-CGAW	Beech 200 Super King Air	Fort Alice Aviation Ltd
	G-CGAX	PZL-Bielsko SZD-55-1 Promyk	I. D. Macro & P. Gold
	G-CGAZ	P & M Aviation Quik R	E. J. Douglas
	G-CGBA	Schleicher ASK-13	The Burn Gliding Club Ltd
	G-CGBB	Schleicher ASK-21	University of Edinburgh Sports Union
	G-CGBC	Balony Kubicek BB26Z balloon	N. Charbonnier
	G-CGBD	PZL-Bielsko SZD-50-3	The Northumbria Gliding Club Ltd
	G-CGBF	Schleicher ASK-21	BBC (London) Club
	G-CGBG	Rolladen-Schneider LS6-18w	C. Villa
	G-CGBH	Raj Hamsa X'Air Hawk	S. E. McEwen
	G-CGBI	VS.349 Spitfire LF.VB	R. W. H. Cole
	G-CGBJ	Grob G.102 Astir CS	Banbury Gliding Club Ltd
	G-CGBK	Grob G.102 Astir CS	B. J. Griffiths
	G-CGBL	Rolladen-Schneider LS7-WL	P. A. Roche
	G-CGBM	Flight Design CTSW	R. J. D. Mellor
	G-CGBN	Schleicher ASK-21	Essex and Suffolk Gliding Club Ltd
	G-CGBO	Rolladen-Schneider LS6	J. R. W. Luxton
	G-CGBR	Rolladen-Schneider LS6-c	V. L. Brown
	G-CGBS	Glaser-Dirks DG-300 Club Elan	A. Gillanders & M. C. Chalmers
	G-CGBU	Centrair 101A Pegase	D. J. Arblaster & R. M. Rowland
	G-CGBV	Schleicher ASK-21	Wolds Gliding Club Ltd
	G-CGBX	Schleicher ASW-22	D. A. Ashby
	G-CGBY	Rolladen-Schneider LS7	I. Ashdown
	G-CGBZ	Glaser-Dirks DG-500 Elan Trainer	Needwood Forest Gliding Club Ltd
	G-CGCA	Schleicher ASW-19B	Deeside Gliding Club (Aberdeenshire) Ltd
	G-CGCC	PZL-Bielsko SZD-51-1 Junior	Coventry Gliding Club Ltd
	G-CGCD	Schempp-Hirth Standard Cirrus	Cirrus Syndicate
	G-CGCE	Magni M16C Tandem Trainer	A. J. A. Fowler
	G-CGCF	Schleicher ASK-23	Needwood Forest Gliding Club Ltd
	G-CGCH	CZAW Sportcruiser	C. Harrison
	G-CGCK	PZL-Bielsko SZD-50-3 Puchacz	Kent Gliding Club Ltd (G-BTJV)
	G-CGCL	Grob G.102 Astir CS	J. A. Williams
	G-CGCM	Rolladen-Schneider LS6-c	G. R. Glazebrook
	G-CGCN	MCR-01 Club	D. J. Smith
	G-CGCO	Schempp-Hirth Cirrus VTC	T. W. Slater
	G-CGCP	Schleicher Ka-6CR	D. & B. Clarke
	G-CGCR	Schleicher ASW-15B	ASW15B 748 Group
	G-CGCS	Glasflugel Club Libelle 205	D. G. Coats

Reg.	Type	Owner or Operator	Notes
G-CGCT	Schempp-Hirth Discus b	P. J. Brown	
G-CGCU	PZL-Bielsko SZD-50-3 Puchacz	Buckminster Gliding Club Ltd	
G-CGCV	Raj Hamsa X'Air Hawk	W. J. Whyte	
G-CGCW	Skyranger Swift 912(1)	C. M. Wilkes	
G-CGCX	Schleicher ASW-15	C. D. Bingham	
G-BGCY	Centrair 101A Pegase	M. S. W. Meagher	
G-CGDA	Rolladen-Schneider LS3-17	A. R. Fish	
G-CGDB	Schleicher K 8B	The Welland Gliding Club Ltd	
G-CGDC	Rotorsport UK MTO Sport	R. E. Derham & T. R. Kingsley	
G-CGDD	Bolkow Phoebus C	G. C. Kench	
G-CGDE	Schleicher Ka 6CR	K6 Syndicate	
G-CGDF	Schleicher Ka 6BR	T. D. Lynch & H. Marshall	
G-CGDG	Cameron C-80 balloon	R. F. Davey	
G-CGDI	EV-97A Eurostar	D. Street	
G-CGDJ	PA-28-161 Warrior II	C. G. D. Jones (G-ETDA)	
G-CGDK	Schleicher K 8B	Vale of Neath Gliding Club	
G-CGDL	P & M Quik R	S. J. Bunce	
G-CGDM	Sonex Sonex	D. Scott	
G-CGDN	Rolladen-Schneider LS3-17	S. J. Pepler	
G-CGDO	Grob G.102 Astir CS	P. Lowe & R. Bostock	
G-CGDP	Thunder Ax10-160 S2 balloon	The Ballooning Business Ltd	
G-CGDR	Schempp-Hirth Discus CS	J. H. C. Friend	
G-CGDS	Schleicher ASW-15B	B. Birk & P. A. Crouch	
G-CGDT	Schleicher ASW-24	Tango 54 Syndicate	
G-CGDU	Schleicher ASK-24	R. J. Brimfield	
G-CGDV	CSA Sportcruiser	D. R. Stevens	
G-CGDW	CSA Sportcruiser	Onega Ltd	
G-CGDX	Orlican Discus CS	Coventry Gliding Club Ltd	
G-CGDY	Schleicher ASW-15B	Cloud Nine Syndicate	
G-CGDZ	Schleicher ASW-24	J. M. Norman	
G-CGEA	Schleicher Ka 6CR	C. M. Alton & P. R. E. Welby-Everard	
G-CGEB	Grob G.102 Astir CS77	T. R. Dews	
G-CGEC	Flight Design CTLS	S. Munday	
G-CGEE	Glasflugel H201B Standard Libelle	C. Metcalfe & J. Kelsey	
G-CGEF	La Mouette Hytrike Srs A	A. Lucchesi & G. Thevenot	
G-CGEG	Schleicher K 8B	Darlton Gliding Club Ltd	
G-CGEH	Schleicher ASW-15B	P. Nayeri	
G-CGEI	Cessna 550 Citation Bravo	S. W. Bond	
G-CGEJ	Alpi Pioneer 200-M	P. S. & N. Bewley	
G-CGEK	Ace Magic Laser	P. L. Wilkinson	
G-CGEL	PZL-Bielsko SZD-50-3	The Northumbria Gliding Club Ltd	
G-CGEM	Schleicher Ka 6CR	GEM Syndicate	
G-CGEN	RAF 2000	D. E. Worley	
G-CGEO	CSA Sportcruiser	The Jester Flying Group	
G-CGEP	Schempp-Hirth Standard Cirrus	D. J. Bundock	
G-CGER	Cameron Z-105 balloon	CV Fly Communication SRL/Italy	
G-CGEU	Flylight Dragonfly	D. Newbrook	
G-CGEV	Heliopolis Gomhouria Mk.6	A. Brier	
G-CGEW	Rotorsport UK MTO Sport	G-CGEW Group	
G-CGEX	P & M Quik GT450	D. L. Clark	
G-CGEY	Julian CD Dingbat	G. Carr	
G-CGEZ	Raj Hamsa X'Air Hawk	M. Howes & B. J. Ellis	
G-CGFB	BB03 Trya/BB103	B. J. Fallows	
G-CGFG	Cessna 152	Cristal Air Ltd	
G-CGFH	Cessna T182T Turbo Skylane	P. P. D. Howard-Johnston	
G-CGFI	MS.885 Super Rallye	AC Civil Engineering Ltd	
G-CGFJ	Cessna 172M	T. I. Murtough	
G-CGFK	Ace Magic Laser	C. J. Boseley	
G-CGFN	Cameron C-60 balloon	R. S. Mohr	
G-CGFO	Ultramagic H-42 balloon	J. A. W. Dyer	
G-CGFP	Pietenpol Aircamper	D. Hetherington	
G-CGFR	Lindstrand LBL HS-120 Airship	Lindstrand Hot Air Balloons Ltd	
G-CGFS	Nanchang CJ-6A	L. C. Myall	
G-CGFU	Schempp-Hirth Mini-Nimbus C	Mini Nimbus Syndicate	
G-CGFY	Lindstrand LBL-105A balloon	J. A. Lawton	
G-CGFZ	Thruster T.600N 450	K. J. Crompton	
G-CGGD	Eurocopter AS365N2 Dauphin 2	Multiflight Ltd	
G-CGGE	Cameron Z-275 balloon	Wickers World Ltd	
G-CGGF	Robinson R44 II	Sky Helicopteros SL	
G-CGGG	Robinson R44	Fly Executive Ltd (G-SJDI)	
G-CGGH	Sky 220-24 balloon	Zebedee Balloon Service Ltd	
G-CGGJ	Schweizer 269C-1	Patriot Aviation Ltd	
G-CGGK	Westland Wasp HAS Mk.1	The Real Aeroplane Co.Ltd	

Notes	Reg.	Type	Owner or Operator
	G-CGGL	Rotorsport UK MTOSport	A. D. Lysser
	G-CGGM	EV-97 TeamEurostar UK	GM Group
	G-CGGN	Dassault Falcon 7X	TAG Aviation (UK) Ltd
	G-CGGO	Robin DR.400-180 Regent	AWE Holdings Ltd
	G-CGGP	Autogyro MTOSport	N. Cowley
	G-CGGS	Robinson R44 II	Oakfield Investments Ltd
	G-CGGT	P & M Quik GT450	M. Earp
	G-CGGV	Rotorsport UK MTO Sport	R. W. Bottom
	G-CGGW	Rotorsport UK MTO Sport	P. Adams
	G-CGGX	TEAM Minimax 91	P. D. Parry
	G-CGGY	UltraMagic N-425 balloon	Anglian Countryside Balloons Ltd
	G-CGGZ	UltraMagic S-90 balloon	P. Lawman
	G-CGHA	P & M Quik R	K. M. Hughes
	G-CGHB	NAMC CJ-6A	M. J. Harvey
	G-CGHC	Pioneer 300 Hawk	M. Bettaglio
	G-CGHD	Cessna 172S	Steptoe & Son Properties Ltd
	G-CGHE	Flight Design CTSW	P & M Aviation Ltd
	G-CGHG	P & M Quik GT450	J. & K. D. McAlpine
	G-CGHH	P & M Quik R	D. J. Tiplady
	G-CGHI	Dassault Falcon 2000	Warton Ltd
	G-CGHJ	Staaken Z-21A Flitzer	D. J. Ashley
	G-CGHK	Alpi Pioneer 300 Hawk	D. J. Ashley
	G-CGHL	Rotorsport UK MTOSport	C. S. Mackenzie
	G-CGHM	PA-28 Cherokee 140	P. Asbridge
	G-CGHN	Aeros Discus/Alize	R. Simpson & N. Sutton
	G-CGHO	P & M Quik R	N. Creveau
	G-CGHR	Magic Laser	N. P. Power
	G-CGHS	DG Flugzeugbau DG-808C	M. A. V. Gatehouse
	G-CGHT	Dyn'Aero MCR-01 Banbi	J. F. McAulay (G-POOP)
	G-CGHU	Hawker Hunter T.Mk.8C	Hawker Hunter Aviation Ltd
	G-CGHW	Czech Sport Aircraft Sportcruiser	Sport Cruiser 290 Group
	G-CGHX	Beagle B.121 Pup	N. F. Foden
	G-CGHY	Raytheon Hawker 800XP	Xclusive Jet Charter Ltd
	G-CGHZ	P & M Quik R	J. Rockey
	G-CGIA	Paramania Action/Bailey Quattro 175	A. E. C. Phillips
	G-CGIB	Magic Cyclone	P and M Aviation Ltd
	G-CGIC	Rotorsport MTO Sport	J. Harmon & K. Snell
	G-CGID	PA-31-350 Navajo Chieftain	T. Michaels
	G-CGIE	Flylight Dragonfly	Flylight Airsports Ltd
	G-CGIF	Flylight Dragonfly	G. Nicholas
	G-CGIG	Lindstrand LBL-90A balloon	Fly Me Home Ltd
	G-CGIH	Cameron C-90 balloon	W. Bracken
	G-CGIJ	Agusta Westland AW139	HM Coastguard
	G-CGIK	Isaacs Spitfire	A. J. Harpley
	G-CGIL	CZAW Sportcruiser	G-CGIL Group
	G-CGIM	Ace Aviation Magic Laser	C. Royle
	G-CGIN	Paramania Action GT/Bailey Quattro 175	A. E. C. Phillips
	G-CGIO	Medway SLA100 Executive	C. J. Draper
	G-CGIP	CZAW Sportcruiser	R. Vincent
	G-CGIR	Remos GX	L. R. Marks & J. A. Pereira
	G-CGIS	Cameron Parachutist 110 SS balloon	K. Gruenauer (G-RIPS)
	G-CGIU	AX1 balloon	M. W. A. Shemilt
	G-CGIV	Kolb Firefly	W. A. Emmerson
	G-CGIW	Sikorsky S-76C-2	Bristow Helicopters (International) Ltd
	G-CGIX	Rotorsport UK MTO Sport	J. K. Houldcroft
	G-CGIY	Piper J3C-65	R. C. Cummings
	G-CGIZ	Flight Design CTSW	J. Hilton
	G-CGJB	Schempp-Hirth Duo Discus T	G. J. Basey
	G-CGJC	Rotorsport UK MTO Sport	J. C. Collingwood
	G-CGJD	Rotorsport UK Calidus	C. Collins
	G-CGJE	VS.361 Spitfire IX	Historic Flight Ltd
	G-CGJF	Fokker E.111 Replica	I. Brewster
	G-CGJH	P & M Quik GT450	B. Montila
	G-CGJI	Best Off Skyranger 912S(1)	Flylight Airsports Ltd
	G-CGJJ	P & M Quik R	A. J. Hubbard
	G-CGJL	CZAW Sportcruiser	G-CGJL Flying Group
	G-CGJM	Skyranger Swift 912S(1)	J. P. Metcalfe
	G-CGJN	Van's RV-7	J. R. & M. G. Jefferies
	G-CGJO	P & M Quik R	C. W. J. Davis
	G-CGJP	Van's RV-10	K. D. Taylor
	G-CGJS	CZAW Sportcruiser	J. M. Tiley
	G-CGJT	CZAW Sportcruiser	D. F. Toller
	G-CGJV	Lindstrand LBL Motorbike SS balloon	Lindstrand Hot Air Balloons Ltd

Reg.	Type	Owner or Operator	Notes
G-CGJW	RAF 2000 GTX-SE	J. J. Wollen	
G-CGJX	SA.341B Gazelle AH Mk.1	B. W. Stuart	
G-CGJY	SA.341D Gazelle HT Mk.3	P. J. Whitaker	
G-CGJZ	SA.341D Gazelle HT Mk.3	A. W. J. Stuart	
G-CGKA	Grob G115E Tutor	Babcock Aerospace Ltd	
G-CGKB	Grob G115E Tutor	Babcock Aerospace Ltd	
G-CGKC	Grob G115E Tutor	Babcock Aerospace Ltd	
G-CGKD	Grob G115E Tutor	Babcock Aerospace Ltd	
G-CGKE	Grob G115E Tutor	Babcock Aerospace Ltd	
G-CGKF	Grob G115E Tutor	Babcock Aerospace Ltd	
G-CGKG	Grob G115E Tutor	Babcock Aerospace Ltd	
G-CGKH	Grob G115E Tutor	Babcock Aerospace Ltd	
G-CGKI	Grob G115E Tutor	Babcock Aerospace Ltd	
G-CGKJ	Grob G115E Tutor	Babcock Aerospace Ltd	
G-CGKK	Grob G115E Tutor	Babcock Aerospace Ltd	
G-CGKL	Grob G115E Tutor	Babcock Aerospace Ltd	
G-CGKM	Grob G115E Tutor	Babcock Aerospace Ltd	
G-CGKN	Grob G115E Tutor	Babcock Aerospace Ltd	
G-CGKO	Grob G115E Tutor	Babcock Aerospace Ltd	
G-CGKP	Grob G115E Tutor	Babcock Aerospace Ltd	
G-CGKR	Grob G115E Tutor	Babcock Aerospace Ltd	
G-CGKS	Grob G115E Tutor	Babcock Aerospace Ltd	
G-CGKT	Grob G115E Tutor	Babcock Aerospace Ltd	
G-CGKU	Grob G115E Tutor	Babcock Aerospace Ltd	
G-CGKV	Grob G115E Tutor	Babcock Aerospace Ltd	
G-CGKW	Grob G115E Tutor	Babcock Aerospace Ltd	
G-CGKX	Grob G115E Tutor	Babcock Aerospace Ltd	
G-CGKY	Cessna 182T	T. A. E. Dobell	
G-CGKZ	Best Off Sky Ranger Swift 912S(1)	A. Worthington	
G-CGLA	Cameron Z-105 balloon	Phoenix Balloons Ltd	
G-CGLB	Airdrome Dream Classic	S. J. Ball	
G-CGLC	Czech Sport Aircraft Sportcruiser	P. Taylor	
G-CGLE	Flylight Dragonfly	B. Skelding	
G-CGLF	Magni M-16C Tandem Trainer	J. S. Walton	
G-CGLG	P & M Quik GT450	A. G. Cummings	
G-CGLH	Rotorsport UK Calidus	A. Marshall	
G-CGLI	Alpi Pioneer 200M	B. A. Lyford	
G-CGLJ	TL 2000UK Sting Carbon	L. A. James	
G-CGLK	Magni M-16C Tandem Trainer	R. M. Savage	
G-CGLL	Rotorsport UK MTO Sport	P. J. Troy-Davies	
G-CGLM	Rotorsport UK MTO Sport	J. Owen	
G-CGLN	Jabiru J430	J. R. Frohnsdorff & C. H. K. Hood	
G-CGLO	P & M Quik R	A. P. Watkins	
G-CGLP	CZAW Sportcruiser	P. S. Tanner	
G-CGLR	Czech Sport Aircraft Sportcruiser	G-CGLR Group	
G-CGLT	Czech Sport Aircraft Sportcruiser	P. J. V. Dibble	
G-CGLV	Beech 58 Baron	Conciair Ltd (G-DAFY)	
G-CGLW	P & M Pegasus Quik	S. Dixon	
G-CGLX	Rotorsport UK MTO Sport	The Gyrocopter Co.Ltd	
G-CGLY	Rotorsport UK Calidus	A. G. A. Edwards	
G-CGLZ	TL 2000UK Sting Carbon	D. Nieman	
G-CGMA	Ace Magic Laser	J. N. Hanson	
G-CGMB	Embraer EMB-135ER	Eastern Airways	
G-CGMC	Embraer EMB-135ER	Eastern Airways	
G-CGMD	Rotorsport UK Calidus	D.W. Leeming	
G-CGME	Ellipse Fuji/Pulma 2000	I. M. Vass	
G-CGMF	Cessna 560XL Citation XLS	Multiflight Charter Services LLP	
G-CGMG	Van's RV-9	D. J. Bone	
G-CGMH	Jodel D150A Mascaret	J. K. Cook	
G-CGMI	P & M Quik GT450	W. G. Reynolds	
G-CGMJ	P & M Quik R	C. D. Waldron	
G-CGMK	Best Off Sky Ranger 582(1)	F. Omaraie-Hamdanie	
G-CGML	TL 2000UK Sting Carbon	G. T. Leedham	
G-CGMM	CZAW Sportcruiser	TAF and Co	
G-CGMN	Best Off Sky Ranger Swift 912S	T. C. Butterworth	
G-CGMO	Ace Magic Laser	G. J. Latham	
G-CGMP	CZAW Sportcruiser	M. Payne	
G-CGMR	Colt Bibendum-110 balloon	Mobberley Balloon Collection (G-GRIP)	
G-CGMS	Sutton/Aquilair KID 1	K. A. Sutton	
G-CGMU	Sikorsky S-92A	HM Coastguard	
G-CGMV	Roko Aero NG 4HD	Eshott NG4 Group	
G-CGMW	Alpi Pioneer 200M	M. S. McCrudden	
G-CGMX	Cameron TR-70 balloon	Cameron Balloons Ltd	

Notes	Reg.	Type	Owner or Operator
	G-CGMZ	P & M Quik R	M. W. Houghton
	G-CGNA	Cameron Super FMG-100 balloon	Cameron Balloons Ltd
	G-CGNC	Rotorsport UK MTO Sport	Comedy South West Ltd
	G-CGND	Robinson R44 II	Ajax Machinery
	G-CGNE	Robinson R44 II	Sandaris Ltd
	G-CGNG	CZAW Sportcruiser	T. Dounias
	G-CGNH	Escapade Jabiru(1)	A. H. Paul
	G-CGNI	Ikarus C42 FB80	G. J. Slater
	G-CGNJ	Cameron Z-105 balloon	Loughborough Students Union Hot Air Balloon Club
	G-CGNK	P & M Quik GT450	G. W. Hillidge
	G-CGNL	Cameron Z-90 balloon	A. M. Holly
	G-CGNM	Magni M-16C Tandem Trainer	Evolo Ltd
	G-CGNN	Montgomerie-Bensen B.8MR	P. M. Ryder
	G-CGNO	P & M Quik GT450	Airways Airsports Ltd
	G-CGNP	Embraer EMB-500 Phenom 100	Flairjet Ltd
	G-CGNR	Van's RV-6	N. Rawlinson
	G-CGNS	Sky 65-24 balloon	R. L. Bovell
	G-CGNT	Avro RJ100	Triangle Regional Aircraft Leasing Ltd
	G-CGNU	Avro RJ100	Triangle Regional Aircraft Leasing Ltd
	G-CGNV	Reality Escapade	M. J. Whatley
	G-CGNW	Scheibe SF-25C Falke	The Royal Air Force Gliding and Soaring Association
	G-CGNX	Rotorsport UK MTO Sport	L. McCallum
	G-CGNY	Cessna 340A	P. W. J. Sharpe-Brash
	G-CGNZ	Europa XS	C. D. Meek
	G-CGOA	Cessna 550 Citation II	Xclusive Jet Charter Ltd (G-JMDW)
	G-CGOB	P & M Quik R	P & M Aviation Ltd
	G-CGOC	Sikorsky S-92A	HM Coastguard
	G-CGOD	Cameron N-77 balloon	G. P. Lane
	G-CGOE	Magni M-16C Tandem Trainer	Gyromania Ltd
	G-CGOG	Evektor EV-97A Eurostar	J. S. Holden
	G-CGOH	Cameron C-80 balloon	Spirit Balloons Ltd
	G-CGOI	Stewart S-51 Mustang (413926 E2-S)	K. E. Armstrong
	G-CGOJ	Jodel D.11	J. A. Macleod
	G-CGOK	Ace Magic Cyclone	V. Grayson
	G-CGOL	Jabiru J430	J. V. Sanders
	G-CGOM	Flight Design MC	P and M Aviation Ltd
	G-CGOO	Sorrell SNS-8 Hyperlight	W. F. Hayward
	G-CGOP	Sikorsky S-76C	Bristow Helicopters Ltd
	G-CGOR	Jodel D.18	R. D. Cook
	G-CGOS	PA-28-161 Warrior III	S. H. B. Smith
	G-CGOT	Rotorsport UK Calidus	P. Slater
	G-CGOU	Sikorsky S-76C	Bristow Helicopters Ltd
	G-CGOV	Raj Hamsa X'Air Falcon 582(2)	A. Hipkin
	G-CGOW	Cameron Z-77 balloon	J. F. Till
	G-CGOX	Raj Hamsa X'Air Hawk	Oscar Xray Group
	G-CGOZ	Cameron GB-1000 free gas balloon	Cameron Balloons Ltd
	G-CGPA	Ace Magic Cyclone	M. A. Sweet
	G-CGPB	Magni M-24C	D. Beevers
	G-CGPC	P & M Pegasus Quik	A. C. Barnes
	G-CGPD	Ultramagic S-90 balloon	S. J. Farrant
	G-CGPE	P & M Quik GT450	E. H. Gatehouse
	G-CGPF	Flylight Dragonfly	K. T. Vinning
	G-CGPG	Rotosport UK MTO Sport	H. A. Batchelor
	G-CGPH	Ultramagic S-50 balloon	The Packhouse Ltd
	G-CGPI	Eurocopter EC135 T2+	Bond Air Services Ltd (G-TAGG)
	G-CGPJ	Robin DR.400-140	W. H. Cole & P. Dass
	G-CGPK	Rotorsport UK MT-03	Ellis Flying Group (G-RIFS)
	G-CGPL	Sonex Sonex	P. C. Askew
	G-CGPN	SOCATA MS.880B Rallye Club	P. White
	G-CGPO	TL2000UK Sting Carbon	G. A. Squires
	G-CGPR	Czech Sport Aircraft Pipersport	J. T. Langford
	G-CGPS	EV-97 Eurostar SL	P. R. Jenson & R. A. Morris
	G-CGPT	Dassault Falcon 900EX	TAG Aviation (UK) Ltd
	G-CGPV	Cameron C-80 balloon	D. G. Such & M. Tomlin
	G-CGPW	Raj Hamsa X'Air Hawk	K. Worthington
	G-CGPX	Zenair CH.601XL Zodiac	A. James
	G-CGPY	Boeing A75L 300 Stearman	M. P. Dentith
	G-CGPZ	Rans S-4 Coyote	C. Saunders
	G-CGRA	Flight Design MC	P & M Aviation Ltd
	G-CGRB	Flight Design CTLS	I. R. Jones
	G-CGRC	P & M Quik R	R. J. Cook
	G-CGRD	Cirrus SR22	Craigard Property Trading Ltd

Reg.	Type	Owner or Operator	Notes
G-CGRE	Cessna F.172H	Parachuting Aircraft Ltd	
G-CGRF	Lindstrand LBL-140A balloon	Lindstrand Hot Air Balloons Ltd	
G-CGRJ	Carnet Paramotor	M. Carnet	
G-CGRL	Robinson R44	A. Williamson	
G-CGRM	VS.329 Spitfire Mk.IIA	J. C. Radford	
G-CGRN	Pazmany PL-4A	G. Hudson	
G-CGRO	Robin DR.400/140B	Exeter Aviation Ltd	
G-CGRP	Pitts P12	R. F. Warner	
G-CGRR	P & M Quik	A. W. Buchan	
G-CGRS	P & M Quik	J. Crosby	
G-CGRU	Sikorsky S-76C	Bristow Helicopters Ltd	
G-CGRV	DG Flugzeugbau DG-1000M	BR Aviation Ltd	
G-CGRW	P & M Quik	W. B. Russell	
G-CGRX	Cessna F.172N	Iscavia Ltd	
G-CGRY	Magni M-24C	K. Herbert	
G-CGRZ	Magni M-24C	J. M. Foster	
G-CGSA	Flylight Dragonfly	W. Lofts	
G-CGSB	Cessna 525A Citationjet CJ2	Sol Aviation Companhia de Aviaco Lda/Portugal	
G-CGSC	Quad City Challenger II	L. Gregory	
G-CGSD	Magni M-16C	The Gyrocopter Company UK Ltd	
G-CGSE	Embraer EMB-135BJ Legacy 650	GE Capital Corporation (Leasing) Ltd	
G-CGSG	Cessna 421C	J. R. Shannon	
G-CGSH	Evektor EV-97 TeamEurostar UK	S. Hoyle	
G-CGSI	Zenair CH.601HDS Zodiac	E. McHugh	
G-CGSJ	Bombardier BD700-1A10 Global Express	TAG Aviation (UK) Ltd	
G-CGSO	P & M Quik GT450	Light Vending Ltd	
G-CGSP	Cessna 152	C. M. de CamposCosta Cabral	
G-CGST	Boeing 737-33A	Aergo Leasing 112 Ltd	
G-CGSU	Cassutt Racer IIIM	D. J. Howell	
G-CGSW	Flylight Motorfloater	M. P. Wimsey	
G-CGSX	Aeroprakt A22-L Foxbat	P. J. Trimble	
G-CGSZ	Schempp-Hirth Ventus 2CM	D. B. Smith	
G-CGTA	Taylorcraft BC-12-65	D. P. Busby	
G-CGTB	Taylorcraft BC-12D	D. P. & D. S. Busby	
G-CGTC	BN-2T-4S Islander	Britten-Norman Aircraft Ltd	
G-CGTD	EV-97 TeamEurostar UK	R. J. Butler	
G-CGTE	Cherry BX-2	D.Roberts	
G-CGTF	AutoGyro MT-03	N. Creveul	
G-CGTG	Skyranger 912S(1)	C. Trollope	
G-CGTK	Magni M-24C	S. Brogden	
G-CGTL	Alpi Pioneer 300 Hawk	M. S. Ashby	
G-CGTM	Cessna 172S	Skytrek Air Services	
G-CGTR	Best Off Sky Ranger Nynja 912S(1)	T. J. Newton	
G-CGTS	Cameron A-140 balloon	A. A. Brown	
G-CGTT	EV-97 Eurostar SL	D. L. Walker	
G-CGTU	P & M Quik GT450	I. G. R. Christie	
G-CGTV	MXP-740 Savannah VG Jabiru(1)	B. L. Cook & P. Etherington	
G-CGTW	Flylight MotorFloater	S. J. Varden	
G-CGTX	CASA 1-131E Jungmann Srs 2000	G. Hunter & T. A. S. Rayner	
G-CGTY	Cameron Z-250 balloon	The Cotswold Balloon Co.Ltd	
G-CGTZ	Reality Escapade Kid	E. O. Otun	
G-CGUD	Lindstrand LBL-77A balloon	I. J. Sharpe	
G-CGUE	Aroprakt A-22-L Foxbat	A. T. Hayward	
G-CGUG	P & M Quik R	J. D. Lawrance	
G-CGUI	Clutton FRED Srs.II	I. Pearson	
G-CGUK	VS.300 Spitfire 1A	Peter Monk Ltd	
G-CGUL	Gulfstream V-SP	Gama Aviation Ltd	
G-CGUN	Alpha R2160	Quo Vadis UK Ltd	
G-CGUO	DH.83C Fox Moth	R. I. Souch	
G-CGUP	P & M Quik GT450	D. J. Allen	
G-CGUR	P & M QuikR	S. D. Couch	
G-CGUS	Embraer ERJ-145MP	ECC Leasing Co.Ltd	
G-CGUT	Balloon Works Firefly 9B-15	J. N. Uhrmann	
G-CGUU	Sky Ranger Nynja 912S(1)	J. A. Hunt	
G-CGUV	Balloon Works Firefly 9B-15	J. N. Uhrmann	
G-CGUW	Tecnam P2002-EA Sierra	D. J. Burton	
G-CGUX	Sikorsky S-92A	Bristow Helicopters Ltd	
G-CGUY	Rotorsport UK Calidus	R. F. Harrison	
G-CGUZ	Cessna 525A CitationJet CJ2	Gama Aviation Ltd	
G-CGVA	Aeroprakt A-22-L Foxbat	T. R. C. Griffin	
G-CGVC	PA-28-181 Archer III	Western Air (Thruxton) Ltd	
G-CGVD	Van's RV-12	RV12 Flying Group	

Notes	Reg.	Type	Owner or Operator
	G-CGVE	Raj Hamsa X'Air Hawk	P. Millership
	G-CGVF	Magni M-24C	J. C. Collingwood
	G-CGVG	Flight Design CTSW	J. T. James
	G-CGVH	Flylight Motorfloater	P. F. Mayes
	G-CGVI	Tanarg/Bionix 15 912S(1)	Flylight Airsports Ltd
	G-CGVJ	Europa XS	D. Glowa
	G-CGVK	Autogyro UK Calidus	B & H Mouldings Ltd
	G-CGVM	Lindstrand LBL-35A Cloudhopper balloon	Airship and Balloon Co.Ltd
	G-CGVN	Lindstrand LBL-90A balloon	Lindstrand Hot Air Balloons Ltd
	G-CGVO	Alpi Pioneer 400	F. A. Cavaciuti
	G-CGVP	EV-97 Eurstar	G. R. Pritchard
	G-CGVR	Flight Design CTLS	P & M Aviation Ltd
	G-CGVS	Raj Hamsa X'Air Hawk	J. Anderson
	G-CGVT	EV-97 TeamEurostar UK	Mainair Microlight School Ltd
	G-CGVU	Avro RJ85	Trident Turboprop (Dublin) Ltd
	G-CGVV	Cameron Z-90 Balloon	Cameron Balloons Ltd
	G-CGVW	Sikorsky S-76C-2	Bristow Helicopters (International) Ltd
	G-CGVX	Europa	M. P. Sambrook
	G-CGVY	Cameron Z-77 balloon	M. P. Hill
	G-CGVZ	Zenair CH.601XL Zodiac	K. A. Dilks
	G-CGWA	Ikarus C42 FB80 Bravo	M. A. Bull
	G-CGWB	Agusta AW139	CHC Scotia Ltd/HM Coastguard
	G-CGWC	Ultramagic H-31 balloon	G. Everett
	G-CGWD	Robinson R-44	J. M. Henderson
	G-CGWE	EV-97A Eurostar	W. S. Long
	G-CGWF	Van's RV-7	M. S. Hill
	G-CGWG	Van's RV-7	G. Waters
	G-CGWH	CZAW Sportcruiser	P. J. F. Spedding
	G-CGWI	Supermarine Aircraft Spitfire Mk.26	I. J. Hutchison
	G-CGWK	Ikarus C42 FB80	GS Aviation (Europe) Ltd
	G-CGWL	Sky Ranger Nynja 912S(1)	Exodus Airsports Ltd
	G-CGWM	Dragonfly Lite	P. A. Gardner
	G-CGWN	Dragonfly Lite	P. M. Finlay
	G-CGWO	Tecnam P2002-JF Sierra	Shropshire Aero Club Ltd
	G-CGWP	Aeroprakt A22-L Foxbat	P. K. Goff
	G-CGWR	Nord NC.856A Norvigie	R. B. McLain
	G-CGWS	Raj Hamsa X'Air Hawk	T. Collins
	G-CGWT	Best Off Sky Ranger Swift 912(1)	N. A. & P. A. Allwood
	G-CGWU	UltraMagic S-90 balloon	K. Graham
	G-CGWV	Embraer EMB-145MP	Eastern Airways
	G-CGWW	Cameron A-120 balloon	Bristol Airways Ltd (G-VIKY)
	G-CGWX	Cameron C-90 balloon	J. D. A. Shields
	G-CGWY	Avro RJ70	Ansett Aircraft Spares & Services Ltd
	G-CGWZ	P & M QuikR	N. D. Leak
	G-CGXB	Glasair Super IIS RG	P. J. Brion
	G-CGXC	Flylight Dragonfly	Flylight Airsports Ltd
	G-CGXE	P & M Quik GT450	A, G. Hughes
	G-CGXF	North Wing Stratus/Skycycle	G. W. Cameron
	G-CGXG	Yakovlev Yak-3M	Chameleon Technologies Ltd
	G-CGXI	Ikarus C42 FB80	G. V. Aggett
	G-CGXJ	Schweizer 269C-1	Milford Aviation
	G-CGXK	Eurocopter EC.135T1	Bond Air Services Ltd
	G-CGXL	Robin DR.400/180	J. L. Jones (G-GLKE)
	G-CGXN	American Legend Cub	Beaver (UK) Ltd
	G-CGXO	Lindstrand LBL-105A balloon	Aerosaurus Balloons Ltd
	G-CGXP	Grob G.109B	Gransden Grob XP
	G-CGXR	Van's RV-9A	Solway Flyers 2010 Ltd
	G-CGXS	Avro RJ-85	Trident Aviation Leasing Services (Jersey) Ltd (G-JAYV)
	G-CGXT	Kowacs Midgie	J. P. Kovacs
	G-CGXV	P & M Quik R	D. W. Allen
	G-CGXW	Grob G.109B	I. B. Kennedy
	G-CGXX	ICP MXP-740 Savannah HKS(1)	P. Hayward
	G-CGXY	Flylight Dragonfly	A. I. Lea
	G-CGXZ	AutoGyro MTO Sport	G-CGXZ Flying Group
	G-CGYA	Stoddard-Hamilton Glasair III	Aerocars Ltd
	G-CGYB	EV-97 TeamEurostar UK	J. Waite
	G-CGYC	Aeropro Eurofox 912(S)	D. C. Fairbrass
	G-CGYD	Fairey Firefly TT.1	Propshop Ltd
	G-CGYE	Schroeder Fire Balloons G balloon	M. Cutraro
	G-CGYF	Gloster Gamecock II	Retro Track & Air (UK) Ltd
	G-CGYG	Aeropro Eurofox 912(S)	R. M. Cornwell

Reg.	Type	Owner or Operator	Notes
G-CGYH	Magni M-24C	A. Parker	
G-CGYI	Van's RV-12	R. A. Smith	
G-CGYJ	VS.361 Spitfire HF.IX	K. M. Perkins	
G-CGYK	Embraer EMB-145MP	ECC Leasing Co.Ltd	
G-CGYM	AT-16 Harvard IIB	Reflight Airworks Ltd	
G-CGYN	DH.82A Tiger Moth	Reflight Airworks Ltd	
G-CGYO	Van's RV-6A	D. G. Lewendon	
G-CGYP	Best Off Sky Ranger 912(2)	M. J. Reeve	
G-CGYR	Avro RJ-85	Trident Turboprop (Dublin) Ltd	
G-CGYS	Avro RJ-85	Trident Aviation Leasing Services (Jersey) Ltd	
G-CGYT	Flylight Dragonfly	G-CGYT Syndicate	
G-CGYY	MXP-740 Savannah VG Jabiru(1)	Carlisle Skyrangers	
G-CGYZ	P & M Quik GT450	Fly Hire Ltd	
G-CGZA	Kolb Twinstar Mk.3 Xtra	A. Wilson	
G-CGZB	Avro RJ-85	Trident Aviation Leasing Services (Jersey) Ltd	
G-CGZD	Eurocopter EC135 P2	Bond Air Services Ltd	
G-CGZE	Rotorsport UK MTO Sport	The Gyrocopter Company UK Ltd	
G-CGZF	EV-97 TeamEurostar UK	24/7 Rescue and Recovery (Membury) Ltd	
G-CGZG	AutoGyro MTO Sport	D. C. Dewey	
G-CGZI	SOCATA TB-21 Trinidad TC	K. B. Hallam	
G-CGZJ	ITV Dakota XL	C. J. Lines	
G-CGZL	Flylight Motor Floater Fox 16T	Flylight Airsports Ltd	
G-CGZM	AutoGyro MTO Sport	A. K. & J. A. Hughes	
G-CGZN	Dudek Synthesis 31/Nirvana Carbon	M. J. Parker	
G-CGZO	Avro RJ-85	Trident Aviation Leasing Services (Jersey) Ltd	
G-CGZP	Curtiss P-40F Kittyhawk (41-19841 X-17)	The Fighter Collection	
G-CGZS	Sikorsky S-92A	Bristow Helicopters Ltd	
G-CGZT	Aeroprakt A22-L Foxbat	R. Stalker	
G-CGZV	Europa XS	R. W. Collings	
G-CGZY	EV-97 TeamEurostar UK	Exodus Airsports Ltd	
G-CGZZ	Kubicek BB22E balloon	A. M. Holly	
G-CHAB	Schleicher Ka 6CR	W. J. Hunter	
G-CHAC	PZL-Bielsko SZD-50-3 Puchacz	Peterborough and Spalding Gliding Club Ltd	
G-CHAD	Aeroprakt A.22 Foxbat	DJB Foxbat	
G-CHAE	Glasflugel H205 Club Libelle	J. C. Cavill & R. S. Hanslip	
G-CHAF	PZL-Bielsko SZD-50-3 Puchacz	Seahawk Gliding Club	
G-CHAH	Shaw Europa	T. Higgins	
G-CHAI	Bombardier CL.601-3R	Hangar 8 Management Ltd (G-FBFI)	
G-CHAM	Cameron 90 Pot SS balloon	Pendle Balloon Company	
G-CHAN	Robinson R22 Beta	Artall Air LLP	
G-CHAO	Rolladen-Schneider LS6-b	A. R. J. Hughes	
G-CHAP	Robinson R44	Brierley Lifting Tackle Co Ltd	
G-CHAR	Grob G.109B	The Royal Air Force Gliding and Soaring Association	
G-CHAS	PA-28-181 Archer II	G-CHAS Flying Group	
G-CHAW	Replica Fokker EIII	S. W. C. Duckworth	
G-CHAX	Schempp-Hirth Standard Cirrus	C. Keating & R. Jarvis	
G-CHAY	Rolladen-Schneider LS7	N. J. Leaton	
G-CHBA	Rolladen-Schneider LS7	LS7 729 Group	
G-CHBB	Schleicher ASW-24	London Gliding Club Propietary Ltd	
G-CHBC	Rolladen-Schneider LS6-c	A. Crowden	
G-CHBD	Glaser-Dirks DG-200	Bravo Delta Group	
G-CHBE	Glaser-Dirks DG-300 Club Elan	DG 356 Group	
G-CHBF	Schempp-Hirth Nimbus 2C	J. A. Clark	
G-CHBG	Schleicher ASW-24	Imperial College of Science, Technology and Medicine	
G-CHBH	Grob G.103C Twin III Acro	Imperial College of Science, Technology and Medicine	
G-CHBK	Grob G.103 Twin Astir II	S. Naylor	
G-CHBL	Grob G.102 Astir CS77	C. Morris	
G-CHBM	Grob G.102 Astir CS77	P. W. Brown	
G-CHBN	Westland Gazelle AH Mk.1	MW Helicopters Ltd	
G-CHBO	Schleicher Ka 6CR	M. I. Perrier & H. Southworth	
G-CHBP	Glaser-Dirks DG-500	A. Taverna	
G-CHBR	Westland Gazelle AH Mk.1	MW Helicopters Ltd	
G-CHBS	PZL-Bielsko SZD-41A Jantar Standard 1	P. J. Chaisty & D. Hendry	
G-CHBT	Grob G.102 Astir CS Jeans	Astir Syndicate	
G-CHBU	Centrair ASW-20F	M. Staljan, S. Brogger & C. Behrendt	
G-CHBV	Schempp-Hirth Nimbus 2B	G. J. Evison, J. Lynas & R. Strarup	
G-CHBW	Jurca Spitfire	T. A. Major	
G-CHBX	Lindstrand LBL-77A balloon	Lindstrand Hot Air Balloons Ltd	

Notes	Reg.	Type	Owner or Operator
	G-CHBZ	TL2000UK Sting Carbon	C. R. Ashley
	G-CHCF	AS.332L-2 Super Puma	CHC Scotia Ltd
	G-CHCG	AS.332L-2 Super Puma	CHC Scotia Ltd
	G-CHCH	AS.332L-2 Super Puma	CHC Scotia Ltd
	G-CHCI	AS.332L-2 Super Puma	CHC Scotia Ltd
	G-CHCJ	EC.225LP Super Puma	CHC Scotia Ltd
	G-CHCK	Sikorsky S-92A	CHC Scotia Ltd
	G-CHCL	EC.225LP Super Puma	CHC Scotia Ltd
	G-CHCM	EC.225LP Super Puma	CHC Scotia Ltd
	G-CHCN	EC.225LP Super Puma	CHC Scotia Ltd
	G-CHCO	AS.365N2 Dauphin 2	CHC Scotia Ltd
	G-CHCP	Agusta AB.139	CHC Scotia Ltd
	G-CHCR	AS.365N2 Dauphin 2	British International Helicopter Services Ltd
	G-CHCS	Sikorsky S-92A	CHC Scotia Ltd
	G-CHCT	Agusta AB.139	CHC Scotia Ltd
	G-CHCU	AS.332L2 Super Puma II	CHC Scotia Ltd
	G-CHCX	EC.225LP Super Puma	CHC Scotia Ltd
	G-CHCZ	Sikorsky S-92A	CHC Scotia Ltd
	G-CHDA	Pilatus B4-PC11AF	F. P. & C. M. E. Bois
	G-CHDB	PZL-Bielsko SZD-51-1 Junior	Stratford on Avon Gliding Club Ltd
	G-CHDD	Centrair 101B Pegase 90	591 Glider Syndicate
	G-CHDE	Pilatus B4-PC11AF	A. A. Jenkins
	G-CHDF	Lindstrand LBL-450A balloon	Lindstrand Hot Air Balloons Ltd
	G-CHDJ	Schleicher ASW-20CL	G. E. G. Lambert & L. M. M. Sebreights
	G-CHDL	Schleicher ASW-20	137 Syndicate
	G-CHDM	P & M QuikR	A. Sheveleu
	G-CHDN	Schleicher K 8B	Upward Bound Trust
	G-CHDP	PZL-Bielsko SZD-50-3 Puchacz	Heron Gliding Club
	G-CHDR	DG-300 Elan	R. Robins
	G-CHDU	PZL-Bielsko SZD-51-1 Junior	Cambridge Gliding Club Ltd
	G-CHDV	Schleicher ASW-19B	ASW Aviation
	G-CHDX	Rolladen-Schneider LS7-WL	D. Holborn & R. T. Halliburton
	G-CHDY	Schleicher K 8B	V. Mallon
	G-CHEB	Shaw Europa	I. C. Smit & P. Whittingham
	G-CHEC	PZL-Bielsko SZD-55-1	D. Pye
	G-CHEE	Schempp-Hirth Discus b	A. Henderson
	G-CHEF	Glaser-Dirks DG-500 Elan Trainer	Yorkshire Gliding Club (Proprietary) Ltd
	G-CHEG	AB Sportine Aviacija LAK-12	Z. Kmita, R. Hannigan & S. Grant
	G-CHEH	Rolladen-Schneider LS7-WL	P. Candler
	G-CHEJ	Schleicher ASW-15B	A. F. F. Webb
	G-CHEK	PZL-Bielsko SZD-51-1	Cambridge Gliding Club Ltd
	G-CHEL	Colt 77B balloon	Chelsea Financial Services PLC
	G-CHEM	PA-34-200T Seneca II	London Executive Aviation Ltd
	G-CHEN	Schempp-Hirth Discus b	G-CHEN Group
	G-CHEO	Schleicher ASW-20	The Eleven Group
	G-CHEP	PZL-Bielsko SZD-50-3 Puchacz	Peterborough and Spalding Gliding Club Ltd
	G-CHER	PA-38-112 Tomahawk II	Carlisle Flight Training Ltd
	G-CHEW	Rolladen-Schneider LS6-c18	D. N. Tew
	G-CHEX	Aero Designs Pulsar	D. R. Piercey
	G-CHEY	PA-31T2 Cheyenne IIXL	Provident Partners Ltd
	G-CHFA	Schempp-Hirth Ventus b/16.6	A. K. Lincoln
	G-CHFB	Schleicher Ka-6CR	P. J. Galloway
	G-CHFF	Schempp-Hirth Standard Cirrus	Foxtrot 2 Group
	G-CHFH	PZL-Bielsko SZD-50-3	Trent Valley Aerotowing Club Ltd
	G-CHFV	Schempp-Hirth Ventus B/16.6	A. Cliffe & B. Pearson
	G-CHFW	Schleicher K 8B	Oxford Gliding Co.Ltd
	G-CHFX	Schempp-Hirth Nimbus 4T	S. G. Jones
	G-CHGB	Grob G.102 Astir CS	G. Jaques, P. Hollamby & G. Clark
	G-CHGF	Schleicher ASW-15B	HGF Flying Group
	G-CHGG	Schempp-Hirth Standard Cirrus	S. Shah
	G-CHGK	Schempp-Hirth Discus bT	HGK Syndicate
	G-CHGL	Bell 206B JetRanger II	Vantage Aviation Ltd (G-BPNG/G-ORTC)
	G-CHGO	AB Sportine Aviacija LAK-12	P. Raymond & J-M Peuffier
	G-CHGP	Rolladen-Schneider LS6-c	D. R. Elrington
	G-CHGR	AB Sportline Aviacija LAK-12	M. R. Garwood
	G-CHGS	Schempp-Hirth Discus b	G-CHGS Syndicate
	G-CHGT	FFA Diamant 16.5	T. E. Lynch
	G-CHGV	Glaser-Dirks DG500/22 Elan	Hotel Golf Victor Syndicate
	G-CHGW	Centrair ASW-20F	S. C. Moss
	G-CHGX	AB Sportine LAK-12 Lietuva	M. Jenks
	G-CHGZ	Schempp-Hirth Discus bT	G-CHGZ Syndicate
	G-CHHH	Rolladen-Schneider LS6-c	P. H. Rackham

Reg.	Type	Owner or Operator
G-CHHI	Van's RV-7	M. G. Jefferies
G-CHHK	Schleicher ASW-19B	M. Walker
G-CHHM	AB Sportline LAK-12 Lietuva	D. Martin
G-CHHN	Schempp-Hirth Ventus b/16.6	N. A. C. Norman & R. K. Forrest
G-CHHO	Schempp-Hirth Discus bT	97Z Syndicate
G-CHHP	Schempp-Hirth Discus b	F. R. Knowles
G-CHHR	PZL-Bielsko SZD-55-1 Promyk	R. T. & G. Starling
G-CHHS	Schleicher ASW-20	P.J. Rocks & D. Britt
G-CHHT	Rolladen-Schneider LS6-c	F. Roles
G-CHHU	Rolladen-Schneider LS6-c	J. M. Hall & P. Shuttleworth
G-CHHW	AB Sportine LAK-12	A. J. Dibdin
G-CHHX	Wassmer WA.26P Squale	M. H. Gagg
G-CHIK	Cessna F.152	Stapleford Flying Club Ltd (G-BHAZ)
G-CHIP	PA-28-181 Archer II	J. A. Divis
G-CHIS	Robinson R22 Beta	Staffordshire Helicopters Training Ltd
G-CHIX	Robin DR.400/500	P. A. & R. Stephens
G-CHJC	Rolladen-Schneider LS6-c	F. J. Davies
G-CHJD	Schleicher Ka 6E	A. G. Linfield
G-CHJE	Schleicher K 8B	J. J. Sconce
G-CHJF	Rolladen-Schneider LS6-c	J. L. Bridge
G-CHJH	Schempp-Hirth Discus bT	Hotel Juliet Hotel Group
G-CHJL	Schempp-Hirth Discus bT	Discus JL Group
G-CHJN	Schempp-Hirth Standard Cirrus	P. M. Hardingham
G-CHJP	Schleicher Ka-6CR	D. M. Cornelius
G-CHJR	Glasflugel H201B Standard Libelle	B. O. Marcham & B. Magnani
G-CHJT	Centrair ASW-20F	R. J. Pirie & M. S. R. Broadway
G-CHJV	Grob G.102 Astir CS	Cotswold Gliding Club
G-CHJX	Rolladen-Schneider LS6-c	M. R. Haynes & P. Robinson
G-CHJY	Schempp-Hirth Standard Cirrus	Cirrus Group
G-CHKA	Orlican Discus CS	R. W. & M. P. Weaver
G-CHKB	Grob G.102 Astir CS77	G-CHKB Group
G-CHKC	Schempp-Hirth Standard Cirrus	A. Taylor
G-CHKD	Schempp-Hirth Standard Cirrus	R. Jeffcoate
G-CHKK	Schleicher K8B	R. E. Johnston
G-CHKL	Cameron 120 Kookaburra SS balloon	Eagle Ltd/Australia
G-CHKM	Grob G.102 Astir CS Jeans	Essex and Suffolk Gliding Club Ltd
G-CHKN	Kiss 400-582(1)	P. J. Higgins
G-CHKR	Jastreb Standard Cirrus G/81	N. A. White
G-CHKS	Jastreb Standard Cirrus G/81	G. G. Butler
G-CHKU	Schempp-Hirth Standard Cirrus	T. J. Wheeler & T. M. O'Sullivan
G-CHKV	Scheibe Zugvogel IIIA	Dartmoor Gliding Society Ltd
G-CHKX	Rolladen-Schneider LS4-B	J. McMackin
G-CHKY	Schempp-Hirth Discus b	C. V. Hill & O. J. Anderson
G-CHKZ	CARMAM JP 15-36AR Aiglon	T. A. & A. J. Hollings
G-CHLB	Rolladen-Schneider LS4-b	E. G. Leach & K. F. Rogers
G-CHLC	Pilatus B4-PC11AF	E. Lockhart
G-CHLH	Schleicher K 8B	Shenington Gliding Club
G-CHLK	Glasflugel H.301 Libelle	G. L. J. Barrett
G-CHLL	Lindstrand LBL-90A balloon	P. J. Hollingsworth
G-CHLM	Schleicher ASW-19B	R. A. Colbeck
G-CHLN	Schempp-Hirth Discus CS	Portsmouth Naval Gliding Centre
G-CHLO	Grob G.109B	F. Waller
G-CHLP	Schleicher ASK-21	Southdown Gliding Club Ltd
G-CHLS	Schempp-Hirth Discus b	R. A. Lennard
G-CHLV	Schleicher ASW-19B	P. J. Belcher & R. I. Brickwood
G-CHLX	Schleicher ASH-25	A. di Stasi
G-CHLY	Schempp-Hirth Discus CS	S. J. Pearce
G-CHMA	PZL-Bielsko SZD-51-1 Junior	The Welland Gliding Club Ltd
G-CHMB	Glaser-Dirks DG-300 Elan	A. D. & P. Langlands
G-CHMG	ICA IS-28B2	A. Sutton, R. Maksymowicz & A. J. Palfreyman
G-CHMH	Schleicher K8B	Shenington Gliding Club
G-CHMK	Rolladen-Schneider LS6-18W	A. S. Decloux
G-CHML	Schempp-Hirth Discus CS	I. D. Bateman
G-CHMM	Glasflugel 304B	Delta 19 Group
G-CHMO	Orlican Discus CS	S. Barter
G-CHMP	Bellanca 7ACA Champ	I. J. Langley
G-CHMS	Glaser-Dirks DG-100	D. A. Fall
G-CHMT	Glasflugel Mosquito B	J. Taberham
G-CHMU	CARMAM JP-15/36AR Aiglon	HMU Group
G-CHMV	Schleicher ASK-13	The Windrushers Gliding Club Ltd
G-CHMX	Rolladen-Schneider LS4-a	K. P. Nakhla & L Couval
G-CHMY	Schempp-Hirth Standard Cirrus	HMY Syndicate

Notes	Reg.	Type	Owner or Operator
	G-CHMZ	Fedorov ME7 Mechta	R. Andrews
	G-CHNA	Glaser-Dirks DG-500/20 Elan	G-CHNA Group
	G-CHNC	Schleicher ASK-19B	T. J. Highton
	G-CHNE	Schempp-Hirth Nimbus 2B	P. J. Uden
	G-CHNF	Schempp-Hirth Duo Discus	Booker Gliding Club Ltd
	G-CHNH	Schempp-Hirth Nimbus 2C	C. J. Pollard
	G-CHNK	PZL-Bielsko SZD-51-1 Junior	Booker Gliding Club Ltd
	G-CHNM	Standard Cirrus G/81	The 55 Syndicate
	G-CHNT	Schleicher ASW-15	S. J. Lintott & I. Dawkins
	G-CHNU	Schempp-Hirth Nimbus 4DT	D. E. Findon
	G-CHNV	Rolladen-Schneider LS4-b	S. K. Armstrong & P. H. Dixon
	G-CHNW	Schempp-Hirth Duo Discus	G-CHNW Group
	G-CHNY	Centrair 101A Pegase	M. O. Breen
	G-CHNZ	Centrair 101A Pegase	R. H. Partington
	G-CHOD	Schleicher ASW-20	S. E. Archer-Jones
	G-CHOF	CARMAM M100S	M. A. Farrelly
	G-CHOG	AB Sportine LAK-12	J. M. Pursey
	G-CHOP	Westland-Bell 47G-3B1	Leamington Hobby Centre Ltd
	G-CHOR	Schempp-Hirth Discus b	The Windrushers Gliding Club Ltd
	G-CHOT	Grob G.102 Astir CS77	Southdown Gliding Club Ltd
	G-CHOV	PZL-Bielsko SZD-51-1 Junior	Coventry Gliding Club Ltd
	G-CHOX	Shaw Europa XS	Chocs Away Ltd
	G-CHOY	Schempp-Hirth Mini Nimbus C	A. H. Sparrow
	G-CHOZ	Rolladen-Schneider LS6-18W	R. E. Scott
	G-CHPA	Robinson R22 Beta	Rivermead Aviation Ltd/Switzerland
	G-CHPC	Schleicher ASW-20 CL	B. L. Liddard & P. J. Williams
	G-CHPD	Rolladen-Schneider LS6-c18	C. J. & K. A. Teagle
	G-CHPE	Schleicher ASK-13	Dumfries and District Gliding Club
	G-CHPH	Schempp-Hirth Discus CS	I. N & S. G. Hunt
	G-CHPI	DHC.1 Chipmunk Mk.22	K. F. Tomsett
	G-CHPK	Van's RV-8	Viscount A. C. Andover (G-JILS)
	G-CHPL	Rolladen-Schneider LS4-b	Southdown Gliding Club Ltd
	G-CHPO	Schleicher Ka-6CR	N. Robinson
	G-CHPR	Robinson R22 Beta	C. Gozzi
	G-CHPT	Fedorov ME7 Mechta	Midland Gliding Club Ltd
	G-CHPV	Schleicher ASK-21	Scottish Gliding Union Ltd
	G-CHPW	Schleicher ASK-21	Scottish Gliding Union Ltd
	G-CHPX	Schempp-Hirth Discus CS	G-CHPX Group
	G-CHPY	DHC.1 Chipmunk 22 (WB652:V)	Devonair Executive Business Travel Ltd
	G-CHRC	Glaser-Dirks DG500/20 Elan	DG500-390 Syndicate
	G-CHRG	PZL-Bielsko SZD-51-1 Junior	Scottish Gliding Union Ltd
	G-CHRH	Schempp-Hirth Discus 2cT	C. Hyett
	G-CHRJ	Schleicher K 8B	Shenington Gliding Club
	G-CHRK	Centrair 101 Pegase	P. T. Bushill & M. Morris
	G-CHRL	Schempp-Hirth Standard Cirrus	D. J. Allen
	G-CHRN	Schleicher ASK-18	Stratford on Avon Gliding Club Ltd
	G-CHRS	Orlican Discus CS	M. Santopinto
	G-CHRW	Schempp-Hirth Duo Discus	802 Syndicate
	G-CHRX	Schempp-Hirth Discus a	N. Worrell & G. S. Bird
	G-CHSA	Rolladen-Schneider LS6-18W	D. A. Benton
	G-CHSB	Glaser-Dirks DG-303 Elan	C. M. Hawkes
	G-CHSD	Schempp-Hirth Discus b	G-CHSD Group
	G-CHSE	Grob G.102 Astir CS77	G. J. Armes
	G-CHSG	Scheibe SF27A	HSG Syndicate
	G-CHSK	Schleicher ASW-20CL	A. J. Watson & C. C. Ramshorn
	G-CHSM	Schleicher ASK-13	Stratford on Avon Gliding Club Ltd
	G-CHSN	Schleicher Ka-6CR	Needwood Forest Gliding Club Ltd
	G-CHSO	Schempp-Hirth Discus b	Midland Gliding Club Ltd
	G-CHSU	Eurocopter EC 135T1	Eurocopter UK Ltd
	G-CHSX	Scheibe SF-27A	Essex & Suffolk Gliding Club Ltd
	G-CHSZ	Rolladen-Schneider LS8-a	I. G. Garden
	G-CHTA	AA-5A Cheetah	R. C. G. Lywood (G-BFRC)
	G-CHTB	Schempp-Hirth Janus	Janus G-CHTB Syndicate
	G-CHTC	Schleicher ASW-15B	G-CHTC Group
	G-CHTD	Grob G.102 Astir CS	S. Waldie
	G-CHTE	Grob G.102 Astir CS77	HTE Group
	G-CHTF	AB Sportline LAK-12	M. Tolson
	G-CHTM	Rolladen-Schneider LS8-18	M. J. Chapman
	G-CHTR	Grob G.102 Astir CS	I. P. & D. M. Wright
	G-CHTS	Rolladen-Schneider LS8-18	P. T. Cunnison
	G-CHTN	Schleicher ASW-22	R. C. Hodge
	G-CHTU	Schempp-Hirth Cirrus	Open Cirrus Group

Reg.	Type	Owner or Operator	Notes
G-CHTV	Schleicher ASK-21	Cambridge Gliding Club Ltd	
G-CHTY	LET L-13 Blanik	Vectis Gliding Club Ltd	
G-CHUA	Schleicher ASW-19B	G. D. Vaughan	
G-CHUD	Schleicher ASK-13	London Gliding Club Propietary Ltd	
G-CHUE	Schleicher ASW-27	M. J. Smith	
G-CHUF	Schleicher ASK-13	The Welland Gliding Club Ltd	
G-CHUG	Shaw Europa	C. M. Washington	
G-CHUH	Schempp-Hirth Janus	Janus D31 Syndicate	
G-CHUJ	Centrair ASW-20F	P. D. Ruskin	
G-CHUK	Cameron O-77 balloon	R. P. E. Phillips	
G-CHUL	Schempp-Hirth Cirrus	I. Ashton	
G-CHUN	Grob G.102 Astir CS Jeans	Staffordshire Gliding Club Ltd	
G-CHUO	Federov ME7 Mechta	J. D. A. Cooper & W. H. Ollis	
G-CHUR	Schempp-Hirth Cirrus	M. Rossiter & A. G. Thomas	
G-CHUS	Scheibe SF27A Zugvogel V	SF27 HUS Syndicate	
G-CHUT	Centrair ASW-20F	S. R. Phelps	
G-CHUU	Schleicher ASK-13	Upward Bound Trust	
G-CHUY	Schempp-Hirth Ventus cT	M. A. & M. N. Challans	
G-CHUZ	Schempp-Hirth Discus bT	P. A. Gelsthorpe	
G-CHVF	Rolladen-Schneider LS8-18	J. Haigh & R. B. Coote	
G-CHVG	Schleicher ASK-21	Rattlesden Gliding Club Ltd	
G-CHVH	Pilatus B4-PC11AF	London Gliding Club Proprietary Ltd	
G-CHVK	Grob G.102 Astir CS	P. G. Goulding	
G-CHVL	Rolladen-Schneider LS8-18	Cumulus Gliding Syndicate	
G-CHVM	Glaser-Dirks DG-300	Glider Syndicate 303	
G-CHVN	Bombardier CL600-2B16 Challenger	Hangar 8 AOC Ltd	
G-CHVO	Schleicher ASK-13	R. Brown	
G-CHVP	Schleicher ASW-20	P. J. Williams	
G-CHVR	Schempp-Hirth Discus b	Yorkshire Gliding Club (Proprietary) Ltd	
G-CHVT	Schempp-Hirth Ventus 2b	Victor Tango Group	
G-CHVU	Rolladen-Schneider LS8-a	European Soaring Club	
G-CHVV	Rolladen-Schneider LS4-b	A. J. Bardgett	
G-CHUW	Rolladen-Schneider LS8-18	S8 Group	
G-CHVX	Centrair ASW-20F	Banbury Gliding Club Ltd	
G-CHVW	Scleicher ASK-13	Rattlesden Gliding Club Ltd	
G-CHVZ	Schempp-Hirth Standard Cirrus	ABC Soaring	
G-CHWA	Schempp-Hirth Ventus 2c	C. Garton	
G-CHWB	Schempp-Hirth Duo Discus	Lasham Gliding Society Ltd	
G-CHWC	Glasflugel Standard Libelle 201B	Whiskey Charlie Group	
G-CHWD	Schempp-Hirth Standard Cirrus	M. R. Hoskins	
G-CHWF	Jastreb Standard Cirrus G/81	M. D. Langford & M. C. Mann	
G-CHWG	Glasflugel Standard Libelle 201B	M. Kalweit	
G-CHWH	Schempp-Hirth Ventus cT	H. R. Browning	
G-CHWL	Rolladen-Schneider LS8-a	W. M. Coffee	
G-CHWP	Glaser-Dirks DG-100G Elan	K. H. Bates	
G-CHWS	Rolladen-Schneider LS8-18	G. E. & H. B. Chalmers	
G-CHWT	Schleicher K 8B	Shenington Gliding Club	
G-CHWW	Grob G.103A Twin II Acro	Crown Service Gliding Club	
G-CHWY	Schempp-Hirth Standard Cirrus	D. D. Copeland	
G-CHXA	Scheibe Zugvogel IIIB	G-CHXA Group	
G-CHXB	Grob G.102 Astir CS77	T. S. Miller	
G-CHXD	Schleicher ASW-27	J. Quartermaine & M. Jerman	
G-CHXE	Schleicher ASW-19B	M. J. Hargreaves	
G-CHXH	Schempp-Hirth Discus b	Deesside Gliding Club (Aberdeenshire) Ltd	
G-CHXJ	Schleicher ASK-13	Cotswold Gliding Club	
G-CHXM	Grob G.102 Astir CS	Bristol University Gliding Club	
G-CHXO	Schleicher ASH-25	The Eleven Group	
G-CHXP	Schleicher ASK-13	The Vale of the White Horse Gliding Centre Ltd	
G-CHXR	Schempp-Hirth Ventus cT	560 Group	
G-CHXT	Rolladen-Schneider LS-4a	H. Hingley	
G-CHXU	Schleicher ASW-19B	D. P. Binney	
G-CHXV	Schleicher ASK-13	Aquila Gliding Club Ltd	
G-CHXW	Rolladen-Schneider LS8-18	W. Aspland	
G-CHXX	Schempp-Hirth Standard Cirrus	A. Coatsworth & R. M. Wooten	
G-CHXZ	Rolladen-Schneider LS4	G-CHXZ Group	
G-CHYA	Rolladen-Schneider LS6c-18	Y. Melou	
G-CHYD	Schleicher ASW-24	E. S. Adlard	
G-CHYE	DG-505 Elan Orion	The Bristol Gliding Club Proprietary Ltd	
G-CHYF	Rolladen-Schneider LS8-18	R. E. Francis	
G-CHYH	Rolladen-Schneider LS3-17	B. Silke	
G-CHYJ	Schleicher ASK-21	Highland Gliding Club Ltd	
G-CHYK	Centrair ASW-20FL	Kilo Twenty Group	

Notes	Reg.	Type	Owner or Operator
	G-CHYP	PZL-Bielsko SZD-50-3 Puchacz	Rattlesden Gliding Club Ltd
	G-CHYR	Schleicher ASW-27	A. J. Manwaring & A. R. Hutchings
	G-CHYS	Schleicher ASK-21	Army Gliding Association
	G-CHYT	Schleicher ASK-21	Army Gliding Association
	G-CHYU	Schempp-Hirth Discus CS	Army Gliding Association
	G-CHYW	Schleicher K 8B	Lincolnshire Gliding Club Ltd
	G-CHYX	Schleicher K 8B	Oxford University Gliding Club
	G-CHYY	Schempp-Hirth Nimbus 3DT	G-CHYY Syndicate
	G-CHZB	PZL-Swidnik PW-5 Smyk	The Burn Gliding Club Ltd
	G-CHZD	Schleicher ASW-15B	C. P. Ellison & S. Barber
	G-CHZE	Schempp-Hirth Discus CS	HZE Glider Syndicate
	G-CHZG	Rolladen-Schneider LS8-18	M. J. & T. J. Webb
	G-CHZH	Schleicher Ka 6CR	M. E. de Torre
	G-CHZJ	Schempp-Hirth Standard Cirrus	P. Fletcher & R. H. D. Adams
	G-CHZM	Rolladen-Schneider LS4-a	J. M. Bevan
	G-CHZN	Robinson R22 Beta	Polar Helicopters Ltd (G-GHZM/G-FENI)
	G-CHZO	Schleicher ASW-27	A. A. Gilmore
	G-CHZR	Schleicher ASK-21	K21 HZR Group
	G-CHZU	Schempp-Hirth Standard Cirrus	N. S. Murning
	G-CHZV	Schempp-Hirth Standard Cirrus	S. M. Sheard
	G-CHZX	Schleicher K 8B	S. M. Chapman & S. Potter
	G-CHZY	Rolladen-Schneider LS4-a	N. P. Wedi
	G-CHZZ	Schleicher ASW-20L	LD Syndicate
	G-CIAO	I.I.I. Sky Arrow 1450-L	G. Arscott
	G-CIAS	BN-2B-21 Islander	Channel Island Air Search Ltd (G-BKJM)
	G-CIBO	Cessna 180K	CIBO Ops Ltd
	G-CIDD	Bellanca 7ECA Citabria	M. J. Medland
	G-CIEL	Cessna 560XL Citation Excel	Enerway Ltd
	G-CIGY	Westland-Bell 47G-3B1	M. L. Romeling (G-BGXP)
	G-CIRI	Cirrus SR20	Cirrus Flyers Group
	G-CIRU	Cirrus SR20	Cirrent BV/Netherlands
	G-CITJ	Cessna 525 CitationJet	Centreline Air Charter Ltd
	G-CITY	PA-31-350 Navajo Chieftain	Blue Sky Investments Ltd
	G-CIVA	Boeing 747-436	British Airways
	G-CIVB	Boeing 747-436	British Airways
	G-CIVC	Boeing 747-436	British Airways
	G-CIVD	Boeing 747-436	British Airways
	G-CIVE	Boeing 747-436	British Airways
	G-CIVF	Boeing 747-436	British Airways
	G-CIVG	Boeing 747-436	British Airways
	G-CIVH	Boeing 747-436	British Airways
	G-CIVI	Boeing 747-436	British Airways
	G-CIVJ	Boeing 747-436	British Airways
	G-CIVK	Boeing 747-436	British Airways
	G-CIVL	Boeing 747-436	British Airways
	G-CIVM	Boeing 747-436	British Airways
	G-CIVN	Boeing 747-436	British Airways
	G-CIVO	Boeing 747-436	British Airways
	G-CIVP	Boeing 747-436	British Airways
	G-CIVR	Boeing 747-436	British Airways
	G-CIVS	Boeing 747-436	British Airways
	G-CIVT	Boeing 747-436	British Airways
	G-CIVU	Boeing 747-436	British Airways
	G-CIVV	Boeing 747-436	British Airways
	G-CIVW	Boeing 747-436	British Airways
	G-CIVX	Boeing 747-436	British Airways
	G-CIVY	Boeing 747-436	British Airways
	G-CIVZ	Boeing 747-436	British Airways
	G-CIXB	Grob G.109B	G-CIXB Syndicate
	G-CIZZ	Beech 58 Baron	Bonanza Flying Club Ltd
	G-CJAB	Dornier 328-300 JET	Corporate Jet Realisations Ltd
	G-CJAD	Cessna 525 CitationJet	Carisle Bay Ltd
	G-CJAI	P & M Quik GT450	J. C. Kitchen
	G-CJAL	Schleicher Ka 6E	JAL Syndicate
	G-CJAO	Schempp-Hirth Discus b	A. Lyth & J. Weddell
	G-CJAP	Ikarus C42 FB80	J. A. Paley
	G-CJAR	Schempp-Hirth Discus bT	S. P. Withey
	G-CJAS	Glasflugel Standard Libelle 201B	M. J. Collett
	G-CJAT	Schleicher K8B	Wolds Gliding Club Ltd
	G-CJAV	Schleicher ASK-21	Wolds Gliding Club Ltd
	G-CJAW	Glaser-Dirks DG-200/17	P. D. Harvey

Reg.	Type	Owner or Operator	Notes
G-CJAX	Schleicher ASK-21	Wolds Gliding Club Ltd	
G-CJAY	Mainair Pegasus Quik GT450	J. C. Kitchen	
G-CJAZ	Grob G.102 Astir CS Jeans	The Bath, Wilts and North Dorset Gliding Club	
G-CJBB	Rolladen-Schneider LS8-a	C. Bruce	
G-CJBC	PA-28 Cherokee 180	J. B. Cave	
G-CJBH	Eiriavion PIK-20D	537 Syndicate	
G-CJBJ	Schempp-Hirth Standard Cirrus	S. T. Dutton	
G-CJBK	Schleicher ASW-19B	D. Caielli, P. Deane & G. Nixon	
G-CJBM	Schleicher ASK-21	Midland Gliding Club Ltd	
G-CJBO	Rolladen-Schneider LS8-18	L7 Syndicate	
G-CJBR	Schempp-Hirth Discus b	G-CJBR Group	
G-CJBT	Schleicher ASW-19B	G. Dennis	
G-CJBW	Schempp-Hirth Discus bT	G-CJBW Syndicate	
G-CJBX	Rolladen-Schneider LS4-a	P. W. Lee	
G-CJBY	AB Sportine LAK-12	P. G. Steggles & N. Clarke	
G-CJBZ	Grob G.102 Astir CS	The Royal Air Force Gliding Association	
G-CJCA	Schleicher ASW-15B	S. Briggs	
G-CJCD	Schleicher ASW-24	M. D. Evershed	
G-CJCF	Grob G.102 Astir CS77	The Northumbria Gliding Club Ltd	
G-CJCG	PZL-Swidnik PW-5 Smyk	M. Evans & T. J Wallace	
G-CJCJ	Schempp-Hirth Standard Cirrus	R. Johnson & R. Carter	
G-CJCK	Schempp-Hirth Discus bT	P. J. Tiller & T. Wright	
G-CJCM	Schleicher ASW-27	J. R. Klunder & K. E. Singer	
G-CJCN	Schempp-Hirth Standard Cirrus 75	F. J. Bradley	
G-CJCT	Schempp-Hirth Nimbus 4T	D. S. Innes	
G-CJCU	Schempp-Hirth Standard Cirrus B	R. A. Davenport	
G-CJCW	Grob G.102 Astir CS77	G. E. Iles & N. G. Smith	
G-CJCX	Schempp-Hirth Discus bT	C. W. M. Claxton	
G-CJCY	Rolladen-Schneider LS8-18	R. Visona & R. Zaccour	
G-CJCZ	Schleicher Ka 6CR	N. Barnes	
G-CJDB	Cessna 525 Citationjet	Breed Aircraft Ltd	
G-CJDC	Schleicher ASW-27	J. J. Marshall	
G-CJDD	Glaser-Dirks DG-200/17	Juliet Delta Delta Group	
G-CJDE	Rolladen-Schneider LS8-18	B. Kerby & M. Davies	
G-CJDF	Schleicher ASH-25E	522 Syndicate	
G-CJDG	Rolladen-Schneider LS6-b	R. H. & A. Moss	
G-CJDJ	Rolladen-Schneider LS3	J. C. Burdett	
G-CJDK	Rolladen-Schneider LS8-18	B. Bredenbeck	
G-CJDM	Schleicher ASW-15B	C. J. H. Donnelly	
G-CJDN	Cameron C-90 balloon	N. Ivison	
G-CJDP	Glaser-Dirks DG-200/17	The Owners of JDP	
G-CJDR	Schleicher ASW-15	M. J. Waters	
G-CJDS	Schempp-Hirth Standard Cirrus 75	P. Nicholls	
G-CJDT	Rolladen-Schneider LS8-a	J. N. & L. Rebbeck	
G-CJDV	DG Flugzeugbau DG-300 Elan Acro	J. M. Gilbey & B. D. Michael	
G-CJDX	Wassmer WA-28	R. Hutchinson	
G-CJDY	Rolladen-Schneider LS8-18	P. O. R. Paterson	
G-CJDZ	Schempp-Hirth Nimbus 4T	P. J. Harvey	
G-CJEA	Rolladen-Schneider LS8-18	P. Morgan	
G-CJEB	Schleicher ASW-24	P. C. Scholz	
G-CJEC	PZL-Bielsko SZD-50-3 Puchasz	Cambridge Gliding Club Ltd	
G-CJED	Schempp-Hirth Nimbus 3/24.5	J. Edyvean	
G-CJEE	Schleicher ASW-20L	B. Pridgeon	
G-CJEH	Glasflugel Mosquito B	M. J. Vickery	
G-CJEL	Schleicher ASW-24	N. K. Shepherd & S. J. Lintott	
G-CJEM	Schempp-Hirth Duo Discus	Duo Discus 572 Flying Group	
G-CJEP	Rolladen-Schneider LS4-b	C. F. Carter & N. Backes	
G-CJER	Schempp-Hirth Standard Cirrus 75	Cirrus Group	
G-CJEU	Glasflugel Standard Libelle	D. B. Johns	
G-CJEV	Schempp-Hirth Standard Cirrus	J. & S. R. Nash	
G-CJEW	Schleicher Ka 6CR	CJEW Syndicate	
G-CJEX	Schempp-Hirth Ventus 2a	D. S. Watt	
G-CJEZ	Glaser-Dirks DG-100	R. Kehr	
G-CJFA	Schempp-Hirth Standard Cirrus	P. M. Sheahan	
G-CJFC	Schempp-Hirth Discus CS	The Royal Air Force Gliding and Soaring Association	
G-CJFE	Schempp-Hirth Janus CE	The Royal Air Force Gliding and Soaring Association	
G-CJFH	Schempp-Hirth Duo Discus	The Royal Air Force Gliding and Soaring Association	
G-CJFJ	Schleicher ASW-20CL	R. J. Stirk	
G-CJFK	Schleicher ASW-20L	G-CJFK Flying Group	

Notes	Reg.	Type	Owner or Operator
	G-CJFM	Schleicher ASK-13	Darlton Gliding Club Ltd
	G-CJFR	Schempp-Hirth Ventus cT	L. Rayment, D. Ryall & D. W. Smith
	G-CJFT	Schleicher K-8B	The Surrey Hills Gliding Club Ltd
	G-CJFU	Schleicher ASW-19B	M. T. Stanley
	G-CJFX	Rolladen-Schneider LS8-a	P. E. Baker
	G-CJFZ	Fedorov ME7 Mechta	R. J. Colbourne
	G-CJGB	Schleicher K 8B	Richard Walker and Partners
	G-CJGD	Sleicher K 8B	R. E. Pettifer & C. A. McLay
	G-CJGE	Schleicher ASK-21	M. R. Wall
	G-CJGF	Schempp-Hirth Ventus c	J.G. Fisher
	G-CJGG	P & M Quik GT450	J. M. Pearce
	G-CJGH	Schempp-Hirth Nimbus 2C	G-CJGH Syndicate
	G-CJGJ	Schleicher ASK-21	Midland Gliding Club Ltd
	G-CJGK	Eiri PIL-200	The Four Aces
	G-CJGL	Schempp-Hirth Discus CS	The Royal Air Force Gliding and Soaring Association
	G-CJGM	Schempp-Hirth Discus CS	The Royal Air Force Gliding and Soaring Association
	G-CJGN	Schempp-Hirth Standard Cirrus	P. A. Shuttleworth
	G-CJGR	Schempp-Hirth Discus bT	S. P. Wareham & D. A. Smith
	G-CJGS	Rolladen-Schneider LS8-18	T. Stupnik
	G-CJGU	Schempp-Hirth Mini-Nimbus B	N. D. Ashton
	G-CJGW	Schleicher ASK-13	Darlton Gliding Club Ltd
	G-CJGX	Schleicher K 8B	Andreas K8 Group
	G-CJGY	Schempp-Hirth Standard Cirrus	P. J. Shout
	G-CJGZ	Glasflugel Standard Libelle 201B	A. & D. M. Cornish
	G-CJHD	Schleicher Ka 6E	The Royal Air Force Gliding and Soaring Association
	G-CJHE	Astir CS77	Aero Club de Portugal
	G-CJHG	Grob G.102 Astir CS	P. L. E. Zelazowski
	G-CJHJ	Glasflugel Standard Libelle 201B	N. P. Marriott
	G-CJHK	Schleicher K8B	Stratford on Avon Gliding Club Ltd
	G-CJHL	Schleicher Ka 6E	J. R. Gilbert
	G-CJHM	Schempp-Hirth Discus b	J. C. Thwaites
	G-CJHN	Grob G.102 Astir CS Jeans	J. C. Hurne
	G-CJHO	Schleicher ASK-18	RAF Gliding and Soaring Association
	G-CJHP	Flight Design CTSW	S. J. Reader
	G-CJHR	Centrair SNC34C Alliance	The Borders (Milfield) Gliding Club Ltd
	G-CJHS	Schleicher ASW-19B	JHS Syndicate
	G-CJHU	Rolladen-Schneider LS8-18	S. P. Ball
	G-CJHW	Glaser-Dirks DG-200	A. W. Thornhill & S. Webster
	G-CJHX	Bolkow Phoebus C	J. Hewitt
	G-CJHY	Rolladen-Schneider LS8-18	L. E. N. Tanner & N. Wall
	G-CJHZ	Schleicher ASW-20	T. J. Stanley
	G-CJJB	Rolladen-Schneider LS4	M. Tomlinson
	G-CJJD	Schempp-Hirth Discus bT	C. E. Turner & D. Wilson
	G-CJJE	Schempp-Hirth Discus a	A. Soffici
	G-CJJF	Schleicher ASW-27	A. R. Armstrong
	G-CJJH	DG Flugzeugbau DG-800S	J. S. Weston
	G-CJJJ	Schempp-Hirth Standard Cirrus	R. McLuckie
	G-CJJK	Rolladen-Schneider LS8-18	A. D. Roch
	G-CJJL	Schleicher ASW-19B	G-CJJL Group
	G-CJJP	Schempp-Hirth Duo Discus	N. Clements
	G-CJJT	Schleicher ASW-27	Portsmouth Naval Gliding Centre
	G-CJJU	Rolladen-Schneider LS8-a	A. J. French
	G-CJJX	Schleicher ASW-15B	STJ Syndicate
	G-CJJZ	Schempp-Hirth Discus bT	S. J. C. Parker
	G-CJKA	Schleicher ASK-21	East Sussex Gliding Club Ltd
	G-CJKB	PZL-Swidnik PW-5 Smyk	J. C. Gibson
	G-CJKD	Rolladen-Schneider LS8-18	D. G. Glover & A. Cockerell
	G-CJKE	PZL-Swidnik PW-5 Smyk	The Burn Gliding Club Ltd
	G-CJKF	Glaser-Dirks DG-200	D. O. Sandells & R. K. Stafford
	G-CJKG	Schleicher ASK-18	The Royal Air Force Gliding and Soaring Association
	G-CJKJ	Schleicher ASK-21	The Royal Air Force Gliding and Soaring Association
	G-CJKK	Schleicher ASK-21	Army Gliding Association
	G-CJKM	Glaser-Dirks DG200/17	G. F. Coles & E. W. Russell
	G-CJKN	Rolladen-Schneider LS8-18	D. A. Booth
	G-CJKO	Schleicher ASK-21	The Royal Air Force Gliding and Soaring Association
	G-CJKP	Rolladen-Schneider LS4-b	D. M. Hope

Reg.	Type	Owner or Operator	Notes
G-CJKS	Schleicher ASW-19B	R. J. P. Lancaster	
G-CJKT	Schleicher ASK-13	The Royal Air Force Gliding and Soaring Association	
G-CJKU	Schleicher ASK-18	The Royal Air Force Gliding and Soaring Association	
G-CJKV	Grob G.103A Twin II Acro	The Welland Gliding Club Ltd	
G-CJKW	Grob G.102 Astir CS77	The Bath, Wilts and North Dorset Gliding Club Ltd	
G-CJKY	Schempp-Hirth Ventus cT	G. V. Matthews & M. P. Osborn	
G-CJKZ	Schleicher ASK-21	The Royal Air Force Gliding and Soaring Association	
G-CJLA	Schempp-Hirth Ventus 2cT	E. C. & P. M. Neighbour	
G-CJLC	Schempp-Hirth Discus CS	The Royal Air Force Gliding and Soaring Association	
G-CJLF	Schleicher ASK-13	Army Gliding Association	
G-CJLG	PZL-Bielsko SZD-51-1 Junior	Army Gliding Association	
G-CJLH	Rolladen-Schneider LS4	JLH Syndicate	
G-CJLJ	Rolladen-Schneider LS4-b	Army Gliding Association	
G-CJLK	Rolladen-Schneider LS7	D. N. Munro & J. P. W. Roche-Kelly	
G-CJLL	Robinson R44 II	AT and P Rentals Ltd	
G-CJLN	Rolladen-Schneider LS8-18	The Royal Air Force Gliding and Soaring Association	
G-CJLO	Schleicher ASK-13	Bowland Forest Gliding Club Ltd	
G-CJLP	Schempp-Hirth Discus CS	The Royal Air Force Gliding and Soaring Association	
G-CJLR	Grob G.102 Astir CS	The Royal Air Force Gliding and Soaring Association	
G-CJLS	Schleicher K-8B	The Royal Air Force Gliding and Soaring Association	
G-CJLV	Schleicher Ka 6E	J. M. & J. C. Cooper	
G-CJLW	Schempp-Hirth Discus CS	The Royal Air Force Gliding and Soaring Association	
G-CJLY	Schleicher ASW-27	L. M. Astle & P. C. Piggott	
G-CJLZ	Grob G.103A Twin II Acro	21 Syndicate	
G-CJMA	Schleicher ASK-18	The Royal Air Force Gliding and Soaring Association	
G-CJMD	Embraer RJ135BJ	Corporate Jet Management Ltd	
G-CJMG	PZL-Bielsko SZD-51-1 Junior	Kent Gliding Club Ltd	
G-CJMJ	Schleicher ASK-13	The Royal Air Force Gliding and Soaring Association	
G-CJMK	Schleicher ASK-18	The Royal Air Force Gliding and Soaring Association	
G-CJML	Grob G.102 Astir CS77	The Royal Air Force Gliding and Soaring Association	
G-CJMN	Schempp-Hirth Nimbus 2	R. A. Holroyd	
G-CJMO	Rolladen-Schneider LS8-18	D. J. Langrick	
G-CJMP	Schleicher ASK-13	East Sussex Gliding Club Ltd	
G-CJMS	Schleicher ASK-21	The Royal Air Force Gliding and Soaring Association	
G-CJMT	Rolladen-Schneider LS8-18	D. P. & K. M. Draper	
G-CJMU	Rolladen-Schneider LS8-18	J. G. Guy	
G-CJMV	Schempp-Hirth Nimbus-2C	G. Tucker & K. R. Walton	
G-CJMW	Schleicher ASK-13	The Royal Air Force Gliding and Soaring Association	
G-CJMX	Schleicher ASK-13	Shalbourne Soaring Society Ltd	
G-CJMY	PZL-Bielsko SZD-51-1 Junior	Highland Gliding Club Ltd	
G-CJMZ	Schleicher ASK-13	The Royal Air Force Gliding and Soaring Association	
G-CJNA	Grob G.102 Astir CS Jeans	Shenington Gliding Club	
G-CJNB	Rolladen-Schneider LS8-18	Tatenhill Aviation Ltd	
G-CJNE	Schempp-Hirth Discus 2a	R. Priest	
G-CJNF	Schempp-Hirth Discus 2a	J. N. Rebbeck	
G-CJNG	Glasflugel Standard Libelle 201B	C. A. Willson	
G-CJNJ	Rolladen-Schneider LS8-18	A. B. Laws	
G-CJNK	Rolladen-Schneider LS8-18	Army Gliding Association	
G-CJNN	Schleicher K 8B	Buckminster Gliding Club Ltd	
G-CJNO	Glaser-Dirks DG-300 Elan	Yankee Kilo Group	
G-CJNP	Rolladen-Schneider LS6-b	E. & P. S. Fink	
G-CJNR	Glasflugel Mosquito B	S. L. Barnes & C. R. North	
G-CJNT	Schleicher ASW-19B	M. D. Borrowdale	
G-CJNX	LET L-13 Blanik	Vectis Gliding Club Ltd	
G-CJNZ	Glaser-Dirks DG-100	T. Tordoff & R. Jones	

Notes	Reg.	Type	Owner or Operator
	G-CJOA	Schempp-Hirth Discus b	The Royal Air Force Gliding and Soaring Association
	G-CJOB	Schleicher K 8B	JQB Syndicate
	G-CJOC	Schempp-Hirth Discus bT	287 Syndicate
	G-CJOD	Rolladen-Schneider LS8-18	The Royal Air Force Gliding and Soaring Association
	G-CJOE	Schempp-Hirth Standard Cirrus	D. I. Bolsdon & P. T. Johnson
	G-CJOG	Grob G.103A Twin II Acro	Acro Syundicate
	G-CJOH	AB Sportine LAK-12 Lietuva	J. M. Sherman
	G-CJOJ	Schleicher K 8B	P. W. Burgess
	G-CJON	Grob G.102 Astir CS77	The Royal Air Force Gliding and Soaring Association
	G-CJOO	Schempp-Hirth Duo Discus	185 Syndicate
	G-CJOP	Centrair 101A Pegase	P. A. Woodcock
	G-CJOR	Schempp-Hirth Ventus 2cT	A. M. George & N. A. Maclean
	G-CJOS	Schempp-Hirth Standard Cirrus	G-CJOS Group
	G-CJOU	AB Sportline Aviacija LAK-17A	B. Dorozko
	G-CJOV	Schleicher ASW-27	J. W. White
	G-CJOW	Schempp-Hirth Cirrus VTC	North Wales Gliding Club Ltd
	G-CJOX	Schleicher ASK-21	Southdown Gliding Club Ltd
	G-CJOZ	Schleicher K 8B	Derbyshire and Lancashire Gliding Club Ltd
	G-CJPA	Schempp-Hirth Duo Discus	Coventry Gliding Club Ltd
	G-CJPC	Schleicher ASK-13	Shalbourne Soaring Society Ltd
	G-CJPJ	Grob G.104 Speed Astir IIB	R. J. L. Maisonpierre
	G-CJPL	Rolladen-Schneider LS8-18	I. A. Reekie
	G-CJPM	Grob G.102 Astir CS Jeans	G-CJPM Syndicate
	G-CJPO	Schleicher ASK-18	The Royal Air Force Gliding and Soaring Association
	G-CJPP	Schempp-Hirth Discus b	Scottish Gliding Union Ltd
	G-CJPR	Rolladen-Schneider LS8-18	D. M. Byass & J. A. McCoshim
	G-CJPT	Schleicher ASW-27	R. C. Willis-Fleming
	G-CJPV	Schleicher ASK-13	The Royal Air Force Gliding and Soaring Association
	G-CJPW	Glaser-Dirks DG-200	A. Brownbridge & A. Kitchen
	G-CJPX	Schleicher ASW-15	R. Hayden & P. Daly
	G-CJPY	Schleicher ASK-13	The Royal Air Force Gliding and Soaring Association
	G-CJPZ	Schleicher ASK-18	The Royal Air Force Gliding and Soaring Association
	G-CJRA	Rolladen-Schneider LS8-18	J. Williams
	G-CJRB	Schleicher ASW-19B	J. W. Baxter
	G-CJRC	Glaser-Dirks DG-300 Elan	P. J. Sillett
	G-CJRD	Grob G.102 Astir CS	A. J. Hadwin & S. J. Kape
	G-CJRE	Scleicher ASW-15	R. A. Starling
	G-CJRF	PZL-Bielsko SZD-50-3 Puchacz	Wolds Gliding Club Ltd
	G-CJRG	Schempp-Hirth Standard Cirrus	N. J. Laux
	G-CJRH	Schleicher ASW-27	C. Jackson & P. C. Jarvis
	G-CJRJ	PZL-Bielsko SZD-50-3 Puchacz	Derbyshire & Lancashire Gliding Club Ltd
	G-CJRL	Glaser-Dirks DG-100G Elan	P. Lazenby
	G-CJRM	Grob G.102 Astir CS	M. Spittal
	G-CJRN	Glaser-Dirks DG-200/17	T. G. Roberts
	G-CJRR	Schempp-Hirth Discus bT	N. A. Hays
	G-CJRT	Schempp-Hirth Standard Cirrus	JRT Syndicate
	G-CJRU	Schleicher ASW-24	S. A. Kerby
	G-CJRV	Schleicher ASW-19B	M. Roome
	G-CJRX	Schleicher ASK-13	The Royal Air Force Gliding and Soaring Association
	G-CJSA	Nanchang NAMC CJ-6A	Bogaerts Aviation BVBA
	G-CJSC	Schempp-Hirth Nimbus-3DT	S. G. Jones
	G-CJSD	Grob G.102 Astir CS	The Royal Air Force Gliding and Soaring Association
	G-CJSE	Schempp-Hirth Discus b	Imperial College of Science, Technology and Medicine
	G-CJSG	Schleicher Ka 6E	A. J. Emck
	G-CJSH	Grob G.102 Club Astir IIIB	Lasham Gliding Society Ltd
	G-CJSJ	Rolladen-Schneider LS7-WL	S. P. Woolcock
	G-CJSK	Grob G.102 Astir CS	Sierra Kilo Group
	G-CJSL	Schempp-Hirth Ventus cT	D. Latimer
	G-CJSN	Schleicher K 8B	Cotswold Gliding Club
	G-CJSS	Schleicher ASW-27	G. K. & S. R. Drury
	G-CJST	Rolladen-Schneider LS1-c	W. A. Bowness & E. Richar
	G-CJSU	Rolladen-Schneider LS8-18	J. G. Bell

Reg.	Type	Owner or Operator	Notes
G-CJSV	Schleicher ASK-13	The Royal Air Force Gliding and Soaring Association	
G-CJSW	Rolladen-Schneider LS4-a	C. Benoit	
G-CJSX	AMS-Flight DG-500	Oxford Gliding Company Ltd	
G-CJSZ	Schleicher ASK-18	C. Weston	
G-CJTB	Schleicher ASW-24	V17 Syndicate	
G-CJTH	Schleicher ASW-24	R. J. & J. E. Lodge	
G-CJTJ	Schempp-Hirth Mini-Nimbus B	A. Richards	
G-CJTK	DG Flugzeugbau DG-300 Elan Acro	A. Jorgensen	
G-CJTL	Rolladen-Schneider LS8-18	J. M. & R. S. Hood	
G-CJTM	Rolladen-Schneider LS8-18	A. D. Holmes	
G-CJTN	Glaser-Dirks DG-300 Elan	A. D. Noble & P. W. Schartau	
G-CJTO	Glasflugel H303A Mosquito	Tango Oscar Group	
G-CJTP	Schleicher ASW-20L	C. A. Sheldon	
G-CJTR	Rolladen-Schneider LS7-WL	D53 Syndicate	
G-CJTS	Schempp-Hirth Cirrus VTC	G-CJTS Cirrus Group	
G-CJTU	Schempp-Hirth Duo Discus T	G-CJTU Syndicate	
G-CJTW	Glasflugel Mosquito B	S. Urry	
G-CJTY	Rolladen-Schneider LS8-a	BBC (London) Club	
G-CJUB	Schempp-Hirth Discus CS	Coventry Gliding Club Ltd	
G-CJUD	Denney Kitfox Mk 3	P. J. And B-J Chandler	
G-CJUF	Schempp-Hirth Ventus 2cT	M. H. B. Pope	
G-CJUG	Issoire E78B Silene	J. M. Sanders	
G-CJUJ	Schleicher ASW-27	P. A. Ivens	
G-CJUK	Grob G.102 Astir CS	P. Freer & S. J. Calvert	
G-CJUM	Schempp-Hirth Duo Discus T	2 UP Group	
G-CJUN	Schleicher ASW-19B	M. P. S. Roberts	
G-CJUP	Schempp-Hirth Discus 2b	The Discuss 2 Uniform Papa Group	
G-CJUR	Valentin Mistral C	M. J. W. Harris	
G-CJUS	Grob G.102 Astir CS	East Sussex Gliding Club Ltd	
G-CJUU	Schempp-Hirth Standard Cirrus	H. R. Fraser	
G-CJUV	Schempp-Hirth Discus b	Lasham Gliding Society Ltd	
G-CJUX	Aviastroitel AC-4C	R. J. Walton	
G-CJUZ	Schleicher ASW-19B	K. W. Clarke	
G-CJVA	Schempp-Hirth Ventus 2cT	M. S. Armstrong	
G-CJVB	Schempp-Hirth Discus bT	C. J. Edwards	
G-CJVC	PZL-Bielsko SZD-51-1 Junior	York Gliding Centre Ltd	
G-CJVE	Eiriavion PIK-20D	S. R. Wilkinson	
G-CJVF	Schempp-Hirth Discus CS	J. Hodgson	
G-CJVG	Schempp-Hirth Discus bT	S. J. Bryan & P. J. Bramley	
G-CJVJ	AB Sportine LAK-17A	J. A. Sutton	
G-CJVL	DG-300 Elan	A. T. Vidion & A. Griffiths	
G-CJVM	Schleicher ASW-27	G. K. Payne	
G-CJVP	Glaser-Dirks DG-200	M. S. Howey & S. Leadbeater	
G-CJVS	Schleicher ASW-28	Zulu Glasstek Ltd	
G-CJVU	Standard Cirrus CS-11-75L	Cirrus 75 Syndicate	
G-CJVV	Schempp-Hirth Janus C	J50 Syndicate	
G-CJVW	Schleicher ASW-15	Victor Whiskey Group	
G-CJVX	Schempp-Hirth Discus CS	G-CJVX Syndicate	
G-CJVZ	Schleicher ASK-21	Yorkshire Gliding Club (Proprietary) Ltd	
G-CJWA	Schleicher ASW-28	P. R. Porter & M. J. Taylor	
G-CJWB	Schleicher ASK-13	East Sussex Gliding Club Ltd	
G-CJWD	Schleicher ASK-21	London Gliding Club Proprietary Ltd	
G-CJWF	Schleicher ASW-27	B. A. Fairston & A. Stotter	
G-CJWG	Schempp-Hirth Nimbus 3	880 Group	
G-CJWJ	Schleicher ASK-13	The Royal Air Force Gliding and Soaring Association	
G-CJWK	Schempp-Hirth Discus bT	722 Syndicate	
G-CJWM	Grob G.103 Twin Astir II	Norfolk Gliding Club Ltd	
G-CJWP	Bolkow Phoebus B1	A. Fidler	
G-CJWR	Grob G.102 Astir CS	Cairngorm Gliding Club	
G-CJWT	Glaser-Dirks DG-200	K. R. Nash	
G-CJWU	Schempp-Hirth Ventus bT	B. C. P. & C. Crook	
G-CJWX	Schempp-Hirth Ventus 2cT	M. M. A. Lipperheide & S. G. Olender	
G-CJXA	Schempp-Hirth Nimbus 3	Y44 Syndicate	
G-CJXB	Centrair 201B Marianne	Marianne Syndicate	
G-CJXC	Wassmer WA28	A. P. Montague	
G-CJXG	Eiriavion PIK-20D	W5 Group	
G-CJXL	Schempp-Hirth Discus CS	J. Hall & M. J. Hasluck	
G-CJXM	Schleicher ASK-13	The Windrushers Gliding Club	
G-CJXN	Centrair 201B	R. D. Trussell	
G-CJXP	Glaser-Dirks DG-100	N. L. Morris	

Notes	Reg.	Type	Owner or Operator
	G-CJXR	Schempp-Hirth Discus b	Cambridge Gliding Club Ltd
	G-CJXT	Schleicher ASW-24B	P. McAuley
	G-CJXW	Schempp-Hirth Duo Discus T	R. A. Beatty
	G-CJXX	Pilatus B4-PC11AF	N. H. Buckenham
	G-CJXY	Neukom Elfe S4A	J. Hunt
	G-CJYC	Grob G.102 Astir CS	R. A. Christie
	G-CJYD	Schleicher ASW-27	J. E. Gatfield
	G-CJYE	Schleicher ASK-13	North Wales Gliding Club Ltd
	G-CJYF	Schempp Hirth Discus CS	W. J. Winthrop
	G-CJYL	AB Sportine Aviacija LAK-12	A. Camerotto
	G-CJYO	Glaser-Dirks DG-100G Elan	A. M. Booth
	G-CJYP	Grob G.102 Club Astir II	Astir Syndicate BGA4891
	G-CJYR	Schempp-Hirth Duo Discus T	G-CJYR Group
	G-CJYS	Schempp-Hirth Mini Nimbus C	A. Jenkins
	G-CJYU	Schempp-Hirth Ventus 2cT	The Royal Air Force Gliding and Soaring Association
	G-CJYV	Schleicher K8B	Club Agrupacion de Pilotos del Sureste/Spain
	G-CJYW	Schleicher K8B	Club Agrupacion de Pilotos del Sureste/Spain
	G-CJYX	Rolladen-Schneider LS3-17	D. Meyer-Beeck & V. G. Diaz
	G-CJZB	DG-500 Elan Orion	Bicester JZB Syndicate
	G-CJZE	Schleicher ASK-13	Needwood Forest Gliding Club Ltd
	G-CJZG	Schempp-Hirth Discus bT	I. K. G. Mitchell
	G-CJZH	Schleicher ASW-20 CL	C. P. Gibson & C. A. Hunt
	G-CJZK	DG-505 Elan Orion	Devon and Somerset Gliding Club Ltd
	G-CJZL	Schempp-Hirth Mini Nimbus B	P. A. Dunthorne
	G-CJZM	Schempp-Hirth Ventus 2a	S. Crabb
	G-CJZN	Schleicher ASW-28	P. J. Coward
	G-CJZY	Grob G.102 Standard Astir III	Lasham Gliding Society Ltd
	G-CJZZ	Rolladen-Schneider LS7	J. H. Tucker
	G-CKAC	Glaser-Dirks DG-200	M. G. Stringer
	G-CKAE	Centrair 101A Pegase	Rattlesden Gliding Club Ltd
	G-CKAK	Schleicher ASW-28	S. J. Kelman
	G-CKAL	Schleicher ASW-28	D. A. Smith & P. A. Ivens
	G-CKAM	Glasflugel Club Libelle 205	P. A. Cronk & R. C. Tallowin
	G-CKAN	PZL-Bielsko SZD-50-3 Puchacz	The Bath Wilts and North Dorset Gliding Club Ltd
	G-CKAP	Schempp-Hirth Discus CS	KAP Syndicate
	G-CKAR	Schempp-Hirth Duo Discus T	977 Syndicate
	G-CKAS	Schempp-Hirth Ventus 2cT	KAS Club
	G-CKAU	DG Flugzeugbau DG-303 Elan Acro	G. Earle
	G-CKAW	AMS-Flight DG-505 Elan	Midland Gliding Club Ltd
	G-CKAX	AMS-Flight DG-500 Elan Orion	York Gliding Centre Ltd
	G-CKAY	Grob G.102 Astir CS	D. Ryder & P. Carrington
	G-CKBA	Centrair 101A Pegase	KBA Pegase 101A Syndicate
	G-CKBC	Rolladen-Schneider LS6-c	A. W. Lyth
	G-CKBD	Grob G.102 Astir CS	R. A. Morriss
	G-CKBF	AMS-Flight DG-303 Elan	A. L. Garfield
	G-CKBG	Schempp-Hirth Ventus 2cT	71 Syndicate
	G-CKBH	Rolladen-Schneider LS6	F. C. Ballard & P. Walker
	G-CKBK	Schempp-Hirth Ventus 2cT	D. Rhys-Jones
	G-CKBL	Grob G.102 Astir CS	Norfolk Gliding Club Ltd
	G-CKBM	Schleicher ASW-28	C. S. & M. E. Newland-Smith
	G-CKBN	PZL-Bielsko SZD-55-1 Promyk	N. D. Pearson
	G-CKBS	Glaser-Dirks DG-600	C. R. R. Audissou
	G-CKBT	Schempp-Hirth Standard Cirrus	P. R. Johnson
	G-CKBU	Schleicher ASW-28	G. C. Metcalfe
	G-CKBV	Schleicher ASW-28	P. Whipp
	G-CKBX	Schleicher ASW-27	M. Wright & T. J. Davies
	G-CKCB	Rolladen-Schneider LS4-a	The Bristol Gliding Club Proprietary Ltd
	G-CKCD	Schempp-Hirth Ventus 2cT	R. S. Jobar & S. G. Jones
	G-CKCE	Schempp-Hirth Ventus 2cT	M. W. Cater & J. P. Walker
	G-CKCH	Schempp-Hirth Ventus 2cT	J. J. Pridal & L. R. Marks
	G-CKCJ	Schleicher ASW-28	S. L. Withall
	G-CKCK	Enstrom 280FX	Rhoburt Ltd
	G-CKCM	Glasflugel Standard Libelle 201B	G. A. Cox
	G-CKCN	Schleicher ASW-27	W. J. Head
	G-CKCP	Grob G.102 Astir CS	Norfolk Gliding Club Ltd
	G-CKCR	AB Sportine Aviacija LAK-17A	M. Kessler/Italy
	G-CKCT	Schleicher ASK-21	Kent Gliding Club Aircraft Ltd
	G-CKCV	Schempp-Hirth Duo Discus T	WE4 Group
	G-CKCW	Glaser-Dirks DG200/17	R. W. Adamson & K. A. B. Morgan
	G-CKCY	Schleicher ASW-20	J. Sugden

Reg.	Type	Owner or Operator	Notes
G-CKCZ	Schleicher ASK-21	Booker Gliding Club Ltd	
G-CKDA	Schempp-Hirth Ventus 2B	D. J. Eade	
G-CKDB	Schleicher Ka 6CR	Banbury Gliding Club Ltd	
G-CKDC	Centrair ASW-20F	M. Staljan, S. Brogger & C. Behrendt	
G-CKDF	Schleicher ASK-21	Portsmouth Naval Gliding Centre	
G-CKDK	Rolladen-Schneider LS4-a	M. C. & P. A. Ridger	
G-CKDN	Schleicher ASW-27B	J. S. McCullagh	
G-CKDO	Schempp-Hirth Ventus 2cT	M. W. Edwards	
G-CKDP	Schleicher ASK-21	Kent Gliding Club Aircraft Ltd	
G-CKDR	PZL-Bielsko SZD-48-3 Jantar Standard 3	G. Hyrkowski	
G-CKDS	Schleicher ASW-27	A. W. Gillett & G. D. Morris	
G-CKDU	Glaser-Dirks DG-200/17	P. G. Noonan	
G-CKDV	Schempp-Hirth Ventus B/16.6	M. A. Codd	
G-CKDW	Schleicher ASW-27	C. Colton	
G-CKDX	Glaser-Dirks DG-200	Delta X Ray Group	
G-CKDY	Glaser-Dirks DG-100	503 Group	
G-CKDZ	Schempp-Hirth Standard Cirrus 75	Charlie 75	
G-CKEA	Schempp-Hirth Cirrus 18	C. M. Reed	
G-CKEB	Schempp-Hirth Standard Cirrus	A. J. Mugleston	
G-CKED	Schleicher ASW-27B	M. H. Bull	
G-CKEE	Grob G.102 Astir CS	Essex and Suffolk Gliding Club Ltd	
G-CKEJ	Schleicher ASK-21	London Gliding Club Proprietary Ltd	
G-CKEK	Schleicher ASK-21	Devon and Somerset Gliding Club Ltd	
G-CKEM	Robinson R44	True Course Helicopter Ltd	
G-CKEP	Rolladen-Schneider LS6-b	T. W. M. Beck	
G-CKER	Schleicher ASW-19B	G-CKER Syndicate	
G-CKES	Schempp-Hirth Cirrus 18	D. Judd & N. Hawley	
G-CKET	Rolladen-Schneider LS8-8	M. B. Jefferyes & J. C. Taylor	
G-CKEV	Schempp-Hirth Duo Discus	The Royal Air Force Gliding and Soaring Association	
G-CKEY	PA-28-161 Warrior II	Warwickshire Aviation Ltd	
G-CKEZ	DG Flugzeugbau LS8	D. A. Jesty	
G-CKFA	Schempp-Hirth Standard Cirrus 75	G. C. Bell	
G-CKFB	Schempp-Hirth Discus-2T	P. L. & P. A. G. Holland	
G-CKFC	Schempp-Hirth Ventus 2cT	P. Lecci	
G-CKFD	Schleicher ASW-27B	W. T. Craig	
G-CKFE	Eiriavion PIK-20D	M. J. McSorley	
G-CKFG	Grob G.103A Twin II Acro	The Surrey Hills Gliding Club Ltd	
G-CKFH	Schempp-Hirth Mini Nimbus	G-CKFH Flying Group	
G-CKFJ	Schleicher ASK-13	York Gliding Centre Ltd	
G-CKFK	Schempp-Hirth Standard Cirrus 75	P. R. Wilkinson	
G-CKFL	Rolladen-Schneider LS4	D. O'Brien & D. R. Taylor	
G-CKFN	DG Flugzeugbau DG1000	Yorkshire Gliding Club (Proprietary) Ltd	
G-CKFP	Schempp-Hirth Ventus 2cxT	C. R. Sutton	
G-CKFR	Schleicher ASK-13	Club Acrupacion de Pilotos del Sureste/Spain	
G-CKFT	Schempp-Hirth Duo Discus T	Duo Discus Syndicate	
G-CKFV	DG Flugzeugbau LS8-t	G. A. Rowden & K. I. Arkley	
G-CKFY	Schleicher ASK.21	Cambridge Gliding Club	
G-CKGA	Schempp-Hirth Ventus 2cxT	D. R. Campbell	
G-CKGC	Schempp-Hirth Ventus 2cxT	C. P. A. Jeffery	
G-CKGD	Schempp-Hirth Ventus 2cxT	C. Morris	
G-CKGF	Schempp-Hirth Duo Discus T	Duo 233 Group	
G-CKGH	Grob G.102 Club Astir II	I. M. Gavan	
G-CKGK	Schleicher ASK-21	The Royal Air Force Gliding & Soaring Association	
G-CKGL	Schempp-Hirth Ventus 2cT	Kilo Golf Lima Syndicate	
G-CKGM	Centrair 101A Pegase	S. France	
G-CKGU	Schleicher ASW-19B	ASW 19 KGU Group	
G-CKGV	Schleicher ASW-20	A. H. Reynolds	
G-CKGX	Schleicher ASK-21	Coventry Gliding Club Ltd	
G-CKGY	Scheibe Bergfalke IV	B. R. Pearson	
G-CKHA	PZL SZD-51-1 Junior	Devon & Somerset Gliding Club Ltd	
G-CKHB	Rolladen-Schneider LS3	C. J. Cole	
G-CKHC	DG Flugzeugbau DG.505	G-CKHC Group	
G-CKHD	Schleicher ASW-27B	N. D Tillett	
G-CKHE	AB Sportine Aviacija LAK-17AT	N. J. Gough & A. J. Garrity	
G-CKHG	Schleicher ASW-27B	R. A. F. King	
G-CKHH	Schleicher ASK-13	Lincolnshire Gliding Club Ltd	
G-CKHK	Schempp-Hirth Duo Discus T	Duo Discus Syndicate	
G-CKHM	Centrair 101A Pegase 90	A. J. Rowlands	
G-CKHN	PZL SZD-51-1 Junior	The Nene Valley Gliding Club Ltd	
G-CKHR	PZL-Bielsko SZD-51-1 Junior	Wolds Gliding Club Ltd	

Notes	Reg.	Type	Owner or Operator
	G-CKHS	Rolladen-Schneider LS7-WL	M. Lawson & D. Wallis
	G-CKHV	Glaser-Dirks DG-100	G-CKHV Trust
	G-CKHW	PZL SZD-50-3 Puchacz	Derbyshire and Lancashire Gliding Club Ltd
	G-CKJB	Schempp-Hirth Ventus bT	J. R. Matthews & J. R. Rayner
	G-CKJC	Schempp-Hirth Nimbus 3T	A. C. Wright
	G-CKJD	Schempp-Hirth Cirrus 75-VTC	P. J. P. Vanden Boer
	G-CKJE	DG Flugzeugbau LS8-18	M. D. Wells
	G-CKJF	Schempp-Hirth Standard Cirrus	G-CKJF Group
	G-CKJG	Schempp-Hirth Cirrus VTC	S. J. Wright
	G-CKJH	Glaser-Dirks DG.300 Elan	Yorkshire Gliding Club
	G-CKJJ	DG Flugzeugbau DG-500 Elan Orion	Ulster Gliding Club Ltd
	G-CKJL	Scleicher ASK-13	Lincolnshire Gliding Club Ltd
	G-CKJM	Schempp-Hirth Ventus cT	G-CKJM Group
	G-CKJN	Schleicher ASW-20	R. Logan
	G-CKJP	Schleicher ASK-21	The Royal Air Force Gliding and Soaring Association
	G-CKJS	Schleicher ASW-28-18E	G-CKJS Syndicate
	G-CKJV	Schleicher ASW-28-18E	A. C. Price
	G-CKJZ	Schempp-Hirth Discus bT	G-CKJZ Group
	G-CKKB	Centrair 101A Pegase	D. M. Rushton
	G-CKKC	DG Flugzeugbau DG-300 Elan Acro	Charlie Kilo Kilo Charlie Syndicate
	G-CKKE	Schempp-Hirth Duo Discus T	The Foxtrot Group
	G-CKKF	Schempp-Hirth Ventus 2cT	A. R. MacGregor
	G-CKKH	Schleicher ASW-27	P. L. Hurd
	G-CKKK	AB Sportine Aviacija LAK-17A	C. J. Nicolas
	G-CKKP	Schleicher ASK-21	Bowland Forest Gliding Club Ltd
	G-CKKR	Schleicher ASK-13	Banbury Gliding Club Ltd
	G-CKKV	DG Flugzeugbau DG-1000S	Lasham Gliding Society Ltd
	G-CKKX	Rolladen-Schneider LS4-A	B. W. Svenson
	G-CKKY	Schempp-Hirth Duo Discus T	P. D. Duffin
	G-CKLA	Schleicher ASK-13	Booker Gliding Club Ltd
	G-CKLC	Glasflugel H206 Hornet	L. P. Woodage
	G-CKLD	Schempp-Hirth Discus 2cT	J. P. Galloway
	G-CKLF	Schempp-Hirth Janus	T. J. Highton & C. J. Lawrence
	G-CKLG	Rolladen-Schneider LS4	P. M. Scheiwiller
	G-CKLN	Rolladen-Schneider LS4-A	Army Gliding Association
	G-CKLP	Scleicher ASW-28-18	J. T. Birch
	G-CKLR	Pezetel SZD-55-1	Zulu Five Gliding Group (G-CKLM)
	G-CKLS	Rolladen-Schneider LS4	Wolds Gliding Club Ltd
	G-CKLT	Schempp-Hirth Nimbus 3/24.5	G. N. Thomas
	G-CKLV	Schempp-Hirth Discus 2cT	S. Baker
	G-CKLW	Schleicher ASK-21	Yorkshire Gliding Club
	G-CKLY	DG Flugzeugbau DG-1000T	G-CKLY Group
	G-CKMA	DG Flugzeugbau LS8-T	W. J. Morecraft
	G-CKMB	AB Sportline Aviacija LAK-19T	D. J. McKenzie
	G-CKMD	Schempp-Hirth Standard Cirrus	S. A. Crabb
	G-CKME	DG Flugzeugbau LS8-T	S. M. Smith
	G-CKMF	Centrair 101A Pegase	D. L. M. Jamin
	G-CKMG	Glaser-Dirks DG-101G Elan	G. G. Dale
	G-CKMI	Schleicher K8C	V. Mallon
	G-CKMJ	Schleicher Ka 6CR	V. Mallon
	G-CKML	Schempp-Hirth Duo Discus T	KML Group
	G-CKMM	Schleicher ASW-28-18E	R. G. Munro
	G-CKMO	Rolladen-Schneider LS7-WL	G. E. M. Turpin
	G-CKMP	AB Sportine Aviacija LAK-17A	J. L. McIver
	G-CKMT	Grob G103C	Essex & Suffolk Gliding Club Ltd
	G-CKMV	Rolladen-Schneider LS3-17	S. Procter & M. P. Woolmer
	G-CKMW	Schleicher ASK-21	The Royal Air Force Gliding & Soaring Association
	G-CKMZ	Schleicher ASW-28-18	J. R. Martindale
	G-CKNB	Schempp-Hirth Standard Cirrus	A. Booker
	G-CKNC	Caproni Calif A21S	J. J. & M. E. Pritchard
	G-CKND	DG Flugzeugbau DG-1000T	KND Group
	G-CKNE	Schempp-Hirth Standard Cirrus 75-VTC	G. D. E. Macdonald
	G-CKNF	DG Flugzeugbau DG-1000T	Six November Fox
	G-CKNG	Schleicher ASW-28-18E	M. P. Brockinhton
	G-CKNK	Glaser-Dirks DG.500	Cotswold Gliding Club
	G-CKNL	Schleicher ASK-21	Buckminster Gliding Club Ltd
	G-CKNM	Scleicher ASK-18	I. L. Pattingale
	G-CKNO	Schempp-Hirth Ventus 2cxT	C. McEwen
	G-CKNR	Schempp-Hirth Ventus 2cxT	R. J. Nicholls
	G-CKNS	Rolladen-Schneider LS4-A	I. R. Willows
	G-CKNV	Schleicher ASW-28-18E	D. G. Brain

Reg.	Type	Owner or Operator	Notes
G-CKOD	Schempp-Hirth Discus BT	A. L. Harris & M. W. Talbot	
G-CKOE	Schleicher ASW-27-18	R. C. Bromwich	
G-CKOH	DG Flugzeugbau DG-1000T	Oscar Hotel Group	
G-CKOI	AB Sportine Aviacija LAK-17AT	C. G. Corbett	
G-CKOK	Schempp-Hirth Discus 2cT	B. D. Scougall	
G-CKOL	Schempp-Hirth Duo Discus T	Oscar Lima Syndicate	
G-CKOM	Schleicher ASW-27-18	L. M. P. Wells	
G-CKON	Schleicher ASW-27-18E	J. P. Gorringe	
G-CKOO	Schleicher ASW-27-18E	A. Darlington, J. P. Lewis & C. T. P. Williams	
G-CKOR	Glaser-Dirks DG-300 Elan	J. A. Sparrow	
G-CKOT	Schleicher ASK-21	Ulster Gliding Club Ltd	
G-CKOU	AB Sportine Aviacija LAK-19T	C. J. Davison	
G-CKOW	DG-505 Elan Orion	Southdown Gliding Club Ltd	
G-CKOX	AMS-Flight DG-505 Elan Orion	Seahawk Gliding Club	
G-CKOY	Schleicher ASW-27-18E	G-CKOY Group	
G-CKOZ	Schleicher ASW-27-18E	E. W. Johnston	
G-CKPA	AB Sportline Aviacija LAK-19T	O. R. Momege	
G-CKPE	Schempp-Hirth Duo Discus	Portsmouth Naval Gliding Centre	
G-CKPG	Schempp-Hirth Discus 2cT	G. Knight & P. Rowden	
G-CKPJ	Neukom S-4D Elfe	S. Szladowski	
G-CKPK	Schempp-Hirth Ventus 2cxT	I. C. Lees	
G-CKPM	DG Flugzeugbau LS8-T	8T Soaring	
G-CKPN	PZL-Bielsko SZD-51-1 Junior	Rattlesden Gliding Club Ltd	
G-CKPO	Schempp-Hirth Duo Discus xT	KPO Syndicate	
G-CKPP	Schleicher ASK-21	The Gliding Centre	
G-CKPU	Schleicher ASW-27-18E	A. J. Kellerman	
G-CKPV	Schempp-Hirth HS.7 Mini-Nimbus B	D. K. McCarthy	
G-CKPX	ZS Jezow PW-6U	J. C. Gibson	
G-CKPY	Schempp-Hirth Duo Discus xT	Duo-Discus Syndicate	
G-CKPZ	Schleicher ASW-20	T. Davies	
G-CKRB	Schleicher ASK-13	Derbyshire and Lancashire Gliding Club Ltd	
G-CKRC	Schleicher ASW-28-18E	M. Woodcock	
G-CKRD	Schleicher ASW-27-18E	R. F. Thirkell	
G-CKRF	DG-300 Elan	G. A. King	
G-CKRH	Grob G.103 Twin Astir II	Staffordshire Gliding Club Ltd	
G-CKRI	Schleicher ASK-21	Kent Gliding Club Aircraft Ltd	
G-CKRJ	Schleicher ASW-27-18E	J. C. Thompson	
G-CKRN	Grob G.102 Astir CS	Yorkshire Gliding Club (Proprietary) Ltd	
G-CKRO	Schempp-Hirth Duo Discus T	Duo Discus Syndicate KRO	
G-CKRR	Schleicher ASW-15B	S. A. Day	
G-CKRS	FFA Diamant 16.5	G-CKRS Syndicate	
G-CKRU	ZS Jezow PW-6U	Cotswold Gliding Club	
G-CKRV	Schleicher ASW-27-18E	J. Cruttenden & J. Taylor	
G-CKRW	Schleicher ASK-21	The Royal Air Force Gliding and Soaring Association	
G-CKRX	Jezow PW-6U	Cotswold Gliding Club	
G-CKSC	Czech Sport Aircraft Sportcruiser	Czechmate Syndicate	
G-CKSD	Rolladen-Schneider LS8-a	N. Kelly & J. Roberts	
G-CKSH	PZL-Bielsko SZD-30 Pirat	J. K. Hoffmann	
G-CKSK	Pilatus B4-PC11	R. Mauthner	
G-CKSL	Schleicher ASW-15B	Sierra Lima Group	
G-CKSM	Schempp-Hirth Duo Discus T	J. H. May & S. P. Ball	
G-CKSX	Schleicher ASW-27-18E	M. C. Foreman	
G-CKSY	Rolladen-Schneider LS-7-WL	C. M. Lewis	
G-CKTB	Schempp-Hirth Ventus 2cT	M. H. Player	
G-CKTC	Schleicher Ka 6CR	Tango Charlie Group	
G-CKZT	PA-28-235 Cherokee Pathfinder	U. Chakravorty	
G-CLAC	PA-28-161 Warrior II	G-CLAC Group	
G-CLAR	EC.225LP Super Puma	CHC Scotia Ltd	
G-CLAV	Shaw Europa	G. Laverty	
G-CLAX	Jurca MJ.5 Sirocco F2/39	G. D. Claxton (G-AWKB)	
G-CLAY	Bell 206B JetRanger 3	Claygate Distribution Ltd (G-DENN)	
G-CLDS	Rotorsport UK Calidus	Rotorsport UK Ltd	
G-CLEA	PA-28-161 Warrior II	G-CLEA Group	
G-CLEE	Rans S.6-ES Coyote II	J. Bell	
G-CLEG	Flight Design CTSW	C. A. S. Powell	
G-CLEM	Bölkow Bö.208A2 Junior	G-CLEM Group (G-ASWE)	
G-CLEO	Zenair CH.601HD	K. M. Bowen	
G-CLES	Scheicher ASW-27-18E	A. P. Brown & N. D. Tillett	
G-CLEU	Glaser-Dirks DG-200	S. F. Tape	
G-CLFB	Rolladen-Schneider LS4-A	B. Harker	

Notes	Reg.	Type	Owner or Operator
	G-CLFC	Mainair Blade	G. N. Cliffe & G. Marshall
	G-CLFH	Schleicher ASW-20C	T. Fordwich-Gorefly & P. Armstrong
	G-CLFX	Schempp-Hirth Duo Discus T	A. L. Baillie
	G-CLFZ	Schleicher ASW-18E	C. F. Cownden & J. P. Davies
	G-CLGC	Schempp-Hirth Duo Discus	London Gliding Club Proprietary Ltd
	G-CLGL	Schempp-Hirth Ventus 2c	M. J. Collett and A. Hegner
	G-CLGR	Glasflugel Club Libelle 205	A. A. Gillon
	G-CLGT	Rolladen-Schneider LS4	C. B. & N. M. Hill
	G-CLGU	Schleicher ASW-27-18	T. J. Scott
	G-CLGW	Centrair 101A Pegase	M. White
	G-CLGZ	Schempp-Hirth Duo Discus T	D. R. Irving
	G-CLHF	Scheibe Bergfalke IV	Andreas Gliding Club Ltd
	G-CLHG	Schempp-Hirth Discus b	S. J. Edinborough
	G-CLIC	Cameron A-105 balloon	R. S. Mohr
	G-CLIF	Ikarus C42 FB UK	C. Sims
	G-CLIN	Ikarus C42 FB100	G. C. Linley
	G-CLJE	Schleicher ASH-25M	G. F. Mann
	G-CLOE	Sky 90-24 balloon	J. Skinner
	G-CLOS	PA-34-200 Seneca II	R. A. Doherty
	G-CLOT	Robinson R44	Tracey Plant Ltd
	G-CLOW	Beech 200 Super King Air	Clowes (Estates) Ltd
	G-CLRK	Sky 77-24 balloon	William Clark & Son (Parkgate) Ltd
	G-CLUE	PA-34-200T Seneca II	P. Pigg
	G-CLUX	Cessna F.172N	J. & K. Aviation
	G-CLWN	Cameron Clown SS balloon	Magical Adventures Ltd (G-UBBE)
	G-CMAS	Embraer EMB-135BJ Legacy	Execujet (UK) Ltd
	G-CMBR	Cessna 172S	C. M. B. Reid
	G-CMBS	MDH MD-900 Explorer	Cambridgeshire Constabulary
	G-CMCC	Robinson R44 II	C. McCann
	G-CMED	SOCATA TB9 Tampico	D. Primorac
	G-CMGC	PA-25 Pawnee 235	Midland Gliding Club Ltd (G-BFEX)
	G-CMLS	Cirrus SR20	S. R. Kay
	G-CMOR	Skyranger 912(2)	N. R. Henry
	G-CMOS	Cessna T.303 Crusader	C. J. Moss
	G-CMSN	Robinson R22 Beta	Kuki Helicopter Sales Ltd (G-MGEE//G-RUMP)
	G-CMWK	Grob G.102 Astir CS	S. J. Saunders
	G-CMXX	Robinson R44 II	Northern Excavators Ltd
	G-CNAB	Avtech Jabiru UL	E. Bentley
	G-CNCN	Rockwell Commander 112CA	G. R. Frost
	G-CNHB	Van's RV-7	M. E. Wood
	G-CNUK	Dassault Falcon 7X	TAG Aviation (UK) Ltd
	G-COAI	Cranfield A.1	Cranfield University (G-BCIT)
	G-COBI	Beech 300 Super King Air	Cobham Flight Inspection Ltd
	G-COBM	Beech 300 Super King Air	Cobham Flight Inspection Ltd
	G-COBO	ATR-72-212A	Aurigny Air Services Ltd
	G-COBS	Diamond DA.42 M-NG	Diamond Aircraft UK Ltd
	G-COCO	Cessna F.172M	P. C. Sheard & R. C. Larder
	G-CODY	Kolb Twinstar Mk.3 Extra	J. W. Codd
	G-COIN	Bell 206B JetRanger 2	J. P. Niehorster
	G-COLA	Beech F33C Bonanza	Airport Direction Ltd (G-BUAZ)
	G-COLH	PA-28 Cherokee 140	Full Sutton Flying Centre Ltd (G-AVRT)
	G-COLI	Rotorsport UK MT-03	C. Gilholm
	G-COLR	Colt 69A balloon ★	British School of Ballooning/Lancing
	G-COLS	Van's RV-7A	C. Terry
	G-COMB	PA-30 Twin Comanche 160B	M. R. Booker (G-AVBL)
	G-COML	Eurocopter EC120B	Combilift
	G-COMP	Cameron N-90 balloon	Computacenter Ltd
	G-CONA	Flight Design CTLS	S. Connah (G-CGED)
	G-CONB	Robin DR.400/180	M. D. Souster (G-BUPX)
	G-CONC	Cameron N-90 balloon	A. A. Brown
	G-CONL	SOCATA TB10 Tobago	J. M. Huntington
	G-CONN	Eurocopter EC.120B Colibri	M. J. Connors (G-BZMK)
	G-CONR	Champion 7GCBC Scout	N. O'Brien
	G-CONV	Convair CV-440-54 ★	Reynard Nursery/Carluke
	G-COOK	Cameron N-77 balloon	IAZ (International) Ltd
	G-COOT	Taylor Coot A	P. M. Napp
	G-COPS	Piper J-3C-65 Cub	R. W. Sproat
	G-CORA	Shaw Europa XS	A. P. Gardner (G-ILUM)
	G-CORB	SOCATA TB20 Trinidad	G. D. Corbin

Reg.	Type	Owner or Operator	Notes
G-CORD	Slingsby T.66 Nipper 3	A. V. Lamprell (G-AVTB)	
G-CORL	AS.350B3 Ecureuil	Abbeyflight Ltd	
G-CORW	PA-28-180 Cherokee C	R. P. Osborne & C. A. Wilson (G-AVRY)	
G-COSF	PA-28-161 Warrior II	PA-28 Warrior Ltd	
G-COSY	Lindstrand LBL-56A balloon	M. H. Read & J. E. Wetters	
G-COTH	MD-900 Explorer	Police Aviation Services Ltd	
G-COTT	Cameron 60 Cottage SS balloon	Dragon Balloon Co Ltd	
G-COUZ	X'Air 582(2)	D. J. Couzens	
G-COVA	PA-26-161 Warrior III	Coventry (Civil) Aviation Ltd (G-CDCL)	
G-COVB	PA-28-161 Warrior III	Coventry (Civil) Aviation Ltd	
G-COVE	Avtech Jabiru UL	A. A. Rowson	
G-COVZ	Cessna F.150M	R. A. Doherty (G-BCRT)	
G-COXS	Aeroprakt A.22 Foxbat	S. Cox	
G-COXY	Kiss 400-582 (1)	J. R. Pearce	
G-COZI	Rutan Cozy III	R. Machin	
G-CPAO	Eurocopter EC.135P2+	Cheshire Police Authority	
G-CPAS	Eurocopter EC.135P2+	Cleveland Police Authority	
G-CPCD	CEA DR.221	P. J. Taylor	
G-CPDA	DH.106 Comet 4C (XS235) ★	C. Walton Ltd/Bruntingthorpe	
G-CPDW	Avions Mudry CAP.10B	Hilfa Ltd	
G-CPET	Boeing 757-236	British Airways	
G-CPEU	Boeing 757-236	Thomson Airways Ltd	
G-CPEV	Boeing 757-236	Thomson Airways Ltd	
G-CPFC	Cessna F.152 II	Falcon Flying Services Ltd	
G-CPFM	PA-28-161 Warrior II	M. O'Rourke (G-BNNS)	
G-CPHA	Robinson R44 II	Heli Air Ltd	
G-CPMK	DHC.1 Chipmunk 22 (WZ847)	P. A. Walley	
G-CPMS	SOCATA TB20 Trinidad	Charlotte Park Management Services Ltd	
G-CPOL	AS.355F1 Twin Squirrel	MW Helicopters Ltd	
G-CPPM	North American Harvard II	S. D. Wilch	
G-CPRR	Cessna 680 Citation Sovereign	Eurojet Aviation Ltd	
G-CPSH	Eurocopter EC 135T1	Thames Valley Police Authority	
G-CPSS	Cessna 208B Grand Caravan	Army Parachute Association	
G-CPTM	PA-28-151 Warrior	T. J. & C. Mackay (G-BTOE)	
G-CPXC	Avions Mudry CAP-10C	Medcentres Property Portfolio Ltd	
G-CRAB	Skyranger 912 (1)	J. O. Williams	
G-CRAR	CZAW Sportcruiser	J. S. Kinsey	
G-CRBV	Balóny Kubíček BB26 balloon	Charter Ballooning Ltd	
G-CRDY	Agusta-Bell 206A JetRanger	Jac-Heli SARL (G-WHAZ)	
G-CRES	Denney Kitfox Mk 3	J. McGoldrick	
G-CREY	SeaRey Amphibian	A. F. Reid & P. J. Gallagher	
G-CRIC	Colomban MC.15 Cri-Cri	R. S. Stoddart-Stones	
G-CRIK	Colomban MC.15 Cri-Cri	C. R. Harrison	
G-CRIL	Rockwell Commander 112B	Rockwell Aviation Group	
G-CRIS	Taylor JT.1 Monoplane	C. R. Steer	
G-CRJW	Schleicher ASW-27-18	R. J. Welford	
G-CRLA	Cirrus SR20	Aero Club Heidelberg EV/Germany	
G-CROB	Shaw Europa XS T-G	R. G. Hallam	
G-CROL	Maule MXT-7-180	W. E. Willets	
G-CROP	Cameron Z-105 balloon	PSH Skypower Ltd	
G-CROW	Robinson R44	Longmoore Ltd	
G-CROY	Shaw Europa	M. T. Austin	
G-CRPH	Airbus A.320-231	Thomas Cook Airlines Ltd	
G-CRSR	Czech Sport Aircraft Sportcruiser	G-CRSR Flying Group	
G-CRST	Agusta A.109E Power	Castle Air Ltd (G-WRBI)	
G-CRUI	CZAW Sportcruiser	J. Massey	
G-CRUM	Westland Scout AH.1 (XV137)	G-CRUM Group	
G-CRUZ	Cessna T.303	Bank Farm Ltd	
G-CRWZ	CZAW Sportcruiser	P. B. Lowry	
G-CRZA	CZAW Sportcruiser	A. J. Radford	
G-CSAM	Van's RV-9A	B. G. Murray	
G-CSAV	Thruster T.600N 450	D. J. N. Brown	
G-CSAW	CZAW Sportcruiser	B. C. Fitzgerald-O'Connor	
G-CSBD	PA-28-236 Dakota	S. B. & S-J. Dunnett (G-CSBO)	
G-CSBM	Cessna F.150M	Hinton Pilot Flight Training Ltd	
G-CSCS	Cessna F.172N	C.Sullivan	
G-CSDJ	Avtech Jabiru UL	G-CSDJ Group	
G-CSDR	Corvus CA22	Crusader Syndicate	
G-CSFC	Cessna 150L	Foxtrot Charlie Flying Group	

Notes	Reg.	Type	Owner or Operator
	G-CSFD	Ultramagic M-90 balloon	L. A. Watts
	G-CSFT	PA-23 Aztec 250D ★	Aces High Ltd (G-AYKU)
	G-CSGT	PA-28-161 Warrior II	C. P. Awdry (G-BPHB)
	G-CSIX	PA-32 Cherokee Six 300	A. J. Hodge
	G-CSMK	Aerotechnik EV-97 Eurostar	R. Frey
	G-CSPR	Van's RV-6A	P. J. Pengilly
	G-CSTL	Bell 206B-3 JetRanger III	Castle Air Ltd (G-HIER/G-BRFD)
	G-CSUE	ICP MXP-740 Savannah Jabiru (5)	J. R. Stratton
	G-CSVS	Boeing 757-236	European Air Transport Leipzig GmbH (G-IEAC)
	G-CSZM	Zenair CH.601XL Zodiac	C. Budd
	G-CTAG	Rolladen-Schneider LS8-18	C. D. R. Tagg
	G-CTAM	Cirrus SR22	M. R. Munn
	G-CTAV	Aerotechnik EV-97 Eurostar	P. Simpson
	G-CTCD	Diamond DA42 Twin Star	CTC Aviation Group PLC
	G-CTCE	Diamond DA42 Twin Star	CTC Aviation Group PLC
	G-CTCF	Diamond DA42 Twin Star	CTC Aviation Group PLC
	G-CTCG	Diamond DA42 Twin Star	I. Annenskiy
	G-CTCH	Diamond DA42 Twin Star	CTC Aviation Group PLC
	G-CTCL	SOCATA TB10 Tobago	Gift Aviation Club (G-BSIV)
	G-CTDH	Flight Design CT2K	A. D. Thelwall
	G-CTDW	Flight Design CTSW	S. L. Morris
	G-CTED	Van's RV-7A	E. W. Lyon
	G-CTEL	Cameron N-90 balloon	M. R. Noyce
	G-CTEN	Cessna 750 Citation X	Pendley Aviation LLP
	G-CTIO	SOCATA TB20 Trinidad	I. R. Hunt
	G-CTIX	VS.509 Spitfire T.IX (PT462)	A. A. Hodgson
	G-CTKL	Noorduyn AT-16 Harvard IIB (54137)	M. R. Simpson
	G-CTLS	Flight Design CTLS	D. J. Haygreen
	G-CTNG	Cirrus SR20	K. D. Brown & K. S. Mitchell
	G-CTOY	Denney Kitfox Mk 3	B. McNeilly
	G-CTPW	Bell 206B JetRanger 3	Aviation Rentals
	G-CTRL	Robinson R22 Beta	Central Helicopters Ltd
	G-CTUG	PA-25 Pawnee 235	The Borders (Milfield) Gliding Club Ltd
	G-CTWO	Schempp-Hirth Standard Cirrus	R. J. Griffin
	G-CTZO	SOCATA TB20 Trinidad GT	G-CTZO Group
	G-CUBA	PA-32R-301T Turbo Saratoge	M. Atlass
	G-CUBB	PA-18 Super Cub 180	Bidford Gliding Ltd
	G-CUBE	Skyranger 912 (2)	A. I. Medler
	G-CUBI	PA-18 Super Cub 125	G. T. Fisher
	G-CUBJ	PA-18 Super Cub 150 (18-5395:CDG)	A. L. Grisay
	G-CUBN	PA-18 Super Cub 150	N. J. R. Minchin
	G-CUBP	PA-18 Super Cub 150	D. W. Berger
	G-CUBS	Piper J-3C-65 Cub	S. M. Rolfe (G-BHPT)
	G-CUBW	WAG-Aero Acro Trainer	B. G. Plumb & ptnrs
	G-CUBY	Piper J-3C-65 Cub	C. A. Bloom (G-BTZW)
	G-CUCU	Colt 180A balloon	S. R. Seage
	G-CUDY	Enstrom 480B	D'Arcy Holdings Ltd (G-REAN)
	G-CUGC	Schleicher ASW-19B	Cambridge University Gliding Club (G-CKEX)
	G-CUIK	QAC Quickie Q.200	C. S. Rayner
	G-CUMU	Schempp-Hirth Discus b	C. E. Fernando
	G-CUPP	Pitts S-2A	Avmarine Ltd
	G-CURV	Avid Speedwing	K. S. Kelso
	G-CUTE	Dyn'Aéro MCR-01	E. G. Shimmin
	G-CUTH	P & M Quik R	A. R. & S. Cuthbertson
	G-CVAL	Ikarus C42 FB100	G. W. F. Morton
	G-CVBF	Cameron A-210 balloon	Virgin Balloon Flights Ltd
	G-CVII	Dan Rihn DR.107 One Design	One Design Group
	G-CVIX	DH.110 Sea Vixen D.3 (XP924)	Drilling Systems Ltd
	G-CVMI	PA-18 Super Cub 150	D. Heslop & T. P. Spurge
	G-CVPM	VPM M-16 Tandem Trainer	P. L. Newman
	G-CVST	Jodel D.140E	D. Runnalls & R. Sheridan
	G-CVXN	Cessna F.406 Caravan	Caledonian Airborne Systems Ltd (G-SFPA)
	G-CVZT	Schempp-Hirth Ventus 2cT	C. D. Sterritt & M. W. Conboy
	G-CWAG	Sequoia F. 8L Falco	D. R. Austin
	G-CWAL	Raj Hamsa X'Air 133	L. R. Morris
	G-CWAY	Ikarus C42 FB100	M. Conway
	G-CWBM	Phoenix Currie Wot	G-CWBM Group (G-BTVP)
	G-CWEB	P & M Quik GT450	M & K. A. Forsyth

Reg.	Type	Owner or Operator	Notes
G-CWFA	PA-38-112 Tomahawk	M. Hoecker (G-BTGC)	
G-CWFC	PA-38-112 Tomahawk ★	Cardiff-Wales Flying Club Ltd (G-BRTA)	
G-CWIC	Mainair Pegasus Quik	G-CWIC Group	
G-CWIK	Mainair Pegasus Quik	C. D. Jackson	
G-CWIS	Diamond DA.20 Star	R. A. Eve	
G-CWLC	Schleicher ASH-25	G-CWLC Group	
G-CWMC	P & M Quik GT450	A. R. Hughes	
G-CWMT	Dyn'Aéro MCR-01 Bambi	J. Jones	
G-CWOT	Currie Wot	D. Doyle & H. Duggan	
G-CWVY	Mainair Pegasus Quik	G-CWVY Group	
G-CXCX	Cameron N-90 balloon	Cathay Pacific Airways (London) Ltd	
G-CXDZ	Cassutt Speed Two	J. A. H. Chadwick	
G-CXIP	Thruster T.600N	India Papa Syndicate	
G-CXLS	Cessna 560 XL Citation XLS	Aviation Beauport Ltd (G-PKRG)	
G-CXSM	Cessna 172R	S. Eustathiou (G-BXSM)	
G-CYGI	HAPI Cygnet SF-2A	B. Brown	
G-CYLL	Sequoia F.8L Falco	N. J. Langrick & A. J. Newall	
G-CYLS	Cessna T.303	Oasis 303 Ltd (G-BKXI)	
G-CYMA	GA-7 Cougar	Cyma Petroleum (UK) Ltd (G-BKOM)	
G-CYPM	Cirrus SR22	R. M. Steeves	
G-CYRA	Kolb Twinstar Mk. 3 (Modified)	S. J. Fox (G-MYRA)	
G-CYRL	Cessna 182T	D. R. Rayne	
G-CYRS	Bell 206L Long Ranger	HJS Helicopters Ltd	
G-CZAC	Zenair CH.601XL	D. Pitt	
G-CZAG	Sky 90-24 balloon	S. Paszkowicz	
G-CZAW	CZAW Sportcruiser	Sprite Aviation Services Ltd	
G-CZCZ	Avions Mudry CAP-10B	M. Farmer	
G-CZMI	Skyranger 912 (2)	L. M. Bassett	
G-CZNE	BN-2B-20 Islander	Skyhopper LLP (G-BWZF)	
G-CZOS	Cirrus SR20	Cirrus UK Training Ltd	
G-CZSC	CZAW Sportcruiser	F. J. Wadia	
G-DAAH	PA-28RT-201T Turbo Arrow IV	P. Randall	
G-DAAT	Eurocopter EC 135T2	Bond Air Services Ltd	
G-DAAZ	PA-28RT-201T Turbo Arrow IV	Calais Ltd	
G-DABS	Robinson R22 Beta II	B16 Ltd	
G-DACA	P.57 Sea Prince T.1 (WF118) ★	P. G. Vallance Ltd/Charlwood	
G-DACF	Cessna 152 II	T. M. & M. L. Jones (G-BURY)	
G-DADA	Rotorsport UK MT-03	J. C. Hilton-Johnson	
G-DADG	PA-18-150 Super Cub	F. J. Cox	
G-DADJ	Glaser-Dirks DG-200	T. Forsey	
G-DADZ	CZAW Sportcruiser	Meon Flying Group	
G-DAGF	EAA Acrosport II	D. A. G. Fraser	
G-DAGJ	Zenair CH.601HD Zodiac	D. A. G. Johnson	
G-DAIR	Luscombe 8A Silvaire	D. F. Soul (G-BURK)	
G-DAIV	Ultramagic H-77 balloon	D. Harrison-Morris	
G-DAJB	Boeing 757-2T7	Monarch Airlines Ltd	
G-DAJC	Boeing 757-31K	Thomas Cook Airlines Ltd	
G-DAKK	Douglas C-47A	General Technics Ltd	
G-DAKM	Diamond DA40D Star	K. MacDonald	
G-DAKO	PA-28-236 Dakota	Methods Consulting Ltd	
G-DAME	Vans RV-7	A. D. Heath	
G-DAMY	Shaw Europa	U. A. Schliessler & R. J. Kelly	
G-DANA	Jodel DR.200 (replica)	Cheshire Eagles (G-DAST)	
G-DAND	SOCATA TB10 Tobago	Portway Aviation Ltd	
G-DANT	Rockwell Commander 114	J Terreaux	
G-DANY	Avtech Jabiru UL	D. A. Crosbie	
G-DAPH	Cessna 180K	T. W. Harris	
G-DASA	Dassault Falcon 50	Bramptonia Ltd (G-ITIH)	
G-DASH	Rockwell Commander 112	D. & M. Nelson (G-BDAJ)	
G-DASS	Ikarus C.42 FB100	D. D. J. Rossdale	
G-DATG	Cessna F.182P	Oxford Aeroplane Co Ltd	
G-DAVB	Aerosport Scamp	D. R. Burns	
G-DAVD	Cessna FR.172K	D. M. Driver & S. Copeland	
G-DAVE	Jodel D.112	D. Evans	
G-DAVG	Robinson R44 II	AG Aviation Ltd (G-WOWW)	
G-DAVM	Akrotech Europe CAP.10B	D. Moorman	
G-DAVS	AB Sportine Aviacija LAK-17AT	G-DAVS Syndicate	
G-DAVV	Robinson R44 Raven II	A. Rahman	

Notes	Reg.	Type	Owner or Operator
	G-DAVZ	Cessna 182T Skylane	D. J. & P. J. Lawrence
	G-DAWZ	Glasflugel 304 CZ	G. Rogers
	G-DAYS	Shaw Europa	D. A. Gittins
	G-DAYZ	Pietenpol Air Camper	N. S. Lomax
	G-DAZZ	Van's RV-8	Wishanger RV8
	G-DBCA	Airbus A.319-131	bmi british midland
	G-DBCB	Airbus A.319-131	bmi british midland
	G-DBCC	Airbus A.319-131	bmi british midland
	G-DBCD	Airbus A.319-131	bmi british midland
	G-DBCE	Airbus A.319-131	bmi british midland
	G-DBCF	Airbus A.319-131	bmi british midland
	G-DBCG	Airbus A.319-131	bmi british midland
	G-DBCH	Airbus A.319-131	bmi british midland
	G-DBCI	Airbus A.319-131	bmi british midland
	G-DBCJ	Airbus A.319-131	bmi british midland
	G-DBCK	Airbus A.319-131	bmi british midland
	G-DBDB	VPM M-16 Tandem Trainer	D. R. Bolsover (G-IROW)
	G-DBIN	Medway SLA 80 Executive	P. L. P. Rooms & S. P. Hoskins
	G-DBJD	PZL-Bielsko SZD-9BIS Bocian 1D	Bertie the Bocian Glider Syndicate
	G-DBKL	VS.379 Spitfire F.Mk.XIV	P. M. Andrews
	G-DBLA	Boeing 767-35EER	Thomson Airways Ltd
	G-DBLX	Aviat A-18 Husky	Aviat Aircraft (UK) Ltd
	G-DBMK	Ikarus C42 FB100 VLA	GDBMK Ltd (G-MROY)
	G-DBND	Schleicher Ka 6CR	A. H. Hall
	G-DBNH	Schleicher Ka 6CR	The Bath, Wilts and North Dorset Gliding Club Ltd
	G-DBNP	Slingsby T.50 Skylark 4	D. H. Smith
	G-DBOD	Cessna 172S	Goodwood Road Racing Co.Ltd
	G-DBOL	Schleicher Ka 6CR	A. C. Thorne
	G-DBRT	Slingsby T.51 Dart	C. W. Logue
	G-DBRU	Slingsby T.51 Dart	L. J. Stephenson
	G-DBRY	Slingsby T.51 Dart	D. J. Knights
	G-DBSA	Slingsby T.51 Dart	G. Burton
	G-DBSL	Slingsby T.51 Dart	G-DBSL Group
	G-DBSR	Kubicek BB26Z balloon	G. J. Bell
	G-DBTF	Schleicher Ka 6CR	T. Fletcher
	G-DBTJ	Schleicher Ka 6CR	I. G. Robinson
	G-DBUZ	Schleicher Ka 6CR	J. J. Hartwell
	G-DBVB	Schleicher K7	Dartmoor Gliding Society Ltd
	G-DBVH	Slingsby T.51 Dart 17R	P. G. Addy
	G-DBVR	Schleicher Ka 6CR	J. R. Ross & J. M. Brooke
	G-DBVX	Schleicher Ka 6CR	R. Lynch
	G-DBVY	LET L-13 Blanik	Victor Yankee Group
	G-DBVZ	Schleicher Ka 6CR	G-DBVZ Group
	G-DBWC	Schleicher Ka 6CR	K6CR-GBWC Group
	G-DBWJ	Slingsby T.51 Dart 17R	M. F. Defendi
	G-DBWM	Slingsby T.51 Dart 17R	P. L. Poole
	G-DBWO	Slingsby T.51 Dart	G. Winch
	G-DBWP	Slingsby T.51 Dart 17R	R. Johnson
	G-DBWS	Slingsby T.51 Dart 17R	R. D. Broome
	G-DBXE	Slingsby T.51 Dart	Group G-DBXE
	G-DBXG	Slingsby T.51 Dart 17R	J. M. Whelan
	G-DBXT	Schleicher Ka 6CR	C. I. Knowles
	G-DBYC	Slingsby T.51 Dart 17R	R. L. Horsnell & N. A. Jaffray
	G-DBYG	Slingsby T.51 Dart 17R	W. T. Emery
	G-DBYL	Schleicher Ka 6CR	Channel Gliding Club Ltd
	G-DBYM	Schleicher Ka 6CR	K. S. Smith
	G-DBYU	Schleicher Ka-6CR	G. B. Sutton
	G-DBYX	Schleicher Ka-6E	J. R. Dent
	G-DBZF	Slingsby T.51 Dart 17R	S. Rhenius & D. Charles
	G-DBZX	Schleicher Ka 6CR	Leeds University Union Gliding Society
	G-DCAE	Schleicher Ka 6E	N. Rolfe
	G-DCAG	Schleicher Ka 6E	715 Syndicate
	G-DCAM	Eurocopter AS.355NP Ecureuil 2	Cameron Charters LLP
	G-DCAO	Schempp-Hirth SHK-1	M. G. Entwisle & A. K. Bartlett
	G-DCAS	Schleicher Ka 6E	R. F. Tindall
	G-DCAZ	Slingsby T.51 Dart 17R	D. A. Bullock & Man L. C.
	G-DCBA	Slingsby T.51 Dart 17R	M. Parsons
	G-DCBI	Schweizer 269C-1	Helicentre Holdings Ltd
	G-DCBM	Schleicher Ka 6CR	R. J. Shepherd
	G-DCBW	Schleicher ASK-13	Stratford on Avon Gliding Club Ltd
	G-DCBY	Schleicher Ka 6CR	Talgarth 475

Reg.	Type	Owner or Operator	Notes
G-DCCA	Schleicher Ka 6E	R. K. Forrest	
G-DCCB	Schempp-Hirth SHK-1	CCB Syndicate	
G-DCCD	Schleicher Ka 6E	Charlie Charlie Delta Group	
G-DCCE	Schleicher ASK-13	Oxford Gliding Co.Ltd	
G-DCCF	Schleicher ASK-13	Norfolk Gliding Club Ltd	
G-DCCG	Schleicher Ka 6E	R. J. Playle	
G-DCCL	Schleicher Ka 6E	G-DCCL Group	
G-DCCM	Schleicher ASK-13	The Burn Gliding Club Ltd	
G-DCCP	Schleicher ASK-13	Lima 99 Syndicate	
G-DCCR	Schleicher Ka 6E	A. Shaw	
G-DCCT	Schleicher ASK-13	Stratford on Avon Gliding Club Ltd	
G-DCCU	Schleicher Ka 6E	J. L. Hasker	
G-DCCV	Schleicher Ka 6E	C. H. Page & J. A. Wade	
G-DCCW	Schleicher ASK-13	Needwood Forest Gliding Club Ltd	
G-DCCX	Schleicher ASK-13	Trent Valley Gliding Club Ltd	
G-DCCY	Schleicher ASK-13	Devon and Somerset Gliding Club Ltd	
G-DCCZ	Schleicher ASK-13	The Windrushers Gliding Club Ltd	
G-DCDA	Schleicher Ka 6E	D. Close, A. Smith & J. Tonkin	
G-DCDC	Lange E1 Antares	J. D. Williams	
G-DCDF	Schleicher Ka 6E	CDF Syndicate	
G-DCDG	FFA Diamant 18	J. Cashin & D. McCarty	
G-DCDH	Schempp-Hirth Cirrus	DCDH Syndicate	
G-DCDO	Ikarus C42 FB80	C42 Dodo Syndicate	
G-DCDW	Diamant 18	D. R. Chapman	
G-DCDZ	Schleicher Ka 6E	J. R. J. Minns	
G-DCEB	PZL-Bielsko SZD-9BIS Bocian 1E	The Bath, Wilts and North Dorset Gliding Club Ltd	
G-DCEC	Schempp-Hirth Cirrus	Cirrus 18 Group	
G-DCEM	Schleicher Ka 6E	E. W. Black	
G-DCEN	PZL-Bielsko SZD-30 Pirat	D. P. Aherne	
G-DCEO	Schleicher Ka 6E	C. L. Lagden & J. C. Green	
G-DCEW	Schleicher Ka 6E	J. W. Richardson and Partners Group	
G-DCEX	Schleicher ASK-13	R. B. Walker	
G-DCFA	Schleicher ASK-13	Booker Gliding Club Ltd	
G-DCFE	Schleicher ASK-13	Loughborough Students Union Gliding Club	
G-DCFF	Schleicher K 8B	Derbyshire and Lancashire Gliding Club Ltd	
G-DCFG	Schleicher ASK-13	The Nene Valley Gliding Club Ltd	
G-DCFK	Schempp-Hirth Cirrus	M. P. Webb	
G-DCFL	Schleicher Ka 6E	L. M. Causer	
G-DCFS	Glasflugel Standard Libelle 201B	P. J. Flack	
G-DCFW	Glasflugel Standard Libelle 201B	D. J. Edwardes & T. J. Price	
G-DCFX	Glasflugel Standard Libelle 201B	K. D. Fishenden	
G-DCFY	Glasflugel Standard Libelle 201B	C. W. Stevens	
G-DCGB	Schleicher Ka 6E	P. M. Turner & S. C. Male	
G-DCGD	Schleicher Ka 6E	Charlie Golf Delta Group	
G-DCGE	Schleicher Ka 6E	C. V. Hill & P. C. Hazlehurst	
G-DCGH	Schleicher K 8B	K7 (1971) Syndicate	
G-DCGM	FFA Diamant 18	J. G. Batch	
G-DCGO	Schleicher ASK-13	Oxford Gliding Company Ltd	
G-DCGY	Schempp-Hirth Cirrus	R. A. J. Jones & G. Nevisky	
G-DCHB	Schleicher Ka 6E	D. L. Jones	
G-DCHC	Bolkow Phoebus C	D. A. Gardner & D. C. Ephraim	
G-DCHJ	Bolkow Phoebus C	D. C. Austin	
G-DCHL	PZL-Bielsko SZD-30	A. P. P. Scorer & A. Stocks	
G-DCHT	Schleicher ASW-15	P. G. Roberts & J. M. Verrill	
G-DCHU	Schleicher K 8B	Highland Gliding Club K8 Syndicate	
G-DCHW	Schleicher ASK-13	Dorset Gliding Club Ltd	
G-DCHZ	Schleicher Ka 6E	V. Harrington	
G-DCJB	Bolkow Phoebus C	R. Idle	
G-DCJF	Schleicher K-8B	G. Smith	
G-DCJJ	Bolkow Phoebus C	P. N. Maddocks	
G-DCJK	Schempp-Hirth SHK-1	R. H. Short	
G-DCJM	Schleicher K-8B	Midland Gliding Club Ltd	
G-DCJN	Schempp-Hirth SHK-1	R. J. Makin	
G-DCJR	Schempp-Hirth Cirrus	J. C. K. Brown	
G-DCJY	Schleicher Ka 6CR	CJY Syndicate	
G-DCKD	PZL-Bielsko SZD-30	Dartmoor Gliding Society Ltd	
G-DCKK	Cessna F.172N	KK Group	
G-DCKL	Schleicher Ka 6E	BGA1603 Owners Syndicate	
G-DCKN	PZL-Bielsko SZD-9bis Bocian 1E	DCKN Bocian Syndicate	
G-DCKP	Schleicher ASW-15	ASW 15-BGA1606 Partnership	
G-DCKR	Schleicher ASK-13	Midland Gliding Club Ltd	

Notes	Reg.	Type	Owner or Operator
	G-DCKV	Schleicher ASK-13	Black Mountains Gliding Club
	G-DCKY	Glasflugel Standard Libelle 201B	G. Herbert
	G-DCKZ	Schempp-Hirth Standard Cirrus	G. I. Bustin
	G-DCLA	Schempp-Hirth Standard Cirrus	S. A. Lees
	G-DCLM	Glasflugel Standard Libelle 201B	C. J. Heide & J. H. Newberry
	G-DCLO	Schempp-Hirth Cirrus	Bravo Delta Group
	G-DCLP	Glasflugel Standard Libelle 201B	D. Heaton
	G-DCLT	Schleicher K7	A. H. Watkins
	G-DCLV	Glasflugel Standard Libelle 201B	K. Vanderputten
	G-DCLZ	Schleicher Ka 6E	G-DCLZ Flying Group
	G-DCMF	PZL-Bielsko SZD-32A Foka 5	K. Szent-Wanyi
	G-DCMG	Schleicher K7	J. P. Bakker
	G-DCMI	Mainair Pegasus Quik	T. F. Fitzsimons
	G-DCMK	Schleicher ASK-13	The South Wales Gliding Club Ltd
	G-DCMN	Schleicher K 8B	The Bristol Gliding Club Proprietary Ltd
	G-DCMO	Glasflugel Standard Libelle 201B	M. E. Wolff & L. C. Wood
	G-DCMR	Glasflugel Standard Libelle 201B	G-DCMR Group
	G-DCMS	Glasflugel Standard Libelle 201B	Libelle 602 Syndicate
	G-DCMV	Glasflugel Standard Libelle 201B	L. B. Roberts
	G-DCMW	Glasflugel Standard Libelle 201B	T. Rose
	G-DCNC	Schempp-Hirth Standard Cirrus	Cirrus 273 Syndicate
	G-DCND	PZL-Bielsko SZD-9bis Bocian 1E	Angus Gliding Club Ltd
	G-DCNE	Glasflugel Standard Libelle 201B	25 Syndicate
	G-DCNG	Glasflugel Standard Libelle 201B	M. C. J. Gardner
	G-DCNJ	Glasflugel Standard Libelle 201B	R. Thornley
	G-DCNM	PZL-Bielsko SZD-9bis Bocian 1E	Bocian Syndicate
	G-DCNP	Glasflugel Standard Libelle 201B	I. G. Carrick & D. J. Miles
	G-DCNS	Slingsby T.59A Kestrel	J. R. Greenwell
	G-DCNW	Slingsby T.59F Kestrel	S. R. Watson
	G-DCNX	Slingsby T.59F Kestrel	M. Boxall
	G-DCOJ	Slingsby T.59A Kestrel	T. W. Treadaway
	G-DCON	Robinson R44	D. Connolly/Ireland
	G-DCOR	Schempp-Hirth Standard Cirrus	J. D. Drury
	G-DCOY	Schempp-Hirth Standard Cirrus	A. D. Walsh & M. R. Latham
	G-DCPA	MBB BK.117C-1C	Veritair Aviation Ltd (G-LFBA)
	G-DCPB	Eurocopter MBB-BK 117C-2	Devon & Cornwall Constabulary
	G-DCPD	Schleicher ASW-17	A. J. Hewitt
	G-DCPG	Schleicher K7	A. L. Maitland & D. N. Mackay
	G-DCPJ	Schleicher KA6E	G-DCPJ Group
	G-DCPM	Glasflugel Standard Libelle 201B	N. Godson & P. E. Jessop
	G-DCPU	Schempp-Hirth Standard Cirrus	P. J. Ketelaar
	G-DCPV	PZL-Bielsko SZD-30 Pirat	CPV Group
	G-DCRB	Glasflugel Standard Libelle 201B	A. I. Mawer
	G-DCRH	Schempp-Hirth Standard Cirrus	P. E. Thelwall
	G-DCRN	Schempp-Hirth Standard Cirrus	J. Craig & L. Runhaar
	G-DCRO	Glasflugel Standard Libelle 201B	G-DCRO Group
	G-DCRS	Glasflugel standard Libelle 201B	J. R. Hiley & M. W. Fisher
	G-DCRT	Schleicher ASK-13	Bowland Forest Gliding Club Ltd
	G-DCRV	Glasflugel Standard Libelle 201B	M. Carnet
	G-DCRW	Glasflugel Standard Libelle 201B	P. J. Trevethick
	G-DCSB	Slingsby T.59F Kestrel	W. Fischer
	G-DCSD	Slingsby T.59D Kestrel	L. P. Davidson
	G-DCSE	Robinson R44	Heli Air Ltd
	G-DCSF	Slingsby T.59F Kestrel 19	R. Birch & S. Glassett
	G-DCSG	Robinson R44	Voute Sales Ltd (G-TRYG)
	G-DCSI	Robinson R44 II	Enable International Ltd (G-TGDL)
	G-DCSJ	Glasflugel Standard Libelle 201B	P. J. Gill
	G-DCSK	Slingsby T.59D Kestrel	Kestrel CSK Group
	G-DCSN	Pilatus B4-PC11AF	J. S. Firth
	G-DCSP	Pilatus B4-PC11	G-DCSP Group
	G-DCSR	Glasflugel Standard Libelle 201B	Glasgow and West of Scotland Gliding Club
	G-DCTB	Schempp-Hirth Standard Cirrus	I. M. Young & S. McCurdy
	G-DCTE	Schleicher ASW-17	C. A. & S. C. Noujaim
	G-DCTJ	Slingsby T.59D Kestrel	R. M. Theil
	G-DCTL	Slingsby T.59D Kestrel	E. S. E. Hibbard
	G-DCTM	Slingsby T.59D Kestrel	C. Roney
	G-DCTO	Slingsby T.59D Kestrel	K. A. Moules
	G-DCTP	Slingsby T.59D Kestrel	D. C. Austin
	G-DCTR	Slingsby T.59D Kestrel	M. W. Hands
	G-DCTT	Schempp-Hirth Standard Cirrus	E. Sparrow
	G-DCTU	Glasflugel Standard Libelle 201B	F. K. Hutchinson & P. M. Davies
	G-DCTV	PZL-Bielsko SZD-30	Black Mountains Gliding Club

Reg.	Type	Owner or Operator	Notes
G-DCTX	PZL-Bielsko SZD-30	Dave King, John Cooper, Ben Fantham Group	
G-DCUB	Pilatus B4-PC11	Staffordshire Gliding Club Ltd	
G-DCUC	Pilatus B4-PC11	G. M. Cumner	
G-DCUD	Yorkshire Sailplanes YS53 Sovereign	T. J. Wilkinson	
G-DCUJ	Glasflugel Standard Libelle 201B	T. G. B. Hobbis	
G-DCUO	Pilatus B4-PC11	Cotswold Gliding Club	
G-DCUS	Schempp-Hirth Cirrus VTC	R. C. Graham	
G-DCUT	Pilatus B4 PC11AF	A. L. Walker	
G-DCVB	LET L-13 Blanik	Blanik Syndicate	
G-DCVE	Schempp-Hirth Cirrus VTC	H. Whybrow	
G-DCVG	Pilatus B4-PC11AF	M. Kempf	
G-DCVK	Pilatus B4-PC11AF	J. P. Marriott	
G-DCVL	Glasflugel Standard Libelle 201B	J. Williams	
G-DCVR	PZL-Bielsko SZD-30 Pirat	M. T. Pitorak	
G-DCVS	PZL-Bielsko SZD-36A	I. A. Burgin	
G-DCVV	Pilatus B4-PC11AF	Syndicate CVV	
G-DCVW	Slingsby T.59D Kestrel	J. J. Green	
G-DCVY	Slingsby T.59D Kestrel	N. Dickenson	
G-DCWA	Slingsby T.59D Kestrel	D. J. Jeffries	
G-DCWB	Slingsby T.59D Kestrel	Kestrel 677 Syndicate	
G-DCWD	Slingsby T.59D Kestrel	Deeside Kestrel Group	
G-DCWE	Glasflugel Standard Libelle 201B	T. W. J. Stoker	
G-DCWF	Slingsby T.59D Kestrel	P. F. Nicholson	
G-DCWG	Glasflugel Standard Libelle 201B	Libelle 322 Group	
G-DCWH	Schleicher ASK-13	York Gliding Centre Ltd	
G-DCWJ	Schleicher K7	Angus Gliding Club K7 Syndicate	
G-DCWR	Schempp-Hirth Cirrus VTC	CWR Group	
G-DCWS	Schempp-Hirth Cirrus VTC	Cirrus G-DCWS Syndicate	
G-DCWT	Glasflugel Standard Libelle 201B	B. J. Darton	
G-DCWX	Glasflugel Standard Libelle	C. A. Weyman	
G-DCWY	Glasflugel Standard Libelle 201B	S. J. Taylor	
G-DCWZ	Glasflugel Standard Libelle 201B	F. de Groote/Belgium	
G-DCXI	Slingsby T.61F Venture T.2	611 Vintage Flight (G-BUDB)	
G-DCXK	Glasflugel Standard Libelle 201B	J. M. Whelan	
G-DCXL	Jodel D.140C	A. C. D. Norris/France	
G-DCXM	Slingsby T.59D Kestrel	R. P. Beck & T. Potter	
G-DCXV	Yorkshire Sailplanes YS-53 Sovereign	T53 Syndicate	
G-DCYA	Pilatus B4 PC-11	B4-072 Group	
G-DCYD	PZL-Bielsko SZD-30 Pirat	J. P. Thompson & E. Vyorlova	
G-DCYG	Glasflugel H201B Standard Libelle	R. Barsby & A. C. S. Lintott	
G-DCYM	Schempp-Hirth Standard Cirrus	K. M. Fisher	
G-DCYO	Schempp-Hirth Standard Cirrus	G. M. Maguire & P. Summers	
G-DCYP	Schempp-Hirth Standard Cirrus	A. F. Scott	
G-DCYT	Schempp-Hirth Standard Cirrus	R. Robertson	
G-DCYZ	Schleicher K 8B	Oxford Gliding Co.Ltd	
G-DCZD	Pilatus B4 PC-11	S. E. Marples	
G-DCZE	PZL-Bielsko SZD-30	L. A. Bean	
G-DCZG	PZL-Bielsko SZD-30	J. T. Pajdak	
G-DCZJ	PZL-Bielsko SZD-30	B. L. C. Gordon	
G-DCZN	Schleicher ASW-15B	G-DCZN Group	
G-DCZR	Slingsby T.59D Kestrel	R. P. Brisbourne	
G-DCZU	Slingsby T.59D Kestrel	M. P. Edwards	
G-DCZZ	Slingsby T.59D Kestrel	C. J. Lowrie	
G-DDAC	PZL-Bielsko SZD-36A	R. J. A. Colenso	
G-DDAJ	Shempp-Hirth Nimbus 2	North Devon Gliding Club Nimbus Group	
G-DDAK	Schleicher K-7	Vale of Neath Gliding Club	
G-DDAN	PZL-Bielsko SZD-30	J. M. A. Shannon	
G-DDAP	SZL-Bielsko SZD-30	Delta Alpha Papa Group	
G-DDAS	Schempp-Hirth Standard Cirrus	G. Goodenough	
G-DDAU	PZL-Bielsko SZD-30	Buckminster Gliding Club Ltd	
G-DDAV	Robinson R44 II	Heli Air Ltd	
G-DDAW	Schleicher Ka 6CR	R. G. Charlesson	
G-DDAY	PA-28R-201T Turbo Arrow III	G-DDAY Group (G-BPDO)	
G-DDBB	Slingsby T.51 Dart 17R	M. D. J. Ladley	
G-DDBC	Pilatus B4-PC11	J. H. France & G. R. Harris	
G-DDBD	Shaw Europa XS	B. Davies	
G-DDBG	ICA IS-29D	P. S. Whitehead	
G-DDBK	Slingsby T.59D Kestrel	523 Syndicate	
G-DDBN	Slingsby T.59D Kestrel	I. B. Kennedy	
G-DDBP	Glasflugel Club Libelle 205	J. P. Beach	
G-DDBS	Slingsby T.59D Kestrel	M. Bond	

Notes	Reg.	Type	Owner or Operator
	G-DDBV	PZL-Bielsko SZD-30	L. Clarke
	G-DDCA	PZL-Bielsko SZD-36A Cobra 15	J. Young & J. R. Aylesbury
	G-DDCC	Glasflugel Standard Libelle 201B	G-DDCC Syndicate
	G-DDCW	Schleicher Ka 6CR	B. W. Rendall
	G-DDDA	Schempp-Hirth Standard Cirrus	A. J. Davis
	G-DDDB	Schleicher ASK-13	Shenington Gliding Club
	G-DDDD	Evektor EV-97 TeamEurostar UK	G-DDDD Syndicate
	G-DDDE	PZL-Bielsko SZD-38A Jantar 1	Jantar One Syndicate
	G-DDDJ	Learjet 45	RCS Trading Corporation Ltd
	G-DDDL	Schleicher K8B	York Gliding Centre Ltd
	G-DDDM	Schempp-Hirth Cirrus	DDM Syndicate
	G-DDDR	Schempp-Hirth Standard Cirrus	J. D. Ewence
	G-DDDY	P & M Quik GT450	J. W. Dodson
	G-DDEA	Slingsby T.59D Kestrel	A. Pickles
	G-DDEB	Slingsby T.59D Kestrel	J. L. Smoker
	G-DDEG	ICA IS-28B2	P. S. Whitehead
	G-DDEO	Glasflugel H205 Club Libelle	N. J. Mitchell
	G-DDEP	Schleicher Ka-6CR	M. D. Brooks
	G-DDEV	Schleicher Ka-6CR	A. N. & L. M. Morley
	G-DDEW	ICA-Brasov IS-29D	G. V. Prater
	G-DDEX	LET-13 Blanik	Blanik DEX Group
	G-DDFC	Schempp-Hirth Standard Cirrus	C. E. & I. Helme
	G-DDFE	Molino PIK-20B	M. A. Roff-Jarrett
	G-DDFK	Molino PIK-20B	B. H. & M. J. Fairclough
	G-DDFL	PZL-Bielsko SZD-38A Jantar 1	G-DDFL Group
	G-DDFN	Glaser-Dirks DG-100	K. Smith
	G-DDFR	Grob G.102 Astir CS	The Windrushers Gliding Club Ltd
	G-DDFV	PZL-Bielsko SZD-38A Jantar 1	G. S. J. Bambrook & A. Purcell
	G-DDFW	PZL-Bielsko SZD-30	Lincolnshire Gliding Club Ltd
	G-DDGA	Schleicher K-8B	The Welland Gliding Club Ltd
	G-DDGE	Schempp-Hirth Standard Cirrus	A. S. Cobbett
	G-DDGG	Schleicher Ka 6E	N. F. Holmes & F. D. Platt
	G-DDGH	PZL-Bielsko SZD-30 Pirat	M. Ling
	G-DDGJ	Champion 8KCAB	Western Air (Thruxton) Ltd
	G-DDGK	Schleicher Ka 6CR	R. G. Olsen
	G-DDGV	Breguet 905S Fauvette	J. N. Lee
	G-DDGX	Schempp-Hirth Standard Cirrus 75	USKGC Group
	G-DDGY	Schempp-Hirth Nimbus 2B	Nimbus 195 Group
	G-DDHA	Schleicher K 8B	Shalborne Soaring Society Ltd
	G-DDHC	PZL-Bielsko SZD-41A	P. J. Kelly
	G-DDHE	Slingsby T.53B	Aviation Preservation Society of Scotland
	G-DDHG	Schleicher Ka 6CR	Angus Gliding Club Ltd
	G-DDHH	Eiriavion PIK-20B	D. M. Steed
	G-DDHJ	Glaser-Dirks DG-100	G. E. McLaughlin
	G-DDHK	Glaser-Dirks DG-100	B. J. & C. M. Griffin
	G-DDHL	Glaser-Dirks DG-100	DHL Syndicate
	G-DDHN	Eiriavion PIK-20B	G. Bass and Partners
	G-DDHT	Schleicher Ka 6E	S. Foster
	G-DDHW	Schempp-Hirth Nimbus 2	M. J. Carruthers & D. Thompson
	G-DDHX	Schempp-Hirth Standard Cirrus B	J. Franke
	G-DDHZ	PZL-Bielsko SZD-30	Peterborough and Spalding Gliding Club
	G-DDIG	Rockwell Commander 114	Daedalus Flying Group (G-CCDT)
	G-DDJB	Schleicher K-8B	Portsmouth Naval Gliding Centre
	G-DDJD	Grob G.102 Astir CS	P. E. Gascoigne
	G-DDJF	Schempp-Hirth Duo Discus T	R. J. H. Fack
	G-DDJK	Schleicher ASK-18	Booker Gliding Club Ltd
	G-DDJN	Eiriavion PIK-20B	M. Ireland & S. Lambourne
	G-DDJR	Schleicher Ka 6CR	Syndicate K6
	G-DDJX	Grob G.102 Astir CS	Trent Valley Gliding Club Ltd
	G-DDKC	Schleicher K 8B	Yorkshire Gliding Club (Proprietary) Ltd
	G-DDKD	Glasflugel Hornet	Hornet Syndicate
	G-DDKE	Schleicher ASK-13	The South Wales Gliding Club Ltd
	G-DDKG	Schleicher Ka 6CR	C. B. Woolf
	G-DDKL	Schempp-Hirth Nimbus 2	G. J. Croll
	G-DDKM	Glasflugel Hornet	R. S. Lee
	G-DDKN	Schleicher Ka 6CR	A. Ciccone
	G-DDKR	Grob G.102 Astir CS	Oxford Gliding Co.Ltd
	G-DDKS	Grob G.102 Astir CS	Oxford Gliding Co.Ltd
	G-DDKT	Eiriavion PIK-20B	F. P. Wilson
	G-DDKU	Grob G.102 Astir CS	Delta Kilo Uniform Syndicate
	G-DDKV	Grob G.102 Astir CS	T. J. Ireson
	G-DDKW	Grob G.102 Astir CS	Southdown Gliding Club Ltd

Reg.	Type	Owner or Operator	Notes
G-DDKX	Grob G.102 Astir CS	L. R. Bennett	
G-DDLA	Pilatus B4 PC-11	P. R. Seddon	
G-DDLB	Schleicher ASK-18	The Vale of the White Horse Gliding Centre Ltd	
G-DDLC	Schleicher ASK-13	Lasham Gliding Society Ltd	
G-DDLE	Schleicher Ka 6E	P. J. Abbott & J. Banks	
G-DDLG	Schempp-Hirth Standard Cirrus 75	S. Naylor	
G-DDLH	Grob G.102 Astir CS77	M. D. & M. E. Saunders	
G-DDLJ	Eiriavion PIK-20B	M. S. Parkes	
G-DDLM	Grob G.102 Astir CS	K. Dyer & D. Hilton	
G-DDLP	Schleicher Ka 6CR	J. R. Crosse	
G-DDLS	Schleicher K 8B	North Devon Gliding Club	
G-DDLT	ICA IS-28B2	M. P. Wiseman	
G-DDLY	Eiriavion PIK-20D	M. Conrad	
G-DDMB	Schleicher K 8B	Crown Service Gliding Club	
G-DDMD	Glaser-Dirks DG-100	K. G. Guest	
G-DDMG	Schleicher K 8B	Dorset Gliding Club Ltd	
G-DDMH	Grob G.102 Astir CS	C. K. Lewis	
G-DDMK	Schempp-Hirth SHK-1	D. Breeze	
G-DDML	Schleicher K-7	Dumfries and District Gliding Club	
G-DDMM	Schempp-Hirth Nimbus 2	T. Linee	
G-DDMN	Glasflugel Mosquito	DMN Group	
G-DDMO	Schleicher Ka 6E	S. D. Hawkin	
G-DDMP	Grob G.102 Astir CS	Kingswood Syndicate	
G-DDMR	Grob G.102 Astir CS	Mendip Gliding Club Ltd	
G-DDMS	Glasflugel Standard Libelle 201B	G-DDMS Group	
G-DDMU	Eiriavion PIK-20D	J. Mjels	
G-DDMV	NA T-6G Texan (493209)	C. Dabin	
G-DDMX	Schleicher ASK-13	Dartmoor Gliding Society Ltd	
G-DDNC	Grob G.102 Astir CS	W. J. Veitch	
G-DDND	Pilatus B4-PC11AF	DND Group	
G-DDNE	Grob G.102 Astir CS77	621 Astir Syndicate	
G-DDNF	PZL-Bielsko SZD-9bis Bocian 1D	Portmoak Bocian (DNF) Syndicate	
G-DDNG	Schempp-Hirth Nimbus 2	Nimbus 265 Syndicate	
G-DDNJ	Schleicher ASK-18	Derbyshire and Lancashire Gliding Club Ltd	
G-DDNK	Grob G.102 Astir CS	G-DDNK Group	
G-DDNT	PZL-Bielsko SZD-30	R. K. Lashly	
G-DDNU	PZL-Bielsko SZD-42-1 Jantar 2	C. D. Rowland & D. Chalmers-Brown	
G-DDNV	Schleicher ASK-13	Channel Gliding Club Ltd	
G-DDNW	Schleicher Ks 6CR	K. Marchant & C. Styles	
G-DDNX	Schleicher Ka 6CR	Black Mountains Gliding Club	
G-DDNZ	Schleicher K 8B	Southampton University Gliding Club	
G-DDOA	Schleicher ASK-13	Essex and Suffolk Gliding Club Ltd	
G-DDOB	Grob G.102 Astir CS77	C. E. Hutson	
G-DDOC	Schleicher Ka 6CR	W. St. G. V. Stoney	
G-DDOE	Grob G.102 Astir CS77	Heron Gliding Club	
G-DDOF	Schleicher Ka 6CR	A. J. Watson	
G-DDOG	SA Bulldog Srs 120/121 (XX524:04)	Deltaero Ltd	
G-DDOK	Schleicher Ka 6E	R. S. Hawley & S. Y. Duxbury	
G-DDOR	Grob G.102 Astir CS77	V. A. Watt	
G-DDOU	Eiriavion PIK-20D	DQU Syndicate	
G-DDOX	Schleicher K-7	The Nene Valley Gliding Club Ltd	
G-DDPA	Schleicher ASK-18	J. P. Kirby	
G-DDPH	Schempp-Hirth Mini-Nimbus B	J. W. Murdoch	
G-DDPK	Glasflugel H303A Mosquito	G. Lawley	
G-DDPL	Eiriavion PIK-20D	437 Syndicate	
G-DDPO	Grob G.102 Astrir CS77	Dorset Gliding Club Ltd	
G-DDPY	Grob G.102 Astir CS77	C. A. Bailey	
G-DDRA	Schleicher Ka 6CR	K6CR Group Shobdon	
G-DDRB	Glaser-Dirks DG-100	DRB Syndicate	
G-DDRD	Schleicher Ka 6CR	Essex and Suffolk Gliding Club Ltd	
G-DDRE	Schleicher Ka 6CR	J. H. Jowett & I. D. King	
G-DDRJ	Schleicher ASK-13	Lasham Gliding Society Ltd	
G-DDRL	Scheibe SF26A	T. A. Lipinski	
G-DDRM	Schleicher K 7	K7 DRM Syndicate	
G-DDRN	Glasflugel H303A Mosquito	A. & V. R. Roberts	
G-DDRO	Grob G.103 Twin Astir	Astir 258 Syndicate	
G-DDRP	Pilatus B4-PC11	DRP Syndicate	
G-DDRT	Eiriavion PIK-20D	PIK 688 Syndicate	
G-DDRU	Grob G.102 Astir CS77	I. P. Stork	
G-DDRV	Schleicher K 8B	DRV Syndicate	
G-DDRW	Grob G.102 Astir CS	I. W. & J. R. King	
G-DDRY	Schleicher Ka 6CR	M. K. Bradford	

Notes	Reg.	Type	Owner or Operator
	G-DDRZ	Schleicher K-8B	East Sussex Gliding Club Ltd
	G-DDSB	Schleicher Ka-6E	G. B. Griffiths
	G-DDSF	Schleicher K-8B	University of Edinburgh Sports Union
	G-DDSG	Schleicher Ka 6CR	S. Montandon
	G-DDSH	Grob G.102 Astir CS77	Astir 648 Syndicate
	G-DDSJ	Grob G.103 Twin Astir II	Herefordshire Gliding Club Ltd
	G-DDSL	Grob G.103 Twin Astir	DSL Group
	G-DDSP	Schempp-Hirth Mini Nimbus B	270 Syndicate
	G-DDST	Schleicher ASW-20L	D. J. Miller
	G-DDSU	Grob G.102 Astir CS77	Bowland Forest Gliding Club Ltd
	G-DDSV	Pilatus B4-PC11AF	G. M. Drinkell & S. J. Brenton
	G-DDSX	Schleicher ASW-19B	T. Johns, J. F. L. Scaife & J. F. Stoneman
	G-DDSY	Schleicher Ka-6CR	G. Jones & P. J. Shuff
	G-DDTA	Glaser-Dirks DG-200	G. A. Nash
	G-DDTC	Schempp-Hirth Janus B	Darlton Gliding Club Ltd
	G-DDTE	Schleicher ASW-19B	G. R. Purcell
	G-DDTG	Schempp-Hirth SHK-1	A. P. Benbow
	G-DDTK	Glasflugel Mosquito B	P. France
	G-DDTM	Glaser-Dirks DG-200	R. S. Skinner
	G-DDTN	Schleicher K 8B	C. G. & G. N. Thomas
	G-DDTP	Schleicher ASW-20	T. S. & S. M. Hills
	G-DDTS	CARMAM M-100S	I. A. Macadam
	G-DDTU	Schempp-Hirth Nimbus 2B	Nimbus Syndicate
	G-DDTV	Glasflugel Mosquito B	S. R. Evans
	G-DDTW	PZL-Bielsko SZD-30 Pirat	NDGC Pirat Syndicate
	G-DDTX	Glasflugel Mosquito B	P. T. S. Nash
	G-DDTY	Glasflugel H303 Mosquito B	W. H. L. Bullimore
	G-DDUB	Glasflugel H303 Mosquito B	Mosquito Group
	G-DDUE	Schleicher ASK-13	Army Gliding Association
	G-DDUF	Schleicher K 8B	M. Staljan
	G-DDUH	Scheibe L-Spatz 55	R. J. Aylesbury & J. Young
	G-DDUK	Schleicher K-8B	The Bristol Gliding Club Propietary Ltd
	G-DDUL	Grob G.102 Astir CS77	G. R. Davey
	G-DDUR	Schleicher Ka 6CR	B. N. Bromley & M. Witthread
	G-DDUS	Schleicher Ka 6E	W. Ellis
	G-DDUT	Schleicher ASW-20	M. E. Doig & E. T. J. Murphy
	G-DDUY	Glaser-Dirks DG-100	R. L. & K. P. McLean
	G-DDVB	Schleicher ASK-13	Essex and Suffolk Gliding Club Ltd
	G-DDVC	Schleicher ASK-13	Staffordshire Gliding Club Ltd
	G-DDVG	Schleicher Ka-6CR	G-DDVG Banana Group
	G-DDVH	Schleicher Ka 6E	M. A. K. Cropper
	G-DDVK	PZL-Bielsko SZD-48 Jantar Standard 2	D. S. Sigournay
	G-DDVL	Schleicher ASW-19	A. C. M. Phillips & P. K. Newman
	G-DDVM	Glasflugel H205 Club Libelle	M. A. Field
	G-DDVN	Eiriavion PIL-20D-78	T. P. Bassett & A. D. Butler
	G-DDVP	Schleicher ASW-19	VP Syndicate
	G-DDVS	Schempp-Hirth Standard Cirrus	J. C. & T. J. Milner
	G-DDVV	Schleicher ASW-20L	A. M. Hooper
	G-DDVX	Schleicher ASK-13	Shenington Gliding Club
	G-DDVY	Schempp-Hirth Cirrus	M. G. Ashton & G. Martin
	G-DDVZ	Glasflugel H303 Mosquito B	B. H. Shaw & R. Spreckley
	G-DDWB	Glasflugel H303 Mosquito B	D. T. Edwards
	G-DDWC	Schleicher Ka 6E	D. E. Jones
	G-DDWG	Schleicher K-8B	Dartmoor Gliding Society Ltd
	G-DDWJ	Glaser-Dirks DG-200	A. P. Kamp & P. R. Desmond
	G-DDWL	Glasflugel Mosquito B	H. A. Stanford
	G-DDWN	Schleicher K7 Rhonadler	L. R. & J. E. Merritt
	G-DDWP	Glasflugel Mosquito B	I. H. Murdoch
	G-DDWR	Glasflugel Mosquito B	C. D. Lovell
	G-DDWS	Eiriavion PIK-20D	D. G. Slocombe
	G-DDWT	Slingsby T.65C Vega	A. P. Grimley
	G-DDWU	Grob G.102 Astir CS	G-DDWU Syndicate
	G-DDWW	Slingsby T.65A Vega	D. M. Thomas
	G-DDWZ	Schleicher ASW-19B	P. Woodcock
	G-DDXA	Glasflugel H303 Mosquito B	G-DDXA Group
	G-DDXB	Schleicher ASW-20	81 Syndicate
	G-DDXD	Slingsby T.65A Vega	G-DDXD Flying Group
	G-DDXE	Slingsby T.65A Vega	H. K. Rattray
	G-DDXF	Slingsby T.65A Vega	B. A. Walker
	G-DDXG	Slingsby T.65A Vega	DXG Group
	G-DDXH	Schleicher Ka 6E	D. E. Findon
	G-DDXJ	Grob G.102 Astir CS77	M. T. Stickland

Reg.	Type	Owner or Operator	Notes
G-DDXK	Centrair ASW-20F	E. & A. Townsend	
G-DDXL	Schempp-Hirth Standard Cirrus	C. J. Button	
G-DDXN	Glaser-Dirks DG-200	J. A. Johnston	
G-DDXT	Schempp-Hirth Mini-Nimbus C	G-DDXT Mini-Nimbus	
G-DDXW	Glasflugel Mosquito B	I. W. Myles & J. E. Shaw	
G-DDXX	Schleicher ASW-19B	M. Dixon	
G-DDYC	Schleicher Ka 6CR	F. J. Bradley	
G-DDYE	Schleicher ASW-20L	828 Syndicate	
G-DDYF	Grob G.102 Astir CS77	York Gliding Centre Ltd	
G-DDYH	Glaser-Dirks DG-200	P. Johnson	
G-DDYJ	Schleicher Ka 6CR	Upward Bound Trust	
G-DDYL	CARMAM JP 15-36AR	P. A. Pickering	
G-DDYR	Schleicher K7	University of the West of England Gliding Club	
G-DDYU	Schempp-Hirth Nimbus -2C	K. Richards	
G-DDYX	Schleicher ASW-20	M. D. Wright	
G-DDZA	Slingsby T.65A Vega	K-H. Kuntze	
G-DDZB	Slingsby T.65A Vega	A. A. Black	
G-DDZF	Schempp-Hirth Standard Cirrus	L. S., J. M. & R. S. Hood	
G-DDZG	Schleicher ASW-19B	M. P. Theo	
G-DDZJ	Grob G.102 Astir CS Jeans	Mendip Astir Syndicate	
G-DDZN	Slingsby T.65A Vega	D. A. White	
G-DDZP	Slingsby T.65A Vega	M. T. Crews	
G-DDZR	IS-28B2	The Furness Gliding Club Proprietary Ltd	
G-DDZT	Eiriavion PIK-20D	PIK-20D 106 Group	
G-DDZU	Grob G.102 Astir CS	P. Clarke	
G-DDZV	Scheibe SF-27A	N. Newham	
G-DDZW	Schleicher Ka 6CR	S. W. Naylor	
G-DDZY	Schleicher ASW-19B	M. C. Fairman	
G-DEAE	Schleicher ASW-20L	R. Burghall	
G-DEAF	Grob G.102 Astir CS77	The Borders (Milfield) Gliding Club Ltd	
G-DEAG	Slingsby T.65A Vega	D. L. King	
G-DEAH	Schleicher Ka 6E	M. Lodge	
G-DEAJ	Schempp-Hirth Nimbus 2	R. M. Crockett	
G-DEAK	Glasflugel H303 Mosquito B	T. A. L. Barnes	
G-DEAM	Schempp-Hirth Nimbus 2B	Alpha Mike Syndicate	
G-DEAN	Solar Wings Pegasus XL-Q	Y. G. Richardson (G-MVJV)	
G-DEAR	Eiriavion PIK-20D	G-DEAR Group	
G-DEAT	Eiriavion PIK-20D	A. Spencer & D. Bieniasz	
G-DEAU	Schleicher K7	The Welland Gliding Club Ltd	
G-DEAV	Schempp-Hirth Mini-Nimbus C	G. D. H. Crawford	
G-DEAW	Grob G.102 Astir CS77	EAW Group	
G-DEBR	Shaw Europa	P. Curley	
G-DEBT	Pioneer 300	N. J. T. Tonks	
G-DEBX	Schleicher ASW-20	S. M. Economou & R. M Harris	
G-DECC	Schleicher Ka 6CR	Redwing	
G-DECF	Schleicher Ka 6CR	ECF Group	
G-DECJ	Slingsby T.65A Vega	J. E. B. Hart	
G-DECK	Cessna T.210N	A. V. Harmer	
G-DECL	Slingsby T.65A Vega	J. E. Strzebrakowski	
G-DECM	Slingsby T.65A Vega	F. Wilson	
G-DECO	Dyn'Aéro MCR-01 Club	G-DECO Flying Group	
G-DECP	Rolladen-Schneider LS3-17	M. H. Ewer & K. Fear	
G-DECR	P & M Quik R	D. V. Lawrence	
G-DECS	Glasflugel H303 Mosquito B	A. C. Cummins & K. L. Fixter	
G-DECW	Schleicher ASK-21	Norfolk Gliding Club Ltd	
G-DECZ	Schleicher ASK-21	Booker Gliding Club Ltd	
G-DEDG	Schleicher Ka 6CR	S. J. Wood	
G-DEDH	Glasflugel H303 Mosquito B	B. L. Liddiard	
G-DEDJ	Glasflugel H303 Mosquito B	D. Martin & R. Bollow	
G-DEDK	Schleicher K7 Rhonadler	North Wales Gliding Club Ltd	
G-DEDM	Glaser-Dirks DG-200	A. H. G. St.Pierre	
G-DEDN	Glaser-Dirks DG-100G	DG 280 Syndicate	
G-DEDU	Schleicher ASK-13	Channel Gliding Club Ltd	
G-DEDX	Slingsby T.65D Vega	G. Kirkham	
G-DEDY	Slingsby T.65D Vega	T. McKinley	
G-DEDZ	Slingsby T.65C Vega	Echo Delta Zulu Group	
G-DEEA	Slingsby T.65C Vega	Borders Sports Vega Syndicate (337)	
G-DEEC	Schleicher ASW-20L	D. Beams	
G-DEED	Schleicher K-8B	The Windrushers Gliding Club Ltd	
G-DEEF	Rolladen-Schneider LS3-17	Echo Echo Foxtrot Group	
G-DEEG	Slingsby T.65C Vega	Vega Syndicate	

Notes	Reg.	Type	Owner or Operator
	G-DEEO	Schleicher ASW-19	K. Kiely
	G-DEEJ	Schleicher ASW-20L	G-DEEJ Group
	G-DEEK	Schempp-Hirth Nimbus 2C	R. Cassidy & W. P. Stephen
	G-DEEM	Schleicher K-8	The South Wales Gliding Club Ltd
	G-DEEN	Schempp-Hirth Standard Cirrus 75	G-DEEN Flying Group
	G-DEEO	Grob G.102 Club Astir II	G-DEEO Group
	G-DEEP	Wassmer WA.26P Squale	B. J. Key & A. S. Jones
	G-DEES	Rolladen-Schneider LS3-17	J. B. Illidge
	G-DEEW	Schleicher Ka 6CR	S. M. Dodds
	G-DEEX	Rolladen-Schneider LS3-17	The LS3 Flyers
	G-DEEZ	Denney Kitfox Mk.3	J. D. & D. Cheesman
	G-DEFA	Schleicher ASW-20L	Eight Eighties Syndicate
	G-DEFB	Schempp-Hirth Nimbus 2C	N. Revell
	G-DEFE	Centrair ASW-20F	W. A. Horne & D. A. Mackenzie
	G-DEFF	Schempp-Hirth Nimbus 2C	J. W. L. Clarke and P. J. D. Smith
	G-DEFN	Scheibe L-Spatz 55	P. L. E. Duguay
	G-DEFS	Rolladen-Schneider LS3	P. R. Thomas
	G-DEFT	Flight Design CTSW	D. Arnold
	G-DEFV	Schleicher ASW-20	A. R. McKillen
	G-DEFW	Slingsby T.65C Sport Vega	Darlton Gliding Club Ltd
	G-DEFY	Robinson R22 Beta	P. M. M. P. Silveira/Portugal
	G-DEFZ	Rolladen-Schneider LS3-a	EFZ Syndicate
	G-DEGD	Schleicher ASW-17S	H. Wucherer
	G-DEGE	Rolladen-Schneider LS3-a	EGE Glider Syndicate
	G-DEGF	Slingsby T.65D Vega	Shalbourne Soaring Society Ltd
	G-DEGH	Slingsby T.65C Vega	K. Dykes, M. J. Davies & R. A. Starling
	G-DEGJ	Slingsby T.65C Vega	Cotswold Vega Syndicate
	G-DEGK	Schempp-Hirth Standard Cirrus	P. H. Robinson
	G-DEGN	Grob G.103 Twin Astir II	Staffordshire Gliding Club Ltd
	G-DEGP	Schleicher ASW-20L	S. Pozerskis
	G-DEGR	Breguet 905 Fauvette	L. P. Woodage
	G-DEGS	Schempp-Hirth Nimbus 2CS	R. C. Nichols
	G-DEGT	Slingsby T.65D Vega	Vega Syndicate EGT
	G-DEGW	Schempp-Hirth Mini-Nimbus C	I. F. Barnes and Partners
	G-DEGX	Slingsby T.65C Vega	Haddenham Vega Syndicate
	G-DEGZ	Schleicher ASK-21	Black Mountains Gliding Club
	G-DEHC	Eichelsdorfer SB-5B	J. A. Castle
	G-DEHG	Slingsby T.65C Vega	Vega Syndicate
	G-DEHH	Schempp-Hirth Ventus a	J. A. White
	G-DEHK	Rolladen-Schneider LS4	S. Eyles
	G-DEHM	Schleicher Ka 6E	J. B. Symonds
	G-DEHO	Schleicher ASK-21	Lasham Gliding Society Ltd
	G-DEHP	Schempp-Hirth Nimbus 2C	D. J. King
	G-DEHT	Schempp-Hirth Nimbus 2C	Nimbus 2C Syndicate
	G-DEHU	Glasflugel 304	F. Townsend
	G-DEHV	Schleicher ASW-20L	M. A. & B. A. Roberts
	G-DEHW	ICA IS-28B2	Y6 Group/Netherlands
	G-DEHY	Slingsby T.65D Vega	Vega Syndicate
	G-DEHZ	Schleicher ASW-20L	D. Crimmins
	G-DEJA	ICA IS-28B2	M. H. Simms
	G-DEJB	Slingsby T.65C Vega	D. Tait & I. G. Walker
	G-DEJC	Slingsby T.65C Vega	I. Powis
	G-DEJD	Slingsby T.65D Vega	R. L. & K. P. McLean
	G-DEJE	Slingsby T.65C Vega	Crown Service Gliding Club
	G-DEJF	Schleicher K 8B	Cotswold Gliding Club
	G-DEJH	Eichelsdorfer SB-5E	S. E. Richardson & B. J. Dawson
	G-DEJR	Schleicher ASW-19B	193 Syndicate
	G-DEJY	PZL-Bielsko SZD-9bis Bocian 1D	G-DEJY Group
	G-DEJZ	Scheibe SF26A	J. M. Collin
	G-DEKA	Cameron Z-90 balloon	P. G. Bogliaccino
	G-DEKC	Schleicher Ka 6E	S. L. Benn
	G-DEKF	Grob G.102 Club Astir III	The Bristol Gliding Club Proprietary Ltd
	G-DEKG	Schleicher ASK-21	Army Gliding Association
	G-DEKJ	Schempp-Hirth Ventus b	I. J. Metcalfe
	G-DEKS	Scheibe SF27A Zugvogel V	J. C. Johnson
	G-DEKT	Wassmer WA.30	D. C. Reynolds
	G-DEKU	Schleicher ASW-20L	A. J. Gillson
	G-DEKV	Rolladen-Schneider LS4	S. L. Helstrip
	G-DEKW	Schempp-Hirth Nimbus 2B	V. Luscombe-Mahoney
	G-DELA	Schleicher ASW-19B	ELA Syndicate
	G-DELB	Robinson R-22 Beta ★	Aero Venture
	G-DELD	Slingsby T65C Vega	ELD Syndicate

Reg.	Type	Owner or Operator	Notes
G-DELF	Aero L-29A Delfin	B. R. Green	
G-DELG	Schempp-Hirth Ventus b/16.6	A. G. Machin	
G-DELN	Grob G.102 Astir CS Jeans	Bowland Forest Gliding Club Ltd	
G-DELO	Slingsby T.65D Vega	I. Sim	
G-DELR	Schempp-Hirth Ventus b	I. D. Smith	
G-DELZ	Schleicher ASW-20L	D. A. Fogden	
G-DEME	Glaser-Dirks DG-200/17	E. D. Casagrande	
G-DEMF	Rolladen-Schneider LS4	R. N. Johnston & M. C. Oggelsby.	
G-DEMG	Rolladen-Schneider LS4	R. C. Bowsfield	
G-DEMH	Cessna F.172M (modified)	M. Hammond (G-BFLO)	
G-DEMJ	Slingsby T65C Sport Vega	W. G. Johnson	
G-DEMM	AS.350B2 Ecureuil	Three Counties Helicopter Co.Ltd	
G-DEMN	Slingsby T.65D Vega	C. D. Sword	
G-DEMP	Slingsby T.65C Vega	The Surrey Hills Gliding Club Ltd	
G-DEMR	Slingsby T.65C Vega	J. Wozny	
G-DEMT	Rolladen-Schneider LS4	M. R. Fox	
G-DEMU	Glaser-Dirks DG-202/17	A. Butterfield & N. Swinton	
G-DEMZ	Slingsby T65A Vega	Vega Syndicate (G-BGCA)	
G-DENB	Cessna F.150G	C. R. Haden (G-ATZZ)	
G-DENC	Cessna F.150G	G-DENC Cessna Group (G-AVAP)	
G-DEND	Cessna F.150M	R. N. Tate (G-WAFC/G-BDFI)	
G-DENE	PA-28 Cherokee 140	D. V. Magee (G-ATOS)	
G-DENI	PA-32 Cherokee Six 300	A. Bendkowski (G-BAIA)	
G-DENJ	Schempp-Hirth Ventus b/16.6	S. Boyden	
G-DENO	Glasflugel Standard Libelle 201B	D. M. Bland	
G-DENS	Binder CP.301S Smaragd	Garston Smaragd Group	
G-DENU	Glaser-Dirks DG-100G	435 Syndicate	
G-DENV	Schleicher ASW-20L	R. D. Hone	
G-DENX	PZL-Bielsko SZD-48 Jantar Standard 2	J. M. Hire	
G-DEOA	Rolladen-Schneider LS4	A. A. Jenkins & R. L. Smith	
G-DEOB	PZL-Bielsko SZD-30	R. M. Golding	
G-DEOD	Grob G.102 Astir CS77	D. S. Fenton	
G-DEOE	Schleicher ASK-13	Essex Gliding Club Ltd	
G-DEOF	Schleicher ASK-13	Essex Gliding Club Ltd	
G-DEOJ	Centrair ASW-20FL	R. Grey & J. Sanders	
G-DEOK	Centrair 101A Pegase	The Pegase Group	
G-DEOM	Carman M100S	S. W. Hutchinson	
G-DEON	Schempp-Hirth Nimbus 3	117 Syndicate	
G-DEOT	Grob G.103A Twin II Acro	R. Tyrrell	
G-DEOU	Pilatus B4-PC11	D. J. Blackman	
G-DEOV	Schempp-Hirth Janus C	Burn Gliding Club Ltd	
G-DEOW	Schempp-Hirth Janus C	383 Syndicate	
G-DEOX	Carmam M-200 Foehn	B. S. Goodspeed	
G-DEOZ	Schleicher K 8B	Cotswold Gliding Club	
G-DEPD	Schleicher ASK-21	EPD Glider Syndicate	
G-DEPE	Schleicher ASW-19B	P. A. Goulding	
G-DEPF	Centrair ASW-20FL	323 Syndicate	
G-DEPG	CARMAM M100S	J. D. Owen	
G-DEPM	Scheibe SF-34	M. H. Sims	
G-DEPP	Schleicher ASK-13	Mendip Gliding Club Ltd	
G-DEPS	Schleicher ASW-20L	C. Beveridge	
G-DEPT	Schleicher K-8B	C. S. Warren	
G-DEPU	Glaser-Dirks DG-101G Elan	J. F. Rogers	
G-DEPX	Schempp-Hirth Ventus b/16.6	M. E. S. Thomas	
G-DERA	Centrair ASW-20FL	R. J. Lockett	
G-DERH	Schleicher ASK-21	The Burn Gliding Club Ltd	
G-DERJ	Schleicher ASK-21	The Royal Air Force Gliding and Soaring Association	
G-DERR	Schleicher ASW-19B	D. Clarke	
G-DERS	Schleicher ASW-19B	G-DERS Flying Group	
G-DERV	Cameron Truck SS balloon	J. M. Percival	
G-DERX	Centrair 101A Pegase	A. Delaney & J. Innes	
G-DESB	Schleicher ASK-21	The Old Boys	
G-DESC	Rolladen-Schneider LS4	J. Crawford & J. M. Staley	
G-DESH	Centrair 101A	J. E. Moore	
G-DESJ	Schleicher K8B	Bowland Forest Gliding Club Ltd	
G-DESO	Glaser-Dirks DG-300 Elan	G. R. P. Brown	
G-DESU	Schleicher ASK-21	Banbury Gliding Club Ltd	
G-DETA	Schleicher ASK-21	P. Hawkins	
G-DETD	Schleicher K8B	Cotswold Gliding Club	
G-DETG	Rolladen-Schneider LS4	K. J. Woods	
G-DETJ	Centrair 101A	S. C. Phillips	

Notes	Reg.	Type	Owner or Operator
	G-DETK	PZL-Bielsko SZD-48 Jantar Standard 2	I. W. Paterson
	G-DETM	Centrair 101A	D. Bowden
	G-DETV	Rolladen-Schneider LS4	P. Fabian
	G-DETY	Rolladen-Schneider LS4	D. T. Staff
	G-DETZ	Schleicher ASW-20CL	The 20 Syndicate
	G-DEUC	Schleicher ASK-13	The Bristol Gliding Club Proprietary Ltd
	G-DEUD	Schleicher ASW-20C	R. Tietema
	G-DEUF	PZL-Bielsko SZD-50-3	Puchacz Group
	G-DEUH	Rolladen-Schneider LS4	A. R. Turner & F. J. Parkinson
	G-DEUJ	Schempp-Hirth Ventus b/16.6	S. C. Renfrew
	G-DEUK	Centrair ASW-20FL	P. A. Clark
	G-DEUS	Schempp-Hirth Ventus b/16.6	R. J. Whitaker
	G-DEUV	PZL-Bielsko SZD-42-2 Jantar 2B	G. V. McKirdy
	G-DEUX	AS.355F Ecureuil 2	Elmridge Ltd
	G-DEUY	Schleicher ASW-20BL	ASW20BL-G-DUEY Group
	G-DEVF	Schempp-Hirth Nimbus 3T	A. G. Leach
	G-DEVH	Schleicher Ka 10	C. W. & K. T. Matten
	G-DEVJ	Schleicher ASK-13	Lasham Gliding Society Ltd
	G-DEVK	Grob G.102 Astir CS	Peterborough and Spalding Gliding Club Ltd
	G-DEVL	Eurocopter EC 120B	Saxon Logistics Ltd
	G-DEVM	Centrair 101A	Seahawk Gliding Club
	G-DEVO	Centrair 101A	D. G. Every & P. Allingham
	G-DEVP	Schleicher ASK-13	Lasham Gliding Society Ltd
	G-DEVS	PA-28 Cherokee 180	180 Group/Blackbushe (G-BGVJ)
	G-DEVV	Schleicher ASK-23	Midland Gliding Club Ltd
	G-DEVW	Schleicher ASK-23	London Gliding Club Proprietary Ltd
	G-DEVX	Schleicher ASK-23	London Gliding Club Proprietary Ltd
	G-DEVY	Schleicher ASK-23	London Gliding Club Proprietary Ltd
	G-DEWE	P & M Flight Design CTSW	Comunica Industries International Ltd
	G-DEWG	Grob G.103A Twin II Acro	J. P. Ryan
	G-DEWI	Rotorsport UK MTO Sport	D. V. Nockels
	G-DEWP	Grob G.103A Twin II Acro	Cambridge Gliding Club Ltd
	G-DEWR	Grob G.103A Twin II Acro	The Bristol Gliding Club Proprietary Ltd
	G-DEWY	Alpi Pioneer 300	W. D. Dewey (G-SRAW)
	G-DEWZ	Grob G.103A Twin II Acro	T. R. Dews
	G-DEXA	Grob G.103A Twin II Acro	Trent Valley Aerotowing Club Ltd
	G-DEXP	ARV Super 2	M. Davies
	G-DEXT	Robinson R44 II	Berkley Properties Ltd
	G-DFAF	Schleicher ASW-20L	A. S. Miller
	G-DFAR	Glasflugel H205 Club Libelle	Alpha Romeo Syndicate
	G-DFAT	Schleicher ASK-13	Dorset Gliding Club Ltd
	G-DFAV	ICA IS-32A	Ibis 32 Syndicate
	G-DFAW	Schempp-Hirth Ventus b/16.6	P. R. Stafford-Allen
	G-DFBD	Schleicher ASW-15B	D. A. Wilson
	G-DFBE	Rolladen-Schneider LS6	J. B. Van Woerden
	G-DFBJ	Schleicher K 8B	Bidford Gliding & Flying Club Ltd
	G-DFBM	Schempp-Hirth Nimbus 3/24.5	D. Gardiner
	G-DFBO	Schleicher ASW-20BL	454 Syndicate
	G-DFBR	Grob G.102 Astir CS77	773 Syndicate
	G-DFBY	Schempp-Hirth Discus b	D. Latimer
	G-DFCD	Centrair 101A	G. J. Bass
	G-DFCK	Schempp-Hirth Ventus b	S. A. Adlard
	G-DFCL	Schleicher K 8B	Bidford Gliding Ltd
	G-DFCM	Glaser-Dirks DG-300	A. Davis & I. D. Roberts
	G-DFCW	Schleicher ASK-13	Lasham Gliding Society Ltd
	G-DFCY	Schleicher ASW-15	M. R. Shaw
	G-DFDF	Grob G.102 Astir CS	The Bristol Gliding Club Proprietary Ltd
	G-DFDW	Glaser-Dirks DG-300	C. M. Hadley
	G-DFEB	Grob G.102 Club Astir III	Lasham Gliding Society Ltd
	G-DFEO	Schleicher ASK-13	Lasham Gliding Society Ltd
	G-DFEX	Grob G.102 Astir CS77	J. Taylor
	G-DFFP	Schleicher ASW-19B	J. M. Hutchinson
	G-DFGJ	Schleicher Ka 6CR	K6 Syndicate
	G-DFGT	Glaser-Dirks DG-300 Elan	T. J. Gray
	G-DFHS	Schempp-Hirth Ventus cT	154 Group
	G-DFHY	Scheibe SF-27A	J. M. Pursey
	G-DFJJ	Schempp-Hirth Ventus cT	S. G. Jones
	G-DFJO	Schempp-Hirth Ventus cT	T. P. Jenkinson
	G-DFKH	Schleicher Ka 6CR	I. A. Megarry
	G-DFKI	Westland Gazelle HT.2	Bourne Park Aviation Group (G-BZOT)
	G-DFKX	Schleicher Ka 6CR	J. E. Herring

Reg.	Type	Owner or Operator	Notes
G-DFLL	PZL-Bielsko SZD-9bis Bocian 10	The Bath, Wilts and North Dorset Gliding Club Ltd	
G-DFMG	Schempp-Hirth Discus b	M. T. Davis & J. Melvin	
G-DFOG	Rolladen-Schneider LS7	J. J. Shaw	
G-DFOX	AS.355F1 Twin Squirrel	Potter Aviation Ltd (G-NAAS/G-BPRG/G-NWPA)	
G-DFRA	Rolladen-Schneider LS6-b	79 Syndicate	
G-DFSA	Grob G.102 Astir CS	Astir 498 Syndicate	
G-DFTJ	PZL-Bielsko SZD-48-1 Jantar Standard 2	P. Nock	
G-DFUN	Van's RV-6	G-DFUN Flying Group	
G-DFWJ	Rolladen-Schneider LS7-WL	G-DFWJ Group	
G-DGAW	Schleicher Ka 6CR	H. C. Yorke & D. Searle	
G-DGCL	Glaser-Dirks DG.800B	C. J. Lowrie	
G-DGDJ	Rolladen-Schneider LS4-a	450 Syndicate	
G-DGFD	Robinson R44 II	FD Aviarion Ltd (G-CGNF)	
G-DGFY	Flylight Dragonfly	M. R. Sands	
G-DGHI	Dyn'Aéro MCR-01 Club	D. G. Hall	
G-DGIK	DG Flugzeugbau DG.1000S	R. P. Davis	
G-DGIO	Glaser-Dirks DG-100G Elan	EDP Group	
G-DGIV	Glaser-Dirks DG.800B	S. M. Tilling & J. Vella-Grech	
G-DGOD	Robinson R22 Beta	Mid-Atlantic Helicopters Ltd	
G-DGRA	DG Flugzeugbau DG-808C	R. Arkle	
G-DGSC	CZAW Sportcruiser	D. J. Gunn	
G-DGSM	Glaser-Dirks DG-400-17	T. E. Snoddy & L. J. McKelvie	
G-DHAA	Glasflugel H201B Standard Libelle	D. J. Jones & R. N. Turner	
G-DHAD	Glasflugel H201B Standard Libelle	R. Hines	
G-DHAH	Aeronca 7BCM Champion	G. D. Horn (G-JTYE)	
G-DHAL	Schleicher ASK-13	The Windrushers Gliding Club Ltd	
G-DHAP	Schleicher Ka 6E	M.Fursedon & T. Turner	
G-DHAT	Glaser-Dirks DG-200/17	G-DHAT Group	
G-DHCA	Grob G.103 Twin Astir	A. Jordan & P. Burton	
G-DHCC	DHC.1 Chipmunk 22 (WG321:G)	Eureka Aviation BVBA/Belgium	
G-DHCE	Schleicher ASW-19B	G-DHCE Syndicate	
G-DHCF	PZL-Bielsko SZD-50-3	Shalbourne Soaring Society Ltd	
G-DHCJ	Grob G.103A Twin II Acro	Peterborough and Spalding Gliding Club Ltd	
G-DHCL	Schempp-Hirth Discus b	C. E. Broom & L. Chicot	
G-DHCO	Glasflugel Standard Libelle 201B	M. J. Birch	
G-DHCR	PZL-Bielsko SZD-51-1	East Sussex Gliding Club Ltd	
G-DHCU	DG-300 Club Elan	R. B. Hankey & M. S. Smith	
G-DHCV	Schleicher ASW-19B	Birkett Air Services Ltd	
G-DHCW	PZL-Bielsko SZD-51-1	Deeside Gliding Club (Aberdeenshire) Ltd	
G-DHCX	Schleicher ASK-21	Devon and Somerset Gliding Club Ltd	
G-DHCZ	DHC.2 Beaver 1	Propshop Ltd (G-BUCJ)	
G-DHDH	Glaser-Dirks DG-200	J. T. Newbery	
G-DHDV	DH.104 Dove 8 (VP981)	Air Atlantique Ltd	
G-DHEB	Schleicher Ka 6CR	J. Burrow	
G-DHEM	Schempp-Hirth Discus CS	473 Syndicate	
G-DHER	Schleicher ASW-19B	B. Meech	
G-DHES	Centrair 101A	C. J. Cole & D. R. Bennett	
G-DHET	Rolladen-Schneider LS6-c18	M. P. Brooks	
G-DHEV	Schempp-Hirth Cirrus	HEV Group	
G-DHGL	Schempp-Hirth Discus b	R. G. Corbin & S. E. Buckley	
G-DHGS	Robinson R22 Beta	Fly Executive Ltd	
G-DHJH	Airbus A.321-211	Thomas Cook Airlines Ltd	
G-DHJZ	Airbus A.320-214	Thomas Cook Airlines Ltd	
G-DHKL	Schempp-Hirth Discus bT	M. A. Thorne	
G-DHLE	Boeing 767-3JHF	DHL Air Ltd	
G-DHLF	Boeing 767-3JHF	DHL Air Ltd	
G-DHLG	Boeing 767-3JHF	DHL Air Ltd	
G-DHMP	Schempp-Hirth Discus b	HMP Discus Syndicate	
G-DHNX	Rolladen-Schneider LS4-b	C. S. Crocker & K. J. Screen	
G-DHOC	Scheibe Bergfalke II-55	R. Karch	
G-DHOK	Schleicher ASW-20CL	S. D. Minson	
G-DHOP	Van's RV-9A	A. S. Orme	
G-DHOX	Schleicher ASW-15B	P. Ridgill & A. Griffiths	
G-DHPA	Issoire E-78 Silene	P. Woodcock	
G-DHPM	OGMA DHC.1 Chipmunk 20 (1365)	P. Meyrick	
G-DHPR	Schempp-Hirth Discus b	G. J. Bowser	
G-DHRG	Airbus A.320-214	Thomas Cook Airlines Ltd	
G-DHRR	Schleicher ASK-21	Lakes Gliding Club	
G-DHSJ	Schempp-Hirth Discus b	A. A. Jenkins	

Notes	Reg.	Type	Owner or Operator
	G-DHSL	Schempp-Hirth Ventus 2c	H. G. Woodsend
	G-DHSR	AB Sportine LAK-12 Lietuva	G. Forster
	G-DHSS	DH.112 Venom FB.50 (WR360:K)	Aviation and Computer Consultancy Ltd
	G-DHTG	Grob G.102 Astir CS	Trent Valley Gliding Club Ltd
	G-DHTM	DH.82A Tiger Moth (replica)	C. R. Hardiman
	G-DHTT	DH.112 Venom FB.50 (WR421)	Aviation and Computer Consultancy Ltd (G-BMOC)
	G-DHUB	PZL-Bielsko SZD-48-3	C. J. M. Chatburn
	G-DHUK	Schleicher Ka 6CR	Essex Gliding Club Ltd
	G-DHUU	DH.112 Venom FB.50 (WR410)	Aviation and Computer Consultancy Ltd (G-BMOD)
	G-DHVM	DH.112 Venom FB.50 (WR470)	Air Atlantique Ltd/Coventry (G-GONE)
	G-DHYL	Schempp-Hirth Ventus 2a	M. J. Cook
	G-DHZF	DH.82A Tiger Moth (N9192)	C. A.Parker & M. R. Johnson (G-BSTJ)
	G-DIAM	Diamond DA40D Star	Ichthis Naftiliaki Ltd
	G-DIAT	PA-28 Cherokee 140	Hinton Pilot Flight Training Ltd (G-BCGK)
	G-DICK	Thunder Ax6-56Z balloon	R. D. Sargeant
	G-DIDG	Van's RV-7	E. T. & D. K. Steele
	G-DIDY	Thruster T600T 450	D. R. Sims
	G-DIGG	Robinson R44 II	Thames Materials Ltd
	G-DIGI	PA-32 Cherokee Six 300	D. Stokes
	G-DIGN	Robin DR.400/180 Regent	D. M. Green
	G-DIKY	Murphy Rebel	R. J. P. Herivel
	G-DIME	Rockwell Commander 114	H. B. Richardson
	G-DINA	AA-5B Tiger	Portway Aviation Ltd
	G-DINO	Pegasus Quantum 15	F. Strath (G-MGMT)
	G-DIPI	Cameron 80 Tub SS balloon	C. G. Dobson
	G-DIPM	PA-46-350P Malibu Mirage	MAS Mix Ltd
	G-DIRK	Glaser-Dirks DG.400	D. J. Blackman
	G-DISA	SA Bulldog Srs 120/125	British Disabled Flying Association
	G-DISK	PA-24 Comanche 250	A. M. & Harrhy (G-APZG)
	G-DISO	Jodel 150	P. F. Craven
	G-DIWY	PA-32 Cherokee Six 300	IFS Chemicals Ltd
	G-DIXY	PA-28-181 Archer III	Modern Air (UK) Ltd
	G-DIZI	Escapade	J. A. & J. M. Iszard
	G-DIZO	Jodel D.120A	D. Aldersea (G-EMKM)
	G-DIZY	PA-28R-201T Turbo Arrow III	Dizy Aviation Ltd
	G-DIZZ	Hughes 369HE	Hopkinsons Fairdeals Remarking LLP
	G-DJAA	Schempp-Hirth Janus B	Bidford Gliding & Flying Club Ltd
	G-DJAB	Glaser-Dirks DG-300 Elan	I. G. Johnston
	G-DJAC	Schempp-Hirth Duo Discus	G-DJAC Group
	G-DJAD	Schleicher ASK-21	The Borders (Milfield) Gliding Club Ltd
	G-DJAE	Cessna 500 Citation	R. C. Lyne (G-JEAN)
	G-DJAH	Schempp-Hirth Discus b	K. Neave & C. F. M. Smith
	G-DJAN	Schempp-Hirth Discus b	N. F. Perren
	G-DJAY	Avtech Jabiru UL-450	G. S. Stokes
	G-DJBC	Ikarus C42 FB100	D. Meegan
	G-DJCR	Varga 2150A Kachina	D. J. C. Robertson (G-BLWG)
	G-DJET	Diamond DA42 Twin Star	Papa Bravo Aviation Ltd
	G-DJGG	Schleicher ASW-15B	A. A. Cole
	G-DJHP	Valentin Mistral C	P. B. Higgs
	G-DJJA	PA-28-181 Archer II	Interactive Aviation Ltd
	G-DJLL	Schleicher ASK-13	Bidford Gliding & Flying Club Ltd
	G-DJMC	Schleicher ASK-21	The Royal Air Force Gliding and Soaring Association
	G-DJMD	Schempp-Hirth Discus b	G-DJMD Flying Group
	G-DJMM	Cessna 172S	J. Browne & M. Manston
	G-DJNC	ICA-Brasov IS-28B2	Delta Juliet November Group
	G-DJNH	Denney Kitfox Mk 3	S. M. Morgan & M. J. Turner
	G-DJST	Ixess 912(1)	D. J. Stimpson
	G-DJWS	Schleicher ASW-15B	B. Pridgeon
	G-DKBA	DKBA AT 0301-0 balloon	I. Chadwick
	G-DKDP	Grob G.109	Grob 4
	G-DKEM	Bell 407	True Course Helicopter Ltd
	G-DKEN	Rolladen-Schneider LS4-a	K. L. Sangster and B. Lytollis
	G-DKEY	PA-28-161 Warrior II	PA-28 Warrior Ltd
	G-DKFU	Schempp-Hirth Ventus 2cxT	W. F. Payton (G-CKFU)
	G-DKGF	Viking Dragonfly ★	(stored)/Enstone
	G-DKNY	Robinson R44 II	Williamair Ltd

Reg.	Type	Owner or Operator	Notes
G-DKTA	PA-28-236 Dakota	G. Beattie & C. J. T. Kitchen	
G-DLAA	Cessna 208 Caravan 1	Aerodynamics Ltd	
G-DLAC	Cessna 208B Grand Caravan	Aerodynamics Ltd	
G-DLAL	Beech E90 King Air	Aerodynamics Ltd	
G-DLCB	Shaw Europa	K. Richards	
G-DLDL	Robinson R22 Beta	Cambridge Aviation Ltd	
G-DLEE	SOCATA TB9 Tampico Club	D. A. Lee (G-BPGX)	
G-DLOM	SOCATA TB20 Trinidad	J. N. A. Adderley	
G-DLTC	Hawker 900XP	Hangar 8 Management Ltd	
G-DLTR	PA-28 Cherokee 180E	R. A. Brown (G-AYAV)	
G-DMAC	Avtech Jabiru SP-430	C. J. Pratt	
G-DMAH	SOCATA TB20 Trinidad	William Cook Aviation Ltd	
G-DMBO	Van's RV-7	C. J. Goodwin	
G-DMCA	Douglas DC-10-30 ★	Forward fuselage/Manchester Airport Viewing Park	
G-DMCI	Ikarus C42 FB100	D. McCartan	
G-DMCS	PA-28R Cherokee Arrow 200-II	Arrow Associates (G-CPAC)	
G-DMCT	Flight Design CT2K	A. M. Sirant	
G-DMND	Diamond DA42 Twin Star	MC Air Ltd	
G-DMRS	Robinson R44 II	Nottinghamshire Helicopters (2004) Ltd	
G-DMSS	Westland Gazelle HT.3 (XW858:C)	G. Wood	
G-DMWW	CFM Shadow Srs DD	G-DMWW Flying Group	
G-DNBH	Raj Hamsa X'Air Hawk	D. N. B. Hearn	
G-DNGA	Balóny Kubiček BB.20	G. J. Bell	
G-DNGR	Colt 31A balloon	G. J. Bell	
G-DKNY	Ikarus C42 FB80	D. N. K. & M. A. Symon	
G-DNOP	PA-46-350P Malibu Mirage	Campbell Aviation Ltd	
G-DOCA	Boeing 737-436	British Airways	
G-DOCB	Boeing 737-436	British Airways	
G-DOCE	Boeing 737-436	British Airways	
G-DOCF	Boeing 737-436	British Airways	
G-DOCG	Boeing 737-436	British Airways	
G-DOCH	Boeing 737-436	British Airways	
G-DOCL	Boeing 737-436	British Airways	
G-DOCN	Boeing 737-436	British Airways	
G-DOCO	Boeing 737-436	British Airways	
G-DOCS	Boeing 737-436	British Airways	
G-DOCT	Boeing 737-436	British Airways	
G-DOCU	Boeing 737-436	British Airways	
G-DOCV	Boeing 737-436	British Airways	
G-DOCW	Boeing 737-436	British Airways	
G-DOCX	Boeing 737-436	British Airways	
G-DOCY	Boeing 737-436	British Airways (G-BVBY)	
G-DOCZ	Boeing 737-436	British Airways (G-BVBZ)	
G-DODB	Robinson R22 Beta	Heliyorks Ltd	
G-DODD	Cessna F.172P-II	K. Watts	
G-DODG	Aerotechnik EV-97A Eurostar	K. G. Vaughan	
G-DOEA	AA-5A Cheetah	Fairway Flying Services (G-RJMI)	
G-DOFY	Bell 206B JetRanger 3	Castle Air Ltd	
G-DOGE	SA Bulldog Srs 100/101	W. P. Cooper (G-AZHX)	
G-DOGG	SA Bulldog Srs 120/121 (XX638)	P. Sengupta	
G-DOGI	Robinson R22 Beta	Southern Heliservices Ltd (G-BVGS)	
G-DOGZ	Horizon 1	M. J. Nolan	
G-DOIG	CZAW Sportcruiser	J. H. Doyle	
G-DOIN	Skyranger 912(S)1	A. G. Borer	
G-DOIT	AS.350B1 Ecureuil	FBS Ltd	
G-DOLF	AS.365N3 Dauphin II	Profred Partners LLP	
G-DOLI	Cirrus SR20	Furness Asset Management Ltd	
G-DOLY	Cessna T.303	KW Aviation Ltd (G-BJZK)	
G-DOME	PA-28-161 Warrior III	Target Aviation Ltd	
G-DOMS	Aerotechnik EV-97A Eurostar	R. K. & C. A. Stewart	
G-DONI	AA-5B Tiger	W. P. Moritz (G-BLLT)	
G-DONS	PA-28RT-201T Turbo Arrow IV	C. E. Griffiths	
G-DONT	Xenair CH.601XL Zodiac	A. C. J. Butcher	
G-DOOM	Cameron Z-105 balloon	Test Flight	
G-DORM	Robinson R44 II	Aero-Heli Ltd	
G-DORN	EKW C-3605	R. G. Gray	
G-DORS	Eurocopter EC 135T2+	Premier Fund Leasing	

Notes	Reg.	Type	Owner or Operator
	G-DORY	Cameron Z-315 balloon	P. Baker
	G-DOSA	Diamond DA42 Twin Star	DO Systems Ltd
	G-DOSB	Diamond DA42 Twin Star	DO Systems Ltd
	G-DOSC	Diamond DA42 Twin Star	DO Systems Ltd
	G-DOTT	CFM Streak Shadow	R. J. Bell
	G-DOTW	Savannah VG Jabiru(1)	I. S. Wright
	G-DOTY	Van's RV-7	H. A. Daines
	G-DOVE	Cessna 182Q	G. Wills
	G-DOVE†	D. H. 104 Devon C.2 ★	E. Surrey College/Gatton Point, Redhill (G-KOOL)
	G-DOVS	Robinson R44 II	D. B. Hamilton
	G-DOWN	Colt 31A balloon	M. Williams
	G-DOZI	Ikarus C.42 FB100	D. A. Izod
	G-DOZZ	Best Off Sky Ranger Swift 912S(1)	J. P. Doswell
	G-DPEP	Aero AT-3 R100	Limerick Flying Club (Coonagh) Ltd
	G-DPJR	Sikorsky S-76B	Blackbird Logistics Ltd (G-JCBA)
	G-DPPF	Augusta A.109E Power	Dyfed-Powys Police Authority
	G-DPYE	Robin DR400/500	C. R. J. Walker
	G-DRAM	Cessna FR.172F (floatplane)	H. R. Mitchell
	G-DRAT	Slingsby T.51 Dart 17R	W. R. Longstaff
	G-DRAW	Colt 77A balloon	A. G. Odell
	G-DRBG	Cessna 172M	Henlow Flying Club Ltd (G-MUIL)
	G-DRCS	Schleicher ASH-25E	C. R. Smithers
	G-DREG	Supercharser	N. R. Beale
	G-DREI	Fokker DR.1 Triplane Replica	P. M. Brueggemann
	G-DREX	Cameron Saturn-110 balloon	M. A. Trimble
	G-DRFC	ATR-42-300	Blue Islands Ltd
	G-DRGC	P & M Quik GT450	D. R. G. Cornwell
	G-DRGS	Cessna 182S	Walter Scott & Partners Ltd
	G-DRIV	Robinson R44 II	MFH Helicopters Ltd
	G-DRLH	Eurocopter EC 120B Colibri	R. L. Hartshorn
	G-DRMM	Shaw Europa	T. J. Harrison
	G-DROL	Robinson R44 II	M. R. Lord (G-OPDG)
	G-DROP	Cessna U.206C	K. Brady (G-UKNO/G-BAMN)
	G-DRPK	Reality Escapade	P. A. Kirkham
	G-DRRT	Slingsby T.51 Dart 17R	1516 Dart Syndicate (G-DBXH)
	G-DRSV	CEA DR.315 (modified)	R. S. Voice
	G-DRYI	Cameron N-77 balloon	C. A. Butter
	G-DRYS	Cameron N-90 balloon	C. A. Butter
	G-DRZF	CEA DR.360	P. K. Kaufeler
	G-DSFT	PA-28R Cherokee Arrow 200-II	J. Jones (G-LFSE/G-BAXT)
	G-DSGC	PA-25 Pawnee 235C	Devon & Somerset Gliding Club Ltd
	G-DSID	PA-34-220T Seneca III	I. S. Gillbe
	G-DSKI	Aerotechnik EV-97 Eurostar	G-DSKI Group
	G-DSKY	Diamond DA.42 Twin Star	Papa Bravo Aviation Ltd (G-CDSZ)
	G-DSLL	Pegasus Quantum 15-912	R. G. Jeffery
	G-DSMA	P & M Aviation Quik R	Forestair Dragoons Ltd
	G-DSPI	Robinson R44	Central Helicopters Ltd (G-DPSI)
	G-DSPK	Cameron Z-140	Bailey Balloons Ltd
	G-DSPL	Diamond DA40 Star	Dynamic Signal Processing Ltd (G-GBOS)
	G-DSPZ	Robinson R44 II	Focal Point Communications Ltd
	G-DSVN	Rolladen-Schneider LS8-18	A. R. Paul
	G-DTAR	P & M Aviation Quik GT450	D. Tarvit
	G-DTCP	PA-32R-300 Cherokee Lance	R. S. Cook (G-TEEM)
	G-DTFF	Cessna T.182T Turbo Skylane	Ridgway Aviation Ltd
	G-DTFL	PA-46-500TP Malibu Meridian	Tyrone Fabrication Ltd
	G-DTOY	Ikarus C.42.FB100	C. W. Laske
	G-DTSM	EV-97 TeamEurostar UK	J. R. Stothart
	G-DTUG	Wag-Aero Super Sport	D. A. Bullock
	G-DTWO	Schempp-Hirth Discus 2A	O. Walters
	G-DUBI	Lindstrans LBL-120A balloon	A. Nimmo
	G-DUDE	Van's RV-8	W. M. Hodgkins
	G-DUDI	Rotorsport UK MTO Sport	Cloud 9 Gyro Flight Ltd
	G-DUDZ	Robin DR.400/180	D. H. Pattison (G-BXNK)
	G-DUFF	Rand Robinson KR-2	J. I. B. Duff
	G-DUGE	Ikarus C42 FB UK	D. Stevenson
	G-DUGI	Lindstrand LBL-90A balloon	J. A. Folkes
	G-DUKY	Robinson R44	English Braids Ltd

G-DUMP – G-ECDX

Reg.	Type	Owner or Operator	Notes
G-DUMP	Customcraft A-25 balloon	P. C. Bailey	
G-DUNK	Cessna F172M Skyhawk	Devon and Somerset Flight Training Ltd	
G-DUNS	Lindstrand LBL-90A balloon	A. Murphy	
G-DUOT	Schempp-Hirth Duo Discus T	G-DUOT Group	
G-DURO	Shaw Europa	W. R. C. Williams-Wynne	
G-DURX	Thunder 77A balloon	R. C. and M. A. Trimble	
G-DUSK	DH.115 Vampire T.11 (XE856) ★	Bournemouth Aviation Museum	
G-DUST	Stolp SA.300 Starduster Too	N. M. Robinson	
G-DUTY	Hughes 369E	Toure International Ltd	
G-DUVL	Cessna F.172N	G-DUVL Flying Group	
G-DVAA	Eurocopter EC135 T2+	Devon Air Ambulance Trading Co.Ltd	
G-DVBF	Lindstrand LBL-210A balloon	Virgin Balloon Flights	
G-DVMI	Van's RV-7	G-DVMI Group	
G-DVON	DH.104 Devon C.2 (VP955)	C. L. Thatcher	
G-DWCE	Robinson R44 II	Jim Davies Civil Engineering Ltd	
G-DWEM	Eurocopter EC135 T2	Bond Air Services Ltd (G-SSXX/G-SSSX)	
G-DWIA	Chilton D.W.1A	D. Elliott	
G-DWIB	Chilton D.W.1B (replica)	J. Jennings	
G-DWJM	Cessna 550 Citation II	TL Aviation Instrad LLP (G-BJIR)	
G-DWMS	Avtech Jabiru UL-450	B. J. Weighell	
G-DWPH	Ultramagic M-77 balloon	Ultramagic SA/Spain	
G-DXCC	Ultramagic M-77 balloon	A. Murphy	
G-DXLT	Schempp-Hirth Duo Discus xLT	G-DXLT Group	
G-DYCE	Robinson R44 II	Moorland Windows	
G-DYKE	Dyke JD.2 Delta	M. S. Bird	
G-DYMC	Aerospool Dynamic WT9 UK	S. Hoyle	
G-DYNA	Dynamic WT9 UK	Yeoman Light Aircraft Co.Ltd	
G-DYNM	Aerospool Dynamic WT9 UK	November Mike Group	
G-DZDZ	Rolladen-Schneider LS4	I. MacArthur	
G-DZKY	Diamond DA.40D Star	Dusky Aviation Ltd (G-CEZP)	
G-DZZY	Champion 8KCAB	Paul's Planes Ltd	
G-EAGA	Sopwith Dove (replica)	A. Wood	
G-EAOU†	Vickers Vimy (replica)(NX71MY)	Greenco (UK) Ltd	
G-EASD	Avro 504L	G. M. New	
G-EASQ†	Bristol Babe (replica) (BAPC87) ★	Bristol Aero Collection (stored)/Kemble	
G-EAVX	Sopwith Pup (B1807)	K. A. M. Baker	
G-EBED†	Vickers 60 Viking (replica) (BAPC114)★	Brooklands Museum of Aviation/Weybridge	
G-EBHX	DH.53 Humming Bird	The Shuttleworth Collection	
G-EBIA	RAF SE-5A (F904)	The Shuttleworth Collection	
G-EBIB	RAF SE-5A ★	Science Museum/South Kensington	
G-EBIC	RAF SE-5A (F938) ★	RAF Museum/Hendon	
G-EBIR	DH.51	The Shuttleworth Collection	
G-EBJE	Avro 504K (E449) ★	RAF Museum/Hendon	
G-EBJG	Parnall Pixie IIIH	Midland Aircraft Preservation Society	
G-EBJI	Hawker Cygnet (replica)	C. J. Essex	
G-EBJO	ANEC IIH	The Shuttleworth Collection	
G-EBKY	Sopwith Pup (9917)	The Shuttleworth Collection	
G-EBLV	DH.60 Cirrus Moth	British Aerospace PLC	
G-EBMB	Hawker Cygnet I ★	RAF Museum/Cosford	
G-EBNV	English Electric Wren	The Shuttleworth Collection	
G-EBQP	DH.53 Humming Bird (J7326) ★	P. L. Kirk & T. G. Pankhurst	
G-EBWD	DH.60X Hermes Moth	The Shuttleworth Collection	
G-EBZM	Avro 594 Avian IIIA ★	Manchester Museum of Science & Industry	
G-EBZN	DH.60X Moth	J. Hodgkinson (G-UAAP)	
G-ECAC	Alpha R21620U	Bulldog Aviation Ltd	
G-ECAD	Cessna FA.152	Bulldog Aviation Ltd (G-JEET/G-BHMF)	
G-ECAE	Royal Aircraft Factory SE.5A	H. A. D. Monro	
G-ECAM	EAA Acrosport II	C. England	
G-ECAN	DH.84 Dragon	Norman Aircraft Trust	
G-ECBH	Cessna F.150K	ECBH Flying Group	
G-ECBI	Schweizer 269C-1	Iris Aviation Ltd	
G-ECDB	Schleicher Ka 6E	C. W. R. Neve	
G-ECDS	DH.82A Tiger Moth	N. C. Wilson	
G-ECDX	DH.71 Tiger Moth (replica)	M. D. Souch	

G-ECEA – G-EEBF

BRITISH CIVIL REGISTRATIONS

Notes	Reg.	Type	Owner or Operator
	G-ECEA	Schempp-Hirth Cirrus	CEA Group
	G-ECGC	Cessna F.172N	S. Din
	G-ECGO	Bölkow Bö.208C1 Junior	A Flight Aviation Ltd
	G-ECJM	PA-28R-201T Turbo Arrow III	Regishire Ltd (G-FESL/G-BNRN)
	G-ECKB	Escapade 912(2)	C. M. & C. P. Bradford
	G-ECLW	Glasflugel Standard Libelle 201B	R. G. Parker
	G-ECMC	Robinson R22 Beta	Bulldog Aviation Ltd (G-LSWL)
	G-ECMK	PA-18-150 Super Cub	111 Supercub Group
	G-ECOA	DHC.8-402 Dash Eight	Flybe.com
	G-ECOB	DHC.8-402 Dash Eight	Flybe.com
	G-ECOC	DHC.8-402 Dash Eight	Flybe.com
	G-ECOD	DHC.8-402 Dash Eight	Flybe.com
	G-ECOE	DHC.8-402 Dash Eight	Flybe.com
	G-ECOF	DHC.8-402 Dash Eight	Flybe.com
	G-ECOG	DHC.8-402 Dash Eight	Flybe.com
	G-ECOH	DHC.8-402 Dash Eight	Flybe.com
	G-ECOI	DHC.8-402 Dash Eight	Flybe.com
	G-ECOJ	DHC.8-402 Dash Eight	Flybe.com
	G-ECOK	DHC.8-402 Dash Eight	Flybe.com
	G-ECOL	Schempp-Hirth Nimbus 2B	M. Upex & L. I. Rigby
	G-ECOM	DHC.8-402 Dash Eight	Flybe.com
	G-ECON	Cessna 172M	Aviation Rentals (G-JONE)
	G-ECOO	DHC.8-402 Dash Eight	Flybe.com
	G-ECOP	DHC.8-402 Dash Eight	Flybe.com
	G-ECOR	DHC.8-402 Dash Eight	Flybe.com
	G-ECOT	DHC.8-402 Dash Eight	Flybe.com
	G-ECOU	AS.355F2 Twin Squirrel	Rulegate Ltd
	G-ECOX	Grega GN.1 Air Camper	H. C. Cox
	G-ECPA	Glasflugel H201B Standard Libelle	M. J. Witton
	G-ECSW	Pilatus B4-PC11AF	I. H. Keyser
	G-ECTF	Comper CLA.7 Swift Replica	P. R. Cozens
	G-ECUB	PA-18 Super Cub 150	G-ECUB Flying Group (G-CBFI)
	G-ECVB	Pietenpol Air Camper	G. Edwards
	G-ECXL	PZL-Bielsko SZD-30 Pirat	Charlie X-Ray Lima Group
	G-ECZA	BN-21-21 Islander	B-N Group Ltd (G-BDPN)
	G-EDAV	SA Bulldog Srs 120/121 (XX534:B)	Edwalton Aviation Ltd
	G-EDAY	BAe Jetstream 3101	Skylease Sweden AB
	G-EDBD	PZL-Bielsko SZD-30 Pirat	S. P. Burgess
	G-EDCJ	Cessna 525 CitationJet	Jetphase Ltd
	G-EDCL	Cessna 525 CitationJet	Air Charter Scotland (Holdings) Ltd
	G-EDCM	Cessna 525 CitationJet	Air Charter Scotland (Holdings) Ltd
	G-EDCS	Raytheon 400A	Mountain Aviation Ltd
	G-EDDD	Schempp-Hirth Nimbus 2	C. A. Mansfield (G-BKPM)
	G-EDDS	CZAW Sportcruiser	E. H. Bishop
	G-EDDV	PZL-Bielsko SZD-38A Jantar 1	S. R. Bruce
	G-EDEE	Comco Ikarus C.42 FB100	Microavionics
	G-EDEL	PA-32-300 Cherokee Six D	I. Blamire
	G-EDEN	SOCATA TB10 Tobago	Group Eden
	G-EDEO	Beech B.24R Sierra 200	G-EDEO Group
	G-EDFS	Pietenpol Air Camper	V. J. Comfort
	G-EDGA	PA-28-161 Warrior II	The RAF Halton Aeroplane Club Ltd
	G-EDGE	Jodel 150	A. D. Edge
	G-EDGJ	PA-28-161 Warrior II	Medcentres Property Portfolio Ltd
	G-EDGJ	Zivko Edge 360	D. G. Jenkins
	G-EDGY	Flight Test Edge 540	C. R. A. Scrope
	G-EDLY	Airborne Edge 912/Streak IIIB	M. & P. L. Eardley
	G-EDMC	Pegasus Quantum 15-912	A. Vaughan
	G-EDNA	PA-38-112 Tomahawk	P. J. Montgomery
	G-EDRE	Lindstrand LBL 90A balloon	Edren Homes Ltd
	G-EDRV	Van's RV-6A	G-EDRV Flying Group
	G-EDTO	Cessna FR.172F	N. G. Hopkinson
	G-EDVK	RH78 Tiger Light	M. Peters (G-MZGT)
	G-EDVL	PA-28R Cherokee Arrow 200-II	J. S. Devlin & Z. Islam (G-BXIN)
	G-EDYO	PA-32-260 Cherokee Six	R. Bursey & A. D. Paton
	G-EEAD	Slingsby T.65A Vega	D. S. Smith
	G-EEBA	Slingsby T.65A Vega	J. A. Cowie & K. Robertson
	G-EEBB	Sikorsky S-76C	Haughey Air Ltd
	G-EEBD	Scheibe Bergfalke IV	F. A. P. M. Otten
	G-EEBE	Issoire E-78B Silene	Silene Syndicate
	G-EEBF	Schempp-Hirth Mini Nimbus C	M. Pingel

Reg.	Type	Owner or Operator	Notes
G-EEBK	Schempp-Hirth Mini Nimbus C	G. S. Bell	
G-EEBL	Schleicher ASK-13	Derbyshire and Lancashire Gliding Club Ltd	
G-EEBM	Grob G.102 Astir CS77	Yorkshire Gliding Club (Proprietary) Ltd	
G-EEBN	Centrair ASW-20FL	S. MacArthur & R. Carlisle	
G-EEBR	Glaser-Dirks DG200/17	N. J. L. Busvine	
G-EEBS	Scheibe Zugvogel IIIA	J. A. Stockford	
G-EEBZ	Schleicher ASK-13	Booker Gliding Club Ltd	
G-EECC	Aerospool Dynamic WT9 UK	C. V. Ellingworth	
G-EECK	Slingsby T65A Vega	The ECK Syndicate	
G-EECO	Lindstrand LBL-25A balloon	A. Jay	
G-EEDE	Centrair ASW-20F	G. M. Cumner	
G-EEEK	Extra EA.300/200	A. R. Willis	
G-EEER	Schempp-Hirth Mini Nimbus C	D. J. Uren	
G-EEEZ	Champion 8KCAB	Les Wallen Manufacturing Ltd	
G-EEFA	Cameron Z-90 balloon	A. Murphy	
G-EEFK	Centrair ASW-20FL	A. P. Balkwill & G. B. Monslow	
G-EEFT	Schempp-Hirth Nimbus 2B	S. A. Adlard	
G-EEGL	Christen Eagle II	M. P. Swoboda & S. L. Nicholson	
G-EEGU	PA-28-161 Warrior II	Premier Flight Training Ltd	
G-EEJE	PA-31 Navajo B	Geeje Ltd	
G-EEKA	Glaser-Dirks DG-202/17	M. J. R. Lindsay & P. Hayward	
G-EEKY	PA-28 Cherokee 140B	Cherokee Aviation Ltd	
G-EELS	Cessna 208B Caravan 1	Glass Eels Ltd	
G-EELT	Rolladen-Schneider LS4	ELT Syndicate	
G-EELY	Schleicher Ka 6CR	K6 ELY Syndicate	
G-EENA	PA-32R-301 Saratoga SP	Gamit Ltd	
G-EENE	Rolladen-Schneider LS4	R. A. Hine	
G-EENI	Shaw Europa	M. P. Grimshaw	
G-EENK	Schleicher ASK-21	Essex Gliding Club Ltd	
G-EENN	Schempp-Hirth Nimbus 3	M. W. Dickson	
G-EENT	Glasflugel 304	M. Hastings & P. D. Morrison	
G-EENW	Schleicher ASW-20L	G-EENW Group	
G-EENZ	Schleicher ASW-19B	O. L. Pugh	
G-EEPJ	Pitts S-1S Special	P. Westerby-Jones	
G-EERH	Ruschmeyer R.90-230RG	D. Sadler	
G-EERV	Van's RV-6	M. Crunden & C. B. Stirling	
G-EERY	Robinson R22	EGB (Helicopters) Ltd	
G-EESA	Shaw Europa	C. Deith (G-HIIL)	
G-EESY	Rolladen-Schneider LS4	G. S. Morley	
G-EETG	Cessna 172Q Cutlass	Tango Golf Flying Group	
G-EEUP	SNCAN Stampe SV.4C	A. M. Wajih	
G-EEVL	Grob G.102 Astir CS77	G. D. E. Macdonald	
G-EEWS	Cessna T.210N	A. N. Macdonald & S. M. Jack	
G-EEWZ	Mainair Pegasus Quik	A. J. Roche	
G-EEYE	Mainair Blade 912	B. J. Egerton	
G-EEZO	DG Flugzeugbau DG-808C	G-ZO Syndicate	
G-EEZR	Robinson R44	Geezer Aviation LLP	
G-EEZS	Cessna 182P	D. A. G. Johnson	
G-EEZZ	Zenair CH.601XL Zodiac	K. W. Allan	
G-EFAM	Cessna 182S Skylane	G-EFAM Flying Group	
G-EFAT	Robinson R44 II	U. Momberg	
G-EFBP	Cessna FR.172K	A. Webster	
G-EFCM	PA-28-180 Cherokee D	ATC Trading Ltd	
G-EFFI	Rotorway Executive 162F	P. D. Annison	
G-EFGH	Robinson R22 Beta	Ryvoan Aviation Ltd	
G-EFIR	PA-28-181 Archer II	Leicestershire Aero Club Ltd	
G-EFJD	MBB Bo.209 Monsun	E. J. Smith	
G-EFLT	Glasflugel Standard Libelle 201B	P. A. Pearson	
G-EFLY	Centrair ASW-20FL	I. D. & J. H. Atherton	
G-EFOF	Robinson R22 Beta	NT Burton Aviation	
G-EFOX	Eurofox 912(2)	R. M. Cornwell	
G-EFSM	Slingsby T.67M Firefly 260	A. J. Macdonald (G-BPLK)	
G-EFTE	Bölkow Bö.207	B. Morris & R. L. Earl	
G-EFTF	AS.350B Ecureuil	T. J. French (G-CWIZ/G-DJEM/G-ZBAC/ G-SEBI/G-BMCU)	
G-EFUN	Bishop & Castelli E-Go	A. W. Bishop & G. Castelli	
G-EFVS	Wassmer WA.52 Europa	D. F. Hurn	
G-EGAG	SOCATA TB20 Trinidad	D. & E. Booth	
G-EGAL	Christen Eagle II	Eagle Partners	
G-EGBS	Van's RV-9A	Shobdon RV-9A Group	

BRITISH CIVIL REGISTRATIONS

Notes	Reg.	Type	Owner or Operator
	G-EGEG	Cessna 172R	C. D. Lever
	G-EGEL	Christen Eagle II	G-EGEL Flying Group
	G-EGGI	Ikarus C.42FB UK	A. G. & G. J. Higgins
	G-EGGS	Robin DR.400/180	G-EGGS Syndicate
	G-EGGZ	Best Off Sky Ranger Swift 912S(1)	J. C. Sheardown
	G-EGHH	Hawker Hunter F.58 (J-4083)	Heritage Aviation Developments Ltd
	G-EGIA	UltraMagic M-65C balloon	Balloon Promotion SAS/Italy
	G-EGIL	Christen Eagle II	Smoke On Go Ltd
	G-EGJA	SOCATA TB20 Trinidad	N. Koutras
	G-EGKE	SOCATA Rallye 180TS	Suffolk Soaring Tug Group
	G-EGLE	Christen Eagle II	D. Thorpe t/a Eagle Group
	G-EGLG	PA-31 Turbo Navajo C	H. Merkado (G-OATC/G-OJPW/G-BGCC)
	G-EGLL	PA-28-161 Warrior II	Airways Aero Associations Ltd (G-BLEJ)
	G-EGLS	PA-28-181 Archer III	O. Sylvester
	G-EGLT	Cessna 310R	Reconnaissance Ventures Ltd (G-BHTV)
	G-EGPG	PA-18-135 Super Cub	G. Cormack (G-BWUC)
	G-EGSJ	Jabiru J400	Seething Jabiru Group (G-MGRK)
	G-EGTB	PA-28-161 Warrior II	Aviation Advice & Consulting Ltd (G-BPWA)
	G-EGTC	Robinson R44	MFH Helicopters Ltd (G-CCNK)
	G-EGTR	PA-28-161 Cadet	Aviation Rentals (G-BRSI)
	G-EGUR	Jodel D.140B	S. H. Williams
	G-EGVO	Dassault Falcon 900EX	TAG Aviation (UK) Ltd
	G-EGWN	American Champion 7ECA	The Royal Air Force Halton Aeroplane Club Ltd
	G-EHAA	MDH MD.900 Explorer	Police Aviation Services Ltd (G-GNAA)
	G-EHAV	Glasflugel Standard Libelle 201B	A. Liran & M. Truelove
	G-EHBJ	CASA 1.131E Jungmann 2000	E. P. Howard
	G-EHCB	Schempp-Hirth Nimbus 3DT	G-EHCB Group
	G-EHCC	PZL-Bielsko SZD-50-3 Puchacz	Heron Gliding Club
	G-EHCZ	Schleicher K8B	The Surrey Hills Gliding Club Ltd
	G-EHDS	CASA 1.131E Jungmann 2000	C. W. N. & A. A. M. Huke (G-DUDS)
	G-EHGF	PA-28-181 Archer II	G. P. Robinson
	G-EHGW	Cessna 550 Citation Bravo	Eurojet Aviation Ltd (G-FCDB)
	G-EHIC	Jodel D.140B	India Charlie Consortium
	G-EHLX	PA-28-181 Archer II	ASG Leasing Ltd
	G-EHMF	Isaacs Fury II	M. W. Bodger
	G-EHMJ	Beech S35 Bonanza	A. J. Daley
	G-EHMM	Robin DR.400/180R	Booker Gliding Club Ltd
	G-EHMS	MD Helicopters MD-900	Virgin HEMS (London) Ltd
	G-EHTT	Schleicher ASW-20CL	HTT Syndicate
	G-EHUP	Aérospatiale SA.341G Gazelle 1	MW Helicopters Ltd
	G-EHXP	Rockwell Commander 112A	A. L. Stewart
	G-EIBM	Robinson R22 Beta	HJS Helicopters Ltd (G-BUCL)
	G-EICK	Cessna 172S	Centenary Flying Group
	G-EIER	Marganski Swift S-1	D. Poll & C Cain
	G-EIGG	BAe Jetstream 3102	Linksair Ltd
	G-EIKY	Shaw Europa	J. D. Milbank
	G-EINI	Europa XS	K. J. Burns (G-KDCC)
	G-EIRE	Cessna T.182T	J. Byrne
	G-EISG	Beech A36 Bonanza	R. J. & B. Howard
	G-EISO	SOCATA MS.892A Rallye Commodore 150	EISO Group
	G-EITE	Luscombe 8F Silvaire	S. R. H. Martin
	G-EIWT	Cessna FR.182RG	J. R. Pybus
	G-EIZO	Eurocopter EC 120B	R. M. Bailey
	G-EJAC	Mudry CAP.232	G. C. J. Cooper, P. Varinot & E. Vazeille (G-OGBR)
	G-EJAE	GlaserDirks DG-200	D. L. P. H. Waller
	G-EJAR	Airbus A.319-111	EasyJet Airline Co Ltd
	G-EJBI	Bolkow Bo.207	J. O'Donnell & J. L. Bone
	G-EJEL	Cessna 550 Citation II	Futura Trading SAS
	G-EJGO	Z.226HE Trener	S. K. T. & C. M. Neofytou
	G-EJHH	Schempp-Hirth Standard Cirrus	D. M. Cornelius
	G-EJIM	Schempp-Hirth Discus 2cT	J. Lynchehaun
	G-EJJB	Airbus A.319-111	EasyJet Airline Co Ltd
	G-EJOC	AS.350B Ecureuil	Air and Ground Aviation Ltd (G-GEDS/G-HMAN/G-SKIM/G-BIVP)
	G-EJRC	Robinson R44 II	Perry Farming Co.
	G-EJRS	PA-28-161 Cadet	Carlisle Flight Traing Ltd
	G-EJTC	Robinson R44	N. Parkhouse

Reg.	Type	Owner or Operator	Notes
G-EJWI	Flight Design CTLS	E. Wright	
G-EKEY	Schleicher ASW-20 CL	K. W. Payne	
G-EKIM	Alpi Pioneer 300	M. Langmead	
G-EKIR	PA-28-262 Cadet	Aeros Leasing Ltd	
G-EKKL	PA-28-161 Warrior II	Apollo Aviation Advisory Ltd/Shoreham	
G-EKMN	Zlin Z.242L	TGD Leasing Ltd	
G-EKOS	Cessna FR.182 RG	S. Charlton	
G-ELAM	PA-30 Twin Comanche160B	Hangar 39 Ltd (G-BAWU/G-BAWV)	
G-ELDR	PA-32 Cherokee Six 260	Demero Ltd	
G-ELEE	Cameron Z-105 balloon	D. Eliot	
G-ELEN	Robin DR.400/180	Avalon Aero Holdings Ltd	
G-ELIS	PA-34-200T Seneca II	Bristol Flying Centre Ltd (G-BOPV)	
G-ELIZ	Denney Kitfox Mk 2	A. J. Ellis	
G-ELKA	Christen Eagle II	J. T. Matthews	
G-ELKS	Avid Speedwing Mk 4	H. S. Elkins	
G-ELLA	PA-32R-301 Saratoga IIHP	C. C. W. Hart	
G-ELLE	Cameron N-90 balloon	D. J. Stagg	
G-ELLI	Bell 206B JetRanger 3	Italian Clothes Ltd	
G-ELMH	NA AT-6D Harvard III (42-84555:EP-H)	M. Hammond	
G-ELMO	Robinson R44 II	Locumlink Associates Ltd/Ireland	
G-ELSE	Diamond DA42 Twin Star	R. Swann	
G-ELSI	Tanarg/Ixess 15 912S(1)	D. Daniel	
G-ELTE	Agusta A109A II	Henfield Lodge Ltd (G-BWZI)	
G-ELUE	PA-28-161 Warrior II	Freedom Aviation Ltd	
G-ELUN	Robin DR.400/180R	Cotswold DR.400 Syndicate	
G-ELUT	PA-28R Cherokee Arrow 200-II	Green Arrow Europe Ltd	
G-ELWK	Van's RV-12	J. Devlin	
G-ELZN	PA-28-161 Warrior II	ZN Flying Group	
G-ELZY	PA-28-161 Warrior II	Redhill Air Services Ltd	
G-EMAA	Eurocopter EC 135T2	Bond Air Services Ltd	
G-EMAC	Robinson R22 Beta	Unique Helicopters (NI) Ltd (G-CBDB)	
G-EMAX	PA-31-350 Navajo Chieftain	Atlantic Bridge Aviation Ltd	
G-EMBC	Embraer RJ145EP	Port One Ltd	
G-EMBI	Embraer RJ145EP	bmi regional	
G-EMBJ	Embraer RJ145EP	bmi regional	
G-EMBN	Embraer RJ145EP	bmi regional	
G-EMBO	Embraer RJ145EP	Aircraft Solutions ERJ-145LLC	
G-EMBP	Embraer RJ145EU	bmi regional	
G-EMBW	Embraer RJ145EU	Aircraft Solutions ERJ-145 LLC	
G-EMBX	Embraer RJ145EU	Aircraft Solutions ERJ-145 LLC	
G-EMBY	Embraer RJ145EU	Aircraft Solutions ERJ-145 LLC	
G-EMCA	Commander Aircraft 114B	S. Roberts	
G-EMDM	Diamond DA40-P9 Star	D. J. Munson	
G-EMHC	Agusta A109E Power	East Midlands Helicopters	
G-EMHK	MBB Bö.209 Monsun 150FV	T. A. Crone (G-BLRD)	
G-EMID	Eurocopter EC 135P2	East Midlands Air Support Unit	
G-EMIN	Shaw Europa	S. A. Lamb	
G-EMJA	CASA 1.131E Jungmann 2000	C. R. Maher	
G-EMLE	Aerotechnik EV-97 Eurostar	A. R. White	
G-EMLS	Cessna T210L Turbo Centurion	I. K. F. Simcock	
G-EMLY	Pegasus Quantum 15	S. J. Reid	
G-EMMM	Diamond DA40 Star	A. J. Leigh	
G-EMMS	PA-38-112 Tomahawk	Ravenair Aircraft Ltd/Liverpool	
G-EMMY	Rutan Vari-Eze	M. J. Tooze	
G-EMOL	Schweizer 269C-1	Bournemouth Helicopters Ltd	
G-EMSA	Czech Sport Aircraft Sportcruiser	A. C. & M. A. Naylor	
G-EMSB	PA-22-160 Tri-Pacer	M. S. Bird (G-ARHU)	
G-EMSI	Shaw Europa	P. W. L. Thomas	
G-EMSY	DH.82A Tiger Moth	G-EMSY Group (G-ASPZ)	
G-ENBD	Lindstrand LBL-120A balloon	A. Nimmo	
G-ENBW	Robin DR.400-180R	Bicester Robin Crew	
G-ENCE	Partenavia P.68B	Bicton Aviation (G-OROY/G-BFSU)	
G-ENEA	Cessna 182P	Air Ads Ltd	
G-ENEE	CFM Streak Shadow SA	S. D. J. Harvey	
G-ENES	Bell 206B JetRanger III	Celtic Energy Ltd	
G-ENGO	Steen Skybolt	R. G. Fulton	
G-ENGR	Head AX8-105 balloon	Royal Engineers Balloon Club	
G-ENHP	Enstrom 480B	H. J. Pelham	

Notes	Reg.	Type	Owner or Operator
	G-ENIA	Staaken Z-21 Flitzer	A. F. Wankowski
	G-ENID	Reality Escapade	Q. Irving
	G-ENIE	Tipsy T.66 Nipper 3	R. J. Ripley
	G-ENII	Cessna F.172M	J. Howley
	G-ENIO	Pitts S-2C Special	Advanced Flying (London) Ltd
	G-ENNA	PA-28-161 Warrior II	Falcon Flying Serices Ltd (G-ESFT)
	G-ENNI	Robin R.3000/180	I. F. Doubtfire
	G-ENNK	Cessna 172S	Pooler-LMT Ltd
	G-ENNY	Cameron V-77 balloon	J. H. Dobson
	G-ENOA	Cessna F.172F	M. K. Acors (G-ASZW)
	G-ENRE	Avtech Jabiru UL	P. R. Turton
	G-ENRI	Lindstrand LBL-105A balloon	P. G. Hall
	G-ENST	CZAW Sportcruiser	L. M. Radcliffe, C. Slater & D. G. Price
	G-ENTL	P & M Quik R	A. Kurt-Elli
	G-ENTS	Van's RV-9A	L. G. Johnson
	G-ENTT	Cessna F.152 II	C. & A. R. Hyett (G-BHHI)
	G-ENTW	Cessna F.152 II	Firecrest Aviation Ltd, C. Oates & C. Castledine (G-BFLK)
	G-ENVO	MBB Bo.105CBS-4	F. C. Owen
	G-ENVY	Mainair Blade 912	P. J. Lomax & J. A. Robinson
	G-ENXA	Falcon 900EX	Enex Aviation Ltd
	G-ENZO	Cameron Z-105 balloon	Garelli VI SPA
	G-EOFS	Shaw Europa	A. Fletcher & G. Plenderleith
	G-EOFW	Pegasus Quantum 15-912	G-EOFW Microlight Group
	G-EOGE	Gefa-Flug AS105GD airship (hot air)	George Brazil Airship Ltd
	G-EOHL	Cessna 182L	G. P. James
	G-EOID	Aeroprakt A22-L Foxbat	M. D. Northwood
	G-EOIN	Zenair CH.701UL	I. J. M. Donnelly
	G-EOJB	Robinson R44 II	G. J. Braithwaite (G-EDES)
	G-EOLD	PA-28-161 Warrior II	M. A. Ward
	G-EOLX	Cessna 172N	Westward Airways (Lands End) Ltd
	G-EOMA	Airbus A.330-243	Monarch Airlines Ltd
	G-EOMK	Robin DR400/180	MK Group
	G-EOPH	Cameron C-90 balloon	A. J. Cherrett
	G-EORG	PA-38-112 Tomahawk	Control Developments (UK) Ltd
	G-EORJ	Shaw Europa	P. E. George
	G-EPAR	Robinson R22 Beta II	Jepar Rotorcraft
	G-EPDI	Cameron N-77 balloon	R. Moss
	G-EPIC	Jabiru UL-450	T. Chadwick
	G-EPOC	Jabiru UL-450	S. Cope
	G-EPOX	Aero Designs Pulsar XP	D. R. Stansfield
	G-EPSN	Ultramagic M-105 balloon	G. Everett
	G-EPTR	PA-28R Cherokee Arrow 200-II	ACS Aviation Ltd
	G-ERCO	Ercoupe 415D	A. R. & M. V. Tapp
	G-ERDA	Staaken Z-21A Flitzer	J. Cresswell
	G-ERDS	DH.82A Tiger Moth	W. A. Gerdes
	G-ERFS	PA-28-161 Warrior II	Medcentres Property Portfolio Ltd
	G-ERIC	Rockwell Commander 112TC	J. A. L. Irwin
	G-ERIE	Raytheon Beech 400A	Platinum Executive Aviation Ltd
	G-ERIK	Cameron N-77 balloon	T. M. Donnelly
	G-ERIW	Staaken Z-21 Flitzer	R. I. Wasey
	G-ERJA	Embraer RJ145EP	Falak Fin Nine Ltd
	G-ERJC	Embraer RJ145EP	Falak Fin Ten Ltd
	G-ERMO	ARV Super 2	S. Vince (G-BMWK)
	G-ERNI	PA-28-181 Archer II	J. Gardener & N. F. P. Hopwood (G-OSSY)
	G-EROB	Europa XS	R. J. Bull (G-RBJW)
	G-EROL	Westland SA.341G Gazelle 1	MW Helicopters Ltd (G-NONA/G-FDAV/G-RIFA/ G-ORGE/G-BBHU)
	G-EROM	Robinson R22 Beta	EBG (Helicopters) Ltd
	G-EROS	Cameron H-34 balloon	Evening Standard Co Ltd
	G-ERRY	AA-5B Tiger	The GERRY Group (G-BFMJ)
	G-ERTE	Skyranger 912S (1)	A. P. Trumper
	G-ERTI	Staaken Z-21A Flitzer	B. S. Carpenter
	G-ERYR	P & M Aviation Quik GT450	R. D. Ellis
	G-ESCA	Escapade Jabiru (1)	G. W. E. & R. H. May
	G-ESCC	Escapade 912	G. & S. Simons
	G-ESCP	Escapade 912(1)	R. G. Hughes
	G-ESEX	Eurocopter EC 135T2	Essex Police Authority

Reg.	Type	Owner or Operator	Notes
G-ESGA	Reality Escapade	I. Bamford	
G-ESKA	Escapade 912	J. H. Beard	
G-ESME	Cessna R.182 II (15211)	G. C. Cherrington (G-BNOX)	
G-ESSL	Cessna 182R Skylane II	Euro Seaplane Services Ltd	
G-ESTA	Cessna 550 Citation II	Executive Aviation Services Ltd (G-GAUL)	
G-ESTR	Van's RV-6	R. M. Johnson	
G-ESUS	Rotorway Executive 162F	J. Tickner	
G-ETAT	Cessna 172S Skyhawk	ADR Aviation	
G-ETBY	PA-32 Cherokee Six 260	G-ETBY Group (G-AWCY)	
G-ETDC	Cessna 172P	The Moray Flying Club	
G-ETFF	Robinson R44	Ridgway Aviation (G-HSLJ)	
G-ETHY	Cessna 208	N. A. Moore	
G-ETIM	Eurocopter EC 120B	Agricultural Machinery Ltdl	
G-ETIN	Robinson R22 Beta	J. M. Lynch	
G-ETIV	Robin DR.400/180	L. A. Seers	
G-ETME	Nord 1002 Pingouin (KG+EM)	108 Flying Group	
G-ETNT	Robinson R44	Irwin Plant Hire	
G-ETOU	Agusta A.109S Grand	P. J. Ogden	
G-ETPS	Hawker Hunter FGA.9 (XE601)	FGA 9 Ltd	
G-ETUS	Bell 206B-2 JetRanger II	D & G Cars Ltd (G-JBHH/G-SCOO/G-CORC/ G-CJHI/G-BBFB)	
G-ETVS	Alpi Pioneer 300 Hawk	V. Serazzi	
G-EUAB	Europa XS	A. D. Stephens	
G-EUAN	Jabiru UL-D	M. Wade & M. Lusted	
G-EUFO	Rolladen-Schneider LS7-WL	J. R. Bane & M. G. Woollard	
G-EUJG	Avro 594 Avian IIIA	R. I. & D. E. Souch	
G-EUKS	Westland Widgeon III	R. I. Souch	
G-EUNA	Airbus A.318-112	British Airways	
G-EUNB	Airbus A.318-112	British Airways	
G-EUNG	Europa NG	D. I. Stanbridge	
G-EUNI	Beech B200 Super King Air	Universita Telematica E-Campus (G-TAGH)	
G-EUOA	Airbus A.319-131	British Airways	
G-EUOB	Airbus A.319-131	British Airways	
G-EUOC	Airbus A.319-131	British Airways	
G-EUOD	Airbus A.319-131	British Airways	
G-EUOE	Airbus A.319-131	British Airways	
G-EUOF	Airbus A.319-131	British Airways	
G-EUOG	Airbus A.319-131	British Airways	
G-EUOH	Airbus A.319-131	British Airways	
G-EUOI	Airbus A.319-131	British Airways	
G-EUOJ	Airbus A.319-131	British Airways	
G-EUOK	Airbus A.319-131	British Airways	
G-EUOL	Airbus A.319-131	British Airways	
G-EUPA	Airbus A.319-131	British Airways	
G-EUPB	Airbus A.319-131	British Airways	
G-EUPC	Airbus A.319-131	British Airways	
G-EUPD	Airbus A.319-131	British Airways	
G-EUPE	Airbus A.319-131	British Airways	
G-EUPF	Airbus A.319-131	British Airways	
G-EUPG	Airbus A.319-131	British Airways	
G-EUPH	Airbus A.319-131	British Airways	
G-EUPJ	Airbus A.319-131	British Airways	
G-EUPK	Airbus A.319-131	British Airways	
G-EUPL	Airbus A.319-131	British Airways	
G-EUPM	Airbus A.319-131	British Airways	
G-EUPN	Airbus A.319-131	British Airways	
G-EUPO	Airbus A.319-131	British Airways	
G-EUPP	Airbus A.319-131	British Airways	
G-EUPR	Airbus A.319-131	British Airways	
G-EUPS	Airbus A.319-131	British Airways	
G-EUPT	Airbus A.319-131	British Airways	
G-EUPU	Airbus A.319-131	British Airways	
G-EUPV	Airbus A.319-131	British Airways	
G-EUPW	Airbus A.319-131	British Airways	
G-EUPX	Airbus A.319-131	British Airways	
G-EUPY	Airbus A.319-131	British Airways	
G-EUPZ	Airbus A.319-131	British Airways	
G-EURT	Eurocopter EC155 B1	William Ewart Properties Ltd (G-EWAT)	
G-EUSO	Robin DR.400/140 Major	Weald Air Services Ltd	
G-EUUA	Airbus A.320-232	British Airways	

Notes	Reg.	Type	Owner or Operator
	G-EUUB	Airbus A.320-232	British Airways
	G-EUUC	Airbus A.320-232	British Airways
	G-EUUD	Airbus A.320-232	British Airways
	G-EUUE	Airbus A.320-232	British Airways
	G-EUUF	Airbus A.320-232	British Airways
	G-EUUG	Airbus A.320-232	British Airways
	G-EUUH	Airbus A.320-232	British Airways
	G-EUUI	Airbus A.320-232	British Airways
	G-EUUJ	Airbus A.320-232	British Airways
	G-EUUK	Airbus A.320-232	British Airways
	G-EUUL	Airbus A.320-232	British Airways
	G-EUUM	Airbus A.320-232	British Airways
	G-EUUN	Airbus A.320-232	British Airways
	G-EUUO	Airbus A.320-232	British Airways
	G-EUUP	Airbus A.320-232	British Airways
	G-EUUR	Airbus A.320-232	British Airways
	G-EUUS	Airbus A.320-232	British Airways
	G-EUUT	Airbus A.320-232	British Airways
	G-EUUU	Airbus A.320-232	British Airways
	G-EUUV	Airbus A.320-232	British Airways
	G-EUUW	Airbus A.320-232	British Airways
	G-EUUX	Airbus A.320-232	British Airways
	G-EUUY	Airbus A.320-232	British Airways
	G-EUUZ	Airbus A.320-232	British Airways
	G-EUXC	Airbus A.321-231	British Airways
	G-EUXD	Airbus A.321-231	British Airways
	G-EUXE	Airbus A.321-231	British Airways
	G-EUXF	Airbus A.321-231	British Airways
	G-EUXG	Airbus A.321-231	British Airways
	G-EUXH	Airbus A.321-231	British Airways
	G-EUXI	Airbus A.321-231	British Airways
	G-EUXJ	Airbus A.321-231	British Airways
	G-EUXK	Airbus A.321-231	British Airways
	G-EUXL	Airbus A.321-231	British Airways
	G-EUXM	Airbus A.321-231	British Airways
	G-EUYA	Airbus A.320-232	British Airways
	G-EUYB	Airbus A.320-232	British Airways
	G-EUYC	Airbus A.320-232	British Airways
	G-EUYD	Airbus A.320-232	British Airways
	G-EUYE	Airbus A.320-232	British Airways
	G-EUYF	Airbus A.320-232	British Airways
	G-EUYG	Airbus A.320-232	British Airways
	G-EUYH	Airbus A.320-232	British Airways
	G-EUYI	Airbus A.320-232	British Airways
	G-EUYJ	Airbus A.320-232	British Airways
	G-EUYK	Airbus A.320-232	British Airways
	G-EUYL	Airbus A.320-232	British Airways
	G-EUYM	Airbus A.320-232	British Airways
	G-EUYN	Airbus A.320-232	British Airways
	G-EVAJ	Best Off Skyranger 912S(1)	A. B. Gridley
	G-EVBF	Cameron Z-350 balloon	Virgin Balloon Flights
	G-EVET	Cameron 80 Concept balloon	L. O. & H. Vaughan
	G-EVEV	Robinson R44 II	M. P. Wilkinson
	G-EVEY	Thruster T.600N 450-JAB	The G-EVEY Flying Group
	G-EVIE	PA-28-181 Warrior II	Tayside Aviation Ltd (G-ZULU)
	G-EVIG	Evektor EV-97 TeamEurostar UK	A. S. Mitchell
	G-EVII	Schempp-Hirth Ventus 2cT	Active Aviation Ltd
	G-EVIP	Agusta A.109E Power Elite	Castle Air Ltd (G-JJJL/G-CEJS)
	G-EVLE	Rearwin 8125 Cloudster	M. C. Hiscock (G-BVLK)
	G-EVPH	Aerotechnik EV-97 Eurostar	A. H. Woolley
	G-EVPI	Evans VP-1 Srs 2	C. P. Martyr
	G-EVRD	Beech 390 Premier 1	Commercial Aviation Charters Ltd
	G-EVRO	Aerotechnik EV-97 Eurostar	J. G. McMinn
	G-EVSL	Aerotechnik EV-97 Eurostar SL	C. M. Theakstone
	G-EVTO	PA-28-161 Warrior II	Redhill Air Services Ltd
	G-EWAD	Robinson R44 II	Excel Law Ltd
	G-EWAN	Prostar PT-2C	C. G. Shaw
	G-EWAW	Bell 206B-3 JetRanger 3	J. Tobias (G-DORB)
	G-EWBC	Avtec Jabiru SK	E. W. B. Comber
	G-EWES	Pioneer 300	D. A. Ions

Reg.	Type	Owner or Operator	Notes
G-EWEW	AB Sportine Aviacija LAK-19T	G. Paul	
G-EWHT	Robinson R-2112	Cotswold Aviation Services	
G-EWIZ	Pitts S-2E Special	Pelham Ltd	
G-EWME	PA-28 Cherokee 235	C. J. Mewis & E. S. Ewen	
G-EWZZ	CZAW Sportcruiser	G. Fraser	
G-EXAM	PA-28RT-201T Turbo Arrow IV	RR. S. Urquhart & A. Cameron	
G-EXEC	PA-34-200 Seneca	Sky Air Travel Ltd	
G-EXES	Shaw Europa XS	D. Barraclough	
G-EXEX	Cessna 404	Reconnaissance Ventures Ltd	
G-EXGC	Extra EA.300/200	P. J. Bull	
G-EXHL	Cameron C-70 balloon	R. K. Gyselynck	
G-EXII	Extra EA.300	A. D. Hoy	
G-EXIL	Extra EA.300/S	C. W. Burkett & S. French	
G-EXIT	MS.893E Rallye 180GT	G-EXIT Group	
G-EXLL	Zenair CH.601	J. L. Adams	
G-EXLT	Extra EA.300/LT	J. W. Marshall	
G-EXPD	Stemme S.10-VT	Global Gliding Expeditions	
G-EXPL	Champion 7GCBC Citabria	P. Koehmann	
G-EXRS	Bombardier BD-700-1A10 Global Express	Ocean Sky Aircraft Management Ltd	
G-EXTR	Extra EA.260	S. J. Carver	
G-EXXL	Zenair CH.601XL Zodiac	B. McFadden	
G-EYAK	Yakovlev Yak-50 (50 yellow)	P. N. A. Whitehead	
G-EYAS	Denney Kitfox Mk 2	R. E. Hughes	
G-EYCO	Robin DR.400/180	M. J. Hanlon	
G-EYNL	MBB Bö.105DBS/5	Alan Mann Aviation Group Ltd	
G-EYOR	Van's RV-6	S. I. Fraser	
G-EYRE	Bell 206L-1 LongRanger	European Aviation and Technical Services Ltd	
G-EZAA	Airbus A.319-111	easyJet Airline Co Ltd	
G-EZAB	Airbus A.319-111	easyJet Airline Co Ltd	
G-EZAC	Airbus A.319-111	easyJet Airline Co Ltd	
G-EZAD	Airbus A.319-111	easyJet Airline Co Ltd	
G-EZAF	Airbus A.319-111	easyJet Airline Co Ltd	
G-EZAG	Airbus A.319-111	easyJet Airline Co Ltd	
G-EZAI	Airbus A.319-111	easyJet Airline Co Ltd	
G-EZAJ	Airbus A.319-111	easyJet Airline Co Ltd	
G-EZAK	Airbus A.319-111	easyJet Airline Co Ltd	
G-EZAL	Airbus A.319-111	easyJet Airline Co Ltd	
G-EZAM	Airbus A.319-111	easyJet Airline Co Ltd (G-CCKA)	
G-EZAN	Airbus A.319-111	easyJet Airline Co Ltd	
G-EZAO	Airbus A.319-111	easyJet Airline Co Ltd	
G-EZAP	Airbus A.319-111	easyJet Airline Co Ltd	
G-EZAR	Pegasus Quik	D. McCormack	
G-EZAS	Airbus A.319-111	easyJet Airline Co Ltd	
G-EZAT	Airbus A.319-111	easyJet Airline Co Ltd	
G-EZAU	Airbus A.319-111	easyJet Airline Co Ltd	
G-EZAV	Airbus A.319-111	easyJet Airline Co Ltd	
G-EZAW	Airbus A.319-111	easyJet Airline Co Ltd	
G-EZAX	Airbus A.319-111	easyJet Airline Co Ltd	
G-EZAY	Airbus A.319-111	easyJet Airline Co Ltd	
G-EZAZ	Airbus A.319-111	easyJet Airline Co Ltd	
G-EZBA	Airbus A.319-111	easyJet Airline Co Ltd	
G-EZBB	Airbus A.319-111	easyJet Airline Co Ltd	
G-EZBC	Airbus A.319-111	easyJet Airline Co Ltd	
G-EZBD	Airbus A.319-111	easyJet Airline Co Ltd	
G-EZBE	Airbus A.319-111	easyJet Airline Co Ltd	
G-EZBF	Airbus A.319-111	easyJet Airline Co Ltd	
G-EZBG	Airbus A.319-111	easyJet Airline Co Ltd	
G-EZBH	Airbus A.319-111	easyJet Airline Co Ltd	
G-EZBI	Airbus A.319-111	easyJet Airline Co Ltd	
G-EZBJ	Airbus A.319-111	easyJet Airline Co Ltd	
G-EZBK	Airbus A.319-111	easyJet Airline Co Ltd	
G-EZBL	Airbus A.319-111	easyJet Airline Co Ltd	
G-EZBM	Airbus A.319-111	easyJet Airline Co Ltd	
G-EZBN	Airbus A.319-111	easyJet Airline Co Ltd	
G-EZBO	Airbus A.319-111	easyJet Airline Co Ltd	
G-EZBR	Airbus A.319-111	easyJet Airline Co Ltd	
G-EZBT	Airbus A.319-111	easyJet Airline Co.Ltd	
G-EZBU	Airbus A.319-111	easyJet Airline Co.Ltd	

Notes	Reg.	Type	Owner or Operator
	G-EZBV	Airbus A.319-111	easyJet Airline Co.Ltd
	G-EZBW	Airbus A.319-111	easyJet Airline Co.Ltd
	G-EZBX	Airbus A.319-111	easyJet Airline Co.Ltd
	G-EZBY	Airbus A.319-111	easyJet Airline Co.Ltd
	G-EZBZ	Airbus A.319-111	easyJet Airline Co.Ltd
	G-EZDA	Airbus A.319-111	easyJet Airline Co.Ltd
	G-EZDB	Airbus A.319-111	easyJet Airline Co.Ltd
	G-EZDC	Airbus A.319-111	easyJet Airline Co Ltd (G-CCKB)
	G-EZDD	Airbus A.319-111	easyJet Airline Co.Ltd
	G-EZDE	Airbus A.319-111	easyJet Airline Co.Ltd
	G-EZDF	Airbus A.319-111	easyJet Airline Co.Ltd
	G-EZDG	Rutan Vari-Eze	D. M. Gale (G-EZOS)
	G-EZDH	Airbus A.319-111	easyJet Airline Co.Ltd
	G-EZDI	Airbus A.319-111	easyJet Airline Co.Ltd
	G-EZDJ	Airbus A.319-111	easyJet Airline Co.Ltd
	G-EZDK	Airbus A.319-111	easyJet Airline Co.Ltd
	G-EZDL	Airbus A.319-111	easyJet Airline Co.Ltd
	G-EZDM	Airbus A.319-111	easyJet Airline Co.Ltd
	G-EZDN	Airbus A.319-111	easyJet Airline Co.Ltd
	G-EZDO	Airbus A.319-111	easyJet Airline Co.Ltd
	G-EZDP	Airbus A.319-111	easyJet Airline Co.Ltd
	G-EZDR	Airbus A.319-111	easyJet Airline Co.Ltd
	G-EZDS	Airbus A.319-111	easyJet Airline Co.Ltd
	G-EZDT	Airbus A.319-111	easyJet Airline Co.Ltd
	G-EZDU	Airbus A.319-111	easyJet Airline Co.Ltd
	G-EZDV	Airbus A.319-111	easyJet Airline Co.Ltd
	G-EZDW	Airbus A.319-111	easyJet Airline Co.Ltd
	G-EZDX	Airbus A.319-111	easyJet Airline Co.Ltd
	G-EZDY	Airbus A.319-111	easyJet Airline Co.Ltd
	G-EZDZ	Airbus A.319-111	easyJet Airline Co Ltd
	G-EZEA	Airbus A.319-111	easyJet Airline Co Ltd
	G-EZEB	Airbus A.319-111	easyJet Airline Co Ltd
	G-EZEC	Airbus A.319-111	easyJet Airline Co Ltd
	G-EZED	Airbus A.319-111	easyJet Airline Co Ltd
	G-EZEF	Airbus A.319-111	easyJet Airline Co Ltd
	G-EZEG	Airbus A.319-111	easyJet Airline Co Ltd
	G-EZEL	Westland SA.341G Gazelle 1	W. R. Pitcher (G-BAZL)
	G-EZEP	Airbus A.319-111	easyJet Airline Co Ltd
	G-EZES	Airbus A.319-111	easyJet Airline Co Ltd
	G-EZET	Airbus A.319-111	easyJet Airline Co Ltd
	G-EZEU	Airbus A.319-111	easyJet Airline Co Ltd
	G-EZEV	Airbus A.319-111	easyJet Airline Co Ltd
	G-EZEW	Airbus A.319-111	easyJet Airline Co Ltd
	G-EZEZ	Airbus A.319-111	easyJet Airline Co Ltd
	G-EZFA	Airbus A.319-111	easyJet Airline Co Ltd
	G-EZFB	Airbus A.319-111	easyJet Airline Co.Ltd
	G-EZFC	Airbus A.319-111	easyJet Airline Co.Ltd
	G-EZFD	Airbus A.319-111	easyJet Airline Co.Ltd
	G-EZFE	Airbus A.319-111	easyJet Airline Co.Ltd
	G-EZFF	Airbus A.319-111	easyJet Airline Co.Ltd
	G-EZFG	Airbus A.319-111	easyJet Airline Co.Ltd
	G-EZFH	Airbus A.319-111	easyJet Airline Co.Ltd
	G-EZFI	Airbus A.319-111	easyJet Airline Co.Ltd
	G-EZFJ	Airbus A.319-111	easyJet Airline Co.Ltd
	G-EZFK	Airbus A.319-111	easyJet Airline Co.Ltd
	G-EZFL	Airbus A.319-111	easyJet Airline Co.Ltd
	G-EZFM	Airbus A.319-111	easyJet Airline Co.Ltd
	G-EZFN	Airbus A.319-111	easyJet Airline Co.Ltd
	G-EZFO	Airbus A.319-111	easyJet Airline Co.Ltd
	G-EZFP	Airbus A.319-111	easyJet Airline Co.Ltd
	G-EZFR	Airbus A.319-111	easyJet Airline Co.Ltd
	G-EZFS	Airbus A.319-111	easyJet Airline Co.Ltd
	G-EZFT	Airbus A.319-111	easyJet Airline Co.Ltd
	G-EZFU	Airbus A.319-111	easyJet Airline Co.Ltd
	G-EZFV	Airbus A.319-111	easyJet Airline Co.Ltd
	G-EZFW	Airbus A.319-111	easyJet Airline Co.Ltd
	G-EZFX	Airbus A.319-111	easyJet Airline Co.Ltd
	G-EZFY	Airbus A.319-111	easyJet Airline Co.Ltd
	G-EZFZ	Airbus A.319-111	easyJet Airline Co.Ltd
	G-EZGA	Airbus A.319-111	easyJet Airline Co.Ltd
	G-EZGB	Airbus A.319-111	easyJet Airline Co.Ltd
	G-EZGC	Airbus A.319-111	easyJet Airline Co.Ltd

Reg.	Type	Owner or Operator	Notes
G-EZGD	Airbus A.319-111	easyJet Airline Co.Ltd	
G-EZGE	Airbus A.319-111	easyJet Airline Co.Ltd	
G-EZGF	Airbus A.319-111	easyJet Airline Co.Ltd	
G-EZGG	Airbus A.319-111	easyJet Airline Co.Ltd	
G-EZGH	Airbus A.319-111	easyJet Airline Co.Ltd	
G-EZGI	Airbus A.319-111	easyJet Airline Co.Ltd	
G-EZGJ	Airbus A.319-111	easyJet Airline Co.Ltd	
G-EZGK	Airbus A.319-111	easyJet Airline Co.Ltd	
G-EZGL	Airbus A.319-111	easyJet Airline Co.Ltd	
G-EZGM	Airbus A.319-111	easyJet Airline Co.Ltd	
G-EZGN	Airbus A.319-111	easyJet Airline Co.Ltd	
G-EZGO	Airbus A.319-111	easyJet Airline Co.Ltd	
G-EZGP	Airbus A.319-111	easyJet Airline Co.Ltd	
G-EZGR	Airbus A.319-111	easyJet Airline Co.Ltd	
G-EZIC	Airbus A.319-111	easyJet Airline Co Ltd	
G-EZID	Airbus A.319-111	easyJet Airline Co Ltd	
G-EZIE	Airbus A.319-111	easyJet Airline Co Ltd	
G-EZIG	Airbus A.319-111	easyJet Airline Co Ltd	
G-EZIH	Airbus A.319-111	easyJet Airline Co Ltd	
G-EZII	Airbus A.319-111	easyJet Airline Co Ltd	
G-EZIJ	Airbus A.319-111	easyJet Airline Co Ltd	
G-EZIK	Airbus A.319-111	easyJet Airline Co Ltd	
G-EZIL	Airbus A.319-111	easyJet Airline Co Ltd	
G-EZIM	Airbus A.319-111	easyJet Airline Co Ltd	
G-EZIN	Airbus A.319-111	easyJet Airline Co Ltd	
G-EZIO	Airbus A.319-111	easyJet Airline Co Ltd	
G-EZIP	Airbus A.319-111	easyJet Airline Co Ltd	
G-EZIR	Airbus A.319-111	easyJet Airline Co Ltd	
G-EZIS	Airbus A.319-111	easyJet Airline Co Ltd	
G-EZIT	Airbus A.319-111	easyJet Airline Co Ltd	
G-EZIU	Airbus A.319-111	easyJet Airline Co Ltd	
G-EZIV	Airbus A.319-111	easyJet Airline Co Ltd	
G-EZIW	Airbus A.319-111	easyJet Airline Co Ltd	
G-EZIX	Airbus A.319-111	easyJet Airline Co Ltd	
G-EZIY	Airbus A.319-111	easyJet Airline Co Ltd	
G-EZIZ	Airbus A.319-111	easyJet Airline Co Ltd	
G-EZMH	Airbus A.319-111	easyJet Airline Co Ltd (G-CCKD)	
G-EZMS	Airbus A.319-111	easyJet Airline Co Ltd	
G-EZNC	Airbus A.319-111	easyJet Airline Co Ltd (G-CCKC)	
G-EZPG	Airbus A.319-111	easyJet Airline Co Ltd	
G-EZSM	Airbus A.319-111	easyJet Airline Co Ltd (G-CCKE)	
G-EZTA	Airbus A.320-214	easyJet Airline Co.Ltd	
G-EZTB	Airbus A.320-214	easyJet Airline Co.Ltd	
G-EZTC	Airbus A.320-214	easyJet Airline Co.Ltd	
G-EZTD	Airbus A.320-214	easyJet Airline Co.Ltd	
G-EZTE	Airbus A.320-214	easyJet Airline Co.Ltd	
G-EZTF	Airbus A.320-214	easyJet Airline Co.Ltd	
G-EZTG	Airbus A.320-214	easyJet Airline Co.Ltd	
G-EZTH	Airbus A.320-214	easyJet Airline Co.Ltd	
G-EZTI	Airbus A.320-214	easyJet Airline Co.Ltd	
G-EZTJ	Airbus A.320-214	easyJet Airline Co.Ltd	
G-EZTK	Airbus A.320-214	easyJet Airline Co.Ltd	
G-EZTL	Airbus A.320-214	easyJet Airline Co.Ltd	
G-EZTM	Airbus A.320-214	easyJet Airline Co.Ltd	
G-EZTN	Airbus A.320-214	easyJet Airline Co.Ltd	
G-EZTR	Airbus A.320-214	easyJet Airline Co.Ltd	
G-EZTT	Airbus A.320-214	easyJet Airline Co.Ltd	
G-EZTV	Airbus A.320-214	easyJet Airline Co.Ltd	
G-EZTW	Airbus A.320-214	easyJet Airline Co.Ltd	
G-EZTX	Airbus A.320-214	easyJet Airline Co.Ltd	
G-EZTY	Airbus A.320-214	easyJet Airline Co.Ltd	
G-EZTZ	Airbus A.320-214	easyJet Airline Co.Ltd	
G-EZUA	Airbus A.320-214	easyJet Airline Co.Ltd	
G-EZUB	Zenair CH.601HD Zodiac	R. A. C. Stephens	
G-EZUC	Airbus A.320-214	easyJet Airline Co.Ltd	
G-EZUD	Airbus A.320-214	easyJet Airline Co.Ltd	
G-EZUE	Airbus A.320-214	easyJet Airline Co.Ltd	
G-EZUF	Airbus A.320-214	easyJet Airline Co.Ltd	
G-EZUG	Airbus A.320-214	easyJet Airline Co.Ltd	
G-EZUH	Airbus A.320-214	easyJet Airline Co.Ltd	
G-EZUI	Airbus A.320-214	easyJet Airline Co.Ltd	
G-EZUJ	Airbus A.320-214	easyJet Airline Co.Ltd	

Notes	Reg.	Type	Owner or Operator
	G-EZUK	Airbus A.320-214	easyJet Airline Co.Ltd
	G-EZVS	Colt 77B balloon	A. J. Lovell
	G-EZXO	Colt 56A balloon	I. Lilja
	G-EZZA	Shaw Europa XS	J. C. R. Davey
	G-EZZE	CZAW Sportcruiser	G. Verity
	G-EZZL	Westland Gazelle HT.3	Regal Group UK (G-CBKC)
	G-EZZY	Evektor EV-97 Eurostar	D. P. Creedy
	G-FACE	Cessna 172S	Oxford Aviation Services Ltd
	G-FAIR	SOCATA TB10 Tobago	Fairwings Ltd
	G-FAJC	Alpi Pioneer 300 Hawk	M. Clare
	G-FAJM	Robinson R44 II	Ryvoan Aviation Ltd
	G-FALC	Aeromere F.8L Falco	D. M. Burbridge (G-AROT)
	G-FAME	Starstreak Shadow SA-II	S. R. Whitehead
	G-FAMH	Zenair CH.701	F. Omaraie-Hamdanie
	G-FANC	Fairchild 24R-46 Argus III	A. T. Fines
	G-FANL	Cessna FR.172K XP-II	J. A. Rees
	G-FARA	BAe Jetstream 3102	Spitfire Investments Ltd
	G-FARE	Robinson R44 II	Toriamos Ltd/Ireland
	G-FARL	Pitts S-1E Special	T. I. Williams
	G-FARO	Aero Designs Star-Lite SL.1	S. C. Goozee
	G-FARR	Jodel 150	G. H. Farr
	G-FARY	QAC Quickie Tri-Q	A. Bloomfield and A. Underwood
	G-FASH	Hughes 369D	The Packshot Company Ltd (G-ERIS/G-PJMD/ G-BMJV)
	G-FATB	Rockwell Commander 114B	James D. Pearce & Co
	G-FATE	Falco F8L	G-FATE Flying Group
	G-FAVC	DH.80A Puss Moth	Liddell Aircraft Ltd
	G-FAVS	PA-32-300 Cherokee Six	Favourites Racing Ltd (G-BKEK)
	G-FBAT	Aeroprakt A.22 Foxbat	J. Jordan
	G-FBEA	Embraer ERJ190-200LR	Flybe.com
	G-FBEB	Embraer ERJ190-200LR	Flybe.com
	G-FBEC	Embraer ERJ190-200LR	Flybe.com
	G-FBED	Embraer ERJ190-200LR	Flybe.com
	G-FBEE	Embraer ERJ190-200LR	Flybe.com
	G-FBEF	Embraer ERJ190-200LR	Flybe.com
	G-FBEG	Embraer ERJ190-200LR	Flybe.com
	G-FBEH	Embraer ERJ190-200LR	Flybe.com
	G-FBEI	Embraer ERJ190-200LR	Flybe.com
	G-FBEJ	Embraer ERJ190-200LR	Flybe.com
	G-FBEK	Embraer ERJ190-200LR	Flybe.com
	G-FBEL	Embraer ERJ190-200LR	Flybe.com
	G-FBEM	Embraer ERJ190-200LR	Flybe.com
	G-FBEN	Embraer ERJ190-200LR	Flybe.com
	G-FBII	Ikarus C.42 FB100	F. Beeson
	G-FBJA	Embraer ERJ170-200STD	Flybe.com
	G-FBJB	Embraer ERJ170-200STD	Flybe.com
	G-FBJC	Embraer ERJ170-200STD	Flybe.com
	G-FBJD	Embraer ERJ170-200STD	Flybe.com
	G-FBJL	Dassault Falcon 2000	TAG Aviation (UK) Ltd
	G-FBKA	Cessna 510 Citation Mustang	Blink Ltd
	G-FBKB	Cessna 510 Citation Mustang	Blink Ltd
	G-FBKC	Cessna 510 Citation Mustang	Blink Ltd
	G-FBKD	Cessna 510 Citation Mustang	Blink Ltd
	G-FBLI	Cessna 510 Citation Mustang	Blink Ltd
	G-FBLK	Cessna 510 Citation Mustang	Blink Ltd
	G-FBNK	Cessna 510 Citation Mustang	Blink Ltd
	G-FBOY	Skystar Kitfox Mk 7	A. Bray
	G-FBPL	PA-34-200 Seneca	Purple Horse Sales and Hire Ltd (G-BBXK)
	G-FBRN	PA-28-181 Archer II	Herefordshire Aero Club Ltd
	G-FBTT	Aeroprakt A22-L Foxbat	T. D. Reid
	G-FBWH	PA-28R Cherokee Arrow 180	F. A. Short
	G-FCAV	Schleicher ASK-13	M. F. Cuming
	G-FCBI	Schweizer 269C-1	Lift West Ltd
	G-FCCC	Schleicher ASK-13	Shenington Gliding Club
	G-FCED	PA-31T2 Cheyenne IIXL	Provident Partners Ltd
	G-FCFC	Bombardier BD700-1A10 Global Express	Ocean Sky (UK) Ltd
	G-FCKD	Eurocopter EC 120B	Pacific Helicopters Ltd
	G-FCLA	Boeing 757-28A	Thomas Cook Airlines Ltd

Reg.	Type	Owner or Operator	Notes
G-FCLB	Boeing 757-28A	Thomas Cook Airlines Ltd	
G-FCLC	Boeing 757-38A	Thomas Cook Airlines Ltd	
G-FCLD	Boeing 757-25F	Thomas Cook Airlines Ltd	
G-FCLE	Boeing 757-28A	Thomas Cook Airlines Ltd	
G-FCLF	Boeing 757-28A	Thomas Cook Airlines Ltd	
G-FCLH	Boeing 757-28A	Thomas Cook Airlines Ltd	
G-FCLI	Boeing 757-28A	Thomas Cook Airlines Ltd	
G-FCLJ	Boeing 757-2Y0	Thomas Cook Airlines Ltd	
G-FCLK	Boeing 757-2Y0	Thomas Cook Airlines Ltd	
G-FCOM	Slingsby T.59F Kestrel	P. A. C. Wheatcroft & A. G. Truman	
G-FCON	Schempp-Hirth Standard Cirrus	M. G. Sankey & I. Keen	
G-FCSL	PA-32-350 Navajo Chieftain	Culross Aerospace Ltd (G-CLAN)	
G-FCSP	Robin DR.400/180	S. Eustace	
G-FCUK	Pitts S-1C Special	D. Stephens	
G-FCUM	Robinson R44 II	The Grange Country Club Ltd	
G-FDDY	Schleicher Ka 6CR	M. D. Brooks	
G-FDPS	Aviat Pitts S-2C Special	Flights and Dreams Ltd	
G-FDZA	Boeing 737-8K5	Thomson Airways Ltd	
G-FDZB	Boeing 737-8K5	Thomson Airways Ltd	
G-FDZD	Boeing 737-8K5	Thomson Airways Ltd	
G-FDZE	Boeing 737-8K5	Thomson Airways Ltd	
G-FDZF	Boeing 737-8K5	Thomson Airways Ltd	
G-FDZG	Boeing 737-8K5	Thomson Airways Ltd	
G-FDZJ	Boeing 737-8K5	Thomson Airways Ltd	
G-FDZR	Boeing 737-8K5	Thomson Airways Ltd	
G-FDZS	Boeing 737-8K5	Thomson Airways Ltd	
G-FDZT	Boeing 737-8K5	Thomson Airways Ltd	
G-FDZU	Boeing 737-8K5	Thomson Airways Ltd	
G-FDZW	Boeing 737-8K5	Thomson Airways Ltd	
G-FDZX	Boeing 737-8K5	Thomson Airways Ltd	
G-FDZY	Boeing 737-8K5	Thomson Airways Ltd	
G-FDZZ	Boeing 737-8K5	Thomson Airways Ltd	
G-FEAB	PA-28-181 Archer III	Feabrex Ltd	
G-FEBB	Grob G.104 Speed Astir IIB	M. Ogbe	
G-FEBJ	Schleicher ASW-19B	A. P. Hatton	
G-FECO	Grob G.102 Astir CS77	C. Peterson	
G-FEDA	Eurocopter EC 120B	J. Henshall	
G-FEET	Mainair Pegasus Quik	M. P. Duckett	
G-FELC	Cirrus SR22	F. Rossello	
G-FELD	Rotorsport UK MTO Sport	S. Pearce	
G-FELL	Shaw Europa	M. C. Costin & J. A. Inglis	
G-FELM	PA-28-180 Cherokee C	F. P. M. Vaille	
G-FELT	Cameron N-77 balloon	Allan Industries Ltd	
G-FELX	CZAW Sportcruiser	T. F. Smith	
G-FERN	Mainair Blade 912	M. H. Moulai	
G-FERV	Rolladen-Schneider LS4	R. J. J. Bennett	
G-FESS	Pegasus Quantum 15-912	P. M. Fessi (G-CBBZ)	
G-FEVS	PZL-Bielsko SZD-50-3 Puchacz	The Borders (Milfield) Gliding Club Ltd	
G-FEWG	Fuji FA.200-160	Caseright Ltd (G-BBNV)	
G-FEZZ	Bell 206B JetRanger II	R. J. Myram	
G-FFAB	Cameron N-105 balloon	B. J. Hammond	
G-FFAF	Cessna F.150L	R. Henderson	
G-FFBG	Cessna F.182Q	W. G. E. James	
G-FFEN	Cessna F.150M	B. Emerson & J. Tuckwell	
G-FFFT	Lindstrand LBL-31A balloon	W. Rousell & J. Tyrrell	
G-FFIT	Pegasus Quik	R. G. G. Pinder	
G-FFOX	Hawker Hunter T.7B (WV318:D)	WV318 Group	
G-FFRA	Dassault Falcon 20DC	FR Aviation Ltd	
G-FFRI	AS.355F1 Twin Squirrel	Sterling Helicopters Ltd (G-GLOW/G-PAPA/ G-CNET/G-MCAH)	
G-FFTI	SOCATA TB20 Trinidad	R. Lenk	
G-FFUN	Pegasus Quantum 15	J. R. F. Hollingshead	
G-FFWD	Cessna 310R	T. S. Courtman (G-TVKE/G-EURO)	
G-FGAZ	Schleicher Ka 6E	C. M. Billings, B. A. & M. A. Roberts	
G-FGID	Vought FG-1D Corsair (KD345:130-A)	Patina Ltd	
G-FGSI	Montgomerie-Bensen B8MR	F. G. Shepherd	
G-FGSK	Cameron 120 Beer Crate SS balloon	Ballon-Sport und Luftwerbung Dresden GmbH/ Germany	

Notes	Reg.	Type	Owner or Operator
	G-FHAS	Scheibe SF.25E Super Falke	D. C. Mason
	G-FIAT	PA-28 Cherokee 140	Demero Ltd & Transcourt Ltd (G-BBYW)
	G-FIBS	AS.350BA Ecureuil	Elitop SRL/Italy
	G-FICS	Flight Design CTSW	J. R. Phillips
	G-FIFA	Cessna 404 Titan	RVL Aviation Ltd (G-TVIP/G-KIWI/G-BHNI)
	G-FIFE	Cessna FA.152	Tayside Aviation Ltd (G-BFYN)
	G-FIFI	SOCATA TB20 Trinidad	F. A. Saker (G-BMWS)
	G-FIFT	Ikarus C.42 FB 100	A. R. Jones
	G-FIGA	Cessna 152	Merseyflight Ltd
	G-FIGB	Cessna 152	A. J. Gomes
	G-FIGP	Boeing 737-2E7	European Skybus Ltd (G-BMDF)
	G-FIII	Extra EA.300/L	J. S. Allison (G-RGEE)
	G-FIJJ	Cessna F.177RG	D. R. Vale (G-AZFP)
	G-FIJV	Lockheed L.188CF Electra	Atlantic Airlines Ltd
	G-FILE	PA-34-200T Seneca	Bristol Flying Centre Ltd
	G-FINA	Cessna F.150L	A. G. Freeman (G-BIFT)
	G-FIND	Cessna F.406	Reconnaissance Ventures Ltd
	G-FINT	Piper L-4B Grasshopper	G. & H. M. Picarella
	G-FINZ	I.I.I Sky Arrow 650T	W. N. Blair-Hickman
	G-FIRM	Cessna 550 Citation Bravo	The Cambridge Aero Club Ltd
	G-FIRS	Robinson R22 Beta II	Helitrain Ltd
	G-FIRZ	Murphy Renegade Spirit UK	S. Koutsoukos
	G-FITY	Europa XS	D. C. A. Moore & M. Fielder
	G-FIXX	Van's RV-7	Hambilton Engineering Ltd
	G-FIZU	Lockheed L.188CF Electra	Atlantic Airlines Ltd
	G-FIZY	Shaw Europa XS	R. Eyles & R. C. Winter (G-DDSC)
	G-FIZZ	PA-28-161 Warrior II	G-FIZZ Group
	G-FJET	Cessna 550 Citation II	London Executive Aviation Ltd (G-DCFR/ G-WYLX/G-JETD)
	G-FJMS	Partenavia P.68B	J. B. Randle (G-SVHA)
	G-FJTH	Aeroprakt A.22 Foxbat	B. Gurling
	G-FKNH	PA-15 Vagabond	M. J. Mothershaw
	G-FKOS	PA-28-181 Archer II	M. K. Johnson
	G-FLAG	Colt 77A balloon	B. A. Williams
	G-FLAV	PA-28-161 Warrior II	The Crew Flying Group
	G-FLBA	DHC.8-402 Dash Eight	Flybe.com
	G-FLBB	DHC.8-402 Dash Eight	Flybe.com
	G-FLBC	DHC.8-402 Dash Eight	Flybe.com
	G-FLBD	DHC.8-402 Dash Eight	Flybe.com
	G-FLBE	DHC.8-402 Dash Eight	Flybe.com
	G-FLBK	Cessna 510 Citation Mustang	Blink Ltd
	G-FLCA	Fleet Model 80 Canuck	E. C. Taylor
	G-FLCT	Hallam Fleche	R. G. Hallam
	G-FLDG	Skyranger 912	A. J. Gay
	G-FLEA	SOCATA TB10 Tobago	TB Group
	G-FLEE	ZJ-Viera	P. C. Piggott
	G-FLEW	Lindstrand LBL-90A balloon	A. Nimmo
	G-FLEX	Mainair Pegasus Quik	L. A. Read
	G-FLGT	Lindstrand LBL-105A balloon	Ballongaventyr I. Skane AB/Sweden
	G-FLIK	Pitts S-1S Special	R. P. Millinship
	G-FLIP	Cessna FA.152	Cristal Air Ltd (G-BOES)
	G-FLIS	Magni M.16C	M. L. L. Temple
	G-FLIT	Rotorway Executive 162F	R. S. Snell
	G-FLIZ	Staaken Z-21 Flitzer	M. J. Clark
	G-FLKE	Scheibe SF.25C Falke	The Royal Air Force Gliding & Soaring Association
	G-FLKS	Scheibe SF.25C Falke	London Gliding Club Propietary Ltd
	G-FLKY	Cessna 172S	M. E. Falkingham
	G-FLOR	Shaw Europa	A. F. C. van Eldik
	G-FLOW	Cessna 172N	P. H. Archard
	G-FLOX	Shaw Europa	DPT Group
	G-FLPI	Rockwell Commander 112	J. P. Thorpe
	G-FLSH	Yak-52	M. A. Wright
	G-FLTA	BAe 146-200	Westall Ltd
	G-FLTC	BAe 146-300	E3205 Trading Ltd (G-JEBH/G-BVTO/G-NJID)
	G-FLTF	BAe 146-300	Rangefield Holdings Ltd (G-DEBE)
	G-FLTZ	Beech 58 Baron	Calder Group Ltd (G-PSVS)
	G-FLUZ	Rolladen-Schneider LS8-18	D. M. King
	G-FLYA	Mooney M.20J	B. Willis

Reg.	Type	Owner or Operator	Notes
G-FLYB	Ikarus C.42 FB100	G-FLYB Group	
G-FLYC	Ikarus C.42 FB100	Solent Flight Ltd	
G-FLYF	Mainair Blade 912	Cool Water Direct Ltd	
G-FLYG	Slingsby T.67C	G. Laden	
G-FLYH	Robinson R22 Beta	J. R. Huggins (G-BXMR)	
G-FLYI	PA-34-200 Seneca II	Falcon Flying Services Ltd (G-BHVO)	
G-FLYM	Ikarus C42 FB100	R. S. O'Carroll	
G-FLYP	Beagle B.206 Srs 2	Key Publishing Ltd (G-AVHO)	
G-FLYT	Shaw Europa	K. F. & R. Richardson	
G-FLYX	Robinson R44 II	R. D. Hagger	
G-FLYY	BAC.167 Strikemaster 80A	B. T. Barber	
G-FLZA	Staaken Z-21A Flitzer	G. R. Pybus	
G-FLZR	Staaken Z-21 Flitzer	I. V. Staines	
G-FMAM	PA-28-151 Warrior (modified)	Lima Tango Flying Group (G-BBXV)	
G-FMBS	Inverted US 12	W. P. Wright	
G-FMGG	Maule M5-235C Lunar Rocket	S. Bierbaum (G-RAGG)	
G-FMKA	Diamond HK.36TC Super Dimona	G. P. Davis	
G-FMSG	Cessna FA.150K	G. Owen/Gamston (G-POTS/G-AYUY)	
G-FNAV	PA-31-350 Navajo Chieftain	Flight Calibration Services Ltd (G-BFFR)	
G-FNEY	Cessna F.177RG	F. Ney	
G-FNLD	Cessna 172N	Papa Hotel Flying Group	
G-FOFO	Robinson R44 II	Kuki Helicopter Sales Ltd	
G-FOGG	Cameron N-90 balloon	J. P. E. Money-Kyrle	
G-FOGI	Shaw Europa XS	B. Fogg	
G-FOGY	Robinson R22 Beta	Helicentre Holdings Ltd	
G-FOKK	Fokker DR1 (replica)	P. D. & S. E. Ford	
G-FOKR	Fokker E.III Replica	D. Stephens	
G-FOLD	Light Aero Avid Speedwing	B. W. & G. Evans	
G-FOLI	Robinson R22 Beta II	G. M. Duckworth	
G-FOLY	Aerotek Pitts S-2A Modified	C. T. Charleston	
G-FOPP	Lancair 320	Airsport (UK) Ltd	
G-FORA	Schempp-Hirth Ventus cT	G. Bailey & J. D. Sorrell	
G-FORC	SNCAN Stampe SV.4C	C. C. Rollings & F. J. Hodson	
G-FORD	SNCAN Stampe SV.4C	P. H. Meeson	
G-FORM	Learjet 45	Broomco 3598 Ltd	
G-FORZ	Pitts S-1S Special	N. W. Parkinson	
G-FOSY	MS.880B Rallye Club	A. G. Foster (G-AXAK)	
G-FOWL	Colt 90A balloon	M. R. Stokoe	
G-FOWS	Cameron N-105 balloon	Ezmerelda Balloon Syndicate	
G-FOXA	PA-28-161 Cadet	Leicestershire Aero Club Ltd	
G-FOXB	Aeroprakt A.22 Foxbat	G. D. McCullough	
G-FOXC	Denney Kitfox Mk 3	T. Willford	
G-FOXD	Denney Kitfox Mk 2	P. P. Trangmar	
G-FOXE	Denney Kitfox Mk 2	K. M. Pinkar	
G-FOXF	Denney Kitfox Mk 4	M. S. Goodwin	
G-FOXG	Denney Kitfox Mk 2	J. U. McKercher	
G-FOXI	Denney Kitfox	I. M. Walton	
G-FOXL	Zenair CH.601XL Zodiac	R. W. Taylor	
G-FOXM	Bell 206B JetRanger 2	Tyringham Charter & Group Services (G-STAK/G-BNIS)	
G-FOXS	Denney Kitfox Mk 2	S. P. Watkins & C. C. Rea	
G-FOXX	Denney Kitfox	A. W. Hodder	
G-FOXZ	Denney Kitfox	S. C. Goozee	
G-FOZY	Van's RV-7	M. G. Forrest (G-COPZ)	
G-FOZZ	Beech A36 Bonanza	Go To Air Ltd	
G-FPIG	PA-28-151 Warrior	G. F. Strain (G-BSSR)	
G-FPLD	Beech 200 Super King Air	Cobham Flight Inspection Ltd	
G-FPLE	Beech 200 Super King Air	Cobham Flight Inspection Ltd	
G-FPSA	PA-28-161 Warrior II	Interactive Dynamics Ltd (G-RSFT/G-WARI)	
G-FRAD	Dassault Falcon 20E	Cobham Leasing Ltd (G-BCYF)	
G-FRAF	Dassault Falcon 20E	FR Aviation Ltd	
G-FRAG	PA-32 Cherokee Six 300E	T. A. Houghton	
G-FRAH	Dassault Falcon 20DC	FR Aviation Ltd	
G-FRAI	Dassault Falcon 20E	FR Aviation Ltd	
G-FRAJ	Dassault Falcon 20E	FR Aviation Ltd	
G-FRAK	Dassault Falcon 20DC	FR Aviation Ltd	
G-FRAL	Dassault Falcon 20DC	FR Aviation Ltd	

Notes	Reg.	Type	Owner or Operator
	G-FRAN	Piper J-3C-90 Cub(480321:H-44)	Essex L-4 Group (G-BIXY)
	G-FRAO	Dassault Falcon 20DC	FR Aviation Ltd
	G-FRAP	Dassault Falcon 20DC	FR Aviation Ltd
	G-FRAR	Dassault Falcon 20DC	FR Aviation Ltd
	G-FRAS	Dassault Falcon 20C	FR Aviation Ltd
	G-FRAT	Dassault Falcon 20C	FR Aviation Ltd
	G-FRAU	Dassault Falcon 20C	FR Aviation Ltd
	G-FRAW	Dassault Falcon 20ECM	FR Aviation Ltd
	G-FRAY	Cassutt IIIM (modified)	C. I. Fray
	G-FRCE	Folland Gnat T.Mk.1	Red Gnat Ltd
	G-FRDY	Dynamic WT9 UK	Peter Dodd Consultants
	G-FRGN	PA-28-236 Dakota	P. J. Vacher
	G-FRGT	P & M Quik GT450	G-FRGT Group
	G-FRIK	P & M Quik GT450	G-FRIK Group
	G-FRIL	Lindstrand LBL-105A balloon	S. Travaglia
	G-FRJB	Britten Sheriff SA-1 ★	Aeropark
	G-FRNK	Skyranger 912(2)	D. L. Foxley & G. Lace
	G-FROM	Ikarus C.42 FB100	G-FROM Group
	G-FRSX	VS.388 Seafire F.46 (LA564)	Seafire Displays Ltd
	G-FRYI	Beech 200 Super King Air	London Executive Aviation Ltd (G-OAVX/ G-IBCA/G-BMCA)
	G-FRYL	Beech 390 Premier 1	Hawk Air Ltd/Farnborough
	G-FRZN	Agusta A109S Grand	Iceland Foods Ltd
	G-FSEU	Beech 200 Super King Air	Air Mercia Ltd
	G-FSHA	Denney Kitfox Mk 2	P. P. Trangmar
	G-FSZY	TB-10 Tobago	P. J. Bentley
	G-FTAX	Cessna 421C	Gold Air International Ltd (G-BFFM)
	G-FTIL	Robin DR.400/180R	RAF Wyton Flying Club Ltd
	G-FTIN	Robin DR.400/100	YP Flying Group
	G-FTSE	BN-2A Mk.III-2 Trislander	Aurigny Air Services Ltd (G-BEPI)
	G-FTSL	Canadair CL.600-2B16 604	Farglobe transport Services Ltd
	G-FUEL	Robin DR.400/180	R. Darch
	G-FUFU	Agusta A.109 Grand	Air Harrods Ltd
	G-FUKM	Westland Gazelle AH.1 (ZA730)	Falcon Aviation Ltd
	G-FULL	PA-28R Cherokee Arrow 200-II	Stapleford Flying Club Ltd (G-HWAY/G-JULI)
	G-FULM	Sikorsky S-76C	Air Harrods Ltd
	G-FUND	Thunder Ax7-65Z balloon	G. B. Davies
	G-FUNK	Yakovlev Yak-50	Redstar Aero Services Ltd
	G-FUNN	Plumb BGP-1	P. E. Barker
	G-FURI	Isaacs Fury II	S. M. Johnston
	G-FURZ	Best Off Sky Ranger Nynja 912S(1)	S. R. Swift
	G-FUSE	Cameron N-105 balloon	S. A. Lacey
	G-FUZZ	PA-18 Super Cub 95 (51-15319)	G. W. Cline
	G-FVEE	Monnett Sonerai 1	J. S. Baldwin
	G-FVEL	Cameron Z-90 balloon	Fort Vale Engineering Ltd
	G-FWAY	Lindstrand LBL-90A balloon	Fairway Furniture Ltd
	G-FWKS	Tanarg/Ixess 15 912S(1)	M. A. Coffin (G-SYUT)
	G-FWPW	PA-28-236 Dakota	P. A. & F. C. Winters
	G-FXBT	Aeroprakt A.22 Foxbat	R. H. Jago
	G-FXII	VS.366 Spitfire F.XII (EN224)	Air Leasing Ltd
	G-FYAN	Williams Westwind MLB	M. D. Williams
	G-FYAO	Williams Westwind MLB	M. D. Williams
	G-FYAU	Williams Westwind Mk 2 MLB	M. D. Williams
	G-FYAV	Osprey Mk 4E2 MLB	C. D. Egan & C. Stiles
	G-FYBX	Portswood Mk XVI MLB	I. Chadwick
	G-FYCL	Osprey Mk 4G MLB	P. J. Rogers
	G-FYCV	Osprey Mk 4D MLB	M. Thomson
	G-FYDF	Osprey Mk 4DV	K. A. Jones
	G-FYDI	Williams Westwind Two MLB	M. D. Williams
	G-FYDN	European 8C MLB	P. D. Ridout
	G-FYDO	Osprey Mk 4D MLB	N. L. Scallan
	G-FYDP	Williams Westwind Three MLB	M. D. Williams
	G-FYDS	Osprey Mk 4D MLB	N. L. Scallan
	G-FYEK	Unicorn UE.1C MLB	D. & D. Eaves
	G-FYEO	Eagle Mk 1 MLB	M. E. Scallan
	G-FYEV	Osprey Mk 1C MLB	M. E. Scallan

Reg.	Type	Owner or Operator	Notes
G-FYEZ	Firefly Mk 1 MLB	M. E. & N. L. Scallan	
G-FYFI	European E.84DS MLB	M. Stelling	
G-FYFJ	Williams Westland 2 MLB	M. D. Williams	
G-FYFN	Osprey Saturn 2 MLB	J. & M. Woods	
G-FYFW	Rango NA-55 MLB	Rango Balloon and Kite Company	
G-FYFY	Rango NA-55RC MLB	Rango Balloon and Kite Company	
G-FYGC	Rango NA-42B MLB	L. J. Wardle	
G-FYGJ	Airspeed 300 MLB	N. Wells	
G-FYGM	Saffrey/Smith Princess MLB	A. Smith	
G-FZZA	General Avia F22-A	APB Leasing Ltd	
G-FZZI	Cameron H-34 balloon	Magical Adventures Ltd	
G-GABI	Lindstrand LBL-35A Cloudhopper balloon	R. D. Sargeant	
G-GABS	Cameron TR-70 balloon	N. M. Gabriel	
G-GABY	Bombardier BD-700-1A10 Global Express	Ocean Sky (UK) Ltd	
G-GACA	P.57 Sea Prince T.1 (WP308:572CU) ★	P. G. Vallance Ltd/Charlwood	
G-GACB	Robinson R44 II	A. C. Barker	
G-GAEA	Aquila AT01	Stamp Aviation Ltd	
G-GAEB	Aquila AT01	Stamp Aviation Ltd	
G-GAFA	PA-34-200T Seneca II	Oxford Aviation Academy (Oxford) Ltd	
G-GAFT	PA-44-180 Seminole	Bravo Aviation Ltd	
G-GAII	Hawker Hunter GA.11 (XE685)	GA11 Ltd	
G-GAJB	AA-5B Tiger	G-GAJB Group (G-BHZN)	
G-GALA	PA-28 Cherokee 180E	FlyBPL.com	
G-GALB	PA-28-161 Warrior II	LB Aviation Ltd	
G-GALL	PA-38-112 Tomahawk	M. Lowe & K. Hazelwood (G-BTEV)	
G-GALX	Dassault Falcon 900 EX	Charter Air Ltd	
G-GAME	Cessna T.303	J. & R. K. Hyatt	
G-GAND	Agusta-Bell 206B Jet Ranger	The Henderson Group (G-AWMK)	
G-GANE	Sequoia F.8L Falco	S. J. Gane	
G-GAOH	Robin DR.400 / 2 +2.	S. D. Baker & M. Stott	
G-GAOM	Robin DR.400 / 2+2	P. M. & P. A. Chapman	
G-GASP	PA-28-181 Archer II	G-GASP Flying Group	
G-GASS	Thunder Ax7-77 balloon	Servowarm Balloon Syndicate	
G-GAST	Van's RV-8	G. M. R. Abrey	
G-GATE	Robinson R44 II	J. W. Gate	
G-GATT	Robinson R44 II	B. W. Faulkner	
G-GAVH	P & M Quik	G. Hardman	
G-GAWA	Cessna 140	C140 Group (G-BRSM)	
G-GAZA	Aérospatiale SA.341G Gazelle 1	The Auster Aircraft Co Ltd (G-RALE/G-SFTG)	
G-GAZN	P & M Quik GT450	P. C. Bishop	
G-GAZO	Ace Magic Cyclone	G. J. Pearce	
G-GAZZ	Aérospatiale SA.341G Gazelle 1	Cheqair Ltd	
G-GBAO	Robin R1180TD	J. Toulorge	
G-GBBB	Schleicher ASH-25	ASH25 BB Glider Syndicate	
G-GBBT	Ultramagic M-90 balloon	British Telecommunications PLC	
G-GBCC	Ikarus C42 FB100	I. R. Westrope	
G-GBEE	Mainair Pegasus Quik	M. G. Evans	
G-GBFF	Cessna F.172N	Aviation Rentals	
G-GBFR	Cessna F.177RG	Airspeed Aviation Ltd	
G-GBGA	Scheibe SF.25C Falke	Bidford Gliding Ltd	
G-GBGB	Ultramagic M.105 balloon	Universal Car Services Ltd	
G-GBGF	Cameron Dragon SS balloon	Magical Adventures Ltd (G-BUVH)	
G-GBHI	SOCATA TB10 Tobago	Robert Purvis Plant Hire Ltd	
G-GBJP	Mainair Pegasus Quantum 15	M. P. Chew	
G-GBJS	Robin HR200/100S Club	Freedom Aviation Ltd	
G-GBLP	Cessna F.172M	Aviate Scotland Ltd (G-GWEN)	
G-GBMR	Beech B200 Super King Air	M and R Aviation LLP	
G-GBOB	Alpi Pioneer 300 Hawk	R. E. Burgess	
G-GBPP	Rolladen-Schneider LS6-c18	G. J. Lyons & R. Sinden	
G-GBRB	PA-28 Cherokee 180C	Bravo Romeo Group	
G-GBRU	Bell 206B JetRanger 3	R. A. Fleming Ltd (G-CDGV)	
G-GBRV	Van's RV-9A	G. Carter & K. L. Chorley (G-THMB)	
G-GBSL	Beech 76 Duchess	M. H. Cundsy (G-BGVG)	
G-GBTA	Boeing 737-436	British Airways (G-BVHA)	
G-GBTB	Boeing 737-436	British Airways (G-BVHB)	
G-GBTL	Cessna 172S	Bohana Technology Ltd	
G-GBUE	Robin DR.400/120A	J. A. Kane (G-BPXD)	
G-GBUN	Cessna 182T	G. M. Bunn	
G-GBVX	Robin DR400/120A	The Leuchars Flying Co.Ltd	

Notes	Reg.	Type	Owner or Operator
	G-GBXF	Robin HR200/120	B. A. Mills
	G-GBXS	Europa XS	Europa Group
	G-GCAC	Europa XS T-G	J. L. Gunn
	G-GCAT	PA-28 Cherokee 140B	Group Cat (G-BFRH)
	G-GCCL	Beech 76 Duchess	Aerolease Ltd
	G-GCDA	Cirrus SR20	Aircraft Grouping Ltd
	G-GCDB	Cirrus SR20	Aircraft Grouping Ltd
	G-GCDC	Cirrus SR20	Stamp Aviation Ltd
	G-GCDD	Cirrus SR20	Stamp Aviation Ltd
	G-GCEA	Pegasus Quik	S. F. Beardsell
	G-GCFM	Diamond DA.40D Star	VifoGmbhsrl/Germany
	G-GCIY	Robin DR.400-140B	Exavia Ltd
	G-GCJA	Rolladen-Schneider LS8-18	N. T. Mallender
	G-GCKI	Mooney M.20K	B. Barr
	G-GCMM	Agusta A109E	Hadleigh Assets
	G-GCMW	Grob G.102 Astir CS	M. S. F. Wood
	G-GCUF	Robin DR400/160	S. T. Bates
	G-GCYC	Cessna F.182Q	A. G. Dodd
	G-GDAV	Robinson R44 II	G. H. Weston
	G-GDEF	Robin DR.400/120	J. M. Shackleton
	G-GDER	Robin R.1180TD	Berkshire Aviation Services Ltd
	G-GDFB	Boeing 737-33A	Jet 2
	G-GDFC	Boeing 737-8K2	Jet 2
	G-GDFD	Boeing 737-8K5	Jet 2
	G-GDFE	Boeing 737-3Q8	Jet 2
	G-GDFF	Boeing 737-85P	Jet 2
	G-GDFH	Boeing 737-3Y5	Jet 2
	G-GDJF	Robinson R44 II	Berkley Properties Ltd (G-DEXT)
	G-GDKR	Robin DR400/140B	L. J. Milbank
	G-GDMW	Beech 76 Duchess	Flew LLP
	G-GDOG	PA-28R Cherokee Arrow 200-II	The Mutley Crew Group (G-BDXW)
	G-GDSG	Agusta A109E Power	Pendley Farm
	G-GDRV	Van's RV-6	J. R. S. Heaton & R. Feather
	G-GDTL	Airbus A.320-231	MyTravel Airways
	G-GDTU	Avions Mudry CAP-10B	D. C. Cooper & A. L. Farr
	G-GECO	Hughes 369HS	N. Duggan (G-ATVEE/G-GCXK)
	G-GEEP	Robin R.1180TD	The Aiglon Flying Group
	G-GEHL	Cessna 172S	Ebryl Ltd
	G-GEHP	PA-28RT-201 Arrow IV	Aeros Leasing Ltd
	G-GEIR	Embraer EMB-505 Phenom 300	ECC Leasing Co.Ltd
	G-GEMM	Cirrus SR20	Schmolke Grosskuechensysteme GmbH
	G-GEMS	Thunder Ax8-90 Srs 2 balloon	Kraft Bauprojekt GmbH/Germany
	G-GEMX	P&M Quik GT450	A. R. Oliver
	G-GEOF	Pereira Osprey 2	G. Crossley
	G-GEOS	Diamond HK.36 TTC-ECO	University Court (School of Geosciences) of the Super Dimona University of Edinburgh
	G-GERS	Robinson R44 II	M. Virdee
	G-GERT	Van's RV-7	Barnstormers
	G-GERY	Stoddard-Hamilton Glastar	S. G. Brown
	G-GEZZ	Bell 206B JetRanger II	Rivermead Aviation Ltd
	G-GFAA	Slingsbt T.67A	Aircraft Grouping Ltd (G-BJXA)
	G-GFCA	PA-28-161 Cadet	Aeros Leasing Ltd
	G-GFCB	PA-28-161 Cadet	A. J. Warren
	G-GFCD	PA-34-220T Seneca III	Stonehurst Aviation Ltd (G-KIDS)
	G-GFDA	Diamond DA.42 Twin Star	Saltaire Motor Co.Ltd (G-CEFX)
	G-GFEA	Cessna 172S	Allan Jefferies (G-CEDY)
	G-GFEY	PA-34-200T Seneca II	G-GFEY Owners Club
	G-GFFE	Boeing 737-528	Pineapple Ltd
	G-GFIA	Cessna 152	Aircraft Grouping Ltd
	G-GFIB	Cessna F.152	Flight Academy Barton Ltd (G-BPIO)
	G-GFIC	Cessna 152	Command Aviation Ltd (G-BORI)
	G-GFID	Cessna 152 II	Silverstar Maintenance Services Ltd (G-BORJ)
	G-GFIE	Cessna 152	Aircraft Grouping Ltd (G-CEUS)
	G-GFIF	Cessna FA.152	J. Viner (G-JONI/G-BFTU)
	G-GFIG	Cessna 152	J. Viner (G-BNOZ)
	G-GFKY	Zenair CH.250	R. G. Kelsall
	G-GFLY	Cessna F.150L	Alan Mann Aviation Group Ltd
	G-GFNO	Robin ATL	B. F. Walker

Reg.	Type	Owner or Operator	Notes
G-GFOX	Aeroprakt A.22 Foxbat	I. A. Love & G. F. Elvis	
G-GFRA	PA-28RT-201T Turbo Arrow IV	NSP Ltd (G-LROY/G-BNTS)	
G-GFRD	Robin ATL L	H. Joosten & S. Kumpen	
G-GFRO	Robin ATL	B. F. Walker	
G-GFSA	Cessna 172R Skyhawk	Aircraft Grouping Ltd	
G-GFTA	PA-28-161 Warrior III	One Zero Three Ltd	
G-GFTB	PA-28-161 Warrior III	One Zero Three Ltd	
G-GGDV	Schleicher Ka 6E	A. J. L. Poundsbery	
G-GGGG	Thunder Ax7-77A balloon	T. A. Gilmour	
G-GGHZ	Robin ATL	Modesto's Bakeries Ltd	
G-GGJK	Robin DR.400/140B	Headcorn Jodelers	
G-GGLE	PA-22 Colt 108 (tailwheel)	J. Guillemot & B. L. Morgan	
G-GGOW	Colt 77A balloon	R. Foster	
G-GGRR	SA Bulldog Srs 120/121 (XX614:V)	C. G. Sims (G-CBAM)	
G-GGTT	Agusta-Bell 47G-4A	P. R. Smith	
G-GGWW	Beech 76 Duchess	Avto Engineering Holding Group (G-BGRG)	
G-GHEE	Aerotechnik EV-97 Eurostar	C. J. Ball	
G-GHER	AS.355N Ecureuil II	Gallagher Air LLP	
G-GHIA	Cameron N-120 balloon	J. A. Marshall	
G-GHKX	PA-28-161 Warrior II	Aviation Rentals	
G-GHOW	Cessna F.182Q	J. F. Busby	
G-GHRW	PA-28RT-201 Arrow IV	Bonus Aircraft Ltd (G-ONAB/G-BHAK)	
G-GHZJ	SOCATA TB9 Tampico	P. K. Hayward	
G-GIBB	Robinson R44 II	Tingdene Aviation Ltd	
G-GIBP	Moravan Zlin Z.526 Trener Master	D. G. Cowden	
G-GIDY	Shaw Europa XS	Gidy Group	
G-GIGA	Vulcanair P68C	Apem Aviation Ltd	
G-GIGI	MS.893A Rallye Commodore	D. J. Moore (G-AYVX)	
G-GIGZ	Van's RV-8	The Giggzy Group	
G-GILI	Robinson R44	Twylight Management Ltd	
G-GIPC	PA-32R-301 Saratoga SP	S. Empson	
G-GIRY	AG-5B Tiger	Romeo Yankee Flying Group	
G-GIST	Luscombe 8E Silvaire	J. B. Brown (G-AKUH)	
G-GIVE	Cameron A-300 balloon	Cameron Flights Southern Ltd	
G-GIWT	Shaw Europa XS	A. Twigg	
G-GJCD	Robinson R22 Beta	J. C. Lane	
G-GJMB	Bombardier CL-600-2B19 Challenger 850	Corporate Jet Management Ltd (G-CJMB)	
G-GKAT	Enstrom 280C	D. G. Allsop & A. J. Clark	
G-GKEV	Alpi Pioneer 300	A. P. Sellars	
G-GKFC	RL-5A LW Sherwood Ranger	P. A. Durrans (G-MYZI)	
G-GKKI	Avions Mudry CAP 231EX	L. Love	
G-GKRC	Cessna 180K	S. J. Beaty	
G-GKUE	SOCATA TB-9 Tampico Club	I. Parkinson	
G-GLAD	Gloster G.37 Gladiator II (N5903:H)	Patina Ltd	
G-GLAK	AB Sportine LAK-12	L. M. Middleton	
G-GLAW	Cameron N-90 balloon	R. A. Vale	
G-GLED	Cessna 150M	Firecrest Aviation Ltd and H. Vara	
G-GLHI	Skyranger 912	S. F. Winter	
G-GLIB	Robinson R44	G. P. Glibbery	
G-GLID	Schleicher ASW-28-18E	S. Bovin and Compagnie Belge d'Assurances Aviation	
G-GLII	Great Lakes 2T-1A-2	T. J. Richardson	
G-GLOC	Extra EA.300/200	The Cambridge Aero Club Ltd	
G-GLST	Great Lakes Sport Trainer	D. A. Graham	
G-GLTT	PA-31-350 Navajo Chieftain	Blue Sky Investments Ltd	
G-GLUC	Van's RV-6	Speedfreak Ltd	
G-GLUE	Cameron N-65 balloon	L. J. M. Muir & G. D. Hallett	
G-GMAA	Learjet 45	Gama Aviation Ltd	
G-GMAB	BAe 125 Srs 1000A	Gama Aviation Ltd (G-BUWX)	
G-GMAC	Gulfstream G-IVSP	Gama Aviation Ltd	
G-GMAX	SNCAN Stampe SV.4C	Glidegold Ltd (G-BXNW)	
G-GMCM	AS.350B3 Ecureuil	T. J. Morris Ltd	
G-GMED	PA-42-720 Cheyenne IIA	Air Medical Fleet Ltd	
G-GMIB	Robin DR400/500	St. David's Farm & Equine Practice	
G-GMKD	Robin HR200/120B	J. Owens	

Notes	Reg.	Type	Owner or Operator
	G-GMKE	Robin HR200/120B	Pilot Flying Group
	G-GMPB	BN-2T-4S Defender 4000	Greater Manchester Police Authority (G-BWPU)
	G-GMPX	MDH MD-900 Explorer	Greater Manchester Police Authority
	G-GMSI	SOCATA TB9 Tampico	M. L. Rhodes
	G-GNJW	Ikarus C.42	N. C. Pearse
	G-GNRV	Van's RV-9A	N. K. Beavins
	G-GNTB	SAAB SF.340A	Loganair Ltd
	G-GNTF	SAAB SF.340A	Loganair Ltd
	G-GOAC	PA-34-200T Seneca II	Oxford Aviation Academy (Oxford) Ltd
	G-GOAL	Lindstrand LBL-105A balloon	I. Chadwick
	G-GOBD	PA-32R-301 Saratoga IIHP	F. & M. Garventa (G-OARW)
	G-GOBT	Colt 77A balloon	British Telecom PLC
	G-GOCX	Cameron N-90 balloon	R. D. Parry/Hong Kong
	G-GOES	Robinson R44-II	Fordville Ltd
	G-GOGB	Lindstrand LBL ,90A	J. Dyer (G-CDFX)
	G-GOGW	Cameron N-90 balloon	S. E. Carroll
	G-GOLF	SOCATA TB10 Tobago	B. Lee
	G-GOOF	Flylight Dragonfly	P. C. Bailey
	G-GORE	CFM Streak Shadow	M. S. Clinton
	G-GORV	Van's RV-8	G-GORV Group
	G-GOSL	Robin DR.400/180	R. M. Gosling (G-BSDG)
	G-GOSS	Jodel DR.221	Avon Flying Group
	G-GOTC	GA-7 Cougar	Western Air (Thruxton) Ltd and Bucklefield Business Developments Ltd
	G-GOTH	PA-28-161 Warrior III	Stamp Aviation Ltd
	G-GOUP	Robinson R22 Beta	M. A. Bennett (G-DIRE)
	G-GOWF	Eurocopter EC.135 T2+	Bond Air Services Ltd
	G-GPAG	Van's RV-6	P. A. Green
	G-GPAT	Beech 76 Duchess	Folada Aero & Technical Services Ltd
	G-GPEG	Sky 90-24 balloon	N. T. Parry
	G-GPMW	PA-28RT-201T Turbo Arrow IV	Calverton Flying Group Ltd
	G-GPPN	Cameron TR-70 balloon	Backetorp Byggconsult AB
	G-GPSF	Jabiru J430	P. S. Furlow
	G-GREY	PA-46-350P Malibu Mirage	S. T. Day & S. C. Askham
	G-GRIN	Van's RV-6	Burel Air Ltd
	G-GRIZ	PA-18-135 Super Cub (modified)	P. N. Elkington (G-BSHV)
	G-GRMN	Aerospool Dynamic WT9 UK	R. M. North
	G-GRND	Agusta A109S	Galegrove 2 LBG
	G-GROE	Grob G.115A	H. Merkado
	G-GROL	Maule MXT-7-180	D. C. Croll & ptnrs
	G-GROW	Cameron N-77 balloon	Derbyshire Building Society
	G-GRPA	Ikarus C.42 FB100	R. Wood
	G-GGRH	Robinson R44	Heli Air Ltd
	G-GRRR	SA Bulldog Srs 120/122	Horizons Europe Ltd (G-BXGU)
	G-GRSR	Schempp-Hirth Discus bT	SR Group
	G-GRVE	Van's RV-6	G-GRVE Group
	G-GRVY	Van's RV-8	P. H. Yarrow
	G-GRWL	Lilliput Type 4 balloon	A. E. & D. E. Thomas
	G-GRWW	Robinson R44 II	G. R. Williams (G-HEEL)
	G-GRYN	Rotorsport UK Calidus	K. Hedger
	G-GRYZ	Beech F33A Bonanza	J. Kawadri & M. Kaveh
	G-GRZD	Gulfstream V-SP	TAG Aviation (UK) Ltd
	G-GRZZ	Robinson R44 II	Graegill Aviation Ltd
	G-GSAL	Fokker E.III Reolica	Grass Strip Aviation Ltd
	G-GSCV	Ikarus C42 FB UK	Jabeque Ltd
	G-GSGZ	Mudry CAP.232	J. Paulson
	G-GSMT	Rotorsport UK MTOSport	Rotorsport UK Ltd
	G-GSPG	Hughes 369HS	S. Giddings Aviation
	G-GSPY	Robinson R44 II	Percy Wood Leisure Ltd
	G-GSRV	Robin DR.400/500	R. G. Fairall
	G-GSSC	Boeing 747-47UF	Global Supply Systems Ltd
	G-GSSD	Boeing 747-87UF	Global Supply Systems Ltd/British Airways Cargo
	G-GSSE	Boeing 747-87UF	Global Supply Systems Ltd/British Airways Cargo
	G-GSSF	Boeing 747-87UF	Global Supply Systems Ltd/British Airways Cargo
	G-GSSO	Gulfstream GV-SP	TAG Aviation (UK) Ltd
	G-GSST	Grob G.102 Astir CS77	770 Group
	G-GSYJ	Diamond DA42 Twin Star	Crosby Aviation (Jersey) Ltd

Reg.	Type	Owner or Operator	Notes
G-GSYS	PA-34-220T Seneca V	SYS (Scaffolding Contractors) Ltd	
G-GTAX	PA-31-350 Navajo Chieftain	Hadagain Investments Ltd (G-OIAS)	
G-GTEE	P & M Quik GT450	Fly Hire Ltd	
G-GTFC	P & M Quik	A. J. Fell	
G-GTGT	P & M Quik GT.450	W. G. Minns	
G-GTHM	PA-38-112 Tomahawk	R. J. Grainger	
G-GTJD	P & M Quik GT450	F. E. Hall	
G-GTJM	Eurocopter EC 120B Colibri	D. Robson	
G-GTOM	Alpi Pioneer 300	S. C. Oliphant	
G-GTSO	P & M Quik GT450	C. Bayliss	
G-GTTP	P & M Quik GT450	J. A. Lockert	
G-GTVM	Beech 58 Baron	Baron Flying Club Ltd	
G-GTWO	Schleicher ASW-15	J. M. G. Carlton & R. Jackson	
G-GUCK	Beech C23 Sundowner 180	J. T. Francis (G-BPYG)	
G-GULP	I.I.I. Sky Arrow 650T	S. Marriott	
G-GULZ	Christen Eagle II	T. N. Jinks	
G-GUMS	Cessna 182P	L. W. Scattergood (G-CBMN)	
G-GUNS	Cameron V-77 balloon	V. Grenier	
G-GUNZ	Van's RV-8	R. Ellingworth & A. G. Thomas	
G-GURN	PA-31 Navajo C	Batair Ltd (G-BHGA)	
G-GURU	PA-28-161 Warrior II	P. J. Wiseman	
G-GUSS	PA-28-151 Warrior	M. J. Cleaver & J. M. Newman (G-BJRY)	
G-GUYS	PA-34-200T Seneca	G. B. Faulkner (G-BMWT)	
G-GVPI	Evans VP-1 srs.2	G. Martin	
G-GWIZ	Colt Clown SS balloon	Magical Adventures Ltd	
G-GWYN	Cessna F.172M	Magic Carpet Flying Co	
G-GXAL	Remos GX	A. B. Atkinson	
G-GYAK	Yakovlev Yak-50	M. W. Levy & M. V. Rijske	
G-GYAT	Gardan GY-80 Horizon 180	Rochester GYAT Flying Group Club	
G-GYAV	Cessna 172N	Southport & Merseyside Aero Club (1979) Ltd	
G-GYBO	Gardan GY-80 Horizon 160	A. L. Fogg	
G-GYRO	Campbell Cricket	J. W. Pavitt	
G-GYTO	PA-28-161 Warrior III	Smart People Don't Buy Ltd	
G-GZDO	Cessna 172N	Cambridge Hall Aviation	
G-GZIP	Rolladen-Schneider LS8-18	D. S. S. Haughton	
G-GZRP	PA-42-720 Cheyenne IIIA	Air Medical Fleet Ltd	
G-HAAH	Schempp-Hirth Ventus 2cT	The V66 Syndicate	
G-HAAT	MDH MD.900 Explorer	Police Aviation Services Ltd (G-GMPS)	
G-HABI	Best Off SkyRanger 912S(1)	J. Habicht	
G-HABS	Cessna 172S	Apem Aviation Ltd (G-RGAP)	
G-HABT	Supermarine Aircraft Spitfire Mk.26	M. R. Overall	
G-HACE	Van's RV-6A	D. C. McElroy	
G-HACK	PA-18 Super Cub 150	Intrepid Aviation Co	
G-HADD	P & M Quik R	T. J. Barker	
G-HAEF	EV-97 TeamEurostar UK	RAF Microlight Flying Association	
G-HAFG	Cessna 340A	Pavilion Aviation Ltd	
G-HAFT	Diamond DA42 Twin Star	Atlantic Flight Training Ltd	
G-HAGL	Robinson R44 II	Devon Helicopters Ltd	
G-HAIB	Aviat A-1B Husky	H. Brockmueller	
G-HAIG	Rutan LongEz	C. Docherty	
G-HAIR	Robin DR.400/180	S. P. Copson	
G-HAJJ	Glaser-Dirks DG.400	W. G. Upton & J. G. Kosak	
G-HALC	PA-28R Cherokee Arrow 200	Halcyon Aviation Ltd	
G-HALJ	Cessna 140	Hangar 1 Ltd	
G-HALL	PA-22 Tri-Pacer 160	F. P. Hall (G-ARAH)	
G-HALP	SOCATA TB10 Tobago	D. H. Halpern	
G-HALT	Mainair Pegasus Quik	J. McGrath	
G-HAMI	Fuji FA.200-180	K. G. Cameron & M. P. Antoniak & P. Fairlie (G-OISF/G-BAPT)	
G-HAMM	Yakovlev Yak-50	Propeller Studios Ltd	
G-HAMP	Bellanca 7ACA Champ	R. J. Grimstead	
G-HAMR	PA-28-161 Warrior II	Electric Scribe 2000 Ltd	
G-HAMS	Pegasus Quik	D. R. Morton	
G-HANA	Westland WS-58 Wessex HC.2	R. A. Fidler	

Notes	Reg.	Type	Owner or Operator
	G-HANG	Diamond DA42 Twin Star	Atlantic Flight Training Ltd
	G-HANS	Robin DR.400 2+2	J. S. Russell
	G-HANY	Agusta-Bell 206B JetRanger 3	Beech Holdings Ltd (G-ESAL/G-BHXW/G-JEKP)
	G-HAPE	Pietenpol Aircamper	J. P. Chape
	G-HAPI	Lindstrand LBL-105A balloon	Adventure Balloons Ltd
	G-HAPY	DHC.1 Chipmunk 22A (WP803)	Astrojet Ltd
	G-HARD	Dyn'Aéro MCR-01 ULC	N. A. Burnet
	G-HARE	Cameron N-77 balloon	D. H. Sheryn & C. A. Buck
	G-HARI	Raj Hamsa X'Air V2 (2)	J. Blackburn
	G-HARK	Canadair CL.600-2B16	Corbridge Ltd
	G-HARN	PA-28-181 Archer II	K. Saxton (G-DENK/G-BXRJ)
	G-HARR	Robinson R22 Beta	Unique Helicopters Ltd
	G-HART	Cessna 152 (tailwheel)	Air Atlantique Ltd (G-BPBF)
	G-HARY	Alon A-2 Aircoupe	M. B. Willis (G-ATWP)
	G-HATF	Thorp T-18CW	A. T. Fraser
	G-HATZ	Hatz CB-1	S. P. Rollason
	G-HAUL	Westland WG.30 Srs 300 ★	IHM/Weston-super-Mare
	G-HAUS	Hughes 369HM	The Uniform Group (G-KBOT/G-RAMM)
	G-HAUT	Schempp-Hirth Mini Nimbus C	530 Syndicate
	G-HAVI	Eurocopter EC.130B4	J. & J. Havakin
	G-HAYY	Czech Sport Aircraft Sportcruiser	B. R. W. Hay
	G-HAZE	Thunder Ax8-90 balloon	T. G. Church
	G-HBBC	DH.104 Dove 8	Roger Gawn 2007 Family Trust (G-ALFM)
	G-HBBH	Ikarus C42 FB100	Golf Bravo Hotel Group
	G-HBEK	Agusta A109C	HPM Investments Ltd (G-RNLD/G-DATE)
	G-HBJT	Eurocopter EC.155B1	Starspeed Ltd
	G-HBMW	Robinson R22	Durham Flying Syndicate (G-BOFA)
	G-HBOB	Eurocopter EC135 T2+	Bond Air Services Ltd/Thames Valley Air Ambulance
	G-HBOS	Scheibe SF-25C Rotax-Falke	Coventry Gliding Club Ltd
	G-HBRO	Eurocopter AS.355NP Ecureuil 2	Henry Brothers (Magherafelt) Ltd
	G-HBUG	Cameron N-90 balloon	Black Horse Ballooning Club (G-BRCN)
	G-HCAC	Schleicher Ka 6E	Ka 6E 994 Group
	G-HCFC	Agusta A.109E Power	Castle Air Ltd
	G-HCGD	Learjet 45	TAG Aviation (UK) Ltd
	G-HCSA	Cessna 525A CJ2	Bookajet Aircraft Management Ltd
	G-HDAE	DHC.1 Chipmunk 22	Airborne Classics Ltd
	G-HDEF	Robinson R44 II	Arena Aviation Ltd (G-LOCO/G-TEMM)
	G-HDEW	PA-32R-301 Saratoga SP	A. H. Biddulph & P. R. Ellis
	G-HDIX	Enstrom 280FX	Clovetree Ltd
	G-HDTV	Agusta A109A-II	Castle Air Ltd (G-BXWD)
	G-HEAD	Colt Flying Head SS balloon	Ikeair
	G-HEAN	AS.355NP Ecureuil 2	Brookview Developments Ltd
	G-HEBB	Schleicher ASW-27-18E	E. Y. Heinonen
	G-HEBI	BN-2B-26 Islander	Hebridean Air Services Ltd (G-BSPT)
	G-HEBS	BN-2B-26 Islander	Hebridean Air Services Ltd (G-BUBJ)
	G-HEBZ	BN-2A-26 Islander	Cormack (Aircraft Services) Ltd (G-BELF)
	G-HECB	Fuji FA.200-160	H. E. W. E. Bailey (G-BBZO)
	G-HEHE	Eurocopter EC.120B Colibri	HE Group Ltd
	G-HEKK	RAF 2000 GTX-SE gyroplane	C. J. Watkinson (G-BXEB)
	G-HEKL	Percival Mew Gull Replica	Innomech Ltd
	G-HELA	SOCATA TB10 Tobago	PMF Group
	G-HELE	Bell 206B JetRanger 3	B. E. E. Smith (G-OJFR)
	G-HELN	Piper PA-18-95 Super Cub	Helen Group
	G-HELV	DH.115 Vampire T.55 (XJ771)	Aviation Heritage Ltd
	G-HEMZ	Agusta A109S Grand	Sloane Helicopters Ltd
	G-HENT	SOCATA Rallye 110ST	F. Monds
	G-HENY	Cameron V-77 balloon	R. S. D'Alton
	G-HEOI	Eurocopter EC135 P2+	Staffordshire & West Mercia Police Authorities
	G-HERB	PA-28R-201 Arrow III	Icarus Flyers Ltd
	G-HERC	Cessna 172S	Cambridge Aero Club Ltd
	G-HERD	Lindstrand LBL-77B balloon	S. W. Herd
	G-HERT	BAE Herti	BAe Systems (Operations) Ltd
	G-HEVN	SOCATA TB200 Tobago XL	Valley Flying Co.Ltd
	G-HEWI	Piper J-3C-90 Cub	Denham Grasshopper Group (G-BLEN)
	G-HEWS	Hughes 369D ★	Spares' use
	G-HEXE	Colr 17A balloon	A. Dunnington
	G-HEYY	Cameron 72 Bear SS balloon	Magical Adventures Ltd

Reg.	Type	Owner or Operator	Notes
G-HFBM	Curtiss Robin C-2	D. M. Forshaw	
G-HFCA	Cessna A.150L	T. H. Scott	
G-HFCB	Cessna F.150L	P. R. Mortimer	
G-HFCL	Cessna F.152	MK Aero Support Ltd (G-BGLR)	
G-HFCT	Cessna F.152	Stapleford Flying Club Ltd	
G-HFLY	Robinson R44 II	Helifly (UK) Ltd	
G-HFRH	DHC-1 Chipmunk 22	Sunrise Global Aviation Ltd	
G-HGAS	Cameron N-77 balloon	N. J. Tovey	
G-HGPI	SOCATA TB20 Trinidad	M. J. Jackson	
G-HGRB	Robinson R44	Ramsgill Aviation Ltd (G-BZIN)	
G-HHAA	HS. Buccaneer S.2B (XX885)	Hawker Hunter Aviation Ltd	
G-HHAC	Hawker Hunter F.58 (J-4021)	Hawker Hunter Aviation Ltd (G-BWIU)	
G-HHDR	Cessna 182T	D. R. & H. Howell	
G-HHII	Hawker Hurricane 2B (BE505: XP-L)	Hangar 11 Collection (G-HRLO)	
G-HHOG	Robinson R44 II	Fast Helicopters Ltd	
G-HHPM	Cameron Z-105 balloon	J. Armstrong	
G-HIBM	Cameron N-145 balloon	Alba Ballooning Ltd	
G-HICU	Schleicher ASW-27-18E	G. Smith & N. Hoare	
G-HIEL	Robinson R22 Beta	Crown Helicopters Ltd	
G-HIJK	Cessna 421C	DO Systems Ltd (G-OSAL)	
G-HIJN	Ikarus C.42 FB80	J. R. North	
G-HILI	Van's RV-3B	A. G. & E. A. Hill	
G-HILO	Rockwell Commander 114	J. G. Gleeson & J. J. Toomey	
G-HILS	Cessna F.172H	G-HILS Aviation Group (G-AWCH)	
G-HILT	SOCATA TB10 Tobago	S. Harrison	
G-HILY	Zenair CH.600 Zodiac	K. V. Hill & D. Woolliscroft (G-BRII)	
G-HILZ	Van's RV-8	A. G. & E. A. Hill	
G-HIMM	Cameron Z-105 balloon	C. M. D. Haynes	
G-HIND	Maule MT-7-235	M. A. Ashmole	
G-HINZ	Avtec Jabiru SK	P. J. Jackson	
G-HIPO	Robinson R22 Beta	SI Plan Electronics (Research) Ltd (G-BTGB)	
G-HIRE	GA-7 Cougar	London Aerial Tours Ltd (G-BGSZ)	
G-HITM	Raj Hamsa X'Air 582 (1)	S. E. Bettley	
G-HITT	Hawker Hurricane 1	Hawker Hurricane Ltd	
G-HIUP	Cameron A-250 balloon	J. D. & K. Griffiths	
G-HIVA	Cessna 337A	G. J. Banfield (G-BAES)	
G-HIVE	Cessna F.150M	M. P. Lynn (G-BCXT)	
G-HIYA	Best Off Skyranger 912(2)	R. D. & C. M. Parkinson	
G-HIZZ	Robinson R22 II	Flyfare (G-CNDY/G-BXEW)	
G-HJSM	Schempp-Hirth Nimbus 4DM	60 Syndicate (G-ROAM)	
G-HJSS	AIA Stampe SV.4C (modified)	H. J. Smith (G-AZNF)	
G-HJZN	Jabiru J430	H. D. Jones	
G-HKAA	Schempp-Hirth Duo Discus T	A. Aveling	
G-HKCF	Enstrom 280C-UK	HKC Helicopter Services (G-MHCF/G-GSML/ G-BNNV)	
G-HKHM	Hughes 369B	Heli Air Ltd	
G-HLCF	Starstreak Shadow SA-II	F. E. Tofield	
G-HLEE	Best Off Sky Ranger J2.2(1)	P. G. Hill	
G-HLEL	American Blimp Corp. A-60+ airship	Lightship Europe Ltd	
G-HLMB	Schempp-Hirth Ventus 2b	U. Hofinghoff	
G-HLOB	Cessna 172S	Goodwood Road Racing Co.Ltd	
G-HMBJ	Rockwell Commander 114B	D. W. R. Best	
G-HMCA	EV-97 TeamEurostar UK	RAF Microlight Flying Association	
G-HMCB	Skyranger Swift 912S(1)	R. W. Goddin	
G-HMCD	Ikarus C42 FB80	RAF Microlight Flying Association	
G-HMCE	Ikarus C42 FB80	RAF Microlight Flying Association	
G-HMED	PA-28-161 Warrior III	Eglinton Flying Club Ltd	
G-HMEI	Dassault Falcon 900	Executive Jet Group Ltd	
G-HMHM	Rotorsport UK MTO Sport	S. D. Evans	
G-HMJB	PA-34-220T Seneca III	W. B. Bateson	
G-HMPS	CZAW Sportcruiser	H. & P. Shedden	
G-HMPT	Agusta-Bell 206B JetRanger 2	Yorkshire Helicopters	
G-HNGE	Ikarus C42 FB100	Compton Abbas Airfield Ltd	
G-HNTR	Hawker Hunter T.7 (XL571:V) ★	Yorkshire Air Museum/Elvington	

Notes	Reg.	Type	Owner or Operator
	G-HOBO	Denney Kitfox Mk 4	J. P. Donovan
	G-HOCA	Robinson R44 II	Howcan Air Services Ltd
	G-HOCK	PA-28 Cherokee 180	G-HOCK Flying Club (G-AVSH)
	G-HOFF	P & M Aviation Quik GT450	L. Mazurek
	G-HOFM	Cameron N-56 balloon	Magical Adventures Ltd
	G-HOGS	Cameron 90 Pig SS balloon	Magical Adventures Ltd
	G-HOJO	Schempp-Hirth Discus 2a	S. G. Jones
	G-HOLA	PA-28-201T Turbo Dakota	J. Prescott (G-BNYB)
	G-HOLD	Robinson R44 II	Mignini and Petrini Spa/Italy
	G-HOLE	P & M Quik GT450	C. J. R. Hardman (G-CEBD)
	G-HOLI	Ultramagic M-77 balloon	G. Everett
	G-HOLM	Eurocopter EC.120B Colibri	Oxford Air Services Ltd
	G-HOLY	ST.10 Diplomate	M. K. Barsham
	G-HONG	Slingsby T.67M Firefly 200	Jewel Aviation and Technology Ltd
	G-HONI	Robinson R22 Beta	Patriot Aviation Ltd (G-SEGO)
	G-HONK	Cameron O-105 balloon	M. A. Green
	G-HONY	Lilliput Type 1 Srs A balloon	A. E. & D. E. Thomas
	G-HOOD	SOCATA TB20 Trinidad GT	M. J. Hoodless
	G-HOPA	Lindstrand LBL-35A balloon	S. F. Burden/Netherlands
	G-HOPE	Beech F33A Bonanza	Hope Aviation
	G-HOPR	Lindstrand LBL-25A balloon	K. C. Tanner
	G-HOPY	Van's RV-6A	R. C. Hopkinson
	G-HORK	Pioneer 300 Hawk	R. Y. Kendal
	G-HOSS	Beech F33A	T. D. Broadhurst
	G-HOTA	EV-97 TeamEurostar UK	W. Chang
	G-HOTB	Eurocopter EC155 B1	Noirmont (EC155) Ltd (G-CEXZ)
	G-HOTM	Cameron C-80 balloon	M. N. Macleod
	G-HOTZ	Colt 77B balloon	C. J. & S. M. Davies
	G-HOUS	Colt 31A balloon ★	The British Balloon Museum and Library
	G-HOWE	Thunder Ax7-77 balloon	C. Suggitt
	G-HOWI	Cessna F.182Q	H. Poulson
	G-HOWL	RAF 2000 GTX-SE gyroplane	C. J. Watkinson
	G-HOXN	Van's RV-9	XRay November Flying Club
	G-HPAD	Bell 206B JetRanger 2	Helipad Ltd (G-CITZ/G-BRTB)
	G-HPEN	Ultramagic M-120 balloon	G. Holtam
	G-HPFT	Cessna 150F	Hinton Pilot Flight Training Ltd (G-ATKF)
	G-HPOL	MDH MD-902 Explorer	Humberside Police Authority
	G-HPPY	Learjet 40	European Skyjets Ltd
	G-HPSF	Rockwell Commander 114B	R. W. Scandrett
	G-HPSL	Rockwell Commander 114B	M. B. Endean
	G-HPUX	Hawker Hunter T.7 (XL587)	Hawker Hunter Aviation Ltd
	G-HPWA	Van's RV-8	M. de Ferranti
	G-HRAF	Schleicher ASK-13	Upward Bound Trust (G-DETS)
	G-HRBS	Robinson R22 Beta	Fly Executive Ltd
	G-HRCC	Robin HR200/100	P. R and J. S. Johnson
	G-HRHE	Robinson R22 Beta	Irwin Plant Sales (G-BTWP)
	G-HRIO	Robin HR.100/120	R. Mullender
	G-HRLI	Hawker Hurricane 1 (V7497)	Hawker Restorations Ltd
	G-HRLK	SAAB 91D/2 Safir	Sylmar Aviation & Services Ltd (G-BRZY)
	G-HRLM	Brügger MB.2 Colibri	M. W. Bodger & M. H. Hoffmann
	G-HRND	Cessna 182T	Dingle Star Ltd
	G-HRNT	Cessna 182S	J. Jeanneret-Grosjean
	G-HROI	Rockwell Commander RC.112	Intereuropean Aviation Ltd
	G-HRPN	Robinson R44 II	M. Lazzari
	G-HRVD	CCF Harvard IV	Anglia Flight (G-BSBC)
	G-HRVS	Van's RV-8	D. J. Harvey & M. S. Pettit
	G-HRYZ	PA-28-180 Cherokee Archer	Lees Avionics Ltd (G-WACR/G-BCZF)
	G-HSAR	Agusta A.109E Power	Caste Air Ltd
	G-HSBC	Lindstrand LBL-69X balloon	A. Nimmo
	G-HSEB	Pegasus Quantum 15-912	S.West (G-BYNO)
	G-HSKE	Aviat A-18 Husky	R. B. Armitage & S. L. Davis
	G-HSKI	Aviat A-1B	C. J. R. Flint
	G-HSOO	Hughes 369HE	Kuki Helicopter Sales Ltd & S. J. Nicholls (G-BFYJ)
	G-HSTH	Lindstrand LBL. HS-110 balloon	Lindstrand Hot Air Balloons Ltd
	G-HSXP	Raytheon Hawker 850XP	Fowey Services Ltd
	G-HTAX	PA-31-350 Navajo Chieftain	Hadagain Investments Ltd
	G-HTBT	Rotorsport UK Calidus	T. J. Troy-Davies

Reg.	Type	Owner or Operator	Notes
G-HTEL	Robinson R44	A. G. & R. S. Higgins	
G-HTFU	Gippsland GA8-TC 320 Airvan	Skydive London Ltd	
G-HTML	P & M Aviation Quik R	A. P. Whitmarsh	
G-HTRL	PA-34-220T Seneca III	Air Medical Fleet Ltd (G-BXXY)	
G-HTWE	Rans S6-116	H. C. C. Coleridge	
G-HUBB	Partenavia P.68B	Ravenair Aircraft Ltd	
G-HUBY	Embraer EMB-135BJ Legacy	London Executive Aviation Ltd	
G-HUCH	Cameron 80 Carrots SS balloon	Magical Adventures Ltd (G-BYPS)	
G-HUES	Hughes 369HS	D. G. Beecroft & A. Gilligan (G-GASC/ G-WELD/G-FROG)	
G-HUEW	Shaw Europa XS	C. R. Wright	
G-HUEY	Bell UH-1H	MX Jets Ltd	
G-HUFF	Cessna 182P	Highfine Ltd	
G-HUKA	MDH Hughes 369E	B. P. Stein (G-OSOO)	
G-HULK	Skyranger 912(2)	L. C. Stockman	
G-HULL	Cessna F.150M	Hull Aero Club Ltd	
G-HUMH	Van's RV-9A	H. A. Daines	
G-HUND	Aviat A-1B Husky	U Ladurner	
G-HUNI	Bellanca 7GCBC Scout	R. G. Munro	
G-HUPW	Hawker Hurricane 1 (R4118:UP-W)	Minmere Farm Partnership	
G-HURI	CCF Hawker Hurricane XIIA (Z5140/HA-C)	Historic Aircraft Collection Ltd	
G-HURN	Robinson R22 Beta	Sloane Helicopters Ltd	
G-HUSK	Aviat A-1B	G. D. Ettlmayr	
G-HUTE	Aerochute Dual	W. A. Kimberlin	
G-HUTT	Denney Kitfox Mk.2	H. D. Colliver	
G-HUTY	Van's RV-7	S. A. Hutt	
G-HVAN	RL-5A LW Sherwood Ranger ST	P. S. Taylor	
G-HVBF	Lindstrand LBL-210A balloon	Virgin Balloon Flights	
G-HVER	Robinson R44 II	Equation Associates Ltd	
G-HVRD	PA-31-350 Navajo Chieftain	N. Singh (G-BEZU)	
G-HVRZ	Eurocopter EC 120B	EDM Helicopters Ltd	
G-HWAA	Eurocopter EC 135T2	Bond Air Services Ltd	
G-HXTD	Robin DR.400/180	P. Malone	
G-HYLL	Robinson R44	Holbeck GHYLL Country House Hotel Ltd (G-KLAS)	
G-HYLT	PA-32R-301 Saratoga SP	T. G. Gordon	
G-HYST	Enstrom 280FX Shark	M. Jop	
G-IACA	Sikorsky S-92A	Bristow Helicopters Ltd	
G-IACB	Sikorsky S-92A	Bristow Helicopters Ltd	
G-IACC	Sikorsky S-92A	Bristow Helicopters Ltd	
G-IACD	Sikorsky S-92A	Bristow Helicopters Ltd	
G-IACE	Sikorsky S-92A	Bristow Helicopters Ltd	
G-IACF	Sikorsky S-92A	Bristow Helicopters Ltd	
G-IAJJ	Robinson R44 II	O'Connor Utilities Ltd	
G-IAJS	Ikarus C.42 FB UK	A. J. Slater	
G-IANB	Glaser-Dirks DG-800B	I. S. Bullous	
G-IANC	SOCATA TB10 Tobago	P. D. Seed (G-BIAK)	
G-IANH	SOCATA TB10 Tobago	R. J. Wright	
G-IANI	Shaw Europa XS T-G	I. F. Rickard & I. A. Watson	
G-IANJ	Cessna F.150K	J. A. & D. T. A. Rees (G-AXVW)	
G-IANN	Kolb Twinstar Mk 3	I. Newman	
G-IANV	Diamond DA42 Twin Star	Plane Talking Ltd	
G-IANW	AS.350B3 Ecureuil	Milford Aviation Services Ltd	
G-IANZ	P & M Quik GT450	Forward Agronomy Ltd	
G-IARC	Stoddard-Hamilton Glastar	A. A. Craig	
G-IASM	Beech 200 Super King Air	TAG Aviation (Stansted) Ltd (G-OEAS)	
G-IBAZ	Ikarus C.42 FB100	B. R. Underwood	
G-IBBC	Cameron 105 Sphere SS balloon	Balloon Preservation Group	
G-IBBS	Shaw Europa	R. H. Gibbs	
G-IBED	Robinson R22A	Brian Seedle Helicopters Blackpool (G-BMHN)	
G-IBFC	BFC Challenger II	K. V. Hill	
G-IBFP	VPM .M.16 Tandem Trainer	B. F. Pearson	
G-IBFW	PA-28R-201 Arrow III	Archer Four Ltd	
G-IBHH	Hughes 269C	Alpha Properties (London) Ltd (G-BSCD)	

Notes	Reg.	Type	Owner or Operator
	G-IBIG	Bell 206B JetRanger 3	Big Heli-Charter Ltd (G-BORV)
	G-IBII	Pitts S-2A Special	Aerobatic Displays Ltd (G-XATS)
	G-IBLP	P & M Quik GT450	B. L. Prime
	G-IBME	SA.342J Gazelle	Gazelle Management Services LLP
	G-IBMS	Robinson R44	Beoley Mill Software Ltd
	G-IBNH	Westland Gazelle HT Mk.2 (XW853)	Buckland Newton Hire Ltd (G-SWWM)
	G-IBSY	VS.349 Spitfire Mk.VC	Fairfax Spitfires Ltd (G-VMIJ)
	G-IBUZ	CZAW Sportcruiser	G. L. Fearon
	G-IBZS	Cessna 182S	S. O. Bjerkeset
	G-ICAS	Pitts S-2B Special	J. C. Smith
	G-ICBM	Stoddard-Hamilton Glasair III Turbine	G. V. Walters & D. N. Brown
	G-ICDM	Jabiru UL-450	D. J. R. Wenham (G-CEKM)
	G-ICES	Thunder Ax6-56 balloon ★	British Balloon Museum & Library Ltd
	G-ICKY	Lindstrand LBL-77A balloon	R. J. Percival & J. Tyrrell
	G-ICMT	Evektor EV-97 Eurostar	R. Haslam
	G-ICOI	Lindstrand LBL-105A balloon	F. Schroeder/Germany
	G-ICOM	Cessna F.172M	C. G. Elesmore (G-BFXI)
	G-ICON	Rutan LongEz	S. J. & M. A. Carradice
	G-ICRS	Ikarus C.42 FB UK Cyclone	Ikarus Flying Group Ltd
	G-ICSG	AS.355F1 Twin Squirrel	RCR Aviation Ltd (G-PAMI/G-BUSA)
	G-ICWT	Pegasus Quantum 15-912	D. H. Evans
	G-IDAB	Cessna 550 Citation Bravo	Mail Handling International Ltd
	G-IDAY	Skyfox CA-25N Gazelle	G. G. Johnstone
	G-IDEB	AS.355F1 Ecureuil 2	MW Helicopters Ltd (G-ORMA/G-SITE/G-BPHC)
	G-IDER	Orlican Discus CS	A. J. Preston & D. B. Keith
	G-IDII	Dan Rihn DR.107 One Design	C. Darlow
	G-IDOL	Evektor EV-97 Eurostar	J. L. Almey
	G-IDRO	Bombardier BD700-1A10 Global Express	Corporate Jet Management Ltd
	G-IDUP	Enstrom 280C Shark	Antique Buildings Ltd (G-BRZF)
	G-IDWR	Hughes 369HS	Copley Electrical Contractors (G-AXEJ)
	G-IEIO	PA-34-200T Seneca II	Sky Zone Servicos Aereos Lda
	G-IEJH	Jodel 150A	A. Turner & D. Worth (G-BPAM)
	G-IEYE	Robin DR.400/180	G. Wood
	G-IFAB	Cessna F.182Q	Bristol & West Aeroplane Club Ltd
	G-IFBP	AS.350B2 Ecureuil	Frank Bird Aviation
	G-IFDM	Robinson R44	MFH Helicopters Ltd
	G-IFFR	PA-32 Cherokee Six 300	Brendair (G-BWVO)
	G-IFFY	Flylight Dragonfly	R. D. Leigh
	G-IFIF	Cameron TR-60 balloon	M. G. Howard
	G-IFIT	PA-31-350 Navajo Chieftain	Dart Group PLC (G-NABI/G-MARG)
	G-IFLE	Aerotechnik EV-97 TeamEurostar UK	M. R. Smith
	G-IFLI	AA-5A Cheetah	C. M. Petherbridge
	G-IFLP	PA-34-200T Seneca II	ACS Aviation Ltd
	G-IFRH	Agusta A109C	Helicopter Services Ltd
	G-IFTE	HS.125 Srs 700B	Albion Aviation Management Ltd (G-BFVI)
	G-IFTF	BAe 125 Srs 800B	Albion Aviation Management Ltd (G-RCEJ/ G-GEIL)
	G-IFWD	Schempp-Hirth Ventus cT	J. C. Ferguson & C. J. Hamilton
	G-IGEL	Cameron N-90 balloon	Computacenter Ltd
	G-IGGL	SOCATA TB10 Tobago	G-IGGL Flying Group (G-BYDC)
	G-IGHH	Enstrom 480	Raw Sports Ltd
	G-IGHT	Van's RV-8	E. A. Yates
	G-IGIA	AS.350B3 Ecureuil	Faloria Ltd
	G-IGIE	SIAI Marchetti SF.260	Flew LLP
	G-IGII	Shaw Europa	C. D. Peacock
	G-IGLE	Cameron V-90 balloon	G-IGLE Group
	G-IGLI	Schempp-Hirth Duo Discus T	C. Fox
	G-IGLL	AutoGyro MTO Sport	I. M. Donnellan
	G-IGLY	P & M Aviation Quik GT450	K. G. Grayson & R. D. Leigh
	G-IGLZ	Champion 8KCAB	Woodgate Aviation (IOM) Ltd
	G-IGPW	Eurocopter EC 120B	Helihopper Ltd (G-CBRI)
	G-IGTE	SIAI Marchetti F.260	D. Fletcher & J. J. Watts
	G-IGWT	Bombardier CL600-2B19	Skywings Ltd
	G-IGZZ	Robinson R44 II	Rivermead Aviation Ltd
	G-IHOP	Cameron Z-31 balloon	N. W. Roberts
	G-IHOT	Aerotechnik EV-97 Eurostar UK	Exodos Airsports Ltd

Reg.	Type	Owner or Operator	Notes
G-IIAC	Aeronca 11AC Chief	F. & M. R. Overall (G-BTPY)	
G-IIAI	Mudry CAP.232	J. Bennett	
G-IIAN	Aero Designs Pulsar	I. G. Harrison	
G-IICI	Aviat Pitts S-2C Special	Aerobatics Leicester Ltd	
G-IICT	Schempp-Hirth Ventus 2Ct	P. McLean	
G-IICX	Schempp-Hirth Ventus 2cxT	S. G. Jones	
G-IIDI	Extra EA.300/L	Power Aerobatics Ltd (G-XTRS)	
G-IIDY	Aerotek Pitts S-2B Special	The S-2B Group (G-BPVP	
G-IIEX	Extra EA.300/L	S. G. Jones	
G-IIFM	Edge 360	F. L. McGee	
G-IIFX	Marganski MDM-1	Swift Aerobatic Display Team	
G-IIGI	Van's RV-4	T. D. R. Hardy	
G-IIHI	Extra 300/SC	YAK UK Ltd	
G-IIID	Dan Rihn DR.107 One Design	D. A. Kean	
G-IIIE	Aerotek Pitts S-2B Special	D. S. A. Gomes da Silva	
G-IIIG	Boeing Stearman A75N1	O. Josse & S. Bolyn /Belgium (G-BSDR)	
G-IIII	Aerotek Pitts S-2B Special	Aerospace Optics Ltd	
G-IIIK	Extra EA.300/SC	Extra 300SC LLP	
G-IIIL	Pitts S-1T Special	Empyreal Airways Ltd	
G-IIIM	Stolp SA.100 Starduster	H. Mackintosh	
G-IIIO	Schempp-Hirth Ventus 2CM	S. J. Clark	
G-IIIP	Pitts S-1D Special	R. S. Grace (G-BLAG)	
G-IIIR	Pitts S-1S Special	R. O. Rogers	
G-IIIS	Sukhoi Su-26M2	Airtime Aerobatics Ltd	
G-IIIT	Aerotek Pitts S-2A Special	Aerobatic Displays Ltd	
G-IIIV	Pitts Super Stinker 11-260	S. D. Barnard & A. N. R. Houghton	
G-IIIX	Pitts S-1S Special	D. S. T. Eggleton (G-LBAT/G-UCCI/G-BIYN)	
G-IIIZ	Sukhoi Su-26M	P. M. M. Bonhommy	
G-IIJC	Midget Mustang	Longacre Aviation Ltd (G-CEKU)	
G-IIMI	Extra EA.300/L	Firebird Aerobatics Ltd	
G-IIMT	Midget Mustang	P. J. Hebdon	
G-IINI	Van's RV-9A	A. Payne & P. Young	
G-IIOO	Schleicher ASW-27-18E	M. Clarke	
G-IIPB	DR.107 One Design	P. D. Baisden	
G-IIPT	Robinson R22 Beta	Highmark Aviation Ltd (G-FUSI)	
G-IIPZ	Mudry CAP.232	S. P. R. Madle & J. Murfitt	
G-IIRG	Stoddard-Hamilton Glasair IIS RG	A. C. Lang	
G-IIRI	Xtreme Air Sbach 300	One Sky Aviation LLP	
G-IIRP	Mudry CAP.232	R. J. Pickin	
G-IIRV	Van's RV-7	D. S. Watson	
G-IIRW	Van's RV-8	R. Winward	
G-IITC	Mudry CAP.232	T. W. Cassells	
G-IIVI	CAP-232	Skylane Aviation Ltd	
G-IIXF	Van's RV-7	C. A. & S. Noujaim	
G-IIXI	Extra EA.300/L	B. Nielsen	
G-IIXX	Parsons 2-seat gyroplane	J. M. Montgomerie	
G-IIYK	Yakovlev Yak-50	D. A. Hammant	
G-IIZI	Extra EA.300	Power Aerobatics Ltd	
G-IJAC	Light Aero Avid Speedwing Mk 4	I. J. A. Charlton	
G-IJAG	Cessna 182T Skylane	AG Group	
G-IJBB	Enstrom 480	R. P. Bateman (G-LIVA/G-PBTT)	
G-IJMC	Magni M-16 Tandem Trainer	R. F. G. Moyle (G-POSA/G-BVJM)	
G-IJMI	Extra EA.300/L	DEP Promotions Ltd	
G-IJNK	Robinson R44	Hi-Range Ltd (G-KTOL/G-DCOM)	
G-IJOE	PA-28RT-201T Turbo Arrow IV	J. H. Bailey	
G-IKAH	Slingsby T.51 Dart 17R	K. A. Hale	
G-IKAP	Cessna T.303	T. M. Beresford	
G-IKBP	PA-28-161 Warrior II	F. J. Page	
G-IKEA	Cameron 120 Ikea SS balloon	IKEA Ltd	
G-IKES	Stoddard-Hamilton GlaStar	M. Stow	
G-IKEV	Jabiru UL-450	D. I. Taylor	
G-IKON	Van's RV-4	S. Sampson	
G-IKOS	Cessna 550 Citation Bravo	Medox Enterprises Ltd	
G-IKRK	Shaw Europa	K. R. Kesterton	
G-IKRS	Ikarus C.42 FK UK Cyclone	K. J. Warburton	
G-IKUS	Ikarus C.42 FB UK Cyclone	C. I. Law	
G-ILBO	Rolladen-Schneider LS3-A	J. P. Gilbert	
G-ILDA	VS.361 Spitfire HF.IX (SM520 : KJ-1)	Spitfire Display Ltd (G-BXHZ)	
G-ILEE	Colt 56A balloon	G. I. Lindsay	

Notes	Reg.	Type	Owner or Operator
	G-ILES	Cameron O-90 balloon	G. N. Lantos
	G-ILIB	PZL-Bielsko SZD-36A	D. Poll
	G-ILLE	Boeing Stearman A75L3 (379)	M. Minkler
	G-ILLG	Robinson R44 II	C. B. Ellis
	G-ILLY	PA-28-181 Archer II	R. A. & G. M. Spiers
	G-ILPD	SIAI Marchetti F.260C	M. Mignini/Italy
	G-ILRS	Ikarus C.42 FB UK Cyclone	Knitsley Mill Leisure Ltd
	G-ILSE	Corby CJ-1 Starlet	S. Stride
	G-ILTS	PA-32 Cherokee Six 300	P. G. Teasdale & Foremans Aviation Ltd (G-CVOK)
	G-ILUA	Alpha R2160I	A. R. Haynes
	G-IMAB	Europa XS	T. J. Price
	G-IMAC	Canadair CL-600-2A12 Challenger	Gama Aviation Ltd
	G-IMAD	Cessna 172P	Leus Aviation Ltd
	G-IMAG	Colt 77A balloon ★	Balloon Preservation Group
	G-IMBI	QAC Quickie 1	J. D. King (G-BWIT)
	G-IMBL	Bell 407	Northern Flights Ltd
	G-IMBY	Pietenpol AirCamper	C. Brockis
	G-IMCD	Van's RV-7	I. G. McDowell
	G-IMEA	Beech 200 Super King Air	MIAW LLP (G-OWAX)
	G-IMEC	PA-31 Navajo C	Planeco Ltd (G-BFOM)
	G-IMEL	Rotary Air Force RAF 2000 GTX-SE	P. F. Murphy
	G-IMHK	P & M Quik R	J. Waite
	G-IMME	Zenair CH.701 STOL	M. Spearman
	G-IMMI	Escapade Kid	J. Pearce
	G-IMMY	Robinson R44	Tony Cain Leisure Services
	G-IMNY	Escapade 912	D. S. Bremner
	G-IMOK	Hoffmann HK-36R Super Dimona	A. L. Garfield
	G-IMPS	Skyranger Nynja 912S	S. J. Brooks & B. J. Killick
	G-IMPX	Rockwell Commander 112B	Impatex Computer Systems Ltd
	G-IMPY	Light Aero Avid Flyer C	T. R. C. Griffin
	G-IMUP	Tanarg/Ixess 15 912S (1)	P. D. Hill
	G-INCA	Glaser-Dirks DG.400	K. D. Hook
	G-INCE	Skyranger 912(2)	N.P. Sleigh
	G-INDC	Cessna T.303	J-Ross Developments Ltd
	G-INDI	Pitts S-2C Special	L. Coesens
	G-INDX	Robinson R44	Kinetic Computers Ltd
	G-INDY	Robinson R44	Lincoln Aviation
	G-INGA	Thunder Ax8-84 balloon	M. L. J. Ritchie
	G-INGE	Thruster T.600N	M. J. O'Carroll
	G-INGS	American Champion 8KCAB	Scotflight Ltd
	G-INII	Pitts S-1 Special	C. Davidson (G-BTEF)
	G-INJA	Ikarus C42 FB UK	C. E. Walls
	G-INNI	Jodel D.112	S. Barry
	G-INNY	SE-5A (replica) (F5459:Y)	M. J. Speakman
	G-INSR	Cameron N-90 balloon	P. J. Waller and The Smith and Pinching Group Ltd
	G-INTS	Van's RV-4	N. J. F. Campbell
	G-INTV	AS.355F2 Ecureuil 2	Arena Aviation Ltd (G-JETU)
	G-IOCO	Beech 58 Baron	Anchor Shipping Agents SpA/Italy
	G-IOFR	Lindstrand LBL-105A balloon	RAF Halton Hot Air Balloon Club
	G-IOIA	I.I.I. Sky Arrow 650T	P.J. Lynch, P.G. Ward, N.J.C. Ray
	G-IOMI	Cameron Z-105 balloon	Elgas SRL/Italy
	G-IOOI	Robin DR.400/160	N. B. Mason
	G-IOOP	Christen Eagle II	A. P. S. Maynard
	G-IOOZ	Agusta A109S Grand	Hundred Percent Aviation Ltd
	G-IOPT	Cessna 182P	Indy Oscar Group
	G-IORG	Robinson R22 Beta	Staffordshire Helicopters Training Ltd
	G-IORV	Van's RV-10	A. F. S. & B. L. Caldecourt
	G-IOSI	Jodel DR.1051	D. C. & M. Brooks
	G-IOSL	Van's RV-9	S. Leach (G-CFIX)
	G-IOSO	Jodel DR.1050	A. E. Jackson
	G-IOWE	Shaw Europa XS	P. G. Leonard
	G-IPAD	Cessna F.172M	D. G. Smith (G-BCCD)
	G-IPAT	Jabiru SP	H. Adams
	G-IPAX	Cessna 560XL Citation Excel	Pacific Aviation Ltd
	G-IPEP	Beech 95-B55 Baron	P. E. T. Price (G-FABM)
	G-IPJF	Robinson R44 II	Specialist Group International Ltd (G-RGNT/G-DMCG)

Reg.	Type	Owner or Operator	Notes
G-IPKA	Alpi Pioneer 300	M. E. Hughes	
G-IPOD	Europa XS	Ultraflight Ltd (G-CEBV)	
G-IPSI	Grob G.109B	D. G. Margetts (G-BMLO)	
G-IPUP	Beagle B.121 Pup 2	Swift Flying Group	
G-IRAF	RAF 2000 GTX-SE gyroplane	P. Robichaud	
G-IRAL	Thruster T600N 450	J. Giraldez	
G-IRAP	Bombardier BD-700-1A10 Global Express	TAG Aviation (UK) Ltd (G-CJME)	
G-IRAR	Van's RV-9	J. Maplethorpe	
G-IREN	SOCATA TB-20 Trinidad GT	Chios Aeroclub	
G-IRGJ	Champion 7ECA Citabria Aurora	T. A. Mann	
G-IRIS	AA-5B Tiger	C. Nichol (G-BIXU)	
G-IRJX	Avro RJX-100 ★	Manchester Heritage Museum	
G-IRKB	PA-28R-201 Arrow III	M. Ruter	
G-IRLE	Schempp-Hirth Ventus cT	D. J. Scholey	
G-IRLY	Colt 90A balloon	C. E. R. Smart	
G-IRLZ	Lindstrand LBL-60X balloon	A. M. Holly	
G-IROE	Flight Design CTSW	S. Roe	
G-IRON	Shaw Europa XS	T. M. Clark	
G-IROS	Rotorsport UK Calidus	JB Aviation Ltd	
G-IRPC	Cessna 182Q	A. T. Jeans (G-BSKM)	
G-IRPW	Europa XS	R. P. Wheelwright	
G-IRSH	Embraer EMB-135RJ	Legemb Ltd	
G-IRTM	DG Flugzeugbau DG-1000M	ATSI Ltd	
G-IRYC	Schweizer 269-1	Virage Helicopter Acadewmy LLP	
G-ISAR	Cessna 421C	Rescue Global Management Services Ltd (G-BHKJ)	
G-ISAX	PA-28-181 Archer III	M. S. Kontowtt	
G-ISBD	Alpi Pioneer 300 Hawk	B. Davies	
G-ISCA	PA-28RT-201 Arrow IV	D. J. & P. Pay	
G-ISCD	Czech Sport Aircraft Sportcruiser	P. W. Shepherd	
G-ISDB	PA-28-161 Warrior II	Action Air Services Ltd (G-BWET)	
G-ISDN	Boeing Stearman A75N1	D. R. L. Jones	
G-ISEH	Cessna 182R	S. J. Nash (G-BIWS)	
G-ISEL	Best Off Skyranger 912 (2)	P. A. Robertson	
G-ISEW	P & M Quik GT450	J. D. Doran	
G-ISFC	PA-31-310 Turbo Navajo B	T. M. Latiff (G-BNEF)	
G-ISHA	PA-28-161 Warrior III	LAC Flying School	
G-ISHK	Cessna 172S	Matchpage Ltd	
G-ISLB	BAe Jetstream 3201	Blue Islands Ltd	
G-ISLC	BAe Jetstream 3202	Blue Islands Ltd	
G-ISLD	BAe Jetstream 3202	Blue Islands Ltd	
G-ISLF	Aerospatiale ATR-42-500	Blue Islands Ltd	
G-ISMA	Van's RV-7	S. Marriott (G-STAF)	
G-ISMO	Robinson R22 Beta	Moy Motorsport Ltd	
G-ISMS	Sorrell SNS-7 Hyperbipe	D. G. Curran (G-HIPE)	
G-ISON	AirBike UK Elite	AirBike UK Ltd	
G-ISPH	Bell 206B JetRanger 2	Blades Aviation (UK) LLP (G-OPJM)	
G-ISST	Eurocopter EC 155B1	Bristow Helicopters Ltd	
G-ISSU	Eurocopter EC 155B1	Bristow Helicopters Ltd	
G-ISSV	Eurocopter EC 155B1	Bristow Helicopters Ltd	
G-ISSY	Eurocopter EC 120B	D. R. Williams (G-CBCG)	
G-ISZA	Aerotek Pitts S-2A Special	F. L. McGee (G-HISS/G-BLVU)	
G-ITAF	SIAI-Marchetti SF.260AM	N. A. Whatling	
G-ITBT	Alpi Pioneer 300 Hawk	F. Paolini	
G-ITII	Aerotech Pitts S-2A Special	P. J. Kirkpatrick	
G-ITIM	Dassault Falcon 7X	TAG Aviation (UK) Ltd	
G-ITOI	Cameron N-90 balloon	Flying Pictures Ltd	
G-ITPH	Robinson R44 II	Helicopter Services Europe Ltd	
G-ITVM	Lindstrand LBL-105A balloon	Elmer Balloon Team	
G-ITWB	DHC.1 Chipmunk 22	I. T. Whitaker-Bethe	
G-IUAN	Cessna 525 CitationJet	R. F. Celada SPA/Italy	
G-IUII	Aerostar Yakovlev Yak-52	D. J. C. Davidson	
G-IUMB	Schleicher ASW-20L	M. S. Szymkowicz	
G-IVAC	Airtour AH-77B balloon	T. D. Gibbs	
G-IVAL	CAB CAP-10B	I. Valentine	
G-IVAN	Shaw TwinEze	A. M. Aldridge	
G-IVAR	Yakovlev Yak-50	A. H. Soper	

Notes	Reg.	Type	Owner or Operator
	G-IVEN	Robinson R44 II	OKR Group/Ireland
	G-IVER	Shaw Europa XS	I. Phillips
	G-IVES	Shaw Europa	M. W. Olliver (G-JOST)
	G-IVET	Shaw Europa	K. J. Fraser
	G-IVII	Vqn's RV-7	M. A. N. Newall
	G-IVIV	Robinson R44	D. Brown
	G-IVJM	Agusta A109E Power	Air Harrods Ltd (G-MOMO)
	G-IVOR	Aeronca 11AC Chief	South Western Aeronca Group
	G-IVYS	Parsons 2-seat gyroplane	R. M. Harris
	G-IWIN	Raj Hamsa X'Air Hawk	H. R. Bethune
	G-IWIZ	Flylight Dragonfly	S. Wilson
	G-IWON	Cameron V-90 balloon	D. P. P. Jenkinson (G-BTCV)
	G-IWRB	Agusta A109A-II	Maison Air Ltd (G-VIPT)
	G-IXII	Christen Eagle II	Eagle Flying Group (G-BPZI)
	G-IXXI	Schleicher ASW-27-18E	G. P. Stingemore
	G-IYCO	Robin DR.400/500	Timgee Holdings Ltd
	G-IZAP	Learjet 45	Premiair Business Aviation Ltd (G-OLDK)
	G-IZII	Marganski Swift S-1	G. C. Westgate
	G-IZIP	Learjet 45	Premiair Business Aviation Ltd (G-OLDW)
	G-IZIT	Rans S.6-116 Coyote II	D. J. Flower
	G-IZZI	Cessna T.182T	D. J. & E-S Lucey
	G-IZZS	Cessna 172S	Air Claire Ltd
	G-IZZY	Cesna 172R	P. A. Adams & T. S. Davies (G-BXSF)
	G-IZZZ	Champion 8KCAB	Phoenix Flyers Ltd
	G-JAAB	Avtech Jabiru UL	R. Holt
	G-JABB	Avtech Jabiru UL	R. J. Sutherland
	G-JABE	Jabiru Aircraft Jabiru UL-D	H. M. Manning and P. M. Jones
	G-JABI	Jabiru Aircraft Jabiru J400	Anvilles Flying Group
	G-JABJ	Jabiru Aircraft Jabiru J400	L. B. W. & F. H. Hancock
	G-JABS	Avtech Jabiru UL-450	Jabiru Flying Group
	G-JABU	Jabiru J430	S. D. Miller
	G-JABY	Avtech Jabiru UL-450	P. R. Smith
	G-JABZ	Avtech Jabiru UL-450	J. T. Grant
	G-JACA	PA-28-161 Warrior II	The Pilot Centre Ltd
	G-JACB	PA-28-181 Archer III	P. R. Coe (G-PNNI)
	G-JACH	PA-28-181 Archer III	Goldcrest 2001 Ltd (G-IDPH)
	G-JACI	Bell 206L-4 LongRanger IV	Morgan Airborne LLP
	G-JACK	Cessna 421C	JCT 600 Ltd
	G-JACO	Avtech Jabiru UL	C. D. Matthews/Ireland
	G-JACS	PA-28-181 Archer III	Modern Air (UK) Ltd
	G-JADJ	PA-28-181 Archer III	ACS Aviation Ltd
	G-JADW	Ikarus C42 FB80	J. W. & D. A. Wilding
	G-JAEE	Van's RV-6A	J. A. E. Edser
	G-JAES	Bell 206B JetRanger 3	Audisio Automobili Cuneo SRL/Italy (G-STOX/G-BNIR)
	G-JAFT	Diamond DA.42 Twin Star	Atlantic Flight Training Ltd
	G-JAGS	Cessna FRA.150L	RAF Marham Flying Club (G-BAUY)
	G-JAIR	Mainair Blade	G. Spittlehouse
	G-JAJA	Robinson R44 II	J. D. Richardson
	G-JAJB	AA-5A Cheetah	Active Aviation Ltd
	G-JAJK	PA-31-350 Navajo Chieftain	Blue Sky Investments Ltd (G-OLDB/G-DIXI)
	G-JAJP	Avtech Jabiru UL	J. Anderson
	G-JAKF	Robinson R44 Raven II	J. G. Froggatt
	G-JAKI	Mooney M.20R	J. M. Moss & D. M. Abrahamson
	G-JAKS	PA-28 Cherokee 160	K. Harper (G-ARVS)
	G-JAMA	Schweizer 269C-1	R. J. Scott
	G-JAME	Zenair CH 601UL	A. Batters (G-CDFZ)
	G-JAMP	PA-28-151 Warrior	Lapwing Flying Group Ltd (G-BRJU)
	G-JAMY	Shaw Europa XS	J. P. Sharp
	G-JAMZ	P & M QuikR	S. Cuthbertson
	G-JANA	PA-28-181 Archer II	S. Hoo-Hing
	G-JANB	Colt Flying Bottle SS balloon	Justerini & Brooks Ltd
	G-JANI	Robinson R44	JT Helicopters Ltd
	G-JANN	PA-34-220T Seneca III	D. J. Whitcombe
	G-JANS	Cessna FR.172J	C. M. Aizlewood
	G-JANT	PA-28-181 Archer II	Janair Aviation Ltd
	G-JAOC	Best Off Sky Ranger Swift 912S(1)	A. C. Bell

Reg.	Type	Owner or Operator	Notes
G-JAPK	Grob G.130A Twin II Acro	Cairngorm Gliding Club	
G-JARM	Robinson R44	J. Armstrong	
G-JASE	PA-28-161 Warrior II	Mid-Anglia School of Flying	
G-JASS	Beech B200 Super King Air	Platinum Executive Aviation LLP	
G-JAVO	PA-28-161 Warrior II	Victor Oscar Ltd (G-BSXW)	
G-JAWC	Pegasus Quantum 15-912	M. J. Robbins	
G-JAWZ	Pitts S-1S Special	A. R. Harding	
G-JAXS	Avtech Jabiru UL	J. P. Pullin	
G-JAYI	Auster J/1 Autocrat	Aviation Heritage Ltd	
G-JAYS	Skyranger 912S(1)	R. A. Green	
G-JAYZ	CZAW Sportcruiser	J. Williams	
G-JBAS	Neico Lancair 200	A. Slater	
G-JBBZ	AS.350B3 Ecureuil	BZ Air Ltd	
G-JBDB	Agusta-Bell 206B JetRanger	Dicksons Van World Ltd (G-OOPS/G-BNRD)	
G-JBDH	Robin DR.400/180	W. A. Clark	
G-JBEN	Mainair Blade 912	G. J. Bentley	
G-JBII	Robinson R22 Beta	Alan Mann Aviation Group Ltd (G-BXLA)	
G-JBIS	Cessna 550 Citation II	247 Jet Ltd	
G-JBIZ	Cessna 550 Citation II	247 Jet Ltd	
G-JBKA	Robinson R44	J. G. Harrison	
G-JBLZ	Cessna 550 Citation Bravo	247 Jet Ltd	
G-JBRE	Rotorsport UK MT-03	J. B. R. Elliot & D. F. Sargant	
G-JBRG	Agusta A109A II	Interceptor Aviation Ltd (G-TMUR/G-CEPO)	
G-JBRN	Cessna 182S	Williams Industrial Services Ltd (G-RITZ)	
G-JBRS	Van's RV-8	C. Jobling	
G-JBSP	Avtech Jabiru SP-470	C. R. James	
G-JBTR	Van's RV-8	R. A. Ellis	
G-JBUZ	Robin DR400/180R Remorqueur	D. A. Saywell	
G-JCAP	Robinson R22 Beta	R. D. Masters	
G-JCAR	PA-46-350P Malibu Mirage	Aquarelle Investments Ltd	
G-JCAS	PA-28-181 Archer II	Charlie Alpha Ltd	
G-JCBB	Gulfstream V-SP	J. C. Bamford Excavators Ltd	
G-JCBJ	Sikorsky S-76C	J. C. Bamford Excavators Ltd	
G-JCBX	Dassault Falcon 900EX	J. C. Bamford Excavators Ltd	
G-JCJC	Colt Flying Jeans SS balloon	Magical Adventures Ltd	
G-JCKT	Stemme S.10VT	J. C. Taylor	
G-JCMW	Rand KR-2	A. Levitt	
G-JCOP	Eurocopter AS.350B3 Ecureuil	Optimum Ltd	
G-JCUB	PA-18 Super Cub 135	Vintage Aircraft Flying Group	
G-JCWM	Robinson R44 II	M. L. J. Goff	
G-JDBC	PA-34-200T Seneca II	Bowdon Aviation Ltd (G-BDEF)	
G-JDEE	SOCATA TB20 Trinidad	JDEE Group	
G-JDEL	Jodel 150	K. F. & R. Richardson (G-JDLI)	
G-JDJM	PA-28 Cherokee 140	Hare Flying Group (G-HSJM/G-AYIF)	
G-JDPB	PA-28R-201T Turbo Arrow III	BC Arrow Ltd (G-DNCS)	
G-JDRD	Alpi Pioneer 300	R. J. Doughton	
G-JEAF	Fokker F.27 Friendship Mk.500	Executive Jet Support Ltd	
G-JEAJ	BAe 146-200	Trident Aviation Leasing Services (Jersey) Ltd (G-OLCA)	
G-JECE	DHC.8-402 Dash Eight	Flybe.com	
G-JECF	DHC.8-402 Dash Eight	Flybe.com	
G-JECG	DHC.8-402 Dash Eight	Flybe.com	
G-JECH	DHC.8-402 Dash Eight	Flybe.com	
G-JECI	DHC.8-402 Dash Eight	Flybe.com	
G-JECJ	DHC.8-402 Dash Eight	Flybe.com	
G-JECK	DHC.8-402 Dash Eight	Flybe.com	
G-JECL	DHC.8-402 Dash Eight	Flybe.com	
G-JECM	DHC.8-402 Dash Eight	Flybe.com	
G-JECN	DHC.8-402 Dash Eight	Flybe.com	
G-JECO	DHC.8-402 Dash Eight	Flybe.com	
G-JECP	DHC.8-402 Dash Eight	Flybe.com	
G-JECR	DHC.8-402 Dash Eight	Flybe.com	
G-JECX	DHC.8-402 Dash Eight	Flybe.com	
G-JECY	DHC.8-402 Dash Eight	Flybe.com	
G-JECZ	DHC.8-402 Dash Eight	Flybe.com	
G-JEDH	Robin DR.400/180	J. B. Hoolahan	
G-JEDI	DHC.8-402 Dash Eight	A and L CF June (2) Ltd	
G-JEDJ	DHC.8-402 Dash Eight	Flybe.com	

Notes	Reg.	Type	Owner or Operator
	G-JEDK	DHC.8-402 Dash Eight	Flybe.com
	G-JEDL	DHC.8-402 Dash Eight	Flybe.com
	G-JEDM	DHC.8-402 Dash Eight	Flybe.com
	G-JEDN	DHC.8-402 Dash Eight	Flybe.com
	G-JEDO	DHC.8-402 Dash Eight	Flybe.com
	G-JEDP	DHC.8-402 Dash Eight	Flybe com
	G-JEDR	DHC.8-402 Dash Eight	Flybe com
	G-JEDS	Andreasson BA-4B	S. B. Jedburgh (G-BEBT)
	G-JEDT	DHC.8-402 Dash Eight	Flybe com
	G-JEDU	DHC.8-402 Dash Eight	Flybe com
	G-JEDV	DHC.8-402 Dash Eight	Flybe.com
	G-JEDW	DHC.8-402 Dash Eight	Flybe.com
	G-JEEP	Evektor EV-97 Eurostar	G-JEEP Group (G-CBNK)
	G-JEFA	Robinson R44	Simlot Ltd
	G-JEJE	RAF 2000 GTX-SE gyroplane	M. R. Spray
	G-JEJH	Jodel DR.1050 Ambassadeur	Bredon Hill Flying Group
	G-JEMA	BAe ATP	PTB (Emerald) Pty Ltd
	G-JEMC	BAe ATP	PTB (Emerald) Pty Ltd
	G-JEMI	Lindstrand LBL-90A balloon	J. A. Lawton
	G-JEMM	Jodel DR.1050	D. W. Garbe
	G-JENA	Mooney M.20K	Jena Air Force
	G-JENI	Cessna R.182	R. A. Bentley
	G-JENK	Ikarus C42 FB80	P. J. Oakey
	G-JERO	Shaw Europa XS	P. Jenkinson and N. Robshaw
	G-JESE	AS.355F2 Ecureuil 2	Arena Aviation Ltd (G-EMHH/G-BYKH)
	G-JESI	AS.350B Ecureuil	Staske Construction Ltd (G-JOSS/G-WILX/ G-RAHM/G-UNIC/G-COLN/G-BHIV)
	G-JESS	PA-28R-201T Turbo Arrow III	R. E. Trawicki (G-REIS)
	G-JETA	Cessna 550 Citation II	Icon Two Ltd (G-RDBS)
	G-JETC	Cessna 550 Citation II	Interceptor Aviation Ltd (G-JCFR)
	G-JETH	Hawker Sea Hawk FGA.6 (XE489) ★	P. G. Vallance Ltd/Charlwood
	G-JETJ	Cessna 550 Citation II	G-JETJ Ltd (G-EJET/G-DJBE)
	G-JETM	Gloster Meteor T.7 (VZ638) ★	P. G. Vallance Ltd/Charlwood
	G-JETO	Cessna 550 Citation II	Air Charter Scotland Ltd (G-RVHT)
	G-JETX	Bell 206B JetRanger 3	L. B. Oldham
	G-JETZ	Hughes 369E	GJP Helicopters Ltd
	G-JEZA	Agusta AW.139	CHC Scotia Ltd
	G-JEZZ	Skyranger 582	N. J. Brownlow & P. W. Day
	G-JFAN	P & M Quik R	J. F. A. Nicol
	G-JFDI	Dynamic WT9 UK	M. S. Gregory
	G-JFER	Rockwell Commander 114B	J. C. & J. A. Ferguson (G-HPSE)
	G-JFLO	Aerospool Dynamic WT9 UK	J. Flood
	G-JFLY	Schleicher ASW-24	Cambridge Gliding Club Ltd
	G-JFMK	Zenair CH.701SP	J. D. Pearson
	G-JFRV	Van's RV-7A	J. H. Fisher
	G-JFWI	Cessna F.172N	Staryear Ltd
	G-JGBI	Bell 206L-4 LongRanger	Dorbcrest Homes Ltd
	G-JGCA	VS.361 Spitfire LF.IXe (TE517)	P. M. Andrews (G-CCIX/G-BIXP)
	G-JGMN	CASA 1.131E Jungmann 2000	P. D. Scandrett
	G-JGSI	Pegasus Quantum 15-912	A. Fern
	G-JHAC	Cessna FRA.150L	J. H. A. Clarke (G-BACM)
	G-JHDD	Czech Sport Aircraft Sportcruiser	D. Draper & J. W. Hagley
	G-JHEW	Robinson R22 Beta	Heli Air Ltd
	G-JHKP	Shaw Europa XS	J. D. Heykoop
	G-JHNY	Cameron A.210 balloon	Floarting Sensations Ltd
	G-JHPC	Cessna 182T	JHP Aviation Ltd
	G-JHYS	Shaw Europa	B. C. Moorhouse
	G-JIBO	BAe Jetstream 3102	Links Asset Management Ltd (G-OJSA/G-BTYG)
	G-JIFI	Schempp-Hirth Duo Discus T	D. K. McCarthy
	G-JIII	Stolp SA.300 Starduster Too	VTIO Co
	G-JIIL	Pitts S-2A Special	A. G. Griffiths
	G-JILY	Robinson R44	R. R. Orr
	G-JIMB	Beagle B.121 Pup 1	K. D. H. Gray & P. G. Fowler (G-AWWF)
	G-JIMC	Van's RV-7	J. Chapman
	G-JIMH	Cessna F.152 II	D. J. Howell (G-SHAH)
	G-JIMM	Shaw Europa XS	J. Riley
	G-JIMP	Messerschmitt Bf 109G-2	G. B. E. Pearce
	G-JIMZ	Van's RV-4	J.W.Hale

Reg.	Type	Owner or Operator	Notes
G-JINI	Cameron V-77 balloon	I. R. Warrington	
G-JINX	Silence SA.180 Twister	P. M. Wells	
G-JIVE	MDH Hughes 369E	Sleekform Ltd (G-DRAR)	
G-JJAB	Jabiru J400	K. Ingebrigtsen	
G-JJAN	PA-28-181 Archer II	J. S. Develin & Z. Islam	
G-JJEN	PA-28-181 Archer III	K. M. R. Jenkins	
G-JJFB	Eurocopter EC.120B Colibri	J. G. Rhoden	
G-JJIL	Extra EA.300/L	Link Goals SP ZOO	
G-JJSI	BAe 125 Srs 800B	Gama Leasing Ltd (G-OMGG)	
G-JJWL	Robinson R44	Willbeth Ltd	
G-JKAY	Robinson R44	Jamiroquai Ltd	
G-JKEL	Van's RV-7	J. D. Kelsall (G-LNNE)	
G-JKKK	Cessna 172S	P. Eaton	
G-JKMH	Diamond DA42 Twin Star	ADR Aviation	
G-JKMJ	Diamond DA42 Twin Star	Medox Enterprises Ltd	
G-JKRV	Schempp-Hirth Arcus T	G-JKRV Syndicate	
G-JLAT	Aerotechnik EV-97 Eurostar	J. Latimer	
G-JLCA	PA-34-200T Seneca II	Tayside Aviation Ltd (G-BOKE)	
G-JLEE	Agusta-Bell 206B JetRanger 3	J. S. Lee (G-JOKE/G-CSKY/G-TALY)	
G-JLHS	Beech A36 Bonanza	I. G. Meredith	
G-JLIN	PA-28-161 Cadet	JH Sandham Aviation	
G-JLLT	Aerotechnik EV-97 Eurostar	J. Latimer	
G-JLRW	Beech 76 Duchess	Airways Flight Training	
G-JMAA	Boeing 757-3CQ	Thomas Cook Airlines Ltd	
G-JMAB	Boeing 757-3CQ	Thomas Cook Airlines Ltd	
G-JMAC	BAe Jetstream 4100 ★	Jetstream Club, Liverpool Marriott Hotel South, Speke (G-JAMD/G-JXLI)	
G-JMAL	Jabiru UL-D	A. D. Sutton	
G-JMCD	Boeing 757-25F	Thomas Cook Airlines Ltd	
G-JMCE	Boeing 757-25F	Thomas Cook Airlines Ltd	
G-JMCG	Boeing 757-2G5	Thomas Cook Airlines Ltd	
G-JMCL	Boeing 737-322	Atlantic Airlines Ltd	
G-JMCN	Robinson R44 II	J. E. McCann	
G-JMDI	Schweizer 269C	D. A. Sempers (G-FLAT)	
G-JMED	Learjet 35A	Air Medical Fleet Ltd, Argyll Ltd & Provident Partners Ltd	
G-JMJR	Cameron Z-90	J. M. Reck/France	
G-JMKE	Cessna 172S	115CR (146) Ltd	
G-JMKM	AutoGyro MTO Sport	K. O. Maurer	
G-JMMX	Dassault Falcon 900EX	Jaymax Jersey Ltd	
G-JMON	Agusta A109A-II	Elmridge Ltd (G-RFDS/G-BOLA)	
G-JMOS	PA-34-220T Seneca V	Moss Aviation LLP	
G-JMRV	Van's RV-7	J. W. Marshall	
G-JMTS	Robin DR.400/180	G-JMTS Group	
G-JNAS	AA-5A Cheetah	C. J. Williams	
G-JNET	Robinson R22 Beta	R. L. Hartshorn	
G-JNMA	VS.379 Spitfire FR.Mk.XIVe	P. M. Andrews	
G-JNNB	Colt 90A balloon	N. A. P. Godfrey	
G-JNSC	Schempp-Hirth Janus CT	D. S. Bramwell	
G-JNUS	Schempp-Hirth Janus C	N. A. Peatfield	
G-JOAL	Beech B200 Super King Air	South Coast Air Charter LLP	
G-JOBA	P & M Quik GT450	B. Hall	
G-JOBS	Cessna T182T	Tech Travel Ltd (G-BZVF)	
G-JODL	Jodel D.1050/M	D. Silsbury	
G-JOEL	Bensen B.8MR	C. Quinn	
G-JOEY	BN-2A Mk III-2 Trislander	Aurigny Air Services (G-BDGG)	
G-JOHA	Cirrus SR20	N. Harris	
G-JOJO	Cameron A-210 balloon	A. C. Rawson & J. J. Rudoni	
G-JOKR	Extra EA.300/L	C. Jefferies	
G-JOLY	Cessna 120	B. V. Meade	
G-JONB	Robinson R22 Beta	J. Bignall	
G-JONG	Rotorway Executive 162F	J. V. George	
G-JONH	Robinson R22 Beta	Polar Helicopters Ltd	
G-JONL	CZAW Sportcruiser	J. R. Linford	
G-JONM	PA-28-181 Archer III	J. H. Massey	
G-JONO	Colt 77A balloon ★	British Balloon Museum and Library	

Notes	Reg.	Type	Owner or Operator
	G-JONT	Cirrus SR22	J. A. Green
	G-JONX	Aeropro Eurofox 912(1)	J. M. Walsh
	G-JONY	Cyclone AX2000 HKS	K. R. Matheson
	G-JONZ	Cessna 172P	Truman Aviation Ltd
	G-JONT	Cirrus SR22	J. A. Green
	G-JOOL	Mainair Blade 912	P. C. Collins
	G-JOPT	Cessna 560 Citation V	Air Charter Scotland Ltd
	G-JORD	Robinson R44 II	Overby Ltd
	G-JOTA	Beech B.90 King Air	Jota Aircraft Leasing Ltd (G-OJRO)
	G-JOYT	PA-28-181 Archer II	John K. Cathcart Ltd (G-BOVO)
	G-JOYZ	PA-28-181 Archer III	S. W. & J. E. Taylor
	G-JPAL	AS.355N Twin Squirrel	JPM Ltd
	G-JPAT	Robin HR.200/100	L. Girardier & A. J. McCulloch
	G-JPBA	Van's RV-6	S. B. Austin
	G-JPEG	BN-2A-20 Islander	Apem Aviation Ltd (G-BEDW)
	G-JPIP	Schempp-Hirth Discus bT	S. Cervantes
	G-JPJR	Robinson R44 II	Longstop Investments Ltd
	G-JPMA	Avtech Jabiru UL	Jabiru Aviation Merseyside
	G-JPOT	PA-32R-301 Saratoga SP	P.J.Wolstencroft (G-BIYM)
	G-JPRO	P.84 Jet Provost T.5A (XW433)	Air Atlantique Ltd
	G-JPSZ	Dassault Falcon 900EX Easy	Sorven Aviation Ltd
	G-JPTT	Enstrom 480	P. G. Lawrence (G-PPAH)
	G-JPTV	P.84 Jet Provost T.5A (XW354)	Century Aviation Ltd
	G-JPVA	P.84 Jet Provost T.5A (XW289)	H. Cooke (G-BVXT)
	G-JPWM	Skyranger 912 (2)	R. S. Waters & M. Pittock
	G-JRED	Robinson R44	J. Reddington Ltd
	G-JREE	Maule MX-7-180	C. R. P. Briand
	G-JRKD	Jodel D.18	R. K. Davies
	G-JRME	Jodel D.140E	J. E. & L. L. Rex
	G-JRSL	Agusta A109E Power	Perment Ltd
	G-JSAK	Robinson R22 Beta II	Tukair Aircraft Charter
	G-JSAT	BN-2T Turbine Islander	Rhine Army Parachute Association/Germany (G-BVFK)
	G-JSEY	Bollonbau Worner NL-STU/1000	M. Leblanc
	G-JSKN	Eurocopter EC225LP Super Puma	CHC Scotia Ltd
	G-JSON	Cameron N-105 balloon	Up and Away Ballooning Ltd
	G-JSPL	Avtech Jabiru SPL-450	A. E. Stowe
	G-JSRV	Van's RV-6	J. Stringer
	G-JSSD	HP.137 Jetstream 3001 ★	Museum of Flight/East Fortune
	G-JTEM	Van's RV-7	J. C. Bacon
	G-JTJT	Robinson R44	Skyrunner Aviation Ltd
	G-JTNC	Cessna 500 Citation	Eurojet Aviation Ltd (G-OEJA/G-BWFL)
	G-JTPC	Aeromot AMT-200 Super Ximango	G. J. & J. T. Potter
	G-JTSA	Robinson R44 II	S. Novotny
	G-JUDD	Avtech Jabiru UL-450H	G. S. Elder
	G-JUDE	Robin DR.400/180	Bravo India Flying Group Ltd
	G-JUDY	AA-5A Cheetah	Gray Hooper Holt LLP
	G-JUGE	Aerotechnik EV-97 TeamEurostar UK	L. J. Appleby
	G-JUGS	Autogyro MTOSport	S. J. M. Hornsby
	G-JUIN	Cessna T.303 Crusader	F. Kratky
	G-JULE	P & M Quik GT450	G. Almond
	G-JULL	Stemme S.10VT	J. P. C. Fuchs
	G-JULU	Cameron V-90 balloon	J. M. Searle
	G-JULZ	Shaw Europa	J. S. Firth
	G-JUNG	CASA 1.131E Jungmann 1000 (E3B-143)	A. Burroughes
	G-JUPP	PA-32RT-300 Lance II	M. N. Jupp (G-BNJF)
	G-JURG	Rockwell Commander 114A	Wright Aviation Dunchurch Ltd
	G-JUST	Beech F33A Bonanza	P. Thompson
	G-JVBF	Lindstrand LBL-210A balloon	Virgin Balloon Flights
	G-JVBP	Aerotechnik EV-97 Team Eurostar UK	B. J. Partridge & J. A. Valentine
	G-JVJK	Alpi Pioneer 300 Hawk	D. R. Vale
	G-JWBI	Agusta-Bell 206B JetRanger 2	J. W. Bonser (G-RODS/G-NOEL/G-BCWN)
	G-JWCM	SA Bulldog Srs 120/1210	Goon Aviation Ltd
	G-JWDB	Ikarus C.42 FB80	A. R. Hughes
	G-JWDS	Cessna F.150G	G. Sayer (G-AVNB)

Reg.	Type	Owner or Operator	Notes
G-JWEB	Robinson R44	P. T. Birdsall	
G-JWIV	Jodel DR.1051	C. M. Fitton	
G-JWJW	CASA 1-131E Jungmann Srs.2000	J. W. & J. T. Whicher	
G-JWNW	Magni M-16C Tandem Trainer	A. G. Jones	
G-JWXS	Shaw Europa XS T-G	J. Wishart	
G-JXTA	BAe Jetstream 3103	Jetstream Executive Travel Ltd	
G-JXTC	BAe Jetstream 3108★	University of Glamorgan instructional airframe (G-LOGT/G-BSFH)	
G-JYAK	Yakovlev Yak-50 (93 white outline)	J. W. Stow	
G-JYRO	Rotorsport UK MT-03	A. Richards	
G-KAAT	MDH MD-902 Explorer	Police Aviation Services Ltd (G-PASS)	
G-KAEW	Fairey Gannet AEW Mk.3	M. Stott	
G-KAFT	Diamond DA40D Star	Atlantic Flight Training Ltd	
G-KAIR	PA-28-181 Archer II	Blue Sky Investments Ltd	
G-KALS	Bombardier BD-100-1A10	Concolor Ltd	
G-KAMP	PA-18 Super Cub 135	G. Cormack	
G-KAMY	AT-6D Harvard II	Orion Enterprises Ltd	
G-KANE	Aerospatiale SA.341G Gazelle 1	MW Helicopters Ltd (G-GAZI)	
G-KANL	Bombardier BD-700-1A10 Global Express	Ocean Sky (UK) Ltd	
G-KANZ	Westland Wasp HAS.1	T. J. Manna	
G-KAOM	Scheibe SF.25C Falke	Falke G-KAOM Syndicate	
G-KAOS	Van's RV-7	J. L. Miles	
G-KAPW	P.56 Provost T.1 (XF603)	The Shuttleworth Collection	
G-KARA	Brügger MB.2 Colibri	C. L. Hill (G-BMUI)	
G-KARI	Fuji FA.200-160	C. P. Rowley	
G-KARK	Dyn'Aéro MCR-01 Club	R. Bailes-Brown	
G-KART	PA-28-161 Warrior II	N. Clark	
G-KASW	Rotorsport UK Calidus	K. C. Wigley	
G-KASX	VS.384 Seafire Mk.XVII (SX336)	T. J. Manna (G-BRMG)	
G-KATE	Westland WG.30 Srs 100 ★	(stored)/Yeovil	
G-KATI	Rans S.7 Courier	T. S. D. Lyle	
G-KATS	PA-28 Cherokee 140	G-KATS Group (G-BIRC)	
G-KATT	Cessna 152 II	Skytaxi KFT (G-BMTK)	
G-KATZ	Flight Design CT2K	A. N. D. Arthur	
G-KAWA	Denney Kitfox Mk 2	L. E. Donaldson	
G-KAXF	Hawker Hunter F.6A (N-294)	Stichting Dutch Hawker Hunter Foundation/Netherlands	
G-KAXT	Westland Wasp HAS.1 (XT787)	Kennet Aviation	
G-KAYH	Extra EA.300/L	R. C. Howe/Netherlands	
G-KAYI	Cameron Z-90 balloon	Snow Business International Ltd	
G-KAZA	Sikorsky S-76C	Bristow Helicopters Ltd	
G-KAZB	Sikorsky S-76C	Bristow Helicopters Ltd	
G-KAZI	Mainair Pegasus Quantum 15-912	Fairlight Engineering Ltd	
G-KBOJ	Autogyro MTOSport	K. M. G. Barnett	
G-KBOX	Flight Design CTSW	C. R. Mason	
G-KBWP	Schempp-Hirth Arcus T	B. F. & P. Walker	
G-KCHG	Schempp-Hirth Ventus Ct	Ventus KJW Syndicate	
G-KCIG	Sportavia RF-5B	Deeside Fournier Group	
G-KCIN	PA-28-161 Cadet	Jetstream Executive Travel Ltd (G-CDOX)	
G-KCWJ	Schempp-Hirth Duo Discus T	8F Group	
G-KDEY	Scheibe SF.25E Super Falke	Falke Syndicate	
G-KDIX	Jodel D.9 Bébé	J. A. Sykes	
G-KDMA	Cessna 560 Citation V	Gamston Aviation Ltd	
G-KDOG	SA Bulldog Srs 120/121 (XX624:E)	Gamit Ltd	
G-KEAM	Schleicher ASH 26E	I. W. Paterson	
G-KEDK	Discus BT	G. N. Fraser	
G-KEEF	Commander Aircraft 112A	K. D. Pearse	
G-KEEN	Stolp SA.300 Starduster Too	Sharp Aerobatics Ltd/Netherlands	
G-KEES	PA-28 Cherokee 180	C. N. Ellerbrook	
G-KEJY	Aerotechnik EV-97 TeamEurostar UK	Kemble Eurostar 1	
G-KELI	Robinson R44 Raven II	KN Network Services Ltd	
G-KELL	Van's RV-6	R. G. Stephens/Ireland	
G-KELS	Van's RV-7	J. Verroen	
G-KELV	Diamond DA42 Twin Star	K. K. Freeman (G-CTCH)	

Notes	Reg.	Type	Owner or Operator
	G-KELX	Van's RV-6	A. L. Burton (G-HAMY)
	G-KELZ	Van's RV-8	M. O'Leary (G-DJRV)
	G-KEMC	Grob G.109	Norfolk Gliding Club Ltd
	G-KEMI	PA-28-181 Archer III	Modern Air (UK) Ltd
	G-KEMY	Cessna 182T	Allen Aircraft Rental Ltd
	G-KENB	Air Command 503 Commander	K. Brogden
	G-KENG	Rotorsport UK MT-03	K. A. Graham
	G-KENI	Rotorway Executive	P. A. Taylor
	G-KENM	Luscombe 8EF Silvaire	M. G. Waters
	G-KENW	Robin DR400/500	K. J. White
	G-KENZ	Rutan Vari-Eze	K. M. McConnel I (G-BNUI)
	G-KEPE	Schempp-Hirth Nimbus 3DT	Nimbus Syndicate
	G-KEPP	Rans S.6-ES Coyote II	R. G. Johnston
	G-KERK	Piper J-3C-65 Cub	C. C. Kirk (G-OINK/G-BILD)
	G-KESS	Glaser-Dirks DG-400	M. T. Collins & T. Flude
	G-KEST	Steen Skybolt	G-KEST Syndicate
	G-KESY	Slingsby T.59D Kestrel	A. J. Whiteman & P. J. R. Hogarth
	G-KETH	Agusta-Bell 206B JetRanger 2	DAC Leasing Ltd
	G-KEVB	PA-28-181 Archer III	Palmair Ltd
	G-KEVG	Rotorsport UK MT-03	K. J. Robinson & R. N. Bodley
	G-KEVI	Jabiru J400	P. Horth & P. G. Macintosh
	G-KEVK	Flight Design CTSW	K. Kirby
	G-KEVL	Rotorway Executive 162F	K. D. Longhurst (G-CBIK)
	G-KEVZ	P & M Quik R	K. Mallin
	G-KEWT	Ultramagic M.90 balloon	R. F. Penney
	G-KEYS	PA-23 Aztec 250F	Giles Aviation Ltd
	G-KEYY	Cameron N-77 balloon	B. N. Trowbridge (G-BORZ)
	G-KFAN	Scheibe SF.25B Falke	R. G. & J. A. Boyes
	G-KFLY	Flight Design CTSW	G-KFLY Group (G-LFLY)
	G-KFOX	Denney Kitfox	I. R. Lawrence & R. Hampshire
	G-KFZI	KFZ-1 Tigerfalck	L. R. Williams
	G-KGAO	Scheibe SF.25C Falke 1700	Falke 2000 Group
	G-KHCC	Schempp-Hirth Ventus Bt	J. L. G. McLane
	G-KHCG	AS.355F2 Ecureuil II	London Helicopter Centres Ltd (G-SDAY/ G-SYPA/G-BPRE)
	G-KHEH	Grob G.109B	N. A. Tziros
	G-KHOM	Aeromot AMT-200 Super Ximango	Bowland Ximango Group
	G-KHOP	Zenair CH.601HDS Zodiac	K. Hopkins
	G-KHRE	MS.893E Rallye 150SV	Kingsmuir Group
	G-KICK	Pegasus Quantum 15-912	G. van der Gaag
	G-KIDD	Jabiru J430	R. L. Lidd (G-CEBB)
	G-KIEV	DKBA AT 0300-0 balloon	The Volga Balloon Team
	G-KIGR	Schleicher ASH-25E	G-KIGR ASH Syndicate
	G-KIII	Extra EA.300/L	Extra 200 Ltd
	G-KIKX	Cessna T.206H Turbo Stationair	Airkix Aircraft Ltd
	G-KIMA	Zenair CH.601XL Zodiac	L. D. Johnston
	G-KIMB	Robin DR.340/140	R. M. Kimbell
	G-KIMH	Rotorsport UK MTO Sport	P. B. Harrison
	G-KIMK	Partenavia P.68B	M. Konstantinovic (G-BCPO)
	G-KIMM	Shaw Europa XS	P. A. D. Clarke
	G-KIMY	Robin DR.400/140B	S. G. Jones
	G-KIRB	Europa XS	P. Handford (G-OIZI)
	G-KIRC	Pietenpol Air Camper	M. Kirk (G-BSVZ)
	G-KIRK	Piper J-3C-65 Cub	M. Kirk
	G-KISS	Rand-Robinson KR-2	E. A. Rooney
	G-KITF	Denney Kitfox	T. Wright
	G-KITH	Alpi Pioneer 300	K. G. Atkinson
	G-KITI	Pitts S-2E Special	B. R. Cornes
	G-KITS	Shaw Europa	J. R. Evernden
	G-KITT	Curtiss P-40M Kittyhawk (49)	P.A. Teichman
	G-KITY	Denney Kitfox Mk 2	Kitfox KFM Group
	G-KIZZ	Kiss 450-582	D. L. Price
	G-KJBS	CSA Sportcruiser	S. M. Lowe
	G-KKAM	Schleicher ASW-22BLE	D. P. Taylor
	G-KKAZ	Airbus A.320-214	Thomas Cook Airlines Ltd
	G-KKER	Avtech Jabiru SPL-450	E. A. Pearson

Reg.	Type	Owner or Operator	Notes
G-KKEV	DHC.8-402 Dash Eight	Flybe.com	
G-KLAW	Christen Eagle II	R. S. Goodwin & B. Lovering	
G-KLNB	Beech 300 Super King Air	Saxonair Charter Ltd	
G-KLNJ	Robinson R44 II	Saxonair Charter Ltd	
G-KLNK	Eurocopter EC135 P2+	Saxonair Charter Ltd (G-VGMB)	
G-KLNP	Eurocopter EC120B Colibri	Saxonair Charter Ltd	
G-KLNR	Hawker 400A	Saxonair Charter Ltd	
G-KLNW	Cessna 510 Citation Mustang	Saxonair Charter Ltd	
G-KLYE	Best Off Sky Ranger Swift 912S(1)	J. F. Murphy	
G-KMFW	Glaser-Dirks DG-800B	SSMT Group	
G-KMRV	Van-s RV-9A	G. K. Mutch	
G-KNCG	PA-32-301FT 6X	MJC Aviation Ltd	
G-KNEE	Ultramagic M-77C balloon	M. A. Green	
G-KNEK	Grob G.109B	Syndicate 109	
G-KNIB	Robinson R22 Beta II	C. G. Knibb	
G-KNIX	Cameron Z-315 balloon	Cameron Flights Southern Ltd	
G-KNOW	PA-32 Cherokee Six 300	A. S. Bansal	
G-KNYT	Robinson R44	Aircol	
G-KOBH	Schempp-Hirth Discus bT	C. F. M. Smith & K. Neave	
G-KOCO	Cirrus SR22	R. Fitzgerald	
G-KODA	Cameron O-77 balloon	K. Stamurs	
G-KOFM	Glaser-Dirks DG.600/18M	A. Mossman	
G-KOKL	Hoffmann H-36 Dimona	Dimona Syndicate	
G-KOLB	Kolb Twinstar Mk 3A	M. P. Wiseman	
G-KOLI	WSK PZL-110 Koliber 150	J. R. Powell	
G-KONG	Slingsby T.67M Firefly 200	R. C. Morton	
G-KOTA	PA-28-236 Dakota	H. C. L. & P. Greatrex	
G-KOYY	Schempp-Hirth Nimbus 4T	R. Kalin	
G-KPEI	Cessna 560XL Citation	Queensway Aviation Ltd	
G-KPLG	Schempp-Hirth Ventus 2cM	M. F. Lassan & A. C. Broadbridge	
G-KPTN	Dassault Falcon 50	TAG Aviation (UK) Ltd	
G-KRES	Stoddard-Hamilton Glasair IIS RG	A. D. Murray	
G-KRIB	Robinson R44 II	Cribarth Helicopters	
G-KRII	Rand-Robinson KR-2	M. R. Cleveley	
G-KRMA	Cessna 425 Corsair	Speedstar Holdings Ltd	
G-KRNW	Eurocopter EC 135T2	Bond Air Services Ltd	
G-KRUZ	CZAW Sportcruiser	A. W. Shellis & P. Whittingham	
G-KSFR	Bombardier BD-100-1A10 Challenger	The Lily Partnership LLP	
G-KSHI	Beech A36 Bonanza	Hangar 11 Collection	
G-KSIR	Stoddard-Hamilton Glasair IIS RG	K. M. Bowen	
G-KSIX	Schleicher Ka 6E	C. D. Sterritt	
G-KSKS	Cameron N-105 balloon	Kiss the Sky Ballooning	
G-KSKY	Sky 77-24 balloon	J. W. Dale	
G-KSSH	MDH MD-900 Explorer	Police Aviation Services Ltd (G-WMID)	
G-KSVB	PA-24 Comanche 260	Knockin Flying Club Ltd	
G-KSWI	Hughes 369E	K. S. Williams (G-OOCS/G-ODTB/G-BXUR)	
G-KTEE	Cameron V-77 balloon	A. Ruitenburg	
G-KTIA	Hawker 900XP	TAG Aviation (UK) Ltd	
G-KTKT	Sky 260-24 balloon	Adventure Balloons Ltd	
G-KTTY	Denney Kitfox Model 3	S. D. Morris (G-LESJ)	
G-KTWO	Cessna 182T	S. J. G. Mole	
G-KUGG	Schleicher ASW-27-18E	R. E. D. Bailey	
G-KUIK	Mainair Pegasus Quik	P. Nugent	
G-KUIP	CZAW Sportcruiser	A. J. Kuipers	
G-KUKI	Robinson R22 Beta	HJS Helicopters Ltd	
G-KULA	Best Off Skyranger 912ULS	G. S. Cridland	
G-KUPP	Flight Design CTSW	S. J. Peet	
G-KURK	Piper J3C-65 Cub	G. V. E. Kirk (G-BJTO)	
G-KUTI	Flight Design CTSW	D. F. & S. M. Kenny	
G-KUTU	Quickie Q.2	R. Nash & J. Parkinson	
G-KUUI	J-3C-65 Cub	V. S. E. Norman	
G-KVBF	Cameron A-340HL balloon	Virgin Balloon Flights	

Notes	Reg.	Type	Owner or Operator
	G-KVIP	Beech 200 Super King Air	Capital Air Charter Ltd
	G-KWAK	Scheibe SF.25C	Mendip Gliding Club Ltd
	G-KWIC	Mainair Pegasus Quik	B. F. Levy
	G-KWIN	Dassault Falcon 2000EX	Quinn Aviation Ltd
	G-KWKI	QAC Quickie Q.200	R. Greatrex
	G-KWKR	P and M Aviation QuikR	L. G. White
	G-KWLI	Cessna 421C	Langley Aviation Ltd (G-DARR/G-BNEZ)
	G-KXXI	Schleicher ASK-21	C. G. Bell
	G-KYLE	Thruster T600N 450	MKS Syndicate
	G-KYTE	Piper PA-28-161 Warrior II	G. Whitlow (G-BRRN)
	G-LABS	Shaw Europa	C. T. H. Pattinson
	G-LACA	PA-28-161 Warrior II	J. H. Mitchell
	G-LACB	PA-28-161 Warrior II	LAC Flying School
	G-LACC	Cameron C-90 balloon	Directorate Army Aviation
	G-LACD	PA-28-181 Archer III	Target Aviation Ltd (G-BYBG)
	G-LACI	Cessna 172S Skyhawk	L. Endresz
	G-LACR	Denney Kitfox	C. M. Rose
	G-LADD	Enstrom 480	Foscombe Transport LLP
	G-LADS	Rockwell Commander 114	D. F. Soul
	G-LADZ	Enstrom 480	Falcon Helicopters Ltd
	G-LAFF	Cameron TR-84 Srs.2 balloon	Balloonists Supporting Barretstown
	G-LAFT	Diamond DA40D Star	Atlantic Flight Training Ltd
	G-LAGR	Cameron N-90 balloon	J. R. Clifton
	G-LAID	Robinson R44 II	SARL Tolla Ciel
	G-LAIN	Robinson R22 Beta	Patriot Aviation Ltd
	G-LAIR	Stoddard-Hamilton Glasair IIS FT	A. I.O'Broin & S. T. Raby
	G-LAKE	Lake LA-250 Renegade	Lake Aviation Ltd
	G-LAKI	Jodel DR.1050	G. Cameron (G-JWBB)
	G-LALE	Embraer EMB-135BJ Legacy	London Executive Avition Ltd
	G-LAMM	Shaw Europa	S. A. Lamb
	G-LAMP	Cameron 110 Lampbulb SS balloon	S. A. Lacey
	G-LAMS	Cessna F.152 II	APB Leasing Ltd
	G-LANC	Avro 683 Lancaster X (KB889) ★	Imperial War Museum/Duxford
	G-LAND	Robinson R22 Beta	Heli Air Ltd
	G-LANE	Cessna F.172N	A. Holmes
	G-LANS	Cessna 182T	AK Enterprises Ltd
	G-LAOL	PA-28RT-201 Arrow IV	Arrow Flying Group
	G-LAPS	Lindstrand LBL 203T gas balloon	Lindstrand Aeroplatforms Ltd
	G-LARA	Robin DR.400/180	K. D. & C. A. Brackwell
	G-LARE	PA-39 Twin Comanche 160 C/R	Glareways (Neasden) Ltd
	G-LARK	Helton Lark 95	N. Huxtable & K Keen
	G-LARR	AS.350B3 Squirrel	Larsen Manufacturing Ltd
	G-LARY	Robinson R44 II	Air 86 SARL/France (G-CCRZ)
	G-LASN	Skyranger J2.2(1)	A. J. Coote
	G-LASR	Stoddard-Hamilton Glasair II	G. Lewis
	G-LASS	Rutan Vari-Eze	J. Mellor
	G-LASU	Eurocopter EC 135T2	Lancashire Constabulary Air Support Unit
	G-LATE	Falcon 2000EX	Hangar 8 Management Ltd
	G-LAVE	Cessna 172R	M. L. Roland (G-BYEV)
	G-LAWX	Sikorsky S-92A	Air Harrods Ltd
	G-LAZL	PA-28-161 Warrior II	Highland Aviation Training Ltd
	G-LAZR	Cameron O-77 balloon	Wickers World Ltd
	G-LAZZ	Stoddard-Hamilton Glastar	A. N. Evans
	G-LBAI	Eurocopter EC.155B1	Polaris Aviation Ltd
	G-LBDC	Bell 206B JetRanger III	Fresh Direct Travel Ltd
	G-LBMM	PA-28-161 Warrior II	M. A. Jones
	G-LBRC	PA-28RT-201 Arrow IV	D. J. V. Morgan
	G-LBUK	Lindstrand LBL-77A balloon	Morrison Design Ltd
	G-LBUZ	Aerotechnick EV-97A Eurostar	D. P. Tassart
	G-LCGL	Comper CLA.7 Swift (replica)	R. A. Fleming
	G-LCKY	Flight Design CTSW	G. D. Honey
	G-LCMW	TL 2000UK Sting Carbon	M. J. White & L. Chadwick
	G-LCOC	BN-2A Mk III Trislander	Blue Island Air
	G-LCOK	Colt 69A balloon	Hot-Air Balloon Co Ltd (G-BLWI)
	G-LCPL	AS.365N-2 Dauphin 2	Charterstyle Ltd
	G-LCUB	PA-18 Super Cub 95	The Tiger Club 1990 Ltd (G-AYPR)

Reg.	Type	Owner or Operator	Notes
G-LCYA	Dassault 900EX	Airport Management and Investment Ltd	
G-LCYD	Embraer ERJ170-100STD	BA Cityflyer Ltd	
G-LCYE	Embraer ERJ170-100STD	BA Cityflyer Ltd	
G-LCYF	Embraer ERJ170-100STD	BA Cityflyer Ltd	
G-LCYG	Embraer ERJ170-100STD	BA Cityflyer Ltd	
G-LCYH	Embraer ERJ170-100STD	BA Cityflyer Ltd	
G-LCYI	Embraer ERJ170-100STD	BA Cityflyer Ltd	
G-LCYJ	Embraer ERJ190-100SR	BA Cityflyer Ltd	
G-LCYK	Embraer ERJ190-100SR	BA Cityflyer Ltd	
G-LCYL	Embraer ERJ190-100SR	BA Cityflyer Ltd	
G-LCYM	Embraer ERJ190-100SR	BA Cityflyer Ltd	
G-LCYN	Embraer ERJ190-100SR	BA Cityflyer Ltd	
G-LCYO	Embraer ERJ190-100SR	BA Cityflyer Ltd	
G-LCYP	Embraer ERJ190-100SR	BA Cityflyer Ltd	
G-LDAH	Skyranger 912 (2)	P. D. Brookes & L. Dickinson	
G-LDER	Schleicher ASW-2	P. Shrosbree & D. Starer	
G-LDFM	Cessna 560XL Citation Excel	Granard Ltd	
G-LDVO	Europa Aviation Europa XS	D. J. Park	
G-LDWS	Jodel D.150	D. H. Wilson Spratt (G-BKSS)	
G-LDYS	Colt 56A balloon	M. J. Myddelton	
G-LEAA	Cessna 510 Citation Mustang	London Executive Aviation Ltd	
G-LEAB	Cessna 510 Citation Mustang	London Executive Aviation Ltd	
G-LEAC	Cessna 510 Citation Mustang	London Executive Aviation Ltd	
G-LEAF	Cessna F.406	Reconnaisance Ventures Ltd	
G-LEAH	Alpi Pioneer 300	A. Bortolan	
G-LEAI	Cessna 510	London Executive Aviation Ltd	
G-LEAM	PA-28-236 Dakota	G-LEAM Group (G-BHLS)	
G-LEAP	BN-2T Turbine Islander	Skydive Swansea Ltd	
G-LEAR	Learjet 35A	Agrevia Holdings Ltd (G-ZEST)	
G-LEAS	Sky 90-24 balloon	C. I. Humphrey	
G-LEAU	Cameron N-31 balloon	P. L. Mossman	
G-LEAX	Cessna 560XL Citation XLS	London Executive Aviation Ltd	
G-LEBE	Shaw Europa	P. Atkinson	
G-LECA	AS.355F1 Twin Squirrel	Western Power Distribution (South West) PLC (G-BNBK)	
G-LEDE	Zenair CH.601UL Zodiac	P. Boyle	
G-LEDR	Westland Gazelle HT.2	R. D. Leader (G-CBSB)	
G-LEED	Denney Kitfox Mk 2	S. J. Walker	
G-LEEE	Avtech Jabiru UL-450	J. P. Mimnagh	
G-LEEH	Ultramagic M-90 balloon	Sport Promotion SRL/Italy	
G-LEEJ	Hughes 369HS	L. Jones	
G-LEEK	Reality Escapade	Phoenix Group	
G-LEEN	Aero Designs Pulsar XP	R. B. Hemsworth (G-BZMP/G-DESI)	
G-LEES	Glaser-Dirks DG.400 (800)	Active Aviation Ltd	
G-LEEZ	Bell 206L-1 LongRanger 2	Pennine Helicopters Ltd (G-BPCT)	
G-LEGC	Embraer EMB-135BJ Legacy	Delos Engineering Corporation	
G-LEGG	Cessna F.182Q	W. A. L. Mitchell (G-GOOS)	
G-LEGO	Cameron O-77 balloon	P. M. Traviss	
G-LEGY	Flight Design CTLS	P. J. Clegg	
G-LELE	Lindstrand LBL-31A balloon	D. S. Wilson	
G-LEMI	Van's RV-8	The Lord Rotherwick	
G-LEMM	Ultramagic Z-90 balloon	M. Maranoni/Italy	
G-LENF	Mainair Blade 912S	G. D. Fuller	
G-LENI	AS.355F1 Twin Squirrel	Grid Defence Systems Ltd (G-ZFDB/G-BLEV)	
G-LENN	Cameron V-56 balloon	D. J. Groombridge	
G-LENS	Thunder Ax7-77Z balloon	R. S. Breakwell	
G-LENX	Cessna 172N	November XRay Ltd	
G-LEOD	Pietenpol Aircamper	I. D. McCleod	
G-LEOS	Robin DR.400/120	R. J. O. Walker	
G-LESH	BB Microlight BB03 Trya/Alien	L. R. Hodgson	
G-LESZ	Denney Kitfox Mk 5	J. C. Holland	
G-LETS	Vans RV-7	M. O'Hearne	
G-LEVI	Aeronca 7AC Champion	G-LEVI Group	
G-LEVO	Robinson R44 II	Leavesley Aviation Ltd	
G-LEXX	Van's RV-8	S. Emery	
G-LEXY	Van's RV-8	P. J. Clegg & M. J. Wood	
G-LEZE	Rutan LongEz	Bill Allen's Autos Ltd	
G-LFES	AB Sportine LAK-17B FES	P. C. Piggott	
G-LFIX	VS.509 Spitfire T.IX (ML407)	C. S. Grace	

Reg.	Type	Owner or Operator
G-LFOR	Piper J3C-65 Cub	A. Hoskins & J. C. Gowdy
G-LFPT	Cessna 510 Citation Mustang	Ambeo PLC
G-LFRS	MBB-BK 117 C-2	Eurocopter UK Ltd
G-LFSA	PA-38-112 Tomahawk	Liverpool Flying School Ltd (G-BSFC)
G-LFSB	PA-38-112 Tomahawk	J. D. Burford
G-LFSC	PA-28 Cherokee 140	P. G. Smith (G-BGTR)
G-LFSG	PA-28 Cherokee 180E	Liverpool Flying School Ltd (G-AYAA)
G-LFSH	PA-38-112 Tomahawk	Liverpool Flying School Ltd (G-BOZM)
G-LFSI	PA-28 Cherokee 140	Flying Group G-LFSI (G-AYKV)
G-LFSJ	PA-28-161 Warrior II	FlyBPL.com
G-LFSM	PA-38-112 Tomahawk	Liverpool Flying School Ltd (G-BWNR)
G-LFSN	PA-38-112 Tomahawk	Liverpool Flying School Ltd (G-BNYV)
G-LFSR	PA-28RT-201 Arrow IV	Liverpool Flying School Ltd (G-JANO)
G-LFVB	VS.349 Spitfire LF.Vb (EP120)	Patina Ltd
G-LGAR	Learjet 60	TAG Aviation (UK) Ltd
G-LGCA	Robin DR.400/180R	London Gliding Club Proprietary Ltd
G-LGCB	Robin DR.400/180R	London Gliding Club Proprietary Ltd
G-LGCC	Robin DR 400/180R	London Gliding Club Proprietary Ltd (G-BNXI)
G-LGEZ	Rutan Long-EZ	P. C. Elliott
G-LGKD	Gulfstream 550	TAG Aviation (UK) Ltd
G-LGLG	Cameron Z-210 balloon	Flying Circus SRL/Spain
G-LGNA	SAAB SF.340B	Loganair Ltd/Flybe.com
G-LGNB	SAAB SF.340B	Loganair Ltd/Flybe.com
G-LGNC	SAAB SF.340B	Loganair Ltd/Flybe.com
G-LGND	SAAB SF.340B	Loganair Ltd/Flybe.com (G-GNTH)
G-LGNE	SAAB SF.340B	Loganair Ltd/Flybe.com (G-GNTI)
G-LGNF	SAAB SF.340B	Loganair Ltd/Flybe.com (G-GNTJ)
G-LGNG	SAAB SF.340B	Loganair Ltd/Flybe.com
G-LGNH	SAAB SF.340B	Loganair Ltd/Flybe.com
G-LGNI	SAAB SF.340B	Loganair Ltd/Flybe.com
G-LGNJ	SAAB SF.340B	Loganair Ltd/Flybe.com
G-LGNK	SAAB SF.340B	Loganair Ltd/Flybe.com
G-LGNL	SAAB SF.340B	Loganair Ltd/Flybe.com
G-LGNM	SAAB SF.340B	Loganair Ltd/Flybe.com
G-LGNN	SAAB SF.340B	Loganair Ltd/Flybe.com
G-LGOC	Aero AT-3 R100	London Transport Flying Club Ltd
G-LHCA	Robinson R22 Beta	London Helicopter Centres Ltd
G-LHCB	Robinson R22 Beta	London Helicopter Centres Ltd (G-SIVX)
G-LHCI	Bell 47G-5	Heli-Highland Ltd (G-SOLH/G-AZMB)
G-LHEL	AS.355F2 Twin Squirrel	Beechview Aviation Ltd
G-LHER	Czech Sport Aircraft Piper Sport	M. P. Lhermette
G-LHMS	Eurocopter EC 120B Colibri	Hadley Helicopters Ltd
G-LHXL	Robinson R44	Lloyd Helicopters Europe Ltd
G-LIBB	Cameron V-77 balloon	R. J. Mercer
G-LIBI	Glasflugel Standard Libelle 201B	G. Spreckley
G-LIBL	Glasflugel Standard Libelle 201B	P. A. Pearson
G-LIBS	Hughes 369HS	R. J. H. Strong
G-LIBY	Glasflugel Standard Libelle 201B	R. P. Hardcastle
G-LICK	Cessna 172N II	Sky Back Ltd (G-BNTR)
G-LIDA	Hoffmann H36 Dimona	Bidford Airfield Ltd
G-LIDE	PA-31-350 Navajo Chieftain	Blue Sky Investments Ltd
G-LIDY	Schleicher ASW-27B	T. Stuart
G-LIGA	Kubicek BB-S/Fish balloon	I. Charbonnier
G-LIKE	Europa	N. G. Henry (G-CHAV)
G-LILA	Bell 206L-1 LongRanger 2	Lothian Helicopters Ltd (G-NEUF/G-BVVV)
G-LILP	Shaw Europa XS	G. L. Jennings
G-LILY	Bell 206B JetRanger 3	T. S. Brown (G-NTBI)
G-LIMO	Bell 206L-1 LongRanger	Heliplayer Ltd
G-LIMP	Cameron C-80 balloon	T. & B. Chamberlain
G-LINE	AS.355N Twin Squirrel	National Grid Electricity Transmission PLC
G-LINN	Shaw Europa XS	T. Pond
G-LINS	Robinson R22 Beta	Rotorum (G-DMCD/G-OOLI)
G-LIOA	Lockheed 10A ElectraH (NC5171N) ★	Science Museum/South Kensington
G-LION	PA-18 Super Cub 135 (R-167)	JG Jones Haulage Ltd
G-LIOT	Cameron O-77 balloon	N. D. Eliot
G-LIPE	Robinson R22 Beta	Heliservices (G-BTXJ)
G-LIPS	Cameron 90 Lips SS balloon	Reach For The Sky Ltd (G-BZBV)
G-LISS	AutoGyro UK Calidus	J. M. & M. J. Newman
G-LITE	Rockwell Commander 112A	B. G. Rhodes

Reg.	Type	Owner or Operator	Notes
G-LITS	P & M Quik R	A. Dixon	
G-LITZ	Pitts S-1E Special	H. J. Morton	
G-LIVH	Piper J-3C-65 Cub (330238:A-24)	U. E. Allman	
G-LIVS	Schleicher ASH-26E	P. O. Sturley	
G-LIVY	Beech B.200 Super King Air	Dragonfly Aviation Services LLP (G-PSTR)	
G-LIZI	PA-28 Cherokee 160	G-LIZI Group (G-ARRP)	
G-LIZY	Westland Lysander III (V9673) ★	G. A. Warner/Duxford	
G-LIZZ	PA-E23 Aztec 250E	I. Kazi & T. J. Nathan (G-BBWM)	
G-LJCC	Murphy Rebel	P. H. Hyde	
G-LKTB	PA-28-181 Archer III	L. D. Charles & J. J. Kennedy	
G-LLCH	Cessna 172S	N. A. Smith (G-PLBI)	
G-LLEW	Aeromot AMT-200S Super Ximango	Echo Whiskey Ximango Syndicate	
G-LLIZ	Robinson R44 II	W. R. Harford	
G-LLLL	Rolladen-Schneider LS8-18	P. C. Fritche	
G-LLMW	Diamond DA42 Twin Star	Ming W. L.	
G-LLOY	Alpi Pioneer 300	A. R. Lloyd	
G-LMBO	Robinson R44	Thurston Helicopters Ltd	
G-LMLV	Dyn'Aéro MCR-01	G-LMLV Flying Group	
G-LNAA	MDH MD-900 Explorer	Police Aviation Services Ltd	
G-LNCT	MDH MD-900 Explorer	Police Aviation Services Ltd	
G-LNDS	Robinson R44	MC Air Ltd	
G-LNIG	Flylight Dragonfly	N. R. Henry	
G-LNKS	BAe Jetstream 3102	K. Ibbotson (G-JURA)	
G-LOAD	Dan Rihn DR.107 One Design	M. J. Clark	
G-LOAM	Flylight MotorFloater	M. F. Cowlishaw	
G-LOAN	Cameron N-77 balloon	P. Lawman	
G-LOBO	Cameron O-120 balloon	Solo Aerostatics	
G-LOCH	Piper J-3C-65 Cub	M. C. & M. R. Greenland	
G-LOFB	Lockheed L.188CF Electra	Atlantic Airlines Ltd	
G-LOFC	Lockheed L.188CF Electra	Atlantic Airlines Ltd	
G-LOFE	Lockheed L.188CF Electra	Atlantic Airlines Ltd	
G-LOFM	Maule MX-7-180A	Air Atlantique Ltd	
G-LOFT	Cessna 500 Citation I	Fox Tango (Jersey) Ltd	
G-LOIS	Avtech Jabiru UL	D. W. Newman	
G-LOKI	Ultramagic M-77C balloon	L. J. M. Muir & G. D. Hallett	
G-LOLA	Beech A36 Bonanza	K. Payne	
G-LONE	Bell 206L-1 LongRanger	Central Helicopters Ltd	
G-LOOC	Cessna 172S	Goodwood Road Racing Co.Ltd	
G-LOON	Cameron C-60 balloon	C. Wolstenholme	
G-LOOP	Pitts S-1C Special	D. Shutter	
G-LORC	PA-28-161 Cadet	Sherburn Aero Club Ltd	
G-LORD	PA-34-200T Seneca II	H. E. Held-Ruf	
G-LORN	Avions Mudry CAP-10B	D. G. R. & P. M. Wansbrough	
G-LORR	PA-28-181 Archer III	Shropshire Aero Club Ltd	
G-LORT	Light Aero Avid Speedwing 4	L. M. Thomas	
G-LORY	Thunder Ax4-31Z balloon	A. J. Moore	
G-LOSI	Cameron Z-105 balloon	Aeropubblicita Vicenza SRL/Italy	
G-LOSM	Gloster Meteor NF.11 (WM167)	Aviation Heritage Ltd	
G-LOST	Denney Kitfox Mk 3	J. H. S. Booth	
G-LOSY	Aerotechnik EV-97 Eurostar	C. D. Reeves	
G-LOTA	Robinson R44	Rahtol Ltd	
G-LOTI	Bleriot XI (replica) ★	Brooklands Museum Trust Ltd	
G-LOVB	BAe Jetstream 3102	Sky Aeronautical Ltd (G-BLCB)	
G-LOWS	Sky 77-24 balloon	A. J. Byrne & D. J. Bellinger	
G-LOWZ	P & M Quik GT450	P. R. Biggs	
G-LOYA	Cessna FR.172J	K. A. D. Mitchell (G-BLVT)	
G-LOYD	Aérospatiale SA.341G Gazelle 1	I. G. Lloyd (G-SFTC)	
G-LOYN	Robinson R44 II	C. J. Siva-Jothy	
G-LPAD	Lindstrand LBL-105A balloon	Line Packaging & Display Ltd	
G-LPIN	P & M Aviation Quik R	Arnold Gilpin Associates Ltd	
G-LREE	Grob G.109B	G-LREE Group	
G-LRGE	Lindstrand LBL-330A balloon	Adventure Balloons Ltd	
G-LRSN	Robinson R44	D. M. McGarrity	

Notes	Reg.	Type	Owner or Operator
	G-LSAA	Boeing 757-236	Jet 2 (G-BNSF)
	G-LSAB	Boeing 757-27B	Jet 2 (G-OAHF)
	G-LSAC	Boeing 757-23A	Jet 2
	G-LSAD	Boeing 757-236	Jet 2 (G-OOOS/G-BRJD)
	G-LSAE	Boeing 757-27B	Jet 2
	G-LSAG	Boeing 757-21B	Jet 2
	G-LSAH	Boeing 757-21B	Jet 2
	G-LSAI	Boeing 757-21B	Jet 2
	G-LSAJ	Boeing 757-236	Jet 2 (G-CDUP/G-OOOT/G-BRJJ)
	G-LSAK	Boeing 757-23N	Jet 2
	G-LSAL	Boeing 757-204	Jet 2 (G-BYAI)
	G-LSAM	Boeing 757-204	Jet 2 (G-BYAH)
	G-LSCM	Cessna 172S	G. A. Luscombe
	G-LSCP	Rolladen-Schneider LS6-18W	L. G. Blows & M. F. Collins
	G-LSED	Rolladen-Schneider LS6-c	McKnight/Baker Syndicate
	G-LSFB	Rolladen-Schneider LS7-WL	P. Thomson
	G-LSFI	AA-5A Cheetah	J. Ibbotson (G-BGSK)
	G-LSFR	Rolladen-Schneider LS4	A. Mulder
	G-LSFT	PA-28-161 Warrior II	Biggin Hill Flying Club Ltd (G-BXTX)
	G-LSGB	Rolladen-Schneider LS6-b	T. J. Brenton
	G-LSGM	Rolladen-Schneider LS3-17	M. R. W. Crook
	G-LSHI	Colt 77A balloon	J. H. Dobson
	G-LSIF	Rolladen-Schneider LS1-f	R. C. Godden
	G-LSIV	Rolladen-Schneider LS4	264 Syndicate
	G-LSIX	Rolladen-Schneider LS6-18W	D. P. Masson & A. V. W. Nunn
	G-LSJE	Escapade Jabiru(1)	L. S. J. Webb
	G-LSKV	Rolladen-Schneider LS8-18	D. Pitman
	G-LSKY	Mainair Pegasus Quik	G. R. Hall & P. R. Brooker
	G-LSLS	Rolladen-Schneider LS4	288 Syndicate
	G-LSMB	Dassault Falcon 2000EX	Aviation Beauport Ltd
	G-LSPH	Van's RV-8	R. S. Partridge-Hicks
	G-LSTR	Stoddard-Hamilton Glastar	A. Vaughan
	G-LSVI	Rolladen-Schneider LS6-c18	J. Saakwa-Mante
	G-LTFB	PA-28 Cherokee 140	Polishing Consulting Ltd (G-AVLU)
	G-LTFC	PA-28 Cherokee 140B	N. M. G. Pearson (G-AXTI)
	G-LTRF	Sportavia Fournier RF-7	D. Radewald (G-EHAP)
	G-LTSB	Cameron LTSB-90 balloon	ABC Flights Ltd
	G-LTWA	Robinson R44	L. T. W. Alderman
	G-LUBB	Cessna 525 Citationjet	Hangar 8 Management Ltd
	G-LUBE	Cameron N-77 balloon	A. C. K. Rawson
	G-LUBY	Jabiru J430	K. Luby
	G-LUCI	Robinson R44 II	ABO Services Ltd (G-CULF)
	G-LUCK	Cessna F.150M	MK Consulting Engineers Ltd
	G-LUCL	Colomban MC-30 Luciole	R. C. Teverson
	G-LUDM	Van's RV-8	D. F. Sargant
	G-LUED	Aero Designs Pulsar	J. C. Anderson
	G-LUEK	Cessna 182T	B. F. Lueken
	G-LUEY	Rans S-7S Courier	S. Garfield
	G-LUKE	Rutan LongEz	R. A. Pearson
	G-LUKY	Robinson R44	Hack Aviation and Executive Aviation Services Ltd
	G-LULA	Cameron C-90 balloon	S. D. Davis
	G-LULU	Grob G.109	A. P. Bowden
	G-LULV	Diamond DA-42 Twin Star	Deltabond Ltd
	G-LUNE	Mainair Pegasus Quik	D. Muir
	G-LUNG	Rotorsport UK MT-03	P. Krysiak & R. H. Sawyer
	G-LUNY	Pitts S-1S Special	G-LUNY Group
	G-LUON	Schleicher ASW-27-18E	P. C. Naegeli
	G-LUPY	Marganski Swift S-1	P. R. J. Conran
	G-LUSC	Luscombe 8E Silvaire	M. Fowler
	G-LUSH	PA-28-151 Warrior	S. S. Bamrah
	G-LUSI	Luscombe 8F Silvaire	P. H. Isherwood
	G-LUSK	Luscombe 8F Silvaire	M. A. Lamprell & P. J. Laycock (G-BRGG)
	G-LUST	Luscombe 8E Silvaire	C. J. Watson
	G-LUXE	BAe 146-301	BAE Systems (Operations) Ltd (G-SSSH)
	G-LUXY	Cessna 551 Citation IISP	Longhan Ltd
	G-LVBF	Lindstrand LBL-330A balloon	Virgin Balloon Flights
	G-LVDC	Bell 206L Long Ranger III	Freshair UK Ltd (G-OFST/G-BXIB)
	G-LVES	Cessna 182S	R. W. & A. M. Glaves (G-ELIE)
	G-LVLV	Canadair CL.604 Challenger	Gama Aviation Ltd

Reg.	Type	Owner or Operator	Notes
G-LVPL	Edge XT912 B/Streak III/B	C. D. Connor	
G-LWDC	Canadair CL600-2A12 Challenger	African Petroleum Ltd	
G-LWNG	Aero Designs Pulsar	A. B. Wood (G-OMKF)	
G-LXUS	Alpi Pioneer 300	W. C. Walters	
G-LYAK	IDA Bacau Yakovlev Yak-52	M. Laub	
G-LYDA	Hoffmann H-36 Dimona	G-LYDA Flying Group	
G-LYDF	PA-31-350 Navajo Chieftain	Atlantic Bridge Aviation Ltd	
G-LYDS	Schempp-Hirth Nimbus 3T	D. H. Smith	
G-LYFA	IDABacau Yakovlev Yak-52	Fox Alpha Group	
G-LYNC	Robinson R22 Beta II	Subacoustech Ltd	
G-LYND	PA-25 Pawnee 235	York Gliding Centre Ltd (G-ASFX/G-BSFZ)	
G-LYNI	Aerotechnik EV-97 Eurostar	G. Evans	
G-LYNK	CFM Shadow Srs DD	B. A. Richards	
G-LYNX	Westland WG.13 Lynx (ZB500)	IHM/Weston-super-Mare	
G-LYPG	Avtech Jabiru UL	A. J. Geary	
G-LYSA	Schleicher ASW-20L	L. A. Humphries	
G-LYTE	Thunder Ax7-77 balloon	G. M. Bulme	
G-LZED	AutoGyro MTO Sport	L. Zivanovic	
G-LZII	Laser Z200	K. G. Begley	
G-LZZY	PA-28RT-201T Turbo Arrow IV	A. C. Gradidge (G-BMHZ)	
G-MAAM	CFM Shadow Srs.C	S. J. Halliwell (G-MTCA)	
G-MAAN	Shaw Europa XS	P. S. Mann	
G-MAAX	Bell 206L-1 LongRanger 2	Lothian Helicopters Ltd (G-EYLE/G-OCRP/G-BWCU)	
G-MABE	Cessna F.150L	I. D. McClelland (G-BLJP)	
G-MACA	Robinson R22 Beta	Jepar Rotorcraft	
G-MACE	Hughes 369E	West Country Helicopters Ltd	
G-MACH	SIAI-Marchetti SF.260	Cheyne Motors Ltd	
G-MACK	PA-28R Cherokee Arrow 200-II	M. D. Hinge	
G-MACN	Cirrus SR22	J. D. M. Tickell	
G-MACP	Bombardier CL600-2B16 Challenger	Ocean Sky Aircraft Management Ltd (G-CGFF/G-OCSF)	
G-MADV	P & M Quik GT450	D. A. Valentine	
G-MAFA	Cessna F.406	Directflight Ltd (G-DFLT)	
G-MAFB	Cessna F.406	Directflight Ltd	
G-MAFE	Dornier 228-202K	FR Aviation Ltd (G-OALF/G-MLDO)	
G-MAFF	BN-2T Turbine Islander	FR Aviation Ltd (G-BJEO)	
G-MAFI	Dornier 228-202K	FR Aviation Ltd	
G-MAFT	Diamond DA.40 Star	Atlantic Flight Training Ltd	
G-MAGC	Cameron Grand Illusion SS balloon	Magical Adventures Ltd	
G-MAGG	Pitts S-1SE Special	O. T. Elmer	
G-MAGK	Schleicher ASW-20L	A. G. K. Mackenzie	
G-MAGL	Sky 77-24 balloon	RCM SRL/Luxembourg	
G-MAGZ	Robin DR.400/500	T. J. Thomas	
G-MAIE	PA-32RT-301T Turbo Saratoga II TC	Sub Marine Services Ltd	
G-MAIK	PA-34-220T Seneca V	Air Prive SA	
G-MAIN	Mainair Blade 912	G. L. Logan	
G-MAIR	PA-34-200T Seneca II	Bristol Flying Centre Ltd	
G-MAJA	BAe Jetstream 4102	Eastern Airways	
G-MAJB	BAe Jetstream 4102	Eastern Airways (G-BVKT)	
G-MAJC	BAe Jetstream 4102	Eastern Airways (G-LOGJ)	
G-MAJD	BAe Jetstream 4102	Eastern Airways (G-WAWR)	
G-MAJE	BAe Jetstream 4102	Eastern Airways (G-LOGK)	
G-MAJF	BAe Jetstream 4102	Eastern Airways (G-WAWL)	
G-MAJG	BAe Jetstream 4102	Eastern Airways (G-LOGL)	
G-MAJH	BAe Jetstream 4102	Eastern Airways (G-WAYR)	
G-MAJI	BAe Jetstream 4102	Eastern Airways (G-WAND)	
G-MAJJ	BAe Jetstream 4102	Eastern Airways (G-WAFT)	
G-MAJL	BAe Jetstream 4102	Eastern Airways	
G-MAJR	DHC.1 Chipmunk 22 (WP805)	Chipmunk Shareholders	
G-MAJS	Airbus A.300B4-605R	Monarch Airlines Ltd	
G-MAJU	BAe Jetstream 4100	Eastern Airways	
G-MAJW	BAe Jetstream 4100	Eastern Airways	
G-MAJY	BAe Jetstream 4100	Eastern Airways	
G-MAJZ	BAe Jetstream 4100	Eastern Airways	
G-MAKE	Rotorsport UK Calidus	P. M. Ford	
G-MAKI	Robinson R44	Hoe Leasing Ltd	

Notes	Reg.	Type	Owner or Operator
	G-MAKK	Aeroprakt A22-L Foxbat	M. A. McKillop
	G-MAKS	Cirrus SR22	C. S. Mullan
	G-MALA	PA-28-181 Archer II	M. & D. Anstee (G-BIIU)
	G-MALC	AA-5 Traveler	B. P. Hogan (G-BCPM)
	G-MALS	Mooney M.20K-231	P. Mouterde
	G-MALT	Colt Flying Hop SS balloon	P. J. Stapley
	G-MANC	BAe ATP	Trident Aviation Leasing Services (Jersey) Ltd (G-LOGF)
	G-MANH	BAe ATP	Atlantic Airlines Ltd (G-LOGC/G-OLCC)
	G-MANN	Aérospatiale SA.341G Gazelle 1	MW Helicopters Ltd
	G-MANO	BAe ATP	Atlantic Airlines Ltd (G-UIET)
	G-MANW	Tri-R Kis	M. T. Manwaring
	G-MANX	FRED Srs 2	S. Styles
	G-MANZ	Robinson R44 II	Steve Hill Ltd
	G-MAPP	Cessna 402B	Reconnaisance Ventures Ltd
	G-MAPR	Beech A36 Bonanza	M. J. B. Cozens
	G-MARA	Airbus A.321-231	Monarch Airlines Ltd
	G-MARE	Schweizer 269C	The Earl of Caledon
	G-MARO	Skyranger J2.2 (2)	J. F. Northey
	G-MARZ	Thruster T.600N 450	S. W. Plume
	G-MASC	Jodel 150A	K. F. & R. Richardson
	G-MASF	PA-28-181 Archer II	Mid-Anglia School of Flying
	G-MASH	Westland-Bell 47G-4A	Kinetic Avionics Ltd (G-AXKU)
	G-MASI	P & M Quik GT450	D. M. Merritt-Holman
	G-MASS	Cessna 152 II	MK Aero Support Ltd (G-BSHN)
	G-MATE	Moravan Zlin Z.50LX	S. A. W. Becker
	G-MATS	Colt GA-42 airship	P. A. Lindstrand
	G-MATT	Robin R.2160	Flew LLP (G-BKRC)
	G-MATY	Robinson R22 Beta	MT Aviation
	G-MATZ	PA-28 Cherokee 140	Midland Air Training School (G-BASI)
	G-MAUK	Colt 77A balloon	B. Meeson
	G-MAUS	Shaw Europa XS	A. P. Ringrose
	G-MAVI	Robinson R22 Beta	Northumbria Helicopters Ltd
	G-MAVV	Aero AT-3 R100	Medcentres Property Portfolio Ltd
	G-MAXG	Pitts S-1S Special	MAXG Group
	G-MAXI	PA-34-200T Seneca II	Draycott Seneca Syndicate Ltd
	G-MAXS	Mainair Pegasus Quik 912S	W. J. Walker
	G-MAXV	Van's RV-4	R. S. Partridge-Hicks
	G-MAYB	Robinson R44	Highmark Aviation Ltd
	G-MAYE	Bell 407	M. Maye
	G-MAZA	Rotorsport UK MT-03	N. Crownshaw & M. Manson
	G-MAZY†	DH.82A Tiger Moth ★	Newark Air Museum
	G-MBAA	Hiway Skytrike Mk 2	M. J. Aubrey
	G-MBAB	Hovey Whing-Ding II	M. J. Aubrey
	G-MBAD	Weedhopper JC-24A	M. Stott
	G-MBAF	R. J. Swift 3	C. G. Wrzesien
	G-MBAW	Pterodactyl Ptraveller	J. C. K. Scardifield
	G-MBBB	Skycraft Scout 2	A. J. & B. Chalkley
	G-MBBJ	Hiway Demon	M. J. Aubrey
	G-MBBM	Eipper Quicksilver MX	J. Brown
	G-MBCJ	Mainair Sports Tri-Flyer	R. A. Smith
	G-MBCK	Eipper Quicksilver MX	P. Rowbotham
	G-MBCL	Sky-Trike/Typhoon	P. J. Callis
	G-MBCX	Airwave Nimrod 165	M. Maylor
	G-MBDG	Eurowing Goldwing	A. J. Glynn
	G-MBDL	AES Lone Ranger ★	North East Aircraft Museum
	G-MBDM	Southdown Sigma Trike	A. R. Prentice
	G-MBET	MEA Mistral Trainer	B. H. Stephens
	G-MBGF	Twamley Trike	T. B. Woolley
	G-MBHE	American Aerolights Eagle	R. J. Osborne
	G-MBHK	Flexiform Skytrike	K. T. Vinning
	G-MBHZ	Pterodactyl Ptraveller	J. C. K. Scardifield
	G-MBIA	Flexiform Sealander Skytrike	I. P. Cook
	G-MBIT	Hiway Demon Skytrike	K. S. Hodgson
	G-MBIZ	Mainair Tri-Flyer	D. M. A. Templeman/E. F. C. Clapham/ S. P. Slade/W. B. S. Dobie
	G-MBJF	Hiway Skytrike Mk II	C. H. Bestwick
	G-MBJK	American Aerolights Eagle	B. W. Olley
	G-MBJL	Airwave Nimrod	A. G. Lowe
	G-MBJM	Striplin Lone Ranger	C. K. Brown
	G-MBKY	American Aerolight Eagle	M. J. Aubrey

Reg.	Type	Owner or Operator	Notes
G-MBKZ	Hiway Skytrike	S. I. Harding	
G-MBLU	Southdown Lightning L.195	C. R. Franklin	
G-MBMG	Rotec Rally 2B	J. R. Pyper	
G-MBOF	Pakes Jackdaw	L. G. Pakes	
G-MBOH	Microlight Engineering Mistral	N. A. Bell	
G-MBPB	Pterodactyl Ptraveller	N. A. Bell	
G-MBPJ	Moto-Delta	J. B. Jackson	
G-MBPX	Eurowing Goldwing	A. R. Channon	
G-MBRB	Electraflyer Eagle 1	R. C. Bott	
G-MBRD	American Aerolights Eagle	R. J. Osborne	
G-MBRH	Ultraflight Mirage Mk II	R. W. F. Boarder	
G-MBSJ	American Aerolights Eagle 215B	T. J. Gayton-Polley	
G-MBSX	Ultraflight Mirage II	C. J. Draper	
G-MBTH	Whittaker MW4	M. W. J. Whittaker	
G-MBTJ	Solar Wings Microlight	H. A. Comber	
G-MBTW	Raven Vector 600	W. A. Fuller	
G-MBUZ	Wheeler Scout Mk II	A. C. Thorne	
G-MBYI	Ultraflight Lazair	C. M. Mackinnon	
G-MBYM	Eipper Quicksilver MX	M. P. Harper & L. L. Perry	
G-MBZO	Tri-Pacer 330	A. N. Burrows	
G-MBZV	American Aerolights Eagle	M. J. Aubrey	
G-MCAB	Gardan GY-201 Minicab	P. G. Hooper	
G-MCAI	Robinson R44 II	M. C. Allen	
G-MCAN	Agusta A109S Grand	Cannon Air LLP	
G-MCAP	Cameron C-80 balloon	L. D. Pickup	
G-MCCF	Thruster T.600N	C. C. F. Fuller	
G-MCCY	IDA Bacau Yakolev Yak-52	D. P. McCoy/Ireland	
G-MCDB	VS.361 Spitfire LF.IX	M. Collenette	
G-MCEL	Pegasus Quantum 15-912	F. Hodgson	
G-MCJL	Pegasus Quantum 15-912	Lincoln Enterprises Ltd	
G-MCLY	Cessna 172P	McAully Flying Group Ltd	
G-MCMC	SOCATA TBM-700	SogestaoAdministraca Gerencia SA	
G-MCMS	Aero Designs Pulsar	R. J. Bost	
G-MCOW	Lindstrand LBL-77A balloon	S. & S. Villiers	
G-MCOX	Fuji FA.200-180AO	W. Surrey Engineering (Shepperton) Ltd	
G-MCPI	Bell 206B JetRanger 3	Castle Air Charters Ltd (G-ONTB)	
G-MCPR	PA-32-301T Turbo Saratoga	M. C. Plomer-Roberts (G-MOLL)	
G-MCRO	Dyn'Aero MCR-01	G. Hawkins	
G-MCUB	Escapade	W. H. Bliss	
G-MCXV	Colomban MC.15 Cri-Cri	P. C. Appleton	
G-MDAC	PA-28-181 Archer II	S. A. Nicklen	
G-MDAY	Cessna 170B	M. Day	
G-MDBA	Dassault Falcon 2000	Execujet (UK) Ltd	
G-MDBC	Pegasus Quantum 15-912	J. H. Bradbury	
G-MDBD	Airbus A.330-243	Thomas Cook Airlines Ltd	
G-MDDT	Robinson R44 II	M. D. Tracey	
G-MDGE	Robinson R22 Beta	C. J. Siva-Jothy (G-OGOG/G-TILL)	
G-MDJE	Cessna 208 Caravan 1 (amphibian)	Loch Lomond Seaplanes Ltd	
G-MDJN	Beech 95-B55 Baron	WAFO Schnecken und Zylinder GmbH (G-SUZI/G-BAXR)	
G-MDKD	Robinson R22 Beta	Euro Systems Projects Ltd	
G-MDPI	Agusta A109A-II	Langfast Ltd (G-PERI/G-EXEK/G-SLNE/ G-EEVS/G-OTSL)	
G-MEDF	Airbus A.321-231	bmi British Midland	
G-MEDG	Airbus A.321-231	bmi British Midland	
G-MEDH	Airbus A.320-232	bmi British Midland	
G-MEDJ	Airbus A.321-232	bmi British Midland	
G-MEDK	Airbus A.320-232	bmi British Midland	
G-MEDL	Airbus A.321-231	bmi British Midland	
G-MEDM	Airbus A.321-231	bmi British Midland	
G-MEDN	Airbus A.321-231	bmi British Midland	
G-MEDU	Airbus A.321-231	bmi British Midland	
G-MEDX	Agusta A109E Power	Sloane Helicopters Ltd	
G-MEEE	Schleicher ASW-20L	T. E. Macfadyen	
G-MEET	Learjet 40	TAG Aviation (UK) Ltd	
G-MEGA	PA-28R-201T Turbo Arrow III	H. de Vries	
G-MEGG	Shaw Europa XS	M. E. Mavers	
G-MEGN	Beech B200 Super King Air	Dragonfly Aviation Services LLP	
G-MEGS	Cessna 172S	The Cambridge Aero Club Ltd	

Notes	Reg.	Type	Owner or Operator
	G-MEHR	Robinson R44 II	M. Karimi
	G-MELL	CZAW Sportcruiser	G. A. & J. A. Mellins
	G-MELS	PA-28-181 Archer III	P. J. Sowood
	G-MELT	Cessna F.172H	Falcon Aviation Ltd (G-AWTI)
	G-MEME	PA-28R-201 Arrow III	Henry J. Clare Ltd
	G-MENU	Robinson R44 II	Eagles in Flight Ltd
	G-MEOW	CFM Streak Shadow	G. J. Moor
	G-MEPU	Rotorsport UK MT-03	M. C. Elliott
	G-MERC	Colt 56A balloon	A. F. & C. D. Selby
	G-MERE	Lindstrand LBL-77A balloon	R. D. Baker
	G-MERF	Grob G.115A	G-MERF Group
	G-MERL	PA-28RT-201 Arrow IV	W. T. Jenkins
	G-MESH	CZAW Sportcruiser	M. E. S. Heaton
	G-METH	Cameron C-90 balloon	A. & D. Methley
	G-MEUP	Cameron A-120 balloon	I. Bentley
	G-MFAC	Cessna F.172H	Cezzy Flying Group (G-AVGZ)
	G-MFEF	Cessna FR.172J	M. & E. N. Ford
	G-MFHI	Shaw Europa	Hi Fliers
	G-MFLA	Robin HR200/120B	Multiflight Ltd (G-HHUK)
	G-MFLB	Robin HR200/120B	Multiflight Ltd (G-BXOR)
	G-MFLC	Robin HR200/120B	Multiflight Ltd (G-BXGW)
	G-MFLE	Robin HR200/120B	Multiflight Ltd (G-BYLH)
	G-MFLI	Cameron V-90 balloon	J. M. Percival
	G-MFLJ	P & M Quik GT450	M. F. Jakeman
	G-MFLM	Cessna F.152 II	Multiflight Ltd (G-BFFC)
	G-MFLY	Mainair Rapier	J. J. Tierney
	G-MFMF	Bell 206B JetRanger 3	Western Power Distribution (South West) PLC (G-BJNJ)
	G-MFMM	Scheibe SF.25C Falke	J. E. Selman
	G-MGAG	Aviasud Mistral 532GB	S. B. Love
	G-MGAN	Robinson R44	FlyBPL.com
	G-MGAP	Pipistrel Virus 912 SW100	MGAP (UK) LLP
	G-MGCA	Jabiru Aircraft Jabiru UL	K. D. Pearce
	G-MGCB	Pegasus XL-Q	M. G. Gomez
	G-MGCK	Whittaker MW6-S FT	A. Chidlow & M. W. J. Whittaker
	G-MGDL	Pegasus Quantum 15	M. J. Buchanan
	G-MGEC	Rans S.6-ESD-XL Coyote II	Mike and Andy Group
	G-MGEF	Pegasus Quantum 15	G. D. Castell
	G-MGFK	Pegasus Quantum 15	F. A. A. Kay
	G-MGGG	Pegasus Quantum 15	R. A. Beauchamp
	G-MGGT	CFM Streak Shadow SAM	D. R. Stansfield
	G-MGGV	Pegasus Quantum 15-912	K. Loder
	G-MGIC	Ace Magic Cyclone	K. A. Armstrong
	G-MGMM	PA-18 Super Cub 150	Alice's Flying Group
	G-MGND	Rans S.6-ESD Coyote IIXL	T. W. Mian
	G-MGNE	Embraer EMB-505 Phenom 300	Flairjet Ltd
	G-MGOD	Medway Raven	A. Wherrett/N. R. Andrew/D. J. Millward
	G-MGOO	Renegade Spirit UK Ltd	J. Aley
	G-MGPA	Ikarus C42 FB100	S. Ashley
	G-MGPD	Pegasus XL-R	H. T. Mounfield
	G-MGPH	CFM Streak Shadow	V. C. Readhead (G-RSPH)
	G-MGPX	Kolb Twinstar Mk.3 Extra	S. P. Garton
	G-MGRH	Quad City Challenger II	A. Hepburn
	G-MGTG	Pegasus Quantum 15	R. B. Milton (G-MZIO)
	G-MGTR	Hunt Wing	A. C. Ryall
	G-MGTV	Thruster T.600N 450	R. Bingham
	G-MGTW	CFM Shadow Srs DD	G. T. Webster
	G-MGUN	Cyclone AX2000	D. A. Perkins
	G-MGUY	CFM Shadow Srs BD	Shadow Flight Centre Ltd
	G-MGWH	Thruster T300	J. J. Hill
	G-MGWI	Robinson R44	Ed Murray and Sons Ltd (G-BZEF)
	G-MHAR	PA-42-720 Cheyenne IIIA	BAE Systems (Operations) Ltd
	G-MHCE	Enstrom F-28A	C. Roumet (G-BBHD)
	G-MHCJ	Enstrom F-28C-UK	Paradise Helicopters (G-CTRN)
	G-MHCM	Enstrom 280FX	Kingswood Bank LLP (G-IBWF/G-ZZWW/G-BSIE)
	G-MHGS	Stoddard-Hamilton Glastar	M. Henderson
	G-MHJK	Diamond DA42 Twin Star	Plane Talking Ltd
	G-MHMH	Agusta-Bell 206B JetRanger II	Helicopter Hire LLP (G-HOLZ/G-CDBT)
	G-MHMR	Pegasus Quantum 15-912	Hadair

Reg.	Type	Owner or Operator	Notes
G-MHRV	Van's RV-6A	M. R. Harris	
G-MICE	Cessna 510 Citation Mustang	Fteron Ltd	
G-MICH	Robinson R22 Beta	Tiger Helicopters Ltd (G-BNKY)	
G-MICI	Cessna 182S	Steve Parrish Racing (G-WARF)	
G-MICK	Cessna F.172N	Branscombe Airfield Ltd	
G-MICY	Everett Srs 1 gyroplane	D. M. Hughes	
G-MIDD	PA-28 Cherokee 140	Midland Air Training School (G-BBDD)	
G-MIDG	Midget Mustang	C. E. Bellhouse	
G-MIDO	Airbus A.320-232	bmi british midland	
G-MIDS	Airbus A.320-232	bmi british midland	
G-MIDT	Airbus A.320-232	bmi british midland	
G-MIDX	Airbus A.320-232	bmi british midland	
G-MIDY	Airbus A.320-232	bmi british midland	
G-MIFF	Robin DR.400/180	G. E. Snushall	
G-MIGG	WSK-Mielec LiM-5 (1211) ★	D. Miles (G-BWUF)	
G-MIII	Extra EA.300/L	Angels High Ltd	
G-MIKE	Brookland Hornet	M. H. J. Goldring	
G-MIKI	Rans S.6-ESA Coyote II	S. P. Slade	
G-MIKS	Robinson R44 II	M. Glastyonbury	
G-MILA	Cessna F.172N	P. J. Miller	
G-MILD	Scheibe SF.25C Falke	The Borders (Milfield) Gliding Club Ltd	
G-MILE	Cameron N-77 balloon	Miles Air Ltd	
G-MILF	Harmon Rocket II	E. Stinton	
G-MILN	Cessna 182Q	G-MILN Group	
G-MILO	Cessna T.303 Crusader	Oasis Flight Ltd	
G-MIME	Shaw Europa	P. Lewis & N. G. Ley	
G-MIND	Cessna 404	Reconnaissance Ventures Ltd	
G-MINN	Lindstrand LBL-90A balloon	S. M. & D. Johnson (G-SKKC/G-OHUB)	
G-MINS	Nicollier HN.700 Menestrel II	R. Fenion	
G-MINT	Pitts S-1S Special	T. R. G. Barnby	
G-MIOO	M.100 Student ★	Museum of Berkshire Aviation/Woodley (G-APLK)	
G-MIRA	Jabiru SP-340	C. P. L. Helson/Belgium (G-LUMA)	
G-MIRM	Stinson HW-75 Voyager	M. Howells (G-BMSA/G-BCUM)	
G-MIRN	Remos GX	M. Kurkic	
G-MISH	Cessna 182R	Graham Churchill Plant Ltd (G-RFAB/G-BIXT)	
G-MISJ	CZAW Sportcruiser	M. T. Dawson	
G-MISK	Robinson R44	C. A. Rosenberg (G-BYCE)	
G-MISS	Taylor JT.2 Titch	D. Beale	
G-MITE	Raj Hamsa X'Air Falcon	R. Hooper & T. G. V. Oyston & R. Hooper	
G-MITZ	Cameron N-77 balloon	Colt Car Co Ltd	
G-MJAD	Eipper Quicksilver MX	J. McCullough	
G-MJAE	American Aerolights Eagle	T. B. Woolley	
G-MJAJ	Eurowing Goldwing	M. J. Aubrey	
G-MJAM	Eipper Quicksilver MX	J. C. Larkin	
G-MJAN	Hiway Skytrike	G. M. Sutcliffe	
G-MJBK	Swallow B	M. A. Newbould	
G-MJBL	American Aerólights Eagle	B. W. Olley	
G-MJCU	Tarjani	J. K. Ewing	
G-MJDE	Huntair Pathfinder	P. Rayson	
G-MJDJ	Hiway Skytrike Demon	A. J. Cowan	
G-MJEO	American Aerolights Eagle	A. M. Shaw	
G-MJER	Flexiform Striker	D. S. Simpson	
G-MJFM	Huntair Pathfinder	M. J. Aubrey	
G-MJFX	Skyhook TR-1	M. R. Dean	
G-MJFZ	Hiway Demon/Tri-flyer	A. W. Lowrie	
G-MJHC	Ultrasports Tripacer 330	G. J. Simoni	
G-MJHR	Southdown Lightning	B. R. Barnes	
G-MJHV	Hiway Demon 250	A. G. Griffiths	
G-MJIA	Flexiform Striker	D. G. Ellis	
G-MJIC	Ultrasports Puma 330	T. J. Gayton-Polley	
G-MJIR	Eipper Quicksilver MX	H. Feeney	
G-MJJA	Huntair Pathfinder	J. M. Watkins & R. D. Bateman	
G-MJJK	Eipper Quicksilver MXII	J. McCullough	
G-MJKB	Striplin Skyranger	A. P. Booth	
G-MJKO	Goldmarque 250 Skytrike	M. J. Barry	
G-MJKP	Super Scorpion/Sky-Trike ★	Aero Venture	
G-MJKX	Ultralight Skyrider Phantom	L. R. Graham	
G-MJMN	Flexiform Striker/Tri-flyer 330	A. Bishop	
G-MJMR	Solar Wings Typhoon	J. C. S. Jones	
G-MJOC	Huntair Pathfinder	A. J. Glynn	
G-MJOE	Eurowing Goldwing	R. J. Osborne	

Notes	Reg.	Type	Owner or Operator
	G-MJPE	Hiway Demon Skytrike	T. G. Elmhirst
	G-MJPV	Eipper Quicksilver MX	F. W. Ellis
	G-MJRL	Eurowing Goldwing	M. Daniels
	G-MJSF	Skyrider Airsports Phantom	B. J. Towers
	G-MJSL	Dragon 200	M. J. Aubrey
	G-MJSO	Hiway Skytrike	D. C. Read
	G-MJSP	Romain Tiger Cub 440	A. R. Sunley
	G-MJST	Pterodactyl Ptraveller	B. W. Olley
	G-MJSY	Eurowing Goldwing	A. J. Rex
	G-MJSZ	DH Wasp	J. J. Hill
	G-MJTM	Aerostructure Pipistrelle 2B	A. M. Sirant
	G-MJTX	Skyrider Airsports Phantom	P. D. Coppin
	G-MJTY	Huntair Pathfinder Mk.1	A. S. Macdonald
	G-MJTZ	Skyrider Airsports Phantom	B. J. Towers
	G-MJUR	Skyrider Aviation Phantom	M. J. Whiteman-Haywood
	G-MJUW	MBA Tiger Cub 440	D. G. Palmer
	G-MJUX	Skyrider Airsports Phantom	N. Flint
	G-MJVF	CFM Shadow	J. A. Cook
	G-MJVN	Ultrasports Puma 440	R. McGookin
	G-MJVP	Eipper Quicksilver MX II	G. J. Ward
	G-MJVU	Eipper Quicksilver MX II	F. J. Griffith
	G-MJVX	Skyrider Phantom	J. R. Harris
	G-MJVY	Dragon Srs 150	J. C. Craddock
	G-MJWB	Eurowing Goldwing	D. G. Palmer
	G-MJWF	Tiger Cub 440	R. A. & T. Maycock
	G-MJWK	Huntair Pathfinder	V. Tabacek
	G-MJYV	Mainair Triflyer 2 Seat	H. L. Phillips
	G-MJYW	Wasp Gryphon III	P. D. Lawrence
	G-MJYX	Mainair Tri-Flyer/Hiway Demon	K. G. Grayson & R. D. Leigh
	G-MJZK	Southdown Puma Sprint 440	R. J. Osborne
	G-MKAA	Boeing 747-2S4F	Transatlantic Aviation Ltd
	G-MKAK	Colt 77A balloon	A. C. Ritchie
	G-MKAS	PA-28 Cherokee 140	MK Aero Support Ltd (G-BKVR)
	G-MKBA	Boeing 747-2B5F	Belfairs (UK) Ltd
	G-MKCA	Boeing 747-2B5B	Transatlantic Aviation Ltd
	G-MKDA	Boeing 747-2B5F	Transatlantic Aviation Ltd
	G-MKEA	Boeing 747-249F	Belfairs (UK) Ltd
	G-MKER	P & M QuikR	M. C. Kerr
	G-MKEV	EV-96 Eurostar	K. Laud
	G-MKGA	Boeing 747-2R7F	Transatlantic Aviation Ltd
	G-MKHA	Boeing 747-2J6B	MK Airlines Ltd
	G-MKIA	VS.300 Spitfire Mk.1A (P9374)	Mark One Partners LLC
	G-MKKA	Boeing 747-219B	MK Airlines Ltd
	G-MKVB	VS.349 Spitfire LF.VB (BM597)	Historic Aircraft Collection
	G-MKXI	VS.365 Spitfire PR.XI (PL624:R)	P. A. Teichman
	G-MLAL	Jabiru J400	J. M. Pipping
	G-MLAS	Cessna 182E ★	Parachute jump trainer/St. Merryn
	G-MLAW	P & M Quik GT450	S. M. Redding
	G-MLHI	Maule MX-7-180 Star Rocket	Maulehigh (G-BTMJ)
	G-MLJL	Airbus A.330-243	Thomas Cook Airlines Ltd
	G-MLKE	P & M Aviation Quik R	G. Oliver
	G-MLLE	CEA DR.200A-B	A. D. Evans
	G-MLWI	Thunder Ax7-77 balloon	M. L. & L. P. Willoughby
	G-MLXP	Europa XS	M. Davies
	G-MLZZ	Best Off Sky Ranger Swift 912S(1)	T. Couston
	G-MMAC	Dragon Srs.200	J. F. Ashton & J. P. Kirwan
	G-MMAG	MBA Tiger Cub 440	M. J. Aubrey
	G-MMAR	Mainair Gemini/Southdown Puma Sprint	B. A. Fawkes
	G-MMBE	MBA Tiger Cub 440	A. Gannon
	G-MMBL	Southdown Puma	B. J. Farrell
	G-MMBU	Eipper Quicksilver MX II	D. A. Norwood
	G-MMCV	Solar Wings Typhoon III	G. Addison
	G-MMDN	Flexiform Striker	M. G. Griffiths
	G-MMDP	Southdown Sprint X	B. Plunkett
	G-MMEK	Medway Hybred 44XL	M. G. J. Bridges
	G-MMFE	Flexiform Striker	W. Camm
	G-MMFV	Flexiform Striker	R. A. Walton
	G-MMGF	MBA Tiger Cub 440	J. G. Boxall
	G-MMGL	MBA Tiger Cub 440	H. E. Dunning

Reg.	Type	Owner or Operator	Notes
G-MMGS	Solar Wings Panther XL	G. C. Read	
G-MMGT	Solar Wings Typhoon	H. Cook	
G-MMGU	Flexiform Sealander	A. D. Cranfield	
G-MMGV	Whittaker MW5 Sorcerer	M. W. J. Whittaker & G. N. Haffey	
G-MMHE	Gemini Sprint	N. L. Zaman	
G-MMHL	Hiway Super Scorpion	E. J. Blyth	
G-MMHN	MBA Tiger Cub 440	M. J. Aubrey	
G-MMHS	SMD Viper	C. J. Meadows	
G-MMIE	MBA Tiger Cub 440	B. M. Olliver	
G-MMIZ	Lightning MkII	D. Coging	
G-MMJD	Southdown Puma Sprint	M. P. Robertshaw	
G-MMJF	Ultrasports Panther Dual 440	J. Benn	
G-MMJV	MBA Tiger Cub 440	D. G. Palmer	
G-MMKA	Ultrasports Panther Dual	R. S. Wood	
G-MMKM	Flexiform Dual Striker	S. W. Hutchinson	
G-MMKP	MBA Tiger Cub 440	J. W. Beaty	
G-MMKR	Southdown Lightning DS	C. R. Madden	
G-MMKX	Skyrider Phantom 330	G. J. Lampitt	
G-MMLE	Eurowing Goldwing SP	M. J. Aubrey	
G-MMMG	Eipper Quicksilver MXL	J. G. Campbell	
G-MMMH	Hadland Willow	M. J. Hadland	
G-MMML	Dragon 150	M. J. Aubrey	
G-MMMN	Ultrasports Panther Dual 440	C. Downton	
G-MMNB	Eipper Quicksilver MX	M. J. Lindop	
G-MMNC	Eipper Quicksilver MX	W. S. Toulmin	
G-MMNH	Dragon 150	T. J. Barlow	
G-MMNN	Buzzard	E. W. Sherry	
G-MMOB	Southdown Sprint	D. Woolcock	
G-MMOK	Solar Wings Panther XL	R. F. & A. J. Foster	
G-MMPH	Southdown Puma Sprint	J. Siddle	
G-MMPL	Flexiform Dual Striker	P. D. Lawrence	
G-MMPO	Mainair Gemini/Flash	M.A Feber	
G-MMPZ	Teman Mono-Fly	H. Smith	
G-MMRH	Highway Skytrike	A. M. Sirant	
G-MMRL	Solar Wings Panther XL	R. J. Hood	
G-MMRN	Southdown Puma Sprint	D. C. Read	
G-MMRP	Mainair Gemini	J. C. S. Jones	
G-MMRW	Flexiform Dual Striker	M. D. Hinge	
G-MMSA	Ultrasports Panther XL	T. W. Thiele & G. Savage	
G-MMSG	Solar Wings Panther XL-S	R. W. McKee	
G-MMSH	Solar Wings Panther XL	I. J. Drake	
G-MMSO	Mainair Tri-Flyer 440	K. A. Maughan	
G-MMSP	Mainair Gemini/Flash	J. Whiteford	
G-MMTD	Mainair Tri-Flyer 330	W. E. Teare	
G-MMTL	Mainair Gemini	K. Birkett	
G-MMTR	Ultrasports Panther	P. M. Kelsey	
G-MMTY	Fisher FP.202U	M. A. Welch	
G-MMUA	Southdown Puma Sprint	M. R. Crowhurst	
G-MMUM	MBA Tiger Cub 440	Coulson Flying Services Ltd	
G-MMUO	Mainair Gemini/Flash	D. R. Howells & B. D. Bastin	
G-MMUV	Southdown Puma Sprint	D. C. Read	
G-MMUW	Mainair Gemini/Flash	J. C. K. Scardifield	
G-MMUX	Gemini Sprint	A. S. Gillespie	
G-MMVA	Southdown Puma Sprint	C. E. Tomkins	
G-MMVH	Southdown Raven	G. W. & K. M. Carwardine	
G-MMVI	Southdown Puma Sprint	G. R. Williams	
G-MMVS	Skyhook Pixie	B. W. Olley	
G-MMWG	Greenslade Mono-Trike	G-MMWG Group	
G-MMWS	Mainair Tri-Flyer	P. H. Risdale	
G-MMWX	Southdown Puma Sprint	G. A. Webb	
G-MMXL	Mainair Gemini Flash	G. W. Warner	
G-MMXO	Southdown Puma Sprint	D. J. Tasker	
G-MMXU	Mainair Gemini/Flash	T. J. Franklin	
G-MMXV	Mainair Gemini/Flash	M. A. Boffin	
G-MMXW	Mainair Gemini/Sprint	A. Hodgson	
G-MMYL	Cyclone 70	A. W. Nancarrow	
G-MMYO	Southdown Puma Sprint	P. R. Whitehouse	
G-MMZA	Mainair Gemini/Flash	G. T. Johnston	
G-MMZD	Mainair Gemini/Flash	S. McDonnell	
G-MMZK	Mainair Gemini/Flash	G. Jones & B. Lee	
G-MMZV	Mainair Gemini/Flash	N. M. Toulson	
G-MMZW	Southdown Puma Sprint	M. G. Ashbee	

Notes	Reg.	Type	Owner or Operator
	G-MNAE	Mainair Gemini/Flash	G. C. luddington
	G-MNAI	Ultrasports Panther XL-S	R. G. Cameron
	G-MNAZ	Solar Wings Pegasus XL-R	R. W. houldsworth
	G-MNBA	Solar Wings Pegasus XL-R	L. Hughes
	G-MNBB	Solar Wings Pegasus XL-R	D. A. Blackston
	G-MNBC	Solar Wings Pegasus XL-R	R. T. Parry
	G-MNBF	Mainair Gemini/Flash	P. Mokryk & S. King
	G-MNBI	Solar Wings Panther XL-S	M. O'Connell
	G-MNBJ	Skyhook Pixie	G. Sykes
	G-MNBM	Southdown Puma Sprint	C. Hall-Gardiner
	G-MNBN	Mainair Gemini/Flash	I. Bond
	G-MNBP	Mainair Gemini/Flash	G. A. Harper
	G-MNBS	Mainair Gemini/Flash	P. A. Comins
	G-MNBT	Mainair Gemini/Flash	R. R. A. Dean
	G-MNCA	Hiway Demon 175	M. A. Sirant
	G-MNCF	Mainair Gemini/Flash	C. F. Janes
	G-MNCG	Mainair Gemini/Flash	J. E. F. Fletcher
	G-MNCM	CFM Shadow Srs B	K. G. D. Macrae
	G-MNCO	Eipper Quicksilver MXII	S. Lawton
	G-MNCP	Southdown Puma Sprint	D. A. Payne
	G-MNCS	Skyrider Airsports Phantom	K. J. Underwood
	G-MNCU	Medway Hybred 44XL	J. E. Evans
	G-MNCV	Medway Hybred 44XL	M. J. Turland
	G-MNDD	Mainair Scorcher Solo	L. Hurman
	G-MNDE	Medway Half Pint	Delta Echo Half Pint Group
	G-MNDM	Mainair Gemini/Flash	J. C. Birkbeck
	G-MNDU	Midland Sirocco 377GB	M. A. Collins
	G-MNDY	Southdown Puma Sprint	A. M. Coupland
	G-MNEG	Mainair Gemini/Flash	A. Sexton/Ireland
	G-MNEH	Mainair Gemini/Flash	I. Rawson
	G-MNER	CFM Shadow Srs B	F. C. Claydon
	G-MNET	Mainair Gemini/Flash	I. P. Stubbins
	G-MNEV	Mainair Gemini/Flash	M. Gardiner
	G-MNEY	Mainair Gemini/Flash	D. A. Spiers
	G-MNFB	Southdown Puma Sprint	C. Lawrence
	G-MNFF	Mainair Gemini/Flash	C. H. Spencer & R. P. Cook
	G-MNFG	Southdown Puma Sprint	M. Ingleton
	G-MNFL	AMF Chevvron	S. S. M. Turner
	G-MNFM	Mainair Gemini/Flash	P. M. Fidell
	G-MNFN	Mainair Gemini/Flash	J. R. Martin
	G-MNFP	Mainair Gemini/Flash	S. E. Walsh
	G-MNGD	Solar Wings Typhoon/Tri-Pacer	I. White
	G-MNGG	Solar Wings Pegasus XL-R	I. D. Mallinson
	G-MNGK	Mainair Gemini/Flash	G. P. Warnes
	G-MNGM	Mainair Gemini/Flash	R. J. Webb
	G-MNGW	Mainair Gemini/Flash	F. R. Stephens
	G-MNHD	Solar Wings Pegasus XL-R	J. R. Hackett
	G-MNHE	Solar Wings Pegasus XL-R	A. Daujotis
	G-MNHH	Solar Wings Panther XL-S	F. J. Williams
	G-MNHI	Solar Wings Pegasus XL-R	R. W. Matthews
	G-MNHJ	Solar Wings Pegasus XL-R	C. Council
	G-MNHL	Solar Wings Pegasus XL-R	The Microlight School (Lichfield) Ltd
	G-MNHM	Solar Wings Pegasus XL-R	P. A. Howell
	G-MNHN	Solar Wings Pegasus XL-R	M. Devlin
	G-MNHR	Solar Wings Pegasus XL-R	B. D. Jackson
	G-MNHZ	Mainair Gemini/Flash	I. O. S. Ross
	G-MNIA	Mainair Gemini/Flash	A. E. Dix
	G-MNID	Mainair Gemini/Flash	M. I. Potts
	G-MNIG	Mainair Gemini/Flash	A. B. Woods
	G-MNIH	Mainair Gemini/Flash	N. H. S. Insall
	G-MNII	Mainair Gemini/Flash	R. F. Finnis
	G-MNIK	Pegasus Photon	M. Belemet
	G-MNIM	Maxair Hummer	K. Wood
	G-MNIW	Airwave Nimrod/Tri-Flyer	G. S. Highley
	G-MNIZ	Mainair Gemini/Flash	A. G. Power
	G-MNJB	Southdown Raven	W. Flood
	G-MNJD	Southdown Puma Sprint	S. D. Smith
	G-MNJJ	Solar Wings Pegasus Flash	P. A. Shelley
	G-MNJL	Solar Wings Pegasus Flash	S. D. Thomas
	G-MNJN	Solar Wings Pegasus Flash	G. J. Crago
	G-MNJR	Solar Wings Pegasus Flash	M. G. Ashbee
	G-MNJS	Southdown Puma Sprint	E. A. Frost

Reg.	Type	Owner or Operator	Notes
G-MNJX	Medway Hybred 44XL	H. A. Stewart	
G-MNKB	Solar Wings Pegasus Photon	M. E. Gilbert	
G-MNKC	Solar Wings Pegasus Photon	K. B. Woods	
G-MNKD	Solar Wings Pegasus Photon	A. M. Sirant	
G-MNKE	Solar Wings Pegasus Photon	G. Forster	
G-MNKG	Solar Wings Pegasus Photon	S. N. Robson	
G-MNKK	Solar Wings Pegasus Photon	M. E. Gilbert	
G-MNKM	MBA Tiger Cub 440	A. R. Sunley	
G-MNKN	Skycraft Scout Mk.3-3R	M. A. Aubrey	
G-MNKO	Solar Wings Pegasus Flash	T. A. Goundry	
G-MNKP	Solar Wings Pegasus Flash	I. N. Miller	
G-MNKU	Southdown Puma Sprint	S. P. O'Hannrachain	
G-MNKW	Solar Wings Pegasus Flash	S. P. Halford	
G-MNKX	Solar Wings Pegasus Flash	T. A. Newton	
G-MNKZ	Southdown Raven	G. B. Gratton	
G-MNLI	Mainair Gemini/Flash	P. M. Fessi	
G-MNLT	Southdown Raven	J. L. Stachini	
G-MNLY	Mainair Gemini/Flash	P. D. Parry	
G-MNMC	Mainair Gemini Sprint	G. A. Davidson	
G-MNMG	Mainair Gemini/Flash	N. A. M. Beyer-Kay	
G-MNMK	Solar Wings Pegasus XL-R	A. F. Smallacombe	
G-MNMM	Aerotech MW5 Sorcerer	S. F. N. Warnell	
G-MNMU	Southdown Raven	M. J. Curley	
G-MNMV	Mainair Gemini/Flash	S. Staig	
G-MNMW	Aerotech MW6 Merlin	E. F. Clapham	
G-MNMY	Cyclone 70	N. R. Beale	
G-MNNA	Southdown Raven	D. & G. D. Palfrey	
G-MNNF	Mainair Gemini/Flash	W. J. Gunn	
G-MNNG	Solar Wings Photon	K. B. Woods	
G-MNNL	Mainair Gemini/Flash II	C. L. Rumney	
G-MNNM	Mainair Scorcher Solo	L. L. Perry & S. R. Leeper	
G-MNNO	Southdown Raven	M. J. Robbins	
G-MNNS	Eurowing Goldwing	J. S. R. Moodie	
G-MNNY	Solar Wings Pegasus Flash	C. W. Payne	
G-MNPC	Mainair Gemini/Flash	M. S. McGimpsey	
G-MNPZ	Mainair Scorcher Solo	S. Stevens	
G-MNRD	Ultraflight Lazair IIIE	Sywell Lazair Group	
G-MNRE	Mainair Scorcher Solo	A. P. Pearce	
G-MNRI	Hornet Dual Trainer	R. H. Goll	
G-MNRM	Hornet Dual Trainer	I. C. Cannan	
G-MNRS	Southdown Raven	M. C. Newman	
G-MNRT	Midland Ultralights Sirocco	R. F. Hinton	
G-MNRX	Mainair Gemini/Flash II	R. Downham	
G-MNRZ	Mainair Scorcher Solo	R. Pattrick & K. Medd	
G-MNSJ	Mainair Gemini/Flash	P. Cooney	
G-MNSL	Southdown Raven X	P. B. Robinson	
G-MNSY	Southdown Raven X	L. A. Hosegood	
G-MNTD	Aerial Arts Chaser 110SX	B. Richardson	
G-MNTE	Southdown Raven X	E. Foster	
G-MNTK	CFM Shadow Srs B	M. J. Bromley	
G-MNTP	CFM Shadow Srs B	E. G. White	
G-MNTV	Mainair Gemini/Flash II	A.M. Sirant	
G-MNUF	Mainair Gemini/Flash II	K. Jones	
G-MNUI	Skyhook Cutlass Dual	M. Holling	
G-MNUR	Mainair Gemini/Flash II	J. S. Hawkins	
G-MNUU	Southdown Raven X	P. N. Jackson	
G-MNUX	Solar Wings Pegasus XL-R	S. Newlands	
G-MNVB	Solar Wings Pegasus XL-R	M. Cairns	
G-MNVE	Solar Wings Pegasus XL-R	M. P. Aris	
G-MNVG	Solar Wings Pegasus Flash II	D. J. Ward	
G-MNVH	Solar Wings Pegasus Flash II	J. A. Clarke & C. Hall	
G-MNVI	CFM Shadow Srs B	D. R. C. Pugh	
G-MNVJ	CFM Shadow Srs CD	G. Mudd	
G-MNVK	CFM Shadow Srs B	A. K. Atwell	
G-MNVL	Aerial Arts 130SX/Half Pint	P. J. Hopkins	
G-MNVO	Hovey Whing-Ding II	C. Wilson	
G-MNVT	Mainair Gemini/Flash II	ACB Hydraulics	
G-MNVV	Mainair Gemini/Flash II	T. Wilbor	
G-MNVW	Mainair Gemini/Flash II	J. C. Munro-Hunt	
G-MNVZ	Solar Wings Pegasus Photon	J. J. Russ	
G-MNWG	Southdown Raven X	D. Murray	
G-MNWI	Mainair Gemini/Flash II	I. E. Chapman	

Notes	Reg.	Type	Owner or Operator
	G-MNWL	Aerial Arts 130SX	E. H. Snook
	G-MNWO	Mainair Gemini/Flash II	P. Burgess
	G-MNXE	Southdown Raven X	A. E. Silvey
	G-MNXF	Southdown Raven X	D. E. Gwenin
	G-MNXG	Southdown Raven X	E. M. & M. A. Williams
	G-MNXO	Medway Hybred 44XLR	R. P. Taylor
	G-MNXS	Mainair Gemini/Flash II	J. M. Macdonald
	G-MNXU	Mainair Gemini/Flash II	J. M. Hucker
	G-MNXX	CFM Shadow Srs BD	M. Nazm
	G-MNXZ	Whittaker MW5 Sorcerer	A. J. Glynn
	G-MNYA	Solar Wings Pegasus Flash II	C. Trollope
	G-MNYC	Solar Wings Pegasus XL-R	J. S. Hawkins
	G-MNYD	Aerial Arts 110SX Chaser	B. Richardson
	G-MNYE	Aerial Arts 110SX Chaser	R. J. Ripley
	G-MNYF	Aerial Arts 110SX Chaser	R. W. Twamley
	G-MNYM	Southdown Raven X	R. L. Davis
	G-MNYP	Southdown Raven X	A. G. Davies
	G-MNYU	Pegasus XL-R	G. L. Turner
	G-MNYW	Solar Wings Pegasus XL-R	M. P. Waldock
	G-MNYX	Solar Wings Pegasus XL-R	P. F. Mayes
	G-MNZB	Mainair Gemini/Flash II	P. A. Ryder
	G-MNZC	Mainair Gemini/Flash II	C. J. Whittaker
	G-MNZD	Mainair Gemini/Flash II	N. D. Carter
	G-MNZJ	CFM Shadow Srs BD	E. W. Laidlaw
	G-MNZK	Solar Wings Pegasus XL-R	P. J. Appleby
	G-MNZP	CFM Shadow Srs B	J. G. Wakeford
	G-MNZS	Aerial Arts 130SX	N. R. Beale
	G-MNZU	Eurowing Goldwing	P. D. Coppin & P. R. Millen
	G-MNZW	Southdown Raven X	T. A. Willcox
	G-MNZZ	CFM Shadow Srs B	Shadow Aviation Ltd
	G-MOAC	Beech F33A Bonanza	R. M. Camrass
	G-MOAN	Aeromot AMT-200S Super Ximango	A. E. Mayhew
	G-MODE	Eurocopter EC 120B	Cardy Construction Ltd
	G-MOFB	Cameron O-120 balloon	D. M. Moffat
	G-MOFZ	Cameron O-90 balloon	D. M. Moffat
	G-MOGI	AA-5A Cheetah	J. G. Stewart (G-BFMU)
	G-MOGS	CZAW Sportcruiser	J. M. Oliver
	G-MOGY	Robinson R22 Beta	Northumbria Helicopters Ltd
	G-MOKE	Cameron V-77 balloon	G-MOKE ASBC/Luxembourg
	G-MOLO	Pilatus PC-12/47E	Breckenridge Ltd
	G-MOMA	Thruster T.600N 450	Compton Abbas Microlight Group (G-CCIB)
	G-MONI	Monnett Moni	P. N. Stacey
	G-MONJ	Boeing 757-2T7	Monarch Airlines Ltd
	G-MONK	Boeing 757-2T7	Monarch Airlines Ltd
	G-MONR	Airbus A.300-605R	Monarch Airlines Ltd
	G-MONS	Airbus A.300-605R	Monarch Airlines Ltd
	G-MONX	Airbus A.320-212	Monarch Airlines Ltd
	G-MOOR	SOCATA TB10 Tobago	P. D. Kirkham (G-MILK)
	G-MOOS	P.56 Provost T.1 (XF690)	H. Cooke (G-BGKA)
	G-MOOV	CZAW Sportcruiser	G-MOOV Syndicate
	G-MOPS	Best Off Sky Ranger Swift 912S	P. Stretton
	G-MOSA	Morane Saulnier MS317	A. C. Whitehead
	G-MOSJ	Beech C.90GTi King Air	Moss Aviation LLP
	G-MOSS	Beech D55 Baron	D. J. da Costa Marques (G-AWAD)
	G-MOSY	Cameron O-84 balloon	P. L. Mossman
	G-MOTA	Bell 206B JetRanger 3	J. W. Sandle
	G-MOTH	DH.82A Tiger Moth (K2567)	P. T. Szluha
	G-MOTI	Robin DR.400/500	Tango India Flying Group
	G-MOTO	PA-24 Comanche 180	S. M. R. Hickman (G-EDHE/G-ASFH)
	G-MOTW	Meyers OTW-145	J. K. Padden
	G-MOUL	Maule M6-235	M. Klinge
	G-MOUR	HS. Gnat T.1 (XR991)	Heritage Aircraft Ltd
	G-MOUT	Cessna 182T	C. Mountain
	G-MOVI	PA-32R-301 Saratoga SP	G-BOON Ltd (G-MARI)
	G-MOWG	Aeroprakt A22-L Foxbat	J. Smith
	G-MOZI	Glasflugel Mosquito	J. Christensen & P. Smith
	G-MOZZ	Avions Mudry CAP-10B	N. Skipworth
	G-MPAA	PA-28-181 Archer III	MPFC Ltd
	G-MPAC	Ultravia Pelican PL	J. H. Leigh t/a The Clipgate Flying Grp
	G-MPAT	EV-97 TeamEurostar UK	P. J. Dale
	G-MPBH	Cessna FA.152	The Moray Flying Club (1996) Ltd (G-FLIC/ G-BILV)

Reg.	Type	Owner or Operator	Notes
G-MPCD	Airbus A.320-212	Monarch Airlines Ltd	
G-MPHY	Ikarus C42 FB100	P. Murphy	
G-MPIT	CFM Shadow Srs DD	P. Cicconetti (G-MZOM)	
G-MPMP	Bombardier CL600-2B16 Challenger	TAG Aviation (UK) Ltd (G-JMMP)	
G-MPRL	Cessna 210M	Mike Stapleton & Co.Ltd	
G-MPSA	Eurocopter MBB BK-117C-2	Metropolitan Police Authority	
G-MPSB	Eurocopter MBB BK-117C-2	Metropolitan Police Authority	
G-MPSC	Eurocopter MBB BK-117C-2	Metropolitan Police Authority	
G-MPSP	Bombardier CL600-2B16 Challenger	Patronus Aviation Ltd (G-MPCW/G-JMMD)	
G-MPTP	Bombardier CL600-2B16 Challenger	Bluejets Ltd (G-MPJM/G-JMCW)	
G-MPWI	Robin HR.100/210	P. G. Clarkson & S. King	
G-MRAJ	Hughes 369E	A. Jardine	
G-MRAM	Mignet HM.1000 Balerit	R. A. Marven	
G-MRDC	Robinson R44 II	E. M. Montefusco	
G-MRDS	CZAW Sportcruiser	P. Wood	
G-MRED	Christavia Mk 1	The Barton Group	
G-MRJJ	Mainair Pegasus Quik	J.H. Sparks	
G-MRJK	Airbus A.320-214	Monarch Airlines Ltd	
G-MRJP	Silence Twister	M. D. Carruthers	
G-MRKS	Robinson R44	TJD Trade Ltd (G-RAYC)	
G-MRKT	Lindstrand LBL-90A balloon	Marketplace Public Relations (London) Ltd	
G-MRLL	NA P-51D Mustang (413521:5Q-B)	M. Hammond	
G-MRLN	Sky 240-24 balloon	Merlin Balloons	
G-MRMJ	Eurocopter AS.365N3 Dauphin 2	Whirligig Ltd	
G-MROC	Pegasus Quantum 15-912	M. A. Metzler	
G-MROD	Van's RV-7A	K. R. Emery	
G-MROO	Cessna 525A Citationjet CJ2	Air Charters Scotland Ltd (G-EEBJ)	
G-MRPH	Murphy Rebel	P. & B. S. Metson	
G-MRRR	Hughes 369E	J. Paxton	
G-MRRY	Robinson R44 II	F. V. Neefs	
G-MRSN	Robinson R22 Beta	Yorkshire Helicopters Ltd	
G-MRST	PA-28 RT-201 Arrow IV	Calverton Flying Group Ltd	
G-MRTN	SOCATA TB10 Tobago	C. Karaiskakis (G-BHET)	
G-MRTY	Cameron N-77 balloon	R. A. Vale & ptnrs	
G-MRVK	Czech Sport Aircraft Pipersport	M. Farrugia	
G-MRVL	Van's RV-7	L. W. Taylor	
G-MSAL	MS.733 Alcyon (143)	M. Isbister t/a Alcyon Flying Group	
G-MSFC	PA-38-112 Tomahawk	Sherwood Flying Club Ltd	
G-MSFT	PA-28-161 Warrior II	Western Air (Thruxton) Ltd (G-MUMS)	
G-MSIX	Glaser-Dirks DG.800B	G-MSIX Group	
G-MSKY	Ikarus C42 FB100 VLA	P. M. Yeoman & J. S. Mason	
G-MSON	Cameron Z-90 balloon	K. D. Peirce	
G-MSOO	Revolution Mini 500 helicopter	R. H. Ryan	
G-MSPT	Eurocopter EC 135T2	M Sport Ltd	
G-MSPY	Pegasus Quantum 15-912	B. E. Wagenhauser	
G-MSTG	NA P-51D Mustang (414419:LH-F)	M. Hammond	
G-MSTR	Cameron 110 Monster SS Balloon	Monster Syndicate (G-OJOB)	
G-MTAB	Mainair Gemini/Flash II	L. Clarkson	
G-MTAC	Mainair Gemini/Flash II	R. Massey	
G-MTAF	Mainair Gemini/Flash II	A. G. Lister	
G-MTAG	Mainair Gemini/Flash II	M. J. Cowie & J. P. Hardy	
G-MTAH	Mainair Gemini/Flash II	A. J. Rowe	
G-MTAI	Solar Wings Pegasus XL-R	S. T. Elkington	
G-MTAP	Southdown Raven X	M. C. Newman	
G-MTAS	Whittaker MW5 Sorcerer	R. J. Scott	
G-MTAV	Solar Wings Pegasus XL-R	S. Fairweather	
G-MTAW	Solar Wings Pegasus XL-R	M. G. Ralph	
G-MTAX	Solar Wings Pegasus XL-R	J. Pool	
G-MTAY	Solar Wings Pegasus XL-R	S. A. McLatchie	
G-MTAZ	Solar Wings Pegasus XL-R	M. O'Connell	
G-MTBB	Southdown Raven X	A. Miller	
G-MTBD	Mainair Gemini/Flash II	J. G. Jones	
G-MTBE	CFM Shadow Srs BD	S. K. Brown	
G-MTBH	Mainair Gemini/Flash II	P. & T. Sludds	
G-MTBJ	Mainair Gemini/Flash II	P. J. & R. M. Perry	
G-MTBL	Solar Wings Pegasus XL-R	R. N. Whiting	
G-MTBN	Southdown Raven X	A. J. & S. E. Crosby-Jones	
G-MTBO	Southdown Raven X	J. Liversuch	
G-MTBP	Aerotech MW5 Sorcerer	L. J. Greenhough	

Notes	Reg.	Type	Owner or Operator
	G-MTBR	Aerotech MW5 Sorcerer	R. Poulter
	G-MTBS	Aerotech MW5 Sorcerer	D. J. Pike
	G-MTCK	SW Pegasus Flash	A. M. Chilingirov
	G-MTCM	Southdown Raven X	J. C. Rose
	G-MTCP	Aerial Arts Chaser 110SX	B. Richardson
	G-MTCU	Mainair Gemini/Flash II	T. J. Philip
	G-MTDD	Aerial Arts Chaser 110SX	B. Richardson
	G-MTDE	American Aerolights 110SX	J. T. Meager
	G-MTDF	Mainair Gemini/Flash II	P. G. Barnes
	G-MTDK	Aerotech MW-5B Sorcerer	C. C. Wright
	G-MTDO	Eipper Quicksilver MXII	D. L. Ham
	G-MTDR	Mainair Gemini/Flash II	D. J. Morriss
	G-MTDU	CFM Shadow Srs BD	A. Harris
	G-MTDW	Mainair Gemini/Flash II	S. R. Leeper
	G-MTDY	Mainair Gemini/Flash II	S. Penoyre
	G-MTEB	Solar Wings Pegasus XL-R	D. P. Gawlowski
	G-MTEC	Solar Wings Pegasus XL-R	R. W. Glover
	G-MTEE	Solar Wings Pegasus XL-R	The Microlight School (Lichfield) Ltd
	G-MTEK	Mainair Gemini/Flash II	G. M. Wrigley & M. O'Hearne
	G-MTER	Solar Wings Pegasus XL-R	G. Carr
	G-MTES	Solar Wings Pegasus XL-R	N. P. Read
	G-MTET	Solar Wings Pegasus XL-R	K. Gilsenan
	G-MTEU	Solar Wings Pegasus XL-R	T. E. Thomas
	G-MTEY	Mainair Gemini/Flash II	A. Wells
	G-MTFA	Pegasus XL-R	S. Hindle
	G-MTFC	Medway Hybred 44XLR	J. K. Masters
	G-MTFG	AMF Chevvron 232	J. Batchelor
	G-MTFM	Solar Wings Pegasus XL-R	P. R. G. Morley
	G-MTFN	Aerotech MW5 Sorcerer	S. M. King
	G-MTFT	Solar Wings Pegasus XL-R	S. J. Ward
	G-MTFU	CFM Shadow Srs CD	G. J. Jones & D. C. Lees
	G-MTGA	Mainair Gemini/Flash	I. White
	G-MTGB	Thruster TST Mk 1	M. J. Aubrey
	G-MTGC	Thruster TST Mk 1	G. M. Cruise-Smith
	G-MTGD	Thruster TST Mk 1	B. A. Janaway
	G-MTGF	Thruster TST Mk 1	B. Swindon
	G-MTGH	Mainair Gemini/Flash II	M. Nazm
	G-MTGL	Solar Wings Pegasus XL-R	R. & P. J. Openshaw
	G-MTGM	Solar Wings Pegasus XL-R	I. J. Steele
	G-MTGO	Mainair Gemini/Flash	J. Ouru
	G-MTGR	Thruster TST Mk 1	M. R. Grunwell
	G-MTGS	Thruster TST Mk 1	R. J. Nelson
	G-MTGV	CFM Shadow Srs BD	V. R. Riley
	G-MTGW	CFM Shadow Srs BD	C. W. Willis
	G-MTHH	Solar Wings Pegasus XL-R	J. Palmer
	G-MTHJ	Solar Wings Pegasus XL-R	M. R. Harrison
	G-MTHN	Solar Wings Pegasus XL-R	M. T. Seal
	G-MTHT	CFM Shadow Srs BD	A. P. Jones
	G-MTHV	CFM Shadow Srs BD	P. G. Kavanagh
	G-MTHZ	Mainair Gemini/Flash IIA	A. Kiselovs
	G-MTIA	Mainair Gemini/Flash IIA	G. W. Jennings
	G-MTIB	Mainair Gemini/Flash IIA	M. D. Maclagan
	G-MTIE	Solar Wings Pegasus XL-R	P. Wibberley
	G-MTIJ	Solar Wings Pegasus XL-R	M. J. F. Gilbody
	G-MTIK	Southdown Raven X	G. A. Oldershaw
	G-MTIL	Mainair Gemini/Flash IIA	M. Ward
	G-MTIM	Mainair Gemini/Flash IIA	T. M. Swan
	G-MTIO	Solar Wings Pegasus XL-R	A. R. Wade
	G-MTIR	Solar Wings Pegasus XL-R	P. Jolley
	G-MTIS	Solar Wings Pegasus XL-R	Upottery Aerotow Club
	G-MTIW	Solar Wings Pegasus XL-R	G. S. Francis
	G-MTIX	Solar Wings Pegasus XL-R	S. Pickering
	G-MTIZ	Solar Wings Pegasus XL-R	S. L. Blount
	G-MTJB	Mainair Gemini/Flash IIA	B. Skidmore
	G-MTJC	Mainair Gemini/Flash IIA	T. A. Dockrell
	G-MTJE	Mainair Gemini/Flash IIA	S. R. Eskins
	G-MTJG	Medway Hybred 44XLR	M. A. Trodden
	G-MTJH	SW Pegasus Flash	C. G. Ludgate
	G-MTJL	Mainair Gemini/Flash IIA	J. Hunter
	G-MTJS	Solar Wings Pegasus XL-Q	R. J. H. Hayward
	G-MTJT	Mainair Gemini/Flash IIA	D. F. Greatbanks
	G-MTJV	Mainair Gemini/Flash IIA	R. W. Hocking

Reg.	Type	Owner or Operator	Notes
G-MTJX	Hornet Dual Trainer/Raven	J. P. Kirwan	
G-MTKA	Thruster TST Mk 1	M. J. Coles & S. R. Williams	
G-MTKB	Thruster TST Mk 1	M. Hanna	
G-MTKD	Thruster TST Mk 1	E. Spain/Ireland	
G-MTKG	Solar Wings Pegasus XL-R	G. D. Barrell	
G-MTKH	Solar Wings Pegasus XL-R	B. P. Hoare	
G-MTKI	Solar Wings Pegasus XL-R	M. Wady	
G-MTKR	CFM Shadow Srs BD	D. P. Eichhorn	
G-MTKW	Mainair Gemini/Flash IIA	J. H. McIvor	
G-MTKZ	Mainair Gemini/Flash IIA	I. S. McNeill	
G-MTLB	Mainair Gemini/Flash IIA	M. J. Jones	
G-MTLC	Mainair Gemini/Flash IIA	R. J. Alston	
G-MTLG	Solar Wings Pegasus XL-R	G. J. Simoni	
G-MTLL	Mainair Gemini/Flash IIA	M. S. Lawrence	
G-MTLM	Thruster TST Mk 1	R.J. Nelson	
G-MTLN	Thruster TST Mk 1	P. W. Taylor	
G-MTLT	Solar Wings Pegasus XL-R	K. M. Mayling	
G-MTLV	Solar Wings Pegasus XL-R	P. Cave	
G-MTLX	Medway Hybred 44XLR	D. A. Coupland	
G-MTLY	Solar Wings Pegasus XL-R	I. Johnston	
G-MTLZ	Whittaker MW5 Sorceror	J. O'Keeffe	
G-MTMA	Mainair Gemini/Flash IIA	G-MTMA Flying Group	
G-MTMC	Mainair Gemini/Flash IIA	Rovogate Ltd	
G-MTME	Solar Wings Pegasus XL-R	R. J. Turner	
G-MTMF	Solar Wings Pegasus XL-R	H. T. M. Smith	
G-MTMG	Solar Wings Pegasus XL-R	C. W. & P. E. F. Suckling	
G-MTML	Mainair Gemini/Flash IIA	J. F. Ashton	
G-MTMP	Hornet Dual Trainer/Raven	P. G. Owen	
G-MTMR	Hornet Dual Trainer/Raven	D. J. Smith	
G-MTMT	Mainair Gemini/Flash IIA	C. Pickvance	
G-MTMV	Mainair Gemini/Flash IIA	G. J. Small	
G-MTMW	Mainair Gemini/Flash IIA	F. Lees	
G-MTMX	CFM Shadow Srs BD	D. R. White	
G-MTNC	Mainair Gemini/Flash IIA	M. G. Titmus & M. E. Cook	
G-MTND	Medway Hybred 44XLR	Butty Boys Flying Group	
G-MTNE	Medway Hybred 44XLR	A. G. Rodenburg	
G-MTNF	Medway Hybred 44XLR	P. A. Bedford	
G-MTNG	Mainair Gemini/Flash IIA	A. N. Bellis	
G-MTNI	Mainair Gemini/Flash IIA	F. J. Clarehugh	
G-MTNJ	Mainair Gemini/Flash IIA	S. M. Cook	
G-MTNL	Mainair Gemini/Flash IIA	R. A. Matthews	
G-MTNM	Mainair Gemini/Flash IIA	P. M. Cary	
G-MTNO	Solar Wings Pegasus XL-Q	A. F. Batchelor	
G-MTNP	Solar Wings Pegasus XL-Q	R. J. Kelly	
G-MTNR	Thruster TST Mk 1	A. M. Sirant	
G-MTNT	Thruster TST Mk 1	M. McKenzie	
G-MTNU	Thruster TST Mk 1	T. H. Brearley	
G-MTNV	Thruster TST Mk 1	J. B. Russell	
G-MTOA	Solar Wings Pegasus XL-R	R. A. Bird	
G-MTOE	Solar Wings Pegasus XL-R	G. W. F. J. Dear	
G-MTOH	Solar Wings Pegasus XL-R	H. Cook	
G-MTON	Solar Wings Pegasus XL-R	D. J. Willett	
G-MTOT	Solar Wings Pegasus XL-R	A. J. Lloyd	
G-MTOY	Solar Wings Pegasus XL-R	G-MTOY Group	
G-MTOZ	Solar Wings Pegasus XL-R	C. P. Davies	
G-MTPB	Mainair Gemini/Flash IIA	G. Bowden	
G-MTPC	Raven X	G. W. Carwardine	
G-MTPE	Solar Wings Pegasus XL-R	J. Bassett	
G-MTPF	Solar Wings Pegasus XL-R	P. M. Watts & A. S. Mitchel	
G-MTPH	Solar Wings Pegasus XL-R	G. Barker & L. Blight	
G-MTPI	Solar Wings Pegasus XL-R	R. J. Bullock	
G-MTPJ	Solar Wings Pegasus XL-R	D. Lockwood	
G-MTPK	Solar Wings Pegasus XL-R	S. H. James	
G-MTPL	Solar Wings Pegasus XL-R	C. J. Jones	
G-MTPM	Solar Wings Pegasus XL-R	D. K. Seal	
G-MTPR	Solar Wings Pegasus XL-R	T. Kenny	
G-MTPT	Thruster TST Mk 1	Chilbolton Thruster Group	
G-MTPU	Thruster TST Mk 1	N. Hay	
G-MTPW	Thruster TST Mk 1	K. Hawthorne	
G-MTPX	Thruster TST Mk 1	T. Snook	
G-MTPY	Thruster TST Mk 1	H. N. Baumgartner	
G-MTRA	Mainair Gemini/Flash IIA	A. Davis	

Notes	Reg.	Type	Owner or Operator
	G-MTRC	Midlands Ultralights Sirocco 377G	D. Thorpe
	G-MTRM	Solar Wings Pegasus XL-R	M. Morris
	G-MTRO	Solar Wings Pegasus XL-R	D. Rowland
	G-MTRS	Solar Wings Pegasus XL-R	J. J. R. Tickle
	G-MTRX	Whittaker MW5 Sorceror	W. Turner
	G-MTRZ	Mainair Gemini/Flash IIA	D. F. G. Barlow
	G-MTSC	Mainair Gemini/Flash IIA	K. Wilson
	G-MTSH	Thruster TST Mk 1	R. R. Orr
	G-MTSJ	Thruster TST Mk 1	C. M. Gall
	G-MTSK	Thruster TST Mk 1	J. S. Pyke
	G-MTSM	Thruster TST Mk 1	R. J. Webb
	G-MTSS	Solar Wings Pegasus XL-R	V. Marchant
	G-MTSY	Solar Wings Pegasus XL-R	N. F. Waldron
	G-MTSZ	Solar Wings Pegasus XL-R	D. L. Pickover
	G-MTTE	Solar Wings Pegasus XL-R	J. N. Fowler
	G-MTTF	Aerotech MW6 Merlin	P. Cotton
	G-MTTI	Mainair Gemini/Flash IIA	R. J. Drake
	G-MTTM	Mainair Gemini/Flash IIA	M. Anderson
	G-MTTN	Ultralight Flight Phantom	F. P. Welsh
	G-MTTP	Mainair Gemini/Flash IIA	A. Ormson
	G-MTTU	Solar Wings Pegasus XL-R	A. Friend
	G-MTTW	Mainair Gemini/Flash IIA	G-MTTW Trustee Group
	G-MTTY	Solar Wings Pegasus XL-Q	N. A. Perry
	G-MTTZ	Solar Wings Pegasus XL-Q	J. Haskett
	G-MTUA	Solar Wings Pegasus XL-R	Fly Hire Ltd
	G-MTUC	Thruster TST Mk 1	S. T. G. Ingram
	G-MTUD	Thruster TST Mk 1	S. Cooper & J. Parker
	G-MTUI	Solar Wings Pegasus XL-R	J. Pool
	G-MTUK	Solar Wings Pegasus XL-R	G. McLaughlin
	G-MTUN	Solar Wings Pegasus XL-Q	M. J. O'Connor
	G-MTUP	Solar Wings Pegasus XL-Q	B. P. Vinall
	G-MTUR	Solar Wings Pegasus XL-Q	G. Ball
	G-MTUS	Solar Wings Pegasus XL-Q	G. Nicol
	G-MTUT	Solar Wings Pegasus XL-Q	R. E. Bull
	G-MTUU	Mainair Gemini/Flash IIA	M. Harris
	G-MTUV	Mainair Gemini/Flash IIA	D. Baker & S. Taylor
	G-MTUY	Solar Wings Pegasus XL-Q	H. C. Lowther
	G-MTVH	Mainair Gemini/Flash IIA	P. H. Statham
	G-MTVI	Mainair Gemini/Flash IIA	R. A. McDowell
	G-MTVJ	Mainair Gemini/Flash IIA	Microlight Flight Lessons
	G-MTVO	Solar Wings Pegasus XL-R	D. A. Payne
	G-MTVP	Thruster TST Mk 1	J. M. Evans
	G-MTVR	Thruster TST Mk 1	D. R. Lucas
	G-MTVT	Thruster TST Mk.1	W. H. J. Knowles
	G-MTVV	Thruster TST Mk 1	J. H. Askew
	G-MTVX	Solar Wings Pegasus XL-Q	D. A. Foster
	G-MTWG	Mainair Gemini/Flash IIA	N. Mackenzie & P. S. Bunting
	G-MTWH	CFM Shadow Srs BD	I. W. Hogg
	G-MTWK	CFM Shadow Srs BD	J. P. Batty & J. R. C. Brightman
	G-MTWR	Mainair Gemini/Flash IIA	J. B. Hodson
	G-MTWS	Mainair Gemini/Flash IIA	M. P. Duncan & C. R. Stewart
	G-MTWX	Mainair Gemini/Flash IIA	J. Donley
	G-MTWY	Thruster TST Mk 1	J. F. Gardner
	G-MTWZ	Thruster TST Mk 1	M. J. Aubrey
	G-MTXA	Thruster TST Mk 1	B. Dennis
	G-MTXB	Thruster TST Mk 1	J. J. Hill
	G-MTXC	Thruster TST Mk.1	W. Macleod
	G-MTXD	Thruster TST Mk 1	K. Myles
	G-MTXJ	Solar Wings Pegasus XL-Q	E. W. Laidlaw
	G-MTXL	Noble Hardman Snowbird Mk IV	P. J. Collins
	G-MTXM	Mainair Gemini/Flash IIA	H. J. Vinning
	G-MTXO	Whittaker MW6	M. W. Shepherd
	G-MTXR	CFM Shadow Srs BD	S. A. O'Neill
	G-MTXU	Snowbird Mk.IV	M. A. Oakley
	G-MTXZ	Mainair Gemini/Flash IIA	J. S. Hawkins
	G-MTYA	Solar Wings Pegasus XL-Q	R. Howieson
	G-MTYC	Solar Wings Pegasus XL-Q	C. I. D. H. Garrison
	G-MTYD	Solar Wings Pegasus XL-Q	R. S. Colebrook
	G-MTYF	Solar Wings Pegasus XL-Q	A. T. Willis
	G-MTYH	Solar Wings Pegasus XL-Q	S. Uzochukwu
	G-MTYI	Solar Wings Pegasus XL-Q	D. Ewing
	G-MTYL	Solar Wings Pegasus XL-Q	E. T. H. Cox

Reg.	Type	Owner or Operator	Notes
G-MTYR	Solar Wings Pegasus XL-Q	D. T. Evans	
G-MTYS	Solar Wings Pegasus XL-Q	R. G. Wall	
G-MTYV	Southdown Raven X	S. R. Jones	
G-MTYW	Raven X	R. Solomons	
G-MTYY	Solar Wings Pegasus XL-R	L. A. Hosegood	
G-MTZA	Thruster TST Mk 1	J. F. Gallagher	
G-MTZB	Thruster TST Mk 1	J. E. Davies	
G-MTZC	Thruster TST Mk 1	R. W. Marshall	
G-MTZE	Thruster TST Mk 1	B. S. P. Finch	
G-MTZF	Thruster TST Mk 1	D. C. Marsh	
G-MTZG	Mainair Gemini/Flash IIA	A. P. Fenn	
G-MTZH	Mainair Gemini/Flash IIA	D. C. Hughes	
G-MTZL	Mainair Gemini/Flash IIA	N. S. Brayn	
G-MTZO	Mainair Gemini/Flash IIA	R. C. Hinds	
G-MTZR	Solar Wings Pegasus XL-Q	P. J. Hatchett	
G-MTZW	Mainair Gemini/Flash IIA	S. I. Hatherall	
G-MTZX	Mainair Gemini/Flash IIA	R. G. Cuckow	
G-MTZY	Mainair Gemini/Flash IIA	K. M. Gough & R. Dunn	
G-MTZZ	Mainair Gemini/Flash IIA	G. J. Cadden	
G-MUCK	Lindstrand LBL 77A	C. J. Wootton	
G-MUDD	Hughes 369E	Derwen Plant Co.Ltd	
G-MUDI	PA-18-150 Super Cub	R. S. Grace (G-BCFO)	
G-MUDY	PA-18-150 Super Cub	C. S. Grace (G-OTUG)	
G-MUIR	Cameron V-65 balloon	L. C. M. Muir	
G-MUKY	Van's RV-8	I. E. K. Mackay	
G-MULT	Beech 76 Duchess	Folada Aero & Technical Services Ltd	
G-MUMM	Colt 180A balloon	D. K. Hempleman-Davis	
G-MUMY	Vans RV-4	S. D. Howes	
G-MUNI	Mooney M.20J	P. R. Williams	
G-MURG	Van's RV-6	Cadmium Lake Ltd	
G-MUSH	Robinson R44 II	Heli Air Ltd/Wellesbourne	
G-MUSO	Rutan LongEz	C. J. Tadjeran/Sweden	
G-MUTT	CZAW Sportcruiser	W. Gillam	
G-MUTZ	Avtech Jabiru J430	N. C. Dean	
G-MUZY	Titan T-51 Mustang	D. Stephens	
G-MVAC	CFM Shadow Srs BD	R. G. Place	
G-MVAH	Thruster TST Mk 1	M. W. H. Henton	
G-MVAI	Thruster TST Mk 1	G. E. Norton	
G-MVAJ	Thruster TST Mk 1	D. Watson	
G-MVAM	CFM Shadow Srs BD	C. P. Barber	
G-MVAN	CFM Shadow Srs BD	R. W. Frost	
G-MVAO	Mainair Gemini/Flash IIA	S. W. Grainger	
G-MVAP	Mainair Gemini/Flash IIA	B. D. Pettit	
G-MVAR	Solar Wings Pegasus XL-R	A. J. Thomas	
G-MVAV	Solar Wings Pegasus XL-R	D. J. Utting	
G-MVAW	Solar Wings Pegasus XL-Q	G. Sharman	
G-MVAX	Solar Wings Pegasus XL-Q	N. M. Cuthbertson	
G-MVAY	Solar Wings Pegasus XL-Q	V. O. Morris	
G-MVBC	Aerial Arts Tri-Flyer 130SX	D. Beer	
G-MVBF	Mainair Gemini/Flash IIA	E. McCallum	
G-MVBG	Mainair Gemini/Flash IIA	D. W. Curtis	
G-MVBI	Mainair Gemini/Flash IIA	S. Irwin	
G-MVBK	Mainair Gemini/Flash IIA	B. R. McLoughlin	
G-MVBL	Mainair Gemini/Flash IIA	S. T. Cain	
G-MVBM	Mainair Gemini/Flash IIA	G. Hall	
G-MVBN	Mainair Gemini/Flash IIA	N. C. Stone	
G-MVBO	Mainair Gemini/Flash IIA	J. A. Brown	
G-MVBP	Thruster TST Mk 1	G-MVBP Group	
G-MVBT	Thruster TST Mk 1	TST Group Flying	
G-MVBZ	Solar Wings Pegasus XL-R	A. G. Butler	
G-MVCA	Solar Wings Pegasus XL-R	R. Walker	
G-MVCC	CFM Shadow Srs BD	R. D. Layton	
G-MVCD	Medway Hybred 44XLR	V. W. Beynon	
G-MVCF	Mainair Gemini/Flash IIA	M. W. Luke	
G-MVCL	Solar Wings Pegasus XL-Q	T. E. Robinson	
G-MVCM	Solar Wings Pegasus XL-Q	P. J. Croney	
G-MVCN	Solar Wings Pegasus XL-Q	C. J. Lamb	
G-MVCR	Solar Wings Pegasus XL-Q	P. Hoeft	
G-MVCS	Solar Wings Pegasus XL-Q	J. J. Sparrow	
G-MVCT	Solar Wings Pegasus XL-Q	G. S. Lampitt	

Notes	Reg.	Type	Owner or Operator
	G-MVCV	Solar Wings Pegasus XL-Q	G. Stewart
	G-MVCW	CFM Shadow Srs BD	D. A. Coupland
	G-MVCY	Mainair Gemini/Flash IIA	A. M. Smith
	G-MVCZ	Mainair Gemini/Flash IIA	P. J. Devine
	G-MVDA	Mainair Gemini/Flash IIA	C. Tweedley
	G-MVDE	Thruster TST Mk 1	G. L. Roberts
	G-MVDF	Thruster TST Mk 1	G-MVDF Syndicate
	G-MVDG	Thruster TST Mk 1	B. M. Grant
	G-MVDH	Thruster TST Mk 1	T. W. Davis
	G-MVDJ	Medway Hybred 44XLR	W. D. Hutchins
	G-MVDK	Aerial Arts Chaser S	S. Adams
	G-MVDL	Aerial Arts Chaser S	N. P. Lloyd
	G-MVDP	Aerial Arts Chaser S	R. G. Mason
	G-MVDT	Mainair Gemini/Flash IIA	D. C. Stephens
	G-MVDV	Solar Wings Pegasus XL-R	K. Mudra
	G-MVDY	Solar Wings Pegasus XL-R	C. G. Murphy
	G-MVDZ	Solar Wings Pegasus XL-R	A. K. Pickering
	G-MVEC	Solar Wings Pegasus XL-R	J. A. Jarvis
	G-MVEG	Solar Wings Pegasus XL-R	A. M. Shaw
	G-MVEH	Mainair Gemini/Flash IIA	E. J. Elliott
	G-MVEI	CFM Shadow Srs BD	I. G. Ferguson
	G-MVEL	Mainair Gemini/Flash IIA	M. R. Starling
	G-MVEN	CFM Shadow Srs BD	T. S. L. Mucklow
	G-MVES	Mainair Gemini/Flash IIA	J. Helm
	G-MVET	Mainair Gemini/Flash IIA	C. Buttery
	G-MVEZ	Solar Wings Pegasus XL-Q	P. W. Millar
	G-MVFA	Solar Wings Pegasus XL-Q	D. J. Bromley
	G-MVFB	Solar Wings Pegasus XL-Q	M. O. Bloy
	G-MVFC	Solar Wings Pegasus XL-Q	J. K. Ewing
	G-MVFD	Solar Wings Pegasus XL-Q	C. D. Humphries
	G-MVFE	Solar Wings Pegasus XL-Q	S. J. Weeks
	G-MVFF	Solar Wings Pegasus XL-Q	A. Makepiece
	G-MVFH	CFM Shadow Srs BD	M. D. Goad
	G-MVFJ	Thruster TST Mk 1	B. E. Reneham
	G-MVFL	Thruster TST Mk 1	E. J. Wallington
	G-MVFM	Thruster TST Mk 1	G. J. Boyer
	G-MVFO	Thruster TST Mk 1	S. R. James Humberstone & A. L. Higgins
	G-MVFT	Solar Wings Pegasus XL-R	J. Bohea
	G-MVFX	Thruster TST Mk 1	A. M. Dalgetty
	G-MVFZ	Solar Wings Pegasus XL-R	R. K. Johnson
	G-MVGA	Aerial Arts Chaser S	N. R. Beale
	G-MVGC	AMF Chevvron 2-32	W. Fletcher
	G-MVGD	AMF Chevvron 2-32	T. R. James
	G-MVGF	Aerial Arts Chaser S	P. J. Higgins
	G-MVGG	Aerial Arts Chaser S	J. A. Horn
	G-MVGH	Aerial Arts Chaser S	J. A. Horn
	G-MVGK	Aerial Arts Chaser S	D. J. Smith
	G-MVGM	Mainair Gemini/Flash IIA	J. K. Clayton
	G-MVGN	Solar Wings Pegasus XL-R	M. J. Smith
	G-MVGO	Solar Wings Pegasus XL-R	J. B. Peacock
	G-MVGP	Solar Wings Pegasus XL-R	J. P. Cox
	G-MVGY	Medway Hybred 44XL	M. Vines
	G-MVGZ	Ultraflight Lazair IIIE	D. M. Broom
	G-MVHD	CFM Shadow Srs BD	D. Raybould
	G-MVHE	Mainair Gemini/Flash IIA	R. J. Lear
	G-MVHG	Mainair Gemini/Flash II	C. A. J. Elder
	G-MVHH	Mainair Gemini/Flash IIA	A. M. Lynch
	G-MVHI	Thruster TST Mk 1	G. L. Roberts
	G-MVHJ	Thruster TST Mk 1	F. Omaraie-Hamdanie
	G-MVHK	Thruster TST Mk 1	D. J. Gordon
	G-MVHL	Thruster TST Mk 1	G. Jones
	G-MVHN	Aerial Arts Chaser S	N. D. Townend
	G-MVHP	Solar Wings Pegasus XL-Q	J. B. Gasson
	G-MVHR	Solar Wings Pegasus XL-Q	J. M. Hucker
	G-MVHS	Solar Wings Pegasus XL-Q	A. P. Clarke
	G-MVIB	Mainair Gemini/Flash IIA	LSA Systems
	G-MVIE	Aerial Arts Chaser S	T. M. Stiles
	G-MVIF	Medway Raven X	A. C. Hing
	G-MVIG	CFM Shadow Srs BD	M. J. Green
	G-MVIH	Mainair Gemini/Flash IIA	T. M. Gilesnan
	G-MVIL	Noble Hardman Snowbird Mk IV	S. J. Reid
	G-MVIN	Noble Hardman Snowbird Mk.IV	C. P. Dawes

Reg.	Type	Owner or Operator	Notes
G-MVIO	Noble Hardman Snowbird Mk.IV	C. R. Taylor	
G-MVIP	AMF Chevvron 232	P. C. Avery	
G-MVIR	Thruster TST Mk 1	T. D. B. Gardner	
G-MVIT	Thruster TST Mk 1	A. C. Bell	
G-MVIU	Thruster TST Mk 1	Anglesey Thrusters Syndicate	
G-MVIV	Thruster TST Mk 1	G. Rainey	
G-MVIX	Mainair Gemini/Flash IIA	S. G. A. Milburn	
G-MVIZ	Mainair Gemini/Flash IIA	D. G. Fisher	
G-MVJC	Mainair Gemini/Flash IIA	B. Temple	
G-MVJD	Solar Wings Pegasus XL-R	D. L. Price	
G-MVJE	Mainair Gemini FlashIIA	M. D. Payne	
G-MVJF	Aerial Arts Chaser S	V. S. Rudham	
G-MVJG	Aerial Arts Chaser S	T. H. Scott	
G-MVJK	Aerial Arts Chaser S	S. P. Maher	
G-MVJM	Microflight Spectrum	S. E. Whitehouse	
G-MVJN	Solar Wings Pegasus XL-Q	A. L. Brown	
G-MVJP	Solar Wings Pegasus XL-Q	S. H. Bakowski	
G-MVJR	Solar Wings Pegasus XL-Q	Group JR	
G-MVJU	Solar Wings Pegasus XL-Q	J. C. Sutton	
G-MVKB	Medway Hybred 44XLR	J. Newby	
G-MVKC	Mainair Gemini/Flash IIA	M. Faulkner	
G-MVKH	Solar Wings Pegasus XL-R	K. M. Elson	
G-MVKJ	Solar Wings Pegasus XL-R	G. V. Warner	
G-MVKK	Solar Wings Pegasus XL-R	G. P. Burns	
G-MVKL	Solar Wings Pegasus XL-R	J. Powell-Tuck	
G-MVKM	Solar Wings Pegasus XL-R	A. J. Clarke	
G-MVKN	Solar Wings Pegasus XL-Q	N. N. James	
G-MVKO	Solar Wings Pegasus XL-Q	A. R. Hughes	
G-MVKP	Solar Wings Pegasus XL-Q	J. Williams	
G-MVKS	Solar Wings Pegasus XL-Q	K. S. Wright	
G-MVKT	Solar Wings Pegasus XL-Q	P. W. Ruffle	
G-MVKU	Solar Wings Pegasus XL-Q	I. K. Priestley	
G-MVKV	Solar Wings Pegasus XL-Q	D. R. Stansfield	
G-MVKW	Solar Wings Pegasus XL-Q	A. T. Scott	
G-MVKZ	Aerial Arts Chaser S	K. P. Smith	
G-MVLA	Aerial Arts Chaser S	K. R. Emery	
G-MVLB	Aerial Arts Chaser S	R. P. Wilkinson	
G-MVLC	Aerial Arts Chaser S	B. R. Barnes	
G-MVLD	Aerial Arts Chaser S	J. D. Doran	
G-MVLE	Aerial Arts Chaser S	R. G. hooker	
G-MVLJ	CFM Shadow Srs B	R. S. Cochrane	
G-MVLL	Mainair Gemini/Flash IIA	S. Coldicott	
G-MVLR	Mainair Gemini/Flash IIA	P. A. Louis	
G-MVLS	Aerial Arts Chaser S	C. Murphy	
G-MVLT	Aerial Arts Chaser S	P. H. Newson	
G-MVLX	Solar Wings Pegasus XL-Q	J. F. Smith	
G-MVLY	Solar Wings Pegasus XL-Q	I. B. Osborn	
G-MVMA	Solar Wings Pegasus XL-Q	G. C. Winter-Goodwin	
G-MVMC	Solar Wings Pegasus XL-Q	I. W. Barlow	
G-MVMG	Thruster TST Mk 1	A. D. McCaldin	
G-MVMK	Medway Hybred 44XLR	D. J. Lewis	
G-MVML	Aerial Arts Chaser S	G. C. Luddington	
G-MVMM	Aerial Arts Chaser S	D. Margereson	
G-MVMR	Mainair Gemini/Flash IIA	P. W. Ramage	
G-MVMT	Mainair Gemini/Flash IIA	R. F. Sanders	
G-MVMV	Aerotech MW5 (K) Sorcerer	J. M. Macdonald	
G-MVMW	Mainair Gemini/Flash IIA	G. Jones	
G-MVMX	Mainair Gemini/Flash IIA	D. J. Rooney	
G-MVNA	Powerchute Raider	J. McGoldrick	
G-MVNB	Powerchute Raider	A. L. Inwood	
G-MVNC	Powerchute Raider	R. S. McFadyen	
G-MVNE	Powerchute Raider	A. E. Askew	
G-MVNL	Powerchute Raider	E. C. Rhodes	
G-MVNM	Gemini/Flash IIA	C. D. Phillips	
G-MVNP	Aerotech MW5 (K) Sorcerer	A. M. Edwards	
G-MVNR	Aerotech MW5 (K) Sorcerer	E. I. Rowlands-Jones	
G-MVNS	Aerotech MW5 (K) Sorcerer	A. M. Sirant	
G-MVNW	Mainair Gemini/Flash IIA	D. J. Gregory	
G-MVNX	Mainair Gemini/Flash IIA	J. P. Neilan	
G-MVNY	Mainair Gemini/Flash IIA	M. K. Buckland	
G-MVNZ	Mainair Gemini/Flash IIA	Microlight Flight Lessons	
G-MVOB	Mainair Gemini/Flash IIA	E. Cave & P. Norton	

Notes	Reg.	Type	Owner or Operator
	G-MVOD	Aerial Arts Chaser 110SX	N. R. Beale
	G-MVOF	Mainair Gemini/Flash IIA	P. J. Nolan
	G-MVOH	CFM Shadow Srs B	I. C. Lewis
	G-MVOJ	Noble Hardman Snowbird Mk IV	C. D. Beetham
	G-MVON	Mainair Gemini/Flash IIA	D. S. Lally
	G-MVOO	AMF Chevvron 2-32	M. K. Field
	G-MVOP	Aerial Arts Chaser S	D. Thorpe
	G-MVOR	Mainair Gemini/Flash IIA	P. T. & R. M. Jenkins
	G-MVOT	Thruster TST Mk 1	R. I. Seed
	G-MVOV	Thruster TST Mk 1	G-MVOV Group
	G-MVPA	Mainair Gemini/Flash IIA	J. E. Milburn
	G-MVPB	Mainair Gemini/Flash IIA	G. A. Harper
	G-MVPC	Mainair Gemini/Flash IIA	W. O. Flannery
	G-MVPD	Mainair Gemini/Flash IIA	P. Thelwel
	G-MVPF	Medway Hybred 44XLR	G. H. Crick
	G-MVPH	Whittaker MW6 Merlin	A. K. Mascord
	G-MVPI	Mainair Gemini/Flash IIA	A. Shand
	G-MVPK	CFM Shadow Srs B	P. Sarfas
	G-MVPM	Whittaker MW6 Merlin	K. W. Curry
	G-MVPN	Whittaker MW6 Merlin	A. M. Field
	G-MVPR	Solar Wings Pegasus XL-Q	C. R. Grainger
	G-MVPS	Solar Wings Pegasus XL-Q	R. J. Hood
	G-MVPX	Solar Wings Pegasus XL-Q	N. Ionita
	G-MVPY	Solar Wings Pegasus XL-Q	G. H. Dawson
	G-MVRA	Mainair Gemini/Flash IIA	F. Flood
	G-MVRB	Mainair Gemini/Flash	G. Callaghan
	G-MVRD	Mainair Gemini/Flash IIA	A. R. Helm
	G-MVRG	Aerial Arts Chaser S	J. P. Kynaston
	G-MVRH	Solar Wings Pegasus XL-Q	K. Farr
	G-MVRI	Solar Wings Pegasus XL-Q	P. Martin
	G-MVRM	Mainair Gemini/Flash IIA	J. S. Stevenson
	G-MVRO	CFM Shadow Srs CD	K. H. Creed
	G-MVRP	CFM Shadow Srs BD	P. J. Tyler
	G-MVRR	CFM Shadow Srs BD	S. P. Christian
	G-MVRS	CFM Shadow Srs BD ★	Aero Venture
	G-MVRT	CFM Shadow Srs BD	P. J. Houtman
	G-MVRW	Solar Wings Pegasus XL-Q	D. L. Hadley
	G-MVRZ	Medway Hybred 44XLR	I. Oswald
	G-MVSE	Solar Wings Pegasus XL-Q	L. B. Richardson
	G-MVSG	Aerial Arts Chaser S	M. Roberts
	G-MVSI	Medway Hybred 44XLR	C. T. H. Tenison
	G-MVSJ	Aviasud Mistral 532	D. W. Curtis
	G-MVSM	Midland Ultralights Sirocco	C. G. Benham
	G-MVSN	Mainair Gemini/Flash IIA	G. B. Wade
	G-MVSO	Mainair Gemini/Flash IIA	A. B. Shayes
	G-MVSP	Mainair Gemini/Flash IIA	D. R. Buchanan
	G-MVST	Mainair Gemini/Flash IIA	M. D. Harper
	G-MVSW	Solar Wings Pegasus XL-Q	K. Perratt
	G-MVSX	Solar Wings Pegasus XL-Q	A. R. Law
	G-MVTA	Solar Wings Pegasus XL-Q	P. Hanby
	G-MVTD	Whittaker MW6 Merlin	G. J. Green
	G-MVTF	Aerial Arts Chaser S 447	S. R. McKiernan
	G-MVTI	Solar Wings Pegasus XL-Q	P. J. Taylor
	G-MVTJ	Solar Wings Pegasus XL-Q	M. P. & R. A. Wells
	G-MVTK	Solar Wings Pegasus XL-Q	A. J. Owen
	G-MVTL	Aerial Arts Chaser S	N. D. Meer
	G-MVTM	Aerial Arts Chaser S	G. L. Davies
	G-MVUA	Mainair Gemini/Flash IIA	E. W. Hughes
	G-MVUB	Thruster T.300	A. K. Grayson
	G-MVUC	Medway Hybred 44XLR	B. Pounder
	G-MVUF	Solar Wings Pegasus XL-Q	G. P. Blakemore
	G-MVUI	Solar Wings Pegasus XL-Q	J. K. Edgecombe & P. E. Hadley
	G-MVUJ	Solar Wings Pegasus XL-Q	J. H. Cooper
	G-MVUO	AMF Chevvron 2-32	W. D. M. Turtle
	G-MVUR	Hornet RS-ZA	G. R. Puffett
	G-MVUS	Aerial Arts Chaser S	H. Poyzer
	G-MVUU	Hornet ZA	K. W. Warn
	G-MVVI	Medway Hybred 44XLR	C. J. Turner
	G-MVVK	Solar Wings Pegasus XL-R	A. J. Weir
	G-MVVO	Solar Wings Pegasus XL-Q	A. L. Scarlett
	G-MVVP	Solar Wings Pegasus XL-Q	I. Pite
	G-MVVT	CFM Shadow Srs BD	W. F. Hayward

Reg.	Type	Owner or Operator	Notes
G-MVVV	AMF Chevvron 2-32	J. S. Firth	
G-MVVZ	Powerchute Raider	A. E. Askew	
G-MVWJ	Powerchute Raider	N. J. Doubek	
G-MVWN	Thruster T.300	Whisky November Group	
G-MVWR	Thruster T.300	G. Rainey	
G-MVWS	Thruster T.300	R. J. Hunphries	
G-MVWW	Aviasud Mistral	Golf Whisky Whisky Group	
G-MVWZ	Aviasud Mistral	C. Buckley	
G-MVXA	Brewster I MW6	J. C. Gates	
G-MVXB	Mainair Gemini/Flash IIA	P. A. Henderson	
G-MVXC	Mainair Gemini/Flash IIA	A. Worthington	
G-MVXJ	Medway Hybred 44XLR	P. J. Wilks	
G-MVXN	Aviasud Mistral	P. W. Cade	
G-MVXP	Aerial Arts Chaser S	P. Blackburn	
G-MVXR	Mainair Gemini/Flash IIA	D. M. Bayne	
G-MVXV	Aviasud Mistral	M. F. E. Chalk	
G-MVXX	AMF Chevvron 232	T. R. James	
G-MVYC	Solar Wings Pegasus XL-Q	P. E. L. Street	
G-MVYD	Solar Wings Pegasus XL-Q	B. Birtle	
G-MVYE	Thruster TST Mk 1	M. J. Aubrey	
G-MVYN	Hornet RS-ZA	M. A. Avossa	
G-MVYR	Medway Hybred 44XLR	K. J. Clarke	
G-MVYS	Mainair Gemini/Flash IIA	P. D. Finch	
G-MVYT	Noble Hardman Snowbird Mk IV	M. A. Oakley	
G-MVYV	Noble Hardman Snowbird Mk IV	D. W. Hayden	
G-MVYW	Noble Hardman Snowbird Mk IV	T. J. Harrison	
G-MVYX	Noble Hardman Snowbird Mk IV	R. McBlain	
G-MVYY	Aerial Arts Chaser S508	R. G. Mason	
G-MVYZ	CFM Shadow Srs BD	T. G. Solomon	
G-MVZA	Thruster T.300	C. C. Belcher	
G-MVZC	Thruster T.300	S. Dougan	
G-MVZD	Thruster T.300	G-MVZD Syndicate	
G-MVZI	Thruster T.300	R. R. R. Whittern	
G-MVZJ	Solar Wings Pegasus XL-Q	G. P. Burns	
G-MVZK	Quad City Challenger II	A. Clift	
G-MVZL	Solar Wings Pegasus XL-Q	P. R. Dobson	
G-MVZM	Aerial Arts Chaser S	J. L. Parker	
G-MVZO	Medway Hybred 44XLR	S. J. Taft	
G-MVZP	Murphy Renegade Spirit UK	The North American Syndicate	
G-MVZS	Mainair Gemini/Flash IIA	R. L. Beese	
G-MVZT	Solar Wings Pegasus XL-Q	C. J. Meadows	
G-MVZU	Solar Wings Pegasus XL-Q	M. G. McMurray	
G-MVZV	Solar Wings Pegasus XL-Q	K. D. Masters	
G-MVZX	Renegade Spirit UK	G. Holmes	
G-MVZZ	AMF Chevvron 232	W. A. L. Mitchell	
G-MWAB	Mainair Gemini/Flash IIA	J. E. Buckley	
G-MWAC	Solar Wings Pegasus XL-Q	H. Lloyd-Hughes	
G-MWAD	Solar Wings Pegasus XL-Q	J. K.Evans	
G-MWAE	CFM Shadow Srs BD	M. D. Brown	
G-MWAF	Solar Wings Pegasus XL-R	J. P. Bonner	
G-MWAJ	Murphy Renegade Spirit UK	L. D. Blair	
G-MWAN	Thruster T.300	E. J. Girling	
G-MWAP	Thruster T.300	The Wanda Flying Group	
G-MWAT	Solar Wings Pegasus XL-Q	D. G. Seymour	
G-MWAV	Solar Wings Pegasus XL-R	T. Woodward	
G-MWAW	Whittaker MW6 Merlin	G. J. Charter	
G-MWBI	Medway Hybred 44XLR	G. E. Coates	
G-MWBJ	Medway Sprint	C. C. Strong	
G-MWBK	Solar Wings Pegasus XL-Q	A. W. Jarvis	
G-MWBL	Solar Wings Pegasus XL-R	J. C. Ring	
G-MWBS	Hornet RS-ZA	P. D. Jaques	
G-MWBW	Hornet RS-ZA	C. G. Bentley	
G-MWBY	Hornet RS-ZA	Forestair Dragoons Ltd	
G-MWCB	Solar Wings Pegasus XL-Q	R. J. Lockyer	
G-MWCC	Solar Wings Pegasus XL-R	I. K. Priestley	
G-MWCE	Mainair Gemini/Flash IIA	B. A. Tooze	
G-MWCF	Solar Wings Pegasus XL-R	R. McKie	
G-MWCG	Microflight Spectrum	C. Ricketts	
G-MWCH	Rans S.6 Coyote	G-MWCH Group	
G-MWCK	Powerchute Kestrel	A. E. Askew	
G-MWCL	Powerchute Kestrel	R. W. Twamley	
G-MWCM	Powerchute Kestrel	G. E. Lockyer	

Notes	Reg.	Type	Owner or Operator
	G-MWCN	Powerchute Kestrel	S. T. P. Askew
	G-MWCO	Powerchute Kestrel	J. R. E. Gladstone
	G-MWCP	Powerchute Kestrel	R. S. McFadyen
	G-MWCS	Powerchute Kestrel	M. A. Avossa
	G-MWCY	Medway Hybred 44XLR	J. K. Masters
	G-MWDB	CFM Shadow Srs BD	M. D. Meade
	G-MWDC	Solar Wings Pegasus XL-R	R. Littler
	G-MWDE	Hornet RS-ZA	H. G. Reid
	G-MWDI	Hornet RS-ZA	R. J. Perrin
	G-MWDK	Solar Wings Pegasus XL-R	T. Wicks
	G-MWDL	Solar Wings Pegasus XL-R	D. J. Windsor
	G-MWDN	CFM Shadow Srs BD	A. S. Wason
	G-MWDS	Thruster T.300	S. Hazelden
	G-MWDZ	Eipper Quicksilver MXL II	S. Cooper & J. Parker
	G-MWEG	Solar Wings Pegasus XL-Q	S. P. Michlig
	G-MWEH	Solar Wings Pegasus XL-Q	K. A. Davidson
	G-MWEK	Whittaker MW5 Sorcerer	D. W. & M. L. Squire
	G-MWEL	Mainair Gemini/Flash IIA	E. St John-Foti
	G-MWEN	CFM Shadow Srs BD	C. Dawn
	G-MWEO	Whittaker MW5 Sorcerer	J. Morton
	G-MWEP	Rans S.4 Coyote	E. J. Wallington
	G-MWER	Solar Wings Pegasus XL-Q	J. A. O'Neill
	G-MWES	Rans S.4 Coyote	J. M. Coffin
	G-MWEY	Hornet RS-ZA	J. Kidd
	G-MWEZ	CFM Shadow Srs CD	G-MWEZ Group
	G-MWFB	CFM Shadow Srs CD	J. S. Morgan
	G-MWFC	TEAM mini-MAX (G-BTXC)	P. C. C. H. Crossley
	G-MWFD	TEAM mini-MAX	J. T. Blackburn
	G-MWFF	Rans S.4 Coyote	P. J. Greenrod
	G-MWFG	Powerchute Kestrel	R. I. Simpson
	G-MWFL	Powerchute Kestrel	M. A. Stevenson
	G-MWFT	MBA Tiger Cub 440	J. R. Ravenhill
	G-MWFU	Quad City Challenger II UK	C. J. Whittaker
	G-MWFV	Quad City Challenger II UK	M. Liptrot
	G-MWFW	Rans S.4 Coyote	M. P. Hallam
	G-MWFX	Quad City Challenger II UK	I. M. Walton
	G-MWFY	Quad City Challenger II UK	C. C. B. Soden
	G-MWFZ	Quad City Challenger II UK	A. Slade
	G-MWGA	Rans S.5 Coyote	P. C. Burns
	G-MWGG	Mainair Gemini/Flash IIA	D. G. Fisher
	G-MWGI	Whittaker MW5 (K) Sorcerer	J. R. Surbey
	G-MWGJ	Whittaker MW5 (K) Sorcerer	I. Pearson
	G-MWGK	Whittaker MW5 (K) Sorcerer	R. J. Cook
	G-MWGL	Solar Wings Pegasus XL-Q	F. McGlynn
	G-MWGN	Rans S.4 Coyote II	V. Hallam
	G-MWGR	Solar Wings Pegasus XL-Q	N. Ionita
	G-MWGU	Powerchute Kestrel	M. Pandolfino
	G-MWGZ	Powerchute Kestrel	J. L. Lynch
	G-MWHC	Solar Wings Pegasus XL-Q	P. J. Lowery
	G-MWHF	Solar Wings Pegasus XL-Q	N. J. Troke
	G-MWHG	Solar Wings Pegasus XL-Q	I. A. Lumley
	G-MWHH	TEAM mini-MAX	I. D. Worthington
	G-MWHI	Mainair Gemini/Flash	P. Harwood
	G-MWHL	Solar Wings Pegasus XL-Q	S. J. Reader
	G-MWHO	Mainair Gemini/Flash IIA	C. Campion-Sheen
	G-MWHP	Rans S.6-ESD Coyote	J. F. Bickerstaffe
	G-MWHR	Mainair Gemini/Flash IIA	B. Brazier
	G-MWHT	Solar Wings Pegasus Quasar	C. G. Jarvis
	G-MWHX	Solar Wings Pegasus XL-Q	N. P. Kelly
	G-MWIA	Mainair Gemini/Flash IIA	G. R. Reynolds
	G-MWIB	Aviasud Mistral	J. Broome
	G-MWIC	Whittaker MW5 Sorcerer	A. M. Witt
	G-MWIE	Solar Wings Pegasus XL-Q	X. S. Norman
	G-MWIF	Rans S.6-ESD Coyote II	K. Kelly
	G-MWIG	Mainair Gemini/Flash IIA	A. P. Purbrick
	G-MWIM	Solar Wings Pegasus Quasar	C. G. Dix
	G-MWIO	Rans S.4 Coyote	K. T. Short
	G-MWIP	Whittaker MW6 Merlin	B. J. Merret & D. Beer
	G-MWIS	Solar Wings Pegasus XL-Q	P. G. Strangward
	G-MWIU	Pegasus Quasar TC	W. Hepburn
	G-MWIW	Solar Wings Pegasus Quasar	W. R. Furness
	G-MWIX	Solar Wings Pegasus Quasar	G. Hawes

Reg.	Type	Owner or Operator	Notes
G-MWIZ	CFM Shadow Srs BD	T. P. Ryan	
G-MWJF	CFM Shadow Srs BD	S. N. White	
G-MWJH	Solar Wings Pegasus Quasar	S. W. Walker	
G-MWJI	Solar Wings Pegasus Quasar	L. Luscombe	
G-MWJJ	Solar Wings Pegasus Quasar	G. F. Campbell & I. A. Gilroy	
G-MWJK	Solar Wings Pegasus Quasar	M. Richardson	
G-MWJN	Solar Wings Pegasus XL-Q	J. C. Corrall	
G-MWJP	Medway Hybred 44XLR	C. D. Simmons	
G-MWJR	Medway Hybred 44XLR	T. G. Almond	
G-MWJT	Solar Wings Pegasus Quasar	D. L. Mitchell	
G-MWJX	Medway Puma Sprint	C. D. Hignell	
G-MWKE	Hornet R-ZA	D. R. Stapleton	
G-MWKO	Solar Wings Pegasus XL-Q	P. M. Golden	
G-MWKX	Microflight Spectrum	C. R. Ions	
G-MWKY	Solar Wings Pegasus XL-Q	D. R. Williams	
G-MWKZ	Solar Wings Pegasus XL-Q	T. G. Burston & I. A. Fox-Mills	
G-MWLA	Rans S.4 Coyote	J. A. R. Hughes	
G-MWLB	Medway Hybred 44XLR	G. P. D. Coan	
G-MWLD	CFM Shadow Srs BD	J. J. Hansen	
G-MWLE	Solar Wings Pegasus XL-R	D. Stevenson	
G-MWLG	Solar Wings Pegasus XL-R	C. Cohen	
G-MWLJ	Solar Wings Pegasus Quasar	P 7 M Aviation Ltd	
G-MWLK	Solar Wings Pegasus Quasar	D. J. Shippen	
G-MWLL	Solar Wings Pegasus XL-Q	A. J. Bacon	
G-MWLM	Solar Wings Pegasus XL-Q	M. C. Wright	
G-MWLN	Whittaker MW6-S Fatboy Flyer	S. J. Field	
G-MWLO	Whittaker MW6 Merlin	G-MWLO Flying Group	
G-MWLP	Mainair Gemini/Flash IIA	C. E. J. Moultrie	
G-MWLS	Medway Hybred 44XLR	M. A. Oliver	
G-MWLU	Solar Wings Pegasus XL-R	T. P. G. Ward	
G-MWLW	TEAM mini-MAX	E. J. Oteng	
G-MWLX	Mainair Gemini/Flash IIA	J. K. Kerr, B. O. Lyell & C. Usher	
G-MWLZ	Rans S.4 Coyote	B. O. McCartan	
G-MWMB	Powerchute Kestrel	E. C. Rhodes	
G-MWMC	Powerchute Kestrel	Talgarreg Flying Club	
G-MWMD	Powerchute Kestrel	D. J. Jackson	
G-MWMF	Powerchute Kestrel	P. J. Blundell	
G-MWMG	Powerchute Kestrel	M. D. Walton	
G-MWMH	Powerchute Kestrel	E. W. Potts	
G-MWMI	SolarWings Pegasus Quasar	R. G. Wyatt	
G-MWML	SolarWings Pegasus Quasar	S. C. Key	
G-MWMM	Mainair Gemini/Flash IIA	R. H. Church	
G-MWMN	Solar Wings Pegasus XL-Q	P. A. Arnold & N. A. Rathbone	
G-MWMO	Solar Wings Pegasus XL-Q	D. S. F. McNair	
G-MWMS	Mainair Gemini/Flash	J. Swindail	
G-MWMV	Solar Wings Pegasus XL-R	M. Nutting	
G-MWMW	Renegade Spirit UK	A. L. & S. Roberts	
G-MWMX	Mainair Gemini/Flash IIA	P. G. Hughes/Ireland	
G-MWMY	Mainair Gemini/Flash IIA	A. D. Bales	
G-MWNB	Solar Wings Pegasus XL-Q	P. F. J. Rogers	
G-MWND	Tiger Cub Developments RL.5A	D. A. Pike	
G-MWNE	Mainair Gemini/Flash IIA	D. Matthews	
G-MWNF	Renegade Spirit UK	R. Haslam	
G-MWNG	Solar Wings Pegasus XL-Q	H. C. TRhomson	
G-MWNK	Solar Wings Pegasus Quasar	G. S. Lynn	
G-MWNL	Solar Wings Pegasus Quasar	Galaxy Microlights	
G-MWNO	AMF Chevvron 232	I. K. Hogg	
G-MWNP	AMF Chevvron 232	M. K. Field	
G-MWNR	Renegade Spirit UK	RJR Flying Group	
G-MWNS	Mainair Gemini/Flash IIA	J. G. Hilliard	
G-MWNT	Mainair Gemini/Flash IIA	November Tango Group	
G-MWNU	Mainair Gemini/Flash IIA	C. C. Muir	
G-MWNX	Powerchute Kestrel	J. H. Greenroyd	
G-MWOC	Powerchute Kestrel	D. M. F. Harvey	
G-MWOD	Powerchute Kestrel	T. Morgan	
G-MWOE	Powerchute Raider	S. T. P. Askew	
G-MWOH	Solar Wings Pegasus XL-R	J. D. Buchanan	
G-MWOI	Solar Wings Pegasus XL-R	B. T. Geoghegan	
G-MWOJ	Mainair Gemini/Flash IIA	C. J. Pryce	
G-MWOO	Renegade Spirit UK	R. C. Wood	
G-MWOR	Solar Wings Pegasus XL-Q	S. E. Smith	
G-MWOV	Whittaker MW6 Merlin	S. Jeffs	

Notes	Reg.	Type	Owner or Operator
	G-MWOY	Solar Wings Pegasus XL-Q	S. P. Griffin
	G-MWPB	Mainair Gemini/Flash IIA	J. Fenton
	G-MWPC	Mainair Gemini/Flash IIA	S. J. Ware
	G-MWPD	Mainair Gemini/Flash IIA	M. R. Picksley
	G-MWPE	Solar Wings Pegasus XL-Q	E. C. R. Hudson
	G-MWPF	Mainair Gemini/Flash IIA	G. P. Taggart
	G-MWPG	Microflight Spectrum	D. Brunton
	G-MWPH	Microflight Spectrum	A. Whittaker
	G-MWPN	CFM Shadow Srs.CD	W. R. H. Thomas
	G-MWPP	CFM Streak Shadow	A. J. Price
	G-MWPR	Whittaker MW6 Merlin	S. F. N. Warnell
	G-MWPS	Renegade Spirit UK	M. D. Stewart
	G-MWPW	AMF Chevvron 2-32C	M. S. Westman
	G-MWPX	Solar Wings Pegasus XL-R	R. J. Wheeler
	G-MWPZ	Renegade Spirit UK	J. Ievers
	G-MWRC	Mainair Gemini/Flash IIA	S. D. Glover
	G-MWRD	Mainair Gemini/Flash IIA	D. Morton
	G-MWRE	Mainair Gemini/Flash IIA	A. Williams
	G-MWRF	Mainair Gemini/Flash IIA	N. Hay
	G-MWRH	Mainair Gemini/Flash IIA	E. G. Astin
	G-MWRJ	Mainair Gemini/Flash IIA	J. M. Breaks
	G-MWRL	CFM Shadow Srs.CD	I. W. Hogg
	G-MWRN	Solar Wings Pegasus XL-R	D. T. Mackenzie
	G-MWRR	Mainair Gemini/Flash IIA	J. Clark t/a G-MWRR Group
	G-MWRS	Ultravia Super Pelican	T. B. Woolley
	G-MWRT	Solar Wings Pegasus XL-R	G. L. Gunnell
	G-MWRU	Solar Wings Pegasus XL-R	R. Barton
	G-MWRY	CFM Shadow Srs CD	A. T. Armstrong
	G-MWSA	TEAM mini-MAX	G. J. Jones
	G-MWSB	Mainair Gemini/Flash IIA	P. J. Bosworth
	G-MWSC	Rans S.6-ESD Coyote II	I. Fernihough
	G-MWSD	Solar Wings Pegasus XL-Q	A. M. Harley
	G-MWSF	Solar Wings Pegasus XL-R	J. J. Freeman
	G-MWSI	Solar Wings Pegasus Quasar TC	K. C. Noakes
	G-MWSJ	Solar Wings Pegasus XL-Q	R. J. Collison
	G-MWSK	Solar Wings Pegasus XL-Q	J. Doogan
	G-MWSL	Mainair Gemini/Flash IIA	C. W. Frost
	G-MWSM	Mainair Gemini/Flash IIA	R. M. Wall
	G-MWSO	Solar Wings Pegasus XL-R	M. A. Clayton
	G-MWSP	Solar Wings Pegasus XL-R	S. I. Hatherall
	G-MWST	Medway Hybred 44XLR	A. Ferguson
	G-MWSU	Medway Hybred 44XLR	T. De Landro
	G-MWSW	Whittaker MW6 Merlin	S. F. N. Warnell
	G-MWSX	Whittaker MW5 Sorcerer	P. J. Hellyer
	G-MWSY	Whittaker MW5 Sorcerer	J. E. Holloway
	G-MWSZ	CFM Shadow Srs CD	M. W. W. Clotworthy
	G-MWTC	Solar Wings Pegasus XL-Q	M. M. Chittenden
	G-MWTI	Solar Wings Pegasus XL-Q	O. G. Johns
	G-MWTJ	CFM Shadow Srs CD	T. D. Wolstenholme
	G-MWTL	Solar Wings Pegasus XL-R	B. Lindsay
	G-MWTN	CFM Shadow Srs CD	M. J. Broom
	G-MWTO	Mainair Gemini/Flash IIA	E. Beckett
	G-MWTP	CFM Shadow Srs CD	R. E. M. Gibson-Bevan
	G-MWTR	Mainair Gemini/Flash IIA	C. Montlake
	G-MWTT	Rans S.6-ESD Coyote II	L. E. Duffin
	G-MWTZ	Mainair Gemini/Flash IIA	C. W. R. Felce
	G-MWUA	CFM Shadow Srs CD	Cloudbase Aviation
	G-MWUB	Solar Wings Pegasus XL-R	T. R. L. Bayley
	G-MWUD	Solar Wings Pegasus XL-R	A. J. Weir
	G-MWUI	AMF Chevvron 2-32C	S. Wilson
	G-MWUK	Rans S.6-ESD Coyote II	G. K. Hoult & S. J. C. Pollock
	G-MWUL	Rans S.6-ESD Coyote II	D. M. Bayne
	G-MWUN	Rans S.6-ESD Coyote II	J. Parke
	G-MWUO	Solar Wings Pegasus XL-Q	A. P. Slade
	G-MWUR	Solar Wings Pegasus XL-R	Nottingham Aerotow Club
	G-MWUS	Solar Wings Pegasus XL-R	H. R. Loxton
	G-MWUU	Solar Wings Pegasus XL-R	B. R. Underwood
	G-MWUV	Solar Wings Pegasus XL-R	C. D. Baines
	G-MWUW	Solar Wings Pegasus XL-R	Ultraflight Microlights Ltd
	G-MWUX	Solar Wings Pegasus XL-Q	B. D. Attwell
	G-MWUY	Solar Wings Pegasus XL-Q	M. J. Sharp
	G-MWUZ	Solar Wings Pegasus XL-Q	S. R. Nanson

Reg.	Type	Owner or Operator	Notes
G-MWVA	Solar Wings Pegasus XL-Q	D. P. Henderson	
G-MWVE	Solar Wings Pegasus XL-R	W. A. Keel-Stocker	
G-MWVF	Solar Wings Pegasus XL-R	J. B. Wright	
G-MWVG	CFM Shadow Srs CD	Shadow Aviation Ltd	
G-MWVH	CFM Shadow Srs CD	M. McKenzie	
G-MWVL	Rans S.6-ESD Coyote II	J. C. Gates	
G-MWVM	Solar Wings Pegasus Quasar II	A. A. Edmonds	
G-MWVN	Mainair Gemini/Flash IIA	J. McCafferty	
G-MWVO	Mainair Gemini/Flash IIA	J. P. Neilan	
G-MWVP	Renegade Spirit UK	P. D. Mickleburgh	
G-MWVT	Mainair Gemini/Flash IIA	R. M. Wigman	
G-MWVY	Mainair Gemini/Flash IIA	A. Mundy	
G-MWVZ	Mainair Gemini/Flash IIA	R. W. Twamley	
G-MWWB	Mainair Gemini/Flash IIA	W. P. Seward	
G-MWWC	Mainair Gemini/Flash IIA	D. & A. Margereson	
G-MWWD	Renegade Spirit	R. A. Arrowsmith	
G-MWWH	Solar Wings Pegasus XL-Q	A. J. Alexander	
G-MWWI	Mainair Gemini/Flash IIA	M. A. S. Nesbitt	
G-MWWK	Mainair Gemini/Flash IIA	S. D. Puddle	
G-MWWN	Mainair Gemini/Flash IIA	R. Whitby	
G-MWWR	Microflight Spectrum	T. H. Evans	
G-MWWS	Thruster T.300	J. Parker	
G-MWWV	Solar Wings Pegasus XL-Q	R. W. Livingstone	
G-MWWZ	Cyclone Chaser S	P. K. Dale	
G-MWXA	Mainair Gemini/Flash IIA	M. Briongos	
G-MWXF	Mainair Mercury	D. McAuley	
G-MWXG	Solar Wings Pegasus Quasar IITC	J. E. Moseley	
G-MWXH	Solar Wings Pegasus Quasar IITC	R. P. Wilkinson	
G-MWXJ	Mainair Mercury	P. J. Taylor	
G-MWXK	Mainair Mercury	M. P. Wilkinson	
G-MWXP	Solar Wings Pegasus XL-Q	A. P. Attfield	
G-MWXV	Mainair Gemini/Flash IIA	M. S. Nichols	
G-MWXW	Cyclone Chaser S	K. C. Dodd	
G-MWXX	Cyclone Chaser S 447	P. I. Frost	
G-MWXY	Cyclone Chaser S 447	D. Curtis	
G-MWXZ	Cyclone Chaser S 508	D. L. Hadley	
G-MWYA	Mainair Gemini/Flash IIA	R. F. Hunt	
G-MWYC	Solar Wings Pegasus XL-Q	M. A. Collins	
G-MWYD	CFM Shadow Srs C	F. E. Greenfield	
G-MWYE	Rans S.6-ESD Coyote II	G. A. M. Moffat	
G-MWYG	Mainair Gemini/Flash IIA	S. P. McVeigh	
G-MWYI	Solar Wings Pegasus Quasar II	T. S. Chadfield	
G-MWYJ	Solar Wings Pegasus Quasar II	A. Clarke & L. B. Hughes	
G-MWYL	Mainair Gemini/Flash IIA	A. J. Hinks	
G-MWYM	Cyclone Chaser S 1000	C. J. Meadows	
G-MWYS	CGS Hawk 1 Arrow	Civilair	
G-MWYT	Mainair Gemini/Flash IIA	J. R. Kendall	
G-MWYU	Solar Wings Pegasus XL-Q	L. A. Dotchin	
G-MWYV	Mainair Gemini/Flash IIA	R. Bricknell	
G-MWYY	Mainair Gemini/Flash IIA	R. D. Allard	
G-MWYZ	Solar Wings Pegasus XL-Q	D. P. Graham	
G-MWZA	Mainair Mercury	A. J. Malham	
G-MWZB	AMF Microlight Chevvron 2-32C	E. Ratcliffe	
G-MWZD	Solar Wings Pegasus Quasar IITC	N. W. Mallen	
G-MWZF	Solar Wings Pegasus Quasar IITC	R. G. T. Corney	
G-MWZI	Solar Wings Pegasus XL-R	K. J. Slater	
G-MWZJ	Solar Wings Pegasus XL-R	P. Kitchen	
G-MWZL	Mainair Gemini/Flash IIA	D. Renton	
G-MWZM	TEAM mini-MAX 91	I. D. Worthington	
G-MWZO	Solar Wings Pegasus Quasar IITC	A. Robinson	
G-MWZP	Solar Wings Pegasus Quasar IITC	C. Garton	
G-MWZR	Solar Wings Pegasus Quasar IITC	R. Veart	
G-MWZS	Solar Wings Pegasus Quasar IITC	G. Bennett	
G-MWZU	Solar Wings Pegasus XL-R	A. D. Winebloom	
G-MWZV	Solar Wings Pegasus XL-R	D. J. Newby	
G-MWZY	Solar Wings Pegasus XL-R	S. J. Barkworth	
G-MWZZ	Solar Wings Pegasus XL-R	The Microlight School (Lichfield) Ltd	
G-MXMX	PA-46-350T Malibu Matrix	Feabrex Ltd	
G-MXPH	BAC.167 Strikemaster Mk 84 (311)	R. S. Partridge-Hicks (G-SARK)	
G-MXVI	VS.361 Spitfire LF.XVIe (TE184:D)	S. R. Stead	

Notes	Reg.	Type	Owner or Operator
	G-MYAB	Solar Wings Pegasus XL-R	A. N. F. Stewart
	G-MYAC	Solar Wings Pegasus XL-Q	M. E. Gilman
	G-MYAE	Solar Wings Pegasus XL-Q	C. R. Bunce
	G-MYAF	Solar Wings Pegasus XL-Q	M. Rees
	G-MYAG	Quad City Challenger II	I. Murray
	G-MYAH	Whittaker MW5 Sorcerer	J. Bolton
	G-MYAI	Mainair Mercury	J. Ellerton
	G-MYAJ	Rans S.6-ESD Coyote II	R. M. Moulton
	G-MYAN	Whittaker MW5 (K) Sorcerer	A. F. Reid
	G-MYAO	Mainair Gemini/Flash IIA	R. A. Chapman
	G-MYAR	Thruster T.300	G. Hawkins
	G-MYAS	Mainair Gemini/Flash IIA	J. R. Davis
	G-MYAT	TEAM mini-MAX	M. W. Hands
	G-MYAZ	Renegade Spirit UK	R. Smith
	G-MYBA	Rans S.6-ESD Coyote II	A. M. Hughes
	G-MYBB	Maxair Drifter	M. Ingleton
	G-MYBC	CFM Shadow Srs CD	M. E. Gilbert
	G-MYBE	Solar Wings Pegasus Quasar IITC	G. Bullock & A. Turner
	G-MYBF	Solar Wings Pegasus XL-Q	K. H. Pead
	G-MYBI	Rans S.6-ESD Coyote II	D. Wilkinson
	G-MYBJ	Mainair Gemini/Flash IIA	G. C. Bowers
	G-MYBM	TEAM mini-MAX	B. Hunter
	G-MYBN	Hiway Demon 175	B. R. Lamming
	G-MYBO	Solar Wings Pegasus XL-R	D. Gledhill
	G-MYBR	Solar Wings Pegasus XL-Q	M. J. Larbey & G. T. Hunt
	G-MYBT	Solar Wings Pegasus Quasar IITC	G. A. Rainbow-Ockwell
	G-MYBU	Cyclone Chaser S 447	R. L. Arscott
	G-MYBV	Solar Wings Pegasus XL-Q	L. R. Hodgson
	G-MYBW	Solar Wings Pegasus XL-Q	J. S. Chapman
	G-MYCA	Whittaker MW6 Merlin	R. A. L-V. Harris
	G-MYCB	Cyclone Chaser S 447	P. Sykes
	G-MYCE	Solar Wings Pegasus Quasar IITC	S. W. Barker
	G-MYCJ	Mainair Mercury	C. A. McLean
	G-MYCK	Mainair Gemini/Flash IIA	T. Kelly
	G-MYCL	Mainair Mercury	P. B. Cole
	G-MYCM	CFM Shadow Srs CD	Aviation for Paraplegics & Tetraplegics Trust
	G-MYCN	Mainair Mercury	P. Lowham
	G-MYCO	Renegade Spirit UK	T. P. Williams
	G-MYCP	Whittaker MW6 Merlin	A. C. Jones
	G-MYCR	Mainair Gemini/Flash IIA	A. P. King
	G-MYCS	Mainair Gemini/Flash IIA	Husthwaite Alpha Group
	G-MYCT	TEAM Mini-MAX 91	R. Smith
	G-MYCX	Powerchute Kestrel	S. J. Pugh-Jones
	G-MYDA	Powerchute Kestrel	K. J. Greatrix
	G-MYDC	Mainair Mercury	M. Howard & K. Littlefair
	G-MYDD	CFM Shadow Srs CD	C. H. Gem/Spain
	G-MYDE	CFM Shadow Srs CD	D. N. L. Howell
	G-MYDF	TEAM mini-MAX	J. G. Bright
	G-MYDJ	Solar Wings Pegasus XL-R	Cambridgeshire Aerotow Club
	G-MYDK	Rans S.6-ESD Coyote II	J. W. Caush & W. Doyle
	G-MYDM	Whittaker MW6-S Fatboy Flyer	K. Gregan
	G-MYDN	Quad City Challenger II	T. C. Hooks
	G-MYDP	Kolb Twinstar Mk 3	Norberts Flying Group
	G-MYDR	Thruster Tn.300	H. G. Soper
	G-MYDT	Thruster T.300	J. B. Grotrian
	G-MYDU	Thruster T.300	S. Collins
	G-MYDV	Mainair Gemini /Flash IIA	S. J. Mazilis
	G-MYDX	Rans S.6-ESD Coyote II	V. Donskovas
	G-MYDZ	Mignet HM.1000 Balerit	D. S. Simpson
	G-MYEA	Solar Wings Pegasus XL-Q	A. M. Taylor
	G-MYED	Solar Wings Pegasus XL-R	G-MYED Group
	G-MYEH	Solar Wings Pegasus XL-R	J. Spuffard
	G-MYEI	Cyclone Chaser S447	D. J. Hyatt
	G-MYEJ	Cyclone Chaser S447	A. W. Lowrie
	G-MYEK	Solar Wings Pegasus Quasar IITC	I. D. Edwards
	G-MYEM	Solar Wings Pegasus Quasar IITC	D. J. Moore
	G-MYEN	Solar Wings Pegasus Quasar IITC	T. J. Feeney
	G-MYEO	Solar Wings Pegasus Quasar IITC	A. G. Curtis
	G-MYER	Cyclone AX3/503	T. F. Horrocks
	G-MYES	Rans S.6-ESD Coyote II	S. J. Mathison
	G-MYET	Whittaker MW6 Merlin	G. Campbell
	G-MYEX	Powerchute Kestrel	R. J. Watkin

Reg.	Type	Owner or Operator	Notes
G-MYFA	Powerchute Kestrel	M. Phillips	
G-MYFH	Quad City Challenger II	W. I. McMillan	
G-MYFK	Solar Wings Pegasus Quasar IITC	M. A. Azeem	
G-MYFL	Solar Wings Pegasus Quasar IITC	S. B. Wilkes	
G-MYFO	Cyclone Airsports Chaser S	O. J. Neece	
G-MYFP	Mainair Gemini/Flash IIA	R. C. Reynolds	
G-MYFR	Mainair Gemini/Flash IIA	S. B. Brady	
G-MYFT	Mainair Scorcher	M. R. Kirby	
G-MYFU	Mainair Gemini/Flash IIA	J. Payne	
G-MYFV	Cyclone AX3/503	J. K. Sargent	
G-MYFW	Cyclone AX3/503	Microlight School (Lichfield) Ltd	
G-MYGD	Cyclone AX3/503	K. B. Vickers	
G-MYGF	TEAM mini-MAX	R. D. Barnard	
G-MYGH	Rans S.6ESD Coyote II	N. Blair & D. G. Higgins	
G-MYGK	Cyclone Chaser S 508	P. C. Collins	
G-MYGM	Quad City Challenger II	G. J. Williams & J. White	
G-MYGN	AMF Chevvron 2-32C	P. J. Huston	
G-MYGO	CFM ShadowSrs CD	S. J. Joseph	
G-MYGP	Rans S.6-ESD Coyote II	R. H. Y. Farrer	
G-MYGR	Rans S.6-ESD Coyote II	P. Smith	
G-MYGT	Solar Wings Pegasus XL-R	Condors Aerotow Syndicate	
G-MYGU	Solar Wings Pegasus XL-R	J. A. Sims	
G-MYGV	Solar Wings Pegasus XL-R	J. A. Crofts & G. M. Birkett	
G-MYGZ	Mainair Gemini/Flash IIA	G. J. Molloy	
G-MYHG	Cyclone AX/503	N. P. Thomson & C. Alsop	
G-MYHH	Cyclone AX/503	D. J. Harber	
G-MYHI	Rans S.6-ESD Coyote II	I. J. Steele	
G-MYHJ	Cyclone AX3/503	B. J. Palfreyman	
G-MYHK	Rans S.6-ESD Coyote II	M. R. Williamson	
G-MYHL	Mainair Gemini/Flash IIA	M. Coates & H. B. Blackwell	
G-MYHM	Cyclone AX3/503	G-MYHM Group	
G-MYHN	Mainair Gemini/Flash IIA	H. J. Timms	
G-MYHP	Rans S.6-ESD Coyote II	K. E. Gair & D. M. Smith	
G-MYHR	Cyclone AX3/503	C. W. Williams	
G-MYIA	Quad City Challenger II	I. Pearson	
G-MYIF	CFM Shadow Srs CD	P. J. Edwards	
G-MYIH	Mainair Gemini/Flash IIA	A. N. Huddart	
G-MYII	TEAM mini-MAX	G. H. Crick	
G-MYIK	Kolb Twinstar Mk 3	B. A. Janaway	
G-MYIL	Cyclone Chaser S 508	R. A. Rawes	
G-MYIN	Solar Wings Pegasus Quasar IITC	W. P. Hughes	
G-MYIP	CFM Shadow Srs CD	T. Bailey	
G-MYIR	Rans S.6-ESD Coyote II	P. D. Smalley	
G-MYIS	Rans S.6-ESD Coyote II	I. S. Everett & M. Stott	
G-MYIT	Cyclone Chaser S 508	R. Barringer	
G-MYIV	Mainair Gemini/Flash IIA	P. F. Brightmore	
G-MYIX	Quad City Challenger II	M. Alaman	
G-MYIY	Mainair Gemini/Flash IIA	D. Jackson	
G-MYIZ	TEAM mini-MAX 2	J. C. Longmore	
G-MYJC	Mainair Gemini/Flash IIA	M. N. Irven	
G-MYJD	Rans S.6-ESD Coyote II	A. A. Ross	
G-MYJF	Thruster T.300	P. F. McConville	
G-MYJG	Thruster T.300	J. W. Rice	
G-MYJJ	Solar Wings Pegasus Quasar IITC	T. A. Willcox	
G-MYJK	Solar Wings Pegasus Quasar IITC	The Microlight School (Lichfield) Ltd	
G-MYJM	Mainair Gemini/Flash IIA	F. Tumelty	
G-MYJO	Cyclone Chaser S 508	A. W. Rawlings	
G-MYJS	Solar Wings Pegasus Quasar IITC	J. P. Rooms	
G-MYJT	Solar Wings Pegasus Quasar IITC	S. Ferguson	
G-MYJU	Solar Wings Pegasus Quasar IITC	D. Al-Bassam	
G-MYJZ	Whittaker MW5D Sorcerer	M. A. Summers	
G-MYKA	Cyclone AX3/503	T. Whittall	
G-MYKB	Kolb Twinstar Mk 3	T. Antell	
G-MYKE	CFM Shadow Srs BD	MKH Engineering	
G-MYKF	Cyclone AX3/503	M. A. Collins	
G-MYKG	Mainair Gemini/Flash IIA	B. D. Walker	
G-MYKH	Mainair Gemini/Flash IIA	A. W. Leadley	
G-MYKJ	TEAM mini-MAX	T. de Breffe Gardner	
G-MYKO	Whittaker MW6-S Fat Boy Flyer	J. A. Weston	
G-MYKR	Solar Wings Pegasus Quasar IITC	C. Stallard	
G-MYKS	Solar Wings Pegasus Quasar IITC	D. J. Oskis	
G-MYKT	Cyclone AX3/503	J. D. Sanger & J. E. Seager	

Notes	Reg.	Type	Owner or Operator
	G-MYKV	Mainair Gemini/Flash IIA	P. J. Gulliver
	G-MYKX	Mainair Mercury	D. T. McAfee
	G-MYKZ	TEAM mini-MAX	R. Targonski
	G-MYLB	TEAM mini-MAX	J. G. Burns
	G-MYLC	Solar Wings Pegasus Quantum 15	C. McKay
	G-MYLD	Rans S.6-ESD Coyote II	E. Kaplan
	G-MYLE	Solar Wings Pegasus Quantum 15	Quantum Quartet
	G-MYLF	Rans S.6-ESD Coyote II	A. J. Spencer
	G-MYLG	Mainair Gemini/Flash IIA	N. J. Axworthy
	G-MYLH	Solar Wings Pegasus Quantum 15	G. Carr
	G-MYLI	Solar Wings Pegasus Quantum 15	A. M. Keyte
	G-MYLK	Solar Wings Pegasus Quantum 15	G-MYLK Group
	G-MYLL	Solar Wings Pegasus Quantum 15	I. A. Macadam
	G-MYLM	Solar Wings Pegasus Quasar IITC	P. Osborne & S. B. Walters
	G-MYLN	Kolb Twinstar Mk 3	J. F. Joyes
	G-MYLO	Rans S.6-ESD Coyote II	P. Bowers
	G-MYLP	Kolb Twinstar Mk 3	R. Thompson (G-BVCR)
	G-MYLR	Mainair Gemini/Flash IIA	A. L. Lyall
	G-MYLS	Mainair Mercury	W. K. C. Davies
	G-MYLT	Mainair Blade	T. D. Hall
	G-MYLV	CFM Shadow Srs CD	Aviation for Paraplegics and Tetraplegics Trust
	G-MYLW	Rans S.6-ESD Coyote II	A. D. Dias
	G-MYLX	Medway Raven	K. Hayley
	G-MYLZ	Solar Wings Pegasus Quantum 15	W. G. McPherson
	G-MYMB	Solar Wings Pegasus Quantum 15	D. B. Jones
	G-MYMH	Rans S.6-ESD Coyote II	P. V. Stevens
	G-MYMI	Kolb Twinstar Mk.3	F. J. Brown
	G-MYMJ	Medway Raven	N. Brigginshaw
	G-MYMK	Mainair Gemini/Flash IIA	A. Britton
	G-MYML	Mainair Mercury	D. J. Dalley
	G-MYMM	Ultraflight Fun 18S	N. P. Power
	G-MYMN	Whittaker MW6 Merlin	K. J. Cole
	G-MYMP	Rans S.6-ESD Coyote II	R. L. Flowerday (G-CHAZ)
	G-MYMR	Rans S.6-ESD Coyote II	J. Minogue
	G-MYMS	Rans S.6-ESD Coyote II	P. G. Briscoe
	G-MYMV	Mainair Gemini/Flash IIA	A. J. Evans
	G-MYMW	Cyclone AX3/503	L. J. Perring
	G-MYMX	Solar Wings Pegasus Quantum 15	I. A. Thomson
	G-MYMZ	Cyclone AX3/503	Microlight School (Lichfield) Ltd
	G-MYNB	Solar Wings Pegasus Quantum 15	J. A. Gregorig
	G-MYND	Mainair Gemini/Flash IIA	S. Wild
	G-MYNE	Rans S.6-ESD Coyote II	J. L. Smoker
	G-MYNF	Mainair Mercury	C. I. Hemingway
	G-MYNH	Rans S.6-ESD Coyote II	E. F. & V. M. Clapham
	G-MYNI	TEAM mini-MAX	I. Pearson
	G-MYNK	Solar Wings Pegasus Quantum 15	J. Britton
	G-MYNL	Solar Wings Pegasus Quantum 15	S. J. Whalley
	G-MYNN	Solar Wings Pegasus Quantum 15	V. Loy
	G-MYNO	Solar Wings Pegasus Quantum 15	P. A. C. R. Stephens
	G-MYNP	Solar Wings Pegasus Quantum 15	K. A. Davidson
	G-MYNR	Solar Wings Pegasus Quantum 15	C. A. Reynolds
	G-MYNS	Solar Wings Pegasus Quantum 15	F. J. McVey
	G-MYNT	Solar Wings Pegasus Quantum 15	C. D. Arnold
	G-MYNV	Solar Wings Pegasus Quantum 15	J. Goldsmith-Ryan
	G-MYNX	CFM Streak Shadow SA	S. P. Fletcher
	G-MYNY	Kolb Twinstar Mk 3	I. F. Hill
	G-MYNZ	Solar Wings Pegasus Quantum 15	P. W. Rogers
	G-MYOA	Rans S6-ESD Coyote II	N. S. M. Day
	G-MYOG	Kolb Twinstar Mk 3	T. A. Womersley
	G-MYOH	CFM Shadow Srs CD	D. R. Sutton
	G-MYOL	Air Creation Fun 18S GTBIS	S. N. Bond
	G-MYON	CFM Shadow Srs CD	D. W. & S. E. Suttill
	G-MYOO	Kolb Twinstar Mk 3	P. D. Coppin
	G-MYOR	Kolb Twinstar Mk 3	R. W. Hocking
	G-MYOS	CFM Shadow Srs CD	C. A. & E. J. Bowles
	G-MYOT	Rans S.6-ESD Coyote II	D. E. Wilson
	G-MYOU	Solar Wings Pegasus Quantum 15	D. J. Tasker
	G-MYOV	Mainair Mercury	P. Newton
	G-MYOX	Mainair Mercury	K. Driver
	G-MYOZ	Quad City Challenger II UK	A. R. Thomson
	G-MYPA	Rans S.6-ESD Coyote II	M. A. Azeem
	G-MYPC	Kolb Twinstar Mk 3	S. J. Ball

Reg.	Type	Owner or Operator	Notes
G-MYPE	Mainair Gemini/Flash IIA	C. A. Carstairs	
G-MYPG	Solar Wings Pegasus XL-Q	V. Ashwell	
G-MYPH	Solar Wings Pegasus Quantum 15	P. M. J. White	
G-MYPI	Solar Wings Pegasus Quantum 15	P. L. Jarvis	
G-MYPJ	Rans S.6-ESD Coyote II	K. A. Eden	
G-MYPL	CFM Shadow Srs CD	G. I. Madden	
G-MYPN	Solar Wings Pegasus Quantum 15	P. J. S. Albon	
G-MYPP	Whittaker MW6-S Fat Boy Flyer	G. Everett & D. Smith	
G-MYPR	Cyclone AX3/503	K. D. Parnell	
G-MYPS	Whittaker MW6 Merlin	I. S. Bishop	
G-MYPT	CFM Shadow Srs CD	R. Gray	
G-MYPV	Mainair Mercury	B. Donnan	
G-MYPW	Mainair Gemini/Flash IIA	T. C. Edwards	
G-MYPX	Solar Wings Pegasus Quantum 15	C. Cleveland & M. M. P. Evans	
G-MYPY	Solar Wings Pegasus Quantum 15	C. Cheasman	
G-MYPZ	Quad City Challenger II	E. G. Astin	
G-MYRC	Mainair Blade	M. P. Sanderson	
G-MYRD	Mainair Blade	D. R. Slater	
G-MYRE	Cyclone Chaser S	S. W. Barker	
G-MYRF	Solar Wings Pegasus Quantum 15	P. D. Gregory	
G-MYRG	TEAM mini-MAX	J. Jones	
G-MYRH	Quad City Challenger II	G. Cousins	
G-MYRK	Renegade Spirit UK	D. J. Newton	
G-MYRL	TEAM mini-MAX	J. N. Hanson	
G-MYRM	Solar Wings Pegasus Quantum 15	B. R. & B. Dale	
G-MYRN	Solar Wings Pegasus Quantum 15	J. Houston & I. Waghorn	
G-MYRO	Cyclone AX3/503	R. S. Mole	
G-MYRP	Letov LK-2M Sluka	R. M. C. Hunter	
G-MYRS	Solar Wings Pegasus Quantum 15	J. E. Smith	
G-MYRT	Solar Wings Pegasus Quantum 15	Poet Pilot (UK) Ltd	
G-MYRU	Cyclone AX3/503	W. A. Emmerson	
G-MYRV	Cyclone AX3/503	M. Gardiner	
G-MYRW	Mainair Mercury	G. C. Hobson	
G-MYRY	Solar Wings Pegasus Quantum 15	N. J. Lindsay	
G-MYRZ	Solar Wings Pegasus Quantum 15	R. E. Forbes	
G-MYSA	Cyclone Chaser S 508	S. D. J. Harvey	
G-MYSB	Solar Wings Pegasus Quantum 15	P. H. Woodward	
G-MYSC	Solar Wings Pegasus Quantum 15	K. R. White	
G-MYSD	BFC Challlenger II	C. W. Udale	
G-MYSG	Mainair Mercury	P. T. Flanagan	
G-MYSI	HM14/93	A. R. D. Seaman	
G-MYSJ	Mainair Gemini/Flash IIA	A. Warnock	
G-MYSL	Aviasud Mistral	J. E. Midder	
G-MYSM	CFM Shadow Srs CD	L. W. Stevens	
G-MYSO	Cyclone AX3/50	R. Bowden	
G-MYSP	Rans S.6-ESD Coyote II	A. J. Alexander, B. Knight & K. G. Diamond	
G-MYSR	Solar Wings Pegasus Quatum 15	W. G. Craig	
G-MYSU	Rans S.6-ESD Coyote II	C. N. Nairn	
G-MYSV	Aerial Arts Chaser	S. H. Hailstone	
G-MYSW	Solar Wings Pegasus Quantum 1	C. Gane	
G-MYSX	Solar Wings Pegasus Quantum 1	L. E. Lesurf	
G-MYSY	Solar Wings Pegasus Quantum 15	B. D. S. Vere	
G-MYSZ	Mainair Mercury	W. Fletcher & S. D. J. Harvey	
G-MYTB	Mainair Mercur	P. J. Higgins	
G-MYTD	Mainair Blade	B. E. Warburton & D. B. Meades	
G-MYTE	Rans S.6-ESD Coyote II	R. A. Currinn	
G-MYTH	CFM Shadow Srs CD	S. G. Smith	
G-MYTI	Solar Wings Pegasus Quantum 15	K. M. Gaffney	
G-MYTJ	Solar Wings Pegasus Quantum 15	L. Blight	
G-MYTK	Mainair Mercury	D. A. Holroyd	
G-MYTL	Mainair Blade	I. T. Callagham & J. W. Coventry	
G-MYTN	Solar Wings Pegasus Quantum 15	P. C. Terry	
G-MYTO	Quad City Challenger II	A. Studley	
G-MYTP	Arrowflight Hawk II	R. J. Turner	
G-MYTT	Quad City Challenger II	D. M. Lockley	
G-MYTU	Mainair Blade	P. D. Hadley	
G-MYTV	Hunt Avon Skytrike	M. Carson	
G-MYTY	CFM Streak Shadow Srs M	D. M. Broom	
G-MYUA	Air Creation Fun 18S GTBIS	J. Leden	
G-MYUC	Mainair Blade	A. D. Clayton	
G-MYUD	Mainair Mercury	P. W. Margetson	
G-MYUF	Renegade Spirit	F. Overall	

Notes	Reg.	Type	Owner or Operator
	G-MYUH	Solar Wings Pegasus XL-Q	K. S. Daniels
	G-MYUI	Cyclone AX3/503	R. Foster
	G-MYUL	Quad City Challenger II UK	N. V. & B. M. R. Van Cleve
	G-MYUN	Mainair Blade	G. A. Barratt
	G-MYUO	Solar Wings Pegasus Quantum 15	E. J. Hughes
	G-MYUP	Letov LK-2M Sluka	J. C. Dawson
	G-MYUS	CFM Shadow Srs CD	Aviation for Paraplegics and Tetraplegics Trust
	G-MYUU	Pegasus Quantum 15	J. A. Slocombe
	G-MYUV	Pegasus Quantum 15	D. W. Wilson
	G-MYUW	Mainair Mercury	G. C. Hobson
	G-MYUZ	Rans S.6-ESD Coyote II	A. R. Trace
	G-MYVA	Kolb Twinstar Mk 3	E. Bayliss
	G-MYVB	Mainair Blade	P. Mountain
	G-MYVC	Pegasus Quantum 15	D. P. Clarke
	G-MYVE	Mainair Blade	S. Cooke
	G-MYVG	Letov LK-2M Sluka	C. I. Chegwen
	G-MYVH	Mainair Mercury	R. H. de C. Ribeiro
	G-MYVI	Air Creation Fun 18S GTBIS	Flylight Airsports Ltd
	G-MYVJ	Pegasus Quantum 15	A. I. McPherson & P. W. Davidson
	G-MYVK	Pegasus Quantum 15	O. C. Rash
	G-MYVL	Mainair Mercury	P. J. Judge
	G-MYVM	Pegasus Quantum 15	G. J. Gibson
	G-MYVN	Cyclone AX3/503	F. Watt
	G-MYVO	Mainair Blade	S. S. Raines
	G-MYVP	Rans S.6-ESD Coyote II	K. J. Legg
	G-MYVR	Pegasus Quantum 15	J. M. Webster
	G-MYVV	Medway Hybred 44XLR	S. Perity
	G-MYVY	Mainair Blade	G. Heeks
	G-MYVZ	Mainair Blade	R. Llewellyn
	G-MYWC	Hunt Wing	M. A. Coffin
	G-MYWE	Thruster T.600	W. A. Stephenson
	G-MYWG	Pegasus Quantum 15	S. L. Greene
	G-MYWH	Hunt Wing/Experience	G. N. Hatchett
	G-MYWJ	Pegasus Quantum 15	L. M. Sams & I. Clarkson
	G-MYWK	Pegasus Quantum 15	M. Garvey
	G-MYWL	Pegasus Quantum 15	S. J. Prouse
	G-MYWM	CFM Shadow Srs CD	N. J. McKinley
	G-MYWN	Cyclone Chaser S 508	R. A. Rawes
	G-MYWO	Pegasus Quantum 15	S. Gill & D. Hume
	G-MYWP	Kolb Twinstar Mk 3	P. R. Day
	G-MYWR	Pegasus Quantum 15	R. Horton
	G-MYWS	Cyclone Chaser S 447	M. H. Broadbent
	G-MYWT	Pegasus Quantum 15	P. B. J. Eveleigh
	G-MYWU	Pegasus Quantum 15	J. R. Buttle
	G-MYWV	Rans S.4C Coyote	P. G. Anthony & D. A. Crouchman
	G-MYWW	Pegasus Quantum 15	C. W. Bailie
	G-MYWY	Pegasus Quantum 15	A. S. R. Czajka
	G-MYXA	TEAM mini-MAX 91	D. H. Clack
	G-MYXB	Rans S.6-ESD Coyote II	K. Gerrard
	G-MYXC	Quad City Challenger II	J. N. Anyan
	G-MYXD	Pegasus Quasar IITC	A. Cochrane
	G-MYXE	Pegasus Quantum 15	J. F. Bolton
	G-MYXF	Air Creation Fun GT503	D. J. N. Brown
	G-MYXH	Cyclone AX3/503	S. Bond
	G-MYXI	Aries 1	H. Cook
	G-MYXJ	Mainair Blade	S. N. Robson
	G-MYXK	Quad City Challenger II	P. J. Collins
	G-MYXL	Mignet HM.1000 Baleri	R. W. Hollamby
	G-MYXM	Mainair Blade	S. C. Hodgson
	G-MYXN	Mainair Blade	P. K. Dale
	G-MYXP	Rans S.6-ESD Coyote II	R. S. Amor
	G-MYXS	Kolb Twinstar Mk 3	B. B. Boniface
	G-MYXT	Pegasus Quantum 15	R. E. J. Pattenden
	G-MYXU	Thruster T.300	D. W. Wilson
	G-MYXV	Quad City Challenger II	T. S. Savage
	G-MYXW	Pegasus Quantum 15	J. Uttley
	G-MYXX	Pegasus Quantum 15	G. Fish
	G-MYXY	CFM Shadow Srs CD	A. P. Watkins & C. W. J. Davis
	G-MYXZ	Pegasus Quantum 15	A. K. Hole
	G-MYYA	Mainair Blade	K. J. Watt
	G-MYYB	Pegasus Quantum 15	A. L. Johnson & D. S. Ross
	G-MYYC	Pegasus Quantum 15	S. B. Cooper

Reg.	Type	Owner or Operator	Notes
G-MYYD	Cyclone Chaser S 447	E. Kelly	
G-MYYF	Quad City Challenger II	J. G. & J. A. Smith	
G-MYYG	Mainair Blade	S. D. Pryke	
G-MYYI	Pegasus Quantum 15	C. M. Day	
G-MYYJ	Hunt Wing	R. M. Jarvis	
G-MYYK	Pegasus Quantum 15	J. D. Philp	
G-MYYL	Cyclone AX3/503	R. Ferguson	
G-MYYP	AMF Chevron 2-45CS	J. Cook	
G-MYYR	TEAM mini-MAX 91	L. S. Bailey	
G-MYYS	TEAM mini-MAX	J. Pulford	
G-MYYV	Rans S.6-ESD Coyote IIXL	J. Rochead	
G-MYYW	Mainair Blade	M. D. Kirby	
G-MYYX	Pegasus Quantum 15	B. J. Chapman	
G-MYYY	Mainair Blade	E. D. Lockie	
G-MYYZ	Medway Raven X	J. W. Leaper	
G-MYZB	Pegasus Quantum 15	M. A. Lovatt	
G-MYZC	Cyclone AX3/503	P. E. Owen	
G-MYZE	TEAM mini-MAX	J. Broome	
G-MYZF	Cyclone AX3/503	Microflight (Ireland) Ltd	
G-MYZG	Cyclone AX3/503	I. A. Holden	
G-MYZH	Chargus Titan 38	T. J. Gayton-Polley	
G-MYZJ	Pegasus Quantum 15	D. R. Harper	
G-MYZK	Pegasus Quantum 15	D. Logan	
G-MYZL	Pegasus Quantum 15	A. N. Grant	
G-MYZM	Pegasus Quantum 15	D. Hope	
G-MYZP	CFM Shadow Srs DD	A. Munro	
G-MYZR	Rans S.6-ESD Coyote II	Rans Clan	
G-MYZV	Rans S.6-ESD Coyote II	B. W. Savory	
G-MYZY	Pegasus Quantum 15	C. Chapman	
G-MZAA	Mainair Blade	A. G. Butler	
G-MZAB	Mainair Blade	D. C. Nixon	
G-MZAC	Quad City Challenger II	I. C. Lewis	
G-MZAE	Mainair Blade	D. J. Guild	
G-MZAF	Mainair Blade	N. R. Stockton	
G-MZAG	Mainair Blade	D. R. G. Cornwell	
G-MZAH	Rans S.6-ESD Coyote II	D. R. C. Bell	
G-MZAJ	Mainair Blade	M. P. Daley	
G-MZAK	Mainair Mercury	I. Rawson	
G-MZAM	Mainair Blade	B. M. Marsh & P. David	
G-MZAN	Pegasus Quantum 15	P. M. Leahy	
G-MZAP	Mainair Blade	K. D. Adams	
G-MZAR	Mainair Blade	P. Bowden	
G-MZAS	Mainair Blade	T. Carter	
G-MZAT	Mainair Blade	M. J. Moulton	
G-MZAU	Mainair Blade	A. F. Glover	
G-MZAV	Mainair Blade	G. Taylor	
G-MZAW	Pegasus Quantum 15	C. A. Mackenzie	
G-MZAZ	Mainair Blade	P. J. Pickering	
G-MZBA	Mainair Blade 912	W. H. McMinn	
G-MZBB	Pegasus Quantum 15	T. Campbell	
G-MZBC	Pegasus Quantum 15	B. M. Quinn	
G-MZBD	Rans S-6-ESD-XL Coyote II	J. P. & M. P. Tilzey	
G-MZBF	Letov LK-2M Sluka	V. Simpson	
G-MZBG	Hodder MW6-A	E. I. Rowlands-Jons & M. W. Kilvert	
G-MZBH	Rans S.6-ESD Coyote II	D. Sutherland	
G-MZBK	Letov LK-2M Sluka	A. W. Hodder	
G-MZBL	Mainair Blade	C. J. Rubery	
G-MZBN	CFM Shadow Srs B	W. J. Buskell	
G-MZBO	Pegasus Quantum 15	K. C. Beattie	
G-MZBR	Southdown Raven	D. M. Lane	
G-MZBS	CFM Shadow Srs D	S. K. Ryan	
G-MZBT	Pegasus Quantum 15	A. C. Barlow	
G-MZBU	Rans S.6-ESD Coyote II	R. S. Marriott	
G-MZBV	Rans S.6-ESD Coyote II	C. L. Barham & R. I. Cannan	
G-MZBW	Quad City Challenger II UK	R. M. C. Hunter	
G-MZBY	Pegasus Quantum 15	I. J. Rawlinson	
G-MZBZ	Quad City Challenger II UK	T. R. Gregory	
G-MZCA	Rans S.6-ESD Coyote II	W. Scott	
G-MZCB	Cyclone Chaser S 447	R. W. Keene	
G-MZCC	Mainair Blade 912	K. S. Rissmann	
G-MZCD	Mainair Blade	T. Drury & S. P. Maxwell	

Notes	Reg.	Type	Owner or Operator
	G-MZCE	Mainair Blade	I. C. Hindle
	G-MZCF	Mainair Blade	C. Hannanby
	G-MZCH	Whittaker MW6-S Fatboy Flyer	J. T. Moore
	G-MZCI	Pegasus Quantum 15	P. H. Risdale
	G-MZCJ	Pegasus Quantum 15	C. R. Madden
	G-MZCK	AMF Chevvron 2-32C	M. Daly
	G-MZCM	Pegasus Quantum 15	J. E. Bullock
	G-MZCN	Mainair Blade	P. Mulvey
	G-MZCR	Pegasus Quantum 15	J. E. P. Stubberfield
	G-MZCS	TEAM mini-MAX	R. F. Morton
	G-MZCT	CFM Shadow Srs CD	W. G. Gill
	G-MZCU	Mainair Blade	C. E. Pearce
	G-MZCV	Pegasus Quantum 15	I. Davidson
	G-MZCW	Pegasus Quantum 15	K. L. Baldwin
	G-MZCY	Pegasus Quantum 15	G. Murphy
	G-MZDA	Rans S.6-ESD Coyote IIXL	R. Plummer
	G-MZDB	Pegasus Quantum 15	Scottish Aerotow Club
	G-MZDC	Pegasus Quantum 15	M. T. Jones
	G-MZDD	Pegasus Quantum 15	A. J. Todd
	G-MZDE	Pegasus Quantum 15	R. G. Hedley
	G-MZDF	Mainair Blade	M. Liptrot
	G-MZDG	Rans S.6-ESD Coyote IIXL	B. Smith
	G-MZDH	Pegasus Quantum 15	N. W. Barnett
	G-MZDJ	Medway Raven X	R. Bryan & S. Digby
	G-MZDK	Mainair Blade	P. Combellack
	G-MZDL	Whittaker MW6-S Fatboy Flyer	N. Hogarth
	G-MZDM	Rans S.6-ESD Coyote II	M. E. Nicholas
	G-MZDN	Pegasus Quantum 15	P. G. Ford
	G-MZDP	AMF Chevvron 2-32	J. Pool
	G-MZDS	Cyclone AX3/503	S. F. N. Warnell
	G-MZDT	Mainair Blade	G. A. Davidson & I. Lee
	G-MZDU	Pegasus Quantum 15	G. Breen/Portugal
	G-MZDV	Pegasus Quantum 15	S. A. Mallett
	G-MZDX	Letov LK-2M Sluka	J. L. Barker
	G-MZDY	Pegasus Quantum 15	R. Bailey
	G-MZDZ	Hunt Wing	E. W. Laidlaw
	G-MZEA	BFC Challenger II	G. S. Cridland
	G-MZEB	Mainair Blade	R. A. Campbell
	G-MZEC	Pegasus Quantum 15	A. B. Godber
	G-MZED	Mainair Blade	G. G. Wilson & N. P. Gallon
	G-MZEE	Pegasus Quantum 15	J. L. Brogan
	G-MZEG	Mainair Blade	R. Jacques
	G-MZEH	Pegasus Quantum 15	P. S. Hall
	G-MZEJ	Mainair Blade	P. G. Thomas
	G-MZEK	Mainair Mercury	G. Crane
	G-MZEL	Cyclone Airsports AX3/503	L. M. Jackson & R. I. Simpson
	G-MZEM	Pegasus Quantum 15	L. H. Black
	G-MZEN	Rans S.6-ESD Coyote II	P. R. Hutty
	G-MZEO	Rans S.6-ESD Coyote IIXL	R. W. Lenthall
	G-MZEP	Mainair Rapier	A. G. Bird
	G-MZER	Cyclone AX2000	J. H. Keep
	G-MZES	Letov LK-2N Sluka	J. L. Self
	G-MZEU	Rans S.6-ESD Coyote IIXL	N. Grugan
	G-MZEV	Mainair Rapier	W. T. Gardner
	G-MZEW	Mainair Blade	T. D. Holder
	G-MZEX	Pegasus Quantum 15	J. P. Quinlan
	G-MZEY	Micro Bantam B.22	P. J. Glover
	G-MZEZ	Pegasus Quantum 15	M. J. Ing
	G-MZFA	Cyclone AX2000	G. S. Highley
	G-MZFB	Mainair Blade	A. J. Plant
	G-MZFC	Letov LK-2M Sluka	F. Overall
	G-MZFD	Mainair Rapier	R. J. Allerton
	G-MZFE	Hunt Wing	G. J. Latham
	G-MZFF	Hunt Wing	B. J. Adamson
	G-MZFG	Pegasus Quantum 15	A. M. Prentice
	G-MZFH	AMF Chevvron 2-32C	A. Greenwell
	G-MZFL	Rans S.6-ESD Coyote IIXL	H. Adams
	G-MZFM	Pegasus Quantum 15	M. McLaughlin
	G-MZFN	Rans S.6.ESD Coyote IIXL	C. J. & W. R. Wallbank
	G-MZFO	Thruster T.600N	S. J. P. Stevenson
	G-MZFS	Mainair Blade	S. L. Rowlands
	G-MZFT	Pegasus Quantum 15	C. Childs

Reg.	Type	Owner or Operator	Notes
G-MZFU	Thruster T.600N	P. G. Hullett	
G-MZFX	Cyclone AX2000	Avon Aerotow Group	
G-MZFY	Rans S.6-ESD Coyote IIXL	L. G. Tserkezos	
G-MZFZ	Mainair Blade	D. J. Bateman	
G-MZGA	Cyclone AX2000	K. G. Grayson & R. D. Leigh	
G-MZGB	Cyclone AX2000	P. Hegarty	
G-MZGC	Cyclone AX2000	C. E. Walls	
G-MZGD	Rans S.5 Coyote II	P. J. Greenrod	
G-MZGF	Letov LK-2M Sluka	G. Lombardi & R. C. Hinkins	
G-MZGG	Pegasus Quantum 15	P. J. Hopkins	
G-MZGH	Hunt Wing/Avon 462	J. H. Cole	
G-MZGI	Mainair Blade 912	H. M. Roberts	
G-MZGJ	Kolb Twinstar Mk 1	L. G. G. Faulkner	
G-MZGK	Pegasus Quantum 15	C. D. Cross & S. H. Moss	
G-MZGL	Mainair Rapier	D. Thrower	
G-MZGM	Cyclone AX2000	A. F. Smallacombe	
G-MZGN	Pegasus Quantum 15	B. J. Youngs	
G-MZGO	Pegasus Quantum 15	S. F. G. Allen	
G-MZGP	Cyclone AX2000	Buchan Light Aeroplane Club	
G-MZGR	TEAM mini-MAX	K. G. Seeley	
G-MZGS	CFM Shadow Srs BD	C. S. Nagy	
G-MZGU	Arrowflight Hawk II (UK)	J. N. Holden	
G-MZGV	Pegasus Quantum 15	H. Millington	
G-MZGW	Mainair Blade	R. Almond	
G-MZGX	Thruster T.600N	K. J. Underwood	
G-MZGY	Thruster T.600N 450	P. E. Young	
G-MZHA	Thruster T.600N	P. Stark	
G-MZHB	Mainair Blade	D. W. Curtis	
G-MZHD	Thruster T.600N	B. E. Foster	
G-MZHF	Thruster T.600N	R. Benner & K. Harmston	
G-MZHG	Whittaker MW6-T Merlin	D. R. Thompson	
G-MZHI	Pegasus Quantum 15	F. R. Macdonald	
G-MZHJ	Mainair Rapier	G. Standish & R. Jones	
G-MZHK	Pegasus Quantum 15	R. Hussain	
G-MZHM	Team Himax 1700R	M. H. McKeown	
G-MZHN	Pegasus Quantum 15	F. W. Ferichs	
G-MZHO	Quad City Challenger II	J. Pavelin	
G-MZHP	Pegasus Quantum 15	P. C. J. Coidan	
G-MZHR	Cyclone AX2000	D. K. Wedge	
G-MZHS	Thruster T.600T	J. R. Davis	
G-MZHT	Whittaker MW6 Merlin	G. J. Chadwick	
G-MZHV	Thruster T.600T	H. G. Denton	
G-MZHW	Thruster T.600N	H. & G. Willingham	
G-MZHY	Thruster T.600N	J. P. & R. E. Jones	
G-MZIB	Pegasus Quantum 15	S. Murphy	
G-MZID	Whittaker MW6 Merlin	C. P. F. Sheppard	
G-MZIE	Pegasus Quantum 15	Flylight Airsports Ltd	
G-MZIF	Pegasus Quantum 15	D. Parsons	
G-MZIH	Mainair Blade	N. J. Waller	
G-MZIJ	Pegasus Quantum 15	D. L. Wright	
G-MZIK	Pegasus Quantum 15	C. M. Wilkinson	
G-MZIL	Mainair Rapier	A. J. Owen & J. C. Price	
G-MZIM	Mainair Rapier	M. J. McKegney	
G-MZIR	Mainair Blade	S. Connor	
G-MZIS	Mainair Blade	M. K. Richings	
G-MZIT	Mainair Blade 912	P. M. Horn	
G-MZIU	Pegasus Quantum 15	A. P. Douglas-Dixon	
G-MZIV	Cyclone AX2000	C. J. Tomlin	
G-MZIW	Mainair Blade	S. R. Pickering	
G-MZIX	Mignet HM.1000 Balerit	P. E. H. Scott	
G-MZIY	Rans S.6-ESD Coyote II	G. Munro	
G-MZIZ	Renegade Spirit UK (G-MWGP)	B. L. R. J. Keeping	
G-MZJA	Mainair Blade	P. L. Dowd	
G-MZJD	Mainair Blade	D. A. Meek	
G-MZJE	Mainair Rapier	G. Ramsay & G. Shand	
G-MZJF	Cyclone AX2000	D. J. Lewis & V. E. Booth	
G-MZJG	Pegasus Quantum 15	K. M. C. Compton	
G-MZJH	Pegasus Quantum 15	P. Copping	
G-MZJJ	Maverick	G. S. Jackson	
G-MZJK	Mainair Blade	P. G. Angus	
G-MZJL	Cyclone AX2000	M. H. Owen	
G-MZJM	Rans S.6-ESD Coyote IIXL	K. A. Hastie	

Notes	Reg.	Type	Owner or Operator
	G-MZJO	Pegasus Quantum 15	D. J. Cook
	G-MZJP	Whittaker MW6-S Fatboy Flyer	R. C. Funnell & D. J. Burton
	G-MZJR	Cyclone AX2000	N. A. Martin
	G-MZJS	Meridian Maverick	M. F. Farrer
	G-MZJT	Pegasus Quantum 15	N. Hammerton
	G-MZJV	Mainair Blade 912	M. A. Roberts
	G-MZJW	Pegasus Quantum 15	M. J. J. Clutterbuck
	G-MZJX	Mainair Blade	N. Cowell & D. Nicholls
	G-MZJY	Pegasus Quantum 15	M. F. Turff
	G-MZJZ	Mainair Blade	A. Openshaw
	G-MZKA	Pegasus Quantum 15	S. P. Tkaczyk
	G-MZKC	Cyclone AX2000	G-MZKC Group
	G-MZKD	Pegasus Quantum 15	T. M. Frost
	G-MZKE	Rans S.6-ESD Coyote IIXL	P. A. Flaherty
	G-MZKF	Pegasus Quantum 15	J. Mooney
	G-MZKG	Mainair Blade	N. S. Rigby
	G-MZKH	CFM Shadow Srs DD	S. P. H. Calvert
	G-MZKI	Mainair Rapier	D. L. Aspinall
	G-MZKJ	Mainair Blade	The G-MZKJ Group
	G-MZKL	Pegasus Quantum 15	G. Williams
	G-MZKN	Mainair Rapier	J. McAloney
	G-MZKR	Thruster T.600N	R. J. Arnett
	G-MZKS	Thruster T.600N	P. J. Hepburn
	G-MZKT	Thruster T.600N	Great Thornes Flying Group
	G-MZKU	Thruster T.600N	A. S. Day
	G-MZKV	Mainair Blade 912	J. D. Harriman
	G-MZKW	Quad City Challenger II	K. W. Warn
	G-MZKY	Pegasus Quantum 15	P. S. Constable
	G-MZKZ	Mainair Blade	R. P. Wolstenholme
	G-MZLA	Pegasus Quantum 15	A. J. Harris
	G-MZLC	Mainair Blade 912	R. A. L. Harris
	G-MZLD	Pegasus Quantum 15	D. Hamilton
	G-MZLE	Maverick (G-BXSZ)	J. S. Hill
	G-MZLF	Pegasus Quantum 15	S. Seymour
	G-MZLG	Rans S.6-ESD Coyote IIXL	F. Y. Allery
	G-MZLI	Mignet HM.1000 Balerit	A. G. Barr
	G-MZLJ	Pegasus Quantum 15	R. M. Williams
	G-MZLK	Solar Wings Typhoon/Tri-Pacer	A. Leak
	G-MZLL	Rans S.6-ESD Coyote II	J. A. Willats & G. W. Champion
	G-MZLM	Cyclone AX2000	P. E. Hadley
	G-MZLN	Pegasus Quantum 15	P. A. Greening
	G-MZLP	CFM Shadow Srs D	D. J. Gordon
	G-MZLR	Solar Wings Pegasus XL-Q	B. Lorraine
	G-MZLS	Cyclone AX2000	S. Swanick
	G-MZLT	Pegasus Quantum 15	P. E. Woodhead
	G-MZLU	Cyclone AX2000	E. Pashley & A. W. Lees
	G-MZLV	Pegasus Quantum 15	A. Armsby
	G-MZLW	Pegasus Quantum 15	R. W. R. Crevel & D. P. Hampson
	G-MZLX	Micro Aviation B.22S Bantam	V. J. Vaughan
	G-MZLY	Letov LK-2M Sluka	W. McCarthy
	G-MZLZ	Mainair Blade	W. Biddulph
	G-MZMA	Solar Wings Pegasus Quasar IITC	M. L. Pardoe
	G-MZMC	Pegasus Quantum 15	J. J. Baker
	G-MZMD	Mainair Blade 912	S. George
	G-MZME	Medway Eclipser	P. A. Wenham
	G-MZMF	Pegasus Quantum 15	A. J. Tranter
	G-MZMG	Pegasus Quantum 15	A. G. Kemp
	G-MZMH	Pegasus Quantum 15	M. Hurtubise
	G-MZMJ	Mainair Blade	D. Wilson
	G-MZMK	Chevvron 2-32C	P. J. Tyler
	G-MZML	Mainair Blade 912	S. C. Stoodley
	G-MZMM	Mainair Blade 912	J. Lynch
	G-MZMN	Pegasus Quantum 912	R. H. Cheesley
	G-MZMO	TEAM mini-MAX 91	R. E. Main
	G-MZMP	Mainair Blade	A. M. Beale
	G-MZMS	Rans S.6-ESD Coyote II	P. F. Berry
	G-MZMT	Pegasus Quantum 15	Z. Cantel
	G-MZMU	Rans S.6-ESD Coyote II	J. W. Willcox
	G-MZMV	Mainair Blade	P. B. Smith
	G-MZMW	Mignet HM.1000 Balerit	M. E. Whapham
	G-MZMX	Cyclone AX2000	L. A. Lacy
	G-MZMY	Mainair Blade	C. J. Millership

Reg.	Type	Owner or Operator	Notes
G-MZMZ	Mainair Blade	W. A. Stacey	
G-MZNA	Quad City Challenger II UK	S. Hennessy	
G-MZNB	Pegasus Quantum 15	F. Gorse	
G-MZNC	Mainair Blade 912	A. J. Harrison	
G-MZND	Mainair Rapier	D. W. Stamp	
G-MZNG	Pegasus Quantum 15	The Scottish Flying Club	
G-MZNH	CFM Shadow Srs DD	P. A. James	
G-MZNJ	Mainair Blade	R. A. Hardy	
G-MZNM	TEAM mini-MAX	P. J. Fahie	
G-MZNN	TEAM mini-MAX	P. J. Bishop	
G-MZNO	Mainair Blade	I. M. & V. M. Vass	
G-MZNR	Pegasus Quantum 15	E. S. Wills	
G-MZNS	Pegasus Quantum 15	S. Uzochukwu	
G-MZNT	Pegasus Quantum 15-912	J. R. Harnett	
G-MZNU	Mainair Rapier	B. Johnson	
G-MZNV	Rans S.6-ESD Coyote II	A. P. Thomas	
G-MZNX	Thruster T.600N	B. Rogan	
G-MZNY	Thruster T.600N	G. Price	
G-MZNZ	Letov LK-2M Sluka	B. F. Crick	
G-MZOC	Mainair Blade	A. S. Davies	
G-MZOD	Pegasus Quantum 15	M. C. Robinson	
G-MZOE	Cyclone AX2000	G-MZOE Flying Group	
G-MZOF	Mainair Blade	R. M. Ellis	
G-MZOG	Pegasus Quantum 15-912	D. Smith	
G-MZOH	Whittaker MW5D Sorcerer	I. Pearson	
G-MZOI	Letov LK-2M Sluka	B. S. P. Finch	
G-MZOJ	Pegasus Quantum 15	M. K. Ashmore	
G-MZOK	Whittaker MW6 Merlin	G-MZOK Syndicate	
G-MZOP	Mainair Blade 912	K. M. Thorogood	
G-MZOS	Pegasus Quantum 15-912	J. R. Moore	
G-MZOV	Pegasus Quantum 15	Pegasus XL Group	
G-MZOW	Pegasus Quantum 15-912	G. P. Burns	
G-MZOX	Letov LK-2M Sluka	D. L. Hadley	
G-MZOY	TEAM Mini-MAX	P. R. & S. E. Whitehouse	
G-MZOZ	Rans S.6-ESD Coyote IIXL	S. G. & D. C. Emmons	
G-MZPH	Mainair Blade	J. D. Hoyland	
G-MZPJ	TEAM mini-MAX	P. R. Jenson	
G-MZPW	Pegasus Quasar IITC	N. S. Payne	
G-MZRC	Pegasus Quantum 15	M. Hopkins	
G-MZRM	Pegasus Quantum 15	R. Milwain	
G-MZRS	CFM Shadow Srs CD	M. Booth	
G-MZSC	Pegasus Quantum 15-912	J. Urrutia	
G-MZTS	Aerial Arts Chaser S	D. G. Ellis (G-MVDM)	
G-MZUB	Rans S.6-ESD Coyote IIXL	N. D. Townend	
G-MZZT	Kolb Twinstar Mk 3	D. E. Martin	
G-MZZY	Mainair Blade 912	A. Mucznik	
G-NAAA	MBB Bö.105DBS/4	Bond Air Services Ltd (G-BUTN/G-AZTI)	
G-NAAL	Bombardier CL600-2B16 Challenger	Hangar 8 Management Ltd	
G-NACA	Norman NAC-2 Freelance 180	A. R. Norman	
G-NACI	Norman NAC-1 Srs 100	L. J. Martin & D. G. French (G-AXFB)	
G-NACL	Norman NAC-6 Fieldmaster	EPA Aircraft Co Ltd (G-BNEG)	
G-NACO	Norman NAC-6 Fieldmaster	EPA Aircraft Co Ltd	
G-NACP	Norman NAC-6 Fieldmaster	EPA Aircraft Co Ltd	
G-NADO	Titan Tornado SS	Euro Aviation LLP	
G-NADS	TEAM mini-MAX 91	R. L. Williams	
G-NADZ	Van's RV-4	R. A. Pritchard (G-BROP)	
G-NAGG	Rotorsport UK MT-03	C. A. Clements	
G-NANI	Robinson R44 II	MOS Gmbh	
G-NANO	Avid Speed Wing	T. M. C. Handley	
G-NAPP	Van's RV-7	E. Fogarty	
G-NARG	Tanarg/Ixess 15 912S (1)	K. Kirby	
G-NARO	Cassutt Racer	C. Ball & R. Supply (G-BTXR)	
G-NARR	Stolp SA300 Starduster Too	G. J. D. Thomson	
G-NATT	Rockwell Commander 114A	Northgleam Ltd	
G-NATY	HS. Gnat T.1 (XR537) ★	Drilling Systems Ltd	
G-NBDD	Robin DR.400/180	B. & S. E. Chambers	
G-NBEL	AS.355F1 Ecureuil 2	Latitude Aviation Ltd (G-SKYW/G-TBIS/G-TALI)	
G-NBSI	Cameron N-77 balloon	Nottingham Hot-Air Balloon Club	
G-NCCC	Bombardier CL600-2B16	TAG Aviation (UK) Ltd	

Notes	Reg.	Type	Owner or Operator
	G-NCFC	PA-38-112 Tomahawk II	A. M. Heynen
	G-NCUB	Piper J-3C-65 Cub	R. J. Willies (G-BGXV)
	G-NDAA	MBB Bö.105DBS-4	Bond Air Services Ltd (G-WMAA/G-PASB/ G-BDMC)
	G-NDAD	Medway SLA100 Executive	K. Angel
	G-NDOL	Europa	S. Longstaff
	G-NDOT	Thruster T.600N	P. C. Bailey
	G-NDPA	Ikarus C42 FB UK	P. A. Pilkington
	G-NEAL	PA-32-260 Cherokee Six	I. Parkinson (G-BFPY)
	G-NEAT	Europa	P. F. D. Foden
	G-NEAU	Eurocopter EC 135T2	Northumbria Police Authority
	G-NEEL	Rotorway Executive 90	I. C. Bedford
	G-NEIL	Thunder Ax3 balloon	R. M. Powell
	G-NELI	PA-28R Cherokee Arrow 180	MK Aero Support Ltd
	G-NEMO	Raj Hamsa X'Air Jabiru (4)	G. F. Allen
	G-NEON	PA-32 Cherokee Six 300B	P. J. P. Coutney
	G-NEPB	Cameron N-77 balloon	The Post Office
	G-NESA	Shaw Europa XS	A. M. Kay
	G-NESE	Tecnam P2002-JF	N. & S. Easton
	G-NESH	Robinson R44 II	M. Tancock
	G-NEST	Christen Eagle II	P. J. Nonat
	G-NESV	Eurocopter EC 135T1	Eurocopter UK Ltd
	G-NESW	PA-34-220T Seneca III	G. C. U. Guida
	G-NESY	PA-18 Super Cub 95	V. Featherstone
	G-NETR	AS.355F1 Twin Squirrel	PLM Dollar Group Ltd (G-JARV/G-OGHL)
	G-NETT	Cessna 172S	Aero-Club Rhein-Nahe EV
	G-NETY	PA-18 Super Cub 150	N. B. Mason
	G-NEWS	Bell 206B-3 JetRanger III	Apple International Inc.Ltd & JAC Heli
	G-NEWT	Beech 35 Bonanza	J. S. Allison (G-APVW)
	G-NEWZ	Bell 206B JetRanger 3	Guay Tulliemet Aviation Ltd
	G-NFLA	BAe Jetstream 3102	Cranfield University (G-BRGN/G-BLHC)
	G-NFLC	HP.137 Jetstream 1H (G-AXUI) ★	Instructional airframe/Perth
	G-NFLY	Tecnam P2002-EA Sierra	C. N. Hodgson
	G-NFNF	Robin DR.400/180	M. Child, W. Cobb & J. Archer
	G-NFON	Van's RV-8	N. F. O'Neill
	G-NGLS	Aerospool Dynamic WT9 UK	The Nigels Ltd
	G-NHAA	AS.365N-2 Dauphin 2	The Great North Air Ambulance Service (G-MLTY)
	G-NHAB	AS.365N-2 Dauphin 2	The Great North Air Ambulance Service (G-DAUF)
	G-NHAC	AS.365N-2 Dauphin 2	The Great North Air Ambulance Service
	G-NHRH	PA-28 Cherokee 140	C. J. Milsom
	G-NHRJ	Shaw Europa XS	D. A. Lowe
	G-NICC	Aerotechnik EV-97 Team Eurostar UK	Pickup and Son Ltd
	G-NICI	Robinson R44	David Fishwick Vehicles Sales Ltd
	G-NICK	PA-18 Super Cub	M. W. Zipfell
	G-NICS	Best Off Sky Ranger Swift 912S(1)	N. G. Heywood
	G-NIDG	Aerotechnik EV-97 Eurostar	Skydrive Ltd
	G-NIEN	Van's RV-9A	NIEN Group
	G-NIFE	SNCAN Stampe SV.4A (156)	Tiger Airways
	G-NIGC	Avtech Jabiru UL-450	W. D. Brereton
	G-NIGE	Luscombe 8E Silvaire	Garden Party Ltd (G-BSHG)
	G-NIGL	Shaw Europa	N. M. Graham
	G-NIGS	Thunder Ax7-65 balloon	S. D. Annett
	G-NIKE	PA-28-181 Archer II	Key Properties Ltd
	G-NIKK	Diamond Katana DA20-C1	Cubair Flight Training Ltd
	G-NIKO	Airbus A.321-211	Thomas Cook Airlines Ltd
	G-NIKX	Robinson R-44 II	P. R. Holloway
	G-NIMA	Balóny Kubiček BB30Z balloon	C. Williamson
	G-NIMB	Schempp-Hirth Nimbus 2C	M. J. Slade
	G-NIME	Cessna T.206H Turbo Stationair	Whitby Seafoods Ltd
	G-NINA	PA-28-161 Warrior II	A. P. Gorrod (G-BEUC)
	G-NINC	PA-28-180 Cherokee	P. A. Layzell
	G-NIND	PA-28-180 Cherokee	Aquarelle Investments Ltd
	G-NINE	Murphy Renegade 912	R. C. McCarthy
	G-NIOG	Robinson R44 II	Helicopter Sharing Ltd
	G-NIOS	PA-32R-301 Saratoga SP	Plant Aviation
	G-NIPA	Slingsby T.66 Nipper 3	R. J. O. Walker (G-AWDD)
	G-NIPP	Slingsby T.66 Nipper 3	R. J. Porter (G-AVKJ)

Reg.	Type	Owner or Operator	Notes
G-NIPR	Slingsby T.66 Nipper 3	P. A. Gibbs (G-AVXC)	
G-NIPS	Tipsy T.66 Nipper 2	B. W. Faulkner	
G-NIPY	Hughes 369HS	Jet Aviation (Northwest) Ltd	
G-NISA	Robinson R44 II	G. P. Jones (G-HTMT)	
G-NISH	Van's RV-8	N. H. F. Hampton & S. R. Whitling	
G-NITA	PA-28 Cherokee 180	T. Clifford (G-AVVG)	
G-NIVA	Eurocopter EC 155B1	Lanthwaite Aviation Ltd	
G-NIVT	Schempp-Hirth Nimbus 4T	G-NIVT Gliding Group	
G-NJBA	Rotorway Executive 162F	British Waterproofing Ltd	
G-NJET	Schempp-Hirth Ventus cT	V. S. Bettle	
G-NJPW	P & M Quik GT450	N. J. P. West	
G-NJSH	Robinson R22 Beta	A. J. Hawes	
G-NJSP	Jabiru J430	N. J. S. Pitman	
G-NJTC	Aeroprakt A22-L Foxbat	B. Jackson & T. F. Casey	
G-NLCH	Lindstrand LBL-35A balloon	S. A. Lacey	
G-NLEE	Cessna 182Q	C. G. D. Jones (G-TLTD)	
G-NLMB	Zenair CH.601UL Zodiac	N. Lamb	
G-NLPA	Hawker 750	Hangar 8 Management Ltd	
G-NLYB	Cameron N-105 balloon	P. H. E. Van Overwalle/Belgium	
G-NMAK	Airbus A.319-115	Twinjet Aircraft Sales Ltd	
G-NMBG	Jabiru J400	P. R. Hendry-Smith & H. I. Smith	
G-NMID	Eurocopter EC 135T2	Derbyshire Constabulary	
G-NMOS	Cameron C-80 balloon	C. J. Thomas & M. C. East	
G-NMRV	Van's RV-6	T. W. Gale & S. R. Whitling	
G-NNAC	PA-18 Super Cub 135	PAW Flying Services Ltd	
G-NNON	Mainair Blade	D. R. Kennedy	
G-NOAH	Airbus A.319-115CJ	Acropolis Aviation Ltd	
G-NOCK	Cessna FR.182RG II	M. K. Aves (G-BGTK)	
G-NODE	AA-5B Tiger	Ultranomad Sro	
G-NOIR	Bell 222	Heron Helicopters Ltd (G-OJLC/G-OSEB/ G-BNDA)	
G-NOMO	Cameron O-31 balloon	Balloon Promotion SAS/Italy	
G-NOMZ	Balony Kubicek BB-S Gnome SS balloon	A. M. Holly	
G-NONE	Dyn'Aéro MCR-01 ULC	T. W. Lorimer	
G-NONI	AA-5 Traveler	November India Group (G-BBDA)	
G-NOOK	Mainair Blade 912S	D. J. S. Sevin	
G-NOOR	Commander 114B	As-Al Ltd	
G-NORA	Ikarus C.42 FB UK	N. A. Rathbone	
G-NORB	Saturne S110K hang glider	R. N. Pearce	
G-NORD	SNCAN NC.854	A. D. Pearce	
G-NORK	Bell 206B-3 JetRanger III	R. S. Forsyth	
G-NOSE	Cessna 402B	Reconnaissance Ventures Ltd (G-MPCU)	
G-NOTE	PA-28-181 Archer III	J. Beach	
G-NOTS	Skyranger 912S(1)	E. A. J. Chalk	
G-NOTT	Nott ULD-2 balloon	J. R. P. Nott	
G-NOUS	Cessna 172S	Flyglass Ltd	
G-NOWW	Mainair Blade 912	C. Bodill	
G-NOXY	Robinson R44	S. A. Knox (G-VALV)	
G-NPKJ	Van's RV-6	M. R. Turner	
G-NPPL	Comco Ikarus C.42 FB.100	Papa Lima Group	
G-NRIA	Beech 23 Musketeer	Respondmatte Flugeliclub	
G-NROY	PA-32RT-300 Lance II	B. Nedjati-Gilani (G-LYNN/G-BGNY)	
G-NRRA	SIAI-Marchetti SF.260 ★	G. Boot	
G-NSBB	Ikarus C.42 FB-100 VLA	B. Bayes & N. E. Sams	
G-NSEW	Robinson R44	G-NSEW Ltd	
G-NSJS	Cessna 680 Citation Sovereign	Ferncroft Ltd	
G-NSKB	Aeroprakt A22-L Foxbat	N. F. Smith	
G-NSOF	Robin HR.200/120B	Modi Aviation Ltd	
G-NSTG	Cessna F.150F	Westair Flying Services Ltd (G-ATNI)	
G-NTWK	AS.355F2 Twin Squirrel	PLM Dollar Group (G-FTWO/G-OJOR/G-BMUS)	
G-NUDD	Embraer EMB-500 Phenom 100	Flairjet Ltd	
G-NUDE	Robinson R44	The Last Great Journey Ltd (G-NSYT)	

Notes	Reg.	Type	Owner or Operator
	G-NUFC	Best Off Skyranger 912S(1)	C. R. Rosby
	G-NUGC	Grob G.103A Twin II Acro	The University of Nottingham Students Union
	G-NUKA	PA-28-181 Archer II	N. Ibrahim
	G-NULA	Flight Design CT2K	L. I. Bailey
	G-NUNI	Lindstrand LBL-77A balloon	J. A. Folkes
	G-NUTA	Christen Eagle II	Blue Eagle Group
	G-NUTT	Mainair Pegasus Quik	NUTT Syndicate
	G-NVBF	Lindstrand LBL-210A balloon	Virgin Balloon Flights
	G-NWAA	Eurocopter EC 135T2	Bond Air Services Ltd
	G-NWFA	Cessna 150M	North Weald Flying Group Ltd (G-CFBD)
	G-NWFC	Cessna 172P	North Weald Flying Group Ltd
	G-NWFG	Cessna 172P	North Weald Flying Group Ltd
	G-NWFS	Cessna 172P	North Weald Flying Group Ltd (G-TYMS)
	G-NWOI	Eurocopter EC135 P2+	North Wales Police Authority
	G-NWPR	Cameron N-77 balloon	D. B. Court
	G-NWPS	Eurocopter EC 135T1	Santander Asset Finance PLC
	G-NXOE	Cessna 172S	Goodwood Road Racing Co.Ltd
	G-NXUS	Nexus Mustang	G. W. Miller
	G-NYMB	Schempp-Hirth Nimbus 3	Nimbus Syndicate
	G-NYMF	PA-25 Pawnee 235D	Bristol Gliding Club Pty Ltd
	G-NYNA	Van's RV-9A	B. Greathead & S. Hiscox
	G-NYNE	Schleicher ASW-27-18E	R. C. W. Ellis
	G-NZGL	Cameron O-105 balloon	R. A. Vale & ptnrs
	G-NZSS	Boeing Stearman N2S-5 (343251:27)	R. W. Davies
	G-OAAA	PA-28-161 Warrior II	Red Hill Air Services Ltd
	G-OAAF	BAe ATP	Atlantic Airlines Ltd (G-JEMB)
	G-OABB	Jodel D.150	K. Manley
	G-OABC	Colt 69A balloon	P. A. C. Stuart-Kregor
	G-OABO	Enstrom F-28A	C. R. Taylor (G-BAIB)
	G-OABR	AG-5B Tiger	A. J. Neale
	G-OACA	PA-44-180 Seminole	H. Merkado (G-GSFT)
	G-OACE	Valentin Taifun 17E	I. F. Wells
	G-OACF	Robin DR.400/180	A. C. Fletcher
	G-OACI	MS.893E Rallye 180GT	Full Sutton Flying Centre Ltd
	G-OADY	Beech 76 Duchess	Multiflight Ltd
	G-OAER	Lindstrand LBL-105A balloon	M. P. Rowley
	G-OAFF	Cessna 208 Caravan 1	Army Parachute Association
	G-OAFR	Cameron Z-105 balloon	PSH Skypower Ltd
	G-OAGI	FLS Aerospace Sprint 160	Black Art Composites Ltd (G-FLSI)
	G-OAGL	Bell 206B JetRanger 3	AGL Helicopters (G-CORN/G-BHTR)
	G-OAHC	Beech F33C Bonanza	Cirrus Aviation Ltd (G-BTTF)
	G-OAJB	Cyclone AX2000	A. J. Allan (G-MZFJ)
	G-OAJC	Robinson R44	Adare International Transport Ltd
	G-OAJL	Ikarus C.42 FB100	G. D. M. McCullogh
	G-OAJS	PA-39 Twin Comanche 160 C/R	S. Vansteenkiste (G-BCIO)
	G-OAKI	BAe Jetstream 3102	Jetstream Executive Travel Ltd
	G-OALD	SOCATA TB20 Trinidad	Gold Aviation
	G-OALH	Tecnam P92-EA Echo	K. D. Pearce
	G-OAMF	Pegasus Quantum 15-912	G. A. Viquerat
	G-OAMI	Bell 206B JetRanger 2	Leamington Hobby Centre Ltd (G-BAUN)
	G-OAML	Cameron AML-105 balloon	Stratton Motor Co (Norfolk) Ltd
	G-OAMP	Cessna F.177RG	J-F. Pitot (G-AYPF)
	G-OANI	PA-28-161 Warrior II	J. F. Mitchell
	G-OANN	Zenair CH.601HD	Zodiac Group Mona
	G-OAPE	Cessna T.303	C. Twiston-Davies & P. L. Drew
	G-OAPR	Brantly B.2B	Helicopter International Magazine
	G-OAPW	Glaser-Dirks DG.400	P. L. Poole
	G-OARA	PA-28R-201 Arrow III	Obmit Ltd
	G-OARC	PA-28RT-201 Arrow IV	Plane Talking Ltd (G-BMVE)
	G-OARI	PA-28R-201 Arrow III	Abraxas Aviation Ltd
	G-OARO	PA-28R-201 Arrow III	Wycombe Air Centre Ltd
	G-OARS	Cessna 172S	AK Enterprises Ltd
	G-OART	PA-23 Aztec 250D	A. N. J. & S. L. Palmer (G-AXKD)
	G-OARU	PA-28R-201 Arrow III	Plane Talking Ltd
	G-OARV	ARV Super 2	I. F. Davidson
	G-OASH	Robinson R22 Beta	J. C. Lane

Reg.	Type	Owner or Operator	Notes
G-OASJ	Thruster T.600N 450	A. E. Turner	
G-OASP	AS.355F2 Twin Squirrel	Helicopter Services Ltd	
G-OASW	Schleicher ASW-27	M. P. W. Mee	
G-OATE	Mainair Pegasus Quantum 15-912	S. J. Goate	
G-OATV	Cameron V-77 balloon	A. W. & E. P. Braund-Smith	
G-OATZ	Van's RV-12	J. Jones & J. W. Armstrong	
G-OAVA	Robinson R22 Beta	J. Sargent	
G-OAWL	Agusta AW.139	Profred Partners LLP	
G-OAWS	Colt 77A balloon	P. Lawman	
G-OBAB	Lindstrand LBL-35A Cloudhopper balloon	B. A. Bower	
G-OBAK	PA-28R-201T Turbo Arrow III	G-OBAK Group Aviation	
G-OBAL	Mooney M.20J	G-OBAL Group	
G-OBAN	Jodel D.140B	S. R. Cameron (G-ATSU)	
G-OBAP	Zenair CH.701SP	J. M. Gale & A. D. Janaway	
G-OBAX	Thruster T.600N 450-JAB	G. B. Denton	
G-OBAZ	Best Off Skyranger 912(2)	B. J. Marsh	
G-OBBO	Cessna 182S	A. E. Kedros	
G-OBDA	Diamond Katana DA20-A1	Oscar Papa Ltd	
G-OBDN	PA-28-161 Warrior II	R. M. Bennett	
G-OBEE	Boeing Stearman A75N-1 (3397:174)	P. G. Smith	
G-OBEI	SOCATA TB200 Tobago XL	K. Stoter	
G-OBEN	Cessna 152 II	Globibussola Lda (G-NALI/G-BHVM)	
G-OBET	Sky 77-24 balloon	P. M. Watkins & S. M. Carden	
G-OBFE	Sky 120-24 balloon	J. Sonnabend	
G-OBFS	PA-28-161 Warrior III	Claris Aviation Ltd	
G-OBIB	Colt 120A balloon	M. W. A. Shemilt	
G-OBIL	Robinson R22 Beta	Fly Executive Ltd	
G-OBIO	Robinson R22 Beta	Burbage Farms Ltd	
G-OBJB	Lindstrand LBL-90A balloon	B. J. Bower	
G-OBJH	Colt 77A balloon	Hayrick Ltd	
G-OBJM	Taylor JT.1 Monoplane	B. J. Main	
G-OBJP	Pegasus Quantum 15-912	S. J. Baker	
G-OBJT	Shaw Europa	B. J. Tarmar (G-MUZO)	
G-OBLC	Beech 76 Duchess	Pridenote Ltd	
G-OBLU	Cameron H-34 balloon	John Aimo Balloons SAS/Italy	
G-OBMI	Mainair Blade	S. R. Kirkham & D. F. Reeves	
G-OBMP	Boeing 737-3Q8	bmi Baby	
G-OBMS	Cessna F.172N	A. J. Ransome, D. Beverley and K. Brown	
G-OBMW	AA-5 Traveler	Fretcourt Ltd (G-BDFV)	
G-OBNA	PA-34-220T Seneca V	Palmair Ltd	
G-OBNC	BN-2B-20 Islander	Britten-Norman Aircraft Ltd	
G-OBOF	Remos GX	D. Hawkins	
G-OBPP	Schleicher ASG-29E	M. H. Patel	
G-OBRA	Cameron Z-315 balloon	Cameron Flights Southern Ltd	
G-OBRO	Alpi Pioneer 200M	A. Brown	
G-OBRY	Cameron N-180 balloon	A. C. K. Rawson & J. J. Rudoni	
G-OBSM	Robinson R44 Raven	Flight Solutions Ltd (G-CDSE)	
G-OBTS	Cameron C-80 balloon	C. F. Cushion	
G-OBUP	DG Flugzeugbau DG-808C	R. A. Roberts	
G-OBUU	Replica Comper CLA Swift	J. A. Pothecary & R. H. Hunt	
G-OBUY	Colt 69A balloon	Balloon Preservation Flying Group	
G-OBUZ	Van's RV-6	A. F. Hall	
G-OBWP	BAe ATP	Trident Aviation Leasing Services (Jersey) Ltd (G-BTPO)	
G-OBYD	Boeing 767-304ER	Thomsonfly Ltd	
G-OBYF	Boeing 767-304ER	Thomsonfly Ltd	
G-OBYG	Boeing 767-3Q8ER	Thomsonfly Ltd	
G-OBYH	Boeing 767-304ER	Thomsonfly Ltd	
G-OBYT	Agusta-Bell 206A JetRanger	R. J. Everett (G-BNRC)	
G-OBZR	Aerostyle Breezer LSA	D. Curtin & S. Greenall	
G-OCAD	Sequoia F.8L Falco	Falco Flying Group	
G-OCAM	AA-5A Cheetah	R. E. Dagless (G-BLHO)	
G-OCBI	Schweizer 269C-1	Alpha Properties (London) Ltd	
G-OCBT	IDA Bacau Yakovlev Yak-52	Cambridge Business Travel	
G-OCCD	Diamond DA40D Star	Flying Pictures Ltd	
G-OCCF	Diamond DA40D Star	Plane Talking Ltd	
G-OCCG	Diamond DA40D Star	Plane Talking Ltd	
G-OCCH	Diamond DA40D Star	Innovative Aviation (Leeds) Ltd	
G-OCCK	Diamond DA40D Star	Aviation Rentals	
G-OCCL	Diamond DA40D Star	Aviation Rentals	

Notes	Reg.	Type	Owner or Operator
	G-OCCN	Diamond DA40D Star	Aviation Rentals
	G-OCCO	Diamond DA40D Star	Plane Talking Ltd
	G-OCCP	Diamond DA40D Star	Plane Talking Ltd
	G-OCCR	Diamond DA40D Star	P. Plaisted
	G-OCCS	Diamond DA40D Star	Plane Talking Ltd
	G-OCCT	Diamond DA40D Star	Plane Talking Ltd
	G-OCCU	Diamond DA40D Star	Chalrey Ltd
	G-OCCX	Diamond DA42 Twin Star	Plane Talking Ltd
	G-OCCZ	Diamond DA42 Twin Star	Aviation Rentals
	G-OCDC	Best Off Sky Ranger Nynja 912S(1)	C. D. Church
	G-OCDP	Flight Design CTSW	M. A. Beadman
	G-OCDW	Jabiru UL	H. Burroughs
	G-OCEG	Beech B.200 Super King Air	Cega Aviation Ambulance UK Ltd.
	G-OCFC	Robin R.2160	Cornwall Flying Club Ltd
	G-OCFD	Bell 206B JetRanger 3	Rushmere Helicopters LLP (G-WGAL/G-OICS)
	G-OCFM	PA-34-200 Seneca II	Stapleford Flying Club Ltd (G-ELBC/G-BANS)
	G-OCGC	Robin DR.400-180R	Cambridge Gliding Club Ltd
	G-OCHM	Robinson R44	Westleigh Developments Ltd
	G-OCJZ	Cessna 525A Citationjet CJ2	Go West Ltd
	G-OCLC	Aviat A-1B Husky	S. Patrick
	G-OCMM	Agusta A109A II	Castle Air Ltd (G-BXCB/G-ISEB/G-IADT/G-HBCA)
	G-OCMS	EV-97 TeamEurostar UK	C. M. Saysell
	G-OCMT	EV-97 TeamEurostar UK	P. Crowhurst
	G-OCOK	American Champion 8KCAB Super Decathlon	J. D. May
	G-OCON	Robinson R44	Da Vinci Helicopters Ltd
	G-OCOV	Robinson R22 Beta	Heli Air Ltd
	G-OCPC	Cessna FA.152	E. & M. O'Toole
	G-OCRI	Colomban MC.15 Cri-Cri	M. J. J. Dunning
	G-OCRL	Europa	R. J. Lewis (G-OBEV)
	G-OCRZ	CZAW Sportcruiser	P. Marsden
	G-OCST	Agusta-Bell 206B JetRanger 3	Lift West Ltd (G-BMKM)
	G-OCTI	PA-32 Cherokee Six 260	D. G. Williams (G-BGZX)
	G-OCTS	Cameron Z-90 balloon	Collett Transport Services Ltd
	G-OCTU	PA-28-161 Cadet	Plane Talking Ltd
	G-OCUB	Piper J-3C-90 Cub	Zebedee Flying Group
	G-OCZA	CZAW Sportcruiser	S. M. Dawson
	G-ODAC	Cessna F.152 II	T. M. Jones (G-BITG)
	G-ODAD	Colt 77A balloon	J. H. Dobson
	G-ODAF	Lindstrand LBL-105A balloon	T. J. Horne
	G-ODAG	Cessna 525A Citationjet CJ2	Air Charter Scotland Ltd
	G-ODAK	PA-28-236 Dakota	Airways Aero Associations Ltd
	G-ODAY	Cameron N-56 balloon	British Balloon Museum & Library
	G-ODAZ	Robinson R44 II	S. L. Walton
	G-ODBN	Lindstrand LBL Flowers SS balloon	Magical Adventures Ltd
	G-ODCC	Bell 206L-3 Long Ranger III	DCC Aviation
	G-ODCH	Schleicher ASW-20L	P. J. Stratten
	G-ODCR	Robinson R44 II	D. Lynn
	G-ODDS	Aerotek Pitts S-2A	A. C. Cassidy
	G-ODDY	Lindstrand LBL-105A balloon	P. & T. Huckle
	G-ODDZ	Schempp-Hirth Duo Discus T	P. A. King
	G-ODEB	Cameron A-250 balloon	A. Derbyshire
	G-ODEE	Van's RV-6	D. Cook
	G-ODEL	Falconar F-11-3	G. F. Brummell
	G-ODGS	Avtech Jabiru UL-450	S. R. Eskins
	G-ODHB	Robinson R44	A. J. Mossop
	G-ODHL	Cameron N-77 balloon	DHL International (UK) Ltd
	G-ODIN	Avions Mudry CAP-10B	CAP Ten
	G-ODJD	Raj Hamsa X'Air 582 (7)	S. Richens
	G-ODJF	Lindstrand LBL-90B balloon	Helena Dos Santos SA/Portugal
	G-ODJG	Shaw Europa	K. R. Challis & C. S. Andersson
	G-ODJH	Mooney M.20C	R. M. Schweitzer/Netherlands (G-BMLH)
	G-ODOC	Robinson R44	Gas & Air Ltd
	G-ODOG	PA-28R Cherokee Arrow 200-II	M. Brancart (G-BAAR)
	G-ODPJ	VPM M-16 Tandem Trainer	K. J. Robinson & S. Palmer (G-BVWX)
	G-ODRD	PA-32R-301T Saratoga II	Interceptor Properties Ltd
	G-ODSK	Boeing 737-37Q	bmi Baby
	G-ODTW	Shaw Europa	D. T. Walters
	G-ODUD	PA-28-181 Archer II	S. Barlow, R. N. Ingle & R. J. Murray (G-IBBO)
	G-ODUO	Schempp-Hirth Duo Discus	3D Syndicate
	G-ODUR	Raytheon Hawker 900XP	Hangar 8 Ltd

Reg.	Type	Owner or Operator	Notes
G-ODVB	CFM Shadow Srs DD	L. J. E. Moss	
G-ODXB	Lindstrand LBL-120A balloon	A. Nimmo	
G-OEAC	Mooney M.20J	S. Lovatt	
G-OEAT	Robinson R22 Beta	C. Y. O. Seeds Ltd (G-RACH)	
G-OEBC	Ultramagic N-300 balloon	European Balloon Display Co.Ltd	
G-OECM	Commander 114B	ECM (Vehicle Delivery Service) Ltd	
G-OECO	Flylight Dragonfly	P. A. & M. W. Aston	
G-OEDB	PA-38-112 Tomahawk	M. A. Petrie (G-BGGJ)	
G-OEDP	Cameron N-77 balloon	M. J. Betts	
G-OEGG	Cameron Egg-65 SS balloon	Calorie Watch Balloon Team	
G-OEGL	Christen Eagle II	The Eagle Flight Syndicate	
G-OEKS	Ikarus C42 FB80	J. D. Smith	
G-OELD	Pegasus Quantum 15-912	R. P. Butler	
G-OELZ	Wassmer WA.52 Europa	G-OELZ Group	
G-OEMT	MBB BK-117 C-1	Sterling Helicopters Ltd	
G-OERR	Lindstrand LBL-60A balloon	P. C. Gooch	
G-OERS	Cessna 172N	E. R. Stevens (G-SSRS)	
G-OESY	Easy Raider J2.2 (1)	J. Gray	
G-OETI	Bell 206B JetRanger 3	T. A. Wells (G-RMIE/G-BPIE)	
G-OETV	PA-31-350 Navajo Chieftain	Hinde Holdings Ltd	
G-OEVA	PA-32-260 Cherokee Six	M. G. Cookson (G-FLJA/G-AVTJ)	
G-OEWD	Raytheon 390 Premier 1	Bookajet Aircraft Management Ltd	
G-OEZI	Easy Raider J2.2(2)	C. D. Pidler	
G-OEZY	Shaw Europa	A. W. Wakefield	
G-OFAA	Cameron Z-105 balloon	R. A. Schwab	
G-OFAL	Ozone Roadster/Bailey Quattro	Malcolm Roberts Heating, Plumbing and Electrical Ltd	
G-OFAS	Robinson R22 Beta	Alan Mann Aviation Group Ltd	
G-OFBU	Ikarus C.42 FB UK	Old Sarum C42 Group	
G-OFCM	Cessna F.172L	Sirius Aviation Ltd (G-AZUN)	
G-OFDT	Mainair Pegasus Quik	D. Bardsley & J. Smith	
G-OFER	PA-18 Super Cub 150	M. S. W. Meagher	
G-OFFA	Pietenpol Air Camper	OFFA Group	
G-OFFO	Extra EA.300/L	2 Excel Aviation Ltd	
G-OFGC	Aeroprakt A22-L Foxbat	J. M. Fearn	
G-OFIT	SOCATA TB10 Tobago	GFI Aviation Group (G-BRIU)	
G-OFIX	Grob G.109B	T. R. Dews	
G-OFJC	Eiriavion PIK-20E	G. Bailey, J. D. Sorrell & D. Thomas	
G-OFLI	Colt 105A balloon	Virgin Airship & Balloon Co Ltd	
G-OFLT	EMB-110P1 Bandeirante ★	Rescue trainer/Aveley, Essex (G-MOBL/G-BGCS)	
G-OFLY	Cessna 210M	A. P. Mothew	
G-OFMC	Avro RJ100	Ford Motor Co.Ltd (G-CDUI)	
G-OFOA	BAe 146-100	Formula One Administration Ltd (G-BKMN/G-ODAN)	
G-OFOM	BAe 146-100	Formula One Management Ltd (G-BSLP/G-BRLM)	
G-OFOX	Denney Kitfox	P. R. Skeels	
G-OFRB	Everett gyroplane	T. N. Holcroft-Smith	
G-OFRY	Cessna 152	Devon and Somerset Flight Training Ltd	
G-OFSP	CZAW Sportcruiser	F. S. Pullman	
G-OFTC	Agusta A109E Power	Castle Air Ltd	
G-OFTI	PA-28 Cherokee 140	G-OFTI Group	
G-OGAR	PZL SZD-45A Ogar	P. Rasmussen t/a Perranporth Ogar Flying Group	
G-OGAS	Westland WG.30 Srs 100 ★	(stored)/Yeovil (G-BKNW)	
G-OGAY	Baloney Kubicek BB-26 balloon	J. W. Soukup	
G-OGAZ	Aérospatiale SA.341G Gazelle 1	Killochries Fold (G-OCJR/G-BRGS)	
G-OGBD	Boeing 737-3L9	bmi Baby	
G-OGCA	PA-28-161 Warrior II	Cardiff-Wales Aviation Services Ltd	
G-OGEM	PA-28-181 Archer II	GEM Integrated Solutions Ltd	
G-OGEO	Aérospatiale SA.341G Gazelle 1	George Steel Contract Services (G-BXJK)	
G-OGES	Enstrom 280FX	G. E. Werkle (G-CBYL)	
G-OGET	PA-39 Twin Comanche	D. Saxton (G-AYXY)	
G-OGFS	BAe.125 Srs 800B	Aircraft Holdings Ltd (G-GRGA/G-DCTA/G-OSPG/G-ETOM/G-BVFC/G-TPHK/G-FDSL)	
G-OGGB	Grob G.102 Astir CS	Golf Brave Group	
G-OGGM	Cirrus SR22	Morson Human Resources Ltd	
G-OGGS	Thunder Ax8-84 balloon	G. Gamble & Sons (Quorn) Ltd	
G-OGGY	Aviat A.1B	C. A. I. Hickling	

Notes	Reg.	Type	Owner or Operator
	G-OGIL	Short SD3-30 Variant 100 ★	North East Aircraft Museum/Usworth (G-BITV)
	G-OGJC	Robinson R44 II	G. Corbett
	G-OGJM	Cameron C-80 balloon	G. F. Madelin
	G-OGJP	Commander 114B	MJ Church Plant Ltd
	G-OGJS	Puffer Cozy	G. J. Stamper
	G-OGKB	Sequoia Falco F8L	G. K. Brothwood
	G-OGLY	Cameron Z-105 balloon	H. M. Ogston
	G-OGOD	P & M Quik GT450	J. R. Elcocks
	G-OGOS	Everett gyroplane	N. A. Seymour
	G-OGSA	Avtech Jabiru SPL-450	G-OGSA Group
	G-OGSK	Embraer EMB-135BJ Legacy	TAG Aviation (UK) Ltd
	G-OGTS	Air Command 532 Elite	GTS Engineering (Coventry) Ltd
	G-OHAC	Cessna F.182Q	Maguirelzatt LLP
	G-OHAL	Pietenpol Air Camper	UK Pietenpol Club Flying Group
	G-OHAM	Robinson R44 II	Hamsters Wheel Productions Ltd (G-GBEN/ G-CDJZ)
	G-OHAV	ATG Ltd HAV-3	Hybrid Air Vehicles Ltd
	G-OHCP	AS.355F1 Twin Squirrel	Staske Construction Ltd (G-BTVS/G-STVE/ G-TOFF/G-BKJX)
	G-OHDC	Colt Film Cassette SS balloon ★	Balloon Preservation Group
	G-OHGA	Hughes O-6A	MSS Holdings (UK) Ltd
	G-OHGC	Scheibe SF.25C Falke	Heron Gliding Club
	G-OHIG	EMB-110P1 Bandeirante ★	Air Salvage International/Alton (G-OPPP)
	G-OHIO	Dyn'Aero MCR-01	J. M. Keane
	G-OHIY	Van's RV-10	M. A. Hutton
	G-OHJE	Alpi Pioneer 300 Hawk	H. J. Edwards
	G-OHJV	Robinson R44	HJV Ltd
	G-OHKS	Pegasus Quantum 15-912	S. J. Farr
	G-OHLI	Robinson R44 II	NCS Partnership
	G-OHMS	AS.355F1 Twin Squirrel	Western Power Distribution (South West) PLC
	G-OHNO	Yakovlev Yak-55	S. Whatmough
	G-OHOV	Rotorway Executive 162F	M. G. Bird
	G-OHPC	Cessna 208 Caravan 1	S. Ulrich
	G-OHVR	Robinson R44 II	Transparent Film Products Ltd
	G-OHWV	Raj Hamsa X'Air 582(6)	C. W. Bridge
	G-OHYE	Thruster T.600N 450	G-OHYE Group (G-CCRO)
	G-OIBM	Rockwell Commander 114	H. A. Barrs (G-BLVZ)
	G-OIBO	PA-28 Cherokee 180	Azure Flying Club Ltd (G-AVAZ)
	G-OICO	Lindstrand LBL-42A balloon	B. Esposito
	G-OIFM	Cameron 90 Dude SS balloon	Magical Adventures Ltd
	G-OIHC	PA-32R-301 Saratoga IIHP	N. J. Lipczynski (G-PUSK)
	G-OIIO	Robinson R22 Beta	Whizzard Helicopters (G-ULAB)
	G-OIMC	Cessna 152 II	East Midlands Flying School Ltd
	G-OINN	UltraMagic H-31 balloon	G. Everett
	G-OIOB	Mudry CAP.10B	J. Ceotto
	G-OIOZ	Thunder Ax9-120 S2 balloon	R. H. Etherington
	G-OISO	Cessna FRA.150L	Pilot Flying Group (G-BBJW)
	G-OITV	Enstrom 280C-UK-2	C. W. Brierley Jones (G-HRVY/G-DUGY/G-BEEL)
	G-OIVN	Liberty XL-2	I. Shaw
	G-OJAB	Avtech Jabiru SK	Flying Spanners Group
	G-OJAC	Mooney M.20J	Hornet Engineering Ltd
	G-OJAE	Hughes 269C	R. W. Cutler
	G-OJAG	Cessna 172S	Chalrey Ltd
	G-OJAN	Robinson R22 Beta	J. C. Lane (G-SANS/G-BUHX)
	G-OJAS	Auster J/1U Workmaster	D. S. Hunt
	G-OJAZ	Robinson R44	P. C. Twigg
	G-OJBB	Enstrom 280FX	Pendragon (Design & Build) Ltd
	G-OJBM	Cameron N-90 balloon	P. Spinlove
	G-OJBS	Cameron N-105A balloon	Up & Away Ballooning Ltd
	G-OJBW	Lindstrand LBL J & B Bottle SS balloon	N. A. P. Godfrey
	G-OJCW	PA-32RT-300 Lance II	P. G. Dobson
	G-OJDA	EAA Acrosport II	D. B. Almey
	G-OJDC	Thunder Ax7-77 balloon	A. Heginbottom
	G-OJDS	Ikarus C.42 FB 80	L. C. Wellington-Graham
	G-OJEG	Airbus A.321-231	Monarch Airlines Ltd
	G-OJEH	PA-28-181 Archer II	P. C. & M. A. Greenaway
	G-OJEN	Cameron V-77 balloon	C. & C. Westwood
	G-OJGC	Van's RV-4	J. G. Claridge
	G-OJGT	Maule M.5-235C	Newnham Joint Flying Syndicate

Reg.	Type	Owner or Operator	Notes
G-OJHC	Cessna 182P	Stapleford Flying Club Ltd	
G-OJHL	Shaw Europa	M. D. Burns & G. Rainey	
G-OJIL	PA-31-350 Navajo Chieftain	Redhill Aviation Ltd	
G-OJIM	PA-28R-201T Turbo Arrow III	G-OJIM Flyers Ltd	
G-OJJV	P & M Pegasus Quik	J. J. Valentine	
G-OJKM	Rans S.7 Courier	G. Lewis & J. Mellor	
G-OJLD	Van's RV-7	J. L. Dixon	
G-OJLH	TEAM mini-MAX 91	J. Riley & D. J. Warren (G-MYAW)	
G-OJMB	Airbus A.330-243	Thomas Cook Airlines Ltd	
G-OJMC	Airbus A.330-243	Thomas Cook Airlines Ltd	
G-OJMF	Enstrom 280FX	Manchester Helicopter Centre Ltd (G-DDOD)	
G-OJMR	Airbus A.300B4-605R	Monarch Airlines Ltd	
G-OJMS	Cameron Z-90 balloon	Joinerysoft Ltd	
G-OJNB	Linsdstrand LBL-21A balloon	N. A. P. Godfrey	
G-OJNE	Schempp-Hirth Nimbus 3T	J. N. Ellis	
G-OJOD	Jodel D.18	D. Hawkes & C. Poundes	
G-OJON	Taylor JT.2 Titch	Freelance Aviation Ltd	
G-OJPS	Bell 206B JetRanger 2	Milford Aviation (G-UEST/G-ROYB/G-BLWU)	
G-OJRH	Robinson R44	J. R. Holgate	
G-OJRM	Cessna T.182T	Colne Airways Ltd	
G-OJSA	BAe Jetstream 3102	Diamond Air Charter Ltd	
G-OJSF	PA-23 Aztec 250F	Comed Aviation Ltd (G-SFHR/G-BHSO)	
G-OJSH	Thruster T.600N 450 JAB	G-OJSH Group	
G-OJVA	Van's RV-6	J. A. Village	
G-OJVH	Cessna F.150H	p. a. James & N. McGowan (G-AWJZ)	
G-OJVL	Van's RV-6	S. E. Tomlinson	
G-OJWB	Hawker 800XP	Langford Lane Ltd	
G-OJWS	PA-28-161 Warrior II	P. J. Ward	
G-OKAG	PA-28R Cherokee Arrow 180	Alpha-Golf Flying Group	
G-OKAY	Pitts S-1E Special	S. R. S. Evans	
G-OKBT	Colt 25A Mk II balloon	British Telecommunications PLC	
G-OKCC	Cameron N-90 balloon	D. J. Head	
G-OKCP	Lindstrand LBL Battery SS balloon	C. L. Thompson (G-MAXX)	
G-OKED	Cessna 150L	L. J. Pluck	
G-OKEM	Mainair Pegasus Quik	W. J. Hardy	
G-OKEN	PA-28R-201T Turbo Arrow III	K. Woodcock	
G-OKER	Van's RV-7	R. M. Johnson	
G-OKEV	Shaw Europa	K. A. Kedward	
G-OKEW	UltraMagic M-65C balloon	Hampshire Balloons Ltd	
G-OKEY	Robinson R22 Beta	Alan Mann Aviation Group Ltd	
G-OKID	Reality Escapade Kid	P. M. Francis	
G-OKIM	Best Off Sykyranger 912 (2)	K. P. Taylor	
G-OKIS	Tri-R Kis	M. R. Cleveley	
G-OKKI	Bombardier BD700-1A10 Global Express	Ocean Sky (UK) Ltd	
G-OKMA	Tri-R Kis	K. Miller	
G-OKPW	Tri-R Kis	K. P. Wordsworth	
G-OKTI	Aquila AT01	P. H. Ferdinand	
G-OKYA	Cameron V-77 balloon	R. J. Pearce	
G-OKYM	PA-28 Cherokee 140	North Wales Air Academy Ltd (G-AVLS)	
G-OLAA	Alpi Pioneer 300 Hawk	G. G. Hammond	
G-OLAU	Robinson R22 Beta	MPW Aviation Ltd	
G-OLAW	Lindstrand LBL-25A balloon	George Law Plant	
G-OLCP	AS.355N Twin Squirrel	Charterstyle Ltd (G-CLIP)	
G-OLDG	Cessna T.182T	Gold Aviation Ltd (G-CBTJ)	
G-OLDH	Aérospatiale SA.341G Gazelle 1	Gold Aviation Ltd (G-UTZY/G-BKLV)	
G-OLDM	Pegasus Quantum 15-912	J. W. Holme	
G-OLDO	Eurocopter EC.120B Colibri	Gold Aviation Ltd (G-HIGI)	
G-OLDP	Mainair Pegasus Quik	A. G. Woodward	
G-OLDT	Learjet 45	Gold Aviation Ltd	
G-OLDX	Cessna 182T	Gold Air International Ltd (G-IBZT)	
G-OLEE	Cessna F.152	Redhill Air Services Ltd	
G-OLEM	Jodel D.18	G. E. Roe (G-BSBP)	
G-OLEW	Vans RV-7A	A. Burani	
G-OLEZ	Piper J-3C-65 Cub	L. Powell (G-BSAX)	
G-OLFA	AS.350B3 Ecureuil	Heliaviation Ltd	
G-OLFB	Pegasus Quantum 15-912	J. G. & P. Callan	
G-OLFF	Cameron Z-120 balloon	A. Nimmo	
G-OLFO	Robinson R44	Crinstown Aviation Ltd	
G-OLFT	Rockwell Commander 114	D. A. Tubby (G-WJMN)	
G-OLFZ	P & M Quik GT450	A. J. Boyd	

Notes	Reg.	Type	Owner or Operator
	G-OLGA	CFM Starstreak Shadow SA-II	G. Taylor
	G-OLJT	Mainair Gemini Flash IIA	M. H. Moulai
	G-OLLI	Cameron O-31 SS balloon	The British Balloon Museum & Library Ltd
	G-OLLS	Cessna U.206H Floatplane	Loch Lomond Seaplanes Ltd
	G-OLMA	Partenavia P.68B Victor	C. M. Evans (G-BGBT)
	G-OLNT	SA.365N1 Dauphin 2	LNT Aviation Ltd (G-POAV/G-BOPI)
	G-OLOW	Robinson R44	C. O. Semik
	G-OLRT	Robinson R22 Beta	The Henderson Group
	G-OLSA	Breezer LSA	RGV Aviation Ltd
	G-OLSF	PA-28-161 Cadet	Flew LLP (G-OTYJ)
	G-OLUG	Cameron Z-120 balloon	K. H. Gruenauer
	G-OMAF	Dornier 228-200	FR Aviation Ltd
	G-OMAG	Cessna 182B	Bodmin Light Aeroplane Services Ltd
	G-OMAL	Thruster T.600N 450	M. Howland
	G-OMAO	SOCATA TB-20 Trinidad	Alpha Oscar Group (G-GDGR)
	G-OMAS	Cessna A.150M	M. A. Segar (G-BTFS)
	G-OMAT	PA-28 Cherokee 140	Midland Air Training School (G-JIMY/G-AYUG)
	G-OMAX	Brantly B.2B	A. Murzyn (G-AVJN)
	G-OMBI	Cessna 525B Citationjet CJ3	Ravenheat Manufacturing Ltd
	G-OMCC	AS.350B Ecureuil	MJH Capital Ltd (G-JTCM/G-HLEN/G-LOLY)
	G-OMDB	Van's V-6A	D. A. Roseblade
	G-OMDD	Thunder Ax8-90 S2 balloon	M. D. Dickinson
	G-OMDH	Hughes 369E	Stilgate Ltd
	G-OMDR	Agusta-Bell 206B JetRanger 3	Castle Air Ltd (G-HRAY/G-VANG/G-BIZA)
	G-OMEA	Cessna 560XL Citation XLS	Marshall Executive Aviation
	G-OMEL	Robinson R44	Helitrain Ltd (G-BVPB)
	G-OMEM	Eurocopter EC 120B	Aero Maintenance Ltd (G-BXYD)
	G-OMEN	Cameron Z-90 balloon	M. G. Howard
	G-OMER	Avtech Jabiru UL-450	G. D. Omer (G-GPAS)
	G-OMEX	Zenair CH.701 UL	S. J. Perry
	G-OMEZ	Zenair CH.601HDS	GOMEZ Group
	G-OMGH	Robinson R44 II	Universal Energy Ltd
	G-OMGR	Cameron Z-105 balloon	Omega Resource Group PLC
	G-OMHC	PA-28RT-201 Arrow IV	Halfpenny Green Flight Centre Ltd
	G-OMHD	EE Canberra PR.Mk.9 (XH134)	Midair SA
	G-OMHI	Mills MH-1	J. P. Mills
	G-OMHP	Avtech Jabiru UL	J. Livingstone
	G-OMIA	MS.893A Rallye Commodore 180	L. Portelli
	G-OMIK	Shaw Europa	M. J. Clews
	G-OMIW	Pegasus Quik	M. I. Woodward
	G-OMJA	PA-28-181 Archer II	R. D. Masters & S. Walker
	G-OMJT	Rutan LongEz	M. J. Timmons
	G-OMLS	Bell 206B JetRanger 2	P. A. Leverton
	G-OMMG	Robinson R22 Beta	CDS Aviation Ltd (G-BPYX)
	G-OMMM	Colt 90A balloon	A. & M. Frayling
	G-OMNI	PA-28R Cherokee Arrow 200D	Cotswold Aviation Services Ltd (G-BAWA)
	G-OMOO	Ultramagic T-150 balloon	Robert Wiseman Dairies PLC
	G-OMPW	Mainair Pegasus Quik	M. P. Wimsey
	G-OMRB	Cameron V-77 balloon	I. J. Jevons
	G-OMRH	Cessna 550 Citation Bravo	McAir Services LLP
	G-OMRP	Flight Design CTSW	M. E. Parker
	G-OMSA	Flight Design CTSW	Microlight Sport Aviation Ltd
	G-OMST	PA-28-161 Warrior III	Mid-Sussex Timber Co Ltd (G-BZUA)
	G-OMSV	Beech B.200GT King Air	JPM Ltd
	G-OMUM	Rockwell Commander 114	M. Lai & G. Syrakis
	G-OMYA	Airbus A.320-214	Thomas Cook Airlines Ltd (G-BXKB)
	G-OMYJ	Airbus A.321-211	Thomas Cook Airlines Ltd (G-OOAF/G-UNID/
			G-UKLO)
	G-OMYT	Airbus A.330-243	Thomas Cook Airlines Ltd (G-MOJO)
	G-ONAA	North American Rockwell OV-10B Bravo	Invicta Aviation Ltd
	G-ONAF	Naval Aircraft Factory N3N-3 (4406:12)	N3N-3 Group
	G-ONAL	Beech 200 Super King Air	Unity Aviation Ltd (G-HAMA)
	G-ONAT	Grob G.102 Astir CS77	N. A. Toogood
	G-ONAV	PA-31-310 Turbo Navajo C	Panther Aviation Ltd (G-IGAR)
	G-ONCB	Lindstrand LBL-31A balloon	M. R. Noyce & R. P. E. Phillips
	G-ONCS	Slingsby T.66 Nipper 3	Ardleigh Flying Group (G-AZBA)
	G-ONEP	Robinson R44 II	Neptune Property Developments Ltd
	G-ONES	Slingsby T.67M Firefly 200	Aquaman Aviation Ltd
	G-ONET	PA-28 Cherokee 180E	Hatfield Flying Club Ltd (G-AYAU)
	G-ONEZ	Glaser-Dirks DG-200/17	One Zulu Group

Reg.	Type	Owner or Operator	Notes
G-ONFL	Murphy Maverick 430	G. J. Johnson (G-MYUJ)	
G-ONGC	Robin DR.400/180R	Norfolk Gliding Club Ltd	
G-ONHH	Forney F-1A Aircoupe	R. D. I. Tarry (G-ARHA)	
G-ONIG	Murphy Elite	N. S. Smith	
G-ONIX	Cameron C-80 balloon	D. J. Griffin	
G-ONKA	Aeronca K	N. J. R. Minchin	
G-ONNE	Westland Gazelle HT.3 (XW858:C)	A. M. Parkes (G-DMSS)	
G-ONON	RAF 2000 GTX-SE gyroplane	M. P. Lhermette	
G-ONPA	PA-31-350 Navajo Chieftain	Synergy Aircraft Leasing Ltd	
G-ONSO	Pitts S-1C Special	A. P. S. Maynard (G-BRRS)	
G-ONTV	Agusta-Bell 206B JetRanger 3	Castle Air Ltd	
G-ONUN	Van's RV-6A	K. R. H. Wingate	
G-OOAN	Boeing 767-39HER	Thomson Airways Ltd (G-UKLH)	
G-OOAR	Airbus A.320-214	Thomson Airways Ltd	
G-OOBA	Boeing 757-26N	Thomson Airways Ltd	
G-OOBB	Boeing 757-28A	Thomson Airways Ltd	
G-OOBC	Boeing 757-28A	Thomson Airways Ltd	
G-OOBD	Boeing 757-28A	Thomson Airways Ltd	
G-OOBE	Boeing 757-28A	Thomson Airways Ltd	
G-OOBF	Boeing 757-28A	Thomson Airways Ltd	
G-OOBG	Boeing 757-236	Thomson Airways Ltd	
G-OOBH	Boeing 757-236	Thomson Airways Ltd	
G-OOBI	Boeing 757-2B7	Thomson Airways Ltd	
G-OOBJ	Boeing 757-2B7	Thomson Airways Ltd	
G-OOBK	Boeing 767-324ER	Thomsonf AirwaysLtd	
G-OOBL	Boeing 767-324ER	Thomson Airways Ltd	
G-OOBM	Boeing 767-324ER	Thomson Airways Ltd	
G-OOBN	Boeing 757-2G5	Thomson Airways Ltd	
G-OOBP	Boeing 757-2G5	Thomson Airways Ltd	
G-OOBR	Boeing 757-204	Thomson Airways Ltd (G-BYAN)	
G-OOCH	Ultramagic H-42 balloon	P. C. Gooch	
G-OODE	SNCAN Stampe SV.4C (modified)	G-OODE Flying Group (G-AZNN)	
G-OODI	Pitts S-1D Special	C. Hutson & R. S. Wood (G-BBBU)	
G-OODM	Cessna 525A Citation CJ2	Air Charter Scotland Ltd	
G-OODW	PA-28-181 Archer II	Redhill Air Services Ltd	
G-OOER	Lindstrand LBL-25A balloon	Airborne Adventures Ltd	
G-OOEX	Cirrus SR22T	Data Interchange PLC	
G-OOEY	Balony Kubicek BB-222 balloon	A. W. Holly	
G-OOFE	Thruster T.600N 450	R. P. Tribe	
G-OOFT	PA-28-161 Warrior III	Plane Talking Ltd	
G-OOGA	GA-7 Cougar	MK Aero Support Ltd	
G-OOGI	GA-7 Cougar	Plane Talking Ltd (G-PLAS/G-BGHL)	
G-OOGO	GA-7 Cougar	M. M. Naviede	
G-OOGS	GA-7 Cougar	P. Pigg (G-BGJW)	
G-OOGY	P & M Quik R	Cambridge Road Professional Services Ltd	
G-OOIO	AS.350B3 Ecureuil	Hovering Ltd	
G-OOJC	Bensen B.8MR	S. Henley	
G-OOJP	Commander 114B	R. J. Rother	
G-OOLE	Cessna 172M	P. S. Eccersley (G-BOSI)	
G-OOMF	PA-18-150 Super Cub	C. G. Bell	
G-OONA	Robinson R44 II	Malaika Developments LLP	
G-OONE	Mooney M.20J	Go One Aviation Ltd	
G-OONK	Cirrus SR22	N. P. Kingdon	
G-OONY	PA-28-161 Warrior II	D. A. Field	
G-OONZ	P & M Quik	A. Barrett	
G-OOON	PA-34-220T Seneca III	Pelican Air Ltd	
G-OOOX	Boeing 757-2Y0	Thomson Airways Ltd	
G-OOPE	Airbus A.321-211	Thomson Airways Ltd (G-OOAE/ G-UNIF)	
G-OOPH	Airbus A.321-211	Thomson Airways Ltd (G-OOAH/G-UNIE)	
G-OOPP	Airbus A.320-214	Thomson Airways Ltd (G-OOAS)	
G-OOPT	Airbus A.320-214	Thomson Airways Ltd (G-OOAT)	
G-OOPU	Airbus A.320-214	Thomson Airways Ltd (G-OOAU)	
G-OORV	Van's RV-6	T. I. Williams	
G-OOSE	Rutan Vari-Eze	B. O. Smith & J. A. Towers	
G-OOSH	Zenair CH.601UL Zodiac	A. G. Ransom	
G-OOSY	DH.82A Tiger Moth	Flying Tigers	
G-OOTC	PA-28R-201T Turbo Arrow III	D. G. & C. M. King (G-CLIV)	
G-OOTT	Eurocopter AS.350B3 Ecureuil	R. J. Green	
G-OOTW	Cameron Z-275 balloon	Airborne Balloon Flights Ltd	
G-OOUK	Cirrus SR22	R. S. Tomlinson	
G-OOWS	Eurocopter AS.350B3 Ecureuil	Millburn World Travel Services Ltd	

Notes	Reg.	Type	Owner or Operator
	G-OOXP	Aero Designs Pulsar XP	P. C. Avery
	G-OPAG	PA-34-200 Seneca II	A. H. Lavender (G-BNGB)
	G-OPAH	Eurocopter EC135 T2 +	VLL Ltd (G-RWLA)
	G-OPAM	Cessna F.152 II (tailwheel)	PJC Leasing Ltd (G-BFZS)
	G-OPAT	Beech 76 Duchess	R. D. J. Axford (G-BHAO)
	G-OPAZ	Pazmany PL.2	P. M. Harrison
	G-OPCG	Cessna 182T	P. L. Nolan
	G-OPEJ	TEAM Minimax 91A	P. E. Jackson
	G-OPEN	Bell 206B	Gazelle Aviation LLP
	G-OPEP	PA-28RT-201T Turbo Arrow IV	SAM Ltd
	G-OPET	PA-28-181 Archer II	Cambrian Flying Group Ltd
	G-OPFA	Pioneer 300	S. Eddison & R. Minett
	G-OPFR	Diamond DA.42 Twin Star	P. F. Rothwell
	G-OPFT	Cessna 172R Skyhawk	AJW Construction Ltd
	G-OPHT	Schleicher ASH-26E	J. S. Wand
	G-OPIC	Cessna FRA.150L	A. V. Harmer (G-BGNZ)
	G-OPIK	Eiri PIK-20E	G-OPIK Syndicate
	G-OPIT	CFM Streak Shadow Srs SA	I. J. Guy
	G-OPJD	PA-28RT-201T Turbo Arrow IV	J. M. McMillan
	G-OPJK	Shaw Europa	P. J. Kember
	G-OPJS	Pietenpol Air Camper	P. J. Shenton
	G-OPKF	Cameron 90 Bowler SS balloon	D. K. Fish
	G-OPLC	DH.104 Dove 8	Columba Aviation Ltd (G-BLRB)
	G-OPME	PA-23 Aztec 250D	A. A. Mattacks & R. G. Pardo (G-ODIR/G-AZGB)
	G-OPMP	Robinson R44 II	Phillips Commercials Ltd (G-HHHH)
	G-OPMT	Lindstrand LBL-105A balloon	K. R. Karlstrom
	G-OPNH	Stoddard-Hamilton Glasair IIRG	A. J. E. & A. E. Smith (G-CINY)
	G-OPRC	Shaw Europa XS	M. J. Ashby-Arnold
	G-OPSF	PA-38-112 Tomahawk	P. I. Higham (G-BGZI)
	G-OPSL	PA-32R-301 Saratoga SP	Defence Vision Systems Pte Ltd (G-IMPW)
	G-OPSS	Cirrus SR20	Dunster House Ltd
	G-OPST	Cessna 182R	M. J. G. Wellings & Welmacs Ltd
	G-OPTF	Robinson R44 II	Heli Air Ltd
	G-OPTI	PA-28-161 Warrior II	A. K. Hulme
	G-OPUB	Slingsby T.67M Firefly 160	P. M. Barker (G-DLTA/G-SFTX)
	G-OPUK	PA-28-161 Warrior III	Dennis and Robinson Ltd
	G-OPUP	Beagle B.121 Pup 2	F. A. Zubiel (G-AXEU)
	G-OPUS	Avtech Jabiru SK	K. W. Whistance
	G-OPVM	Van's RV-9A	P. Mather
	G-OPWS	Mooney M.20K	D. S. Overton
	G-OPYE	Cessna 172S	Far North Aviation
	G-OPYO	Alpi Pioneer 300 Hawk	T. J. Franklin & D. S. Simpson
	G-ORAC	Cameron 110 Van SS balloon	A. G. Kennedy
	G-ORAE	Van's RV-7	R. W. Eaton
	G-ORAF	CFM Streak Shadow	A. P. Hunn
	G-ORAM	Thruster T600N 450	D. W. Wilson
	G-ORAR	PA-28-181 Archer III	P. N. & S. M. Thornton
	G-ORAS	Clutton FRED Srs 2	A. I. Sutherland
	G-ORAU	Evektor EV-97A Eurostar	W. R. C. Williams-Wynne
	G-ORAY	Cessna F.182Q II	Unicorn Consultants Ltd (G-BHDN)
	G-ORBK	Robinson R44 II	T2 Technology Ltd (G-CCNO)
	G-ORBS	Mainair Blade	J. W. Dodson
	G-ORCA	Van's RV-4	J. J. & B. P. Waites
	G-ORCW	Schempp-Hirth Ventus 2cT	R. C. Wilson
	G-ORDB	Cessna 550 Citation Bravo	Equipe Air Ltd
	G-ORDH	AS.355N Twin Squirrel	Harpin Ltd
	G-ORDS	Thruster T.600N 450	G. J. Pill
	G-ORDW	Magni M-24C	A. R. Waitson
	G-ORED	BN-2T Turbine Islander	B-N Group Ltd (G-BJYW)
	G-ORGY	Cameron Z-210 balloon	Cameron Flights Southern Ltd
	G-ORIG	Glaser-Dirks DG.800A	I. Godfrey
	G-ORIX	ARV K1 Super 2	T. M. Lyons (G-BUXH/G-BNVK)
	G-ORJA	Beech B.200 Super King Air	Airwest Ltd
	G-ORJK	Laverda F.8L Falco Srs 4	Viking BV/Netherlands
	G-ORKY	AS.350B2 Ecureuil	Jet Helicopters Ltd
	G-ORLA	P & M Pegasus Quik	J. Summers
	G-ORMB	Robinson R22 Beta	Scotia Helicopters Ltd
	G-ORMG	Cessna 172R II	J. R. T. Royle
	G-ORMW	Ikarus C.42 FB100	B. J. Jenkins
	G-OROD	PA-18 Super Cub 150	B. W. Faulkner

vReg.	Type	Owner or Operator	Notes
G-OROS	Ikarus C.42 FB80	R. I. Simpson	
G-ORPC	Shaw Europa XS	P. W. Churms	
G-ORPR	Cameron O-77 balloon	S. R. Vining	
G-ORRG	Robin DR.400-180 Regent	Radley Robin Group	
G-ORTH	Beech E90 King Air	Gorthair Ltd	
G-ORUG	Thruster T.600N 450	D. J. N. Brown	
G-ORVE	Van's RV-6	R. J. F. Swain & F. M. Sperryn	
G-ORVG	Van's RV-6	RV Group	
G-ORVI	Van's RV-6	J. D. N. Cooke	
G-ORVR	Partenavia P.68B	Ravenair Aircraft Ltd (G-BFBD)	
G-ORVS	Van's RV-9	C. J. Marsh	
G-ORXI	Beech RB390 Premier 1A	Oryx Jet Ltd (G-RIZA)	
G-ORYX	Hawker 900XP	Oryx Jet Ltd	
G-ORZA	Diamond DA42 Twin Star	M. J. Hill (G-FCAC)	
G-OSAT	Cameron Z-105 balloon	Lotus Balloons Ltd	
G-OSAW	QAC Quickie Q.2	S. A. Wilson (G-BVYT)	
G-OSAZ	Robinson R22	Hi-Air (Redditch) Ltd (G-DERB/G-BPYH)	
G-OSCC	PA-32 Cherokee Six 300	BG & G Airlines Ltd (G-BGFD)	
G-OSCO	TEAM mini-MAX 91	V. Grayson	
G-OSDI	Beech 95-58 Baron	A. W. Eldridge & J. A. Heard (G-BHFY)	
G-OSEA	BN-2B-26 Islander	W. T. Johnson & Sons (Huddersfield) Ltd (G-BKOL)	
G-OSEP	Mainair Blade 912	J. D. Smith	
G-OSFB	Diamond HK.36TTC Super Dimona	Oxfordshire Sportflying Ltd	
G-OSFS	Cessan F.177RG	D. G. Wright	
G-OSHK	Schempp-Hirth SHK-1	P. B. Hibbard	
G-OSHL	Robinson R22 Beta	Sloane Helicopters Ltd	
G-OSIC	Pitts S-1C Special	J. A. Dodd (G-BUAW)	
G-OSII	Cessna 172N	India India Flying Group (G-BIVY)	
G-OSIS	Pitts S-1S Special	N. J. Riddin	
G-OSIT	Pitts S-1T Special	C. J. J. Robertson	
G-OSJF	PA-23-250 Aztec F	G-OSJF Owners Group (G-SFHR/G-BHSO)	
G-OSJL	Robinson R44 II	Darlo Air Ltd	
G-OSJN	Shaw Europa XS	N. Landell-Mills & R. J. Tobin	
G-OSKP	Enstrom 480	C. C. Butt	
G-OSKR	Skyranger 912 (2)	K. Clark	
G-OSKY	Cessna 172M	Skyhawk Leasing Ltd	
G-OSLD	Shaw Europa XS	S. Percy & C. Davies	
G-OSLO	Schweizer 269C	A. H. Helicopter Services Ltd	
G-OSMD	Bell 206B JetRanger 2	Overby Ltd (G-LTEK/G-BMIB)	
G-OSND	Cessna FRA.150M	Group G-OSND (G-BDOU)	
G-OSOE	HS.748 Srs 2A	PTB (Emerald) Pty Ltd (G-AYYG)	
G-OSON	P & M QuikR	R. Parr	
G-OSPD	Aerotechnik EV-97 TeamEurostar UK	I. Nicholls	
G-OSPK	Cessna 172S	R. W. Denny	
G-OSPS	PA-18 Super Cub 95	R. C. Lough	
G-OSPY	Cirrus SR20	Cambridge Guarantee Ltd	
G-OSRL	Learjet 45	S. R. Lloyd	
G-OSSA	Cessna Tu.206B	Skydive St.Andrews Ltd	
G-OSST	Colt 77A balloon	A. A. Brown	
G-OSTC	AA-5A Cheetah	5th Generation Designs Ltd	
G-OSTL	Ikarus C.42 FB 100	G-OSTL Syndicate	
G-OSTY	Cessna F.150G	R. F. Newman (G-AVCU)	
G-OSUP	Lindstrand LBL-90A balloon	M. E. Orchard	
G-OSUS	Mooney M.20K	J. B. King	
G-OSUT	Scheibe SF-25C Rotax-Falke	Yorkshire Gliding Club (Pty.) Ltd	
G-OSZA	Aerotek Pitts S-2A	Septieme Ciel	
G-OSZB	Christen Pitts S-2B Special	P. M. Ambrose (G-OGEE)	
G-OSZS	Pitts S-2S Special	L. V. Nieuwenhove	
G-OTAG	Bombardier CL600-2B16 Challenger	TAG Aviation (UK) Ltd	
G-OTAL	ARV Super 2	J. M. Cullen (G-BNGZ)	
G-OTAM	Cessna 172M	G. V. White	
G-OTAN	PA-18 Super Cub 135 (54-2445)	J. Style & M. G. F. Di Prima	
G-OTAZ	Hawker 900XP	Hangar 8 Management Ltd	
G-OTCH	CFM Streak Shadow	B. McFadden	
G-OTCM	Hughes 369E	Trans Holdings Ltd (G-DASY)	
G-OTCV	Skyranger 912S (1)	T. C. Viner	
G-OTCZ	Schempp-Hirth Ventus 2cT	D. H. Conway t/a CZ Group	
G-OTDI	Diamond DA40D Star	Atrium Ltd	
G-OTEC	Tecnam P2002 Sierra Deluxe	C. W. Thirtle	

Notes	Reg.	Type	Owner or Operator
	G-OTEL	Thunder Ax8-90 balloon	J. W. Adkins
	G-OTFL	Eurocopter EC 120B	J. Henshall (G-IBRI)
	G-OTFT	PA-38-112 Tomahawk	P. Tribble (G-BNKW)
	G-OTGA	PA-28R-201 Arrow III	TG Aviation Ltd
	G-OTHE	Enstrom 280C-UK Shark	G. E. Heritage (G-OPJT/G-BKCO)
	G-OTIB	Robin DR.400/180R	The Windrushers Gliding Club Ltd
	G-OTIG	AA-5B Tiger	L. Burke (G-PENN)
	G-OTIM	Bensen B.8MV	T. J. Deane
	G-OTIV	Aerospool Dynamic WT9 UK	D. N. E. d'Ath
	G-OTJH	Pegasus Quantum 15-912	L. R. Gartside
	G-OTJS	Robinson R44 II	TJS Self Drive
	G-OTLC	Grumman AA-5 Traveller	Total Logistics Concepts Ltd (G-BBUF)
	G-OTNA	Robinson R44 Raven II	Abel Developments Ltd
	G-OTOE	Aeronca 7AC Champion	D. Cheney (G-BRWW)
	G-OTOO	Stolp SA.300 Starduster Too	I. M. Castle
	G-OTOP	P & M Quik R	S. D. Pain
	G-OTRV	Van's RV-6	E. N. Burnett
	G-OTRY	Schleicher ASW-24	A. R. Harrison & G. Pursey
	G-OTSP	AS.355F1 Twin Squirrel	MW Helicopters Ltd (G-XPOL/G-BPRF)
	G-OTTY	Rotorsport UK Calidus	J. M. Giles
	G-OTUI	SOCATA TB20 Trinidad	D. J. Wood (G-KKDL/G-BSHU)
	G-OTUN	Aerotechnik EV-97 Eurostar	S. P. Slater
	G-OTUP	Lindstrand LBL-180A balloon	A. N. Sharp
	G-OTVI	Robinson R44 II	Hields Aviation
	G-OTVR	PA-34-220T Seneca V	IAS Medical Ltd
	G-OTWO	Rutan Defiant	B. Wronski
	G-OTYE	Aerotechnik EV-97 Eurostar	A. B. Godber & J. Tye
	G-OTYP	PA-28 Cherokee 180	T. C. Lewis
	G-OUCH	Cameron N-105 balloon	A. C. Elson
	G-OUDA	Aeroprakt A22-L Foxbat	A. R. Cattell
	G-OUGH	Yakovlev Yak-52	I. M. Gough (G-LAOK)
	G-OUHI	Shaw Europa XS	Airplan Flight Equipment Ltd
	G-OUIK	Mainair Pegasus Quik	D. G. Baker
	G-OUMC	Lindstrand LBL-105A balloon	Executive Ballooning
	G-OUNI	Cirrus SR20	Unique Helicopters (NI) Ltd (G-TABI)
	G-OURO	Shaw Europa	I. M. Mackay
	G-OUVI	Cameron O-105 balloon	Bristol University Hot Air Ballooning Society
	G-OVAL	Ikarus C.42 FB100	N. G. Tomes
	G-OVBF	Cameron A-250 balloon	Virgin Balloon Flights
	G-OVBL	Lindstrand LBL-150A balloon	R. J. Henderson
	G-OVET	Cameron O-56 balloon	A. R. Hardwick & E. Fearon
	G-OVFM	Cessna 120	T. B. Parmenter
	G-OVFR	Cessna F.172N	Marine and Aviation Ltd
	G-OVIA	Lindstrand LBL-105A balloon	N. C. Lindsey
	G-OVII	Van's RV-7	T. J. Richardson
	G-OVIN	Rockwell Commander 112TC	G. Vekaria
	G-OVIV	Aerostyle Breezer LSA	P. & V. Lynch
	G-OVLA	Ikarus C.42 FB	Webb Plant Sales
	G-OVMC	Cessna F.152 II	Swiftair Maintenance Ltd
	G-OVNE	Cessna 401A H	Norwich Aviation Museum
	G-OVNR	Robinson R22 Beta	Glenntrade Ltd
	G-OVOL	Skyranger 912S(1)	A. S. Docherty
	G-OVON	PA-18-95 Super Cub	V. F. A. Stanley
	G-OWAI	Schleicher ASK-21	Scottish Gliding Union
	G-OWAL	PA-34-220T Seneca III	R. G. & W. Allison
	G-OWAN	Cessna 210D Centurion	G. Owen
	G-OWAP	PA-28-161 Cherokee Warrior II	Aviation Advice & Consulting (G-BXNH)
	G-OWAR	PA-28-161 Warrior II	Bickertons Aerodromes Ltd
	G-OWAZ	Pitts S-1C Special	P. E. S. Latham (G-BRPI)
	G-OWBR	Tipsy Nipper T.66 series 2	W. J. Y. Ronge
	G-OWEL	Colt 105A balloon	S. R. Seager
	G-OWEN	K & S Jungster	R. C. Owen
	G-OWFS	Cessna A.152	Westair Flying Services Ltd (G-DESY/G-BNJE)
	G-OWGC	Slingsby T.61F Venture T.2	Wolds Gliding Club Ltd
	G-OWIL	Cessna 120	R. Flanagan (G-BTYW)
	G-OWLC	PA-31 Turbo Navajo	Channel Airways Ltd (G-AYFZ)
	G-OWMC	Thruster T.600N	Wilts Microlight Centre
	G-OWND	Robinson R44 Astro	R. E. Todd
	G-OWOW	Cessna 152 II	Plane Talking Ltd (G-BMSZ)

Reg.	Type	Owner or Operator	Notes
G-OWRC	Cessna F.152 II	Unimat SA/France	
G-OWRT	Cessna 182G	L. Townsend (G-ASUL)	
G-OWWW	Shaw Europa	R. F. W. Holder	
G-OWYE	Lindstrand LBL-240A balloon	Wye Valley Aviation Ltd	
G-OWYN	Aviamilano F.14 Nibbio	R. Nash	
G-OXBA	Cameron Z-160 balloon	J. E. Rose	
G-OXBC	Cameron A-140 balloon	J. E. Rose	
G-OXBY	Cameron N-90 balloon	C. A. Oxby	
G-OXII	Van's RV-12	J. A. King	
G-OXKB	Cameron 110 Sports Car SS balloon	D. M. Moffat	
G-OXLS	Cessna 560XL Citation XLS	Go XLS Ltd	
G-OXOM	PA-28-161 Cadet	Aviation Rentals (G-BRSG)	
G-OXPS	Falcon XPS	J. C. Greenslade (G-BUXP)	
G-OXRS	Bombardier BD700 1A10 Global Express	Profred Partners LLP	
G-OXVI	VS.361 Spitfire LF.XVIe (TD248:CR-S)	Spitfire Ltd	
G-OYAK	Yakovlev C-11 (9 white)	A. H. Soper	
G-OYES	Mainair Blade 912	B. McAdam & A. Hatton	
G-OYIO	Robin DR.400/120	Exeter Aviation Ltd	
G-OYST	Agusta-Bell 206B JetRanger 2	L. E. V. Knifton (G-JIMW/G-UNIK/G-TPPH/ G-BCYP)	
G-OYTE	Rans S.6ES Coyote II	N. D. Major	
G-OZAR	Enstrom 480	Benham Helicopters Ltd (G-BWFF)	
G-OZBB	Airbus A.320-212	Monarch Airlines Ltd	
G-OZBE	Airbus A.321-231	Monarch Airlines Ltd	
G-OZBF	Airbus A.321-231	Monarch Airlines Ltd	
G-OZBG	Airbus A.321-231	Monarch Airlines Ltd	
G-OZBH	Airbus A.321-231	Monarch Airlines Ltd	
G-OZBI	Airbus A.321-231	Monarch Airlines Ltd	
G-OZBK	Airbus A.320-214	Monarch Airlines Ltd	
G-OZBL	Airbus A.321-231	Monarch Airlines Ltd (G-MIDE)	
G-OZBM	Airbus A.321-231	Monarch Airlines Ltd (G-MIDJ)	
G-OZBN	Airbus A.321-231	Monarch Airlines Ltd (G-MIDK)	
G-OZBO	Airbus A.321-231	Monarch Airlines Ltd (G-MIDM)	
G-OZBP	Airbus A.321-231	Monarch Airlines Ltd (G-TTIB)	
G-OZBR	Airbus A.321-231	Monarch Airlines Ltd	
G-OZBS	Airbus A.321-231	Monarch Airlines Ltd (G-TTIA)	
G-OZBT	Airbus A.321-231	Monarch Airlines Ltd (G-TTIH)	
G-OZBU	Airbus A.321-231	Monarch Airlines Ltd (G-TTII)	
G-OZEE	Light Aero Avid Speedwing Mk 4	G. D. Bailey	
G-OZEF	Shaw Europa XS	Z. M. Ahmad	
G-OZIE	Jabiru J400	S. A. Bowkett	
G-OZIO	Aquila AT01	Caseright Ltd	
G-OZOI	Cessna R.182	J. R. G. & F. L. G. Fleming (G-ROBK)	
G-OZOO	Cessna 172N	R. A. Brown (G-BWEI)	
G-OZOZ	Schempp-Hirth Nimbus 3DT	G-OZOZ Syndicate	
G-OZRH	BAe 146-200	Calder Ltd	
G-OZZE	Lambert Mission M108	A. & J. Oswald	
G-OZZI	Jabiru SK	A. H. Godfrey	
G-OZZO	Avions Mudry CAP.231	R. M. Buchan	
G-PACE	Robin R.1180T	M. T. Fitzpatrick & T. C. Wise	
G-PACL	Robinson R22 Beta	Whizzard Helicopters	
G-PACO	Sikorsky S-76C	Cardinal Helicopter Services	
G-PACT	PA-28-181 Archer III	A. Parsons	
G-PADD	AA-5A Cheetah	Caseright Ltd (G-ESTE/G-GHNC)	
G-PADE	Escapade Jabiru(3)	C. L. G. Innocent	
G-PADI	Cameron V-77 balloon	C. Chardon	
G-PAFC	Cameron C-70 balloon	G. A. Boyle	
G-PAFF	AutoGyro MTO Sport	S. R. Paffett	
G-PAFR	Glaser-Dirks DG-300 Elan	Y. G. J-P. Clave	
G-PAIG	Grob G.109B	M. E. Baker	
G-PAIZ	PA-12 Super Cruiser	B. R. Pearson	
G-PALI	Czech Sport Aircraft Piper Sport	P. A. Langley	
G-PAMY	Robinson R44 II	Batchelor Aviation Ltd	
G-PARG	Pitts S-1C Special	M. Kotsageridis	
G-PARI	Cessna 172RG Cutlass	V. A. Holliday	
G-PASH	AS.355F1 Twin Squirrel	Diamond Aviation Ltd	
G-PASN	Enstrom F-28F	Passion 4 Health International Ltd (G-BSHZ)	

Notes	Reg.	Type	Owner or Operator
	G-PATF	Shaw Europa	E. P. Farrell
	G-PATG	Cameron O-90 balloon	s. Neighbour & N. Symonds
	G-PATI	Cessna F.172M	Nigel Kenny Aviation Ltd (G-WACZ/G-BCUK)
	G-PATM	AS.350B2 Ecureuil	Mealey Construction Ltd
	G-PATN	SOCATA TB10 Tobago	G-PATN Owners Group (G-LUAR)
	G-PATO	Zenair CH.601UL Zodiac	N. D. Townend
	G-PATP	Lindstrand LBL-77A balloon	P. Pruchnickyj
	G-PATS	Shaw Europa	G-PATS Flying Group
	G-PATX	Lindstrand LBL-90A balloon	P. C. Gooch
	G-PATZ	Shaw Europa	H. P. H. Griffin
	G-PAVL	Robin R.3000/120	MintLPG Ltd
	G-PAWL	PA-28 Cherokee 140	G-PAWL Group (G-AWEU)
	G-PAWN	PA-25 Pawnee 260C	A. P. Meredith (G-BEHS)
	G-PAWS	AA-5A Cheetah	M. J. Patrick
	G-PAWZ	Best Off Sky Ranger Swift 912S(1)	L. Moore
	G-PAXX	PA-20 Pacer 135 (modified)	I. P. Burnett
	G-PAYD	Robin DR.400/180	M. J. Bennett
	G-PAZY	Pazmany PL.4A	M. Richardson (G-BLAJ)
	G-PBAT	Czech Sport Aircraft Sportcruiser	P. M. W. Bath
	G-PBEC	Van's RV-7	P. G. Reid
	G-PBEE	Robinson R44	Echo Echo Syndicate
	G-PBEK	Agusta A109A	Castle Air Ltd (G-BXIV)
	G-PBEL	CFM Shadow Srs DD	S. Fairweather
	G-PBIX	VS.361 Spitfire LF XVI E	Pemberton-Billing LLP (G-XVIA)
	G-PBRL	Robinson R22	Cardy Construction Ltd
	G-PBUS	Avtech Jabiru SK	R. D. Bennett
	G-PBYA	Consolidated PBY-5A Catalina (433915)	Catalina Aircraft Ltd
	G-PBYY	Enstrom 280FX	S. Craske (G-BXKV)
	G-PBZN	AS.350B Ecureuil	Quarry and Mining Equipment Ltd (G-MURP)
	G-PCAF	Pietenpol Air Camper	C. C. & F. M. Barley
	G-PCAT	SOCATA TB10 Tobago	S. D. Johnson (G-BHER)
	G-PCCC	Alpi Pioneer 300	R. Pidcock
	G-PCDP	Zlin Z.526F Trener Master	J. Mann
	G-PCMC	P & M Quik R	M. J. & P. J. Canty
	G-PCOP	Beech B200 Super King Air	Albert Batlett and Sons (Airdrie) Ltd
	G-PDGE	Eurocopter EC 120B	A. J. Wicklow
	G-PDGF	AS.350B2 Ecureuil	PLM Dollar Group Ltd (G-FROH)
	G-PDGG	Aeromere F.8L Falco Srs 3	P. D. G. Grist
	G-PDGI	AS.350B1 Ecureuil	PLM Dollar Group Ltd (G-BVJE)
	G-PDGK	SA.365N Dauphin 2	PLM Dollar Group Ltd (G-HEMS)
	G-PDGN	SA.365N Dauphin 2	PLM Dollar Group Ltd (G-TRAF/G-BLDR)
	G-PDGR	AS.350B2 Ecureuil	PLM Dollar Group Ltd (G-RICC/G-BTXA)
	G-PDGT	AS.355F2 Ecureuil 2	PLM Dollar Group Ltd (G-BOOV)
	G-PDHJ	Cessna T.182R	P. G. Vallance Ltd
	G-PDOC	PA-44-180 Seminole	Medicare (G-PVAF)
	G-PDOG	Cessna O-1E Bird Dog (24550)	J. D. Needham
	G-PDSI	Cessna 172N	DA Flying Group
	G-PEAR	P &M Pegasus Quik	C. D. Hayle
	G-PECK	PA-32-300 Cherokee Six D	L. M. Empson (G-ETAV/G-MCAR/G-LADA/ G-AYWK)
	G-PEER	Cessna 525A Citationjet CJ2	Air Charter Scotland (Holdings) Ltd (G-SYGC/ G-HGRC)
	G-PEGA	Pegasus Quantum 15-912	E. Schoonbrood
	G-PEGE	Skyranger 912	A. N. Hughes
	G-PEGI	PA-34-200T Seneca II	ACS Aviation Ltd
	G-PEGY	Shaw Europa	M. Powell
	G-PEGZ	Centrair 101A Pegase	G-PEGZ Group
	G-PEJM	PA-28-181 Archer III	S. J. Clark
	G-PEKT	SOCATA TB20 Trinidad	H. E. Prew-Smith
	G-PENH	Ultramagic M-90 balloon	G. Holtam
	G-PEPA	Cessna 206H	R. D. Lygo (G-MGMG)
	G-PEPE	Cessna 560XL Citation XLS	Fram Partners LLP
	G-PEPS	Robinson R44	PEP Aviation (G-LFBW/G-ODES)
	G-PERB	Agusta AW.139	Bond Offshore Helicopters Ltd
	G-PERC	Cameron N-90 balloon	I. R. Warrington
	G-PERE	Robinson R22 Beta	R. F. McLachlan
	G-PERR	Cameron 60 Bottle SS balloon ★	British Balloon Museum/Newbury

Reg.	Type	Owner or Operator	Notes
G-PEST	Hawker Tempest II (MW401)	Tempest Two Ltd	
G-PETH	PA-24-260C Comanche	J. V. Hutchinson	
G-PETR	PA-28-140 Cherokee	A. A. Gardner (G-BCJL)	
G-PETS	Diamond DA42NG Twin Star	Airways Aircraft Leasing Ltd	
G-PEYO	Gefa-Flug AS 105 GD airship	International Merchandising Promotion and Services SA	
G-PFAA	EAA Biplane Model P	T. A. Fulcher	
G-PFAF	FRED Srs 2	M. S. Perkins	
G-PFAH	Evans VP-1	J. A. Scott	
G-PFAP	Currie Wot/SE-5A (C1904:Z)	J. H. Seed	
G-PFAR	Isaacs Fury II (K2059)	M. A. Watts	
G-PFAT	Monnett Sonerai II	H. B. Carter	
G-PFAW	Evans VP-1	R. F. Shingler	
G-PFCL	Cessna 172S	C. H. S. Carpenter	
G-PFCT	Learjet 45	The Fighter Collection Ltd (G-GOMO/G-OLDF/ G-JRJR)	
G-PFFN	Beech 200 Super King Air	The Puffin Club Ltd	
G-PFSL	Cessna F.152	P. A. Simon	
G-PGAC	MCR-01	G. A. Coatesworth	
G-PGBR	Vulcanair P-68R	Caseright Ltd	
G-PGFG	Tecnam P92-EM Echo	P. G. Fitzgerald	
G-PGGY	Robinson R44	Linic Consultants Ltd	
G-PGHM	Air Creation Kiss 450	P. G. H. Millbank	
G-PGRP	Embraer EMB-135BJ Legacy	ECC Leasing Company Ltd	
G-PGSA	Thruster T.600N	T. Davis	
G-PGSI	Pierre Robin R2160	M. A. Spencer	
G-PHAA	Cessna F.150M	Douglas Held Aviation Ltd (G-BCPE)	
G-PHAB	Cirrus SR22	G3 Aviation Ltd (G-MACL)	
G-PHAT	Cirrus SR20	Hetherington Properties Ltd	
G-PHCJ	Vol Mediterrani VM-1 Esqual C	C. R. James	
G-PHLY	Cessna FRA150L	M. Bonsall	
G-PHMG	Van's RV-8	B. F. Hill	
G-PHNM	Embraer EMB-500 Phenom 100	YC Investments	
G-PHNX	Schempp-Hirth Duo Discus Xt	J. L. Birch & R. Maskell	
G-PHOR	Cessna FRA.150L Aerobat	M. Bonsall (G-BACC)	
G-PHOX	Aeroprakt A22-L Foxbat	J. D. Webb	
G-PHSI	Colt 90A balloon	P. H. Strickland	
G-PHTG	SOCATA TB10 Tobago	A. J. Baggarley	
G-PHUN	Cessna FRA.150L Aerobat	M. Bonsall (G-BAIN)	
G-PHVM	Van's RV-8	G. Howes & V. Millard	
G-PHXS	Shaw Europa XS	P. Handford	
G-PHYL	Denney Kitfox Mk 4	J. S. A. Evans	
G-PHYS	Jabiru SP-470	C. Mayer	
G-PHYZ	Jabiru J430	P. C. Knight	
G-PIAF	Thunder Ax7-65 balloon	L. Battersley	
G-PICX	P & M Aviation QuikR	C. J. Meadows	
G-PIEL	CP.301A Emeraude	P. R. Thorne (G-BARY)	
G-PIES	Thunder Ax7-77Z balloon	S. J. Hollingsworth & M. K. Bellamy	
G-PIET	Pietenpol Air Camper	A. R. Wyatt	
G-PIGG	Lindstrand LBL Pig SS balloon	I. Heidenreich/Germany	
G-PIGI	Aerotechnik EV-97 Eurostar	Pigs Might Fly Group	
G-PIGS	SOCATA Rallye 150ST	Boonhill Flying Group (G-BDWB)	
G-PIGY	Short SC.7 Skyvan Srs 3A Variant 100	Invicta Aviation Ltd	
G-PIII	Pitts S-1D Special	On A Roll Aerobatics Group (G-BETI)	
G-PIIT	Pitts S-2 Special	R. Reid	
G-PIIX	Cessna P.210N	D. L. Harrisberg & R. Dennis (G-KATH)	
G-PIKD	Eiriavion PIK-20D-78	M. C. Hayes	
G-PIKE	Robinson R22 Mariner	Sloane Helicopters Ltd	
G-PIKK	PA-28 Cherokee 140	Coventry Aviators Flying Group (G-AVLA)	
G-PILE	Rotorway Executive 90	J. B. Russell	
G-PILL	Light Aero Avid Flyer Mk 4	D. R. Meston	
G-PILY	Pilatus B4 PC-11	N. Frost & K. E. Fox	
G-PILZ	AutoGyro MT-03	G. Millward	
G-PIMM	Ultramagic M-77 balloon	G. Everett	
G-PIMP	Robinson R44	Maxim Gestioni SRL	
G-PINC	Cameron Z-90 balloon	C. W. Clarke	
G-PING	AA-5A Cheetah	J. A. Newbold	
G-PINO	AutoGyro MTO Sport	P. A. Tolman	
G-PINT	Cameron 65 Barrel SS balloon	D. K. Fish	

Notes	Reg.	Type	Owner or Operator
	G-PINX	Lindstrand Pink Panther SS balloon	Magical Adventures Ltd/USA
	G-PIOM	Robinson R44	Karl Hayes Plant Hire (G-BXUK)
	G-PION	Alpi Pioneer 300	P. F. J. Burton
	G-PIPI	Mainair Pegasus Quik	N. R. Williams
	G-PIPP	PA-32R-301T Saratoga II TC	Poores Travel Consultants Ltd
	G-PIPR	PA-18 Super Cub 95	R. Forfitt & A. J. J. Sproule (G-BCDC)
	G-PIPS	Van's RV-4	P. M. Jarvis
	G-PIPY	Cameron 105 Pipe SS balloon	D. M. Moffat
	G-PITS	Pitts S-2AE Special	P. N. A. & S. N. Whithead
	G-PITT	Pitts S-2 Special	Mansfield Property Consultancy Ltd
	G-PITZ	Pitts S-2A Special	J. A. Coutts
	G-PIXE	Colt 31A balloon	J. F. Trehern
	G-PIXI	Pegasus Quantum 15-912	K. J. Rexter
	G-PIXL	Robinson R44 II	Flying TV Ltd
	G-PIXX	Robinson R44 II	Flying TV Ltd
	G-PIXY	Supermarine Aircraft Spitfire Mk.26	R. Collenette
	G-PJLO	Boeing 767-35EER	Thomson Airways Ltd
	G-PJMT	Lancair 320	V. Hatton & P. Gilroy
	G-PJPJ	Boeing 737-5H6	Celestrial Aviation Trading Ltd (G-GFFJ)
	G-PJSY	Van's RV-6	P. J. York
	G-PJTM	Cessna FR.172K II	R. & J. R. Emery (G-BFIF)
	G-PKPK	Schweizer 269C	C. H. Dobson
	G-PLAD	Kolb Twinstar Mk 3 Extra	P. J. Ladd
	G-PLAJ	BAe Jetstream 3102	Aviation Rentals Ltd
	G-PLAL	Eurocopter EC 135T2	Eurocopter UK Ltd
	G-PLAN	Cessna F.150L	G-PLAN Flying Group
	G-PLAR	Vans RV-9A	M. P. Board
	G-PLAY	Robin R.2112	A. M. and G. F. Granger t/a Alpha Flying Group
	G-PLAZ	Rockwell Commander 112	I. Hunt (G-RDCI/G-BFWG)
	G-PLEE	Cessna 182Q	Peterlee Parachute Centre
	G-PLIP	Diamond DA.40D Star	C. A. & D. R. Ho
	G-PLLT	Lindstrand Box SS balloon	Lindstrand Hot Air Balloons Ltd
	G-PLMH	AS.350B2 Ecureuil	PLM Dollar Group Ltd
	G-PLMI	SA.365C-1 Dauphin	PLM Dollar Group Ltd
	G-PLOP	Magni M-24C	C. A. Ho
	G-PLOW	Hughes 269B	C. Walton Ltd (G-AVUM)
	G-PLPC	Schweizer Hughes 269C	A. R. Baker
	G-PLPL	Agusta A109E Power	Iceland Foods Ltd (G-TMWC)
	G-PLPM	Shaw Europa XS	P. L. P. Mansfield
	G-PLSA	Aero Designs Pulsar XP	Air Ads Ltd (G-NEVS)
	G-PLSR	P & M PulsR	P and M Aviation Ltd
	G-PMAM	Cameron V-65 balloon	P. A. Meecham
	G-PMGG	Agusta-Bell 206A JetRanger	P. M. Gallagher & M. J. Lee (G-EEGO/G-PELS/ G-DNCN)
	G-PMHT	SOCATA TBM850	Ewan Air
	G-PMNF	VS.361 Spitfire HF.IX (TA805:FX-M)	P. R. Monk
	G-PNEU	Colt 110 Bibendum SS balloon	A. M. Holly
	G-PNGC	Schleicher ASK-21	Portsmouth Naval Gliding Centre
	G-PNIX	Cessna FRA.150L	Dukeries Aviation (G-BBEO)
	G-POCO	Cessna 152	K. M. Watts
	G-POET	Robinson R44 II	C. L. Farrell
	G-POGO	Flight Design CT2K	L. I. Bailey
	G-POLA	Eurocopter EC 135 P2+	West Midlands Police Authority
	G-POLI	Robinson R44 II	Luxtronic Ltd
	G-POLL	Skyranger 912 (1)	D. L. Pollitt
	G-POLY	Cameron N-77 balloon	S. Church & S. Jenkins
	G-POND	Oldfield Baby Lakes	U. Reichert/Germany
	G-POOH	Piper J-3C-65 Cub	P. Robinson
	G-POOL	ARV Super 2	P. A. Dawson (G-BNHA)
	G-POPA	Beech A36 Bonanza	C. J. O'Sullivan
	G-POPE	Eiri PIK-20E-1	G-POPE Syndicate
	G-POPI	SOCATA TB10 Tobago	I. S. Hacon & C. J. Earle (G-BKEN)
	G-POPW	Cessna 182S	D. L. Price
	G-POPY	Best Off Sky Ranger Swift 912S(1)	S. G. Penk & S. J. Sant
	G-PORK	AA-5B Tiger	R. A. Lambert (G-BFHS)
	G-POSH	Colt 56A balloon	B. K. Rippon (G-BMPT)

Reg.	Type	Owner or Operator	Notes
G-POUX	Pou du Ciel-Bifly	G. D. Priest	
G-POWC	Boeing 737-33A	Titan Airways Ltd	
G-POWD	Boeing 767-36N	Titan Airways Ltd	
G-POWF	Avro RJ100	Titan Airways Ltd (G-CFAA)	
G-POWG	Cessna 525A Citationjet CJ2	Hagondale Ltd	
G-POWL	Cessna 182R	B. W. Powell	
G-POZA	Escapade Jabiru ULP (1)	M. R. Jones	
G-PPIO	Cameron C-90 balloon	A. Murphy	
G-PPLC	Cessna 560 Citation V	Sterling Aviation	
G-PPLG	Rotorsport UK MT-03	J. E. Butler	
G-PPLL	Van's RV-7A	A. Payne & P. Young	
G-PPLO	Fournier RF-4D	M. Housley	
G-PPOD	Europa Aviation Europa XS	S. Easom	
G-PPPP	Denney Kitfox Mk 3	R. Powers	
G-PPTS	Robinson R44	J. & L. Prowse	
G-PRAG	Brügger MB.2 Colibri	Colibri Flying Group	
G-PRAH	Flight Design CT2K	G. N. S. Farrant	
G-PRDH	AS.355F2 Ecureuil 2	EZ-Int Ltd	
G-PRET	Robinson R44	J. A. Wilson	
G-PREY	Pereira Osprey II	N. S. Dalrymple (G-BEPB)	
G-PREZ	Robin DR.400/500	Regent Group	
G-PRFI	Agusta-Bell 206B Jet Ranger II	P. Fox (G-CPTS)	
G-PRII	Hawker Hunter PR.11 (XG164/A)	Interactive Dynamics Ltd	
G-PRIM	PA-38-112 Tomahawk	Braddock Ltd	
G-PRIV	VS.353 Spitfire PR.IV	P. R. Arnold	
G-PRKR	Canadair CL600-2B16 Challenger 604	TAG Aviation (UK) Ltd	
G-PRLY	Avtech Jabiru SK	N. C. Cowell (G-BYKY)	
G-PROJ	Robinson R44 II	Project Racing Team Ltd	
G-PROO	Hawker 4000 Horizon	Hangar 8 Management Ltd	
G-PROS	Van's RV-7A	S. A. Jarrett	
G-PROV	P.84 Jet Provost T.52A (T.4)	Provost Group	
G-PROW	Aerotechnik EV-97A Eurostar	Nene Valley Microlights Ltd	
G-PRSI	Pegasus Quantum 15-912	G-PRSI Group	
G-PRTT	Cameron N-31 balloon	A. Kaye	
G-PRXI	VS.365 Spitfire PR.XI (PL983)	Propshop Ltd	
G-PSAX	Lindstrand LBL-77B balloon	M. V. Farrant & I. Risbridger	
G-PSFG	Robin R.21601	Mardenair Ltd (G-COVD/G-BYOF)	
G-PSGC	PA-25 Pawnee 260C (modified)	Peterborough & Spalding Gliding Club Ltd (G-BDDT)	
G-PSHK	Schempp-Hirth SHK-1	P. Gentil	
G-PSIR	Jurca MJ.77 Gnatsum (474008 'VF-R')	P. W. Carlton & T. R. Grief	
G-PSKY	Skyranger 912S(1)	P. W. Curnock & J. W. Wilcox	
G-PSNI	Eurocopter EC 135T2	Police Service of Northern Ireland	
G-PSNO	Eurocopter MBB BK-117C-2	Police Service of Northern Ireland	
G-PSON	Colt Cylinder One SS balloon	Balloon Preservation Flying Group	
G-PSRT	PA-28-151 Warrior	P. A. S. Dyke (G-BSGN)	
G-PSST	Hunter F.58A	Heritage Aviation Developments Ltd	
G-PSUE	CFM Shadow Srs CD	D. A. Crosbie (G-MYAA)	
G-PSUK	Thruster T.600N 450	Thruster Syndicate	
G-PTAG	Shaw Europa	R. C. Harrison	
G-PTAR	Best Off Skyranger 912S(1)	P. Vergette	
G-PTDP	Bücker Bü133C Jungmeister	T. J. Reeve (G-AEZX)	
G-PTEA	PA-46-350P Malibu Mirage	P. J. Caiger	
G-PTOO	Bell 206L-4 LongRanger 4	P2 Air Ltd	
G-PTRE	SOCATA TB20 Trinidad	Trantshore Ltd (G-BNKU)	
G-PTRI	Cessna 182T	G-PTRI LLP	
G-PTTS	Aerotek Pitts S-2A	P. & J. Voce	
G-PTWO	Pilatus P2-05 (U-110)	R. G. Meredith	
G-PUDL	PA-18 Super Cub 150	C. M. Edwards	
G-PUDS	Shaw Europa	M. J. Riley	
G-PUFF	Thunder Ax7-77A balloon	Intervarsity Balloon Club	
G-PUGS	Cessna 182H	N. C. & M. F. Shaw	
G-PUKA	Jabiru Aircraft Jabiru J400	D. P. Harris	
G-PULR	Pitts S-2AE	A. Ayre	
G-PUME	AS.332L Super Puma	CHC Scotia Ltd	
G-PUMM	AS.332L Super Puma	CHC Scotia Ltd	
G-PUMN	AS.332L Super Puma	CHC Scotia Ltd	

Notes	Reg.	Type	Owner or Operator
	G-PUMO	AS.332L-2 Super Puma	CHC Scotia Ltd
	G-PUMR	EC.225LP Super Puma	Bond Offshore Helicopters Ltd.
	G-PUMS	AS.332L-2 Super Puma	CHC Scotia Ltd
	G-PUNK	Thunder Ax8-105 balloon	S. C. Kinsey
	G-PUNT	Robinson R44 II	R. D. Cameron
	G-PUPP	Beagle B.121 Pup 2	A. D. Wood (G-BASD)
	G-PUPS	Cameron Z-210 balloon	High On Adventure Balloons Ltd
	G-PUPY	Shaw Europa XS	V. L. Flett
	G-PURE	Cameron can 70 SS balloon	Mobberley Balloon Collection
	G-PURL	PA-32R-301 Saratoga II	A. P.H. & E. Hay
	G-PURP	Lindstrand LBL-90° balloon	C. & P. Mackley
	G-PURR	AA-5A Cheetah	D. H. Green (G-BJDN)
	G-PURS	Rotorway Executive	J. E. Houseman
	G-PUSA	Gefa-Flug AS105GD Hot Air Airship	Skyking Aviation Ltd
	G-PUSI	Cessna T.303	Crusader Craft
	G-PUSS	Cameron N-77 balloon	L. D. Pickup
	G-PUTT	Cameron Golfball 76 SS balloon	Lakeside Lodge Golf Centre
	G-PVBF	Lindstrand LBL-260S balloon	Virgin Balloon Flights
	G-PVCV	Robin DR400/140	Bustard Flying Club Ltd
	G-PVEL	Bombardier BD700-1A11 Global 5000	Ocean Sky (UK) Ltd
	G-PVET	DHC.1 Chipmunk 22 (WB565)	Connect Properties Ltd
	G-PVHT	Dassault Falcon 7X	TAG Aviation (UK) Ltd
	G-PVML	Robin DR400/140B	Weald Air Services Ltd
	G-PVSS	P & M Quik GT450	K. & L. Ramsay
	G-PVST	Thruster T.600N 450	R. J. Davey
	G-PWBE	DH.82A Tiger Moth	M. F. Newman
	G-PWIT	Bell 206L-1 LongRanger	Formal Holdings Ltd (G-DWMI)
	G-PWNS	Cessna 525 Citationjet	Langford Lane Ltd
	G-PWUL	Van's RV-6	D. C. Arnold
	G-PYNE	Thruster T.600N 450	R. Dereham
	G-PYPE	Van's RV-7	R. & L. Pyper
	G-PYRO	Cameron N-65 balloon	A. C. Booth
	G-PZAS	Schleicher ASW-27-18	A. P. C. Sampson
	G-PZAZ	PA-31-350 Navajo Chieftain	Argyll Ltd (G-VTAX/G-UTAX)
	G-RAAA	Bombardier BD700-1A10 Global Express	Ocean Sky (UK) Ltd
	G-RAAF	VS.359 Spitfire VIII	Composite Mast Engineering and Technology Ltd
	G-RAAL	Embraer EMB-500 Phenom 100	Flairjet Ltd
	G-RABS	Alpi Pioneer 300	J. Mullen
	G-RACA	P.57 Sea Prince T.1 (571/CU) ★	(stored)/Long Marston
	G-RACI	Beech C90 King Air (modified)	E Flight SRL/Italy (G-SHAM)
	G-RACO	PA-28R Cherokee Arrow 200-II	Graco Group Ltd
	G-RACR	Ultramagic M-65C balloon	R. A. Vale
	G-RACY	Cessna 182S	N. J. Fuller
	G-RADI	PA-28-181 Archer II	I. Davidson
	G-RADR	Douglas AD-4NA Skyraider (126922:503)	Orion Enterprises Ltd (G-RAID)
	G-RADY	Bombardier CL600-2B19 Challenger 850	TAG Aviation (UK) Ltd
	G-RAEF	Schempp-Hirth SHK-1	R. A. Earnshaw-Fretwell
	G-RAEM	Rutan LongEz	G. F. H. Singleton
	G-RAES	Boeing 777-236	British Airways
	G-RAFA	Grob G.115	RAF College Flying Club Ltd
	G-RAFB	Grob G.115	RAF College Flying Club Ltd
	G-RAFC	Robin R.2112	RAF Charlie Group
	G-RAFE	Thunder Ax7-77 balloon	Giraffe Balloon Syndicate
	G-RAFG	Slingsby T.67C Firefly	G. S. Evans
	G-RAFH	Thruster T.600N 450	G-RAFH Group
	G-RAFR	Skyranger J2.2(1)	M. D. Gregory & B. Lowry
	G-RAFS	Thruster T.600N 450	Caunton GRAFS Syndicate
	G-RAFT	Rutan LongEz	W. S. Allen
	G-RAFV	Avid Speedwing	Fox Victor Group (G-MOTT)
	G-RAFW	Mooney M.20E	Vinola (Knitwear) Manufacturing Co Ltd (G-ATHW)
	G-RAFY	Best Off Sky Ranger Swift 912S(1)	M. A. Evans & C. R. Cawley
	G-RAFZ	RAF 2000 GTX-SE	John Pavitt (Engineers) Ltd
	G-RAGE	Wilson Cassutt IIIM	R. S. Grace (G-BEUN)
	G-RAGS	Pietenpol Air Camper	S. H. Leonard
	G-RAGT	PA-32-301FT Cherokee Six	Oxhill Aviation
	G-RAIG	SA Bulldog Srs 100/101	Power Aerobatics Ltd (G-AZMR)

Reg.	Type	Owner or Operator	Notes
G-RAIR	Schleicher ASH-25	P. T. Reading	
G-RAIX	CCF AT-16 Harvard 4 (KF584)	M. R. Paul (G-BIWX)	
G-RAJA	Raj Hamsa X'Air 582 (2)	K. McKay	
G-RAJJ	BAe 146-200	Cello Aviation Ltd (G-CFDH)	
G-RALA	Robinson R44 Clipper II	Rala Aviation Ltd	
G-RALF	Rotorway Executive 162F	I. C. Bedford (G-BZOM)	
G-RAMA	Cameron C-70 balloon	Poppies (UK) Ltd	
G-RAMI	Bell 206B JetRanger 3	Yorkshire Helicopters	
G-RAMP	Piper J-3C-65 Cub	J. A. Holman & T. A. Hinton	
G-RAMS	PA-32R-301 Saratoga SP	Mike Sierra LLP	
G-RAMY	Bell 206B JetRanger 2	Lincair Ltd	
G-RAPD	Hughes 369E	FS Aviation LLP	
G-RAPH	Cameron O-77 balloon	P. A. Sweatman	
G-RAPI	Lindstrand LBL-105A balloon	P. A. Foot	
G-RARB	Cessna 172N	Prior Group Holdings Ltd	
G-RARE	Thunder Ax5-42 SS balloon ★	Balloon Preservation Group	
G-RASA	Diamond DA42 Twin Star	C. D. Hill	
G-RASC	Evans VP-2	R. F. Powell	
G-RASH	Grob G.109E	G-RASH Syndicate	
G-RATC	Van's RV-4	A. F. Ratcliffe	
G-RATD	Van's RV-8	J. R. Pike	
G-RATE	AA-5A Cheetah	G-RATE Flying Group (G-BIFF)	
G-RATH	Rotorway Executive 162F	W. H. Cole	
G-RATI	Cessna F.172M	D. Daniel (G-PATI/G-WACZ/G-BCUK)	
G-RATV	PA-28RT-201T Turbo Arrow IV	Tango Victor Ltd (G-WILS)	
G-RATZ	Shaw Europa	W. Goldsmith	
G-RAVE	Southdown Raven X	M. J. Robbins (G-MNZV)	
G-RAVN	Robinson R44	Brambledown Aircraft Hire	
G-RAWB	P & M Quik GT450	R. Blatchford	
G-RAWS	Rotorway Executive 162F	R. P. Robinson	
G-RAYA	Denney Kitfox Mk 4	G. M. Park	
G-RAYB	P & M Quik GT450	R. Blatchford	
G-RAYH	Zenair CH.701UL	R. Horner	
G-RAYO	Lindstrand LBL-90A balloon	R. Owen	
G-RAYS	Zenair CH.250	A. D. Lowe	
G-RAYY	Cirrus SR22	Alquiler de Veleros SL/Spain	
G-RAYZ	Tecnam P2002-EA Sierra	R. Wells	
G-RAZY	PA-28-181 Archer II	T. H. Pemberton (G-REXS)	
G-RAZZ	Maule MX-7-180	C. S. Baird	
G-RBBB	Shaw Europa	T. J. Hartwell	
G-RBCA	Agusta A109A II	G-RBCA Ltd (G-TBGL/G-VJCB/G-BOUA)	
G-RBCI	BN-2A Mk.III-2 Trislander	Aurigny Air Services Ltd (G-BDWV)	
G-RBCT	Schempp-Hirth Ventus 2Ct	M. J. Weston & J. D. Huband	
G-RBMV	Cameron O-31 balloon	P. D. Griffiths	
G-RBNS	Embraer EMB-135BJ Legacy 650	Portrack Global Ltd	
G-RBOS	Colt AS-105 airship ★	Science Museum/Wroughton	
G-RBOW	Thunder Ax-7-65 balloon	R. S. McDonald	
G-RBSN	Ikarus C.42 FB80	P. B. & M. Robinson	
G-RCED	Rockwell Commander 114	D. J. and D. Pitman	
G-RCHL	P & M Quik GT450	R. M. Broughton	
G-RCHY	Aerotechnik EV-97 Eurostar	N. McKenzie	
G-RCKT	Harmon Rocket II	K. E. Armstrong	
G-RCMC	Murphy Renegade 912	J. Matcham	
G-RCMF	Cameron V-77 balloon	J. M. Percival	
G-RCML	Sky 77-24 balloon	R. C. M. Sarl/Luxembourg	
G-RCNB	Eurocopter EC 120B	Furbs Pension Fund	
G-RCOM	Bell 206L-3 LongRanger 3	G. R. S. Harrison	
G-RCRC	P & M Quik	R. M. Brown	
G-RCSR	Replica de Havilland DH.88 Comet	K. Fern	
G-RCST	Jabiru J430	G. R. Cotterell	
G-RCUS	Schempp-Hirth Arcus T	R. B. Witter	
G-RCWK	Cessna 182T Skylane	R. C. W. King	
G-RDAD	Reality Escapade ULP(1)	R. W. Burge	
G-RDAY	Van's RV-9	R. M. Day	
G-RDCO	Avtech Jabiru J430	RDCO (International) LLP	
G-RDDT	Schempp-Hirth Duo Discus T	R. Witter	
G-RDEL	Robinson R44	Blond Helicopter SL/Spain	
G-RDFX	Aero AT-3	B. Wilson	
G-RDHS	Shaw Europa XS	R. D. H. Spencer	

Notes	Reg.	Type	Owner or Operator
	G-RDNS	Rans S.6-S Super Coyote	P. G. Cowling & J. S. Crofts
	G-RDPH	P & M Quik R	R. S. Partidge-Hicks
	G-READ	Colt 77A balloon	Intervarsity Balloon Club
	G-REAF	Jabiru J400	R. E. Afia
	G-REAH	PA-32R-301 Saratoga SP	M. Q. Tolbod & S. J. Rogers (G-CELL)
	G-REAR	Lindstrand LBL-69X balloon	A. M. Holly
	G-REAS	Van's RV-6A	T. J. Smith
	G-REBB	Murphy Rebel	M. Stow
	G-RECO	Jurca MJ-5L Sirocco	J. D. Tseliki
	G-REDC	Pegasus Quantum 15-912	S. Houghton
	G-REDE	Eurocopter AS.365N3 Dauphin 2	Bond European Aviation Leasing Ltd
	G-REDF	Eurocopter AS.365N3 Dauphin 2	Bond European Aviation Leasing Ltd
	G-REDG	Eurocopter AS.365N3 Dauphin 2	Bond Offshore Helicopters Ltd
	G-REDH	Eurocopter AS.365N3 Dauphin 2	Bond Offshore Helicopters Ltd
	G-REDJ	Eurocopter AS.332L-2 Super Puma	International Aviation Leasing Ltd
	G-REDK	Eurocopter AS.332L-2 Super Puma	International Aviation Leasing Ltd
	G-REDM	Eurocopter AS.332L-2 Super Puma	International Aviation Leasing Ltd
	G-REDN	Eurocopter AS.332L-2 Super Puma	International Aviation Leasing Ltd
	G-REDO	Eurocopter AS.332L-2 Super Puma	International Aviation Leasing Ltd
	G-REDP	Eurocopter AS.332L-2 Super Puma	International Aviation Leasing Ltd
	G-REDR	Eurocopter AS.225LP Super Puma	International Aviation Leasing Ltd
	G-REDT	Eurocopter EC.225LP Super Puma	International Aviation Leasing LLP
	G-REDV	Eurocopter EC.225LP Super Puma	Bond Offshore Helicopters Ltd
	G-REDW	Eurocopter EC.225LP Super Puma	Bond Offshore Helicopters Ltd
	G-REDX	Experimental Aviation Berkut	G. V. Waters
	G-REDY	Robinson R22 Beta	L. Iampieri
	G-REDZ	Thruster T.600T 450	N. S. Dell
	G-REEC	Sequoia F.8L Falco	J. D. Tseliki
	G-REED	Mainair Blade 912S	I. C. Macbeth
	G-REEF	Mainair Blade 912S	G. Mowll
	G-REEM	AS.355F1 Twin Squirrel	Heliking Ltd (G-EMAN/G-WEKR/G-CHLA)
	G-REER	Centrair 101A Pegase	R. L. Howorth & G. C. Stinchcombe
	G-REES	Jodel D.140C	G-REES Flying Group
	G-REGC	Zenair CH.601XL Zodiac	G. P. Coutie
	G-REGE	Robinson R44	Rotorvation Helicopters
	G-REGI	Cyclone Chaser S508	G. S. Stokes (G-MYZW)
	G-REGS	Thunder Ax7-77 balloon	D. R. Rawlings
	G-REJP	Europa XS	A. Milner
	G-REKO	Pegasus Quasar IITC	M. Sims (G-MWWA)
	G-RELL	D.62B Condor	P. S. Grellier (G-OPJH/G-AVDW)
	G-REMH	Bell 206B-3 JetRanger III	Nottinghamshire Helicopters (2008) Ltd
	G-RENO	SOCATA TB10 Tobago	V. W. Ood
	G-RESC	MBB BK.117C-1	Sterling Helicopters Ltd
	G-RESG	Dyn'Aéro MCR-01 Club	R. E. S. Greenwood
	G-REST	Beech P35 Bonanza	C. R. Taylor (G-ASFJ)
	G-RETA	CASA 1.131 Jungmann 2000	Richard Shuttleworth Trustees (G-BGZC)
	G-REVE	Van's RV-6	J. D. Winder
	G-REVO	Skyranger 912(2)	H. Murray
	G-REYS	Canadair CL600-2B16 Challenger 604	TAG Aviation
	G-RFIO	Aeromot AMT-200 Super Ximango	M. D. Evans
	G-RFLY	Extra EA.300/L	H. B. Sauer
	G-RFOX	Denney Kitfox Mk 3	B. & P. J. Chandler
	G-RFSB	Sportavia RF-5B	G-RFSB Group
	G-RFUN	Robinson R44	Brooklands Developments Ltd
	G-RGSG	Raytheon Hawker 900XP	Hangar 8 Management Ltd
	G-RGTS	Schempp-Hirth Discus b	G. R. & L. R. Green
	G-RGUS	Fairchild 24A-46A Argus III (44-83184)	T. R. Coulton & J. L. Bryan
	G-RGZT	Cirrus SR20	D. A. Whalley
	G-RHAM	Skyranger 582(1)	I. Smart & T. Driffield
	G-RHCB	Schweizer 269C-1	Lift West Ltd
	G-RHHT	PA-32RT-300 Lance II	M. R. Boutel
	G-RHMS	Embraer EMB-135BJ Legacy	Astra Fire Ltd
	G-RHOS	ICP MXP-740 Savannah VG Jabiru(1)	J. C. Munro-Hunt
	G-RHYM	PA-31-310 Turbo Navajo B	2 Excel Aviation Ltd (G-BJLO)
	G-RHYS	Rotorway Executive 90	A. K. Voase
	G-RIAM	SOCATA TB10 Tobago	H. Varia
	G-RIBA	P & M Quik GT450	R. J. Murphy

Reg.	Type	Owner or Operator	Notes
G-RICK	Beech 95-B55 Baron	J. Jack (G-BAAG)	
G-RICO	AG-5B Tiger	I. J. Ward	
G-RICS	Shaw Europa	The Flying Property Doctor	
G-RIDA	Eurocopter AS.355NP Ecureuil 2	National Grid Electricity Transmission PLC	
G-RIDE	Stephens Akro	R. Mitchell	
G-RIDG	Van's RV-7	C. Heathcote	
G-RIEF	DG Flugzeugbau DG-1000T	EF Gliding Group	
G-RIET	Hoffmann H.36 Dimona	Dimona Gliding Group	
G-RIEV	Rolladen-Schneider LS8-18	R. D. Grieve	
G-RIFB	Hughes 269C	AA Consultants Ltd	
G-RIFN	Avion Mudry CAP-10B	D. E. Starkey & R. A. J. Spurrell	
G-RIFO	Schempp-Hirth Standard Cirrus 75-VTC	L. de Marchi (G-CKGT)	
G-RIFY	Christen Eagle II	C. J. Gow	
G-RIGB	Thunder Ax7-77 balloon	N. J. Bettin	
G-RIGH	PA-32R-301 Saratoga IIHP	G. M. R. Graham	
G-RIGS	PA-60 Aerostar 601P	G. G. Caravati & P. G. Penati/Italy	
G-RIHN	Dan Rihn DR.107 One Design	P. J. Burgess	
G-RIII	Vans RV-3B	R. S. Grace & D. H. Burge	
G-RIIV	Van's RV-4	D. J. Taylor	
G-RIKI	Mainair Blade 912	RIKI Group	
G-RIKS	Shaw Europa XS	R. Morris	
G-RIKY	Mainair Pegasus Quik	P. J. Bent	
G-RILA	Flight Design CTSW	P. Mahony	
G-RILY	Monnett Sonnerai 2L	A Sharp	
G-RIMB	Lindstrand LBL-105A balloon	D. Grimshaw	
G-RIME	Lindstrand LBL-25A balloon	N. Ivison	
G-RIMM	Westland Wasp HAS.1 (XT435:430)	G. P. Hinkley	
G-RINN	Mainair Blade	P. Hind	
G-RINO	Thunder Ax7-77 balloon	D. J. Head	
G-RINS	Rans S.6-ESD Coyote II	R. W. Hocking	
G-RINT	CFM Streak Shadow	D. Grint	
G-RINZ	Van's RV-7	P. Chaplin (G-UZZL)	
G-RIPA	Partenavia P68 Observer 2	Apem Ltd	
G-RIPH	VS.384 Seafire F.XVII	Seafire Displays Ltd (G-CDTM)	
G-RISA	PA-28-180 Cherokee C	D. B. Riseborough (G-ATZK)	
G-RISE	Cameron V-77 balloon	D. L. Smith	
G-RISH	Rotorway Exeecutive 162F	C. S. Rische	
G-RISK	Hughes 369E	Wavendon Social Housing Ltd	
G-RISY	Van's RV-7	G-RISY Group	
G-RITT	Pegasus Quik	I. A. Macadam	
G-RIVE	Jodel D.153	P. Fines	
G-RIVR	Thruster T.600N 450	Thruster Air Services Ltd	
G-RIVT	Van's RV-6	N. Reddish	
G-RIXA	J-3C-65 Cub	J. J. Rix	
G-RIXS	Shaw Europa XS	R. Iddon	
G-RIXY	Cameron Z-77 balloon	Rix Petroleum Ltd	
G-RIZE	Cameron O-90 balloon	S. F. Burden/Netherlands	
G-RIZI	Cameron N-90 balloon	R. Wiles	
G-RIZZ	PA-28-161 Warrior II	Modi Aviation Ltd	
G-RJAH	Boeing Stearman A75N1	R. J. Horne	
G-RJAM	Sequoia F.8L Falco	A. L. Hall-Carpenter	
G-RJCC	Cessna 172S	R. J. Chapman	
G-RJCP	Rockwell Commander 114B	Heltor Ltd	
G-RJCS	Hughes 369E	Exsol Ltd	
G-RJMS	PA-28R-201 Arrow III	M. G. Hill	
G-RJRJ	Evektor EV-97A Eurostar	D. P. Myatt	
G-RJWW	Maule M5-235C Lunar Rocket	D. E. Priest (G-BRWG)	
G-RJWX	Shaw Europa XS	J. R. Jones	
G-RJXA	Embraer RJ145EP	bmi regional	
G-RJXB	Embraer RJ145EP	bmi regional	
G-RJXC	Embraer RJ145EP	bmi regional	
G-RJXD	Embraer RJ145EP	bmi regional	
G-RJXE	Embraer RJ145EP	bmi regional	
G-RJXF	Embraer RJ145EP	bmi regional	
G-RJXG	Embraer RJ145EP	bmi regional	
G-RJXH	Embraer RJ145EP	bmi regional	
G-RJXI	Embraer RJ145EP	bmi regional	
G-RJXJ	Embraer RJ135LR	bmi regional	
G-RJXK	Embraer RJ135LR	bmi regional	
G-RJXL	Embraer RJ135LR	bmi regional	
G-RJXM	Embraer RJ145MP	bmi regional	

Notes	Reg.	Type	Owner or Operator
	G-RXJP	Embraer RJ135ER	bmi regional (G-CDFS)
	G-RJXR	Embraer RJ145EP	bmi regional (G-CCYH)
	G-RKEL	Agusta-Bell 206B JetRanger 3	Nunkeeling Ltd
	G-RKKT	Cessna FR.172G	K. L. Irvine (G-AYJW)
	G-RLEF	Hawker Hurricane XII	P. J. Lawton
	G-RLMW	Tecnam P2002-EA Sierra	G. J. Slater
	G-RLON	BN-2A Mk III-2 Trislander	Aurigny Air Services Ltd (G-ITEX/G-OCTA/ G-BCXW)
	G-RLWG	Ryan ST3KR	R. A. Fleming
	G-RMAC	Shaw Europa	P. J. Lawless
	G-RMAN	Aero Designs Pulsar	M. B. Redman
	G-RMAX	Cameron C-80 balloon	J. Kenny
	G-RMCM	EV-97 TeamEurostar UK	Nene Valley Microlights Ltd
	G-RMCS	Cessna 182R	R. W. C. Sears
	G-RMHE	Aerospool Dynamic WT9 UK	R. M. Hughes-Ellis
	G-RMIT	Van's RV-4	J. P. Kloos
	G-RMMA	Dassault Falcon 900EX	Execujet (UK) Ltd
	G-RMMT	Europa XS	N. Schmitt
	G-RMPI	Whittaker MW5D Sorcerer	N. R. Beale
	G-RMPS	Van's RV-12	K. D. Boardman
	G-RMPY	Aerotechnik EV-97 Eurostar	N. R. Beale
	G-RMRV	Van's RV-7A	R. Morris
	G-RMTO	Rotorsport UK MTO Sport	J. R. S. Heaton
	G-RMUG	Cameron Nescafe Mug 90 SS balloon	The British Balloon Museum & Library Ltd
	G-RNAC	IDA Bacau Yakovlev Yak-52	RNAEC Group
	G-RNAS	DH.104 Sea Devon C.20 (XK896) ★	Airport Fire Service/Filton
	G-RNBW	Bell 206B JetRanger 2	Rainbow Helicopters Ltd
	G-RNCH	PA-28-181 Archer II	Carlisle Flight Training Ltd
	G-RNDD	Robin DR.400/500	Witham (Specialist Vehicles) Ltd
	G-RNGO	Robinson R22 Beta II	M. Flandina
	G-RNHF	Hawker Sea Fury T.Mk.20 (VX281)	Naval Aviation Ltd (G-BCOW)
	G-RNIE	Cameron 70 Ball SS balloon	N. J. Bland
	G-RNLI	VS.236 Walrus I (W2718) ★	Walrus Aviation Ltd
	G-RNRM	Cessna A.185F	Skydive St. Andrews Ltd
	G-RNRS	SA Bulldog Srs.100/101	Power Aerobatics Ltd (G-AZIT)
	G-ROAD	Robinson R44 II	IntecPC Ltd
	G-ROBD	Shaw Europa	M. P. Wiseman
	G-ROBG	P & M Quik GT450	Exodus Airsports Ltd
	G-ROBJ	Robin DR.500/200i	D. R. L. Jones
	G-ROBN	Pierre Robin R1180T	N. D. Anderson
	G-ROBT	Hawker Hurricane I (P2902:DX-X)	R. A. Roberts
	G-ROBY	Colt 17A balloon	Virgin Airship & Balloon Co Ltd
	G-ROBZ	Grob G109B	Bravo Zulu Group
	G-ROCH	Cessna T.303	R. S. Bentley
	G-ROCK	Thunder Ax7-77 balloon	M. A. Green
	G-ROCO	ACLA Sirocco	D. C. Arnold
	G-ROCR	Schweizer 269C	Hayles Aviation
	G-ROCT	Robinson R44 II	A. von Liechtenstein
	G-RODC	Steen Skybolt	D. G. Girling
	G-RODD	Cessna 310R II	R. J. Herbert Engineering Ltd (G-TEDD/G-MADI)
	G-RODG	Avtech Jabiru UL	G-RODG Group
	G-RODI	Isaacs Fury (K3731)	M. Housley
	G-RODJ	Ikarus C42 FB80	T. J. Jenkins
	G-RODO	Shaw Europa XS	R. M. Carson (G-ROWI)
	G-RODZ	Van's RV-3A	M. H. Hoffmann
	G-ROEI	Avro Roe 1 Replica	Brooklands Museum Trust Ltd
	G-ROGY	Cameron 60 Concept balloon	S. A. Laing
	G-ROKO	Roko-Aero NG-4HD	M. Coaten & D. S. Watson
	G-ROKT	Cessna FR.172E	G-ROKT Flying Club Ltd
	G-ROLF	PA-32R-301 Saratoga SP	P. F. Larkins
	G-ROLL	Pitts S-2A Special	Aerobatic Displays Ltd
	G-ROLY	Cessna F.172N	M. Bonsall (G-BHIH)
	G-ROME	I.I.I. Sky Arrow 650TC	Sky Arrow (Kits) UK Ltd
	G-ROMP	Extra 230H	G. G. Ferriman
	G-ROMW	Cyclone AX2000	K. V. Falvey
	G-RONA	Shaw Europa	C. M. Noakes
	G-RONG	PA-28R Cherokee Arrow 200-II	D. Griffiths & S. P. Rooney

Reg.	Type	Owner or Operator	Notes
G-RONI	Cameron V-77 balloon	R. E. Simpson	
G-RONS	Robin DR.400/180	R. & K. Baker	
G-RONW	FRED Srs 2	F. J. Keitch	
G-ROOB	Embraer EMB-500 Phenom 100	Hangar 8 Management Ltd	
G-ROOK	Cessna F.172P	Rolim Ltd	
G-ROOV	Shaw Europa XS	P. W. Hawkins & K. Siggery	
G-RORB	Spitfire Mk.26	Golf Romeo Bravo Club	
G-RORI	Folland Gnat T.1 (01)	Heritage Aircraft Ltd	
G-RORY	Piaggio FWP.149D	M. Edwards (G-TOWN)	
G-ROSI	Thunder Ax7-77 balloon	J. E. Rose	
G-ROTG	Robinson R44 II	Aldwick Court Farm	
G-ROTS	CFM Streak Shadow Srs SA	J. Edwards	
G-ROUP	Cessna F.172M	Perranporth Flying School Ltd (G-BDPH)	
G-ROUS	PA-34-200T Seneca II	Oxford Aviation Training Ltd	
G-ROVE	PA-18 Super Cub 135	S. J. Gaveston	
G-ROVY	Robinson R22 Beta	Fly Executive Ltd	
G-ROWA	Aquila AT01	Chicory Crops Ltd	
G-ROWE	Cessna F.182P	D. Rowe	
G-ROWL	AA-5B Tiger	T. A. Timms	
G-ROWR	Robinson R44	R. A. Oldworth	
G-ROWS	PA-28-151 Warrior	Air Academy	
G-ROXI	Cameron C-90 balloon	A. Murphy	
G-ROYC	Avtech Jabiru UL450	M. W. Hanley	
G-ROYM	Robinson R44 II	Business Agility Ltd	
G-ROZI	Robinson R44	Rotormotive Ltd	
G-ROZZ	Ikarus C.42 FB 80	A. J. Blackwell	
G-RPAF	Europa XS	G-RPAF Group	
G-RPCC	Europa XS	R. P. Churchill-Coleman	
G-RPEZ	Rutan LongEz	M. P. Dunlop	
G-RPPO	Groppo Trail	G. N. Smith	
G-RPRV	Van's RV-9A	M. G. Titmus	
G-RRAK	Enstrom 480B	B. Satherley (G-RIBZ)	
G-RRAT	CZAW Sportcruiser	G. Sipson	
G-RRCU	CEA DR.221B Dauphin	Merlin Flying Club Ltd	
G-RRED	PA-28-181 Archer II	J. P. Reddington	
G-RRFC	SOCATA TB20 Trinidad GT	C. A. Hawkins	
G-RRFF	VS.329 Spitfire Mk.IIB	P. Maksimczyk	
G-RRGN	VS.390 Spitfire PR.XIX (PS853)	Rolls-Royce PLC (G-MXIX)	
G-RROB	Robinson R44 II	Something Different Charters LLP	
G-RRRZ	Van's RV-8	D. J. C. Davidson	
G-RRSR	Piper J-3C-65 Cub (480173:57-H)	R. W. Roberts	
G-RRVX	Van's RV-10	R. E. Garforth	
G-RSAF	BAC.167 Strikemaster 80A	Viper Classics Ltd	
G-RSCU	Agusta A.109E	Sloane Helicopters Ltd	
G-RSHI	PA-34-220T Seneca V	R. S. Hill and Sons	
G-RSKR	PA-28-161 Warrior II	ACS Engineering Ltd (G-BOJY)	
G-RSKY	Skyranger 912(2)	C. G. Benham & C. H. Tregonning	
G-RSMC	Medway SLA 100 Executive	W. S. C. Toulmin	
G-RSSF	Denney Kitfox Mk 2	R. W. Somerville	
G-RSWO	Cessna 172R	M. L. Rothe	
G-RSWW	Robinson R22 Beta	Tiger Helicopters Ltd	
G-RSXL	Cessna 560 Citation XLS	Aircraft Leasing Overseas Ltd	
G-RTBI	Thunder Ax6-56 balloon	P. J. Waller	
G-RTFM	Jabiru J400	I. A. Macphee	
G-RTHS	Rans S-6-ES Coyote II	T. Harrison-Smith	
G-RTIN	Rotorsport UK MT-03	P. McCrory	
G-RTMS	Rans S.6 ES Coyote II	C. J. Arthur	
G-RTMY	Ikarus C.42 FB 100	Mike Yankee Group	
G-RTRT	PZL-104MA Wilga 2000	E. A. M. Austin	
G-RTRV	V an's RV-9A	R. Taylor	
G-RUBB	AA-5B Tiger	D. E. Gee	
G-RUBE	Embraer EMB-135BJ Legacy	Autumn Breeze International Ltd	
G-RUBO	Embraer EMB-500 Phenom 100	Hangar 8 Management Ltd	
G-RUBY	PA-28RT-201T Turbo Arrow IV	Arrow Aircraft Group (G-BROU)	
G-RUCK	Bell 206B-3 JetRanger III	J. A. Ruck	
G-RUES	Robin HR.100/210	R. H. R. Rue	
G-RUFF	Mainair Blade 912	C. W. THompson	

Notes	Reg.	Type	Owner or Operator
	G-RUFS	Avtech Jabiru UL	M. Bastin
	G-RUGS	Campbell Cricket Mk 4 gyroplane	J. L. G. McLane
	G-RUIA	Cessna F.172N	D. C. Parry
	G-RULE	Robinson R44 Raven II	Huckair
	G-RUMI	Noble Harman Snowbird Mk.IV	G. Crossley (G-MVOI)
	G-RUMM	Grumman F8F-2P Bearcat (121714:201B)	Patina Ltd
	G-RUMN	AA-1A Trainer	M. T. Manwaring
	G-RUMW	Grumman FM-2 Wildcat (JV579:F)	Patina Ltd
	G-RUNT	Cassutt Racer IIIM	D. P. Lightfoot
	G-RUPS	Cameron TR-70 balloon	R. M. Stanley
	G-RUSL	Van's RV-6A	G. R. Russell
	G-RUSO	Robinson R22 Beta	R. M. Barnes-Gorell
	G-RUSS	Cessna 172N ★	Leisure Lease (stored)/Southend
	G-RUVE	Van's RV-8	J. P. Brady & D. J. Taylor
	G-RUVI	Zenair CH.601UL	P. G. Depper
	G-RUVY	Van's RV-9A	R. D. Taylor
	G-RUZZ	Robinson R44 II	Russell Harrison PLC
	G-RVAB	Van's RV-7	I. M. Belmore & A. T. Banks
	G-RVAC	Van's RV-7	A. F. S. & B. Caldecourt
	G-RVAL	Van's RV-8	R. N. York
	G-RVAN	Van's RV-6	D. Broom
	G-RVAT	Van's RV-8	T. R. Grief
	G-RVAW	Van's RV-6	C. Rawlings & R. J. Tomlinson
	G-RVBA	Van's RV-8A	D. P. Richard
	G-RVBC	Van's RV-6A	B. J. Clifford
	G-RVBF	Cameron A-340 balloon	Virgin Balloon Flights
	G-RVBI	Van's RV-8	M. A. N. Newall
	G-RVCE	Van's RV-6A	M. D. Barnard & C. Voelger
	G-RVCH	Van's RV-8A	C. R. Harrison
	G-RVCL	Van's RV-6	M. A. Wyer
	G-RVDG	Van's RV-9	D. M. Gill
	G-RVDH	Van's RV-8	D. J. Harrison (G-ONER)
	G-RVDJ	Van's RV-6	J. D. Jewitt
	G-RVDP	Van's RV-4	O. Florin
	G-RVDR	Van's RV-6A	P. R. Redfern
	G-RVDX	Van's RV-4	M. R. Tingle (G-FTUO)
	G-RVEE	Van's RV-6	J. C. A. Wheeler
	G-RVEI	Van's RV-8	D. Stephens
	G-RVEM	Van's RV-7A	E. M. Farquharson & G. J. Newby (G-CBJU)
	G-RVER	Van's RV-4	R. D. E. Holah
	G-RVET	Van's RV-6	D. R. Coleman
	G-RVGA	Van's RV-6A	R. Emery
	G-RVGO	Van's RV-10	D. C. Arnold
	G-RVIA	Van's RV-6A	K. R. W. Scull & J. Watkins
	G-RVIB	Van's RV-6	K. Martin & P. Gorman
	G-RVIC	Van's RV-6A	I. T. Corse
	G-RVII	Van's RV-7	P. H. C. Hall
	G-RVIN	Van's RV-6	R. G. Jines
	G-RVIO	Van's RV-10	R. C. Hopkinson
	G-RVIS	Van's RV-8	I. V. Sharman
	G-RVIT	Van's RV-6	P. J. Shotbolt
	G-RVIV	Van's RV-4	S. B. Robson
	G-RVIW	Van's RV-9	G. S. Scott
	G-RVIX	Van's RV-9A	J. R. Holt & C. S. Simmons
	G-RVIZ	Van's RV-12	J. E. Singleton
	G-RVJM	Van's RV-6	M. D. Challoner
	G-RVJO	Van's RV-9A	J. C. Simpson
	G-RVJP	Van's RV-9A	R. M. Palmer
	G-RVJW	Van's RV-4	J. M. Williams
	G-RVLC	Van's RV-9A	L. J. Clark
	G-RVMB	Van's RV-9A	M. James & R. W. Littledale
	G-RVMT	Van's RV-6	M. J. Aldridge
	G-RVMZ	Van's RV-8	A. E. Kay
	G-RVNA	PA-38-112 Tomahawk	Ravenair Aircraft Ltd (G-DFLY)
	G-RVNB	PA-38-112 Tomahawk	Ravenair Aircraft Ltd (G-SUKI/G-BPNV)
	G-RVNC	PA-38-112 Tomahawk	Ravenair Aircraft Ltd (G-BTJK)
	G-RVND	PA-38-112 Tomahawk	Ravenair Aircraft Ltd (G-BTAS)
	G-RVNE	Partenavia P.68B	Ravenair Aircraft Ltd (G-SAMJ)
	G-RVNH	Van's RV-9A	N. R. Haines
	G-RVNI	Van's RV-6A	G-RVNI Group

Reg.	Type	Owner or Operator	Notes
G-RVNS	Van's RV-4	B. R. Hunter (G-CBGN)	
G-RVPH	Van's RV-8	J. C. P. Herbert	
G-RVPL	Van's RV-8	B. J. Summers	
G-RVPM	Van's RV-4	P. J. McMahon (G-RVDS)	
G-RVPW	Van's RV-6A	P. Waldron	
G-RVRA	PA-28 Cherokee 140	Par Contractors Ltd (G-OWVA)	
G-RVRB	PA-34-200T Seneca II	Ravenair Aircraft Ltd (G-BTAJ)	
G-RVRC	PA-23 Aztec 250E	C. J. Williams (G-BNPD)	
G-RVRD	PA-23 Aztec 250E	Ravenair Aircraft Ltd (G-BRAV/G-BBCM)	
G-RVRE	Partenavia P.68B	Ravenair Aircraft Ltd	
G-RVRI	Cessna 172N Skyhawk	Truro Aerodrome Ltd (G-CCCC)	
G-RVRJ	PA-E23 Aztec 250E	Ravenair Aircraft Ltd (G-BBGB)	
G-RVRK	PA-38-112 Tomahawk	Ravenair Aircraft Ltd (G-BGZW)	
G-RVRL	PA-38-112 Tomahawk	Ravenair Aircraft Ltd (G-BGZW/G-BGBY)	
G-RVRM	PA-38-112 Tomahawk	Ravenair Aircraft Ltd (G-BGEK)	
G-RVRN	PA-28-161 Warrior II	Ravenair Aircraft Ltd (G-BPID)	
G-RVRO	PA-38-112 Tomahawk II	Ravenair Aircraft Ltd (G-BOUD)	
G-RVRP	Van's RV-7	R. C. Parris	
G-RVRR	PA-38-112 Tomahawk	Ravenair Aircraft Ltd (G-BRHT)	
G-RVRT	PA-28-140 Cherokee C	Ravenair Aircraft Ltd (G-AYKX)	
G-RVRU	PA-38-112 Tomahawk	Ravenair Aircraft Ltd (G-NCFE/G-BKMK)	
G-RVRV	Van's RV-4	P. Jenkins	
G-RVRW	PA-23 Aztec 250E	Ravenair Aircraft Ltd (G-BAVZ)	
G-RVRX	Partenavia P.68B	Ravenair Aircraft Ltd (G-PART)	
G-RVRY	PA-38-112 Tomahawk	Ravenair Aircraft Ltd (G-BTND)	
G-RVRZ	PA-23-250 Aztec E	Ravenair Aircraft Ltd (G-NRSC/G-BSFL)	
G-RVSA	Van's RV-6A	W. H. Knott	
G-RVSD	Van's RV-9A	S. W. Damarell	
G-RVSG	Van's RV-9A	S. Gerrish	
G-RVSH	Van's RV-6A	S. J. D. Hall	
G-RVSR	Van's RV-8	R. K. & S. W. Elders	
G-RVSX	Van's RV-6	R. L. & V. A. West	
G-RVTE	Van's RV-6	E. McShane & T. Feeny	
G-RVTN	Van's RV-10	C. I. Law	
G-RVTT	Van's RV-7	A. Phillips	
G-RVUK	Van's RV-7	P. D. G. Grist	
G-RVVI	Van's RV-6	John Reynolds Racing Ltd	
G-RVVY	Van's RV-10	P. R. Marskell	
G-RWAY	Rotorway Executive 162F	C. R. Johnson (G-URCH)	
G-RWEW	Robinson R44	Northern Heli Charters	
G-RWGS	Robinson R44 II	R. W. G. Simpson	
G-RWIA	Robinson R22 Beta	GPS Fabrications Ltd (G-BOEZ)	
G-RWIN	Rearwin 175	A. B. Bourne & N. D. Battye	
G-RWLY	Shaw Europa XS	C. R. Arcle	
G-RWMW	Zenair CH.601XL Zodiac	R. W. H. Watson & M. Whyte (G-DROO)	
G-RWSS	Denney Kitfox Mk 2	R. W. Somerville	
G-RWWW	WS-55 Whirlwind HCC.12 (XR486)★	IHM/Weston-super-Mare	
G-RXUK	Lindstrand LBL-105A balloon	R. K. Scott & E. C. Fouracre	
G-RYAL	Avtech Jabiru UL	D. J. Piper	
G-RYDR	Rotorsport UK MT-03	A. D. McCutcheon	
G-RYNS	PA-32-301FT Cherokee Six	D. A. Earle	
G-RYPE	DG Flugzeugbau DG-1000T	DG-1000T Partners	
G-RYPH	Mainair Blade 912	I. A. Cunningham	
G-RYZZ	Robinson R44 II	Rivermead Aviation Ltd	
G-RZEE	Schleicher ASW-19B	L. Y. Smith	
G-RZLY	Flight Design CTSW	J. D. Macnamara	
G-SAAA	Flight Design CTSW	P. J. Watson & A. J. Kolleng	
G-SABA	PA-28R-201T Turbo Arrow III	C. A. Burton (G-BFEN)	
G-SABB	Eurocopter EC 135T1	Bond Air Services Ltd	
G-SABI	Dassault Falcon 900EX	TAG Aviation (UK) Ltd	
G-SABR	NA F-86A Sabre (8178:FU-178)	Golden Apple Operations Ltd	
G-SACH	Stoddard-Hamilton Glastar	R. S. Holt	
G-SACI	PA-28-161 Warrior II	PJC (Leasing) Ltd	
G-SACM	TL2000UK Sting Carbon	M. Clare	
G-SACO	PA-28-161 Warrior II	Stapleford Flying Club Ltd	
G-SACR	PA-28-161 Cadet	Sherburn Aero Club Ltd	
G-SACS	PA-28-161 Cadet	Sherburn Aero Club Ltd	
G-SACT	PA-28-161 Cadet	Sherburn Aero Club Ltd	

Notes	Reg.	Type	Owner or Operator
	G-SACX	Aero AT-3 R100	Sherburn Aero Club Ltd
	G-SACY	Aero AT-3 R100	Sherburn Aero Club Ltd
	G-SADC	Gulfstream G450	Ocean Sky (UK) Ltd
	G-SAFE	Cameron N-77 balloon	P. J. Waller
	G-SAFI	CP.1320 Super Emeraude	C. S. Carleton-Smith
	G-SAFR	SAAB 91D Safir	Sylmar Aviation & Services Ltd
	G-SAGA	Grob G.109B	G-GROB Ltd/Booker
	G-SAGE	Luscombe 8A Silvaire	C. Howell (G-AKTL)
	G-SAHI	Trago Mills SAH-1	Hotel India Group
	G-SAIG	Robinson R44 II	Torfield Aviation Ltd
	G-SAIR	Cessna 421C	Air Support Aviation Services Ltd (G-OBCA)
	G-SAJA	Schempp-Hirth Discus 2	J. G. Arnold
	G-SALA	PA-32 Cherokee Six 300E	R. M. J. Harrison & J. W. A. Portch
	G-SALE	Cameron Z-90 balloon	R. D. Baker
	G-SAMG	Grob G.109B	The Royal Air Force Gliding and Soaring Association
	G-SAMY	Shaw Europa	K. R. Tallent
	G-SAMZ	Cessna 150D	Fly More Aviation Ltd (G-ASSO)
	G-SANL	Bombardier BD700-1A10 Global Express	Sanctuary Aviation LLP
	G-SAOC	Schempp-Hirth Discus 2cT	The Royal Air Force Gliding and Soaring Association
	G-SAPM	SOCATA TB20 Trinidad	G-SAPM Ltd (G-EWFN)
	G-SARA	PA-28-181 Archer II	Apollo Aviation Advisory Ltd
	G-SARB	Sikorsky S-92A	CHC Scotia Ltd (HM Coastguard)
	G-SARC	Sikorsky S-92A	CHC Scotia Ltd (HM Coastguard)
	G-SARD	Agusta Westland AW139	CHC Scotia Ltd (HM Coastguard)
	G-SARJ	P & M Quik GT450	A. R. Jones
	G-SARM	Ikarus C.42 FB80	G-SARM Group
	G-SARV	Van's RV-4	Hinton Flying Group
	G-SASA	Eurocopter EC 135T1	Bond Air Services Ltd
	G-SASB	Eurocopter EC 135T2+	Bond Air Services Ltd
	G-SASC	Beech B200C Super King Air	Gama Aviation Ltd
	G-SASD	Beech B200C Super King Air	Gama Aviation Ltd
	G-SASG	Schleicher ASW-27-18E	F. B. Jeynes
	G-SASH	MDH MD.900 Explorer	Yorkshire Air Ambulance Ltd
	G-SASI	CZAW Sportcruiser	A. S. Arundell
	G-SASK	PA-31P Pressurised Navajo	Middle East Business Club Ltd (G-BFAM)
	G-SASM	Westland Scout AH.Mk.1	C. J. Marsden
	G-SASY	Eurocopter EC.130 B4	R. J. H. Smith
	G-SATN	PA-25-260 Pawnee C	The Royal Gliding and Soaring Association
	G-SAUO	Cessna A.185F	T. G. Lloyd
	G-SAUK	Rans S6-ES	M. D. Tulloch
	G-SAVY	Savannah VG Jabiru(1)	C. S. Hollingworth & S. P. Yardley
	G-SAWI	PA-32RT-300T Turbo Lance II	Regularity Ltd
	G-SAXT	Schempp-Hirth Duo Discus Xt	The Royal Air Force Gliding and Soaring Association
	G-SAYS	RAF 2000 GTX-SE gyroplane	D. Beevers
	G-SAZY	Avtech Jabiru J400	S.M. Pink
	G-SAZZ	CP.328 Super Emeraude	D. J. Long
	G-SBAE	Cessna F.172P	Warton Flying Club
	G-SBDB	Remos GX	G-SBDB Group
	G-SBHH	Schweizer 269C	Ag-Raum GmbH/Germany (G-XALP)
	G-SBIZ	Cameron Z-90 balloon	Snow Business International Ltd
	G-SBKR	SOCATA TB10 Tobago	S. C. M. Bagley
	G-SBKS	Cessna 206H Stationair	Alard Properties Ltd
	G-SBLT	Steen Skybolt	Skybolt Group
	G-SBOL	Steen Skybolt	M. P. Barley
	G-SBRK	Aero AT-3 R100	Sywell Aerodrome Ltd
	G-SBUS	BN-2A-26 Islander	Isles of Scilly Skybus Ltd (G-BMMH)
	G-SCAN	Vinten-Wallis WA-116/100	K. H. Wallis
	G-SCBI	SOCATA TB20 Trinidad	Ace Services
	G-SCCZ	CZAW Sportcruiser	J. W. Ellis
	G-SCHI	AS.350B2 Ecureuil	Patriot Aviation Ltd
	G-SCHO	Robinson R22 Beta	Blades Aviation (UK) LLP
	G-SCII	Agusta A109C	C and M Coldstores (G-JONA)
	G-SCIP	SOCATA TB20 Trinidad GT	The Studio People Ltd
	G-SCLX	FLS Aerospace Sprint 160	E. J. F. McEntee (G-PLYM)
	G-SCNN	Schempp-Hirth Standard Cirrus	G. C. Short
	G-SCOL	Gippsland GA-8 Airvan	Parachuting Aircraft Ltd
	G-SCPD	Escapade 912 (1)	R. W. L. Breckell

Reg.	Type	Owner or Operator	Notes
G-SCPI	CZAW Sportcruiser	I. M. Speight & P. R. W. Goslin	
G-SCPL	PA-28 Cherokee 140	Aeros Leasing Ltd (G-BPVL)	
G-SCRZ	CZAW Sportcruiser	P. H. Grant	
G-SCSC	CZAW Sportcruiser	G-SCSC Group	
G-SCTA	Westland Scout AH.1	G. R. Harrison	
G-SCUB	PA-18 Super Cub 135 (542447)	M. E. Needham	
G-SCUL	Rutan Cozy	K. R. W. Scull	
G-SCVF	Czech Sprt Aircraft Sportcruiser	V. Flintham	
G-SCZR	CZAW Sportcruiser	R. Manning	
G-SDAT	Flight Design CTSW	A. R. Wade	
G-SDCI	Bell 206B JetRanger 2	S. D. Coomes (G-GHCL/G-SHVV)	
G-SDEC	American Champion 8KCAB	D. Boag	
G-SDEV	DH. 104 Sea Devon C.20 (XK895)	Aviation Heritage Ltd	
G-SDFM	Aerotechnik EV-97 Eurostar	G-SDFM Group	
G-SDNI	VS.361 Spitfire LF.IX E	P. M. Andrews	
G-SDOB	Tecnam P2002-EA Sierra	S. P. S. Dornan	
G-SDOI	Aeroprakt A.22 Foxbat	S. A. Owen	
G-SDOZ	Tecnam P92-EA Echo Super	Cumbernauld Flyers G-SDOZ	
G-SEAI	Cessna U.206G (amphibian)	K. O'Conner	
G-SEAJ	Cessna 525 Citationjet	CJ 525 Ltd	
G-SEAT	Colt 42A balloon	R. M. Horn	
G-SEBN	Skyranger 912S(1)	C. M. James	
G-SEDO	Cameron N-105 balloon	Wye Valley Aviation Ltd	
G-SEED	Piper J-3C-65 Cub	J. H. Seed	
G-SEEE	Pegasus Quik GT450	I. M. Spence	
G-SEEK	Cessna T.210N	A. Hopper	
G-SEFI	Robinson R44 II	Kermann Avionics Sales Ltd	
G-SEHK	Cessna 182T	S. Holland	
G-SEIL	BN-2B-27 Islander	MV Capital Ltd (G-BIIP)	
G-SEJW	PA-28-161 Warrior II	Blue Sky Investments Ltd	
G-SELA	Cessna 152	L. W. Scattergood (G-FLOP)	
G-SEGA	Cameron Sonic 90 SS balloon	M. E. White	
G-SELB	PA-28-161 Warrior II	L. W. Scattergood (G-LFSK)	
G-SELC	Diamond DA42 Twin Star	Stapleford Flying Club Ltd	
G-SELF	Shaw Europa	N. D. Crisp & ptnrs	
G-SELL	Robin DR.400/180	C. R. Beard Farmers Ltd	
G-SELY	Agusta-Bell 206B JetRanger 3	DSC North Ltd	
G-SEMI	PA-44-180 Seminole	J. Benfell & M. Djukic (G-DENW)	
G-SEMR	Cessna T206H Turbo Stationair	Semer LLP	
G-SENA	Rutan LongEz	G. Bennett	
G-SEND	Colt 90A balloon	Air du Vent/France	
G-SENE	PA-34-200T Seneca II	M. O'Hara	
G-SENS	Eurocopter EC.135T2+	Eurocopter UK Ltd	
G-SENX	PA-34-200T Seneca II	First Air Ltd (G-DARE/G-WOTS/G-SEVL)	
G-SEPT	Cameron N-105 balloon	A. G. Merry	
G-SERE	Diamond DA42 Twin Star	Sere Ltd	
G-SERL	SOCATA TB10 Tobago	R. J. Searle (G-LANA)	
G-SERV	Cameron N-105 balloon	PSH Skypower Ltd	
G-SESA	RAF SE.5A 75 replica	D. J. Calvert	
G-SETI	Cameron Sky 80-16 balloon	R. P. Allan	
G-SEUK	Cameron TV-80 ss balloon	Mobberley Balloon Collection	
G-SEVA	SE-5A (replica) (F141:G)	I. D. Gregory	
G-SEVE	Cessna 172N	MK Aero Support Ltd	
G-SEVN	Van's RV-7	N. Reddish	
G-SEXE	Scheibe SF.25C Falke	Repulor Ltd	
G-SEXX	PA-28-161 Warrior II	Weald Air Services Ltd	
G-SEXY	AA-1 Yankee ★	Jetstream Club, Liverpool Marriott Hotel South, Speke (G-AYLM)	
G-SFAR	Ikarus C42 FB100	Hadair	
G-SFLA	Ikarus C42 FB80	Solent Flight Ltd	
G-SFLB	Ikarus C42 FB80	Solent Flight Ltd	
G-SFLY	Diamond DA40 Star	L. & N. P. L. Turner	
G-SFPB	Cessna F.406	Reims Aviation Industries SA/France	
G-SFRI	Bombardier CL600-2B16 Challenger	Perfect Aviation UK Ltd	
G-SFRY	Thunder Ax7-77 balloon	M. Rowlands	
G-SFSL	Cameron Z-105 balloon	A. J. Gregory	
G-SFTZ	Slingsby T.67M Firefly 160	Western Air (Thruxton) Ltd	
G-SGEN	Ikarus C.42 FB 80	G. A. Arturi	

Notes	Reg.	Type	Owner or Operator
	G-SGRP	Agusta AW.109SP Grand New	WA Developments International Ltd
	G-SGSE	PA-28-181 Archer II	U. Patel (G-BOJX)
	G-SHAA	Enstrom 280-UK	C. J. Vincent
	G-SHAF	Robinson R44 II	Tresillian Leisure Ltd
	G-SHAK	Cameron Cabin SS balloon	Magical Adventures Ltd (G-ODIS)
	G-SHAL	Bombardier CL-600-2B19	TAG Aviation (UK) Ltd
	G-SHAN	Cessna 182T Skylane	M. Herzog
	G-SHAR	Robinson R44 II	J. E. R. Gardner
	G-SHAY	PA-28R-201T Turbo Arrow III	Alpha Yankee Flying Group (G-BFDG/G-JEFS)
	G-SHED	PA-28-181 Archer II	G-SHED Flying Group (G-BRAU)
	G-SHEE	P & M Quik GT450	L. Cottle
	G-SHEF	Bombardier BD700-1A10 Global Express	Gama Aviation Ltd
	G-SHEZ	Mainair Pegasus Quik	R. Wells
	G-SHHH	Glaser-Dirks DG-100G	P. J. Masson
	G-SHIM	CFM Streak Shadow	K. R. Anderson
	G-SHIP	PA-23 Aztec 250F ★	Midland Air Museum/Coventry
	G-SHMI	Evektor EV-97 Team EuroStar UK	Poet Pilot (UK) Ltd
	G-SHMK	Cirrus SR22T	Avicon
	G-SHOG	Colomban MC.15 Cri-Cri	K. D. & C. S. Rhodes (G-PFAB)
	G-SHOW	MS.733 Alycon	J. Wesson
	G-SHRK	Enstrom 280C-UK	Flighthire Ltd/Belgium (G-BGMX)
	G-SHRN	Schweizer 269C-1	CSL Industrial Ltd
	G-SHRT	Robinson R44 II	Air and Ground Aviation Ltd
	G-SHSH	Shaw Europa	S. G. Hayman & J. Price
	G-SHSI	Embraer EMB-135BJ Legacy	Pramilia Holdings Inc
	G-SHSP	Cessna 172S	Shropshire Aero Club Ltd
	G-SHUC	Rans S-6-ESD Coyote II	T. A. England (G-MYKN)
	G-SHUF	Mainair Blade	G. Holdcroft
	G-SHUG	PA-28R-201T Turbo Arrow III	G-SHUG Ltd
	G-SHUU	Enstrom 280C-UK-2	D. Ellis (G-OMCP/G-KENY/G-BJFG)
	G-SHUV	Aerosport Woody Pusher	J. R. Wraigh
	G-SHWK	Cessna 172S	Cambridge Aero Club Ltd
	G-SIAI	SIAI-Marchetti SF.260W	Air Training Services
	G-SIBK	Raytheon Beech A36 Bonanza	B. & S. J. Shaw
	G-SICA	BN-2B-20 Islander	Shetland Leasing and Property Development Ltd (G-SLAP)
	G-SICB	BN-2B-20 Islander	Shetlands Islands Council (G-NESU/G-BTVN)
	G-SIGN	PA-39 Twin Comanche 160 C/R	D. Buttle
	G-SIIE	Christen Pitts S-2B Special	J. & T. J. Bennett (G-SKYD)
	G-SIII	Extra EA.300	Fun Flight Ltd
	G-SIIS	Pitts S-1S Special	R. P. Marks (G-RIPE)
	G-SIJJ	North American P-51D-NA Mustang (472035)	P. A. Teichman
	G-SIJW	SA Bulldog Srs 120/121 (XX630:5)	M. Miles
	G-SILS	Pietenpol Skyscout	D. Silsbury
	G-SILY	Pegasus Quantum 15	S. D. Sparrow
	G-SIMI	Cameron A-315 balloon	Balloon Safaris
	G-SIMM	Ikarus C.42 FB 100 VLA	D. Simmons
	G-SIMP	Avtech Jabiru SP	A. C. A. Hayes
	G-SIMS	Robinson R22 Beta	CDS Aviation Ltd
	G-SIMY	PA-32-300 Cherokee Six	I. Simpson (G-OCPF/G-BOCH)
	G-SINK	Schleicher ASH-25	G-SINK Group
	G-SIPA	SIPA 903	A. C. Leak & G. S. Dilland (G-BGBM)
	G-SIPP	Lindstrand lbl-35a Cloudhopper balloon	N. Bourke
	G-SIRA	Embraer EMB-135BJ Legacy	ECC Leasing Company Ltd
	G-SIRD	Robinson R44 II	Peglington Productions Ltd
	G-SIRE	Best Off Sky Ranger Swift 912S(1)	A. B. King
	G-SIRJ	Cessna 680 Citation Sovereign	Bookajet Ltd
	G-SIRO	Dassault Falcon 900EX	Condor Aviation LLP
	G-SIRS	Cessna 560XL Citation Excel	London Executive Aviation Ltd
	G-SISI	Schempp-Hirth Duo Discus	Glider Sierra India
	G-SISU	P & M Quik GT450	Executive and Business Aviation Support Ltd
	G-SITA	Pegasus Quantum 15-912	A. F. S. McDougall
	G-SIVJ	Westland Gazelle HT.2	Skytrace (UK) Ltd (G-CBSG)
	G-SIVK	MBB Bolkow Bo.105DBS-4	C. J. Siva-Jothy (G-PASX)
	G-SIVR	MDH MD.900 Explorer	C. J. Siva-Jothy
	G-SIVW	Lake LA-250 Renegade	C. J. Siva-Jothy
	G-SIXC	Douglas DC-6B★	The DC-6 Diner/Coventry
	G-SIXD	PA-32 Cherokee Six 300D	M. B. Paine & I. Gordon

Reg.	Type	Owner or Operator	Notes
G-SIXT	PA-28-161 Warrior II	Airways Aero Associations Ltd (G-BSSX)	
G-SIXX	Colt 77A balloon	P. & M. Still	
G-SIXY	Van's RV-6	C. J. Hall & C. R. P. Hamlett	
G-SIZZ	Jabiru J400	K. J. Betteley	
G-SJBI	Pitts S-2C Special	S. L. Walton	
G-SJCH	BN-2T-4S Defender 4000	Hampshire Police Authority (G-BWPK)	
G-SJES	Evektor EV-97 TeamEurostar UK	Purple Aviation Ltd	
G-SJKR	Lindstrand LBL-90A balloon	S. J. Roake	
G-SJMH	Robin DR.400-140B	C. S. & J. A. Bailey	
G-SJPI	Dynamic WT9 UK	S. J. Phillips	
G-SJSS	Bombardier CL600-2B16	TAG Aviation (UK) Ltd	
G-SKAN	Cessna F.172M	M. Richardson & J. Williams (G-BFKT)	
G-SKAZ	Aero AT-3 r100	G-SKAZ Flying Group	
G-SKCI	Rutan Vari-Eze	C. Hannan	
G-SKEN	Cessna 182T	Kenward Orthopaedic Ltd	
G-SKEW	Mudry CAP-232	J. H. Askew	
G-SKIE	Steen Skybolt	K. G. G. Howe and M. J. Coles	
G-SKKY	Cessna 172S Skyhawk	Skyquest Ltd	
G-SKNT	Pitts S-2A	First Light Aviation Ltd (G-PEAL)	
G-SKOT	Cameron V-42 balloon	S. A. Laing	
G-SKPG	Best Off Skyranger 912 (2)	P. Gibbs	
G-SKPH	Yakovlev Yak-50	R. S. Partridge-Hicks & I. C. Austin (G-BWWH)	
G-SKPP	Eurocopter EC.120B Colbri	Bournemouth Helicopters Ltd (G-MKII)	
G-SKRA	Best Off Skyranger 912S (1)	P. A. Banks	
G-SKRG	Best Off Skyranger 912 (2)	I. D. Town	
G-SKSW	Best Off Sky Ranger Swift 912S	M. D. & S. M. North	
G-SKUA	Stoddard-Hamilton Glastar	F. P. Smiddy (G-LEZZ/G-BYCR)	
G-SKYC	Slingsby T.67M Firefly	T. W. Cassells (G-BLDP)	
G-SKYE	Cessna TU.206G	RAF Sport Parachute Association	
G-SKYF	SOCATA TB10 Tobago	W. L. McNeil	
G-SKYJ	Cameron Z-315 balloon	Cameron Flights Southern Ltd	
G-SKYK	Cameron A-275 balloon	Cameron Flights Southern Ltd	
G-SKYL	Cessna 182S	Skylane Aviation Ltd	
G-SKYN	AS.355F1 Twin Squirrel	Arena Aviation Ltd (G-OGRK/G-BWZC/G-MODZ)	
G-SKYO	Slingsby T.67M-200	R. H. Evelyn	
G-SKYR	Cameron A-180 balloon	Cameron Flights Southern Ltd	
G-SKYT	I.I.I. Sky Arrow 650TC	W. M. Bell & S. J. Brooks	
G-SKYU	Cameron A-210 balloon	Cameron Flights Southern Ltd	
G-SKYV	PA-28RT-201T Turbo Arrow IV	North Yorks Properties Ltd (G-BNZG)	
G-SKYW	AS355F1	Skywalker Aviation Ltd (G-BTIS/G-TALI)	
G-SKYX	Cameron A-210 balloon	Cameron Flights Southern Ltd	
G-SKYY	Cameron A-275 balloon	Cameron Flights Southern Ltd	
G-SLAC	Cameron N-77 balloon	A. Barnes	
G-SLAK	Thruster T.600N 450	M. P. Williams (G-CBXH)	
G-SLAR	Agusta A109C	Adraian Raymond Ltd (G-OWRD/G-USTC/ G-LAXO)	
G-SLCE	Cameron C-80 balloon	A. M. Holly	
G-SLCT	Diamond DA42NG Twin Star	Stapleford Flying Club Ltd	
G-SLEA	Mudry/CAARP CAP-10B	M. J. M. Jenkins & N. R. Thorburn	
G-SLII	Cameron O-90 balloon	J. Edwards	
G-SLIP	Easy Raider	D. R. Squires	
G-SLMG	Diamond HK.36 TTC Super Dimona	G-SLMG Syndicate	
G-SLNM	EV-97 TeamEurostar UK	N. W. Mayes	
G-SLNT	Flight Design CTSW	K. Kirby	
G-SLNW	Robinson R22 Beta	Heli-4 Charter LLP (G-LNIC)	
G-SLTN	SOCATA TB20 Trinidad	Paikea Aviation Ltd	
G-SLYN	PA-28-161 Warrior II	Flew LLP	
G-SMAN	Airbus A.330-243	Monarch Airlines Ltd	
G-SMAS	BAC.167 Strikemaster 80A (1104)	M. A. Petrie	
G-SMBM	Pegasus Quantum 15-912	N. Charles & P. A. Henretty	
G-SMDH	Shaw Europa XS	S. W. Pitt	
G-SMDJ	AS.350B2 Ecureuil	Denis Ferranti Hoverknights Ltd	
G-SMIG	Cameron O-65 balloon	R. D. Parry	
G-SMMA	Cessna F.406 Caravan II	Secretary of State for Scotland per Environmental and Rural Affairs Department	
G-SMMB	Cessna F.406 Caravan II	Secretary of State for Scotland per Environmental and Rural Affairs Department	
G-SMRS	Cessna 172F	M. R. Sarling	

Notes	Reg.	Type	Owner or Operator
	G-SMRT	Lindstrand LBL-260A balloon	Cameron Flights Southern Ltd
	G-SMTH	PA-28 Cherokee 140	R. W. Harris & A. Jahanfar (G-AYJS)
	G-SMYK	PZL-Swidnik PW-5 Smyk	PW-5 Syndicate
	G-SNAL	Cessna 182T	N. S. Lyndhurst
	G-SNEV	CFM Streak Shadow SA	J. D. Reed
	G-SNIF	Cameron A-300 balloon	A. C. K. Rowson & Sudoni
	G-SNOG	Kiss 400-582 (1)	B. H. Ashman
	G-SNOP	Shaw Europa	Bob Crowe Aircraft Sales Ltd (G-DESL/G-WWWG)
	G-SNOW	Cameron V-77 balloon	G. G. Cannon & P. Haworth
	G-SNOZ	Shaw Europa	P. O. Bayliss (G-DONZ)
	G-SNSA	Agusta AW139	CHC Scotia Ltd
	G-SNSB	Agusta AW139	CHC Scotia Ltd
	G-SNUZ	PA-28-161 Warrior II	Freedom Aviation Ltd
	G-SNZY	Learjet 45	European Skyjets Ltd
	G-SOAF	BAC.167 Strikemaster Mk. 82A (425)	Strikemaster Flying Club
	G-SOAR	Eiri PIK-20E	L. J. Kaye
	G-SOAY	Cessna T.303	Wrekin Construction Co Ltd
	G-SOBI	PA-28-181 Archer II	Sherburn Aero Club Ltd
	G-SOCK	Mainair Pegasus Quik	K. R. McCartney
	G-SOCT	Yakovlev Yak-50 (AR-B)	C. R. Turton
	G-SOHO	Diamond DA40D Star	Soho Aviation Ltd
	G-SOKO	Soko P-2 Kraguj (30149)	P. C. Avery (G-BRXK)
	G-SOLA	Aero Designs Star-Lite SL.1	G. P. Thomas
	G-SONA	SOCATA TB10 Tobago	J. Freeman (G-BIBI)
	G-SONE	Cessna 525A Citationjet	CJ 525 Ltd
	G-SONX	Sonex	M. Chambers
	G-SOOA	Cessna172S	Goodwood Road Racing Co.Ltd
	G-SOOC	Hughes 369HS	R.J.H. Strong (G-BRRX)
	G-SOOS	Colt 21A balloon	P. J. Stapley
	G-SOOT	PA-28 Cherokee 180	J. A. Bridger (G-AVNM)
	G-SOPH	Skyranger 912(2)	S. Marathe
	G-SOPP	Enstrom 280FX	F. J. Sopp (G-OSAB)
	G-SORA	Glaser-Dirks DG.500/22	C. A. Boyle, C. P. Arthur, B. Douglas & R. Jackson
	G-SORT	Cameron N-90 balloon	A. Brown
	G-SOUL	Cessna 310R	Reconnaissance Ventures Ltd
	G-SOVB	Learjet 45	Murray Air Ltd (G-OLDJ)
	G-SPAM	Avid Aerobat (modified)	M. Durcan
	G-SPAO	Eurocopter EC135	Bond Air Services Ltd
	G-SPAT	Aero AT-3 R100	S2T Aero Ltd
	G-SPCZ	CZAW Sportcruiser	R. J. Robinson
	G-SPDR	DH.115 Sea Vampire T.22 (N6-766)	M. J. Cobb
	G-SPDY	Raj Hamsa X'Air Hawk	G. H. Gilmour-White
	G-SPED	Alpi Pioneer 300	M. Taylor
	G-SPEE	Robinson R22 Beta	Heliclub de laValle du Loing (G-BPJC)
	G-SPEL	Sky 220-24 balloon	Cameron Flights Southern Ltd
	G-SPEY	Agusta-Bell 206B JetRanger 3	Castle Air Ltd (G-BIGO)
	G-SPFX	Rutan Cozy	B. D. Tutty
	G-SPHU	Eurocopter EC 135T2+	Bond Air Services Ltd
	G-SPIN	Pitts S-2A Special	P. Avery
	G-SPIT	VS.379 Spitfire FR.XIV (MV268)	Patina Ltd (G-BGHB)
	G-SPJE	Robinson R44 II	Abel Alarm Co.Ltd
	G-SPMM	Best Off Sky Ranger Swift 912S(1)	L. Chesworth & M. L. Sumner
	G-SPOG	Jodel DR.1050	P. D. Thomas (G-AXVS)
	G-SPTR	Robinson R44 II	Heli Air Ltd
	G-SPUR	Cessna 550 Citation II	London Executive Aviation Ltd
	G-SPVK	AS.350B3 Ecureuil	Stratos Aviation LLP (G-CERU)
	G-SPYS	Robinson R44 II	SKB Partners LLP
	G-SRAH	Schempp-Hirth Mini-Nimbus C	P. Hawkins
	G-SRBN	Embraer EMB-500 Phenom 100	Hangar 8 Management Ltd
	G-SRDG	Dassault Falcon 7X	Triair (Bermuda) Ltd
	G-SRII	Easy Raider 503	K. Myles
	G-SROE	Westland Scout AH.1 (XP907)	Saunders-Roe Helicopter Ltd
	G-SRPH	Robinson R44	Rooney Helicopter Hire
	G-SRRA	Tecnam P2002-EA Sierra	J. Dunn
	G-SRUM	Aero AT-3 R100	Medcentres Property Portfolio Ltd
	G-SRVA	Cirrus SR20	Harineras del Mediterraneo SL

Reg.	Type	Owner or Operator	Notes
G-SRVO	Cameron N-90 balloon	Servo & Electronic Sales Ltd	
G-SRWN	PA-28-161 Warrior II	S. Smith (G-MAND/G-BRKT)	
G-SRYY	Shaw Europa XS	I. O'Brien	
G-SRZZ	Cirrus SR22	M. P. Bowcock	
G-SSCL	MDH Hughes 369E	Shaun Stevens Contractors Ltd	
G-SSDR	Scooter	J. Attard	
G-SSIX	Rans S.6-116 Coyote II	R. I. Kelly	
G-SSKY	BN-2B-26 Islander	Isles of Scilly Skybus Ltd (G-BSWT)	
G-SSSC	Sikorsky S-76C	CHC Scotia Ltd	
G-SSSD	Sikorsky S-76C	CHC Scotia Ltd	
G-SSSE	Sikorsky S-76C	CHC Scotia Ltd	
G-SSTI	Cameron N-105 balloon	A. A. Brown	
G-SSWV	Sportavia Fournier RF-5B	Fournier Flying Group	
G-STAA	Robinson R44	Free Flight Pilot Association (G-HALE)	
G-STAV	Cameron O-84 balloon	Blenheim Scout Group	
G-STAY	Cessna FR.172K	J. M. Wilkins	
G-STBA	Boeing 777-336ER	British Airways	
G-STBB	Boeing 777-36NER	British Airways	
G-STBC	Boeing 777-36NER	British Airways	
G-STBD	Boeing 777-36NER	British Airways	
G-STBE	Boeing 777-36NER	British Airways	
G-STCH	Fiesler Fi 156A-1 Storch (GM+AI)	P. R. Holloway	
G-STDL	Phillips ST.2 Speedtwin	Speedtwin Developments Ltd (G-DPST)	
G-STEA	PA-28R Cherokee Arrow 200	D. W. Breden	
G-STEE	EV-97 Eurostar	S. A. Ivell	
G-STEM	Stemme S.10V	G-STEM Group	
G-STEN	Stemme S.10 (4)	G-STEN Syndicate	
G-STEP	Schweizer 269C	M. Johnson	
G-STER	Bell 206B JetRanger 3	Maintopic Ltd	
G-STEU	Rolladen-Schneider LS6-18W	F. K. Russell	
G-STEV	Jodel DR.221	S. W. Talbot	
G-STGR	Agusta 109S Grand	WA Developments International Ltd	
G-STHA	PA-31-350 Navajo Chieftain	Hinde Holdings Ltd (G-GLUG/G-BLOE/G-NITE)	
G-STIN	TL 2000UK Sting Carbon	N. A. Smith	
G-STIX	Van's RV-7	R. D. S. Jackson	
G-STME	Stemme S 10-VT	R. A. Roberts	
G-STMP	SNCAN Stampe SV.4A	A. C. Thorne	
G-STNG	TL2000UK Sting Carbon	Geesting 3 Syndicate	
G-STNR	IDA Bacau Yakovlev Yak-52	S. M. Norman (G-BWOD)	
G-STNS	Agusta A109A-II	Heliflight (UK) Ltd	
G-STOD	ICP MXP-740 Savannah VG Jabiru(1)	S. B. Todd	
G-STOK	Colt 77B balloon	A. C. Booth	
G-STON	AS355N Ecureuil II	Gryphon Aviation LLP	
G-STOO	Stolp Starduster Too	K. F. Crumplin	
G-STOP	Robinson R44 Raven II	HLQ Services Ltd/Ireland	
G-STOW	Cameron 90 Wine Box SS balloon	Flying Enterprises	
G-STPI	Cameron A-210 balloon	The Ballooning Business Ltd	
G-STRF	Boeing 737-76N	Celestial Aviation Trading 6 Ltd	
G-STRG	Cyclone AX2000	Pegasus Flight Training (Cotswolds)	
G-STRI	Boeing 737-33A	AWAS (UK) Leasing Four Ltd	
G-STRJ	Boeing 737-33A	AWAS (UK) Leasing Four Ltd	
G-STRK	CFM Streak Shadow SA	E. J. Hadley	
G-STRL	AS.355N Twin Squirrel	Harrier Enterprises Ltd	
G-STRM	Cameron N-90 balloon	A. Brown	
G-STRW	Boeing 757-28A	CGTSN Ltd	
G-STSN	Stinson 108-3 Voyager	M. S. Colebrook (G-BHMR)	
G-STUA	Aerotek Pitts S-2A Special (modified)	G-STUA Group	
G-STUB	Christen Pitts S-2B Special	A. F. D. Kingdon	
G-STUF	Learjet 40	Concierge Aviation Ltd	
G-STUI	Pitts S-2AE	S. L. Goldspink	
G-STUN	TL2000UK Sting Carbon	D. Russell (G-KEVT)	
G-STUY	Robinson R44 II	Central Helicopters Ltd	
G-STVT	CZAW Sportcruiser	S. Taylor	
G-STWO	ARV Super 2	P. M. Paul	
G-STZZ	TL2000UK Sting Carbon	W. R. Field	
G-SUCH	Cameron V-77 balloon	D. G. Such (G-BIGD)	
G-SUCK	Cameron Z-105 balloon	R. P. Wade	
G-SUCT	Robinson R22	Irwin Plant Sales	
G-SUEB	PA-28-181 Archer III	ACS Aviation Ltd	

Notes	Reg.	Type	Owner or Operator
	G-SUED	Thunder Ax8-90 balloon	E. C. Lubbock & S. A. Kidd (G-PINE)
	G-SUEI	Diamond DA.42 Twin Star	Sue Air
	G-SUEL	P & M Quik GT450	J. M. Ingram
	G-SUER	Bell 206B JetRanger	Aerospeed Ltd (G-CBYX)
	G-SUET	Bell 206B JetRanger	Aerospeed Ltd (G-BLZN)
	G-SUEW	Airbus A.320-214	Thomas Cook Airlines Ltd
	G-SUEX	Agusta-Bell 206B JetRanger 2	Aerospeed Ltd (G-AYBC/G-BTWW)
	G-SUEY	Bell 206L-1 Long Ranger	Aerospeed Ltd
	G-SUEZ	Agusta-Bell 206B JetRanger 2	Aerospeed Ltd
	G-SUFK	Eurocopter EC 135P2+	Suffolk Police Authority
	G-SUGA	Embraer EMB-135BJ Legacy 650	Amsair Aircraft Ltd
	G-SUKY	P & M Quik R	S. J. Reid
	G-SUMX	Robinson R22 Beta	J. A. Bickerstaffe
	G-SUMZ	Robinson R44 II	Frankham Bros Ltd
	G-SUNN	Robinson R44	R. Purchase
	G-SUPA	PA-18 Super Cub 150	R. D. Masters
	G-SURG	PA-30 Twin Comanche 160B	A. R. Taylor (G-VIST/G-AVHG)
	G-SURY	Eurocopter EC 135T2	South East Air Support Unit
	G-SUSE	Shaw Europa XS	P. R. Tunney
	G-SUSI	Cameron V-77 balloon	J. H. Dryden
	G-SUSX	MDH MD-902 Explorer	South East Air Support Unit
	G-SUTD	Jabiru UL-D	W. J. Lister
	G-SUTN	I.I.I. Sky Arrow 650TC	D. J. Goldsmith
	G-SUZN	PA-28-161 Warrior II	St. George Flight Training Ltd
	G-SVAS	PA-18-150 Super Cub	Richard Shuttleworth Trustees
	G-SVDG	Jabiru SK	R. Tellegen
	G-SVEA	PA-28-161 Warrior II	G-SVEA Group
	G-SVEN	Centrair 101A Pegase	G7 Group
	G-SVET	Yakovlev Yak-50	Yak-50 Group
	G-SVEY	Vulcanair P-68TC Observer 2	C Aviation Ltd
	G-SVIP	Cessna 421B Golden Eagle II	R. P. Bateman
	G-SVIV	SNCAN Stampe SV.4C	J. E. Keighley
	G-SVNC	Rolladen-Schneider LS4	M. C. Jenkins
	G-SVPN	PA-32R-301T Turbo Saratoga	LAC Marine Ltd
	G-SVSB	Cessna 680 Citation Sovereign	Ferron Trading Ltd
	G-SWAK	Oldfield Baby Lakes	White Mountain Aviation & Alpacas
	G-SWAT	Robinson R44 II	Unique Helicopters (NI) Ltd
	G-SWAY	PA-18-150 Super Cub	R. Lillywhite
	G-SWCT	Flight Design CTSW	J. A. Shufflebotham
	G-SWEE	Beech 95-B55 Baron	Orman (Carrolls Farm) Ltd (G-AZDK)
	G-SWEL	Hughes 369HS	M. A. Crook & A. E. Wright (G-RBUT)
	G-SWIF	VS.541 Swift F.7 (XF114) ★	Solent Sky, Southampton
	G-SWIG	Robinson R44	S. Goddard
	G-SWIP	Silence Twister	Zulu Glasstek Ltd (G-RIOT)
	G-SWLL	Aero AT-3 R100	Sywell Aerodrome Ltd
	G-SWON	Pitts S-1S Special	S. L. Goldspink
	G-SWOT	Currie Wot (C3011:S)	P. N. Davis
	G-SWPR	Cameron N-56 balloon	A. Brown
	G-SWSW	Schempp-Hirth Ventus bT	R. Kalin
	G-SWYM	CZAW Sportcruiser	R. W. Beal
	G-SXIX	Rans S.19	J. L. Almey
	G-SXTY	Learjet 60	TAG Aviation (UK) Ltd
	G-SYCO	Europa	P. J. Tiller
	G-SYEL	Aero AT-3 R100	Sywell Aerodrome Ltd
	G-SYFW	Focke-Wulf Fw.190 replica (2+1)	J. C. Metcalf
	G-SYGA	Beech B200 Super King Air	Synergy Aircraft Leasing Ltd (G-BPPM)
	G-SYLJ	Embraer RJ135BJ	TAG Aviation (UK) Ltd
	G-SYLV	Cessna 208B Grand Caravan	WAS Aircraft Leasing Ltd
	G-SYPS	MDH MD.900 Explorer	South Yorkshire Police Authority
	G-SYWL	Aero AT-3 R100	Sywell Aerodrome Ltd
	G-TAAB	Cirrus SR22	TAA UK Ltd
	G-TAAC	Cirrus SR20	TAA UK Ltd
	G-TABB	Schempp-Hirth Ventus 2cT	G. Tabbner
	G-TABS	EMB-110P1 Bandeirante	Alan Mann Aviation Group Ltd (G-PBAC)
	G-TABY	Cirrus SR20	N. Carter
	G-TACK	Grob G.109B	A. P. Mayne
	G-TAFC	Maule M7-2358 Super Rocket	The Amphibious Flying Club Ltd

BRITISH CIVIL REGISTRATIONS — G-TAFF – G-TCBA

Reg.	Type	Owner or Operator	Notes
G-TAFF	CASA 1.131E Jungmann 1000	A. J. E. Smith (G-BFNE)	
G-TAFI	Bücker Bü 133C Jungmeister	R. P. Lamplough	
G-TAGE	Bombardier CL600-2B16 Challenger	Aviation (UK) Ltd	
G-TAGF	Dassault Falcon 900DX	TAG Aviation (UK) Ltd	
G-TAGR	Europa	C. G. Sutton	
G-TAIR	PA-34-200T Seneca II	AWA Aeronautical Web Academy Ida	
G-TAJF	Lindstrand LBL-77A balloon	T. A. J. Fowles	
G-TAKE	AS.355F1 Ecureuil II	Arena Aviation Ltd (G-OITN)	
G-TALA	Cessna 152 II	Tatenhill Aviation Ltd (G-BNPZ)	
G-TALB	Cessna 152 II	Tatenhill Aviation Ltd (G-BORO)	
G-TALC	Cessna 152	Tatenhill Aviation Ltd (G-BPBG)	
G-TALD	Cessna F.152	Tatenhill Aviation Ltd (G-BHRM)	
G-TALE	PA-28-181 Archer II	Tatenhill Aviation Ltd (G-BJOA)	
G-TALF	PA-24-250 Comanche	Tatenhill Aviation Ltd (G-APUZ)	
G-TALG	PA-28-151 Warrior	Tatenhill Aviation Ltd (G-BELP)	
G-TALH	PA-28-181 Archer II	Tatenhill Aviation Ltd (G-CIFR)	
G-TALN	Rotorway A600 Talon	Southern Helicopters Ltd	
G-TAMC	Schweizer 269D	Alan Mann Aviation Group Ltd	
G-TAMD	Schweizer 269D	Total Air Management Services Ltd	
G-TAMR	Cessna 172S	Caledonian Air Surveys Ltd	
G-TAMS	Beech A23-24 Musketeer Super	Aerograde Ltd	
G-TANA	Tanarg 912S(2)/Ixess 15	A. P. Marks	
G-TANG	Tanarg 912S(2)/Ixess 15	N. L. Stammers	
G-TANJ	Raj Hamsa X'Air 582(5)	M. M. & P. M. Stoney	
G-TANK	Cameron N-90 balloon	D. J., A. H. & A. M. Mercer	
G-TANS	SOCATA TB20 Trinidad	B. J. Ryan	
G-TANY	EAA Acrosport 2	P. J. Tanulak	
G-TAPE	PA-23 Aztec 250D	Ravenair Aircraft Ltd	
G-TAPS	PA-28RT-201T Turbo Arrow IV	P. G. Doble	
G-TARN	Pietenpol Air Camper	P. J. Heilbron	
G-TARR	P & M Quik	A. Edwards	
G-TART	PA-28-236 Dakota	N. K. G. Prescot	
G-TASH	Cessna 172N (modified)	N. Pletl	
G-TASK	Cessna 404	Reconnaissance Ventures Ltd	
G-TATO	Robinson R22	Skyrunner Aviation Ltd	
G-TATR	Replica Travelair R Type	R. A. Seeley	
G-TATS	AS.350BA Ecureuil	T. J. Hoare	
G-TATT	Gardan GY-20 Minicab	Tatt's Group	
G-TAYC	Gulfstream G450	TAG Aviation (UK) Ltd	
G-TAYI	Grob G.115	K. P. Widdowson & K. Hackshall (G-DODO)	
G-TAYS	Cessna F.152 II	Tayside Aviation Ltd (G-LFCA)	
G-TAZZ	Dan Rihn DR.107 One Design	N. J. Riddin	
G-TBAE	BAe 146-200	BAE Systems (Corporate Travel Ltd) (G-HWPB/G-BSRU/G-OSKI/G-JEAR)	
G-TBAG	Murphy Renegade II	M. R. Tetley	
G-TBBC	Pegasus Quantum 15-912	J. Horn	
G-TBEA	Cessna 525A Citation CJ2	Centreline Air Charter Ltd	
G-TBGT	SOCATA TB10 Tobago GT	P. G. Sherry & A. J. Simmonds	
G-TBHH	AS355F2 Twin Squirrel	Alpha Properties (London) Ltd (G-HOOT/G-SCOW/G-POON/G-MCAL)	
G-TBIC	BAe 146-200	Casco Ltd	
G-TBIO	SOCATA TB10 Tobago	R. G. L. Solomon and J. S. Ritchie	
G-TBJP	Mainair Pegasus Quik	R. J. Price	
G-TBLB	P & M Quik GT450	B. L. Benson	
G-TBLY	Eurocopter EC 120B	AD Bly Aircraft Leasing Ltd	
G-TBMR	P & M Aviation Quik GT450	B. Robertson	
G-TBMW	Murphy Renegade Spirit	S. J. & M. J. Spavins (G-MYIG)	
G-TBOK	SOCATA TB10 Tobago	TB10 Ltd	
G-TBSV	SOCATA TB20 Trinidad GT	Condron Concrete Ltd	
G-TBTB	Robinson R44	ARB Helicopters (G-CDUN)	
G-TBTN	SOCATA TB10 Tobago	Airways International Ltd (G-BKIA)	
G-TBXX	SOCATA TB20 Trinidad	Aeroplane Ltd	
G-TBZO	SOCATA TB20 Trinidad	R. P. Lewis	
G-TCAC	Airbus A.320-232	Thomas Cook Airlines Ltd (G-ERAA)	
G-TCAD	Airbus A.320-214	Thomas Cook Airlines Ltd	
G-TCAL	Robinson R44 II	C. M. Gough-Cooper	
G-TCAN	Colt 69A balloon	H. C. J. Williams	
G-TCAS	Cameron Z-275 balloon	The Ballooning Business Ltd	
G-TCBA	Boeing 757-28A	Thomas Cook Airlines Ltd (G-OOOY)	

Notes	Reg.	Type	Owner or Operator
	G-TCBB	Boeing 757-236	Thomas Cook Airlines Ltd
	G-TCBC	Boeing 757-236	Thomas Cook Airlines Ltd
	G-TCCA	Boeing 767-31K	Thomas Cook Airlines Ltd (G-SJMC)
	G-TCCB	Boeing 767-31KER	Thomas Cook Airlines Ltd (G-DIMB)
	G-TCDA	Airbus A.321-211	Thomas Cook Airlines Ltd (G-JOEE)
	G-TCEE	Hughes 369HS	Aviation Styling Ltd (G-AZVM)
	G-TCHI	VS.509 Spitfire Tr.9	M. B. Phillips
	G-TCHO	VS Spitfire Mk.IX	B. Phillips
	G-TCNM	Tecnam P92-EA Echo	F. G. Walker
	G-TCNY	Mainair Pegasus Quik	L. A. Maynard
	G-TCSM	Bell 206B-3 JetRanger III	Aerial Helicopters Ltd (G-CDYS/G-BOTM)
	G-TCTC	PA-28RT-200 Arrow IV	P. Salemis
	G-TCUB	Piper J-3C-65 Cub (modified)	C. Kirk
	G-TCXA	Airbus A.330-243	Thomas Cook Airlines Ltd
	G-TDKI	CZAW Sportcruiser	D. R. Kendall
	G-TDOG	SA Bulldog Srs 120/121 (XX538:O)	G. S. Taylor
	G-TDRA	Cessna 172S Skyhawk	TDR Aviation Ltd
	G-TDSA	Cessna F.406 Caravan II	Nor Leasing
	G-TDVB	Dyn' Aero MCR-01ULC	D. V. Brunt
	G-TDYN	Aerospool Dynamic WT9 UK	A. A. & L. J. Rice
	G-TEAS	Tanarg/Ixess 15 912S(1)	G. T. Lewis
	G-TEBZ	PA-28R-201 Arrow III	Bowen-Air Ltd
	G-TECC	Aeronca 7AC Champion	N. J. Orchard-Armitage
	G-TECH	Rockwell Commander 114	Karrek Financial Management Ltd (G-BEDH)
	G-TECI	Tecnam P2002-JF	Polarb Air Ltd
	G-TECK	Cameron V-77 balloon	M. W. A. Shemilt
	G-TECM	Tecnam P92-EM Echo	N. G. H. Staunton
	G-TECO	Tecnam P92-EM Echo	A. N. Buchan
	G-TECS	Tecnam P2002-EA Sierra	D. A. Lawrence
	G-TECT	Tecnam P2006T	Polarb Air Ltd
	G-TEDB	Cessna F.150L	E. L. Bamford (G-AZLZ)
	G-TEDI	Best Off Skyranger J2.2(1)	J. E. McGee
	G-TEDW	Kiss 450-582 (2)	K. Buckley
	G-TEDY	Evans VP-1	N. K. Marston (G-BHGN)
	G-TEFC	PA-28 Cherokee 140	Foxtrot Charlie Flyers
	G-TEGS	Bell 206B JetRanger III	E. Drinkwater
	G-TEHL	CFM Streak Shadow	L. T. Flower (G-MYJE)
	G-TEKK	Tecnam P2006T	Aeros Holdings Ltd
	G-TELC	Rotorsport UK MT-03	C. M. Jones
	G-TELY	Agusta A109A-II	Castle Air Ltd
	G-TEMB	Tecnam P2000-EA Sierra	M. B. Hill
	G-TEMP	PA-28 Cherokee 180	F. Busch International Ltd (G-AYBK)
	G-TEMT	Hawker Tempest II (MW763)	Tempest Two Ltd
	G-TENG	Extra EA.300/L	D. McGinn
	G-TENT	Auster J/1N Alpha	R. Callaway-Lewis (G-AKJU)
	G-TERN	Shaw Europa	J. Smith
	G-TERR	Mainair Pegasus Quik	T. R. Thomas
	G-TERY	PA-28-181 Archer II	J. R. Bratherton (G-BOXZ)
	G-TESI	Tecnam P2002 EA Sierra	C. C. Burgess
	G-TESR	Tecnam P2002-RG Sierra	Tecnam UK Ltd
	G-TEST	PA-34-200 Seneca	Stapleford Flying Club Ltd (G-BLCD)
	G-TEWS	PA-28-140 Cherokee	D. Barron & S. G. Brown (G-KEAN/G-AWTM)
	G-TEXN	North American T-6G Texan (3072:72)	Thunderprop Ltd (G-BHTH)
	G-TEZZ	CZAW Sportcruiser	T. D. Baker
	G-TFIX	Mainair Pegasus Quantum 15-912	T. G. Jones
	G-TFLX	P & M Quik GT450	L. A. Wood
	G-TFLY	Air Creation Kiss 450-582 (1)	A. J. Ladell
	G-TFOG	Best Off Skyranger 912(2)	T. J. Fogg
	G-TFOX	Denney Kitfox Mk.2	R. Janek
	G-TFRB	Air Command 532 Elite	F. R. Blennerhassett
	G-TFUN	Valentin Taifun 17E	North West Taifun Group
	G-TFYN	PA-32RT-300 Lance II	R. C. Poolman
	G-TGER	AA-5B Tiger	D. T. Pangbourne (G-BFZP)
	G-TGGR	Eurocopter EC 120B	Messiah Corporation Ltd
	G-TGRA	Agusta A109A	Tiger Helicopters Ltd
	G-TGRD	Robinson R22 Beta II	Tiger Helicopters Ltd (G-OPTS)
	G-TGRE	Robinson R22A	Tiger Helicopters Ltd (G-SOLD)
	G-TGRS	Robinson R22 Beta	Tiger Helicopters Ltd (G-DELL)
	G-TGRZ	Bell 206B JetRanger 3	Tiger Helicopters Ltd (G-BXZX)

Reg.	Type	Owner or Operator	Notes
G-TGTT	Robinson R44 II	London Helicopter Centres Ltd (G-STUS)	
G-TGUN	Aero AT-3 R100	Medcentres Property Portfolio Ltd	
G-THAT	Raj Hamsa X'Air Falcon 912 (1)	E. E. Colley	
G-THEO	TEAM mini-MAX 91	D. W. Melville	
G-THFC	Embraer RJ135BJ Legacy	Raz Air Ltd (G-RRAZ/G-RUBN)	
G-THFW	Bell 206B-3 JetRanger III	Fly Heli Wales Ltd	
G-THIN	Cessna FR.172E	I. C. A. Ussher (G-BXYY)	
G-THLA	Robinson R22 Beta	Thurston Helicopters Ltd & J. W. F. Tuke	
G-THNX	Cessna 525 Citationjet	Synery Aviation Ltd (G-BVCM)	
G-THOM	Thunder Ax-6-56 balloon	T. H. Wilson	
G-THOC	Boeing 737-59D	TAG Aviation (Stansted) Ltd (G-BVKA)	
G-THOO	Boeing 737-33V	Thomsonfly Ltd (G-EZYK)	
G-THOP	Boeing 737-3U3	Thomsonfly Ltd	
G-THOT	Avtech Jabiru SK	S. G. Holton	
G-THRE	Cessna 182S	J. P. Monjalet	
G-THRM	Schleicher ASW-27	C. G. Starkey (G-CJWC)	
G-THSL	PA-28R-201 Arrow III	D. M. Markscheffe	
G-TIAC	Tiger Cub RL5A LW Sherwood Ranger	The Light Aircraft Co.Ltd	
G-TICH	Taylor JT.2 Titch	R. Davitt	
G-TIDS	Jodel 150	M. R. Parker	
G-TIFG	Ikarus C42 FB80	The Ikarus Flying Group	
G-TIGA	DH.82A Tiger Moth	D. E. Leatherland (G-AOEG)	
G-TIGC	AS.332L Super Puma	Bristow Helicopters Ltd (G-BJYH)	
G-TIGE	AS.332L Super Puma	Bristow Helicopters Ltd (G-BJYJ)	
G-TIGF	AS.332L Super Puma	Bristow Helicopters Ltd	
G-TIGG	AS.332L Super Puma	Bristow Helicopters Ltd	
G-TIGJ	AS.332L Super Puma	Bristow Helicopters Ltd	
G-TIGS	AS.332L Super Puma	Bristow Helicopters Ltd	
G-TIGV	AS.332L Super Puma	Bristow Helicopters Ltd	
G-TIII	Aerotek Pitts S-2A Special	Treble India Group	
G-TILE	Robinson R22 Beta	Fenland Helicopters Ltd	
G-TIMB	Rutan Vari-Eze	P. G. Kavanagh (G-BKXJ)	
G-TIMC	Robinson R44	T. Clark Aviation LLP (G-CDUR)	
G-TIMH	Robinson R22	Central Helicopters Ltd	
G-TIMK	PA-28-181 Archer II	Minimal Risk Consultancy Ltd	
G-TIMM	Folland Gnat T.1 (XM693)	Heritage Aircraft Ltd	
G-TIMP	Aeronca 7BCM Champion	R. B. Valler	
G-TIMS	Falconar F-12A	T. Sheridan	
G-TIMX	Head AX8-88B balloon	T. S. Crowdy	
G-TIMY	Gardan GY-80 Horizon 160	R. G. Whyte	
G-TINA	SOCATA TB10 Tobago	A. Lister	
G-TING	Cameron O-120 balloon	Floating Sensations Ltd	
G-TINK	Robinson R22 Beta	Airtask Group PLC	
G-TINS	Cameron N-90 balloon	J. R. Clifton	
G-TINT	Aerotechnik EV-97 Team Eurostar UK	I. A. Cunningham	
G-TINY	Z.526F Trener Master	D. Evans	
G-TIPJ	Cameron Z-77 balloon	J. R. Lawson	
G-TIPS	Nipper T.66 Srs.3	F. V. Neefs	
G-TIVS	Rans S.6-ES Coyote II	A. P. Michell	
G-TIVV	Aerotechnik EV-97 Team Eurostar UK	I. Shulver	
G-TIZZ	Westland SA.341C Gazelle HT.2	Falcon Aviation Flying Group (G-CBSD)	
G-TJAG	PA-34-220T Seneca V	Morgan Airborne LLP	
G-TJAL	Jabiru SPL-430	D. W. Cross	
G-TJAV	Mainair Pegasus Quik	T. Scott	
G-TJAY	PA-22 Tri-Pacer 135	D. Pegley	
G-TJDM	Van's RV-6A	J. D. Michie	
G-TKAY	Shaw Europa	A. M. Kay	
G-TKEV	P & M Quik R	O. P. Gall	
G-TKIS	Tri-R Kis	T. J. Bone	
G-TKNO	UltraMagic S-50 balloon	P. Dickinson	
G-TLAC	Sherwood Ranger ST	The Light Aircraft Co.Ltd	
G-TLDL	Medway SLA 100 Executive	D. T. Lucas	
G-TLET	PA-28-161 Cadet	ADR Aviation (G-GFCF/G-RHBH)	
G-TLFK	Cessna 680 Citation Sovereign	International Jetclub Ltd	
G-TLST	TL 2000UK Sting Carbon	I. Foster	
G-TLTL	Schempp-Hirth Discus CS	E. K. Armitage	

Notes	Reg.	Type	Owner or Operator
	G-TMAN	Roadster/Adventure Funflyer Quattro	P. A. Mahony
	G-TMAX	Evektor EV-97 Sportstar Max	Cosmik Aviation Ltd
	G-TMCB	Best Off Skyranger 912 (2)	P. R. Hanman
	G-TMCC	Cameron N-90 balloon	M. S. Jennings
	G-TMOL	SOCATA TB20 Trinidad	Blackbrooks LLP
	G-TMRB	Short SD3-60 Variant 100	HD Air Ltd (G-SSWB/G-BMLE)
	G-TNGO	Van's RV-6	R. Marsden
	G-TNJB	P & M Quik R	C. J. Shorter
	G-TNRG	Tanarg/Ixess 15 912S(2)	J. W. Mann
	G-TNTN	Thunder Ax6-56 balloon	H. M. Savage & J. F. Trehern
	G-TOAD	Jodel D.140B	J. H. Stevens & J. Whittle
	G-TOBA	SOCATA TB10 Tobago	E. Downing
	G-TOBI	Cessna F.172K	TOBI Group (G-AYVB)
	G-TODD	ICA IS-28M2A	C. I. Roberts & C. D. King
	G-TODG	Flight Design CTSW	S. J. Sykes
	G-TOFT	Colt 90A balloon	C. S. Perceval
	G-TOGO	Van's RV-6	I. R. Thomas
	G-TOHS	Cameron V-31 balloon	J. P. Moore
	G-TOLI	Robinson R44 II	Coleman Cantle Partnership
	G-TOLL	PA-28R-201 Arrow III	Arrow Aircraft Ltd
	G-TOLS	Robinson R44	K. N. Tolley (G-CBOT)
	G-TOLY	Robinson R22 Beta	Helicopter Services Ltd (G-NSHR)
	G-TOMC	NA AT-6D Harvard III	A. A. Marshall
	G-TOMJ	Flight Design CT2K	K. Brown
	G-TOMX	MCR-01 VLA Sportster	P. T. Knight
	G-TOMZ	Denney Kitfox Mk.2	S. J. Spavins
	G-TONE	Pazmany PL-4	P. I. Morgans
	G-TONN	Mainair Pegasus Quik	D. R. Richards
	G-TONS	Slingsby T.67M-200	D. I. Stanbridge
	G-TOOB	Schempp-Hirth Discus 2b	M. F. Evans & P. Davis
	G-TOOL	Thunder Ax8-105 balloon	D. V. Howard
	G-TOPC	AS.355F1 Twin Squirrel	Kinetic Avionics Ltd
	G-TOPK	Shaw Europa XS	P. J. Kember
	G-TOPO	PA-23-250 Turbo Aztec	Blue Sky Investments Ltd (G-BGWW)
	G-TOPS	AS.355F1 Twin Squirrel	Sterling Helicopters (G-BPRH)
	G-TORC	PA-28R Cherokee Arrow 200	Haimoss Ltd
	G-TORE	P.84 Jet Provost T.3A ★	Instructional airframe/City University, Islington
	G-TORI	Zenair CH.701SP	M. J. Maddock (G-CCSK)
	G-TORK	Cameron Z-105 balloon	M. E. Dunstan-Sewell
	G-TORN	Flight Design CTSW	J. A. Moss
	G-TOSH	Robinson R22 Beta	Heli Air Ltd
	G-TOTN	Cessna 210M	Quay Financial Strategies Ltd (G-BVZM)
	G-TOTO	Cessna F.177RG	TOTO Flying Group (G-OADE/G-AZKH)
	G-TOUR	Robin R.2112	A. Carnegie
	G-TOWS	PA-25 Pawnee 260	Lasham Gliding Society Ltd
	G-TOYD	Boeing 737-33V	bmi Baby (G-EZYT)
	G-TOYF	Boeing 737-36N	bmi Baby (G-IGOO/G-SMDB)
	G-TOYG	Boeing 737-36N	bmi Baby (G-IGOJ)
	G-TOYH	Boeing 737-36N	bmi Baby (G-IGOY)
	G-TOYI	Boeing 737-3Q8	bmi Baby
	G-TOYJ	Boeing 737-36M	bmi Baby
	G-TOYK	Boeing 737-33R	bmi Baby
	G-TOYL	Boeing 737-36N	bmi Baby (G-THOL/G-IGOK)
	G-TOYM	Boeing 737-36Q	bmi Baby (G-OHAJ)
	G-TOYZ	Bell 206B JetRanger 3	Potter Aviation Ltd (G-RGER)
	G-TPAL	P & M Aviation Quik GT450	R. Robertson
	G-TPSL	Cessna 182S	A. N. Purslow
	G-TPSY	Champion 8KCAB Super Decathlon	G. R. Potts (G-CEOE)
	G-TPTP	Robinson R44	A. N. Purslow
	G-TPWL	P & M Quik GT450	The G-TPWL Group
	G-TPWX	Heliopolis Gomhouria Mk.6 (TP+WX)	W. H. Greenwood
	G-TRAC	Robinson R44	C. J. Sharples
	G-TRAM	Pegasus Quantum 15-912	G-TRAM Group
	G-TRAN	Beech 76 Duchess	Multiflight Ltd (G-NIFR)
	G-TRAT	Pilatus PC-12/45	Sky Elite Ltd
	G-TRAW	Augusta A.109E	Castle Air Ltd
	G-TRAX	Cessna F.172M	Skytrax Aviation Ltd
	G-TRBO	Schleicher ASW-28-18E	A. Cluskey

Reg.	Type	Owner or Operator	Notes
G-TRCY	Robinson R44	Sugarfree Air Ltd	
G-TREC	Cessna 421C	Sovereign Business Integration PLC (G-TLOL)	
G-TREE	Bell 206B JetRanger 3	Bush Woodlands	
G-TREK	Jodel D.18	R. H. Mole	
G-TREX	Alpi Pioneer 300	S. R. Winter	
G-TRIB	Lindstrand LBL HS-110 airship	S. L. Bell	
G-TRIC	DHC.1 Chipmunk 22 (18013:013)	A. A. Fernandez (G-AOSZ)	
G-TRIG	Cameron Z-90 balloon	Hedge Hoppers Balloon Group	
G-TRIM	Monnett Moni	E. A. Brotherton-Ratcliffe	
G-TRIN	SOCATA TB20 Trinidad	M. Hardy & M. J. Porter	
G-TRJB	Beech A36 Bonanza	G. A. J. Bowles	
G-TRNG	Agusta A109E Power	Castle Air Ltd (G-NWOY/G-JMXA)	
G-TROY	NA T-28A Fennec (51-7692)	S. G. Howell & S. Tilling	
G-TRTM	DG Flugzeugbau DG-808C	D. T. S. Walsh	
G-TRUE	MDH Hughes 369E	N. E. Bailey	
G-TRUK	Stoddard-Hamilton Glasair RG	M. P. Jackson	
G-TRUX	Colt 77A balloon	Servowarm Baloon Syndicate	
G-TRYK	Kiss 400-582 (1)	M. A. Pantling	
G-TRYX	Enstrom 480B	Atryx Aviation LLP	
G-TSAC	Tecnam P2002-EA Sierra	A. G. Cozens	
G-TSDS	PA-32R-301 Saratoga SP	I. R. Jones (G-TRIP/G-HOSK)	
G-TSGA	PA-28R-201 Arrow III	TSG Aviation Ltd (G-ONSF/G-EMAK)	
G-TSGE	Cirrus SR20	Renneta Ltd	
G-TSGJ	PA-28-181 Archer II	Golf Juliet Flying Club	
G-TSHO	Ikarus C42 FB80	A. P. Shoobert	
G-TSIM	Titan T-51 Mustang	B. J. Chester-Master	
G-TSIX	AT-6C Harvard IIA (111836:JZ-6)	Century Aviation Ltd	
G-TSJF	Cessna 525B CitationJet CJ3	Lunar Jet Ltd	
G-TSKD	Raj Hamsa X'Air Jabiru J.2.2.	T. Sexton & K. B. Dupuy	
G-TSKS	EV-97 TeamEurostar UK	Purple Aviation Ltd	
G-TSKY	Beagle B.121 Pup 2	R. G. Hayes (G-AWDY)	
G-TSLC	Schweizer 269C-1	Bournemouth Helicopters Ltd	
G-TSLS	Bombardier BD-700-1A11 Global 5000	TAG Aviation (UK) Ltd	
G-TSOB	Rans S.6-ES Coyote II	S. Luck	
G-TSOL	EAA Acrosport 1	J. A. Wojda (G-BPKI)	
G-TSUE	Shaw Europa	H. J. C. Maclean	
G-TSWI	Lindstrand LBL-90A balloon	R. J. Gahan	
G-TTAT	ICP MXP-740 Savannah VG Jabiru(1)	A. N. Green	
G-TTDD	Zenair CH.701 STOL	D. B. Dainton & V. D. Asque	
G-TTFG	Colt 77B balloon	T. J. & M. J. Turner (G-BUZF)	
G-TTMB	Bell 206B JetRanger 3	Sky Charter UK Ltd (G-RNME/G-CBDF)	
G-TTOB	Airbus A.320-232	British Airways PLC	
G-TTOE	Airbus A.320-232	British Airways PLC	
G-TTOY	CFM Streak Shadow SA	J. Softley	
G-TTRL	Van's RV-9A	J. E. Gattrell	
G-TUBB	Avtech Jabiru UL	A. H. Bower	
G-TUCK	Van's RV-8	N. G. R. Moffat	
G-TUGG	PA-18 Super Cub 150	Ulster Gliding Club Ltd	
G-TUGI	CZAW Sportcruiser	T. J. Wilson	
G-TUGS	PA-25-235 Pawnee D	J. A. Stephen (G-BFEW)	
G-TUGY	Robin DR.400/180	TUGY Group	
G-TUGZ	Robin DR.400/180R	Buckminster Gliding Club Ltd	
G-TUNE	Robinson R22 Beta	Heli Air Ltd (G-OJVI)	
G-TURF	Cessna F.406	Reconnaissance Ventures Ltd	
G-TUTU	Cameron O-105 balloon	A. C. K. Rawson & J. J. Rudoni	
G-TVAM	MBB Bo105DBS-4	South Georgis Heritage Trust (G-SPOL)	
G-TVBF	Lindstrand LBL-310A balloon	Virgin Balloons Flights	
G-TVCO	Gippsland GA-8 Airvan	Zyox Ltd	
G-TVHB	Eurocopter EC 135 P2+	Thames Valley Police Authority	
G-TVHD	AS.355F2 Ecureuil 2	Arena Aviation Ltd	
G-TVII	Hawker Hunter T.7 (XX467:86)	G-TVII Group/Exeter	
G-TVIJ	CCF Harvard IV (T-6J) (28521:TA-521)	R. W. Davies (G-BSBE)	
G-TVSI	Campbell Cricket Replica	C. Smith	
G-TWAZ	Rolladen-Schneider LS7-WL	S. Derwin	
G-TWEL	PA-28-181 Archer II	International Aerospace Engineering Ltd	
G-TWEY	Colt 69A balloon	N. Bland	
G-TWIN	PA-44-180 Seminole	Bonus Aircraft Ltd	

Notes	Reg.	Type	Owner or Operator
	G-TWIS	Silence Twister	C. S. & K. D. Rhodes
	G-TWIZ	Rockwell Commander 114	B. C. & P. M. Cox
	G-TWLV	Van's RV-12	G-TWLV Group
	G-TWNN	Beech 76 Duchess	Folada Aero and Technical Services Ltd
	G-TWOA	Schempp-Hirth Discus 2a	A. J. McNamara
	G-TWOC	Schempp-Hirth Ventus 2cT	D. Heslop
	G-TWOO	Extra EA.300/200	Extra 200 Aviation Ltd (G-MRKI)
	G-TWRL	Pitts S-1S Special	C. Dennis
	G-TWSR	Silence Twister	J. A. Hallam
	G-TWSS	Silence Twister	A. P. Hatton
	G-TWTR	Robinson R44 II	Heli Aviation Ltd
	G-TWTW	Denney Kitfox Mk.2	R. M. Bremner
	G-TXAN	AT-6D Harvard III (FX301)	P. J. Lawton (G-JUDI)
	G-TYAK	IDA Bacau Yakovlev Yak-52	S. J. Ducker
	G-TYER	Robin DR.400/500	Robin Group
	G-TYGA	AA-5B Tiger	G-TYGA Group (G-BHNZ)
	G-TYGR	Best Off Skyranger 912S (1)	M. J. Poole
	G-TYKE	Avtech Jabiru UL-450	S. C. Reeve
	G-TYMO	DH.82A Tiger Moth	N. Rose
	G-TYNA	PA-28-181 Archer II	Winged Bull Aviation
	G-TYNE	SOCATA TB20 Trinidad	N. V. Price
	G-TYPH	BAe.146-200	BAE Systems (Corporate Air Travel) Ltd (G-BTVT)
	G-TYRE	Cessna F.172M	J. S. C. English
	G-TZEE	SOCATA TB10 Tobago	Zytech Ltd
	G-TZII	Thorp T.211B	M. J. Newton
	G-UACA	Skyranger R.100	R. G. Openshaw
	G-UAKE	NA P-51D-5-NA Mustang	P. S. Warner
	G-UANO	DHC.1 Chipmunk 22	Advanced Flight Training Ltd (G-BYYW)
	G-UANT	PA-28 Cherokee 140	Air Navigation & Trading Co Ltd
	G-UAPA	Robin DR.400/140B	Carlos Saraive Lda/Portugal
	G-UAPO	Ruschmeyer R.90-230RG	P. Randall
	G-UAVA	PA-30 Twin Comanche	Small World Aviation Ltd
	G-UCAM	PA-31-350 Navajo Chieftain	Blue Sky Investments Ltd (G-NERC/G-BBXX)
	G-UCCC	Cameron 90 Sign SS balloon	Unipart Group of Companies Ltd
	G-UCLU	Schleicher ASK-21	University College London Union
	G-UDET	Replica Fokker E.111	M. J. Clark
	G-UDGE	Thruster T.600N	G-UDGE Syndicate (G-BYPI)
	G-UDMS	PA-46R-350T Malibu Matrix	J. C. M. Critchley & S. Harding
	G-UDOG	SA Bulldog Srs 120/121 (XX518:S)	Gamit Ltd
	G-UFAW	Raj Hamsa X'Air 582 (5)	P. Batchelor
	G-UFCB	Cessna 172S	The Cambridge Aero Club Ltd
	G-UFCC	Cessna 172S	Oxford Aviation Services Ltd
	G-UFCF	Cessna 172S	Innovative Converged Devices Ltd
	G-UFCG	Cessna 172S	Ulster Flying Club (1961) Ltd
	G-UFCH	Cessna 172S	Air-Unlimited Sweden AB/Sweden
	G-UFCI	Cessna 172S	Ulster Flying Club (1961) Ltd
	G-UFCJ	Cessna 172S	Air-Unlimited Sweden AB/Sweden (G-RMIN)
	G-UFCL	Tecnam P2002-JF Sierra	Ulster Flying Club (1961) Ltd
	G-UFCM	Tecnam P2002-JF Sierra	Ulster Flying Club (1961) Ltd
	G-UFLY	Cessna F.150H	Westair Flying Services Ltd (G-AVVY)
	G-UFOE	Grob G.115	Swiftair Maintenance Ltd
	G-UHIH	Bell UH-1H Iroquois (21509)	MSS Holdings Ltd
	G-UHOP	UltraMagic H-31 balloon	S. J. Roake
	G-UIKR	P & M Quik R	A. M. Sirant
	G-UILA	Aquila AT01	Aquila Sport Aeroplanes LLP
	G-UILD	Grob G.109B	K. Butterfield
	G-UILE	Lancair 320	R. J. Martin
	G-UILT	Cessna T.303	Rock Seat Ltd (G-EDRY)
	G-UIMB	Guimbal Cabri G2	Helitrain Ltd
	G-UINN	Stolp SA.300 Starduster Too	J. D. H. Gordon

Reg.	Type	Owner or Operator	Notes
G-UJAB	Avtech Jabiru UL	C. A. Thomas	
G-UJGK	Avtech Jabiru UL	W. G. Upton & J. G. Kosak	
G-UKAW	Agusta A.109E	Agusta Westland Ltd	
G-UKOZ	Avtech Jabiru SK	D. J. Burnett	
G-UKPS	Cessna 208 Caravan 1	UK Parachute Services Ltd	
G-UKRB	Colt 105A balloon	Virgin Airship & Balloon Co Ltd	
G-UKUK	Head Ax8-105 balloon	P. A. George	
G-ULAS	DHC.1 Chipmunk 22 (WK517)	ULAS Flying Club Ltd/Denham	
G-ULES	AS.355F2 Twin Squirrel	Select Plant Hire Company Ltd (G-OBHL/-HARO/G-DAFT/G-BNNN)	
G-ULHI	SA Bulldog Srs.100/101	Power Aerobatics Ltd (G-OPOD/G-AZMS)	
G-ULIA	Cameron V-77 balloon	J. T. Wilkinson	
G-ULPS	Everett Srs 1 gyroplane	C. J. Watkinson (G-BMNY)	
G-ULSY	Ikarus C.42 FB 80	B. W. Rooke	
G-ULTA	Ultramagic M-65C	G. A. Board	
G-ULTR	Cameron A-105 balloon	P. Glydon	
G-UMAS	Rotorsport UK MT-03	BAE Systems (Operations) Ltd	
G-UMBO	Thunder Ax7-77A balloon	Virgin Airship & Balloon Co Ltd	
G-UMKA	Dassault Falcon 7X	Ocean Sky (UK) Ltd	
G-UMMI	PA-31-310 Turbo Navajo	J. A. & D. T. A. Rees (G-BGSO)	
G-UMMS	EV-97 TeamEurostar UK	A. C. Lees (G-ODRY)	
G-UMMY	Best Off Skyranger J2.2(2)	A. R. Williams	
G-UMPY	Shaw Europa	GDBMK Ltd	
G-UNDD	PA-23 Aztec 250E	G. J. & D. P. Deadman (G-BATX)	
G-UNER	Lindstrand LBL-90A balloon	St. Dunstans	
G-UNES	Van's RV-6	R. C. Dyer	
G-UNGE	Lindstrand LBL-90A balloon	Silver Ghost Balloon Club (G-BVPJ)	
G-UNGO	Pietenpol Air Camper	A. R. Wyatt	
G-UNIN	Schempp-Hirth Ventus b	U9 Syndicate	
G-UNIV	Montgomerie-Parsons 2-seat gyroplane	University of Glasgow (G-BWTP)	
G-UNIX	VPM M16 Tandem Trainer	A. P. Wilkinson	
G-UNNA	Jabiru UL-450WW	N. D. A. Graham	
G-UNRL	Lindstrand LBL-RR21 balloon	Alton Aviation Ltd	
G-UORO	Shaw Europa	D. Dufton	
G-UPFS	Waco UPS-7	D. N. Peters & N. R. Finlayson	
G-UPHI	Best Off Skyranger Swift 912S(1)	Flylight Airsports Ltd	
G-UPID	Bowers Fly Baby 1A	R. D. Taylor	
G-UPOI	Cameron TR-84 S1 balloon	Beatwax Ltd	
G-UPPI	BAC 167 Strikemaster Mk.80A	G. P. Williams (G-CBPB)	
G-UPTA	Skyranger 912S (1)	D. Minnock	
G-UPUP	Cameron V-77 balloon	S. F. Burden/Netherlands	
G-UPUZ	Lindstrand LBL-120A balloon	C.J. Sanger-Davies	
G-UROP	Beech 95-B55 Baron	S. C. Smith	
G-URRR	Air Command 582 Sport	L. Armes	
G-URRU	Bombardier CL600-2B16 Challenger	Executive Jet Charter Ltd	
G-URSA	Sikorsky S-76C	Premiair Aviation Services Ltd (G-URSS)	
G-URUH	Robinson R44	Heli Air Ltd	
G-URUS	Maule MX7-180B Super Rocket	Broomco Ltd	
G-USAA	Cessna F.150G	A. Naish (G-OIDW)	
G-USAR	Cessna 441 Conquest	I. Annenskiy	
G-USIL	Thunder Ax7-77 balloon	Window On The World Ltd	
G-USKY	Aviat A-1B Husky	B. Walker and Co (Dursley) Ltd	
G-USMC	Cameron Chestie 90 SS balloon	J. W. Soukup	
G-USRV	Van's RV-6	C. Cartwright & B. Vincent	
G-USSY	PA-28-181 Archer II	The Leicestershire Aero Club Ltd	
G-USTH	Agusta A109A-II	Stratton Motor Co.(Norfolk) Ltd	
G-USTS	Agusta A109A-II	MB Air Ltd (G-MKSF)	
G-USTY	FRED Srs 2	A. S. Watts	
G-UTRA	Ultramagic M-77 balloon	Ultrait Ltd	
G-UTSI	Rand-Robinson KR-2	K. B. Gutridge	
G-UTSY	PA-28R-201 Arrow III	J. P. Quoniam	
G-UTTS	Robinson R44	HS (Holdings) Ltd (G-ROAP)	
G-UTZI	Robinson R44 II	S. K. Miles/Spain	

Notes	Reg.	Type	Owner or Operator
	G-UURO	Aerotechnik EV-97 Eurostar	Romeo Oscar Syndicate
	G-UVBF	Lindstrand LBL-400A balloon	Virgin Balloon Flights
	G-UVIP	Cessna 421C	MM Air Ltd (G-BSKH)
	G-UVNR	BAC.167 Strikemaster Mk 87	P. Turek (G-BXFS)
	G-UYAD	Bombardier CL600-2B16	Coldstream SARL/Luxembourg
	G-UZEL	Aérospatiale SA.341G Gazelle 1	Fairalls of Godstone Ltd (G-BRNH)
	G-UZLE	Colt 77A balloon	G. B. Davies
	G-UZUP	Aerotechnik EV-97A Eurostar	G-UZUP EV-97 Flying Group
	G-VAAC	PA-28-181 Archer III	A. J. Catzelfis (G-CCDN)
	G-VAAV	P & M Quik R	A. Voyce
	G-VAIR	Airbus A.340-313	Virgin Atlantic Airways Ltd *Maiden Tokyo*
	G-VALS	Pietenpol Air Camper	J. R. D. Bygraves
	G-VALY	SOCATA TB21 Trinidad GT Turbo	R. J. Thwaites and Westflight Aviation Ltd
	G-VALZ	Cameron N-120 balloon	J. D. & K. Griffiths
	G-VANA	Gippsland GA-8 Airvan	P. Marsden
	G-VAND	Gippsland GA-8 Airvan	Go Adventure Ireland Ltd
	G-VANN	Van's RV-7A	D. N. & J. A. Carnegie
	G-VANS	Van's RV-4	R. J. Marshall
	G-VANX	Gippsland GA-8 Airvan	Airkix Aircraft Ltd
	G-VANZ	Van's RV-6A	S. J. Baxter
	G-VARG	Varga 2150A Kachina	J. Denton
	G-VART	Rotorway Executive 90	I. R. Brown & K. E. Parker (G-BSUR)
	G-VAST	Boeing 747-41R	Virgin Atlantic Airways Ltd *Ladybird*
	G-VATL	Airbus A.340-642	Virgin Atlantic Airways Ltd *Miss Kitty,born October 2003*
	G-VBCA	Cirrus SR22	C. A. S. Atha
	G-VBFA	Ultramagic N-250 balloon	Virgin Balloon Flights
	G-VBFB	Ultramagic N-355 balloon	Virgin Balloon Flights
	G-VBFC	Ultramagic N-250 balloon	Virgin Balloon Flights
	G-VBFD	Ultramagic N-250 balloon	Virgin Balloon Flights
	G-VBFE	Ultramagic N-255 balloon	Virgin Balloon Flights
	G-VBFF	Lindstrand LBL-360A balloon	Virgin Balloon Flights
	G-VBFG	Cameron Z-350 balloon	Virgin Balloon Flights
	G-VBFH	Cameron Z-350 balloon	Virgin Balloon Flights
	G-VBFI	Cameron Z-350 balloon	Virgin Balloon Flights
	G-VBFJ	Cameron Z-350 balloon	Virgin Balloon Flights
	G-VBFK	Cameron Z-350 balloon	Virgin Balloon Flights
	G-VBFL	Cameron Z-400 balloon	Virgin Balloon Flights
	G-VBFM	Cameron Z-375 balloon	Virgin Balloon Flights
	G-VBFN	Cameron Z-375 balloon	Virgin Balloon Flights
	G-VBFO	Cameron Z-375 balloon	Virgin Balloon Flights
	G-VBFP	Ultramagic N-425 balloon	Virgin Balloon Flights
	G-VBFR	Cameron Z-375 balloon	Virgin Balloon Flights
	G-VBFS	Cameron Z-375 balloon	Virgin Balloon Flights
	G-VBFT	Cameron Z-375 balloon	Virgin Balloon Flights
	G-VBFU	Cameron A-400 balloon	Virgin Balloon Flights
	G-VBFV	Cameron Z-400 balloon	Virgin Balloon Flights
	G-VBFW	Cameron Z-77 balloon	Virgin Balloon Flights
	G-VBFX	Cameron Z-400 balloon	Virgin Balloon Flights
	G-VBFY	Cameron Z-400 balloon	Virgin Balloon Flights
	G-VBFZ	Cameron A-300 balloon	Virgin Balloon Flights
	G-VBIG	Boeing 747-4Q8	Virgin Atlantic Airways Ltd *Tinkerbelle*
	G-VBLU	Airbus A.340-642	Virgin Atlantic Airways Ltd *Soul Sister*
	G-VBPM	Cirrus SR22	Pestrin Ltd
	G-VBUG	Airbus A.340-642	Virgin Atlantic Airways Ltd
	G-VCIO	EAA Acro Sport II	C. M. Knight
	G-VCJH	Robinson R22 Beta	Hughes Plant Ltd
	G-VCML	Beech 58 Baron	St. Angelo Aviation Ltd
	G-VCXT	Schempp-Hirth Ventus 2cT	R. F. Aldous/Germany
	G-VDIR	Cessna T.310R	J. Driver
	G-VDOG	Cessna 305C Bird Dog (24582)	D. K. Shead
	G-VECD	Robin R.1180T	B. Lee
	G-VECG	Robin R.2160	I. A. Anderson
	G-VECT	Cessna 560XL Citation Excel	Fly Vectra Ltd

Reg.	Type	Owner or Operator	Notes
G-VEGA	Slingsby T.65A Vega	R. A. Rice (G-BFZN)	
G-VEIL	Airbus A.340-642	Virgin Atlantic Airways Ltd *Queen of the Skies*	
G-VEIT	Robinson R44 II	Field Marshall Helicopters Ltd	
G-VELA	SIAI-Marchetti S.205-22R	D. A. Clarke & N. D. Dixon	
G-VELD	Airbus A.340-313	Virgin Atlantic Airways Ltd *African Queen*	
G-VELO	Velocity 173RG	J. Bergin	
G-VENC	Schempp-Hirth Ventus 2cT	J. B. Giddins	
G-VENI	DH.112 Venom FB.50 (VV612)	Aviation and Computer Consultancy Ltd	
G-VENM	DH.112 Venom FB.50 (WK436)	Aviation Heritage Ltd (G-BLIE)	
G-VERA	Gardan GY-201 Minicab	D. K. Shipton	
G-VERU	Agusta A109S Grand	MRY Ltd	
G-VETA	Hawker Hunter T.Mk.7	Viper ClassicS Ltd (G-BVWN)	
G-VETS	Enstrom 280C-UK Shark	B. G. Rhodes (G-FSDC/G-BKTG)	
G-VEYE	Robinson R22	K. A. Jones (G-BPTP)	
G-VEZE	Rutan Vari-Eze	Go Eze Flying	
G-VFAB	Boeing 747-4Q8	Virgin Atlantic Airways Ltd *Lady Penelope*	
G-VFAR	Airbus A.340-313	Virgin Atlantic Airways Ltd *Diana*	
G-VFAS	PA-28R-200 Cherokee Arrow	P. Wood (G-MEAH/G-BSNM)	
G-VFIT	Airbus A.340-642	Virgin Atlantic Airways Ltd *Dancing Queen*	
G-VFIZ	Airbus A.340-642	Virgin Atlantic Airways Ltd *Bubbles*	
G-VFOX	Airbus A.340-642	Virgin Atlantic Airways Ltd Queen of Cuba	
G-VGAG	Cirrus SR20 GTS	Alfred Graham Ltd	
G-VGAL	Boeing 747-443	Virgin Atlantic Airways Ltd *Jersey Girl*	
G-VGAS	Airbus A.340-542	Virgin Atlantic Airways Ltd *Varga Girl*	
G-VGMC	Eurocopter AS.355N Ecureuil II	Cheshire Helicopters Ltd (G-HEMH)	
G-VGMG	Eurocopter AS.350B Ecureuil II	Arianne Developments Ltd (G-KELY/G-WKRD/ G-BUJG/G-HEAR)	
G-VGOA	Airbus A.340-642	Virgin Atlantic Airways Ltd *Indian Princess*	
G-VGVG	Savannah VG Jabiru(1)	M. A. Jones	
G-VHOT	Boeing 747-4Q8	Virgin Atlantic Airways Ltd *Tubular Belle*	
G-VICC	PA-28-161 Warrior II	Freedom Aviation Ltd (G-JFHL)	
G-VICI	DH.112 Venom FB.50 (J-1573)	Aviation and Computer Consultancy Ltd	
G-VICM	Beech F33C Bonanza	Velocity Engineering Ltd	
G-VICS	Commander 114B	N. Griffin	
G-VICT	PA-31-310 Turbo Navajo	Aviation Leasing ACS (G-BBZI)	
G-VIEW	Vinten-Wallis WA-116/100	K. H. Wallis	
G-VIIA	Boeing 777-236	British Airways	
G-VIIB	Boeing 777-236	British Airways	
G-VIIC	Boeing 777-236	British Airways	
G-VIID	Boeing 777-236	British Airways	
G-VIIE	Boeing 777-236	British Airways	
G-VIIF	Boeing 777-236	British Airways	
G-VIIG	Boeing 777-236	British Airways	
G-VIIH	Boeing 777-236	British Airways	
G-VIIJ	Boeing 777-236	British Airways	
G-VIIK	Boeing 777-236	British Airways	
G-VIIL	Boeing 777-236	British Airways	
G-VIIM	Boeing 777-236	British Airways	
G-VIIN	Boeing 777-236	British Airways	
G-VIIO	Boeing 777-236	British Airways	
G-VIIP	Boeing 777-236	British Airways	
G-VIIR	Boeing 777-236	British Airways	
G-VIIS	Boeing 777-236	British Airways	
G-VIIT	Boeing 777-236	British Airways	
G-VIIU	Boeing 777-236	British Airways	
G-VIIV	Boeing 777-236	British Airways	
G-VIIW	Boeing 777-236	British Airways	
G-VIIX	Boeing 777-236	British Airways	
G-VIIY	Boeing 777-236	British Airways	
G-VIIZ	CZAW Sportcruiser	Skyview Systems Ltd	
G-VIKE	Bellanca 1730A Viking	S. J. Doughty	
G-VILA	Avtech Jabiru UL	G. T. Clipstone (G-BYIF)	
G-VILL	Lazer Z.200 (modified)	The G-VILL Group (G-BOYZ)	
G-VILP	Embraer EMB-135BJ Legacy 650	Etlagh Aviation Ltd	
G-VIPA	Cessna 182S	Stallingborough Aviation Ltd	
G-VIPH	Agusta A109C	Cheqair Ltd(G-BVNH/G-LAXO)	
G-VIPI	BAe 125 Srs 800B	Yeates of Leicester Ltd	
G-VIPP	PA-31-350 Navajo Chieftain	Capital Air Charter Ltd	

Notes	Reg.	Type	Owner or Operator
	G-VIPR	Eurocopter EC 120B Colibri	Amey Aviation LLP
	G-VIPU	PA-31-350 Navajo Chieftain	Capital Air Charter Ltd
	G-VIPV	PA-31-350 Navajo Chieftain	Capital Air Charter Ltd
	G-VIPW	PA-31-350 Navajo Chieftain	Capital Air Charter Ltd
	G-VIPX	PA-31-350 Navajo Chieftain	Capital Air Charter Ltd
	G-VIPY	PA-31-350 Navajo Chieftain	Capital Air Charter Ltd
	G-VIRU	Agusta A109E Power	MRY Ltd
	G-VITA	Dassault Falcon 7X	Casanova Air 7X Ltd
	G-VITE	Robin R.1180T	G-VITE Flying Group
	G-VITL	Lindstrand LBL-105A balloon	Vital Resources
	G-VIVA	Thunder Ax7-65 balloon	R. J. Mitchener
	G-VIVI	Taylor JT.2 Titch	D. G. Tucker
	G-VIVM	P.84 Jet Provost T.5	K. Lyndon-Dykes (G-BVWF)
	G-VIVO	Nicollier HN700 Menestrel II	D. G. Tucker
	G-VIVS	PA-28-151 Cherokee Warrior	S. J. Harrison & V. A. Donnelly
	G-VIXN	DH.110 Sea Vixen FAW.2 (XS587) ★	P. G. Vallance Ltd/Charlwood
	G-VIXX	Alpi Pioneer 300	B. F. Walker (G-CESE/G-CERJ)
	G-VIZA	LBL-260A balloon	A. Nimmo
	G-VIZZ	Sportavia RS.180 Sportsman	Exeter Fournier Group
	G-VJET	Avro 698 Vulcan B.2 (XL426) ★	Vulcan Restoration Trust
	G-VJMJ	Agusta-Bell 206B JetRanger II	Total Digital Solutions Ltd (G-PEAK/G-BLJE)
	G-VKGO	Embraer EMB-500 Phenom 100	M-Kick LP
	G-VKIT	Shaw Europa	T. H. Crow
	G-VKSS	Airbus A.330-343	Virgin Atlantic Airways Ltd *Mademoiselle Rouge*
	G-VKUP	Cameron Z-90 balloon	Global Brands Ltd
	G-VLCC	Schleicher ASW-27-18E	Viscount Cobham
	G-VLCN	Avro 698 Vulcan B.2 (XH558) ★	Vulcan to the Sky Trust/Bruntingthorpe
	G-VLIP	Boeing 747-443	Virgin Atlantic Airways Ltd *Hot Lips*
	G-VMCG	PA-38-112 Tomahawk	P. J. Montgomery (G-BSVX)
	G-VMEG	Airbus A.340-642	Virgin Atlantic Airways Ltd *Mystic Maiden*
	G-VMIJ	VS 349 Spitfire Mk.VC	I. D. Ward
	G-VMJM	SOCATA TB10 Tobago	S. C. Brown (G-BTOK)
	G-VMVM	Cessna Z-77 balloon	Virgin Balloon Flights
	G-VNAP	Airbus A.340-642	Virgin Atlantic Airways Ltd *Sleeping Beauty*
	G-VNOM	DH.112 Venom FB.50 (J-1632) ★	de Havilland Heritage Museum/London Colney
	G-VNON	Escapade Jabiru (3)	P. A. Vernon
	G-VNTS	Schempp-Hirth Ventus bT	911 Syndicatem
	G-VOAR	PA-28-181 Archer III	Solent Flight Ltd
	G-VOCE	Robinson R22	J. J. Voce (G-BSCL)
	G-VODA	Cameron N-77 balloon	I. Harris
	G-VOGE	Airbus A.340-642	Virgin Atlantic Airways Ltd *Cover Girl*
	G-VOID	PA-28RT-201 Arrow IV	Doublecube Aviation LLP
	G-VOIP	Westland SA.341G Gazelle	Q. Milne (G-HOBZ/G-CBSJ)
	G-VOLO	Alpi Pioneer 300	J. Buglass
	G-VONA	Sikorsky S-76A	Von Essen Aviation Ltd (G-BUXB)
	G-VONB	Sikorsky S-76B	Von Essen Aviation Ltd (G-POAH)
	G-VONC	Sikorsky S-76B	Von Essen Aviation Ltd
	G-VOND	Bell 222	Von Essen Aviation Ltd (G-OWCG/G-VERT/ G-JLBZ/G-BNGB)
	G-VONE	Eurocopter AS355N Twin Squirrel	Von Essen Aviation Ltd (G-LCON)
	G-VONG	AS.355F1 Twin Squirrel	Von Essen Aviation Ltd (G-OILX/G-RMGN/ G-BMCY)
	G-VONH	AS.355F1 Twin Squirrel	Von Essen Aviation Ltd (G-BKUL/G-FFHI/ G-GWHH)
	G-VONK	AS.355F1 Squirrel	Airbourne Solutions Ltd (G-BLRI/G-NUTZ)
	G-VONS	PA-32R-301T Saratoga IITC	W. S. Stanley
	G-VOOM	Pitts S-1S Special	P. G. Roberts
	G-VORN	Aerotechnik EV-97 Eurostar	J. Parker (G-ODAV)
	G-VPAT	Evans VP-1 Srs 2	A. P. Twort
	G-VPPL	SOCATA TB20 Trinidad	P. Murer, L. Printie & P. J. Wood (G-BPAS)
	G-VPSJ	Shaw Europa	J. D. Bean
	G-VRCW	Cessna P.210N	M. Mignini/Italy
	G-VRED	Airbus A.340-642	Virgin Atlantic Airways Ltd *Scarlet Lady*

Reg.	Type	Owner or Operator	Notes
G-VRMM	Van's RV-9	D. J. Rose	
G-VROC	Boeing 747-41R	Virgin Atlantic Airways Ltd *Mustang Sally*	
G-VROE	Avro 652A Anson T.21 (WD413)	Air Atlantique Ltd/Coventry (G-BFIR)	
G-VROS	Boeing 747-443	Virgin Atlantic Airways Ltd *English Rose*	
G-VROY	Boeing 747-443	Virgin Atlantic Airways Ltd *Pretty Woman*	
G-VRVB	Van's RV-8	R. J. Verrall (G-CETI)	
G-VSGE	Cameron O-105 balloon	G. Sbocchelli	
G-VSHY	Airbus A.340-642	Virgin Atlantic Airways Ltd *Madam Butterfly*	
G-VSIX	Schempp-Hirth Ventus 2cT	V6 Group	
G-VSSH	Airbus A.340-642	Virgin Atlantic Airways Ltd *Sweet Dreamer*	
G-VSTR	Stolp SA-900 V-Star	R. L. Hanreck	
G-VSUN	Airbus A.340-313	Virgin Atlantic Airways Ltd *Rainbow Lady*	
G-VSXY	Airbus A.330-343	Virgin Atlantic Airways Ltd *Beauty Queen*	
G-VTAL	Beech V35 Bonanza	E. D. Ovenden	
G-VTCT	Schempp-Hirth Ventus-2cT	V26 Syndicate	
G-VTGE	Bell 206L LongRanger	Vantage Helicopters Ltd (G-ELIT)	
G-VTII	DH.115 Vampire T.11 (XX507:74)	Vampire Preservation Group, Bournemouth	
G-VTOL	Hawker Siddeley Harrier T.52 ★	Brooklands Museum of Aviation/Weybridge	
G-VTOP	Boeing 747-4Q8	Virgin Atlantic Airways Ltd *Virginia Plain*	
G-VTUS	Schempp-Hirth Ventus 2cT	Ventus 02 Syndicate	
G-VTWO	Schempp-Hirth Ventus 2c	F. & B. Birlison	
G-VUEA	Cessna 550 Citation II	AD Aviation Ltd (G-BWOM)	
G-VUEZ	Cessna 550 Citation II	AD Aviation Ltd	
G-VULC	Avro 698 Vulcan B.2A (XM655) ★	Radarmoor Ltd/Wellesbourne	
G-VVBA	AS.355F2 Ecureuil II	Hinde Holdings Ltd (G-DBOK)	
G-VVBE	Robinson R22 Beta	Hinde Holdings Ltd (G-OTOY/G-BPEW)	
G-VVBF	Colt 315A balloon	Virgin Balloon Flights	
G-VVBK	PA-34-200T Seneca II	Ravenair Aircraft Ltd (G-BSBS/G-BDRI)	
G-VVBL	Robinson R44 II	Hinde Holdings Ltd	
G-VVBO	Bell 206L-3 LongRanger III	Hinde Holdings Ltd	
G-VVIP	Cessna 421C	Cranfield Aerospace Ltd (G-BMWB)	
G-VVPA	Bombardier CL600-2B16	TAG Aviation (UK) Ltd	
G-VVTV	Diamond DA42 Twin Star	A. D. R. Northeast	
G-VVVV	Skyranger 912 (2)	J. Thomas	
G-VVWW	Enstrom 280C Shark	P. J. Odendaal	
G-VWEB	Airbus A.340-642	Virgin Atlantic Airways Ltd *Surfer Girl*	
G-VWIN	Airbus A.340-642	Virgin Atlantic Airways Ltd *Lady Luck*	
G-VWKD	Airbus A.340-642	Virgin Atlantic Airways Ltd *Miss Behavin'*	
G-VWOW	Boeing 747-41R	Virgin Atlantic Airways Ltd *Cosmic Girl*	
G-VXLG	Boeing 747-41R	Virgin Atlantic Airways Ltd *Ruby Tuesday*	
G-VYAK	Yakovlev Yak-18T	A. I. McRobbie	
G-VYGA	Airbus A.330-243	Air Tanker Ltd	
G-VYOU	Airbus A.340-642	Virgin Atlantic Airways Ltd *Emmeline Heaney born August 2006*	
G-VYPO	DH.115 Sea Vampire T.35 (N6-766)	N. Rose (G-SPDR)	
G-VZIM	Alpha R2160	I. M. Hollingsworth	
G-VZON	ATR-72-212A	Aurigny Air Services Ltd	
G-WAAN	MBB Bö.105DB	PLM Dollar Group Ltd (G-AZOR)	
G-WAAS	MBB Bö.105DBS-4	Bond Air Services Ltd (G-ESAM/G-BUIB/ G-BDYZ)	
G-WABB	Dassault Falcon 900EX	TAG Aviation (UK) Ltd	
G-WABH	Cessna 172S Skyhawk	Blackhawk Aviation Ltd	
G-WACB	Cessna F.152 II	Wycombe Air Centre Ltd	
G-WACE	Cessna F.152 II	Wycombe Air Centre Ltd	
G-WACF	Cessna 152 II	Wycombe Air Centre Ltd	
G-WACG	Cessna 152 II	Wycombe Air Centre Ltd	
G-WACH	Cessna FA.152 II	Wycombe Air Centre Ltd	
G-WACI	Beech 76 Duchess	Wycombe Air Centre Ltd	
G-WACJ	Beech 76 Duchess	Wycombe Air Centre Ltd	
G-WACL	Cessna F.172N	A. G. Arthur (G-BHGG)	
G-WACO	Waco UPF-7	R. F. L. Cuypers/Belgium	
G-WACT	Cessna F.152 II	Durham Tees Flight Training Ltd (G-BKFT)	
G-WACU	Cessna FA.152	Wycombe Air Centre Ltd (G-BJZU)	

Notes	Reg.	Type	Owner or Operator
	G-WACW	Cessna 172P	Technical Power & Maintenance Ltd
	G-WACY	Cessna F.172P	Wycombe Air Centre Ltd
	G-WADI	PA-46-350P Malibu Mirage	Air Malibu AG/Liechtenstein
	G-WADS	Robinson R22 Beta	Whizzard Helicopters (G-NICO)
	G-WAGA	Wag-Aero Wagabond	A. I. Sutherland (G-BNJA)
	G-WAGG	Robinson R22 Beta II	N. J. Wagstaff Leasing
	G-WAGN	Stinson 108-3 Voyager	S. E. H. Ellcome
	G-WAGS	Robinson R44 II	Wagstaff Homes Ltd
	G-WAHL	QAC Quickie	A. A. A. Wahlberg
	G-WAIN	Cessna 550 Citation Bravo	Williams Aviation Ltd
	G-WAIR	PA-32-301 Saratoga	Finningley Aviation
	G-WAIT	Cameron V-77 balloon	C. P. Brown
	G-WAKE	Mainair Blade 912	J. E. Rourke
	G-WAKY	Cyclone AX2000	R. Knight & R. Hinton
	G-WALI	Robinson R44 II	Casdron Enterprises Ltd
	G-WALY	Maule MX-7-180	J. R. Colthurst
	G-WALZ	Best Off Sky Ranger Nynja 912S(1)	R. J. Thomas
	G-WAMS	PA-28R-201 Arrow	Stapleford Flying Club Ltd
	G-WANT	Robinson R22 Beta	M. Lombardi
	G-WAPA	Robinson R44 II	Heli Air Ltd
	G-WARA	PA-28-161 Warrior III	Aviation Rentals
	G-WARB	PA-28-161 Warrior III	OSF Ltd
	G-WARD	Taylor JT.1 Monoplane	R. P. J. Hunter
	G-WARE	PA-28-161 Warrior II	N. M. G. Pearson
	G-WARH	PA-28-161 Warrior III	KN Singles & Twins Aviation Consultants BV
	G-WARO	PA-28-161 Warrior III	T. G. D. Leasing Ltd
	G-WARP	Cessna 182F Sylane	R. D. Fowden (G-ASHB)
	G-WARR	PA-28-161 Warrior II	B. Huda
	G-WARS	PA-28-161 Warrior III	Blaneby Ltd
	G-WARU	PA-28-161 Warrior III	Smart People Don't Buy Ltd
	G-WARV	PA-28-161 Warrior III	Plane Talking Ltd
	G-WARW	PA-28-161 Warrior III	Lomac Aviators Ltd
	G-WARX	PA-28-161 Warrior III	C. M. A. Clark
	G-WARY	PA-28-161 Warrior III	Target Aviation Ltd
	G-WARZ	PA-28-161 Warrior III	Target Aviation Ltd
	G-WASN	Eurocopter EC.135 T2+	Bond Air Services Ltd
	G-WASS	Eurocopter EC.135 T2+	Bond Air Services Ltd
	G-WATJ	Beech B200GT Super King Air	Saxonhenge Ltd
	G-WATR	Christen A1 Husky	S. N. Gregory
	G-WAVA	Robin HR.200/120B	Smart People Don't Buy Ltd
	G-WAVE	Grob G.109B	C. G. Wray
	G-WAVI	Robin HR.200/120B	Plane Talking Ltd (G-BZDG)
	G-WAVN	Robin HR.200/120B	Plane Talking Ltd (G-VECA)
	G-WAVS	PA-28-161 Warrior III	TGD Leasing Ltd (G-WARC)
	G-WAVT	Robin R.2160i	TGD Leasing Ltd (G-CBLG)
	G-WAVV	Robon HR200/120B	TGD Leasing Ltd (G-GORF)
	G-WAVY	Grob G.109B	G-WAVY Group
	G-WAWW	P & M Quik GT450	Oztubs Ltd
	G-WAYS	Lindstrand LBL-105A balloon	Lindstrand Hot Air Balloons Ltd
	G-WAZP	Skyranger 912 (2)	L. V. McClune
	G-WAZZ	Pitts S-1S Special	J. P. Taylor (G-BRRP)
	G-WBEV	Cameron N-77 balloon	T. J. & M. Turner (G-PVCU)
	G-WBLY	Mainair Pegasus Quik	A. J. Lindsey
	G-WBTS	Falconar F-11	W. C. Brown (G-BDPL)
	G-WBVS	Diamond DA.4D Star	G. W. Beavis
	G-WCAO	Eurocopter EC 135T2	Avon & Somerset Constabulary & Gloucestershire Constabulary
	G-WCAT	Colt Flying Mitt SS balloon	I. Chadwick
	G-WCCI	Embraer RJ135BJ Legacy	Altarello Ltd (G-REUB)
	G-WCCP	Beech B200 Super King Air	William Cook Aviation Ltd
	G-WCEI	MS.894E Rallye 220GT	R. A. L. Lucas (G-BAOC)
	G-WCKD	Eurocopter EC130 B4	Batchelor Aviation Ltd (G-CFWX)
	G-WCKM	Best Off Sky Ranger 912(1)	J. Depree & B. Janson
	G-WCRD	Aérospatiale SA.341G Gazelle	MW Helicopters Ltd
	G-WCUB	PA-18 Super Cub 150	P. A. Walley
	G-WCUP	Cameron Z-77 balloon	A. M. Holly
	G-WDEB	Thunder Ax-7-77 balloon	A. Heginbottom
	G-WDEV	Westland SA.341G Gazelle 1	Cropspray Ltd (G-IZEL/G-BBHW)
	G-WDGC	Rolladen-Schneider LS8-18	W. D. G. Chappel (G-CEWJ)

Reg.	Type	Owner or Operator	Notes
G-WDKR	AS.355F1 Ecureuil 2	Cheshire Helicopters Ltd (G-NEXT/G-OMAV)	
G-WEAT	Robinson R44 II	R. F. Brook	
G-WEBI	Hughes 369E	M. Webb	
G-WEBY	Ace Magic Cyclone	B. W. Webster	
G-WEBS	American Champion 7ECA Citabria	P. J. Webb	
G-WEED	Ace Magic Laser	R. D. Leigh	
G-WEEK	Skyranger 912(2)	D. J. Prothero	
G-WEFR	Alpi Pioneer 200-M	Cardiff Backpacker Caerdydd Ltd	
G-WEGO	Robinson R44 II	Helimove Ltd	
G-WELY	Agusta A109E Power	Titan Airways Ltd	
G-WENA	AS.355F2 Ecureuil II	Multiflight Ltd (G-CORR/G-MUFF/G-MOBI)	
G-WEND	PA-28RT-201 Arrow IV	Tayside Aviation Ltd	
G-WERY	SOCATA TB20 Trinidad	WERY Flying Group	
G-WESX	CFM Streak Shadow	M. Catania	
G-WETI	Cameron N-31 balloon	C. A. Butter & J. J. T. Cooke	
G-WFFW	PA-28-161 Warrior II	S. Letheren & D. Jelly	
G-WFLY	Mainair Pegasus Quik	D. E. Lord	
G-WFOX	Robinson R22 Beta II	Rotorfun Aviation	
G-WGCS	PA-18 Super Cub 95	S. C. Thompson	
G-WGHB	Canadair T-33AN Silver Star 3	Parkhouse Aviation	
G-WGSC	Pilatus PC-6/B2-H4 Turbo Porter	D. M. Penny	
G-WGSI	Tanarg/Ixess 13 912S(1)	J. A. Ganderton	
G-WHAL	QAC Quickie	A. A. M. Wahiberg	
G-WHAM	AS.350B3 Ecureuil	Horizon Helicopter Hire Ltd	
G-WHAT	Colt 77A balloon	M. A. Scholes	
G-WHEE	Pegasus Quantum 15-912	Airways Airsports Ltd	
G-WHEN	Tecnam P92-EM Echo	N. Harrison	
G-WHIM	Colt 77A balloon	D. L. Morgan	
G-WHOG	CFM Streak Shadow	B. R. Cannell	
G-WHOO	Rotorway Executive 162F	J. White	
G-WHRL	Schweizer 269C	M. Gardiner	
G-WHST	AS.350B2 Ecureuil	Keltruck Ltd (G-BWYA)	
G-WHYS	ICP MXP-740 Savannah VG Jabiru(1)	D. J. Whysall	
G-WIBB	Jodel D.18	C. J. Bragg	
G-WIBS	CASA 1-131E Jungmann 2000	C. Willoughby	
G-WICH	Clutton FRED Srs II	L. A. Tomlinson	
G-WIFE	Cessna R.182 RG II	Wife 182 Group (G-BGVT)	
G-WIFI	Cameron Z-90 balloon	Trigger Concepts Ltd	
G-WIGY	Pitts S-1S Special	R. E. Welch (G-ITTI)	
G-WIII	Schempp-Hirth Ventus bT	P. Turner & B. Goodyer	
G-WIIZ	Augusta-Bell 206B JetRanger 2	Tiger Helicopters Ltd (G-DBHH/G-AWVO)	
G-WIKI	Europa XS	J. Greenhaigh	
G-WILB	Ultramagic M-105 balloon	A. S. Davidson, B. N. Trowbridge & W. C. Bailey	
G-WILD	Pitts S-1T Special	The Wild Bunch	
G-WILG	PZL-104 Wilga 35	M. H. Bletsoe-Brown (G-AZYJ)	
G-WILT	Ikarus C.42 FB 100	A. E. Lacy-Hulbert	
G-WIMP	Colt 56A balloon	T. & B. Chamberlain	
G-WINA	Cessna 560XL Citation XL	Inclination 1 LLP	
G-WINE	Thunder Ax7-77Z balloon ★	Balloon Preservation Group/Lancing	
G-WINH	EV-97 TeamEurostar UK	H. M. Wooldridge	
G-WINI	SA Bulldog Srs.120/121 (XX546:03)	A. Bole (G-CBCO)	
G-WINK	AA-5B Tiger	B. St. J. Cooke	
G-WINN	Stolp SA.300 Starduster Too	H. Feeney	
G-WINR	Robinson R22	Heli Air Ltd (G-BTHG)	
G-WINS	PA-32 Cherokee Six 300	Cheyenne Ltd	
G-WINT	Pilatus PC-12/47	Air Winton Ltd	
G-WIRL	Robinson R22 Beta	Rivermead Aviation Ltd/Switzerland	
G-WISE	PA-28-181 Archer III	M. Arnold	
G-WISZ	Steen Skybolt	G. S. Reid	
G-WIWI	Sikorsky S-76C	Air Harrods Ltd	
G-WIXI	Avions Mudry CAP-10B	A. R. Harris	
G-WIZI	Enstrom 280FX	AAA Pest Control GmbH	
G-WIZR	Robinson R22 Beta II	Physio Supplies Ltd	
G-WIZS	Mainair Pegasus Quik	G. R. Barker	
G-WIZY	Robinson R22 Beta	Subacoustech Ltd (G-BMWX)	
G-WIZZ	Agusta-Bell 206B JetRanger 2	Rivermead Aviation Ltd	

Notes	Reg.	Type	Owner or Operator
	G-WJAC	Cameron TR-70 balloon	S. J. & J. A. Bellaby
	G-WJAN	Boeing 757-21K	Thomas Cook Airlines Ltd
	G-WJCJ	Eurocopter EC 155B1	Starspeed Ltd
	G-WJCM	CASA 1.131E Jungmann 2000 (S5+B06)	M. L. J. Goff (G-BSFB)
	G-WKNS	Shaw Europa XS	A. L. Wickens
	G-WLAC	PA-18 Super Cub 150	White Waltham Airfield Ltd (G-HAHA/G-BSWE)
	G-WLDN	Robinson R44 Raven	Fly Executive Ltd
	G-WLGC	PA-28-181 Archer III	E. F. Mangion (G-FLUX)
	G-WLKI	Lindstrand LBL-105A balloon	C. Wilkinson
	G-WLLS	Rolladen-Schneider LS8-18	L & A Wells
	G-WLMS	Mainair Blade 912	G. Zerrun
	G-WLSN	Best Off Skyranger 912S (1)	A. Wilson & ptnrs
	G-WLVS	Dassault Falcon 2000EX	Trinity Aviation Ltd
	G-WMAS	Eurocopter EC 135T1	Bond Air Services Ltd
	G-WMLT	Cessna 182Q	P. J. Kloosterman (G-BOPG)
	G-WMTM	AA-5B Tiger	Falcon Flying Group
	G-WNCH	Beech B200 Super King Air	Winch Air Ltd (G-OMGI)
	G-WNSA	Sikorsky S-92A	CHC Scotia Ltd
	G-WNTR	PA-28-161 Warrior II	Fleetlands Flying Group (G-BFNJ)
	G-WOCO	Waco YMF-5C	Classic Aviation Ltd
	G-WOFM	Agusta A109E Power	Quinnasette Ltd (G-NWRR)
	G-WOLF	PA-28 Cherokee 140	K. C. Fitch
	G-WONE	Schempp-Hirth Ventus 2cT	J. P. Wright
	G-WONN	Eurocopter EC135 T2	Bond Air Services Ltd
	G-WOOD	Beech 95-B55A Baron	M. S. Choskey (G-AYID)
	G-WOOF	Enstrom 480	Netcopter.co.uk Ltd & Curvature Ltd
	G-WOOL	Colt 77A balloon	Whacko Balloon Group
	G-WOOO	CZAW Sportcruiser	F. Sayyah & A. Palmer
	G-WORM	Thruster T.600N	Medway Airsports
	G-WOSY	MBB Bö.105DBS/4	Redwood Aviation Ltd (G-PASD/G-BNRS)
	G-WOTW	Ultramagic M-77 balloon	Window on the World Ltd
	G-WOWA	DHC.8-311 Dash Eight	Eastern Airways (G-BRYS)
	G-WOWB	DHC.8-311 Dash Eight	Eastern Airways (G-BRYT)
	G-WOWE	DHC.8-311 Dash Eight.	Eastern Airways (G-BRYI)
	G-WOWI	Van's RV-7	P. J. Wood
	G-WPAS	MDH MD-900 Explorer	Police Aviation Services Ltd
	G-WPDA	Eurocopter EC135 P1	WPD Helicopter Unit
	G-WPDB	Eurocopter EC135 P1	WPD Helicopter Unit
	G-WREN	Pitts S-2A Special	Modi Aviation Ltd
	G-WRFM	Enstrom 280C-UK Shark	A. J. Clark (G-CTSI/G-BKIO)
	G-WRIT	Thunder Ax7-77A balloon	G. Pusey
	G-WRLY	Robinson R22 Beta	Burman Aviation Ltd (G-OFJS/G-BNXJ)
	G-WRWR	Robinson R22 Beta II	MFH Helicopters Ltd
	G-WSKY	Enstrom 280C-UK-2 Shark	B. J. Rutterford (G-BEEK)
	G-WSMW	Robinson R44	M. Wass (G-SGPL)
	G-WSSX	Ikarus C42 FB100	J. M. Crane
	G-WTAV	Robinson R44 II	William Taylor Aviation Ltd
	G-WTEC	Cirrus SR22	B. J. White
	G-WTWO	Aquila AT01	J. P. Wright
	G-WUFF	Shaw Europa	M. A. Barker
	G-WULF	WAR Focke-Wulf Fw.190 (8+)	S. Laver
	G-WVBF	Lindstrand LBL-210A balloon	Virgin Balloon Flights Ltd
	G-WVIP	Beech B.200 Super King Air	Capital Air Charter Ltd
	G-WWAL	PA-28R Cherokee Arrow 180	White Waltham Airfield Ltd (G-AZSH)
	G-WWAY	Piper PA-28-181 Archer II	R. A. Witchell
	G-WWBC	Airbus A.330-243	bmi british midland
	G-WWBD	Airbus A.330-243	bmi british midland
	G-WWBM	Airbus A.330-243	bmi british midland
	G-WWLF	Extra EA.300/L	P. Sapignoli
	G-WWZZ	CZAW Sportcruiser	L. Hogan

Reg.	Type	Owner or Operator	Notes
G-WYAT	CFM Streak Shadow Srs SA	K. Kerr	
G-WYDE	Schleicher ASW-20BL	461 Syndicate	
G-WYKD	Tanarg/Ixess 15 912S(2)	D. L. Turner	
G-WYND	Wittman W.8 Tailwind	R. S. Marriott	
G-WYNE	BAe 125 Srs 800B	Global Flight Solutions Ltd (G-CJAA/G-HCFR/ G-SHEA/G-BUWC)	
G-WYNT	Cameron N-56 balloon	O. James	
G-WYPA	MBB Bö.105DBS/4	Police Aviation Services Ltd	
G-WYSZ	Robin DR.400/100	R. S. M. Fendt (G-FTIM)	
G-WYVN	DG Flugzeugbau DG-1000S	Army Gliding Association	
G-WZOL	RL.5B LWS Sherwood Ranger	D. Lentell (G-MZOL)	
G-WZOY	Rans S.6-ES Coyote II	S. P. Read	
G-WZRD	Eurocopter EC 120B Colibri	Conductia Enterprises Ltd	
G-XAIM	Ultramagic H-31 balloon	G. Everett	
G-XALT	PA-38-112 Tomahawk	P. J. Crowther	
G-XALZ	Rans S6S-116 Super Six	M. R. McNeil	
G-XARV	ARV Super 2	D. J. Burton (G-OPIG/G-BMSJ)	
G-XAVB	Cessna 510 Citation Mustang	Aviation Beauport Ltd	
G-XAVI	PA-28-161 Warrior II	J. R. Santamaria (G-SACZ)	
G-XAXA	BN-2A-26 Islander	Blue Island Air (G-LOTO/G-BDWG)	
G-XAYR	Raj Hamsa X'Air 582 (6)	P. Jordanou	
G-XBAL	Skyringer Nynja 912S(1)	W. G. Gill & N. D. Ewer	
G-XBCI	Bell 206B JetRanger 3	BCI Helicopter Charters Ltd	
G-XBEL	Cessna 560XL Citation XLS	Aviation Beauport Ltd	
G-XBGA	Glaser-Dirks DG500/22 Elan	N. Kelly	
G-XBJT	Aerotechnik EV-97 Eurostar	B. J. Tyre (G-WHOA/G-DATH)	
G-XBLU	Cessna 680 Citation Sovereign	Datel Holdings Ltd	
G-XBOX	Bell 206B JetRanger 3	Castle Air Ltd (G-OOHO/G-OCHC/G-KLEE/ G-SIZL/G-BOSW)	
G-XCBI	Schweizer 269C-1	B. Durkan	
G-XCCC	Extra EA.300/L	P. T. Fellows	
G-XCIT	Alpi Pioneer 300	A. Thomas	
G-XCRJ	Van's RV-9A	R. Jones	
G-XCUB	PA-18 Super Cub 150	M. C. Barraclough	
G-XDUO	Schempp-Hirth Duo Discus xT	G-XDUO Group	
G-XDWE	P & M Quik GT450	R. J. Harper	
G-XELA	Robinson R44 II	A. Yew	
G-XELL	Schleicher ASW-27-18E	S. R. Ell	
G-XENA	PA-28-161 Warrior II	P. Brewer	
G-XERO	CZAW Sportcruiser	M. R. Mosley	
G-XFLY	Lambert Mission M212-100	Lambert Aircraft Engineering BVBA	
G-XHOT	Cameron Z-105 balloon	S. F. Burden	
G-XIII	Van's RV-7	Icarus Flying Group	
G-XIIX	Robinson R22 Beta ★	(Static exhibit)/Blackbushe	
G-XINE	PA-28-161 Warrior II	P. Tee (G-BPAC)	
G-XIOO	Raj Hamsa X'Air 133 (1)	M. Ridgway	
G-XIXI	Evektor EV-97 TeamEurostar UK	J. A. C. Cockfield	
G-XIXX	Glaser-Dirks DG-300 Elan	S. D. Black	
G-XJCB	Sikorsky S-76C	J. C. Bamford Excavators Ltd	
G-XJJM	P & M Pegasus Quik	Mainair Microlight Centre Ltd	
G-XJON	Schempp-Hirth Ventus 2b	J. C. Bastin	
G-XKKA	Diamond KH36 Super Dimona	G-XKKA Group	
G-XLAM	Best Off Skyranger 912S	X-LAM Skyranger Syndicate	
G-XLGB	Cessna 560XL Citation Excel	Tosh Air Ltd	
G-XLII	Schleicher ASW-27-18E	P. M. Wells	
G-XLLL	AS.355F1 Twin Squirrel	MW Helicopters Ltd (G-PASF/G-SCHU)	
G-XLNT	Zenair CH.601XL	Zenair G-XLNT Group	
G-XLTG	Cessna 182S	T. I. M. Paul	
G-XLXL	Robin DR.400/160	L. R. Marchant (G-BAUD)	

Notes	Reg.	Type	Owner or Operator
	G-XMGO	Aeromot AMT-200S Super Ximango	G. McLean & R. P. Beck
	G-XMII	Eurocopter EC 135T1	Merseyside Police Authority
	G-XOAR	Schleicher ASW-27-18E	R. A. Browne
	G-XOIL	AS.355N Twin Squirrel	Firstearl Marine and Aviation Ltd (G-LOUN)
	G-XONE	Canadair CL600-2B16	Gama Aviation Ltd
	G-XPBI	Letov LK-2M Sluka	R. M. C. Hunter
	G-XPDA	Cameron Z-120 balloon	M. Cowling
	G-XPII	Cessna R.172K	The Hawk Flying Group (G-DIVA)
	G-XPWW	Cameron TR-77 balloon	Chalmers Ballong Corps/Sweden
	G-XPXP	Aero Designs Pulsar XP	B. J. Edwards
	G-XRAF	Raj Hamsa X'Air 582(5)	J. Ryan
	G-XRAY	Rand-Robinson KR-2	R. S. Smith
	G-XRED	Pitts S-1C Special	J. E. Rands (G-SWUN/G-BSXH)
	G-XRLD	Cameron A-250 balloon	The Cotswold Balloon Co.Ltd
	G-XRVB	Van's RV-8	P. G. Winters
	G-XRVX	Van's RV-10	N. K. Lamping
	G-XRXR	Raj Hamsa X'Air 582 (1)	R. J. Philpotts
	G-XSAM	Van's RV-9A	D. G. Lucas & S. D. Austen
	G-XSDJ	Europa XS	D. N. Joyce
	G-XSEA	Van's RV-8	H. M. Darlington
	G-XSEL	Silence Twister	Skyview Systems Ltd
	G-XSRF	Europa XS	R. L. W. Frank
	G-XTEE	Edge XT912-B/Streak III	Airborne Australia UK
	G-XTHT	Edge XT912-B/Streak III-B	H. A. Taylor
	G-XTME	Xtremeair XA42	Xtreme Aerobatics Ltd
	G-XTNI	AirBorne XT912-B/Streak	A. J. Parry
	G-XTOR	BN-2A Mk III-2 Trislander	Aurigny Air Services Ltd (G-BAXD)
	G-XTRA	Extra EA.230	C. Butler
	G-XTUN	Westland-Bell 47G-3B1 (XT223)	P. A. Rogers (G-BGZK)
	G-XVAX	Tecnam P2006T	J. Byrne
	G-XVOM	Van's RV-6	A. Baker-Munton
	G-XWEB	Best Off Skyranger 912 (2)	K. B. Woods
	G-XWON	Rolladen-Schneider LS8-18	P. K Carpenter
	G-XXBH	Agusta-Bell 206B JetRanger 3	Coln Aviation Ltd (G-BYBA/G-BHXV/G-OWJM)
	G-XXEB	Sikorsky S-76C	The Queen's Helicopter Flight
	G-XXIV	Agusta-Bell 206B JetRanger 3	Bart Fifty Nine Ltd
	G-XXIX	Schleicher ASW-27-18E	P. R. & A. H. Pentecost
	G-XXRG	Avid Speed Wing Mk.4	R. J. Grainger (G-BWLW)
	G-XXRS	Bombardier BD-700 Global Express	TAG Aviation (UK) Ltd
	G-XXRV	Van's RV-9	D. R. Gilbert & D. Slabbert
	G-XXTB	SOCATA TB20 Trinidad	N. Schaefer (G-KPTT)
	G-XXTR	Extra EA.300/L	Shoreham Extra Group (G-ECCC)
	G-XXVB	Schempp-Hirth Ventus b	R. Johnson
	G-XXZZ	Learjet 60	Gama Aviation Ltd
	G-XYAK	IDA Bacau Yakovlev Yak-52 (69 blue)	R. Davies
	G-XYJY	Best Off Skyranger 912 (2)	A. V. Francis
	G-XYZT	Aeromot AMT-200S Super Ximango	M. Zacharia & B. Chalabi
	G-XZXZ	Robinson R44 II	Ashley Martin Ltd
	G-YAAK	Yakovlev Yak-50	R. J. Luke (G-BWJT)
	G-YAAZ	Gulfstream 550	Ocean Sky (UK) Ltd
	G-YADA	Ikarus C42 FB100	Ikarus Flying Syndicate (Carlisle)
	G-YAGT	Bombardier CL600-2B16 Challenger	Ocean Sky Aircraft Management Ltd
	G-YAKA	Yakovlev Yak-50	M. Chapman
	G-YAKB	Aerostar Yakovlev Yak-52	M. J. Gadsby
	G-YAKC	Yakovlev Yak-52	T. J. Wilson
	G-YAKF	Aerostar Yakovlev Yak-52	B. Gwynett
	G-YAKH	IDA Bacau Yakovlev Yak-52	Plus 7 minus 5 Ltd
	G-YAKI	IDA Bacau Yakovlev Yak-52 (100 blue)	Yak One Ltd
	G-YAKK	Yakovlev Yak-50	A. P. Wilson
	G-YAKM	IDA Bacau Yakovlev Yak-50 (61 red)	Airborne Services Ltd

Reg.	Type	Owner or Operator	Notes
G-YAKN	IDA Bacau Yakovlev Yak-52 (66 red)	Airborne Services Ltd	
G-YAKP	Yakovlev Yak-9	M. V. Rijkse & N. M. R. Richards	
G-YAKR	IDA Bacau Yakovlev Yak-52 (03 white)	G-YAKR Group	
G-YAKT	IDA Bacau Yakovlev Yak-52	G-YAKT Group	
G-YAKU	IDA Bacau Yakovlev Yak-50 (49 red)	D. J. Hopkinson (G-BXND)	
G-YAKV	IDA Bacau Yakovlev Yak-52 (31 grey)	P. D. Scandrett	
G-YAKX	IDA Bacau Yakovlev Yak-52 (27 red)	The X-Flyers Ltd	
G-YAKY	Aerostar Yakovlev Yak-52	W. T. Marriott	
G-YAKZ	IDA Bacau Yakovlev Yak-50 (33 red)	Airborne Services Ltd	
G-YANK	PA-28-181 Archer II	G-YANK Flying Group	
G-YARR	Mainair Rapier	D. Yarr	
G-YARV	ARV Super 2	A. M. Oliver (G-BMDO)	
G-YAWW	PA-28RT-201T Turbo Arrow IV	Barton Aviation Ltd	
G-YBAA	Cessna FR.172J	A. Evans	
G-YCII	LET Yakovlev C-11 (11 yellow)	R. W. Davies	
G-YCUB	PA-18 Super Cub 150	F. W. Rogers	
G-YCUE	Agusta A109A	Oldham Broadway Developments Ltd	
G-YEHA	Schleicher ASW-27	B. L. Cooper	
G-YELL	Murphy Rebel	A. H. Godfrey	
G-YELO	Rotorsport UK MT-03	M. Black	
G-YEOM	PA-31-350 Navajo Chieftain	A. B. Yeoman	
G-YEWS	Rotorway Executive 152	R. Turrell & P. Mason	
G-YFLY	VPM M-16 Tandem Trainer	A. J. Unwin (G-BWGI)	
G-YFUT	Yakovlev Yak-52	R. Oliver	
G-YFZT	Cessna 172S	AB Integro	
G-YIII	Cessna F.150L	Merlin Flying Club Ltd	
G-YIPI	Cessan FR.172K	A. J. G. Davis	
G-YIRO	Campbell Cricket Mk.4	R. Boese (G-KGED)	
G-YJET	Montgomerie-Bensen B.8MR	A. Shuttleworth (G-BMUH)	
G-YKCT	Aerostar Yakovlev Yak-52	F. Koldehofe	
G-YKSO	Yakovlev Yak-50	Classic Displays Ltd	
G-YKSS	Yakovlev Yak-55	T. Ollivier	
G-YKSZ	Aerostar Yakovlev Yak-52 (01 yellow)	Tzarina Group	
G-YKYK	Aerostar Yakovlev Yak-52	K. J. Pilling	
G-YMBO	Robinson R22M Mariner	Rotorfun Aviation	
G-YMFC	Waco YMF	S. J. Brenchley	
G-YMMA	Boeing 777-236ER	British Airways	
G-YMMB	Boeing 777-236ER	British Airways	
G-YMMC	Boeing 777-236ER	British Airways	
G-YMMD	Boeing 777-236ER	British Airways	
G-YMME	Boeing 777-236ER	British Airways	
G-YMMF	Boeing 777-236ER	British Airways	
G-YMMG	Boeing 777-236ER	British Airways	
G-YMMH	Boeing 777-236ER	British Airways	
G-YMMI	Boeing 777-236ER	British Airways	
G-YMMJ	Boeing 777-236ER	British Airways	
G-YMMK	Boeing 777-236ER	British Airways	
G-YMML	Boeing 777-236ER	British Airways	
G-YMMN	Boeing 777-236ER	British Airways	
G-YMMO	Boeing 777-236ER	British Airways	
G-YMMP	Boeing 777-236ER	British Airways	
G-YMMR	Boeing 777-236ER	British Airways	
G-YMMS	Boeing 777-236ER	British Airways	
G-YMMT	Boeing 777-236ER	British Airways	
G-YMMU	Boeing 777-236ER	British Airways	
G-YNOT	D.62B Condor	T. Littlefair (G-AYFH)	
G-YNYS	Cessna 172S Skyhawk	T. V. Hughes	
G-YOBI	Schleicher ASH-25	J. Kangurs	
G-YODA	Schempp-Hirth Ventus 2cT	A. Charlier	
G-YOGI	Robin DR.400/140B	M. M. Pepper (G-BDME)	
G-YOLK	P & M Aviation Quik GT450	M. Austin	
G-YORK	Cessna F.172M	EIMH-Flying Group	

Notes	Reg.	Type	Owner or Operator
	G-YOTS	IDA Bacau Yakovlev Yak-52	YOTS Group
	G-YOYO	Pitts S-1E Special	J. D. L. Richardson (G-OTSW/G-BLHE)
	G-YPDN	Rotorsport UK MT-03	T. M. Jones
	G-YPOL	MDH MD-900 Explorer	West Yorkshire Police Authority
	G-YPRS	Cessna 550 Citation Bravo	Executive Aviation Services Ltd (G-IPAC/G-IPAL)
	G-YPSY	Andreasson BA-4B	D. J. Howell
	G-YRAF	RAF 2000 GTX-SE gyroplane	J. R. Cooper
	G-YRAX	Magni M-24C	C. M. Jones
	G-YRIL	Luscombe 8E Silvaire	C. Potter
	G-YRKS	Robinson R44	Storetec Services Ltd
	G-YROA	Rotorsport UK MTO Sport	J. P. R. McLaren
	G-YROC	Rotorsport UK MT-03	C. V. Catherall
	G-YROH	Rotorsport UK MTO Sport	J. W. G. Andrews
	G-YROI	Air Command 532 Elite	W. B. Lumb
	G-YROJ	RAF 2000 GTX-SE gyroplane	J. R. Mercer
	G-YROM	Rotorsport UK MT-03	A. Wallace
	G-YRON	Magni M-16C Tandem Trainer	A. J. Brent & A. D. Mann
	G-YROO	RAF 2000 GTX-SE gyroplane	D. R. C. Bell
	G-YROP	Magni M-16C Tandem Trainer	Magni Guernsey Flying Group
	G-YROR	Magni M.24C	R. M. Stanley
	G-YROX	Rotorsport UK MT-03	Surplus Art
	G-YROY	Montgomerie-Bensen B.8MR	S. S. Wilson
	G-YROZ	Rotorsport UK Calidus	P. Chaplin
	G-YRRO	AutoGyro Calidus	W. C. Walters
	G-YRUS	Jodel D.140E	W. E. Massam (G-YRNS)
	G-YSMO	Mainair Pegasus Quik	F. Poirot
	G-YSTT	PA-32R-301 Saratoga II HP	A. W. Kendrick
	G-YTLY	Rans S-6-ES Coyote II	Royal Aeronautical Society
	G-YUGE	Schempp-Hirth Ventus cT	E. P. Lambert (G-CFNN)
	G-YUGO	HS.125 Srs 1B/R-522 ★	Fire Section/Dunsfold (G-ATWH)
	G-YULL	PA-28 Cherokee 180E	ASG Leasing Ltd (G-BEAJ)
	G-YUMM	Cameron N-90 balloon	H. Stringer
	G-YUMN	Dassault Falcon 2000	Gama Aviation Ltd
	G-YUPI	Cameron N-90 balloon	MCVH SA/Belgium
	G-YURO	Shaw Europa ★	Yorkshire Air Museum/Elvington
	G-YVES	Alpi Pioneer 300	G-YVES Group
	G-YYAK	Aerostar SA Yak-52	A. Bonnet
	G-YYRO	Magni M-16C Tandem Trainer	J. A. McGill
	G-YYYY	MH.1521C-1 Broussard	Aerosuperbatics Ltd
	G-YZYZ	Mainair Blade 912	P. G. Eastlake
	G-ZAAP	CZAW Sportcruiser	H. Page
	G-ZAAZ	Van's RV-8	P. A. Soper
	G-ZABC	Sky 90-24 balloon	P. Donnelly
	G-ZACE	Cessna 172S	Sywell Aerodrome Ltd
	G-ZACH	Robin DR.400/100	A. P. Wellings (G-FTIO)
	G-ZADA	Best Off Skyranger 912S(1)	B. Bisley
	G-ZAIR	Zenair CH 601HD	J. R. Standring
	G-ZANG	PA-28 Cherokee 140	A. M. Khan
	G-ZANY	Diamond DA40D Star	Altair Aviation Ltd
	G-ZAPH	Bell 206B JetRanger 3	WPD Helicopter Unit (G-DBMW)
	G-ZAPK	BAe 146-200QC	Titan Airways Ltd (G-BTIA/G-PRIN)
	G-ZAPN	BAe 146-200QC	Titan Airways Ltd (G-BPBT)
	G-ZAPO	BAe 146-200QC	Trident Aviation Leasing Services (Jersey) Ltd (G-BWLG/G-PRCS)
	G-ZAPV	Boeing 737-3Y0	Titan Airways Ltd (G-IGOC)
	G-ZAPW	Boeing 737-3L9	Titan Airways Ltd (G-BOZB/G-IGOX)
	G-ZAPX	Boeing 757-256	Titan Airways Ltd
	G-ZAPY	Robinson R22 Beta	Heli Air Ltd (G-INGB)
	G-ZAPZ	Boeing 737-33A	Titan Airways Ltd
	G-ZARI	AA-5B Tiger	ZARI Aviation Ltd (G-BHVY)
	G-ZARV	ARV Super 2	P. R. Snowden
	G-ZAVI	Ikarus C42 FB100	B. & J. M. Cooper
	G-ZAZA	PA-18 Super Cub 95	G. J. Harry, The Viscount Goschen

Reg.	Type	Owner or Operator	Notes
G-ZAZZ	Lindstrand LBL-120A balloon	Idea Balloon SAS Di Stefano Travaglia and Co./Italy	
G-ZBED	Robinson R22 Beta	P. D. Spinks	
G-ZBLT	Cessna 182S Skylane	Cessna 182S Group/Ireland	
G-ZBOP	PZL-Bielsko SZD-36A Cobra 15	S. Bruce	
G-ZEBO	Thunder Ax8-105 S2 balloon	S. M. Waterton	
G-ZEBY	PA-28 Cherokee 140	G. Gee (G-BFBF)	
G-ZECH	CZAW Sportcruiser	P. J. Reilly	
G-ZEIN	Slingsby T.67M Firefly 260	R. C. P. Brookhouse	
G-ZELE	Westland Gazelle HT.Mk.2	London Helicopter Centres Ltd (G-CBSA)	
G-ZENA	Zenair CH.701UL	A. N. Aston	
G-ZENI	Zenair CH.601HD Zodiac	P. P. Plumley	
G-ZENN	Schempp-Hirth Ventus 2cT	Z. Marczynski	
G-ZENR	Zenair CH.601HD Zodiac	A. D. Revill (G-BRJB)	
G-ZENY	Zenair CH.601HD Zodiac	T. R. & B. K. Pugh	
G-ZEPI	Colt GA-42 gas airship	P. A. Lindstrand (G-ISPY/G-BPRB)	
G-ZERO	AA-5B Tiger	Emery-Little Insurance Brokers Ltd	
G-ZETA	Lindstrand LBL-105A balloon	S. Travaglia/Italy	
G-ZEXL	Extra EA.300/L	2 Excel Aviation Ltd	
G-ZFOX	Denney Kitfox Mk.2	S. M. Hall	
G-ZGZG	Cessna 182T	J. Noble	
G-ZHKF	Escapade 912(2)	C. D. & C. M. Wills	
G-ZHWH	Rotorway Executive 162F	B. Alexander	
G-ZIGI	Robin DR.400/180	D. C. R. Writer	
G-ZIGY	Europa XS	K. D. Weston	
G-ZIII	Pitts S-2B	W. A. Cruickshank (G-CDBH)	
G-ZINC	Cessna 182S	Zinc Ahead Ltd (G-VALI)	
G-ZING	Learjet 35A	Agrevia Holdings Ltd (G-ZENO/G-GAYL)	
G-ZINT	Cameron Z-77 balloon	D. Ricci	
G-ZIPA	Rockwell Commander 114A	Roissy Technical Services Ltd (G-BHRA)	
G-ZIPE	Agusta A109E Power Elite	Noble Foods Ltd	
G-ZIPI	Robin DR.400/180	A. J. Cooper	
G-ZIPR	Hawker 750	Premiair Business Aviation Ltd	
G-ZIPY	Wittman W.8 Tailwind	K. J. Nurcombe	
G-ZIRA	Z-1RA Stummelflitzer	D. H. Pattison	
G-ZITZ	AS.355F2 Twin Squirrel	Heli Aviation Ltd	
G-ZIZI	Cessna 525 CitationJet	Ortac Air Ltd	
G-ZIZZ	Agusta A.109 II	Fortis Property Investment LLP	
G-ZJET	Cessna 510 Citation Mustang	C. J. Reston	
G-ZLLE	Aérospatiale SA.341G Gazelle	MW Helicopters Ltd	
G-ZLOJ	Beech A36 Bonanza	W. D. Gray	
G-ZMAM	PA-28-181 Archer II	Z. Mahmood (G-BNPN)	
G-ZMED	Learjet 35A	Air Medical Fleet Ltd, Argyll Ltd (G-JETL)	
G-ZODY	Zenair CH.601UL Zodiac	Sarum AX2000 Group	
G-ZOGT	Cirrus SR20	M. Banbury	
G-ZONX	Moulai Sonex	FFFF Flyers Group	
G-ZOOG	Tecnam P2006T	Polarb Air Ltd	
G-ZOOH	Balony Kubicek BB20XR balloon	Balony Kubicek Spol Sro	
G-ZOOL	Cessna FA.152	W. J. D. Tollett (G-BGXZ)	
G-ZORO	Shaw Europa	N. T. Read	
G-ZOSA	Champion 7GCAA	R. McQueen	
G-ZRZZ	Cirrus SR22	EKM Systems Ltd	
G-ZSDB	PA-28-236 Dakota	Dakota Air Services LLP (G-BPCX)	
G-ZSIX	Schleicher ASW-27-18E	S. J. Riddington	
G-ZSKD	Cameron Z-90 balloon	M. J. Gunston	
G-ZSKY	Best Off Sky Ranger Swift 912S(1)	J. E. Lipinski	
G-ZTED	Shaw Europa	J. J. Kennedy	
G-ZTWO	Staaken Z-2 Flitzer	S. J. Randle	

Notes	Reg.	Type	Owner or Operator
	G-ZUMI	Van's RV-8	D. R. CairnsT
	G-ZVIP	Beech 200 Super King Air	Capital Air Charter Ltd (G-SAXN/G-OMNH)
	G-ZVKO	Edge 360	P. J. Tomlinson
	G-ZWIP	Silence Twister	Zulu Glasstek Ltd (G-TWST)
	G-ZXCL	Extra EA.300/L	2 Excel Aviation Ltd
	G-ZXEL	Extra EA.300/L	2 Excel Aviation Ltd
	G-ZXLL	Extra EA.300/L	2 Excel Aviation Ltd
	G-ZXZX	Learjet 45	Gama Aviation Ltd
	G-ZYAK	IDA Bacau Yakovlev YAK-52	J. A. H. Van Rossom
	G-ZZAC	Aerotechnik EV-97 Eurostar	Cosmik Aviation Ltd
	G-ZZAJ	Schleicher ASH-26E	A.T. Johnstone
	G-ZZDD	Schweizer 269C	Fly 7 Helicopters LLP (G-OCJK)
	G-ZZDG	Cirrus SR20 G2	Little Mouse Productions Ltd
	G-ZZEL	Westland Gazelle AH.1	Tregenna Castle Hotel Ltd
	G-ZZIJ	PA-28-180 Cherokee C	G-ZZIJ Group (G-AVGK)
	G-ZZLE	Westland Gazelle AH.2	Estates (UK) Management Ltd (G-CBSE)
	G-ZZMM	Enstrom 480B	Fly 7 Helicopters LLP (G-TOIL)
	G-ZZOE	Eurocopter EC 120B	J. F. H. James
	G-ZZOW	Medway Eclipse	M. Belemet
	G-ZZSA	Eurocopter EC.225LP Super Puma	Bristow Helicopters Ltd
	G-ZZSB	Eurocopter EC.225LP Super Puma	Bristow Helicopters Ltd
	G-ZZSC	Eurocopter EC.225LP Super Puma	Bristow Helicopters Ltd
	G-ZZSD	Eurocopter EC.225LP Super Puma	Bristow Helicopters Ltd
	G-ZZSE	Eurocopter EC.225LP Super Puma	Bristow Helicopters Ltd
	G-ZZSF	Eurocopter EC.225LP Super Puma	Bristow Helicopters Ltd
	G-ZZSG	Eurocopter EC.225LP Super Puma	Bristow Helicopters Ltd
	G-ZZSI	Eurocopter EC.225LP Super Puma	Bristow Helicopters Ltd (G-CGES)
	G-ZZTT	Schweizer 269C	Heli Andaluz SL/Spain
	G-ZZXX	P & M Quik GT450	R. G. Street
	G-ZZZA	Boeing 777-236	British Airways
	G-ZZZB	Boeing 777-236	British Airways
	G-ZZZC	Boeing 777-236	British Airways
	G-ZZZS	Eurocopter EC.120B Colibri	London Helicopter Centres Ltd

ISLE OF MAN REGISTER

Notes	Reg.	Type	Owner or Operator
	M-AAAD	Bombardier CL600-2B16 Challenger	Gulf Wings (IOM) Ltd
	M-AAES	Bombardier CL600-2B16 Challenger	Eliston Enterprises Ltd
	M-ABCD	Dassault Falcon 2000	ASP Aviation Ltd
	M-ABCM	Bombardier BD100-1A10 Challenger 300	Cameron Industries Inc
	M-ABCU	Bombardier CL600-2B16 Challenger	MeHoria Ltd
	M-ABDL	Hawker 4000	SB Leasing Ireland Ltd
	M-ABDP	Hawker 800XP	Kitlan Ltd
	M-ABDQ	Eurocopter EC.135 P2+	Knightspeed Ltd
	M-ABDS	Cessna 208B Grand Caravan	Randgold Resources Ltd
	M-ABDU	Pilatus PC-12/47E	Guernsey PC-12 Ltd
	M-ABEB	Dassault Falcon 900EX	Dassault Aviation SA
	M-ABEG	Aerospatiale ATR-72-202	Aircraft Solutrions Lux SARL
	M-ABEM	Airbus A.320-214	CIT Aerospace International
	M-ACPT	BAe. 125 Srs.1000	Remo Investments Ltd
	M-ACRO	Eurocopter AS.350B3 Ecureuil	F. Allani
	M-ADAM	Pilatus PC-12/47	ADAM Aircraft Services Ltd
	M-AFAJ	Dassault Falcon 900EX	Elan Finance Management SA
	M-AGGY	Cessna 550 Citation II	Maudib GmbH Deutschland
	M-AGIC	Cessna 680 Citation Sovereign	Trustair Ltd
	M-AIRS	Learjet 60	Maiton Air LLP
	M-AIRU	Bombardier CL600-2B16 Challenger	Setfair Holdings Ltd
	M-AJDM	Cessna 525A Citationjet CJ2	Mazia Investments Ltd
	M-AJOR	Hawker 900XP	INEOS Aviation LLP
	M-AJWA	Bombardier BD700-1A11 Global Express	Global Express Management Ltd
	M-AKAK	Embraer 135BJ Legacy	AAK Company
	M-AKAR	Sikorsky S-76C	Starspeed Ltd
	M-AKVI	Bombardier BD100-1A10 Challenger 300	AK VI Ltd

BRITISH CIVIL REGISTRATIONS

Isle of Man

Reg.	Type	Owner or Operator	Notes
M-ALCB	Pilatus PC-12/47E	M. S. Bartlett	
M-ALEX	Learjet 60	Berta Finance Ltd	
M-ALII	Bombardier CL600-2B16 Challenger 604	Western Gulf Assets Ltd	
M-ALMA	Dassault Falcon 7X	Armad Ltd	
M-ALRV	Dassault Falcon 2000EX	Lodgings 2000 LP	
M-ALUN	BAe 125 Srs.700A	Briarwood Products Ltd	
M-AMAN	Pilatus PC-12	Pilatus PC-12 Centre UK Ltd	
M-AMND	Dassault Falcon 2000EX	Doha Capital Ltd	
M-ANGO	Bombardier CL600-2B16 Challenger	Waylawn Ltd	
M-ANIE	Gulfstream 550	Pobedy Corporation	
M-ANTA	Bombardier CL600-2B190 Challenger 85	Tathra International Holdings Inc	
M-APWC	Learjet 60	Trans Aviation Ltd	
M-ARIA	Hawker 850XP	Swiss Aviation IM Ltd	
M-ARIE	Pilatus PC-12/47E	Guernsey PC-12 Ltd	
M-ARTY	Pilatus PC-12/47E	Creston (UK) Ltd	
M-ASHI	Bombardier CL600-2B16 Challenger	Beckett Holding Ltd	
M-ASRI	Bombardier BD700-1A10 Global Express	YYA Aviation Ltd	
M-ASRY	Bombardier BD100-1A10 Challenger 300	Celina Aviation Ltd	
M-ATAK	Bombardier BD700-1A10 Global 5000	Greenway Investment Assets Ltd	
M-ATHS	Pilatus PC-12/47E	Altis Partners (Aviation) Ltd	
M-ATOS	Dassault Falcon 900EX	Banton Overseas Ltd	
M-ATPS	Gulfstream V-SP	Tarona Ltd	
M-AUTO	Leajet 60	Federation Internationalede l'Automobile	
M-AXIM	CessnaT.206H Turbo Stationair	C. D. B. Cope	
M-AZAG	BAe.125 Srs.800B	Mazag	
M-AZIZ	Boeing 737-505	Azizi Group Ltd	
M-BEST	Cessna 750 Citation X	Lanara Ltd	
M-BETS	Rockwell Commander 695A	Aldersey Aviation Ltd	
M-BIGG	Bombardier CL600-2B16 Challenger	Signal Aviation Ltd	
M-BONO	Cessna 172N Skyhawk II	J. McCandless	
M-BTLT	Bombardier BD100-1A10 Challenger 300	Bombardier Transportation GmbH	
M-BWFC	Cessna 560XL Citation XLS	Limonia Ltd	
M-BXRH	Cessna 185A	R. E. M. Holmes	
M-CCCP	Bombardier BD700-1A11 Global 5000	Heda Airlines Ltd	
M-CELT	Dassault Falcon 7X	Cravant Ltd	
M-CHEM	Dassault Falcon 200EX	Hampshire Aviation LLP	
M-CHLG	Bombardier CL600-1A11 Challenger	Albion Holdings Ltd	
M-CICO	Dassault Falcon 50	BZ Air Ltd	
M-CIMO	Dassault Falcon 2000EX	Dassault Aviation SA	
M-CLAB	Bombardier BD100-1A10 Challenger 300	Shamrock Trading Ltd	
M-CMAF	Embraer EMB-135BJ	ATS 1011 Leasing Ltd	
M-COOL	Cessna 510 Citation Mustang	E. Keats	
M-DADI	Dassault Falcon 900DX	Rubicon Capital Consulting Co.Ltd	
M-DARA	Dassault Falcon 200LX	Trident Investment Ltd	
M-DAVE	Pilatus PC-12/47E	Pilatus PC-12 Centre UK Ltd	
M-DBOY	Agusta A.109C	Herair Ltd	
M-DEJB	Dassault Falcon 200	Baron Aircraft Management SA	
M-DINO	Cessna 525 Citationjet CJ1	J. N. Bentley	
M-DKVL	Gulfstream 450	Fiordani Holding Ltd	
M-DSCL	Embraer 135BJ Legacy	Legacy Aviation Ltd	
M-EAGL	Dassault Falcon 900EX	Faycroft Finance	
M-EANS	Bombardier BD100-1A10 Challenger 300	YH Aviation Ltd	
M-ECJI	Dassault Falcon 10	Fleet International Aviation and Finance Ltd	
M-EDOK	Bombardier BD100-1A10 Challenger 300	Jarvirne Ltd	
M-EGGA	Beech B200 Super King Air	Langley Aviation Ltd	
M-ELON	Cessna 525B Citationjet CJ3	Sleepwell Aviation Ltd	
M-EMLI	Agusta A109E Power	Tycoon Aviation Ltd	
M-ERCI	Bombardier CL600-2B16 Challenger	J & S Holding Ltd	
M-ERIL	Pilatus PC-12/47E	Confidentia Aviation Ltd	
M-ERRY	Sikorsky S-76B	Trustair Ltd	
M-ESGR	Embraer ERJ135 Legacy	Hermes Executive Aviation Ltd	
M-ETIS	Boeing 727-2XB	Azer Management Ltd	
M-EVAN	Bombardier BD100-1A10Challenger 300	Marcus Evans (Aviation) Ltd	
M-EXPL	Eurocopter AS.355N Ecureuil 2	Select Plant Hire Co.Ltd	
M-FAHD	Boeing 727-76	Prime Air Corporation	
M-FALC	Falcon 900EX	Noclaf Ltd	

305

Isle of Man

Notes	Reg.	Type	Owner or Operator
	M-FBVZ	Bombardier CL600-2B16 Challenger	Qaltin Enterprises Ltd
	M-FINK	BAe. 125 Srs.1000B	B. T. Fink
	M-FIVE	Beech B300 Super King Air 350	Larvotto LP
	M-FLYI	Beech B300 Super King Air 350	Avtrade Ltd
	M-FMHG	Gulfstream IV SP	Future Aviation Ltd
	M-FOUR	Beech G36 Bonanza	Quadra Aviation LP
	M-FROG	Beech 390 Premier 1	White and Cope Aviation LLP
	M-FRZN	Hawker 850XP	Iceland Foods Ltd
	M-FUAD	Gulfstream 550	Future Pipe Aviation Ltd
	M-FZMH	Bombardier CL600-2B19 Global Express	AK VI Ltd
	M-GACB	Dassault Falcon 10	Valiant Aviation Ltd
	M-GBAL	Bombardier BD700-1A10 Global Express	Noclaf Ltd
	M-GCCC	Beech B.350i King Air	NG2 SA
	M-GFOR	Gulfstream IV	Star Oriental International Ltd
	M-GLEX	Bombardier BD700-1A10 Global Express	Pytonian Trade & Invest SA
	M-GLOB	Bombardier BD700-1A10 Global Express	Colvic Investment Holdings Ltd
	M-GOLF	Cessna FR.182RG	P. R. Piggin & C. J. Harding
	M-GOLX	Dassault Falcon 2000EX	LX Aviation (SPL) Ltd
	M-GPIK	Dassault Falcon 50EX	Dassault Falcon Leasing Ltd
	M-GRAN	Bombardier BD700-1A11 Global 5000	Starflight Investments Ltd
	M-GSKY	Bombardier BD700-1A10 Global Express	Jerand Holdings Ltd
	M-GVSP	Gulfstream 550	Business Universe Ltd
	M-GYQM	Bombardier BD700-1A10 Global Express	Head Win Group Ltd
	M-GZOO	Gulfstream 200	Sentrus Overseas Ltd
	M-HARP	Pilatus PC-12/47E	Harpin Ltd
	M-HAWK	Hawker 800XP	INEOS Aviation LLP
	M-HDAM	BAe 125 Srs.800B	ABG Air Ltd
	M-HELI	Eurocopter EC.155-B1	Flambards Ltd
	M-HNOY	Bombardier CL600-2B16 Challenger 605	Merhav Aviation LP
	M-HOIL	Learjet 60	Begal Air Ltd
	M-HOTB	Gulfstream V SP	Darwin Air Ltd
	M-HSNT	Bombardier BD100-1A10 Challenger 300	Unisky Ltd
	M-HSXP	Hawker 800XP	HEWE Ltd
	M-IABU	Airbus A.340-313	Klaret Aviation Ltd
	M-ICKY	Pilatus PC12/45	Saxon Logistics Ltd
	M-IDAS	Agusta A109E Power	Trustair Ltd
	M-IFES	Bombardier CL600-1A11 Challenger	Inflite Aviation (IOM) Ltd
	M-IFLY	Pilatus PC-12/47E	N. J. Vetch
	M-IGHT	Learjet 60	High Wing Aviation Ltd
	M-IGOR	Learjet 60	Condamine Enterprises Ltd
	M-IKAT	Dassault Falcon 2000EX	F2000 LX Ltd
	M-IKEL	Dassault Falcon 2000LX	Second Aircraft Co.Ltd
	M-IMAK	Embraer EMB-135BJ Legacy 600	Donard Trading Ltd
	M-INOR	Hawker 900XP	INEOS Aviation LLP
	M-IPHS	Gulfstream 550	Islands Aviation Ltd
	M-IRNE	Hawker 850XP	R. N. Edmiston
	M-ISKY	Cessna 550 Citation Bravo	MYSKY LLP
	M-ISLA	Bombardier CL600-2B19 Challenger 850	Knightsdene Ltd
	M-ISLE	Cessna 680 Citation Sovereign	Bakewell Industries Ltd
	M-IVSP	Gulfstream IV SP	Travcorp Air Transportation Ltd
	M-JACK	Beech B200GT King Air	Jetstream Aviation Ltd
	M-JANP	Bombardier BD700-1A10 Global Express	Joannou and Paraskevaides (Aviation) Ltd
	M-JCPO	HS.125 Srs.700A	Saucar Ltd
	M-JETI	BAe 125 Srs 800B	Cassel Invest Ltd
	M-JETT	Dassault Falcon 200	Piraeus Leasing Chrimatodotikes Mishoseis SA
	M-JETZ	Dassault Falcon 2000EX	Avtorita Holdings Ltd
	M-JJTL	Pilatus PC-12/47E	L. Uggia, J. P. Huth & K. Giannamore
	M-JMMM	Dassault Falcon 900B	Executive Aviation (SPV) Ltd
	M-JNJL	Bombardier BD700-1A11 Global Express	Global Thirteen Worldwide Resources Ltd
	M-JOLY	Hawker 900XP	Rooksmead Capital Ltd
	M-JSMN	Bombardier BD700-1A11 Global 5000	Jasmin Aviation Ltd
	M-JSTA	Bombardier CL600-2B16 Challenger	Jetsteff Aviation Ltd

Reg.	Type	Owner or Operator
M-KATE	Airbus A.319-133	Sophar Property Holding
M-KELY	Embraer EMB-500 Phenom 100	Kelly Air Ltd
M-KENF	Hawker 4000 Horizon	Avalanche Aviation Ltd
M-KING	Beech C.90A King Air	Villocq Investments Ltd
M-KPCO	Embraer EMB-135BJ Legacy	M-KPCO Holding Co.Ltd
M-KRRR	Learjet 55	R. Rogner
M-LCJP	Hawker 900XP	Yolenal Ltd
M-LEKT	Robin DR.400/180	T. D. Allan, P. & J. P. Bromley
M-LEYS	Beech C.90GT King Air	Heres Aviation Ltd
M-LIFE	Bombardier BD100-1A10 Challenger 300	NY Jets Transporter Ltd
M-LION	Hawker 900XP	Lion Invest and Trade Ltd
M-LJGI	Dassault Falcon 2000Easy	Ven Air
M-LRJT	Learjet 40	Chemiplastica Aviation Ltd
M-LUNA	Eurocopter MBB BK-117C-2	Flambards Ltd
M-LVIA	Eurocopter AS.365N3 Dauphin 2	Flambards Ltd
M-MACH	Embraer EMB-500 Phenom 100	Mach Air Ltd
M-MANX	Cessna 425 Conquest	Suas Investments Ltd
M-MDDE	CL-600-2B16 Challenger	Fielding Overseas Ltd
M-MHDH	Cessna 510 Citation Mustang	Herrenknecht Aviation GmbH
M-MHMH	Cessna 525B Citationjet CJ3	Herrenknecht Aviation GmbH
M-MIDO	Raytheon Hawker 800XP	Barbican Holdings Ltd
M-MIKE	Cessna 525B Citationjet CJ3	M. F. Jacobson
M-MMAS	Bombardier BD700-1A10 Global Express	Jana Aviation Ltd
M-MNAA	Bombardier BD700-1A10 Global Express	JAPAT AG (Isle of Man)
M-MNBB	Dassault Falcon 7X	JAPAT AG (Isle of Man)
M-MNDD	Dassault Falcon 900EX	JAPAT AG (Isle of Man)
M-MOMO	Gulfstream V SP	Fayair (Jersey) Co Ltd
M-MRBB	Learjet 45	Boultbee Aviation 3 LLP
M-MSGG	Gulfstream G200	ARTOC Prague
M-MTPO	Bombardier CL600-2A12 Challenger	Marimax Jets Ltd
M-MTRM	Beech 390 Premier 1A	Rumit Aviation Ltd
M-NEWT	Bombardier BD100-1A10 Challenger	Stirling Aviation Properties LLP
M-NGSN	Pilatus PC-12/47E	N. Stolt-Nielson
M-NHOI	Bombardier CL600-2B16 Challenger	Hatta Investments Ltd
M-NICE	Gulfstream 200	M-NICE Ltd
M-NINE	Beech G58 Baron	Larvotto LP
M-NLYY	PA-42-1000 Cheyenne 400LS	Factory Leasing Ltd
M-NOEL	Bombardier BD100-1A10 Challenger	ABS Service Ltd
M-NOLA	Bombardier CL600-2B16 Challenger	Nola Aviation Ltd
M-ODKZ	Dassault Falcon 900EX	Skylane LP
M-OGUL	Agusta A109S Grand	Medway Leasing Ltd
M-OLAR	Liberty XL-2	C. Partington
M-OLEG	Embraer 135BJ Legacy	Hermitage Air Ltd
M-OLLE	Hawker 750	Dunard Engineering Ltd
M-OLTT	Pilatus PC-12/47E	One Luxury Travel LLP
M-OMAN	Dassault Falcon 7X	RUWI Ltd
M-OMOO	Sikorsky S-76C	Seaplus 2 (IOM) Ltd
M-ONAV	Hawker 900XP	Monavia Ltd
M-ONDE	Eurocopter MBB BK.117C2	Peyton Ltd
M-ONEM	Gulfstream 550	G550 Ltd
M-ONEY	Agusta A109E Power	Tycoon Aviation Ltd
M-ONTY	Sikorsky S-76C	Trustair Ltd
M-OODY	Cessna 525B Citationjet CJ3	Futures Aviation Services Ltd
M-OOSE	PA-46-500TP Malibu Meridian	Global Domain Names Ltd
M-OOUN	Hawker 800XP	United Airgroup Corporation
M-OPAL	Pilatus PC-12/47E	G-GYC Ltd
M-OPED	PA-32-301XTC Saratoga	Hock Lai Cham
M-OSPB	Gulfstream G200	G200 Ltd
M-OTOR	Beech C90A King Air	Pektron Group Ltd
M-OUSE	Cessna 510 Citation Mustang	Mouse (IOM) Ltd
M-OUTH	Diamond DA.42 Twin Star	Sky Fly LP Inc
M-OZZA	Bombardier BD100-1A10 Challenger 300	Casam International Ltd
M-PACF	Eurocopter EC135 P2+	Starspeed Ltd
M-PARK	Cessna 525 CitationJet	Parkridge (Aviation) Ltd
M-PBKI	Gulfstream IV SP	GIV-SP Air Service Ltd
M-PHML	American General AG-5B Tiger	I. J. Ross & J. R. Shannon
M-POWR	Beech C.90A King Air	Northside Aviation Ltd
M-PREI	Raytheon RB390 Premier 1	Craft Air SA
M-PRIT	Pilatus PC-12/47E	J. Pritchard

Notes	Reg.	Type	Owner or Operator
	M-PRVT	Cessna 750 Citation X	Unifox Holdings Ltd
	M-RACE	Hawker 850XP	First Aircraft Leasing Co.Ltd
	M-RBUS	Airbus A.319-115CJ	Belville Investment Ltd
	M-RCCG	Embraer EMB-135BJ Legacy 650	Russian Copper Co. Holdings Ltd
	M-RIDE	BD-700-1A11 Global 5000	Jesper Continental SA
	M-RKAY	Raytheon 390 Premier 1A	Sunseeker Corporate Aviation Ltd
	M-RKSL	Bombardier BD700-1A10 Global Express	Angel Aviation Ltd
	M-RLDR	Pilatus PC-12/45	RDLR Air Ltd
	M-RLIV	Bombardier CL600-2B16 Challenger	Mobyhold Ltd
	M-ROLL	Dassault Falcon 7X	Pacelli Beteiligungs GmbH and Co KG
	M-RONE	Dassault Falcon 2000EX	Ocean Sky Aircraft Management Ltd
	M-ROWL	Dassault Falcon 900EX	M. Rowley
	M-RUAT	Bombardier BD700-1A10 Global Express	Vipjet Ltd
	M-RURU	Falcon 900B	Rozita Ltd
	M-RWGW	Learjet 45	Woodlands Air LLP
	M-SAIL	Pilatus PC-12/47E	G. G. & L. G. Gordon
	M-SAIR	Falcon 900B	W. A. Developments International Ltd
	M-SAPT	Hawker 900XP	Sapetro Aviation Ltd
	M-SBAH	Embraer ERJ190ECJ Lineage 1000	National Lineage M-SBAH Holding Co.Ltd
	M-SCMG	Dassault Falcon 7X	BlueSky International Management Ltd
	M-SGCR	Cessna 550 Citation Bravo	Labraid Ltd
	M-SHEP	SOCATA TBM-850	L. W. & J. K. Shephard
	M-SKSM	Bombardier BD700-1A11 Global	Tesker Management Ltd
	M-SKZL	Bombardier CL600-2B16 Challenger	Kerzner Investment Management Ltd
	M-SMJJ	Cessna 414A	Gull Air Ltd
	M-SMKM	Cirrus SR20	K. Mallet
	M-SNAP	Cessna 560XL Citation XLS	AMS Ltd
	M-SNER	Dassault Falcon 2000EX	Wincor Aviation Establishment
	M-SPEC	Beech B350 Super King Air	Specsavers Aviation Ltd
	M-SPEX	Beech B350 Super King Air	Specsavers Aviation Ltd
	M-SPOR	Beech B200 King Air	Select Plant Hire Co.Ltd
	M-SQAR	Gulfstream V-SP	M Square Aviation Ltd
	M-SRNE	Eurocopter MBB-BK.117C-2	Serena Aviation Ltd
	M-STCO	Dassault Falcon F2000EX	STC (Bermuda) Ltd
	M-STEP	Gulfstream G150	ArtJet Ltd
	M-SUEC	PA-32-301XTC Saratoga	H. L. Chan
	M-SVGN	Cessna 680 Citation Sovereign	Vocalion Ltd
	M-SYGB	Beech B.200GT Super King Air	Rialus Ltd
	M-TAKE	Bombardier CL600-2B19 Challenger 850	Caropan Company SA
	M-TANA	Dassault Falcon 2000	F2000 Ltd
	M-TEAM	Cessna 525B Citationjet CJ1+	Mistral Aviation Ltd
	M-TKFR	Gulfstream V SP	Tele-Fonika Kable Sp
	M-TNTJ	Learjet 55	TNT Airways SA
	M-TOMS	Pilatus PC-12/47E	C J Airways Ltd
	M-TOPI	Bombardier CL600-2B16 Challenger	Gladiator Flight Ltd
	M-TRIX	Bombardier CL600-2B16 Challenger	Universal Air Services Ltd
	M-TSRI	Beech C.90GT King Air	Timpson Ltd
	M-UKHA	Hawker 800XP	Nebula III Ltd
	M-UNIS	Bombardier BD700-1A10 Global Express	Lapwing Ltd
	M-UPCO	Cessna 525B CitationJet CJ3	Ulla Popken GmbH
	M-URKA	Sikorsky S-76B	Starspeed Ltd
	M-URUS	Boeing 737-7GC	Ingram Services Ltd
	M-USCA	SOCATA TBM-850	Sterna Aviation Ltd
	M-USHY	Cessna 441 Conquest	Flying Dogs Ltd
	M-USTG	Cessna 510 Citation Mustang	OSM Aviation Ltd
	M-VANG	Bombardier BD700-1A10 Global Express	Elderberry Ltd
	M-VBBQ	Beech 390 Premier 1A	Asia Universal Jet Ltd
	M-VBPO	Beech 390 Premier 1A	Asia Universal Jet Ltd
	M-VQBI	Bombardier BD700-1A10 Global Express	Altitude X3 Ltd
	M-VRNY	Gulfstream 550	Mirtos Ltd
	M-VSSK	Bombardier CL600-2B16 Challenger	Clear Horizon Ltd
	M-WHAT	Eurocopter EC.135T2+	Starspeed Ltd
	M-WIND	Dassault Falco 2000	Dassault Aviation SA
	M-WING	Dassault Falcon 900EX	Certeco Aviation Ltd
	M-WLLM	Beech C.90GTI King Air	Wilpot Ltd
	M-WMWM	Cessna 525A Citationjet CJ2	Standard Aviation Ltd
	M-WOOD	Cessna 550 Citation Bravo	Horizon Air LLP

Reg.	Type	Owner or Operator	Notes
M-XHEC	Eurocopter EC155B	Flambards Ltd	
M-YAAA	Bombardier BD700-1A10 Global Express	Glenn Eagles Research LLP	
M-YAIR	Hawker 390 Premier 1A	RB209 IOM Ltd	
M-YBBJ	Boeing 737-7HE BBJ	Hamilton Jets Ltd	
M-YBJK	Gulfstream 550	AC Executive Aircraft (2011) Ltd	
M-YBST	Bombardier CL600-2B16 Challenger	Kilmarnock Management Ltd	
M-YBUB	Pilatus PC-12/45	H. Nathanson	
M-YCUP	Embraer EMB-135BJ Legacy	Reatex Invest SA	
M-YEDC	Cessna 525B CitationJet CJ3	Air Charter Scotland Ltd	
M-YEDT	Gulfstream 100	Opal Consulting LLC	
M-YFLY	Bombardier BD100-1A10 Challenger 300	Apollo Traders Ltd	
M-YGIV	Gulfstream IV	Al-Sahab Ltd	
M-YGLK	Gulfstream 450	Overseas Operation Ltd	
M-YHOP	Agusta A109S Grand	Lemsage Ltd	
M-YJET	Dassault Falcon 2000Easy	My Jet Ltd	
M-YLEO	Pilatus PC-12/47E	Guernsey PC-12 Ltd	
M-YNJC	Embraer RJ135BJ Legacy	Hermes Executive Aviation Ltd	
M-YNNS	Dassault Falcon 7X	NS Falcon Ltd	
M-YONE	Bombardier CL600-2B16 Challenger	Inflite Aviation (IOM) Ltd	
M-YRGN	Embraer ERJ-170-200LR	Celestial Aviation Trading 71 Ltd	
M-YRGO	Embraer ERJ-170-200LR	ECC Leasing Co.Ltd	
M-YRGP	Embraer ERJ-170-200LR	ECC Leasing Co.Ltd	
M-YRGR	Airbus A.310-324F	Nilgiri Hills Leasing Ltd	
M-YRGS	Airbus A.310-324F	Kaveri Leasing Ltd	
M-YRGT	Airbus A.310-324F	Godvari Leasing Ltd	
M-YSAI	Bombardier BD700-1A10 Global 5000	Capital Investment Worldwide	
M-YSKY	Raytheon 390 Premier 1A	RB209 IOM Ltd	
M-YTOY	Embraer EMB-500 Phenom 100	TD Aviation IOM Ltd	
M-YULI	Bombardier BD700-1A11 Global Express	Primevalue Trading Ltd	
M-YUNI	Bombardier CL600-2B16 Challenger	Unitrans Management Ltd	
M-YWAY	Gulfstream IV SP	Blue Sky Leasing Ltd	
M-YZZT	Cirrus SR22T	Stamp Aviation Ltd	
M-ZELL	Cessna 208 Caravan	Ridler Verwaltungs und Vermittlungs GmbH	
M-ZUMO	Pilatus PC-12/47	C. C. H. Way Ltd	

G-ADJJ DH.82 Tiger Moth. *Tom Cole*

G-AJEE Auster J/1 Autocrat. *Peter R. March*

G-AKIN M.38 Messenger 2A. *Allan Wright*

G-ASSS Cessna 172E. *Tom Cole*

G-BYXN Grob G.115E Tutor. *Peter R. March*

G-CFVC Schleicher ASK-13. *Peter R. March*

G-CGIW Sikorsky S-76C. *Peter R. March*

G-DHCZ DHC.2 Beaver 1. *Tom Cole*

G-ECAN DH.84 Dragon. *Peter R. March*

G-ECOG DHC.8 Dash Eight 402 of Flybe. *Allan Wright*

G-FAVC DH.80A Puss Moth. *Peter R. March*

G-GMPB BN-2T-4S Defender 4000. *Allan Wright*

G-JMCL Boeing 737-322. *Peter R. March*

G-LCYO Embraer ERJ190-100SR of BA Cityflyer. *Allan Wright*

G-NSOF Robin HR.200/120B. *Allan Wright*

G-RIHN Dan Rihn DR.107 One Design. *Tom Cole*

G-RSCU Agusta A.109E. *Peter R. March*

G-RVMZ Van's RV-8. *Peter R. March*

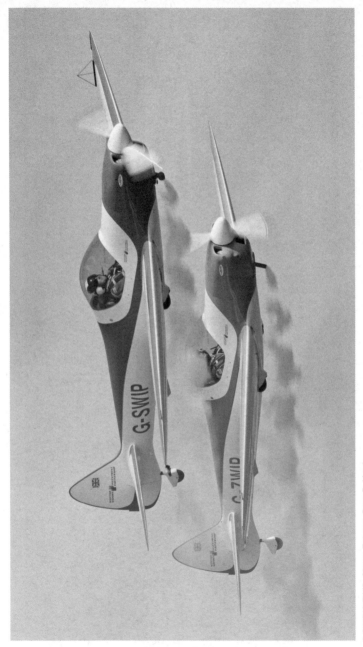

G-SWIP/G-ZWIP Silence Twisters. *Peter R. March*

G-TMOL TB20 Trinidad. *Allan Wright*

G-TRYX Enstrom 480B. *Allan Wright*

G-WIGY Pitts S-1S Special. *Allan Wright*

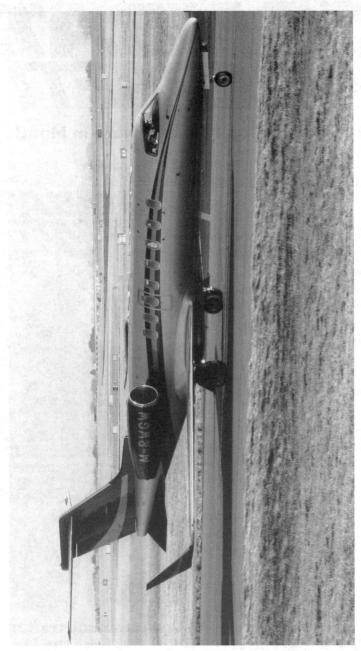

M-RWGW Learjet 45. *Allan Wright*

COMBAT AIRCRAFT MONTHLY

The World's Top Military Aviation Monthly

Renowned as the world's top military aviation magazine, *Combat Aircraft Monthly* is the magazine of choice for modern military aviation. Produced in US and Europe editions, the magazine covers military aviation subjects from around the world, from combat accounts from the cockpit over Afghanistan to air force overviews and emerging aerospace industry stories. *Combat Aircraft Monthly* delivers all the latest news, with added value from expert analysis, opinion and views from the front line of military aviation.

Combat Aircraft Monthly is the military aviation magazine that sets the pace, often with world exclusives, the best and most authoritative features every month, and all supported by imagery from the world's leading aviation photographers. With each issue packed with extensive news coverage and exciting features, *Combat Aircraft Monthly* delivers everything for the military aviation enthusiast in one magazine!

SUBSCRIBE ONLINE: www.combataircraft.net
SUBS HOTLINE: 0844 245 6931 for the UK
+44 1795 592 814 for overseas enquiries

Military to Civil Cross-Reference

Serial carried	Civil identity	Serial carried	Civil identity
001	G-BYPY	1377 (Portuguese AF)	G-BARS
1	G-BPVE	1747 (Portuguese AF)	G-BGPB
6G-ED (Luftwaffe)	G-BZOB	2345 (RFC)	G-ATVP
9 (Soviet AF)	G-OYAK	3066	G-AETA
09 (DOSAAF)	G-BVMU	3072:72 (USN)	G-TEXN
10 (DOSAAF)	G-BTZB	3349 (RCAF)	G-BYNF
10 (DOSAAF)	G-CBMD	3397:174 (USN)	G-OBEE
11 (Soviet AF)	G-YCII	4034 (Luftwaffe)	G-CDTI
26 (USAAC)	G-BAVO	4406:12 (USN)	G-ONAF
26 (DOSAAF)	G-BVXK	4513:1 (French AF)	G-BFYO
27 (Soviet AF)	G-YAKX	5964 (RFC)	G-BFVH
27 (USN)	G-BRVG	6136:205 (USN)	G-BRUJ
27 (USAAC)	G-AGYY	7198/18 (Luftwaffe)	G-AANJ
27 (Soviet AF)	G-YAKX	7797 (USAAF)	G-BFAF
42 (Soviet AF)	G-CBRU	8178:FU-178 (USAF)	G-SABR
43:SC (USAF)	G-AZSC	8449M (RAF)	G-ASWJ
44 (DOSAAF)	G-BXAK	9917	G-EBKY
49 (USAAF)	G-KITT	01420 (Polish AF but in Korean colours)	G-BMZF
50 (DOSAAF)	G-CBPM	14863 (USAAF)	G-BGOR
50 (DOSAAF)	G-CBRW	16693:693 (RCAF)	G-BLPG
50 (DOSAAF)	G-EYAK	18013:013 (RCAF)	G-TRIC
52 (DOSAAF)	G-BWVR	18393:393 (RCAF)	G-BCYK
55 (DOSAAF)	G-BVOK	18671:671 (RCAF)	G-BNZC
67 (DOSAAF)	G-CBSL	20310:310 (RCAF)	G-BSBG
68 (Chinese AF)	G-BVVG	21261:261 (RCAF)	G-TBRD
69 (Russian AF)	G-XYAK	21509 (US Army)	G-UHIH
78 (French Army)	G-BIZK	24550 (US Army)	G-PDOG
82:8 (French AF)	G-CCVH	24582 (US Army)	G-VDOG
93 (DOSAAF)	G-JYAK	28521:TA-521 (USAF)	G-TVIJ
100 (DOSAAF)	G-YAKI	30146 (Yugoslav Army)	G-BSXD
112 (USAAC)	G-BSWC	30149 (Yugoslav Army)	G-SOKO
113 (Kuwait AF)	G-CFBK	31145:G-26 (USAAF)	G-BBLH
118 (USAAC)	G-BSDS	3-1923 (USAAF)	G-BRHP
124 (French Army)	G-BOSJ	31952 (USAAF)	G-BRPR
143 (French AF)	G-MSAL	39624:D-39 (USAAF)	G-BVMH
156 (French AF)	G-NIFE	40467:19 (USN)	G-BTCC
161 (Irish Air Corps)	G-CCCA	56321:U-AB (Royal Norwegian AF)	G-BKPY
168 (RFC)	G-BFDE	80105 (US Air Service)	G-CCBN
174 (Royal Netherlands Navy)	G-BEPV	80425:WT-4 (USN)	G-RUMT
177 (Irish Air Corps)	G-BLIW	111836:JZ-6 (USN)	G-TSIX
311 (Singapore AF)	G-MXPH	115042:TA-042 (USAF)	G-BGHU
347	G-AWYI	115227 (USN)	G-BKRA
379 (USAAC)	G-ILLE	115302:TP (USMC)	G-BJTP
422/15 (Luftwaffe)	G-AVJO	115373 (USAAF)	G-AYPM
423 / 427 (Royal Norwegian AF)	G-AMRK	115684 (USAAF)	G-BKVM
425 (Oman AF)	G-SOAF	121714:201-B (USN)	G-RUMM
441 (USN)	G-BTFG	124485:DF-A (USAAF)	G-BEDF
450/17 (Luftwaffe)	G-BVGZ	126922:503 (USN)	G-RADR
503 (Hungarian AF)	G-BRAM	150225:123 (USMC)	G-AWOX
540 (USAAF)	G-BCNX	18-2001 (USAAF)	G-BIZV
669 (USAAC)	G-CCXA	18-5395:CDG (French Army)	G-CUBJ
781-32 (Spanish AF)	G-BPDM	238410:A-44 (USAAF)	G-BHPK
854 (USAAC)	G-BTBH	314887 (USAAF)	G-AJPI
897:E (USN)	G-BJEV	315509:W7-S (USAAF)	G-BHUB
99+26 (Luftwaffe)	G-BZGL	329405:A-23 (USAAF)	G-BCOB
99+32 (Luftwaffe)	G-BZGK	329417 (USAAF)	G-BDHK
1018 (Polish AF)	G-ISKA	329471:F-44 (USAAF)	G-BGXA
1102:102 (USN)	G-AZLE	329601:D-44 (USAAF)	G-AXHR
1104 (Royal Saudi AF)	G-SMAS	329854:R-44 (USAAF)	G-BMKC
1125 (Kuwaiti AF)	G-CFBK	329934:B-72 (USAAF)	G-BCPH
1130 (Royal Saudi AF)	G-VPER	330238:A-24 (USAAF)	G-LIVH
1164:64 (USAAC)	G-BKGL	330485:C-44 (USAAF)	G-AJES
1211(North Korean AF)	G-MIGG	343251:27 (USAAC)	G-NZSS
1342 (Soviet AF)	G-BTZD	413521:5Q-B (USAAF)	G-MRLL
1363 (Portuguese AF)	G-DHPM	413704: 87-H (USAAF)	G-BTCD
1373 (Portuguese AF)	G-CBJG	413926: E2-S (USAAF)	G-CGOI

Serial carried	Civil identity	Serial carried	Civil identity
414419:LH-F (USAAF)	G-MSTG	F8010:Z	G-BDWJ
433915 (USAAF)	G-PBYA	F8614	G-AWAU
436021 (USAAF)	G-BWEZ	G-48-1 (Class B)	G-ALSX
454467:J-44 (USAAF)	G-BILI	H5199	G-ADEV
454537:J-04 (USAAF)	G-BFDL	J-1573 (Swiss AF)	G-VICI
461748:Y (USAF)	G-BHDK	J-1605 (Swiss AF)	G-BLID
472035 (USAAF)	G-SIJJ	J-1632 (Swiss AF)	G-VNOM
472216:HO-M (USAAF)	G-BIXL	J-1758 (Swiss AF)	G-BLSD
474008:VF-R (USAAF)	G-PSIR	J-4021 (Swiss AF)	G-HHAC
479744:M-49 (USAAF)	G-BGPD	J-4083 (Swiss AF)	G-EGHH
479766:D-63 (USAAF)	G-BKHG	J7326	G-EBQP
480015:M-44 (USAAF)	G-AKIB	J9941:57	G-ABMR
480133:B-44 (USAAF)	G-BDCD	K1786	G-AFTA
480173:57-H (USAAF)	G-RRSR	K1930	G-BKBB
480321:H-44 (USAAF)	G-FRAN	K2048	G-BZNW
480480:E-44 (USAAF)	G-BECN	K2050	G-ASCM
480636:A-58 (USAAF)	G-AXHP	K2059	G-PFAR
480723:E5-J (USAAF)	G-BFZB	K2075	G-BEER
480752:E-39 (USAAF)	G-BCXJ	K2227	G-ABBB
493209 (US ANG)	G-DDMV	K2567	G-MOTH
542447 (USAF)	G-SCUB	K2572	G-AOZH
2632019 (Chinese AF)	G-BXZB	K2585	G-ANKT
41-33275:CE (USAAF)	G-BICE	K2587	G-BJAP
42-25068:WZ (USAAF)	G-CDVX	K3241	G-AHSA
42-35870:129 (USN)	G-BWLJ	K3661	G-BURZ
42-58678:IY (USAAF)	G-BRIY	K3731	G-RODI
42-78044 (USAAF)	G-BRXL	K4259:71	G-ANMO
42-84555:EP-H (USAAF)	G-ELMH	K5054	G-BRDV
43-35943 (USN)	G-BKRN	K5414:XV	G-AENP
44-79609:44-S (USAAF)	G-BHXY	K5600	G-BVVI
44-80594 (USAAF)	G-BEDJ	K5673	G-BZAS
44-83184 (USAAF)	G-RGUS	K5674	G-CBZP
51-7692 (French AF)	G-TROY	K7985	G-AMRK
51-11701A:AF258 (USAF)	G-BSZC	K8203	G-BTVE
51-15319 (USAAF)	G-FUZZ	K8303:D	G-BWWN
54-2445 (USAF)	G-OTAN	L2301	G-AIZG
A-10 (Swiss AF)	G-BECW	L6906	G-AKKY
A16-199:SF-R (RAAF)	G-BEOX	N-294 (RNeth AF)	G-KAXF
A17-48 (RAAF)	G-BPHR	N500	G-BWRA
A-57 (Swiss AF)	G-BECT	N1854	G-AIBE
A-806 (Swiss AF)	G-BTLL	N1977:8 (French AF)	G-BWMJ
A8226	G-BIDW	N3200	G-CFGJ
B595:W	G-BUOD	N3788	G-AKPF
B1807	G-EAVX	N4877:MK-V	G-AMDA
B2458:R	G-BPOB	N5182	G-APUP
B6401	G-AWYY	N5195	G-ABOX
C1904:Z	G-PFAP	N5199	G-BZND
C3009	G-BFWD	N5719	G-CBHO
C3011:S	G-SWOT	N5903:H	G-GLAD
C4918	G-BWJM	N6-766 (Royal Australian Navy)	G-VYPO
C4994	G-BLWM	N6290	G-BOCK
C5430	G-CCXG	N6452	G-BIAU
C9533:M	G-BUWE	N6466	G-ANKZ
D-692	G-BVAW	N6537	G-AOHY
D5397/17 (Luftwaffe)	G-BFXL	N6720:VX	G-BYTN
D7889	G-AANM	N6797	G-ANEH
D8084	G-ACAA	N6847	G-APAL
D8096:D	G-AEPH	N6965:FL-J	G-AJTW
E-15 (Royal Netherlands AF)	G-BIYU	N9191	G-ALND
E3B-143 (Spanish AF)	G-JUNG	N9192:RCO-N	G-DHZF
E3B-153:781-75 (Spanish AF)	G-BPTS	P2902:DX-X	G-ROBT
E3B-350:05-97 (Spanish AF)	G-BHPL	P6382:C	G-AJRS
E449	G-EBJE	P9374	G-MKIA
E8894	G-CDLI	R-151 (RNethAF)	G-BIYR
F141:G	G-SEVA	R-163 (RNethAF)	G-BIRH
F235:B	G-BMDB	R-167 (RNethAF)	G-LION
F904	G-EBIA	R1914	G-AHUJ
F938	G-EBIC	R3821:UX-N	G-BPIV
F943	G-BIHF	R4118:UP-W	G-HUPW
F943	G-BKDT	R4922	G-APAO
F5447:N	G-BKER	R4959:59	G-ARAZ
F5459:Y	G-INNY	R5136	G-APAP

Serial carried	Civil identity	Serial carried	Civil identity
R5172:FIJ-E	G-AOIS	FJ777 (RCAF)	G-BIXN
R5250	G-AODT	FR886	G-BDMS
S1287	G-BEYB	FS628	G-AIZE
S1579:571	G-BBVO	FT391	G-AZBN
S1581:573	G-BWWK	FX301:FD-NQ	G-TXAN
T5854	G-ANKK	FZ626:YS-DH	G-AMPO
T5879:RUC-W	G-AXBW	HB275	G-BKGM
T6562	G-ANTE	HB751	G-BCBL
T6953	G-ANNI	HD-75 (R Belgian AF)	G-AFDX
T7230	G-AFVE	HG691	G-AIYR
T7281	G-ARTL	HM580	G-ACUU
T7793	G-ANKV	JF343:JW-P	G-CCZP
T7794	G-ASPV	JV579:F	G-RUMW
T7798	G-ANZT	KB889:NA-I	G-LANC
T7842	G-AMTF	KD345:130-A	G-FGID
T7909	G-ANON	KF584:RAI-X	G-RAIX
T8191	G-BWMK	KF729	G-BJST
T9707	G-AKKR	KG651	G-AMHJ
T9738	G-AKAT	KK116	G-AMPY
T9768	G-AIUA	KN353	G-AMYJ
U-0247 (Class B identity)	G-AGOY	LB264	G-AIXA
U-80 (Swiss AF)	G-BUKK	LB312	G-AHXE
U-95 (Swiss AF)	G-BVGP	LB323	G-AHSD
U-99 (Swiss AF)	G-AXMT	LB367	G-AHGZ
U-108 (Swiss AF)	G-BJAX	LB375	G-AHGW
U-110 (Swiss AF)	G-PTWO	LF858	G-BLUZ
V-54 (Swiss AF)	G-BVSD	LZ766	G-ALCK
V3388	G-AHTW	MB293	G-CFGI
V7497	G-HRLI	MH434:ZD-B	G-ASJV
V9312	G-CCOM	MJ627:9G-P	G-BMSB
V9367:MA-B	G-AZWT	ML407:OU-V	G-LFIX
V9673:MA-J	G-LIZY	MP425	G-AITB
W2718	G-RNLI	MS824 (French AF)	G-AWBU
W5856:A2A	G-BMGC	MT197	G-ANHS
W9385:YG-L	G-ADND	MT438	G-AREI
X4276	G-CDGU	MT818	G-AIDN
Z2033:N/275	G-ASTL	MV268:JE-J	G-SPIT
Z5140:HA-C	G-HURI	MW401	G-PEST
Z5207	G-BYDL	MW763:HF-A	G-TEMT
Z5252:GO-B	G-BWHA	NJ633	G-AKXP
Z7015:7-L	G-BKTH	NJ673	G-AOCR
Z7197	G-AKZN	NJ695	G-AJXV
Z7288	G-AHGD	NJ719	G-ANFU
AB196	G-CCGH	NJ889	G-AHLK
AP506	G-ACWM	NL750	G-AOBH
AP507:KX-P	G-ACWP	NL985	G-BWIK
AR213:PR-D	G-AIST	NM181	G-AZGZ
AR501:NN-A	G-AWII	NX534	G-BUDL
BB697	G-ADGT	NX611:LE-C/DX-C	G-ASXX
BB807	G-ADWO	PL965:R	G-MKXI
BE505:XP-L	G-HHII	PL983	G-PRXI
BI-005 (RNethAF)	G-BUVN	PS853:C	G-RRGN
BM597:JH-C	G-MKVB	PT462:SW-A	G-CTIX
CW-BG (Luftwaffe)	G-BXBD	PT879	G-BYDE
DE208	G-AGYU	RG333	G-AIEK
DE470	G-ANMY	RG333	G-AKEZ
DE623	G-ANFI	RH377	G-ALAH
DE673	G-ADNZ	RL962	G-AHED
DE992	G-AXXV	RM221	G-ANXR
DF112	G-ANRM	RN218:N	G-BBJI
DF128:RCO-U	G-AOJJ	RR232	G-BRSF
DF155	G-ANFV	RT486:PF-A	G-AJGJ
DF198	G-BBRB	RT520	G-ALYB
DG590	G-ADMW	RT610	G-AKWS
EM720	G-AXAN	RX168	G-BWEM
EN224	G-FXII	SM520:KJ-1	G-ILDA
EP120:AE-A	G-LFVB	SM969:D-A	G-BRAF
ES.1-4 (Spanish AF)	G-BUTX	SX336:105-VL	G-KASX
FB226:MT-A	G-BDWM	TA634:8K-K	G-AWJV
FE695:94	G-BTXI	TA719:6T	G-ASKC
FE788	G-CTKL	TA805:FX-M	G-PMNF
FH153	G-BBHK	TD248:CR-S	G-OXVI

Serial carried	Civil identity	Serial carried	Civil identity
TE184:D	G-MXVI	WF877	G-BPOA
TE517	G-JGCA	WG308:8	G-BYHL
TJ534	G-AKSY	WG316	G-BCAH
TJ569	G-AKOW	WG321:G	G-DHCC
TJ652	G-AMVD	WG348	G-BBMV
TJ672:TS-D	G-ANIJ	WG350	G-BPAL
TJ704:JA	G-ASCD	WG407:67	G-BWMX
TS798	G-AGNV	WG422:16	G-BFAX
TW439	G-ANRP	WG465	G-BCEY
TW467	G-ANIE	WG469:72	G-BWJY
TW511	G-APAF	WG472	G-AOTY
TW536:TS-V	G-BNGE	WG719	G-BRMA
TW591:N	G-ARIH	WJ358	G-ARYD
TW641	G-ATDN	WJ368	G-ASZX
TX213	G-AWRS	WJ945:21	G-BEDV
TX310	G-AIDL	WK163	G-BVWC
VF512:PF-M	G-ARRX	WK436	G-VENM
VF516	G-ASMZ	WK512:A	G-BXIM
VF526:T	G-ARXU	WK514	G-BBMO
VF581	G-ARSL	WK517	G-ULAS
VL348	G-AVVO	WK522	G-BCOU
VL349	G-AWSA	WK549	G-BTWF
VM360	G-APHV	WK577	G-BCYM
VN799	G-CDSX	WK585	G-BZGA
VP955	G-DVON	WK586:V	G-BXGX
VP981	G-DHDV	WK590:69	G-BWVZ
VR192	G-APIT	WK609:93	G-BXDN
VR249:FA-EL	G-APIY	WK611	G-ARWB
VR259:M	G-APJB	WK624	G-BWHI
VS356	G-AOLU	WK628	G-BBMW
VS610:K-L	G-AOKL	WK630	G-BXDG
VS623	G-AOKZ	WK633:A	G-BXEC
VV612	G-VENI	WK640:C	G-BWUV
VX113	G-ARNO	WK642:94	G BXDP
VX118	G-ASNB	WL626:P	G-BHDD
VX147	G-AVIL	WM167	G-LOSM
VX281	G-RNHF	WP308:572CU	G-GACA
VX927	G-ASYG	WP321	G-BRFC
VZ638:HF	G-JETM	WP788	G-BCHL
VZ728	G-AGOS	WP790:T	G-BBNC
WA576	G-ALSS	WP795:901	G-BVZZ
WA577	G-ALST	WP800:2	G-BCXN
WA591:FMK-Q	G-BWMF	WP803	G-HAPY
WB565:X	G-PVET	WP805:D	G-MAJR
WB569:R	G-BYSJ	WP808	G-BDEU
WB571:34	G-AOSF	WP809:78 RN	G-BVTX
WB585:M	G-AOSY	WP840:9	G-BXDM
WB588:D	G-AOTD	WP857:24	G-BDRJ
WB615:E	G-BXIA	WP859:E	G-BXCP
WB652:V	G-CHPY	WP860:6	G-BXDA
WB654:U	G-BXGO	WP896	G-BWVY
WB671:910	G-BWTG	WP901:B	G-BWNT
WB697:95	G-BXCT	WP903	G-BCGC
WB702	G-AOFE	WP925:C	G-BXHA
WB703	G-ARMC	WP928:D	G-BXGM
WB711	G-APPM	WP929:F	G-BXCV
WB726:E	G-AOSK	WP930:J	G-BXHF
WB763:14	G-BBMR	WP970:12	G-BCOI
WD286	G-BBND	WP971	G-ATHD
WD292	G-BCRX	WP983:B	G-BXNN
WD305	G-ARGG	WP984:H	G-BWTO
WD310:B	G-BWUN	WR360:K	G-DHSS
WD327	G-ATVF	WR410:N	G-BLKA
WD331:J	G-BXDH	WR410	G-DHUU
WD363:5	G-BCIH	WR421	G-DHTT
WD373:12	G-BXDI	WR470	G-DHVM
WD379:K	G-APLO	WT333	G-BVXC
WD390:68	G-BWNK	WT933	G-ALSW
WD413	G-VROE	WV198:K	G-BJWY
WE569	G-ASAJ	WV318:D	G-FFOX
WE724:062	G-BUCM	WV322:Y	G-BZSE
WF118	G-DACA	WV372:R	G-BXFI

Serial carried	Civil identity	Serial carried	Civil identity
WV493:29	G-BDYG	XP924	G-CVIX
WV740	G-BNPH	XR240	G-BDFH
WV783	G-ALSP	XR241	G-AXRR
WZ507:74	G-VTII	XR246	G-AZBU
WZ662	G-BKVK	XR486	G-RWWW
WZ711	G-AVHT	XR502:Z	G-CCUP
WZ847:F	G-CPMK	XR537:T	G-NATY
WZ868:H	G-ARMF	XR538:01	G-RORI
WZ872:E	G-BZGB	XR595:M	G-BWHU
WZ879	G-BWUT	XR673:L	G-BXLO
WZ882:K	G-BXGP	XR724	G-BTSY
XA880	G-BVXR	XR944	G-ATTB
XD693:Z-Q	G-AOBU	XR991	G-MOUR
XE489	G-JETH	XS111	G-TIMM
XE601	G-ETPS	XS165:37	G-ASAZ
XE685:861/VL	G-GAII	XS235	G-CPDA
XE856	G-DUSK	XS587	G-VIXN
XE956	G-OBLN	XS765	G-BSET
XF114	G-SWIF	XT223	G-XTUN
XF597:AH	G-BKFW	XT420:606	G-CBUI
XF603	G-KAPW	XT435:430	G-RIMM
XF690	G-MOOS	XT634	G-BYRX
XF785	G-ALBN	XT671	G-BYRC
XF836:J-G	G-AWRY	XT787	G-KAXT
XG160:U	G-BWAF	XT788:316	G-BMIR
XG164:A	G-PRII	XT793:456	G-BZPP
XG452	G-BRMB	XV130:R	G-BWJW
XH134	G-OMHD	XV134:P	G-BWLX
XH558	G-VLCN	XV137	G-CRUM
XJ389	G-AJJP	XV268	G-BVER
XJ398	G-BDBZ	XW289:73	G-JPVA
XJ615	G-BWGL	XW293:Z	G-BWCS
XJ729	G-BVGE	XW310	G-BWGS
XJ771	G-HELV	XW324:K	G-BWSG
XK417	G-AVXY	XW325:E	G-BWGF
XK895:19/CU	G-SDEV	XW333:79	G-BVTC
XK896	G-RNAS	XW354	G-JPTV
XK940:911	G-AYXT	XW422:3	G-BWEB
XL426	G-VJET	XW423:14	G-BWUW
XL500	G-KAEW	XW433	G-JPRO
XL502	G-BMYP	XW613	G-BXRS
XL571:V	G-HNTR	XW635	G-AWSW
XL573	G-BVGH	XW784:VL	G-BBRN
XL577:V	G-BXKF	XW853	G-IBNH
XL587	G-HPUX	XW854:46/CU	G-TIZZ
XL602	G-BWFT	XW858:C	G-ONNE
XL621	G-BNCX	XW866:E	G-BXTH
XL714	G-AOGR	XX406:P	G-CBSH
XL809	G-BLIX	XX432	G-CDNO
XL929	G-BNPU	XX467:86	G-TVII
XL954	G-BXES	XX513:10	G-CCMI
XM223:J	G-BWWC	XX514	G-BWIB
XM370:10	G-BVSP	XX515:4	G-CBBC
XM424	G-BWDS	XX518:S	G-UDOG
XM479:54	G-BVEZ	XX521:H	G-CBEH
XM553	G-AWSV	XX524:04	G-DDOG
XM575	G-BLMC	XX525:8	G-CBJJ
XM655	G-VULC	XX528:D	G-BZON
XM685:513/PO	G-AYZJ	XX534:B	G-EDAV
XM819	G-APXW	XX537:C	G-CBCB
XN351	G-BKSC	XX538:O	G-TDOG
XN437	G-AXWA	XX543:F	G-CBAB
XN441	G-BGKT	XX546:03	G-WINI
XN459:N	G-BWOT	XX549:6	G-CBID
XN498	G-BWSH	XX550:Z	G-CBBL
XN637:03	G-BKOU	XX551:E	G-BZDP
XP242	G-BUCI	XX554	G-BZMD
XP254	G-ASCC	XX561:7	G-BZEP
XP279	G-BWKK	XX611:7	G-CBDK
XP282	G-BGTC	XX612:A, 03	G-BZXC
XP355	G-BEBC	XX614:V	G-GGRR
XP907	G-SROE	XX619:T	G-CBBW

Serial carried	Civil identity	Serial carried	Civil identity
XX621:H	G-CBEF	ZA652	G-BUDC
XX622:B	G-CBGZ	ZA730	G-FUKM
XX624:E	G-KDOG	ZB500	G-LYNX
XX626:02, W	G-CDVV	ZB627:A	G-CBSK
XX628:9	G-CBFU	ZB646:59/CU	G-CBGZ
XX629:V	G-BZXZ	2+1:7334 Luftwaffe	G-SYFW
XX630:5	G-SIJW	3+ (Luftwaffe)	G-BAYV
XX631:W	G-BZXS	4+ (Luftwaffe)	G-BSLX
XX636:Y	G-CBFP	4-97/MM52801 (Italian)	G-BBII
XX638	G-DOGG	07 (Russian AF)	G-BMJY
XX658:07	G-BZPS	8+ (Luftwaffe)	G-WULF
XX667:16	G-BZFN	F+IS (Luftwaffe)	G-BIRW
XX668:1	G-CBAN	BU+CC (Luftwaffe)	G-BUCC
XX692:A	G-BZMH	BU+CK (Luftwaffe)	G-BUCK
XX693:07	G-BZML	CF+HF (Luftwaffe)	EI-AUY
XX694:E	G-CBBS	DM+BK (Luftwaffe)	G-BPHZ
XX695:3	G-CBBT	GM+AI (Luftwaffe)	G-SCTH
XX698:9	G-BZME	LG+01 (Luftwaffe)	G-AYSJ
XX699:F	G-CBCV	LG+03 (Luftwaffe)	G-AEZX
XX700:17	G-CBEK	KG+EM (Luftwaffe)	G-ETME
XX702:P	G-CBCR	NJ+C11 (Luftwaffe)	G-ATBG
XX704	G-BCUV	S4+A07 (Luftwaffe)	G-BWHP
XX707:4	G-CBDS	S5+B06 (Luftwaffe)	G-WJCM
XX885	G-HHAA	6J+PR (Luftwaffe)	G-AWHB
XZ239	G-BZYD	57-H (USAAC)	G-AKAZ
XZ934:U	G-CBSI	97+04 (Luftwaffe)	G-APVF
XZ937:Y	G-CBKA	+14 (Luftwaffe)	G-BSMD
ZA250	G-VTOL	146-11083 (5)	
ZA634:C	G-BUHA	G-BNAI	

G-RADR/126922 Douglas AD-4NA Skyraider. *Allan Wright*

Republic of Ireland Civil Registrations

Reg.	Type (†False registration)	Owner or Operator	Notes
EI-ABI	DH.84 Dragon	Aer Lingus Charitable Foundation (EI-AFK)	
EI-AED	Cessna 120	E. McNeill & P. O'Reilly	
EI-AEE	Auster 3/1 Autocrat	B. J. Hogan	
EI-AEF	Cessna 120	J. Halligan	
EI-AFE	Piper J3C-65 Cub	4 of Cubs Flying Group	
EI-AFF	B.A. Swallow 2	J. J. Sullivan & ptnrs	
EI-AGD	Taylorcraft Plus D	B. & K. O'Sullivan	
EI-AGJ	Auster J/1 Autocrat	T. G. Rafter	
EI-AHI	DH.82A Tiger Moth	High Fidelity Flyers	
EI-AKM	Piper J-3C-65 Cub	J. A. Kent	
EI-ALP	Avro 643 Cadet	J.C. O'Loughlin (stored)	
EI-AMK	Auster J/1 Autocrat	J. J. Sullivan	
EI-AMY	Auster J/1N Alpha	T. Lennon	
EI-ANT	Champion 7ECA Citabria	T. Croke & ptnrs	
EI-ANY	PA-18 Super Cub 95	Bogavia Group	
EI-AOB	PA-28 Cherokee 140	Knock Flying Group	
EI-APS	Schleicher ASK.14	E. Shiel & ptnrs	
EI-ARW	Jodel D.R.1050	J. Davy	
EI-ASR	McCandless Gyroplane Mk 4	J. J. Fasenfeld	
EI-AST	Cessna F.150H	Ormond Flying Club	
EI-ATJ	B.121 Pup Srs 2	L. O'Leary	
EI-AUM	Auster J/1 Autocrat	T. G. Rafter	
EI-AUO	Cessna FA.150K Aerobat	S. Burke & L. Bagnell	
EI-AUS	Auster J/5F Aiglet Trainer	T. Stevens & ptnrs	
EI-AVB	Aeronca 7AC Champion	T. Brett	
EI-AVM	Cessna F.150L	Tojo Air Leasing	
EI-AWD	PA-22 Tri-Pacer 160	J. P. Montcalm	
EI-AWH	Cessna 210J	Rathcoole Flying Club	
EI-AWP	DH.82A Tiger Moth	A. P. Bruton	
EI-AWR	Malmö MFI-9 Junior	A. Szorfy	
EI-AYB	GY-80 Horizon 180	J. B. Smith	
EI-AYI	MS.880B Rallye Club	J. McNamara	
EI-AYN	BN-2A-8 Islander	Aer Arann	
EI-AYR	Schleicher ASK-16	B. O'Broin & ptnrs	
EI-AYT	MS.894A Rallye Minerva	K. A. O'Connor	
EI-AYY	Evans VP-1	R. Dowd	
EI-BAJ	Stampe SV.4C	Dublin Tiger Group	
EI-BAR	Thunder Ax8-105 balloon	J. Burke & ptnrs	
EI-BAT	Cessna F.150M	K. Kacprzak	
EI-BAV	PA-22 Colt 108	E. Finnamore	
EI-BBC	PA-28 Cherokee 180C	Vero Beach	
EI-BBD	Evans VP-1	Volksplane Group	
EI-BBE	Champion 7FC Tri-Traveler (tailwheel)	P. Ryan	
EI-BBI	MS.892 Rallye Commodore	Ossory Flying & Gliding Club	
EI-BBO	MS.893E Rallye 180GT	G. P. Moorhead	
EI-BBV	Piper J-3C-65 Cub	F. Cronin	
EI-BCE	BN-2A-26 Islander	Aer Arann	
EI-BCF	Bensen B.8M	P. Flanagan	
EI-BCJ	Aeromere F.8L Falco 1 Srs 3	M. P. McLoughlin	
EI-BCK	Cessna F.172N II	K. A. O'Connor	
EI-BCL	Cessna 182P	A. D. Brennan	
EI-BCM	Piper J-3C-65 Cub	M. Bergin & Partners	
EI-BCN	Piper J-3C-65 Cub	H. Diver	
EI-BCO	Piper J-3C-65 Cub	J. Molloy	
EI-BCP	D.62B Condor	T. Delaney	
EI-BCW	MS.880B Rallye Club	Kilkenny Flying Club	
EI-BDL	Evans VP-2	P. Buggle	
EI-BDM	PA-23 Aztec 250D	G. A. Costello	
EI-BDR	PA-28 Cherokee 180	Cherokee Group	
EI-BEN	Piper J-3C-65 Cub	Capt. J. J. Sullivan	
EI-BEP	MS.892A Rallye 150	H. Lynch & J. O'Leary	
EI-BFF	Beech A.23 Musketeer	J. Lankfer	
EI-BFI	MS.880B Rallye 100ST	J. O'Neill	
EI-BFO	Piper J-3C-90 Cub	D. Gordon	
EI-BGA	SOCATA Rallye 100ST	J. J. Frew	

Notes	Reg.	Type	Owner or Operator
	EI-BGC	MS.880B Rallye Club	P. Moran
	EI-BGD	MS.880B Rallye Club	N. Kavanagh
	EI-BGJ	Cessna F.152 II	Sligo Aero Club
	EI-BGS	MS.893E Rallye	M. Farrelly
	EI-BGT	Colt 77A balloon	M. J. Mills
	EI-BGU	MS.880B Rallye Club	M. F. Neary
	EI-BHF	MS.892A Rallye Commodore 150	B. Mullen
	EI-BHI	Bell 206B JetRanger 2	G. Tracey
	EI-BHM	Cessna F.337G	City of Dublin VE College
	EI-BHN	MS.893A Rallye Commodore 180T	T. Garvan
	EI-BHV	Champion 7EC Traveler	P. O'Donnell & ptnrs
	EI-BHW	Cessna F.150F	R. Sharpe
	EI-BIB	Cessna F.152	Sligo Aeronautical Club Ltd
	EI-BID	PA-18 Super Cub 95	S. Coghlan & P. Ryan
	EI-BIG	Zlin 526	P. von Lonkhuyzen
	EI-BIK	PA-18 Super Cub 180	Dublin Gliding Club
	EI-BIM	MS.880B Rallye Club	D. Millar
	EI-BIO	Piper J-3C-65 Cub	H. Duggan & Partners
	EI-BIR	Cessna F.172M	Figile Flying Group
	EI-BIS	Robin R.1180TD	Robin Aiglon Group
	EI-BIV	Bellanca 8KCAB	Aerocrat Pilots Ltd
	EI-BIW	MS.880B Rallye Club	E. J. Barr
	EI-BJB	Aeronca 7AC Champion	A. W. Kennedy
	EI-BJC	Aeronca 7AC Champion	A. E. Griffin
	EI-BJI	Cessna FR.172E	Irish Parachute Club
	EI-BJK	MS.880B Rallye 110ST	M. Keenen
	EI-BJM	Cessna A.152	K. A. O'Connor
	EI-BJO	Cessna R.172K	The XP Group
	EI-BKC	Aeronca 15AC Sedan	G. Hendrick & M. Farrell
	EI-BKF	Cessna F.172H	D. Darby
	EI-BKK	Taylor JT.1 Monoplane	R. Klimcke
	EI-BLD	Bolkow Bö.105DB	Irish Helicopters
	EI-BLE	Eipper Quicksilver Microlight	R. Smith & P. St. George
	EI-BLN	Eipper Quicksilver MX	O. J. Conway & ptnrs
	EI-BMA	MS.880B Rallye Club	W. Rankin & M. Kelleher
	EI-BMB	MS.880B Rallye 100T	Glyde Court Developments
	EI-BMF	Laverda F.8L Falco srs IV	M. Slazenger
	EI-BMH	MS.880B Rallye Club	N. S. Bracken
	EI-BMI	SOCATA TB9 Tampico	A. Breslin
	EI-BMM	Cessna F.152 II	P. Redmond
	EI-BMN	Cessna F.152 II	K. A. O'Connor
	EI-BMU	Monnet Sonerai IIL	A. Fenton
	EI-BMV	Grumman AA-5 Traveler	E. Tierney & K. A. Harold
	EI-BNF	Eurowing Goldwing Canard	T. Morelli
	EI-BNH	Hiway Skytrike	M. Martin
	EI-BNJ	Evans VP-2	G. Cashman
	EI-BNK	Cessna U.206F	Irish Parachute Club
	EI-BNL	Rand-Robinson KR-2	K. Hayes
	EI-BNP	Rotorway 133	R. L. Renfroe
	EI-BNT	Cvjetkovic CA-65	B. Tobin & ptnrs
	EI-BNU	MS.880B Rallye Club	J. Cooke
	EI-BOA	Pterodactyl Ptraveller	A. Murphy
	EI-BOE	SOCATA TB10 Tobago	Tobago Group
	EI-BOH	Eipper Quicksilver	J. Leech
	EI-BOV	Rand-Robinson KR-2	G. O'Hara & G. Callan
	EI-BOX	Jordan Duet	Dr. K. Riccius
	EI-BPE	Viking Dragonfly	G. G. Bracken
	EI-BPL	Cessna F.172K	Phoenix Flying
	EI-BPN	Flexiform Striker	P. H. Collins
	EI-BPP	Quicksilver MX	J. A. Smith
	EI-BPT	Skyhook Sabre	T. McGrath
	EI-BRS	Cessna P.172D	P. Mathews
	EI-BRU	Evans VP-1	Home Bru Flying Group
	EI-BRW	Hovey Deltabird	A & E Aerosport
	EI-BSB	Wassmer Jodel D.112	S. Byrne
	EI-BSC	Cessna F.172N	M. Foreman
	EI-BSG	Bensen B.80	J. Todd
	EI-BSK	SOCATA TB9 Tampico	T. Drury
	EI-BSL	PA-34-220T Seneca III	P. Sreenan
	EI-BSN	Cameron O-65 balloon	C. O'Neill & T. Hooper
	EI-BSO	PA-28 Cherokee 140B	S. Brazil

Reg.	Type	Owner or Operator	Notes
EI-BSW	Solar Wings Pegasus XL-R	E. Fitzgerald	
EI-BSX	Piper J-3C-65 Cub	J. & T. O'Dwyer	
EI-BUA	Cessna 172M	K. A. O'Connor	
EI-BUC	Jodel D.9 Bébé	B. Lyons & M. Blake	
EI-BUF	Cessna 210N	210 Group	
EI-BUG	SOCATA ST.10 Diplomate	J. Cooke	
EI-BUJ	MS.892A Rallye Commodore 150	T. Cunniffe	
EI-BUL	Whittaker MW5 Sorcerer	J. Culleton	
EI-BUN	Beech 76 Duchess	K. A. O'Connor	
EI-BUT	MS.893A Commodore 180	T. Keating	
EI-BVJ	AMF Chevvron 232	A. Dunn	
EI-BVK	PA-38-112 Tomahawk	M. Martin	
EI-BVT	Evans VP-2	P. Morrison	
EI-BVY	Zenith 200AA-RW	J. Matthews & M. Skelly	
EI-BYA	Thruster TST Mk 1	E. Fagan	
EI-BYG	SOCATA TB9 Tampico	M. McGinn	
EI-BYL	Zenith CH.250	M. McLoughlin	
EI-BYO	Aérospatiale ATR-42-310	Aer Arann	
EI-BYX	Champion 7GCAA	P. J. Gallagher	
EI-BYY	Piper J-3C-85 Cub	The Cub Club	
EI-CAC	Grob G.115A	C. Phillips	
EI-CAD	Grob G.115A	C. Phillips	
EI-CAE	Grob G.115A	O. O'Reilly	
EI-CAN	Aerotech MW5 Sorcerer	V. A. Vaughan	
EI-CAP	Cessna R.182RG	K. K. Skorupski	
EI-CAU	AMF Chevvron 232	J. Tarrant	
EI-CAX	Cessna P.210N	K. A. O'Connor	
EI-CBK	Aérospatiale ATR-42-310	Aer Arann	
EI-CCF	Aeronca 11AC Chief	G. McGuinness	
EI-CCJ	Cessna 152 II	P. Cahill	
EI-CCK	Cessna 152 II	P. Cahill	
EI-CCL	Cessna 152 II	P. Cahill	
EI-CCM	Cessna 152 II	E. Hopkins	
EI-CDD	Boeing 737-548	Castle 2003-2 Ireland/Pulkovo Airlines	
EI-CDE	Boeing 737-548	Castle 2003-2 Ireland/Pulkovo Airlines	
EI-CDF	Boeing 737-548	Jetscope Aviation Ireland/Pulkovo Airlines	
EI-CDG	Boeing 737-548	Nordic Aviation Contractor (Ireland) Ltd/Pulkovo Airlines	
EI-CDH	Boeing 737-548	Jetscope Aviation Ireland/Pulkovo Airlines	
EI-CDP	Cessna 182L	Irish Parachute Club	
EI-CDV	Cessna 150G	K. A. O'Connor	
EI-CEG	MS.893A Rallye 180GT	M. Jarrett	
EI-CEN	Thruster T.300	P. A. J. Murphy	
EI-CES	Taylorcraft BC-65	G. Higgins & Others	
EI-CFF	PA-12 Super Cruiser	J. & T. O'Dwyer	
EI-CFG	CP.301B Emeraude	F. Doyle	
EI-CFH	PA-12 Super Cruiser	G. Treacy	
EI-CFO	Piper J-3C-65 Cub	J. T. Wilson & ptnrs	
EI-CFP	Cessna 172P (floatplane)	K. A. O'Connor	
EI-CFY	Cessna 172N	K. A. O'Connor	
EI-CGC	Stinson 108-3	A. D. Weldon & L. Shoebridge	
EI-CGD	Cessna 172M	G. Cashman	
EI-CGF	Luton LA-5 Major	P. White	
EI-CGG	Erco Ercoupe 415C	Irish Ercoupe Group	
EI-CGH	Cessna 210N	J. Smith	
EI-CGJ	Solar Wings Pegasus XL-R	A. P. Hearty	
EI-CGN	Solar Wings Pegasus XL-R	V. Power	
EI-CGP	PA-28 Cherokee 140C	L. A. Tattan	
EI-CGT	Cessna 152 II	J. Rafter	
EI-CHK	Piper J-3C-65 Cub	N. Higgins	
EI-CHR	CFM Shadow Srs BD	B. Kelly	
EI-CHT	Solar Wings Pegasus XL-R	J. Grattan	
EI-CIF	PA-28 Cherokee 180C	AA Flying Group	
EI-CIG	PA-18 Super Cub 150	K. A. O'Connor	
EI-CIM	Avid Flyer Mk IV	P. Swan	
EI-CIN	Cessna 150K	K. A. O'Connor	
EI-CIV	PA-28 Cherokee 140	L. A. Tatton	
EI-CJJ	Slingsby T-31M	J. J. Sullivan	
EI-CJR	SNCAN Stampe SV.4A	P. McKenna	
EI-CJS	Jodel D.120A	A. Flood	

REPUBLIC OF IRELAND

Notes	Reg.	Type	Owner or Operator
	EI-CJT	Slingsby Motor Cadet III	J. Tarrant
	EI-CJV	Moskito 2	M. Peril & ptnrs
	EI-CKG	Avon Hunt Weightlift	B. Kenny
	EI-CKH	PA-18 Super Cub 95	G. Brady
	EI-CKI	Thruster TST Mk 1	S. Woodgates
	EI-CKJ	Cameron N-77 balloon	A. F. Meldon
	EI-CKU	Solar Wings Pegasus SLR	M. O'Regan
	EI-CKZ	Jodel D.18	J. O'Brien
	EI-CLA	HOAC Katana DV.20	J. Cooke
	EI-CLQ	Cessna F.172N	E. Finnamore
	EI-CMB	PA-28 Cherokee 140	K. Furnell & Partners
	EI-CMK	Goldwing ST	M. Gavigan
	EI-CML	Cessna 150M	K. A. O'Connor
	EI-CMN	PA-12 Super Cruiser	A. McNamee & ptnrs
	EI-CMR	Rutan LongEz	F. & C. O'Caoimh
	EI-CMT	PA-34-200T Seneca II	Atlantic Flight Training
	EI-CMU	Mainair Mercury	Bill O'Neill
	EI-CMV	Cessna 150L	K. A. O'Connor
	EI-CMW	Rotorway Executive	B. McNamee
	EI-CNA	Letov LK-2M Sluka	G. Doody
	EI-CNC	TEAM mini-MAX	A. M. S. Allen
	EI-CNG	Air & Space 18A gyroplane	P. Joyce
	EI-CNU	Pegasus Quantum 15-912	M. Ffrench
	EI-COE	Shaw Europa	F. Flynn
	EI-COG	Gyroscopic Rotorcraft gyroplane	R. C. Fidler & D. Bracken
	EI-COM	Whittaker MW6-S Fatboy Flyer	M. Watson
	EI-COO	Carlson Sparrow II	D. Logue
	EI-COT	Cessna F.172N	Tojo Air Leasing
	EI-COY	Piper J-3C-65 Cub	W. Flood
	EI-COZ	PA-28 Cherokee 140C	L. A. Tattan
	EI-CPE	Airbus A.321-211	Aer Lingus St Enda
	EI-CPG	Airbus A.321-211	Aer Lingus St Aidan
	EI-CPH	Airbus A.321-211	Aer Lingus St Dervilla
	EI-CPI	Rutan LongEz	D. J. Ryan
	EI-CPN	Auster J/4	E. Fagan
	EI-CPP	Piper J-3C-65 Cub	E. Fitzgerald
	EI-CPT	Aérospatiale ATR-42-320	Aer Arann
	EI-CPX	I.I.I. Sky Arrow 650T	M. McCarthy
	EI-CRB	Lindstrand LBL-90A balloon	J. & C. Concannon
	EI-CRE	McD Douglas MD-83	AAR Ireland/Meridiana
	EI-CRG	Robin DR.400/180R	D. & B. Lodge
	EI-CRH	McD Douglas MD-83	Airplanes 111/Meridiana
	EI-CRR	Aeronca 11AC Chief	L. Maddock & ptnrs
	EI-CRU	Cessna 152	W. Reilly
	EI-CRV	Hoffman H-36 Dimona	The Dimona Group
	EI-CRW	McD Douglas MD-83	Airplanes IAL/Meridiana
	EI-CRX	SOCATA TB-9 Tampico	Hotel Bravo Flying Club
	EI-CRY	Medway Eclipser	G. A. Murphy
	EI-CSG	Boeing 737-8AS	CIT Aerospace International
	EI-CTI	Cessna FRA.150L	J. Logan & T. Bradford
	EI-CTL	Aerotech MW-5B Sorcerer	M. Wade
	EI-CUA	Boeing 737-4K5	Aerco Ireland/Blue Panorama
	EI-CUD	Boeing 737-4Q8	Castle 2003-2 Ireland/Blue Panorama
	EI-CUJ	Cessna 172N	M. Nally
	EI-CUM	Airbus A.320-232	Wilmington Trust SP Services (Dublin) Ltd/Windjet
	EI-CUN	Boeing 737-4K5	Aerco Ireland/Blue Panorama
	EI-CUP	Cessna 335	J. Greany
	EI-CUS	AB-206B JetRanger 3	R. Lyons
	EI-CUT	Maule MX-7-180A	Cosair
	EI-CUW	BN-2B-20 Islander	Aer Arann
	EI-CVA	Airbus A.320-214	Aer Lingus St Schira
	EI-CVB	Airbus A.320-214	Aer Lingus St Mobhi
	EI-CVC	Airbus A.320-214	Aer Lingus St Kealin
	EI-CVD	Airbus A.320-214	Aer Lingus St Kevin
	EI-CVL	Ercoupe 415CD	V. O'Rourke
	EI-CVM	Schweizer S.269C	B. Moloney
	EI-CVW	Bensen B.8M	F. Kavanagh
	EI-CVY	Brock KB-2 Gyro	G. Smyth
	EI-CWE	Boeing 737-42C	Air One
	EI-CWX	Boeing 737-4Y0	Air One
	EI-CXC	Raj Hamsa X'Air 502T	R. Dunleavy

Reg.	Type	Owner or Operator	Notes
EI-CXK	Boeing 737-4S3	Transaero	
EI-CXN	Boeing 737-329	Transaero	
EI-CXO	Boeing 767-3G5ER	Blue Panorama	
EI-CXR	Boeing 737-329	Transaero	
EI-CXS	Sikorsky S-61N	CHC Ireland Ltd	
EI-CXV	Boeing 737-8CX	MASL Ireland(14)Ltd/MIAT Mongolian Airlines	
EI-CXY	Evektor EV-97 Eurostar	G. Doody & ptnrs	
EI-CXZ	Boeing 767-216ER	Transaero	
EI-CZA	ATEC Zephyr 2000	P. Whitehouse-Tedd	
EI-CZC	CFM Streak Shadow Srs II	M. Culhane & D. Burrows	
EI-CZD	Boeing 767-216ER	Transaero	
EI-CZH	Boeing 767-3G5ER	ILFC Aircraft 76B-29435 Ltd/Blue Panorama	
EI-CZK	Boeing 737-4Y0	Transaero	
EI-CZN	Sikorsky S-61N	CHC Ireland	
EI-CZP	Schweizer 269C-1	T. Ng Kam	
EI-DAA	Airbus A.330-202	Aer Lingus St Keeva	
EI-DAC	Boeing 737-8AS	Ryanair	
EI-DAD	Boeing 737-8AS	Ryanair	
EI-DAE	Boeing 737-8AS	Ryanair	
EI-DAF	Boeing 737-8AS	Ryanair	
EI-DAG	Boeing 737-8AS	Ryanair	
EI-DAH	Boeing 737-8AS	Ryanair	
EI-DAI	Boeing 737-8AS	Ryanair	
EI-DAJ	Boeing 737-8AS	Ryanair	
EI-DAK	Boeing 737-8AS	Ryanair	
EI-DAL	Boeing 737-8AS	Ryanair	
EI-DAM	Boeing 737-8AS	Ryanair	
EI-DAN	Boeing 737-8AS	Ryanair	
EI-DAO	Boeing 737-8AS	Ryanair	
EI-DAP	Boeing 737-8AS	Ryanair	
EI-DAR	Boeing 737-8AS	Ryanair	
EI-DAS	Boeing 737-8AS	Ryanair	
EI-DBF	Boeing 767-3Q8ER	ACG Acquisition Ireland/Transaero	
EI-DBG	Boeing 767-3Q8ER	VEBL-767-300 Ltd/Transaero	
EI-DBH	CFM Streak Shadow SA-11	M. O'Mahony	
EI-DBI	Raj Hamsa X'Air Mk.2 Falcon	E. Hamilton	
EI-DBJ	Huntwing Pegasus XL Classic	P. A. McMahon	
EI-DBK	Boeing 777-243ER	GECAS Technical Services/Alitalia	
EI-DBL	Boeing 777-243ER	GECAS Technical Services/Alitalia	
EI-DBM	Boeing 777-243ER	GECAS Technical Services/Alitalia	
EI-DBO	Air Creation Kiss 400	E. Spain	
EI-DBP	Boeing 767-35H	Centennial Aviation (Ireland) Ltd/Alitalia	
EI-DBU	Boeing 767-37EER	Pegasus Aviation Ireland/Transaero	
EI-DBV	Rand Kar X' Air 602T	S. Scanlon	
EI-DBW	Boeing 767-201	Orix Aircraft Management Ltd/Transaero	
EI-DCA	Raj Hamsa X'Air	S. Cahill	
EI-DCF	Boeing 737-8AS	Ryanair	
Ei-DCG	Boeing 737-8AS	Ryanair	
EI-DCH	Boeing 737-8AS	Ryanair	
EI-DCI	Boeing 737-8AS	Ryanair	
EI-DCJ	Boeing 737-8AS	Ryanair	
EI-DCK	Boeing 737-8AS	Ryanair	
EI-DCL	Boeing 737-8AS	Ryanair	
EI-DCM	Boeing 737-8AS	Ryanair	
EI-DCN	Boeing 737-8AS	Ryanair	
EI-DCO	Boeing 737-8AS	Ryanair	
EI-DCP	Boeing 737-8AS	Ryanair	
EI-DCR	Boeing 737-8AS	Ryanair	
EI-DCW	Boeing 737-8AS	Ryanair	
EI-DCX	Boeing 737-8AS	Ryanair	
EI-DCY	Boeing 737-8AS	Ryanair	
EI-DCZ	Boeing 737-8AS	Ryanair	
EI-DDA	Robinson R44 II	Eirecopter Helicopters Ltd	
EI-DDC	Cessna F.172M	Trim Flying Club	
EI-DDD	Aeronca 7AC	J. Sullivan & M. Quinn	
EI-DDH	Boeing 777-243ER	GECAS Technical Services/Alitalia	
EI-DDI	Schweizer S.269C-1	B. Hade	
EI-DDJ	Raj Hamsa X'Air 582	J. P. McHugh	
EI-DDK	Boeing 737-4S3	Transaero	
EI-DDP	Southdown International microlight	M. Mannion	
EI-DDR	Bensen B.8V	P. MacCabe & K. Renolds	

Notes	Reg.	Type	Owner or Operator
	EI-DDW	Boeing 767-3S1ER	Alitalia
	EI-DDX	Cessna 172S	Atlantic Flight Training
	EI-DDY	Boeing 737-4Y0	Aerco Ireland/Transaero
	EI-DEA	Airbus A.320-214	Aer Lingus St Fidelma
	EI-DEB	Airbus A.320-214	Aer Lingus St Nathy
	EI-DEC	Airbus A.320-214	Aer Lingus St Fergal
	EI-DEE	Airbus A.320-214	Aer Lingus St Fintan
	EI-DEF	Airbus A.320-214	Aer Lingus St Declan
	EI-DEG	Airbus A.320-214	Aer Lingus St Fachtna
	EI-DEH	Airbus A.320-214	Aer Lingus St Malachy
	EI-DEI	Airbus A.320-214	Aer Lingus St Kilian
	EI-DEJ	Airbus A.320-214	Aer Lingus St Oliver Plunkett
	EI-DEK	Airbus A.320-214	Aer Lingus St Eunan
	EI-DEL	Airbus A.320-214	Aer Lingus St Ibar
	EI-DEM	Airbus A.320-214	Aer Lingus St Canice
	EI-DEN	Airbus A.320-214	Aer Lingus St Kieran
	EI-DEO	Airbus A.320-214	Aer Lingus St Senan
	EI-DEP	Airbus A.320-214	Aer Lingus St Eugene
	EI-DER	Airbus A.320-214	Aer Lingus St Mel
	EI-DES	Airbus A.320-214	Aer Lingus St Pappin
	EI-DET	Airbus A.320-214	Aer Lingus St Brendan
	EI-DEZ	Airbus A.319-112	Meridiana
	EI-DFA	Airbus A.319-112	Meridiana
	EI-DFH	Embraer ERJ-170-100LR	Alitalia Express
	EI-DFI	Embraer ERJ-170-100LR	Alitalia Express
	EI-DFJ	Embraer ERJ-170-100LR	Alitalia Express
	EI-DFK	Embraer ERJ-170-100LR	Alitalia Express
	EI-DFL	Embraer ERJ-170-100LR	Alitalia Express
	EI-DFM	Evektor EV-97 Eurostar	G. Doody
	EI-DFN	Airbus A.320-211	Windjet
	EI-DFO	Airbus A.320-211	Windjet
	EI-DFP	Airbus A.319-112	Meridiana
	EI-DFS	Boeing 767-33AER	Transaero
	EI-DFX	Air Creation Kiss 400	L. Daly
	EI-DFY	Raj Hamsa R100 (2)	P. McGirr & R Gillespie
	EI-DGA	Urban Air UFM-11UK Lambada	Dr. P. & D. Durkin
	EI-DGG	Raj Hamsa X'Air 582	P. A. Weldon
	EI-DGH	Raj Hamsa X'Air 582	M. Garvey & T. McGowan
	EI-DGJ	Raj Hamsa X'Air 582	N. Brereton
	EI-DGK	Raj Hamsa X'Air 133	B. Chambers
	EI-DGP	Urban Air UFM-11 Lambada	R. Linehan
	EI-DGT	Urban Air UFM-11UK Lambada	P. Walsh & Partners
	EI-DGV	ATEC Zephyr 2000	K. Higgins
	EI-DGW	Cameron Z-90 balloon	J. Leahy
	EI-DGX	Cessna 152 II	K. A. O'Connor
	EI-DGY	Urban Air UFM-11 Lambada	D. McMorrow
	EI-DHA	Boeing 737-8AS	Ryanair
	EI-DHB	Boeing 737-8AS	Ryanair
	EI-DHC	Boeing 737-8AS	Ryanair
	EI-DHD	Boeing 737-8AS	Ryanair
	EI-DHE	Boeing 737-8AS	Ryanair
	EI-DHF	Boeing 737-8AS	Ryanair
	EI-DHG	Boeing 737-8AS	Ryanair
	EI-DHH	Boeing 737-8AS	Ryanair
	EI-DHI	Boeing 737-8AS	Ryanair
	EI-DHJ	Boeing 737-8AS	Ryanair
	EI-DHK	Boeing 737-8AS	Ryanair
	EI-DHL	Airbus A.300B4-203F	European Air Transport/DHL
	EI-DHM	Boeing 737-8AS	Ryanair
	EI-DHN	Boeing 737-8AS	Ryanair
	EI-DHO	Boeing 737-8AS	Ryanair
	EI-DHP	Boeing 737-8AS	Ryanair
	EI-DHR	Boeing 737-8AS	Ryanair
	EI-DHS	Boeing 737-8AS	Ryanair
	EI-DHT	Boeing 737-8AS	Ryanair
	EI-DHV	Boeing 737-8AS	Ryanair
	EI-DHW	Boeing 737-8AS	Ryanair
	EI-DHX	Boeing 737-8AS	Ryanair
	EI-DHY	Boeing 737-8AS	Ryanair
	EI-DHZ	Boeing 737-8AS	Ryanair
	EI-DIA	Solar Wings Pegasus XL-Q	P. Byrne

Reg.	Type	Owner or Operator	Notes
EI-DIF	PA-31-350 Navajo Chieftain	Flightwise Aviation Ltd & Partners	
EI-DIP	Airbus A.330-202	Alitalia	
EI-DIR	Airbus A.330-202	Alitalia	
EI-DIY	Van's RV-4	J. A. Kent	
EI-DJL	Boeing 767-330ER	Blue Panorama	
EI-DJM	PA-28-161 Warrior II	Waterford Aero Club	
EI-DJS	Boeing 737-3YO	KD Avia	
EI-DJX	Farrington Twinstarr	F. Kavanagh	
EI-DJY	Grob G.115	Atlantic Flight Training	
EI-DJZ	Lindstrand LBL-31A Cloudhopper	M. E. White	
EI-DKC	Solar Wings Quasar	K. Daly	
EI-DKE	Air Creation Kiss 450-582	J. Bennett	
EI-DKI	Robinson R22 Beta	P. Gilboy	
EI-DKJ	Thruster T.600N	C. Brogan	
EI-DKK	Raj Hamsa X'Air Jabiru	M. Tolan	
EI-DKL	Boeing 757-231	Blue Panorama	
EI-DKN	ELA Aviacion ELA-07 gyrocopter	S. Brennan	
EI-DKT	Raj Hamsa X'Air 582 (11)	S. O'Reilly	
EI-DKU	Air Creation Kiss 450-582 (1)	P. Kirwan	
EI-DKW	Evektor EV-97 Eurostar	Ormand Flying Club	
EI-DKY	Raj Hamsa X'Air 582	M. Clarke	
EI-DKZ	Reality Aircraft Escapade 912 (1)	J. Deegan	
EI-DLB	Boeing 737-8AS	Ryanair	
EI-DLC	Boeing 737-8AS	Ryanair	
EI-DLD	Boeing 737-8AS	Ryanair	
EI-DLE	Boeing 737-8AS	Ryanair	
EI-DLF	Boeing 737-8AS	Ryanair	
EI-DLG	Boeing 737-8AS	Ryanair	
EI-DLH	Boeing 737-8AS	Ryanair	
EI-DLI	Boeing 737-8AS	Ryanair	
EI-DLJ	Boeing 737-8AS	Ryanair	
EI-DLK	Boeing 737-8AS	Ryanair	
EI-DLL	Boeing 737-8AS	Ryanair	
EI-DLM	Boeing 737-8AS	Ryanair	
EI-DLN	Boeing 737-8AS	Ryanair	
EI-DLO	Boeing 737-8AS	Ryanair	
EI-DLR	Boeing 737-8AS	Ryanair	
EI-DLS	Boeing 737-8AS	Ryanair	
EI-DLT	Boeing 737-8AS	Ryanair	
EI-DLV	Boeing 737-8AS	Ryanair	
EI-DLW	Boeing 737-8AS	Ryanair	
EI-DLX	Boeing 737-8AS	Ryanair	
EI-DLY	Boeing 737-8AS	Ryanair	
EI-DLZ	Boeing 737-8AS	Ryanair	
EI-DMA	MS.892E Rallye 150	J. Lynn & Partners	
EI-DMB	Best Off Skyranger 912S (1)	Fun 2 Fly Ltd	
EI-DMC	Schweizer 269C-1	B. Hade	
EI-DMG	Cessna 441	Dawn Meats Group	
EI-DMR	Boeing 737-436	Air One	
EI-DMU	Whittaker MW6S Merlin	G. W. Maher	
EI-DNA	Boeing 757-231	Blue Panorama	
EI-DNM	Boeing 737-4S3	Transaero	
EI-DNN	Bede BD-5G	H. John & E. M. Cox	
EI-DNO	Bede BD-5G	R. A. Gardiner	
EI-DNP	Airbus A.320-212	Wind Jet	
EI-DNR	Raj Hamsa X'Air 582 (5)	N. Furlong & J. Grattan	
EI-DNU	Schweizer 269C-1	Skywest Aviation Ltd	
EI-DNV	Urban Air UFM-11UK Lambada	F. Maughan	
EI-DNW	Skyranger J2.2 (1)	M. Kerrison	
EI-DNZ	Boeing 737-3T0	BCI Aircraft Leasing/Avolar	
EI-DOB	Zenair CH-701	D. O'Brien	
EI-DOE	Airbus A.320-211	Wind Jet	
EI-DOH	Boeing 737-31S	Transaero	
EI-DOP	Airbus A.320-232	Wind Jet	
EI-DOT	Bombardier CL-600-2D24	Air One	
EI-DOU	Bombardier CL-600-2D24	Air One	
EI-DOW	Mainair Blade 912	G. D. Fortune	
EI-DOX	Solar Wings XL-R	T. Noonan	
EI-DOY	PZL Koliber 150A	V. O'Brien & Partners	
EI-DPA	Boeing 737-8AS	Ryanair	
EI-DPB	Boeing 737-8AS	Ryanair	

Notes	Reg.	Type	Owner or Operator
	EI-DPC	Boeing 737-8AS	Ryanair
	EI-DPD	Boeing 737-8AS	Ryanair
	EI-DPE	Boeing 737-8AS	Ryanair
	EI-DPF	Boeing 737-8AS	Ryanair
	EI-DPG	Boeing 737-8AS	Ryanair
	EI-DPH	Boeing 737-8AS	Ryanair
	EI-DPI	Boeing 737-8AS	Ryanair
	EI-DPJ	Boeing 737-8AS	Ryanair
	EI-DPK	Boeing 737-8AS	Ryanair
	EI-DPL	Boeing 737-8AS	Ryanair
	EI-DPM	Boeing 737-8AS	Ryanair
	EI-DPN	Boeing 737-8AS	Ryanair
	EI-DPO	Boeing 737-8AS	Ryanair
	EI-DPP	Boeing 737-8AS	Ryanair
	EI-DPR	Boeing 737-8AS	Ryanair
	EI-DPS	Boeing 737-8AS	Ryanair
	EI-DPT	Boeing 737-8AS	Ryanair
	EI-DPV	Boeing 737-8AS	Ryanair
	EI-DPW	Boeing 737-8AS	Ryanair
	EI-DPX	Boeing 737-8AS	Ryanair
	EI-DPY	Boeing 737-8AS	Ryanair
	EI-DPZ	Boeing 737-8AS	Ryanair
	EI-DRA	Boeing 737-852	Aeromexico
	EI-DRB	Boeing 737-852	Aeromexico
	EI-DRC	Boeing 737-852	Aeromexico
	EI-DRD	Boeing 737-852	Aeromexico
	EI-DRE	Boeing 737-752	Aeromexico
	EI-DRH	Mainair Blade	J. McErlain
	EI-DRI	Bombardier CL-600-2D24	Air One
	EI-DRJ	Bombardier CL-600-2D24	Air One
	EI-DRK	Bombardier CL-600-2D24	Air One
	EI-DRL	Raj Hamsa X'Air Jabiru	J. O'Connor
	EI-DRM	Urban Air UFM-10 Samba	M. Tormey
	EI-DRT	Air Creation Tanarg 912	L. Daly
	EI-DRU	Tecnam P92/EM Echo	P. Gallogly
	EI-DRW	Evektor EV-97R Eurostar	Eurostar Flying Club
	EI-DRX	Raj Hamsa X'Air 582 (5)	M. Sheelan & D. McShane
	EI-DSA	Airbus A.320-216	Alitalia
	EI-DSB	Airbus A.320-216	Alitalia
	EI-DSC	Airbus A.320-216	Alitalia
	EI-DSD	Airbus A.320-216	Alitalia
	EI-DSE	Airbus A.320-216	Alitalia
	EI-DSF	Airbus A.320-216	Alitalia
	EI-DSG	Airbus A.320-216	Alitalia
	EI-DSH	Airbus A.320-216	Alitalia
	EI-DSI	Airbus A.320-216	Alitalia
	EI-DSJ	Airbus A.320-216	Alitalia
	EI-DSK	Airbus A.320-216	Alitalia
	EI-DSL	Airbus A.320-216	Alitalia
	EI-DSM	Airbus A.320-216	Alitalia
	EI-DSN	Airbus A.320-216	Alitalia
	EI-DSO	Airbus A.320-216	Alitalia
	EI-DSP	Airbus A.320-216	Alitalia
	EI-DSR	Airbus A.320-216	Alitalia
	EI-DSS	Airbus A.320-216	Alitalia
	EI-DST	Airbus A.320-216	Alitalia
	EI-DSU	Airbus A.320-216	Alitalia
	EI-DSV	Airbus A.320-216	Alitalia
	EI-DSW	Airbus A.320-216	Alitalia
	EI-DSX	Airbus A.320-216	Alitalia
	EI-DSY	Airbus A.320-216	Alitalia
	EI-DSZ	Airbus A.320-216	Alitalia
	EI-DTA	Airbus A.320-216	Alitalia
	EI-DTB	Airbus A.320-216	Alitalia
	EI-DTC	Airbus A.320-216	Alitalia
	EI-DTD	Airbus A.320-216	Alitalia
	EI-DTE	Airbus A.320-216	Alitalia
	EI-DTF	Airbus A.320-216	Alitalia
	EI-DTG	Airbus A.320-216	Alitalia
	EI-DTH	Airbus A.320-216	Alitalia
	EI-DTI	Airbus A.320-216	Alitalia

Reg.	Type	Owner or Operator	Notes
EI-DTJ	Airbus A.320-216	Alitalia	
EI-DTK	Airbus A.320-216	Alitalia	
EI-DTL	Airbus A.320-216	Alitalia	
EI-DTM	Airbus A.320-216	Alitalia	
EI-DTN	Airbus A.320-216	Alitalia	
EI-DTO	Airbus A.320-216	Alitalia	
EI-DTS	PA-18 Super Cub	P. Dunne, K. Synnott & M. Murphy	
EI-DTT	ELA-07 R-100 Gyrocopter	N. Steele	
EI-DTU	Boeing 737-5Y0	Transaero	
EI-DTV	Boeing 737-5Y0	Transaero	
EI-DTW	Boeing 737-5Y0	Transaero	
EI-DTX	Boeing 737-5Q8	Transaero	
EI-DUA	Boeing 757-256	Kras Air/AiRUnion	
EI-DUC	Boeing 757-256	Kras Air/AiRUnion	
EI-DUD	Boeing 757-256	Kras Air/AiRUnion	
EI-DUF	AS.365N	Dauphin 2 Aviation Ltd	
EI-DUH	Scintex CP.1310C3 Emeraude	W. Kennedy	
EI-DUJ	Evektor EV-97 Eurostar	E. Fitzpatrick	
EI-DUK	Bombardier CL-600-2D24	myAir	
EI-DUL	Alpi Aviation Pioneer	J. Hackett	
EI-DUO	Airbus A.330-203	Aer Lingus	
EI-DUS	Boeing 737-32B	Mistral Air	
EI-DUV	Beech 55	J. Given	
EI-DUZ	Airbus A.330-203	Aer Lingus	
EI-DVA	Boeing 737-33A	Mistral Air	
EI-DVC	Boeing 737-33A	Mistral Air	
EI-DVD	Airbus A.319-113	WindJet SpA	
EI-DVE	Airbus A.320-214	Aer Lingus	
EI-DVF	Airbus A.320-214	Aer Lingus	
EI-DVG	Airbus A.320-214	Aer Lingus	
EI-DVH	Airbus A.320-214	Aer Lingus	
EI-DVI	Airbus A.320-214	Aer Lingus	
EI-DVJ	Airbus A.320-214	Aer Lingus	
EI-DVK	Airbus A.320-214	Aer Lingus	
EI-DVL	Airbus A.320-214	Aer Lingus	
EI-DVM	Airbus A.320-214	Aer Lingus	
EI-DVN	Airbus A.320-214	Aer Lingus	
EI-DVO	Barnett j4b2	T. Brennan	
EI-DVP	CL-600-2D24	Air One	
EI-DVR	CL-600-2D24	Air One	
EI-DVS	CL-600-2D24	Air One	
EI-DVT	CL-600-2D24	Air One	
EI-DVU	Airbus A.319-113	WindJet SpA	
EI-DVZ	Robinson R44 II	D. McAuliffe	
EI-DWA	Boeing 737-8AS	Ryanair	
EI-DWB	Boeing 737-8AS	Ryanair	
EI-DWC	Boeing 737-8AS	Ryanair	
EI-DWD	Boeing 737-8AS	Ryanair	
EI-DWE	Boeing 737-8AS	Ryanair	
EI-DWF	Boeing 737-8AS	Ryanair	
EI-DWG	Boeing 737-8AS	Ryanair	
EI-DWH	Boeing 737-8AS	Ryanair	
EI-DWI	Boeing 737-8AS	Ryanair	
EI-DWJ	Boeing 737-8AS	Ryanair	
EI-DWK	Boeing 737-8AS	Ryanair	
EI-DWL	Boeing 737-8AS	Ryanair	
EI-DWM	Boeing 737-8AS	Ryanair	
EI-DWO	Boeing 737-8AS	Ryanair	
EI-DWP	Boeing 737-8AS	Ryanair	
EI-DWR	Boeing 737-8AS	Ryanair	
EI-DWS	Boeing 737-8AS	Ryanair	
EI-DWT	Boeing 737-8AS	Ryanair	
EI-DWV	Boeing 737-8AS	Ryanair	
EI-DWW	Boeing 737-8AS	Ryanair	
EI-DWX	Boeing 737-8AS	Ryanair	
EI-DWY	Boeing 737-8AS	Ryanair	
EI-DWZ	Boeing 737-8AS	Ryanair	
EI-DXA	Ikarus C42	M. Kirrane	
EI-DXC	Boeing 737-4Q8	Air One	
EI-DXL	CFM Shadow	F. Lynch	
EI-DXM	Raj Hamsa X'Air 582	B. Nugent	

Notes	Reg.	Type	Owner or Operator
	EI-DXN	Zenair CH.601HD	N. Gallagher
	EI-DXP	Cyclone AX3/503	J. McCann
	EI-DXS	CFM Shadow	R. W. Frost
	EI-DXT	UrbanAir UFM-10 Samba	N. Irwin
	EI-DXU	ELA-07 R115	R. Savage
	EI-DXV	Thruster T.600N	P. Higgins
	EI-DXX	Raj Hamsa X'AIR 582(5)	D. Hanly & C. Wright
	EI-DXY	Airbus A.320-212	Rossiya
	EI-DXZ	UrbanAir UFM-10 Samba	D. O'Leary
	EI-DYA	Boeing 737-8AS	Ryanair
	EI-DYB	Boeing 737-8AS	Ryanair
	EI-DYC	Boeing 737-8AS	Ryanair
	EI-DYD	Boeing 737-8AS	Ryanair
	EI-DYE	Boeing 737-8AS	Ryanair
	EI-DYF	Boeing 737-8AS	Ryanair
	EI-DYH	Boeing 737-8AS	Ryanair
	EI-DYI	Boeing 737-8AS	Ryanair
	EI-DYJ	Boeing 737-8AS	Ryanair
	EI-DYK	Boeing 737-8AS	Ryanair
	EI-DYL	Boeing 737-8AS	Ryanair
	EI-DYM	Boeing 737-8AS	Ryanair
	EI-DYN	Boeing 737-8AS	Ryanair
	EI-DYO	Boeing 737-8AS	Ryanair
	EI-DYP	Boeing 737-8AS	Ryanair
	EI-DYR	Boeing 737-8AS	Ryanair
	EI-DYS	Boeing 737-8AS	Ryanair
	EI-DYT	Boeing 737-8AS	Ryanair
	EI-DYV	Boeing 737-8AS	Ryanair
	EI-DYW	Boeing 737-8AS	Ryanair
	EI-DYX	Boeing 737-8AS	Ryanair
	EI-DYY	Boeing 737-8AS	Ryanair
	EI-DYZ	Boeing 737-8AS	Ryanair
	EI-DZA	Colt 21A balloon	P. Baker
	EI-DZB	Colt 21A balloon	P. Baker
	EI-DZE	UrbanAir UFM-10 Samba	P. Keane
	EI-DZF	Pipistrel Sinus 912	Light Sport Aviation Ltd
	EI-DZH	Boeing 767-3Q8ER	Rossiya
	EI-DZK	Robinson R22B2 Beta	Skywest Aviation Ltd
	EI-DZL	Urban Air Samba XXL	M. Tormey
	EI-DZM	Robinson R44 II	A. & G. Thomond Builders Ltd
	EI-DZN	Bell 222	B. McCarty & A. Dalton
	EI-DZO	Dominator Gyroplane Ultrawhite	P. O'Reilly
	EI-DZR	Airbus A.320-212	Rossiya
	EI-DZS	BRM Land Africa	M. Whyte
	EI-EAB	Airbus A.300B4-203F	European Air Transport/DHL
	EI-EAC	Airbus A.300B4-203F	European Air Transport/DHL
	EI-EAD	Airbus A.300B4-203F	European Air Transport/DHL
	EI-EAG	Pipistrel Virus 912	R. Armstrong
	EI-EAJ	RAF-2000GTX-SE	J. P. Henry
	EI-EAK	Airborne Windsports Edge XT	M. O'Brien
	EI-EAM	Cessna 172R	Atlantic Flight Training Ltd
	EI-EAP	Mainair Blade	H. D. Lynch
	EI-EAR	Boeing 767-3Q8ER	Rossiya
	EI-EAV	Airbus A.330-302	Aer Lingus
	EI-EAW	Airborne Windsports Edge XT582	F. Heary
	EI-EAX	Raj Hamsa X'Air 582 (2)	M. Murphy
	EI-EAY	Raj Hamsa X'Air 582 (5)	R. Smith
	EI-EAZ	Cessna 172R	Atlantic Flight Training Ltd
	EI-EBA	Boeing 737-8AS	Ryanair
	EI-EBB	Boeing 737-8AS	Ryanair
	EI-EBC	Boeing 737-8AS	Ryanair
	EI-EBD	Boeing 737-8AS	Ryanair
	EI-EBE	Boeing 737-8AS	Ryanair
	EI-EBF	Boeing 737-8AS	Ryanair
	EI-EBG	Boeing 737-8AS	Ryanair
	EI-EBH	Boeing 737-8AS	Ryanair
	EI-EBI	Boeing 737-8AS	Ryanair
	EI-EBK	Boeing 737-8AS	Ryanair
	EI-EBL	Boeing 737-8AS	Ryanair
	EI-EBM	Boeing 737-8AS	Ryanair
	EI-EBN	Boeing 737-8AS	Ryanair

Reg.	Type	Owner or Operator	Notes
EI-EBO	Boeing 737-8AS	Ryanair	
EI-EBP	Boeing 737-8AS	Ryanair	
EI-EBR	Boeing 737-8AS	Ryanair	
EI-EBS	Boeing 737-8AS	Ryanair	
EI-EBT	Boeing 737-8AS	Ryanair	
EI-EBV	Boeing 737-8AS	Ryanair	
EI-EBW	Boeing 737-8AS	Ryanair	
EI-EBX	Boeing 737-8AS	Ryanair	
EI-EBY	Boeing 737-8AS	Ryanair	
EI-EBZ	Boeing 737-8AS	Ryanair	
EI-ECB	Boeing 767-3Q8ER	ILFC Ireland	
EI-ECC	Cameron Z-90 balloon	J. J. Daly	
EI-ECG	BRM Land Africa	J. McGuinness	
EI-ECK	Raj Hamsa X'Air Hawk	N. Geh	
EI-ECO	Raj Hamsa X'Air Hawk	J. McLaughlin	
EI-ECP	Raj Hamsa X'Air Hawk	R. Gillespie & Partners	
EI-ECR	Cessna 525	Aircraft International Renting Ltd	
EI-ECV	Raj Hamsa X'Air Hawk	D. P. Myers	
EI-ECW	BRM Land Africa	Seosamh Mac Eochgain	
EI-ECX	Airbus A.319-132	ILFC Ireland Ltd	
EI-ECY	Airbus A.319-132	ILFC Ireland Ltd	
EI-ECZ	Raj Hamsa X'Air Hawk	M. Tolan	
EI-EDA	Raj Hamsa X'Air Hawk	A. Clarke	
EI-EDB	Cessna 152	K. O'Connor	
EI-EDC	Cessna FA.152	K. O'Connor	
EI-EDI	Ikarus C42	M. Owens	
EI-EDJ	CZAW Sportcruiser	Croftal Ltd	
EI-EDM	Airbus A.319-132	Wind Jet Ireland Ltd	
EI-EDP	Airbus A.320-214	Aer Lingus	
EI-EDR	PA-28R Cherokee Arrow 200	Dublin Flyers	
EI-EDS	Airbus A.320-214	Aer Lingus	
EI-EDV	Cessna 172S	R. Carey	
EI-EDY	Airbus A.330-302	Aer Lingus	
EI-EDZ	Boeing 737-8K5	Transaero	
EI-EEA	Boeing 737-8K5	Transaero	
EI-EEB	Boeing 737-73S	Pembroke 7006 Leasing Ltd/AIRES Colombia	
EI-EED	Boeing 767-31AER	Blue Panorama	
EI-EEF	Raj Jamsa X'Air Jabiru(3)	P. J. Sheehy	
EI-EEG	Raj Hamsa X'Air Hawk	C. Kiernan	
EI-EEH	BRM Land Africa	P. Higgins	
EI-EEI	Airbus A.320-232	ILFC Aircraft 32A-661 Ltd/Avia Nova	
EI-EEL	Airbus A.320-232	ILFC Ireland Ltd	
EI-EEO	Van's RV-7	A. Butler	
EI-EES	ELA-07R	D. Doyle & Partners	
EI-EEU	Osprey II	P. Forde & S. Coughlan	
EI-EEV	Boeing 737-73S	Pembroke 7006 Leasing Ltd/AIRES Colombia	
EI-EEW	Boeing 737-375	Blue Panorama	
EI-EEX	Airbus A.320-231	AWAS Ireland Leasing Eight Ltd	
EI-EEY	Airbus A.320-231	AWAS Ireland Leasing Eight Ltd	
EI-EEZ	Bombardier CL-600-2B19	Airlink Airways Ltd	
EI-EFA	Boeing 737-8AS	Ryanair	
EI-EFB	Boeing 737-8AS	Ryanair	
EI-EFC	Boeing 737-8AS	Ryanair	
EI-EFD	Boeing 737-8AS	Ryanair	
EI-EFE	Boeing 737-8AS	Ryanair	
EI-EFF	Boeing 737-8AS	Ryanair	
EI-EFG	Boeing 737-8AS	Ryanair	
EI-EFH	Boeing 737-8AS	Ryanair	
EI-EFI	Boeing 737-8AS	Ryanair	
EI-EFJ	Boeing 737-8AS	Ryanair	
EI-EFK	Boeing 737-8AS	Ryanair	
EI-EFL	Boeing 737-8AS	Ryanair	
EI-EFM	Boeing 737-8AS	Ryanair	
EI-EFN	Boeing 737-8AS	Ryanair	
EI-EFO	Boeing 737-8AS	Ryanair	
EI-EFP	Boeing 737-8AS	Ryanair	
EI-EFR	Boeing 737-8AS	Ryanair	
EI-EFS	Boeing 737-8AS	Ryanair	
EI-EFT	Boeing 737-8AS	Ryanair	
EI-EFV	Boeing 737-8AS	Ryanair	
EI-EFW	Boeing 737-8AS	Ryanair	

Notes	Reg.	Type	Owner or Operator
	EI-EFX	Boeing 737-8AS	Ryanair
	EI-EFY	Boeing 737-8AS	Ryanair
	EI-EFZ	Boeing 737-8AS	Ryanair
	EI-EGA	Boeing 737-8AS	Ryanair
	EI-EGB	Boeing 737-8AS	Ryanair
	EI-EGC	Boeing 737-8AS	Ryanair
	EI-EGD	Boeing 737-8AS	Ryanair
	EI-EGG	Robinson R44 Raven	B. Haugh
	EI-EHG	Robinson R22 Beta	G. Jordan
	EI-EHH	Aerospatiale ATR-42-300	Aer Arran
	EI-EHK	Magni Gyro M-22 Voyager	M. Concannon
	EI-EHL	Air Creation Tanarg/Ixess 15 912S	S. Woods
	EI-EHM	Rand KR-2T	A. Lagun
	EI-EHP	Robinson R44	P. Tallis
	EI-EHV	CZAW Sportcruiser	G. Doody & Partners
	EI-EHY	Urban Air Samba XXL	J. K. Woodville
	EI-EIA	Airbus A.320-216	Alitalia
	EI-EIB	Airbus A.320-216	Alitalia
	EI-EIC	Airbus A.320-216	Alitalia
	EI-EID	Airbus A.320-216	Alitalia
	EI-EIE	Airbus A.320-216	Alitalia
	EI-EIG	Airbus A.320-216	Alitalia
	EI-EJG	Airbus A.330-202	Alitalia
	EI-EJH	Airbus A.330-202	Alitalia
	EI-EJI	Airbus A.330-202	Alitalia
	EI-EJJ	Airbus A.330-202	Alitalia
	EI-EJK	Airbus A.330-202	Alitalia
	EI-EJL	Airbus A.330-202	Alitalia
	EI-EJR	Robinson R44	Gerair Ltd
	EI-EKA	Boeing 737-8AS	Ryanair
	EI-EKB	Boeing 737-8AS	Ryanair
	EI-EKC	Boeing 737-8AS	Ryanair
	EI-EKD	Boeing 737-8AS	Ryanair
	EI-EKE	Boeing 737-8AS	Ryanair
	EI-EKF	Boeing 737-8AS	Ryanair
	EI-EKG	Boeing 737-8AS	Ryanair
	EI-EKH	Boeing 737-8AS	Ryanair
	EI-EKI	Boeing 737-8AS	Ryanair
	EI-EKJ	Boeing 737-8AS	Ryanair
	EI-EKK	Boeing 737-8AS	Ryanair
	EI-EKL	Boeing 737-8AS	Ryanair
	EI-EKM	Boeing 737-8AS	Ryanair
	EI-EKN	Boeing 737-8AS	Ryanair
	EI-EKO	Boeing 737-8AS	Ryanair
	EI-EKP	Boeing 737-8AS	Ryanair
	EI-EKR	Boeing 737-8AS	Ryanair
	EI-EKS	Boeing 737-8AS	Ryanair
	EI-EKT	Boeing 737-8AS	Ryanair
	EI-EKV	Boeing 737-8AS	Ryanair
	EI-EKW	Boeing 737-8AS	Ryanair
	EI-EKX	Boeing 737-8AS	Ryanair
	EI-EKY	Boeing 737-8AS	Ryanair
	EI-EKZ	Boeing 737-8AS	Ryanair
	EI-ELA	Airbus A.330-302	Aer Lingus
	EI-ELB	Raj Hamsa X'Air 582 (1)	M. Smullen
	EI-ELC	Ikarus C42B	J. Roddy
	EI-ELD	Airbus A.320-232	Avia Nova
	EI-ELE	Airbus A.320-232	Avia Nova
	EI-ELG	Airbus A.340-311	ILFC Ireland Ltd
	EI-ELL	Medway Eclipser	P. McMahon
	EI-ELM	PA-18-95 Super Cub	S. Coughlan
	EI-ELN	Airbus A.320-232	Avia Nova
	EI-ELV	Pegasus XL-R	D. Minnock
	EI-ELZ	Boeing 737-4Q8	Mistral Air
	EI-EMA	Boeing 737-8AS	Ryanair
	EI-EMB	Boeing 737-8AS	Ryanair
	EI-EMC	Boeing 737-8AS	Ryanair
	EI-EMD	Boeing 737-8AS	Ryanair
	EI-EME	Boeing 737-8AS	Ryanair
	EI-EMF	Boeing 737-8AS	Ryanair
	EI-EMH	Boeing 737-8AS	Ryanair

Reg.	Type	Owner or Operator	Notes
EI-EMI	Boeing 737-8AS	Ryanair	
EI-EMJ	Boeing 737-8AS	Ryanair	
EI-EMK	Boeing 737-8AS	Ryanair	
EI-EML	Boeing 737-8AS	Ryanair	
EI-EMM	Boeing 737-8AS	Ryanair	
EI-EMN	Boeing 737-8AS	Ryanair	
EI-EMO	Boeing 737-8AS	Ryanair	
EI-EMP	Boeing 737-8AS	Ryanair	
EI-EMR	Boeing 737-8AS	Ryanair	
EI-EMS	McD Douglas MD-11F	Cagoitalia	
EI-EMT	PA-16 Clipper	J. Dolan	
EI-EMU	Cessna F.152	K. O'Connor	
EI-EMV	CZAW Sportcruiser	L. Doherty & partners	
EI-ENA	Boeing 737-8AS	Ryanair	
EI-ENB	Boeing 737-8AS	Ryanair	
EI-ENC	Boeing 737-8AS	Ryanair	
EI-ENE	Boeing 737-8AS	Ryanair	
EI-ENF	Boeing 737-8AS	Ryanair	
EI-ENG	Boeing 737-8AS	Ryanair	
EI-ENH	Boeing 737-8AS	Ryanair	
EI-ENI	Boeing 737-8AS	Ryanair	
EI-ENJ	Boeing 737-8AS	Ryanair	
EI-ENK	Boeing 737-8AS	Ryanair	
EI-ENL	Boeing 737-8AS	Ryanair	
EI-ENM	Boeing 737-8AS	Ryanair	
EI-ENN	Boeing 737-8AS	Ryanair	
EI-ENO	Boeing 737-8AS	Ryanair	
EI-ENP	Boeing 737-8AS	Ryanair	
EI-ENR	Boeing 737-8AS	Ryanair	
EI-ENS	Boeing 737-8AS	Ryanair	
EI-ENT	Boeing 737-8AS	Ryanair	
EI-ENV	Boeing 737-8AS	Ryanair	
EI-ENW	Boeing 737-8AS	Ryanair	
EI-ENX	Boeing 737-8AS	Ryanair	
EI-ENY	Boeing 737-8AS	Ryanair	
EI-ENZ	Boeing 737-8AS	Ryanair	
EI-EOA	Raj Hamsa X'Air Jabiru	B. Lynch Jnr	
EI-EOB	Cameron Z-69 balloon	J. Leahy	
EI-EOC	Van's RV-6	D. McCann	
EI-EOE	Boeing 737-505	Engaly Ltd	
EI-EOF	Jabiru SP430	J. Bermingham	
EI-EOH	BRM Land Africa	P. J. Piling	
EI-EOI	Take Off Merlin 1100	N. Fitzmaurice	
EI-EOJ	Boeing 737-8BK	Air Italy Polska	
EI-EOO	Ikarus C42 FB UK	B. Gurnett & Partners	
EI-EOU	Evektor EV-97 Eurostar SL	E. McEvoy	
EI-EOW	Flight Design CTSW	J. Moriarty	
EI-EOZ	Boeing 737-3Q8	Celestial Aviation Trading 21 Ltd	
EI-EPA	Boeing 737-8AS	Ryanair	
EI-EPB	Boeing 737-8AS	Ryanair	
EI-EPC	Boeing 737-8AS	Ryanair	
EI-EPD	Boeing 737-8AS	Ryanair	
EI-EPE	Boeing 737-8AS	Ryanair	
EI-EPF	Boeing 737-8AS	Ryanair	
EI-EPG	Boeing 737-8AS	Ryanair	
EI-EPH	Boeing 737-8AS	Ryanair	
EI-EPI	Medway Hybred 44XLR	H. J. Long	
EI-EPJ	Mainair/Gemini Flash IIA	L. Flannery	
EI-EPK	Pegasus Quantum 15-912	R. A. Atkinson	
EI-EPL	Boeing 737-505	Jeritt Ltd	
EI-EPN	Jodel DR.1050	Conor Airpark Developments Ltd	
EI-EPP	PA-22-160	P. McCabe	
EI-EPR	Airbus A.319-111	RBS Aerospace Ltd	
EI-EPW	MXP-740 Savannah Jabiru(5)	C. Kiernan	
EI-EPX	Airbus A.320-214	Calliope Ltd	
EI-EPY	UFM-11 Lambada	P. Kearney	
EI-EPZ	Jodel DR.1050M1	A. Dunne & Partners	
EI-ERD	Boeing 737-36N	Aircraft Finance Trust Ireland Ltd	
EI-ERE	Pegasus Quantum 15-912	M. Carter	
EI-ERF	Boeing 757-256	I-Fly	

Notes	Reg.	Type	Owner or Operator
	EI-ERH	Airbus A.320-232	Avia Nova
	EI-ERI	Air Creation Clipper/Kiss 400-582(1)	E. Redmond
	EI-ERJ	Southdown Raven X	M. Hanley
	EI-ERL	Best Off Sky Ranger 912	B. Chambers
	EI-ERM	Ikarus C42B	C42 Club
	EI-ERN	Magni Gyro M-16 Tandem Trainer	M. Tormey
	EI-ERO	Pegasus XL-R	M. Doyle
	EI-ERP	Boeing 737-3S3	Transaero
	EI-ERZ	Flight Design CT-2K	M. Bowden
	EI-ESB	Urban Air Samba XXL	G. Creegan
	EI-ESC	BRM Land Africa	D. Killian
	EI-ESD	Mainair Blade	O. Farrell
	EI-ESE	Zenair CH.601XL Zodiac	O. Haslett & Partners
	EI-ESF	PA-22-160	J. Dolan
	EI-ESG	Airbus A.319-132	Windjet
	EI-ESL	Boeing 737-8AS	Ryanair
	EI-ESM	Boeing 737-8AS	Ryanair
	EI-ESN	Boeing 737-8AS	Ryanair
	EI-ESO	Boeing 737-8AS	Ryanair
	EI-ESP	Boeing 737-8AS	Ryanair
	EI-ESR	Boeing 737-8AS	Ryanair
	EI-ESS	Boeing 737-8AS	Ryanair
	EI-EST	Boeing 737-8AS	Ryanair
	EI-ESV	Boeing 737-8AS	Ryanair
	EI-ESW	Boeing 737-8AS	Ryanair
	EI-ESX	Boeing 737-8AS	Ryanair
	EI-ESY	Boeing 737-8AS	Ryanair
	EI-ESZ	Boeing 737-8AS	Ryanair
	EI-ETB	Ikarus C42B	P. Higgins & Partners
	EI-ETG	Airbus A.319-111	Bank of America Leasing Ireland Co.Ltd
	EI-ETH	Airbus A.321-211	Wilmington Trust SP Services (Dublin) Ltd
	EI-ETI	Airbus A.330-322	Constitution Aircraft Leasing (Ireland) 3 Ltd
	EI-EXC	Robinson R44	S. Geany
	EI-EZL	Airbus A.330-223	CIT Aerospace International Ltd
	EI-EZN	Airbus A.320-232	Meridiana
	EI-EZO	Airbus A.320-232	Meridiana
	EI-EZR	Airbus A.320-214	Meridiana
	EI-EZS	Airbus A.320-214	Meridiana
	EI-EZT	Airbus A.320-214	Meridiana
	EI-FAB	Eurocopter EC.120B	Billy Jet Ltd
	EI-FII	Cessna 172RG	K. O'Connor
	EI-FXA	Aérospatiale ATR-42-300	Air Contractors (Ireland) Ltd
	EI-FXB	Aérospatiale ATR-42-300	Air Contractors (Ireland) Ltd
	EI-FXC	Aérospatiale ATR-42-300	Air Contractors (Ireland) Ltd
	EI-FXD	Aérospatiale ATR-42-300	Air Contractors (Ireland) Ltd
	EI-FXE	Aérospatiale ATR-42-300	Air Contractors (Ireland) Ltd
	EI-FXG	Aérospatiale ATR-72-202	Air Contractors (Ireland) Ltd
	EI-FXH	Aérospatiale ATR-72-202	Air Contractors (Ireland) Ltd
	EI-FXI	Aérospatiale ATR-72-202	Air Contractors (Ireland) Ltd
	EI-FXJ	Aerospatiale ATR-72-202	Air Contractors (Ireland) Ltd
	EI-FXK	Aerospatiale ATR-72-202	Air Contractors (Ireland) Ltd
	EI-GCE	Sikorsky S-61N	CHC Ireland Ltd
	EI-GDL	Gulfstream GV-SP (G550)	Westair Aviation
	EI-GER	Maule MX7-180A	R. Lanigan & J.Patrick
	EI-GJL	AS.365N3	AIBP
	EI-GKL	Robinson R22 Beta	Eamonn Duffy (Rosemount) Ltd
	EI-GLA	Schleicher ASK-21	Dublin Gliding Club Ltd
	EI-GLB	Schleicher ASK-21	Dublin Gliding Club Ltd
	EI-GLC	Centrair 101A Pegase	Dublin Gliding Club Ltd
	EI-GLD	Schleicher ASK-13	Dublin Gliding Club Ltd
	EI-GLF	Schleicher K-8B	Dublin Gliding Club Ltd
	EI-GLG	Schleicher Ka 6CR	C. Sinclair
	EI-GLH	AB Sportine LAK-17A	S. Kinnear
	EI-GLL	Glaser-Dirks DG-200	P. Denman & C. Craig
	EI-GLM	Schleicher Ka-6CR	P. Denman, C. Craig & J. Finnan
	EI-GLN	Glasflugel H201 Standard Libelle	S. Coveney
	EI-GLO	Scheibe Zugvogel IIIB	J. Walsh, J. Murphy & N. Short
	EI-GLP	Olympia 2B	J. Cashin
	EI-GLS	Rolladen-Schneider LS-7	M. McHugo
	EI-GLT	Schempp-Hirth Discus b	D. Thomas
	EI-GLU	Schleicher Ka-6CR	K. Cullen & Partners

Reg.	Type	Owner or Operator	Notes
EI-GLV	Schleicher ASW-19B	C. Sinclair & B. O'Neill	
EI-GMB	Schleicher ASW-17	ASW-17 Group	
EI-GMC	Schleicher ASK-18	The Eighteen Group	
EI-GMD	Phoebus C	F. McDonnell & Partners	
EI-GMF	Schleicher ASK-13	Dublin Gliding Club Ltd	
EI-GML	Grob G.103 Twin Astir	D. McCarthy	
EI-GMN	DG Flugzeugbau DG-808C	K. Houlihan	
EI-GPT	Robinson R22 Beta	Treaty Plant & Tool (Hire & Sales)	
EI-GPZ	Robinson R44 II	G & P Transport	
EI-GSE	Cessna F.172M	K. A. O'Connor	
EI-GSM	Cessna 182S	Westpoint Flying Group	
EI-GVM	Robinson R22 Beta	G. V. Maloney	
EI-GWY	Cessna 172R	Atlantic Flight Training	
EI-HAZ	Robinson R44	Forestbrook Developments Ltd	
EI-HCS	Grob G.109B	H. Sydner	
EI-HUM	Van's RV-7	G. Humphreys	
EI-IAN	Pilatus PC-6/B2-H4	Irish Parachute Club	
EI-IGP	Boeing 737-7GL	Air Italy	
EI-IGR	Boeing 737-36N	Air Italy	
EI-IGS	Boeing 737-36N	Air Italy	
EI-IGT	Boeing 737-73V	Air Italy	
EI-IGU	Boeing 737-73V	Air Italy	
EI-IKB	Airbus A.320-214	Alitalia	
EI-IKF	Airbus A.320-214	Alitalia	
EI-IKG	Airbus A.320-214	Alitalia	
EI-IKL	Airbus A.320-214	Alitalia	
EI-IKU	Airbus A.320-214	Alitalia	
EI-ILS	Eurocopter EC.135T2+	Irish Helicopters Ltd	
EI-IMB	Airbus A.319-112	Alitalia	
EI-IMC	Airbus A.319-112	Alitalia	
EI-IMD	Airbus A.319-112	Alitalia	
EI-IME	Airbus A.319-112	Alitalia	
EI-IMF	Airbus A.319-112	Alitalia	
EI-IMG	Airbus A.319-112	Alitalia	
EI-IMH	Airbus A.319-112	Alitalia	
EI-IMI	Airbus A.319-112	Alitalia	
EI-IMJ	Airbus A.319-112	Alitalia	
EI-IML	Airbus A.319-112	Alitalia	
EI-IMM	Airbus A.319-112	Alitalia	
EI-IMN	Airbus A.319-111	Alitalia	
EI-IMO	Airbus A.319-112	Alitalia	
EI-IMP	Airbus A.319-111	Alitalia	
EI-IMR	Airbus A.319-111	Alitalia	
EI-IMS	Airbus A.319-111	Alitalia	
EI-ING	Cessna F.172P	21st Century Flyers	
EI-IRV	AS.350B Ecureuil	S. Harris	
EI-ISD	Boeing 777-243ER	Alitalia	
EI-IXB	Airbus A.321-112	Alitalia	
EI-IXC	Airbus A.321-112	Alitalia	
EI-IXD	Airbus A.321-112	Alitalia	
EI-IXF	Airbus A.321-112	Alitalia	
EI-IXG	Airbus A.321-112	Alitalia	
EI-IXH	Airbus A.321-112	Alitalia	
EI-IXI	Airbus A.321-112	Alitalia	
EI-IXJ	Airbus A.321-112	Alitalia	
EI-IXO	Airbus A.321-112	Alitalia	
EI-IXU	Airbus A.321-112	Alitalia	
EI-IXV	Airbus A.321-112	Alitalia	
EI-IXZ	Airbus A.321-112	Alitalia	
EI-JAR	Robinson R44	Donnie, Rita, Carly & Tracy Horan	
EI-JIM	Urban Air Samba XLA	J. Smith	
EI-JIV	L.382G-44K-30 Hercules	Air Contractors (Ireland)	
EI-JJJ	Hawker 900XP	Airlink Airways Ltd	
EI-JOR	Robinson R44 II	Skywest Aviation Ltd	
EI-JPK	Tecnam P2002-JF	Limerick Flying Club (Coonagh) Ltd	
EI-KDH	PA-28-181 Archer II	K. O'Driscoll & D. Harris	
EI-KEL	Eurocopter EC.135T2+	Bond Air Services (Ireland) Ltd	
EI-KEV	Raj Hamsa X'Air Jabiru(3)	P. Kearney	
EI-LAD	Robinson R44 II	J. Harney & Partners	
EI-LAX	Airbus A.330-202	Aer Lingus St Mella	
EI-LCM	TBM-700N	G. Power	

345

Notes	Reg.	Type	Owner or Operator
	EI-LEM	SOCATA TB9 Tampico	M. Fleing
	EI-LFC	Tecnam P.2002-JF	Limerick Flying Club (Coonagh) Ltd
	EI-LIR	Airbus A.319-132	Belle Air
	EI-LIS	Airbus A.320-214	Belle Air
	EI-LMK	Agusta A. 109S	Skyheli Ltd
	EI-LOW	AS.355N	Executive Helicopter Maintenance Ltd
	EI-MCF	Cessna 172R	K. O'Connor
	EI-MCG	Cessna 172R	Galway Flying Club
	EI-MED	Cessna 550	Airlink Airways Ltd
	EI-MEJ	Bell 206B JetRanger	Gaelic Helicopters
	EI-MER	Bell 206B JetRanger III	Gaelic Helicopters
	EI-MES	Sikorsky S-61N	CHC Ireland
	EI-MIK	Eurocopter EC 120B	Executive Helicopter Maintenance Ltd
	EI-MIP	SA.365N Dauphin 2	CHC Ireland
	EI-MIR	Roko Aero NG 4HD	H. Goulding
	EI-MJC	Cessna 525B	Munster Jet Partnership Ltd
	EI-MPW	Robinson R44	Connacht Helicopters
	EI-MSG	Agusta A.109E	Beckdrive Ltd
	EI-MTZ	Urban Air Samba XXL	M. Motz
	EI-MUL	Robinson R44	J. T. Clarke
	EI-NFW	Cessna 172S	Galway Flying Club
	EI-NJA	Robinson R44 II	Nojo Aviation Ltd
	EI-NTH	Agusta A.109E	O'Flynn Construction Co.
	EI-NVL	Jora spol S. R. O. Jora	A. McAllister & partners
	EI-ODD	Bell 206B JetRanger	Dwyer Nolan Developments Ltd
	EI-OFM	Cessna F.172N	C. Phillips
	EI-OOR	Cessna 172S	Sligo Flying Schol Ltd
	EI-OZB	Airbus A.300B4-103F	European Air Transport/DHL
	EI-OZC	Airbus A.300B4-103F	European Air Transport/DHL
	EI-OZD	Airbus A.300B4-203F	European Air Transport/DHL
	EI-OZE	Airbus A.300B4-203F	European Air Transport/DHL
	EI-OZF	Airbus A.300B4-203F	European Air Transport/DHL
	EI-OZG	Airbus A.300B4-203F	European Air Transport/DHL
	EI-OZH	Airbus A.300B4-203F	European Air Transport/DHL
	EI-OZI	Airbus A.300B4-203F	European Air Transport/DHL
	EI-PCI	Bell 206B JetRanger	Malcove Ltd
	EI-PJD	AS.350B2 Twin Squirrel	New World Plant
	EI-PMI	Agusta-Bell 206B JetRanger III	Ping Golf Equipment
	EI-POP	Cameron Z-90 balloon	The Travel Department
	EI-RCA	Roko Aero NG4UL	Racecrest Ltd
	EI-RCG	Sikorsky S-61N	CHC Ireland
	EI-RDA	Embraer ERJ170-200LR	Alitalia Cityliner
	EI-RDB	Embraer ERJ170-200LR	Alitalia Cityliner
	EI-REH	Aérospatiale ATR-72-201	Aer Arann
	EI-REI	Aérospatiale ATR-72-201	Aer Arann
	EI-REJ	Aérospatiale ATR-72-201	Air Contractgors (Ireland) Ltd
	EI-REL	Aerospatiale ATR-72-212	Aer Arann
	EI-REM	Aerospatiale ATR-72-212	Aer Arann
	EI-REO	Aerospatiale ATR-72-212	Aer Arann
	EI-REP	Aerospatiale ATR-72-212	Aer Arann
	EI-REX	Learjet 60	Airlink Airways
	EI-RHM	Bell 407	A. Morrin
	EI-RJA	Avro RJ85	Cityjet
	EI-RJB	Avro RJ85	Cityjet Bere Island
	EI-RJC	Avro RJ85	Cityjet
	EI-RJD	Avro RJ85	Cityjet
	EI-RJE	Avro RJ85	Cityjet
	EI-RJF	Avro RJ85	Cityjet
	EI-RJG	Avro RJ85	Cityjet
	EI-RJH	Avro RJ85	Cityjet
	EI-RJI	Avro RJ85	Cityjet
	EI-RJJ	Avro RJ85	Cityjet
	EI-RJK	Avro RJ85	Cityjet
	EI-RJL	Avro RJ85	Cityjet
	EI-RJM	Avro RJ85	Cityjet
	EI-RJN	Avro RJ85	Cityjet
	EI-RJO	Avro RJ85	Cityjet
	EI-RJP	Avro RJ85	Cityjet Clare Island
	EI-RJR	Avro RJ85	Cityjet
	EI-RJS	Avro RJ85	Cityjet Dursey Island

Reg.	Type	Owner or Operator	Notes
EI-RJT	Avro RJ85	Cityjet	
EI-RJU	Avro RJ85	Cityjet	
EI-RJV	Avro RJ85	Cityjet	
EI-RJW	Avro RJ85	Cityjet Garinish Island	
EI-RJX	Avro RJ85	Cityjet	
EI-RJY	Avro RJ85	Cityjet	
EI-RJZ	Avro RJ85	Cityjet	
EI-RMC	Bell 206B JetRanger	Westair Aviation	
EI-RNA	Embraer ERJ190-100STD	Alitalia Cityliner	
EI-RNB	Embraer ERJ190-100STD	Alitalia Cityliner	
EI-RNC	Embraer ERJ190-100STD	Alitalia Cityliner	
EI-ROB	Robin R.1180TD	Extras Ltd	
EI-ROK	Roko Aero NG 4UL	K. Harley	
EI-RUB	Boeing 737-85P	Transaero	
EI-SAC	Cessna 172P	Sligo Aero Club	
EI-SAF	Airbus A.300B4-203F	European Air Transport/DHL	
EI-SAR	Sikorsky S-61N	CHC Ireland	
EI-SAT	Steen Skybolt	Capt. B. O'Sullivan	
EI-SEA	SeaRey	J. Brennan	
EI-SKB	PA-44-180 Seminole	Shemburn Ltd	
EI-SKC	PA-44-180 Seminole	Shemburn Ltd	
EI-SKD	PA-44-180 Seminole	Shemburn Ltd	
EI-SKE	Robin DR400/140B	Shemburn Ltd	
EI-SKP	Cessna F.172P	Shemburn Ltd	
EI-SKR	PA-44-180 Seminole	Shemburn Ltd	
EI-SKS	Robin R.2160	Shemburn Ltd	
EI-SKT	PA-44-180 Seminole	Shemburn Ltd	
EI-SKU	PA-28RT-201 Arrow IV	Shemburn Ltd	
EI-SKV	Robin R.2160	Shemburn Ltd	
EI-SKW	PA-28-161 Warrior II	Shemburn Ltd	
EI-SLA	Aérospatiale ATR-42-310	Air Contractors (Ireland) Ltd	
EI-SLF	Aérospatiale ATR-72-201	Air Contractors (Ireland) Ltd	
EI-SLG	Aérospatiale ATR-72-202	Air Contractors (Ireland) Ltd	
EI-SLH	Aerospatiale ATR-72-202	Air Contractors (Ireland) Ltd	
EI-SLJ	Aerospatiale ATR-72-201	Air Contractors (Ireland) Ltd	
EI-SLK	Aerospatiale ATR-72-212	Air Contractors (Ireland) Ltd	
EI-SLL	Aerospatiale ATR-72-212	Air Contractors (Ireland) Ltd/Aer Arran	
EI-SLM	Aerospatiale ATR-72-212	Air Contractors (Ireland) Ltd/Aer Arran	
EI-SLN	Aerospatiale ATR-72-212	Air Contractors (Ireland) Ltd/Aer Arran	
EI-SMK	Zenair CH701	S. King	
EI-SPB	Cessna T206H	P. Morrissey	
EI-SQG	Agusta A109E	Quinn Group	
EI-STA	Boeing 737-31S	Air Contractors (Ireland) Ltd/Europe Airpost	
EI-STT	Cessna 172M	Trim Flying Club	
EI-SUB	Robinson R44	EI-SUB Ltd	
EI-SYM	Van's RV-7	E. Symes	
EI-TAB	Airbus A.320-233	Wilmington Trust SP Services/TACA	
EI-TAD	Airbus A.320-233	Alvi Leasing/TACA	
EI-TAG	Airbus A.320-233	Wilmington Trust SP Services/TACA	
EI-TDV	Dassault Falcon 2000LX	Herodias Executive Aircraft	
EI-TGF	Robinson R22 Beta	Skyexpress Ltd	
EI-TIM	Piper J-5A	N. & P. Murphy	
EI-TKI	Robinson R22 Beta	J. McDaid	
EI-TON	M. B. Cooke 582 (5)	T. Merrigan	
EI-UFO	PA-22 Tri-Pacer 150 (tailwheel)	W. Treacy	
EI-UNA	Boeing 767-3P6ER	Transaero	
EI-UNB	Boeing 767-3P6ER	Transaero	
EI-UNC	Boeing 767-319ER	Transaero	
EI-UND	Boeing 767-2P6ER	Transaero	
EI-UNE	Boeing 767-3Q8ER	Transaero	
EI-UNF	Boeing 767-3P6ER	Transaero	
EI-UNG	Boeing 737-524	Transaero	
EI-UNH	Boeing 737-524	Transaero	
EI-UNI	Robinson R44 II	Unipipe (Irl) Ltd	
EI-UNJ	Boeing 737-86J	Transaero	
EI-UNK	Boeing 737-86J	Transaero	
EI-UNL	Boeing 777-312	Transaero	
EI-UNN	Boeing 777-312	Transaero	
EI-UNR	Boeing 777-212ER	Transaero	
EI-UNS	Boeing 777-212ER	Transaero	
EI-UNT	Boeing 777-212ER	Transaero	

Notes	Reg.	Type	Owner or Operator
	EI-UNU	Boeing 777-222ER	Transaero
	EI-UNV	Boeing 777-222ER	Transaero
	EI-UNW	Boeing 777-222	Transaero
	EI-UNX	Boeing 777-222	Transaero
	EI-UNY	Boeing 777-222	Transaero
	EI-UNZ	Boeing 777-222	Transaero
	EI-UPE	McD Douglas MD-11F	Alitalia
	EI-UPI	McD Douglas MD-11F	Alitalia
	EI-VII	Vans RV-7	B. Sheane
	EI-VLN	PA-18A-150	D. O'Mahony
	EI-WAC	PA-23 Aztec 250E	Westair Aviation
	EI-WAT	Tecnam P.2002-JF	Waterford Aero Club Ltd
	EI-WAV	Bell 430	Westair Aviation
	EI-WFD	Tecnam P.2002-JF	Waterford Aero Club Ltd
	EI-WFI	Bombardier CL600-2B16 Challenger	Midwest Atlantic/Westair
	EI-WIG	Sky Ranger 912	M. Brereton
	EI-WJN	HS.125 Srs 700A	Westair Aviation
	EI-WMN	PA-23 Aztec 250F	Westair Aviation
	EI-WWI	Robinson R44 II	J. Murtagh
	EI-WXA	Avro RJ85	Cityjet Ltd
	EI-WXB	Avro RJ85	Cityjet Ltd
	EI-WXP	Hawker 800XP	Westair Aviation Ltd
	EI-XLA	Urban Air Samba XLA	K. Dardis
	EI-XLB	Boeing 747-446	Transaero
	EI-XLC	Boeing 747-446	Transaero
	EI-XLD	Boeing 747-446	Transaero
	EI-XLF	Boeing 747-446	Transaero
	EI-XLG	Boeing 747-446	Transaero
	EI-XLH	Boeing 747-446	Transaero
	EI-XLI	Boeing 747-446	Transaero
	EI-XLJ	Boeing 747-446	Transaero
	EI-XLK	Boeing 747-412	Transaero
	EI-XLL	Boeing 747-412	Transaero
	EI-XLM	Boeing 747-412	Transaero
	EI-XLS	Cessna 560XL	Airlink Airways Ltd
	EI-YLG	Robin HR.200/120B	Leinster Aero Club
	EI-ZZZ	Bell222	Executive Helicopter Maintenance Ltd

EI-CDD Boeing 737-548 of Rossiya. *Allan Wright*

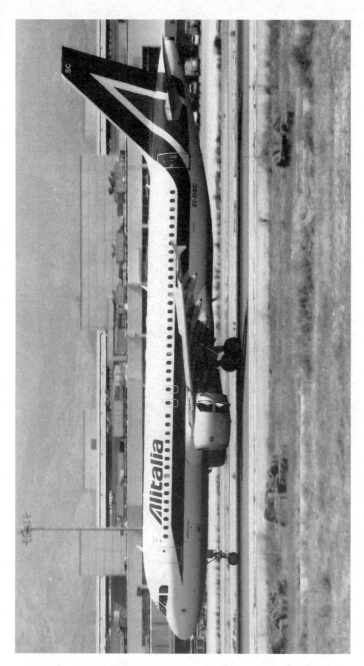

EI-DSC Airbus A.320-216 of Alitalia. *Allan Wright*

A6-EDR Airbus A.380-861 of Emirates Airlines. *Allan Wright*

Overseas Airliner Registrations

(Aircraft included in this section are those most likely to be seen at UK and nearby European airports or overflying UK airspace.)

Reg.	Type	Owner or Operator	Notes

A6 (Arab Emirates)

Reg.	Type	Owner or Operator	Notes
A6-AFA	Airbus A.330-343X	Etihad Airways	
A6-AFB	Airbus A.330-343X	Etihad Airways	
A6-AFC	Airbus A.330-343X	Etihad Airways	
A6-AFD	Airbus A.330-343X	Etihad Airways	
A6-AFE	Airbus A.330-343X	Etihad Airways	
A6-AFF	Airbus A.330-343X	Etihad Airways	
A6-EAA	Airbus A.330-243	Emirates Airlines *Spirit of Birmingham*	
A6-EAD	Airbus A.330-243	Emirates Airlines	
A6-EAE	Airbus A.330-243	Emirates Airlines	
A6-EAF	Airbus A.330-243	Emirates Airlines	
A6-EAG	Airbus A.330-243	Emirates Airlines	
A6-EAH	Airbus A.330-243	Emirates Airlines	
A6-EAI	Airbus A.330-243	Emirates Airlines	
A6-EAJ	Airbus A.330-243	Emirates Airlines	
A6-EAK	Airbus A.330-243	Emirates Airlines	
A6-EAL	Airbus A.330-243	Emirates Airlines	
A6-EAM	Airbus A.330-243	Emirates Airlines	
A6-EAN	Airbus A.330-243	Emirates Airlines	
A6-EAO	Airbus A.330-243	Emirates Airlines	
A6-EAP	Airbus A.330-243	Emirates Airlines	
A6-EAQ	Airbus A.330-243	Emirates Airlines	
A6-EAR	Airbus A.330-243	Emirates Airlines	
A6-EAS	Airbus A.330-243	Emirates Airlines	
A6-EBA	Boeing 777-31HER	Emirates Airlines	
A6-EBB	Boeing 777-36NER	Emirates Airlines	
A6-EBC	Boeing 777-36NER	Emirates Airlines	
A6-EBD	Boeing 777-31HER	Emirates Airlines	
A6-EBE	Boeing 777-36NER	Emirates Airlines	
A6-EBF	Boeing 777-31HER	Emirates Airlines	
A6-EBG	Boeing 777-36NER	Emirates Airlines	
A6-EBH	Boeing 777-31HER	Emirates Airlines	
A6-EBI	Boeing 777-36NER	Emirates Airlines	
A6-EBJ	Boeing 777-36NER	Emirates Airlines	
A6-EBK	Boeing 777-31HER	Emirates Airlines	
A6-EBL	Boeing 777-31HER	Emirates Airlines	
A6-EBM	Boeing 777-31HER	Emirates Airlines	
A6-EBN	Boeing 777-36NER	Emirates Airlines	
A6-EBO	Boeing 777-36NER	Emirates Airlines	
A6-EBP	Boeing 777-31HER	Emirates Airlines	
A6-EBQ	Boeing 777-36NER	Emirates Airlines	
A6-EBR	Boeing 777-31HER	Emirates Airlines	
A6-EBS	Boeing 777-31HER	Emirates Airlines	
A6-EBT	Boeing 777-31HER	Emirates Airlines	
A6-EBU	Boeing 777-31HER	Emirates Airlines	
A6-EBV	Boeing 777-31HER	Emirates Airlines	
A6-EBW	Boeing 777-36NER	Emirates Airlines	
A6-EBX	Boeing 777-31HER	Emirates Airlines	
A6-EBY	Boeing 777-36NER	Emirates Airlines	
A6-EBZ	Boeing 777-31HER	Emirates Airlines	
A6-ECA	Boeing 777-36NER	Emirates Airlines	
A6-ECB	Boeing 777-31HER	Emirates Airlines	
A6-ECC	Boeing 777-36NER	Emirates Airlines	
A6-ECD	Boeing 777-36NER	Emirates Airlines	
A6-ECE	Boeing 777-31HER	Emirates Airlines	
A6-ECF	Boeing 777-31HER	Emirates Airlines	
A6-ECG	Boeing 777-31HER	Emirates Airlines	
A6-ECH	Boeing 777-31HER	Emirates Airlines	
A6-ECI	Boeing 777-31HER	Emirates Airlines	
A6-ECJ	Boeing 777-31HER	Emirates Airlines	
A6-ECK	Boeing 777-31HER	Emirates Airlines	
A6-ECL	Boeing 777-31NER	Emirates Airlines	
A6-ECM	Boeing 777-31NER	Emirates Airlines	
A6-ECN	Boeing 777-31NER	Emirates Airlines	

Notes	Reg.	Type	Owner or Operator
	A6-ECO	Boeinb 777-31NER	Emirates Airlines
	A6-ECP	Boeing 777-31NER	Emirates Airlines
	A6-ECQ	Boeing 777-31HER	Emirates Airlines
	A6-ECR	Boeing 777-31HER	Emirates Airlines
	A6-ECS	Boeing 777-31HER	Emirates Airlines
	A6-ECT	Boeing 777-31HER	Emirates Airlines
	A6-ECU	Boeing 777-31HER	Emirates Airlines
	A6-ECV	Boeing 777-31HER	Emirates Airlines
	A6-ECW	Boeing 777-31HER	Emirates Airlines
	A6-ECX	Boeing 777-31HER	Emirates Airlines
	A6-ECY	Boeing 777-31HER	Emirates Airlines
	A6-ECZ	Boeing 777-31HER	Emirates Airlines
	A6-EDA	Airbus A.380-861	Emirates Airlines
	A6-EDB	Airbus A.380-861	Emirates Airlines
	A6-EDC	Airbus A.380-861	Emirates Airlines
	A6-EDD	Airbus A.380-861	Emirates Airlines
	A6-EDE	Airbus A.380-861	Emirates Airlines
	A6-EDF	Airbus A.380-861	Emirates Airlines
	A6-EDG	Airbus A.380-861	Emirates Airlines
	A6-EDH	Airbus A.380-861	Emirates Airlines
	A6-EDI	Airbus A.380-861	Emirates Airlines
	A6-EDJ	Airbus A.380-861	Emirates Airlines
	A6-EDK	Airbus A.380-861	Emirates Airlines
	A6-EDL	Airbus A.380-861	Emirates Airlines
	A6-EDM	Airbus A.380-861	Emirates Airlines
	A6-EDN	Airbus A.380-861	Emirates Airlines
	A6-EDO	Airbus A.380-861	Emirates Airlines
	A6-EDP	Airbus A.380-861	Emirates Airlines
	A6-EDQ	Airbus A.380-861	Emirates Airlines
	A6-EDR	Airbus A.380-861	Emirates Airlines
	A6-EDS	Airbus A.380-861	Emirates Airlines
	A6-EDT	Airbus A.380-861	Emirates Airlines
	A6-EDU	Airbus A.380-861	Emirates Airlines
	A6-EDV	Airbus A.380-861	Emirates Airlines
	A6-EDW	Airbus A.380-861	Emirates Airlines
	A6-EDX	Airbus A.380-861	Emirates Airlines
	A6-EDY	Airbus A.380-861	Emirates Airlines
	A6-EDZ	Airbus A.380-861	Emirates Airlines
	A6-EGA	Boeing 777-31HER	Emirates Airlines
	A6-EGB	Boeing 777-31HER	Emirates Airlines
	A6-EGC	Boeing 777-31HER	Emirates Airlines
	A6-EGD	Boeing 777-31HER	Emirates Airlines
	A6-EGE	Boeing 777-31HER	Emirates Airlines
	A6-EGF	Boeing 777-31HER	Emirates Airlines
	A6-EGG	Boeing 777-31HER	Emirates Airlines
	A6-EGH	Boeing 777-31HER	Emirates Airlines
	A6-EGI	Boeing 777-31HER	Emirates Airlines
	A6-EGJ	Boeing 777-31HER	Emirates Airlines
	A6-EGK	Boeing 777-31HER	Emirates Airlines
	A6-EGL	Boeing 777-31HER	Emirates Airlines
	A6-EGM	Boeing 777-31HER	Emirates Airlines
	A6-EGN	Boeing 777-31HER	Emirates Airlines
	A6-EGO	Boeing 777-31HER	Emirates Airlines
	A6-EGP	Boeing 777-31HER	Emirates Airlines
	A6-EGQ	Boeing 777-31HER	Emirates Airlines
	A6-EGR	Boeing 777-31HER	Emirates Airlines
	A6-EHA	Airbus A.340-541	Etihad Airways
	A6-EHB	Airbus A.340-541	Etihad Airways
	A6-EHC	Airbus A.340-541	Etihad Airways
	A6-EHD	Airbus A.340-541	Etihad Airways
	A6-EHE	Airbus A.340-642	Etihad Airways
	A6-EHF	Airbus A.340-642	Etihad Airways
	A6-EHH	Airbus A.340-642	Etihad Airways
	A6-EHI	Airbus A.340-642	Etihad Airways
	A6-EHJ	Airbus A.340-642	Etihad Airways
	A6-EHK	Airbus A.340-642	Etihad Airways
	A6-EHL	Airbus A.340-642	Etihad Airways
	A6-EKQ	Airbus A.330-243	Emirates Airlines
	A6-EKR	Airbus A.330-243	Emirates Airlines
	A6-EKS	Airbus A.330-243	Emirates Airlines
	A6-EKT	Airbus A.330-243	Emirates Airlines
	A6-EKU	Airbus A.330-243	Emirates Airlines
	A6-EKV	Airbus A.330-243	Emirates Airlines
	A6-EKW	Airbus A.330-243	Emirates Airlines

Reg.	Type	Owner or Operator	Notes
A6-EKX	Airbus A.330-243	Emirates Airlines	
A6-EKY	Airbus A.330-243	Emirates Airlines	
A6-EKZ	Airbus A.330-243	Emirates Airlines	
A6-EMD	Boeing 777-21H	Emirates Airlines	
A6-EME	Boeing 777-21H	Emirates Airlines	
A6-EMF	Boeing 777-21H	Emirates Airlines	
A6-EMG	Boeing 777-21HER	Emirates Airlines	
A6-EMH	Boeing 777-21HER	Emirates Airlines	
A6-EMI	Boeing 777-21HER	Emirates Airlines	
A6-EMJ	Boeing 777-21HER	Emirates Airlines	
A6-EMK	Boeing 777-21HER	Emirates Airlines	
A6-EML	Boeing 777-21HER	Emirates Airlines	
A6-EMM	Boeing 777-31H	Emirates Airlines	
A6-EMN	Boeing 777-31H	Emirates Airlines	
A6-EMO	Boeing 777-31H	Emirates Airlines	
A6-EMP	Boeing 777-31H	Emirates Airlines	
A6-EMQ	Boeing 777-31H	Emirates Airlines	
A6-EMR	Boeing 777-31H	Emirates Airlines	
A6-EMS	Boeing 777-31H	Emirates Airlines	
A6-EMT	Boeing 777-31H	Emirates Airlines	
A6-EMU	Boeing 777-31H	Emirates Airlines	
A6-EMV	Boeing 777-31H	Emirates Airlines	
A6-EMW	Boeing 777-31H	Emirates Airlines	
A6-EMX	Boeing 777-31H	Emirates Airlines	
A6-ERA	Airbus A.340-541	Emirates Airlines	
A6-ERB	Airbus A.340-541	Emirates Airlines	
A6-ERC	Airbus A.340-541	Emirates Airlines	
A6-ERD	Airbus A.340-541	Emirates Airlines	
A6-ERE	Airbus A.340-541	Emirates Airlines	
A6-ERF	Airbus A.340-541	Emirates Airlines	
A6-ERG	Airbus A.340-541	Emirates Airlines	
A6-ERH	Airbus A.340-541	Emirates Airlines	
A6-ERI	Airbus A.340-541	Emirates Airlines	
A6-ERJ	Airbus A.340-541	Emirates Airlines	
A6-ERM	Airbus A.340-313X	Emirates Airlines	
A6-ERN	Airbus A.340-313X	Emirates Airlines	
A6-ERO	Airbus A.340-313X	Emirates Airlines	
A6-ERP	Airbus A.340-313X	Emirates Airlines	
A6-ERQ	Airbus A.340-313X	Emirates Airlines	
A6-ERR	Airbus A.340-313X	Emirates Airlines	
A6-ERS	Airbus A.340-313X	Emirates Airlines	
A6-ERT	Airbus A.340-313X	Emirates Airlines	
A6-ETA	Boeing 777-3FXER	Etihad Airways	
A6-ETB	Boeing 777-3FXER	Etihad Airways	
A6-ETC	Boeing 777-3FXER	Etihad Airways	
A6-ETD	Boeing 777-3FXER	Etihad Airways	
A6-ETE	Boeing 777-3FXER	Etihad Airways	
A6-ETF	Boeing 777-3FXER	Etihad Airways	
A6-ETG	Boeing 777-3FXER	Etihad Airways	
A6-ETH	Boeing 777-3FXER	Etihad Airways	
A6-ETI	Boeing 777-3FXER	Etihad Airways	
A6-ETJ	Boeing 777-3FXER	Etihad Airways	
A6-ETK	Boeing 777-3FXER	Etihad Airways	
A6-EWA	Boeing 777-21HLR	Emirates Airlines	
A6-EWB	Boeing 777-21HLR	Emirates Airlines	
A6-EWC	Boeing 777-21HLR	Emirates Airlines	
A6-EWD	Boeing 777-21HLR	Emirates Airlines	
A6-EWE	Boeing 777-21HLR	Emirates Airlines	
A6-EWF	Boeing 777-21HLR	Emirates Airlines	
A6-EWG	Boeing 777-21HLR	Emirates Airlines	
A6-EWH	Boeing 777-21HER	Emirates Airlines	
A6-EWI	Boeing 777-21HER	Emirates Airlines	
A6-EWJ	Boeing 777-21HLR	Emirates Airlines	
A6-EYD	Airbus A.330-243	Etihad Airways	
A6-EYE	Airbus A.330-243	Etihad Airways *Blue Moon Rising*	
A6-EYF	Airbus A.330-243	Etihad Airways	
A6-EYG	Airbus A.330-243	Etihad Airways	
A6-EYH	Airbus A.330-243	Etihad Airways	
A6-EYI	Airbus A.330-243	Etihad Airways	
A6-EYJ	Airbus A.330-243	Etihad Airways	
A6-EYK	Airbus A.330-243	Etihad Airways	
A6-EYL	Airbus A.330-243	Etihad Airways	
A6-EYM	Airbus A.330-243	Etihad Airways	

Notes	Reg.	Type	Owner or Operator
	A6-EYN	Airbus A.330-243	Etihad Airways
	A6-EYO	Airbus A.330-243	Etihad Airways
	A6-EYP	Airbus A.330-243	Etihad Airways
	A6-EYQ	Airbus A.330-243	Etihad Airways
	A6-EYR	Airbus A.330-243	Ethiad Airways
	A6-EYS	Airbus A.330-243	Ethiad Airways
	A6-HAZ	Airbus A.300B4-622RF	Maximus Air Cargo
	A6-SUL	Airbus A.300B4-622RF	Maximus Air Cargo

A7 (Qatar)

	Reg.	Type	Owner or Operator
	A7-ACA	Airbus A.330-202	Qatar Airways *Al Wajba*
	A7-ACB	Airbus A.330-202	Qatar Airways *Al Majida*
	A7-ACC	Airbus A.330-202	Qatar Airways *Al Shahaniya*
	A7-ACD	Airbus A.330-202	Qatar Airways *Al Wusell*
	A7-ACE	Airbus A.330-202	Qatar Airways *Al Dhakira*
	A7-ACF	Airbus A.330-202	Qatar Airways *Al Kara'anah*
	A7-ACG	Airbus A.330-202	Qatar Airways *Al Wabra*
	A7-ACH	Airbus A.330-202	Qatar Airways *Al Mafjar*
	A7-ACI	Airbus A.330-202	Qatar Airways *Muathier*
	A7-ACJ	Airbus A.330-202	Qatar Airways *Zikreet*
	A7-ACK	Airbus A.330-202	Qatar Airways
	A7-ACL	Airbus A.330-202	Qatar Airways
	A7-ACM	Airbus A.330-202	Qatar Airways
	A7-AEA	Airbus A.330-302	Qatar Airways *Al Muntazah*
	A7-AEB	Airbus A.330-302	Qatar Airways *Al Sayliyah*
	A7-AEC	Airbus A.330-302	Qatar Airways *Al Markhiya*
	A7-AED	Airbus A.330-302	Qatar Airways *Al Nu'uman*
	A7-AEE	Airbus A.330-302	Qatar Airways *Semaisma*
	A7-AEF	Airbus A.330-302	Qatar Airways *Al Rumellah*
	A7-AEG	Airbus A.330-302	Qatar Airways *Al Duhell*
	A7-AEH	Airbus A.330-302	Qatar Airways
	A7-AEI	Airbus A.330-302	Qatar Airways
	A7-AEJ	Airbus A.330-302	Qatar Airways
	A7-AEM	Airbus A.330-302	Qatar Airways
	A7-AEN	Airbus A.330-302	Qatar Airways
	A7-AEO	Airbus A.330-302	Qatar Airways
	A7-AFL	Airbus A.330-202	Qatar Airways *Al Messilah*
	A7-AFM	Airbus A.330-202	Qatar Airways *Al Udaid*
	A7-AFP	Airbus A.330-202	Qatar Airways *Al Shamal*
	A7-AGA	Airbus A.340-642	Qatar Airways
	A7-AGB	Airbus A.340-642	Qatar Airways
	A7-AGC	Airbus A.340-642	Qatar Airways
	A7-AGD	Airbus A.340-642	Qatar Airways
	A7-AKA	Airbus A.380-861	Qatar Airways
	A7-AKB	Airbus A.380-861	Qatar Airways
	A7-BAA	Boeing 777-3DZ ER	Qatar Airways
	A7-BAB	Boeing 777-3DZ ER	Qatar Airways
	A7-BAC	Boeing 777-3DZ ER	Qatar Airways
	A7-BAE	Boeing 777-3DZ ER	Qatar Airways
	A7-BAF	Boeing 777-3DZ ER	Qatar Airways
	A7-BAG	Boeing 777-3DZ ER	Qatar Airways
	A7-BAH	Boeing 777-3DZ ER	Qatar Airways
	A7-BAI	Boeing 777-3DZ ER	Qatar Airways
	A7-BAJ	Boeing 777-3DZ ER	Qatar Airways
	A7-BAK	Boeing 777-3DZ ER	Qatar Airways
	A7-BAL	Boeing 777-3DZ ER	Qatar Airways
	A7-BAM	Boeing 777-3DZ ER	Qatar Airways
	A7-BAN	Boeing 777-3DZ ER	Qatar Airways
	A7-BAO	Boeing 777-3DZ ER	Qatar Airways
	A7-BAP	Boeing 777-3DZ ER	Qatar Airways *Al Qattard*
	A7-BAQ	Boeing 777-3DZ ER	Qatar Airways
	A7-BAS	Boeing 777-3DZ ER	Qatar Airways
	A7-BBA	Boeing 777-2DZ LR	Qatar Airways
	A7-BBB	Boeing 777-2DZ LR	Qatar Airways
	A7-BBC	Boeing 777-2DZ LR	Qatar Airways
	A7-BBD	Boeing 777-2DZ LR	Qatar Airways
	A7-BBE	Boeing 777-2DZ LR	Qatar Airways
	A7-BBF	Boeing 777-2DZ LR	Qatar Airways
	A7-BBG	Boeing 777-2DZ LR	Qatar Airways
	A7-BBH	Boeing 777-2DZ LR	Qatar Airways *A.Calail*
	A7-BBI	Boeing 777-2DZ LR	Qatar Airways *Jaow Alsalam*
	A7-BBJ	Boeing 777-2DZ LR	Qatar Airways

A9C (Bahrain)

A9C-KA	Airbus A.330-243 (501)	Gulf Air
A9C-KB	Airbus A.330-243 (502)	Gulf Air
A9C-KC	Airbus A.330-243 (503)	Gulf Air
A9C-KD	Airbus A.330-243 (504)	Gulf Air
A9C-KE	Airbus A.330-243 (505)	Gulf Air
A9C-KF	Airbus A.330-243 (506)	Gulf Air *Aldafra*
A9C-KG	Airbus A.330-243	Gulf Air
A9C-KH	Airbus A.330-243	Gulf Air
A9C-KI	Airbus A.330-243	Gulf Air
A9C-KJ	Airbus A.330-243	Gulf Air
A9C-LG	Airbus A.340-313X (407)	Gulf Air
A9C-LH	Airbus A.340-313X (408)	Gulf Air
A9C-LI	Airbus A.340-313X (409)	Gulf Air
A9C-LJ	Airbus A.340-313X (410)	Gulf Air

A40 (Oman)

A40-DA	Airbus A.330-243	Oman Air
A40-DB	Airbus A.330-343	Oman Air
A40-DC	Airbus A.330-243	Oman Air
A40-DD	Airbus A.330-343	Oman Air
A40-DE	Airbus A.330-343	Oman Air
A40-DF	Airbus A.330-243	Oman Air
A40-DG	Airbus A.330-243	Oman Air

AP (Pakistan)

AP-BDZ	Airbus A.310-308	Pakistan International Airlines
AP-BEB	Airbus A.310-308	Pakistan International Airlines
AP-BEC	Airbus A.310-308	Pakistan International Airlines
AP-BEG	Airbus A.310-308	Pakistan International Airlines
AP-BEQ	Airbus A.310-308	Pakistan International Airlines
AP-BEU	Airbus A.310-308	Pakistan International Airlines
AP-BGJ	Boeing 777-240ER	Pakistan International Airlines
AP-BGK	Boeing 777-240ER	Pakistan International Airlines
AP-BGL	Boeing 777-240ER	Pakistan International Airlines
AP-BGY	Boeing 777-240LR	Pakistan International Airlines
AP-BGZ	Boeing 777-240LR	Pakistan International Airlines
AP-BHV	Boeing 777-340ER	Pakistan International Airlines
AP-BHW	Boeing 777-340ER	Pakistan International Airlines
AP-BHX	Boeing 777-240ER	Pakistan International Airlines
AP-BID	Boeing 777-240ER	Pakistan International Airlines
AP-BIE	Airbus A.319-112	AirBlue
AP-BIF	Airbus A.319-112	AirBlue
AP-EDB	Airbus A.319-111	AirBlue
AP-EDC	Airbus A.319-111	AirBlue

B (China/Taiwan/Hong Kong)

B-HKE	Boeing 747-412	Cathay Pacific Airways
B-HKF	Boeing 747-412	Cathay Pacific Airways
B-HKH	Boeing 747-412BCF (SCD)	Cathay Pacific Airways
B-HKJ	Boeing 747-412BCF	Cathay Pacific Airways
B-HKT	Boeing 747-412BCF	Cathay Pacific Airways
B-HKU	Boeing 747-412	Cathay Pacific Airways
B-HKV	Boeing 747-412	Cathay Pacific Airways
B-HKX	Boeing 747-412BCF	Cathay Pacific Airways
B-HOP	Boeing 747-467	Cathay Pacific Airways
B-HOR	Boeing 747-467	Cathay Pacific Airways
B-HOS	Boeing 747-467	Cathay Pacific Airways
B-HOT	Boeing 747-467	Cathay Pacific Airways
B-HOV	Boeing 747-467	Cathay Pacific Airways
B-HOW	Boeing 747-467	Cathay Pacific Airways
B-HOX	Boeing 747-467	Cathay Pacific Airways
B-HOY	Boeing 747-467	Cathay Pacific Airways
B-HOZ	Boeing 747-467BCF	Cathay Pacific Airways
B-HUA	Boeing 747-467	Cathay Pacific Airways
B-HUB	Boeing 747-467	Cathay Pacific Airways

Notes	Reg.	Type	Owner or Operator
	B-HUD	Boeing 747-467	Cathay Pacific Airways
	B-HUE	Boeing 747-467	Cathay Pacific Airways
	B-HUF	Boeing 747-467	Cathay Pacific Airways
	B-HUG	Boeing 747-467	Cathay Pacific Airways
	B-HUH	Boeing 747-467F (SCD)	Cathay Pacific Airways
	B-HUI	Boeing 747-467	Cathay Pacific Airways
	B-HUJ	Boeing 747-467	Cathay Pacific Airways
	B-HUK	Boeing 747-467F (SCD)	Cathay Pacific Airways
	B-HUL	Boeing 747-467F (SCD)	Cathay Pacific Airways
	B-HUO	Boeing 747-467F (SCD)	Cathay Pacific Airways
	B-HUP	Boeing 747-467F (SCD)	Cathay Pacific Airways
	B-HUQ	Boeing 747-467F (SCD)	Cathay Pacific Airways
	B-HXA	Airbus A.340-313X	Cathay Pacific Airways
	B-HXB	Airbus A.340-313X	Cathay Pacific Airways
	B-HXC	Airbus A.340-313X	Cathay Pacific Airways
	B-HXD	Airbus A.340-313X	Cathay Pacific Airways
	B-HXE	Airbus A.340-313X	Cathay Pacific Airways
	B-HXF	Airbus A.340-313X	Cathay Pacific Airways
	B-HXG	Airbus A.340-313X	Cathay Pacific Airways
	B-HXH	Airbus A.340-313X	Cathay Pacific Airways
	B-HXI	Airbus A.340-313X	Cathay Pacific Airways
	B-HXJ	Airbus A.340-313X	Cathay Pacific Airways
	B-HXK	Airbus A.340-313X	Cathay Pacific Airways
	B-KAE	Boeing 747-412BCF	Cathay Pacific Airways
	B-KAF	Boeing 747-412BCF	Cathay Pacific Airways
	B-KAH	Boeing 747-412BCF	Cathay Pacific Airways
	B-KAI	Boeing 747-412BCF	Cathay Pacific Airways
	B-KPA	Boeing 777-367ER	Cathay Pacific Airways
	B-KPB	Boeing 777-367ER	Cathay Pacific Airways
	B-KPC	Boeing 777-367ER	Cathay Pacific Airways
	B-KPD	Boeing 777-367ER	Cathay Pacific Airways
	B-KPE	Boeing 777-367ER	Cathay Pacific Airways
	B-KPF	Boeing 777-367ER	Cathay Pacific Airways
	B-KPG	Boeing 777-367ER	Cathay Pacific Airways
	B-KPH	Boeing 777-367ER	Cathay Pacific Airways
	B-KPI	Boeing 777-367ER	Cathay Pacific Airways
	B-KPJ	Boeing 777-367ER	Cathay Pacific Airways
	B-KPK	Boeing 777-367ER	Cathay Pacific Airways
	B-KPL	Boeing 777-367ER	Cathay Pacific Airways
	B-KPM	Boeing 777-367ER	Cathay Pacific Airways
	B-KPN	Boeing 777-367ER	Cathay Pacific Airways
	B-KPO	Boeing 777-367ER	Cathay Pacific Airways
	B-KPP	Boeing 777-367ER	Cathay Pacific Airways
	B-KPQ	Boeing 777-367ER	Cathay Pacific Airways
	B-KPR	Boeing 777-367ER	Cathay Pacific Airways
	B-KPS	Boeing 777-367ER	Cathay Pacific Airways
	B-KPT	Boeing 777-367ER	Cathay Pacific Airways
	B-KPU	Boeing 777-367ER	Cathay Pacific Airways
	B-KPV	Boeing 777-367ER	Cathay Pacific Airways
	B-KPW	Boeing 777-367ER	Cathay Pacific Airways
	B-KPX	Boeing 777-367ER	Cathay Pacific Airways
	B-KPY	Boeing 777-367ER	Cathay Pacific Airways
	B-KPZ	Boeing 777-367ER	Cathay Pacific Airways
	B-KQA	Boeing 777-367ER	Cathay Pacific Airways
	B-KQB	Boeing 777-367ER	Cathay Pacific Airways
	B-LIA	Boeing 747-467ERF	Cathay Pacific Airways
	B-LIB	Boeing 747-467ERF	Cathay Pacific Airways
	B-LIC	Boeing 747-467ERF	Cathay Pacific Airways
	B-LID	Boeing 747-467ERF	Cathay Pacific Airways
	B-LIE	Boeing 747-467ERF	Cathay Pacific Airways
	B-LIF	Boeing 747-467ERF	Cathay Pacific Airways
	B-LJA	Boeing 747-867F	Cathay Pacific Airways
	B-LJB	Boeing 747-867F	Cathay Pacific Airways
	B-LJE	Boeing 747-867F	Cathay Pacific Airways
	B-LNC	Airbus A.330-223	Hong Kong Airlines
	B-LND	Airbus A.330-223	Hong Kong Airlines
	B-LNE	Airbus A.330-223	Hong Kong Airlines
	B-LNF	Airbus A.330-223	Hong Kong Airlines
	B-LNG	Airbus A.330-223	Hong Kong Airlines
	B-LNI	Airbus A.330-223	Hong Kong Airlines
	B-LNJ	Airbus A.330-223	Hong Kong Airlines
	B-2385	Airbus A.340-313X	Air China
	B-2386	Airbus A.340-313X	Air China
	B-2387	Airbus A.340-313X	Air China

Reg.	Type	Owner or Operator	Notes
B-2388	Airbus A.340-313X	Air China	
B-2389	Airbus A.340-313X	Air China	
B-2390	Airbus A.340-313X	Air China	
B-2409	Boeing 747-412F (SCD)	Air China Cargo	
B-2455	Boeing 747-412BCF	Air China Cargo	
B-2456	Boeing 747-4J6BCF	Air China Cargo	
B-2457	Boeing 747-412BCF	Air China Cargo	
B-2458	Boeing 747-4J6BCF	Air China Cargo	
B-2460	Boeing 747-4J6BCF	Air China Cargo	
B-2475	Boeing 747-4FTF (SCD)	Air China Cargo	
B-2476	Boeing 747-4FTF (SCD)	Air China Cargo	
B-2477	Boeing 747-433SF	Air China Cargo	
B-2478	Boeing 747-433SF	Air China Cargo	
B-6070	Airbus A.330-243	Air China	
B-6071	Airbus A.330-243	Air China	
B-6072	Airbus A.330-243	Air China	
B-6073	Airbus A.330-243	Air China	
B-6075	Airbus A.330-243	Air China	
B-6076	Airbus A.330-243	Air China	
B-6079	Airbus A.330-243	Air China	
B-6080	Airbus A.330-243	Air China	
B-6081	Airbus A.330-243	Air China	
B-6082	Airbus A.330-243	China Eastern Airlines	
B-6090	Airbus A.330-243	Air China	
B-6091	Airbus A.330-243	Air China	
B-6092	Airbus A.330-243	Air China	
B-6093	Airbus A.330-243	Air China	
B-6099	Airbus A.330-243	China Eastern Airlines	
B-6113	Airbus A.330-243	Air China	
B-6115	Airbus A.330-243	Air China	
B-6117	Airbus A.330-243	Air China	
B-6121	Airbus A.330-243	China Eastern Airlines	
B-6122	Airbus A.330-243	China Eastern Airlines	
B-6123	Airbus A.330-243	China Eastern Airlines	
B-6130	Airbus A.330-243	Air China	
B-6131	Airbus A.330-243	Air China	
B-6132	Airbus A.330-243	Air China	
B-6505	Airbus A.330-243	Air China	
B-6533	Airbus A.330-243	Air China	
B-6536	Airbus A.330-243	Air China	
B-6537	Airbus A.330-243	China Eastern Airlines	
B-6538	Airbus A.330-243	China Eastern Airlines	
B-16101	McD Douglas MD-11F	EVA Air Cargo	
B-16107	McD Douglas MD-11F	EVA Air Cargo	
B-16108	McD Douglas MD-11F	EVA Air Cargo	
B-16109	McD Douglas MD-11F	EVA Air Cargo	
B-16110	McD Douglas MD-11F	EVA Air Cargo	
B-16111	McD Douglas MD-11F	EVA Air Cargo	
B-16112	McD Douglas MD-11F	EVA Air Cargo	
B-16113	McD Douglas MD-11F	EVA Air Cargo	
B-16403	Boeing 747-45E	EVA Airways	
B-16405	Boeing 747-45E	EVA Airways	
B-16408	Boeing 747-45E	EVA Airways	
B-16409	Boeing 747-45E	EVA Airways	
B-16410	Boeing 747-45E	EVA Airways	
B-16411	Boeing 747-45E	EVA Airways	
B-16412	Boeing 747-45E	EVA Airways	
B-16701	Boeing 777-35EER	EVA Airways	
B-16702	Boeing 777-35EER	EVA Airways	
B-16703	Boeing 777-35EER	EVA Airways	
B-16705	Boeing 777-35EER	EVA Airways	
B-16706	Boeing 777-35EER	EVA Airways	
B-16707	Boeing 777-35EER	EVA Airways	
B-16708	Boeing 777-35EER	EVA Airways	
B-16709	Boeing 777-35EER	EVA Airways	
B-16710	Boeing 777-35EER	EVA Airways	
B-16711	Boeing 777-35EER	EVA Airways	
B-16712	Boeing 777-35EER	EVA Airways	
B-16713	Boeing 777-35EER	EVA Airways	
B-16715	Boeing 777-35EER	EVA Airways	
B-16716	Boeing 777-35EER	EVA Airways	
B-16717	Boeing 777-35EER	EVA Airways	
B-18701	Boeing 747-409F (SCD)	China Airlines	

Notes	Reg.	Type	Owner or Operator
	B-18702	Boeing 747-409F (SCD)	China Airlines
	B-18706	Boeing 747-409F (SCD)	China Airlines
	B-18707	Boeing 747-409F (SCD)	China Airlines
	B-18708	Boeing 747-409F (SCD)	China Airlines
	B-18709	Boeing 747-409F (SCD)	China Airlines
	B-18710	Boeing 747-409F (SCD)	China Airlines
	B-18711	Boeing 747-409F (SCD)	China Airlines
	B-18712	Boeing 747-409F (SCD)	China Airlines
	B-18715	Boeing 747-409F (SCD)	China Airlines
	B-18716	Boeing 747-409F (SCD)	China Airlines
	B-18717	Boeing 747-409F (SCD)	China Airlines
	B-18718	Boeing 747-409F (SCD)	China Airlines
	B-18719	Boeing 747-409F (SCD)	China Airlines
	B-18720	Boeing 747-409F (SCD)	China Airlines
	B-18721	Boeing 747-409F (SCD)	China Airlines
	B-18722	Boeing 747-409F (SCD)	China Airlines
	B-18723	Boeing 747-409F (SCD)	China Airlines
	B-18725	Boeing 747-409F (SCD)	China Airlines
	B-18801	Airbus A.340-313X	China Airlines
	B-18802	Airbus A.340-313X	China Airlines
	B-18803	Airbus A.340-313X	China Airlines
	B-18805	Airbus A.340-313X	China Airlines
	B-18806	Airbus A.340-313X	China Airlines
	B-18807	Airbus A.340-313X	China Airlines

C (Canada)

	Reg.	Type	Owner or Operator
	C-FCAB	Boeing 767-375ER (681)	Air Canada
	C-FCAE	Boeing 767-375ER (682)	Air Canada
	C-FCAF	Boeing 767-375ER (683)	Air Canada
	C-FCAG	Boeing 767-375ER (684)	Air Canada
	C-FDAT	Airbus A.310-308 (305)	Air Transat
	C-FITL	Boeing 777-333ER (731)	Air Canada
	C-FITU	Boeing 777-333ER (732)	Air Canada
	C-FITW	Boeing 777-3Q8ER (733)	Air Canada
	C-FIUA	Boeing 777-233LR (701)	Air Canada
	C-FIUF	Boeing 777-233LR (702)	Air Canada
	C-FIUJ	Boeing 777-233LR (703)	Air Canada
	C-FIUL	Boeing 777-333ER (734)	Air Canada
	C-FIUR	Boeing 777-333ER (735)	Air Canada
	C-FIUV	Boeing 777-333ER	Air Canada
	C-FIUW	Boeing 777-333ER	Air Canada
	C-FIVK	Boeing 777-233LR	Air Canada
	C-FIVM	Boeing 777-333ER	Air Canada
	C-FIVQ	Boeing 777-333ER	Air Canada
	C-FIVR	Boeing 777-333ER	Air Canada
	C-FIVS	Boeing 777-333ER	Air Canada
	C-FMWP	Boeing 767-333ER (631)	Air Canada
	C-FMWQ	Boeing 767-333ER (632)	Air Canada
	C-FMWU	Boeing 767-333ER (633)	Air Canada
	C-FMWV	Boeing 767-333ER (634)	Air Canada
	C-FMWY	Boeing 767-333ER (635)	Air Canada
	C-FMXC	Boeing 767-333ER (636)	Air Canada
	C-FNND	Boeing 777-233LR	Air Canada
	C-FNNH	Boeing 777-233LR	Air Canada
	C-FOCA	Boeing 767-375ER (640)	Air Canada
	C-FPCA	Boeing 767-375ER (637)	Air Canada
	C-FRAM	Boeing 777-333ER	Air Canada
	C-FTCA	Boeing 767-375ER (638)	Air Canada
	C-FXCA	Boeing 767-375ER (639)	Air Canada
	C-GBZR	Boeing 767-38EER (645)	Air Canada
	C-GCTS	Airbus A.330-342	Air Transat
	C-GDUZ	Boeing 767-38EER (646)	Air Canada
	C-GEOQ	Boeing 767-375ER (647)	Air Canada
	C-GEOU	Boeing 767-375ER (648)	Air Canada
	C-GFAF	Airbus A.330-343X (931)	Air Canada
	C-GFAH	Airbus A.330-343X (932)	Air Canada
	C-GFAJ	Airbus A.330-343X (933)	Air Canada
	C-GFAT	Airbus A.310-304 (301)	Air Transat
	C-GFUR	Airbus A.330-343X (934)	Air Canada
	C-GGTS	Airbus A.330-243 (101)	Air Transat
	C-GHKR	Airbus A.330-343X (935)	Air Canada
	C-GHKW	Airbus A.330-343X (936)	Air Canada

Reg.	Type	Owner or Operator	Notes
C-GHKX	Airbus A.330-343X (937)	Air Canada	
C-GHLA	Boeing 767-35HER (656)	Air Canada	
C-GHLK	Boeing 767-35HER (657)	Air Canada	
C-GHLM	Airbus A.330-343X (938)	Air Canada	
C-GHLQ	Boeing 767-333ER (658)	Air Canada	
C-GHLT	Boeing 767-333ER (659)	Air Canada	
C-GHLU	Boeing 767-333ER (660)	Air Canada	
C-GHLV	Boeing 767-333ER (661)	Air Canada	
C-GHOZ	Boeing 767-375ER (685)	Air Canada	
C-GHPD	Boeing 767-3Y0ER (687)	Air Canada	
C-GHPE	Boeing 767-33AER	Air Canada	
C-GHPF	Boeing 767-3Y0ER (689)	Air Canada	
C-GHPN	Boeing 767-33AER	Air Canada	
C-GITS	Airbus A.330-243 (102)	Air Transat	
C-GKTS	Airbus A.330-342 (100)	Air Transat	
C-GLAT	Airbus A.310-308 (302)	Air Transat	
C-GLCA	Boeing 767-375ER (641)	Air Canada	
C-GPAT	Airbus A.310-308 (303)	Air Transat	
C-GPTS	Airbus A.330-243 (103)	Air Transat	
C-GSAT	Airbus A.310-308 (304)	Air Transat	
C-GSCA	Boeing 767-375ER (642)	Air Canada	
C-GTSD	Airbus A.330-343	Air Transat	
C-GTSF	Airbus A.310-304 (345)	Air Transat	
C-GTSH	Airbus A.310-304 (343)	Air Transat	
C-GTSJ	Airbus A.330-243	Air Transat	
C-GTSK	Airbus A.310-304	Air Transat	
C-GTSN	Airbus A.330-243	Air Transat	
C-GTSO	Airbus A.330-342	Air Transat	
C-GTSR	Airbus A.330-243	Air Transat	
C-GTSW	Airbus A.310-304	Air Transat	
C-GTSX	Airbus A.310-304	Air Transat	
C-GTSY	Airbus A.310-304 (344)	Air Transat	
C-GTSZ	Airbus A.330-243	Air Transat	

Note: Airline fleet number when carried on aircraft is shown in parentheses.

CN (Morocco)

CN-RGA	Boeing 747-428	Royal Air Maroc	
CN-RGE	Boeing 737-86N	Royal Air Maroc	
CN-RGF	Boeing 737-86N	Royal Air Maroc	
CN-RGG	Boeing 737-86N	Royal Air Maroc	
CN-RGH	Boeing 737-86N	Royal Air Maroc	
CN-RGI	Boeing 737-86N	Royal Air Maroc	
CN-RMF	Boeing 737-4B6	Royal Air Maroc	
CN-RMG	Boeing 737-4B6	Royal Air Maroc	
CN-RMV	Boeing 737-5B6	Royal Air Maroc	
CN-RMW	Boeing 737-5B6	Royal Air Maroc	
CN-RMY	Boeing 737-5B6	Royal Air Maroc	
CN-RNB	Boeing 737-5B6	Royal Air Maroc	
CN-RNC	Boeing 737-4B6	Royal Air Maroc	
CN-RND	Boeing 737-4B6	Royal Air Maroc	
CN-RNG	Boeing 737-5B6	Royal Air Maroc	
CN-RNH	Boeing 737-5B6	Royal Air Maroc	
CN-RNJ	Boeing 737-8B6	Royal Air Maroc	
CN-RNK	Boeing 737-8B6	Royal Air Maroc	
CN-RNL	Boeing 737-7B6	Royal Air Maroc	
CN-RNM	Boeing 737-7B6	Royal Air Maroc	
CN-RNP	Boeing 737-8B6	Royal Air Maroc	
CN-RNQ	Boeing 737-7B6	Royal Air Maroc	
CN-RNR	Boeing 737-7B6	Royal Air Maroc	
CN-RNS	Boeing 767-3B6ER	Royal Air Maroc	
CN-RNT	Boeing 767-3B6ER	Royal Air Maroc	
CN-RNU	Boeing 737-8B6	Royal Air Maroc	
CN-RNV	Boeing 737-7B6	Royal Air Maroc	
CN-RNW	Boeing 737-8B6	Royal Air Maroc	
CN-RNX	Airbus A.321-211	Royal Air Maroc	
CN-RNY	Airbus A.321-211	Royal Air Maroc	
CN-RNZ	Boeing 737-8B6	Royal Air Maroc	
CN-ROA	Boeing 737-8B6	Royal Air Maroc	
CN-ROB	Boeing 737-8B6	Royal Air Maroc	
CN-ROC	Boeing 737-8B6	Royal Air Maroc	
CN-ROD	Boeing 737-7B6	Royal Air Maroc	
CN-ROE	Boeing 737-8B6	Royal Air Maroc	

Notes	Reg.	Type	Owner or Operator
	CN-ROF	Airbus A.321-211	Royal Air Maroc
	CN-ROG	Boeing 767-328ER	Royal Air Maroc
	CN-ROH	Boeing 737-8B6	Royal Air Maroc
	CN-ROJ	Boeing 737-8B6	Royal Air Maroc
	CN-ROK	Boeing 737-8B6	Royal Air Maroc
	CN-ROL	Boeing 737-8B6	Royal Air Maroc
	CN-ROM	Airbus A.321-211	Royal Air Maroc
	CN-ROP	Boeing 737-8B6	Royal Air Maroc
	CN-ROR	Boeing 737-8B6	Royal Air Maroc
	CN-ROS	Boeing 737-8B6	Royal Air Maroc
	CN-ROT	Boeing 737-8B6	Royal Air Maroc
	CN-ROU	Boeing 737-8B6	Royal Air Maroc
	CN-ROV	Boeing 767-3Q8ER	Royal Air Maroc
	CN-ROW	Boeing 767-343ER	Royal Air Maroc
	CN-ROY	Boeing 737-8B6	Royal Air Maroc
	CN-ROZ	Boeing 737-8B6	Royal Air Maroc

CS (Portugal)

Notes	Reg.	Type	Owner or Operator
	CS-TFT	Boeing 767-3YOER	Euro Atlantic Airways
	CS-TFW	Airbus A.340-542	Arik Air
	CS-TFX	Airbus A.340-542	Arik Air *Captain Bob Hayes,OON*
	CS-TGU	Airbus A.310-304	SATA International *Terceira*
	CS-TGV	Airbus A.310-304	SATA International
	CS-TJE	Airbus A.321-211	TAP Portugal *Pero Vaz de Caminha*
	CS-TJF	Airbus A.321-211	TAP Portugal *Luis Vaz de Camoes*
	CS-TJG	Airbus A.321-211	TAP Portugal *Amelia Rodrigues*
	CS-TKI	Airbus A.310-304	White Airways *FlyRed*
	CS-TKJ	Airbus A.320-212	SATA International *Pico*
	CS-TKK	Airbus A.320-214	SATA International *Corvo*
	CS-TKL	Airbus A.320-214	SATA International *Sao Jorge*
	CS-TKM	Airbus A.310-304	SATA International *Autonomia*
	CS-TKN	Airbus A.310-325	SATA International *Macaronesia*
	CS-TKO	Airbus A.320-214	SATA International
	CS-TLO	Boeing 767-383ER	Euro Atlantic Airways
	CS-TMW	Airbus A.320-214	TAP Portugal *Luisa Todi*
	CS-TNG	Airbus A.320-214	TAP Portugal *Mouzinho da Silveira*
	CS-TNH	Airbus A.320-214	TAP Portugal *Almada Negreiros*
	CS-TNI	Airbus A.320-214	TAP Portugal *Aquilino Ribiera*
	CS-TNJ	Airbus A.320-214	TAP Portugal *Florbela Espanca*
	CS-TNK	Airbus A.320-214	TAP Portugal *Teofilo Braga*
	CS-TNL	Airbus A.320-214	TAP Portugal *Vitorino Nermesio*
	CS-TNM	Airbus A.320-214	TAP Portugal *Natalia Correia*
	CS-TNN	Airbus A.320-214	TAP Portugal *Gil Vicente*
	CS-TNP	Airbus A.320-214	TAP Portugal *Alexandre O'Neill*
	CS-TNQ	Airbus A.320-214	TAP Portugal *Jose Regio*
	CS-TNR	Airbus A.320-214	TAP Portugal
	CS-TNS	Airbus A.320-214	TAP Portugal *D.Alfonso Henriques*
	CS-TNT	Airbus A.320-214	TAP Portugal
	CS-TNU	Airbus A.320-214	TAP Portugal
	CS-TNV	Airbus A.320-214	TAP Portugal
	CS-TOA	Airbus A.340-312	TAP Portugal *Fernao Mendes Pinto*
	CS-TOB	Airbus A.340-312	TAP Portugal *D Joao de Castro*
	CS-TOC	Airbus A.340-312	TAP Portugal *Wenceslau de Moraes*
	CS-TOD	Airbus A.340-312	TAP Portugal *D Francisco de Almeida*
	CS-TOE	Airbus A.330-223	TAP Portugal *Pedro Alvares Cabal*
	CS-TOF	Airbus A.330-223	TAP Portugal *Infante D Henrique*
	CS-TOG	Airbus A.330-223	TAP Portugal *Bartolomeu de Gusmão*
	CS-TOH	Airbus A.330-223	TAP Portugal *Nuno Gongalves*
	CS-TOI	Airbus A.330-223	TAP Portugal *Damiao de Gois*
	CS-TOJ	Airbus A.330-223	TAP Portugal *D.Ja-o II 'O Principe Perfeito*
	CS-TOK	Airbus A.330-223	TAP Portugal *Padre Antonio Vieira*
	CS-TOL	Airbus A.330-202	TAP Portugal *Joao Goncalves Zarco*
	CS-TOM	Airbus A.330-202	TAP Portugal *Vasco da Gama*
	CS-TON	Airbus A.330-202	TAP Portugal *Ja-o XXI*
	CS-TOO	Airbus A.330-202	TAP Portugal *Fernao de Magalhaes*
	CS-TOP	Airbus A.330-202	TAP Portugal *Pedro Nunes*
	CS-TQD	Airbus A.320-214	TAP Portugal
	CS-TQL	Airbus A.340-312	HiFly
	CS-TQS	Airbus A.320-211	White Airways
	CS-TQU	Boeing 737-8K2	Euro Atlantic Airways
	CS-TTA	Airbus A.319-111	TAP Portugal *Vieira da Silva*
	CS-TTB	Airbus A.319-111	TAP Portugal *Gago Coutinho*

Reg.	Type	Owner or Operator	Notes
CS-TTC	Airbus A.319-111	TAP Portugal *Fernando Pessoa*	
CS-TTD	Airbus A.319-111	TAP Portugal *Amadeo de Souza-Cardoso*	
CS-TTE	Airbus A.319-111	TAP Portugal *Francisco d'Ollanda*	
CS-TTF	Airbus A.319-111	TAP Portugal *Calouste Gulbenkian*	
CS-TTG	Airbus A.319-111	TAP Portugal *Humberto Delgado*	
CS-TTH	Airbus A.319-111	TAP Portugal *Antonio Sergio*	
CS-TTI	Airbus A.319-111	TAP Portugal *Eca de Queiros*	
CS-TTJ	Airbus A.319-111	TAP Portugal *Eusebio*	
CS-TTK	Airbus A.319-111	TAP Portugal *Miguel Torga*	
CS-TTL	Airbus A.319-111	TAP Portugal *Almeida Garrett*	
CS-TTM	Airbus A.319-111	TAP Portugal *Alexandre Herculano*	
CS-TTN	Airbus A.319-111	TAP Portugal *Camilo Castelo Branco*	
CS-TTO	Airbus A.319-111	TAP Portugal *Antero de Quental*	
CS-TTP	Airbus A.319-111	TAP Portugal *Josefa d'Obidos*	
CS-TTQ	Airbus A.319-112	TAP Portugal *Agostinho da Silva*	
CS-TTR	Airbus A.319-112	TAP Portugal	
CS-TTS	Airbus A.319-112	TAP Portugal *Guilhermina Suggia*	

CU (Cuba)

CU-T1250	Ilyushin IL-96-300	Cubana	
CU-T1251	Ilyushin IL-96-300	Cubana	
CU-T1254	Ilyushin IL-96-300	Cubana	

D (Germany)

D-AALA	Boeing 777-FZN	AeroLogic	
D-AALB	Boeing 777-FZN	AeroLogic	
D-AALC	Boeing 777-FZN	AeroLogic	
D-AALD	Boeing 777-FZN	AeroLogic	
D-AALE	Boeing 777-FZN	AeroLogic	
D-AALF	Boeing 777-FZN	AeroLogic	
D-AALG	Boeing 777-FZN	AeroLogic	
D-AALH	Boeing 777-FZN	AeroLogic	
D-AALI	Boeing 777-FZN	AeroLogic	
D-AALJ	Boeing 777-FZN	AeroLogic	
D-AALK	Boeing 777-FZN	AeroLogic	
D-AALL	Boeing 777-FZN	AeroLogic	
D-AALM	Boeing 777-FZN	AeroLogic	
D-AALN	Boeing 777-FZN	AeroLogic	
D-AALO	Boeing 777-FZN	AeroLogic	
D-ABAF	Boeing 737-86J	Air Berlin	
D-ABAG	Boeing 737-86J	Air Berlin	
D-ABAP	Boeing 737-86J	Air Berlin	
D-ABAQ	Boeing 737-86J	Air Berlin	
D-ABAR	Boeing 737-86J	Air Berlin	
D-ABAS	Boeing 737-86J	Air Berlin	
D-ABBB	Boeing 737-86J	Air Berlin	
D-ABBC	Boeing 737-86J	Air Berlin	
D-ABBD	Boeing 737-86J	Air Berlin	
D-ABBE	Boeing 737-86J	Air Berlin	
D-ABBF	Boeing 737-86J	Air Berlin	
D-ABBG	Boeing 737-86J	Air Berlin	
D-ABBI	Boeing 737-86J	Air Berlin	
D-ABBJ	Boeing 737-86Q	Air Berlin	
D-ABBK	Boeing 737-8BK	Air Berlin	
D-ABBS	Boeing 737-76N	Air Berlin	
D-ABBT	Boeing 737-76N	Air Berlin	
D-ABBU	Boeing 737-8Q8	Air Berlin	
D-ABBV	Boeing 737-7Q8	Air Berlin	
D-ABBW	Boeing 737-7Q8	Air Berlin	
D-ABBX	Boeing 737-808	Air Berlin	
D-ABBY	Boeing 737-808	Air Berlin	
D-ABCA	Airbus A.321-211	Air Berlin	
D-ABCB	Airbus A.321-211	Air Berlin	
D-ABCC	Airbus A.321-211	Air Berlin	
D-ABCF	Airbus A.321-211	Air Berlin	
D-ABCG	Airbus A.321-211	Air Berlin	
D-ABCH	Airbus A.321-211	Air Berlin	
D-ABCI	Airbus A.321-231	Air Berlin	
D-ABCJ	Airbus A.321-231	Air Berlin	
D-ABDP	Airbus A.320-214	Air Berlin	

D

Notes	Reg.	Type	Owner or Operator
	D-ABDQ	Airbus A.320-214	Air Berlin
	D-ABDR	Airbus A.320-214	Air Berlin
	D-ABDS	Airbus A.320-214	Air Berlin
	D-ABDU	Airbus A.320-214	Air Berlin
	D-ABDW	Airbus A.320-214	Air Berlin
	D-ABDX	Airbus A.320-214	Air Berlin
	D-ABDY	Airbus A.320-214	Air Berlin
	D-ABEA	Boeing 737-330	Lufthansa *Saarbrücken*
	D-ABEB	Boeing 737-330	Lufthansa *Xanten*
	D-ABEC	Boeing 737-330	Lufthansa *Karlsrühe*
	D-ABED	Boeing 737-330	Lufthansa *Hagen*
	D-ABEE	Boeing 737-330	Lufthansa *Ulm*
	D-ABEF	Boeing 737-330	Lufthansa *Weiden i.d.Obf.*
	D-ABEH	Boeing 737-330	Lufthansa *Bad Kissingen*
	D-ABEI	Boeing 737-330	Lufthansa *Bamberg*
	D-ABEK	Boeing 737-330	Lufthansa *Wuppertal*
	D-ABEL	Boeing 737-330	Lufthansa *Pforzheim*
	D-ABEM	Boeing 737-330	Lufthansa *Eberswalde*
	D-ABEN	Boeing 737-330	Lufthansa *Neubrandenburg*
	D-ABEO	Boeing 737-330	Lufthansa *Plauen*
	D-ABEP	Boeing 737-330	Lufthansa *Naumburg (Saale)*
	D-ABER	Boeing 737-330	Lufthansa *Merseburg*
	D-ABES	Boeing 737-330	Lufthansa *Koethen/Anhalt*
	D-ABET	Boeing 737-330	Lufthansa *Gelsenkirchen*
	D-ABEU	Boeing 737-330	Lufthansa *Goslar*
	D-ABEW	Boeing 737-330	Lufthansa *Detmold*
	D-ABFA	Airbus A.320-214	Air Berlin
	D-ABFB	Airbus A.320-214	Air Berlin
	D-ABFC	Airbus A.320-214	Air Berlin
	D-ABFE	Airbus A.320-214	Air Berlin
	D-ABFF	Airbus A.320-214	Air Berlin
	D-ABFG	Airbus A.320-214	Air Berlin
	D-ABFK	Airbus A.320-214	Air Berlin
	D-ABFL	Airbus A.320-214	Air Berlin
	D-ABFM	Airbus A.320-214	Air Berlin
	D-ABFN	Airbus A.320-214	Air Berlin
	D-ABFO	Airbus A.320-214	Air Berlin
	D-ABFP	Airbus A.320-214	Air Berlin
	D-ABFT	Airbus A.320-214	Air Berlin
	D-ABFU	Airbus A.320-214	Air Berlin
	D-ABFY	Airbus A.320-214	Air Berlin
	D-ABGH	Airbus A.319-112	Air Berlin
	D-ABGJ	Airbus A.319-112	Air Berlin
	D-ABGK	Airbus A.319-112	Air Berlin
	D-ABGN	Airbus A.319-112	Air Berlin
	D-ABGO	Airbus A.319-112	Air Berlin
	D-ABGP	Airbus A.319-112	Air Berlin
	D-ABGQ	Airbus A.319-112	Air Berlin
	D-ABGR	Airbus A.319-112	Air Berlin
	D-ABGS	Airbus A.319-112	Air Berlin
	D-ABIA	Boeing 737-530	Lufthansa *Greifswald*
	D-ABIB	Boeing 737-530	Lufthansa *Esslingen*
	D-ABIC	Boeing 737-530	Lufthansa *Krefeld*
	D-ABID	Boeing 737-530	Lufthansa *Aachen*
	D-ABIE	Boeing 737-530	Lufthansa *Hildesheim*
	D-ABIF	Boeing 737-530	Lufthansa *Landau*
	D-ABIH	Boeing 737-530	Lufthansa *Bruchsal*
	D-ABII	Boeing 737-530	Lufthansa *Lörrach*
	D-ABIK	Boeing 737-530	Lufthansa *Rastatt*
	D-ABIL	Boeing 737-530	Lufthansa *Memmingen*
	D-ABIM	Boeing 737-530	Lufthansa *Salzgitter*
	D-ABIN	Boeing 737-530	Lufthansa *Langenhagen*
	D-ABIO	Boeing 737-530	Lufthansa *Wesel*
	D-ABIP	Boeing 737-530	Lufthansa *Oberhausen*
	D-ABIR	Boeing 737-530	Lufthansa *Anklam*
	D-ABIS	Boeing 737-530	Lufthansa *Rendsburg*
	D-ABIT	Boeing 737-530	Lufthansa *Neumünster*
	D-ABIU	Boeing 737-530	Lufthansa *Limburg a.d. Lahn*
	D-ABIW	Boeing 737-530	Lufthansa *Bad Nauheim*
	D-ABIX	Boeing 737-530	Lufthansa *Iserlohn*
	D-ABIY	Boeing 737-530	Lufthansa *Lingen*
	D-ABJB	Boeing 737-530	Lufthansa *Rheine*
	D-ABKA	Boeing 737-82R	Air Berlin
	D-ABKB	Boeing 737-86J	Air Berlin

Reg.	Type	Owner or Operator	Notes
D-ABKC	Boeing 737-86J	Air Berlin	
D-ABKD	Boeing 737-86J	Air Berlin	
D-ABKI	Boeing 737-86J	Air Berlin	
D-ABKJ	Boeing 737-86J	Air Berlin	
D-ABKK	Boeing 737-86J	Air Berlin	
D-ABKM	Boeing 737-86J	Air Berlin	
D-ABKN	Boeing 737-86J	Air Berlin	
D-ABKO	Boeing 737-86J	Air Berlin	
D-ABKP	Boeing 737-86J	Air Berlin	
D-ABKQ	Boeing 737-86J	Air Berlin	
D-ABKS	Boeing 737-86J	Air Berlin	
D-ABKT	Boeing 737-86J	Air Berlin	
D-ABKU	Boeing 737-86J	Air Berlin	
D-ABKW	Boeing 737-86J	Air Berlin	
D-ABKY	Boeing 737-86J	Air Berlin	
D-ABLA	Boeing 737-76J	Air Berlin	
D-ABLB	Boeing 737-76J	Air Berlin	
D-ABLC	Boeing 737-76J	Air Berlin	
D-ABLD	Boeing 737-76J	Air Berlin	
D-ABLE	Boeing 737-76J	Air Berlin	
D-ABLF	Boeing 737-76J	Air Berlin	
D-ABMB	Boeing 737-86J	Air Berlin	
D-ABMC	Boeing 737-86J	Air Berlin	
D-ABOA	Boeing 757-330	Condor	
D-ABOB	Boeing 757-330	Condor	
D-ABOC	Boeing 757-330	Condor	
D-ABOE	Boeing 757-330	Condor	
D-ABOF	Boeing 757-330	Condor	
D-ABOG	Boeing 757-330	Condor	
D-ABOH	Boeing 757-330	Condor	
D-ABOI	Boeing 757-330	Condor	
D-ABOJ	Boeing 757-330	Condor	
D-ABOK	Boeing 757-330	Condor	
D-ABOL	Boeing 757-330	Condor	
D-ABOM	Boeing 757-330	Condor	
D-ABON	Boeing 757-330	Condor	
D-ABQA	DHC.8Q-402 Dash Eight	Air Berlin	
D-ABQB	DHC.8Q-402 Dash Eight	Air Berlin	
D-ABQC	DHC.8Q-402 Dash Eight	Air Berlin	
D-ABQD	DHC.8Q-402 Dash Eight	Air Berlin	
D-ABQE	DHC.8Q-402 Dash Eight	Air Berlin	
D-ABQF	DHC.8Q-402 Dash Eight	Air Berlin	
D-ABQG	DHC.8Q-402 Dash Eight	Air Berlin	
D-ABQH	DHC.8Q-402 Dash Eight	Air Berlin	
D-ABQI	DHC.8Q-402 Dash Eight	Air Berlin	
D-ABQJ	DHC.8Q-402 Dash Eight	Air Berlin	
D-ABTA	Boeing 747-430 (SCD)	Lufthansa *Sachsen*	
D-ABTB	Boeing 747-430 (SCD)	Lufthansa *Brandenburg*	
D-ABTC	Boeing 747-430 (SCD)	Lufthansa *Mecklenburg-Vorpommern*	
D-ABTD	Boeing 747-430 (SCD)	Lufthansa *Hamburg*	
D-ABTE	Boeing 747-430 (SCD)	Lufthansa *Sachsen-Anhalt*	
D-ABTF	Boeing 747-430 (SCD)	Lufthansa *Thüringen*	
D-ABTH	Boeing 747-430 (SCD)	Lufthansa *Duisburg*	
D-ABTK	Boeing 747-430 (SCD)	Lufthansa *Kiel*	
D-ABTL	Boeing 747-430 (SCD)	Lufthansa *Dresden*	
D-ABUA	Boeing 767-330ER	Condor	
D-ABUB	Boeing 767-330ER	Condor	
D-ABUC	Boeing 767-330ER	Condor	
D-ABUD	Boeing 767-330ER	Condor	
D-ABUE	Boeing 767-330ER	Condor	
D-ABUF	Boeing 767-330ER	Condor	
D-ABUH	Boeing 767-330ER	Condor	
D-ABUI	Boeing 767-330ER	Condor	
D-ABUK	Boeing 767-343ER	Condor	
D-ABUZ	Boeing 767-330ER	Condor	
D-ABVA	Boeing 747-430	Lufthansa *Berlin*	
D-ABVB	Boeing 747-430	Lufthansa *Bonn*	
D-ABVC	Boeing 747-430	Lufthansa *Baden-Württemberg*	
D-ABVD	Boeing 747-430	Lufthansa *Bochum*	
D-ABVE	Boeing 747-430	Lufthansa *Potsdam*	
D-ABVF	Boeing 747-430	Lufthansa *Frankfurt am Main*	
D-ABVH	Boeing 747-430	Lufthansa *Düsseldorf*	
D-ABVK	Boeing 747-430	Lufthansa *Hannover*	
D-ABVL	Boeing 747-430	Lufthansa *Muenchen*	

D

Notes	Reg.	Type	Owner or Operator
	D-ABVM	Boeing 747-430	Lufthansa *Hessen*
	D-ABVN	Boeing 747-430	Lufthansa *Dortmund*
	D-ABVO	Boeing 747-430	Lufthansa *Mulheim a.d.Ruhr*
	D-ABVP	Boeing 747-430	Lufthansa *Bremen*
	D-ABVR	Boeing 747-430	Lufthansa *Koln*
	D-ABVS	Boeing 747-430	Lufthansa *Saarland*
	D-ABVT	Boeing 747-430	Lufthansa *Rheinland Pfalz*
	D-ABVU	Boeing 747-430	Lufthansa *Bayern*
	D-ABVW	Boeing 747-430	Lufthansa *Wolfsburg*
	D-ABVX	Boeing 747-430	Lufthansa *Schleswig-Holstein*
	D-ABVY	Boeing 747-430	Lufthansa *Nordrhein Westfalen*
	D-ABVZ	Boeing 747-430	Lufthansa *Niedersachsen*
	D-ABWH	Boeing 737-330	Lufthansa *Rothenburg o. d. Taube*
	D-ABXA	Airbus A.330-223	Air Berlin
	D-ABXB	Airbus A.330-223	Air Berlin
	D-ABXL	Boeing 737-330	Lufthansa *Neuss*
	D-ABXM	Boeing 737-330	Lufthansa *Herford*
	D-ABXN	Boeing 737-330	Lufthansa *Böblingen*
	D-ABXO	Boeing 737-330	Lufthansa *Schwäbisch-Gmünd*
	D-ABXP	Boeing 737-330	Lufthansa *Fulda*
	D-ABXR	Boeing 737-330	Lufthansa *Celle*
	D-ABXS	Boeing 737-330	Lufthansa *Sindelfingen*
	D-ABXT	Boeing 737-330	Lufthansa *Reutlingen*
	D-ABXU	Boeing 737-330	Lufthansa *Seeheim-Jugenheim*
	D-ABXW	Boeing 737-330	Lufthansa *Hanau*
	D-ABXX	Boeing 737-330	Lufthansa *Bad Homburg v.d. Höhe*
	D-ABXY	Boeing 737-330	Lufthansa *Hof*
	D-ABXZ	Boeing 737-330	Lufthansa *Bad Mergentheim*
	D-ABYA	Boeing 747-830	Lufthansa
	D-ABYC	Boeing 747-830	Lufthansa
	D-ABYD	Boeing 747-830	Lufthansa
	D-ABYE	Boeing 747-830	Lufthansa
	D-ABYF	Boeing 747-830	Lufthansa
	D-ACKA	Canadair CRJ900ER	Lufthansa Regional *Pfaffenhofen a.d.ilm*
	D-ACKB	Canadair CRJ900ER	Lufthansa Regional *Schliersee*
	D-ACKC	Canadair CRJ900ER	Lufthansa Regional *Mettmann*
	D-ACKD	Canadair CRJ900ER	Lufthansa Regional *Wittlich*
	D-ACKE	Canadair CRJ900ER	Lufthansa Regional *Weningerode*
	D-ACKF	Canadair CRJ900ER	Lufthansa Regional *Prenzlau*
	D-ACKG	Canadair CRJ900ER	Lufthansa Regional *Glucksburg*
	D-ACKH	Canadair CRJ900ER	Lufthansa Regional *Radebuel*
	D-ACKI	Canadair CRJ900ER	Lufthansa Regional *Tuttlingen*
	D-ACKJ	Canadair CRJ900ER	Lufthansa Regional *Ilmenau*
	D-ACKK	Canadair CRJ900ER	Lufthansa Regional *Furstenwalde*
	D-ACKL	Canadair CRJ900ER	Lufthansa Regional *Bad Bergzabern*
	D-ACNA	Canadair CRJ900ER	Lufthansa Regional
	D-ACNB	Canadair CRJ900ER	Lufthansa Regional
	D-ACNC	Canadair CRJ900ER	Lufthansa Regional
	D-ACND	Canadair CRJ900ER	Lufthansa Regional
	D-ACNE	Canadair CRJ900ER	Lufthansa Regional
	D-ACNF	Canadair CRJ900ER	Lufthansa Regional
	D-ACNG	Canadair CRJ900ER	Lufthansa Regional
	D-ACNH	Canadair CRJ900ER	Lufthansa Regional
	D-ACNI	Canadair CRJ900ER	Lufthansa Regional
	D-ACNJ	Canadair CRJ900ER	Lufthansa Regional
	D-ACNK	Canadair CRJ900ER	Lufthansa Regional
	D-ACNL	Canadair CRJ900ER	Lufthansa Regional
	D-ACNM	Canadair CRJ900ER	Lufthansa Regional
	D-ACNN	Canadair CRJ900ER	Lufthansa Regional
	D-ACNO	Canadair CRJ900ER	Lufthansa Regional
	D-ACNP	Canadair CRJ900ER	Lufthansa Regional
	D-ACNQ	Canadair CRJ900ER	Lufthansa Regional
	D-ACNR	Canadair CRJ900ER	Lufthansa Regional
	D-ACNT	Canadair CRJ900ER	Lufthansa Regional
	D-ACNU	Canadair CRJ900ER	Lufthansa Regional
	D-ACNV	Canadair CRJ900ER	Lufthansa Regional
	D-ACNW	Canadair CRJ900ER	Lufthansa Regional
	D-ACNX	Canadair CRJ900ER	Lufthansa Regional
	D-ACPA	Canadair CRJ700ER	Lufthansa Regional *Westerland/Sylt*
	D-ACPB	Canadair CRJ700ER	Lufthansa Regional *Rudesheim a. Rhein*
	D-ACPC	Canadair CRJ700ER	Lufthansa Regional *Espelkamp*
	D-ACPD	Canadair CRJ700ER	Lufthansa Regional *Vilshofen*
	D-ACPE	Canadair CRJ700ER	Lufthansa Regional *Belzig*
	D-ACPF	Canadair CRJ700ER	Lufthansa Regional *Uhingen*

Reg.	Type	Owner or Operator	Notes
D-ACPG	Canadair CRJ700ER	Lufthansa Regional *Leinfelden-Echterdingen*	
D-ACPH	Canadair CRJ700ER	Lufthansa Regional *Eschwege*	
D-ACPI	Canadair CRJ700ER	Lufthansa Regional *Viernheim*	
D-ACPJ	Canadair CRJ700ER	Lufthansa Regional *Neumarkt i. d. Oberfalz*	
D-ACPK	Canadair CRJ700ER	Lufthansa Regional *Besigheim*	
D-ACPL	Canadair CRJ700ER	Lufthansa Regional *Halberstadt*	
D-ACPM	Canadair CRJ700ER	Lufthansa Regional *Heidenheim an der Brenz*	
D-ACPN	Canadair CRJ700ER	Lufthansa Regional *Quedlinburg*	
D-ACPO	Canadair CRJ700ER	Lufthansa Regional *Spaichingen*	
D-ACPP	Canadair CRJ700ER	Lufthansa Regional *Torgau*	
D-ACPQ	Canadair CRJ700ER	Lufthansa Regional *Lübbecke*	
D-ACPR	Canadair CRJ700ER	Lufthansa Regional *Weinheim an der Bergstrasse*	
D-ACPS	Canadair CRJ700ER	Lufthansa Regional *Berchtesgarten*	
D-ACPT	Canadair CRJ700ER	Lufthansa Regional *Altötting*	
D-ADHA	DHC.8Q-402 Dash Eight	Lufthansa Regional	
D-ADHB	DHC.8Q-402 Dash Eight	Lufthansa Regional	
D-ADHC	DHC.8Q-402 Dash Eight	Lufthansa Regional	
D-ADHD	DHC.8Q-402 Dash Eight	Lufthansa Regional	
D-ADHE	DHC.8Q-402 Dash Eight	Lufthansa Regional	
D-ADHP	DHC.8Q-402 Dash Eight	Lufthansa Regional	
D-ADHQ	DHC.8Q-402 Dash Eight	Lufthansa Regional	
D-ADHR	DHC.8Q-402 Dash Eight	Lufthansa Regional	
D-ADHS	DHC.8Q-402 Dash Eight	Lufthansa Regional	
D-ADHT	DHC.8Q-402 Dash Eight	Lufthansa Regional	
D-AEBA	Embraer ERJ190-200LR	Lufthansa Regional	
D-AEBB	Embraer ERJ190-200LR	Lufthansa Regional	
D-AEBC	Embraer ERJ190-200LR	Lufthansa Regional	
D-AEBD	Embraer ERJ190-200LR	Lufthansa Regional	
D-AEBE	Embraer ERJ190-200LR	Lufthansa Regional	
D-AEBF	Embraer ERJ190-200LR	Lufthansa Regional	
D-AEBG	Embraer ERJ190-200LR	Lufthansa Regional	
D-AEBH	Embraer ERJ190-200LR	Lufthansa Regional	
D-AEBI	Embraer ERJ190-200LR	Lufthansa Regional	
D-AEBJ	Embraer ERJ190-200LR	Lufthansa Regional	
D-AEBK	Embraer ERJ190-200LR	Lufthansa Regional	
D-AECA	Embraer ERJ190-100LR	Lufthansa Regional *Deidesheim*	
D-AECB	Embraer ERJ190-100LR	Lufthansa Regional *Meiben*	
D-AECC	Embraer ERJ190-100LR	Lufthansa Regional *Eisleben*	
D-AECD	Embraer ERJ190-100LR	Lufthansa Regional *Schkeuditz*	
D-AECE	Embraer ERJ190-100LR	Lufthansa Regional *Kronach*	
D-AECF	Embraer ERJ190-100LR	Lufthansa Regional	
D-AECG	Embraer ERJ190-100LR	Lufthansa Regional	
D-AECH	Embraer ERJ190-100LR	Lufthansa Regional	
D-AECI	Embraer ERJ190-100LR	Lufthansa Regional	
D-AEMA	Embraer ERJ190-200LR	Lufthansa Regional	
D-AEMB	Embraer ERJ190-200LR	Lufthansa Regional	
D-AEMC	Embraer ERJ190-200LR	Lufthansa Regional	
D-AEMD	Embraer ERJ190-200LR	Lufthansa Regional	
D-AEME	Embraer ERJ190-200LR	Lufthansa Regional	
D-AEMF	Embraer ERJ190-100LR	Lufthansa Regional	
D-AEMG	Embraer ERJ190-100LR	Lufthansa Regional	
D-AERK	Airbus A.330-322	Air Berlin	
D-AERQ	Airbus A.330-322	Air Berlin	
D-AFKA	Fokker 100	Contact Air/Lufthansa Regional	
D-AFKB	Fokker 100	Contact Air/Lufthansa Regional	
D-AFKC	Fokker 100	Contact Air/Lufthansa Regional	
D-AFKD	Fokker 100	Contact Air/Lufthansa Regional	
D-AFKE	Fokker 100	Contact Air/Lufthansa Regional	
D-AFKF	Fokker 100	Contact Air/Lufthansa Regional	
D-AGEC	Boeing 737-76J	Air Berlin	
D-AGEE	Boeing 737-35B	Germania	
D-AGEL	Boeing 737-75B	Air Berlin	
D-AGEN	Boeing 737-75B	Air Berlin	
D-AGEP	Boeing 737-75B	Air Berlin	
D-AGEQ	Boeing 737-75B	Germania	
D-AGER	Boeing 737-75B	Germania	
D-AGES	Boeing 737-75B	Air Berlin	
D-AGET	Boeing 737-75B	Germania	
D-AGEU	Boeing 737-75B	Air Berlin	
D-AGPH	Fokker 100	Contact Air/Swiss	
D-AGPK	Fokker 100	Contact Air/Swiss	
D-AGWA	Airbus A.319-132	Germanwings	
D-AGWB	Airbus A.319-132	Germanwings	
D-AGWC	Airbus A.319-132	Germanwings	

D

Notes	Reg.	Type	Owner or Operator
	D-AGWD	Airbus A.319-132	Germanwings
	D-AGWE	Airbus A.319-132	Germanwings
	D-AGWF	Airbus A.319-132	Germanwings
	D-AGWG	Airbus A.319-132	Germanwings
	D-AGWH	Airbus A.319-132	Germanwings
	D-AGWI	Airbus A.319-132	Germanwings
	D-AGWJ	Airbus A.319-132	Germanwings
	D-AGWK	Airbus A.319-132	Germanwings
	D-AGWL	Airbus A.319-132	Germanwings
	D-AGWM	Airbus A.319-132	Germanwings
	D-AGWN	Airbus A.319-132	Germanwings
	D-AGWO	Airbus A.319-132	Germanwings
	D-AGWP	Airbus A.319-132	Germanwings
	D-AGWQ	Airbus A.319-132	Germanwings
	D-AGWR	Airbus A.319-132	Germanwings
	D-AGWS	Airbus A.319-132	Germanwings
	D-AGWT	Airbus A.319-132	Germanwings
	D-AHFA	Boeing 737-8K5	Air Berlin
	D-AHFH	Boeing 737-8K5	TUIfly
	D-AHFI	Boeing 737-8K5	TUIfly
	D-AHFK	Boeing 737-8K5	TUIfly
	D-AHFL	Boeing 737-8K5	TUIfly
	D-AHFM	Boeing 737-8K5	TUIfly
	D-AHFO	Boeing 737-8K5	Air Berlin
	D-AHFP	Boeing 737-8K5	TUIfly
	D-AHFR	Boeing 737-8K5	TUIfly
	D-AHFS	Boeing 737-86N	Air Berlin
	D-AHFT	Boeing 737-8K5	TUIfly
	D-AHFV	Boeing 737-8K5	TUIfly
	D-AHFW	Boeing 737-8K5	Air Berlin
	D-AHFX	Boeing 737-8K5	TUIfly
	D-AHFY	Boeing 737-8K5	TUIfly
	D-AHFZ	Boeing 737-8K5	TUIfly
	D-AHHA	Airbus A.319-111	Hamburg Airways
	D-AHHB	Airbus A.319-112	Hamburg Airways
	D-AHHC	Airbus A.320-214	Hamburg Airways
	D-AHIA	Boeing 737-73S	Air Berlin
	D-AHLK	Boeing 737-8K5	TUIfly
	D-AHXA	Boeing 737-7K5	Air Berlin
	D-AHXB	Boeing 737-7K5	Air Berlin
	D-AHXC	Boeing 737-7K5	Air Berlin
	D-AHXD	Boeing 737-7K5	Air Berlin
	D-AHXE	Boeing 737-7K5	Air Berlin
	D-AHXF	Boeing 737-7K5	Air Berlin
	D-AHXG	Boeing 737-7K5	Air Berlin
	D-AHXH	Boeing 737-7K5	Air Berlin
	D-AHXJ	Boeing 737-7K5	Air Berlin
	D-AIBA	Airbus A.319-114	Lufthansa
	D-AIBB	Airbus A.319-114	Lufthansa
	D-AIBC	Airbus A.319-114	Lufthansa
	D-AIBD	Airbus A.319-114	Lufthansa *Pirmasens*
	D-AIBE	Airbus A.319-114	Lufthansa *Schonfeld*
	D-AIBF	Airbus A.319-112	Lufthansa
	D-AIBG	Airbus A.319-112	Lufthansa
	D-AIBH	Airbus A.319-112	Lufthansa
	D-AIBI	Airbus A.319-112	Lufthansa
	D-AIBJ	Airbus A.319-112	Lufthansa
	D-AICA	Airbus A.320-212	Condor
	D-AICC	Airbus A.320-212	Condor
	D-AICD	Airbus A.320-212	Condor
	D-AICE	Airbus A.320-212	Condor
	D-AICF	Airbus A.320-212	Condor
	D-AICG	Airbus A.320-212	Condor
	D-AICH	Airbus A.320-212	Condor
	D-AICI	Airbus A.320-212	Condor
	D-AICJ	Airbus A.320-212	Condor
	D-AICK	Airbus A.320-212	Condor
	D-AICL	Airbus A.320-212	Condor
	D-AICN	Airbus A.320-214	Condor
	D-AIDA	Airbus A.321-231	Lufthansa
	D-AIDB	Airbus A.321-231	Lufthansa
	D-AIDC	Airbus A.321-231	Lufthansa
	D-AIDD	Airbus A.321-231	Lufthansa
	D-AIDE	Airbus A.321-231	Lufthansa

Reg.	Type	Owner or Operator	Notes
D-AIDF	Airbus A.321-231	Lufthansa	
D-AIDG	Airbus A.321-231	Lufthansa	
D-AIDH	Airbus A.321-231	Lufthansa	
D-AIDI	Airbus A.321-231	Lufthansa	
D-AIDJ	Airbus A.321-231	Lufthansa	
D-AIDK	Airbus A.321-231	Lufthansa	
D-AIDL	Airbus A.321-231	Lufthansa	
D-AIDM	Airbus A.321-231	Lufthansa	
D-AIDN	Airbus A.321-231	Lufthansa	
D-AIDO	Airbus A.321-231	Lufthansa	
D-AIDP	Airbus A.321-231	Lufthansa	
D-AIDQ	Airbus A.321-231	Lufthansa	
D-AIFA	Airbus A.340-313X	Lufthansa Dorsten	
D-AIFC	Airbus A.340-313X	Lufthansa Gander/Halifax	
D-AIFD	Airbus A.340-313X	Lufthansa Giessen	
D-AIFE	Airbus A.340-313X	Lufthansa Passau	
D-AIFF	Airbus A.340-313X	Lufthansa Delmenhorst	
D-AIGA	Airbus A.340-311	Lufthansa Oldenburg	
D-AIGB	Airbus A.340-311	Lufthansa Recklinghausen	
D-AIGC	Airbus A.340-311	Lufthansa Wilhelmshaven	
D-AIGD	Airbus A.340-311	Lufthansa Remscheid	
D-AIGF	Airbus A.340-311	Lufthansa Gottingen	
D-AIGH	Airbus A.340-311	Lufthansa Koblenz	
D-AIGI	Airbus A.340-311	Lufthansa Worms	
D-AIGK	Airbus A.340-311	Lufthansa Bayreuth	
D-AIGL	Airbus A.340-313X	Lufthansa Herne	
D-AIGM	Airbus A.340-313X	Lufthansa Görlitz	
D-AIGN	Airbus A.340-313X	Lufthansa Solingen	
D-AIGO	Airbus A.340-313X	Lufthansa Offenbach	
D-AIGP	Airbus A.340-313X	Lufthansa Paderborn	
D-AIGS	Airbus A.340-313X	Lufthansa Bergisch-Gladbach	
D-AIGT	Airbus A.340-313X	Lufthansa Viersen	
D-AIGU	Airbus A.340-313X	Lufthansa Castrop-Rauxei	
D-AIGV	Airbus A.340-313X	Lufthansa Dinslaken	
D-AIGW	Airbus A.340-313X	Lufthansa Gladbeck	
D-AIGX	Airbus A.340-313X	Lufthansa Duren	
D-AIGY	Airbus A.340-313X	Lufthansa Lünen	
D-AIGZ	Airbus A.340-313X	Lufthansa Villingen-Schwenningen	
D-AIHA	Airbus A.340-642	Lufthansa Nurnberg	
D-AIHB	Airbus A.340-642	Lufthansa Bremerhaven	
D-AIHC	Airbus A.340-642	Lufthansa Essen	
D-AIHD	Airbus A.340-642	Lufthansa Stuttgart	
D-AIHE	Airbus A.340-642	Lufthansa Leverkusen	
D-AIHF	Airbus A.340-642	Lufthansa Lübeck	
D-AIHH	Airbus A.340-642	Lufthansa	
D-AIHI	Airbus A.340-642	Lufthansa	
D-AIHK	Airbus A.340-642	Lufthansa	
D-AIHL	Airbus A.340-642	Lufthansa	
D-AIHM	Airbus A.340-642	Lufthansa	
D-AIHN	Airbus A.340-642	Lufthansa	
D-AIHO	Airbus A.340-642	Lufthansa	
D-AIHP	Airbus A.340-642	Lufthansa	
D-AIHQ	Airbus A.340-642	Lufthansa	
D-AIHR	Airbus A.340-642	Lufthansa	
D-AIHS	Airbus A.340-642	Lufthansa	
D-AIHT	Airbus A.340-642	Lufthansa	
D-AIHU	Airbus A.340-642	Lufthansa	
D-AIHV	Airbus A.340-642	Lufthansa	
D-AIHW	Airbus A.340-642	Lufthansa	
D-AIHX	Airbus A.340-642	Lufthansa	
D-AIHY	Airbus A.340-642	Lufthansa	
D-AIHZ	Airbus A.340-642	Lufthansa	
D-AIKA	Airbus A.330-343X	Lufthansa Minden	
D-AIKB	Airbus A.330-343X	Lufthansa Cuxhaven	
D-AIKC	Airbus A.330-343X	Lufthansa Hamm	
D-AIKD	Airbus A.330-343X	Lufthansa Siegen	
D-AIKE	Airbus A.330-343X	Lufthansa Landshut	
D-AIKF	Airbus A.330-343X	Lufthansa Witten	
D-AIKG	Airbus A.330-343X	Lufthansa Ludwigsburg	
D-AIKH	Airbus A.330-343X	Lufthansa	
D-AIKI	Airbus A.330-343X	Lufthansa	
D-AIKJ	Airbus A.330-343X	Lufthansa	
D-AIKK	Airbus A.330-343X	Lufthansa	
D-AIKL	Airbus A.330-343X	Lufthansa	

Notes	Reg.	Type	Owner or Operator
	D-AIKM	Airbus A.330-343X	Lufthansa
	D-AIKN	Airbus A.330-343X	Lufthansa
	D-AIKO	Airbus A.330-343X	Lufthansa
	D-AIKP	Airbus A.330-343X	Lufthansa
	D-AIKQ	Airbus A.330-343X	Lufthansa
	D-AIKR	Airbus A.330-343X	Lufthansa
	D-AILA	Airbus A.319-114	Lufthansa *Frankfurt (Oder)*
	D-AILB	Airbus A.319-114	Lufthansa *Lutherstadt Wittenburg*
	D-AILC	Airbus A.319-114	Lufthansa *Russelsheim*
	D-AILD	Airbus A.319-114	Lufthansa *Dinkelsbühl*
	D-AILE	Airbus A.319-114	Lufthansa *Kelsterbach*
	D-AILF	Airbus A.319-114	Lufthansa Italia
	D-AILH	Airbus A.319-114	Lufthansa Italia *Norderstedt*
	D-AILI	Airbus A.319-114	Lufthansa Italia *Roma*
	D-AILK	Airbus A.319-114	Lufthansa *Landshut*
	D-AILL	Airbus A.319-114	Lufthansa *Marburg*
	D-AILM	Airbus A.319-114	Lufthansa *Friedrichshafen*
	D-AILN	Airbus A.319-114	Lufthansa *Idar-Oberstein*
	D-AILP	Airbus A.319-114	Lufthansa *Tubingen*
	D-AILR	Airbus A.319-114	Lufthansa *Tegernsee*
	D-AILS	Airbus A.319-114	Lufthansa *Heide*
	D-AILT	Airbus A.319-114	Lufthansa *Straubing*
	D-AILU	Airbus A.319-114	Lufthansa *Verden*
	D-AILW	Airbus A.319-114	Lufthansa *Donaueschingen*
	D-AILX	Airbus A.319-114	Lufthansa *Feilbach*
	D-AILY	Airbus A.319-114	Lufthansa *Schweinfurt*
	D-AIMA	Airbus A.380-841	Lufthansa *Frankfurt am Main*
	D-AIMB	Airbus A.380-841	Lufthansa
	D-AIMC	Airbus A.380-841	Lufthansa
	D-AIMD	Airbus A.380-841	Lufthansa
	D-AIME	Airbus A.380-841	Lufthansa *Johannesburg*
	D-AIMF	Airbus A.380-841	Lufthansa *Zurich*
	D-AIMG	Airbus A.380-841	Lufthansa
	D-AIMH	Airbus A.380-841	Lufthansa
	D-AIMI	Airbus A.380-841	Lufthansa
	D-AIMJ	Airbus A.380-841	Lufthansa
	D-AIMK	Airbus A.380-841	Lufthansa
	D-AIPA	Airbus A.320-211	Lufthansa *Buxtehude*
	D-AIPB	Airbus A.320-211	Lufthansa *Heidelberg*
	D-AIPC	Airbus A.320-211	Lufthansa *Braunschweig*
	D-AIPD	Airbus A.320-211	Lufthansa *Freiburg*
	D-AIPE	Airbus A.320-211	Lufthansa *Kassel*
	D-AIPF	Airbus A.320-211	Lufthansa *Deggendorf*
	D-AIPH	Airbus A.320-211	Lufthansa *Munster*
	D-AIPK	Airbus A.320-211	Lufthansa *Wiesbaden*
	D-AIPL	Airbus A.320-211	Lufthansa *Ludwigshafen am Rhein*
	D-AIPM	Airbus A.320-211	Lufthansa *Troisdorf*
	D-AIPP	Airbus A.320-211	Lufthansa *Stamberg*
	D-AIPR	Airbus A.320-211	Lufthansa *Kaufbeuren*
	D-AIPS	Airbus A.320-211	Lufthansa *Augsburg*
	D-AIPT	Airbus A.320-211	Lufthansa *Cottbus*
	D-AIPU	Airbus A.320-211	Lufthansa *Dresden*
	D-AIPW	Airbus A.320-211	Lufthansa *Schwerin*
	D-AIPX	Airbus A.320-211	Lufthansa *Mannheim*
	D-AIPY	Airbus A.320-211	Lufthansa *Magdeburg*
	D-AIPZ	Airbus A.320-211	Lufthansa *Erfurt*
	D-AIQA	Airbus A.320-211	Lufthansa *Mainz*
	D-AIQB	Airbus A.320-211	Lufthansa *Bielefeld*
	D-AIQC	Airbus A.320-211	Lufthansa *Zwickau*
	D-AIQD	Airbus A.320-211	Lufthansa *Jena*
	D-AIQE	Airbus A.320-211	Lufthansa *Gera*
	D-AIQF	Airbus A.320-211	Lufthansa *Halle (Saale)*
	D-AIQH	Airbus A.320-211	Lufthansa *Dessau*
	D-AIQK	Airbus A.320-211	Lufthansa *Rostock*
	D-AIQL	Airbus A.320-211	Lufthansa *Stralsund*
	D-AIQM	Airbus A.320-211	Lufthansa *Nordenham*
	D-AIQN	Airbus A.320-211	Lufthansa *Laupheim*
	D-AIQP	Airbus A.320-211	Lufthansa *Suhl*
	D-AIQR	Airbus A.320-211	Lufthansa *Lahr/Schwarzwald*
	D-AIQS	Airbus A.320-211	Lufthansa *Eisenach*
	D-AIQT	Airbus A.320-211	Lufthansa *Gotha*
	D-AIQU	Airbus A.320-211	Lufthansa *Backnang*
	D-AIQW	Airbus A.320-211	Lufthansa *Kleve*
	D-AIRA	Airbus A.321-131	Lufthansa *Finkenwerder*

Reg.	Type	Owner or Operator	Notes
D-AIRB	Airbus A.321-131	Lufthansa *Baden-Baden*	
D-AIRC	Airbus A.321-131	Lufthansa *Erlangen*	
D-AIRD	Airbus A.321-131	Lufthansa *Coburg*	
D-AIRE	Airbus A.321-131	Lufthansa *Osnabrueck*	
D-AIRF	Airbus A.321-131	Lufthansa *Kempten*	
D-AIRH	Airbus A.321-131	Lufthansa *Garmisch-Partenkirchen*	
D-AIRK	Airbus A.321-131	Lufthansa *Freudenstadt/Schwarzwald*	
D-AIRL	Airbus A.321-131	Lufthansa *Kulmbach*	
D-AIRM	Airbus A.321-131	Lufthansa *Darmstadt*	
D-AIRN	Airbus A.321-131	Lufthansa *Kaiserslautern*	
D-AIRO	Airbus A.321-131	Lufthansa *Konstanz*	
D-AIRP	Airbus A.321-131	Lufthansa *Lüneburg*	
D-AIRR	Airbus A.321-131	Lufthansa *Wismar*	
D-AIRS	Airbus A.321-131	Lufthansa *Husum*	
D-AIRT	Airbus A.321-131	Lufthansa *Regensburg*	
D-AIRU	Airbus A.321-131	Lufthansa *Würzburg*	
D-AIRW	Airbus A.321-131	Lufthansa *Heilbronn*	
D-AIRX	Airbus A.321-131	Lufthansa *Weimar*	
D-AIRY	Airbus A.321-131	Lufthansa *Flensburg*	
D-AISB	Airbus A.321-231	Lufthansa *Hamein*	
D-AISC	Airbus A.321-231	Lufthansa *Speyer*	
D-AISD	Airbus A.321-231	Lufthansa *Chemnitz*	
D-AISE	Airbus A.321-231	Lufthansa *Neustadt an der Weinstrasse*	
D-AISF	Airbus A.321-231	Lufthansa *Lippstadt*	
D-AISG	Airbus A.321-231	Lufthansa *Dormagen*	
D-AISH	Airbus A.321-231	Lufthansa	
D-AISI	Airbus A.321-231	Lufthansa	
D-AISJ	Airbus A.321-231	Lufthansa	
D-AISK	Airbus A.321-231	Lufthansa	
D-AISL	Airbus A.321-231	Lufthansa *Arnsberg*	
D-AISN	Airbus A.321-231	Lufthansa *Goppingen*	
D-AISO	Airbus A.321-231	Lufthansa	
D-AISP	Airbus A.321-231	Lufthansa	
D-AISQ	Airbus A.321-231	Lufthansa	
D-AISR	Airbus A.321-231	Lufthansa	
D-AIST	Airbus A.321-231	Lufthansa	
D-AISU	Airbus A.321-231	Lufthansa *Nordlingen*	
D-AISV	Airbus A.321-231	Lufthansa *Bingen*	
D-AISW	Airbus A.321-231	Lufthansa	
D-AISX	Airbus A.321-231	Lufthansa	
D-AISZ	Airbus A.321-231	Lufthansa	
D-AIZA	Airbus A.320-214	Lufthansa	
D-AIZB	Airbus A.320-214	Lufthansa	
D-AIZC	Airbus A.320-214	Lufthansa	
D-AIZD	Airbus A.320-214	Lufthansa	
D-AIZE	Airbus A.320-214	Lufthansa	
D-AIZF	Airbus A.320-214	Lufthansa	
D-AIZG	Airbus A.320-214	Lufthansa	
D-AIZH	Airbus A.320-214	Lufthansa	
D-AIZI	Airbus A.320-214	Lufthansa	
D-AIZJ	Airbus A.320-214	Lufthansa	
D-AIZK	Airbus A.320-214	Lufthansa	
D-AIZL	Airbus A.320-214	Lufthansa	
D-AIZM	Airbus A.320-214	Lufthansa	
D-AKNK	Airbus A.319-112	Germanwings	
D-AKNL	Airbus A.319-112	Germanwings	
D-AKNM	Airbus A.319-112	Germanwings	
D-AKNN	Airbus A.319-112	Germanwings	
D-AKNO	Airbus A.319-112	Germanwings	
D-AKNP	Airbus A.319-112	Germanwings	
D-AKNQ	Airbus A.319-112	Germanwings	
D-AKNR	Airbus A.319-112	Germanwings *Spirit of T-Com*	
D-AKNS	Airbus A.319-112	Germanwings *Spirit of T Mobile*	
D-AKNT	Airbus A.319-112	Germanwings *City of Hamburg*	
D-AKNU	Airbus A.319-112	Germanwings	
D-AKNV	Airbus A.319-112	Germanwings	
D-ALCA	McD Douglas MD-11F	Lufthansa Cargo	
D-ALCB	McD Douglas MD-11F	Lufthansa Cargo	
D-ALCC	McD Douglas MD-11F	Lufthansa Cargo	
D-ALCD	McD Douglas MD-11F	Lufthansa Cargo	
D-ALCE	McD Douglas MD-11F	Lufthansa Cargo	
D-ALCF	McD Douglas MD-11F	Lufthansa Cargo	
D-ALCG	McD Douglas MD-11F	Lufthansa Cargo	
D-ALCH	McD Douglas MD-11F	Lufthansa Cargo	

Notes	Reg.	Type	Owner or Operator
	D-ALCI	McD Douglas MD-11F	Lufthansa Cargo
	D-ALCJ	McD Douglas MD-11F	Lufthansa Cargo
	D-ALCK	McD Douglas MD-11F	Lufthansa Cargo
	D-ALCL	McD Douglas MD-11F	Lufthansa Cargo
	D-ALCM	McD Douglas MD-11F	Lufthansa Cargo
	D-ALCN	McD Douglas MD-11F	Lufthansa Cargo
	D-ALCO	McD Douglas MD-11F	Lufthansa Cargo
	D-ALCP	McD Douglas MD-11F	Lufthansa Cargo
	D-ALCR	McD Douglas MD-11F	Lufthansa Cargo
	D-ALCS	McD Douglas MD-11F	Lufthansa Cargo
	D-ALEA	Boeing 757-236SF	DHL Express
	D-ALEB	Boeing 757-236SF	DHL Express
	D-ALEC	Boeing 757-236SF	DHL Express
	D-ALED	Boeing 757-236SF	DHL Express
	D-ALEE	Boeing 757-236SF	DHL Express
	D-ALEF	Boeing 757-236SF	DHL Express
	D-ALEG	Boeing 757-236SF	DHL Express
	D-ALEH	Boeing 757-236SF	DHL Express
	D-ALEI	Boeing 757-236SF	DHL Express
	D-ALEJ	Boeing 757-23APF	DHL Express
	D-ALEK	Boeing 757-236SF	DHL Express
	D-ALIE	Embraer RJ170-100LR	Cirrus Airlines
	D-ALIN	BAe 146-300	WDL Aviation
	D-ALPA	Airbus A.330-223	Air Berlin
	D-ALPB	Airbus A.330-223	Air Berlin
	D-ALPC	Airbus A.330-223	Air Berlin
	D-ALPD	Airbus A.330-223	Air Berlin
	D-ALPE	Airbus A.330-223	Air Berlin
	D-ALPF	Airbus A.330-223	Air Berlin
	D-ALPG	Airbus A.330-223	Air Berlin
	D-ALPH	Airbus A.330-223	Air Berlin
	D-ALPI	Airbus A.330-223	Air Berlin
	D-ALPJ	Airbus A.330-223	Air Berlin
	D-ALSA	Airbus A.321-211	Air Berlin
	D-ALSB	Airbus A.321-211	Air Berlin
	D-ALSC	Airbus A.321-211	Air Berlin
	D-ALSD	Airbus A.321-211	Air Berlin
	D-ALTE	Airbus A.320-214	Air Berlin
	D-ALTF	Airbus A.320-214	Air Berlin
	D-ALTJ	Airbus A.320-214	Air Berlin
	D-ALTK	Airbus A.320-214	Air Berlin
	D-ALTL	Airbus A.320-214	Air Berlin
	D-AMAJ	BAe 146-200	WDL Aviation
	D-AMAX	BAe 146-300	WDL Aviation
	D-AMGL	BAe 146-200	WDL Aviation
	D-AOLB	SAAB 2000	OLT
	D-AOLC	SAAB 2000	OLT
	D-AOLG	Fokker 100	OLT
	D-AOLH	Fokker 100	OLT
	D-AOLT	SAAB 2000	OLT *Emden*
	D-APBB	Boeing 737-8FH	PrivatAir/Lufthansa
	D-APBC	Boeing 737-8BK	PrivatAir/Lufthansa
	D-APBD	Boeing 737-8BK	PrivatAir/Lufthansa
	D-ASTA	Airbus A.319-112	Germania *Dr.Heinrich Bischoff*
	D-ASTB	Airbus A.319-112	Germania
	D-ASTY	Airbus A.319-112	Germania
	D-ASTZ	Airbus A.319-112	Germania
	D-ATUA	Boeing 737-8K5	TUIfly
	D-ATUB	Boeing 737-8K5	TUIfly
	D-ATUC	Boeing 737-8K5	TUIfly
	D-ATUD	Boeing 737-8K5	TUIfly
	D-ATUE	Boeing 737-8K5	TUIfly
	D-ATUF	Boeing 737-8K5	TUIfly
	D-ATUG	Boeing 737-8K5	TUIfly
	D-ATUH	Boeing 737-8K5	TUIfly
	D-ATUI	Boeing 737-8K5	TUIfly
	D-ATUJ	Boeing 737-8K5	TUIfly
	D-ATUK	Boeing 737-8K5	TUIfly
	D-ATUL	Boeing 737-8K5	TUIfly
	D-AVRA	Avro RJ85	Lufthansa Regional
	D-AVRB	Avro RJ85	Lufthansa Regional
	D-AVRJ	Avro RJ85	Lufthansa Regional
	D-AVRP	Avro RJ85	Lufthansa Regional
	D-AVRQ	Avro RJ85	Lufthansa Regional

Reg.	Type	Owner or Operator	Notes
D-AVRR	Avro RJ85	Lufthansa Regional	
D-AWBA	Bae 146-300	WDL Aviation	
D-AWUE	BAe 146-200	WDL Aviation	
D-AXLD	Boeing 737-8FH	XL Airways Germany	
D-AXLE	Boeing 737-8Q8	XL Airways Germany	
D-AXLF	Boeing 737-8Q8	XL Airways Germany	
D-AXLG	Boeing 737-8Q8	XL Airways Germany	
D-BGAE	Dornier 328JET	Cirrus Airlines	
D-BGAL	Dornier 328JET	Cirrus Airlines	
D-BGAQ	Dornier 328JET	Cirrus Airlines	
D-CCAS	Short SD3-60-300	Night Express	
D-CCIR	Dornier 328-130	Cirrus Airlines	
D-CIRB	Dornier 328-110	Cirrus Airlines	
D-CIRC	Dornier 328-110	Cirrus Airlines	
D-CIRD	Dornier 328-110	Cirrus Airlines	
D-CIRI	Dornier 328-110	Cirrus Airlines	
D-CIRK	Dornier 328-110	Cirrus Airlines	
D-CIRP	Dornier 328-110	Cirrus Airlines	
D-CMNX	Dornier Do.228	Manx2	
D-COLE	SAAB SF.340A	OLT *Bremen*	
D-COSA	Dornier 328-110	Cirrus Airlines	
D-CPRW	Dornier 328-110	Cirrus Airlines	
D-CRAS	Short SD3-60-300	Night Express	
D-IEXB	Beech 99	Night Express	
D-IFLM	Dornier Do.228	Manx2	
D-ILKA	Dornier Do.228	Manx2	

EC (Spain)

EC-ELT	BAe 146-200QT	Pan Air/TNT Airways	
EC-FCB	Airbus A.320-211	Vueling Airlines	
EC-FDB	Airbus A.320-211	Vueling Airlines	
EC-FLP	Airbus A.320-211	Vueling Airlines	
EC-FNR	Airbus A.320-211	Vueling Airlines	
EC-FQY	Airbus A.320-211	Vueling Airlines	
EC-FVY	BAe 146-200QT	Pan Air/TNT Airways	
EC-FZE	BAe 146-200QT	Pan Air/TNT Airways	
EC-GCV	McD Douglas MD-82	Spanair *Sunburst (ceased operations)*	
EC-GGS	Airbus A.340-313	Iberia *Concha Espina*	
EC-GHX	Airbus A.340-313	Iberia *Rosalia de Castro*	
EC-GJT	Airbus A.340-313	Iberia *Rosa Chacel*	
EC-GLE	Airbus A.340-313	Iberia *Concepcion Arenal*	
EC-GPB	Airbus A.340-313X	Iberia *Teresa de Avila*	
EC-GQG	McD Douglas MD-83	Spanair *Sunrise (ceased operations)*	
EC-GQO	BAe 146-200QT	Pan Air/TNT Airways	
EC-GRG	Airbus A.320-211	Vueling Airlines	
EC-GRH	Airbus A.320-211	Vueling Airlines	
EC-GUP	Airbus A.340-313X	Iberia *Agustina De Aragon*	
EC-GUQ	Airbus A.340-313X	Iberia *Beatriz Galindo*	
EC-GVE	Swearingen SA227AC Metro III	Aeronova	
EC-GVO	McD Douglas MD-83	Spanair *Sunspot (ceased operations)*	
EC-GXU	McD Douglas MD-83	Spanair *Sunray (ceased operations)*	
EC-GYI	Canadair CRJ200ER	Air Nostrum/Iberia Regional	
EC-GZA	Canadair CRJ200ER	Air Nostrum/Iberia Regional	
EC-HAG	Airbus A.320-214	Iberia *Senorio de Bertiz*	
EC-HCH	Swearingen SA227AC Metro III	Aeronova	
EC-HDH	BAe 146-200QT	Pan Air/TNT Airways	
EC-HDK	Airbus A.320-214	Iberia *Mar Ortigola*	
EC-HDQ	Airbus A.340-313X	Iberia *Sor Juana Ines de la Cruz*	
EC-HDS	Boeing 757-256	Iberia *Paraguay*	
EC-HDT	Airbus A.320-214	Iberia *Museo Guggenheim Bilbao*	
EC-HEK	Canadair CRJ200ER	Air Nostrum/Iberia Regional	
EC-HGR	Airbus A.319-111	Iberia *Ribeira Sacra*	
EC-HGS	Airbus A.319-111	Iberia *Bardenas Reales*	
EC-HGT	Airbus A.319-111	Iberia *Icnitas de Enciso*	
EC-HGU	Airbus A.340-313X	Iberia *Maria de Molina*	
EC-HGV	Airbus A.340-313X	Iberia *Maria Guerrero*	
EC-HGX	Airbus A.340-313X	Iberia *Maria Pita*	
EC-HGZ	Airbus A.320-214	Iberia *Boi Taull*	
EC-HHA	Airbus A.320-214	Vueling Airlines	
EC-HHI	Canadair CRJ200ER	Air Nostrum/Iberia Regional	
EC-HHV	Canadair CRJ200ER	Air Nostrum/Iberia Regional	
EC-HJH	BAe 146-200QT	Pan Air/TNT Airways	

Notes	Reg.	Type	Owner or Operator
	EC-HJP	Boeing 737-85P	Air Europa
	EC-HJQ	Boeing 737-85P	Air Europa
	EC-HKO	Airbus A.319-111	Iberia *Gorbia*
	EC-HKQ	Boeing 737-85P	Air Europa *San Pedro Alcantara*
	EC-HKR	Boeing 737-85P	Air Europa
	EC-HPM	Airbus A.321-231	Spanair *Camillo José Cela (ceased operations)*
	EC-HPR	Canadair CRJ200ER	Air Nostrum/Iberia Regional
	EC-HQI	Airbus A.320-214	Vueling Airlines *Merce Sune*
	EC-HQJ	Airbus A.320-214	Vueling Airlines
	EC-HQL	Airbus A.320-214	Vueling Airlines *Click on Vueling*
	EC-HQZ	Airbus A.321-231	Spanair *(ceased operations)*
	EC-HRG	Airbus A.321-231	Spanair *Placido Domingo (ceased operations)*
	EC-HRP	Airbus A.320-232	Spanair *Juan de Avalos (ceased operations)*
	EC-HSF	Airbus A.320-214	Iberia *Mar Menor*
	EC-HSH	Canadair CRJ200ER	Air Nostrum/Iberia Regional
	EC-HTA	Airbus A.320-214	Iberia *Cadaques*
	EC-HTB	Airbus A.320-214	Iberia *Playa de las Americas*
	EC-HTC	Airbus A.320-214	Iberia *Alpujarra*
	EC-HTD	Airbus A.320-214	Vueling Airlines *Unos Vuelan,otros Vueling*
	EC-HTZ	Canadair CRJ200ER	Air Nostrum/Iberia Regional
	EC-HUH	Airbus A.321-211	Iberia *Benidorm*
	EC-HUI	Airbus A.321-211	Iberia *Comunidad Autonoma de la Rioja*
	EC-HUJ	Airbus A.320-214	Iberia *Getaria*
	EC-HUK	Airbus A.320-214	Iberia *Laguna Negra*
	EC-HUL	Airbus A.320-214	Iberia *Monasterio de Rueda*
	EC-HXA	Airbus A.320-232	Spanair *(ceased operations)*
	EC-HXM	Canadair CRJ200ER	Air Nostrum/Iberia Regional
	EC-HYC	Airbus A.320-214	Iberia *Cuidad de Ceuta*
	EC-HYD	Airbus A.320-214	Iberia *Maspalomas*
	EC-HYG	Canadair CRJ200ER	Air Nostrum/Iberia Regional
	EC-HZH	Swearingen SA227AC Metro III	Aeronova
	EC-HZR	Canadair CRJ200ER	Air Nostrum/Iberia Regional
	EC-HZS	Boeing 737-86Q	Air Europa
	EC-IAA	Canadair CRJ200ER	Air Nostrum/Iberia Regional
	EC-IAZ	Airbus A.320-232	Spanair *(ceased operations)*
	EC-IBM	Canadair CRJ200ER	Air Nostrum/Iberia Regional
	EC-ICF	Airbus A.340-313X	Iberia *Maria Zambrano*
	EC-ICL	Airbus A.320-232	Spanair *(ceased operations)*
	EC-ICQ	Airbus A.320-211	Vueling Airlines *Iker Ochandorena*
	EC-ICR	Airbus A.320-211	Vueling Airlines
	EC-ICS	Airbus A.320-211	Vueling Airlines
	EC-ICT	Airbus A.320-211	Vueling Airlines
	EC-IDA	Boeing 737-86Q	Air Europa
	EC-IDC	Canadair CRJ200ER	Air Nostrum/Iberia Regional
	EC-IDF	Airbus A.340-313X	Iberia *Mariana Pineda*
	EC-IDT	Boeing 737-86Q	Air Europa
	EC-IEF	Airbus A.320-214	Iberia *Castillo de Loarre*
	EC-IEG	Airbus A.320-214	Iberia *Costa Brava*
	EC-IEI	Airbus A.320-214	Iberia *Monasterio de Valldigna*
	EC-IEJ	Airbus A.320-232	Spanair *(ceased operations)*
	EC-IGK	Airbus A.321-211	Iberia *Costa Calida*
	EC-IGO	Canadair CRJ200ER	Air Nostrum/Iberia Regional
	EC-IIG	Airbus A.321-211	Iberia *Ciudad de Siguenza*
	EC-IIH	Airbus A.340-313X	Iberia *Maria Barbara de Braganza*
	EC-III	Boeing 737-86Q	Air Europa
	EC-IIZ	Airbus A.320-232	Spanair *(ceased operations)*
	EC-IJE	Canadair CRJ200ER	Air Nostrum/Iberia Regional
	EC-IJF	Canadair CRJ200ER	Air Nostrum/Iberia Regional
	EC-IJN	Airbus A.321-211	Iberia *Merida*
	EC-IJS	Canadair CRJ200ER	Air Nostrum/Iberia Regional
	EC-IJU	Airbus A.321-231	Spanair *(ceased operations)*
	EC-IKZ	Canadair CRJ200ER	Air Nostrum/Iberia Regional
	EC-ILF	Canadair CRJ200ER	Air Nostrum/Iberia Regional
	EC-ILH	Airbus A.320-232	Spanair *(ceased operations)*
	EC-ILO	Airbus A.321-211	Iberia *Cueva de Nerja*
	EC-ILP	Airbus A.321-211	Iberia *Peniscola*
	EC-ILQ	Airbus A.320-214	Iberia *La Pedrera*
	EC-ILR	Airbus A.320-214	Iberia *San Juan de la Pena*
	EC-ILS	Airbus A.320-214	Iberia *Sierra de Cameros*
	EC-IMB	Airbus A.320-232	Spanair *(ceased operations)*
	EC-INB	Airbus A.321-231	Spanair *(ceased operations)*
	EC-INF	Canadair CRJ200ER	Air Nostrum/Iberia Regional
	EC-INM	Airbus A.320-232	Spanair *(ceased operations)*
	EC-INO	Airbus A.340-642	Iberia *Gaudi*

Reg.	Type	Owner or Operator	Notes
EC-INZ	Airbus A.320-214	Orbest	
EC-IOB	Airbus A.340-642	Iberia *Julio Romanes de Torres*	
EC-IOH	Airbus A.320-232	Spanair *(ceased operations)*	
EC-IPI	Airbus A.320-232	Spanair *(ceased operations)*	
EC-IRI	Canadair CRJ200ER	Air Nostrum/Iberia Regional	
EC-IQR	Airbus A.340-642	Iberia *Salvador Dali*	
EC-ISE	Boeing 737-86Q	Air Europa	
EC-ISN	Boeing 737-86Q	Air Europa	
EC-ITN	Airbus A.321-211	Iberia *Empuries*	
EC-ITU	Canadair CRJ200ER	Air Nostrum/Iberia Regional	
EC-IVG	Airbus A.320-232	Spanair *(ceased operations)*	
EC-IVH	Canadair CRJ200ER	Air Nostrum/Iberia Regional	
EC-IXD	Airbus A.321-211	Iberia *Vall d'Aran*	
EC-IYG	Airbus A.320-232	Spanair *(ceased operations)*	
EC-IZD	Airbus A.320-214	Vueling Airlines	
EC-IZH	Airbus A.320-214	Iberia *San Pere de Roda*	
EC-IZK	Airbus A.320-232	Spanair *(ceased operations)*	
EC-IZP	Canadair CRJ200ER	Air Nostrum/Iberia Regional	
EC-IZR	Airbus A.320-214	Iberia *Urkiola*	
EC-IZX	Airbus A.340-642	Iberia *Mariano Benlliure*	
EC-IZY	Airbus A.340-642	Iberia *I. Zuloaga*	
EC-JAP	Boeing 737-85P	Air Europa	
EC-JAZ	Airbus A.319-111	Iberia *Las Medulas*	
EC-JBA	Airbus A.340-642	Iberia *Joaquin Rodrigo*	
EC-JBJ	Boeing 737-85P	Air Europa	
EC-JBK	Boeing 737-85P	Air Europa	
EC-JBL	Boeing 737-85P	Air Europa	
EC-JCG	Canadair CRJ200ER	Air Nostrum/Iberia Regional	
EC-JCL	Canadair CRJ200ER	Air Nostrum/Iberia Regional	
EC-JCM	Canadair CRJ200ER	Air Nostrum/Iberia Regional	
EC-JCO	Canadair CRJ200ER	Air Nostrum/Iberia Regional	
EC-JCU	Swearingen SA227AC Metro III	Aeronova	
EC-JCY	Airbus A.340-642	Iberia *Andrés Segovia*	
EC-JCZ	Airbus A.340-642	Iberia *Vicente Aleixandre*	
EC-JDL	Airbus A.319-111	Iberia *Los Llanos de Aridane*	
EC-JDM	Airbus A.321-211	Iberia *Cantabria*	
EC-JDR	Airbus A.321-211	Iberia	
EC-JEE	Canadair CRJ200ER	Air Nostrum/Iberia Regional	
EC-JEF	Canadair CRJ200ER	Air Nostrum/Iberia Regional	
EC-JEI	Airbus A.319-111	Iberia *Xátiva*	
EC-JEJ	Airbus A.321-211	Iberia *Rio Frio*	
EC-JEN	Canadair CRJ200ER	Air Nostrum/Iberia Regional	
EC-JFF	Airbus A.320-214	Vueling Airlines *Vueling the world*	
EC-JFG	Airbus A.320-214	Vueling Airlines	
EC-JFH	Airbus A.320-214	Vueling Airlines	
EC-JFN	Airbus A.320-214	Iberia *Sirrea de las Nieves*	
EC-JFX	Airbus A.340-642	Iberia *Jacinto Benavente*	
EC-JGM	Airbus A.320-214	Vueling Airlines *The joy of vueling*	
EC-JGS	Airbus A.321-211	Iberia *Guadelupe*	
EC-JHK	Boeing 737-85P	Air Europa	
EC-JHL	Boeing 737-85P	Air Europa	
EC-JHP	Airbus A.330-343X	Orbest	
EC-JJD	Airbus A.320-232	Spanair *(ceased operations)*	
EC-JJS	McD Douglas MD-83	Swiftair	
EC-JLE	Airbus A.340-642	Iberia *Santiago Ramon y Cajal*	
EC-JLI	Airbus A.321-211	Iberia *Delta del Llobregrat*	
EC-JMR	Airbus A.321-211	Iberia *Aranjuez*	
EC-JNB	Canadair CRJ900ER	Air Nostrum/Iberia Regional	
EC-JNC	Airbus A.320-214	Spanair *Juan Antonio Samaranch (ceased operations)*	
EC-JNF	Boeing 737-85P	Air Europa *Mutua Madrilega*	
EC-JNI	Airbus A.321-211	Iberia *Palmeral de Eiche*	
EC-JNQ	Airbus A.340-642	Iberia *Antonio Machado*	
EC-JNX	Canadair CRJ200ER	Air Nostrum/Iberia Regional	
EC-JOD	Canadair CRJ200ER	Air Nostrum/Iberia Regional	
EC-JOY	Canadair CRJ200ER	Air Nostrum/Iberia Regional	
EC-JPF	Airbus A.330-202	Air Europa	
EC-JPU	Airbus A.340-642	Iberia *Pio Baroja*	
EC-JQG	Airbus A.330-202	Air Europa *Estepona – Costa del Sol*	
EC-JQQ	Airbus A.330-202	Air Europa	
EC-JQV	McD Douglas MD-83	Swiftair	
EC-JQZ	Airbus A.321-211	Iberia *Generalife*	
EC-JRE	Airbus A.321-211	Iberia *Villa de Uncastillo*	
EC-JSB	Airbus A.320-214	Iberia *Benalmadena*	

Notes	Reg.	Type	Owner or Operator
	EC-JSK	Airbus A.320-214	Iberia *Ciudad Encantada*
	EC-JSY	Airbus A.320-214	Vueling Airlines
	EC-JTQ	Airbus A.320-214	Vueling Airlines *Vueling, que es gerundio*
	EC-JTR	Airbus A.320-214	Vueling Airlines *No Vueling no party*
	EC-JTS	Canadair CRJ900ER	Air Nostrum/Iberia Regional
	EC-JTT	Canadair CRJ900ER	Air Nostrum/Iberia Regional
	EC-JTU	Canadair CRJ900ER	Air Nostrum/Iberia Regional
	EC-JVE	Airbus A.319-111	Iberia *Puerto de la Cruz*
	EC-JXJ	Airbus A.319-111	Vueling Airlines *Un Vueling s'il vous plait*
	EC-JXV	Airbus A.319-111	Iberia *Concejo de Cabrales*
	EC-JXZ	Canadair CRJ900ER	Air Nostrum/Iberia Regional
	EC-JYA	Canadair CRJ900ER	Air Nostrum/Iberia Regional
	EC-JYV	Canadair CRJ900ER	Air Nostrum/Iberia Regional
	EC-JYX	Airbus A.320-214	Vueling Airlines *Elisenda Masana*
	EC-JZI	Airbus A.320-214	Vueling Airlines *Vueling in love*
	EC-JZL	Airbus A.330-202	Air Europa
	EC-JZM	Airbus A.321-211	Iberia *Águila Imperial Ibérica*
	EC-JZQ	Airbus A.320-214	Vueling Airlines *I want to Vueling*
	EC-JZS	Canadair CRJ900ER	Air Nostrum/Iberia Regional
	EC-JZT	Canadair CRJ900ER	Air Nostrum/Iberia Regional
	EC-JZU	Canadair CRJ900ER	Air Nostrum/Iberia Regional
	EC-JZV	Canadair CRJ900ER	Air Nostrum/Iberia Regional
	EC-KBJ	Airbus A.319-111	Iberia *Lince Iberico*
	EC-KBU	Airbus A.320-214	Vueling Airlines
	EC-KBX	Airbus A.319-111	Iberia *Oso Pardo*
	EC-KCG	Boeing 737-85P	Air Europa
	EC-KCL	Airbus A.340-311	Iberia
	EC-KCU	Airbus A.320-216	Vueling Airlines
	EC-KCX	McD Douglas MD-83	Swiftair
	EC-KDG	Airbus A.320-214	Vueling Airlines
	EC-KDH	Airbus A.320-214	Vueling Airlines *Ain't no Vueling high enough*
	EC-KDI	Airbus A.319-111	Iberia *Cigu-a Negra*
	EC-KDT	Airbus A.320-216	Vueling Airlines
	EC-KDX	Airbus A.320-216	Vueling Airlines *Francisco Jose Ruiz Cortizo*
	EC-KEC	Airbus A.320-232	Spanair *(ceased operations)*
	EC-KFI	Airbus A.320-216	Vueling Airlines
	EC-KFT	Airbus A.319-111	Iberia *Nutria*
	EC-KHJ	Airbus A.320-214	Iberia
	EC-KHM	Airbus A.319-111	Iberia *Buho Real*
	EC-KHN	Airbus A.320-216	Vueling Airlines
	EC-KJD	Airbus A.320-216	Vueling Airlines
	EC-KJE	McD Douglas MD-87	Spanair *(ceased operations)*
	EC-KKS	Airbus A.319-111	Iberia *Halcon Peregrino*
	EC-KKT	Airbus A.320-214	Vueling Airlines *Vueling Together*
	EC-KLB	Airbus A.320-214	Vueling Airlines *Vuela Punto*
	EC-KLT	Airbus A.320-214	Vueling Airlines
	EC-KMD	Airbus A.319-111	Iberia *Petirrojo*
	EC-KME	Airbus A.319-111	Iberia *Grulla*
	EC-KMI	Airbus A.320-216	Vueling Airlines *How are you? I'm Vueling!*
	EC-KNM	Airbus A.320-214	Iberia *Hoces de Cabriel*
	EC-KOH	Airbus A.320-214	Iberia
	EC-KOM	Airbus A.330-202	Air Europa
	EC-KOU	Airbus A.340-313	Iberia
	EC-KOX	Airbus A.320-232	Spanair *(ceased operations)*
	EC-KOY	Airbus A.319-111	Iberia *Vencejo*
	EC-KPX	Airbus A.320-232	Spanair
	EC-KQC	Boeing 747-412	Pullmantur Air
	EC-KRH	Airbus A.320-214	Vueling Airlines *Vueling me softly*
	EC-KRJ	Embraer RJ190-200SR	Air Europa
	EC-KSE	Airbus A.340-313X	Iberia
	EC-KSM	Boeing 747-412	Pullmantur Air
	EC-KTG	Airbus A.330-203	Air Europa
	EC-KUB	Airbus A.319-111	Iberia
	EC-KXD	Embraer RJ190-200SR	Air Europa
	EC-KXN	Boeing 747-4H6	Pullmantur Air
	EC-KYO	Embraer RJ190-200SR	Air Europa
	EC-KYP	Embraer RJ190-200SR	Air Europa
	EC-KYZ	Airbus A.320-214	Orbest
	EC-KZG	Airbus A.320-214	Orbest
	EC-KZI	Airbus A.340-642	Iberia *Miguel Hernandez*
	EC-LAA	Airbus A.320-214	Vueling Airlines
	EC-LAB	Airbus A.320-214	Vueling Airlines
	EC-LAJ	Airbus A.320-214	Orbest

Reg.	Type	Owner or Operator	Notes
EC-LBC	Boeing 757-208ET	Mint Airways	
EC-LCQ	Embraer ERJ190-20LR	Air Europa	
EC-LCZ	Airbus A.340-642	Iberia	
EC-LEA	Airbus A.320-214	Iberia *Formentera*	
EC-LEI	Airbus A.319-111	Iberia *Vison Europeo*	
EC-LEK	Embraer ERJ190-200LR	Air Europa	
EC-LEQ	Airbus A.330-343E	Orbest	
EC-LEU	Airbus A.340-642	Iberia	
EC-LEV	Airbus A.340-642	Iberia	
EC-LEY	McD Douglas MD-83	Swiftair	
EC-LFS	Airbus A.340-642	Iberia	
EC-LFZ	Embraer ERJ190-200LR	Air Europa	
EC-LHL	Boeing 757-28A	Mint Airways	
EC-LHM	Airbus A.340-313X	Iberia	
EC-LIN	Embraer ERJ190-200LR	Air Europa	
EC-LJR	Canadair CRJ1000ER	Air Nostrum/Iberia Regional	
EC-LJS	Canadair CRJ1000ER	Air Nostrum/Iberia Regional	
EC-LJT	Canadair CRJ1000ER	Air Nostrum/Iberia Regional	
EC-LJX	Canadair CRJ1000ER	Air Nostrum/Iberia Regional	
EC-LKE	Airbus A.330-243	Air Europa	
EC-LKF	Canadair CRJ1000ER	Air Nostrum/Iberia Regional	
EC-LKG	Airbus A.320-214	Iberia *Santiago de Compostela*	
EC-LKH	Airbus A.320-214	Vueling Airlines	
EC-LKM	Embraer ERJ190-200LR	Air Europa	
EC-LKS	Airbus A.340-313	Iberia *Placido Domingo*	
EC-LKX	Embraer ERJ190-200LR	Air Europa	
EC-LLJ	Airbus A.320-216	Vueling Airlines *Luke-SkyVueling*	
EC-LLM	Airbus A.320-216	Vueling Airlines *Be happy, be Vueling*	
EC-LLR	Embraer ERJ190-200LR	Air Europa	
EC-LLX	Airbus A.320-214	Orbest	
EC-LML	Airbus A.320-216	Vueling Airlines	
EC-LMN	Airbus A.330-243	Air Europa	
EC-LMR	BAe 146-300QT	Panair/TNT Airways	
EC-LNA	Boeing 747-446	Pullmantur Air	
EC-LNH	Airbus A.330-243	Air Europa	
EC-LOB	Airbus A.320-232	Vueling Airlines	
EC-LOC	Airbus A.320-232	Vueling Airlines *Vueling on heaven's door*	
EC-LOF	BAe 146-300QT	Panair/TNT Airways	
EC-LOJ	Canadair CRJ1000ER	Air Nostrum/Iberia Regional	
EC-LOP	Airbus A.320-214	Vueling Airlines	
EC-LOV	Canadair CRJ1000ER	Air Nostrum/Iberia Regional	

EK (Armenia)

EK-32007	Airbus A.319-111	Armavia	
EK-32008	Airbus A.320-211	Armavia	

EP (Iran)

EP-IAA	Boeing 747SP-86	Iran Air	
EP-IAB	Boeing 747SP-86	Iran Air *Khorasan*	
EP-IAC	Boeing 747SP-86	Iran Air	
EP-IAD	Boeing 747SP-86	Iran Air	
EP-IAG	Boeing 747-286B	Iran Air	
EP-IAH	Boeing 747-286B	Iran Air *Khuzestan*	
EP-IAI	Boeing 747-230B	Iran Air	
EP-IAM	Boeing 747-186B	Iran Air	
EP-IBA	Airbus A.300B4-605R	Iran Air	
EP-IBB	Airbus A.300B4-605R	Iran Air	
EP-IBC	Airbus A.300B4-605R	Iran Air	
EP-IBD	Airbus A.300B4-605R	Iran Air	
EP-MHO	Airbus A.310-304	Mahan Air	
EP-MNO	Airbus A.310-304	Mahan Air	
EP-MNP	Airbus A.310-308	Mahan Air	
EP-MNV	Airbus A.310-304	Mahan Air	
EP-MNX	Airbus A.310-304ET	Mahan Air	

ER (Moldova)

ER-AXP	Airbus A.320-211	Air Moldova	
ER-AXT	Airbus A.320-231	Air Moldova	

Notes	Reg.	Type	Owner or Operator
	ER-AXV	Airbus A.320-211	Air Moldova
	ER-ECB	Embraer RJ190-100AR	Air Moldova

ES (Estonia)

	ES-ABJ	Boeing 737-33R	Estonian Air
	ES-ABL	Boeing 737-5L9	Estonian Air *Linda*
	ES-ABO	Boeing 737-505	Estonian Air
	ES-ACB	Canadair CRJ900ER	Estonian Air
	ES-ACC	Canadair CRJ900ER	Estonian Air
	ES-LBD	Boeing 737-35B	Tor Air

ET (Ethiopia)

	ET-AJS	Boeing 757-260PF	Ethiopian Airlines
	ET-AJX	Boeing 757-260F	Ethiopian Airlines
	ET-AKC	Boeing 757-260	Ethiopian Airlines
	ET-AKE	Boeing 757-260	Ethiopian Airlines
	ET-AKF	Boeing 757-260	Ethiopian Airlines
	ET-ALC	Boeing 767-33AER	Ethiopian Airlines
	ET-ALH	Boeing 767-3BGER	Ethiopian Airlines
	ET-ALJ	Boeing 767-360ER	Ethiopian Airlines
	ET-ALL	Boeing 767-3BGER	Ethiopian Airlines
	ET-ALO	Boeing 767-360ER	Ethiopian Airlines
	ET-ALP	Boeing 767-360ER	Ethiopian Airlines
	ET-ALZ	Boeing 757-231	Ethiopian Airlines
	ET-AME	Boeing 767-306ER	Ethiopian Airlines
	ET-AMF	Boeing 767-3BGER	Ethiopian Airlines
	ET-AMG	Boeing 767-3BGER	Ethiopian Airlines
	ET-AMK	Boeing 757-28A	Ethiopian Airlines
	ET-AML	McD Douglas MD-11F	Ethiopian Airlines
	ET-AMQ	Boeing 767-33AER	Ethiopian Airlines
	ET-AMT	Boeing 757-23N	Ethiopian Airlines
	ET-AMU	Boeing 757-23N	Ethiopian Airlines
	ET-AND	McD Douglas MD-11F	Ethiopian Airlines
	ET-ANU	Boeing 767-3Q8ER	Ethiopian Airlines

EW (Belarus)

	EW-100PJ	Canadair CRJ200LR	Belavia
	EW-250PA	Boeing 737-524	Belavia
	EW-251PA	Boeing 737-5Q8	Belavia
	EW-252PA	Boeing 737-524	Belavia
	EW-253PA	Boeing 737-524	Belavia
	EW-254PA	Boeing 737-3Q8	Belavia
	EW-276PJ	Canadair CRJ200ER	Belavia
	EW-277PJ	Canadair CRJ200ER	Belavia
	EW-282PA	Boeing 737-3Q8	Belavia
	EW-283PA	Boeing 737-3Q8	Belavia
	EW-290PA	Boeing 737-5Q8	Belavia
	EW-294PA	Boeing 737-505	Belavia
	EW-303PJ	Canadair CRJ200LR	Belavia
	EW-308PA	Boeing 737-3K2	Belavia

EZ (Turkmenistan)

	EZ-A010	Boeing 757-23A	Turkmenistan Airlines
	EZ-A011	Boeing 757-22K	Turkmenistan Airlines
	EZ-A012	Boeing 757-22K	Turkmenistan Airlines
	EZ-A014	Boeing 757-22K	Turkmenistan Airlines

F (France)

	F-GEXB	Boeing 747-4B3	Air France Cargo
	F-GFKH	Airbus A.320-211	Air France *Ville de Bruxelles*
	F-GFKJ	Airbus A.320-211	Air France *Pays de Roissy*
	F-GFKM	Airbus A.320-211	Air France *Ville de Luxembourg*
	F-GFKR	Airbus A.320-211	Air France *Ville de Barceloune*
	F-GFKS	Airbus A.320-211	Air France *Ville de Marseilles*

Reg.	Type	Owner or Operator	Notes
F-GFKV	Airbus A.320-211	Air France *Ville de Bordeaux*	
F-GFKY	Airbus A.320-211	Air France *Ville de Toulouse*	
F-GFKZ	Airbus A.320-211	Air France *Ville de Turin*	
F-GHQG	Airbus A.320-211	Air France	
F-GHQJ	Airbus A.320-211	Air France	
F-GHQK	Airbus A.320-211	Air France	
F-GHQL	Airbus A.320-211	Air France	
F-GHQO	Airbus A.320-211	Air France	
F-GHQP	Airbus A.320-211	Air France	
F-GHQQ	Airbus A.320-211	Air France	
F-GHQR	Airbus A.320-211	Air France	
F-GISC	Boeing 747-428	Air France	
F-GISD	Boeing 747-428	Air France	
F-GITD	Boeing 747-428	Air France	
F-GITE	Boeing 747-428	Air France	
F-GITF	Boeing 747-428	Air France	
F-GITH	Boeing 747-428	Air France	
F-GITI	Boeing 747-428	Air France	
F-GITJ	Boeing 747-428	Air France	
F-GIUA	Boeing 747-428ERF (SCD)	Air France Cargo	
F-GIUC	Boeing 747-428ERF (SCD)	Air France Cargo	
F-GIUD	Boeing 747-428ERF (SCD)	Air France Cargo	
F-GJVB	Airbus A.320-211	Air France	
F-GJVF	Airbus A.320-211	Aigle Azur	
F-GJVG	Airbus A.320-211	Air France	
F-GJVW	Airbus A.320-211	Air France	
F-GKHK	Airbus A.320-212	XL Airways France	
F-GKPD	Aerospatiale ATR-72-202	Airlinair/Air France	
F-GKXA	Airbus A.320-211	Air France	
F-GKXD	Airbus A.320-214	Air France	
F-GKXE	Airbus A.320-214	Air France	
F-GKXF	Airbus A.320-214	Air France	
F-GKXG	Airbus A.320-214	Air France	
F-GKXH	Airbus A.320-214	Air France	
F-GKXI	Airbus A.320-214	Air France	
F-GKXJ	Airbus A.320-214	Air France	
F-GKXK	Airbus A.320-214	Air France	
F-GKXL	Airbus A.320-214	Air France	
F-GKXM	Airbus A.320-214	Air France	
F-GKXN	Airbus A.320-214	Air France	
F-GKXO	Airbus A.320-214	Air France	
F-GKXP	Airbus A.320-214	Air France	
F-GKXR	Airbus A.320-214	Air France	
F-GKXS	Airbus A.320-214	Air France	
F-GKXT	Airbus A.320-214	Air France	
F-GKXU	Airbus A.320-214	Air France	
F-GKXV	Airbus A.320-214	Air France	
F-GKXY	Airbus A.320-214	Air France	
F-GKXZ	Airbus A.320-214	Air France	
F-GLZC	Airbus A.340-312	Air France	
F-GLZH	Airbus A.340-312	Air France	
F-GLZI	Airbus A.340-312	Air France	
F-GLZJ	Airbus A.340-313X	Air France	
F-GLZK	Airbus A.340-313X	Air France	
F-GLZL	Airbus A.340-313X	Air France	
F-GLZM	Airbus A.340-313X	Air France	
F-GLZN	Airbus A.340-313X	Air France	
F-GLZO	Airbus A.340-313X	Air France	
F-GLZP	Airbus A.340-313X	Air France	
F-GLZR	Airbus A.340-313X	Air France	
F-GLZS	Airbus A.340-313X	Air France	
F-GLZT	Airbus A.340-313X	Air France	
F-GLZU	Airbus A.340-313X	Air France	
F-GMZA	Airbus A.321-111	Air France	
F-GMZB	Airbus A.321-111	Air France	
F-GMZC	Airbus A.321-111	Air France	
F-GMZD	Airbus A.321-111	Air France	
F-GMZE	Airbus A.321-111	Air France	
F-GNII	Airbus A.340-313X	Air France	
F-GPEK	Boeing 757-236	Open Skies	
F-GPMA	Airbus A.319-113	Air France	
F-GPMB	Airbus A.319-113	Air France	
F-GPMC	Airbus A.319-113	Air France	
F-GPMD	Airbus A.319-113	Air France	

Notes	Reg.	Type	Owner or Operator
	F-GPME	Airbus A.319-113	Air France
	F-GPMF	Airbus A.319-113	Air France
	F-GPOC	Aerospatiale ATR-72-202	Airlinair/Air France
	F-GPOD	Aerospatiale ATR-72-202	Airlinair/Air France
	F-GPYA	Aerospatiale ATR-42-500	Airlinair/Air France
	F-GPYD	Aerospatiale ATR-42-500	Airlinair/Air France
	F-GPYF	Aerospatiale ATR-42-500	Airlinair/Air France
	F-GPYK	Aerospatiale ATR-42-500	Airlinair/Air France
	F-GPYL	Aerospatiale ATR-42-500	Airlinair/Air France
	F-GPYM	Aerospatiale ATR-42-500	Airlinair/Air France
	F-GPYO	Aerospatiale ATR-42-500	Airlinair/Air France
	F-GRGA	Embraer RJ145EU	Regional Airlines/Air France
	F-GRGB	Embraer RJ145EU	Regional Airlines/Air France
	F-GRGC	Embraer RJ145EU	Regional Airlines/Air France
	F-GRGD	Embraer RJ145EU	Regional Airlines/Air France
	F-GRGE	Embraer RJ145EU	Regional Airlines/Air France
	F-GRGF	Embraer RJ145EU	Regional Airlines/Air France
	F-GRGG	Embraer RJ145EU	Regional Airlines/Air France
	F-GRGH	Embraer RJ145EU	Regional Airlines/Air France
	F-GRGI	Embraer RJ145EU	Regional Airlines/Air France
	F-GRGJ	Embraer RJ145EU	Regional Airlines/Air France
	F-GRGK	Embraer RJ145EU	Regional Airlines/Air France
	F-GRGL	Embraer RJ145EU	Regional Airlines/Air France
	F-GRGM	Embraer RJ145EU	Regional Airlines/Air France
	F-GRGP	Embraer RJ135ER	Regional Airlines/Air France
	F-GRGQ	Embraer RJ135ER	Regional Airlines/Air France
	F-GRGR	Embraer RJ135ER	Regional Airlines/Air France
	F-GRHA	Airbus A.319-111	Air France
	F-GRHB	Airbus A.319-111	Air France
	F-GRHC	Airbus A.319-111	Air France
	F-GRHD	Airbus A.319-111	Air France
	F-GRHE	Airbus A.319-111	Air France
	F-GRHF	Airbus A.319-111	Air France
	F-GRHG	Airbus A.319-111	Air France
	F-GRHH	Airbus A.319-111	Air France
	F-GRHI	Airbus A.319-111	Air France
	F-GRHJ	Airbus A.319-111	Air France
	F-GRHK	Airbus A.319-111	Air France
	F-GRHL	Airbus A.319-111	Air France
	F-GRHM	Airbus A.319-111	Air France
	F-GRHN	Airbus A.319-111	Air France
	F-GRHO	Airbus A.319-111	Air France
	F-GRHP	Airbus A.319-111	Air France
	F-GRHQ	Airbus A.319-111	Air France
	F-GRHR	Airbus A.319-111	Air France
	F-GRHS	Airbus A.319-111	Air France
	F-GRHT	Airbus A.319-111	Air France
	F-GRHU	Airbus A.319-111	Air France
	F-GRHV	Airbus A.319-111	Air France
	F-GRHX	Airbus A.319-111	Air France
	F-GRHY	Airbus A.319-111	Air France
	F-GRHZ	Airbus A.319-111	Air France
	F-GRJG	Canadair CRJ100ER	Brit Air/Air France
	F-GRJI	Canadair CRJ100ER	Brit Air/Air France
	F-GRJJ	Canadair CRJ100ER	Brit Air/Air France
	F-GRJK	Canadair CRJ100ER	Brit Air/Air France
	F-GRJL	Canadair CRJ100ER	Brit Air/Air France
	F-GRJM	Canadair CRJ100ER	Brit Air/Air France
	F-GRJN	Canadair CRJ100ER	Brit Air/Air France
	F-GRJO	Canadair CRJ100ER	Brit Air/Air France
	F-GRJP	Canadair CRJ100ER	Brit Air/Air France
	F-GRJQ	Canadair CRJ100ER	Brit Air/Air France
	F-GRJR	Canadair CRJ100ER	Brit Air/Air France
	F-GRJT	Canadair CRJ100ER	Brit Air/Air France
	F-GRJU	Canadair CRJ100ER	Brit Air/Air France
	F-GRSQ	Airbus A.330-243	XL Airways France
	F-GRXA	Airbus A.319-111	Air France
	F-GRXB	Airbus A.319-111	Air France
	F-GRXC	Airbus A.319-111	Air France
	F-GRXD	Airbus A.319-111	Air France
	F-GRXE	Airbus A.319-111	Air France
	F-GRXF	Airbus A.319-111	Air France
	F-GRXG	Airbus A.319-115LR	Air France Dedicate
	F-GRXH	Airbus A.319-115LR	Air France Dedicate

Reg.	Type	Owner or Operator	Notes
F-GRXJ	Airbus A.319-115LR	Air France	
F-GRXK	Airbus A.319-115LR	Air France Dedicate	
F-GRXL	Airbus A.319-111	Air France	
F-GRXM	Airbus A.319-111	Air France	
F-GRXN	Airbus A.319-115LR	Air France Dedicate	
F-GRZA	Canadair CRJ700	Brit Air/Air France	
F-GRZB	Canadair CRJ700	Brit Air/Air France	
F-GRZC	Canadair CRJ700	Brit Air/Air France	
F-GRZD	Canadair CRJ700	Brit Air/Air France	
F-GRZE	Canadair CRJ700	Brit Air/Air France	
F-GRZF	Canadair CRJ700	Brit Air/Air France	
F-GRZG	Canadair CRJ700	Brit Air/Air France	
F-GRZH	Canadair CRJ700	Brit Air/Air France	
F-GRZI	Canadair CRJ700	Brit Air/Air France	
F-GRZJ	Canadair CRJ700	Brit Air/Air France	
F-GRZK	Canadair CRJ700	Brit Air/Air France	
F-GRZL	Canadair CRJ700	Brit Air/Air France	
F-GRZM	Canadair CRJ700	Brit Air/Air France	
F-GRZN	Canadair CRJ700	Brit Air/Air France	
F-GRZO	Canadair CRJ700	Brit Air/Air France	
F-GSEU	Airbus A.330-243	XL Airways France	
F-GSPA	Boeing 777-228ER	Air France	
F-GSPB	Boeing 777-228ER	Air France	
F-GSPC	Boeing 777-228ER	Air France	
F-GSPD	Boeing 777-228ER	Air France	
F-GSPE	Boeing 777-228ER	Air France	
F-GSPF	Boeing 777-228ER	Air France	
F-GSPG	Boeing 777-228ER	Air France	
F-GSPH	Boeing 777-228ER	Air France	
F-GSPI	Boeing 777-228ER	Air France	
F-GSPJ	Boeing 777-228ER	Air France	
F-GSPK	Boeing 777-228ER	Air France	
F-GSPL	Boeing 777-228ER	Air France	
F-GSPM	Boeing 777-228ER	Air France	
F-GSPN	Boeing 777-228ER	Air France	
F-GSPO	Boeing 777-228ER	Air France	
F-GSPP	Boeing 777-228ER	Air France	
F-GSPQ	Boeing 777-228ER	Air France	
F-GSPR	Boeing 777-228ER	Air France	
F-GSPS	Boeing 777-228ER	Air France	
F-GSPT	Boeing 777-228ER	Air France	
F-GSPU	Boeing 777-228ER	Air France	
F-GSPV	Boeing 777-228ER	Air France	
F-GSPX	Boeing 777-228ER	Air France	
F-GSPY	Boeing 777-228ER	Air France	
F-GSPZ	Boeing 777-228ER	Air France	
F-GSQA	Boeing 777-328ER	Air France	
F-GSQB	Boeing 777-328ER	Air France	
F-GSQC	Boeing 777-328ER	Air France	
F-GSQD	Boeing 777-328ER	Air France	
F-GSQE	Boeing 777-328ER	Air France	
F-GSQF	Boeing 777-328ER	Air France	
F-GSQG	Boeing 777-328ER	Air France	
F-GSQH	Boeing 777-328ER	Air France	
F-GSQI	Boeing 777-328ER	Air France	
F-GSQJ	Boeing 777-328ER	Air France	
F-GSQK	Boeing 777-328ER	Air France	
F-GSQL	Boeing 777-328ER	Air France	
F-GSQM	Boeing 777-328ER	Air France	
F-GSQN	Boeing 777-328ER	Air France	
F-GSQO	Boeing 777-328ER	Air France	
F-GSQP	Boeing 777-328ER	Air France	
F-GSQR	Boeing 777-328ER	Air France	
F-GSQS	Boeing 777-328ER	Air France	
F-GSQT	Boeing 777-328ER	Air France	
F-GSQU	Boeing 777-328ER	Air France	
F-GSQV	Boeing 777-328ER	Air France	
F-GSQX	Boeing 777-328ER	Air France	
F-GSQY	Boeing 777-328ER	Air France	
F-GSTA	Airbus A.300-608ST Beluga (1)	Airbus Transport International	
F-GSTB	Airbus A.300-608ST Beluga (2)	Airbus Transport International	
F-GSTC	Airbus A.300-608ST Beluga (3)	Airbus Transport International	
F-GSTD	Airbus A.300-608ST Beluga (4)	Airbus Transport International	
F-GSTF	Airbus A.300-608ST Beluga (5)	Airbus Transport International	

Notes	Reg.	Type	Owner or Operator
	F-GTAD	Airbus A.321-211	Air France
	F-GTAE	Airbus A.321-211	Air France
	F-GTAH	Airbus A.321-211	Air France
	F-GTAI	Airbus A.321-211	Air France
	F-GTAJ	Airbus A.321-211	Air France
	F-GTAK	Airbus A.321-211	Air France
	F-GTAL	Airbus A.321-211	Air France
	F-GTAM	Airbus A.321-211	Air France
	F-GTAN	Airbus A.321-211	Air France
	F-GTAO	Airbus A.321-211	Air France
	F-GTAP	Airbus A.321-212	Air France
	F-GTAQ	Airbus A.321-211	Air France
	F-GTAR	Airbus A.321-211	Air France
	F-GTAS	Airbus A.321-211	Air France
	F-GTAT	Airbus A.321-211	Air France
	F-GTAU	Airbus A.321-211	Air France,
	F-GTAV	Airbus A.321-211	Air France
	F-GTAX	Airbus A.321-211	Air France
	F-GTAY	Airbus A.321-211	Air France
	F-GTAZ	Airbus A.321-211	Air France
	F-GTUI	Boeing 747-422	Corsair
	F-GUAA	Airbus A.321-211	Aigle Azur
	F-GUAM	Embraer RJ145MP	Regional Airlines/Air France
	F-GUBA	Embraer RJ145MP	Regional Airlines/Air France
	F-GUBB	Embraer RJ145MP	Regional Airlines/Air France
	F-GUBC	Embraer RJ145MP	Regional Airlines/Air France
	F-GUBD	Embraer RJ145MP	Regional Airlines/Air France
	F-GUBE	Embraer RJ145MP	Regional Airlines/Air France
	F-GUBF	Embraer RJ145MP	Regional Airlines/Air France
	F-GUBG	Embraer RJ145MP	Regional Airlines/Air France
	F-GUEA	Embraer RJ145MP	Regional Airlines/Air France
	F-GUFD	Embraer RJ145MP	Regional Airlines/Air France
	F-GUGA	Airbus A.318-111	Air France
	F-GUGB	Airbus A.318-111	Air France
	F-GUGC	Airbus A.318-111	Air France
	F-GUGD	Airbus A.318-111	Air France
	F-GUGE	Airbus A.318-111	Air France
	F-GUGF	Airbus A.318-111	Air France
	F-GUGG	Airbus A.318-111	Air France
	F-GUGH	Airbus A.318-111	Air France
	F-GUGI	Airbus A.318-111	Air France
	F-GUGJ	Airbus A.318-111	Air France
	F-GUGK	Airbus A.318-111	Air France
	F-GUGL	Airbus A.318-111	Air France
	F-GUGM	Airbus A.318-111	Air France
	F-GUGN	Airbus A.318-111	Air France
	F-GUGO	Airbus A.318-111	Air France
	F-GUGP	Airbus A.318-111	Air France
	F-GUGQ	Airbus A.318-111	Air France
	F-GUGR	Airbus A.318-111	Air France
	F-GUMA	Embraer RJ145MP	Regional Airlines/Air France
	F-GUOB	Boeing 777-F28	Air France Cargo
	F-GUOC	Boeing 777-F28	Air France Cargo
	F-GUPT	Embraer RJ145MP	Regional Airlines/Air France
	F-GVHD	Embraer RJ145MP	Regional Airlines/Air France
	F-GVZL	Aerospatiale ATR-72-500	Airlinair/Air France
	F-GVZM	Aerospatiale ATR-72-212	Airlinair/Air France
	F-GVZN	Aerospatiale ATR-72-500	Airlinair/Air France
	F-GXAH	Airbus A.319-132	Aigle Azur
	F-GYAI	Airbus A.320-211	Air Mediterranée
	F-GYAJ	Airbus A.321-211	Air Mediterranée
	F-GYAN	Airbus A.321-111	Air Mediterranée
	F-GYAO	Airbus A.321-111	Air Mediterranée
	F-GYAP	Airbus A.321-111	Air Mediterranée
	F-GYAQ	Airbus A.321-211	Air Mediterranée
	F-GYAR	Airbus A.321-211	Air Mediterranée
	F-GYAZ	Airbus A.321-111	Air Mediterranée
	F-GZCA	Airbus A.330-203	Air France
	F-GZCB	Airbus A.330-203	Air France
	F-GZCC	Airbus A.330-203	Air France
	F-GZCD	Airbus A.330-203	Air France
	F-GZCE	Airbus A.330-203	Air France
	F-GZCF	Airbus A.330-203	Air France
	F-GZCG	Airbus A.330-203	Air France

Reg.	Type	Owner or Operator	Notes
F-GZCH	Airbus A.330-203	Air France	
F-GZCI	Airbus A.330-203	Air France	
F-GZCJ	Airbus A.330-203	Air France	
F-GZCK	Airbus A.330-203	Air France	
F-GZCL	Airbus A.330-203	Air France	
F-GZCM	Airbus A.330-203	Air France	
F-GZCN	Airbus A.330-203	Air France	
F-GZCO	Airbus A.330-203	Air France	
F-GZHA	Boeing 737-8GJ	Transavia France	
F-GZHB	Boeing 737-8GJ	Transavia France	
F-GZHC	Boeing 737-8GJ	Transavia France	
F-GZHD	Boeing 737-8K2	Transavia France	
F-GZHE	Boeing 737-8K2	Transavia France	
F-GZHF	Boeing 737-8HX	Transavia France	
F-GZHN	Boeing 737-8K2	Transavia France	
F-GZHV	Boeing 737-85H	Transavia France	
F-GZNA	Boeing 777-328ER	Air France	
F-GZNB	Boeing 777-328ER	Air France	
F-GZNC	Boeing 777-328ER	Air France	
F-GZND	Boeing 777-328ER	Air France	
F-GZNE	Boeing 777-328ER	Air France	
F-GZNF	Boeing 777-328ER	Air France	
F-GZNG	Boeing 777-328ER	Air France	
F-GZNH	Boeing 777-328ER	Air France	
F-GZNI	Boeing 777-328ER	Air France	
F-GZNJ	Boeing 777-328ER	Air France	
F-GZNK	Boeing 777-328ER	Air France	
F-GZNL	Boeing 777-328ER	Air France	
F-GZNM	Boeing 777-328ER	Air France	
F-GZNN	Boeing 777-328ER	Air France	
F-HAVI	Boeing 757-26D	Open Skies *Violette*	
F-HAVN	Boeing 757-230	Open Skies	
F-HAXL	Boeing 737-8Q8	XL Airways France	
F-HBAB	Airbus A.321-211	Aigle Azur	
F-HBAF	Airbus A.321-211	Aigle Azur	
F-HBAL	Airbus A.319-111	Aigle Azur	
F-HBAO	Airbus A.320-214	Aigle Azur	
F-HBAP	Airbus A.320-214	Aigle Azur	
F-HBII	Airbus A.320-214	Aigle Azur	
F-HBIL	Airbus A.330-243	Corsair	
F-HBLA	Embraer RJ190-100LR	Regional Airlines/Air France	
F-HBLB	Embraer RJ190-100LR	Regional Airlines/Air France	
F-HBLC	Embraer RJ190-100LR	Regional Airlines/Air France	
F-HBLD	Embraer RJ190-100LR	Regional Airlines/Air France	
F-HBLE	Embraer RJ190-100LR	Regional Airlines/Air France	
F-HBLF	Embraer RJ190-100LR	Regional Airlines/Air France	
F-HBLG	Embraer RJ190-100LR	Regional Airlines/Air France	
F-HBLH	Embraer RJ190-100LR	Regional Airlines/Air France	
F-HBLI	Embraer RJ190-100LR	Regional Airlines/Air France	
F-HBLJ	Embraer RJ190-100LR	Regional Airlines/Air France	
F-HBMI	Airbus A.319-114	Aigle Azur	
F-HBNA	Airbus A.320-214	Air France	
F-HBNB	Airbus A.320-214	Air France	
F-HBNC	Airbus A.320-214	Air France	
F-HBND	Airbus A.320-214	Air France	
F-HBNE	Airbus A.320-214	Air France	
F-HBNF	Airbus A.320-214	Air France	
F-HBNG	Airbus A.320-214	Air France	
F-HBNH	Airbus A.320-214	Air France	
F-HBNI	Airbus A.320-214	Air France	
F-HBNJ	Airbus A.320-214	Air France	
F-HBNK	Airbus A.320-214	Air France	
F-HBNL	Airbus A.320-214	Air France	
F-HBNM	Airbus A.320-214	Air France	
F-HBNN	Airbus A.320-214	Air France	
F-HBXA	Embraer RJ170-100LR	Regional Airlines/Air France	
F-HBXB	Embraer RJ170-100LR	Regional Airlines/Air France	
F-HBXC	Embraer RJ170-100LR	Regional Airlines/Air France	
F-HBXD	Embraer RJ170-100LR	Regional Airlines/Air France	
F-HBXE	Embraer RJ170-100LR	Regional Airlines/Air France	
F-HBXF	Embraer RJ170-100LR	Regional Airlines/Air France	
F-HBXG	Embraer RJ170-100LR	Regional Airlines/Air France	
F-HBXH	Embraer RJ170-100LR	Regional Airlines/Air France	
F-HBXI	Embraer RJ170-100LR	Regional Airlines/Air France	

Notes	Reg.	Type	Owner or Operator
	F-HBXJ	Embraer RJ170-100LR	Regional Airlines/Air France
	F-HBXK	Embraer RJ170-100LR	Regional Airlines/Air France
	F-HCAI	Airbus A.321-111	Aigle Azur
	F-HCAT	Airbus A.330-243	Corsair
	F-HCOA	Boeing 737-5LP	Air Mediterranee
	F-HCZI	Airbus A.319-112	Aigle Azur
	F-HEPA	Airbus A.320-214	Air France
	F-HEPB	Airbus A.320-214	Air France
	F-HEPC	Airbus A.320-214	Air France
	F-HEPD	Airbus A.320-214	Air France
	F-HEPE	Airbus A.320-214	Air France
	F-HJER	Boeing 737-86N	XL Airways France
	F-HJUL	Boeing 737-8Q8	XL Airways France
	F-HKIS	Boeing 747-422	Corsair
	F-HLOV	Boeing 747-422	Corsair
	F-HMLA	Canadair CRJ1000	Brit Air/Air France
	F-HMLC	Canadair CRJ1000	Brit Air/Air France
	F-HMLD	Canadair CRJ1000	Brit Air/Air France
	F-HMLE	Canadair CRJ1000	Brit Air/Air France
	F-HMLF	Canadair CRJ1000	Brit Air/Air France
	F-HMLG	Canadair CRJ1000	Brit Air/Air France
	F-HMLH	Canadair CRJ1000	Brit Air/Air France
	F-HMLI	Canadair CRJ1000	Brit Air/Air France
	F-HMLJ	Canadair CRJ1000	Brit Air/Air France
	F-HMLK	Canadair CRJ1000	Brit Air/Air France
	F-HMLL	Canadair CRJ1000	Brit Air/Air France
	F-HPJA	Airbus A.380-861	Air France
	F-HPJB	Airbus A.380-861	Air France
	F-HPJC	Airbus A.380-861	Air France
	F-HPJD	Airbus A.380-861	Air France
	F-HPJE	Airbus A.380-861	Air France
	F-HPJF	Airbus A.380-861	Air France
	F-HPJG	Airbus A.380-861	Air France
	F-HPJH	Airbus A.380-861	Air France
	F-HPJI	Airbus A.380-861	Air France
	F-HPJJ	Airbus A.380-861	Air France
	F-HPJK	Airbus A.380-861	Air France
	F-HSEA	Boeing 747-422	Corsair
	F-HSUN	Boeing 747-422	Corsair
	F-OHGV	Airbus A.320-232	Royal Jordanian *Irbid*
	F-OHGX	Airbus A.320-232	Royal Jordanian *Madaba*
	F-OJHH	Airbus A.310-304ET	Mahan Air
	F-OJHI	Airbus A.310-304ET	Mahan Air
	F-OMRN	Airbus A.320-232	Middle East Airlines
	F-OMRO	Airbus A.320-232	Middle East Airlines
	F-ORAD	Airbus A.320-233	Belle Air
	F-ORAE	Airbus A.320-233	Belle Air
	F-ORAG	Airbus A.319-132	Belle Air
	F-ORMA	Airbus A.330-243	Middle East Airlines
	F-ORME	Airbus A.321-231	Middle East Airlines
	F-ORMF	Airbus A.321-231	Middle East Airlines
	F-ORMG	Airbus A.321-231	Middle East Airlines

HA (Hungary)

	HA-LKE	Boeing 737-86Q	Travel Service Airlines
	HA-LOA	Boeing 737-7Q8	Malev *(ceased operations)*
	HA-LOB	Boeing 737-7Q8	Malev *(ceased operations)*
	HA-LOC	Boeing 737-8Q8	Malev *(ceased operations)*
	HA-LOD	Boeing 737-6Q8	Malev *(ceased operations)*
	HA-LOE	Boeing 737-6Q8	Malev *(ceased operations)*
	HA-LOF	Boeing 737-6Q8	Malev *(ceased operations)*
	HA-LOG	Boeing 737-6Q8	Malev *(ceased operations)*
	HA-LOH	Boeing 737-8Q8	Malev *(ceased operations)*
	HA-LOI	Boeing 737-7Q8	Malev *(ceased operations)*
	HA-LOJ	Boeing 737-6Q8	Malev *(ceased operations)*
	HA-LOK	Boeing 737-8Q8	Malev *(ceased operations)*
	HA-LOL	Boeing 737-7Q8	Malev *(ceased operations)*
	HA-LOM	Boeing 737-8Q8	Malev *(ceased operations)*
	HA-LON	Boeing 737-6Q8	Malev *(ceased operations)*
	HA-LOP	Boeing 737-7Q8	Malev *(ceased operations)*
	HA-LOR	Boeing 737-7Q8	Malev *(ceased operations)*
	HA-LOS	Boeing 737-7Q8	Malev *(ceased operations)*

Reg.	Type	Owner or Operator	Notes
HA-LOU	Boeing 737-8Q8	Malev (ceased operations)	
HA-LPD	Airbus A.320-233	Wizz Air	
HA-LPE	Airbus A.320-233	Wizz Air	
HA-LPF	Airbus A.320-233	Wizz Air	
HA-LPI	Airbus A.320-233	Wizz Air	
HA-LPJ	Airbus A.320-232	Wizz Air	
HA-LPK	Airbus A.320-231	Wizz Air	
HA-LPL	Airbus A.320-232	Wizz Air	
HA-LPM	Airbus A.320-232	Wizz Air	
HA-LPN	Airbus A.320-232	Wizz Air	
HA-LPO	Airbus A.320-232	Wizz Air	
HA-LPQ	Airbus A.320-232	Wizz Air	
HA-LPR	Airbus A.320-232	Wizz Air	
HA-LPS	Airbus A.320-232	Wizz Air	
HA-LPT	Airbus A.320-232	Wizz Air	
HA-LPU	Airbus A.320-232	Wizz Air	
HA-LPV	Airbus A.320-232	Wizz Air	
HA-LPW	Airbus A.320-232	Wizz Air	
HA-LPX	Airbus A.320-232	Wizz Air	
HA-LPY	Airbus A.320-232	Wizz Air	
HA-LPZ	Airbus A.320-232	Wizz Air	
HA-LWA	Airbus A.320-232	Wizz Air	
HA-LWB	Airbus A.320-232	Wizz Air	
HA-LWC	Airbus A.320-232	Wizz Air	
HA-LWD	Airbus A.320-232	Wizz Air	
HA-LWE	Airbus A.320-232	Wizz Air	
HA-LWF	Airbus A.320-232	Wizz Air	
HA-LWG	Airbus A.320-232	Wizz Air	
HA-LWH	Airbus A.320-232	Wizz Air	
HA-LWI	Airbus A.320-214	Wizz Air	
HA-LWJ	Airbus A.320-214	Wizz Air	
HA-LWK	Airbus A.320-232	Wizz Air	
HA-LWL	Airbus A.320-232	Wizz Air	

HB (Switzerland)

Reg.	Type	Owner or Operator	Notes
HB-AEO	Dornier Do.328-110	Sky Work Airlines	
HB-AER	Dornier Do.328-110	Sky Work Airlines	
HB-AES	Dornier Do.328-110	Sky Work Airlines	
HB-IEE	Boeing 757-23A	PrivatAir	
HB-IHX	Airbus A.320-214	Edelweiss Air Calvaro	
HB-IHY	Airbus A.320-214	Edelweiss Air Upali	
HB-IHZ	Airbus A.320-214	Edelweiss Air Viktoria	
HB-IIR	Boeing 737-86Q	PrivatAir/Swiss International	
HB-IJB	Airbus A.320-214	Swiss International Embrach	
HB-IJD	Airbus A.320-214	Swiss International	
HB-IJE	Airbus A.320-214	Swiss International Arosa	
HB-IJF	Airbus A.320-214	Swiss International	
HB-IJH	Airbus A.320-214	Swiss International	
HB-IJI	Airbus A.320-214	Swiss International Basodino	
HB-IJJ	Airbus A.320-214	Swiss International Les Diablerets	
HB-IJK	Airbus A.320-214	Swiss International Wissigstock	
HB-IJL	Airbus A.320-214	Swiss International Pizol	
HB-IJM	Airbus A.320-214	Swiss International Schilthorn	
HB-IJN	Airbus A.320-214	Swiss International Vanil Noir	
HB-IJO	Airbus A.320-214	Swiss International Lissengrat	
HB-IJP	Airbus A.320-214	Swiss International Nollen	
HB-IJQ	Airbus A.320-214	Swiss International Agassizhorn	
HB-IJR	Airbus A.320-214	Swiss International Dammastock	
HB-IJS	Airbus A.320-214	Swiss International Creux du Van	
HB-IJU	Airbus A.320-214	Swiss International Bietschhorn	
HB-IJV	Airbus A.320-214	Swiss International Wildspitz	
HB-IJW	Airbus A.320-214	Swiss International Bachtel	
HB-IJX	Airbus A.320-214	Swiss International Davos	
HB-IOC	Airbus A.321-111	Swiss International Eiger	
HB-IOD	Airbus A.321-111	Swiss International	
HB-IOF	Airbus A.321-111	Swiss International	
HB-IOH	Airbus A.321-111	Swiss International Piz Palu	
HB-IOK	Airbus A.321-111	Swiss International Biefertenstock	
HB-IOL	Airbus A.321-111	Swiss International Kaiseregg	
HB-IOM	Airbus A.321-212	Swiss International	
HB-IOP	Airbus A.320-214	Air Berlin/Belair	
HB-IOQ	Airbus A.320-214	Air Berlin/Belair	

Notes	Reg.	Type	Owner or Operator
	HB-IOR	Airbus A.320-214	Air Berlin/Belair
	HB-IOS	Airbus A.320-214	Air Berlin/Belair
	HB-IOW	Airbus A.320-214	Air Berlin/Belair
	HB-IOX	Airbus A.319-112	Air Berlin/Belair
	HB-IOY	Airbus A.319-112	Air Berlin/Belair
	HB-IOZ	Airbus A.320-214	Air Berlin/Belair
	HB-IPR	Airbus A.319-112	Swiss International *Commune de Champagne*
	HB-IPS	Airbus A.319-112	Swiss International *Weiach*
	HB-IPT	Airbus A.319-112	Swiss International *Stadel*
	HB-IPU	Airbus A.319-112	Swiss International *Hochfelden*
	HB-IPV	Airbus A.319-112	Swiss International *Rumlang*
	HB-IPX	Airbus A.319-112	Swiss International *Steinmaur*
	HB-IPY	Airbus A.319-112	Swiss International *Hori*
	HB-IQA	Airbus A.330-223	Swiss International/Brussels Airlines
	HB-IQI	Airbus A.330-223	Edelweiss Air *Kiburi*
	HB-IXN	Avro RJ100	Swiss European Airlines *Balmhorn 3699m*
	HB-IXO	Avro RJ100	Swiss European Airlines *Brisen 2404m*
	HB-IXP	Avro RJ100	Swiss European Airlines *Chestenberg 647m*
	HB-IXQ	Avro RJ100	Swiss European Airlines *Corno Gries 2969m*
	HB-IXR	Avro RJ100	Swiss European Airlines *Hoho Winde 1204m*
	HB-IXS	Avro RJ100	Swiss European Airlines *Mont Velan 3731m*
	HB-IXT	Avro RJ100	Swiss European Airlines *Ottenberg 681m*
	HB-IXU	Avro RJ100	Swiss European Airlines *Pfannenstiel 853m*
	HB-IXV	Avro RJ100	Swiss European Airlines *Saxer First 2151m*
	HB-IXW	Avro RJ100	Swiss European Airlines *Shafarnisch 2107m*
	HB-IXX	Avro RJ100	Swiss European Airlines *Silberen 2319m*
	HB-IYQ	Avro RJ100	Swiss European Airlines *Piz Buin 3312m*
	HB-IYR	Avro RJ100	Swiss European Airlines *Vrenelisgärtli 2904m*
	HB-IYS	Avro RJ100	Swiss European Airlines *Churfirsten 2306m*
	HB-IYT	Avro RJ100	Swiss European Airlines *Bluemlisalp 3663m*
	HB-IYU	Avro RJ100	Swiss European Airlines *Rot Turm 2002m*
	HB-IYV	Avro RJ100	Swiss European Airlines *Pizzo Barone 2864m*
	HB-IYW	Avro RJ100	Swiss European Airlines *Spitzmeilen 2501m*
	HB-IYY	Avro RJ100	Swiss European Airlines *Titlis 3238m*
	HB-IYZ	Avro RJ100	Swiss European Airlines *Tour d'Ai 2331m*
	HB-JGA	DHC.8Q-402 Dash Eight	Sky Work Airlines
	HB-JHA	Airbus A.330-343	Swiss International
	HB-JHB	Airbus A.330-343	Swiss International *Sion*
	HB-JHC	Airbus A.330-343	Swiss International *Bellinzona*
	HB-JHD	Airbus A.330-343	Swiss International *St.Gallen*
	HB-JHE	Airbus A.330-343	Swiss International *Fribourg*
	HB-JHF	Airbus A.330-343	Swiss International
	HB-JHG	Airbus A.330-343	Swiss International *Glarus*
	HB-JHH	Airbus A.330-343	Swiss International *Neuchatel*
	HB-JHI	Airbus A.330-343	Swiss International *Geneve*
	HB-JHJ	Airbus A.330-343	Swiss International *Appenzell*
	HB-JHK	Airbus A.330-343	Swiss International
	HB-JHL	Airbus A.330-343	Swiss International
	HB-JHQ	Airbus A.330-343	Edelweiss Air *Chamsin*
	HB-JIJ	DHC.8Q-402 Dash Eight	Sky Work Airlines
	HB-JIK	DHC.8Q-402 Dash Eight	Sky Work Airlines
	HB-JIW	Airbus A.320-214	Hello
	HB-JIX	Airbus A.320-214	Hello
	HB-JIY	Airbus A.320-214	Hello
	HB-JIZ	Airbus A.320-214	Hello
	HB-JLP	Airbus A.320-214	Swiss International *Allschwil*
	HB-JLQ	Airbus A.320-214	Swiss International *Bllach*
	HB-JMA	Airbus A.340-313X	Swiss International *Matterhorn*
	HB-JMB	Airbus A.340-313X	Swiss International *Zurich*
	HB-JMC	Airbus A.340-313X	Swiss International *Basel*
	HB-JMD	Airbus A.340-313X	Swiss International *Liestal*
	HB-JME	Airbus A.340-313X	Swiss International *Dom*
	HB-JMF	Airbus A.340-313X	Swiss International *Liskamm*
	HB-JMG	Airbus A.340-313X	Swiss International *Luzern*
	HB-JMH	Airbus A.340-313X	Swiss International *Chur*
	HB-JMI	Airbus A.340-313X	Swiss International *Schaffhausen*
	HB-JMJ	Airbus A.340-313X	Swiss International *City of Basel*
	HB-JMK	Airbus A.340-313X	Swiss International *Aarau*
	HB-JML	Airbus A.340-313X	Swiss International *Liestal*
	HB-JMM	Airbus A.340-313X	Swiss International
	HB-JMN	Airbus A.340-313X	Swiss International
	HB-JMO	Airbus A.340-313X	Swiss International
	HB-JOZ	Airbus A.320-214	Air Berlin/Belair
	HB-JVC	Fokker 100	Helvetic Airways

Reg.	Type	Owner or Operator	Notes
HB-JVE	Fokker 100	Helvetic Airways	
HB-JVF	Fokker 100	Helvetic Airways	
HB-JVG	Fokker 100	Helvetic Airways	
HB-JVH	Fokker 100	Helvetic Airways	
HB-JVI	Fokker 100	Helvetic Airways	
HB-JZF	Airbus A.319-111	easyJet Switzerland	
HB-JZI	Airbus A.319-111	easyJet Switzerland	
HB-JZJ	Airbus A.319-111	easyJet Switzerland	
HB-JZK	Airbus A.319-111	easyJet Switzerland	
HB-JZL	Airbus A.319-111	easyJet Switzerland	
HB-JZM	Airbus A.319-111	easyJet Switzerland	
HB-JZN	Airbus A.319-111	easyJet Switzerland	
HB-JZO	Airbus A.319-111	easyJet Switzerland	
HB-JZP	Airbus A.319-111	easyJet Switzerland	
HB-JZQ	Airbus A.319-111	easyJet Switzerland	
HB-JZR	Airbus A.320-214	easyJet Switzerland	
HB-JZS	Airbus A.319-111	easyJet Switzerland	
HB-JZT	Airbus A.319-111	easyJet Switzerland	
HB-JZU	Airbus A.319-111	easyJet Switzerland	
HB-JZV	Airbus A.319-111	easyJet Switzerland	
HB-JZW	Airbus A.319-111	easyJet Switzerland	
HB-JZX	Airbus A.320-214	easyJet Switzerland	
HB-JZY	Airbus A.320-214	easyJet Switzerland	
HB-JZZ	Airbus A.320-214	easyJet Switzerland	

HL (Korea)

Reg.	Type	Owner or Operator	Notes
HL7400	Boeing 747-4B5F	Korean Air Cargo	
HL7403	Boeing 747-4B5F	Korean Air Cargo	
HL7404	Boeing 747-4B5	Korean Air	
HL7413	Boeing 747-48EBCF	Asiana Airlines Cargo	
HL7414	Boeing 747-48EBCF	Asiana Airlines Cargo	
HL7415	Boeing 747-48EBCF	Asiana Airlines Cargo	
HL7417	Boeing 747-48EBCF	Asiana Airlines Cargo	
HL7419	Boeing 747-48EF (SCD)	Asiana Airlines Cargo	
HL7420	Boeing 747-48EF (SCD)	Asiana Airlines Cargo	
HL7434	Boeing 747-4B5F	Korean Air Cargo	
HL7436	Boeing 747-48EF (SCD)	Asiana Airlines Cargo	
HL7437	Boeing 747-4B5F	Korean Air Cargo	
HL7438	Boeing 747-4B5ERF	Korean Air Cargo	
HL7439	Boeing 747-4B5ERF	Korean Air Cargo	
HL7448	Boeing 747-4B5F (SCD)	Korean Air Cargo	
HL7449	Boeing 747-4B5F (SCD)	Korean Air Cargo	
HL7460	Boeing 747-4B5	Korean Air	
HL7461	Boeing 747-4B5	Korean Air	
HL7462	Boeing 747-4B5F	Korean Air Cargo	
HL7466	Boeing 747-4B5F	Korean Air Cargo	
HL7467	Boeing 747-4B5F	Korean Air Cargo	
HL7472	Boeing 747-4B5	Korean Air	
HL7473	Boeing 747-4B5	Korean Air	
HL7482	Boeing 747-4B5BCF	Korean Air Cargo	
HL7483	Boeing 747-4B5BCF	Korean Air Cargo	
HL7484	Boeing 747-4B5BCF	Korean Air Cargo	
HL7485	Boeing 747-4B5BCF	Korean Air Cargo	
HL7486	Boeing 747-4B5BCF	Korean Air Cargo	
HL7487	Boeing 747-4B5	Korean Air	
HL7488	Boeing 747-4B5	Korean Air	
HL7489	Boeing 747-4B5	Korean Air	
HL7490	Boeing 747-4B5	Korean Air	
HL7491	Boeing 747-4B5	Korean Air	
HL7492	Boeing 747-4B5	Korean Air	
HL7493	Boeing 747-4B5	Korean Air	
HL7494	Boeing 747-4B5	Korean Air	
HL7495	Boeing 747-4B5	Korean Air	
HL7498	Boeing 747-4B5	Korean Air	
HL7499	Boeing 747-4B5ERF	Korean Air Cargo	
HL7500	Boeing 777-28EER	Asiana Airlines	
HL7526	Boeing 777-2B5ER	Korean Air	
HL7530	Boeing 777-2B5ER	Korean Air	
HL7531	Boeing 777-2B5ER	Korean Air	
HL7574	Boeing 777-2B5ER	Korean Air	
HL7575	Boeing 777-2B5ER	Korean Air	
HL7596	Boeing 777-28EER	Asiana Airlines	

Notes	Reg.	Type	Owner or Operator
	HL7597	Boeing 777-28EER	Asiana Airlines
	HL7598	Boeing 777-2B5ER	Korean Air
	HL7600	Boeing 747-4B5ERF	Korean Air Cargo
	HL7601	Boeing 747-4B5ERF	Korean Air Cargo
	HL7602	Boeing 747-4B5ERF	Korean Air Cargo
	HL7603	Boeing 747-4B5ERF	Korean Air Cargo
	HL7605	Boeing 747-4B5ERF	Korean Air Cargo
	HL7606	Boeing 747-4B5BCF	Korean Air Cargo
	HL7607	Boeing 747-4B5	Korean Air
	HL7608	Boeing 747-4B5BCF	Korean Air Cargo
	HL7616	Boeing 747-446F	Asiana Airlines Cargo
	HL7700	Boeing 777-28EER	Asiana Airlines
	HL7714	Boeing 777-2B5ER	Korean Air
	HL7715	Boeing 777-2B5ER	Korean Air
	HL7721	Boeing 777-2B5ER	Korean Air
	HL7732	Boeing 777-28EER	Asiana Airlines
	HL7733	Boeing 777-2B5ER	Korean Air
	HL7734	Boeing 777-2B5ER	Korean Air
	HL7739	Boeing 777-28EER	Asiana Airlines
	HL7742	Boeing 777-28EER	Asiana Airlines
	HL7743	Boeing 777-2B5ER	Korean Air
	HL7750	Boeing 777-2B5ER	Korean Air
	HL7751	Boeing 777-2B5ER	Korean Air
	HL7752	Boeing 777-2B5ER	Korean Air
	HL7755	Boeing 777-28EER	Asiana Airlines
	HL7756	Boeing 777-28EER	Asiana Airlines
	HL7764	Boeing 777-2B5ER	Korean Air
	HL7765	Boeing 777-2B5ER	Korean Air
	HL7766	Boeing 777-2B5ER	Korean Air
	HL7775	Boeing 777-28EER	Asiana Airlines
	HL7791	Boeing 777-28EER	Asiana Airlines

HS (Thailand)

	HS-TGA	Boeing 747-4D7	Thai Airways International *Srisuriyothai*
	HS-TGB	Boeing 747-4D7	Thai Airways International *Si Satchanulai*
	HS-TGF	Boeing 747-4D7	Thai Airways International *Sri Ubon*
	HS-TGG	Boeing 747-4D7	Thai Airways International *Pathoomawadi*
	HS-TGH	Boeing 747-4D7	Thai Airways International *Chaiprakarn*
	HS-TGJ	Boeing 747-4D7	Thai Airways International *Hariphunchai*
	HS-TGK	Boeing 747-4D7	Thai Airways International *Alongkorn*
	HS-TGL	Boeing 747-4D7	Thai Airways International *Theparat*
	HS-TGM	Boeing 747-4D7	Thai Airways International *Chao Phraya*
	HS-TGN	Boeing 747-4D7	Thai Airways International *Simongkhon*
	HS-TGO	Boeing 747-4D7	Thai Airways International *Bowonrangsi*
	HS-TGP	Boeing 747-4D7	Thai Airways International *Thepprasit*
	HS-TGR	Boeing 747-4D7	Thai Airways International *Siriwatthana*
	HS-TGT	Boeing 747-4D7	Thai Airways International *Watthanothai*
	HS-TGW	Boeing 747-4D7	Thai Airways International *Visuthakasatriya*
	HS-TGX	Boeing 747-4D7	Thai Airways International *Sirisobhakya*
	HS-TGY	Boeing 747-4D7	Thai Airways International *Dararasmi*
	HS-TGZ	Boeing 747-4D7	Thai Airways International *Phimara*
	HS-TNA	Airbus A.340-642	Thai Airways International *Watthana Nakhon*
	HS-TNB	Airbus A.340-642	Thai Airways International *Saraburi*
	HS-TNC	Airbus A.340-642	Thai Airways International *Chon Buri*
	HS-TND	Airbus A.340-642	Thai Airways International *Phetchaburi*
	HS-TNE	Airbus A.340-642	Thai Airways International *Nonthaburi*
	HS-TNF	Airbus A.340-642	Thai Airways International

HZ (Saudi Arabia)

	HZ-AKA	Boeing 777-268ER	Saudi Arabian Airlines
	HZ-AKB	Boeing 777-268ER	Saudi Arabian Airlines
	HZ-AKC	Boeing 777-268ER	Saudi Arabian Airlines
	HZ-AKD	Boeing 777-268ER	Saudi Arabian Airlines
	HZ-AKE	Boeing 777-268ER	Saudi Arabian Airlines
	HZ-AKF	Boeing 777-268ER	Saudi Arabian Airlines
	HZ-AKG	Boeing 777-268ER	Saudi Arabian Airlines
	HZ-AKH	Boeing 777-268ER	Saudi Arabian Airlines
	HZ-AKI	Boeing 777-268ER	Saudi Arabian Airlines
	HZ-AKJ	Boeing 777-268ER	Saudi Arabian Airlines
	HZ-AKK	Boeing 777-268ER	Saudi Arabian Airlines

Reg.	Type	Owner or Operator	Notes
HZ-AKL	Boeing 777-268ER	Saudi Arabian Airlines	
HZ-AKM	Boeing 777-268ER	Saudi Arabian Airlines	
HZ-AKN	Boeing 777-268ER	Saudi Arabian Airlines	
HZ-AKO	Boeing 777-268ER	Saudi Arabian Airlines	
HZ-AKP	Boeing 777-268ER	Saudi Arabian Airlines	
HZ-AKQ	Boeing 777-268ER	Saudi Arabian Airlines	
HZ-AKR	Boeing 777-268ER	Saudi Arabian Airlines	
HZ-AKS	Boeing 777-268ER	Saudi Arabian Airlines	
HZ-AKT	Boeing 777-268ER	Saudi Arabian Airlines	
HZ-AKU	Boeing 777-268ER	Saudi Arabian Airlines	
HZ-AKV	Boeing 777-268ER	Saudi Arabian Airlines	
HZ-AKW	Boeing 777-268ER	Saudi Arabian Airlines	
HZ-ANA	McD Douglas MD-11F	Saudi Arabian Airlines Cargo	
HZ-ANB	McD Douglas MD-11F	Saudi Arabian Airlines Cargo	
HZ-ANC	McD Douglas MD-11F	Saudi Arabian Airlines Cargo	
HZ-AND	McD Douglas MD-11F	Saudi Arabian Airlines Cargo	

I (Italy)

I-AIGH	Boeing 767-23BER	Air Italy	
I-AIGM	Boeing 737-3Q8	Air Italy	
I-AIMR	Boeing 737-430	Air Italy	
I-BIKA	Airbus A.320-214	Alitalia Johann Sebastian Bach	
I-BIKC	Airbus A.320-214	Alitalia Zefiro	
I-BIKD	Airbus A.320-214	Alitalia Maestrale	
I-BIKE	Airbus A.320-214	Alitalia Franz Liszt	
I-BIKI	Airbus A.320-214	Alitalia Girolamo Frescobaldi	
I-BIKO	Airbus A.320-214	Alitalia George Bizet	
I-BIMA	Airbus A.319-112	Alitalia Isola d'Elba	
I-BIXA	Airbus A.321-112	Alitalia Piazza del Duomo Milano	
I-BIXE	Airbus A.321-112	Alitalia Piazza di Spagna Roma	
I-BIXK	Airbus A.321-112	Alitalia Piazza Ducale Vigevano	
I-BIXL	Airbus A.321-112	Alitalia Piazza del Duomo Lecce	
I-BIXM	Airbus A.321-112	Alitalia Piazza di San Franceso Assisi	
I-BIXN	Airbus A.321-112	Alitalia Piazza del Duomo Catania	
I-BIXP	Airbus A.321-112	Alitalia Carlo Morelli	
I-BIXQ	Airbus A.321-112	Alitalia Domenico Colapietro	
I-BIXR	Airbus A.321-112	Alitalia Piazza dell Campidoglio-Roma	
I-BIXS	Airbus A.321-112	Alitalia Piazza San Martino-Lucca	
I-BIXT	Airbus A.321-112	Alitalia Piazza dei Miracoli Pisa	
I-DACR	McD Douglas MD-82	Alitalia Carrara	
I-DACS	McD Douglas MD-82	Alitalia Maratea	
I-DACV	McD Douglas MD-82	Alitalia	
I-DACZ	McD Douglas MD-82	Alitalia Castelfidardo	
I-DAND	McD Douglas MD-82	Alitalia Bolzano	
I-DANF	McD Douglas MD-82	Alitalia Vicenza	
I-DANG	McD Douglas MD-82	Alitalia	
I-DANH	McD Douglas MD-82	Alitalia Messina	
I-DANQ	McD Douglas MD-82	Alitalia Lecce	
I-DANU	McD Douglas MD-82	Alitalia Trapani	
I-DANW	McD Douglas MD-82	Alitalia Siena	
I-DATC	McD Douglas MD-82	Alitalia Foggia	
I-DATE	McD Douglas MD-82	Alitalia Grosseto	
I-DATG	McD Douglas MD-82	Alitalia Arezzo	
I-DATI	McD Douglas MD-82	Alitalia Siracusa	
I-DATQ	McD Douglas MD-82	Alitalia Modena	
I-DAVT	McD Douglas MD-82	Alitalia Como	
I-DEIG	Boeing 767-33AER	Alitalia Francesco Agello	
I-DISA	Boeing 777-243ER	Alitalia Taromina	
I-DISB	Boeing 777-243ER	Alitalia Portor Rotondo	
I-DISE	Boeing 777-243ER	Alitalia Portofino	
I-DISU	Boeing 777-243ER	Alitalia Madonna di Campiglio	
I-EEZE	Airbus A.320-214	Meridiana Fly	
I-EEZF	Airbus A.320-214	Meridiana Fly	
I-EEZG	Airbus A.320-214	Meridiana Fly	
I-EEZH	Airbus A.320-214	Meridiana Fly	
I-EEZI	Airbus A.320-214	Meridiana Fly	
I-EEZJ	Airbus A.330-223	Meridiana Fly	
I-EEZK	Airbus A.320-214	Meridiana Fly	
I-EEZM	Airbus A.330-223	Meridiana Fly	
I-EEZP	Airbus A.320-233	Meridiana Fly	
I-EEZQ	Airbus A.319-112	Meridiana Fly	
I-NEOS	Boeing 737-86N	Neos	

Notes	Reg.	Type	Owner or Operator
	I-NEOT	Boeing 737-86N	Neos
	I-NEOU	Boeing 737-86N	Neos
	I-NEOW	Boeing 737-86N	Neos
	I-NEOX	Boeing 737-86N	Neos
	I-NEOZ	Boeing 737-86N	Neos *Monte Rosa*
	I-NDMJ	Boeing 767-306ER	Neos
	I-NDOF	Boeing 767-306ER	Neos
	I-SMEB	McD Douglas MD-82	Meridiana Fly
	I-SMEL	McD Douglas MD-82	Meridiana Fly
	I-SMEM	McD Douglas MD-82	Meridiana Fly
	I-SMEN	McD Douglas MD-83	Meridiana Fly
	I-SMEP	McD Douglas MD-82	Meridiana Fly
	I-SMER	McD Douglas MD-82	Meridiana Fly
	I-SMES	McD Douglas MD-82	Meridiana Fly
	I-SMET	McD Douglas MD-82	Meridiana Fly
	I-SMEV	McD Douglas MD-82	Meridiana Fly
	I-SMEZ	McD Douglas MD-83	Meridiana Fly
	I-WEBA	Airbus A.320-214	Air One
	I-WEBB	Airbus A.320-214	Air One

JA (Japan)

	JA01KZ	Boeing 747-481F	Nippon Cargo Airlines
	JA02KZ	Boeing 747-481F	Nippon Cargo Airlines
	JA03KZ	Boeing 747-4KZF	Nippon Cargo Airlines
	JA04KZ	Boeing 747-4KZF	Nippon Cargo Airlines
	JA05KZ	Boeing 747-4KZF	Nippon Cargo Airlines *NCA Apollo*
	JA06KZ	Boeing 747-4KZF	Nippon Cargo Airlines
	JA07KZ	Boeing 747-4KZF	Nippon Cargo Airlines *NCA Andromeda*
	JA08KZ	Boeing 747-4KZF	Nippon Cargo Airlines *NCA Aries*
	JA13KZ	Boeing 747-8KZF	Nippon Cargo Airlines
	JA731A	Boeing 777-381ER	All Nippon Airways
	JA731J	Boeing 777-346ER	Japan Airlines
	JA732A	Boeing 777-381ER	All Nippon Airways
	JA732J	Boeing 777-346ER	Japan Airlines
	JA733A	Boeing 777-381ER	All Nippon Airways
	JA733J	Boeing 777-346ER	Japan Airlines
	JA734A	Boeing 777-381ER	All Nippon Airways
	JA734J	Boeing 777-346ER	Japan Airlines
	JA735A	Boeing 777-381ER	All Nippon Airways
	JA735J	Boeing 777-346ER	Japan Airlines
	JA736A	Boeing 777-381ER	All Nippon Airways
	JA736J	Boeing 777-346ER	Japan Airlines
	JA737J	Boeing 777-346ER	Japan Airlines
	JA738J	Boeing 777-346ER	Japan Airlines
	JA739J	Boeing 777-346ER	Japan Airlines
	JA740J	Boeing 777-346ER	Japan Airlines
	JA741J	Boeing 777-346ER	Japan Airlines
	JA742J	Boeing 777-346ER	Japan Airlines
	JA743J	Boeing 777-346ER	Japan Airlines
	JA751J	Boeing 777-346ER	Japan Airlines
	JA752J	Boeing 777-346ER	Japan Airlines
	JA777A	Boeing 777-381ER	All Nippon Airways
	JA778A	Boeing 777-381ER	All Nippon Airways
	JA779A	Boeing 777-381ER	All Nippon Airways
	JA780A	Boeing 777-381ER	All Nippon Airways
	JA781A	Boeing 777-381ER	All Nippon Airways
	JA782A	Boeing 777-381ER	All Nippon Airways
	JA783A	Boeing 777-381ER	All Nippon Airways
	JA784A	Boeing 777-381ER	All Nippon Airways
	JA785A	Boeing 777-381ER	All Nippon Airways
	JA786A	Boeing 777-381ER	All Nippon Airways
	JA787A	Boeing 777-381ER	All Nippon Airways
	JA788A	Boeing 777-381ER	All Nippon Airways
	JA789A	Boeing 777-381ER	All Nippon Airways

JY (Jordan)

	JY-AGM	Airbus A.310-304	Royal Jordanian *Princess Alia bin Al-Hussein*
	JY-AGN	Airbus A.310-304	Royal Jordanian *Prince Faisal bin Al-Hussein*
	JY-AGQ	Airbus A.310-304F	Royal Jordanian Cargo
	JY-AGR	Airbus A.310-304F	Royal Jordanian Cargo

Reg.	Type	Owner or Operator	Notes
JY-AIE	Airbus A.330-223	Royal Jordanian *Jordan River*	
JY-AIF	Airbus A.330-223	Royal Jordanian *Prince Ali bin Al Hussein*	
JY-AIG	Airbus A.330-223	Royal Jordanian *Prince Feisal Ibn Al-Hussein*	
JY-AYD	Airbus A.320-232	Royal Jordanian *Amman*	
JY-AYF	Airbus A.320-232	Royal Jordanian *Aqaba*	
JY-AYG	Airbus A.321-231	Royal Jordanian *As-Salt*	
JY-AYH	Airbus A.321-231	Royal Jordanian	
JY-AYJ	Airbus A.321-231	Royal Jordanian *Ramtha*	
JY-AYK	Airbus A.321-231	Royal Jordanian	
JY-AYL	Airbus A.319-132	Royal Jordanian	
JY-AYM	Airbus A.319-132	Royal Jordanian	
JY-AYN	Airbus A.319-132	Royal Jordanian	
JY-AYP	Airbus A.319-132	Royal Jordabian *Ajloun*	
JY-AYQ	Airbus A.320-232	Royal Jordanian *Mount Nebo*	
JY-AYR	Airbus A.320-232	Royal Jordanian	
JY-AYS	Airbus A.320-232	Royal Jordanian	

LN (Norway)

Reg.	Type	Owner or Operator	Notes
LN-BRE	Boeing 737-405	SAS *Haakon V Magnusson*	
LN-BRH	Boeing 737-505	SAS *Haakon den Gode*	
LN-BRI	Boeing 737-405	SAS *Harald Haarfagre*	
LN-BRO	Boeing 737-505	SAS *Magnus Haraldsson*	
LN-BRQ	Boeing 737-405	SAS *Harald Graafell*	
LN-BRV	Boeing 737-505	SAS *Haakon Sverresson*	
LN-BRX	Boeing 737-505	SAS *Sigurd Munn*	
LN-BUC	Boeing 737-505	SAS *Magnus Erlingsson*	
LN-BUD	Boeing 737-505	SAS *Inge Krokrygg*	
LN-BUE	Boeing 737-505	SAS *Erling Skjalgsson*	
LN-BUG	Boeing 737-505	SAS *Oystein Haraldsson*	
LN-DYA	Boeing 737-8JP	Norwegian Air Shuttle *Erik Bye*	
LN-DYB	Boeing 737-8JP	Norwegian Air Shuttle *Bjornstjerne Bjornson*	
LN-DYC	Boeing 737-8JP	Norwegian Air Shuttle *Max Manus*	
LN-DYD	Boeing 737-8JP	Norwegian Air Shuttle *Hans Christian Andersen*	
LN-DYE	Boeing 737-8JP	Norwegian Air Shuttle *Arne Jacobsen*	
LN-DYF	Boeing 737-8JPM	Norwegian Air Shuttle *Fridtjof Nansen*	
LN-DYG	Boeing 737-8JP	Norwegian Air Shuttle *Jenny Lind*	
LN-DYH	Boeing 737-8JP	Norwegian Air Shuttle *Soren Kierkegaard*	
LN-DYI	Boeing 737-8JP	Norwegian Air Shuttle *Aasmund Olavson Vinje*	
LN-DYJ	Boeing 737-8JP	Norwegian Air Shuttle *Georg Brandes*	
LN-DYK	Boeing 737-8JP	Norwegian Air Shuttle *Karl Larsson*	
LN-DYL	Boeing 737-8JP	Norwegian Air Shuttle *Amalie Skram*	
LN-DYM	Boeing 737-8JP	Norwegian Air Shuttle *Andre Bjerke*	
LN-DYN	Boeing 737-8JP	Norwegian Air Shuttle *Karen Blixen*	
LN-DYO	Boeing 737-8JP	Norwegian Air Shuttle *Otto Sverdrup*	
LN-DYP	Boeing 737-8JP	Norwegian Air Shuttle *Aksel Sandemose*	
LN-DYQ	Boeing 737-8JP	Norwegian Air Shuttle *Helge Ingstad*	
LN-DYR	Boeing 737-8JP	Norwegian Air Shuttle *Peter C Asbjornsen/Jorgen Moe*	
LN-DYS	Boeing 737-8JP	Norwegian Air Shuttle *Niels Henrik Abel*	
LN-DYT	Boeing 737-8JP	Norwegian Air Shuttle *Kirsten Flagstad*	
LN-DYU	Boeing 737-8JP	Norwegian Air Shuttle *Jorn Utzon*	
LN-DYV	Boeing 737-8JP	Norwegian Air Shuttle *Elsa Beskow*	
LN-DYW	Boeing 737-8JP	Norwegian Air Shuttle	
LN-DYX	Boeing 737-8JP	Norwegian Air Shuttle	
LN-DYY	Boeing 737-8JP	Norwegian Air Shuttle	
LN-KHA	Boeing 737-31S	Norwegian Air Shuttle	
LN-KHB	Boeing 737-31S	Norwegian Air Shuttle	
LN-KHC	Boeing 737-31S	Norwegian Air Shuttle	
LN-KKC	Boeing 737-3Y5	Norwegian Air Shuttle	
LN-KKD	Boeing 737-33V	Norwegian Air Shuttle	
LN-KKI	Boeing 737-3K2	Norwegian Air Shuttle *Helge Ingstad*	
LN-KKJ	Boeing 737-36N	Norwegian Air Shuttle *Sonja Henie*	
LN-KKL	Boeing 737-36N	Norwegian Air Shuttle *Roald Amundsen*	
LN-KKM	Boeing 737-3Y0	Norwegian Air Shuttle *Thor Heyerdahl*	
LN-KKN	Boeing 737-3Y0	Norwegian Air Shuttle *Sigrid Undset*	
LN-KKO	Boeing 737-3Y0	Norwegian Air Shuttle *Henrik Ibsen*	
LN-KKQ	Boeing 737-36Q	Norwegian Air Shuttle *Alf Proysen*	
LN-KKR	Boeing 737-3Y0	Norwegian Air Shuttle	
LN-KKS	Boeing 737-33A	Norwegian Air Shuttle *Edvard Munch*	
LN-KKW	Boeing 737-3K9	Norwegian Air Shuttle	
LN-KKX	Boeing 737-33S	Norwegian Air Shuttle	
LN-NIA	Boeing 737-86JP	Norwegian Air Shuttle	

Reg.	Type	Owner or Operator
LN-NIB	Boeing 737-86J	Norwegian Air Shuttle *Helmer Hanssen*
LN-NOB	Boeing 737-8FZ	Norwegian Air Shuttle *Edward Grieg*
LN-NOC	Boeing 737-81Q	Norwegian Air Shuttle *Ole Bull*
LN-NOD	Boeing 737-8Q8	Norwegian Air Shuttle *Sonje Henie*
LN-NOE	Boeing 737-8Q8	Norwegian Air Shuttle *Henrik Wergeland*
LN-NOF	Boeing 737-86N	Norwegian Air Shuttle *Edvard Munch*
LN-NOG	Boeing 737-86N	Norwegian Air Shuttle *Henrik Ibsen*
LN-NOH	Boeing 737-86N	Norwegian Air Shuttle *Selma Lagerlof*
LN-NOI	Boeing 737-86N	Norwegian Air Shuttle *Sam Eyde*
LN-NOJ	Boeing 737-86N	Norwegian Air Shuttle *Tycho Brahe*
LN-NOL	Boeing 737-8Q8	Norwegian Air Shuttle
LN-NOM	Boeing 737-86N	Norwegian Air Shuttle *Greta Garbo*
LN-NON	Boeing 737-86N	Norwegian Air Shuttle *Anders Celcius*
LN-NOO	Boeing 737-86Q	Norwegian Air Shuttle *Gustav Vigeland*
LN-NOP	Boeing 737-86N	Norwegian Air Shuttle *Camilla Collett*
LN-NOQ	Boeing 737-86N	Norwegian Air Shuttle *Kristian Birkeland*
LN-NOR	Boeing 737-86N	Norwegian Air Shuttle *Povel Ramel*
LN-NOS	Boeing 737-8BK	Norwegian Air Shuttle *Ludvig Holberg*
LN-NOT	Boeing 737-8JP	Norwegian Air Shuttle *Piet Hein*
LN-NOU	Boeing 737-8FZ	Norwegian Air Shuttle *Carl von Linne*
LN-NOV	Boeing 737-8FZ	Norwegian Air Shuttle *Evart Taube*
LN-NOW	Boeing 737-8JP	Norwegian Air Shuttle *Oda Krohg*
LN-NOX	Boeing 737-8JP	Norwegian Air Shuttle *Christian Krohg*
LN-NOY	Boeing 737-8JP	Norwegian Air Shuttle
LN-NOZ	Boeing 737-8JP	Norwegian Air Shuttle
LN-RCN	Boeing 737-883	SAS *Hedrun Viking*
LN-RCT	Boeing 737-683	SAS *Fridlev Viking*
LN-RCU	Boeing 737-683	SAS *Sigfrid Viking*
LN-RCW	Boeing 737-683	SAS *Yngvar Viking*
LN-RCX	Boeing 737-883	SAS *Hottur Viking*
LN-RCY	Boeing 737-883	SAS *Eylime Viking*
LN-RCZ	Boeing 737-883	SAS *Glitne Viking*
LN-RKF	Airbus A.340-313X	SAS *Godfred Viking*
LN-RKG	Airbus A.340-313X	SAS *Gudrod Viking*
LN-RKH	Airbus A.330-343X	SAS *Emund Viking*
LN-RKI	Airbus A.321-231	SAS *Gunnhild Viking*
LN-RKK	Airbus A.321-231	SAS *Viger Viking*
LN-RLE	McD Douglas MD-82	SAS *Ketiil Viking*
LN-RLF	McD Douglas MD-82	SAS *Finn Viking*
LN-RML	McD Douglas MD-82	SAS *Aud Viking*
LN-RMM	McD Douglas MD-82	SAS *Blenda Viking*
LN-RMO	McD Douglas MD-82	SAS *Bergljot Viking*
LN-RMR	McD Douglas MD-82	SAS *Olav Viking*
LN-RMS	McD Douglas MD-82	SAS *Nial Viking*
LN-RMT	McD Douglas MD-82	SAS *Jarl Viking*
LN-RNL	Canadair CRJ900ER	SAS *Fafner Viking*
LN-RNN	Boeing 737-783	SAS *Borgny Viking*
LN-RNO	Boeing 737-783	SAS *Gjuke Viking*
LN-RNU	Boeing 737-783	SAS *Hans Viking*
LN-RNW	Boeing 737-783	SAS *Granmar Viking*
LN-ROP	McD Douglas MD-82	SAS *Bjoern Viking*
LN-ROT	McD Douglas MD-82	SAS *Ingjaid Viking*
LN-ROX	McD Douglas MD-82	SAS *Ulvrik Viking*
LN-RPA	Boeing 737-683	SAS *Arnljot Viking*
LN-RPB	Boeing 737-683	SAS *Bure Viking*
LN-RPE	Boeing 737-683	SAS *Edla Viking*
LN-RPF	Boeing 737-683	SAS *Frede Viking*
LN-RPG	Boeing 737-683	SAS *Geirmund Viking*
LN-RPH	Boeing 737-683	SAS *Hamder Viking*
LN-RPJ	Boeing 737-783	SAS *Grimhild Viking*
LN-RPK	Boeing 737-783	SAS *Heimer Viking*
LN-RPL	Boeing 737-883	SAS *Svanevit Viking*
LN-RPM	Boeing 737-883	SAS *Frigg Viking*
LN-RPN	Boeing 737-883	SAS *Bergfora Viking*
LN-RPO	Boeing 737-883	SAS *Thorleif Viking*
LN-RPR	Boeing 737-883	SAS *Ore Viking*
LN-RPS	Boeing 737-683	SAS *Gautrek Viking*
LN-RPT	Boeing 737-683	SAS *Ellida Viking*
LN-RPU	Boeing 737-683	SAS *Ragna Viking*
LN-RPW	Boeing 737-683	SAS *Alvid Viking*
LN-RPX	Boeing 737-683	SAS *Nanna Viking*
LN-RPY	Boeing 737-683	SAS *Olof Viking*
LN-RPZ	Boeing 737-683	SAS *Bera Viking*
LN-RRA	Boeing 737-783	SAS *Steinar Viking*

Reg.	Type	Owner or Operator	Notes
LN-RRB	Boeing 737-783	SAS Cecilia Viking	
LN-RRC	Boeing 737-683	SAS Sindre Viking	
LN-RRD	Boeing 737-683	SAS Embla Viking	
LN-RRE	Boeing 737-883	SAS Knut Viking	
LN-RRF	Boeing 737-883	SAS Froydis Viking	
LN-RRG	Boeing 737-883	SAS Einar Viking	
LN-RRH	Boeing 737-883	SAS Freja Viking	
LN-RRJ	Boeing 737-883	SAS Frida Viking	
LN-RRK	Boeing 737-883	SAS Gerud Viking	
LN-RRL	Boeing 737-883	SAS Jarlabanke Viking	
LN-RRM	Boeing 737-783	SAS Erland Viking	
LN-RRN	Boeing 737-783	SAS Solveig Viking	
LN-RRO	Boeing 737-683	SAS Bernt Viking	
LN-RRP	Boeing 737-683	SAS Vilborg Viking	
LN-RRR	Boeing 737-683	SAS Torbjorn Viking	
LN-RRS	Boeing 737-883	SAS Ymir Viking	
LN-RRT	Boeing 737-883	SAS Lodyn Viking	
LN-RRU	Boeing 737-883	SAS Vingolf Viking	
LN-RRW	Boeing 737-883	SAS Saga Viking	
LN-RRX	Boeing 737-683	SAS Ragnfast Viking	
LN-RRY	Boeing 737-683	SAS Signe Viking	
LN-RRZ	Boeing 737-683	SAS Gisla Viking	
LN-TUA	Boeing 737-705	SAS Ingeborg Eriksdatter	
LN-TUD	Boeing 737-705	SAS Margrete Skulesdatter	
LN-TUF	Boeing 737-705	SAS Tyra Haraldsdatter	
LN-TUH	Boeing 737-705	SAS Margrete Ingesdatter	
LN-TUI	Boeing 737-705	SAS Kristin Knudsdatter	
LN-TUJ	Boeing 737-705	SAS Eirik Blodoks	
LN-TUK	Boeing 737-705	SAS Inge Bardsson	
LN-TUL	Boeing 737-705	SAS Haakon IV Haakonson	
LN-TUM	Boeing 737-705	SAS Oystein Magnusson	
LN-WDE	DHC.8-402 Dash Eight	Wideroe's Flyveselskap	
LN-WDF	DHC.8-402 Dash Eight	Wideroe's Flyveselskap	
LN-WDG	DHC.8-402 Dash Eight	Wideroe's Flyveselskap	
LN-WDH	DHC.8-402 Dash Eight	Wideroe's Flyveselskap	
LN-WDI	DHC.8-402 Dash Eight	Wideroe's Flyveselskap	
LN-WDJ	DHC.8-402 Dash Eight	Wideroe's Flyveselskap	
LN-WDK	DHC.8-402 Dash Eight	Wideroe's Flyveselskap	
LN-WDL	DHC.8-402 Dash Eight	Wideroe's Flyveselskap	
LN-WFC	DHC.8-311 Dash Eight	Wideroe's Flyveselskap	
LN-WFD	DHC.8-311 Dash Eight	Wideroe's Flyveselskap	
LN-WFH	DHC.8-311 Dash Eight	Wideroe's Flyveselskap	
LN-WFO	DHC.8Q-311 Dash Eight	Wideroe's Flyveselskap	
LN-WFP	DHC.8Q-311 Dash Eight	Wideroe's Flyveselskap	
LN-WFS	DHC.8Q-311 Dash Eight	Wideroe's Flyveselskap	
LN-WFT	DHC.8Q-311 Dash Eight	Wideroe's Flyveselskap	

LX (Luxembourg)

Reg.	Type	Owner or Operator	Notes
LX-ACV	Boeing 747-4B5BCF	Cargolux	
LX-DCV	Boeing 747-4B5CF	Cargolux	
LX-KCV	Boeing 747-4R7F (SCD)	Cargolux City of Dudelange	
LX-LGA	DHC.8Q-402 Dash Eight	Luxair	
LX-LGC	DHC.8Q-402 Dash Eight	Luxair	
LX-LGD	DHC.8Q-402 Dash Eight	Luxair	
LX-LGE	DHC.8Q-402 Dash Eight	Luxair	
LX-LGF	DHC.8Q-402 Dash Eight	Luxair	
LX-LGI	Embraer RJ145LU	Luxair	
LX-LGJ	Embraer RJ145LU	Luxair	
LX-LGL	Embraer RJ135LR	Luxair	
LX-LGQ	Boeing 737-7C9	Luxair Chateau de Burg	
LX-LGR	Boeing 737-7C9	Luxair Chateau de Fischbach	
LX-LGS	Boeing 737-7C9	Luxair Chateau de Senningen	
LX-LGT	Boeing 737-8K5	Luxair	
LX-LGW	Embraer RJ145LU	Luxair	
LX-LGX	Embraer RJ145LU	Luxair	
LX-LGY	Embraer RJ145LU	Luxair	
LX-LGZ	Embraer RJ145LU	Luxair	
LX-OCV	Boeing 747-4R7F (SCD)	Cargolux City of Differdange	
LX-PCV	Boeing 747-4R7F (SCD)	Cargolux City of Diekirch	
LX-RCV	Boeing 747-4R7F (SCD)	Cargolux City of Schengen	
LX-SCV	Boeing 747-4R7F (SCD)	Cargolux City of Niederanven	
LX-STA	Airbus A.320-212	Strategic Airlines	

Notes	Reg.	Type	Owner or Operator
	LX-STB	Airbus A.320-212	Strategic Airlines
	LX-STC	Airbus A.320-211	Strategic Airlines
	LX-TCV	Boeing 747-4R7F (SCD)	Cargolux *City of Sandweiler*
	LX-UCV	Boeing 747-4R7F (SCD)	Cargolux *City of Bertragne*
	LX-VCB	Boeing 747-8R7F	Cargolux *City of Esch-sur-Aizette*
	LX-VCC	Boeing 747-8R7F	Cargolux
	LX-VCD	Boeing 747-8R7F	Cargolux *City of Luxembourg*
	LX-VCE	Boeing 747-8R7F	Cargolux
	LX-VCV	Boeing 747-4R7F (SCD)	Cargolux *City of Walferdange*
	LX-WAE	BAe ATP	West Air Europe
	LX-WAF	BAe ATP	West Air Europe
	LX-WAK	BAe ATP	West Air Europe
	LX-WAN	BAe ATP	West Air Europe
	LX-WAO	BAe ATP	West Air Europe
	LX-WAP	BAe ATP	West Air Europe
	LX-WAS	BAe ATP	West Air Europe
	LX-WAT	BAe ATP	West Air Europe
	LX-WAV	BAe ATP	West Air Europe
	LX-WAW	BAe ATP	West Air Europe
	LX-WAX	BAe ATP	West Air Europe
	LX-WCV	Boeing 747-4R7F (SCD)	Cargolux *City of Petange*
	LX-YCV	Boeing 747-4R7F	Cargolux *City of Contem*
	LX-ZCV	Boeing 747-481BCF	Cargolux

LY (Lithuania)

	LY-FLC	Boeing 737-31S	Small Planet Airlines
	LY-FLE	Boeing 737-3L9	Small Planet Airlines
	LY-FLH	Boeing 737-382	Small Planet Airlines
	LY-FLJ	Boeing 737-3K2	Small Planet Airlines
	LY-SKA	Boeing 737-35B	Aurela
	LY-SKW	Boeing 737-382	Aurela

LZ (Bulgaria)

	LZ-BHB	Airbus A.320-212	BH Air
	LZ-BHC	Airbus A.320-212	BH Air
	LZ-BHD	Airbus A.320-212	BH Air
	LZ-BHE	Airbus A.320-211	BH Air
	LZ-BHF	Airbus A.320-214	BH Air
	LZ-BOU	Boeing 737-3L9	Bulgaria Air
	LZ-BOV	Boeing 737-330	Bulgaria Air
	LZ-BOW	Boeing 737-330	Bulgaria Air
	LZ-FBA	Airbus A.319-112	Bulgaria Air
	LZ-FBB	Airbus A.319-112	Bulgaria Air
	LZ-FBC	Airbus A.320-214	Bulgaria Air
	LZ-FBD	Airbus A.320-214	Bulgaria Air
	LZ-FBE	Airbus A.320-214	Bulgaria Air
	LZ-FBF	Airbus A.319-111	Bulgaria Air
	LZ-LDC	McD Douglas MD-82	Bulgarian Air Charter
	LZ-LDF	McD Douglas MD-82	Bulgarian Air Charter
	LZ-LDK	McD Douglas MD-82	Bulgarian Air Charter
	LZ-LDO	McD Douglas MD-82	Bulgarian Air Charter
	LZ-LDP	McD Douglas MD-82	Bulgarian Air Charter
	LZ-LDW	McD Douglas MD-82	Bulgarian Air Charter
	LZ-LDY	McD Douglas MD-82	Bulgarian Air Charter

N (USA)

	N104UA	Boeing 747-422	United Airlines
	N105UA	Boeing 747-451	United Airlines
	N107UA	Boeing 747-422	United Airlines
	N116UA	Boeing 747-422	United Airlines
	N117UA	Boeing 747-422	United Airlines
	N118UA	Boeing 747-422	United Airlines
	N119UA	Boeing 747-422	United Airlines
	N120UA	Boeing 747-422	United Airlines
	N121UA	Boeing 747-422	United Airlines
	N122UA	Boeing 747-422	United Airlines
	N127UA	Boeing 747-422	United Airlines
	N128UA	Boeing 747-422	United Airlines

Reg.	Type	Owner or Operator	Notes
N152DL	Boeing 767-3P6ER	Delta Air Lines	
N153DL	Boeing 767-3P6ER	Delta Air Lines	
N154DL	Boeing 767-3P6ER	Delta Air Lines	
N155DL	Boeing 767-3P6ER	Delta Air Lines	
N156DL	Boeing 767-3P6ER	Delta Air Lines	
N169DZ	Boeing 767-332ER	Delta Air Lines	
N171DN	Boeing 767-332ER	Delta Air Lines	
N171DZ	Boeing 767-332ER	Delta Air Lines	
N171UA	Boeing 747-422	United Airlines	
N172AJ	Boeing 757-223ET	American Airlines	
N172DN	Boeing 767-332ER	Delta Air Lines	
N172DZ	Boeing 767-332ER	Delta Air Lines	
N173AN	Boeing 757-223ET	American Airlines	
N173DZ	Boeing 767-332ER	Delta Air Lines	
N174AA	Boeing 757-223ET	American Airlines	
N174DN	Boeing 767-332ER	Delta Air Lines	
N174DZ	Boeing 767-332ER	Delta Air Lines	
N174UA	Boeing 747-422	United Airlines	
N175AN	Boeing 757-223ET	American Airlines	
N175DN	Boeing 767-332ER	Delta Air Lines	
N175DZ	Boeing 767-332ER	Delta Air Lines	
N175UA	Boeing 747-422	United Airlines	
N176AA	Boeing 757-223ET	American Airlines	
N176DN	Boeing 767-332ER	Delta Air Lines	
N176DZ	Boeing 767-332ER	Delta Air Lines	
N177AN	Boeing 757-223ET	American Airlines	
N177DN	Boeing 767-332ER	Delta Air Lines	
N177DZ	Boeing 767-332ER	Delta Air Lines	
N177UA	Boeing 747-422	United Airlines	
N178AA	Boeing 757-223ET	American Airlines	
N178DN	Boeing 767-332ER	Delta Air Lines	
N178DZ	Boeing 767-332ER	Delta Air Lines	
N178UA	Boeing 747-422	United Airlines	
N179AA	Boeing 757-223ET	American Airlines	
N179DN	Boeing 767-332ER	Delta Air Lines	
N179UA	Boeing 747-422	United Airlines	
N180DN	Boeing 767-332ER	Delta Air Lines	
N180UA	Boeing 747-422	United Airlines	
N181AN	Boeing 757-223ET	American Airlines	
N181DN	Boeing 767-332ER	Delta Air Lines	
N181UA	Boeing 747-422	United Airlines	
N182AN	Boeing 757-223ET	American Airlines	
N182DN	Boeing 767-332ER	Delta Air Lines	
N182UA	Boeing 747-422	United Airlines	
N183AN	Boeing 757-223ET	American Airlines	
N183DN	Boeing 767-332ER	Delta Air Lines	
N184AN	Boeing 757-223ET	American Airlines	
N184DN	Boeing 767-332ER	Delta Air Lines	
N185AN	Boeing 757-223ET	American Airlines	
N185DN	Boeing 767-332ER	Delta Air Lines	
N186AN	Boeing 757-223ET	American Airlines	
N186DN	Boeing 767-332ER	Delta Air Lines	
N187AN	Boeing 757-223ET	American Airlines	
N187DN	Boeing 767-332ER	Delta Air Lines	
N188AN	Boeing 757-223ET	American Airlines	
N188DN	Boeing 767-332ER	Delta Air Lines	
N189AN	Boeing 757-223ET	American Airlines	
N189DN	Boeing 767-332ER	Delta Air Lines	
N190AA	Boeing 757-223ET	American Airlines	
N190DN	Boeing 767-332ER	Delta Air Lines	
N191AN	Boeing 757-223ET	American Airlines	
N191DN	Boeing 767-332ER	Delta Air Lines	
N192AN	Boeing 757-223ET	American Airlines	
N192DN	Boeing 767-332ER	Delta Air Lines	
N193AN	Boeing 757-223ET	American Airlines	
N193DN	Boeing 767-332ER	Delta Air Lines	
N194AA	Boeing 757-223ET	American Airlines	
N194DN	Boeing 767-332ER	Delta Air Lines	
N195AN	Boeing 757-223ET	American Airlines	
N195DN	Boeing 767-332ER	Delta Air Lines	
N196AA	Boeing 757-223ET	American Airlines	
N196DN	Boeing 767-332ER	Delta Air Lines	
N197AN	Boeing 757-223ET	American Airlines	
N197DN	Boeing 767-332ER	Delta Air Lines	

Notes	Reg.	Type	Owner or Operator
	N197UA	Boeing 747-422	United Airlines
	N198AA	Boeing 757-223ET	American Airlines
	N198DN	Boeing 767-332ER	Delta Air Lines
	N199AN	Boeing 757-223ET	American Airlines
	N199DN	Boeing 767-332ER	Delta Air Lines
	N199UA	Boeing 747-422	United Airlines
	N200UU	Boeing 757-2B7	US Airways
	N201UU	Boeing 757-2B7	US Airways
	N202UW	Boeing 757-2B7	US Airways
	N203UW	Boeing 757-23N	US Airways
	N204UA	Boeing 777-222ER	United Airlines
	N204UW	Boeing 757-23N	US Airways
	N205UW	Boeing 757-23N	US Airways
	N206UA	Boeing 777-222ER	United Airlines
	N206UW	Boeing 757-2B7	US Airways
	N209UA	Boeing 777-222ER	United Airlines
	N216UA	Boeing 777-222ER	United Airlines
	N217UA	Boeing 777-222ER	United Airlines
	N218UA	Boeing 777-222ER	United Airlines
	N219CY	Boeing 767-383ER	ABX Air/DHL
	N219UA	Boeing 777-222ER	United Airlines
	N220UA	Boeing 777-222ER	United Airlines
	N221UA	Boeing 777-222ER	United Airlines
	N222UA	Boeing 777-222ER	United Airlines
	N223UA	Boeing 777-222ER	United Airlines
	N224UA	Boeing 777-222ER	United Airlines
	N225UA	Boeing 777-222ER	United Airlines
	N226UA	Boeing 777-222ER	United Airlines
	N227UA	Boeing 777-222ER	United Airlines
	N228UA	Boeing 777-222ER	United Airlines
	N229UA	Boeing 777-222ER	United Airlines
	N245AY	Boeing 767-201ER	US Airways
	N246AY	Boeing 767-201ER	US Airways
	N248AY	Boeing 767-201ER	US Airways
	N249AU	Boeing 767-201ER	US Airways
	N250AY	Boeing 767-201ER	US Airways
	N251AY	Boeing 767-2B7ER	US Airways
	N252AU	Boeing 767-2B7ER	US Airways
	N253AY	Boeing 767-2B7ER	US Airways
	N255AY	Boeing 767-2B7ER	US Airways
	N256AY	Boeing 767-2B7ER	US Airways
	N269WA	McD Douglas MD-11	World Airways
	N270AY	Airbus A.330-323X	US Airways
	N270WA	McD Douglas MD-11AH	World Airways
	N271AY	Airbus A.330-323X	US Airways
	N271WA	McD Douglas MD-11 (271)	World Airways
	N272AY	Airbus A.330-323X	US Airways
	N272WA	McD Douglas MD-11 (272)	World Airways
	N273AY	Airbus A.330-323X	US Airways
	N273WA	McD Douglas MD-11 (273)	World Airways
	N274AY	Airbus A.330-323X	US Airways
	N274WA	McD Douglas MD-11F (274)	World Airways
	N275AY	Airbus A.330-323X	US Airways
	N275WA	McD Douglas MD-11CF (275)	World Airways
	N276AY	Airbus A.330-323X	US Airways
	N276WA	McD Douglas MD-11F	World Airways
	N277AY	Airbus A.330-323X	US Airways
	N277WA	McD Douglas MD-11 (277)	World Airways
	N278AY	Airbus A.330-323X	US Airways
	N278WA	McD Douglas MD-11 (278)	World Airways
	N279AY	Airbus A.330-243	US Airways
	N279WA	McD Douglas MD-11 (279)	World Airways/Etihad Airways
	N280AY	Airbus A.330-243	US Airways
	N281AY	Airbus A.330-243	US Airways
	N282AY	Airbus A.330-243	US Airways
	N283AY	Airbus A.330-243	US Airways
	N284AY	Airbus A.330-243	US Airways
	N285AY	Airbus A.330-243	US Airways
	N301UP	Boeing 767-34AFER	United Parcel Service
	N302UP	Boeing 767-34AFER	United Parcel Service
	N303UP	Boeing 767-34AFER	United Parcel Service
	N304UP	Boeing 767-34AFER	United Parcel Service
	N305UP	Boeing 767-34AFER	United Parcel Service
	N306UP	Boeing 767-34AFER	United Parcel Service

Reg.	Type	Owner or Operator	Notes
N307UP	Boeing 767-34AFER	United Parcel Service	
N308UP	Boeing 767-34AFER	United Parcel Service	
N309UP	Boeing 767-34AFER	United Parcel Service	
N310UP	Boeing 767-34AFER	United Parcel Service	
N311UP	Boeing 767-34AFER	United Parcel Service	
N312UP	Boeing 767-34AFER	United Parcel Service	
N313UP	Boeing 767-34AFER	United Parcel Service	
N314UP	Boeing 767-34AFER	United Parcel Service	
N315UP	Boeing 767-34AFER	United Parcel Service	
N316UP	Boeing 767-34AFER	United Parcel Service	
N317UP	Boeing 767-34AFER	United Parcel Service	
N318UP	Boeing 767-34AFER	United Parcel Service	
N319UP	Boeing 767-34AFER	United Parcel Service	
N320UP	Boeing 767-34AFER	United Parcel Service	
N322UP	Boeing 767-34AFER	United Parcel Service	
N323UP	Boeing 767-34AFER	United Parcel Service	
N324UP	Boeing 767-34AFER	United Parcel Service	
N325UP	Boeing 767-34AFER	United Parcel Service	
N326UP	Boeing 767-34AFER	United Parcel Service	
N327UP	Boeing 767-34AFER	United Parcel Service	
N328UP	Boeing 767-34AFER	United Parcel Service	
N329UP	Boeing 767-34AER	United Parcel Service	
N330UP	Boeing 767-34AER	United Parcel Service	
N331UP	Boeing 767-34AER	United Parcel Service	
N332UP	Boeing 767-34AER	United Parcel Service	
N334UP	Boeing 767-34AER	United Parcel Service	
N335UP	Boeing 767-34AF	United Parcel Service	
N336UP	Boeing 767-34AF	United Parcel Service	
N337UP	Boeing 767-34AF	United Parcel Service	
N338UP	Boeing 767-34AF	United Parcel Service	
N339UP	Boeing 767-34AF	United Parcel Service	
N340UP	Boeing 767-34AF	United Parcel Service	
N341UP	Boeing 767-34AF	United Parcel Service	
N342AN	Boeing 767-323ER	American Airlines	
N342UP	Boeing 767-34AF	United Parcel Service	
N343AN	Boeing 767-323ER	American Airlines	
N343UP	Boeing 767-34AF	United Parcel Service	
N344AN	Boeing 767-323ER	American Airlines	
N344UP	Boeing 767-34AF	United Parcel Service	
N345AN	Boeing 767-323ER	American Airlines	
N345UP	Boeing 767-34AF	United Parcel Service	
N346AN	Boeing 767-323ER	American Airlines	
N346UP	Boeing 767-34AF	United Parcel Service	
N347AN	Boeing 767-323ER	American Airlines	
N347UP	Boeing 767-34AF	United Parcel Service	
N348AN	Boeing 767-323ER	American Airlines	
N348UP	Boeing 767-34AF	United Parcel Service	
N349AN	Boeing 767-323ER	American Airlines	
N349UP	Boeing 767-34AF	United Parcel Service	
N350AN	Boeing 767-323ER	American Airlines	
N350UP	Boeing 767-34AF	United Parcel Service	
N351AA	Boeing 767-323ER	American Airlines	
N351UP	Boeing 767-34AF	United Parcel Service	
N352AA	Boeing 767-323ER	American Airlines	
N352UP	Boeing 767-34AF	United Parcel Service	
N353AA	Boeing 767-323ER	American Airlines	
N353UP	Boeing 767-34AF	United Parcel Service	
N354AA	Boeing 767-323ER	American Airlines	
N355AA	Boeing 767-323ER	American Airlines	
N357AA	Boeing 767-323ER	American Airlines	
N358AA	Boeing 767-323ER	American Airlines	
N359AA	Boeing 767-323ER	American Airlines	
N360AA	Boeing 767-323ER	American Airlines	
N361AA	Boeing 767-323ER	American Airlines	
N362AA	Boeing 767-323ER	American Airlines	
N363AA	Boeing 767-323ER	American Airlines	
N366AA	Boeing 767-323ER	American Airlines	
N368AA	Boeing 767-323ER	American Airlines	
N369AA	Boeing 767-323ER	American Airlines	
N370AA	Boeing 767-323ER	American Airlines	
N371AA	Boeing 767-323ER	American Airlines	
N372AA	Boeing 767-323ER	American Airlines	
N373AA	Boeing 767-323ER	American Airlines	
N374AA	Boeing 767-323ER	American Airlines	

Notes	Reg.	Type	Owner or Operator
	N376AN	Boeing 767-323ER	American Airlines
	N377AN	Boeing 767-323ER	American Airlines
	N378AN	Boeing 767-323ER	American Airlines
	N379AA	Boeing 767-323ER	American Airlines
	N380AN	Boeing 767-323ER	American Airlines
	N380WA	McD Douglas MD-11F	World Airways
	N381AN	Boeing 767-323ER	American Airlines
	N381WA	McD Douglas MD-11F (381)	World Airways
	N382AN	Boeing 767-323ER	American Airlines
	N382WA	McD Douglas MD-11F	World Airways
	N383AN	Boeing 767-323ER	American Airlines
	N383WA	McD Douglas MD-11F	World Airways
	N384AA	Boeing 767-323ER	American Airlines
	N384WA	McD Douglas MD-11F	World Airways
	N385AM	Boeing 767-323ER	American Airlines
	N386AA	Boeing 767-323ER	American Airlines
	N387AM	Boeing 767-323ER	American Airlines
	N388AA	Boeing 767-323ER	American Airlines
	N389AA	Boeing 767-323ER	American Airlines
	N390AA	Boeing 767-323ER	American Airlines
	N391AA	Boeing 767-323ER	American Airlines
	N392AN	Boeing 767-323ER	American Airlines
	N393AN	Boeing 767-323ER	American Airlines
	N394AN	Boeing 767-323ER	American Airlines
	N394DL	Boeing 767-324ER	Delta Air Lines
	N395AN	Boeing 767-323ER	American Airlines
	N396AN	Boeing 767-323ER	American Airlines
	N397AN	Boeing 767-323ER	American Airlines
	N398AN	Boeing 767-323ER	American Airlines
	N399AN	Boeing 767-323ER	American Airlines
	N408MC	Boeing 747-47UF	Atlas Air/Emirates SkyCargo
	N412MC	Boeing 747-47UF	Atlas Air
	N415MC	Boeing 747-47UF	Atlas Air/Emirates SkyCargo
	N418MC	Boeing 747-47UF	Atlas Air
	N419MC	Boeing 747-48EF	Atlas Air
	N429MC	Boeing 747-481	Atlas Air
	N458MC	Boeing 747-446BCF	Atlas Air
	N459MC	Boeing 747-446BCF	Atlas Air
	N464MC	Boeing 747-446	Atlas Air
	N465MC	Boeing 747-446	Atlas Air
	N470EV	Boeing 747-273C	Evergreen International Airlines
	N471EV	Boeing 747-273C	Evergreen International Airlines
	N475MC	Boeing 747-47U	Atlas Air
	N476MC	Boeing 747-47U	Atlas Air
	N482EV	Boeing 747-212B (SCD)	Evergreen International Airlines
	N485EV	Boeing 747-212B (SCD)	Evergreen International Airlines
	N486EV	Boeing 747-212B (SCD)	Evergreen International Airlines
	N487EV	Boeing 747-230B (SF)	Evergreen International Airlines
	N488EV	Boeing 747-230B (SF)	Evergreen International Airlines
	N489EV	Boeing 747-230B (SF)	Evergreen International Airlines
	N490EV	Boeing 747-230F (SCD)	Evergreen International Airlines
	N493MC	Boeing 747-47UF	Atlas Air
	N496MC	Boeing 747-47UF	Atlas Air
	N497MC	Boeing 747-47UF	Atlas Air/Emirates SkyCargo
	N498MC	Boeing 747-47UF	Atlas Air
	N499MC	Boeing 747-47UF	Atlas Air/Polar Air Cargo
	N517MC	Boeing 747-243F (SCD)	Atlas Air
	N521FE	McD Douglas MD-11F	Federal Express
	N522FE	McD Douglas MD-11F	Federal Express
	N523FE	McD Douglas MD-11F	Federal Express
	N523MC	Boeing 747-2D7B (SF)	Atlas Air
	N524FE	McD Douglas MD-11F	Federal Express
	N524MC	Boeing 747-2D7BF	Atlas Air
	N525FE	McD Douglas MD-11F	Federal Express
	N527FE	McD Douglas MD-11F	Federal Express
	N528FE	McD Douglas MD-11F	Federal Express
	N529FE	McD Douglas MD-11F	Federal Express
	N572FE	McD Douglas MD-11F	Federal Express
	N573FE	McD Douglas MD-11F	Federal Express
	N574FE	McD Douglas MD-11F	Federal Express
	N575FE	McD Douglas MD-11F	Federal Express
	N576FE	McD Douglas MD-11F	Federal Express
	N577FE	McD Douglas MD-11F	Federal Express
	N578FE	McD Douglas MD-11F	Federal Express *Stephen*

Reg.	Type	Owner or Operator	Notes
N579FE	McD Douglas MD-11F	Federal Express *Nash*	
N580FE	McD Douglas MD-11F	Federal Express *Ashton*	
N582FE	McD Douglas MD-11F	Federal Express *Jamie*	
N583FE	McD Douglas MD-11F	Federal Express *Nancy*	
N584FE	McD Douglas MD-11F	Federal Express *Jeffrey Wellington*	
N585FE	McD Douglas MD-11F	Federal Express *Katherine*	
N586FE	McD Douglas MD-11F	Federal Express *Dylan*	
N587FE	McD Douglas MD-11F	Federal Express *Jeanna*	
N588FE	McD Douglas MD-11F	Federal Express *Kendra*	
N589FE	McD Douglas MD-11F	Federal Express *Shaun*	
N590FE	McD Douglas MD-11F	Federal Express	
N591FE	McD Douglas MD-11F	Federal Express *Giovanni*	
N592FE	McD Douglas MD-11F	Federal Express *Joshua*	
N593FE	McD Douglas MD-11F	Federal Express *Harrison*	
N594FE	McD Douglas MD-11F	Federal Express	
N595FE	McD Douglas MD-11F	Federal Express *Avery*	
N596FE	McD Douglas MD-11F	Federal Express	
N597FE	McD Douglas MD-11F	Federal Express	
N598FE	McD Douglas MD-11F	Federal Express	
N599FE	McD Douglas MD-11F	Federal Express *Mariana*	
N601FE	McD Douglas MD-11F	Federal Express *Jim Riedmeyer*	
N602FE	McD Douglas MD-11F	Federal Express *Malcolm Baldridge 1990*	
N603FE	McD Douglas MD-11F	Federal Express *Elizabeth*	
N604FE	McD Douglas MD-11F	Federal Express *Hollis*	
N605FE	McD Douglas MD-11F	Federal Express *April Star*	
N606FE	McD Douglas MD-11F	Federal Express *Charles & Theresa*	
N607FE	McD Douglas MD-11F	Federal Express *Christina*	
N608FE	McD Douglas MD-11F	Federal Express *Karen*	
N609FE	McD Douglas MD-11F	Federal Express *Scott*	
N610FE	McD Douglas MD-11F	Federal Express *Marisa*	
N612FE	McD Douglas MD-11F	Federal Express *Alyssa*	
N613FE	McD Douglas MD-11F	Federal Express *Krista*	
N614FE	McD Douglas MD-11F	Federal Express *Christy Allison*	
N615FE	McD Douglas MD-11F	Federal Express *Max*	
N616FE	McD Douglas MD-11F	Federal Express *Shanita*	
N617FE	McD Douglas MD-11F	Federal Express *Travis*	
N618FE	McD Douglas MD-11F	Federal Express *Justin*	
N619FE	McD Douglas MD-11F	Federal Express *Lyndon*	
N620FE	McD Douglas MD-11F	Federal Express	
N621FE	McD Douglas MD-11F	Federal Express *Connor*	
N623FE	McD Douglas MD-11F	Federal Express *Meghan*	
N624FE	McD Douglas MD-11F	Federal Express	
N625FE	McD Douglas MD-11F	Federal Express	
N628FE	McD Douglas MD-11F	Federal Express	
N631FE	McD Douglas MD-11F	Federal Express	
N641UA	Boeing 767-322ER	United Airlines	
N642FE	McD Douglas MD-11F	Federal Express	
N642UA	Boeing 767-322ER	United Airlines	
N643FE	McD Douglas MD-11F	Federal Express	
N643UA	Boeing 767-322ER	United Airlines	
N644FE	McD Douglas MD-11F	Federal Express	
N644UA	Boeing 767-322ER	United Airlines	
N645FE	McD Douglas MD-11F	Federal Express	
N646UA	Boeing 767-322ER	United Airlines	
N647UA	Boeing 767-322ER	United Airlines	
N648UA	Boeing 767-322ER	United Airlines	
N649UA	Boeing 767-322ER	United Airlines	
N651UA	Boeing 767-322ER	United Airlines	
N652UA	Boeing 767-322ER	United Airlines	
N653UA	Boeing 767-322ER	United Airlines	
N654UA	Boeing 767-322ER	United Airlines	
N655UA	Boeing 767-322ER	United Airlines	
N656UA	Boeing 767-322ER	United Airlines	
N657UA	Boeing 767-322ER	United Airlines	
N658UA	Boeing 767-322ER	United Airlines	
N659UA	Boeing 767-322ER	United Airlines	
N660UA	Boeing 767-322ER	United Airlines	
N661UA	Boeing 767-322ER	United Airlines	
N662UA	Boeing 767-322ER	United Airlines	
N663UA	Boeing 767-322ER	United Airlines	
N700CK	Boeing 747-246B	Kalitta Air	
N701CK	Boeing 747-259B (SF)	Kalitta Air	
N702TW	Boeing 757-2Q8	Delta Air Lines	
N703CK	Boeing 747-212B (SF)	Kalitta Air	

Notes	Reg.	Type	Owner or Operator
	N703TW	Boeing 757-2Q8	Delta Air Lines
	N704CK	Boeing 747-246F	Kalitta Air
	N704X	Boeing 757-2Q8	Delta Air Lines
	N705TW	Boeing 757-231	Delta Air Lines
	N706TW	Boeing 757-2Q8	Delta Air Lines
	N707CK	Boeing 747-246F (SCD)	Kalitta Air
	N707TW	Boeing 757-2Q8	Delta Air Lines
	N708CK	Boeing 747-212B	Kalitta Air
	N709TW	Boeing 757-2Q8	Delta Air Lines
	N710TW	Boeing 757-2Q8	Delta Air Lines
	N711ZX	Boeing 757-231	Delta Air Lines
	N712TW	Boeing 757-2Q8	Delta Air Lines
	N713CK	Boeing 747-2B4B (SF)	Kalitta Air
	N713TW	Boeing 757-2Q8	Delta Air Lines
	N715CK	Boeing 747-209B (SF)	Kalitta Air
	N717TW	Boeing 757-231	Delta Air Lines
	N718TW	Boeing 757-231	Delta Air Lines
	N721TW	Boeing 757-231	Delta Air Lines
	N722TW	Boeing 757-231	Delta Air Lines
	N723TW	Boeing 757-231	Delta Air Lines
	N727TW	Boeing 757-231	Delta Air Lines
	N740CK	Boeing 747-4H6BCF	Kalitta Air
	N740WA	Boeing 747-4H6F	World Airways
	N741CK	Boeing 747-4H6F	Kalitta Air
	N741WA	Boeing 747-4H6F	World Airways
	N742CK	Boeing 747-446BCF	Kalitta Air
	N743CK	Boeing 747-446BCF	Kalitta Air
	N742WA	Boeing 747-412F	World Airways
	N743WA	Boeing 747-412F	World Airways
	N744CK	Boeing 747-446BCF	Kalitta Air
	N745CK	Boeing 747-446BCF	Kalitta Air
	N746CK	Boeing 747-246B	Kalitta Air
	N747CK	Boeing 747-221F	Kalitta Air
	N748CK	Boeing 747-221F	Kalitta Air
	N750AN	Boeing 777-223ER	American Airlines
	N751AN	Boeing 777-223ER	American Airlines
	N752AN	Boeing 777-223ER	American Airlines
	N753AN	Boeing 777-223ER	American Airlines
	N754AN	Boeing 777-223ER	American Airlines
	N755AN	Boeing 777-223ER	American Airlines
	N756AM	Boeing 777-223ER	American Airlines
	N757AN	Boeing 777-223ER	American Airlines
	N758AN	Boeing 777-223ER	American Airlines
	N759AN	Boeing 777-223ER	American Airlines
	N760AN	Boeing 777-223ER	American Airlines
	N761AJ	Boeing 777-223ER	American Airlines
	N762AN	Boeing 777-223ER	American Airlines
	N765AN	Boeing 777-223ER	American Airlines
	N766AN	Boeing 777-223ER	American Airlines
	N767AJ	Boeing 777-223ER	American Airlines
	N768AA	Boeing 777-223ER	American Airlines
	N768UA	Boeing 777-222	United Airlines
	N769UA	Boeing 777-222	United Airlines
	N770AN	Boeing 777-223ER	American Airlines
	N771AN	Boeing 777-223ER	American Airlines
	N771UA	Boeing 777-222	United Airlines
	N772AN	Boeing 777-223ER	American Airlines
	N772UA	Boeing 777-222	United Airlines
	N773AN	Boeing 777-223ER	American Airlines
	N773UA	Boeing 777-222	United Airlines
	N774AN	Boeing 777-223ER	American Airlines
	N774UA	Boeing 777-222	United Airlines
	N775AN	Boeing 777-223ER	American Airlines
	N775UA	Boeing 777-222	United Airlines
	N776AN	Boeing 777-223ER	American Airlines
	N776UA	Boeing 777-222	United Airlines
	N777AN	Boeing 777-223ER	American Airlines
	N777UA	Boeing 777-222	United Airlines
	N778AN	Boeing 777-223ER	American Airlines
	N778UA	Boeing 777-222	United Airlines
	N779AN	Boeing 777-223ER	American Airlines
	N779UA	Boeing 777-222	United Airlines
	N780AN	Boeing 777-223ER	American Airlines
	N780UA	Boeing 777-222	United Airlines

Reg.	Type	Owner or Operator	Notes
N781AN	Boeing 777-223ER	American Airlines	
N781UA	Boeing 777-222	United Airlines	
N782AN	Boeing 777-223ER	American Airlines	
N782UA	Boeing 777-222ER	United Airlines	
N783AN	Boeing 777-223ER	American Airlines	
N783UA	Boeing 777-222ER	United Airlines	
N784AN	Boeing 777-223ER	American Airlines	
N784UA	Boeing 777-222ER	United Airlines	
N785AN	Boeing 777-223ER	American Airlines	
N785UA	Boeing 777-222ER	United Airlines	
N786AN	Boeing 777-223ER	American Airlines	
N786UA	Boeing 777-222ER	United Airlines	
N787AL	Boeing 777-223ER	American Airlines	
N787UA	Boeing 777-222ER	United Airlines	
N788AN	Boeing 777-223ER	American Airlines	
N788UA	Boeing 777-222ER	United Airlines	
N789AN	Boeing 777-223ER	American Airlines	
N790AN	Boeing 777-223ER	American Airlines	
N790CK	Boeing 747-251F	Kalitta Air	
N791AN	Boeing 777-223ER	American Airlines	
N791CK	Boeing 747-251F	Kalitta Air	
N791UA	Boeing 777-222ER	United Airlines	
N792CK	Boeing 747-212F	Kalitta Air	
N792AN	Boeing 777-223ER	American Airlines	
N792UA	Boeing 777-222ER	United Airlines	
N793AN	Boeing 777-223ER	American Airlines	
N793CK	Boeing 747-222B	Kalitta Air	
N793UA	Boeing 777-222ER	United Airlines	
N794AN	Boeing 777-223ER	American Airlines	
N794CK	Boeing 747-222B	Kalitta Air	
N794UA	Boeing 777-222ER	United Airlines	
N795AN	Boeing 777-223ER	American Airlines	
N795CK	Boeing 747-251B	Kalitta Air	
N795UA	Boeing 777-222ER	United Airlines	
N796AN	Boeing 777-223ER	American Airlines	
N796UA	Boeing 777-222ER	United Airlines	
N797AN	Boeing 777-223ER	American Airlines	
N797UA	Boeing 777-222ER	United Airlines	
N798AN	Boeing 777-223ER	American Airlines	
N798UA	Boeing 777-222ER	United Airlines	
N799AN	Boeing 777-223ER	American Airlines	
N799UA	Boeing 777-222ER	United Airlines	
N801DE	McD Douglas MD-11 (801)	World Airways	
N801NW	Airbus A.330-323X	Delta Airlines	
N801SY	Boeing 737-8Q8	Sun Country Airlines	
N802NW	Airbus A.330-323X	Delta Airlines	
N803NW	Airbus A.330-323X	Delta Air Lines	
N804DE	McD Douglas MD-11 (804)	World Airways	
N804NW	Airbus A.330-323X	Delta Air Lines	
N804SY	Boeing 737-8Q8	Sun Country Airlines	
N805NW	Airbus A.330-323X	Delta Air Lines	
N805SY	Boeing 737-8Q8	Sun Country Airlines	
N806NW	Airbus A.330-323X	Delta Air Lines	
N806SY	Boeing 737-8Q8	Sun Country Airlines	
N807NW	Airbus A.330-323X	Delta Air Lines	
N808NW	Airbus A.330-323X	Delta Air Lines	
N809NW	Airbus A.330-323E	Delta Air Lines	
N809SY	Boeing 737-8Q8	Sun Country Airlines	
N810NW	Airbus A.330-323E	Delta Air Lines	
N811NW	Airbus A.330-323E	Delta Air Lines	
N812NW	Airbus A.330-323E	Delta Air Lines	
N813NW	Airbus A.330-323E	Delta Air Lines	
N813SY	Boeing 737-8Q8	Sun Country Airlines	
N814SY	Boeing 737-8BK	Sun Country Airlines	
N815SY	Boeing 737-8BK	Sun Country Airlines	
N816SY	Boeing 737-8Q8	Sun Country Airlines	
N814NW	Airbus A.330-323E	Delta Air Lines	
N815NW	Airbus A.330-323E	Delta Air Lines	
N816NW	Airbus A.330-323E	Delta Air Lines	
N817NW	Airbus A.330-323E	Delta Air Lines	
N818NW	Airbus A.330-323E	Delta Air Lines	
N819NW	Airbus A.330-323E	Delta Air Lines	
N820NW	Airbus A.330-323E	Delta Air Lines	
N821NW	Airbus A.330-323E	Delta Air Lines	

Notes	Reg.	Type	Owner or Operator
	N825MH	Boeing 767-432ER (1801)	Delta Air Lines
	N826MH	Boeing 767-432ER (1802)	Delta Air Lines
	N827MH	Boeing 767-432ER (1803)	Delta Air Lines
	N828MH	Boeing 767-432ER (1804)	Delta Air Lines
	N829MH	Boeing 767-432ER (1805)	Delta Air Lines
	N830MH	Boeing 767-432ER (1806)	Delta Air Lines
	N831MH	Boeing 767-432ER (1807)	Delta Air Lines
	N832MH	Boeing 767-432ER (1808)	Delta Air Lines
	N833MH	Boeing 767-432ER (1809)	Delta Air Lines
	N834MH	Boeing 767-432ER (1810)	Delta Air Lines
	N835MH	Boeing 767-432ER (1811)	Delta Air Lines
	N836MH	Boeing 767-432ER (1812)	Delta Air Lines
	N837MH	Boeing 767-432ER (1813)	Delta Air Lines
	N838MH	Boeing 767-432ER (1814)	Delta Air Lines
	N839MH	Boeing 767-432ER (1815)	Delta Air Lines
	N840MH	Boeing 767-432ER (1816)	Delta Air Lines
	N841MH	Boeing 767-432ER (1817)	Delta Air Lines
	N842MH	Boeing 767-432ER (1818	Delta Air Lines
	N843MH	Boeing 767-432ER (1819)	Delta Air Lines
	N844MH	Boeing 767-432ER (1820)	Delta Air Lines
	N845MH	Boeing 767-432ER (1821)	Delta Air Lines
	N850FD	Boeing 777-2S2LRF	Federal Express
	N851FD	Boeing 777-2S2LRF	Federal Express
	N851NW	Airbus A.330-223	Delta Air Lines
	N852FD	Boeing 777-2S2LRF	Federal Express
	N852GT	Boeing 747-87UF	Atlas Air
	N852NW	Airbus A.330-223	Delta Air Lines
	N853FD	Boeing 777-2S2LRF	Federal Express
	N853GT	Boeing 747-87UF	Atlas Air
	N853NW	Airbus A.330-223	Delta Air Lines
	N854FD	Boeing 777-2S2LRF	Federal Express
	N854NW	Airbus A.330-223	Delta Air Lines
	N855FD	Boeing 777-2S2LRF	Federal Express
	N855NW	Airbus A.330-223	Delta Air Lines
	N856FD	Boeing 777-2S2LRF	Federal Express
	N856NW	Airbus A.330-223	Delta Air Lines
	N857FD	Boeing 777-2S2LRF	Federal Express
	N857NW	Airbus A.330-223	Delta Air Lines
	N858FD	Boeing 777-2S2LRF	Federal Express
	N858NW	Airbus A.330-223	Delta Air Lines
	N859FD	Boeing 777-2S2LRF	Federal Express
	N859NW	Airbus A.330-223	Delta Air Lines
	N860FD	Boeing 777-2S2LRF	Federal Express
	N860NW	Airbus A.330-223	Delta Air Lines
	N861FD	Boeing 777-2S2LRF	Federal Express
	N861NW	Airbus A.330-223	Delta Air Lines
	N862FD	Boeing 777-2S2LRF	Federal Express
	N863FD	Boeing 777-2S2LRF	Federal Express
	N864FD	Boeing 777-2S2LRF	Federal Express
	N880FD	Boeing 777-2S2LRF	Federal Express
	N882FD	Boeing 777-2S2LRF	Federal Express
	N883FD	Boeing 777-2S2LRF	Federal Express
	N884FD	Boeing 777-2S2LRF	Federal Express
	N885FD	Boeing 777-2S2LRF	Federal Express
	N892FD	Boeing 777-2S2LRF	Federal Express
	N937UW	Boeing 757-2B7	US Airways
	N938UW	Boeing 757-2B7	US Airways
	N939UW	Boeing 757-2B7	US Airways
	N940UW	Boeing 757-2B7	US Airways
	N941UW	Boeing 757-2B7	US Airways
	N942UW	Boeing 757-2B7	US Airways
	N1200K	Boeing 767-332ER (200)	Delta Air Lines
	N1201P	Boeing 767-332ER (201)	Delta Air Lines
	N1501P	Boeing 767-3P6ER (1501)	Delta Air Lines
	N1602	Boeing 767-332ER (1602)	Delta Air Lines
	N1603	Boeing 767-332ER (1603)	Delta Air Lines
	N1604R	Boeing 767-332ER (1604)	Delta Air Lines
	N1605	Boeing 767-332ER (1605)	Delta Air Lines
	N1607B	Boeing 767-332ER (1607)	Delta Air Lines
	N1608	Boeing 767-332ER (1608)	Delta Air Lines
	N1609	Boeing 767-332ER (1609)	Delta Air Lines
	N1610D	Boeing 767-332ER (1610)	Delta Air Lines
	N1611B	Boeing 767-332ER (1611)	Delta Air Lines
	N1612T	Boeing 767-332ER (1612)	Delta Air Lines

Reg.	Type	Owner or Operator	Notes
N1613B	Boeing 767-332ER (1613)	Delta Air Lines	
N7375A	Boeing 767-323ER	American Airlines	
N12109	Boeing 757-224	United Airlines	
N12114	Boeing 757-224	United Airlines	
N12116	Boeing 757-224	United Airlines	
N12125	Boeing 757-224	United Airlines	
N13110	Boeing 757-224	United Airlines	
N13113	Boeing 757-224	United Airlines	
N13138	Boeing 757-224	United Airlines	
N14102	Boeing 757-224	United Airlines	
N14106	Boeing 757-224	United Airlines	
N14107	Boeing 757-224	United Airlines	
N14115	Boeing 757-224	United Airlines	
N14118	Boeing 757-224	United Airlines	
N14120	Boeing 757-224	United Airlines	
N14121	Boeing 757-224	United Airlines	
N16065	Boeing 767-332ER (1606)	Delta Air Lines	
N17104	Boeing 757-224	United Airlines	
N17105	Boeing 757-224	United Airlines	
N17122	Boeing 757-224	United Airlines	
N17126	Boeing 757-224	United Airlines	
N17128	Boeing 757-224	United Airlines	
N17133	Boeing 757-224	United Airlines	
N17139	Boeing 757-224	United Airlines	
N18112	Boeing 757-224	United Airlines	
N18119	Boeing 757-224	United Airlines	
N19117	Boeing 757-224	United Airlines	
N19130	Boeing 757-224	United Airlines	
N19136	Boeing 757-224	United Airlines	
N19141	Boeing 757-224	United Airlines	
N21108	Boeing 757-224	United Airlines	
N26123	Boeing 757-224	United Airlines	
N27015	Boeing 777-224ER	United Airlines	
N29124	Boeing 757-224	United Airlines	
N29129	Boeing 757-224	United Airlines	
N33103	Boeing 757-224	United Airlines	
N33132	Boeing 757-224	United Airlines	
N34131	Boeing 757-224	United Airlines	
N34137	Boeing 757-224	United Airlines	
N37018	Boeing 777-224ER	United Airlines	
N39356	Boeing 767-323ER	American Airlines	
N39364	Boeing 767-323ER	American Airlines	
N39365	Boeing 767-323ER	American Airlines	
N39367	Boeing 767-323ER	American Airlines	
N41135	Boeing 757-224	United Airlines	
N41140	Boeing 757-224	United Airlines	
N48127	Boeing 757-224	United Airlines	
N57016	Boeing 777-224ER	United Airlines	
N57111	Boeing 757-224	United Airlines	
N58101	Boeing 757-224	United Airlines	
N59053	Boeing 767-424ER	United Airlines	
N66051	Boeing 767-424ER	United Airlines	
N66056	Boeing 767-424ER	United Airlines	
N66057	Boeing 767-424ER	United Airlines	
N67052	Boeing 767-424ER	United Airlines	
N67058	Boeing 767-424ER	United Airlines	
N67134	Boeing 757-224	United Airlines	
N67157	Boeing 767-224ER	United Airlines	
N67158	Boeing 767-224ER	United Airlines	
N68061	Boeing 767-424ER	United Airlines	
N68155	Boeing 767-224ER	United Airlines	
N68159	Boeing 767-224ER	United Airlines	
N68160	Boeing 767-224ER	United Airlines	
N69020	Boeing 777-224ER	United Airlines	
N69059	Boeing 767-424ER	United Airlines	
N69063	Boeing 767-424ER	United Airlines	
N69154	Boeing 767-224ER	United Airlines	
N73152	Boeing 767-224ER	United Airlines	
N74007	Boeing 777-224ER	United Airlines	
N76010	Boeing 777-224ER	United Airlines	
N76021	Boeing 777-224ER	United Airlines	
N76054	Boeing 767-424ER	United Airlines	
N76055	Boeing 767-424ER	United Airlines	
N76062	Boeing 767-424ER	United Airlines	

Notes	Reg.	Type	Owner or Operator
	N76064	Boeing 767-424ER	United Airlines
	N76065	Boeing 767-424ER	United Airlines
	N76151	Boeing 767-224ER	United Airlines
	N76153	Boeing 767-224ER	United Airlines
	N76156	Boeing 767-224ER	United Airlines
	N77006	Boeing 777-224ER	United Airlines
	N77012	Boeing 777-224ER	United Airlines
	N77014	Boeing 777-224ER	United Airlines
	N77019	Boeing 777-224ER	United Airlines
	N77022	Boeing 777-224ER	United Airlines
	N77066	Boeing 767-424ER	United Airlines
	N78001	Boeing 777-224ER	United Airlines
	N78002	Boeing 777-224ER	United Airlines
	N78003	Boeing 777-224ER	United Airlines
	N78004	Boeing 777-224ER	United Airlines
	N78005	Boeing 777-224ER	United Airlines
	N78008	Boeing 777-224ER	United Airlines
	N78009	Boeing 777-224ER	United Airlines
	N78013	Boeing 777-224ER	United Airlines
	N78017	Boeing 777-224ER	United Airlines
	N78060	Boeing 767-424ER	United Airlines
	N79011	Boeing 777-224ER	United Airlines

OD (Lebanon)

	OD-MEA	Airbus A.330-243	Middle East Airlines
	OD-MEB	Airbus A.330-243	Middle East Airlines
	OD-MEC	Airbus A.330-243	Middle East Airlines
	OD-MRM	Airbus A.320-232	Middle East Airlines
	OD-MRR	Airbus A.320-232	Middle East Airlines
	OD-MRS	Airbus A.320-232	Middle East Airlines
	OD-MRT	Airbus A.320-232	Middle East Airlines
	OD-RMH	Airbus A.321-231	Middle East Airlines
	OD-RMI	Airbus A.321-231	Middle East Airlines
	OD-RMJ	Airbus A.321-231	Middle East Airlines
	OD-TMA	Airbus A.300F4-605R	TMA – Trans Mediterranean Airways

Middle East Airlines also operate Airbus A.321s, Airbus A.320s and an Airbus A.330 on the French Register

OE (Austria)

	OE-IHA	Embraer ERJ190-100LR	Niki *Samba*
	OE-IHB	Embraer ERJ190-100LR	Niki *Lambada*
	OE-IHC	Embraer ERJ190-100LR	Niki *Bossa Nova*
	OE-IHD	Embraer ERJ190-100LR	Niki *Calypso*
	OE-IHE	Embraer ERJ190-100LR	Niki *Rumba*
	OE-IHF	Embraer ERJ190-100LR	Niki *Salsa*
	OE-IHG	Embraer ERJ190-100LR	Niki *Tango*
	OE-LAE	Boeing 767-3Z9ER	Austrian Airlines *Malaysia*
	OE-LAT	Boeing 767-31AER	Austrian Airlines *Enzo Ferrari*
	OE-LAW	Boeing 767-3Z9ER	Austrian Airlines *China*
	OE-LAX	Boeing 767-3Z9ER	Austrian Airlines *Thailand*
	OE-LAY	Boeing 767-3Z9ER	Austrian Airlines *Japan*
	OE-LAZ	Boeing 767-3Z9ER	Austrian Airlines *India*
	OE-LBA	Airbus A.321-111	Austrian Airlines *Salzkammergut*
	OE-LBB	Airbus A.321-111	Austrian Airlines *Pinzgau*
	OE-LBC	Airbus A.321-111	Austrian Airlines *Sudtirol*
	OE-LBD	Airbus A.321-111	Austrian Airlines *Steirisches Weinland*
	OE-LBE	Airbus A.321-111	Austrian Airlines *Wachau*
	OE-LBF	Airbus A.321-111	Austrian Airlines *Wien*
	OE-LBN	Airbus A.320-214	Austrian Airlines *Osttirol*
	OE-LBO	Airbus A.320-214	Austrian Airlines *Pyhrn-Eisenwurzen*
	OE-LBP	Airbus A.320-214	Austrian Airlines *Neusiedler See*
	OE-LBQ	Airbus A.320-214	Austrian Airlines *Wienerwald*
	OE-LBR	Airbus A.320-214	Austrian Airlines *Frida Kahle*
	OE-LBS	Airbus A.320-214	Austrian Airlines *Waldviertel*
	OE-LBT	Airbus A.320-214	Austrian Airlines *Worthersee*
	OE-LBU	Airbus A.320-214	Austrian Airlines *Muhlviertel*
	OE-LBV	Airbus A.320-214	Austrian Airlines *Weinviertel*
	OE-LCN	Canadair CRJ200LR	Austrian Arrows *Bremen*
	OE-LCR	Canadair CRJ200LR	Austrian Arrows *Baden*
	OE-LDA	Airbus A.319-112	Austrian Airlines *Sofia*

OVERSEAS AIRLINERS

OE

Reg.	Type	Owner or Operator	Notes
OE-LDB	Airbus A.319-112	Austrian Airlines *Bucharest*	
OE-LDC	Airbus A.319-112	Austrian Airlines *Kiev*	
OE-LDD	Airbus A.319-112	Austrian Airlines *Moscow*	
OE-LDE	Airbus A.319-112	Austrian Airlines *Baku*	
OE-LDF	Airbus A.319-112	Austrian Airlines *Sarajevo*	
OE-LDG	Airbus A.319-112	Austrian Airlines *Tbilisi*	
OE-LEA	Airbus A.320-214	Niki *Rock 'n Roll*	
OE-LEB	Airbus A.320-214	Niki *Polka*	
OE-LEC	Airbus A.320-214	Niki *Flamenco*	
OE-LEE	Airbus A.320-214	Niki *Reggae*	
OE-LEF	Airbus A.320-214	Niki *Sirtaki*	
OE-LEG	Airbus A.320-214	Niki *Bolero*	
OE-LEH	Airbus A.320-214	Niki *Gospel*	
OE-LEO	Airbus A.320-214	Niki *Soul*	
OE-LES	Airbus A.321-211	Niki *Boogie Woogie*	
OE-LET	Airbus A.321-211	Niki *Heavy Metal*	
OE-LEU	Airbus A.320-214	Niki *Cancan*	
OE-LEW	Airbus A.321-211	Niki *Cancan*	
OE-LEX	Airbus A.320-214	Niki *Jazz*	
OE-LEZ	Airbus A.321-211	Niki *Blues*	
OE-LFG	Fokker 70	Austrian Arrows *Innsbruck*	
OE-LFH	Fokker 70	Austrian Arrows *Salzburg*	
OE-LFI	Fokker 70	Austrian Arrows *Klagenfurt*	
OE-LFJ	Fokker 70	Austrian Arrows *Graz*	
OE-LFK	Fokker 70	Austrian Arrows *Wien*	
OE-LFL	Fokker 70	Austrian Arrows *Linz*	
OE-LFP	Fokker 70	Austrian Airlines *Wels*	
OE-LFQ	Fokker 70	Austrian Airlines *Dornbirn*	
OE-LFR	Fokker 70	Austrian Airlines *Steyr*	
OE-LGA	DHC.8Q-402 Dash Eight	Austrian Arrows *Karnten*	
OE-LGB	DHC.8Q-402 Dash Eight	Austrian Arrows *Tirol*	
OE-LGC	DHC.8Q-402 Dash Eight	Austrian Arrows *Salzburg*	
OE-LGD	DHC.8Q-402 Dash Eight	Austrian Arrows *Steiermark*	
OE-LGE	DHC.8Q-402 Dash Eight	Austrian Arrows *Oberosterreich*	
OE-LGF	DHC.8Q-402 Dash Eight	Austrian Arrows *Niederosterreich*	
OE-LGG	DHC.8Q-402 Dash Eight	Austrian Arrows *Budapest*	
OE-LGH	DHC.8Q-402 Dash Eight	Austrian Arrows *Vorarlberg*	
OE-LGI	DHC.8Q-402 Dash Eight	Austrian Arrows *Eisenstadt*	
OE-LGJ	DHC.8Q-402 Dash Eight	Austrian Arrows *St Pölten*	
OE-LGK	DHC.8Q-402 Dash Eight	Austrian Arrows *Burgenland*	
OE-LGL	DHC.8Q-402 Dash Eight	Austrian Arrows *Altenrhein*	
OE-LGM	DHC.8Q-402 Dash Eight	Austrian Arrows *Villach*	
OE-LGN	DHC.8Q-402 Dash Eight	Austrian Arrows *Gmunden*	
OE-LNJ	Boeing 737-8Z9	Austrian Airlines *Falco*	
OE-LNL	Boeing 737-6Z9	Austrian Airlines *Kahlenberg*	
OE-LNM	Boeing 737-6Z9	Austrian Airlines *Albert Einstein*	
OE-LNN	Boeing 737-7Z9	Austrian Airlines *Maria Callas*	
OE-LNO	Boeing 737-7Z9	Austrian Airlines *Greta Garbo*	
OE-LNP	Boeing 737-8Z9	Austrian Airlines *George Harrison*	
OE-LNQ	Boeing 737-8Z9	Austrian Airlines *Gregory Peck*	
OE-LNR	Boeing 737-8Z9	Austrian Airlines *Frank Zappa*	
OE-LNS	Boeing 737-8Z9	Austrian Airlines *Miles Davis*	
OE-LNT	Boeing 737-8Z9	Austrian Airlines *Kurt Cobain*	
OE-LPA	Boeing 777-2Z9	Austrian Airlines *Melbourne*	
OE-LPB	Boeing 777-2Z9	Austrian Airlines *Sydney*	
OE-LPC	Boeing 777-2Z9ER	Austrian Airlines *Donald Bradman*	
OE-LPD	Boeing 777-2Z9ER	Austrian Airlines *America*	
OE-LVA	Fokker 100	Austrian Arrows *Riga*	
OE-LVB	Fokker 100	Austrian Arrows *Vilnius*	
OE-LVC	Fokker 100	Austrian Arrows *Tirana*	
OE-LVD	Fokker 100	Austrian Arrows *Belgrade*	
OE-LVE	Fokker 100	Austrian Arrows *Zagreb*	
OE-LVF	Fokker 100	Austrian Arrows *Yerevan*	
OE-LVG	Fokker 100	Austrian Arrows *Krakow*	
OE-LVH	Fokker 100	Austrian Arrows *Minsk*	
OE-LVI	Fokker 100	Austrian Arrows *Prague*	
OE-LVJ	Fokker 100	Austrian Arrows *Bratislava*	
OE-LVK	Fokker 100	Austrian Arrows *Timisoara*	
OE-LVL	Fokker 100	Austrian Arrows *Odessa*	
OE-LVM	Fokker 100	Austrian Arrows *Krasnodar*	
OE-LVN	Fokker 100	Austrian Arrows *Dnepropetrovsk*	
OE-LVO	Fokker 100	Austrian Arrows *Chisinau*	

Notes	Reg.	Type	Owner or Operator

OH (Finland)

	OH-AFI	Boeing 757-2K2	Air Finland
	OH-AFJ	Boeing 757-2Q8	Air Finland
	OH-AFL	Boeing 757-204	Air Finland
	OH-BLG	Boeing 717-2CM	Blue 1
	OH-BLH	Boeing 717-2CM	Blue 1
	OH-BLI	Boeing 717-2CM	Blue 1
	OH-BLJ	Boeing 717-23S	Blue 1
	OH-BLM	Boeing 717-23S	Blue 1
	OH-BLN	Boeing 717-2K9	Blue 1
	OH-BLO	Boeing 717-2K9	Blue 1
	OH-BLP	Boeing 717-23S	Blue 1
	OH-BLQ	Boeing 717-2K9	Blue 1
	OH-LBO	Boeing 757-2Q8	Finnair
	OH-LBR	Boeing 757-2Q8	Finnair
	OH-LBS	Boeing 757-2Q8	Finnair
	OH-LBT	Boeing 757-2Q8	Finnair
	OH-LEE	Embraer RJ170-100LR	Finnair
	OH-LEF	Embraer RJ170-100LR	Finnair
	OH-LEG	Embraer RJ170-100LR	Finnair
	OH-LEH	Embraer RJ170-100LR	Finnair
	OH-LEI	Embraer RJ170-100STD	Flybe Nordic
	OH-LEK	Embraer RJ170-100STD	Flybe Nordic
	OH-LEL	Embraer RJ170-100LR	Finnair
	OH-LGC	McD Douglas MD-11	Finnair Cargo
	OH-LKE	Embraer RJ190-100LR	Finnair
	OH-LKF	Embraer RJ190-100LR	Finnair
	OH-LKG	Embraer RJ190-100LR	Finnair
	OH-LKH	Embraer RJ190-100LR	Finnair
	OH-LKI	Embraer RJ190-100LR	Finnair
	OH-LKK	Embraer RJ190-100LR	Finnair
	OH-LKL	Embraer RJ190-100LR	Finnair
	OH-LKM	Embraer RJ190-100LR	Finnair
	OH-LKN	Embraer RJ190-100LR	Finnair
	OH-LKO	Embraer RJ190-100LR	Finnair
	OH-LKP	Embraer RJ190-100LR	Finnair
	OH-LKR	Embraer RJ190-100LR	Finnair
	OH-LQA	Airbus A.340-311	Finnair
	OH-LQB	Airbus A.340-313X	Finnair
	OH-LQC	Airbus A.340-313E	Finnair
	OH-LQD	Airbus A.340-313E	Finnair
	OH-LQE	Airbus A.340-313E	Finnair
	OH-LQF	Airbus A.340-313X	Finnair
	OH-LQG	Airbus A.340-313X	Finnair
	OH-LTM	Airbus A.330-302	Finnair
	OH-LTN	Airbus A.330-302	Finnair
	OH-LTO	Airbus A.330-302	Finnair
	OH-LTP	Airbus A.330-302	Finnair
	OH-LTR	Airbus A.330-302	Finnair
	OH-LTS	Airbus A.330-302	Finnair
	OH-LTT	Airbus A.330-302	Finnair
	OH-LTU	Airbus A.330-302	Finnair
	OH-LVA	Airbus A.319-112	Finnair
	OH-LVB	Airbus A.319-112	Finnair
	OH-LVC	Airbus A.319-112	Finnair
	OH-LVD	Airbus A.319-112	Finnair
	OH-LVE	Airbus A.319-112	Finnair
	OH-LVF	Airbus A.319-112	Finnair
	OH-LVG	Airbus A.319-112	Finnair
	OH-LVH	Airbus A.319-112	Finnair
	OH-LVI	Airbus A.319-112	Finnair
	OH-LVK	Airbus A.319-112	Finnair
	OH-LVL	Airbus A.319-112	Finnair
	OH-LXA	Airbus A.320-214	Finnair
	OH-LXB	Airbus A.320-214	Finnair
	OH-LXC	Airbus A.320-214	Finnair
	OH-LXD	Airbus A.320-214	Finnair
	OH-LXE	Airbus A.320-214	Finnair
	OH-LXF	Airbus A.320-214	Finnair
	OH-LXG	Airbus A.320-214	Finnair
	OH-LXH	Airbus A.320-214	Finnair
	OH-LXI	Airbus A.320-214	Finnair

Reg.	Type	Owner or Operator	Notes
OH-LXK	Airbus A.320-214	Finnair	
OH-LXL	Airbus A.320-214	Finnair	
OH-LXM	Airbus A.320-214	Finnair	
OH-LZA	Airbus A.321-211	Finnair	
OH-LZB	Airbus A.321-211	Finnair	
OH-LZC	Airbus A.321-211	Finnair	
OH-LZD	Airbus A.321-211	Finnair	
OH-LZE	Airbus A.321-211	Finnair	
OH-LZF	Airbus A.321-211	Finnair	

OK (Czech Republic)

OK-ASA	Let L410UVP-E	Manx2	
OK-CEC	Airbus A.321-211	CSA Czech Airlines *Nove Mesto nad Metuji*	
OK-CED	Airbus A.321-211	CSA Czech Airlines *Havlikuv Brod*	
OK-DGL	Boeing 737-55S	CSA Czech Airlines *Tabor*	
OK-GEA	Airbus A.320-214	CSA Czech Airlines *Roznovpod Radhostem*	
OK-GEB	Airbus A.320-214	CSA Czech Airlines *Strakonice*	
OK-HCA	Airbus A.320-214	Holidays Czech Airlines	
OK-HCB	Airbus A.320-214	Holidays Czech Airlines	
OK-LEE	Airbus A.320-214	CSA Czech Airlines	
OK-LEF	Airbus A.320-214	CSA Czech Airlines	
OK-LEG	Airbus A.320-214	CSA Czech Airlines	
OK-MEH	Airbus A.320-214	CSA Czech Airlines	
OK-MEI	Airbus A.320-214	CSA Czech Airlines	
OK-MEJ	Airbus A.320-214	CSA Czech Airlines	
OK-MEK	Airbus A.319-112	CSA Czech Airlines	
OK-MEL	Airbus A.319-112	CSA Czech Airlines	
OK-NEM	Airbus A.319-112	CSA Czech Airlines	
OK-NEN	Airbus A.319-112	CSA Czech Airlines	
OK-NEO	Airbus A.319-112	CSA Czech Airlines	
OK-NEP	Airbus A.319-112	CSA Czech Airlines	
OK-OER	Airbus A.319-112	CSA Czech Airlines	
OK-PET	Airbus A.319-112	CSA Czech Airlines	
OK-RDA	Let L410UVP-E9	Manx2	
OK-REQ	Airbus A.319-112	CSA Czech Airlines	
OK-SWV	Boeing 737-522	Smart Wings	
OK-TCA	Let L410UVP-E	Manx2	
OK-TVB	Boeing 737-8CX	Travel Service Airlines	
OK-TVD	Boeing 737-86N	Travel Service Airlines	
OK-TVL	Boeing 737-8FN	Travel Service Airlines	
OK-TVM	Boeing 737-8FN	Travel Service Airlines	
OK-TVN	Boeing 737-8BK	Travel Service Airlines	
OK-TVO	Boeing 737-8CX	Travel Service Airlines	
OK-TVP	Boeing 737-8K5	Travel Service Airlines	
OK-TVS	Boeing 737-86N	Travel Service Airlines	
OK-TVT	Boeing 737-86N	Travel Service Airlines	
OK-TVU	Boeing 737-86N	Travel Service Airlines	
OK-TVV	Boeing 737-86N	Travel Service Airlines	
OK-UBA	Let 410UVP-E	Manx2	
OK-WGX	Boeing 737-436	Holidays Czech Airlines	
OK-WGY	Boeing 737-436	Holidays Czech Airlines	
OK-XGB	Boeing 737-55S	CSA Czech Airlines *Olomouc*	
OK-XGC	Boeing 737-55S	CSA Czech Airlines *Ceske Budejovice*	
OK-XGD	Boeing 737-55S	CSA Czech Airlines *Poprad*	
OK-XGE	Boeing 737-55S	CSA Czech Airlines *Kosice*	

OM (Slovakia)

OM-AEX	Boeing 737-4YO	AirExplore	
OM-BEX	Boeing 737-382	AirExplore	
OM-BTS	Boeing 737-55S	Slovakian Airlines	
OM-SAA	Boeing 737-476	Samair	
OM-TVA	Boeing 737-86N	Travel Service Airlines	
OM-TVR	Boeing 737-86N	Travel Service Airlines	

OO (Belgium)

OO-DJP	Avro RJ85	Brussels Airlines	
OO-DJQ	Avro RJ85	Brussels Airlines	
OO-DJR	Avro RJ85	Brussels Airlines	

Notes	Reg.	Type	Owner or Operator
	OO-DJS	Avro RJ85	Brussels Airlines
	OO-DJT	Avro RJ85	Brussels Airlines
	OO-DJV	Avro RJ85	Brussels Airlines
	OO-DJW	Avro RJ85	Brussels Airlines
	OO-DJX	Avro RJ85	Brussels Airlines
	OO-DJY	Avro RJ85	Brussels Airlines
	OO-DJZ	Avro RJ85	Brussels Airlines
	OO-DWA	Avro RJ100	Brussels Airlines
	OO-DWB	Avro RJ100	Brussels Airlines
	OO-DWC	Avro RJ100	Brussels Airlines
	OO-DWD	Avro RJ100	Brussels Airlines
	OO-DWE	Avro RJ100	Brussels Airlines
	OO-DWF	Avro RJ100	Brussels Airlines
	OO-DWG	Avro RJ100	Brussels Airlines
	OO-DWH	Avro RJ100	Brussels Airlines
	OO-DWI	Avro RJ100	Brussels Airlines
	OO-DWJ	Avro RJ100	Brussels Airlines
	OO-DWK	Avro RJ100	Brussels Airlines
	OO-DWL	Avro RJ100	Brussels Airlines
	OO-JAA	Boeing 737-8BK	Jetairfly/TUI Airlines Belgium
	OO-JAD	Boeing 737-8K5	Jetairfly/TUI Airlines Belgium
	OO-JAF	Boeing 737-8K5	Jetairfly/TUI Airlines Belgium
	OO-JAH	Boeing 737-8K5	Jetairfly/TUI Airlines Belgium *Perspective*
	OO-JAM	Boeing 737-46J	Jetairfly/TUI Airlines Belgium
	OO-JAN	Boeing 737-76N	Jetairfly/TUI Airlines Belgium
	OO-JAO	Boeing 737-7K5	Jetairfly/TUI Airlines Belgium
	OO-JAP	Boeing 767-38EER	Jetairfly/TUI Airlines Belgium
	OO-JAQ	Boeing 737-8K5	Jetairfly/TUI Airlines Belgium *Vision*
	OO-JAR	Boeing 737-7K5	Jetairfly/TUI Airlines Belgium
	OO-JAS	Boeing 737-7K5	Jetairfly/TUI Airlines Belgium
	OO-JAT	Boeing 737-5K5	Jetairfly/TUI Airlines Belgium
	OO-JAX	Boeing 737-8K5	Jetairfly/TUI Airlines Belgium
	OO-JBG	Boeing 737-8K5	Jetairfly/TUI Airlines Belgium *Gerard Brack*
	OO-LTM	Boeing 737-3M8	Brussels Airlines
	OO-SFM	Airbus A.330-301	Brussels Airlines
	OO-SFN	Airbus A.330-301	Brussels Airlines
	OO-SFO	Airbus A.330-301	Brussels Airlines
	OO-SFV	Airbus A.330-322	Brussels Airlines
	OO-SFW	Airbus A.330-322	Brussels Airlines
	OO-SFY	Airbus A.330-223	Brussels Airlines
	OO-SFZ	Airbus A.330-223	Brussels Airlines
	OO-SNA	Airbus A.320-214	Brussels Airlines
	OO-SNB	Airbus A.320-214	Brussels Airlines
	OO-SSC	Airbus A.319-112	Brussels Airlines
	OO-SSD	Airbus A.319-112	Brussels Airlines
	OO-SSG	Airbus A.319-112	Brussels Airlines
	OO-SSK	Airbus A.319-112	Brussels Airlines
	OO-SSM	Airbus A.319-112	Brussels Airlines
	OO-SSP	Airbus A.319-112	Brussels Airlines
	OO-SSQ	Airbus A.319-112	Brussels Airlines
	OO-SSR	Airbus A.319-112	Brussels Airlines
	OO-SSU	Airbus A.319-111	Brussels Airlines
	OO-SSV	Airbus A.319-111	Brussels Airlines
	OO-TAD	BAe 146-300QT	TNT Airways
	OO-TAE	BAe 146-300QT	TNT Airways
	OO-TAF	BAe 146-300QT	TNT Airways
	OO-TAH	BAe 146-300QT	TNT Airways
	OO-TAJ	BAe 146-300QT	TNT Airways
	OO-TAR	BAe 146-200QT	TNT Airways
	OO-TAS	BAe 146-300QT	TNT Airways
	OO-TAU	BAe 146-200QT	TNT Airways
	OO-TAW	BAe 146-200QT	TNT Airways
	OO-TAY	BAe 146-200QT	TNT Airways
	OO-TAZ	BAe 146-200QC	TNT Airways
	OO-TCH	Airbus A.320-214	Thomas Cook Airlines Belgium *experience*
	OO-TCI	Airbus A.320-214	Thomas Cook Airlines Belgium *relax*
	OO-TCJ	Airbus A.320-214	Thomas Cook Airlines Belgium *inspire*
	OO-TCN	Airbus A.320-212	Thomas Cook Airlines Belgium *dream*
	OO-TCP	Airbus A.320-214	Thomas Cook Airlines Belgium *desire*
	OO-TFA	Boeing 757-28A	TNT Airways
	OO-THA	Boeing 747-4HAERF	TNT Airways
	OO-THB	Boeing 747-4HAERF	TNT Airways
	OO-THC	Boeing 747-4HAERF	TNT Airways/Emirates Airlines
	OO-THD	Boeing 747-4HAERF	TNT Airways/Emirates Airlines

Reg.	Type	Owner or Operator	Notes
OO-TNA	Boeing 737-3T0F	TNT Airways	
OO-TNB	Boeing 737-3T0F	TNT Airways	
OO-TNC	Boeing 737-3T0F	TNT Airways	
OO-TNE	Boeing 737-3Q8	TNT Airways	
OO-TNG	Boeing 737-3Y0QC	TNT Airways	
OO-TNH	Boeing 737-301F	TNT Airways	
OO-TNL	Boeing 737-34SF	TNT Airways	
OO-TNM	Boeing 737-34SF	TNT Airways	
OO-TNN	Boeing 737-45D	TNT Airways	
OO-TNO	Boeing 737-49RF	TNT Airways	
OO-TNP	Boeing 737-45D	TNT Airways	
OO-TNR	Boeing 737-4MOF	TNT Airways	
OO-TNQ	Boeing 737-4MOF	TNT Airways	
OO-TSA	Boeing 777-FHT	TNT Airways	
OO-TSB	Boeing 777-FHT	TNT Airways	
OO-TSC	Boeing 777-FHT	TNT Airways	
OO-TUC	Boeing 767-341ER	Jetairfly/TUI Airlines Belgium *Discover*	
OO-VAC	Boeing 737-8BK	Jetairfly/TUI Airlines Belgium *Rising Sun*	
OO-VEG	Boeing 737-36N	Brussels Airlines	
OO-VEH	Boeing 737-36N	Brussels Airlines	
OO-VEK	Boeing 737-405	Brussels Airlines	
OO-VEN	Boeing 737-36N	Brussels Airlines	
OO-VEP	Boeing 737-43Q	Brussels Airlines	
OO-VES	Boeing 737-43Q	Brussels Airlines	
OO-VET	Boeing 737-4Q8	Brussels Airlines	
OO-VLF	Fokker 50	Cityjet	
OO-VLI	Fokker 50	Cityjet	
OO-VLJ	Fokker 50	Cityjet	
OO-VLL	Fokker 50	Cityjet	
OO-VLM	Fokker 50	Cityjet	
OO-VLN	Fokker 50	Cityjet	
OO-VLO	Fokker 50	Cityjet	
OO-VLP	Fokker 50	Cityjet	
OO-VLQ	Fokker 50	Cityjet	
OO-VLR	Fokker 50	Cityjet	
OO-VLS	Fokker 50	Cityjet	
OO-VLV	Fokker 50	Cityjet	
OO-VLY	Fokker 50	Cityjet	
OO-VLZ	Fokker 50	Cityjet	

OY (Denmark)

OY-BJP	Swearingen SA.227AC Metro III	Benair	
OY-JRU	McD Douglas MD-87	Danish Air Transport	
OY-JTA	Boeing 737-33A	Jet Time	
OY-JTB	Boeing 737-3Y0	Jet Time	
OY-JTC	Boeing 737-3L9	Jet Time	
OY-JTD	Boeing 737-3Y0	Jet Time	
OY-JTE	Boeing 737-3L9	Jet Time	
OY-JTF	Boeing 737-382	Jet Time	
OY-JTY	Boeing 737-7Q8	Jet Time	
OY-JTZ	Boeing 737-73S	Jet Time	
OY-KBA	Airbus A.340-313X	SAS *Adalstein Viking*	
OY-KBB	Airbus A.321-231	SAS *Hjorulf Viking*	
OY-KBC	Airbus A.340-313X	SAS *Fredis Viking*	
OY-KBD	Airbus A.340-313X	SAS *Toste Viking*	
OY-KBE	Airbus A.321-231	SAS *Emma Viking*	
OY-KBF	Airbus A.321-231	SAS *Skapti Viking*	
OY-KBH	Airbus A.321-231	SAS *Sulke Viking*	
OY-KBI	Airbus A.340-313X	SAS *Rurik Viking*	
OY-KBK	Airbus A.321-231	SAS *Arne Viking*	
OY-KBL	Airbus A.321-231	SAS *Gynnbjorn Viking*	
OY-KBM	Airbus A.340-313X	HiFly	
OY-KBN	Airbus A.330-343X	SAS *Eystein Viking*	
OY-KBO	Airbus A.319-131	SAS *Christian Valdemar Viking*	
OY-KBP	Airbus A.319-131	SAS *Viger Viking*	
OY-KBR	Airbus A.319-132	SAS *Finnboge Viking*	
OY-KBT	Airbus A.319-131	SAS *Ragnvald Viking*	
OY-KFA	Canadair CRJ900ER	SAS *Johan Viking*	
OY-KFB	Canadair CRJ900ER	SAS *Alfhild Viking*	
OY-KFC	Canadair CRJ900ER	SAS *Bertil Viking*	
OY-KFD	Canadair CRJ900ER	SAS *Estrid Viking*	
OY-KFE	Canadair CRJ900ER	SAS *Ingemar Viking*	

Notes	Reg.	Type	Owner or Operator
	OY-KFF	Canadair CRJ900ER	SAS *Karl Viking*
	OY-KFG	Canadair CRJ900ER	SAS *Maria Viking*
	OY-KFH	Canadair CRJ900ER	SAS *Ella Viking*
	OY-KFI	Canadair CRJ900ER	SAS *Rolf Viking*
	OY-KFK	Canadair CRJ900ER	SAS *Hardeknud Viking*
	OY-KFL	Canadair CRJ900ER	SAS *Regin Viking*
	OY-KGT	McD Douglas MD-82	SAS *Hake Viking*
	OY-KHE	McD Douglas MD-82	SAS *Saxo Viking*
	OY-KHG	McD Douglas MD-82	SAS *Alle Viking*
	OY-KHM	McD Douglas MD-82	SAS *Mette Viking*
	OY-KHN	McD Douglas MD-82	SAS *Dan Viking*
	OY-KHP	McD Douglas MD-81	SAS *Harild Viking*
	OY-KHU	McD Douglas MD-87	SAS *Ravn Viking*
	OY-KKS	Boeing 737-683	SAS *Ramveig Viking*
	OY-MBT	Canadair CRJ200LR	Cimber Sterling/SAS
	OY-MRE	Boeing 737-7L9	Cimber Sterling
	OY-MRF	Boeing 737-7L9	Cimber Sterling
	OY-MRG	Boeing 737-7L9	Cimber Sterling
	OY-MRH	Boeing 737-7L9	Cimber Sterling
	OY-MRS	Boeing 737-76N	Cimber Sterling
	OY-MRU	Boeing 737-7L9	Cimber Sterling
	OY-NCA	Dornier 328-100	Sun-Air/British Airways
	OY-NCL	Dornier 328-300 JET	Sun-Air/British Airways
	OY-NCM	Dornier 328-300 JET	Sun-Air/British Airways
	OY-NCN	Dornier 328-300 JET	Sun-Air/British Airways
	OY-NCO	Dornier 328-300 JET	Sun-Air
	OY-NCP	Dornier 328-300 JET	Sun-Air/British Airways
	OY-NCS	Dornier 328-100	Sun-Air/British Airways
	OY-NCT	Dornier 328-300 JET	Sun-Air
	OY-PBH	Let L410UVP-E20	Benair
	OY-PBI	Let L410UVP-E20	Benair
	OY-PSA	Boeing 737-8Q8	Primera Air Scandinavia
	OY-PSB	Boeing 737-8Q8	Primera Air Scandinavia
	OY-PSC	Boeing 737-86N	Primera Air Scandinavia
	OY-PSD	Boeing 737-86N	Primera Air Scandinavia
	OY-PSE	Boeing 737-809	Primera Air Scandinavia
	OY-PSF	Boeing 737-7Q8	Primera Air Scandinavia
	OY-RCC	Avro RJ100	Atlantic Airways
	OY-RCD	Avro RJ85	Atlantic Airways
	OY-RCE	Avro RJ85	Atlantic Airways
	OY-RCW	BAe 146-200	Atlantic Airways
	OY-RJA	Canadair CRJ200LR	Cimber Sterling
	OY-RJB	Canadair CRJ200LR	Cimber Sterling/SAS
	OY-RJC	Canadair CRJ200LR	Cimber Sterling/SAS
	OY-RJD	Canadair CRJ200LR	Cimber Sterling
	OY-RJF	Canadair CRJ200LR	Cimber Sterling
	OY-RJG	Canadair CRJ200LR	Cimber Sterling
	OY-RJH	Canadair CRJ200LR	Cimber Sterling
	OY-RJI	Canadair CRJ200LR	Cimber Sterling/SAS
	OY-RJJ	Canadair CRJ200LR	Cimber Sterling
	OY-RUE	McD Douglas MD-83	Danish Air Transport
	OY-SRF	Boeing 767-219 (SF)	Star Air
	OY-SRG	Boeing 767-219 (SF)	Star Air
	OY-SRH	Boeing 767-204 (SF)	Star Air
	OY-SRI	Boeing 767-25E (SF)	Star Air
	OY-SRJ	Boeing 767-25E (SF)	Star Air
	OY-SRK	Boeing 767-204 (SF)	Star Air
	OY-SRL	Boeing 767-232 (SF)	Star Air
	OY-SRM	Boeing 767-25E (SF)	Star Air
	OY-SRN	Boeing 767-219 (SF)	Star Air
	OY-SRO	Boeing 767-25E (SF)	Star Air
	OY-SRP	Boeing 767-232 (SF)	Star Air
	OY-VKA	Airbus A.321-211	Thomas Cook Airlines
	OY-VKB	Airbus A.321-211	Thomas Cook Airlines
	OY-VKC	Airbus A.321-211	Thomas Cook Airlines
	OY-VKD	Airbus A.321-211	Thomas Cook Airlines
	OY-VKE	Airbus A.321-211	Thomas Cook Airlines
	OY-VKF	Airbus A.330-243	Thomas Cook Airlines
	OY-VKG	Airbus A.330-343X	Thomas Cook Airlines
	OY-VKH	Airbus A.330-343X	Thomas Cook Airlines
	OY-VKI	Airbus A.330-343X	Thomas Cook Airlines
	OY-VKM	Airbus A.320-214	Thomas Cook Airlines
	OY-VKS	Airbus A.320-214	Thomas Cook Airlines
	OY-VKT	Airbus A.321-211	Thomas Cook Airlines

Reg.	Type	Owner or Operator	Notes

P4 (Aruba)

P4-EAS	Boeing 757-2G5	Air Astana	
P4-FAS	Boeing 757-2G5	Air Astana	
P4-GAS	Boeing 757-2G5	Air Astana	
P4-KCA	Boeing 767-306ER	Air Astana	
P4-KCB	Boeing 767-306ER	Air Astana	
P4-KCU	Boeing 757-23N	Air Astana	
P4-MAS	Boeing 757-28A	Air Astana	

PH (Netherlands)

PH-AHQ	Boeing 767-383ER	TUI Airlines Nederland/Arkefly	
PH-AHX	Boeing 767-383ER	TUI Airlines Nederland/Arkefly	
PH-AKA	Airbus A.330-303	KLM	
PH-AKB	Airbus A.330-303	KLM	
PH-AKD	Airbus A.330-303	KLM	
PH-AOA	Airbus A.330-203	KLM *Dam – Amsterdam*	
PH-AOB	Airbus A.330-203	KLM *Potsdamer Platz – Berlin*	
PH-AOC	Airbus A.330-203	KLM *Place de la Concorde – Paris*	
PH-AOD	Airbus A.330-203	KLM *Plazza del Duomo – Milano*	
PH-AOE	Airbus A.330-203	KLM *Parliament Square – Edinburgh*	
PH-AOF	Airbus A.330-203	KLM *Federation Square – Melbourne*	
PH-AOH	Airbus A.330-203	KLM *Senaatintori/Senate Square-Helsinki*	
PH-AOI	Airbus A.330-203	KLM *Plaza de la Independencia-Madrid*	
PH-AOK	Airbus A.330-203	KLM *Radhuspladsen-Kobenhavn*	
PH-AOL	Airbus A.330-203	KLM *Picadilly Circus – London*	
PH-BCA	Boeing 737-8K2	KLM *Flamingo*	
PH-BCB	Boeing 737-8BK	KLM *Grote Pijlstormvogel/Great Shearwater*	
PH-BCC	Boeing 737-8BK	KLM	
PH-BCD	Boeing 737-8BK	KLM	
PH-BCE	Boeing 737-8BK	KLM	
PH-BCG	Boeing 737-8BK	KLM	
PH-BFA	Boeing 747-406	KLM *City of Atlanta*	
PH-BFB	Boeing 747-406	KLM *City of Bangkok*	
PH-BFC	Boeing 747-406 (SCD)	KLM *City of Calgary*	
PH-BFD	Boeing 747-406 (SCD)	KLM *City of Dubai*	
PH-BFE	Boeing 747-406 (SCD)	KLM *City of Melbourne*	
PH-BFF	Boeing 747-406 (SCD)	KLM *City of Freetown*	
PH-BFG	Boeing 747-406	KLM *City of Guayaquil*	
PH-BFH	Boeing 747-406 (SCD)	KLM *City of Hong Kong*	
PH-BFI	Boeing 747-406 (SCD)	KLM *City of Jakarta*	
PH-BFK	Boeing 747-406 (SCD)	KLM *City of Karachi*	
PH-BFL	Boeing 747-406	KLM *City of Lima*	
PH-BFM	Boeing 747-406 (SCD)	KLM *City of Mexico*	
PH-BFN	Boeing 747-406	KLM *City of Nairobi*	
PH-BFO	Boeing 747-406 (SCD)	KLM *City of Orlando*	
PH-BFP	Boeing 747-406 (SCD)	KLM *City of Paramaribo*	
PH-BFR	Boeing 747-406 (SCD)	KLM *City of Rio de Janeiro*	
PH-BFS	Boeing 747-406 (SCD)	KLM *City of Seoul*	
PH-BFT	Boeing 747-406 (SCD)	KLM *City of Tokyo*	
PH-BFU	Boeing 747-406 (SCD)	KLM *City of Beijing*	
PH-BFV	Boeing 747-406	KLM *City of Vancouver*	
PH-BFW	Boeing 747-406	KLM *City of Shanghai*	
PH-BFY	Boeing 747-406	KLM *City of Johannesburg*	
PH-BGA	Boeing 737-8K2	KLM *Tureluur/Redshank*	
PH-BGB	Boeing 737-8K2	KLM *Whimbrel/Regenwulg*	
PH-BGC	Boeing 737-8K2	KLM *Pijlstaart/Pintail*	
PH-BGD	Boeing 737-706	KLM *Goldcrest/Goadhaantje*	
PH-BGE	Boeing 737-706	KLM *Ortolan Bunting/Ortolaan*	
PH-BGF	Boeing 737-7K2	KLM *Great White Heron/Grote Ziverreiger*	
PH-BGG	Boeing 737-706	KLM *King Eider/Koening Seider*	
PH-BGH	Boeing 737-7K2	KLM *Grutto/Godwit*	
PH-BGI	Boeing 737-7K2	KLM *Vink/Finch*	
PH-BGK	Boeing 737-7K2	KLM *Noordse Stormvogel/Fulmar*	
PH-BGL	Boeing 737-7K2	KLM *Rietzangler/Warbler*	
PH-BGM	Boeing 737-7K2	KLM *Aabscholver/Cormorant*	
PH-BGN	Boeing 737-7K2	KLM *Jan van Gent/Gannet*	
PH-BGO	Boeing 737-7K2	KLM *Paradijsvogel/Bird of Paradise*	
PH-BGP	Boeing 737-7K2	KLM *Pelikaan/Pelican*	
PH-BGQ	Boeing 737-7K2	KLM *Wielewaal/Golden Oriole*	
PH-BGR	Boeing 737-7K2	KLM *Zwarte Wouw/Black Kite*	

Notes	Reg.	Type	Owner or Operator
	PH-BGT	Boeing 737-7K2	KLM *Zanglijster/Song Thrush*
	PH-BGU	Boeing 737-7K2	KLM *Koekoek/Cuckoo*
	PH-BGW	Boeing 737-7K2	KLM
	PH-BGX	Boeing 737-7K2	KLM *Scholekster/Oystercatcher*
	PH-BQA	Boeing 777-206ER	KLM *Albert Plesman*
	PH-BQB	Boeing 777-206ER	KLM *Borobudur*
	PH-BQC	Boeing 777-206ER	KLM *Chichen-Itza*
	PH-BQD	Boeing 777-206ER	KLM *Darjeeling Highway*
	PH-BQE	Boeing 777-206ER	KLM *Epidaurus*
	PH-BQF	Boeing 777-206ER	KLM *Ferrara City*
	PH-BQG	Boeing 777-206ER	KLM *Galapagos Islands*
	PH-BQH	Boeing 777-206ER	KLM *Hadrian's Wall*
	PH-BQI	Boeing 777-206ER	KLM *Iguazu Falls*
	PH-BQK	Boeing 777-206ER	KLM *Mount Kilimanjaro*
	PH-BQL	Boeing 777-206ER	KLM *Litomysl Castle*
	PH-BQM	Boeing 777-206ER	KLM *Macchu Picchu*
	PH-BQN	Boeing 777-206ER	KLM *Nahanni National Park*
	PH-BQO	Boeing 777-206ER	KLM *Old Rauma*
	PH-BQP	Boeing 777-206ER	KLM *Pont du Gard*
	PH-BVA	Boeing 777-306ER	KLM *National Park De Hoge Veluwe*
	PH-BVB	Boeing 777-306ER	KLM *Fulufjallet National Park*
	PH-BVC	Boeing 777-306ER	KLM *National ParkSian Ka'an*
	PH-BVD	Boeing 777-306ER	KLM *Amboseli National Park*
	PH-BVF	Boeing 777-306ER	KLM *Yakushima*
	PH-BVG	Boeing 777-306ER	KLM
	PH-BVI	Boeing 777-306ER	KLM
	PH-BVK	Boeing 777-306ER	KLM
	PH-BXA	Boeing 737-8K2	KLM *Zwaan/Swan*
	PH-BXB	Boeing 737-8K2	KLM *Valk/Falcon*
	PH-BXC	Boeing 737-8K2	KLM *Korhoen/Grouse*
	PH-BXD	Boeing 737-8K2	KLM *Arend/Eagle*
	PH-BXE	Boeing 737-8K2	KLM *Harvik/Hawk*
	PH-BXF	Boeing 737-8K2	KLM *Zwallou/Swallow*
	PH-BXG	Boeing 737-8K2	KLM *Kraanvogel/Crane*
	PH-BXH	Boeing 737-8K2	KLM *Gans/Goose*
	PH-BXI	Boeing 737-8K2	KLM *Zilvermeeuw*
	PH-BXK	Boeing 737-8K2	KLM *Gierzwallou/Swift*
	PH-BXL	Boeing 737-8K2	KLM *Sperwer/Sparrow*
	PH-BXM	Boeing 737-8K2	KLM *Kluut/Avocet*
	PH-BXN	Boeing 737-8K2	KLM *Merel/Blackbird*
	PH-BXO	Boeing 737-9K2	KLM *Plevier/Plover*
	PH-BXP	Boeing 737-9K2	KLM *Meerkoet/Crested Coot*
	PH-BXR	Boeing 737-9K2	KLM *Nachtegaal/Nightingale*
	PH-BXS	Boeing 737-9K2	KLM *Buizerd/Buzzard*
	PH-BXT	Boeing 737-9K2	KLM *Zeestern/Sea Tern*
	PH-BXU	Boeing 737-8BK	KLM *Albatros/Albatross*
	PH-BXV	Boeing 737-8K2	KLM *Roodborstje*
	PH-BXW	Boeing 737-8K2	KLM *Patrijs/Partridge*
	PH-BXY	Boeing 737-8K2	KLM *Fuut/Grebe*
	PH-BXZ	Boeing 737-8K2	KLM *Uil/Owl*
	PH-CKA	Boeing 747-406ERF	KLM Cargo/Martinair *Eendracht*
	PH-CKB	Boeing 747-406ERF	KLM Cargo/Martinair *Leeuwin*
	PH-CKC	Boeing 747-406ERF	KLM Cargo/Martinair *Oranje*
	PH-CKD	Boeing 747-406F	KLM Cargo/Martinair *Wapen van Amsterdam*
	PH-EZA	Embraer ERJ190-100STD	KLM CityHopper
	PH-EZB	Embraer ERJ190-100STD	KLM CityHopper
	PH-EZC	Embraer ERJ190-100STD	KLM CityHopper
	PH-EZD	Embraer ERJ190-100STD	KLM CityHopper
	PH-EZE	Embraer ERJ190-100STD	KLM CityHopper
	PH-EZF	Embraer ERJ190-100STD	KLM CityHopper
	PH-EZG	Embraer ERJ190-100STD	KLM Cityhopper
	PH-EZH	Embraer ERJ190-100STD	KLM Cityhopper
	PH-EZI	Embraer ERJ190-100STD	KLM Cityhopper
	PH-EZK	Embraer ERJ190-100STD	KLM Cityhopper
	PH-EZL	Embraer ERJ190-100STD	KLM Cityhopper
	PH-EZM	Embraer ERJ190-100STD	KLM CityHopper
	PH-EZN	Embraer ERJ190-100STD	KLM CityHopper
	PH-EZO	Embraer ERJ190-100STD	KLM CityHopper
	PH-EZP	Embraer ERJ190-100STD	KLM CityHopper
	PH-EZR	Embraer ERJ190-100STD	KLM CityHopper
	PH-EZS	Embraer ERJ190-100STD	KLM CityHopper
	PH-HSA	Boeing 737-8K2	Transavia
	PH-HSB	Boeing 737-8K2	Transavia
	PH-HSC	Boeing 737-8K2	Transavia

OVERSEAS AIRLINERS

PH

Reg.	Type	Owner or Operator	Notes
PH-HSD	Boeing 737-8K2	Transavia	
PH-HSE	Boeing 737-8K2	Transavia	
PH-HSW	Boeing 737-8K2	Transavia	
PH-HZD	Boeing 737-8K2	Transavia	
PH-HZE	Boeing 737-8K2	Transavia	
PH-HZF	Boeing 737-8K2	Transavia	
PH-HZG	Boeing 737-8K2	Transavia	
PH-HZI	Boeing 737-8K2	Transavia	
PH-HZJ	Boeing 737-8K2	Transavia	
PH-HZK	Boeing 737-8K2	Transavia	
PH-HZN	Boeing 737-8K2	Transavia	
PH-HZO	Boeing 737-8K2	Transavia	
PH-HZV	Boeing 737-8K2	Transavia	
PH-HZW	Boeing 737-8K2	Transavia	
PH-HZX	Boeing 737-8K2	Transavia	
PH-JCH	Fokker 70	KLM CityHopper	
PH-JCT	Fokker 70	KLM CityHopper	
PH-KCA	McD Douglas MD-11	KLM Amy Johnson	
PH-KCB	McD Douglas MD-11	KLM Maria Montessori	
PH-KCC	McD Douglas MD-11	KLM Marie Curie	
PH-KCD	McD Douglas MD-11	KLM Florence Nightingale	
PH-KCE	McD Douglas MD-11	KLM Audrey Hepburn	
PH-KCF	McD Douglas MD-11	KLM Annie Romein	
PH-KCG	McD Douglas MD-11	KLM Maria Callas	
PH-KCH	McD Douglas MD-11	KLM Anna Pavlova	
PH-KCI	McD Douglas MD-11	KLM Ingrid Bergman	
PH-KCK	McD Douglas MD-11	KLM Marie Servaes	
PH-KZA	Fokker 70	KLM CityHopper	
PH-KZB	Fokker 70	KLM CityHopper	
PH-KZC	Fokker 70	KLM CityHopper	
PH-KZD	Fokker 70	KLM CityHopper	
PH-KZE	Fokker 70	KLM CityHopper	
PH-KZF	Fokker 70	KLM CityHopper	
PH-KZG	Fokker 70	KLM CityHopper	
PH-KZH	Fokker 70	KLM CityHopper	
PH-KZI	Fokker 70	KLM CityHopper	
PH-KZK	Fokker 70	KLM CityHopper	
PH-KZL	Fokker 70	KLM CityHopper	
PH-KZM	Fokker 70	KLM CityHopper	
PH-KZN	Fokker 70	KLM CityHopper	
PH-KZO	Fokker 70	KLM CityHopper	
PH-KZP	Fokker 70	KLM CityHopper	
PH-KZR	Fokker 70	KLM CityHopper	
PH-KZS	Fokker 70	KLM CityHopper	
PH-KZT	Fokker 70	KLM CityHopper	
PH-KZU	Fokker 70	KLM CityHopper	
PH-KZV	Fokker 70	KLM Cityhopper	
PH-KZW	Fokker 70	KLM CityHopper	
PH-MCP	McD Douglas MD-11CF	Martinair Cargo	
PH-MCR	McD Douglas MD-11CF	Martinair Cargo	
PH-MCS	McD Douglas MD-11CF	Martinair Cargo	
PH-MCT	McD Douglas MD-11CF	Martinair Cargo	
PH-MCU	McD Douglas MD-11F	Martinair Cargo	
PH-MCW	McD Douglas MD-11CF	Martinair Cargo	
PH-MCY	McD Douglas MD-11F	Martinair Cargo	
PH-MPR	Boeing 747-412BCF	Martinair Cargo	
PH-MPS	Boeing 747-412BCF	Martinair Cargo	
PH-OFL	Fokker 100	KLM CityHopper	
PH-OFM	Fokker 100	KLM CityHopper	
PH-OFN	Fokker 100	KLM CityHopper	
PH-OFO	Fokker 100	KLM CityHopper	
PH-OFP	Fokker 100	KLM CityHopper	
PH-OYE	Boeing 767-304ER	TUI Airlines Nederland/Arkefly	
PH-OYI	Boeing 767-304ER	TUI Airlines Nederland/Arkefly	
PH-OYJ	Boeing 767-304ER	TUI Airlines Nederland/Arkefly	
PH-TFA	Boeing 737-8FH	TUI Airlines Nederland/Arkefly	
PH-TFB	Boeing 737-8K5	TUI Airlines Nederland/Arkefly	
PH-TFC	Boeing 737-8K5	TUI Airlines Nederland/Arkefly	
PH-TFD	Boeing 737-86N	TUI Airlines Nederland/Arkefly	
PH-TFF	Boeing 737-86N	TUI Airlines Nederland/Arkefly	
PH-WXA	Fokker 70	KLM CityHopper	
PH-WXC	Fokker 70	KLM CityHopper	
PH-WXD	Fokker 70	KLM CityHopper	
PH-XRA	Boeing 737-7K2	Transavia Leontien van Moorsel	

Notes	Reg.	Type	Owner or Operator
	PH-XRB	Boeing 737-7K2	Transavia
	PH-XRC	Boeing 737-7K2	Transavia
	PH-XRD	Boeing 737-7K2	Transavia
	PH-XRE	Boeing 737-7K2	Transavia
	PH-XRV	Boeing 737-7K2	Transavia
	PH-XRW	Boeing 737-7K2	Transavia
	PH-XRX	Boeing 737-7K2	Transavia
	PH-XRY	Boeing 737-7K2	Transavia
	PH-XRZ	Boeing 737-7K2	Transavia

PP/PR/PT (Brazil)

	Reg.	Type	Owner or Operator
	PT-MUA	Boeing 777-32WER	TAM Linhas Aereas
	PT-MUB	Boeing 777-32WER	TAM Linhas Aereas
	PT-MUC	Boeing 777-32WER	TAM Linhas Aereas
	PT-MUD	Boeing 777-32WER	TAM Linhas Aereas
	PT-MVA	Airbus A.330-223	TAM Linhas Aereas
	PT-MVB	Airbus A.330-223	TAM Linhas Aereas
	PT-MVC	Airbus A.330-223	TAM Linhas Aereas
	PT-MVD	Airbus A.330-223	TAM Linhas Aereas
	PT-MVE	Airbus A.330-223	TAM Linhas Aereas
	PT-MVF	Airbus A.330-203	TAM Linhas Aereas
	PT-MVG	Airbus A.330-203	TAM Linhas Aereas
	PT-MVH	Airbus A.330-203	TAM Linhas Aereas
	PT-MVK	Airbus A.330-203	TAM Linhas Aereas
	PT-MVL	Airbus A.330-203	TAM Linhas Aereas
	PT-MVM	Airbus A.330-223	TAM Linhas Aereas
	PT-MVN	Airbus A.330-223	TAM Linhas Aereas
	PT-MVO	Airbus A.330-223	TAM Linhas Aereas
	PT-MVP	Airbus A.330-223	TAM Linhas Aereas
	PT-MVQ	Airbus A.330-223	TAM Linhas Aereas
	PT-MVR	Airbus A.330-223	TAM Linhas Aereas
	PT-MVS	Airbus A.330-223	TAM Linhas Aereas
	PT-MVT	Airbus A.330-223	TAM Linhas Aereas
	PT-MVU	Airbus A.330-223	TAM Linhas Aereas
	PT-MVV	Airbus A.330-223	TAM Linhas Aereas

RA (Russia)

	Reg.	Type	Owner or Operator
	RA-61701	Antonov An-148-100B	Rossiya
	RA-61702	Antonov An-148-100B	Rossiya
	RA-61703	Antonov An-148-100B	Rossiya
	RA-61704	Antonov An-148-100B	Rossiya
	RA-61705	Antonov An-148-100B	Rossiya
	RA-61706	Antonov An-148-100B	Rossiya
	RA-82010	An-124	Polet
	RA-82042	An-124	Volga-Dnepr
	RA-82043	An-124	Volga-Dnepr
	RA-82044	An-124	Volga-Dnepr
	RA-82045	An-124	Volga-Dnepr
	RA-82046	An-124	Volga-Dnepr
	RA-82047	An-124	Volga-Dnepr
	RA-82068	An-124	Polet
	RA-82074	An-124	Volga-Dnepr
	RA-82075	An-124	Polet
	RA-82077	An-124	Polet
	RA-82078	An-124	Volga-Dnepr
	RA-82079	An-124	Volga-Dnepr
	RA-82080	An-124	Polet
	RA-82081	An-124	Volga-Dnepr

S2 (Bangladesh)

	Reg.	Type	Owner or Operator
	S2-ACO	Douglas DC-10-30	Bangladesh Biman City of Shah Makhdum (R.A.)
	S2-ACP	Douglas DC-10-30	Bangladesh Biman The City of Dhaka
	S2-ACQ	Douglas DC-10-30	Bangladesh Biman The City of Hazarat-Shah Jalal (R.A.)
	S2-ACR	Douglas DC-10-30	Bangladesh Biman The New Era
	S2-ADF	Airbus A.310-325	Bangladesh Biman City of Chittagong
	S2-ADK	Airbus A.310-324	Bangladesh Biman
	S2-AFF	Airbus A.310-325	United Airways

Reg.	Type	Owner or Operator	Notes
S2-AFO	Boeing 777-3E9ER	Bangladesh Biman	
S2-AFP	Boeing 777-3E9FR	Bangladesh Biman	
S2-AFT	Airbus A.310-325	Bangladesh Biman	

S5 (Slovenia)

S5-AAD	Canadair CRJ200LR	Adria Airways	
S5-AAE	Canadair CRJ200LR	Adria Airways	
S5-AAF	Canadair CRJ200LR	Adria Airways	
S5-AAG	Canadair CRJ200LR	Adria Airways	
S5-AAI	Canadair CRJ200LR	Adria Airways	
S5-AAJ	Canadair CRJ200LR	Adria Airways	
S5-AAK	Canadair CRJ900LR	Adria Airways	
S5-AAL	Canadair CRJ900LR	Adria Airways	
S5-AAN	Canadair CRJ900LR	Adria Airways	
S5-AAO	Canadair CRJ900LR	Adria Airways	
S5-AAP	Airbus A.319-132	Adria Airways	
S5-AAR	Airbus A.319-132	Adria Airways	
S5-AAS	Airbus A.320-231	Adria Airways	

SE (Sweden)

SE-DIK	McD Douglas MD-82	SAS *Stenkil Viking*	
SE-DIL	McD Douglas MD-82	SAS *Tord Viking*	
SE-DIN	McD Douglas MD-82	SAS *Eskil Viking*	
SE-DIP	McD Douglas MD-87	SAS *Margret Viking*	
SE-DIR	McD Douglas MD-82	SAS *Nora Viking*	
SE-DIS	McD Douglas MD-82	SAS *Sigmund Viking*	
SE-DIU	McD Douglas MD-87	City Airline	
SE-DMB	McD Douglas MD-81	SAS *Bjarne Viking*	
SE-DMC	McD Douglas MD-87	City Airline	
SE-DMK	McD Douglas MD-87	SAS	
SE-DNX	Boeing 737-683	SAS *Torvald Viking*	
SE-DOR	Boeing 737-683	SAS *Elisabeth Viking*	
SE-DTH	Boeing 737-683	SAS *Vile Viking*	
SE-DZB	Embraer RJ145EP	City Airline	
SE-DZK	Boeing 737-804	TUIfly Nordic	
SE-DZN	Boeing 737-804	TUIfly Nordic	
SE-DZV	Boeing 737-804	TUIfly Nordic	
SE-LGX	BAe ATP	West Air Sweden	
SE-LGY	BAe ATP	West Air Sweden	
SE-LHZ	BAe ATP	West Air Sweden	
SE-LNY	BAe ATP	West Air Sweden	
SE-LPU	BAe ATP	West Air Sweden	
SE-MAF	BAe ATP	West Air Sweden	
SE-MAH	BAe ATP	West Air Sweden	
SE-MAJ	BAe ATP	West Air Sweden	
SE-MAR	BAe ATP	West Air Sweden	
SE-MAY	BAe ATP	West Air Sweden	
SE-RAA	Embraer RJ135ER	City Airline *City of Gothenburg*	
SE-RAB	Embraer RJ135LR	City Airline *City of Linkoping*	
SE-RAC	Embraer RJ145LR	City Airline	
SE-RAD	Embraer RJ145EU	City Airline	
SE-RAE	Embraer RJ145EU	City Airline	
SE-RAF	Embraer RJ145LR	City Airline	
SE-RAG	Embraer RJ145LR	City Airline	
SE-RDN	Airbus A.321-231	Novair Airlines	
SE-RDO	Airbus A.321-231	Novair Airlines	
SE-RDP	Airbus A.321-231	Novair Airlines	
SE-REE	Airbus A.330-343X	SAS *Sigrid Viking*	
SE-REF	Airbus A.330-343X	SAS *Erik Viking*	
SE-RFO	Boeing 757-204	TUIfly Nordic	
SE-RFR	Boeing 767-38AER	TUIfly Nordic	
SE-RFS	Boeing 767-304ER	TUIfly Nordic	
SE-RFT	Boeing 737-8K5	TUIfly Nordic	
SE-RFU	Boeing 737-8K5	TUIfly Nordic	
SE-RFV	Boeing 737-86N	TUIfly Nordic	
SE-RIA	Embraer RJ145MP	City Airline	
SE-RIC	Embraer RJ145EU	City Airline	
SE-RJA	Boeing 737-4Q8	Tor Air	
SE-RJM	Airbus A.320-212	Air Sweden	
SE-RJP	McD Douglas MD-82	Air Sweden	

Notes	Reg.	Type	Owner or Operator

SP (Poland)

	SP-LDA	Embraer RJ170 100ST	LOT
	SP-LDB	Embraer RJ170 100ST	LOT
	SP-LDC	Embraer RJ170 100ST	LOT
	SP-LDD	Embraer RJ170 100ST	LOT
	SP-LDE	Embraer RJ170 100LR	LOT
	SP-LDF	Embraer RJ170 100LR	LOT
	SP-LDG	Embraer RJ170 100LR	LOT
	SP-LDH	Embraer RJ170 100LR	LOT
	SP-LDI	Embraer RJ170 100LR	LOT
	SP-LDK	Embraer RJ170 100LR	LOT
	SP-LIA	Embraer RJ170-200STD	LOT
	SP-LIB	Embraer RJ170-200STD	LOT
	SP-LIC	Embraer RJ170-200STD	LOT
	SP-LID	Embraer RJ170-200STD	LOT
	SP-LIE	Embraer RJ170-200STD	LOT
	SP-LIF	Embraer RJ170-200STD	LOT
	SP-LII	Embraer RJ170-200STD	LOT
	SP-LIK	Embraer RJ170-200STD	LOT
	SP-LIL	Embraer RJ170-200STD	LOT
	SP-LIM	Embraer RJ170-200STD	LOT
	SP-LIN	Embraer RJ170-200STD	LOT
	SP-LIO	Embraer RJ170-200STD	LOT
	SP-LKD	Boeing 737-55D	LOT
	SP-LKE	Boeing 737-55D	LOT
	SP-LKF	Boeing 737-55D	LOT
	SP-LLB	Boeing 737-45D	LOT
	SP-LLC	Boeing 737-45D	LOT
	SP-LLE	Boeing 737-45D	LOT
	SP-LLF	Boeing 737-45D	LOT
	SP-LLG	Boeing 737-45D	LOT
	SP-LLK	Boeing 737-4Q8	LOT
	SP-LLL	Boeing 737-4Q8	LOT
	SP-LNA	Embraer RJ190-200LR	LOT
	SP-LNB	Embraer RJ190-200LR	LOT
	SP-LNC	Embraer RJ190-200LR	LOT
	SP-LND	Embraer RJ190-200LR	LOT
	SP-LPA	Boeing 767-35DER	LOT *Warszawa*
	SP-LPB	Boeing 767-35DER	LOT *Gdansk*
	SP-LPC	Boeing 767-35DER	LOT *Poznan*
	SP-LPE	Boeing 767-341ER	LOT
	SP-LPG	Boeing 767-306ER	LOT

SU (Egypt)

	SU-GAC	Airbus A.300B4-203F	EgyptAir Cargo *New Valley*
	SU-GAS	Airbus A.300F4-622RF	EgyptAir Cargo *Cheops*
	SU-GAY	Airbus A.300B4-622RF	EgyptAir Cargo *Seti I*
	SU-GBM	Airbus A.340-212	EgyptAir *Osirus Express*
	SU-GBN	Airbus A.340-212	EgyptAir *Cleo Express*
	SU-GBO	Airbus A.340-212	EgyptAir *Hathor Express*
	SU-GBR	Boeing 777-266ER	EgyptAir *Nefertari*
	SU-GBS	Boeing 777-266ER	EgyptAir *Tyie*
	SU-GBT	Airbus A.321-231	EgyptAir *Red Sea*
	SU-GBU	Airbus A.321-231	EgyptAir
	SU-GBV	Airbus A.321-231	EgyptAir
	SU-GBW	Airbus A.321-231	EgyptAir *The Nile*
	SU-GBX	Boeing 777-266ER	EgyptAir *Neit*
	SU-GBY	Boeing 777-266ER	EgyptAir *Titi*
	SU-GCE	Airbus A.330-243	EgyptAir
	SU-GCF	Airbus A.330-243	EgyptAir
	SU-GCG	Airbus A.330-243	EgyptAir
	SU-GCH	Airbus A.330-243	EgyptAir
	SU-GCI	Airbus A.330-243	EgyptAir
	SU-GCJ	Airbus A.330-243	EgyptAir
	SU-GCK	Airbus A.330-243	EgyptAir
	SU-GDL	Boeing 777-36NER	EgyptAir
	SU-GDM	Boeing 777-36NER	EgyptAir
	SU-GDN	Boeing 777-36NER	Egyptair
	SU-GDO	Boeing 777-36NER	Egyptair
	SU-GDP	Boeing 777-36NER	Egyptair

Reg.	Type	Owner or Operator	Notes
SU-GDR	Boeing 777-36NER	Egyptair	
SU-GDS	Airbus A.330-343X	Egyptair	
SU-GDT	Airbus A.330-343X	Egyptair	
SU-GDU	Airbus A.340-343X	Egyptair	
SU-GDV	Airbus A.330-343X	Egyptair	

SX (Greece)

SX-BHR	Boeing 737-5L9	Air Mediterranee	
SX-BTG	McD Douglas MD-83	Sky Wings Airlines	
SX-BTL	McD Douglas MD-82	Sky Wings Airlines	
SX-BTM	McD Douglas MD-83	Sky Wings Airlines	
SX-BTP	Airbus A.320-231	Sky Wings Airlines	
SX-DGA	Airbus A.321-231	Aegean Airlines	
SX-DGB	Airbus A.320-232	Aegean Airlines	
SX-DGC	Airbus A.320-232	Aegean Airlines	
SX-DGD	Airbus A.320-232	Aegean Airlines	
SX-DGE	Airbus A.320-232	Aegean Airlines	
SX-DGF	Airbus A.319-132	Aegean Airlines	
SX-DGG	Airbus A.319-132	Aegean Airlines	
SX-DGH	Airbus A.319-132	Aegean Airlines	
SX-DGI	Airbus A.320-232	Aegean Airlines	
SX-DVG	Airbus A.320-232	Aegean Airlines *Ethos*	
SX-DVH	Airbus A.320-232	Aegean Airlines *Nostos*	
SX-DVI	Airbus A.320-232	Aegean Airlines *Kinesis*	
SX-DVJ	Airbus A.320-232	Aegean Airlines *Kinesis*	
SX-DVK	Airbus A.320-232	Aegean Airlines	
SX-DVL	Airbus A.320-232	Aegean Airlines	
SX-DVM	Airbus A.320-232	Aegean Airlines	
SX-DVN	Airbus A.320-232	Aegean Airlines	
SX-DVO	Airbus A.321-232	Aegean Airlines *Philoxenia*	
SX-DVP	Airbus A.321-232	Aegean Airlines	
SX-DVQ	Airbus A.320-232	Aegean Airlines	
SX-DVR	Airbus A.320-232	Aegean Airlines	
SX-DVS	Airbus A.320-232	Aegean Airlines	
SX-DVT	Airbus A.320-232	Aegean Airlines	
SX-DVU	Airbus A.320-232	Aegean Airlines *Pheidias*	
SX-DVV	Airbus A.320-232	Aegean Airlines *Cleisthenes*	
SX-DVW	Airbus A.320-232	Aegean Airlines	
SX-DVX	Airbus A.320-232	Aegean Airlines	
SX-DVY	Airbus A.320-232	Aegean Airlines	
SX-DVZ	Airbus A.321-232	Aegean Airlines	
SX-OAF	Airbus A.319-112	Olympic Air	
SX-OAG	Airbus A.319-112	Olympic Air	
SX-OAH	Airbus A.320-232	Olympic Air	
SX-OAJ	Airbus A.319-112	Olympic Air	
SX-OAQ	Airbus A.320-232	Olympic Air	
SX-OAR	Airbus A.320-232	Olympic Air	
SX-OAT	Airbus A.320-214	Olympic Air	
SX-OAU	Airbus A.320-214	Olympic Air	

TC (Turkey)

TC-AAE	Boeing 737-82R	Pegasus Airlines *Hayirli*	
TC-AAF	Boeing 737-58E	Pegasus Airlines	
TC-AAH	Boeing 737-82R	Pegasus Airlines	
TC-AAI	Boeing 737-82R	Pegasus Airlines	
TC-AAJ	Boeing 737-82R	Pegasus Airlines	
TC-AAK	Boeing 737-8FH	Pegasus Airlines	
TC-AAL	Boeing 737-82R	Pegasus Airlines	
TC-AAN	Boeing 737-82R	Pegasus Airlines *Merve*	
TC-AAO	Boeing 737-86N	Pegasus Airlines	
TC-AAR	Boeing 737-86N	Pegasus Airlines	
TC-AAS	Boeing 737-82R	Pegasus Airlines	
TC-AAT	Boeing 737-82R	Pegasus Airlines	
TC-AAU	Boeing 737-82R	Pegasus Airlines *Duru*	
TC-AAV	Boeing 737-82R	Pegasus Airlines	
TC-AAY	Boeing 737-82R	Pegasus Airlines	
TC-AAZ	Boeing 737-82R	Pegasus Airlines *Mina*	
TC-ABK	Airbus A.300B4-203F	ULS Cargo *Adiyaman*	
TC-ABP	Boeing 737-82R	Pegasus Airlines *Nisa*	
TC-ACD	Airbus A.300B4-203F	ACT Cargo	

Notes	Reg.	Type	Owner or Operator
	TC-ACE	Airbus A.300B4-203F	ACT Cargo
	TC-ACP	Boeing 737-82R	Pegasus Airlines
	TC-ACU	Airbus A.300B4-203F	ACT Cargo
	TC-ACZ	Airbus A.300B4-103F	ACT Cargo
	TC-ADP	Boeing 737-82R	Pegasus Airlines *Nisa Nur*
	TC-AEP	Boeing 737-82R	Pegasus Airlines
	TC-AGK	Airbus A.300B4-203F	ULS Cargo
	TC-AGP	Boeing 737-82R	Pegasus Airlines *Sebnem*
	TC-AHP	Boeing 737-82R	Pegasus Airlines *Iram Naz*
	TC-AIP	Boeing 737-82R	Pegasus Airlines *Hante*
	TC-AIS	Boeing 737-82R	Pegasus Airlines
	TC-AJP	Boeing 737-82R	Pegasus Airlines *Masal*
	TC-AMP	Boeing 737-82R	Pegasus Airlines *Nil*
	TC-ANP	Boeing 737-82R	Pegasus Airlines *Sena*
	TC-APD	Boeing 737-42R	Pegasus Airlines
	TC-APH	Boeing 737-8S3	Pegasus Airlines
	TC-APR	Boeing 737-4Y0	Pegasus Airlines
	TC-ARP	Boeing 737-82R	Pegasus Airlines *Nehir*
	TC-ASP	Boeing 737-82R	Pegasus Airlines
	TC-ATB	Airbus A.321-211	Atlasjet Airlines
	TC-ATE	Airbus A.321-211	Atlasjet Airlines
	TC-ATF	Airbus A.321-211	Atlasjet Airlines
	TC-AVP	Boeing 737-82R	Pegasus Airlines
	TC-CCP	Boeing 737-86J	Pegasus Airlines
	TC-ETE	Boeing 757-2Q8	Atlasjet Airlines
	TC-ETF	Airbus A.321-211	Atlasjet Airlines
	TC-ETH	Airbus A.321-211	Atlasjet Airlines
	TC-ETJ	Airbus A.321-211	Atlasjet Airlines
	TC-ETM	Airbus A.321-131	Atlasjet Airlines
	TC-ETN	Airbus A.321-131	Atlasjet Airlines
	TC-ETV	Airbus A.321-211	Atlasjet Airlines
	TC-FBF	Airbus A.320-212	Freebird Airlines
	TC-FBG	Airbus A.321-131	Freebird Airlines
	TC-FBH	Airbus A.320-214	Freebird Airlines
	TC-FBJ	Airbus A.320-232	Freebird Airlines
	TC-FBR	Airbus A.320-232	Freebird Airlines
	TC-FBT	Airbus A.321-131	Freebird Airlines
	TC-FBV	Airbus A.320-214	Freebird Airlines
	TC-JAI	Airbus A.320-232	Turkish Airlines
	TC-JCT	Airbus A.310-304F	Turkish Airlines *Samsun*
	TC-JCV	Airbus A.310-304F	Turkish Airlines *Aras*
	TC-JCY	Airbus A.310-304F	Turkish Airlines *Coruh*
	TC-JCZ	Airbus A.310-304F	Turkish Airlines *Ergene*
	TC-JDG	Boeing 737-4Y0	Turkish Airlines *Marmaris*
	TC-JDH	Boeing 737-4Y0	Turkish Airlines *Amasra*
	TC-JDJ	Airbus A.340-311	Turkish Airlines *Istanbul*
	TC-JDK	Airbus A.340-311	Turkish Airlines *Diyarbakir*
	TC-JDL	Airbus A.340-311	Turkish Airlines *Ankara*
	TC-JDM	Airbus A.340-311	Turkish Airlines *Izmir*
	TC-JDN	Airbus A.340-313X	Turkish Airlines *Adana*
	TC-JDT	Boeing 737-4Y0	Turkish Airlines *Alanya*
	TC-JFC	Boeing 737-8F2	Turkish Airlines *Diyarbakir*
	TC-JFD	Boeing 737-8F2	Turkish Airlines *Rize*
	TC-JFE	Boeing 737-8F2	Turkish Airlines *Hatay*
	TC-JFF	Boeing 737-8F2	Turkish Airlines *Afyon*
	TC-JFG	Boeing 737-8F2	Turkish Airlines *Mardi*
	TC-JFH	Boeing 737-8F2	Turkish Airlines *Igdir*
	TC-JFI	Boeing 737-8F2	Turkish Airlines *Sivas*
	TC-JFJ	Boeing 737-8F2	Turkish Airlines *Agri*
	TC-JFK	Boeing 737-8F2	Turkish Airlines *Zonguldak*
	TC-JFL	Boeing 737-8F2	Turkish Airlines *Ordu*
	TC-JFM	Boeing 737-8F2	Turkish Airlines *Nigde*
	TC-JFN	Boeing 737-8F2	Turkish Airlines *Bitlis*
	TC-JFO	Boeing 737-8F2	Turkish Airlines *Batman*
	TC-JFT	Boeing 737-8F2	Turkish Airlines *Kastamonu*
	TC-JFU	Boeing 737-8F2	Turkish Airlines *Elazig*
	TC-JFV	Boeing 737-8F2	Turkish Airlines *Tunceli*
	TC-JFY	Boeing 737-8F2	Turkish Airlines *Manisa*
	TC-JFZ	Boeing 737-8F2	Turkish Airlines *Bolu*
	TC-JGB	Boeing 737-8F2	Turkish Airlines *Eskisehir*
	TC-JGC	Boeing 737-8F2	Turkish Airlines *Kocaeli*
	TC-JGD	Boeing 737-8F2	Turkish Airlines *Nevsehir*
	TC-JGF	Boeing 737-8F2	Turkish Airlines *Ardahan*
	TC-JGG	Boeing 737-8F2	Turkish Airlines *Erzincan*

Reg.	Type	Owner or Operator	Notes
TC-JGH	Boeing 737-8F2	Turkish Airlines Tokat	
TC-JGI	Boeing 737-8F2	Turkish Airlines Siirt	
TC-JGJ	Boeing 737-8F2	AnadoluJet	
TC-JGK	Boeing 737-8F2	AnadoluJet	
TC-JGL	Boeing 737-8F2	AnadoluJet	
TC-JGM	Boeing 737-8F2	AnadoluJet	
TC-JGN	Boeing 737-8F2	AnadoluJet	
TC-JGO	Boeing 737-8F2	AnadoluJet	
TC-JGP	Boeing 737-8F2	Turkish Airlines Bartin	
TC-JGR	Boeing 737-8F2	Turkish Airlines Usak	
TC-JGS	Boeing 737-8F2	Turkish Airlines Kahramanmaras	
TC-JGT	Boeing 737-8F2	Turkish Airlines Avanos	
TC-JGU	Boeing 737-8F2	Turkish Airlines Bodrum	
TC-JGV	Boeing 737-8F2	Turkish Airlines Cesme	
TC-JGY	Boeing 737-8F2	Turkish Airlines Managvat	
TC-JGZ	Boeing 737-8F2	Turkish Airlines Midyat	
TC-JHA	Boeing 737-8F2	Turkish Airlines Mudanya	
TC-JHB	Boeing 737-8F2	Turkish Airlines Safranbolu	
TC-JHC	Boeing 737-8F2	Turkish Airlines Iskenderun	
TC-JHD	Boeing 737-8F2	Turkish Airlines Serik	
TC-JHE	Boeing 737-8F2	Turkish Airlines Burhaniye	
TC-JHF	Boeing 737-8F2	Turkish Airlines Ayvalik	
TC-JHG	Boeing 737-8GJ	AnadoluJet	
TC-JHH	Boeing 737-8GJ	AnadoluJet	
TC-JHI	Boeing 737-8FH	AnadoluJet	
TC-JHJ	Boeing 737-86Q	AnadoluJet	
TC-JHK	Boeing 737-8F2	Turkish Airlines Yesilkoy	
TC-JHL	Boeing 737-8F2	Turkish Airlines Unye	
TC-JIH	Airbus A.340-313X	Turkish Airlines Kocaeli	
TC-JII	Airbus A.340-313X	Turkish Airlines Aydin	
TC-JIJ	Airbus A.340-313X	Turkish Airlines Selcuk	
TC-JIK	Airbus A.340-313X	Turkish Airlines Kas	
TC-JJE	Boeing 777-3F2ER	Turkish Airlines Dolmabahce	
TC-JJF	Boeing 777-3F2ER	Turkish Airlines Beylerbeyi	
TC-JJG	Boeing 777-3F2ER	Turkish Airlines Yildiz	
TC-JJH	Boeing 777-3F2ER	Turkish Airlines Rumeli	
TC-JJI	Boeing 777-3F2ER	Turkish Airlines Ede	
TC-JJJ	Boeing 777-3F2ER	Turkish Airlines Erzurum	
TC-JJK	Boeing 777-3F2ER	Turkish Airlines Akdeniz	
TC-JJL	Boeing 777-3F2ER	Turkish Airlines Karadeniz	
TC-JJM	Boeing 777-3F2ER	Turkish Airlines Mamara	
TC-JJN	Boeing 777-3F2ER	Turkish Airlines Anadolu	
TC-JJO	Boeing 777-3F2ER	Turkish Airlines Istanbul	
TC-JJP	Boeing 777-3F2ER	Turkish Airlines Ankara	
TC-JKF	Boeing 737-76N	AnadoluJet	
TC-JKG	Boeing 737-76N	AnadoluJet	
TC-JKH	Boeing 737-76N	AnadoluJet	
TC-JKI	Boeing 737-76N	AnadoluJet	
TC-JKJ	Boeing 737-752	Turkish Airlines Eyup	
TC-JKK	Boeing 737-752	Turkish Airlines Fatih	
TC-JKL	Boeing 737-76N	AnadoluJet	
TC-JKM	Boeing 737-76N	AnadoluJet	
TC-JKN	Boeing 737-752	Turkish Airlines Besiktas	
TC-JKO	Boeing 737-752	Turkish Airlines Kadikoy	
TC-JKP	Boeing 737-7GL	AnadoluJet	
TC-JKR	Boeing 737-7GL	AnadoluJet	
TC-JKS	Boeing 737-73V	AnadoluJet	
TC-JKT	Boeing 737-73V	AnadoluJet	
TC-JLJ	Airbus A.320-232	Turkish Airlines Sirnak	
TC-JLK	Airbus A.320-232	Turkish Airlines Kirklareli	
TC-JLL	Airbus A.320-232	Turkish Airlines Duzce	
TC-JLM	Airbus A.319-132	Turkish Airlines Sinop	
TC-JLN	Airbus A.319-132	Turkish Airlines Karabuk	
TC-JLO	Airbus A.319-132	Turkish Airlines Ahlat	
TC-JLP	Airbus A.319-132	Turkish Airlines Koycegiz	
TC-JLR	Airbus A.319-132	Turkish Airlines	
TC-JLS	Airbus A.319-132	Turkish Airlines Salihli	
TC-JLT	Airbus A.319-132	Turkish Airlines Adilcevaz	
TC-JLU	Airbus A.319-132	Turkish Airlines	
TC-JLV	Airbus A.319-132	Turkish Airlines	
TC-JLY	Airbus A.319-132	Turkish Airlines Bergama	
TC-JLZ	Airbus A.319-132	Turkish Airlines	
TC-JMC	Airbus A.321-231	Turkish Airlines Aksaray	
TC-JMD	Airbus A.321-231	Turkish Airlines Cankiri	

TC

Notes	Reg.	Type	Owner or Operator
	TC-JMH	Airbus A.321-232	Turkish Airlines Didim
	TC-JMI	Airbus A.321-232	Turkish Airlines Milas
	TC-JMJ	Airbus A.321-232	Turkish Airlines Tekirdag
	TC-JMK	Airbus A.321-232	Turkish Airlines Uskudar
	TC-JML	Airbus A.321-231	Turkish Airlines Eminonu
	TC-JMM	Airbus A.321-232	Turkish Airlines
	TC-JMN	Airbus A.321-232	Turkish Airlines
	TC-JMO	Airbus A.321-232	Turkish Airlines
	TC-JMP	Airbus A.321-232	Turkish Airlines
	TC-JMQ	Airbus A.321-232	Turkish Airlines
	TC-JNA	Airbus A.330-203	Turkish Airlines Gaziantep
	TC-JNB	Airbus A.330-203	Turkish Airlines Konya
	TC-JNC	Airbus A.330-203	Turkish Airlines Bursa
	TC-JND	Airbus A.330-203	Turkish Airlines Antalya
	TC-JNE	Airbus A.330-203	Turkish Airlines Kayseri
	TC-JNF	Airbus A.330-203	Turkish Airlines Canakkale
	TC-JNG	Airbus A.330-203	Turkish Airlines Eskisehir
	TC-JNH	Airbus A.330-343X	Turkish Airlines Topkapi
	TC-JNI	Airbus A.330-343X	Turkish Airlines Konak
	TC-JNJ	Airbus A.330-343X	Turkish Airlines Kapadokya
	TC-JNK	Airbus A.330-343X	Turkish Airlines Sanliurfa
	TC-JNL	Airbus A.330-343E	Turkish Airlines Trabzon
	TC-JNM	Airbus A.330-343X	Turkish Airlines Samsun
	TC-JNN	Airbus A.330-343	Turkish Airlines Manisa
	TC-JPA	Airbus A.320-232	Turkish Airlines Mus
	TC-JPB	Airbus A.320-232	Turkish Airlines Rize
	TC-JPC	Airbus A.320-232	Turkish Airlines Erzurum
	TC-JPD	Airbus A.320-232	Turkish Airlines Isparta
	TC-JPE	Airbus A.320-232	Turkish Airlines Gumushane
	TC-JPF	Airbus A.320-232	Turkish Airlines Yozgat
	TC-JPG	Airbus A.320-232	Turkish Airlines Osmaniye
	TC-JPH	Airbus A.320-232	Turkish Airlines Kars
	TC-JPI	Airbus A.320-232	Turkish Airlines Dogubeyazit
	TC-JPJ	Airbus A.320-232	Turkish Airlines Edremit
	TC-JPK	Airbus A.320-232	Turkish Airlines Erdek
	TC-JPL	Airbus A.320-232	Turkish Airlines Goreme
	TC-JPM	Airbus A.320-232	Turkish Airlines Harput
	TC-JPN	Airbus A.320-232	Turkish Airlines Sarikamis
	TC-JPO	Airbus A.320-232	Turkish Airlines Kemer
	TC-JPP	Airbus A.320-232	Turkish Airlines Harran
	TC-JPR	Airbus A.320-232	Turkish Airlines Kusadasi
	TC-JPS	Airbus A.320-232	Turkish Airlines Adilcevaz
	TC-JPT	Airbus A.320-232	Turkish Airlines Urgup
	TC-JPU	Airbus A.320-214	Turkish Airlines Salihli
	TC-JPV	Airbus A.320-214	Turkish Airlines Sisli
	TC-JPY	Airbus A.320-214	Turkish Airlines Beykoz
	TC-JRA	Airbus A.321-231	Turkish Airlines Kutayha
	TC-JRB	Airbus A.321-231	Turkish Airlines Sanliurfa
	TC-JRC	Airbus A.321-231	Turkish Airlines Sakarya
	TC-JRD	Airbus A.321-231	Turkish Airlines Balikesir
	TC-JRE	Airbus A.321-231	Turkish Airlines Trabzon
	TC-JRF	Airbus A.321-231	Turkish Airlines Fethiye
	TC-JRG	Airbus A.321-231	Turkish Airlines Finike
	TC-JRH	Airbus A.321-231	Turkish Airlines Yalova
	TC-JRI	Airbus A.321-232	Turkish Airlines Adiyaman
	TC-JRJ	Airbus A.321-232	Turkish Airlines Corum
	TC-JRK	Airbus A.321-231	Turkish Airlines Batman
	TC-JRL	Airbus A.321-231	Turkish Airlines Tarsus
	TC-JRM	Airbus A.321-232	Turkish Airlines Afyonkarahisar
	TC-JRN	Airbus A.321-232	Turkish Airlines Sariyer
	TC-JRO	Airbus A.321-231	Turkish Airlines Uludag
	TC-JRP	Airbus A.321-231	Turkish Airlines Urgup
	TC-JRR	Airbus A.321-231	Turkish Airlines Emirgan
	TC-JRS	Airbus A.321-231	Turkish Airlines Datca
	TC-JRT	Airbus A.321-231	Turkish Airlines Alacati
	TC-JRU	Airbus A.321-231	Turkish Airlines
	TC-JYA	Boeing 737-9F2ER	Turkish Airlines Amasya
	TC-JYB	Boeing 737-9F2ER	Turkish Airlines Denizli
	TC-KZV	Airbus A.300B4-103F	ULS Cargo
	TC-LER	Airbus A.310-308F	ULS Cargo Aras
	TC-MCA	Airbus A.300B4-605R	MNG Cargo
	TC-MCB	Airbus A.300B4-203F	MNG Cargo
	TC-MCF	Boeing 737-4K5F	MNG Cargo
	TC-MNB	Airbus A.300B4-203F	MNG Cargo

Reg.	Type	Owner or Operator	Notes
TC-MNJ	Airbus A.300B4-203F	MNG Cargo	
TC-MNU	Airbus A.300B4-203F	MNG Cargo	
TC-MNV	Airbus A.300B4-605R	MNG Cargo	
TC-OAE	Airbus A.321-231	Onur Air	
TC-OAF	Airbus A.321-231	Onur Air	
TC-OAI	Airbus A.321-231	Onur Air	
TC-OAK	Airbus A.321-231	Onur Air	
TC-OAL	Airbus A.321-231	Onur Air	
TC-OAN	Airbus A.321-231	Onur Air	
TC-OBD	Airbus A.320-232	Onur Air	
TC-OBE	Airbus A.320-232	Onur Air	
TC-OBF	Airbus A.321-231	Onur Air	
TC-OBG	Airbus A.320-233	Onur Air	
TC-OBH	Airbus A.320-233	Onur Air	
TC-OBI	Airbus A.320-233	Onur Air	
TC-OBJ	Airbus A.321-231	Onur Air	
TC-OBL	Airbus A.320-232	Onur Air	
TC-OBM	Airbus A.320-232	Onur Air	
TC-OBN	Airbus A.320-232	Onur Air	
TC-OBO	Airbus A.320-232	Onur Air	
TC-OBP	Airbus A.320-232	Onur Air	
TC-OCD	Airbus A.330-322	Onur Air	
TC-ONJ	Airbus A.321-131	Onur Air	
TC-ONS	Airbus A.321-131	Onur Air	
TC-SNE	Boeing 737-8HX	SunExpress	
TC-SNF	Boeing 737-8HC	SunExpress	
TC-SNG	Boeing 737-8HC	SunExpress	
TC-SNH	Boeing 737-8FH	SunExpress	
TC-SNI	Boeing 737-8FH	SunExpress	
TC-SNJ	Boeing 737-86J	SunExpress	
TC-SNL	Boeing 737-86N	SunExpress	
TC-SNM	Boeing 737-8BK	SunExpress	
TC-SNN	Boeing 737-8HC	SunExpress	
TC-SNO	Boeing 737-8HC	SunExpress	
TC-SNP	Boeing 737-8HC	SunExpress	
TC-SNR	Boeing 737-8HC	SunExpress	
TC-SNT	Boeing 737-8HC	SunExpress	
TC-SNU	Boeing 737-8HC	SunExpress	
TC-SUI	Boeing 737-8CX	SunExpress	
TC-SUL	Boeing 737-85F	SunExpress	
TC-SUM	Boeing 737-85F	SunExpress	
TC-SUO	Boeing 737-86Q	SunExpress	
TC-SUU	Boeing 737-86Q	SunExpress	
TC-SUV	Boeing 737-86N	SunExpress	
TC-SUY	Boeing 737-86N	SunExpress	
TC-SUZ	Boeing 737-8HX	SunExpress	
TC-TJB	Boeing 737-3Q8	Corendon Air	
TC-TJE	Boeing 737-4YO	Corendon Air	
TC-TJF	Boeing 737-4YO	Corendon Air	
TC-TJG	Boeing 737-86J	Corendon Air	
TC-TJH	Boeing 737-86J	Corendon Air	
TC-TJI	Boeing 737-8S3	Corendon Air	
TC-TJJ	Boeing 737-8S3	Corendon Air	
TC-TJK	Boeing 737-8GQ	Corendon Air	
TC-TLA	Boeing 737-4Q8	Tailwind Airlines	
TC-TLB	Boeing 737-4Q8	Tailwind Airlines	
TC-TLC	Boeing 737-4Q8	Tailwind Airlines	
TC-TLD	Boeing 737-4Q8	Tailwind Airlines	
TC-TLE	Boeing 737-4Q8	Tailwind Airlines	
TC-VEL	Airbus A.310-308F	ULS Cargo	

TF (Iceland)

TF-AAA	Boeing 747-236F	Air Atlanta Icelandic/Cargolux	
TF-AAB	Boeing 747-236F	Air Atlanta Icelandic/Saudi Arabian Airlines	
TF-AMI	Boeing 747-412BCF	Air Atlanta Icelandic/Saudi Arabian Airlines	
TF-AMJ	Boeing 747-312	Air Atlanta Icelandic/Saudi Arabian Airlines	
TF-AMS	Boeing 747-481	Air Atlanta Icelandic/Saudi Arabian Airlines	
TF-AMT	Boeing 747-481	Air Atlanta Icelandic/Saudi Arabian Airlines	
TF-AMU	Boeing 747-48E	Air Atlanta Icelandic/Saudi Arabian Airlines	
TF-AMV	Boeing 747-412	Air Atlanta Icelandic/Saudi Arabian Airlines	
TF-AMX	Boeing 747-441BCF	Air Atlanta Icelandic/Saudi Arabian Airlines	
TF-AMY	Boeing 747-446	Air Atlanta Icelandic/Bangladesh Biman	

Notes	Reg.	Type	Owner or Operator
	TF-AMZ	Boeing 747-446	Air Atlanta Icelandic/Saudi Arabian Airlines
	TF-ARJ	Boeing 737-236BF	Air Atlanta Icelandic
	TF-ARU	Boeing 747-344	Air Atlanta Icelandic
	TF-ATX	Boeing 747-236F	Air Atlanta Icelandic
	TF-BBD	Boeing 737-3Y0F	Bluebird Cargo
	TF-BBE	Boeing 737-36EF	Bluebird Cargo
	TF-BBF	Boeing 737-36EF	Bluebird Cargo
	TF-BBG	Boeing 737-36EF	Bluebird Cargo
	TF-BBH	Boeing 737-4YO	Bluebird Cargo
	TF-BBI	Boeing 737-301SF	Bluebird Cargo
	TF-CIB	Boeing 757-204F	Icelandair Cargo/TNT
	TF-FIA	Boeing 757-256	Icelandair
	TF-FIC	Boeing 757-23N	Icelandair
	TF-FID	Boeing 757-23APF	Icelandair Cargo/TNT
	TF-FIE	Boeing 757-23APF	Icelandair Cargo
	TF-FIG	Boeing 757-23APF	Icelandair Cargo
	TF-FIH	Boeing 757-208PCF	Icelandair Cargo
	TF-FII	Boeing 757-208	Icelandair
	TF-FIJ	Boeing 757-208	Icelandair *Surtsey*
	TF-FIN	Boeing 757-208	Icelandair *Bryndis*
	TF-FIO	Boeing 757-208	Icelandair *Valdis*
	TF-FIP	Boeing 757-208	Icelandair *Leifur Eiriksson*
	TF-FIR	Boeing 757-256	Icelandair
	TF-FIU	Boeing 757-256	Icelandair
	TF-FIV	Boeing 757-208	Icelandair *Gudridur Porbjarnardottir*
	TF-FIX	Boeing 757-308	Icelandair *Snorri Porfinnsson*
	TF-FIY	Boeing 757-256	Icelandair
	TF-FIZ	Boeing 757-256	Icelandair
	TF-LLX	Boeing 757-256	Icelandair
	TF-NAC	Boeing 747-428BCF	Air Atlanta Icelandic
	TF-TNM	Boeing 737-34SF	Bluebird Cargo

TS (Tunisia)

	TS-IMB	Airbus A.320-211	Tunis Air *Fahrat Hached*
	TS-IMC	Airbus A.320-211	Tunis Air *7 Novembre*
	TS-IMD	Airbus A.320-211	Tunis Air *Khereddine*
	TS-IME	Airbus A.320-211	Tunis Air *Tabarka*
	TS-IMF	Airbus A.320-211	Tunis Air *Djerba*
	TS-IMG	Airbus A.320-211	Tunis Air *Abou el Kacem Chebbi*
	TS-IMH	Airbus A.320-211	Tunis Air *Ali Belhaouane*
	TS-IMI	Airbus A.320-211	Tunis Air *Jughurta*
	TS-IMJ	Airbus A.319-114	Tunis Air *El Kantaoui*
	TS-IMK	Airbus A.320-211	Tunis Air *Kerkenah*
	TS-IML	Airbus A.320-211	Tunis Air *Gafsa el Ksar*
	TS-IMM	Airbus A.320-211	Tunis Air *Le Bardo*
	TS-IMN	Airbus A.320-211	Tunis Air *Ibn Khaldoun*
	TS-IMO	Airbus A.319-114	Tunis Air *Hannibal*
	TS-IMP	Airbus A.320-211	Tunis Air *La Galite*
	TS-IMQ	Airbus A.319-114	Tunis Air *Alyssa*
	TS-IMR	Airbus A.320-211	Tunis Air *Habib Bourguiba*
	TS-IMS	Airbus A.320-214	Tunis Air *Dougga*
	TS-INA	Airbus A.320-214	Nouvelair
	TS-INB	Airbus A.320-214	Nouvelair
	TS-INC	Airbus A.320-214	Nouvelair
	TS-INF	Airbus A.320-212	Nouvelair
	TS-INH	Airbus A.320-214	Nouvelair
	TS-INI	Airbus A.320-212	Nouvelair
	TS-INL	Airbus A.320-212	Nouvelair
	TS-INN	Airbus A.320-212	Nouvelair
	TS-INO	Airbus A.320-214	Nouvelair
	TS-INP	Airbus A.320-214	Nouvelair
	TS-IOG	Boeing 737-5H3	Tunis Air *Sfax*
	TS-IOH	Boeing 737-5H3	Tunis Air *Hammamet*
	TS-IOI	Boeing 737-5H3	Tunis Air *Mahida*
	TS-IOJ	Boeing 737-5H3	Tunis Air *Monastir*
	TS-IOK	Boeing 737-6H3	Tunis Air *Kairouan*
	TS-IOL	Boeing 737-6H3	Tunis Air *Tozeur-Nefta*
	TS-IOM	Boeing 737-6H3	Tunis Air *Carthage*
	TS-ION	Boeing 737-6H3	Tunis Air *Utique*
	TS-IOP	Boeing 737-6H3	Tunis Air *El Jem*
	TS-IOQ	Boeing 737-6H3	Tunis Air *Bizerte*
	TS-IOR	Boeing 737-6H3	Tunis Air *Tahar Haddad*

Reg.	Type	Owner or Operator	Notes
TS-IPA	Airbus A.300B4-605R	Tunis Air *Sidi Bou Said*	
TS-IPB	Airbus A.300B4-605R	Tunis Air *Tunis*	
TS-IPC	Airbus A.300B4-605R	Tunis Air *Amilcar*	
TS-IQA	Airbus A.321-211	Nouvelair	
TS-IQB	Airbus A.321-211	Nouvelair	

UK (Uzbekistan)

UK-31002	Airbus A.310-324	Uzbekistan Airways *Fergana*	
UK-31003	Airbus A.310-324	Uzbekistan Airways *Bukhara*	
UK-67001	Boeing 767-33PER	Uzbekistan Airways	
UK-67002	Boeing 767-33PER	Uzbekistan Airways	
UK-67003	Boeing 767-33PER	Uzbekistan Airways	
UK-67004	Boeing 767-33PER	Uzbekistan Airways	

UN (Kazakhstan)

Note: Air Astana operates P4- registered Boeing 757s and 767s.

UR (Ukraine)

UR-DAA	Airbus A.320-211	Donbassaero	
UR-DAB	Airbus A.320-231	Donbassaero	
UR-DAC	Airbus A.320-233	Donbassaero	
UR-DAD	Airbus A.320-233	Donbassaero	
UR-DAE	Airbus A.320-212	AeroSvit Airlines	
UR-DAH	Airbus A.320-212	AeroSvit Airlines	
UR-DAI	Airbus A.320-212	AeroSvit Airlines	
UR-DAJ	Airbus A.320-232	Donbassaero	
UR-DAK	Airbus A.320-211	Donbassaero	
UR-GAH	Boeing 737-32Q	Ukraine International *Mayrni*	
UR-GAK	Boeing 737-5Y0	Ukraine International	
UR-GAM	Boeing 737-4Y0	Ukraine International	
UR-GAN	Boeing 737-36N	Ukraine International	
UR-GAO	Boeing 737-4Z9	Ukraine International	
UR-GAP	Boeing 737-4Z9	Ukraine International	
UR-GAQ	Boeing 737-33R	Ukraine International	
UR-GAS	Boeing 737-528	Ukraine International	
UR-GAT	Boeing 737-528	Ukraine International	
UR-GAU	Boeing 737-5Y0	Ukraine International	
UR-GAV	Boeing 737-4C9	Ukraine International	
UR-GAW	Boeing 737-5Y0	Ukraine International	
UR-GAX	Boeing 737-4Y0	Ukraine International	
UR-GAZ	Boeing 737-55D	Ukraine International	
UR-PSA	Boeing 737-8HX	Ukraine International	
UR-PSB	Boeing 737-8HX	Ukraine International	
UR-PSC	Boeing 737-8HX	Ukraine International	
UR-PSD	Boeing 737-89P	Ukraine International	
UR-WUA	Airbus A.320-232	Wizz Air Ukraine	
UR-WUB	Airbus A.320-232	Wizz Air Ukraine	
UR-82007	Antonov An-124	Antonov Airlines	
UR-82008	Antonov An-124	Antonov Airlines	
UR-82009	Antonov An-124	Antonov Airlines	
UR-82027	Antonov An-124	Antonov Airlines	
UR-82029	Antonov An-124	Antonov Airlines	
UR-82060	Antonov An-225	Antonov Airlines	
UR-82072	Antonov An-124	Antonov Airlines	
UR-82073	Antonov An-124	Antonov Airlines	

V5 (Namibia)

V5-NME	Airbus A.340-311	Air Namibia	
V5-NMF	Airbus A.340-311	Air Namibia	

V8 (Brunei)

V8-BLA	Boeing 777-212ER	Royal Brunei Airlines	
V8-BLB	Boeing 777-212ER	Royal Brunei Airlines	
V8-BLC	Boeing 777-212ER	Royal Brunei Airlines	

Notes	Reg.	Type	Owner or Operator
	V8-BLD	Boeing 777-212ER	Royal Brunei Airlines
	V8-BLE	Boeing 777-212ER	Royal Brunei Airlines
	V8-BLF	Boeing 777-212ER	Royal Brunei Airlines

VH (Australia)

	VH-OEB	Boeing 747-48E	QANTAS
	VH-OEE	Boeing 747-438ER	QANTAS
	VH-OEF	Boeing 747-438ER	QANTAS
	VH-OEG	Boeing 747-438ER	QANTAS
	VH-OEH	Boeing 747-438ER	QANTAS
	VH-OEI	Boeing 747-438ER	QANTAS
	VH-OEJ	Boeing 747-438ER	QANTAS
	VH-OJA	Boeing 747-438	QANTAS
	VH-OJB	Boeing 747-438	QANTAS
	VH-OJC	Boeing 747-438	QANTAS
	VH-OJD	Boeing 747-438	QANTAS
	VH-OJE	Boeing 747-438	QANTAS
	VH-OJF	Boeing 747-438	QANTAS
	VH-OJG	Boeing 747-438	QANTAS
	VH-OJH	Boeing 747-438	QANTAS
	VH-OJI	Boeing 747-438	QANTAS
	VH-OJJ	Boeing 747-438	QANTAS
	VH-OJL	Boeing 747-438	QANTAS
	VH-OJM	Boeing 747-438	QANTAS
	VH-OJO	Boeing 747-438	QANTAS
	VH-OJP	Boeing 747-438	QANTAS
	VH-OJQ	Boeing 747-438	QANTAS
	VH-OJS	Boeing 747-438	QANTAS
	VH-OJT	Boeing 747-438	QANTAS
	VH-OJU	Boeing 747-438	QANTAS
	VH-OQA	Airbus A.380-841	QANTAS
	VH-OQB	Airbus A.380-841	QANTAS
	VH-OQC	Airbus A.380-841	QANTAS
	VH-OQD	Airbus A.380-841	QANTAS
	VH-OQE	Airbus A.380-841	QANTAS
	VH-OQF	Airbus A.380-841	QANTAS
	VH-OQG	Airbus A.380-841	QANTAS
	VH-OQH	Airbus A.380-841	QANTAS
	VH-OQI	Airbus A.380-841	QANTAS
	VH-OQJ	Airbus A.380-841	QANTAS
	VH-OQK	Airbus A.380-841	QANTAS
	VH-OQL	Airbus A.380-841	QANTAS
	VH-OQM	Airbus A.380-841	QANTAS
	VH-OQN	Airbus A.380-841	QANTAS

VN (Vietnam)

	VN-A141	Boeing 777-2Q8ER	Vietnam Airlines
	VN-A142	Boeing 777-2Q8ER	Vietnam Airlines
	VN-A143	Boeing 777-26KER	Vietnam Airlines
	VN-A144	Boeing 777-26KER	Vietnam Airlines
	VN-A145	Boeing 777-26KER	Vietnam Airlines
	VN-A146	Boeing 777-26KER	Vietnam Airlines
	VN-A147	Boeing 777-2Q8ER	Vietnam Airlines
	VN-A149	Boeing 777-2Q8ER	Vietnam Airlines
	VN-A150	Boeing 777-2Q8ER	Vietnam Airlines
	VN-A151	Boeing 777-2Q8ER	Vietnam Airlines

VP-B/VP-Q (Bermuda)

	VP-BAV	Boeing 767-36NER	Aeroflot Russian International *L. Tolstoy*
	VP-BAX	Boeing 767-36NER	Aeroflot Russian International *F. Dostoevsky*
	VP-BAY	Boeing 767-36NER	Aeroflot Russian International *I. Turgenev*
	VP-BAZ	Boeing 767-36NER	Aeroflot Russian International *N. Nekrasov*
	VP-BBR	Boeing 757-22L	Azerbaijan Airlines *Garabagh*
	VP-BBS	Boeing 757-22L	Azerbaijan Airlines
	VP-BDI	Boeing 767-38AER	Aeroflot Russian International *A. Pushkin*
	VP-BDK	Airbus A.320-214	Aeroflot Russian International *G. Sviridov*
	VP-BDM	Airbus A.319-111	Aeroflot Russian International *A. Borodin*
	VP-BDN	Airbus A.319-111	Aeroflot Russian International *A. Dargomyzhsky*

Reg.	Type	Owner or Operator	Notes
VP-BDO	Airbus A.319-111	Aeroflot Russian International *I. Stravinsky*	
VP-BDP	McD Douglas MD-11F	Aeroflot Cargo	
VP-BDQ	McD Douglas MD-11F	Aeroflot Cargo	
VP-BDR	McD Douglas MD-11F	Aeroflot Cargo	
VP-BIQ	Airbus A.319-111	Rossiya	
VP-BIT	Airbus A.319-111	Rossiya	
VP-BIU	Airbus A.319-114	Rossiya	
VP-BKC	Airbus A.320-214	Aeroflot Russian International	
VP-BKX	Airbus A.320-214	Aeroflot Russian International *G. Sedov*	
VP-BKY	Airbus A.320-214	Aeroflot Russian International *M. Rostropovich*	
VP-BLX	Airbus A.330-243	Aeroflot Russian International *E. Svetlanov*	
VP-BLY	Airbus A.330-243	Aeroflot Russian International	
VP-BME	Airbus A.320-214	Aeroflot Russian International *N. Mikluho-Maklay*	
VP-BMF	Airbus A.320-214	Aeroflot Russian International *G. Shelihov*	
VP-BPA	Boeing 737-5K5	Transaero	
VP-BPD	Boeing 737-5K5	Transaero	
VP-BQP	Airbus A.320-214	Aeroflot Russian International *A. Rublev*	
VP-BQR	Airbus A.321-211	Aeroflot Russian International *I. Repin*	
VP-BQS	Airbus A.321-211	Aeroflot Russian International *I. Kramskoi*	
VP-BQT	Airbus A.321-211	Aeroflot Russian International *I. Shishkin*	
VP-BQU	Airbus A.320-214	Aeroflot Russian International *A. Nikitin*	
VP-BQV	Airbus A.320-214	Aeroflot Russian International *V. Vasnetsov*	
VP-BQW	Airbus A.320-214	Aeroflot Russian International *V. Vereshchagin*	
VP-BQX	Airbus A.321-211	Aeroflot Russian International *I. Ayvazovsky*	
VP-BRW	Airbus A.321-211	Aeroflot Russian International	
VP-BRX	Airbus A.320-214	Aeroflot Russian International *V. Surikov*	
VP-BRY	Airbus A.320-214	Aeroflot Russian International *K. Brulloff*	
VP-BRZ	Airbus A.320-214	Aeroflot Russian International *V. Serov*	
VP-BUB	Boeing 757-23P	Uzbekistan Airways *Urgench*	
VP-BUD	Boeing 757-23P	Uzbekistan Airways *Shahrisabz*	
VP-BUE	Boeing 767-3CBER	Uzbekistan Airways	
VP-BUF	Boeing 767-33PER	Uzbekistan Airways	
VP-BUH	Boeing 757-231	Uzbekistan Airways	
VP-BUI	Boeing 757-231	Uzbekistan Airways	
VP-BUJ	Boeing 757-231	Uzbekistan Airways	
VP-BUK	Airbus A.319-111	Aeroflot Russian International *Yuri Senkevich*	
VP-BUM	Airbus A.321-211	Aeroflot Russian International *A.Deineka*	
VP-BUN	Airbus A.319-112	Aeroflot Russian International	
VP-BUO	Airbus A.319-111	Aeroflot Russian International *K. Malevich*	
VP-BUP	Airbus A.321-211	Aeroflot Russian International	
VP-BWA	Airbus A.319-111	Aeroflot Russian International *S. Prokofiev*	
VP-BWD	Airbus A.320-214	Aeroflot Russian International *A. Aliabiev*	
VP-BWE	Airbus A.320-214	Aeroflot Russian International *H. Rimsky-Korsakov*	
VP-BWF	Airbus A.320-214	Aeroflot Russian International *D. Shostakovich*	
VP-BWG	Airbus A.319-111	Aeroflot Russian International *A. Aleksandrov*	
VP-BWH	Airbus A.320-214	Aeroflot Russian International *M. Balakirev*	
VP-BWI	Airbus A.320-214	Aeroflot Russian International *A. Glazunov*	
VP-BWJ	Airbus A.319-111	Aeroflot Russian International *S. Taneyev*	
VP-BWK	Airbus A.319-111	Aeroflot Russian International *A. Grechaninov*	
VP-BWL	Airbus A.319-111	Aeroflot Russian International *S. Rakhmaninov*	
VP-BWM	Airbus A.320-214	Aeroflot Russian International *A. Skriabin*	
VP-BWN	Airbus A.321-211	Aeroflot Russian International *P. Chaikovsky*	
VP-BWO	Airbus A.321-211	Aeroflot Russian International *M. Musorgsky*	
VP-BWP	Airbus A.321-211	Aeroflot Russian International *I. Bunin*	
VP-BWU	Boeing 767-3T7ER	Aeroflot Russian International *A. Kuprin*	
VP-BWV	Boeing 767-3T7ER	Aeroflot Russian International *S. Esenin*	
VP-BWW	Boeing 767-306ER	Aeroflot Russian International *A. Blok*	
VP-BWX	Boeing 767-306ER	Transaero	
VP-BYI	Boeing 737-524	Transaero	
VP-BYJ	Boeing 737-524	Transaero	
VP-BYN	Boeing 737-524	Transaero	
VP-BYO	Boeing 737-524	Transaero	
VP-BYP	Boeing 737-524	Transaero	
VP-BYQ	Boeing 737-524	Transaero	
VP-BYT	Boeing 737-524	Aeroflot Russian International *V. Bering*	
VP-BZO	Airbus A.320-214	Aeroflot Russian International *E. Habarov*	
VP-BZP	Airbus A.320-214	Aeroflot Russian International *Yu. Lisiansky*	
VP-BZQ	Airbus A.320-214	Aeroflot Russian International *F. Bellinsgauzen*	
VP-BZR	Airbus A.320-214	Aeroflot Russian International *M. Lazarev*	
VP-BZS	Airbus A.320-214	Rossiya	
VQ-BAQ	Airbus A.319-112	Rossiya	
VQ-BAR	Airbus A.319-112	Rossiya	
VQ-BAS	Airbus A.319-112	Rossiya	
VQ-BAT	Airbus A.319-112	Rossiya	

Notes	Reg.	Type	Owner or Operator
	VQ-BAU	Airbus A.319-112	Rossiya
	VQ-BAV	Airbus A.319-112	Rossiya
	VQ-BAX	Airbus A.320-214	Aeroflot Russian International *G. Nevelskoy*
	VQ-BAY	Airbus A.320-214	Aeroflot Russian International *S. Krasheninnikov*
	VQ-BAZ	Airbus A.320-214	Aeroflot Russian International *V. Obruchev*
	VQ-BBA	Airbus A.319-112	Aeroflot Russian International *S. Cheliuskin*
	VQ-BBB	Airbus A.320-114	Aeroflot Russian International *Yu. Gagarin*
	VQ-BBC	Airbus A.320-214	Aeroflot Russian International
	VQ-BBD	Airbus A.319-112	Aeroflot Russian International *V. Golovnin*
	VQ-BBE	Airbus A.330-243	Aeroflot Russian International *I. Brodsky*
	VQ-BBF	Airbus A.330-243	Aeroflot Russian International *A. Griboedov*
	VQ-BBG	Airbus A.330-243	Aeroflot Russian International *N. Gogol*
	VQ-BBM	Airbus A.320-214	Rossiya
	VQ-BCM	Airbus A.320-214	Aeroflot Russian International
	VQ-BCN	Airbus A.320-214	Aeroflot Russian International
	VQ-BCO	Airbus A.319-111	Aeroflot Russian International
	VQ-BCP	Airbus A.319-112	Aeroflot Russian International *D. Mendeleev*
	VQ-BCQ	Airbus A.330-343	Aeroflot Russian International
	VQ-BCU	Airbus A.330-343	Aeroflot Russian International *W. Majakowski*
	VQ-BCV	Airbus A.330-343	Aeroflot Russian International
	VQ-BDQ	Airbus A.320-214	Rossiya
	VQ-BDR	Airbus A.320-214	Rossiya
	VQ-BDY	Airbus A.320-214	Rossiya
	VQ-BEA	Airbus A.321-211	Aeroflot Russian International *I. Michurin*
	VQ-BED	Airbus A.321-211	Aeroflot Russian International
	VQ-BEE	Airbus A.321-211	Aeroflot Russian International
	VQ-BEF	Airbus A.321-211	Aeroflot Russian International
	VQ-BEG	Airbus A.321-211	Aeroflot Russian International
	VQ-BEH	Airbus A.320-214	Aeroflot Russian International
	VQ-BEI	Airbus A.321-211	Aeroflot Russian International
	VQ-BEJ	Airbus A.320-214	Aeroflot Russian International
	VQ-BEK	Airbus A.330-343	Aeroflot Russian International *A. Tvardovsky*
	VQ-BEL	Airbus A.330-343	Aeroflot Russian International
	VQ-BHK	Airbus A.321-211	Aeroflot Russian International
	VQ-BHL	Airbus A.320-214	Aeroflot Russian International
	VQ-BHM	Airbus A.321-211	Aeroflot Russian International
	VQ-BHN	Airbus A.320-214	Aeroflot Russian International *N. Lobachevsky*
	VQ-BIR	Airbus A.320-214	Aeroflot Russian International
	VQ-BIT	Airbus A.320-214	Aeroflot Russian International
	VQ-BIU	Airbus A.320-214	Aeroflot Russian International
	VQ-BIV	Airbus A.320-214	Aeroflot Russian International *A. Kolmogorov*
	VQ-BIW	Airbus A.320-214	Aeroflot Russian International *V. Glushko*
	VQ-BKS	Airbus A.320-214	Aeroflot Russian International *A. Chizhevsky*
	VQ-BKT	Airbus A.320-214	Aeroflot Russian International
	VQ-BKU	Airbus A.320-214	Aeroflot Russian International
	VQ-BMV	Airbus A.330-343	Aeroflot Russian International
	VQ-BMX	Airbus A.330-343	Aeroflot Russian International
	VQ-BNS	Airbus A.330-343	Aeroflot Russian International
	VQ-BOH	Airbus A.321-211	Aeroflot Russian International
	VQ-BOI	Airbus A.321-211	Aeroflot Russian International
	VQ-BQX	Airbus A.330-343	Aeroflot Russian International
	VQ-BQY	Airbus A.330-343X	Aeroflot Russian International *M. Sholohov*
	VQ-BQZ	Airbus A.330-343	Aeroflot Russian International
	VQ-BRD	Airbus A.320-214	Rossiya

VT (India)

Notes	Reg.	Type	Owner or Operator
	VT-ALA	Boeing 777-237LR	Air-India *State of Andhra Pradesh*
	VT-ALB	Boeing 777-237LR	Air-India *Arunachal Pradesh*
	VT-ALC	Boeing 777-237LR	Air-India *State of Assam*
	VT-ALD	Boeing 777-237LR	Air-India *Gujarat*
	VT-ALE	Boeing 777-237LR	Air India *Haryana*
	VT-ALF	Boeing 777-237LR	Air India *Jharkhand*
	VT-ALG	Boeing 777-237LR	Air India *Kerala*
	VT-ALH	Boeing 777-237LR	Air India *Maharashtra*
	VT-ALJ	Boeing 777-337ER	Air India *Bihar*
	VT-ALK	Boeing 777-337ER	Air India *Chattisgarh*
	VT-ALL	Boeing 777-337ER	Air-India *State of Assam*
	VT-ALM	Boeing 777-337ER	Air India *Himachel Pradesh*
	VT-ALN	Boeing 777-337ER	Air India *Jammu & Kashmir*
	VT-ALO	Boeing 777-337ER	Air India *Karnataka*
	VT-ALP	Boeing 777-337ER	Air India *Madhya Pradesh*
	VT-ALQ	Boeing 777-337ER	Air India *Manpur*

Reg.	Type	Owner or Operator	Notes
VT-ALR	Boeing 777-337ER	Air India *Meghalaya*	
VT-ALS	Boeing 777-337ER	Air India *Mizoram*	
VT-ALT	Boeing 777-337ER	Air India *Nagaland*	
VT-ALU	Boeing 777-337ER	Air India *Orissa*	
VT-ALV	Boeing 777-337ER	Air India	
VT-ALW	Boeing 777-337ER	Air India	
VT-ALX	Boeing 777-337ER	Air India	
VT-JEG	Boeing 777-35RER	Jet Airways	
VT-JEH	Boeing 777-35RER	Jet Airways	
VT-JEK	Boeing 777-35RER	Jet Airways	
VT-JEL	Boeing 777-35RER	Jet Airways	
VT-JEM	Boeing 777-35RER	Jet Airways	
VT-JWD	Airbus A.330-243	Jet Airways	
VT-JWE	Airbus A.330-243	Jet Airways	
VT-JWF	Airbus A.330-243	Jet Airways	
VT-JWG	Airbus A.330-243	Jet Airways	
VT-JWH	Airbus A.330-302	Jet Airways	
VT-JWJ	Airbus A.330-203	Jet Airways	
VT-JWK	Airbus A.330-203	Jet Airways	
VT-JWL	Airbus A.330-203	Jet Airways	
VT-JWM	Airbus A.330-202	Jet Airways	
VT-JWN	Airbus A.330-203	Jet Airways	
VT-JWP	Airbus A.330-203	Jet Airways	
VT-JWQ	Airbus A.330-203	Jet Airways	
VT-VJK	Airbus A.330-223	Kingfisher Airlines	
VT-VJL	Airbus A.330-223	Kingfisher Airlines	
VT-VJN	Airbus A.330-223	Kingfisher Airlines	
VT-VJO	Airbus A.330-223	Kingfisher Airlines	
VT-VJP	Airbus A.330-223	Kingfisher Airlines	

YI (Iraq)

YI-AQS	Boeing 737-48E	Al-Naser Airlines	

YK (Syria)

YK-AKA	Airbus A.320-232	Syrianair *Ugarit*	
YK-AKB	Airbus A.320-232	Syrianair *Ebla*	
YK-AKC	Airbus A.320-232	Syrianair *Afamia*	
YK-AKD	Airbus A.320-232	Syrianair *Mari*	
YK-AKE	Airbus A.320-232	Syrianair *Bosra*	
YK-AKF	Airbus A.320-232	Syrianair *Amrit*	

YL (Latvia)

YL-BBD	Boeing 737-53S	Air Baltic	
YL-BBE	Boeing 737-53S	Air Baltic	
YL-BBI	Boeing 737-33A	Air Baltic	
YL-BBJ	Boeing 737-36Q	Air Baltic	
YL-BBK	Boeing 737-33V	Air Baltic	
YL-BBL	Boeing 737-33V	Air Baltic	
YL-BBM	Boeing 737-522	Air Baltic	
YL-BBN	Boeing 737-522	Air Baltic	
YL-BBP	Boeing 737-522	Air Baltic	
YL-BBQ	Boeing 737-522	Air Baltic	
YL-BBR	Boeing 737-315	Air Baltic	
YL-BBS	Boeing 737-31S	Air Baltic	
YL-BBX	Boeing 737-36Q	Air Baltic	
YL-BBY	Boeing 737-36Q	Air Baltic	
YL-BDC	Boeing 757-256ET	Air Baltic	

YR (Romania)

YR-ASA	Airbus A.318-111	Tarom	
YR-ASB	Airbus A.318-111	Tarom	
YR-ASC	Airbus A.318-111	Tarom	
YR-ASD	Airbus A.318-111	Tarom	
YR-BAC	Boeing 737-377	Blue Air	
YR-BAE	Boeing 737-46N	Blue Air	
YR-BAF	Boeing 737-322	Blue Air	

Notes	Reg.	Type	Owner or Operator
	YR-BAG	Boeing 737-5L9	Blue Air
	YR-BAJ	Boeing 737-430	Blue Air
	YR-BAK	Boeing 737-430	Blue Air
	YR-BAL	Boeing 737-484	Blue Air
	YR-BGA	Boeing 737-38J	Tarom *Alba Iulia*
	YR-BGB	Boeing 737-38J	Tarom *Bucuresti*
	YR-BGD	Boeing 737-38J	Tarom *Deva*
	YR-BGE	Boeing 737-38J	Tarom *Timisoara*
	YR-BGF	Boeing 737-78J	Tarom *Braila*
	YR-BGG	Boeing 737-78J	Tarom *Craiova*
	YR-BGH	Boeing 737-78J	Tarom *Hunedoara*
	YR-BGI	Boeing 737-78J	Tarom *Iasi*
	YR-BGS	Boeing 737-8GJ	Tarom
	YR-HBE	McD Douglas MD-83	Trawel Fly
	YR-HBY	McD Douglas MD-83	Medallion Air
	YR-LCA	Airbus A.310-325	Tarom

YU (Serbia and Montenegro)

	YU-AND	Boeing 737-3H9	JAT Airways *City of Krusevac*
	YU-ANF	Boeing 737-3H9	JAT Airways
	YU-ANI	Boeing 737-3H9	JAT Airways
	YU-ANJ	Boeing 737-3H9	JAT Airways
	YU-ANK	Boeing 737-3H9	JAT Airways
	YU-ANL	Boeing 737-3H9	JAT Airways
	YU-ANV	Boeing 737-3H9	JAT Airways
	YU-ANW	Boeing 737-3H9	JAT Airways
	YU-AON	Boeing 737-3Q4	JAT Airways

Z (Zimbabwe)

	Z-WPE	Boeing 767-2N0ER	Air Zimbabwe *Victoria Falls*
	Z-WPF	Boeing 767-2N0ER	Air Zimbabwe *Chimanimani*

ZK (New Zealand)

	ZK-OKA	Boeing 777-219ER	Air New Zealand
	ZK-OKB	Boeing 777-219ER	Air New Zealand
	ZK-OKC	Boeing 777-219ER	Air New Zealand
	ZK-OKD	Boeing 777-219ER	Air New Zealand
	ZK-OKE	Boeing 777-219ER	Air New Zealand
	ZK-OKF	Boeing 777-219ER	Air New Zealand
	ZK-OKG	Boeing 777-219ER	Air New Zealand
	ZK-OKH	Boeing 777-219ER	Air New Zealand
	ZK-OKM	Boeing 777-319ER	Air New Zealand
	ZK-OKN	Boeing 777-319ER	Air New Zealand
	ZK-OKO	Boeing 777-319ER	Air New Zealand
	ZK-OKP	Boeing 777-319ER	Air New Zealand
	ZK-OKQ	Boeing 777-319ER	Air New Zealand

ZS (South Africa)

	ZS-SLC	Airbus A.340-211	South African Airways
	ZS-SLF	Airbus A.340-211	South African Airways
	ZS-SNA	Airbus A.340-642	South African Airways
	ZS-SNB	Airbus A.340-642	South African Airways
	ZS-SNC	Airbus A.340-642	South African Airways
	ZS-SND	Airbus A.340-642	South African Airways
	ZS-SNE	Airbus A.340-642	South African Airways
	ZS-SNF	Airbus A.340-642	South African Airways
	ZS-SNG	Airbus A.340-642	South African Airways
	ZS-SNH	Airbus A.340-642	South African Airways
	ZS-SNI	Airbus A.340-642	South African Airways
	ZS-SXA	Airbus A.340-313E	South African Airways
	ZS-SXB	Airbus A.340-313E	South African Airways
	ZS-SXC	Airbus A.340-313E	South African Airways
	ZS-SXD	Airbus A.340-313E	South African Airways
	ZS-SXE	Airbus A.340-313E	South African Airways
	ZS-SXF	Airbus A.340-313E	South African Airways
	ZS-SXG	Airbus A.340-313X	South African Airways

Reg.	Type	Owner or Operator	Notes
ZS-SXH	Airbus A.340-313X	South African Airways	
ZS-SXU	Airbus A.330-243	South African Airways	
ZS-SXV	Airbus A.330-243	South African Airways	
ZS-SXW	Airbus A.330-243	South African Airways	
ZS-SXX	Airbus A.330-243	South African Airways	
ZS-SXY	Airbus A.330-243	South African Airways	
ZS-SXZ	Airbus A.330-243	South African Airways	

3B (Mauritius)

3B-NAU	Airbus A.340-312	Air Mauritius *Pink Pigeon*	
3B-NAY	Airbus A.340-313X	Air Mauritius *Cardinal*	
3B-NBD	Airbus A.340-313X	Air Mauritius *Parakeet*	
3B-NBE	Airbus A.340-313X	Air Mauritius *Paille en Queue*	
3B-NBI	Airbus A.340-313E	Air Mauritius *Le Flamboyant*	
3B-NBJ	Airbus A.340-313E	Air Mauritius *Le Chamarel*	

4K (Azerbaijan)

4K-AZ03	Airbus A.319-111	Azerbaijan Airlines	
4K-AZ04	Airbus A.319-111	Azerbaijan Airlines	
4K-AZ05	Airbus A.319-111	Azerbaijan Airlines	
4K-AZ38	Boeing 757-256	Azerbaijan Airlines	
4K-AZ43	Boeing 757-2M6	Azerbaijan Airlines	
4K-AZ54	Airbus A.320-214	Azerbaijan Airlines	
4K-AZ77	Airbus A.320-214	Azerbaijan Airlines	
4K-AZ78	Airbus A.320-214	Azerbaijan Airlines	
4K-AZ79	Airbus A.320-214	Azerbaijan Airlines	
4K-AZ80	Airbus A.320-214	Azerbaijan Airlines	
4K-AZ83	Airbus A.320-214	Azerbaijan Airlines	
4K-AZ84	Airbus A.320-214	Azerbaijan Airlines	

4O (Montenegro)

4O-AOA	Embraer ERJ190-200LR	Montenegro Airlines	
4O-AOB	Embraer ERJ190-200LR	Montenegro Airlines	
4O-AOC	Embraer ERJ190-200LR	Montenegro Airlines	
4O-AOK	Fokker 100	Montenegro Airlines	
4O-AOL	Fokker 100	Montenegro Airlines	
4O-AOM	Fokker 100	Montenegro Airlines	
4O-AOP	Fokker 100	Montenegro Airlines	
4O-AOT	Fokker 100	Montenegro Airlines	

4R (Sri Lanka)

4R-ADA	Airbus A.340-311	SriLankan Airlines	
4R-ADB	Airbus A.340-311	SriLankan Airlines	
4R-ADC	Airbus A.340-311	SriLankan Airlines	
4R-ADE	Airbus A.340-313X	SriLankan Airlines	
4R-ADF	Airbus A.340-313X	SriLankan Airlines	
4R-ADG	Airbus A.340-313X	SriLankan Airlines	
4R-ALA	Airbus A.330-243	SriLankan Airlines	
4R-ALB	Airbus A.330-243	SriLankan Airlines	
4R-ALC	Airbus A.330-243	SriLankan Airlines	
4R-ALD	Airbus A.330-243	SriLankan Airlines	
4R-ALG	Airbus A.330-243	SriLankan Airlines	
4R-ALH	Airbus A.330-243	SriLankan Airlines	

4X (Israel)

4X-ABF	Airbus A.320-232	Israir	
4X-ABG	Airbus A.320-232	Israir	
4X-AXL	Boeing 747-245F (SCD)	El Al Cargo	
4X-EAJ	Boeing 767-330ER	El Al	
4X-EAK	Boeing 767-3Q8ER	El Al	
4X-EAL	Boeing 767-33AER	El Al	
4X-EAP	Boeing 767-3Y0ER	El Al	
4X-EAR	Boeing 767-352ER	El Al	
4X-ECA	Boeing 777-258ER	El Al *Galilee*	

Notes	Reg.	Type	Owner or Operator
	4X-ECB	Boeing 777-258ER	El Al *Negev*
	4X-ECC	Boeing 777-258ER	El Al *Hasharon*
	4X-ECD	Boeing 777-258ER	El Al *Carmel*
	4X-ECE	Boeing 777-258ER	El Al *Sderot*
	4X-ECF	Boeing 777-258ER	El Al *Kiryat Shmona*
	4X-EKA	Boeing 737-858	El Al *Tiberias*
	4X-EKB	Boeing 737-858	El Al *Eilat*
	4X-EKC	Boeing 737-858	El Al *Beit Shean*
	4X-EKD	Boeing 737-758	El Al *Ashkelon*
	4X-EKE	Boeing 737-758	El Al *Nazareth*
	4X-EKF	Boeing 737-858	El Al *Kinneret*
	4X-EKH	Boeing 737-85P	El Al *Yarden*
	4X-EKI	Boeing 737-86N	El Al
	4X-EKJ	Boeing 737-85P	El Al *Degania*
	4X-EKL	Boeing 737-85P	El Al *Nahalal*
	4X-EKO	Boeing 737-86Q	El Al
	4X-EKP	Boeing 737-8Q8	El Al
	4X-EKS	Boeing 737-8Q8	El Al *Caesarea*
	4X-EKT	Boeing 737-8BK	El Al
	4X-ELA	Boeing 747-458	El Al *Tel Aviv-Jaffa*
	4X-ELB	Boeing 747-458	El Al *Haifa*
	4X-ELC	Boeing 747-458	El Al *Beer Sheva*
	4X-ELD	Boeing 747-458	El Al *Jerusalem*
	4X-ELE	Boeing 747-458	El Al *Rishon Letsion*
	4X-ELF	Boeing 747-412F	El Al Cargo
	4X-ELH	Boeing 747-412	El Al

5B (Cyprus)

	5B-DBB	Airbus A.320-231	Cyprus Airways *Akamas*
	5B-DBO	Airbus A.319-132	Cyprus Airways *Nikoklis*
	5B-DBP	Airbus A.319-132	Cyprus Airways *Chalkanor*
	5B-DCF	Airbus A.319-132	Cyprus Airways *Larnaka*
	5B-DCG	Airbus A.320-232	Cyprus Airways *Aphrodite*
	5B-DCH	Airbus A.320-232	Cyprus Airways *Lefkosia*
	5B-DCJ	Airbus A.320-232	Cyprus Airways *Amathus*
	5B-DCK	Airbus A.320-232	Cyprus Airways *Pafos*
	5B-DCL	Airbus A.320-232	Cyprus Airways *Pentadaktylos*
	5B-DCM	Airbus A.320-232	Cyprus Airways *Troodos*
	5B-DCN	Airbus A.319-132	Cyprus Airways *Limassol*

5N (Nigeria)

	5N-MJN	Boeing 737-86N	Arik Air
	5N-MJO	Boeing 737-86N	Arik Air
	5N-MJP	Boeing 737-8JE	Arik Air
	5N-MJQ	Boeing 737-8JE	Arik Air

5Y (Kenya)

	5Y-KQS	Boeing 777-2U8ER	Kenya Airways
	5Y-KQT	Boeing 777-2U8ER	Kenya Airways
	5Y-KQU	Boeing 777-2U8ER	Kenya Airways
	5Y-KQX	Boeing 767-36NER	Kenya Airways
	5Y-KQY	Boeing 767-36NER	Kenya Airways
	5Y-KQZ	Boeing 767-36NER	Kenya Airways
	5Y-KYW	Boeing 767-319ER	Kenya Airways
	5Y-KYX	Boeing 767-3P6ER	Kenya Airways
	5Y-KYZ	Boeing 777-2U8ER	Kenya Airways

7O (Yemen)

	7O-ADP	Airbus A.330-243	Yemenia *Sana'a*
	7O-ADR	Airbus A.310-324	Yemenia
	7O-ADT	Airbus A.330-243	Yemenia *Aden*
	7O-ADV	Airbus A.310-325	Yemenia
	7O-ADW	Airbus A.310-325	Yemenia

7T (Algeria)

Reg.	Type	Owner or Operator	Notes
7T-VJG	Boeing 767-3D6ER	Air Algerie	
7T-VJH	Boeing 767-3D6ER	Air Algerie	
7T-VJI	Boeing 767-3D6ER	Air Algerie	
7T-VJJ	Boeing 737-8D6	Air Algerie *Jugurtha*	
7T-VJK	Boeing 737-8D6	Air Algerie *Mansourah*	
7T-VJL	Boeing 737-8D6	Air Algerie *Illizi*	
7T-VJM	Boeing 737-8D6	Air Algerie	
7T-VJN	Boeing 737-8D6	Air Algerie	
7T-VJO	Boeing 737-8D6	Air Algerie	
7T-VJP	Boeing 737-8D6	Air Algerie	
7T-VJQ	Boeing 737-6D6	Air Algerie *Kasbah d'Alger*	
7T-VJR	Boeing 737-6D6	Air Algerie	
7T-VJS	Boeing 737-6D6	Air Algerie	
7T-VJT	Boeing 737-6D6	Air Algerie	
7T-VJU	Boeing 737-6D6	Air Algerie	
7T-VJV	Airbus A.330-202	Air Algerie *Tinhinan*	
7T-VJW	Airbus A.330-202	Air Algerie *Lalla Setti*	
7T-VJX	Airbus A.330-202	Air Algerie *Mers el Kebir*	
7T-VJY	Airbus A.330-202	Air Algerie *Monts des Beni Chougrane*	
7T-VJZ	Airbus A.330-202	Air Algerie *Teddis*	
7T-VKA	Boeing 737-8D6	Air Algerie	
7T-VKB	Boeing 737-8D6	Air Algerie	
7T-VKC	Boeing 737-8D6	Air Algerie	
7T-VKD	Boeing 737-8D6	Air Algerie	
7T-VKE	Boeing 737-8D6	Air Algerie	
7T-VKF	Boeing 737-8D6	Air Algerie	
7T-VKG	Boeing 737-8D6	Air Algerie	
7T-VKH	Boeing 737-8D6	Air Algerie	
7T-VKI	Boeing 737-8D6	Air Algerie	
7T-VKJ	Boeing 737-8D6	Air Algerie	

9A (Croatia)

Reg.	Type	Owner or Operator	Notes
9A-CTF	Airbus A.320-211	Croatia Airlines *Rijeka*	
9A-CTG	Airbus A.319-112	Croatia Airlines *Zadar*	
9A-CTH	Airbus A.319-112	Croatia Airlines *Zagreb*	
9A-CTI	Airbus A.319-112	Croatia Airlines *Vukovar*	
9A-CTJ	Airbus A.320-214	Croatia Airlines *Dubrovnik*	
9A-CTK	Airbus A.320-214	Croatia Airlines *Split*	
9A-CTL	Airbus A.319-112	Croatia Airlines *Pula*	

9H (Malta)

Reg.	Type	Owner or Operator	Notes
9H-AEF	Airbus A.320-214	Air Malta	
9H-AEG	Airbus A.319-112	Air Malta	
9H-AEH	Airbus A.319-111	Air Malta *Floriana*	
9H-AEJ	Airbus A.319-111	Air Malta *San Pawl il-Bahar*	
9H-AEK	Airbus A.320-214	Air Malta *San Giljan*	
9H-AEL	Airbus A.319-111	Air Malta *Marsaxlokk*	
9H-AEM	Airbus A.319-111	Air Malta *Birgu*	
9H-AEN	Airbus A.320-214	Air Malta	
9H-AEO	Airbus A.320-214	Air Malta	
9H-AEP	Airbus A.320-214	Air Malta	
9H-AEQ	Airbus A.320-214	Air Malta	

9K (Kuwait)

Reg.	Type	Owner or Operator	Notes
9K-ADE	Boeing 747-469 (SCD)	Kuwait Airways *Al-Jabariya*	
9K-ALA	Airbus A.310-308	Kuwait Airways *Al-Jahra*	
9K-ALB	Airbus A.310-308	Kuwait Airways *Gharnada*	
9K-ALC	Airbus A.310-308	Kuwait Airways *Kazma*	
9K-AMA	Airbus A.300B4-605R	Kuwait Airways *Failaka*	
9K-AMB	Airbus A.300B4-605R	Kuwait Airways *Burghan*	
9K-AMC	Airbus A.300B4-605R	Kuwait Airways *Wafra*	
9K-AMD	Airbus A.300B4-605R	Kuwait Airways *Wara*	
9K-AME	Airbus A.300B4-605R	Kuwait Airways *Al-Rawdhatain*	
9K-ANA	Airbus A.340-313	Kuwait Airways *Warba*	
9K-ANB	Airbus A.340-313	Kuwait Airways *Bayan*	

Notes	Reg.	Type	Owner or Operator
	9K-ANC	Airbus A.340-313	Kuwait Airways *Meskan*
	9K-AND	Airbus A.340-313	Kuwait Airways *Al-Riggah*
	9K-AOA	Boeing 777-269ER	Kuwait Airways *Al-Grain*
	9K-AOB	Boeing 777-269ER	Kuwait Airways *Garouh*

9M (Malaysia)

	9M-MPB	Boeing 747-4H6	Malaysian Airlines *Shah Alam*
	9M-MPD	Boeing 747-4H6	Malaysian Airlines
	9M-MPF	Boeing 747-4H6	Malaysian Airlines *Kota Bharu*
	9M-MPK	Boeing 747-4H6	Malaysian Airlines *Johor Bahru*
	9M-MPL	Boeing 747-4H6	Malaysian Airlines *Penang*
	9M-MPM	Boeing 747-4H6	Malaysian Airlines *Melaka*
	9M-MPN	Boeing 747-4H6	Malaysian Airlines *Pangkor*
	9M-MPO	Boeing 747-4H6	Malaysian Airlines *Alor Setar*
	9M-MPP	Boeing 747-4H6	Malaysian Airlines *Putrajaya*
	9M-MPQ	Boeing 747-4H6	Malaysian Airlines *Kuala Lumpur*
	9M-MPR	Boeing 747-4H6F	Malaysian Airlines Cargo
	9M-MPS	Boeing 747-4H6F	Malaysian Airlines Cargo
	9M-MRA	Boeing 777-2H6ER	Malaysian Airlines
	9M-MRB	Boeing 777-2H6ER	Malaysian Airlines
	9M-MRC	Boeing 777-2H6ER	Malaysian Airlines
	9M-MRD	Boeing 777-2H6ER	Malaysian Airlines
	9M-MRE	Boeing 777-2H6ER	Malaysian Airlines
	9M-MRF	Boeing 777-2H6ER	Malaysian Airlines
	9M-MRG	Boeing 777-2H6ER	Malaysian Airlines
	9M-MRH	Boeing 777-2H6ER	Malaysian Airlines
	9M-MRI	Boeing 777-2H6ER	Malaysian Airlines
	9M-MRJ	Boeing 777-2H6ER	Malaysian Airlines
	9M-MRK	Boeing 777-2H6ER	Malaysian Airlines
	9M-MRL	Boeing 777-2H6ER	Malaysian Airlines
	9M-MRM	Boeing 777-2H6ER	Malaysian Airlines
	9M-MRN	Boeing 777-2H6ER	Malaysian Airlines
	9M-MRO	Boeing 777-2H6ER	Malaysian Airlines
	9M-MRP	Boeing 777-2H6ER	Malaysian Airlines
	9M-MRQ	Boeing 777-2H6ER	Malaysian Airlines

9V (Singapore)

	9V-SCA	Boeing 747-412F	Singapore Airlines Cargo
	9V-SCB	Boeing 747-412f	Singapore Airlines Cargo
	9V-SFD	Boeing 747-412F	Singapore Airlines Cargo
	9V-SFF	Boeing 747-412F	Singapore Airlines Cargo
	9V-SFG	Boeing 747-412F	Singapore Airlines Cargo
	9V-SFJ	Boeing 747-412F	Singapore Airlines Cargo
	9V-SFK	Boeing 747-412F	Singapore Airlines Cargo
	9V-SFL	Boeing 747-412F	Singapore Airlines Cargo
	9V-SFM	Boeing 747-412F	Singapore Airlines Cargo
	9V-SFN	Boeing 747-412F	Singapore Airlines Cargo
	9V-SFO	Boeing 747-412F	Singapore Airlines Cargo
	9V-SFP	Boeing 747-412F	Singapore Airlines Cargo
	9V-SFQ	Boeing 747-412F	Singapore Airlines Cargo
	9V-SKA	Airbus A.380-841	Singapore Airlines
	9V-SKB	Airbus A.380-841	Singapore Airlines
	9V-SKC	Airbus A.380-841	Singapore Airlines
	9V-SKD	Airbus A.380-841	Singapore Airlines
	9V-SKE	Airbus A.380-841	Singapore Airlines
	9V-SKF	Airbus A.380-841	Singapore Airlines
	9V-SKG	Airbus A.380-841	Singapore Airlines
	9V-SKH	Airbus A.380-841	Singapore Airlines
	9V-SKI	Airbus A.380-841	Singapore Airlines
	9V-SKJ	Airbus A.380-841	Singapore Airlines
	9V-SKK	Airbus A.380-841	Singapore Airlines
	9V-SKL	Airbus A.380-841	Singapore Airlines
	9V-SKM	Airbus A.380-841	Singapore Airlines
	9V-SKN	Airbus A.380-841	Singapore Airlines
	9V-SKP	Airbus A.380-841	Singapore Airlines
	9V-SKQ	Airbus A.380-841	Singapore Airlines
	9V-SKR	Airbus A.380-841	Singapore Airlines
	9V-SKS	Airbus A.380-841	Singapore Airlines
	9V-SKT	Airbus A.380-841	Singapore Airlines
	9V-SVE	Boeing 777-212ER	Singapore Airlines

Reg.	Type	Owner or Operator	Notes
9V-SVH	Boeing 777-212ER	Singapore Airlines	
9V-SVI	Boeing 777-212ER	Singapore Airlines	
9V-SVJ	Boeing 777-212ER	Singapore Airlines	
9V-SVK	Boeing 777-212ER	Singapore Airlines	
9V-SVL	Boeing 777-212ER	Singapore Airlines	
9V-SVM	Boeing 777-212ER	Singapore Airlines	
9V-SVN	Boeing 777-212ER	Singapore Airlines	
9V-SVO	Boeing 777-212ER	Singapore Airlines	
9V-SWA	Boeing 777-312ER	Singapore Airlines	
9V-SWB	Boeing 777-312ER	Singapore Airlines	
9V-SWD	Boeing 777-312ER	Singapore Airlines	
9V-SWE	Boeing 777-312ER	Singapore Airlines	
9V-SWF	Boeing 777-312ER	Singapore Airlines	
9V-SWG	Boeing 777-312ER	Singapore Airlines	
9V-SWH	Boeing 777-312ER	Singapore Airlines	
9V-SWI	Boeing 777-312ER	Singapore Airlines	
9V-SWJ	Boeing 777-312ER	Singapore Airlines	
9V-SWK	Boeing 777-312ER	Singapore Airlines	
9V-SWL	Boeing 777-312ER	Singapore Airlines	
9V-SWM	Boeing 777-312ER	Singapore Airlines	
9V-SWN	Boeing 777-312ER	Singapore Airlines	
9V-SWO	Boeing 777-312ER	Singapore Airlines	
9V-SWP	Boeing 777-312ER	Singapore Airlines	
9V-SWQ	Boeing 777-312ER	Singapore Airlines	
9V-SWR	Boeing 777-312ER	Singapore Airlines	
9V-SWS	Boeing 777-312ER	Singapore Airlines	
9V-SWT	Boeing 777-312ER	Singapore Airlines	

D-AERK Airbus A.330-322 of Air Berlin. *Allan Wright*

EC-IJF Canadair CRJ200ER of Air Nostrum. *Allan Wright*

EC-KLT Airbus A.320-214 of Vueling Airlines. *Allan Wright*

433

LX-STA Airbus A.320-212 of Strategic Airlines. *Allan Wright*

N181UA Boeing 747-422 of United Airlines. *Peter R. March*

OY-RCW BAe 146-200 of Atlantic Airways. *Allan Wright*

PH-KZO Fokker 70 of KLM Cityhopper. *Allan Wright*

Radio Frequencies

The frequencies used by the larger airfields/airports are listed below. Abbreviations used: TWR – Tower, APP – Approach, A/G – Air-Ground advisory. It is possible that changes will be made from time to time with the frequencies allocated, all of which are quoted in Megahertz (MHz).

Airfield	TWR	APP	A/G	Airfield	TWR	APP	A/G
Aberdeen	118.1	119.05		Jersey	119.45	120.3	
Alderney	125.35	128.65		Kemble			118.9
Andrewsfield			130.55	Land's End	120.25		
Barton			120.25	Lasham			125.25
Barrow			123.2	Leeds Bradford	120.3	123.75	
Beccles			120.375	Leicester			122.125
Belfast International	118.3	128.5		Liverpool	126.35	119.85	
Belfast City	130.75	130.85		London City	118.075	132.7	
Bembridge			123.25	Luton	132.55	129.55	
Biggin Hill	134.8	129.4		Lydd			120.7
Birmingham	118.3	118.05		Manchester	118.625	119.575	
Blackbushe			122.3	Manston	119.925	126.35	
Blackpool	118.4	119.95		Netherthorpe			123.275
Bodmin			122.7	Newcastle	119.7	124.375	
Bourn			124.35	Newquay	123.4	128.725	
Bournemouth	125.6	119.475		North Denes			123.4
Breighton			129.80	North Weald			123.525
Bristol/Filton	132.35	122.725		Norwich	124.25	119.35	
Bristol/Lulsgate	133.85	127.25		Nottingham EMA	124.0	134.175	
Bruntingthorpe			122.825	Old Warden			130.7
Caernarfon			122.25	Oxford	133.425	125.325	
Cambridge	122.2	123.6		Penzance			118.1
Cardiff	125.0	126.625		Perth	119.8		
Carlisle	123.6			Popham			129.8
Clacton			118.15	Prestwick	118.15	120.55	
Compton Abbas			122.7	Redhill	119.6		
Conington			129.725	Rochester			122.25
Cosford	128.65	135.875		Ronaldsway IOM	118.9	120.85	
Coventry	124.8	119.25		Sandown			119.275
Cranfield	134.925	122.85		Sandtoft			130.425
Cumbernauld	120.6			Scilly Isles	123.825		
Denham			130.725	Seething			122.6
Doncaster RHA	128.775	126.225		Sheffield City			128.525
Dundee	122.9			Sherburn			122.6
Dunkeswell			123.475	Shipdham			132.25
Durham Tees Valley	119.8	118.85		Shobdon			123.5
Duxford			122.075	Shoreham	125.4	123.15	
Earls Colne			122.425	Sibson			122.3
Edinburgh	118.7	121.2		Sleap			122.45
Elstree			122.4	Southampton	118.2	128.85	
Exeter	119.8	128.975		Southend	127.725	130.775	
Fairoaks			123.425	Stansted	123.8	120.625	
Farnborough	122.5	134.35		Stapleford			122.8
Fenland			122.925	Sumburgh	118.25	131.3	
Fowlmere			135.7	Swansea			119.7
Gamston			130.475	Sywell			122.7
Gatwick	124.225	126.825		Tatenhill			124.075
Glasgow	118.8	119.1		Thruxton			130.45
Gloucester/Staverton	122.9	128.55		Tollerton			134.875
Goodwood			122.45	Wellesbourne			124.025
Guernsey	119.95	128.65		Welshpool			128.0
Haverfordwest			122.2	White Waltham			122.6
Hawarden	124.95	123.35		Wick			119.7
Henstridge			130.25	Wickenby			122.45
Headcorn			122.0	Wolverhampton			123.3
Heathrow	118.5	119.725		Woodford	120.7	130.75	
Hethel			122.35	Woodvale	119.75	121.0	
Hucknall			130.8	Wycombe Air Park			126.55
Humberside	124.9	119.125		Yeovil	125.4	130.8	
Inverness			122.6				

Airline Flight Codes

Those listed below identify the UK and overseas carriers appearing in the book

Code	Airline	Reg	Code	Airline	Reg	Code	Airline	Reg
AAF	Aigle Azur	F	BRU	Belavia	EW	HLX	Hapag-Lloyd Express	D
AAG	Atlantic Air Transport	G	BTI	Air Baltic	YL	HVN	Vietnam Airlines	VN
AAL	American Airlines	N	BUC	Bulgarian Air Charter	LZ	IBE	Iberia	EC
AAR	Asiana Airlines	HL	BZH	Brit Air	F	ICB	Islandsflug	TF
ABD	Air Atlanta Icelandic	TF	CAI	Corendon Airlines	TC	ICE	Icelandair	TF
ABQ	AirBlue	AP	CAL	China Airlines	B	IOS	Isles of Scilly Skybus	G
ABR	Air Contractors	EI	CCA	Air China	B	IRA	Iran Air	EP
ACA	Air Canada	C	CES	China Eastern	B	IRM	Mahan Air	EP
ADB	Antonov Airlines	UR	CFG	Condor	D	ISS	Meridianafly	I
ADH	Air One	I	CIM	Cimber Sterling	OY	IWD	Orbest	EC
ADR	Adria Airways	S5	CKS	Kalitta Air	N	IYE	Yemenia	7O
AEA	Air Europa	EC	CLH	Lufthansa CityLine	D	JAI	Jet Airways	VT
AEE	Aegean Airlines	SX	CLX	Cargolux	LX	JAL	Japan Airlines	JA
AEW	Aerosvit Airlines	UR	COA	Continental Airlines	N	JAT	JAT Airways	YU
AEY	Air Italy	I	CPA	Cathay Pacific	B	JKK	Spanair	EC
AFL	Aeroflot	RA	CRB	Air Astana	UN	JXX	Iceland Express	TF
AFR	Air France	F	CRK	Hong Kong Airlines	B	JOR	Blue Air	YR
AHY	Azerbaijan Airlines	4K	CRL	Corsair	F	JTG	Jet Time	OY
AIC	Air-India	VT	CSA	CSA Czech Airlines	OK	KAC	Kuwait Airways	9K
AJA	Anadolujet	TC	CTN	Croatia Airlines	9A	KAL	Korean Air	HL
AKL	Air Kilroe	G	CUB	Cubana	CU	KBR	Koral Blue	AP
ALK	SriLankan Airlines	4R	CWC	Centurion Air Cargo	N	KLC	KLM CityHopper	PH
AMC	Air Malta	9H	CYP	Cyprus Airways	5B	KLM	KLM	PH
AMT	ATA Airlines	N	DAH	Air Algerie	7T	KQA	Kenya Airways	5Y
ANA	All Nippon Airways	JA	DAL	Delta Air Lines	N	KZR	Air Astana	UN
ANE	Air Nostrum	EC	DBK	Dubrovnik Airline	9A	KZU	Kuzu Airlines Cargo	TC
ANZ	Air New Zealand	ZK	DHL	DHL Express	D/G/N	LBT	Nouvelair	TS
ARA	Arik Air	5N	DLH	Lufthansa	D	LDA	Lauda Air	OE
ATN	Air Transport International	N	DTR	Danish Air Transport	OY	LGL	Luxair	LX
AUA	Austrian Airlines	OE	EDW	Edelweiss Air	HB	LLC	Small Planet Airlines	LY
AUI	Ukraine International	UR	EIA	Evergreen International	N	LOG	Loganair	G
AUR	Aurigny A/S	G	EIN	Aer Lingus	EI	LOT	Polish Airlines (LOT)	SP
AWC	Titan Airways	G	ELL	Estonian Air	ES	LSK	Aurela	LY
AXM	Air Asia X	9M	ELY	El Al	4X	LZB	Bulgaria Air	LZ
AZA	Alitalia	I	ETD	Etihad Airways	A6	MAH	Malev	HA
AZE	Arcus Air	D	ETH	Ethiopian Airlines	ET	MAS	Malaysian Airlines	9M
AZW	Air Zimbabwe	Z	EUK	Air Atlanta Europe	TF	MAU	Air Mauritius	3B
BAW	British Airways	G	EVA	EVA Airways	B	MEA	Middle East Airlines	OD
BBC	Biman Bangladesh	S2	EWG	Eurowings	D	MGX	Montenegro Airlines	4O
BBD	Bluebird Cargo	TF	EXS	Jet2	G	MLD	Air Moldova	ER
BBO	Baboo	HB	EZE	Eastern Airways	G	MMZ	Euro Atlantic Airways	CS
BCS	European A/T	OO	EZS	easyJet Switzerland	HB	MNB	MNG Airlines	TC
BCY	CityJet	EI	EZY	easyJet	G	MON	Monarch Airlines	G
BDI	BenAir A/S	OY	FDX	Federal Express	N	MPH	Martinair	PH
BEE	Flybe	G	FHE	Hello	HB	MSR	EgyptAir	SU
BEL	Brussels Airlines	OO	FHY	Freebird Airlines	TC	NAX	Norwegian Air Shuttle	LN
BER	Air Berlin	D	FIF	Air Finland	OH	NCA	Nippon Cargo Airlines	JA
BGA	Airbus Tpt International	F	FIN	Finnair	OH	NEX	Northern Executive	G
BGH	Balkan Holidays	LZ	FLI	Atlantic Airways	OY	NLY	Niki	OE
BHP	Belair	HB	GEC	Lufthansa Cargo	D	NMB	Air Namibia	V5
BID	Binair	D	GFA	Gulf Air	A9C	NOA	Olympic Air	SX
BIE	Air Mediterranée	F	GHA	Ghana Airways	9G	NOS	Neos	I
BIH	CHC Scotia	G	GMI	Germania	D	NPT	Atlantic Airlines	G
BLC	TAM Linhas Aereas	PT	GTI	Atlas Air	N	NVR	Novair Airlines	SE
BLF	Blue 1	OH	GWI	Germanwings	D	OAE	Omni Air International	N
BMA	bmi british midland	G	GWL	Great Wall Airlines	B	OAS	Oman Air	A40
BMI	bmi baby	G	GXL	XL Airways Germany	D	OAW	Helvetic Airways	HB
BOS	Open Skies	F	HAY	Hamburg Airways	D	OBS	Orbest	CS
BOX	AeroLogic	D	HCC	Holidays Czech Airlines	OK	OGE	Atlasjet	TC
BPA	Blue Panorama	I	HFY	HiFly	CS	OHY	Onur Air	TC
BRT	BA Citiexpress	G	HLF	Hapag-Lloyd	D	OLT	OLT	D

AIRLINE FLIGHT CODES

PAC	Polar Air Cargo	N	SEU	Star Airlines	F	TSC	Air Transat	C
PGT	Pegasus Airlines	TC	SEY	Air Seychelles	S7	TSO	Transaero	RA
PIA	Pakistan International A/L	AP	SVA	Singapore Airlines	9V	TUA	Turkmenistan Airlines	EZ
PLK	Rossiya	RA	SLL	Slovak Airlines	OM	TUB	TUI Airlines Belgium	OO
POT	Polet	RA	SLM	Surinam Airways	PZ	TUI	TUIfly	D
PRI	Primera Airlines	OY	SQC	Singapore Airlines Cargo	9V	TVF	Transavia France	F
PTG	PrivatAir	D	SRK	SkyWork Airlines	HB	TVS	Travel Service/Smart Wings	OK
PTI	PrivatAir	HB	SRR	Starair	OY	TWI	Tailwind Airlines	TC
QFA	QANTAS	VH	STZ	Strategic Airlines	LX	TYR	Austrian Arrows	OE
QTR	Qatar Airways	A7	SUD	Sudan Airways	ST	UAE	Emirates Airlines	A6
RAE	Regional Airlines	F	SUS	Sun-Air	OY	UAL	United Airlines	N
RAM	Royal Air Maroc	CN	SVA	Saudi Arabian Airlines	HZ	UBD	United Airways	S2
RBA	Royal Brunei Airlines	V8	SVK	Air Slovakia	OM	UDC	Donbassero Airlines	UR
RCF	Aeroflot Cargo	RA	SWN	West Air Sweden	SE	UPS	United Parcel Service	N
REA	Aer Arann	EI	SWR	Swiss	HB	USA	US Airways	N
RJA	Royal Jordanian	JY	SXS	SunExpress	TC	UZB	Uzbekistan Airways	UK
RNV	Armavia	EK	SYR	Syrianair	YK	VDA	Volga-Dnepr	RA
ROT	Tarom	YR	TAP	TAP Portugal	CS	VIR	Virgin Atlantic	G
RUS	Cirrus Airlines	D	TAR	Tunis Air	TS	VKH	Viking Hellas	SX
RYR	Ryanair	EI	TAY	TNT Airways	OO	VLG	Vueling	EC
RZO	SATA International	CS	TCW	Thomas Cook Belgium	OO	VLM	VLM	OO
SAA	South African Airways	ZS	TCX	Thomas Cook Airlines	G	WDL	WDL Aviation	D
SAS	SAS	SE/ OY/ LN	TDK	Transavia Denmark	OY	WIF	Wideroe's	LN
SAY	Scot Airways	G	TFL	Arkefly	PH	WHT	White Airways	CS
SCW	Malmo Aviation	SE	THA	Thai Airways International	HS	WLX	West Air Europe	LX
SCX	Sun Country Airlines	N	THY	Turkish Airlines	TC	WOA	World Airways	N
SDM	Rossiya	RA	TOM	Thomson Airways	G	WZZ	Wizz Air	HA/LZ
SDR	City Airline	SE	TRA	Transavia	PH	XLF	XL Airways France	F

G-YROZ Rotorsport UK Calidus. *Peter R. March*

British Aircraft Preservation Council Register

The British Aircraft Preservation Council was formed in 1967 to co-ordinate the works of all bodies involved in the preservation, restoration and display of historical aircraft. Membership covers the whole spectrum of national, Service, commercial and voluntary groups, and meetings are held regularly at the bases of member organisations. The Council is able to provide a means of communication, helping to resolve any misunderstandings or duplication of effort. Every effort is taken to encourage the raising of standards of both organisation and technical capacity amongst the member groups to the benefit of everyone interested in aviation. To assist historians, the B.A.P.C. register has been set up and provides an identity for those aircraft which do not qualify for a Service serial or inclusion in the UK Civil Register.

Aircraft on the current B.A.P.C. Register are as follows:

Reg.	Type	Owner or Operator	Notes
1	Roe Triplane Type 4 (replica)	Shuttleworth Collection as G-ARSG (not carried)	
2	Bristol Boxkite (replica)	Shuttleworth Collection as G-ASPP (not carried)	
6	Roe Triplane Type IV (replica)	Manchester Museum of Science & Industry	
7	Southampton University MPA	Solent Sky, Southampton	
8	Dixon ornithopter	The Shuttleworth Collection	
9	Humber Monoplane (replica)	Midland Air Museum/Coventry	
10	Hafner R.II Revoplane	Museum of Army Flying/Middle Wallop	
12	Mignet HM.14	Museum of Flight/East Fortune	
13	Mignet HM.14	Brimpex Metal Treatments	
14	Addyman Standard Training Glider	A. Lindsay & N. H. Ponsford	
15	Addyman Standard Training Glider	The Aeroplane Collection	
16	Addyman ultra-light aircraft	N. H. Ponsford	
17	Woodhams Sprite	BB Aviation/Canterbury	
18	Killick MP Gyroplane	A. Lindsay & N. H. Ponsford	
20	Lee-Richards annular biplane (replica)	Visitor Centre Shoreham Airport	
21	Thruxton Jackaroo	M. J. Brett	
22	Mignet HM.14 (G-AEOF)	Aviodome/Netherlands	
23	SE-5A Scale Model	Newark Air Museum	
24	Currie Wot (replica)	Newark Air Museum	
25	Nyborg TGN-III glider	Midland Air Museum	
28	Wright Flyer (replica)	Corn Exchange/Leeds	
29	Mignet HM.14 (replica) (G-ADRY)	Brooklands Museum of Aviation/Weybridge	
32	Crossley Tom Thumb	Midland Air Museum	
33	DFS.108-49 Grunau Baby IIb	–	
34	DFS.108-49 Grunau Baby IIb	D. Elsdon	
35	EoN primary glider	–	
36	Fieseler Fi 103 (V-1) (replica)	Kent Battle of Britain Museum/Hawkinge	
37	Blake Bluetit (G-BXIY)	The Shuttleworth Collection/Old Warden	
38	Bristol Scout replica (A1742)	K. Williams & M. Thorn	
39	Addyman Zephyr sailplane	A. Lindsay & N. H. Ponsford	
40	Bristol Boxkite (replica)	Bristol City Museum	
41	B.E.2C (replica) (6232)	Yorkshire Air Museum/Elvington	
42	Avro 504 (replica) (H1968)	Yorkshire Air Museum/Elvington	
43	Mignet HM.14	Newark Air Museum/Winthorpe	
44	Miles Magister (L6906)	Museum of Berkshire Aviation (G-AKKY)/ Woodley	
45	Pilcher Hawk (replica)	Stanford Hall Museum	
46	Mignet HM.14	Stored	
47	Watkins Monoplane	National Museum of Wales	
48	Pilcher Hawk (replica)	Glasgow Museum of Transport	
49	Pilcher Hawk	Royal Scottish Museum/East Fortune	
50	Roe Triplane Type 1	Science Museum/South Kensington	
51	Vickers Vimy IV	Science Museum/South Kensington	
52	Lilienthal glider	Science Museum Store/Hayes	
53	Wright Flyer (replica)	Science Museum/South Kensington	
54	JAP-Harding monoplane	Science Museum/South Kensington	
55	Levavasseur Antoinette VII	Science Museum/South Kensington	
56	Fokker E.III (210/16)	Science Museum/South Kensington	
57	Pilcher Hawk (replica)	Science Museum/South Kensington	
58	Yokosuka MXY7 Ohka II (15-1585)	F.A.A. Museum/Yeovilton	
59	Sopwith Camel (replica) (D3419)	Aerospace Museum/Cosford	

Notes	Reg.	Type	Owner or Operator
	60	Murray M.1 helicopter	The Aeroplane Collection Ltd
	61	Stewart man-powered ornithopter	Lincolnshire Aviation Museum
	62	Cody Biplane (304)	Science Museum/South Kensington
	63	Hurricane (replica) (P3208)	Kent Battle of Britain Museum/Hawkinge
	64	Hurricane (replica) (P3059)	Kent Battle of Britain Museum/Hawkinge
	65	Spitfire (replica) (N3289)	Kent Battle of Britain Museum/Hawkinge
	66	Bf 109 (replica) (1480)	Kent Battle of Britain Museum/Hawkinge
	67	Bf 109 (replica) (14)	Kent Battle of Britain Museum/Hawkinge
	68	Hurricane (replica) (H3426)	Midland Air Museum
	69	Spitfire (replica) (N3313)	Kent Battle of Britain Museum/Hawkinge
	70	Auster AOP.5 (TJ398)	North East Aircraft Museum/Usworth
	71	Spitfire (replica) (P8140)	Norfolk & Suffolk Aviation Museum
	72	Hurricane (model) (V6779)	Gloucestershire Aviation Collection
	73	Hurricane (replica)	–
	74	Bf 109 (replica) (6357)	Kent Battle of Britain Museum/Hawkinge
	75	Mignet HM.14 (G-AEFG)	N. H. Ponsford
	76	Mignet HM.14 (G-AFFI)	Yorkshire Air Museum/Elvington
	77	Mignet HM.14 (replica) (G-ADRG)	Lower Stondon Transport Museum
	78	Hawker Hind (K5414) (G-AENP)	The Shuttleworth Collection/Old Warden
	79	Fiat G.46-4B (MM53211)	British Air Reserve/France
	80	Airspeed Horsa (KJ351)	Museum of Army Flying/Middle Wallop
	81	Hawkridge Dagling	Russavia Collection
	82	Hawker Hind (Afghan)	RAF Museum/Hendon
	83	Kawasaki Ki-100-1b (24)	Aerospace Museum/Cosford
	84	Nakajima Ki-46 (Dinah III)(5439)	Aerospace Museum/Cosford
	85	Weir W-2 autogyro	Museum of Flight/East Fortune
	86	de Havilland Tiger Moth (replica)	Yorkshire Aircraft Preservation Society
	87	Bristol Babe (replica) (G-EASQ)	Bristol Aero Collection/Kemble
	88	Fokker Dr 1 (replica) (102/17)	F.A.A. Museum/Yeovilton
	89	Cayley glider (replica)	Manchester Museum of Science & Industry
	90	Colditz Cock (replica)	Imperial War Museum/Duxford
	91	Fieseler Fi 103 (V-1)	Lashenden Air Warfare Museum
	92	Fieseler Fi 103 (V-1)	RAF Museum/Hendon
	93	Fieseler Fi 103 (V-1)	Imperial War Museum/Duxford
	94	Fieseler Fi 103 (V-1)	Aerospace Museum/Cosford
	95	Gizmer autogyro	F. Fewsdale
	96	Brown helicopter	North East Aircraft Museum
	97	Luton L.A.4A Minor	North East Aircraft Museum
	98	Yokosuka MXY7 Ohka II (997)	Manchester Museum of Science & Industry
	99	Yokosuka MXY7 Ohka II (8486M)	Aerospace Museum/Cosford
	100	Clarke Chanute biplane gliderr	RAF Museum/Hendon
	101	Mignet HM.14	Newark Air Museum/Winthorpe
	102	Mignet HM.14	Not completed
	103	Hulton hang glider (replica)	Personal Plane Services Ltd
	104	Bleriot XI	Sold in France
	105	Blériot XI (replica)	Arango Collection/Los Angeles
	106	Blériot XI (164)	RAF Museum/Hendon
	107	Blériot XXVII	RAF Museum/Hendon
	108	Fairey Swordfish IV (HS503)	RAF Restoration Centre/Wyton
	109	Slingsby Kirby Cadet TX.1	RAF Museum/Henlow store
	110	Fokker D.VII replica (static) (5125)	Stored
	111	Sopwith Triplane replica (static) (N5492)	F.A.A. Museum/Yeovilton
	112	DH.2 replica (static) (5964)	Museum of Army Flying/Middle Wallop
	113	S.E.5A replica (static) (B4863)	Stored
	114	Vickers Type 60 Viking (static) (G-EBED)	Brooklands Museum of Aviation/Weybridge
	115	Mignet HM.14	Norfolk & Suffolk Aviation Museum/Flixton
	116	Santos-Dumont Demoiselle (replica)	Cornwall Aero Park/Helston
	117	B.E.2C (replica)(1701)	Stored Hawkinge
	118	Albatros D.V (replica) (C19/18)	North Weald Aircraft Restoration Flight
	119	Bensen B.7	North East Aircraft Museum
	120	Mignet HM.14 (G-AEJZ)	South Yorkshire Aviation Museum/Doncaster
	121	Mignet HM.14 (G-AEKR)	South Yorkshire Aviation Society
	122	Avro 504 (replica) (1881)	Stored

Reg.	Type	Owner or Operator	Notes
123	Vickers FB.5 Gunbus (replica)	A. Topen (stored)/Cranfield	
124	Lilienthal Glider Type XI (replica)	Science Museum/South Kensington	
126	D.31 Turbulent (static)	Midland Air Museum/Coventry	
127	Halton Jupiter MPA	The Shuttleworth Collection	
128	Watkinson Cyclogyroplane Mk IV	IHM/Weston-super-Mare	
129	Blackburn 1911 Monoplane (replica)	Cornwall Aero Park/Helston store	
130	Blackburn 1912 Monoplane (replica)	Yorkshire Air Museum	
131	Pilcher Hawk (replica)	C. Paton	
132	Blériot XI (G-BLXI)	Stored	
133	Fokker Dr 1 (replica) (425/17)	Kent Battle of Britain Museum/Hawkinge	
134	Pitts S-2A static (G-CARS)	Toyota Ltd/Sywell	
135	Bristol M.1C (replica) (C4912)	Stored	
136	Deperdussin Seaplane (replica)	National Air Race Museum/USA	
137	Sopwith Baby Floatplane (replica) (8151)	Stored	
138	Hansa Brandenburg W.29 Floatplane (replica) (2292)	Stored	
139	Fokker Dr 1 (replica) 150/17	Stored	
140	Curtiss 42A (replica)	Stored	
141	Macchi M39 (replica)	Switzerland	
142	SE-5A (replica) (F5459)	Stored	
143	Paxton MPA	R. A. Paxton/Gloucestershire	
144	Weybridge Mercury MPA	Cranwell Gliding Club	
145	Oliver MPA	Stored	
146	Pedal Aeronauts Toucan MPA	Stored	
147	Bensen B.7	Norfolk & Suffolk Aviation Museum/Flixton	
148	Hawker Fury II (replica) (K7271)	High Ercall Aviation Museum	
149	Short S.27 (replica)	F.A.A. Museum (stored)/Yeovilton	
150	SEPECAT Jaguar GR.1 (replica) (XX728)	RAF M & R Unit/St. Athan RAF Marketing & Recruitment Unit/St. Athan	
151	SEPECAT Jaguar GR.1 (replica) (XZ363)	RAF M & R Unit/St. Athan	
152	BAe Hawk T.1 (replica) (XX227)	RAF M & R Unit/Bottesford	
153	Westland WG.33	IHM/Weston-super-Mare	
154	D.31 Turbulent	Lincolnshire Aviation Museum/E. Kirkby	
155	Panavia Tornado GR.1 (model) (ZA556)	RAF M & R Unit/St. Athan	
156	Supermarine S-6B (replica)	National Air Race Museum/USA	
157	Waco CG-4A(237123)	Yorkshire Air Museum/Elvington	
158	Fieseler Fi 103 (V-1)	Defence Ordnance Disposal School/Chattenden	
159	Yokosuka MXY7 Ohka II	Defence Ordnance Disposal School/Chattenden	
160	Chargus 18/50 hang glider	Museum of Flight/East Fortune	
161	Stewart Ornithopter Coppelia	Bomber County Museum	
162	Goodhart MPA	Science Museum/Wroughton	
163	AFEE 10/42 Rotabuggy (replica)	Museum of Army Flying/Middle Wallop	
164	Wight Quadruplane Type 1 (replica)	Solent Sky, Southampton	
165	Bristol F.2b (E2466)	RAF Museum/Hendon	
166	Bristol F.2b (D7889)	Stored	
167	Bristol SE-5A	Stored	
168	DH.60G Moth (static replica)	Stored Hawkinge (G-AAAH)	
169	BAC/Sepecat Jaguar GR.1 (XX110)	RAF Training School/Cosford	
170	Pilcher Hawk (replica)	A. Gourlay/Strathallan	
171	BAe Hawk T.1 (model) (XX308)	RAF Marketing & Recruitment Unit/Bottesford	
172	Chargus Midas Super 8 hang glider	Science Museum/Wroughton	
173	Birdman Promotions Grasshopper	Science Museum/Wroughton	
174	Bensen B.7	Science Museum/Wroughton	
175	Volmer VJ-23 Swingwing	Manchester Museum of Science & Industry	
176	SE-5A (replica) (A4850)	South Yorks Aviation Society/Firbeck	
177	Avro 504K (replica) (G-AACA)	Brooklands Museum of Aviation/Weybridge	
178	Avro 504K (replica) (E373)	Bygone Times Antique Warehouse/ Eccleston, Lancs	
179	Sopwith Pup (replica) (A7317)	Midland Air Museum/Coventry	
180	McCurdy Silver Dart (replica)	Reynolds Pioneer Museum/Canada	
181	RAF B.E.2b (replica) (687)	RAF Museum/Hendon	
182	Wood Ornithopter	Manchester Museum of Science & Industry	

Notes	Reg.	Type	Owner or Operator
	183	Zurowski ZP.1 helicopter	Newark Air Museum/Winthorpe
	184	Spitfire IX (replica) (EN398)	Fighter Wing Display Team/North Weald
	185	Waco CG-4A (243809)	Museum of Army Flying/Middle Wallop
	186	DH.82B Queen Bee (LF789)	de Havilland Heritage Museum
	187	Roe Type 1 biplane (replica)	Brooklands Museum of Aviation/Weybridge
	188	McBroom Cobra 88	Science Museum/Wroughton
	189	Bleriot XI (replica)	Stored
	190	Spitfire (replica) (K5054)	P. Smith/Hawkinge
	191	BAe Harrier GR.7 (model) (ZH139)	RAF M & R Unit/St. Athan
	192	Weedhopper JC-24	The Aeroplane Collection
	193	Hovey WD-11 Whing Ding	The Aeroplane Collection
	194	Santos Dumont Demoiselle (replica)	RAF Museum Store/RAF Stafford
	195	Moonraker 77 hang glider	Museum of Flight/East Fortune
	196	Sigma 2M hang glider	Museum of Flight/East Fortune
	197	Scotkites Cirrus III hang glider	Museum of Flight/East Fortune
	198	Fieseler Fi 103 (V-1)	Imperial War Museum/Lambeth
	199	Fieseler Fi 103 (V-1)	Science Museum/South Kensington
	200	Bensen B.7	K. Fern Collection/Stoke
	201	Mignet HM.14	Caernarfon Air Museum
	202	Spitfire V (model) (MAV467)	Maes Artro Craft Centre
	203	Chrislea LC.1 Airguard (G-AFIN)	The Aeroplane Collection
	204	McBroom hang glider	Newark Air Museum
	205	Hurricane (replica) (Z3427)	RAF Museum/Hendon
	206	Spitfire (replica) (MH486)	RAF Museum/Hendon
	207	Austin Whippet (replica) (K.158)	South Yorkshire Aviation Museum/Doncaster
	208	SE-5A (replica) (D276)	Prince's Mead Shopping Precinct/Farnborough
	209	Spitfire IX (replica) (MJ751)	Museum of D-Day Aviation/Shoreham
	210	Avro 504J (replica) (C4451)	Solent Sky, Southampton
	211	Mignet HM.14 (replica) (G-ADVU)	North East Aircraft Museum
	212	Bensen B.8	IHM/Weston-super-Mare
	213	Vertigo MPA	IHM/Weston-super-Mare
	214	Spitfire prototype (replica) (K5054)	Tangmere Military Aviation Museum
	215	Airwave hang-glider prototype	Solent Sky, Southampton
	216	DH.88 Comet (replica) (G-ACSS)	de Havilland Heritage Museum/London Colney
	217	Spitfire (replica) (K9926)	RAF Museum/Bentley Priory
	218	Hurricane (replica) (P3386)	RAF Museum/Bentley Priory
	219	Hurricane (replica) (L1710)	RAF Memorial Chapel/Biggin Hill
	220	Spitfire 1 (replica) (N3194)	RAF Memorial Chapel/Biggin Hill
	221	Spitfire LF.IX (replica) (MH777)	RAF Museum/Northolt
	222	Spitfire IX (replica) (BR600)	RAF Museum/Uxbridge
	223	Hurricane 1 (replica) (V7467)	RAF Museum/Coltishall
	224	Spitfire V (replica) (BR600)	Ambassador Hotel/Norwich
	225	Spitfire IX (replica) (P8448)	RAF Museum/Cranwell
	226	Spitfire XI (replica) (EN343)	RAF Museum/Benson
	227	Spitfire 1A (replica) (L1070)	RAF Museum/Turnhouse
	228	Olympus hang-glider	North East Aircraft Museum/Usworth
	229	Spitfire IX (replica) (MJ832)	RAF Museum/Digby
	230	Spitfire (replica) (AA550)	Eden Camp/Malton
	231	Mignet HM.14 (G-ADRX)	South Copeland Aviation Group
	232	AS.58 Horsa I/II	de Havilland Heritage Museum/London Colney
	233	Broburn Wanderlust sailplane	Museum of Berkshire Aviation/Woodley
	234	Vickers FB.5 Gunbus (replica)	RAF Manston Museum
	235	Fieseler Fi 103 (V-1) (replica)	Eden Camp Wartime Museum
	236	Hurricane (replica) (P2793)	Eden Camp Wartime Museum
	237	Fieseler Fi 103 (V-1)	RAF Museum Store/RAF Stafford
	238	Waxflatter ornithopter	Personal Plane Services Ltd
	239	Fokker D.VIII 5/8 scale replica	Norfolk & Suffolk Aviation Museum/Flixton
	240	Messerschmitt Bf.109G replica	Yorkshire Air Museum/Elvington
	241	Hurricane 1 (replica) (L1679)	Tangmere Military Aviation Museum
	242	Spitfire Vb (replica) (BL924)	Tangmere Military Aviation Museum
	243	Mignet HM.14 (replica) (G-ADYV)	P. Ward
	244	Solar Wings Typhoon	Museum of Flight/East Fortune
	245	Electraflyer Floater hang glider	Museum of Flight/East Fortune
	246	Hiway Cloudbase hang glider	Museum of Flight/East Fortune
	247	Albatross ASG.21 hang glider	Museum of Flight/East Fortune

Reg.	Type	Owner or Operator	Notes
248	McBroom hang glider	Museum of Berkshire Aviation/Woodley	
249	Hawker Fury 1 (replica) (K5673)	Brooklands Museum of Aviation/Weybridge	
250	RAF SE-5A (replica) (F5475)	Brooklands Museum of Aviation/Weybridge	
251	Hiway Spectrum hang glider (replica)	Manchester Museum of Science & Industry	
252	Flexiform Wing hang glider	Manchester Museum of Science & Industry	
253	Mignet HM.14 (G-ADZW)	H. Shore/Sandown	
254	Hawker Hurricane (P3873)	Yorkshire Air Museum/Elvington	
255	NA P-51D Mustang (replica) (463209)	American Air Museum/Duxford	
256	Santos Dumont Type 20 (replica)	Brooklands Museum of Aviation/Weybridge	
257	DH.88 Comet (G-ACSS)	The Galleria/Hatfield	
258	Adams balloon	British Balloon Museum	
259	Gloster Gamecock (replica)	Jet Age Museum Gloucestershire	
260	Mignet HM280	–	
261	GAL Hotspur (replica)	Museum of Army Flying/ Middle Wallop	
262	Catto CP-16	Museum of Flight/East Fortune	
263	Chargus Cyclone	Ulster Aviation Heritage/Langford Lodge	
264	Bensen B.8M	IHM/Weston-super-Mare	
265	Spitfire 1 (P3873)	Yorkshire Air Museum/Elvington	
266	Rogallo hang glider	Ulster Aviation Heritage	
267	Hurricane (model)	Duxford	
268	Spifire (model)	–	
269	Spitfire (model) USAF	Lakenheath	
270	DH.60 Moth (model)	Yorkshire Air Museum	
271	Messerschmitt Me 163B	Shuttleworth Collection/Old Warden	
272	Hurricane (model)	Kent Battle of Britain Museum/Hawkinge	
273	Hurricane (model)	Kent Battle of Britain Museum/Hawkinge	
274	Boulton & Paul P.6 (model)	Boulton & Paul Aircraft Heritage Project	
275	Bensen B.7 gyroglider	Doncaster Museum	
276	Hartman Ornithopter	Science Museum/Wroughton	
277	Mignet HM.14	Visitor Centre Shoreham Airport	
278	Hurricane (model)	Kent Battle of Britain Museum/Hawkinge	
279	Airspeed Horsa	Shawbury	
280	DH.89A Dragon Rapide (model)	–	
281	Boulton & Paul Defiant (model)	–	
282	Manx Elder Duck	Isle of Man Airport Terminal	
283	Spitfire (model	Jurby, Isle of Man	
284	Gloster E.28/39 (model)	Lutterworth Leics	
285	Gloster E.28/39 (model)	Farnborough	
286	Mignet HM.14	Caernarfon Air Museum	
287	Blackburn F.2 Lincock (model)	Street Life Museum/Hull	
288	Hurricane (model)	Wonderland Pleasure Park, Mansfield	
289	Gyro Boat	IHM Weston-super-Mare	
290	Fieseler Fi 103 (V1) (model)	Dover Museum	
291	Hurricane (model)	National Battle of Britain Memorial, Capel-le-Ferne, Kent	
292	Eurofighter Typhoon (model)	RAF Museum/Hendon	
293	Spitfire (model)	RAF Museum/Hendon	
294	Fairchild Argus (model)	Visitor Centre, Thorpe Camp, Woodhall Spa	
295	Da Vinci hang glider (replica)	Skysport Engineering	
296	Army Balloon Factory NuIII (replica)	RAF Museum, Hendon	
297	Spitfire (replica)	Kent Battle of Britain Museum/Hawkinge	
298	Spitfire IX (Model)	RAF Cosford Parade Ground	
299	Spitfire 1 (model).	National Battle of Britain Memorial, Capel-le-Ferne, Kent	
300	Hummingbird (replica)	Shoreham Airport Historical Association	
301	Spitfire V FSM (replica)	Thornaby Aerodrome Memorial, Thornaby-on-Tees	
302	Mignet HM.14 reproduction	Shoreham Airport Historical Association	
303	Goldfinch 161 Amphibian	Norfolk and Suffolk Aviation Museum, Flixton	
305	Mersnier pedal powered airship Reproduction	British Balloon Museum and Library	
306	Lovegrove Autogyro trainer	Norfolk and Suffolk Aviation Museum, Flixton	

Note: Registrations/Serials carried are mostly false identities.

MPA = Man Powered Aircraft, IHM = International Helicopter Museum. The aircraft, listed as 'models' are generally intended for exhibition purposes and are not airworthy although they are full scale replicas. However, in a few cases the machines have the ability to taxi when used for film work

Future Allocations Log

The grid provides the facility to record future registrations as they are issued or seen. To trace a particular code, refer to the left hand column which contains the three letters following the G prefix. The final letter can be found by reading across the columns headed A to Z. For example, the box for G-CGZT is located 6 rows down (CGZ) and then 19 across to the T column.

G-	A	B	C	D	E	F	G	H	I	J	K	L	M	N	O	P	R	S	T	U	V	W	X	Y	Z
CHF																									
CHG																									
CHH																									
CHI																									
CHJ																									
CHK																									
CHL																									
CHM																									
CHN																									
CHO																									
CHP																									
CHR																									
CHS																									
CHT																									
CHU																									
CHV																									
CHW																									
CHX																									
CHY																									
CHZ																									
CIA																									
CIB																									
CIC																									
CID																									
CIE																									
CIF																									
CIG																									
CIH																									
CIJ																									
CIK																									
CIL																									
CIM																									
CIN																									
	A	B	C	D	E	F	G	H	I	J	K	L	M	N	O	P	R	S	T	U	V	W	X	Y	Z

Credit: *Wal Gandy*